■ THE RESOURCE FOR THE INDEPENDENT TRAVELER

"The guides are aimed not only at young budget travelers but at the indepedent traveler; a sort of streetwise cookbook for traveling alone."

—The New York Times

"Unbeatable; good sight-seeing advice; up-to-date info on restaurants, hotels, and inns; a commitment to money-saving travel; and a wry style that brightens nearly every page."

—The Washington Post

"Lighthearted and sophisticated, informative and fun to read. [Let's Go] helps the novice traveler navigate like a knowledgeable old hand."

—Atlanta Journal-Constitution

"A world-wise traveling companion—always ready with friendly advice and helpful hints, all sprinkled with a bit of wit."

—The Philadelphia Inquirer

■ THE BEST TRAVEL BARGAINS IN YOUR PRICE RANGE

"All the dirt, dirt cheap."

—People

"Anything you need to know about budget traveling is detailed in this book."

—The Chicago Sun-Times

"Let's Go follows the creed that you don't have to toss your life's savings to the wind to travel—unless you want to."

—The Salt Lake Tribune

■ REAL ADVICE FOR REAL EXPERIENCES

"The writers seem to have experienced every rooster-packed bus and lunar-surfaced mattress about which they write."

—The New York Times

"A guide should tell you what to expect from a destination. Here Let's Go shines."

—The Chicago Tribune

LET'S GO PUBLICATIONS

TRAVEL GUIDES

Alaska & the Pacific Northwest 2003
Australia 2003
Austria & Switzerland 2003
Britain & Ireland 2003
California 2003
Central America 8th edition
Chile 1st edition **NEW TITLE**
China 4th edition
Costa Rica 1st edition **NEW TITLE**
Eastern Europe 2003
Egypt 2nd edition
Europe 2003
France 2003
Germany 2003
Greece 2003
Hawaii 2003 **NEW TITLE**
India & Nepal 7th edition
Ireland 2003
Israel 4th edition
Italy 2003
Mexico 19th edition
Middle East 4th edition
New Zealand 6th edition
Peru, Ecuador & Bolivia 3rd edition
South Africa 5th edition
Southeast Asia 8th edition
Southwest USA 2003
Spain & Portugal 2003
Thailand 1st edition **NEW TITLE**
Turkey 5th edition
USA 2003
Western Europe 2003

CITY GUIDES

Amsterdam 2003
Barcelona 2003
Boston 2003
London 2003
New York City 2003
Paris 2003
Rome 2003
San Francisco 2003
Washington, D.C. 2003

MAP GUIDES

Amsterdam
Berlin
Boston
Chicago
Dublin
Florence
Hong Kong
London
Los Angeles
Madrid
New Orleans
New York City
Paris
Prague
Rome
San Francisco
Seattle
Sydney
Venice
Washington, D.C.

LET'S GO

INDIA & NEPAL

GABRIEL MELCHIADES STRUCK EDITOR
BART LOUNSBURY ASSOCIATE EDITOR
FATIMAH DAWOOD ASSOCIATE EDITOR
EFRAT KUSSEL UPDATE EDITOR

RESEARCHER-WRITERS

JOE CHASE
MATT DANIELS
DAVID EGAN
MANDY HU
NORA MORRISON
KURT MUELLER

ANDREA VOLFOVA
KATE MCCARTHY
PAUL WARHAM
GRAEME WOOD
NITIN SHAH

JULIE STEPHENS MAP EDITOR
KATHARINE M. HOLT MANAGING EDITOR
JEN TAYLOR TYPESETTER

ST. MARTIN'S PRESS ♏ NEW YORK

HELPING LET'S GO
If you want to share your discoveries, suggestions, or corrections, please drop us a line. We read every piece of correspondence, whether a postcard, a 10-page email, or a coconut. Please note that mail received after May 2003 may be too late for the 2004 book, but will be kept for future editions. **Address mail to:**

Let's Go: India & Nepal
67 Mount Auburn Street
Cambridge, MA 02138
USA

Visit Let's Go at **http://www.letsgo.com,** or send email to:

feedback@letsgo.com
Subject: "Let's Go: India & Nepal"

In addition to the invaluable travel advice our readers share with us, many are kind enough to offer their services as researchers or editors. Unfortunately, our charter enables us to employ only currently enrolled Harvard students.

WHO WE ARE

A NEW LET'S GO FOR 2003

With a sleeker look and innovative new content, we have revamped the entire series to reflect more than ever the needs and interests of the independent traveler. Here are just some of the improvements you will notice when traveling with the new *Let's Go*.

MORE PRICE OPTIONS

Still the best resource for budget travelers, *Let's Go* recognizes that everyone needs the occassional indulgence. Our "Big Splurges" indicate establishments that are actually worth those extra pennies (pulas, pesos, or pounds), and price-level symbols (❶ ❷ ❸ ❹ ❺) allow you to quickly determine whether an accommodation or restaurant will break the bank. We may have diversified, but we'll never lose our budget focus—"Hidden Deals" reveal the best-kept travel secrets.

BEYOND THE TOURIST EXPERIENCE

Our Alternatives to Touism chapter offers ideas on immersing yourself in a new community through study, work, or volunteering.

AN INSIDER'S PERSPECTIVE

As always, every item is written and researched by our on-site writers. This year we have highlighted more viewpoints to help you gain an even more thorough understanding of the places you are visiting.

IN RECENT NEWS. *Let's Go* correspondents around the globe report back on current regional issues that may affect you as a traveler.

CONTRIBUTING WRITERS. Respected scholars and former *Let's Go* writers discuss topics on society and culture, going into greater depth than the usual guidebook summary.

THE LOCAL STORY. From the Parisian monk toting a cell phone to the Russian *babushka* confronting capitalism, *Let's Go* shares its revealing conversations with local personalities—a unique glimpse of what matters to real people.

FROM THE ROAD. Always helpful and sometimes downright hilarious, our researchers' share useful insights on the typical (and atypical) travel experience.

SLIMMER SIZE

Don't be fooled by our new, smaller size. *Let's Go* is still packed with invaluable travel advice, but now it's easier to carry with a more compact design.

FORTY-THREE YEARS OF WISDOM

For over four decades *Let's Go* has provided the most up-to-date information on the hippest cafes, the most pristine beaches, and the best routes from border to border. It all started in 1960 when a few well-traveled students at Harvard University handed out a 20-page mimeographed pamphlet of their tips on budget travel to passengers on student charter flights to Europe. From humble beginnings, *Let's Go* has grown to cover six continents and *Let's Go: Europe* still reigns as the world's best-selling travel guide. This year we've beefed up our coverage of Latin America with *Let's Go: Costa Rica* and *Let's Go: Chile;* on the other side of the globe, we've added *Let's Go: Thailand* and *Let's Go: Hawaii.* Our new guides bring the total number of titles to 61, each infused with the spirit of adventure that travelers around the world have come to count on.

CONTENTS

X

HOW TO USE THIS BOOK

ORGANIZATION. The introductory chapters of this book are to help you get on your way. We have organized our **India** coverage alphabetically by state, starting with the Andaman Islands and ending with West Bengal. **Nepal** coverage begins in the Kathmandu Valley and moves through the Western Hills, the lowland Terai, and the Eastern Hills before culminating at the highest point on earth. The black tabs on the side of the book should help you navigate your way through.

PRICE RANGES AND RANKINGS. Our researchers list establishments in order of value from best to worst. Our absolute favorites are denoted by the Let's Go thumbs-up (👍). Since the best value does not always mean the cheapest price, we have incorporated a system of price ranges in the guide. The table below lists how prices fall within each bracket..

INDIA	❶	❷	❸	❹	❺
ACCOMMODATIONS	Rs1-250	Rs250-500	Rs500-750	Rs750-1000	Rs1000+
FOOD	Rs1-90	Rs90-180	Rs180-270	Rs270-360	Rs360+
NEPAL	❶	❷	❸	❹	❺
ACCOMMODATIONS	Rs1-300	Rs300-600	Rs600-900	Rs900-1200	Rs1200+
FOOD	Rs1-125	Rs125-250	Rs250-375	Rs375-500	Rs500+

PHONE CODES AND TELEPHONE NUMBERS. Area codes for each region appear opposite the name of the region and are denoted by the ☎ icon. Phone numbers in text are also preceded by the ☎ icon.

WHEN TO USE IT

TWO MONTHS BEFORE. The first chapter, **Discover India,** contains highlights of the region, including Suggested Itineraries (see p. 22) that can help you plan your trip. The **Essentials** (see p. 8) section contains practical information on planning a budget, making reservations, renewing a passport, and has other useful tips about traveling in India.

ONE MONTH BEFORE. Take care of insurance, and write down a list of emergency numbers and hotlines. Make a list of packing essentials (see **Packing,** p. 28) and shop for anything you are missing. Read through the coverage and make sure you understand the logistics of your itinerary (catching trains, ferries, etc.). Make any reservations if necessary.

2 WEEKS BEFORE. Leave an itinerary and a photocopy of important documents with someone at home. Take some time to peruse the **Life and Times** (see p. 68) which has info on history, culture, flora and fauna, recent political events, and more.

RESEARCHER-WRITERS

Joe Chase   *Kashmir, Himachal Pradesh*

Having traveled in neighboring Pakistan and with a *Lets Go: Middle East* route
firmly under his belt, Joe set off for the wilds of Kashmir and Himachal Pradesh.
He conquered his fears of Indian mountain roads enough to add lush Manikaran to
our book, and when we finally heard from him, he had been there and back on a
spectacular trek across the barren moonscape of Ladakh. Even a failed Indo-Pak
peace summit didn't deter our valiant political science guru from taking on Srinagar, where he tremendously improved our coverage.

Matt Daniels   *Andhra Pradesh, Karnataka, Gujarat*

Matt tackled his route with the gusto of one who has spent too many years working *Let's Go* desk jobs. He delighted us with descriptions of the famously incendiary Andhra cuisine, sobered us with his reflections on the earthquake-ravaged
Rann of Kutch, and sent back wonderful tales of the Ganesh Utsav. To top (or
chop) it it all, he had his locks tonsured for darshan. We wish Matt the best for his
long stay in India and hope that he sends us some more (and larger) Honda boxer
briefs, or at least some more *betel nut.*

David Egan   *Sikkim, Trekking in Nepal, West Bengal*

Undeterred by the permit problems and strikes that plagued him wherever he
went, David turned *Let's Go* on its head to make his coverage of Sikkim that
much better. This veteran researcher's travels to Turkey and along the Trans-
Siberian Route gave him a nose for adventure, spurring him on to scale new
heights in the Langtang region of the Nepalese Himalayas. With flawless copy
and unflagging spirits, David awakened in us a renewed sense of wanderlust.
Many thanks to Dr. and Mrs. Roy, Dr. and Mrs. Kar, Deki Choden, and Karma
Bhutia, for their help.

Mandy Hu   *Kathmandu Valley, Eastern Nepal*

When Mandy agreed to travel to Nepal, she didn't quite know what she was getting
into, and neither did we when she arrived in Kathmandu the day the entire royal
family was assassinated. This seasoned traveler and country blues guitar enthusi-
ast, suavely dealt with strikes, riots, and curious locals, managing to send back
some fantastic copy and hilarious tales from the road.

Nora Morrison   *Goa, Kerala*

Even though SPF 45 isn't strong enough for this former *Let's Go: Greece* editor,
Nora was unfazed by the sun 'n' sand of her beach-bummer's route. In fact, she
arose dutifully before sunrise in order to catch a few waves at dawn before setting
off on the hippie trails of Anjuna and Calangute. We pictured Nora traveling
through the hibiscus lined waterways of Kerala and startling herds of wild boar on
pre-dawn nature walks, and her incredible descriptions proved us right.

Kurt Mueller   *Delhi, Orissa, Uttar Pradesh*

Never resting for long, Kurt tirelessly hit the subcontinent with a taste for sea-side barbecues and the perfect *thali*. Whether it was Puri's Jagannath festival or the perfect sculptural depiction of *Shiva*, this former *Let's Go* map editor sent in page after page of detailed copy. Coming head to head with a Hindu priest on matters existential, Kurt held his own until August 15th, when he decided to celebrate India's freedom.

Kate McCarthy   *Rajasthan, Northern Madhya Pradesh*

In the swan song of a storied Let's Go career, this editor of *Let's Go: Europe* and former Editor-in-Chief left behind the mortal trappings of office life (including Diet Coke) to be reincarnated in the desert nirvana of northern India. Stopping just long enough in her year-long journey around the world to discover all that Rajasthan had to offer, bionic Katie endured the strange greetings of natives to make sure no palace was left unexplored and no camel left unridden. She always felt that her true calling was as a researcher—and she didn't disappoint, using her finely tuned editorial skills and razor-sharp travel smarts to greatly improve coverage of one of the most popular states in the subcontinent.

Nitin Shah   *Calcutta, Punjab and Haryana, Uttaranchal*

Nitin was such a great RW, we wanted him to send us back more. Although traveling in India was nothing new for him, we were glad to see that he rediscovered his roots while *ashram*- and temple-hopping between one state and another. When the Valley of the Flowers beckoned, Nitin responded with a superb prose ditty on one of the most magnificent treks in Uttaranchal. And as the thermometer rose to 45 in Amritsar, Nitin kept his cool and brought us brilliant coverage of the subcontinent's most brilliant temple.

Andrea Volfova   *Maharashta, Eastern Madhya Pradesh*

A native Czech and former editor of *Let's Go: Eastern Europe*, Andrea combined her European panache with her travel savvy to render the coverage of western India infinitely superior. Even the July monsoon couldn't dampen the spirit of this trooper, who proved her mettle by sending us back fabulous, well-researched copy. Undeterred by roadside Romeos, bouts of pneumonia, and bad phone lines, Andrea got to hobnob with Mumbai's clubbing elite, all while sneaking a daytrip here and there to a nearby spelunking spot or two.

Paul Warham   *Tamil Nadu*

Returning to India for a second-time *bharat darshan*, Paul Indianepaul was pleasantly surprised by how much nicer Tamil Nadu was to him than the gritty cities of Bihar. Using his freshly minted experience as Editor of *Let's Go: India and Nepal*, Paul got to the bottom of every bas-relief and barrel-vaulted temple by day, and kicking back at the end of it with his favourite Kingfisher lager. Once his route was done, Paul came home to head-up off-season editing duties. He won't let go of us, threatening to patent I&N under his name sometime in the near future.

Graeme Wood *Andaman Islands, Bihar, Northeast States*

Sneaking across the allegedly closed Bangladeshi border into India, Graeme started off by showing us that nothing is impossible. He continued to astonish us by enjoying his sojourn in Patna, playing doctor on his own foot, and trysting with India's most isolated outposts in the Northeast. Furthermore, Graeme gave the introductory chapters the overhaul they'd long been needing. Making a brief stopover in Cambridge between Meghalaya and Mozambique, Graeme is well on his way to traveling the majority of the world's inaccessible destinations.

CONTRIBUTING WRITERS

Kurt Mueller has a degree in Visual and Environmental studies from Harvard College and is currently living and working as an artist in Los Angeles, California.

Joanna O'Leary is the editor of *Let's Go: Austria and Switzerland 2003*. She voluteered in a rural village in northern India, working at a daycare and researching health issues.

Sharmila Sen is an assistant professor of English and American literature and language at Harvard University. She is currently writing about borders in Bollywood cinema and working on a book on consumption and representations of India in anglophone texts.

ACKNOWLEDGMENTS

EFRAT THANKS. First and foremost to Alex for helping me make it to the feverish end. To Chris and Caleb for understanding my technologically impaired mind over and over again. To my lovely receptionists: Alex, Adam, Tom, and Megan for keeping me on task. To Anne for making everything run smoothly. And to my family, for a fantastic summer.

GABE THANKS. Bart, Fatimah, and Tania, for doing great work on the book and putting up with my music and numerous yak jokes. Special thanks to Bart for sticking it out to the crazy end. Thanks to Gautam, Megha, and Kiri, who made our place home. And Sharmi......you are the best. And finally, Hot Carl. Thanks and much love to Dad, Mom, Jesse, Miranda and Henry, and all those past and present at 32 Ivaloo.

FATIMAH THANKS. Gabe and Bart for their understanding, dedication and Tibetan pidgeon proverbs, to Sharmi who is most certainly an ME extraordinaire, and to the I&N/SEAS pod for good laughs and good music. Also, much thanks to mom, dad, and the zoo for keeping me sane, paving my way to Nepal and encouraging me to keep writing. Finally, I am forever grateful to Nepal whose people and mountains changed me and left me blessed.

BART THANKS. Gabe for late-night juggling and edifying terminology (I'll have a Cajun whatchamacallit). Fatimah and Tania for making work much more than the mindless task it could have been. Sharmi for her dedication and amiability in the face of us two lunatic editors. Priya for a great summer. SEAS for being the best podmates imaginable—I'll never look at an Indian market the same way again. Haley for gracing us all with her spirit. And Mom, Dad, Natalie, Grandma, and Granddad for encouraging and helping me in everything I do.

Editor
Gabriel Melchaides Struck
Associate Editors
Bart Lounsbury, Fatimah Dawood
Update Editor
Efrat Kussell
Managing Editor
Katherine Holt
Map Editor
D.K. Osseo-Asare

Publishing Director
Matthew Gibson
Editor-in-Chief
Brian R. Walsh
Production Manager
C. Winslow Clayton
Cartography Manager
Julie Stephens
Design Manager
Amy Cain
Editorial Managers
Christopher Blazejewski,
Abigail Burger, Cody Dydek,
Harriett Green, Angela Mi Young Hur,
Marla Kaplan, Celeste Ng
Financial Manager
Noah Askin
Marketing & Publicity Managers
Michelle Bowman, Adam M. Grant
New Media Managers
Jesse Tov, Kevin Yip
Online Manager
Amélie Cherlin
Personnel Managers
Alex Leichtman, Owen Robinson
Production Associates
Caleb Epps, David Muehlke
Network Administrators
Steven Aponte, Eduardo Montoya
Design Associate
Juice Fong
Financial Assistant
Suzanne Siu
Office Coordinators
Alex Ewing, Adam Kline,
Efrat Kussel
Director of Advertising Sales
Erik Patton
Senior Advertising Associates
Patrick Donovan, Barbara Eghan,
Fernanda Winthrop
Advertising Artwork Editor
Leif Holtzman
Cover Photo Research
Laura Wyss
President
Bradley J. Olson
General Manager
Robert B. Rombauer
Assistant General Manager
Anne E. Chisholm

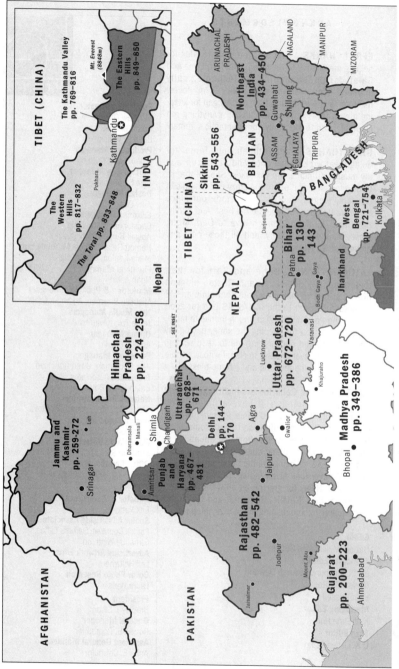

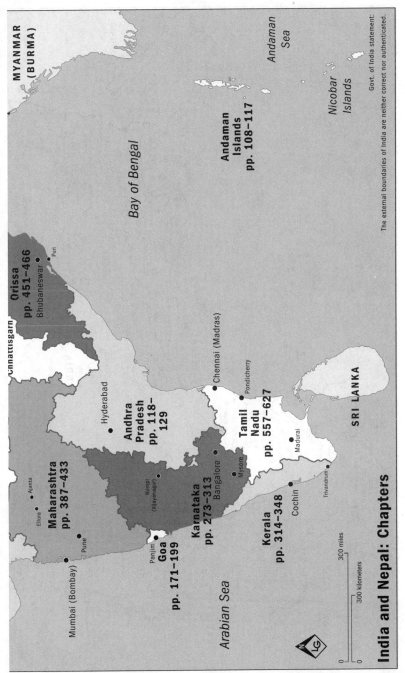

India and Nepal: Chapters

MYANMAR (BURMA)

Andaman Sea

Nicobar Islands

Andaman Islands pp. 108–117

Bay of Bengal

Orissa pp. 451–466

Puri ●

Bhubaneswar ●

Chhattisgarh

Hyderabad ●

Andhra Pradesh pp. 118–129

Chennai (Madras) ●

Pondicherry ●

Tamil Nadu pp. 557–627

Madurai ●

SRI LANKA

Maharashtra pp. 387–433

Ellora ● ● Ajanta

Pune ●

Mumbai (Bombay) ●

Panjim ●

Hampi (Vijayanagar) ●

Goa pp. 171–199

Karnataka pp. 273–313

Bangalore ●

Mysore ●

Kerala pp. 314–348

Cochin ●

Trivandrum ●

Arabian Sea

0 — 300 miles
0 — 300 kilometers

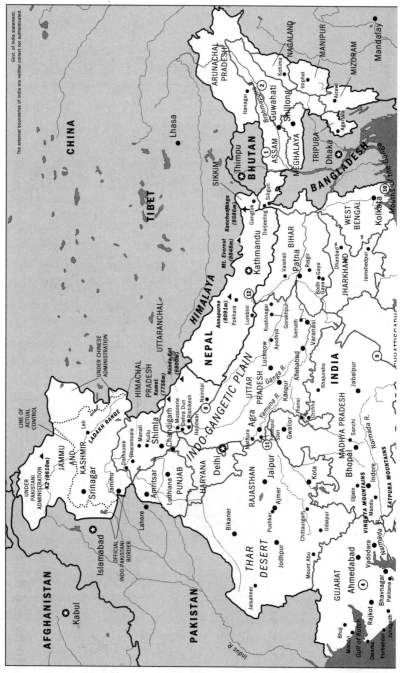

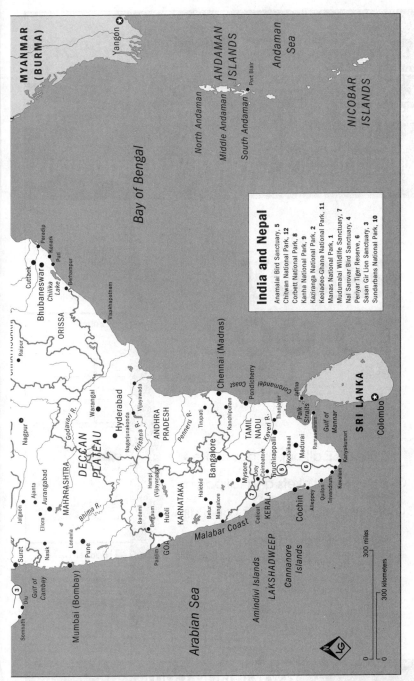

India and Nepal

Anamalai Bird Sanctuary, **5**
Chitwan National Park, **12**
Corbett National Park, **8**
Kanha National Park, **9**
Kaziranga National Park, **2**
Keoladeo-Ghana National Park, **11**
Manas National Park, **1**
Mudumalai Wildlife Sanctuary, **7**
Nal Sarovar Bird Sanctuary, **4**
Periyar Tiger Reserve, **6**
Sasan Gir Lion Sanctuary, **3**
Sundarbans National Park, **10**

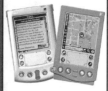
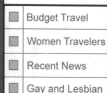

DISCOVER

INDIA & NEPAL

With a population that has just topped one billion, **India** bursts at the seams with dozens of different cultures and a vibrant variety to match the magnitude of its sheer numbers. Birthplace of three of the world's oldest religions—Hinduism, Buddhism, and Jainism—India today accommodates countless others and struggles to maintain its secular facade as the world's largest democracy. For the traveler swept up into this grandest of cultural confluences, India can be as challenging—and as threatening—as it is rewarding and unforgettable. This is not a country that you can sit back and observe; India demands reaction. From the moment you step down from the plane, your senses will be under assault. The sublime beauty of India's natural scenery and towering temples are as likely to overwhelm as the ubiquitous smells of dirt, dust, and dung. *Paan* stains the city streets, *tilak* powder dusts the temple walls, the smell of freshly caught fish permeates the seaside air, and the traffic horns will honk you out of your senses. But the magical swirl of color and life, the mosques and the minarets, the quick and spicy meal at a roadside *dhaba*, and the early morning chime of temple bells make the subcontinent quite unlike anywhere you've ever been before. After a few weeks here, many people are only too happy to escape back to a safer world, where things move at a different pace. But nobody leaves India completely unchanged. Quite a few never leave at all.

Land-locked **Nepal** is a country shaped by its geography, which takes in some of the world's highest peaks as well as some of its greenest valleys. Ancient temple towns and palace squares help to bring true every romantic dream you ever dreamed about the Kathmandu Valley, the political and social center of the country. Soaring high above the valleys and farms, of course, are the mighty Himalayas, which offer better hiking and more spectacular scenery than you'll find anywhere else on the planet.

An open mind and a healthy dose of patience are your best inoculations against the travails of travel in the subcontinent. So, don a pair of non-leather sandals, brush up on those non-verbal communication skills, grab some anti-diarrhea medication, and get ready to roll.

INDIA	NEPAL
✴ **Population (people):** 1 billion	✴ **Population:** 23 million
✴ **Population (cows):** 200 million	✴ **Average annual ascents of Everest**
✴ **Annual mango production:** 10 million tons	**during the 1990s:** 67.2
✴ **Spit produced per annum by paan chewers:** 1.5 million tons.	✴ **National Motto:** "The Motherland is worth more than the Kingdom of Heaven."
✴ **Average Income Per Capita:** US$350	✴ **Number of toes on a yeti's foot:** 4
✴ **Literacy:** 66% male, 38% female	✴ **Average Income Per Capita:** US$165
	✴ **Literacy:** 41% male, 14% female

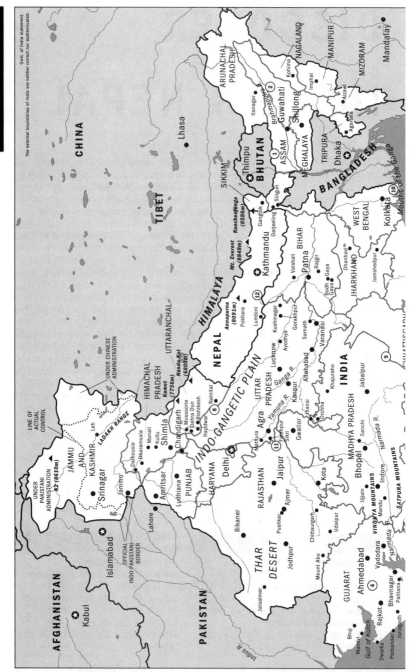

Govt. of India statement:
The external boundaries of India are neither correct nor authenticated.

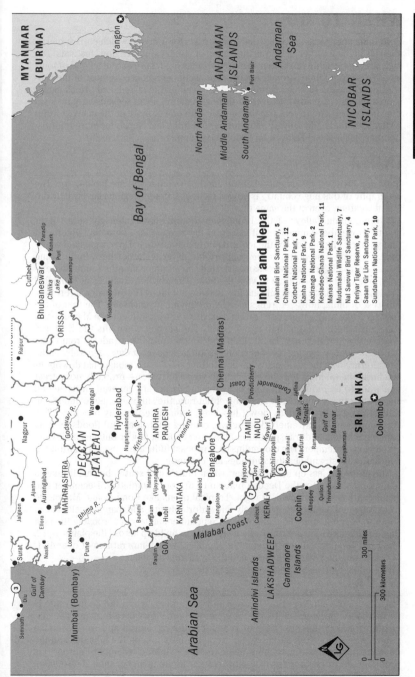

India and Nepal

Anamalai Bird Sanctuary, **5**
Chitwan National Park, **12**
Corbett National Park, **8**
Kanha National Park, **9**
Kaziranga National Park, **2**
Keoladeo-Ghana National Park, **11**
Manas National Park, **1**
Mudumalai Wildlife Sanctuary, **7**
Nal Sarovar Bird Sanctuary, **4**
Periyar Tiger Reserve, **6**
Sasan Gir Lion Sanctuary, **3**
Sundarbans National Park, **10**

WHEN TO GO

Both India and Nepal have high and low periods for tourism, which correspond to changes in the weather as well as the timing of holidays and religious festivals. The high season (roughly November to March) brings higher prices and a flood of tourists; low season (June through August—monsoon season across most of the subcontinent) means reduced services and reduced traffic at reduced prices. Some tourist towns close down altogether during this time. Peak seasons vary by location. It is worth timing your trip to coincide with one or more of the many colorful festivals that take place every year throughout India and Nepal; for more information, see **Holidays and Festivals for 2003,** and a temperature chart, p. 881.

INDIA

India can give you just about whatever kind of weather you are looking for. The geography of this huge country is so diverse that different regions have vastly different weather, even at the same time of year.

The mountain valleys of the Himalayan foothills have intensely cold winter nights (November-January). Fall asleep in the wrong place here, and you might find yourself chipped out of the ice and put in a museum in three thousand years' time. Daytime temperatures are comfortable all year. In northern India, some mountain roads are only accessible during the summer months (June-September), generally the best time to visit the hills. The northern reaches of Himachal Pradesh and Ladakh are in rainshadow and are not hit by the monsoonal torrents. The rest of India, however, relies heavily on the mighty **monsoon.** The first of the country's two major monsoons sweeps across Western India in late May or early June sloshing into Rajasthan and Gujarat. The second wave hits the East and South pouring water over Tamil Nadu and southern Andhra Pradesh from October to November. During the monsoon season it rains most days, generally in the late afternoon as the sun begins to slip. Getting caught in a monsoonal downpour is a little like taking a hot shower with all your clothes on—probably not a treat you want to be indulging in on a daily basis. Storms are generally intense and short: after thirty minutes or so of torrential rain, the sun will emerge and steam things up again—mountain views, however, remain perpetually obscured. The monsoons can be extremely destructive, causing mudslides and floods, cutting communications and transportation lines, and causing power outages and widespread loss of temper. The mountains of Northeast India are especially hard-hit in July and August, and deadly landslides are common.

The monsoon lets up in September, when India's **cool season** begins. It takes a few months more for the Deccan plateau to dry out completely. December and January are cool, even cold, at night. Tropical ovens like Bombay and Madras go from being unbearably hot to merely uncomfortably hot, and many travelers head south to beach haunts like Goa. **Winter** (September-January) is probably the best time to visit India. By February, the heat starts to build up across the plains. April, May, and June are all very cruel months indeed, with temperatures of over 45°C (110°F). And then come the rains, and the cycle repeats itself.

NEPAL

Most tourists visit Nepal in October and November, when the countryside is fresh, the temperatures mild, the air clear, and the views breathtaking. The dry, clean air makes this best time of year for trekking. March and April are also good months to visit: huge rhododendrons are in bloom on the hillsides and the days are long and warm, without being too hot. Winter (December-February) is probably the worst time to visit: snow covers anything higher than 2000-3000m, and even Kathmandu gets damp and cold. The monsoon descends from late June to September. Most of the country is cloud-cast and beset with downpours, but western Nepal is largely in the rainshadow, and tends to be drier. Although the land turns noticeably greener during the monsoon, there are drawbacks: roads get washed out, flights get canceled, and leeches become your closest companions on trekking routes.

THINGS TO DO

From climbing the highest mountains in the world to jostling worshipers at a local temple, from partying on the beach to picnicking in the grounds of a medieval fort, you can do it all in India and Nepal. For a more detailed list of the best things to see and do, refer to the **Let's Go Picks** below and the **Highlights of the Region** box at the beginning of each chapter.

HOLY PLACES

Visit some of the subcontinent's most sacred sites and witness the rituals and traditions that have remained intact for thousands of years. Hinduism's holiest city, **Varanasi** (p. 703), is the chosen home of Lord Shiva himself, and the city where pious Hindus come to live out their last moments of earthly existence. Walk in the footsteps of the 9th-century saint, Shankara, who established India's four major *dhams* (divine abodes): **Badrinath** (p. 652) in the north, **Dwarka** (p. 217) in the west, **Rameswaram** (p. 610) in the south, and **Puri** (p. 460) in the east. Take in some of the finest Hindu temple architecture in India at **Bhubaneswar** (p. 452), or sing songs of praise to Lord Krishna in his playground, **Vrindaban** (p. 686). The holiest city for Sikhs, **Amritsar** (p. 472) houses the beautiful Golden Temple. Free yourself from worldly desire in **Bodh Gaya** (p. 137), where the Buddha attained enlightenment, or circumambulate Nepal's most important stupa in **Boudha** (p. 802). Jains head to **Mount Abu** (p. 517) and its gorgeous Dilwara temples; other religious crowd-pullers include the Sun Temple at **Konark** (p. 458), the Meenakshi Amman Temple in **Madurai** (p. 604), and the Har-ki-Pairi *ghat* in **Haridwar** (p. 639). The bloodthirsty can witness animal sacrifices to the goddess Kali at **Dakshinkali** (p. 816) in Nepal.

TREKKING AND TIGER-SPOTTING

Some of the best trekking in the world is in the Himalayas. Journey past **Mt. Everest, Annapurna,** and the **Langtang Valley** and experience head-spinning scenery as you watch the transition from Nepali villages to Tibetan hamlets (p. 851). The **Kinnaur-Spiti Road** (p. 251) in Himachal Pradesh passes through the most remote regions of India, with great hikes along the way, particularly near **Kalpa** (p. 254). Trek through **Western Sikkim** (p. 550), wander across the desert plateau of **Leh** (p. 261), or marvel at Kashmir's **Nubra Valley** (p. 269). Get up close and personal with rhinos in **Kaziranga National Park** (p. 441) or with black bears in Nepal's **Chitwan National Park** (p. 838). Elephants rumble and trumpet their way through **Jaldapara Wildlife Sanctuary** (p. 741). Tiger-hunters can enjoy the **Periyar Tiger Reserve** (p. 329) and **Corbett National Park** (p. 655), and birders will be sent into paroxysms of twitching by the world-renowned **Keoladeo Ghana National Park** (p. 497).

GOLDEN OLDIES

Delhi's **Red Fort** and **Jama Masjid** (p. 161) are an impressive introduction to the relics of India's Mughal rulers. The abandoned city of **Fatehpur Sikri** (p. 684) is an architectural time-machine that will whisk you back to Mughal times in less time than it takes you to say Shah Jahan. The erotic sculptures of **Khajuraho** (p. 368) attract visitors interested in more than just intricate stonework; the pure-of-heart get their carvings fix at the world-renowned **Ellora** and **Ajanta** caves (p. 426) in Maharashtra. Patan's **Durbar Square** (p. 793), the best of many in Nepal, is full of temples; more sacrilegious practices take place in Hampi's **Vijayanagar ruins** (p. 304), popular with homeless hippies. The **Lake Palace** in Udaipur (p. 512) encapsulates the romantic allure of Rajasthan, but it is just one of many famous forts and palaces in India, including **Gwalior Fort** (p. 384), Jaipur's **City Palace** (p. 491), the windswept **Jaisalmer Fort** (p. 532), Hyderabad's **Golconda Fort** (p. 123), and Mysore's **Maharaja's Palace** (p. 287). Oh, and then there's the **Taj Mahal** (p. 680).

BEACH BUMS

For some serious beach action, head to Goa: from the tourist-trafficked shores of **Anjuna** (p. 184) to the less-crowded beaches of **Benaulim** (p. 196) and **Palolem** (p. 198), Goa has it all. Farther north, **Dwarka's** (p. 217) shores are lapped by the waves of the Arabian Sea. Pretend you're in the south of France on the sands of **Pondicherry** (p. 583) in Tamil Nadu. The white sands of **Kovalam** (p. 320) and **Puri** (p. 460) are outdone only by the pristine shores of **Varkala** (p. 326) and temple-studded **Mahabalipuram** (p. 578). The **Andaman Islands** (p. 108), 1000km off shore in the Bay of Bengal, have been attracting larger numbers of tourists in recent years, but are still as far off the beaten track as you can get without leaving India completely.

DHARMA BUMS

Hippie hang-outs are great places to swap travel yarns, drink some tea, and make arrangements for the next leg of your journey. Among the backpacker meccas of India and Nepal are: **Manali** (p. 247) and **Dharamsala** (p. 231) in Himachal Pradesh, **Pushkar** (p. 500) in Rajasthan, **Anjuna** (p. 184) in Goa, **Kovalam** (p. 320) in Kerala, **Mahabalipuram** (p. 578) in Tamil Nadu, **Puri** (p. 460) in Orissa, **Darjeeling** (p. 744) in West Bengal, **Pokhara** (p. 824) in Nepal's Western Hills, and **Kathmandu's** Thamel district (p. 781), to name a just select few.

NO BUMS

Traveling off season is the best way to avoid the crowds, but some fascinating places see surprisingly little traffic regardless of the season: **Kausani** (p. 670) in Uttaranchal, **Ayodhya** (p. 698) in Uttar Pradesh, **Chamba** (p. 240) in Himachal Pradesh, **Bikaner** (p. 536) in Rajasthan, **Mandvi** (p. 222) and **Bhuj** (p. 218) in Gujarat, **Mandu** (p. 360) in Madhya Pradesh, **Kodaikanal** (p. 617) and **Rameswaram** (p. 610) in Tamil Nadu, and **Kirtipur** (p. 799), **Manakamana** (p. 820), and **Tansen** (p. 821) in Nepal. Other places fail to draw many travelers since they pose threats to personal safety. But if political volatility and the occasional bomb aren't enough to get you ruffled, nothing beats a night on a houseboat in **Srinagar** (p. 270) or the chance to watch the closing of the Indo-Pakistani border at **Wagah** (p. 481).

⧄ LET'S GO PICKS

BEST BENDERS: Freak out at the full-moon raves on Anjuna beach, Goa (p. 184), an experience sure to turn your mind inside out. Or be like the Beatles and join thousands of other body benders for the world-renowned International Yoga Festival along the banks of the Ganga in Rishikesh (p. 644). Twist and wind through vibrant valleys, dry, sandstone plateaux, and breathtaking Himalayan peaks along the Manali-Leh Road (p. 260), one of the highest highways in the world.

BEST PLACES TO GET DOWN: Groove and gyrate into the wee hours at The Ghetto (p. 408), one of Bombay's hippest discos, and at The Club in Bangalore (p. 283), site of MTV's South Asia launch. Or plunge into the coral-studded depths of the Bay of Bengal—teeming with angelfish, sea anemones, silver jacks, and hammerhead sharks—at the Mahatma Gandhi National Marine Park (p. 113) in the Andaman Islands.

BEST WAYS TO GET A BLISTER: Wander through mind-blowing mountainscapes and past meditative monasteries on the Local Trek in Sikkim (p. 552)—a 3-4 day hike that includes a visit to the holy Khechopalri Lake, where all your wishes are guaranteed to come true. Carouse through the lush Langtang Region (p. 864), the least crowded and least cliched of Nepal's classic trinity of treks.

BEST PLACES FOR PACKRATS: If you've ever thought twice about tossing your elephant-shaped foot scrubbers, a visit to the Raja Kelkar Museum (p. 418) in Pune or the Jai Vilas Palace (p. 386) in Gwalior will remind you that you're not alone. Better still, slurp up the sacred spit of the thousands of holy rats that pack the Karni Mata Temple (p. 542) in Deshnok, Rajasthan.

BEST PLACE TO FLAUNT YOUR MOUSTACHE: Compete for the crown of Mr. Desert (p. 532) in Jaisalmer if you think you're the man who best embodies Rajasthani masculinity with your full-bodied bristles.

BEST KEPT SECRET: Artists and pretty people commune in the calm glow of candlelight at the Villa River Cat in the secluded beach town of Mandrem (p. 192). Find it before it gets found out.

BEST TONGUE TWISTERS: The menus might not be the most inventive, but the restaurant names are hard to beat. Try the See Green Little Tibet Cafe Brick Oven Olive Pizza Restaurant in Vagator (p. 188), The Place: Touché the Sizzler (p. 413) in Pune, or the The Rum Doodle 40,000½-Feet Bar and Restaurant (p. 791) in Kathmandu, where you can share a beer or two with the mountain-high.

BEST HIGH: Grass and hippies grow wild in the Himachal hilltop town of Manali (p. 247), at the base of the Himalayas. For a milder buzz, head to the Happy Valley Tea Estate (p. 749) in the hill station retreat of Darjeeling, and watch workers pluck those world-famous leaves before your eyes.

BEST PARTIES IN TOWN: Join 13 million of your closest friends for a dip in the holy Ganga and Yamuna Rivers in Allahabad at the Kumbh Mela (p. 716)—the grandest of Hindu bathing rituals, which only comes around once every 12 years. The largest event of its kind in the world, the International Kite Festival kicks off that month (p. 206) in Ahmedabad. Pack it in at Pushkar in November, when 50,000 hump-backs and 200,000 humans squeeze into one square kilometer for the Pushkar Camel Festival (p. 500).

BEST CHANCE OF GETTING BITTEN: Prowl close to endangered (though still extremely ferocious) tigers at the Chitwan National Park (p. 838) in Nepal or the Periyar Tiger Reserve (p. 329) in Kerala. If they don't get you, head to Kashmir, where *lha-ba* healers will open wide and suck evil spirits out of your soul (p. 264).

BEST REASONS TO GET OUT OF BED IN THE MORNING: Rise at dawn to have buckets of holy water dumped over your head at the Ramanathaswamy Temple (p. 612), a once-in-a-lifetime experience sure to clear your head and absolve you of the sins of the night before. Keep dry and watch the sun crawl above Mt. Everest from the Nepalese town of Nagarkot (p. 814), or trace its ascent over the ancient *ghats* of Varanasi (p. 703), with the chime of temple bells providing the mood music.

ESSENTIALS

FACTS FOR THE TRAVELER

ENTRY REQUIREMENTS

Passport (p. 9): Required for all citizens traveling to India and Nepal.

Visa (p. 10): Required for all travelers, except citizens of India traveling to Nepal and vice versa. Visas for Nepal are issued on arrival.

Inoculations (p. 22): Visitors who have been in Africa, South America, or Trinidad and Tobago within six days of their arrival in India must have a certificate of vaccination against yellow fever.

Special Permits (p. 10) India's island territories and parts of the Northeast States require a special permit in addition to an Indian visa. For more information, see p. 9.

Work Permit (p. 10 and p. 63): Required for all foreigners working in India or Nepal. Hence the name.

EMBASSIES & CONSULATES

INDIAN CONSULAR MISSIONS

Australia: 3-5 Moonah Place, Yarralumla, **Canberra**, ACT 2600 (☎(02) 6273 3999). **Consulates:** 25 Bligh St., Level 27, **Sydney**, NSW 2000 (☎(02) 9223 9500); 195 Adelaide Terrace, Level 1, 724 Curtin Avenue East, Eagle Farm, **Queensland** 4008 (☎(07) 3260 2825); **East Perth**, WA 6004 (☎(08) 9221 1485); 15 Munro St., **Coburg**, Victoria 3058 (☎(03) 9384 0141).

Canada: 10 Springfield Rd., **Ottawa**, Ontario K1M 1C9 (☎613-744-3751). **Consulates:** 2 Bloor St. West, #5000, **Toronto**, Ontario M4W 3E2 (☎416-960-0751); 325 Howe St., 2nd fl., **Vancouver**, BC V6C 1Z7 (☎604-662-8811).

Ireland: 6 Leeson Park, **Dublin** 6 (☎(01) 497 0843).

New Zealand: 180 Molesworth St., P.O. Box 4045, **Wellington** 4045 (☎(04) 473 6390).

South Africa: 852 Schoeman St., Arcadia 0083, P.O. Box 40216, Arcadia, **Pretoria** 0007 (☎(012) 342 5392). **Consulates:** Old Station Building, 160 Pine Road, 4th fl., Durban 4001, P.O. Box 3276, **Durban** 4000 (☎(031) 304 7020); 1 Eton Road, Corner Jan Smuts Ave., Parktown 2193, P.O. Box 6805, **Johannesburg** 2000 (☎(011) 482 8487; www.indconjoburg.co.za).

UK: India House, Aldwych, **London**, WC2 B4NA (☎(020) 7836 8484; www.hcilondon.org). **Consulates:** 20 Augusta St., Jewellery Quarter, Hockley, **Birmingham** B18 6JL (☎(0121) 212 2778); 17 Rutland Sq., **Edinburgh** EH1 2BB (☎(0131) 229 2144; fax 229 2155).

US: 2536 Massachusetts Ave. NW, **Washington, D.C.** 20008 (☎202-939-9806; www.indianembassy.org); **Consulates:** 3 East 64th St., **New York**, NY 10021 (☎212-774-0600); 540 Arguello Blvd., **San Francisco**, CA 94118 (☎415-668-0662); 455 North Cityfront Plaza Dr., #850, **Chicago**, IL 60611 (☎312-595-0405); 1990 Post Oak Blvd., #600, **Houston**, TX 77056 (☎713-626-2355).

NEPALESE CONSULAR MISSIONS

Tourist visas are available upon arrival in Nepal. Don't go through the trouble of arranging a visa in advance unless you need something fancier than a tourist visa. Travelers from Ireland should contact the London embassy. The Sydney office serves New Zealanders. There is no embassy in South Africa.

Australia: 48 Mitchell St., McMahons Point, **Sydney,** NSW 2060 (☎(02) 956 8815); 18-20 Bank Pl., Ste. 23, **Melbourne** 300, Victoria.

Canada: Royal Bank Plaza, 200 Bay St., **Toronto**, Ontario M5R 1V9 (☎416-865-0110).

UK: 12a Kensington Palace Gardens, **London** W8 4QU (☎(020) 7229 1594).

US: 2131 Leroy Pl. NW, **Washington, D.C.** 20008 (☎202-667-4550; **Consulates:** 820 Second Ave., #17B, **New York**, NY 10017 (☎212-370-3988); 1500 Lakehorse Drive, **Chicago**, IL 60610 (☎312-263-1250); 909 Montgomery St., #400, **San Francisco,** CA 94133 (☎415-434-1111); 16250 Dallas Pkwy, #110, **Dallas,** TX 75248 (☎214-931-1212).

CONSULAR SERVICES IN INDIA AND NEPAL

Most countries have embassies in **Delhi** (see p. 153). Many have consulates in **Mumbai** (see p. 398), and a few in **Chennai** (see p. 565) and **Calcutta** (see p. 729). In Nepal, all foreign diplomatic missions are in **Kathmandu** (see p. 779).

TOURIST OFFICES

The Indian government's tourist information offices around the world are a good source of glossy brochures and maps. The **Tourist Information Department** has its main offices in New Delhi (see p. 152) and branches in most major cities. Most states also operate their own independent **Tourist Development Corporations,** offering information on local sights, transportation, guided tours, hotel bookings, etc. Standards vary enormously from one office to another: many are excellent, some are utterly useless. *Let's Go* lists details for both Government of India and state-run Tourist Information Offices in the Practical Information listings for each town.

Australia: Level 1, 17 Castlereagh St., **Sydney**, NSW 2000. (☎02 232 1600).

Canada: 60 Bloor St. (West), Ste. 1003, **Toronto,** Ontario M4W 3B8. (☎416- 962-3787).

UK: 7 Cork St., London W1X 2LW. (☎0207 437 3677).

US: 3550 Wilshire Blvd., Rm. 204, **Los Angeles** CA 90010. (☎213-380-8855); 30 Rockefeller Plaza, Ste. 15, North Mezzanine, **New York** NY 10112. (☎212-586-4903).

DOCUMENTS & FORMALITIES

PASSPORTS

REQUIREMENTS. Unless you are a president, king, queen, or refugee, you will not get far without a passport. India and Nepal won't let you in if your passport is due to expire in less than six months; returning home with an expired passport is illegal and may result in a fine.

PHOTOCOPIES. Before you go, photocopy the page of your passport that contains your photograph, passport number, and other identifying information, along with other important documents (visas, travel insurance policies, airplane tickets, and traveler's check serial numbers). Carry at least one set of copies in a safe place apart from the originals and leave another set at home with someone you can call when you lose everything. Consulates also recommend that you carry an expired passport or an official copy of your birth certificate in your baggage separate from other documents.

ESSENTIALS

LOST PASSPORTS. If you lose your passport, immediately notify the local police and your home country's nearest embassy or consulate. This is when you start to feel really happy about having photocopies of the passport you have just lost (see above). To expedite its replacement, you will need to know all the numbers and dates printed on your old passport, and you will also need to show identification and proof of citizenship. In some cases, a replacement will take weeks to process, and it may be valid only for a limited time. Any visas stamped in your old passport will be irretrievably lost. In an emergency, ask for immediate temporary traveling papers that will allow you to get home. You will occasionally have to surrender your passport to a foreign government official, but if you don't get it back within a reasonable length of time, inform your embassy.

NEW PASSPORTS. Citizens of Australia, Canada, Ireland, New Zealand, the United Kingdom, and the United States can apply for a passport at the nearest post office, passport office, or court of law. Citizens of South Africa can apply for a passport at the nearest office of Foreign Affairs. Any new passport or renewal applications must be filed well in advance of the departure date, although most passport offices offer rush services for a very steep fee. Citizens living abroad who need a passport or renewal services should contact the nearest consular service of their home country.

VISAS, INVITATIONS, & WORK PERMITS

VISAS

All travelers to India and Nepal need a visa. Nepalese visas are issued on arrival and must be bought with US dollars. Indian visas must be arranged in advance, through your nearest embassy or consulate. Entering India or Nepal to study or work requires a special visa. For more information, see **Studying Abroad,** p. 61.

INDIA. Tourist visas permit six months or one year stays and normally allow for multiple entries. Other options include a one-year visa for students, journalists, or business travelers. When applying for a visa, make sure your passport is valid six months beyond the date of intended return.

It is fastest to apply through the embassy in your home country. You'll need to fill out an application form and provide your current passport, at least two passport photos, and a visa processing fee, which varies from country to country. The process can take anywhere between a few hours and a few weeks. **Contact your nearest embassy well in advance of your trip** for more information.

SPECIAL PERMITS. Certain areas require a special permit in addition to an Indian visa. These restricted zones are some of India's most beautiful and interesting areas.

Northeast India: Many areas, such as Assam, Meghalaya, and Tripura, are now open to tourists. A permit is no longer needed for these three states, but it is still a good idea to consult your embassy about the political situation, especially in Assam, before visiting. Owing to tribal insurgencies and fears of a conflict with China, the other 4 northeastern states—**Arunachal Pradesh, Nagaland, Manipur,** and **Mizoram**—require permits. Acquiring one requires patience and perseverance. A minimum of 4 people are required to travel together, and a government-approved travel agency must sponsor the group (Rs300-400). The permits themselves are free and allow 5-15 days of travel, depending on the state. **Restricted area permits are available only at the Ministry of Home Affairs in New Delhi** (see p. 153). Permits can take anywhere from 2 days to a lifetime to process. (For more info., see p. 450.)

West Bengal: Some areas around Darjeeling require a 15-day permit, issued to individuals or groups. The Home Department of West Bengal in Calcutta issues the permits.

Sikkim: Sikkim borders China; and the Indian government regards it as a military buffer zone. All foreigners require a permit. Permits allow travel as far north as Phodang and Yuksam. They can be extended at the Commissioner's Office in Gangtok in special circumstances. For North Sikkim, an inner-line permit is required. This is issued through tour companies to groups of 4 or more. A guide must accompany the group; the minimum charge is US$30-50 per day, including guide. The permit takes at least one work day to process and is available only in Gangtok. See **Sikkim Permits,** p. 545.

Andaman and Nicobar Islands: All foreign visitors to the Andamans require permits (valid for 30 days). These are now issued on arrival. The Nicobar Islands are off-limits to non-Indian citizens. See **The Andaman Islands,** p. 111.

Bhutan: Though officially an independent country, Bhutan's foreign policy and immigration procedures are controlled by India. The number of visas to Bhutan is limited by a quota system and group tours are much more likely to receive one than individuals. Solo travelers are required to spend US$240 per day—this amount decreases slightly with larger groups. To apply for a visa, contact a Bhutanese embassy or a travel agent.

NEPAL. Anybody with a passport and a photo can get a Nepalese visa upon arrival at the airport in Kathmandu or at any of the land border crossings. The fee (US$30 for a 60-day, single-entry visa, more for multiple-entry visas); **this fee must be paid in US dollars.** Any Nepalese consulate or embassy can issue visas for up to 60 days, although this can often be extended once you're in Nepal. The Department of Immigration, Tridevi Marg, Thamel, Kathmandu (☎ (01) 470650 or 494273), grants extensions for up to four months. Apply for a visa extension a day or two before you really need it. Extensions are no longer granted while you wait.

WORK PERMITS. Entering India or Nepal to study or work requires a special visa. For more information, see **Alternatives to Tourism,** p. 63.

SURROUNDING COUNTRIES. Several of the countries surrounding India and Nepal are politically volatile; it's always a good idea to check for up-to-date information before packing your bags and setting out for the border. **As of May 2002, most governments were advising their nationals to avoid all travel to Pakistan.**

Bangladesh: Passengers arriving in Dhaka by air can get a 15-day visa at the airport. Single-entry visas are valid for 90 days. Visa rules change frequently. For the latest contact a Bangladeshi embassy: 56 Ring Rd., Lajpat Nagar III, **Delhi** (☎ (011) 683 4668); 9 Circus Ave., **Calcutta** (☎ (033) 247 5208); Chakrapath, Maharajgunj, **Kathmandu** (☎ (01) 414943); 35 Endevour St., PO Box 5, Red Hill, A.C.T. 2603, **Canberra** (☎ (02) 6295-3328; fax 6295-5331); 275 Bank St., Ste. 302, **Ottawa,** Ontario K2P 2LP (☎ (613) 236-0138; fax 567-3213); 28 Queen's Gate, **London** SW7 53A (☎ (020) 7584 0081; fax 7225 2130); 3510 International Drive NW, **Washington** DC 20008 (☎ (202) 244-0183; fax 244-5366).

Myanmar (Burma): Visas are valid for a single entry of up to 28 days. The embassy in India is at 3/50-F Nyaya Marg, Chanakyapuri, **Delhi** (☎ (011) 600 251) and in Nepal at Chakupat, Patan City Gate, **Kathmandu,** PO Box 2437 (☎ (01) 512788 or 524788). The only border crossings into Myanmar are from Thailand and China.

China: To travel to **Tibet** from Nepal, you need a Chinese visa. These are almost impossible to obtain at the embassy in Kathmandu but are easily available through the embassy in Delhi. Visas are valid for 30 days and can sometimes be extended. In Kathmandu, you need to contact one of the many agencies specializing in tours to Tibet. **Star Tours and Travel,** Thamel, Tridevi Marg (☎ 423742 or 423446), and **Royal Mountain Trekking,** Durbar Marg, have frequent departures for Lhasa, and low prices. Permits take between a few hours and several days to process. The standard deal consists of a 5-day drive to Lhasa and includes all the necessary permits, as well as 4 nights' dorm lodging in Nyalam, Lhatse, Gyantse, and Shigatse. US$240 might seem a lot to pay, but it's the cheapest way of getting into Tibet. Once you are in Lhasa, you are allowed to stay for a maximum for 7 days. You have to reserve your return ticket when you book. A landcruiser back to Kathmandu costs about US$60. **Flying** to Lhasa is also an option, if you have US$390 you want to get rid of. **Do not attempt to enter Tibet on your own.** The Chinese Embassy in India is at 50-D Shantipath, Chanakyapuri, **Delhi** (☎(011) 6871585) and in Nepal, Baluwatar, **Kathmandu** (☎(01) 413916).

Pakistan: A visa is necessary for entry into Pakistan. These are normally valid for one month. Pakistani embassies: 2/50-G Shantipath, Chanakyapuri, **Delhi** (☎(011) 600603) and Maharajganj, **Kathmandu** (☎(01) 374012). **As of May 2002, most governments were advising their nationals to avoid all travel to Pakistan.**

Sri Lanka: For stays of up to 30 days, citizens of most European countries, the US, Canada, and Australia will be granted free visas on arrival with a confirmed ticket on a flight out of the country and enough funds to support themselves during their stay.

Thailand: Citizens from most European countries and the US, Canada, and Australia do not need visas if they plan to be in Thailand for less than 30 days. Visas are necessary for longer stays. In India: 56-N Nyaya Marg, Chanakyapuri, **Delhi** (☎(011) 611 8103). In Nepal: Maharajganj, **Kathmandu** (☎(01) 371408).

IDENTIFICATION

When you travel, always carry two or more forms of identification on your person, including at least one photo ID; a passport combined with a driver's license or birth certificate is usually adequate. Many establishments, especially banks, may require several IDs to cash traveler's checks. Never carry all your forms of ID together; split them up and photocopy them in case of theft or loss.

TEACHER, STUDENT & YOUTH IDENTIFICATION. The **International Student Identity Card (ISIC),** the most widely accepted form of student ID, provides discounts on sights, accommodations, food, and transport. The ISIC is preferable to an institution-specific card (such as a university ID) because it is more likely to be recognized and honored abroad. All cardholders have access to a 24hr. emergency helpline for medical, legal, and financial emergencies (in North America call 877-370-ISIC, elsewhere call US collect +1 715-345-0505), and US cardholders are also eligible for insurance benefits (see **Insurance,** p. 28). Applicants must be degree-seeking students of a secondary or post-secondary school and must be at least 12 years old. Because of the proliferation of fake ISICs, some services (particularly airlines) require additional proof of student identity, such as a school ID or a letter attesting to your student status, signed by your registrar and stamped with your school seal.

The **International Teacher Identity Card (ITIC)** offers teachers the same insurance coverage as well as similar but limited discounts. To receive an ITIC, you must prove that you worked at a recognized educational establishment for at least 18 hours per week. For travelers who are 25 years old or under but are not students, the **International Youth Travel Card** (**IYTC;** formerly the **GO 25** Card) offers many of the same benefits as the ISIC.

Each of these identity cards costs US$22 or equivalent. ISIC and ITIC cards are valid for roughly one and a half academic years; IYTC cards are valid for one year from the date of issue. Many student travel agencies (see p. 42) issue the cards, including STA Travel in Australia and New Zealand; Travel CUTS in Canada; USIT in the Republic of Ireland and Northern Ireland; SASTS in South Africa; Campus

Travel and STA Travel in the UK; and Council Travel and STA Travel in the US. For a listing of issuing agencies, or for more information, contact the **International Student Travel Confederation (ISTC),** Herengracht 479, 1017 BS Amsterdam, Netherlands (☎ +31 20 421 28 00; fax 421 28 10; istcinfo@istc.org; www.istc.org)

MONEY MATTERS

CURRENCY AND EXCHANGE

The charts below are based on May 2002 exchange rates. Check a newspaper or the web (finance.yahoo.com or www.bloomberg.com) for the latest rates.

THE INDIAN RUPEE

The Indian rupee (Rs, IRs in the Nepal section of the book), is divided into 100 paise (p.). Coins are issued in denominations of p.10, 25, 50, Rs1, 2, and 5. Bills come in values of Rs1, 2, 5, 10, 20, 50, 100, and 500.

INDIAN RUPEE (Rs)		
US$1 = Rs49.10	Rs100 = US$2.03
CDN$1 = Rs31.59	Rs100 = CDN$3.16
UK£1 = Rs71.52	Rs100 = UK£1.39
AUS$1 = Rs26.96	Rs100 = AUS$3.71
NZ$1 = Rs22.65	Rs100 = NZ$4.42
SAR1 = Rs4.85	Rs100 = SAR20.63
EUR€1 = Rs44.79	Rs100 = EUR€2.23
NRS1 = Rs0.66	Rs100 = NRS151.68

THE NEPALESE RUPEE

The Nepalese rupee (Rs, NRs in the India section of the book), is divided into 100 paise (p.). Money comes in the following shapes and sizes. Coins: p.1, 2, 5, 10, 25, 50, Rs1, and 2. Bills: Rs1, 2, 5, 10, 25, 50, 100, 500, and 1000. Collect the whole set, and trade them with your friends.

NEPALESE RUPEE (Rs)		
US$1 = Rs77.86	Rs100 = US$1.28
CDN$1 = Rs50.69	Rs100 = CDN$1.97
UK£1 = Rs113.28	Rs100 = UK£0.88
AUS$1 = Rs43.24	Rs100 = AUS$2.31
NZ$1 = Rs36.48	Rs100 = NZ$2.75
SAR1 = Rs7.69	Rs100 = SAR12.97
EUR€1 = Rs71.73	Rs100 = EUR€1.39
IRS1 = Rs1.59	Rs100 = 62.89IRS

Neither the Indian nor the Nepalese rupee may be exported. There are 24hr. branches of the national banks at international airports. British pounds and US dollars are the best currencies to bring with you; others will not always be easy to exchange. Avoid changing money at luxury hotels and restaurants, which often give outrageous rates and high commission rates. The national **State Bank of India** and the **Nepal Bank Ltd.** are generally the best places to change money. Not all branches change foreign currency—it is usually worth tracking down the biggest branch in town. In smaller towns it can be difficult to find any bank set up to deal with foreign currency. Changing money takes a long time and

ESSENTIALS

requires great reserves of patience. You should aim to take part in this farce as seldom as possible. In India, get an **encashment certificate** as proof of the transaction whenever you change money. This is sometimes demanded when paying for plane and train tickets or large bills in rupees, and you will need it if you want to change any left-over rupees back into hard currency before you leave. Foreign banks, like ANZ Grindlays and HSBC, are faster than their competitors. **Bank of Baroda** (in India) offers cash advances on Visa and MasterCard at most of its many locations. Banking hours are short (M-F 10am-2pm, Sa 10am-noon). ATMs are available only in major cities.

Since you lose money on each transaction, it's a good idea convert in large sums. You should carry small denominations (the equivalent of US$50 or less) for when you are forced to exchange money at lousy rates. Coins and small bills are essential for maintaining sanity, since nobody ever admits to having change.

In some places. vendors prefer Western currency will actually be preferred to local money - avoid using Western money when you can. Throwing the big bucks about for preferential treatment attracts thieves and encourages locals to jack up prices.

TRAVELER'S CHECKS

Traveler's checks (**American Express** and **Thomas Cook** are the most widely recognized in India and Nepal) are one of the safest and least troublesome means of carrying funds. Many banks and agencies sell them for a small commission. Check issuers provide refunds if the checks are lost or stolen, and many provide additional services, such as toll-free refund hotlines abroad, emergency message services, and stolen credit card assistance. Banks in some smaller towns may not be able to change traveler's checks.

While traveling, keep check receipts and a record of which checks you've cashed separate from the checks themselves. Also leave a list of check numbers with someone at home. Never countersign checks until you're ready to cash them, and always bring your passport with you to cash them. If your checks are lost or stolen, immediately contact a refund center (of the company that issued your checks) to be reimbursed; they may require a police report verifying the loss or theft. Less-touristed areas may not have refund centers at all, in which case you might have to wait to be reimbursed. Ask about toll-free refund hotlines and the location of refund centers when purchasing checks, and always carry emergency cash.

American Express: Checks available with commission at select banks and all AmEx offices. US residents can also buy checks by phone (☎888-887-8986) or online (www.aexp.com). AAA (see p. 52) offers commission-free checks to its members. Checks available in US, Australian, British, Canadian, Japanese, and Euro currencies. *Cheques for Two* can be signed by either of 2 people traveling together. For more information contact AmEx's service centers: In the US and Canada (☎800-221-7282); in the UK (☎0800 521 313); in Australia (☎800 25 19 02); in New Zealand (☎0800 441 068); in India (☎(011) 614 5920); elsewhere US collect (☎+1 801-964-6665).

Visa: Checks available (generally with commission) at banks worldwide. To find the nearest issuing location call Visa's service centers: In the US (☎800-227-6811); in the UK (☎0800 89 50 78); elsewhere UK collect (☎+44 020 7937 8091). Checks available in US, British, Canadian, Japanese, and Euro currencies.

Travelex/Thomas Cook: In the US and Canada (☎800-287-7362); in the UK (☎0800 62 21 01); in India (☎(011) 335 6571); elsewhere call UK collect (☎+44 1733 31 89 50).

FANTASTIC PLASTIC

Credit cards are gaining acceptance in South Asia, but they are still hardly recognized outside the big cities. In places like Delhi and Mumbai, many expensive hotels and restaurants accept payment by card, but budget hotels will want cash. Where they are accepted, credit cards offer superior exchange rates—up to 5% better than the retail rate used by banks. **American Express, MasterCard** (a.k.a. **Euro-Card** or **Access in Europe**), and **Visa** (a.k.a. **Carte Bleue** or **Barclaycard**) are the cards most likely to be accepted in the subcontinent.

Credit cards are also useful for **cash advances,** which allow you to withdraw rupees from associated banks and ATMs in major cities. However, transaction fees for all credit card advances (up to US$10 per advance, plus 2-3% extra on foreign transactions after conversion, plus possible foreign transaction fees) tend to make credit cards a more costly way of withdrawing cash than ATMs or traveler's checks. In an emergency, however, the transaction fee may prove worth the cost. To be eligible for an advance, you'll need to get a **Personal Identification Number (PIN)** from your credit card company (see **Cash Cards (ATM Cards),** below).

Credit card scams are common in India and Nepal. Be cautious when purchasing items with a credit card. Make sure that the card remains in view at all times to ensure that the vendor does not make extra imprints. Also, if you're planning to ship goods through a shop owner, don't believe him when he says he won't forward the credit slip for payment until you've received the goods. For more info on how to get ripped off, see p. 18.

CASH CARDS (ATM CARDS)

Major cities such as Delhi, Mumbai, Chennai, Calcutta, Kathmandu, and Pokhara, have a sprinkling of ATMs.

The two major international money networks are **Cirrus** (to locate ATMs US ☎800-424-7787 or www.mastercard.com) and **Visa/PLUS** (US ☎800-843-7587 or www.visa.com). Most ATMs charge a small transaction fee.

Visa TravelMoney allows you to access money from any ATM on the Visa/PLUS network. You deposit an amount before you travel (plus a small administrative fee) and can then withdraw up to that sum. TravelMoney cards are available at Travelex/Interpayment locations worldwide; US residents may also obtain them through AAA offices (see p. 52) or by calling ☎877-394-2247. **American Express Express Cash** allows AmEx cardholders to withdraw money from American Express ATMs worldwide. To enroll, US cardholders may call ☎800-227-4669.

HELP—I'VE RUN OUT OF MONEY!

This is not something you want to do. The easiest and cheapest solution is to have someone back home make a deposit to your credit card or cash (ATM) card. Failing that, consider one of the following options.

WIRING MONEY. It is possible to arrange a bank money transfer, which means asking a bank back home to wire money to a bank in India or Nepal. This is the cheapest way to transfer cash, but it's also the slowest (at least two working days). Note that some banks only release your funds in local currency, potentially sticking you with a poor exchange rate. Wiring money to India and Nepal can be a bureaucratic fuss. Foreign banks such as CitiBank and ANZ Grindlays are the most reliable; be precise about the branch you want the money sent to. Money transfer services like Western Union are faster and more convenient—but much pricier. **Western Union** has many locations worldwide. To find one, visit www.westernunion.com, or call ☎800-325-6000 in the **US,** ☎800-235-0000 in **Canada,** ☎0800 83

ESSENTIALS

38 33 in the **UK,** ☎800 501 500 in **Australia,** ☎800 27 0000 in **New Zealand,** ☎0860 100031 in **South Africa,** ☎(011) 336 8771 in **India,** ☎(01) 418738 in **Nepal.** Money transfer services are also at American Express and Thomas Cook offices.

FEDERAL EXPRESS. Some people send money abroad in cash via FedEx to avoid transmission fees and taxes. This method is illegal, and FedEx won't take responsibility if your money is lost. In the **US** and **Canada,** ☎800-463-3339; in the **UK,** ☎0800 12 38 00; in **Ireland,** ☎800 535 800; in **Australia,** ☎13 26 10; in **New Zealand,** ☎0800 733 339; and in **South Africa,** ☎011 923 8000.

US STATE DEPARTMENT (US CITIZENS ONLY). In dire emergencies, good old Uncle Sam will forward money within hours to the nearest consular office, which will then disburse it according to instructions for a US$15 fee. If you wish to use this service, you must contact the **Overseas Citizens Service** division of the US State Department (☎202-647-5225; nights, Sundays, and holidays ☎202-647-4000).

COSTS

The cost of your trip will depend on where you go, how you travel, and where you stay. The single biggest cost of your trip will probably be your round-trip (return) **airfare** to India or Nepal (see **Getting to India and Nepal: By Plane,** p. 40). Once you get there, travel in India or Nepal is extremely cheap: depending on where you visit and your definition of comfort, between US$5-20 per person per day. Spending just a few dollars more on accommodations leads to huge gains in comfort. **Accommodation** starts at about US$2-3 per night for a grim room with shared bathroom and squat toilet. For US$10 you can normally find a decent-sized, clean, well-aired room, often with extra little luxuries such as clean sheets, seat toilets, and toilet paper. International-standard five-star luxury hotels are only in the major cities. A basic **meal** costs under US$1, but quality increases dramatically if you spend a little more.

ECONOMICS AND ETHICS

Foreigners' fat wallets attract obnoxious **touts**, armies of **beggars**, and silver-tongued **con men**. For budget travelers, these shenanigans can be exhausting and infuriating. After a tout has lied to you about a hotel to get you into the one his brother owns, or after a rickshaw-*wallah* has demanded five times the standard fare, you may find yourself arguing over small change simply as a matter of "principle."

However, Western travelers trying to pinch rupees should remember how much their money means to the destitute Indians and Nepalis they are dealing with. Even austere budget travelers spend as much in a day as their hotel watchman or rickshaw-*wallah* earns in a month.

TIPPING, BARGAINING, AND BAKSHEESH

"Baksheesh" is usually translated as a "tip," but this broad concept includes everything from simple gifts to outright bribes. Baksheesh can be a bribe given to a railway porter to find a seat on a "full" train; it can also be the small change given to a beggar. **Small tips** are expected for restaurant service, "coolie" (porter) service, and unofficial tour guides. There is no need to tip taxi or rickshaw drivers. Tips depend on your level of satisfaction and usually run between Rs1 and Rs20, not following any particular percentage rule. Most Indians and Nepalis expect great tips from foreigners, but don't be swayed by pleading groans. If your first offer is met with a quick roll of the head signifying "OK," then you have done well.

THE ART OF THE DEAL In India and Nepal, bargaining isn't just practical knowledge, it's an art form. With a little practice, you may leave the country a master. Vendors and drivers will automatically quote you a price that is much too high; it's up to you to get them down to a reasonable rate. With the following tips and a bit of finesse, you might be able to impress even the most hardened of hawkers:

1. Bargaining needn't be a fierce struggle. Quite the opposite: good-natured wrangling with a cheerful smile may prove your biggest weapon.

2. Use your poker face. The less your face betrays your interest in an item, the better. If you touch an item to inspect it, the vendor will be sure to "encourage" you to name a price or make a purchase. Cooing over that plastic elephant or coming back again and again to admire that marvellous mother-of-pearl Taj Mahal are good ways to ensure that you pay a higher price. Be cool.

3. Know when to bargain. In most cases, it's quite clear when it's appropriate to bargain. Taxi and auto-rickshaw fares and things for sale in outdoor markets are all fair game. Don't bargain on prepared or pre-packaged foods on the street or in restaurants. In some stores, signs will indicate whether fixed prices prevail. When in doubt, ask tactfully, "Is that your lowest price?" or whether there are discounts.

4. Never underestimate the power of peer pressure. Bargaining with more than one person at a time—particularly rickshaw-*wallahs*— always leads to higher prices. Bargaining in the company of other travelers - especially travelers who are discouraging you from buying - can drop a price dramatically.

5. Know when to turn away. Refuse any vendor or rickshaw driver who bargains rudely, and move to another vendor if the one you are dealing with will not be reasonable. However, bargaining without an intention to buy is a major *faux pas*. It is extraordinarily rude to agree on a price and then decline. If you are given a high price, turn away slowly with a smile and a "thank you;" the price may plummet.

6. Start low. Never feel guilty offering a ridiculously low price. That's how bargaining is done.

TOUTS, MIDDLEMEN, AND SCAMS

Touts surround travelers at airports, bus stands and train stations, or accost them on the streets of the tourist ghettos, offering deals on transportation, currency exchange, drugs, or any other service rupees can buy. They are pushy and will try to convince you to buy something you don't want; they count on foreigners to be too naive or too polite to refuse. Many touts are equipped with a guilt-trip line tailored to your demographic group: "My friend, one question: Why don't you white Americans like to talk to us Indians?" Don't let these guilt trips get to you—touts are only interested in your money.

It's hard to find a hotel without a tout getting involved; you'll usually be approached as soon as you get off the plane, bus, or train. Hotels pay touts, taxi drivers, and rickshaw-*wallahs*, commission to gather tourists and then add commission to your hotel bill. If the hotel doesn't pay commission, touts will tell you it's full, closed, or open only to people with three heads; don't believe them. Be firm—decide on your hotel before you arrive in town and have a taxi or rickshaw-*wallah* take you there directly.

In major tourist centers, you'll often meet people who offer tours or invite you to visit their homes or shops. Unless you have asked to go somewhere, you are under no obligation to follow them or pay them.

ESSENTIALS

Many **travel agents** near train stations are little more than touts behind desks. They are notorious for giving out false information, charging hefty commissions, and selling tickets for trains that don't exist. Most Indians buy train tickets directly from the station; you will save money if you follow their lead and **eliminate the middleman.**

Another annoyance at many monuments and temples are the unofficial **guides** who spout drivel at you, refuse to leave you alone, and then have the cheek to demand *baksheesh* for their unwanted services. If you stay calm and say clearly, "No thank you, I do not want a guide," exactly once, then they will leave you alone when you begin to ignore them. It is better to book a guide through a tourist office or other government organization than wait to be approached.

Be cautious about accepting **food or drinks** from a stranger. Con men have drugged travelers and then robbed them. Bear in mind, however, that offers of food and drink are one of the primary forms of Indian hospitality. If you don't feel comfortable accepting food or drink from strangers, a gracious "the doctor told me I shouldn't have that" is a good way to turn down an offer without offending anyone.

WARNING. Locals in Delhi, Jaipur, Agra, and Kathmandu sometimes accost travelers to chat about tourism, your home country, their city, and cricket. Having thus established themselves as friends, they offer their hospitality: "You're a guest in my country. The least I can do is invite you to my place for some food." Nine times out of ten, their "place" is a jewelry, gems, or carpet shop. Eventually, travelers are offered the opportunity to carry US$500 to US$10,000 worth of jewelry abroad to be handed over to an "overseas partner." In return, these dealers offer a 100% commission. The scheme is straightforward. Export laws impose a 250% tariff on gems and jewelry, but foreigners with tourist visas may carry a certain amount of gems and jewelry out of the country. So, by having tourists do their exporting for them at 100% commission, gem dealers save a lot of money. First, however, they will insist you give them your **credit card** number for "insurance purposes," since corrupt customs officials sometimes confiscate valuables. The gem dealers call it "couriering," and insist that it's done all the time. As soon as you hand over your card, they charge hundreds of dollars to your account. **Export schemes** sound too good to be true because they are—stay away from them. If you ever feel uncomfortable in a store, just leave, even if it seems rude or awkward. (Also see **Fantastic Plastic**, p. 15.)

BEGGING

Thirty rupees is more than many Indians see in a week. **Carry coins and one- or two-rupee bills**—these are appropriate baksheesh for beggars. For children, give food instead of money—a gift of biscuits is more likely to benefit the child than cash, which often goes straight into the hands of a ringleader. It is customary to give to beggars at pilgrimage sites, to *sadhus* (wandering Hindu holy men who survive by begging), and to transvestites on trains. Don't give to cute, healthy kids who approach with requests for rupees, coins, or pens. These are not beggars, but regular schoolchildren trying their luck. You can recognize them by their shoes—no legitimate Indian beggar has shoes.

Many Indians are concerned that foreigners' handouts are creating a culture of laziness and low self-esteem. A more responsible way to distribute you charity is to donate to a reputable local aid organization.

SAFETY & SECURITY

PERSONAL SAFETY

India and Nepal are generally safe; rates of crime, especially violent crime, are extremely low. The sheer mass of people in India means that you will almost always be surrounded, and most Indians and Nepalis are well-meaning, often willing to go out of their way to help a foreigner in trouble. What goes on in public is everyone's business, for better or worse.

BLENDING IN. Unless you look South Asian, your chances of blending in are approximately zero. The best you can do is to pretend you know what you're doing and to try not to stand out too much. **Dress modestly.** Don't flaunt money or jewelry in public. Knowing the words for "hello," "thank you," "yes/no," and "where" in the **local language** (see **Appendix,** p. 881), may gain the sympathy of someone who would not help you otherwise. For more information, see **Customs and Etiquette,** p. 93.

The gawking camera-toter is a more obvious target for robbery than the low-profile traveler. Familiarize yourself with your surroundings before setting out; if you must check a map on the street, duck into a shop or restaurant first. If you are traveling alone, be sure someone at home knows your itinerary. If you are female, never admit that you're traveling alone.

EXPLORING. Find out about unsafe neighborhoods from tourist offices, from the manager of your hotel, or from a trustworthy local. Whenever possible, *Let's Go* warns of unsafe areas, but only your eyes can tell you for sure when you've wandered into one. When walking at night, stick to busy, well-lit streets and avoid dark alleyways. Do not cross through parks, parking lots, or other large, deserted areas. Look for children playing, women walking in the open, and other signs of an active community. If you feel uncomfortable, leave quickly and directly, but don't allow fear of the unknown to turn you into a hermit. Careful exploration will build confidence and make your trip more rewarding.

SELF DEFENSE. A good self-defense course will give you concrete ways to react to unwanted advances. **Impact, Prepare, and Model Mugging** can refer you to local self-defense courses in the US (☎ 800-345-5425). Visit the website at www.impact-safety.org for a list of nearby chapters. Workshops (2-3hr.) start at US$50; full courses run US$350-500.

TRANSPORTATION. Planes and trains are the safest way to travel in the subcontinent. Although the railways are extensive, they don't run to some of the smaller towns, and they don't exist at all in Nepal. Buses are the only alternative in these situations. However, road rules are nonexistent, and bus accidents are common, particularly in hilly or mountainous regions. Getting on a bus is the most dangerous thing most tourists do in India **Take trains whenever possible.** Indian bus drivers, who drive sometimes drunk and always recklessly, are guys who have a hard time buying a life insurance policy. Minibuses are deadliest of all and almost never worth the money you'll save over a full-size. When on foot, be very careful of the traffic, which is generally chaotic—most vehicles will not stop for pedestrians. For info on the perils of **hitchhiking,** see p. 47.

WILD WILDLIFE. Watch out for stray animals; rabies (see p. 27) is far more prevalent in India and Nepal than in Western countries. The rhesus **monkeys** that hover in the treetops above temples are aggressive, and they snatch food and bite. If a stray **dog** growls at you, pick up a stone and act like you're about to throw it. Even if you can't find a stone, just pretending to pick one up usually scares them away. Also be wary of **rats,** both indoors and out. Since rats are attracted to crumbs, keep food away from your bed. Finally, India's larger wildlife--**buffalo, elephants, tigers**--can gore, trample, and maul. This will really ruin your holiday.

TERRORISM AND POLITICAL INSTABILITY. Pakistan and India flirt with war every few years over the state of Jammu and Kashmir. Most governments advise their citizens not to travel there even in times of relative peace. Violent secessionist groups **have captured or killed tourists.** For more information, see **Srinagar,** p. 270. Extremist groups based in Pakistan attacked American interests in Calcutta and Karachi in 2002. **Do not linger outside US consulates. (See the warning box,** p. 82.) Hindu-Muslim violence led to 1000 deaths in Gujarat in early 2002 (See **This Year's News,** p. 81). The situation remains unstable, and travelers are advised to avoid Gujarat and areas around the contested holy city of Ayodhya in Uttar Pradesh, until tensions subside. Banditry and organized thuggery continue to make parts of Bihar dangerous. The **ongoing Maoist rebellion in Nepal** makes many areas outside the Kathmandu Valley off-limits for safety-conscious travelers, although tourists have not yet been targeted (see p. 760). The box on **travel advisories** (p. 20) lists offices to contact and webpages to visit for an up-to-date list of government travel advisories.

TRAVEL ADVISORIES. The following government offices provide travel information and advisories by telephone, by fax, or via the web:

Australian Department of Foreign Affairs and Trade: ☎ 1300 55 51 35; fax-back service 02 6261 1299; www.dfat.gov.au.

Canadian Department of Foreign Affairs and International Trade (DFAIT): In Canada and the US call 800-267-6788, elsewhere call +1 613-944-6788; www.dfait-maeci.gc.ca. Call for their free booklet, *Bon Voyage...But.*

New Zealand Ministry of Foreign Affairs: ☎ 04 494 8500; fax 494 8506; www.mft.govt.nz/trav.html.

United Kingdom Foreign and Commonwealth Office: ☎ 020 7008 0232; fax 7008 0155; www.fco.gov.uk.

US Department of State: ☎ 202-647-5225, faxback service 202-647-3000; http://travel.state.gov. For *A Safe Trip Abroad,* call 202-512-1800.

FINANCIAL SECURITY

PROTECTING YOUR VALUABLES. Bring as little with you as possible. Leave expensive watches, jewelry, cameras, and electronic equipment (like your Discman) at home; chances are you'd only break them, lose them, or get sick of lugging them around anyway. Buy a few combination **padlocks** to secure your belongings either in your pack—which you should **never leave unattended**—or in a hostel or train station locker. **Carry as little cash as possible;** instead carry traveler's checks and ATM/credit cards, keeping them in a **money belt**—not a "fanny pack" (or "bumbag")—along with your passport and ID cards. **Keep a small cash reserve separate from your primary stash.** This should consist of about US$150 in hard currency (American dollars or UK pounds) sewn into or stored in the depths of your pack, along with your traveler's check numbers and important photocopies. Keep a small amount of money in your pockets so that you don't need to sift through a thick wad of cash every time you buy a bottle of ThumsUp.

CON ARTISTS & PICKPOCKETS. Con artists often work in groups. Children are among the most effective. They possess innumerable ruses. Beware of certain classics: sob stories that require money, rolls of bills "found" on the street, mustard spilled (or saliva spit) onto your shoulder to distract you while they snatch your bag. Don't hand your passport to someone whose authority you question (ask to accompany them to a police station if they insist), and **don't ever let your passport out of your sight.** Similarly, don't let your bag out of sight; never trust a "station-porter" who insists on carrying your bag or stowing it in the baggage compartment or a "new friend" who offers to guard your bag while you buy a train ticket or use the restroom. Beware of **pickpockets** in city crowds, especially on public transportation. Also, be alert in public telephone booths. If you must say your calling card number, do so very quietly; if you punch it in, make sure no one can look over your shoulder. For more low-down on low-lifes, see **Touts, Middlemen, and Scams,** p. 17.

ACCOMMODATION & TRANSPORTATION. Most **hotels** have locks on the doors, but this doesn't mean you will be the only one with access to your room. Hotel staff can get into your room, and some make a good living by looting backpacks while guests are away. Never leave valuables in your hotel room, even if it's locked. If you are going on a trek, you might want to leave your luggage at a guest house, but don't leave your valuables. If you leave anything, make sure it is securely locked. Many travelers bring their own locks for extra security. Western locks are many times stronger than the ones you can get in India.

Be particularly careful on **buses.** Carry your backpack in front of you where you can see it and don't trust anyone to "watch your bag for a second." If your bag is going on a bus roof rack, make sure it's tied down so that it doesn't fall or get taken off. Thieves thrive on **trains;** professionals wait for tourists to fall asleep and then carry off whatever they can. When alone, **lock and chain** your pack to the bunk. Keep important documents and other valuables on your person and try to sleep on top bunks with your luggage stored above you (if not in bed with you).

If your belongings are stolen in India or Nepal, you'll have to go to the police. There is virtually no chance you will ever see your camera again, but you can at least get an official **police report,** which you will need for an insurance claim.

DRUGS & BOOZE

Marijuana (*ganja*) and hashish (*charas*) are grown throughout the Himalayas and are extremely cheap, but **they are illegal** and considered socially unacceptable by most Indians and Nepalis. An exception is made for *sadhus* (Hindu holy men), since *ganja* is associated with the worship of Shiva. A few ethnic groups in the Himalayas also use *ganja* and *charas* with no stigma. These indulgences do not extend to tourists, however. In fact, penalties are sometimes harsher for foreigners.

India has a 10-year minimum sentence for drug possession or trafficking, but those caught with small amounts of *ganja* are likely to get off with less. If charged with drug possession, you are likely to find yourself required to prove your innocence in an often-corrupt justice system whose rules you won't understand. **We cannot overemphasize how horrible an experience this will be.** Those who attempt to influence a police officer must do so discreetly and indirectly. Drug law enforcement in Nepal is more relaxed, but sentences are still stiff. If you do get into trouble with the law, police are required to contact your country's diplomatic mission. Bear in mind that if you are arrested, diplomats can visit you, provide a list of lawyers, inform your family, and bring you cookies, but they can't get you out of jail.

In the more touristy places, alcohol is easy to come by. Beer is popular, and India and Nepal produce drinkable vodka, gin, rum, whisky, and other liquors. In India, these are classified as IMFL (Indian-Made Foreign Liquor). Beware of home-brewed concoctions, however; every year dodgy batches of toddykill dozens. The

ESSENTIALS

Indian state of Gujarat is officially dry, and its mildly successful prohibitive efforts have recently been copied by Haryana and Manipur. Other areas (Tamil Nadu, Mumbai, and Delhi) have dry days. Liquor permits, available at embassies, consulates, and tourist offices in Delhi, Chennai, Mumbai, and Calcutta, are not essential but may help you get booze with less difficulty in dry areas. There is no standard drinking age in India or Nepal.

HEALTH

Travelers complain most often about their feet and their stomach; so take precautionary measures. Drink three liters of water per day to prevent dehydration and constipation, and wear sturdy, broken-in shoes. During the hot season, take extra precautions against heatstroke and sunburn.

BEFORE YOU GO

In your **passport,** write the names of any people you wish to contact in case of a medical emergency, and also list allergies or medical conditions you want doctors to know about. Matching a prescription to a foreign equivalent is not always easy, safe, or possible. Carry up-to-date, legible prescriptions or a statement from your doctor stating the medication's trade name, manufacturer, generic name, and dosage. While traveling, be sure to keep all medication with you in your carry-on luggage. [For tips on packing a basic **first-aid kit** and other health essentials, see p. 29.]

IMMUNIZATIONS & PRECAUTIONS

In most cases, no inoculations are **required** for entry into India or Nepal, but most travelers get a number of recommended inoculations (see box below). Visitors who have been in Africa, South America, or Trinidad and Tobago within six days of their arrival in India must have a certificate of vaccination against yellow fever. Visit a doctor at least 4-6 weeks before your departure to allow time for the series of vaccinations.

For immunizations and prophylaxis, consult the CDC (see below) in the US or the equivalent in your home country, and check with a doctor.

! **INOCULATION REQUIREMENTS & RECOMMENDATIONS.**
The US Centers for Disease Control:
Hepatitis A: Immune globulin (IG).
Hepatitis B: If you might be exposed to blood, have sexual contact, stay longer than 6 months, or undergo medical treatment. Hepatitis B vaccine is recommended for infants and for children who did not receive the series as infants.
Japanese encephalitis: If you plan to be in a rural area for over 4 weeks.
Rabies: If you plan to touch or kiss Indian animals.
Typhoid: Vaccination is particularly important because strains in India and Nepal are resistant to multiple antibiotics.
Others: Up to date vaccines for tetanus-diphtheria, measles, mumps, and rubella. One-time dose of polio for adults, and haemophilus influenza B (meningitis).

USEFUL ORGANIZATIONS & PUBLICATIONS

The US **Centers for Disease Control and Prevention** (**CDC;** ☎877-FYI-TRIP; toll free fax 888-232-3299; www.cdc.gov/travel) maintain an informative website. The CDC's comprehensive booklet *Health Information for International Travel*, an annual rundown of disease, immunization, and general health advice, is free online or US$25 via the Public Health Foundation (☎877-252-1200). For quick information on health and other travel warnings, call the **Overseas Citizens Services** (☎202-647-5225;

after-hours 202-647-4000), contact a passport agency or an embassy or consulate abroad. US citizens can send a self-addressed, stamped envelope to the Overseas Citizens Services, Bureau of Consular Affairs, #4811, US Department of State, Washington, D.C. 20520. For information on medical evacuation services and travel insurance firms, see the US government's website at http://travel.state.gov/medical.html or the **British Foreign and Commonwealth Office** (www.fco.gov.uk).

MEDICAL ASSISTANCE ON THE ROAD

Tourist centers are full of pharmacies, and many pharmacists (called chemists in India) speak enough English to understand what you need. Most pharmacies sell prescription medicines as over-the-counter drugs. Only a few are open 24hr. In an emergency, head to the nearest major hospital that is open all night and has an in-house pharmacy. Outside the major tourist centers, the going is a bit rougher, although every major town should have at least one pharmacy.

India and Nepal suffer from a lack of doctors and medical equipment. **Public hospitals** are overcrowded, short on staff and supplies, and rarely have English-speaking staff. In many places in India, "hospitals" function essentially as hospices—homes for the dying. There is little point in visiting one of these unless you're looking for stories to tell. Most foreign visitors in India go to more expensive **private hospitals.** These are mainly in the big cities; elsewhere, they are usually known as nursing homes. Small private clinics, usually operated by a single physician, are also widespread and reliable. In Kathmandu, a number of tourist-oriented clinics offer care up to Western standards. For serious medical problems, however, those who can afford it have themselves evacuated to facilities in Singapore or Europe.

You can also contact your **diplomatic mission** and ask for **list of doctors.** Carry these names with your other medical documents. If a **blood transfusion** is necessary, ask whether someone from your diplomatic mission can donate blood or whether family members at home can send blood by air. Also ask whether your diplomatic mission can arrange emergency evacuation. Often, hospital syringes haven't been properly sanitized, carry a few unused syringes with you in case you need some sort of injection. Make sure you also carry a doctor's note explaining that they are for medicinal purposes.

Travel insurance (such as ISIC and ITIC) will cover most **medical expenses** in India or Nepal. Even for long-term stays and major surgery at top hospitals, costs are much lower than back home. Nevertheless, it's a good idea to carry a credit card for immediate payment. Unfortunately, Westerners do not have good reputations for paying their bills fairly and squarely; many hospitals are hesitant to trust them with late payments.

If you are concerned about medical support while traveling, there are special support services. The *MedPass* from **GlobalCare, Inc.,** 2001 Westside Pkwy., #120, Alpharetta, GA 30004, USA (☎800-860-1111; fax 770-677-0455; www.globalems.com), provides 24hr. international medical assistance, support, and medical evacuation resources. The **International Association for Medical Assistance to Travelers** (IAMAT; US ☎716-754-4883, Canada ☎416-652-0137, New Zealand ☎03 352 20 53; www.sentex.net/~iamat) has free membership, lists English-speaking doctors worldwide, and offers detailed info on immunization requirements and sanitation. If your regular **insurance** policy does not cover travel abroad, you may wish to purchase additional coverage (see p. 28).

Those with medical conditions (diabetes, allergies to antibiotics, epilepsy, heart conditions) may want to obtain a **Medic Alert** membership (first year US$35, annually thereafter US$20), which includes a stainless steel ID tag, among other benefits, like a 24hr. collect-call number. Contact the Medic Alert Foundation, 2323 Colorado Ave, Turlock, CA 95382, USA (☎888-633-4298; outside US 209-668-3333; www.medicalert.org).

ONCE IN INDIA AND NEPAL

ENVIRONMENTAL HAZARDS

Air Quality: Some of the world's most polluted cities are on the subcontinent. The exhaust fumes band high industrial emissions affect big and small cities alike. These may aggravate respiratory problems and create new problems for previously healthy travelers. If you suffer from allergies or asthma, take inhalers and/or prescription medication with you, and consult your doctor before you leave.

Heat exhaustion and dehydration: Heat exhaustion, characterized by dehydration and salt deficiency, can lead to fatigue, headaches, and wooziness. Avoid it by drinking plenty of water, eating salty foods (e.g. crackers), and avoiding dehydrating beverages (e.g., alcohol, coffee, tea, caffeinated sodas). Continuous heat stress leads to heatstroke (rising temperature, severe headache, and cessation of sweating). Cool off victims with wet towels and get a doctor.

Sunburn: If you're prone to sunburn, bring sunscreen (it's more expensive and hard to find when traveling), and apply it liberally and often to avoid burns and skin cancer. If you are planning on spending time near water, in the desert, or in the snow, you are at risk of getting burned, even through clouds. If you get sunburned, drink fluids and apply Calamine or aloe lotion.

Heat rashes: For some travelers, a visit to India and Nepal will mean an introduction to **prickly heat,** a rash that develops when sweat is trapped under the skin. Men are susceptible to developing this rash in the groin. To alleviate itch, shower regularly and dry thoroughly. Wear loose-fitting clothes made of absorbent fibers like cotton.

Hypothermia and frostbite: Victims of overexposure to the cold may shiver, feel exhausted, have poor coordination or slurred speech, hallucinate, or suffer amnesia. *Do not let hypothermia victims fall asleep,* or their body temperature will continue to drop and they may die. To avoid hypothermia, keep dry, wear layers, and stay out of the wind. When the temperature is below freezing, watch out for frostbite. If skin turns white, waxy, and cold, do not rub the area. Drink warm beverages, get dry, and slowly warm the area with dry fabric or steady body contact until a doctor can be found.

High altitude: Travelers to high altitudes such as the Himalayas should ascend at a gradual rate, less than 1000 meters per day, to let their bodies adjust to the lower oxygen levels in the air. High elevations can cause insomnia, headaches, nausea and **Acute Mountain Sickness** (AMS; see p. 36). At these levels, UV rays are stronger, and alcohol can give you a potent kick in the head.

INSECT-BORNE DISEASES

Many diseases are transmitted by insects—mainly mosquitoes, fleas, ticks, and lice. Be aware of insects in wet or forested areas, especially while hiking and camping. **Mosquitoes** are most active from dusk to dawn. Wear long pants and long sleeves (preferably light-colored) and try tucking your pants (and your vanity) into your socks. Some travelers also bring along a mosquito net, but this can add extra weight to your pack. Use insect repellents containing DEET, and soak or spray your gear with permethrin (licensed in the US for use on clothing). Consider natural repellents like vitamin B-12 or garlic pills, which make you too smelly for some insects. To stop the itch once you've been bitten, try Calamine lotion or topical cortisones (like Cortaid), or take a bath with a half-cup of baking soda or oatmeal.

Malaria: Transmitted by *Anopheles* mosquitoes that bite at night, malaria is the most serious disease travelers to India and Nepal are likely to contract. The incubation period varies from 6-8 days to several months. Early symptoms include fever, chills, aches, and fatigue, followed by high fever and sweating, sometimes with vomiting and diarrhea. See a doctor for any flu-like sickness that occurs after travel in a risk area. Left untreated, malaria can cause anemia, kidney failure, coma, and death. It is an especially serious threat to pregnant women. To reduce the risk of contracting malaria, use mosquito repellent, particularly in the evenings and when visiting forested areas, and take oral prophylactics, like **mefloquine** (Lariam) or **doxycycline** (ask your doctor for a prescription). Be aware that these drugs can have serious side effects, including slowed heart rate and nightmares.

Dengue fever: An "urban viral infection" transmitted by *Aedes* mosquitoes, which bite during the day. Dengue has flu-like symptoms and a rash 3-4 days after the onset of fever. Symptoms for the first 2-4 days include chills, high fever, headaches, swollen lymph nodes, muscle aches, and in some instances, a pink rash on the face. If you experience these symptoms, see a doctor, drink plenty of liquids, and take fever-reducing medication such as acetaminophen (Tylenol). *Never take aspirin to treat dengue fever.*

Japanese encephalitis: Another mosquito-borne disease, most prevalent during the rainy season in rural areas near rice fields and livestock pens. Aside from delirium, most symptoms are flu-like: chills, headache, fever, vomiting, muscle fatigue. Since the disease carries a high mortality rate, it's essential to go to a hospital as soon as symptoms appear. The JE-VAX vaccine, usually given in 3 shots over a 30-day period, is effective for a year, but it has been associated with serious side effects. According to the CDC, there is little chance of being infected if proper precautions are taken, such as using mosquito repellents containing DEET and sleeping under mosquito nets.

Yellow Fever: Yellow fever occurs only in areas of South America and Africa, but many countries require a certificate of vaccination for travelers arriving from affected regions. **(See Immunizations and Precautions,** p. 22.)

Other insect-borne diseases: Filariasis is a roundworm infestation transmitted by mosquitoes. Infection causes enlargement of extremities and has no vaccine. **Leishmaniasis,** a parasite transmitted by sand-flies, can occur in the subcontinent. Common symptoms are fever, weakness, and swelling of the spleen. There is a treatment, but no vaccine. The **plague** and **relapsing fever,** both transmitted through fleas and ticks, still occur. Treatment is available for both.

FOOD- & WATER-BORNE DISEASES

Food- and water-borne diseases are the biggest cause of illness among travelers to India and Nepal. Prevention is the best cure: be sure that the water you drink is clean and that everything you eat is cooked properly. **Avoid ice and drink only boiled water.** If you're a staunch purist, keep your mouth shut in the shower and don't brush your teeth with tap water or rinse your toothbrush under the faucet. To purify your own water, bring it to a rolling boil for five minutes or filter it with a portable water filter (available at camping good stores) and treat it with **iodine tablets.** Bottled mineral water is sold everywhere in India. Beware of unsealed bottles—these have probably been refilled with tap water. **Carbonated drinks** ("cold drinks") are also safe as long as they are fizzy. **Coffee** and *chai*, which are boiled are usually safe. As tasty as they may be, avoid *lassis* or *nimbu pani* (lemonade) except in the ritziest restaurants; these are often made with ice water. Insist on drinks without ice, even if means quenching your desert thirst with a lukewarm Limca. Keep in mind that water safety is also seasonal, and that it's riskier to drink the water or eat the seafood during **monsoon,** when all the year's crud seeps into the water supply.

Any food cooked immediately before it is served is probably safe. Street vendors and juice stands are rarely sanitary, and although *pani puri* may please a parched palate, the equipment used to make it is open to disease-carrying flies. If possible, eat in restaurants that serve local food and are popular with locals. Touristy restaurants that serve shoddy imitations of Western food are often less clean (and tasty) than *dhabas* that dish out *dal bhat* to truckers all day. Your body will adapt better if you eat at regular times and eat the same sort of foods daily.

The biggest risk to travelers usually comes from **fruit, vegetables,** and **dairy products.** With fruits and vegetables, if you can peel it, you can eat it. Beware of watermelon, which is sometimes injected with impure water, and vegetables like lettuce. Stick to pasteurized dairy products. Other than that, it might take your stomach time to adjust to the spiciness of the food and the variability of ingredients. Adjust to the food slowly, and have high-energy, non-sugary foods with you to keep your strength up; you'll need plenty of protein and carbohydrates. **Wash your hands before you eat;** since sinks and soap may not always be available bring a few packs of baby wipes or a quick-drying purifying liquid hand cleaner. Your bowels will thank you.

■ **Traveler's diarrhea:** Results from drinking **untreated water** or eating **uncooked foods;** a temporary (and fairly common) reaction to the bacteria in new food ingredients. Symptoms include nausea, bloating, urgency, and malaise. Try quick-energy, non-sugary foods with protein and carbohydrates to keep your strength up. Over-the-counter anti-diarrheals (e.g., Imodium) may counteract the problems, but can complicate serious infections. The most dangerous side effect is dehydration; drink 8 oz. of water with ½ tsp. of sugar or honey and a pinch of salt, try uncaffeinated soft drinks, or munch on salted crackers. If you develop a fever or your symptoms don't go away after 4-5 days, consult a doctor. Consult a doctor for treatment of diarrhea in children.

Dysentery: Results from a serious intestinal infection. The most common type is bacillary dysentery, also called shigellosis. Symptoms include bloody diarrhea (sometimes mixed with mucus), fever, and abdominal pain and tenderness. Bacillary dysentery generally only lasts a week, but it is highly contagious. Amoebic dysentery, which develops more slowly, is a more serious disease and may cause long-term damage if left untreated. A stool test can determine which kind you have; seek medical help immediately. Dysentery can be treated with the drugs norfloxacin or ciprofloxacin (commonly known as Cipro). If you are traveling in high-risk (especially rural) regions, consider obtaining a prescription before you leave home.

Cholera: An intestinal disease caused by bacteria in contaminated food. Symptoms include diarrhea, dehydration, vomiting, and muscle cramps. See a doctor immediately; if left untreated, it may be deadly. Antibiotics are available, but the most important treatment is rehydration. Consider getting a (50% effective) vaccine if you have stomach problems (e.g., ulcers) or will be living where the water is not reliable.

Hepatitis A: A viral infection of the liver acquired primarily through contaminated water and food. Symptoms include fatigue, fever, loss of appetite, nausea, dark urine, jaundice, vomiting, aches and pains, and light stools. The risk is highest in rural areas and the countryside, but it is also present in cities. Ask your doctor about the vaccine (Havrix or Vaqta) or an injection of immune globulin (IG; formerly called gamma globulin).

Parasites: Microbes, tapeworms, etc. that hide in unsafe water and food. **Giardiasis,** for example, is acquired by drinking untreated water from streams or lakes. Symptoms include swollen glands or lymph nodes, fever, rashes or itchiness, digestive problems, eye problems, and anemia. Boil water, wear shoes, avoid bugs, and eat only cooked food.

Schistosomiasis: Also known as bilharzia; a parasitic disease caused when the larvae of flatworm penetrate unbroken skin. Symptoms include an itchy localized rash, followed in 4-6 weeks by fever, fatigue, painful urination, diarrhea, loss of appetite, night sweats, and a hive-like rash on the body. If exposed to untreated water, rub the area vigorously with a towel and apply rubbing alcohol. Schistosomiasis can be treated with prescription drugs. In general, swimming in fresh water should be avoided.

Typhoid fever: Caused by the salmonella bacteria; common in villages and rural areas. While mostly transmitted through contaminated food and water, it may also be acquired by direct contact with another person. Early symptoms include fever, headaches, fatigue, loss of appetite, constipation, and sometimes a rash on the abdomen or chest. Antibiotics can treat typhoid, but a vaccination (70-90% effective) is recommended.

OTHER INFECTIOUS DISEASES

Rabies: Transmitted through the saliva of infected animals; fatal if untreated. By the time symptoms appear (thirst and muscle spasms), the disease is in its terminal stage. If you are bitten, wash the wound thoroughly, seek immediate medical care, and try to locate the animal. A rabies vaccine, which consists of 3 shots given over a 21-day period, is available but is only semi-effective.

Hepatitis B: A viral infection of the liver transmitted via bodily fluids or needle-sharing. Symptoms may not surface for years. Vaccinations are recommended for health-care workers, sexually active travelers, and anyone planning to seek medical treatment abroad. The 3-shot vaccination series must begin 6 mo. before traveling.

AIDS, HIV, & STDS

Thanks to prostitution, a needle drugs, and a lack of sex education, HIV and AIDS are spreading fast. The World Health Organization estimates that there are over four million people with HIV/AIDS in India and 25,000 in Nepal. If you need an injection, make sure the needle has been sterilized; to be extra safe, carry your own **syringes** and insist that they be used. Bring a letter from your doctor stating that the syringes are for medical purposes. If you get a shave from a barber, make sure he uses a new blade. The most common mode of transmission is sexual intercourse. Health professions recommend latex condoms. For detailed information on **Acquired Immune Deficiency Syndrome (AIDS)** in India and Nepal, call the **US Centers for Disease Control's** 24hr. hotline at ☎ 800-342-2437, or contact the **Joint United Nations Programme** on HIV/AIDS (UNAIDS), 20, ave. Appia, CH-1211 Geneva 27, Switzerland (☎ +41 22 791 3666; fax 22 791 4187). Council's brochure, "Travel Safe: AIDS and International Travel," is available at all Council Travel offices and on their Web site (www.ciee.org/Isp/safety/travelsafe.htm). The Indian government screens all incoming travelers over 18 years of age with a visa valid for one year or more for HIV. Contact the nearest consulate of India or Nepal for up-to-date information.

Sexually transmitted diseases (STDs) such as gonorrhea, chlamydia, genital warts, syphilis, and herpes are easier to catch than HIV. **Hepatitis** B and C are also serious STDs (see **Other Infectious Diseases,** p. 27). Though condoms may protect you from some STDs, oral or even tactile contact can transmit. Warning signs include swelling, sores, bumps, or blisters on sex organs, the rectum, or the mouth; burning and pain during urination and bowel movements; itching around sex organs; swelling or redness of the throat; and flu-like symptoms. If these symptoms develop, see a doctor immediately.

WOMEN'S HEALTH

Women traveling in unsanitary conditions are vulnerable to **urinary tract** and **bladder infections,** common and uncomfortable bacterial infestations that cause a burning sensation and painful (sometimes frequent) urination. To try to avoid these infections, drink plenty of vitamin C-rich juice and clean water, and urinate frequently, especially right after intercourse. Untreated, these infections can lead to kidney infections, sterility, and even death Mictasol is an effective over the counter remedy. If symptoms persist, see a doctor.

Vaginal yeast infections may flare up in hot and humid climates. Wearing loosely fitting trousers or a skirt and cotton underwear will help, as will over-the-counter remedies like Monistat or Gynelotrimin. Bring supplies from home if you are prone to infection, as they may be difficult to find on the road. In a pinch, some travelers use a natural alternative such as a yogurt and lemon juice douche. Since **tampons, pads,** and reliable **contraceptive devices** are hard to find when traveling and your preferred brand will rarely be available, bring supplies with you.

INSURANCE

Travel insurance covers four basic areas: medical/health problems, property loss, trip cancellation/interruption, and emergency evacuation. Although your regular insurance policies may well extend to travel-related accidents, you may consider purchasing travel insurance if the cost of potential trip cancellation/interruption or emergency medical evacuation is greater than you can absorb. Prices for travel insurance bought separately run about US$50 per week for full coverage. Trip cancellation/interruption may be purchased separately at about US$5.50 per US$100 of coverage.

Medical insurance (especially university policies) often covers costs incurred abroad; check with your provider. **US Medicare** does not cover foreign travel. **Canadians** are protected by their home province's health insurance plan for up to 90 days after leaving the country; check with the provincial Ministry of Health or Health Plan Headquarters for details. **Homeowners' insurance** (or your family's coverage) often covers theft during travel and loss of travel documents (passport, plane ticket, railpass, etc.) up to US$500.

ISIC and **ITIC** (see p. 12) provide basic insurance benefits, including US$100 per day of in-hospital sickness for up to 60 days, US$3000 of accident-related medical reimbursement, and US$25,000 for emergency medical transport. Cardholders have access to a toll-free 24hr. helpline (run by the insurance provider **TravelGuard**) for medical, legal, and financial emergencies overseas (US and Canada ☎877-370-4742, elsewhere call US collect +1 715-345-0505). **American Express** (US ☎800-528-4800) grants most cardholders automatic car rental insurance (collision and theft, but not liability) and ground travel accident coverage of US$100,000 on flight purchases made with the card.

INSURANCE PROVIDERS. Council and **STA** (see p. 42) offer plans that can supplement your basic coverage. Other private insurance providers in the US and Canada include: **Access America** (☎800-284-8300); **Berkely Group/Carefree Travel Insurance** (☎800-323-3149; www.berkely.com); **Globalcare Travel Insurance** (☎800-821-2488; www.globalcare-cocco.com); and **Travel Assistance International** (☎800-821-2828; www.europ-assistance.com). Providers in the **UK** include **Columbus Direct** (☎020 7375 0011). In **Australia,** try **AFTA** (02 9375 4955).

PACKING

One of Indian Railways' sternly comic admonitions sums it up: **Less Luggage, More Comfort.** As a general rule, pack only what you absolutely need, then take half of the clothes and twice the money. The less you have, the less you have to lose (or store or carry on your back).

LUGGAGE. If you plan to cover most of your itinerary by foot, a sturdy **backpack** is unbeatable. (For the basics on buying a pack, see p. 35.) Toting a **suitcase** or **trunk** is fine if you plan to live in one or two cities and explore from there, but a very bad idea if you're going to be moving around a lot. In addition to your main piece of luggage, a **daypack** (a small backpack or courier bag) is a must.

CLOTHING. Bring lightweight clothing that you can wear in layers; avoid jeans in favor of cotton and linen pants. Women should leave the miniskirts and tank tops at home. Wearing shorts is considered disrespectful for women and juvenile for men. Even if you're in the middle of a trek, shorts are still a bad idea—you'll make yourself vulnerable to insects and leeches. Comfortable walking shoes are essential. For heavy-duty trekking, a pair of study lace-up **hiking boots** will help out. A double pair of socks—light polypropylene inside and thick wool outside—will cushion feet and keep them dry. **Rain gear** is a necessity in cooler climates. During the monsoon, a good rain jacket and backpack cover (or even plastic garbage bags) will take care of you and your gear at a moment's notice, which is often all you'll get. If you plan to **trek,** see p. 31. Remember that you will need to be respectfully dressed to visit religious sites and government offices. See **Customs and Etiquette,** p. 93.

SLEEPSACK. Most hotels provide sheets and pillows, but it is still a good idea to bring along a sleepsack. To make your own, fold a full-size sheet in half lengthwise, and then sew it closed. See your mother for further details.

CONVERTERS & ADAPTERS. In India and Nepal, electricity is 220 volts AC, enough to fry any 110V American or Canadian appliances. 220V electrical appliances don't like 110V current, either. Visit a hardware store for an adapter (which changes the shape of the plug) and a converter (which changes the voltage). Don't make the mistake of using only an adapter (unless appliance instructions state otherwise). **New Zealanders** and **South Africans** (who both use 220V at home) as well as **Australians** (who use 240/250V) won't need a converter, but will need a set of adapters to use anything electrical. Don't count on electricity to be regular or dependable, especially in rural areas.

TOILETRIES. Toothbrushes, towels, cold-water soap, talcum powder, deodorant, razors, tampons, and condoms are often available, but may be difficult to find, so bring extras along. **Contact lenses,** on the other hand, may be expensive and difficult to find, so bring enough extra pairs and solution for your entire trip. Also bring your glasses and a copy of your prescription.

FIRST-AID KIT. For a basic first-aid kit, pack: bandages, pain reliever, antibiotic cream, a thermometer, a Swiss Army knife, tweezers, moleskin, decongestant, motion-sickness remedy, diarrhea or upset-stomach medication (Pepto Bismol or Imodium), an antihistamine, sunscreen, insect repellent, burn ointment, and a syringe for emergencies (get an explanatory letter from your doctor).

FILM. Photo film in India and Nepal generally costs US$3-4 for a roll of 24 color exposures, and the quality is usually good. Developing costs under $1, but you might not be thrilled with the results. Less serious photographers may want to bring a **disposable camera** or two rather than an expensive permanent one. Despite disclaimers, airport security X-rays *can* fog film, so buy a lead-lined pouch at a camera store or ask security to hand-inspect it. Always pack film in your carry-on luggage, since higher-intensity X-rays are used on checked luggage.

OTHER USEFUL ITEMS. Bring a strong **padlock** (some hotels don't have locks on room doors, and on trains it's a good idea to lock your bag to something). Other useful items include: sealable plastic bags (for damp clothes, soap, food, shampoo, etc.), an alarm clock, waterproof matches, sun hat, needle and thread, safety pins, sunglasses, compass, flashlight (torch), soap, **earplugs** (oh yes), electrical tape (for patching tears in your pack), and garbage bags, and a small **calculator.**

ACCOMMODATIONS

Cheap accommodation is everywhere in India and Nepal. Wherever you go, it should be easy to find a place to stay without spending more than US$2-3 per night, as long as you don't mind life without air-conditioning. Even up-market hotels are much cheaper than at home. **Prices fluctuate wildly according to season, and the seasons are very different from destination to destination.** Most foreign tourists come to India during the winter months (Nov.-Feb.), so places that draw mostly foreigners have "high season" (and correspondingly high prices) during these months. Indian tourists head for the hills during the sweltering pre-monsoon months (May-July), causing rates to head higher too.

BUDGET HOTELS

The main travelers' centers have **tourist districts,** enclaves of shabby, bare-bones hotels with hard beds and a ceiling fan on overdrive. Managers are usually happy to provide any service rupees can buy. Where tourist districts have developed and the clientele is foreign, competition has made hotels much cheaper, cleaner, and more comfortable. It is rarely necessary to make **reservations,** except at major peak times (such as festivals). However, it can be difficult to find a place to stay in big cities that see few foreign tourists, where the hotels may be full of businessmen or might lack the paperwork to accept foreigners. Budget hotels frequently have **restaurants** attached and sometimes Star TV and air-conditioning. Another attractive feature is **room service,** which usually costs no more than food in the restaurant. If you are a lazy **launderer,** you can surrender your clothes to the local *dhobi* (most hotels have their own and store-front laundries are everywhere).

One thing to look out for when choosing a hotel is the **check-out time**—many cheap hotels have a 24hr. rule, which means if you arrive in the morning after an overnight train you'll be expected to leave as early when you check out. **Don't let touts or rickshaw-wallahs make your lodging plans for you.** These shady characters cart tourists off to whichever hotel offers the biggest commission. For more information, see **Touts, Middlemen, and Scams,** p. 17.

Many budget travelers prefer to bring their own **padlock** for budget hotels; the locally made padlocks are easy to break. You should also carry sheets, towels, soap, and **toilet paper.** Many places have **hot water** only at certain hours of the day or only in buckets. Since the power supply is erratic everywhere in India, **generators** provide a very noisy solution. **Air-cooling,** a system by which air is blown by a fan over a surface of water, is common.

Some hotels have built reputations as places for foreign travelers to hang out and share stories. Some places have even instituted discriminatory **no-Indians policies** to create sanitized, foreigners-only environments for their guests.

Nepal's budget scene is the result of a recent boom, and foreigners are its main targets. Major tourist districts, unlike anything in India, have grown up in Pokhara and Kathmandu, where fierce competition has led to rock-bottom prices and generally better hotels than in India.

HOSTELS

Youth hostels are scattered throughout India, especially in the far north and south. They are extremely cheap and popular with foreign visitors. **YMCAs** and **YWCAs** are only in the big cities and are usually quite expensive, although the women-only policy of YWCAs makes them a safe option for women traveling alone. Hostels in India rarely exclude nonmembers or charge them extra. **Hostels**

in Nepal are nonexistent. In India, the state tourism development corporations have set up large **tourist bungalows** in both popular and less-touristed areas. Combining hotel with tourist office, these places are convenient, but the slight improvement over budget hotels is seldom worth the price.

UPSCALE HOTELS

Nicer hotels offer an escape from life on the road and can help you maintain sanity. Pricier accommodation is available almost anywhere in India, with air-conditioning, 24hr. hot water, and TVs. The rates will seem exorbitant compared to the budget hotels. However, many mid-range hotels are all show: a spacious, carpeted lobby disguises rooms only marginally better than those in budget hotels. Across central and western India, former **palaces** of rajas and maharajas have been turned into mid-range hotels and offer travelers the decadence of a bygone era at a more or less affordable price. Large, expensive hotels such as the Taj, Sheraton, and Oberoi chains and the ITDC's line of Ashoks are in the main cities and tourist centers. In Nepal, more expensive hotels are only in Kathmandu and Pokhara. Even if a night's stay is beyond your budget, the bookstores, restaurants, and pools at these places are still great resources. Larger hotels require payment in **foreign currency;** this rule extends even farther down the price scale in Nepal.

OTHER TYPES OF ACCOMMODATIONS

RELIGIOUS REST HOUSES

Traditional rest houses for Hindu pilgrims known as *dharamsalas* sometimes provide foreign guests spartan accommodation free of charge. You will be expected to give a donation. Sikh *gurudwaras* also have a tradition of hospitality. Be on your best behavior if you stay in these religious places. They are not hotels; many have curfews or other restrictions. Smoking and drinking are not allowed.

HOMESTAYS

Homestays with Indian families provide the paying guest with an opportunity to experience the daily life of the country at first-hand; the Government of India's Tourist Department is promoting the concept aggressively. The **Paying Guest Scheme** is a relatively new phenomenon in India, but it is gaining momentum in a number of states, particularly Tamil Nadu and Rajasthan. Government of India Tourist Offices publish a list of host families and information about the rooms, facilities, and meals provided. Homestays are more expensive than budget hotels, but cheaper than starred hotels. They are rare in Nepal.

TREKKING

Since the first Europeans crossed the Mana La into Tibet during the early 1600's, trekking has become a big business in Nepal and India, and mountain tourism provides numerous jobs to guides, porters, cooks, village lodgers, and shop owners. In 1986, 25,000 people went trekking in Nepal's Annapurna region—that figure has now tripled. Hikers outnumber the indigenous population by two-to-one. Serious mountaineers spend serious money here, but there are plenty of chances for less dedicated travelers to experience the mountains and trails in a more low-key, low-cost, and low-impact way.

ESSENTIALS

Trekking is neither mountaineering nor backpacking. It is simply a journey on foot through the hills that can take a day, a week, a month, or if it suits you, a lifetime. You might be walking from village to village along ancient highways or striking off into more remote areas where accommodation is sparse and a tent the only place to sleep. However you do it, you'll be living off the land, eating local food and meeting local people. A classic "day" involves five to six hours on the trail with frequent stops for tea and photo-taking. Most treks go through populated country, but some venture over high passes and along trails used only by herders on their way to high-altitude pastures. Keep in mind that the Himalayas are the tallest mountains in the world, and even the foothills provide plenty of tough walking. At the end of the day, while you are putting bandages on your blisters, admire the magnificent views; a few aching muscles are a small price to pay.

WHEN TO GO

The post-monsoon reprieve (Oct.-Nov.) is the most popular season for trekking in **Nepal** (see p. 851), and the more popular routes teem with hikers. March to May is Nepal's second and less crowded trekking season. In India, the pre-monsoon (May-June) and post-monsoon (Sept.-Oct.) seasons afford the best hiking in the hill regions of **Kangra, Kullu** (see p. 243), **Shimla** (see p. 224), and **Uttaranchal** (see p. 628). The areas of **Upper Kinnaur** (see p. 251), **Lahaul** (see p. 258), **Spiti** (see p. 252), and **Ladakh** (see p. 267) are in the rainshadow and get none of the monsoon. From December to February, it is too cold for trekking at high altitudes, and snow blocks many passes. The temperatures rise in March and April and make trekking more feasible. The air is usually dusty and dry, but rhododendra, magnolias, and orchids are impressive compensation. In May—the hottest and least predictable of months—the monsoon is just around the corner and most trekking activities taper off as trekkers retreat to higher regions. Despite the stunning views in places like the Valley of Flowers, few choose to endure the cloud-bound, slippery, and leech-beleaguered trail conditions of the monsoon. For the persistent and enterprising, however, trekking during the summer season has at least one benefit—the virtual absence of foreign tourists.

PLANNING A TREK

There are two ways of organizing a trek in the Himalayas. Trekking independently saves money and allows you to set the pace, choose companions, and plan rest days and side trips of personal interest. There is a downside to freedom, though. Arranging your own trek also entails obtaining your own permits, renting equipment, buying supplies, and hiring porters and guides. If you are not blessed with patience and time, a trekking agency can take care of the preparations for you, and their expertise might make it possible to trek through more remote back country. The ease and comfort come will cost you. For more info on planning a trek in Nepal, see **Trekking in Nepal,** p. 851.

PRACTICAL INFORMATION

NEPAL. Villages along Nepal's most popular routes have outdone themselves to accommodate foreigners, and they are lined with tea houses and small hotels offering meals and a place to sleep. In Nepal, English signs advertise **lodging** and **food** at bargain prices (usually under NRs20), and often an English-speaking manager greets the guests. Increasingly, private rooms are available along the most popular routes in Nepal, but dormitory-style accommodation still predominates in the back country and at high elevations. The tea house social scene can be lively, and these lodges are full of potential trekking companions—if you're looking for a good night's sleep, bring along your ear plugs.

TREKKING PERMITS AND OTHER FEES. Permits are no longer required for the Everest, Langtang, and Annapurna trekking areas in Nepal. Permits for other areas can be obtained at immigration offices in Kathmandu (for more information see **Kathmandu, Practical Information: Immigration Office,** p. 775). You can normally complete the process in one day, though long lines at the height of the season can extend the process to 2-3 days. **Your permit will be checked regularly (and stamped) at police check-posts.** If your trek enters a national park, you will have to pay a fee. Trekking permits are not required in India, except in **North Sikkim** (see p. 11), although you will need a permit merely to enter certain regions considered to be "defense areas," such as parts of **Northeast India** (see p. 10) and regions bordering Tibet. **Camping is not allowed in national parks or wildlife sanctuaries.**

INDIA. Trekking in India requires more self-sufficiency than trekking in Nepal. India has no equivalent to Nepal's tea houses; in some areas, there might be an occasional rest house, but these are often out of the way, and food supplies are unreliable. Tents are essential for shelter, and the supplies and equipment you will need to carry are much greater. Because of the heavier load, you'll need porters more often than in Nepal—backpacks become a considerable burden on treks longer than a few days. Population tends to be a lot thinner in the Indian Himalayas than in Nepal, and trekkers often see no one for days. It is important to go with someone who knows the trails.

PORTERS AND GUIDES

One variation on trekking alone is to hire your own porters and guides. You will have a knowledgeable local with you, you won't need to carry as much, and you'll be supporting the local economy. **Porters** carry most of your gear, allowing you the comfort of walking with just a small pack containing the items you will need during the day. Of course, you'll have to make sure that your porter understands what you want him to do and where you want to go. There is always a small chance that your porter will disappear, leaving you with just a pair of sunglasses and a pack of playing cards. Choose your porter carefully; the expense entailed in hiring a porter through a recognized trekking agency is a sound investment.

Guides, who usually speak English, are not necessary on the better-known routes, where it is easy to find your way. Having someone who knows English might prove helpful in negotiations and pre-trek planning, however. A guide can color your experience with his knowledge, and often, guides will take trekkers on unusual side trips to visit friends and family. Guides will not carry anything (that's what porters are for).

Although the trekking service industry in the Indian Himalayas is not as developed as the one in Nepal, you can arrange your own equipment, food, and staff at most hill stations or trailheads. In general, porters and guides are easy to find, but you will want to investigate their honesty and experience. You can be almost certain to get reputable workers through a guest house or trekking agency. Ask to see letters of recommendation from previous trekkers. Guides and porters hired through companies are slightly more expensive but are usually more reliable and better qualified. In the unlikely event that your guide or porter disappears, you will at least have a company to hold responsible once you manage to find your way back down the hillside—an insurance that is worth a few extra rupees per day. If you do hire your own guides and porters, make sure you know exactly what services are covered, where you will go, and what supplies you will need to provide along the way. Most agreements stipulate that guides and porters pay for their own food and housing. As a responsible employer, you should make sure that porters and guides are adequately clothed when trekking at high altitudes by outfitting them with good shoes, a parka, sunglasses, mittens, and a sleeping bag. Establish beforehand if you expect them to return anything. (For more information on porters' living conditions and responsible trekking, consult the **International Porter Protection Group**, www.ippg.net, which has representatives across the world.) The standard salary for a porter carrying 20 kilos is about US$10 per day in Nepal, US$5 per day in India; the salary for guides is higher (US$12-20 per day in India). In addition to these fees, you are expected to tip your staff generously at the end of a trek.

ORGANIZED TREKKING

Many people do not want to spend precious vacation time planning their trek, buying equipment, and hiring porters and guides. You can book treks through a large, international adventure travel company in your home country, in which case everything is arranged before you even leave for the airport. If you wait until you arrive, you can book through a local trekking agency, which usually requires one week's notice. The agent makes reservations for hotels and transportation and provides a complete staff—guide, porters, and cooks—for the trek. You will have to commit to the prearranged itinerary, and you might also be trekking with smelly people you have never met before. Organized treks often veer off from the crowded routes into more remote areas. The group carries its own food, prepared by cooks skilled in the art of kerosene cuisine. The comforts of trekking through an agency can also include tables, chairs, dining tents, and toilet tents. All this comfort and convenience usually costs US$15 to US$150 (usually US$40-50) per person per day. Keep in mind that little of this money reaches people in the trekking region; instead it pads the wallet of the middleman in the city.

PACKING AND EQUIPMENT

What you carry with you on your trek will depend greatly on where you go, the style of trekking you choose, and–if you have arranged a trek through an agency-- what they provide. For the most part, outfitting yourself for a trek is easier in Nepal than in India. Nepalese tea houses relieve you of the need to carry food, cooking supplies, and tents—unless you're going to high altitudes beyond the reach of tea house culture. With all its trekking stores, you could show up naked in Kathmandu and be equipped for the most arduous trek within hours. In India it might be necessary to bring your own gear. For more information on packing, see p. 28. A quick checklist of items to carry along on a trek:

CLOTHING	EQUIPMENT
boots or running shoes	sleeping bag
camp shoes or thongs	water bottle
lots of socks (polypropylene and wool)	flashlight, batteries
down jacket	insulated mat, if camping
woolen shirt	backpack and daypack
shorts/skirt	toilet paper and hand towel
long trousers	lighter, stove, fuel
rainwear and umbrella	sunblock and lip balm
cotton T-shirts or blouses	towel
thermal underwear	water purification system
gloves	sewing kit with safety pins
sun hat and wool hat	small knife
snow gaiters	first-aid kit (see p. 29)
snow goggles/sunglasses	zip-loc bags

IF YOU PLAN TO BUY...

Good camping equipment is sturdy and light. Camping equipment is generally more expensive in Australia, New Zealand, and the UK than in North America.

Sleeping Bag: Most sleeping bags are rated by season ("summer" means 30-40°F at night; "four-season" or "winter" often means below 0°F). They are made either of **down** (warmer and lighter, but more expensive, and miserable when wet) or of **synthetic** material (heavier, more durable, and warmer when wet). Prices range US$80-210 for a summer synthetic to US$250-300 for a good down winter bag. **Sleeping bag pads** include foam pads (US$10-20), air mattresses (US$15-50), and Therm-A-Rest self-inflating pads (US$45-80). Bring a **stuff sack** to store your bag and keep it dry.

Tent: The best tents are free-standing (with their own frames and suspension systems), set up quickly, and require staking only in high winds. Low-profile dome tents are the best all-around. Good 2-person tents start at US$90, 4-person at US$300. Seal the seams of your tent with waterproofer, and make sure it has a rain fly. Other tent accessories include a **battery-operated lantern,** a **plastic groundcloth,** and a **nylon tarp.**

Backpack: Internal-frame packs mold better to your back, keep a lower center of gravity, and flex adequately to allow you to hike difficult trails. **External-frame packs** are more comfortable for long hikes over even terrain, as they keep weight higher and distribute it more evenly. Make sure your pack has a strong, padded hip-belt to transfer weight to your legs. Any serious backpacking requires a pack of at least 4000 in^3 (16,000cc), plus 500 in^3 for sleeping bags in internal-frame packs. Sturdy backpacks cost anywhere from US$125-420—this is one area in which it doesn't pay to economize. Fill up any pack with something heavy and walk around the store with it to get a sense of how it distributes weight before buying it. Either buy a **waterproof backpack cover,** or store all of your belongings in plastic bags inside your pack. This is important.

Boots: Be sure to wear hiking boots with good **ankle support.** They should fit snugly and comfortably over 1-2 pairs of wool socks and thin liner socks. Break in boots over several weeks first in order to spare yourself painful and debilitating blisters.

Other Necessities: Synthetic layers, like those made of polypropylene, and a pile jacket will keep you warm even when wet. A "space blanket" will help you retain your body heat and can double as a groundcloth (US$5-15). Plastic water bottles are virtually shatter- and leak-proof. Bring water-purification tablets for when you can't boil water. If you're trekking without a cook and no decent food option presents itself, you'll need a camp stove (the classic MSR WhisperLite starts at US$60) and fuel. (Gas stations and supply stores are few and far between in the mountains, so have adequate fuel before hitting the trail.) Also don't forget a first-aid kit, pocketknife, insect repellent, calamine lotion, and waterproof matches or a lighter.

HEALTH AND SAFETY

Trekking is hard work, so don't overdo it. Go at a comfortable pace and take rest days when necessary. Make sure your water is safe; boiling is often impractical (and ineffective at high altitudes where water boils at a lower temperature). Chemical treatment is the best option. Iodine solution or iodine-water purification tablets will do the job. Use Tang orange-juice powder or chewable vitamin C tablets to mask the flavor. If you're eating in local inns, go vegetarian and stick to fried food—a good dose of hot oil does wonders for even the most resilient of nasties, and given the rate at which calories burn as you toil uphill, the forbidden delights of the frying pan can be consumed guilt-free. The popular Nepalese trekking routes witness a lot of diarrhea and nausea-induced misery. For more information, see **Health,** p. 22.

ESSENTIALS

Women should not trek alone. It is better to find a group, either on your own, through notice boards, or through a trekking agency. Some agencies now specialize in providing female porters and guides for women.

Knee and ankle sprains are common trekking injuries. Knees in particular can become painfully inflamed. If you are susceptible to knee injuries, bind your knees with a cloth bandage as a preventive measure. Sprained ankles can keep you from walking for days. Good footwear with ankle support is the best prevention. A bad **blister** will ruin your trek. If you feel a "hot-spot" coming on, cover it with moleskin. Keep your feet dry; take your boots and socks off at every rest stop, and change your socks regularly. Once you've got a blister, drain the fluid using a needle sterilized in a metal flame and then dress it.

Cuts to the skin should be cleaned with water and covered with Betadine and a firm bandage. Clean and dress the wound daily. If the wound becomes infected, apply an antibiotic ointment. Although trekkers do not often need serious medical attention, trekking mishaps do occur. If urgent medical attention is needed, **emergency rescue** request messages can be sent by radio at police, army, national park, and other official offices. Helicopter rescue is very expensive (usually US$1000-2000). In Nepal, money must be deposited or guaranteed in Kathmandu before the helicopter will fly. For people on agency treks, the agency will often advance the money. This process is a lot easier if you are registered with your embassy, which you can do quickly and easily in Kathmandu at your embassy.

Acute Mountain Sickness (AMS): If you are trekking to altitudes above 3500m, you will probably experience mild symptoms of altitude sickness, which can worsen into Acute Mountain Sickness (AMS). AMS is the body's reaction to the low oxygen environment of high altitudes, and it can kill you if left untreated. Since the rate of acclimatization is so variable and unpredictable, budget plenty of time for high-altitude portions of your trek. If you're trekking in Nepal, having a trekking permit valid for a week longer than you anticipate is a good idea. Trekkers who fly directly to high altitudes are more likely to be affected by AMS than those who walk up gradually. Susceptibility to AMS is almost impossible to predict—some people have no problems acclimatizing; others take a long time. Despite what you might have read, there are no prescriptions for avoiding AMS. The best advice is to **drink lots of water, take it slow,** and to **sleep low, go high.** Once you're at about 3000m, try to sleep no more than 300m higher than the previous night. If you have to cross a high pass, sleep at the bottom and make it a long day up and over. **Drink lots of fluids.** It's always sensible to be well hydrated, but the need for hydration is especially important at higher altitudes. Note that alcohol impedes acclimatization. **Watch for symptoms.** Typically the first symptom is a mild headache, but there's a whole suite of other symptoms: dizziness, nausea, insomnia, racing heart, fatigue. If you experience any of these, do not sleep at higher altitudes. Don't ascend, and the symptoms will probably pass within 24hr. If your condition continues to deteriorate, you **must** descend. Even a descent of just a few hundred meters can make all the difference. **Most AMS fatalities occur in groups,** since badly affected trekkers don't want to hold up others in the group. Ensure that this does not happen by gaining altitude at a rate suited to the slowest acclimatizer. For more information on AMS and other trekking illnesses visit the **High Altitude Medicine Guide** website at www.high-altitude-medicine.com.

Frostbite and Hypothermia: Frostbite and hypothermia might seem a long way away when you're sweating in sunny valleys, but they're an ever-present danger at high altitudes. All too often people run into problems because they are determined to press on through bad conditions. If the weather turns against you, get to shelter as soon as you can, even if it means retracing your steps. For tips on preventing and combating these conditions, see p. 24.

Sunburn: Ultraviolet light is stronger at higher altitudes, so it's necessary to protect against sunburn with sunblock and a hat. Sunburn can be particularly severe if you're on snow or ice, and because of the angle of reflected light, it can show up in the strangest places, like under your chin or even inside your mouth. You can never have too much sunblock. A good pair of sunglasses with wrap-around protection can help prevent snow blindness, a condition caused by the reflection of UV light off snow or ice.

Leeches: Leeches are rampant during monsoon season. Trekkers often get them on their legs or in their boots. Carry salt with you in a small container for chemical attack on them. Carefully applying a lit cigarette is another effective way of removing them. Unlike ticks, they do not leave any part of themselves behind, so it is safe to pull them off; disinfect the bite anyway. A leech bite isn't painful, and leeches do not transmit diseases. The effect is mostly psychological.

RESPONSIBLE TREKKING

Trekking can help the local economy, but it can hurt the environment. Cultivate respect for the land you are trampling. The ecological balance in the Himalayas is at risk as a result of overgrazing, pollution, and, most importantly, **deforestation.** Never cut vegetation or clear new campsites. Loss of vegetation is the beginning of an ecological spiral that leads to **erosion** and **landslides.** Whenever possible, ask for kerosene or gas to be used for cooking and heating water; blazing campfire hearths are taboo where deforestation is a problem. Even in regions with plentiful trees, gather only dead branches and brush for burning. Limit hot showers to those heated by electricity, solar energy, or back-boilers. Industrious and innovative shower suppliers deserve encouragement.

Trekkers and their waste also contribute to litter, sanitation, and water pollution problems. The rule to follow is: **burn it, bury it, or carry it out.** Toilet paper is generally burned, biodegradables such as food wastes are buried, and non-disposables (plastics, aluminum foil, batteries, glass, cans, etc.) are packed up and carried. Make sure your campsite is at least 150 ft. (50m) from water supplies or bodies of water. If there are no toilet facilities, bury turds (but not paper) at least four inches (10cm) deep and above the high-water line, and 150 ft. or more from any water supplies, campsites, village compounds, and crop fields. Use biodegradable soap and shampoo, and don't rinse directly in streams. If you can't leave the area clean, don't go. On organized treks, make sure that a person from your team is the last to leave camp; guided tour operators seldom do what they promise about garbage disposal.

Trekkers can also have a profound effect on the people they encounter. If you're moved by the plight of the villagers you meet, make a donation at the end of your trip to an aid program involved in education, health care, or environmental issues.

FURTHER RESOURCES

Himalayan Rescue Association (HRA; ☎(01) 262746; hra@aidpost.mos.com.np; www.nepalonline.net/hra), just off Jyatha, south of Thamel, in Kathmandu. A voluntary non-profit organization providing information for trekkers on where and how to trek, trekking hazards, altitude sickness, and how to protect the environment. They also have in-season clinics with volunteer Western doctors during the trekking season in Pheriche on the Everest trek and in Marang on the Annapurna Circuit. Open Su-F 10am-5pm.

Kathmandu Environmental Education Project (KEEP), PO Box 9178, Jyatha, Thamel, Kathmandu (☎(01) 259567; fax 256615; tour@keep.wlink.com.np or keep@info.com.np; www.keepnepal.org). Also off Jyatha, close to the HRA. A non-profit organization that promotes "soft trekking," which minimizes impact on the environment and culture. They offer free advice to trekkers and trekking staff. During the trekking season (Oct.-Dec. and Feb.-May) they have a free talk on eco-tourism at their office at 4pm every Friday. A good place to find trekking companies and a source of up-to-date information. Open Su-F 10am-5pm.

Annapurna Conservation Area Project (ACAP), c/o King Mahendra Trust, P.O. Box 3712, Kathmandu (☎(01) 526571; fax 526570; kmtnc@mos.com.np), in the King Mahendra Trust Office, near Grindlay's bank in Jawalakhel or in the Natural History Museum on Pokhara's Prithvi Narayan campus. Authoritative source on the Annapurna region of Nepal; promotes environmentally sound trekking. Open M-F 9am-5pm.

Nepal Mountaineering Association (NMA), (☎(01) 434525; fax 434578; office@nma.com.np; www.nma.com.np), just south of Nag Pokhari in Naxal, in Kathmandu. Issues permits for the Nepalese Himalayas.

Indian Mountaineering Foundation, 6 Benito Juarez Marg, New Delhi 110021 (☎(011) 4677935 or 4671211; fax 6883412; indmount@vsnl.com; www.indmount.com). Information on treks above 6000m.

Earthwatch, in the US and Canada: 3 Clock Tower Place, Ste. 100, Box 75, Maynard, MA 01754, USA (☎800-776-0188 or 978-461-0081; info@earthwatch.org; www.earthwatch.org); in Europe: 57 Woodstock Rd., Oxford OX2 6HJ, UK (☎018 6531 8838; info@earthwatch.org.uk); in Australia: 126 Bank St., South Melbourne, Victoria 3205, Australia (☎03 9682 6828; earth@earthwatch.org). Supports research, education, and conservation programs in India and Nepal.

KEEPING IN TOUCH

BY MAIL

RECEIVING MAIL IN INDIA AND NEPAL

Airmail letters under 1 oz. take two to three weeks to get to India and Nepal. Envelopes should be marked "air mail" or "par avion." There are several ways to get letters sent to you.

General Delivery: Mail can be sent to India and Nepal via **Poste Restante** to almost any city or town with a post office. Address *Poste Restante* letters in this format: Emi SHIMOKAWA, *Poste Restante*, GPO, Delhi, 110001, India. The mail will go to a special desk in the central post office. It is best to use the largest post office in the area, since mail will often be sent there regardless of what is written on the envelope. Bring your passport to prove your identity to skeptical clerks. If they insist that there is nothing for you, have them check under your first name as well.

American Express: AmEx's travel offices throughout the world will act as a mail service for cardholders if you contact them in advance. Under this free **Client Letter Service,** they will hold mail for up to 30 days and forward on request. Some offices will offer these services to non-cardholders (especially those who have purchased AmEx Traveler's Checks), but call ahead to make sure. *Let's Go* lists AmEx locations for many large cities; for a complete, free list, call 800-528-4800 in the US, or visit http://travel.americanexpress.com/travel/personal/resources/tso/?sitemap.

Other Options: Federal Express (www.fedex.com; Australia ☎13 26 10; US and Canada ☎800-247-4747; New Zealand ☎0800 73 33 39; UK ☎0800 12 38 00) can get a letter from New York to New Delhi in 5 days for a whopping US$41. Rates among non-US locations are equally expensive; London to New Delhi costs £30 and up. By **US Express Mail,** (www.usps.gov) a letter from New York should arrive within 4-5 days and cost US$17. **DHL** (Australia (☎ 13 14 06; UK (☎ 087 0110 0300); US (☎ 800-225-5345); www.dhl.com) operates throughout South Asia; it costs about US$77 to send a small package to India or Nepal. Delivery takes 3-5 business days. Letters from the UK arrive in 3 days or less and cost about £36. DHL packages sent from India or Kathmandu to the US cost US$25-40 and take 3-5 days.

SENDING MAIL HOME

Aerogrammes, printed sheets that fold into envelopes and travel via airmail, are available at post offices. Post offices will refuse to send aerogrammes with enclosures. Allow *at least* two weeks for mail delivery from South Asia. Sending a **package** home will involve getting it cleared by customs, getting it wrapped in cloth and sealed in wax, going to the post office to fill out the customs forms, buying stamps, and finally, seeing it processed. It might take months or even years by surface mail, and all packages run the risk of getting X-rayed or searched. If you need to receive a package from abroad, have it registered—this will reduce the chance that your goods will get stolen.

BY TELEPHONE

Phones are almost everywhere in India and Nepal. The STD/ISD sign (Standard Trunk Dialing/International Subscriber Dialing) means that there's a phone nearby. Some STD/ISD booths are open 24hr. and offer fax services. Incoming calls are usually the cost of a local call, so it's a good idea to place your call and then have someone call you back. Discuss this with the booth operator before you try it; they may refuse to allow this since they don't make any money this way.

PLACING INTERNATIONAL CALLS. To call India or Nepal from home or to place an international call from India or Nepal dial:

1. The **international dialing prefix.** To call out of **Australia,** dial 0011; **Canada** or the **US,** 011; the **Republic of Ireland, New Zealand,** or the **UK,** 00; **South Africa,** 09; **India** or **Nepal,** 00.

2. The **country code** of the country you want to call. To call **Australia,** dial 61; **Canada** or the **US,** 1; the **Republic of Ireland,** 353; **New Zealand,** 64; **South Africa,** 27; the **UK,** 44; **India,** 91; **Nepal,** 977.

3. The **city** or **area code.** *Let's Go* lists phone codes opposite the city or town's name, alongside the following icon: ☎. If the first digit is a zero (e.g. 020 for London), omit it when calling from abroad.

4. The **local number.**

A **calling card** is another (often futile) alternative. Calls are billed either collector to your account. Though calling cards often work in the major tourist centers of India and Nepal, the STD/ISD booths in many smaller cities and villages do not have access to international operators. And even those cards that might potentially work are often disallowed by booth owners, who don't profit on these calls. International **collect calls** cannot be made from India or Nepal to some countries, and booth owners often won't let you try.

CALLING WITHIN INDIA AND NEPAL

To call within India or Nepal, dial the city code and then the number. Long-distance calls are either full price (M-Sa 8am-7pm); half-price (M-Sa 7-8am and 7-8:30pm, Su 7am-8:30pm); one-third price (daily 6-7am and 8:30-11pm); or one-quarter price (daily 11pm-6am).

INDIA PHONE CODES	
Agra	0562
Ahmedabad	079
Amritsar	0183
Bangalore	080
Bhopal	0755
Bhubaneswar	0674
Mumbai (Bombay)	022
Calcutta	033
Chandigarh	0172
Delhi	011
Dharamsala	01892
Guwahati	0361
Hyderabad	040

Jaipur	0141
Khajuraho	07686
Leh	01982
Chennai (Madras)	044
Manali	01902
Patna	0612
Panjim (Panaji)	0832
Shimla	0177
Trivandrum	0471
Varanasi	0542
NEPAL PHONE CODES	
Kathmandu	01
Chitwan	056
Pokhara	061

TIME DIFFERENCES

India is 5½ hr. ahead of GMT, 4½ hr. behind Sydney, and 10½ hr. ahead of New York. Summer puts the northern countries an hour closer to India. India is 15min. behind Nepal.

BY EMAIL AND INTERNET

Thousands of **cybercafes** can be found all over India and Nepal. Outside the major cities, connections are slow, and cybercafes tend to get crowded, so don't count on being able to send digital copies of your holiday snaps home every night unless you have patience and time.

Free **web-based email accounts** (e.g., www.rediff.com and www.yahoo.com) are the fastest and cheapest way to send email in India. **Internet cafes** are in the **Practical Information** sections of major cities.

GETTING TO INDIA AND NEPAL

BY PLANE

A little effort can save you a bundle. Tickets bought from consolidators and standby seating are good deals, but last-minute specials, airfare wars, and charter flights often beat these fares. Hunt, be flexible, and ask persistently about discounts. Students, seniors, and those under 26 should never pay full price.

AIRFARES

Airfares to India and Nepal peak between mid-June and early September; holidays are also expensive. Midweek (M-Th morning) round-trip flights run US$40-50 cheaper than weekend flights. Traveling with an "open return" ticket can be pricier than fixing a return date when buying the ticket. Round-trip flights are by

far the cheapest; "open-jaw" (arriving in and departing from different cities, e.g. London-Delhi and Kathmandu-London) tickets tend to be pricier. Patching one-way flights together is the most expensive way to travel. Flights between capital cities and regional hubs offer the most competitive fares.

If India or Nepal is just one stop on a more extensive globe-trotting trip, consider a round-the-world (RTW) ticket. Tickets usually include at least 5 stops and are valid for about a year (US$1200-5000). Try **Northwest Airlines/KLM** (US ☎800-447-4747; www.nwa.com) or **Star Alliance**, a consortium of 22 airlines including United (US ☎800-241-6522; www.star-alliance.com).

Fares for roundtrip flights to **Delhi** or **Mumbai** from the **US** or **Canada** cost US$900-1200 during the low season/US$1200-1700 during the summer; from **London**, UK£450-750/UK£500-900; From **Australia** and **New Zealand,** peak-season fares (late Nov. to late Jan.) are between AUS$2000-3000 round-trip from the east coast of Australia to Delhi, Calcutta, or Kathmandu. Low-season fares are AUS$1500-2200. Flying from Perth is usually about AUS$150 cheaper than flying from the east coast.

BUDGET & STUDENT TRAVEL AGENCIES

Travelers holding **ISIC** and **IYTC cards** (see p. 12) qualify for big discounts from student travel agencies. Most flights from budget agencies are on major airlines, but in peak season some may sell seats on less reliable chartered aircraft.

USIT world (www.usitworld.com). 50 **usit campus** branches in the UK, including 52 Grosvenor Gardens, **London** SW1W 0AG (☎0870 240 10 10); **Manchester** (☎0161 273 1880); and **Edinburgh** (☎0131 668 3303). 20 **usit NOW** offices in Ireland, including 19-21 Aston Quay, O'Connell Bridge, **Dublin** 2 (☎01 602 1600; www.usitnow.ie), and **Belfast** (☎02 890 327 111; www.usitnow.com). Offices also in Athens, Auckland, Brussels, Frankfurt, Johannesburg, Lisbon, Luxembourg, Madrid, Paris, and Warsaw.

Council Travel (www.counciltravel.com). Countless US offices, including branches in Atlanta, Boston, Chicago, L.A., New York, San Francisco, Seattle, and Washington, D.C. Check the website or call ☎800-2-COUNCIL (226-8624) for the office nearest you. Also an office at 28A Poland St. (Oxford Circus), **London**, W1V 3DB (☎0207 437 77 67).

CTS Travel, 44 Goodge St., **London** W1T 2AD (☎0207 636 0031; fax 0207 637 5328; ctsinfo@ctstravel.co.uk).

STA Travel, 7890 S. Hardy Dr., Ste. 110, Tempe AZ 85284 (24hr. reservations and info ☎800-781-4040; www.sta-travel.com). A student and youth travel organization with over 150 offices worldwide, including Boston, Chicago, L.A., New York, San Francisco, Seattle, and Washington, D.C. Ticket booking, travel insurance, railpasses, and more. In the UK, walk-in office 11 Goodge St., **London** W1T 2PF or call 0207-436-7779. In New Zealand, Shop 2B, 182 Queen St., **Auckland** (☎09 309 0458). In Australia, 366 Lygon St., **Carlton** Victoria 3053 (☎03 9349 4344).

Travel CUTS (Canadian Universities Travel Services Limited), 187 College St., **Toronto,** ON M5T 1P7 (☎416-979-2406; fax 979-8167; www.travelcuts.com). 60 offices across Canada. Also in the UK, 295-A Regent St., **London** W1R 7YA (☎0207-255-1944).

TICKET CONSOLIDATORS

Ticket consolidators, or **"bucket shops,"** buy unsold tickets in bulk and sell them at discounted rates. The best place to look is in the Sunday travel section of any major newspaper (such as the *New York Times*), where many bucket shops place tiny ads. Call quickly, as availability is limited. Not all bucket shops are reliable, so insist on a receipt that gives full details of restrictions, refunds, and tickets, and pay by credit card (in spite of the 2-5% fee) so you can stop payment if you never receive your tickets. For more info, see www.travel-library.com/air-travel/consolidators.html.

ESSENTIALS

FLIGHT PLANNING ON THE INTERNET. The Internet is one of the best places to look for travel bargains—it's fast and convenient, and you can spend as long as you like exploring options without driving your travel agent insane.

Many airline sites offer special last-minute deals on the Web. Other sites do the legwork and compile the deals for you—try www.bestfares.com, www.one-travel.com, www.lowestfare.com, and www.travelzoo.com.

STA (www.sta-travel.com), **Council** (www.counciltravel.com), and **StudentUniverse** (www.studentuniverse.com), and **Orbitz.com** provide quotes on student tickets, while **Expedia** (www.expedia.com) and **Travelocity** (www.travelocity.com) offer full travel services. **Priceline** (www.priceline.com) allows you to specify a price, and obligates you to buy any ticket that meets or beats it; be prepared for antisocial hours and odd routes. **Skyauction** (www.skyauction.com) allows you to bid on both last-minute and advance-purchase tickets.

An indispensable resource on the Internet is the *Air Traveler's Handbook* (www.cs.cmu.edu/afs/cs/user/mkant/Public/Travel/airfare.html), a comprehensive listing of links to everything you need to know before you board a plane.

TRAVELING FROM THE US & CANADA

Travel Avenue (☎ 800-333-3335; www.travelavenue.com) searches for best available published fares and then uses several consolidators to attempt to beat that fare. **NOW Voyager,** 74 Varick St., Ste. 307, New York, NY 10013 (☎ 212-431-1616; fax 219-1793; www.nowvoyagertravel.com) arranges discounted flights, mostly from New York, to major cities around the world. Other consolidators worth trying are **Interworld** (☎ 305-443-4929; fax 443-0351); **Pennsylvania Travel** (☎ 800-331-0947); **Rebel** (☎ 800-227-3235; travel@rebeltours.com; www.rebeltours.com); **Cheap Tickets** (☎ 800-377-1000; www.cheaptickets.com); and **Travac** (☎ 800-872-8800; fax 212-714-9063; www.travac.com). Yet more consolidators on the web include the **Internet Travel Network** (www.itn.com); **Travel Information Services** (www.tiss.com); **TravelHUB** (www.travelhub.com); and **The Travel Site** (www.thetravelsite.com). Keep in mind that these are just suggestions to get you started in your research; *Let's Go* does not endorse any of these agencies. As always, be cautious, and research companies before you hand over your credit card number.

TRAVELING FROM THE UK, AUSTRALIA, & NEW ZEALAND

In London, the **Air Travel Advisory Bureau** (☎ 0207-636-5000; www.atab.co.uk) can provide names of reliable consolidators and discount flight specialists. From Australia and New Zealand, look for consolidator ads in the travel section of the *Sydney Morning Herald* and other papers.

CHARTER FLIGHTS

Charters are flights a tour operator contracts with an airline to fly extra loads of passengers during peak season. Charter flights fly less frequently than major airlines, make refunds particularly difficult, and are almost always fully booked. Schedules and itineraries may also change or be cancelled at the last moment (as late as 48 hours before the trip, and without a full refund), and check-in, boarding, and baggage claim are often much slower. However, they can also be cheaper.

Discount clubs and **fare brokers** offer members savings on last-minute charter and tour deals. Study contracts closely; you don't want to end up with an unwanted overnight layover.

GET CARD.

TRAVEL HARD.

There's only one way to max out your travel experience and make the most of your time on the road: The International Student Identity Card.

 Packed with travel discounts, benefits and services, this card will keep your travel days and your wallet full. Get it before you hit it!

Visit **ISICUS.com** to get the full story on the benefits of carrying the ISIC.

90 minutes, wash & dry (one sock missing).
5 minutes to book online (Detroit to Mom's).

Save money & time on student and faculty
travel at **StudentUniverse.com**

StudentUniverse.com   Real Travel Deals

BY BOAT

For those who have travel time to spare, the **Internet Guide to Freighter Travel** (www.geocities.com/freighterman.geo) provides a comprehensive list of freighter services from ports around the world. **Freighter World Cruises**, 180 S. Lake Ave., Ste. 335, Pasadena, CA 991101 (☎800-531-7774) organizes freighter trips departing from New York and arriving in several ports in India. Ask for a complimentary copy of their *Freighter Space Advisory Bulletin*.

BORDER CROSSINGS

India-Nepal: There are 6 crossings: Mahendranagar, Dhangadi, Nepalganj, **Sunauli** (see p. 834), **Raxaul/Birganj** (see p. 143 and p. 844), and **Kakarbhitta** (see p. 848). Sunauli is a 3hr. bus ride from Gorakhpur in Uttar Pradesh; from there you can catch a 10hr. bus to Pokhara or a 11hr. bus to Kathmandu. Raxaul is a 6hr. bus ride from Patna in Bihar; from Birganj, across the border, it's a 10-12hr. bus ride to Kathmandu. The Kakarbhitta crossing, at the eastern end of Nepal, is easily accessible from **Siliguri,** which is a transit point for Darjeeling. It is not necessary to get a Nepalese visa before you arrive at the border, but you must get your Indian visa ahead of time if you are going from Nepal to India. Visitors can also drive across the border if they possess an international *carnet* (see p. 50*)*.

India-Bangladesh: Trains and buses run from Calcutta to **Bangaon** in West Bengal. From there a rickshaw ride can take you to **Benapol, Bangladesh,** with connections via Khulna or Jessore to Dhaka. The northern border, from Jalpaiguri to Haldibari, is only periodically open and requires an exit permit.The border from Agartala, Tripura, to Akhaura, Bangladesh, sees little traffic.

India-Burma: No land frontier open.

India-Bhutan: If you are lucky enough to get a Bhutanese visa, you must cross the border at **Puntsholing,** a 3-4hr. bus ride from **Siliguri** in West Bengal. Make sure you also have a "transit permit" from the Indian Ministry of External Affairs.

India-China: No land frontier open.

India-Pakistan: Pakistan is not a safe place. Only one road crossing is open along the entire length of the 2000km border. Trains between Amritsar in the Indian Punjab and Lahore in Pakistan stopped running in January 2002, as the result of increased tensions between the two countries. The direct bus service between Delhi and Lahore has also been suspended. As of May 2002, the road crossing at **Wagah** remained open to individuals traveling on foot or by private vehicle. For more information, see **Wagah**, p. 481.

India-Sri Lanka: The boat service from Rameswaram in Tamil Nadu to Talaimannar in Sri Lanka has been indefinitely suspended because of the war in northern Sri Lanka. Travelers must fly to Colombo, Sri Lanka.

Nepal-China: The Arniko Rajmarg (Kathmandu-Kodari Highway) links Kathmandu with the Tibet Autonomous Region of China via the exit point of Kodari. The border is open only to travelers on organized tours. Before crossing into Tibet, check in with your embassy in Kathmandu to make sure that the border situation is stable, as there have occasionally been difficulties for tourists crossing overland into Tibet. For more information on requirements for travel to Tibet, see **Surrounding Countries,** p. 11.

GETTING AROUND
BY PLANE

ESSENTIALS

India and Nepal both have relatively safe extensive air networks. However, air travel is more expensive than surface travel and will not always save you much time. Waiting in airport-office queues, traveling to and from airports (often far from town), and checking-in can all slow you down. Airports in South Asia subject passengers to purgatorial delays. Fly only to escape unbearable cross-country bus or train rides. In the mountains, where the roads are poor—and bus rides therefore dangerous and interminable—the balance may be shifted slightly in favor of air travel.

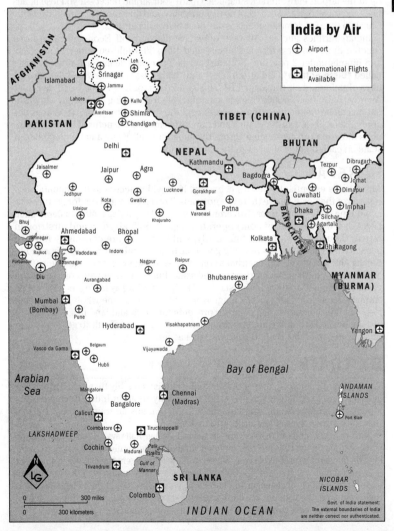

IN INDIA

Though government-run **Indian Airlines** (http://indian-airlines.nic.in/) still maintains the largest flight network, private companies are challenging its former monopoly. **Jet Airways** (www.jetairways.com) is the second largest domestic airline and is slightly ahead of Indian Airlines in quality and service. **Sahara Airlines** (www.saharaairline.com) is the third major domestic carrier. **Reservations** are essential on nearly all flights and must be made well in advance, especially during peak season (Nov.-Mar.), when flights are almost always full. Go to one of the airline offices or use a travel agent to make a booking. *Let's Go* lists airline office contact details in the **Practical Information** listings for most major towns. If you don't get a seat, put your name on the waiting list and show up at the airport early; miracles happen. Guard your airline ticket—if you lose it, airlines and travel agents will accept no responsibility, and there are no refunds available. Check-in time for domestic flights is one hour before departure.

Indian Airlines and Jet Airways offer 25% discount off Economy Class fares (quoted in US dollars) for passengers aged 12 to 30. Children under 12 pay 50%, and infants under 2 pay 10%. Both airlines sell package deals for foreign tourists called **"Discover India"** (Indian Airlines) and **"India Pass"** (Jet Airways) that give 21 days of unlimited air travel for US$750-800, 15 days for US$500-550, or 7 days (Jet Airways only) for US$300. There is a nominal fee for booking each flight. No destination can be visited more than once, except the first and last points (this does not apply if a city is a transfer point), and itineraries must be structured in one continuous direction (no zig-zagging across the subcontinent). Only a limited number of seats on each flight is allotted to these programs.

IN NEPAL

Air travel is essential to Nepal's economy. It provides access to the mountainous regions of the north where there are no roads. Travelers should opt for air travel to avoid long, hellish bus rides. Government-operated **Royal Nepal Airlines Corporation** (RNAC; www.royalnepal.com) operates flights to 35 airports and airstrips in Nepal, though it is suffering financially, and its planes are constantly filled to capacity. Privatization has recently given birth to several new airlines: **Everest Air, Gorkha Airlines** (www.gorkhaairlines.com.np), **Necon Air** (www.neconair.com), and Nepal Airways. All airlines' prices are the same, but the new private companies are generally thought to have better service. **Foreigners must pay for flights with foreign currency.** Domestic flight prices range from US$50-160. On the whole, air travel in Nepal is unpredictable. Bad weather prevents take-offs and landings; long delays are the norm. During the high trekking season it may be difficult to get tickets for popular destinations. Book through a travel agent.

BY TRAIN

The Indian rail network, one of the few things Indians readily thank the British for, is extensive. For budget travelers, rail is *the* way to go in India. Because of its mountains (and freedom from colonization), Nepal has no trains, except for one that runs across the Indian border to Janakpur.

With over 1.6 million workers on its payroll, **Indian Railways** (IR; www.indianrailways.com) is the world's largest employer. Trains are generally the best way to cover long distances at a reasonable cost. Eleven million passengers travel daily over its vast network, which covers over 62,000km. There is a unique culture on the Indian railways—you'll meet locals eager to chat about your country and theirs as landscapes rush by outside the window and *chai-wallahs* sell cups of tea for a few rupees. Indian Railways may not get you there on time, but they will get you there, Indian style.

TYPES OF TRAINS. The two main kinds of trains are **express** (or mail) and **passenger.** The express trains are much faster and a bit more expensive than passenger trains, which shudder and clank along at an average speed of 27.2km per hour, if you're lucky. The extra-special **"super-fast"** trains—*Shatabdi Express, Rajdhani Express*, and *Taj Express*—cover routes between the major cities. These luxury trains come with full air-conditioning and meals, and cost at least four times as much as standard second class fares. A few scenic hill stations, such as Darjeeling, Ooty, and Shimla, are reached by **"toy trains,"** narrow-gauge machines that chug along at a snail's pace and gush billowing clouds of steam.

CLASSES OF COMFORT. Second class unreserved (previously known simply as "Third class") is generally the cheapest fare available, but it is crowded, uncomfortable, and sometimes risky (pickpockets have easy access to your things). The 2nd class unreserved car is usually at the front or back of the train. You will probably have to stand for your entire trip. Ride in this class only if you want a goat in your lap and your face squashed against the window grille. Much better is the **2nd class sleeper** (requires a reservation; see "Buying a Ticket" below), featuring guaranteed seats and modest three-tiered berths for overnight trips. This is the most popular class among budget travelers. The lack of air conditioning is tempered by the cool breeze that streams through the open windows, though it would be a stretch to say that the air is always cool during the summer. **First class,** three to four times the price of 2nd class sleeper, is less crowded and offers a more "protected" experience, with views of the countryside through scratched, amber-tinted windows and private compartments made up of three to four berths. For air-conditioned travel, there are **chair cars** (with reclining seats) built into the "superfast" trains. **A/C 2nd class sleepers** and **A/C 1st class** round out the options at prices ranging from half to 2.5 times 1st class. Women traveling on their own or with children should inquire about ladies' compartments, available on many overnight mail and express trains. Some locals advise women to opt for the open berths in 2nd class reserved (where there are always kind but tough old ladies) rather than the private compartment cars.

BUYING A TICKET. For overnight trips, any travel during the high season (Nov.-Mar.), and all reserved trains (all classes mentioned above, except 2nd class unreserved), make **reservations** and purchase your ticket at least a day or two before traveling (seats on popular trains can sell out a week ahead of time). At computerized stations, you can make a reservation up to 60 days before your date of travel. It is safest to do this at the station (look for the **reservation office**), though travel agents can also get your train tickets for a commission. Expect long delays and anarchic queues at big stations (see **Bureaucracy Blues,** p. 50). At the biggest stations, you can pay in US dollars, pounds sterling, or in rupees (with an encashment certificate or ATM receipt). A **tourist quota** is often set aside for foreigners, and at stations in the major tourist cities there are even separate lines for tourists. Some stations have **ladies' queues** or allow women to jump to the front of the line to avoid the pushing and shoving.

When you arrive at the office, get a reservation slip from the window, and scribble down the train you want. Each route has a name and a number; for route information, arm yourself with a copy of the indispensable *Trains at a Glance* (Rs25), which contains **schedules** for all express and mail trains. The staff at most train station **enquiry counters** are well-informed. A 21st-century alternative to the trusty old *Trains at a Glance* has recently appeared, in the form of two excellent **Web sites** run by the major rail companies. The official websites of India Railways (www.indianrailways.com) and Southern Railway (www.srailway.com) tell you more than you will ever need to know—train names, numbers, and timetables. You can also make on-line reservations.

BUREAUCRACY BLUES Nothing is simple in India. Your railway journey, for example, begins not at the platform, but at the reservation booth, where your will wait for an eternity before you get anywhere near the ticket clerks. The reservation rooms of many train stations in India are stuffy, dust-heavy halls full of ill-tempered officials and unbreathable air. The cruel but far from unusual punishment begins at the counter, where a few people are employed full-time to dole out **reservation request slips.** These precious pieces of paper are not given out lightly—expect a struggle, endure the wait, and treat the slip like a hundred dollar bill. Once you've got your form filled in, you move next door, join the scrum that hums and heaves around the reservation counters, and wait. And wait. In India, waiting in "line" can be a brutal, full-contact sport. After 45 minutes, you make it to one of the counters, out of patience and struggling for breath. You scream your destination through the wire window, smile, and are kindly told to take your slip back outside for an official stamp. Two uniformed men sit in silence, keeping a stern vigil over a small made-in-Manchester metal stamp and a worn-out inkpad. Smile again. With your form now "official," you tramp back inside to rejoin the line for another long wait. Next time up at the window, the cloud of smoke behind the counter kindly directs you to Counter 6, reserved for "foreign tourists, senior citizens, physically handicapped, or freedom fighters." You notice a long line of young, able-bodied Indian civilians already waiting in front of you, and are glad you brought a book.

Foreign passport holders can buy **Indrail Passes,** available for between one week and three months in a variety of classes (paid for in US dollars or pounds sterling). They include all fares, reservation charges, and supplementary charges, but prices are high, and it's hard to get your money's worth. Indrail Passes can save you some hassle—on super-fast trains, pass holders are exempt from reservation fees and extra charges and don't need tickets on shorter journeys. Reservations are still necessary for longer trips.

If you have a reservation, you'll be fine getting to the station just a few minutes before the train arrives. If you're leaving from a major station, check the computer-printed list (usually on the platform or the side of each train car) for your name and seat, and listen for announcements. Don't be surprised if your train is delayed—find a waiting room and ask a coolie (porter) when he thinks your train will arrive. Foreigners can sometimes assume a place in the first class waiting room regardless of what class they're traveling, but be ready to exit graciously if the attendant catches you without the right ticket. Railway **retiring rooms,** cheaper than budget hotels, are available to anyone with a valid ticket or Indrail pass. They operate on a 24hr. basis, and most also rent for 12hr. at a stretch.

If you fail to get a reservation, you can still get on the waiting list (ask about the tourist quota) and hope. In an emergency, find the station master. He probably won't be thrilled to see you, but if anyone can find a seat on a "full" train, he's your man. As a last resort, baksheesh to porters has been known to turn up unreserved berths in unlikely places. If you cancel your reservation more than 24hr. before your trip, you can still get a refund, but you'll be charged Rs10-50 depending on the class; up to four hours before, you'll get 75% back, and after that (sometimes even 12hr. after the train has left), you can still get a refund of up to 50%.

BY BUS

In train-less Nepal, buses are *the* mode of long-distance transportation. In India, they come a close second. Buses are often almost as fast as trains, or even faster. They can climb the hilly areas of India, where trains cannot go, and generally involve far less pre-departure hassle. The main drawback is discomfort, and possible death and dismemberment. Seats are narrow, with very little cushioning and no leg room. There are almost always more passengers than seats, and many pass the trip standing up. Buses also tend to make pit stops every 15 minutes. You will often lose your seat if you get up. But then, you might find yourself unable to stand up at all if you go a whole journey without at least one stroll. At scheduled stops, women have a hard time finding a place to use a toilet; they should ask the conductor to wait longer for them as they search.

Road conditions are bad—expect to hear gears grinding and horns blaring, and to feel sudden lurches as the bus bumps its way along pot-holed roads. The bigger and newer the bus, the more likely you'll arrive alive. No one ever survives **minibus** crashes; avoid these. Riding in the mountains at night is suicidal. **Never ride on the roof of a bus,** no matter how cool the breeze, how gorgeous the scenery, or how many other people are sitting on top. It is illegal and terribly dangerous.

INTERCITY BUSES. Express buses are the norm. They have thinly padded seats, are jam-packed, and stop for anyone and everyone at any point along the route. **Tourist buses** or **"superdeluxe" buses,** usually available only on popular tourist routes on the west coast, have cushioned seats and more space; although they are certainly not luxurious by Greyhound standards, they seat four passengers to an aisle rather than five (or six or seven). They often have fans and sometimes even air-conditioning. In Nepal, and some places in India, there are special **night buses,** which have reclining seats and a bit more leg room, though you shouldn't count on getting any sleep. They stop for *chai* endlessly (just be glad the driver is getting his caffeine). At all costs, **avoid video coaches** unless you enjoy being subjected to black-and-white Hindi films for five hours (or more) at ear-splitting levels. **Luggage** on the roof rack of a bus is usually safe, but bags have been known to disappear at intermediate stops in a flurry of untraceable movement. Make sure your pack is tied down, or ask if you can put it somewhere else—in a compartment at the back, or at the front where you can keep an eye on it. If your luggage goes on the roof, give baksheesh to the person who put it up there.

IN INDIA

In this guide, **bus stands** and **bus stations** are where state (and sometimes private) buses roll in and out; private buses often leave from the particular company's office. **Government buses** are often crowded, so get to the bus stand at least 30 minutes before departure. For longer trips (over 8hr.) it may be necessary to book a day ahead; do this at the bus stand rather than through an agent. Some **private bus companies** offer excellent service; others don't deserve to be licensed at all. There are so many private bus companies that it is difficult to know the quality of an operation until you're already screaming down the highway. As with train tickets, it is unwise to buy bus tickets from random travel agencies.

> **WARNING:** You are more likely to die on an Indian or Nepalese bus than in any other way. When there is a train, take it.

IN NEPAL

Bus travel is widely used in Nepal, although road conditions are poor and the hilly terrain increases travel time. Almost all buses are private, but look out for the **government Sajha buses,** which are generally safer and much more comfortable. For these, you'll probably have to book tickets a day in advance from the bus stand. Booking bus tickets from Kathmandu or Pokhara can be a hassle since the bus stands are so far from the tourist centers; it may be easier to book through a travel agent. Avoid package deals for bus journeys with connections; these are often scams. It's best to buy your second ticket once you arrive.

BY CAR

Driving a car (better yet, a VW Microbus) across Asia was a classic 1960s hippie expedition. Today, it's a nightmare. Besides swerving to avoid cars, motorcycles, rickshaws, people, and cows, there is also a general disregard for traffic regulations. Drivers are reckless and aggressive, constrained only by potholes and the vehicles they drive. Many pedestrians who have just arrived from villages lack basic traffic sense. Not surprisingly, India and Nepal have high rates of road accidents. If you get into a traffic accident in India or Nepal, **leave the scene of the accident immediately and go to the nearest police station.** Also keep in mind that killing a cow in India and Nepal, even by accident, is punishable by law.

RENTING

A car is utterly unnecessary in a large city, where buses, rickshaws, and taxis can get you anywhere cheaply. The cost of renting a four-door sedan is many times the cost of a night's stay at a guest house. Also, some rental companies do not offer insurance; a serious accident can mean spending time in jail or the hospital and shelling out a large sum of money to cover damages. If you absolutely must have a car, keep your **international driving permit** (see below) handy, as well as a lot of money. A safer alternative is to hire a car with a **driver.**

DRIVING PERMITS & CAR INSURANCE

INTERNATIONAL DRIVING PERMIT (IDP). Renting a **car, motor-scooter,** or **motorcycle** usually requires an International Driving Permit (IDP). You must be over 18 and have a driver's license from your own country. Your IDP, valid for one year, must be issued in your own country before you depart. An application usually requires one or two photos, a current local license, an additional form of identification, and a fee. Contact your local automobile club or association for more information.

CAR INSURANCE. Most credit cards cover standard insurance. If you rent, lease, or borrow a car, you will need a **green card,** or **International Insurance Certificate,** to certify that you have liability insurance and that it applies abroad. Green cards can be obtained at car rental agencies, car dealers (for those leasing cars), some travel agents, and some border crossings. Rental agencies may require you to purchase theft insurance in countries that they consider to have a high risk of auto theft. Ask your rental agency about India and Nepal.

BY LOCAL TRANSPORTATION

BUSES. Getting around by **local buses** can be chaotic and confusing. Bus schedules are practically impossible to decipher, and figuring out which bus goes where takes years of patient trial and error. Smile at locals waiting at bus stops and hope they know what they're talking about. In a hurry to wedge themselves into city traffic, bus drivers roll-start, so you might want to learn the skill of leaping on and off the back stairs. Once safely inside, sit or stand until the bus-*wallah*, with his little bus satchel, comes by and clicks a small metal contraption in your face. That means pay up—ask how much it is to your destination, since prices vary by distance. Women get preferential seating; men are expected to give up their seats. Women (and men) should watch out for groping hands in crowded buses.

AUTO-RICKSHAWS AND TEMPOS. To some, these podlike three-wheelers are a powerful symbol of the South Asian experience; to others, they are just dirty diesel fume-belching beasts. Fans argue that they are cheaper than taxis, more con-

TOOT YOUR OWN HORN India is a land of many gods and countless different creeds. But everyone in India follows one religious tenet without fail: always honk your horn. Incessantly. Honk if you are about to pass, honk if you're considering passing, being passed, or just contemplating a general theory of passing. Honk if you are approaching a blind curve, honk if you see a pedestrian, or honk to alert the world to your existence. On a bicycle, you can ring like hell on your tinkling little bell. There are many ways to blow a horn, and the avatars of the horn itself are as numerous and as varied as the moods that honking gives voice to—from the majestic, almost-musical tone of the largest trucks, to the boastful bellow of the buses, the chaotic clarion of the clanking cars, and the eruptive fart of the city scooter.... It is a religion that is easy to follow and fun to obey. So join the party—rent a bike, steal a scooter, buy a truck, whatever. And when it's just you on the one-lane open road, and a crowded bus, an overloaded truck, and a couple of motorcycles—don't hesitate, don't be shy—let them know you're there and just happy to be alive! Toot your own horn, sweetheart. Ain't nobody gonna do it for you.

venient than buses, and small enough to dart through heavy traffic. Much of this, of course, depends on the driver. Detractors criticize rickshaws for the damage they do to the environment and to human ears. Auto-rickshaws seat one to three adults (but often up to 10 school children). Low ceilings, minimal leg room, and narrow seats are all part of the fun. Drivers will often say that it's "broken," but insist that they use the **meter** if you're unsure of the regular cost of going to your destination. Avoid pushy drivers, and always scoff at the first price demanded. If a driver won't go by the meter, aim to bargain at least 30-40% off his original price. **In most cities, it is illegal for rickshaw-wallahs to overcharge for local, daytime service.** A threat to report them to the police can sometimes help to squeeze out a more reasonable fare. Sometimes, if you know what price you should be paying, it is easier to get in the rickshaw without negotiating a charge and then pay at the end of the trip. This may necessitate walking calmly away from a screaming rickshaw-*wallah*, but it can also alleviate the pains of negotiation. Depending on the town, some drivers may add a surcharge to the meter or display a government-issued "fare adjustment card," because the meters are outdated and the price of fuel has risen. **Nighttime fares** can be as much as double the standard rate. Also, **make sure your rickshaw-wallah is not drunk or stoned.**

Rickshaw-*wallahs*, who have the bad reputation of being in **commission** cahoots with hotels, will often inform you that the hotel you want to go to has been shut down or that its staff has been rounded up and deported to the Falkland Islands (see **Touts, Middlemen, and Scams,** p. 17). Chances are that this "insider info" is incorrect. If your driver is persistent, he may just take you to accommodation of his choice anyway, regardless of your protests. If a driver taking you home asks if you need a ride the next day, know that if you flippantly agree he will probably sleep in his rickshaw all night waiting for you to emerge in the morning.

Tempos seat about six people, follow fixed routes, and have low fares; they are of limited use to foreigners, however, because their destinations are never marked, and they are often over-packed anyway.

CYCLE-RICKSHAWS. There are two other kinds of rickshaws in India and Nepal. Calcutta is home to India's last fleet of **hand-pulled rickshaws.** Far more common are **cycle-rickshaws,** where the driver pedals in front and his trusting passengers sit on a cushioned box above the rear axle. These are not always found in metropolitan areas (such as Mumbai), but they ply the countryside wherever there are flat roads. In Nepal, rickshaws are limited to the Terai and parts of Kathmandu, where they cater mainly to tourists. The welcome breeze and open views are the main benefits of a cycle-rickshaw; negative aspects include the longer traveling time and the sorrow of seeing an old man labor away at the wheel (though he definitely wants your business). If he jumps out and starts pushing you up a hill that's too steep to pedal, get out and lend a hand. The worst part of a rickshaw ride is settling the **price,** which is highly negotiable. Foreigners usually pay about Rs10 per kilometer in India—more in touristy places, less in villages—but you will pay much more unless you haggle energetically. Indians seem to get a kick out of seeing foreigners pedaling rickshaws. If you want to make people smile, off to trade places with your wallah and take him down a (not so busy) street.

TAXIS. You will find taxis in the larger cities of India and Nepal; in some cities, such as Mumbai, only taxis (and not rickshaws or auto-rickshaws) are allowed. India's international airports offer reliable **pre-paid taxi services**—you pay at an official counter and give your receipt to a driver in the waiting queue, who takes you where you need to go. Taxis are supposed to have meters, but since these are sometimes out of date, the driver will sometimes add a percentage or wave about an official-looking "fare adjustment card" with up-to-date prices. All this varies from city to city; there are no hard-and-fast rules, but in general you should use the meter rather than negotiate a price. Private companies rent out taxis and **drivers** for longer hours, short trips, or even days; inquire at train stations, airports, tourist offices, or travel agents. This is definitely a better alternative to driving around India or Nepal yourself; the driver looks after petrol costs and repairs, is familiar with the roads, and will take responsibility for the vehicle if the wheels fall off halfway to your destination. With enough passengers to split the costs, this option is usually within reach of the budget traveler. In mountainous regions, **jeeps** (sometimes called Gypsies or Mahindras) function as taxis or mini-buses.

MOTORCYCLES, MOPEDS, AND BICYCLES

MOTORCYCLES. Rental shops are abundant near major tourist stops. An International Driving Permit (see p. 52) is legally required for you to rent a scooter or motorcycle, but it is rarely checked. Motorcycle and scooter engines in India and Nepal are usually 100cc and are not good for long trips. Mopeds are easy to operate, but dangerous in traffic. Scooters have a high center of gravity and small wheels, which make them very dangerous; scooters are also very difficult to operate and must be manually shifted from gear to gear. A popular alternative is to rent Kinetic-Hondas, automatic shifting scooters that are easy to operate and a bit safer on the road.

Motorcycles are **extremely dangerous.** Never ride without a helmet; helmets ensure that your head survives a crash, although it probably won't be attached to your body anymore.

BICYCLES. Because of the over-congested streets, trying to ride a bicycle around the big Indian cities is a dangerous exercise in futility. But on back roads through rural towns and throughout much of Nepal, bicycles are a great alternative to motorcycles or scooters. Most bikes don't have gears, which makes anything hill-shaped pretty hard-going. In tourist centers like Kathmandu and Pokhara, bikes can be rented very cheaply on a day-to-day basis. Clunky Indian bikes are also cheap to buy and resell.

BY BOAT

Ferries run between Mumbai and Goa, and ships travel regularly from Calcutta and Chennai to Port Blair in the Andamans. Ferries are the only way to cross some rivers during the monsoon. White-water rafting is the only boat travel in Nepal.

BY THUMB

Hitchhiking is unheard of and unnecessary in most parts of India and Nepal, since public transportation networks are extensive and cheap. In mountain areas like Kumaon and Himachal Pradesh, where traffic is sparse, jeeps and cargo trucks sometimes take on passengers for a small charge.

> **WARNING.** Let's Go urges you to consider the risks before you hitchhike. We do not recommend, and women should never hitchhike alone.

SPECIFIC CONCERNS

WOMEN TRAVELERS

Incidents of **sexual harassment** are common, especially in northern India, but seldom more serious than verbal advances or groping. Many Indians and Nepalis believe that foreign women are indiscriminately promiscuous. This belief is due partly to stereotypes picked up from American television and movies--they think American life is like *Baywatch*--and partly to the fact that many foreign women do things that "good" Indians and Nepalis do not. The less you look like a tourist, the better off you will be. Look as if you know where you're going (even when you don't) and approach other women (or couples) if you need help or directions. **Dress conservatively, covering legs and shoulders, and always wear a bra.** Don't jump to the conclusion that since Indian women wearing saris reveal their lower backs and stomachs, it's OK to wear shorts—it's definitely not. And don't automatically assume that a T-shirt, which appears to cover the same vital areas as a sari, if not more, is appropriate. The shape of the breast should be left a mystery—most women's chests are covered by more than one layer of clothing. Consider wearing a *salwar kameez*, baggy pants with a loose long-sleeved shirt. Wearing a conspicuous **wedding band** can also help prevent unwanted overtures. Some women find that carrying pictures of a "husband" or "children" can be useful in helping to back up marital status. Even a brief mention of a husband waiting back at the hotel is enough in some places to counteract your potentially vulnerable, unattached appearance. Remember that **non-verbal communication** is different from what you're used to back home—making eye contact, responding when asked a question, even smiling can be perceived as a come-on by South Asian men.

Invest in secure accommodation, particularly family-run guest houses with doors that lock from the inside. Stay in central locations and avoid late-night walks. **Hitchhiking** is never safe for women. Trains often have separate **ladies' compartments** and stations may have **ladies' waiting rooms.** On buses, you should be allowed to sit near the front.

South India is safer for women than the north. In Bihar and eastern Uttar Pradesh, where there is no law and order, foreign women have been raped. The Himalayan regions, however, from Himachal Pradesh to Nepal to Sikkim, are among the safest areas; attitudes toward women are much more liberal among many mountain ethnic groups. In the cosmopolitan circles in major cities (especially in Mumbai), women can usually feel as comfortable as they would in any big city anywhere in the world.

The slightest bit of resistance usually stops most harassers, who have generally encountered few foreign women before. Your best answer to harassment is no answer at all; feigned deafness, sitting motionless and staring straight ahead at nothing in particular can do a world of good. The extremely persistent can sometimes be dissuaded by exactly one firm, loud, and very public *"Mujhe chod dho!"* ("Leave me alone!" in Hindi). If need be, turn to an older woman for help in an uncomfortable situation; her stern rebukes will usually embarrass even the most persistent jerk. Don't hesitate to get the attention of passersby and point at your harasser, as people have a strong sense of public morality. Seek out a policeman if you need one, but keep in mind that some policemen, like other men, may assume that a women traveling alone is looking for sex; don't place all your trust in them, particularly in untouristed areas. Emergency numbers (uniform across India and Nepal) are listed on the inside back cover of this book, as well as in the Practical Information listings of cities. A **Model Mugging self-defense course** (see p. 19) will not only prepare you for a potential attack, but will also raise your awareness of your surroundings as well as your confidence. Also be sure you are aware of the health concerns that women face when traveling (see p. 27).

TRAVELING ALONE

There are many benefits to traveling alone, including independence and greater interaction with locals. On the other hand, any solo traveler is a more vulnerable target of harassment and street theft. Lone travelers need to be well-organized and keep high spirits at all times. The cheerier you are, the more friends you'll make and the more dinner invitations you'll get. Spread good will and smile; locals will help you and watch out for you. Maintain regular contact with someone at home who knows your itinerary.

Alternatively, several services link solo travelers with companions who have similar travel habits and interests; for a bi-monthly newsletter for single travelers seeking a travel partner (subscription US$48), contact the **Travel Companion Exchange,** P.O. Box 833, Amityville, NY 11701 (☎631-454-0880 or 800-392-1256 in the US; www.whytravelalone.com; US$48).

OLDER TRAVELERS

Senior citizens are rarely offered discounts in India or Nepal. Agencies for senior group travel are growing in enrollment and popularity. Those listed below offer travel packages to South Asia aimed specifically at older travelers.

ElderTreks, 597 Markham St., Toronto, ON M6G 2L7 (☎800-741-7956; www.elder-treks.com). Adventure travel programs for the 50+ traveler in India and Nepal.

Elderhostel, 11 Ave. de Lafayette, Boston, MA 02111 (☎877-426-8056; www.elderhostel.org). Organizes 1- to 4-week "educational adventures" in India and Nepal for travelers aged 55 and over.

The Mature Traveler, P.O. Box 15791, Sacramento, CA 95852 (☎800-460-6676). Deals, discounts, and travel packages for the 50+ traveler. Subscription$30.

BISEXUAL, GAY, & LESBIAN TRAVELERS

Homosexuality is taboo in India and Nepal, and in India male homosexual sex is illegal. Most gays and lesbians stay closeted. *Hijras* (male eunuchs) form a subculture of prostitutes in the big cites--especially Mumbai and Hyderabad--but this scene is generally not open to foreigners. Male friends may hold hands or hug in public, but these gestures are not considered sexual. Most gay and lesbian organizations in India and Nepal remain underground, but in the past decade, some groups have gained recognition for their work on sex and gender issues. **Bombay Dost** (www.bombay-dost.com), a quarterly magazine by Pride

Publications, was started by three gay Mumbai men in 1990 and addresses issues such as sexual health and hygiene, attitudes toward sexuality, and gay activism. *Bombay Dost* can be purchased from select newsstands in Mumbai, Delhi, Calcutta, and Hyderabad (see their web page for details), and can be ordered directly from Pride Publications Pvt. Ltd., 105 Veena Beena Shopping Centre, Bandra Station Road, Bandra (West), Mumbai 400 050. The success of Bombay Dost inspired the founding of **The Humsafar Trust** (www.humsafar.org), an organization dedicated to activism, outreach, research, and advocacy for gay men in India. The Internet is a good place to find up-to-date city-specific information on gay happenings and events. **http://members.tripod.com/gaydelhi** has links to a number of sites.

Trikone, P.O. Box 21354, San Jose, CA 95151 (☎415-789-7322; fax 274-2733; trikone-web@trikone.org; www.trikone.org), is a US-based organization for gay and lesbian South Asians. They provide a list of gay and lesbian centers in India.

Footprints Travel, 506 Church St., Ste. 200, Toronto, ON Canada M4Y 2C8 (☎888-962-6211 or 416-962-8111; fax 962-6621; www.footprintstravel.com) offers gay and lesbian travel packages to Nepal.

Out and About (www.planetout.com) offers a bi-weekly newsletter and a comprehensive site addressing gay travel concerns.

Gay's the Word, 66 Marchmont St., London WC1N 1AB (☎+44 20 7278 7654; www.gaystheword.co.uk). The largest gay and lesbian bookshop in the UK, with both fiction and non-fiction titles. Mail-order service available.

Giovanni's Room, 1145 Pine St., Philadelphia, PA 19107 (☎215-923-2960; www.queerbooks.com). An international lesbian/feminist and gay bookstore with mail-order service (carries many of the publications listed below).

International Lesbian and Gay Association (ILGA), 81 rue Marché-au-Charbon, B-1000 Brussels, Belgium (☎+32 2 502 2471; www.ilga.org). Provides political information, such as homosexuality laws of individual countries.

FURTHER READING: BISEXUAL, GAY, & LESBIAN.

Spartacus International Gay Guide 2001-2002. Bruno Gmunder Verlag (US$33).

Ferrari Guides' Gay Travel A to Z, Ferrari Guides' Men's Travel in Your Pocket, and *Ferrari Guides' Inn Places.* Ferrari Publications (US$16-20). Purchase the guides online at www.ferrariguides.com.

The Gay Vacation Guide: The Best Trips and How to Plan Them, Mark Chesnut. Citadel Press (US$15).

TRAVELERS WITH DISABILITIES

Although the incidence of physical disability is higher than in Western countries, **most of South Asia is ill-equipped to deal with travelers with disabilities.** Special facilities are rare, and hospitals, even in the major cities, cannot be relied upon to replace broken braces or prostheses successfully. Public transportation is completely inaccessible and most cities have no sidewalks or ramps. Many sights also require climbing long staircases or hiking. The best option is probably to hire a car and driver; the lower costs of living common throughout the subcontinent make this a more viable option than in other parts of the world.

USEFUL ORGANIZATIONS

Mobility International USA (MIUSA), P.O. Box 10767, Eugene, OR 97440 (☎541-343-1284, voice and TDD; www.miusa.org). Sells *A World of Options: A Guide to International Educational Exchange, Community Service, and Travel for Persons with Disabilities* (US$35).

Society for the Advancement of Travel for the Handicapped (SATH), 347 Fifth Ave., #610, New York, NY 10016 (☎212-447-7284; www.sath.org). An advocacy group that publishes free online travel information and the travel magazine *OPEN WORLD* (US$18, free for members). Annual membership US$45, students and seniors US$30.

TOUR AGENCIES

Accessible Journeys, 35 West Sellers Ave., Ridley Park, PA 19078 (☎800-846-4537; fax 610-521-6959; www.disabilitytravel.com) runs tours for people with disabilities.

Directions Unlimited, 123 Green Ln., Bedford Hills, NY 10507 (☎800-533-5343). Books individual and group vacations for the physically disabled; not an info service.

TRAVELERS WITH CHILDREN

Family vacations often require that you slow your pace, and always require that you plan ahead. If you are traveling with small children, it is crucial to protect them from sunburn, excessive heat, insect bites, and diarrhea, which can cause severe dehydration and can kill children. Older children should carry ID in case of an emergency, and you should arrange a reunion spot in case of separation when sight-seeing. Children under two generally fly for 10% of the adult airfare on international flights (this does not necessarily include a seat). International fares are usually discounted 25% for children from two to 11. Children receive high discounts on flights within India. Finding a private place for **breast feeding** is often a problem while traveling, so pack accordingly.

For more information, consult one of the following books:

Backpacking with Babies and Small Children, Goldie Silverman. Wilderness Press (US$10).

How to Take Great Trips with Your Kids, Sanford and Jane Portnoy. Harvard Common Press (US $10).

Have Kid, Will Travel: 101 Survival Strategies for Vacationing With Babies and Young Children, Claire and Lucille Tristram. Andrews McMeel Publishing (US$9).

Adventuring with Children: An Inspirational Guide to World Travel and the Outdoors, Nan Jeffrey. Avalon House Publishing (US$15).

Trouble Free Travel with Children, Vicki Lansky. Book Peddlers (US$9).

DIETARY CONCERNS

India and Nepal are a paradise for vegetarians. The staple foods of a budget-minded connoisseur (rice and *dal*) will meet the most stringent vegetarian standards. Vegans, however, should be warned that *ghee* (clarified butter) is widely used in Indian cooking, and that cheese often appears in otherwise vegetarian dishes. The Muslim presence makes *halal* food a large part of the cuisine, kosher meals are next to nonexistent in India and Nepal. If you are strict in your observance, you may have to prepare your own food on the road. A good resource is the *Jewish Travel Guide*, by Michael Zaidner (Vallentine Mitchell; US$17).

OTHER RESOURCES

Listed below are other books and Web sites that can serve as jumping off points for your own research.

TRAVEL PUBLISHERS & BOOKSTORES

Rand McNally, P.O. Box 7600, Chicago, IL 60680, USA (☎847-329-8100; www.randmcnally.com), publishes road atlases.

Adventurous Traveler Bookstore, P.O. Box 2221, Williston, VT 05495, USA (☎800-282-3963; www.adventuroustraveler.com).

Travel Books & Language Center, Inc., 4437 Wisconsin Ave. NW, Washington, D.C. 20016 (☎800-220-2665; www.bookweb.org/bookstore/travelbks/). Over 60,000 titles from around the world.

WORLD WIDE WEB

Almost every aspect of budget travel is accessible via the Web. Within 10 minutes at the keyboard, you can make a reservation at a hostel, get advice on travel hotspots from other travelers who have just returned from the region, or find out schedules and fares for the train from Delhi to Mumbai.

Listed here are some budget travel sites to start off your surfing; other relevant Web sites are listed throughout the book. Because Web site turnover is high, use search engines (such as www.google.com) to strike out on your own.

THE ART OF BUDGET TRAVEL

How to See the World: www.artoftravel.com. A compendium of great travel tips, from cheap flights to self-defense to interacting with local culture.

Rec. Travel Library: www.travel-library.com. A fantastic set of links for general information and personal travelogues.

Lycos: http://cityguide.lycos.com. Introductions to India and Nepal, accompanied by links to applicable histories, news, and local tourism sites.

INFORMATION ON INDIA AND NEPAL

Bollywood World: www.bollywoodworld.com. News and gossip from the world of Indian cinema.

Cricket Info: www-ind.cricket.org. Comprehensive cricket news site, with daily updates on all the games and players. Essential reading for bluffers and old-hands alike.

Indian Railways: www.indianrail.gov.in. Online timetables and ticket reservation service.

Music India: www.musicindiaonline.com. First-class resource, featuring hundreds of articles, reviews, and recordings covering all genres of Indian music.

My Travel Guide: www.mytravelguide.com. Country overviews, with everything from history to transportation to live Web cam coverage.

Nepal Homepage: www.info-nepal.com. Cultural, business, and tourism resources.

Nepal News: www.nepalnews.com. An on-line English newspaper detailing current events in Nepal.

Samachar: www.samachar.com provides a digest of articles, updated daily, culled from all the major English-language papers in India.

Times of India: www.timesofindia.com. India's premier English-language newspaper.

Tour India: www.tourindia.com. A useful site on Indian tourism, providing links to the Indian airlines and tourist offices throughout the subcontinent.

Webguide India: www.webguideindia.com. Provides city directories as well as lists of everything from freebies and shopping to schools and cricket in India.

World Travel Guide: www.travel-guides.com/navigate/world.asp. Helpful practical info.

AND OUR PERSONAL FAVORITE...

Let's Go: www.letsgo.com. Our constantly expanding Web site features photos and streaming video, online ordering of all our titles, a travel forum buzzing with stories and tips, and links that will help you find (almost) everything you ever wanted to know about India and Nepal.

ALTERNATIVES TO TOURISM

As fun and exciting as traveling the world (or even just part of it) can be, actually living in a country and working, volunteering, or studying for an extended period of time can often be a more rewarding and complete way to truly appreciate the local culture and environment. This chapter outlines some of the different ways to get to know a new place, whether you want to pay your way through, or just get the personal satisfaction the comes from studying and volunteering.

Volunteering, working, or studying in a foreign country can be extremely rewarding, both financially and personally. And, in most cases, these alternatives to tourism result in a longer, more meaningful experience—something that the average budget traveler often misses out on.

There are many resources and programs available for those looking for non-tourist experiences in India and Nepal. The following list may serve as a starting point for finding out more. A surprising number of alternatives can be arranged informally especially if you're willing to work for room and board (just make sure you have the correct documentation—valid visas, work permits, etc.). We list such out-of-the-way opportunities in the specific city sections when we can, but the best advice is to look and ask around. For an extensive listing of "off-the-beaten-track" and specialty travel opportunities, try the **Specialty Travel Index,** 305 San Anselmo Ave., #313, San Anselmo, CA 94960 (☎ 888-624-4030; www.spectrav.com; US$6). Take your search to the web with the on-line newsletter published by **Transitions Abroad** (www.transabroad.com) and the catalogue of study, internship and teaching opportunities provided by **GoAbroad.com**.

STUDYING ABROAD

Studying abroad—whether for a few weeks or for a few years—is a great way to get to know both a language and a country. Programs range from basic language and culture courses to college-level classes, (often for credit). When choosing a program, find out what kind of students participate in the program and what the accommodations are. In programs that have large groups of students who speak the same language, the opportunity to practice a foreign language or to befriend locals and other international students is diminished. Local universities are often cheaper, though you may not be able to receive academic credit. Some schools offering study abroad programs to foreigners are listed below.

As for accommodations, students in some programs live with families, while in others dorm-like apartments or housing are made available to students. There are benefits and drawbacks to both—living in dorms provides better opportunities to mingle with fellow students, but there is less of a chance to experience the local scene. If you live with a family, there is a potential to build lifelong friendships with natives and to experience day-to-day life in more depth, but conditions can vary greatly from family to family.

UNIVERSITIES AND LANGUAGE PROGRAMS

For semester- or year-long programs for college credit, most American under-graduates usually enroll in programs sponsored by US universities. Many pro-grams offer classes in English and beginner- and lower-level language courses; ask around. For **language study,** *Let's Go* recommends traditional university study-abroad programs, both for summer-study and during the regular school year. Unlike American universities, language schools are frequently indepen-dently-run international or local organizations or divisions of foreign universi-ties that rarely offer college credit. Language schools are a good alternative to university study if you desire a deeper focus on the language or a slightly less-rigorous courseload.

A good resource for finding programs that cater to your particular interests is **www.studyabroad.com,** which has links to a huge number of study-abroad programs in the subcontinent. The following is a list of organizations that can help place students in university programs abroad.

American Institute of Indian Studies, 1130 East 59th St., Chicago, IL 60637. (§773-702-8638; aiis§uchicago.edu; www.indiastudies.org). Open to advanced-level students enrolled at American universities and colleges. Offers courses in Hindi, Bengali, Mar-athi, Telugu, and Tamil at various locations throughout India. Fees are around US$2000 for summer programs, US$6000 for one-year courses.

Applied Hindi Course: Faculty of Asian Studies, National University of Australia, Canberra ACT 0200. (☎+61 2 6249; fax 61 2 6249 0745; richard.barz@anu.edu.au). Runs intensive Hindi courses in Rishikesh, designed for students with the equivalent of at least a year's previous study.

Association of Commonwealth Universities (ACU), John Foster House, 36 Gordon Sq., London WC1H OPF (☎+44 020 7380 6700; www.acu.ac.uk). Publishes information about Commonwealth universities in India and Nepal.

Brethren Colleges Abroad: 605 East College Ave., North Manchester, IN 46962. (☎260-982-5238; fax 260-982-7755; inquiry@bcanet.org). Organizes study-abroad programs at the Cochin University of Science and Technology in Kerala.

Rutgers University India Program: The State University of New Jersey, 102 College Ave., New Brunswick, NJ 08903. (☎732-932-7787; fax 932-8659; ru_abroad@email.rut-gers.edu). Runs study-abroad schemes for college-level students at St. Stephen's Col-lege, Delhi. Costs are around US$6000 per semester.

School for International Training, College Semester Abroad, Admissions, Kipling Rd., P.O. Box 676, Brattleboro, VT 05302 (☎800-336-1616 or 802-257-7751; www.sit.edu). Semester- and year-long programs in India and Nepal run US$10,600-13,700.

Council on International Educational Exchange (CIEE), 633 3rd Ave., 20th fl., New York, NY 10017-6706 (☎800-407-8839; www.ciee.org) sponsors work, volunteer, aca-demic, and internship programs in India.

International Association for the Exchange of Students for Technical Experience (IAESTE), 10400 Little Patuxent Pkwy., Ste. 250, Columbia, MD 21044 (☎410-997-2200; www.aipt.org). 8- to 12-week programs in India for college students who have completed 2 years of technical study. US$25 application fee.

International Partnership for Service Learning, 815 Second Ave., #315, New York, NY 10017. (☎212-986-0989; fax 986-5039; www.ipsl.org), offers a 3-week program in Jan. or Aug., with the option of extending each into a 9-week semester. Both combine volunteer social work (with terminal patients in Missionaries of Charity hospices and in children's rehabilitation centers) with study of language (Bengali) and culture. 3-week program US$5300 (airfare included); semester-long program US$9,200 (including airfare and intercession). Study is done in Calcutta (in small hotels during 3-week program, homestays during the semester), with trips to Agra and Delhi.

Naropa Institute, 2130 Arapahoe Ave., Boulder, CO 80302 (☎444-444-0202; www.naropa.edu/studyabroad/). Runs programs in Boudha, Nepal as well as in Mysore and Auroville; students take classes in art and culture, language, culture, and religion. Open to both undergraduate and graduate students (US$10,350 for tuition, room, and board; does not include international airfare).

Pitzer College, External Studies, 1050 N. Mills Ave., Claremont, CA 91711 (☎909- 621-8104; fax 621-0518; www.pitzer.edu/academics/ilcenter/external_studies). Semester-long program (fall and spring) on Nepali language and culture. Family homestays just outside Kathmandu, with treks in Annapurna Conservation Area and Chitwan National Park. US$6,965 includes airfare, tuition, room and board, and field trip. Financial aid usually transferable.

University of Virginia Semester-in-India Program: Center for South Asian Studies, 110 Minor Hall, PO Box 400169, University of Virginia, Charlottesville, VA 22904. (email: southasia@virginia.edu; www.virginia.edu/~soasia). Language and civilization classes in Jodhpur, Rajasthan run at approx. US$7,500 per semester.

University of Wisconsin-Madison, 500 Lincoln Dr., 252 Bascom Hall, Madison, WI 53706 (☎608-265-6329; fax 262-6998; www.wisc.edu/studyabroad). Has college-year programs in Hyderabad, Madurai, Varanasi, and Kathmandu. The college-year programs concentrate on field work, with a year-long local language class and independently-chosen tutorial. One year of local language study is required. Fees cover academic expenses, administrative costs, a one-way plane ticket to India from the West Coast, room, meals, and pocket expenses: US$13,500 for India and Nepal. A summer performing arts program in Kerala is also offered for US$4500 (Wisconsin residents pay only US$1400).

WORKING

Although it's easy to find a temporary job in India and Nepal—native speakers of English often find that their skills are in high demand—it will rarely be lucrative or glamorous, and it might not even cover your airfare. It is also very difficult to get permission to work at all (both India and Nepal are net exporters of labor, with many going to earn a living in the Middle East). Officially, you can hold a job in most countries only with a **work permit.** Your employer must obtain this document, usually by demonstrating that you have skills that locals lack—not the easiest of tasks. Students can check with their universities' foreign language departments, which may have connections to job openings abroad. Call the embassy or consulate of the country in which you wish to work to get more information about work permits (see **Embassies and Consulates,** p. 8).

Many books list work-abroad opportunities. Note especially the excellent guides put out by **Vacation Work** (www.vacationwork.co.uk). For US college students, recent graduates, and young adults, the simplest way to get legal permission to work abroad is through **Council Exchanges Work Abroad Programs.** Fees are from US$300-425. Council Exchanges can help you obtain a three- to six-month work permit/visa and also provides assistance finding jobs and housing. To avoid scams from fraudulent employment agencies demanding large fees and providing no results, learn more about available opportunities from the following sources.

FROM THE ROAD

VOLUNTEER FOR INDIA

The pervasion of Indian influence into American pop culture in the form of yoga, bindis, and samosas, sparked a generation of visitors eager for an "alternative" vacation. I was among the many caught up in this frenzy and made the two-day journey to India after my freshman year at college. I toured the southern half of the country for two weeks shopping in the markets, sampling the cuisine, and adjusting to what seemed like life as the only white person around. Although my travels were incredible, I longed to do something more meaningful in India. I returned the next year as a volunteer in a rural village in the foothills of the Himalayas on a mission to make a difference, change some lives, and satisfy the other naïve clichés of most first time volunteers. I expected some fulfilling experiences, but no major surprises since I was confident my knowledge of India from my previous travels was complete.

And yet, I was shocked when I entered the village daycare. The tiny shack had a crumbling concrete floor, two drab posters for decoration, and was definitely not child-friendly. My six charges and an older woman filed in and sat on the floor, peering at me expectantly. I would teach the alphabet and the animals in English and Hindi. Soon after starting, I saw that my lesson plans were not challenging enough. Although the kids were very young, the alacrity and accuracy with which they learned was amazing. These were not the intellectually deprived children I thought I would encounter, but rather quite precocious youngsters. I left feeling silly for presuming that their poverty would somehow affect their cognitive capacity.

Archaeological Institute of America, 656 Beacon St., Boston, MA 02215, USA (š617- 353-9361; fax 353-6550; aiaşbu.edu; www.archaeological.org), puts out the *Archaeological Fieldwork Opportunities Bulletin* (US$15 for non-members), which occasionally lists field sites in India. This can be purchased from Kendall/Hunt Publishing, 4050 Westmark Dr., Dubuque, IA 52004, USA (š800-228-0810).

Council, Marketing Services Dept., 205 E. 42nd St., New York, NY 10017, USA (☎888- 268-6245; fax 212-822-2699; www.ciee.org), publishes *International and Volunteer Projects Directory* (US$20) and *Volunteer! The Comprehensive Guide to Voluntary Service in the US and Abroad* (US$12.95).

International Schools Services (ISS), 15 Roszel Rd., Box 5910, Princeton, NJ 08543-5910, USA (☎609-452-0990; fax 609-452-2690; www.iss.edu). Hires teachers for more than 200 overseas schools; candidates should have experience teaching or with international affairs, 2-year committment expected.

InterExchange, 161 Sixth Ave., New York, NY 10013, USA (☎212-924-0446; fax 924-0575; www.interexchange.org).

Office of Overseas Schools, US Department of State, Room H328, SA-1, Washington, D.C. 20522, USA (☎202-261-8200; fax 261-8224; www.state.gov/www/about_state/schools/). Keeps a list of schools abroad and agencies that arrange placement for Americans to teach abroad.

Uniworld Business Publications, Inc., 257 Central Park West, New York, NY 10024, USA (☎212-496-2448; fax 769-0413; www.uniworldbp.com). Check your local library for their Directory of American Firms Operating in Foreign Countries (January 2001; US$350). Now also available in a separate South Asia regional volume (US$49).

VOLUNTEERING

Volunteer jobs are widely available, and the cost of living in India and Nepal is low enough that volunteering is not a great financial setback. Consult the index for details of volunteer opportunities listed in this book. You might receive room and board in exchange for your labor. You may also avoid high application fees charged by placement organizations by contacting workcamps directly. Many volunteer services actually charge you a fee to participate in the program and to do work, and these fees can be surprisingly hefty. Try to do research on a program before committing—talk to people who have previously participated and find out exactly what you're getting into, as living and working conditions can vary greatly. Different programs are geared toward different ages and levels of experience, so be sure to make sure that you are not taking on too much.

Most people choose to go through a parent organization, which takes care of logistical details, and frequently provides a group environment and support system. There are two main types of organizations—religious, and non-sectarian—although there are rarely restrictions on participation for either. Adventurous travelers can search for a non-profit organization once in a country, and then only pay living expenses rather than the costly program fees for organized volunteer projects.

Amizade, Ltd., 367 S. Graham St., Pittsburgh, PA 15232, USA (§888-973-4443; fax 412-648-1492; www.amizade.org). Sends individuals or groups (over age 18) to work on short-term community-oriented projects, such as building schools and health centers, giving vocational training to children, etc. Costs vary from US$500-2500.

Child Family Health International, 953 Mission St., Ste. 220, San Francisco, CA 94103, USA (☎415-957-9000; fax 501-423-6852, www.cfhi.org). Sends pre-med undergraduate and medical students to work with physicians in India, although the focus is more on working with the community and learning about health care rather than actually providing medical assistance. Program fees are around US$1500, but don't include airfare.

Cross-Cultural Solutions, 47 Potter Ave., New Rochelle, NY 10801, USA (☎800-380-4777 or 914-632-0022; fax 914-632-8494, www.crossculturalsolutions.org). Operates short- and long-term humanitarian work in health care, education, and social development. Fees range from US$2100-4200.

Dakshinayan, c/o Siddarth Sanyal A5/108, Clifton Apartments, Charmwood Village, Surajkund Rd., Faridabad 121009, INDIA (from Delhi ☎525 3114; from outside Delhi (0129) 525 3114; mobile phone 98 1119 2133; email sid@linkindia.com; www.linkindia.com/dax). Places volunteers in short or long-term work projects in India

Earthwatch, 3 Clocktower Pl. Ste. 100, Box 75, Maynard, MA 01754, USA (☎800-776-0188 or 978-461-0081; www.earthwatch.org). Arranges 1- to 3-week programs in India and Nepal designed to promote conservation of natural resources. Fees vary based on program location and duration, costs average US$1700 plus airfare.

Elderhostel, Inc., 11 Ave. de Lafayette, Boston, MA 92111-1746, USA (☎877-426-8056; fax 877-426-

Working at the village hospital was equally eye opening. After touring the facility and talking with doctors, I realized that I was not there to inform them about how doctors worked in America but instead learn about Indian medicine, an institution free from the trials of insurance companies and malpractice lawsuits. Though Indian technology was limited (X-rays were dried on the hospital's front lawn), their knowledge was not; in fact their raw diagnostic skills were arguably better than those of American doctors. Indian doctors and nurses worked tirelessly to treat the hordes of people who came to the hospital each day resulting in prestige bordering on divinity because their healing powers made them godly for some patients.

Still, I was never without reminder that I was in a culture far different than my own. Hospital forms I helped nurses file still had space for a patient's caste information, and female doctors wore traditional *saris* under their white coats. The occasional case of tuberculosis or goiter reminded me that I was in a place where malnutrition and lack of vaccinations were a reality.

I often think about all the activities that India made so intriguing, exasperating, and wonderful: traipsing down a mountain each morning to use the bathroom, listening to a child switch from English to Hindi to Nepali without blinking, and fighting off aggressive monkeys. When I accepted such mundane activities as routine, I was no longer a tourist, rather someone privileged to better a country she was, albeit briefly, calling home.

—Joanna O'Learyl

2166; www.elderhostel.org). Sends volunteers age 55 and over around the world to work in construction, research, teaching, and many other projects. Costs average US$100 per day plus airfare.

Habitat for Humanity International, 121 Habitat St., Americus, GA 31709, USA (☎229-924-6935 x2551; www.habitat.org). Volunteers build houses in over 83 countries for anywhere from 2 weeks to 3 years. Short-term program costs range from US$1200-4000.

The Joint Assistance Center, Attn: Prof. P.L. Govil, G17/3 DLF Qutab Enclave Phase I, Gurgaon 122022, Haryana, INDIA (☎(0124) 352141), places volunteers directly in India. **Friends of JAC in the Americas,** P.O. Box 14481, Santa Rosa, CA 95402, USA(☎707-573-1740; fax 528-8917; jacusa@juno.com), assists with placement.

Peace Corps, Office of Volunteer Recruitment and Selection, 1111 20th St., NW, Washington D.C., 20526, USA (☎800-424-8580; www.peacecorps.gov). Opportunities in 70 developing nations, including Nepal.

Service Civil International Voluntary Service (SCI-IVS), SCI USA, 3213 W. Wheeler St., Seattle, WA 98199, USA (☎/fax 206-350-6585; www.sci-ivs.org). Arranges placement in work camps in Nepal for those 18 and over. Registration fee US$65-125.

Volunteers for Peace, 1034 Tiffany Rd., Belmont., VT 05730, USA (☎802-259-2759; www.vfp.org). Arranges placement in work camps in Nepal. Membership required for registration. Annual *International Workcamp Directory* US$20. Programs average US$200-500 for 2-3 weeks.

SPIRITUAL INTERESTS

The birthplace of several major world religions (Hinduism, Buddhism, Jainism, and Sikhism), the countries of South Asia are marked by strong religious beliefs and a profound sense of spirituality. Not surprisingly, India and Nepal attract huge numbers of travelers looking for the meaning of life. Aside from the mainstream traditions in India and Nepal (see **India: Religion,** p. 85, and **Nepal: Religion,** p. 762), some religious communities are open to initiates from abroad.

For **Hinduism,** these often take the form of *ashrams* (retreats), many of which are under the leadership of a modern-day guru—those who have attracted particularly large numbers of foreign devotees are sometimes referred to as "export gurus." Some of the most famous ashrams in India include that of the late **Sri Aurobindo** in Pondicherry (see p. 583), the **Osho Commune** in Pune (see p. 418), and **Sai Baba's** ashrams in Andhra Pradesh and Karnataka. **Rishikesh** (see p. 644) in Uttaranchal is a major center for gurus and students of yoga. If you stay in an ashram, you will usually be required to stay clean and quiet and to avoid meat, alcohol, tobacco, *paan* (betel), and drugs.

Since the 1959 Chinese crackdown in Tibet, India and Nepal have become the most accessible places in the world to study **Tibetan Buddhism. Dharamsala** (see p. 231) in India, the home of the Dalai Lama and the Tibetan government-in-exile, is a popular place to learn about Tibetan culture. There are opportunities for volunteer work among the Tibetan community here (see **Volunteer Opportunities,** p. 238). In Nepal (the Buddha's birthplace), the foremost Tibetan Buddhist center is located at **Boudha** (see **Study and Volunteer Opportunities,** p. 805), just outside Kathmandu. Unlike *lamas* (monks), Western students of Tibetan Buddhism do not usually live in monasteries, though they are expected to live austerely. Public lectures (often in English) and meditation courses are offered at the major Buddhist centers, including **Bodh Gaya** in Bihar (see **Buddhism and Community Service,** p. 141), the site of the Buddha's Enlightenment.

Christianity is India's third largest religion, after Hinduism and Islam. There are long traditions of faith and missionary work in the subcontinent. Many hospitals, schools, and Non-Governmental Organizations (NGOs) are run or supported by local or international Christian organizations. The **Missionaries of Charity,** founded by Mother Teresa, is the most famous of these organizations (see p. 738).

FOR FURTHER READING ON ALTERNATIVES TO TOURISM

Alternatives to the Peace Corps: A Directory of Third World and US Volunteer Opportunities, by Joan Powell. Food First Books, 2000 (US$10).

How to Get a Job in Europe, by Sanborn and Matherly. Surrey Books, 1999 (US$22).

How to Live Your Dream of Volunteering Overseas, by Collins, DeZerega, and Heckscher. Penguin Books, 2002 (US$17).

International Directory of Voluntary Work, by Whetter and Pybus. Peterson's Guides and Vacation Work, 2000 (US$16).

International Jobs, by Kocher and Segal. Perseus Books, 1999 (US$18).

Overseas Summer Jobs 2002, by Collier and Woodworth. Peterson's Guides and Vacation Work, 2002 (US$18).

Work Abroad: The Complete Guide to Finding a Job Overseas, by Hubbs, Griffith, and Nolting. Transitions Abroad Publishing, 2000 (US$16).

Work Your Way Around the World, by Susan Griffith. Worldview Publishing Services, 2001 (US$18).

ALTERNATIVES TO TOURISM

LIFE AND TIMES

INDIA

LAND

The colors of the Indian flag symbolize the coutnry's terrain: green tropical jungle, white Himalayan snow, and orange-red Deccan earth. In fact, the landscape is even more diverse than this comparison suggests. The **Himalayas** (Nepali for "abode of snow") crown the country and form a natural barrier between India and Central Asia, Tibet, and China. The world's highest mountain range, the Himalayas extend over 2000km and are the source of the subcontinent's three great rivers, the **Indus,** the **Ganga,** and the **Brahmaputra.** Fed by rain and glacial melt-off, these rivers and their tributaries nourish the vast, densely-populated **Indo-Gangetic Plain,** which stretches from Rajasthan in the west to Bengal in the east.

The **Vindhyas,** a belt of stepped hills, divide the Indo-Gangetic Plain from the **Deccan Plateau** (Maharashtra, Karnataka, and Andhra Pradesh). The **Arabian Sea** washes the continent to the west, the **Bay of Bengal** is on the east, and the southern tip, Kanyakumari, borders the Indian Ocean. Flanking the **Malabar Coast** of Kerala, Karnataka, and Goa, the **Western Ghats** (a north-south chain of mountains and hills) are separated from the coast by a narrow strip of richly forested coastal plain. The eastern **Coromandel Coast** is broader. The Ghats converge at the **Nilgiri Hills** of Kerala and Tamil Nadu. The **Lakshadweep Islands,** in the Arabian Sea, and the **Andaman and Nicobar Islands,** in the Bay of Bengal, are also Indian territories. For information on India's climate, see **When To Go** (p. 4). For a chart of **average temperatures and rainfall,** see p. 881.

FLORA & FAUNA

India is home to more than 500 species of mammals, 1,000 species of birds, and 6% of the world's reptile species, including 250 kinds of snakes. One of India's national symbols is the majestic (and endangered) **Bengal Tiger.** Poachers brought tigers close to extinction in the years after Independence, but more recently the establishment of national parks, reserves, and conservation projects—notably **Project Tiger** (see p. 367)—have reversed the slide, and the tiger population is now at a stable 3,000-4,000. Other Indian felines include leopards, panthers, and jungle cats. Also endangered is the **One-Horned Rhinoceros,** which once roamed across the subcontinent but now survives in only two places: **Kaziranga National Park** in Assam (see box below) and the **Chitwan National Park** in Nepal (see p. 838). Other mammals include bear, buffalo, bison *(ghaur),* mongoose, and dozens of species of antelope, deer, and gazelle. India also offers some of the best bird-watching spots in the world, including the **Keoladeo Ghana National Park,** near Bharatpur in Rajasthan (see below). Even outside the parks and reserves, colorful species such as peacocks, parrots, mynahs, bee-eaters, and hoopoes are common throughout the country. Also ubiquitous, but more often heard than seen, is the koel, a kind of cuckoo whose plaintive, "coo-ee" call follows you everywhere across southern Asia. Dozens of species of monkey inhabit India, and not just its jungles and forests; the small, long-tailed *langurs* are common in cities and towns, especially in temple precincts, where they are revered as sacred. These beasts are aggressive, diseased scavengers and are best avoided. Elephants are used as work animals, and can also be seen wild in several national parks.

PARK	LOCATION	BEST TIME TO VISIT	INFO.
Bandhavgarh National Park	Jabalpur, Madhya Pradesh (p. 368)	Nov. - Jun.	Highest-density tiger population
Corbett National Park	Uttaranchal (p. 655)	Nov. - Jun.	India's oldest national park; tigers, elephants, leopards
Eravikulam National Park	Munnar, Kerala (p. 342)	Sept. - May	Nilgiri *tahr*, jungle cat, mongoose
Gibbon Wildlife Sanctuary	Jorhat, Assam (p. 442)	Nov. - Apr.	Home to the Indo-US Primate Project
Kanha National Park	Jabalpur, Madhya Pradesh (p. 365)	Nov. - Jun.	Raj-era hunting ground, setting for Kipling's *Jungle Book*; tiger, leopard, boar, bear
Kaziranga National Park	Assam (p. 441)	Nov. - Apr.	Rhino, buffalo, elephant
Keoladeo Ghana National Park	Bharatpur, Rajasthan (p. 496)	Nov. - Jan.	One of the best bird-watching spots in Asia. 400-plus species
Mahatma Gandhi Marine National Park	Andaman Islands (p. 113)	Nov. - May	Diving, snorkeling, fish-watching
Manas National Park	Assam (p. 441)	After the guerrillas leave	Controlled by guerrillas and off-limits to the public
Nameri National Park	Assam (p. 441)	Nov. - Mar.	Elephants, orchids, rare duck, and tiger
Nandankan Zoological Park	Bhubaneswar, Orissa (p. 457)	Year-round	Zoo-cum-wildlife park; rare breeds (such as Bengal White Tiger) squeezed into tiny cages
Orang Wildlife Sanctuary	Assam (p. 441)	Nov. - Mar.	Rhino, elephant
Periyar Tiger Reserve	Kerala (p. 329)	Sept. - Mar.	Elephant, tiger, boating, trekking
Sundarbans National Park	West Bengal (p. 742)	Nov. - Mar.	Tiger, crocodile, deer

ECOLOGY

Air and water pollution in India have gone unchecked for decades. In a country where 300 million people live in poverty, green issues are often an afterthought. However, the vast majority of India's one billion people live in rural areas and depend on nature for their livelihood. Cash crops such as cotton, paper, rubber, tobacco, and spices account for a huge portion of GDP. Illegal logging continues to destroy forests, the natural habitat of species such as the **Bengal Tiger** and the **One-Horned Rhino,** already threatened by poaching. Industrial factories are killing flora, fauna, and even humans with toxic gases and tailings. Mines, highways, and hydroelectric dams have also disrupted India's ecological equilibrium. In the 1970s and 1980s, resistance to the destruction of India's forests was organized into what became known as the Chipko Movement. The name means "embrace"; local villagers and protesters would literally hug the trees to save them from the ax. The movement's success led in 1980 to a moratorium on logging in the Himalayan forests of Uttar Pradesh. Recently in Madhya Pradesh, a well-organized grass-roots movement has opposed government plans for dams along the River Narmada because the dams may damage the environment and displace as many as half a million people. Booker Prize winning novelist Arundhati Roy has been a prominent part of the protest and served a night in jail for contempt of court in March 2002.

HISTORY

ANCIENT HISTORY (3500-1500 BC). India gets its name from the Indus River, along whose banks the first significant civilization on the subcontinent flourished four thousand years ago. During the 1920s, the remains of huge cities were unearthed at **Harappa** and **Mohenjo-Daro** (both in Pakistan).

c.2500 BC
Indus Valley
Civilization at
Harrapa and
Mohenjo-Daro

The Indus Valley civilization prospered for more than a thousand years and comprised perhaps 100 cities, stretching out across half a million square miles. The population of its metropolitan centers—like the one at Harappa—was as high as 35,000. The streets of its cities were laid out in neat grids with elaborate drainage systems, centered on a "Great Bath" used for ritual. The valley dwellers were skilled farmers and created irrigation systems that let them harvest and keep huge stores of wheat and barley. Unearthed artifacts indicate that the Indus people traded by land and sea with Mesopotamia, Egypt, and Assyria. Little else is known about the everyday life of these people; their script, found on numerous seals, remains indecipherable. These seals feature humans, gods, and animals both real and imaginary, and suggest that the Indus people worshipped a mother-goddess and another deity who may be an ancestor of the Hindu god Shiva. Environmental changes were probably what killed the Indus civilization: tectonic plate movements around 1800 BC changed the river's course, flooding the carefully irrigated farmland that had nourished the valley for more than a thousand years.

c. 1500 BC
Aryan migrations
into the north of
India

THE ARYANS (1500-300 BC). As the Indus civilization declined, a new group entered the subcontinent. The Aryans were Indo-European nomads who had been raping and pillaging their way across the continent since being kicked out of the Caucasus around 2000 BC. They spread out in all directions, and a group of them came to the subcontinent by 1500 BC.

A loose band of tribes, each ruled by a *raja* (king), the Aryans spread out from the Punjab and the Indus Valley until they occupied most of northern India. With their snorting horses and their spoke-wheeled chariots, these fight-hungry warriors brought with them a culture and technology that permanently altered the civilizations they ran into (usually by destroying them completely).

The language of the Aryans was **Sanskrit** (in which *arya* means "noble one"), a member of the same Indo-European family that spawned Latin and Greek and is the root of the modern North Indian languages. Aryans worshiped the forces of nature: they performed fire-sacrifices to guarantee the continued sponsorship of **Agni,** the fire god, and **Indra,** god of war and an embodiment of the monsoon.

The Aryans brought to the subcontinent not only their language and religion but also a new social order. Aryan society was divided into three classes or *varna* (colors), probably originally based on race. The social hierarchy, made up of the **brahmin** (priests), the **kshatriya** (warriors), and the **vaishya** (merchants), formed the basis for the caste system (see **Caste,** p. 86).

The environment of India did much to change the cultural practices of the Aryans. As they moved into the Doab, the fertile plain of the Ganga and Yamuna Rivers, the Aryan tribes consolidated themselves into kingdoms and settled down into more permanent towns and villages. By the time they reached Bihar around 1000 BC, they had learned how to make iron tools. This discovery allowed them to clear the forests that covered the region, and they brought large areas under cultivation for the first time.

THE MAURYA EMPIRE (300-200 BC). By the 6th century BC, Aryans occupied the whole of northern India, where 16 separate Aryan kingdoms vied for supremacy. Having finished his conquest of Persia and the Mediterranean, **Alexander the Great** proceeded toward India's northwest frontier in 326 BC. But his troops had already had enough empire-building, and they soon grew tired of the endless marches against unknown enemies. Alexander was forced to turn back when his troops mutinied. Shortly after Alexander's retreat, **Chandragupta Maurya,** an adventurer from eastern India, seized control of the kingdom of Magadha, the most powerful Aryan state, in Bihar. Chandragupta moved quickly to subdue the area around the Ganga valley, and he continued to consolidate his power throughout northern India. Over the next 100 years, the Mauryan Empire, ruling from its capital at Pataliputra—modern day Patna (see p. 130)—came to control the whole of the subcontinent except for its southern tip—the closest anyone would come to wielding power over all of India until modern times.

The Mauryan Empire abandoned its policies of violent military expansion at the height of its power, after the invasion of the Kalinga Kingdom in Orissa, during which more than 100,000 people were killed. This bloody battle horrified the great Mauryan emperor **Ashoka** (r. 269-232 BC) so much that he renounced violence forever and became a Buddhist. With the last of his enemies conveniently dead, Ashoka preached the virtues of peaceful government and set about propagating a policy of non-violence *(ahimsa).* Edicts promoting Buddhism to the status of official creed were inscribed on pillars and stones, and the emperor passed rules to ensure that the vast lands under Mauryan control would be governed according to "moral law." The Mauryan Empire collapsed soon after Ashoka's death, but many of his edict-inscribed pillars still stand.

THE GUPTAS: A GOLDEN AGE (AD 300-500). In AD 319 another Chandragupta came to power in the eastern kingdom of Magadha. No relation to the founder of the Maurya dynasty, **Chandragupta II** (r. 375-415) followed in his namesake's illustrious footsteps and launched an empire of his own. At the peak of its power, the Gupta empire ruled over all of North India.

1500-300 BC
First traces of Hinduism (and its caste system)

c. 570-450 BC
Spread of Jainism and Buddhism. Buddha lived roughly 560-480 BC

INDIA

c. 500 BC
Composition of the Mahabharata and the Ramayana

326 BC
Alexander the Great invades

324-184 BC
Mauryan Empire rules from Magadha, Bihar

269-232 BC
Great Buddhist emperor Ashoka reigns over Mauryan Empire. Pillars engraved with his codes of law constructed all over India

AD 375-415
Reign of Chandragupta II

AD 300-500
Golden Age of
Indian culture: Kali-
dasa flourishes at
court; cave sculp-
tures at Ajanta

Today, the Guptas are remembered for the cultural refinement and religious tolerance that marked their rule, often
referred to as India's "Golden Age." They were great patrons of
the arts and sciences, into which they funneled their wealth
from overseas trade. Engineers built India's first stone dams
and temples, artisans carved the cave-sculptures at **Ajanta** out
of a sheer cliff face (see p. 428), and **Kalidasa,** India's greatest
lyric poet, served at the court of Chandragupta II.

Northern traders and priests had succeeded in converting
much of the South to Hinduism, and southern rulers tended to
model their governments on Aryan political structures. Despite
this apparent Aryanization, South Indian culture remained
independent in most other areas; distinct architectural styles
emerged, and Tamil poet-saints and thinkers, together with the
religious elite, co-inspired the *bhakti* devotional movement
that eventually overtook the north.

AD 630-645
Chinese monk
Xuanzang travels
through India in
search of Buddhist
scriptures; studies
at Nalanda in Bihar

REGIONALISM (AD 500-1192). The Gupta Empire disinte-
grated in the 5th century, when the Huns of Central Asia
invaded. North India fractured into small kingdoms again and
remained divided for most of the next 700 years.

The strongest kingdom in India at the time was the **Chola**
dynasty of Tamil Nadu, which conquered most of the southern
peninsula and sent forces to the Maldives, Sri Lanka, and
Malaysia. After the 8th century, a group of warriors known as
the **Rajputs** dominated northwest India. They set up several
small kingdoms from their base in the **Thar Desert** in Rajasthan
and developed a culture distinguished by chivalric values and a
proud architectural and literary tradition.

AD 712
Arabs conquer
Sind

THE ARRIVAL OF ISLAM (1192-1526). At the beginning of
the 7th century, the Prophet Mohammed received a set of revelations from God; the new faith he founded, **Islam,** spread east-
ward from its birthplace in Arabia to the northwest fringes of
the Indian subcontinent. Although Muslims traded with India
by sea, and many settled along the west coast, Islam made little
impression on the subcontinent until the raids of **Mahmud of
Ghazni,** the king of a Turkish dynasty in Afghanistan. Between
997 and 1030, Mahmud's armies looted and plundered North
India on an almost annual basis, though they never made any
attempt at a more permanent invasion.

AD 997-1030
Mahmud of Ghazni
raids northern
India

But at the end of the 12th century, another Turko-Afghan
king, **Mohammed of Ghur,** had conquest on his mind. In 1192 he
defeated a loose coalition of Rajput armies and conquered the
Ganga Valley. Though Mohammed himself soon headed home
to Afghanistan, he left his slave-general **Qutb-al-Din Aibak** behind
in Delhi to govern on his behalf (see **Qutb Minar,** p. 163). When
Mohammed died in 1206, Qutb-al-Din succeeded him, and proclaimed the birth of the **Delhi Sultanate,** India's first Muslim
kingdom. The Sultanate ruled most of North India for 300 years.
By the early 15th century, independent Muslim kingdoms had
emerged in Bengal, Gujarat, and Central India. The Delhi Sultanate's hold on power was always precarious. The palace was
in constant turmoil, and the sultans' habit of financing their
extravagant life at court with taxes paid by the Hindu masses

1206
Qutb-al-din founds
Delhi Sultanate;
beiginnings of Mus-
lim rule across
northern India

caused frequent revolts and widespread unhappiness. In 1398, the Central Asian conqueror **Tamerlane** crashed the party in Delhi and ruined the court's fun by burning the city to ashes.

Islam won huge numbers of converts, but ultimately, religious fragmentation undermined the centralized political authority of the **Lodis,** the last dynasty of the Delhi Sultanate. Provincial governors seceded in Bihar, Portuguese ships landed in Goa, and in central India the one-eyed, one-armed Rajput leader Rana Sanaga called for foreign intervention to vanquish the Delhi Sultanate.

THE MUGHALS (1526-1700). Rana Sanaga's call was heeded by the Central Asian warlord **Babur** (1483-1530), who counted both Tamerlane and Genghis Khan among his ancestors. A precocious little conqueror, Babur took Samarkand (in modern Uzbekistan) at the age of 13 and Kabul eight years later. In the Battle of Panipat, fought outside Delhi in 1526, Babur prevailed against numerically superior forces and crushed the Lodi dynasty. When Babur's son **Humayun** became sick in 1530, Babur prayed that the sickness would leave his son and afflict him instead. Babur died within weeks, and Humayun was proclaimed emperor over a kingdom that stretched from Bihar to Kabul.

Addicted to opium and astrology, Humayun was never a popular leader; within a decade, revolt was in the air. In 1540 the Afghan warlord Sher Shah deposed Humayun. Shah banished Humayun to the sand dunes of the Sindh desert while he worked to secure his position, but when Shah was killed during a siege of a Rajput stronghold in 1545, Humayun shook the sand out of his robes and headed back to court. With Persian help he retook Delhi, though he was to die four months later after a fatal tumble down the stairs in his library. His son **Akbar** (1542-1605) took the throne in 1555.

Akbar was 13 when he succeeded his father, but he quickly squashed rebellions and cemented Mughal dominion by conquering Rajasthan, Gujarat, Orissa, Kashmir, and Bengal. Akbar also worked to create a **centralized imperial bureaucracy.** To win Hindu support, Akbar married a Rajput princess and appointed Hindus to government posts. He also stopped the bulldozing of Hindu temples and eliminated the *jizya*, a widely despised tax levied on non-Muslims.

Akbar's successors **Jehangir** (r. 1605-27) and **Shah Jahan** (r. 1628-57) built on Akbar's work. Together, their reigns were a golden era for the Mughals. This period also saw the construction of stunningly beautiful buildings, including the marble **Taj Mahal** in Agra (p. 680) and the sandstone **Red Fort** in Delhi (p. 161). But when Shah Jahan fell ill in 1657, his sons went to war, **Aurangzeb** eventually emerging victorious, having murdered his brother and imprisoned his father in the fort at Agra.

Aurangzeb's rule lasted 48 years. Mughal armies conquered huge swathes of southern and eastern India. Fanatically pious, Aurangzeb undid a century of tolerance and understanding and made it difficult for Hindus to advance through the civil service bureaucracy. He banned the repair of Hindu temples and

1398
Tamerlane sacks Delhi

1469-1538
Guru Nanak and the birth of Sikhism

1500
Portuguese traders arrive at Goa

1562-1572
Akbar rules Mughal Empire. Humayun's tomb built in Delhi

1571-1586
Building of Fatehpur Sikri, modern-day Uttar Pradesh

1600
Queen Elizabeth I grants a charter to the East India Company, with instructions to seize control over international trade in Asia

1628-1657
Taj Mahal built during reign of Shah Jahan

I N D I A

brought back the *jizya*; the Hindu majority hated him. By the time Aurangzeb died, well into his eighties, the Mughal empire was already disintegrating. For the next half-century, the Mughals ruled in name only. Delhi was sacked and looted by Persians in 1738 and by Afghans in 1757.

THE BEGINNINGS OF BRITISH INTERFERENCE (1700-1757).

1748-1761
Anglo-French Wars on three continents; British capture French settlements in southeast India

European ships had been sailing the seas for hundreds of years in search of the riches of the East, but they didn't reach India until the 17th century, when the English, Portuguese, Dutch, and French governments chartered trading companies. The gradual decline of Portuguese sea power, together with a Dutch decision to focus on Indonesia, paved the way for the **British East India Company** to assert monopolistic control over South Asia's resources. From Calcutta and Madras, the Company ran a highly profitable trade, exchanging gold and silver for Indian finished goods, especially hand-crafted textiles.

The Company recruited small Indian armies to defend its warehouses with European weapons. These mercenary armies allowed the Company to dominate Bengal in the mid-18th century. It would soon extend its influence even farther.

1757
Battle of Plassey

Led by Robert Clive, the Company allied itself with a coalition of Muslims and Hindus, and after a series of battles culminating at **Plassey** in 1757 established unrivalled authority over much of Eastern India.

1774-1785
Warren Hastings appointed first governor-general

EAST INDIA COMPANY RULE (1757-1857).

During the late 18th century the Company, led first by Warren Hastings and then by Lord Cornwallis, developed a British-dominated bureaucracy to administer its business and government in Indian territories.

1848-1856
Lord Dalhousie appointed governor-general

Between the late 1820s and 1857, the Company attempted to recast Indian society in a European mold. It introduced railways, textile mills, and telegraphs, and outlawed **sati,** in which widows burned themselves on their husbands' funeral pyres, and **thugi,** in which devotees of the goddess Kali committed ritual robbery and murder. In keeping with their goal of improving Indian culture by Westernization, British authorities changed the official language of state from Persian to English in 1847 and funded the development of secondary schools, medical colleges, and universities. In all of these, both the curriculum and language of instruction were English. Millions of Indians resented the British influence, and in the 1850s, the situation turned violent.

1857-1858
Sepoy Mutiny in Lucknow and other cities

SEPOY MUTINY AND AFTERMATH (1857-1858).

In 1857, the Company outfitted its 200,000 *sepoys* (Indian soldiers) with the Lee-Enfield rifle, whose ammunition cartridges were rumored to be lubricated with pig and cow fat. Hindus (for whom cows are sacred) and Muslims (for whom pigs are impure) were incensed when they learned that soldiers had to bite the tip off these cartridges with their teeth before loading them. In the **Sepoy Mutiny** of May 1857, Indian soldiers raised the Mughal flag over Delhi, indiscriminately massacring Europeans as they took control of the city; similar bloodshed occurred in several other cities, most famously in Lucknow (see p. 690). But the victory was short-lived: backed by Sikh regiments, British troops retaliated four months later, recapturing Delhi and Lucknow at the cost of great numbers of Indian lives. By March of 1858, the British had suppressed the Mutiny (the War of Independence, as Indian nationalists call it today).

The revolt alarmed the British and triggered dramatic changes in the way they governed India. An 1858 Act of Parliament stripped the East India Company of its rule; within a year, the Crown was administering India directly as a full-fledged colony. The **Raj** had begun. To ensure tight control over India, Crown authorities increased the number of British troops stationed in South Asia, banned Indians from becoming officers in the army, and staffed the upper echelons of the burgeoning Indian Civil Service with British bureaucrats. The increasingly racist British tended to withdraw from Indian society, setting up hill stations remote from the cities and for the most part abandoning their quest to westernize South Asia.

RAJ VS. SWARAJ (1858-1915). A group of 70 wealthy Indians met in Bombay in 1885 to form the **Indian National Congress,** a political association that demanded reform and independence. As it grew, the Congress split into two wings: the moderates, who advocated reform but were content to remain a part of the Empire, and the extremists, who wanted to put an end to British meddling once and for all. The extremist view began to win widespread support after 1905, when the British viceroy partitioned Bengal into two provinces: one with a Hindu majority, the other Muslim.

The terms of the debate had shifted, and self-rule, or **swaraj,** became the ultimate objective. In the next decade, Indians from all walks of life actively resisted British rule by whatever means possible. Millions of Indians boycotted British-made textiles, opting instead for the rougher, homespun *swadeshi* cloth. Muslims concerned about Hindu domination of Congress founded the **All-India Muslim League** in 1906.

Indian nationalists cooperated with the British during the First World War in the hope that their loyalty would be rewarded with greater freedom. Instead, the British suspended civil liberties and imposed martial law. In 1919, British soldiers led by General Dyer massacred over 300 people when they opened fire on unarmed Indians who had assembled in **Amritsar** to protest.

It was to this atmosphere of violence and unrest that **Mohandas Karamchand Gandhi** (later proclaimed the Mahatma, or "Great Soul," by Bengali poet Rabindranath Tagore) returned in 1915. Born into a Gujarati family in 1869, Gandhi had gone abroad to study law. After studying in England, Gandhi spent 20 years in South Africa, where he devoted his energies to ending racial discrimination against Indians living in that country. Upon his return, he developed *satyagraha*, a kind of non-violent resistance he described as "soul force."

1858
Government transferred from East India Company to direct Crown rule

INDIA

1869
Mohandas Gandhi born in Porbandar, Gujarat

1885
First meeting of Indian National Congress

1877
Victoria declared "Empress of India"

1905
Partition of Bengal

1906
All-India Muslim League founded

1919
Amritsar Massacre

1921
Victoria Memorial
opens in Calcutta

1930
Gandhi's salt
march

1937
First elections held

1942
Congress leaders
imprisoned

1947
Partition and
Independence,
August 14-15. Lord
Mountbatten
leaves his post as
the last viceroy.
Fierce fighting in
Kashmir; millions
migrate across new
borders between
India and Pakistan

THE STRUGGLE FOR FREEDOM (1915-1947). Gandhi enjoyed amazing popularity throughout the 1920s. His religious tolerance earned him support from both Hindus and Muslims, and his rejection of Western products in favor of *swadeshi* goods made him popular among the peasant masses. This popularity paved the way for his leadership of Congress, and he seized the opportunity and reshaped the elite party into a populist one supported by millions of ordinary Indians.

Millions participated in non-violent civil disobedience throughout the 1920s. In 1930 **Jawaharlal Nehru,** the charismatic young leader of the Congress party's radical wing, audaciously declared the 26th of January to be Indian Independence day. Seven weeks later, Gandhi embarked on his famous **salt march.** British authorities had declared it illegal for salt to be sold or manufactured except under the auspices of the heavily taxed official monopoly, leading the very poorest of India's people to suffer the tax's heavy burden. In defiance of the law, Gandhi and his supporters marched 380km from his Sabarmati Ashram in Ahmedabad to the sea, attracting crowds and media coverage along the way. Staff in hand, Gandhi reached the coastal town of Dandi on April 6. Wading into the water, he took a handful of sea-water, poured it onto dry ground, and made salt. The act meant little in itself, but its symbolic value was tremendous. The British authorities responded by arresting 60,000 people, but there was little they could do to control the rising tide of nationalism. In 1932, the army granted its first commissions to Indian officers, and in 1935, the Government of India Act was passed, giving authority over provincial government to elected Indian representatives.

Meanwhile, tension grew between Congress and the Muslim League. Leaders such as **Mohammed Ali Jinnah** advocated aggressive seizure of power as the only way for Muslims to ensure that their rights would be guaranteed in an independent, Hindu-dominated India. In 1940, the League declared the Muslims of India a separate nation and demanded the creation of an independent Muslim state called Pakistan.

By the end of WWII, Britain's new Labour government agreed to grant India full independence. Vicious religious conflicts wracked Calcutta, the Punjab, and the Ganga Valley in 1946 and encouraged the division of India into two sovereign states—one Hindu, one Muslim. Defying geography, the government carved the new state of Pakistan out of Muslim-majority areas in both the east and the west, splitting Bengal and Punjab in two. Independence for India arrived at the same time as **Partition,** as the vast territory that had been the "the jewel in the crown" of the British Empire was divided. The independent nation of **Pakistan** was born on August 14, 1947, and **India** followed suit 24 hours later. The last British viceroy, Lord Mountbatten, stayed on to oversee the exchange of power, but the days of the British Raj were over. Hours before **Independence,** Nehru made one of the most famous speeches of the 20th century to the Constituent Assembly in New Delhi: "At the stroke of the midnight hour, when the world sleeps, India will awake to life and freedom. A moment comes, which comes but rarely in history, when we step from the old to the new, when an age ends, and when the soul of a nation, long suppressed, finds utterance."

PARTITION AND AFTER (1947-1964). As countries were created, so were refugees: millions of desperate Sikhs and Hindus streamed into India, fearing for their lives, while millions of Muslims fled to Pakistan. These massive migrations, probably the largest movements of people in history, touched off stampedes and religious violence on a horrific scale. Well over 500,000 were killed. Five months later, Mahatma Gandhi was assassinated on his way to evening prayers by **Nathuram Godse,** a Hindu extremist angered by Gandhi's cordial relations with the Muslim League.

Nehru's India faced innumerable economic problems. The vast majority of Indians lived in terrible poverty, and huge economic rifts separated the urban middle classes from the village-based majority. Nehru embarked on a series of **five year plans** and successfully solicited foreign aid, but sluggish economic growth failed to keep pace with the needs of an ever-expanding population.

Foreign policy problems plagued Nehru's administration. Independence forced **Kashmir,** a formerly independent kingdom in the Himalayas with a Hindu maharaja and a population that was 75% Muslim, to choose to be part of either India or Pakistan. Border skirmishes with Pakistan led the maharaja to choose India, with Nehru promising a fair plebiscite soon. A brief, undeclared war between India and Pakistan ended in 1949 with a UN cease-fire. The war established a still-disputed "line of control" between Pakistani and Indian Kashmir, but did nothing to solve the problems at the root of the conflict (see **Jammu and Kashmir,** p. 259). At the same time, the new nation bickered about Kashmir's borders with China. They went to war in 1962.

INDIRA'S INDIA (1964-1984). After Nehru's death in 1962, **Lal Bahadur Shastri** became prime minister, but died shortly after a victory in a war against Pakistan. Shastri was succeeded by Nehru's daughter, Indira Gandhi (see **What's in a Name?,** p. 78). As soon as she came to power, Mrs. Gandhi fought with the Congress "old guard" and began to align India with the Soviet Union. Pakistan aligned with the U.S.

In 1971, East Pakistan broke away from West Pakistan, prompting a swift invasion by West Pakistan. The flood of millions of refugees into India inflicted a heavy burden on India's already-strained treasury. India started arming and training Bengali guerrillas, and in December, Pakistani planes attacked Indian airfields. The next day, Indira Gandhi sent troops into both East and West Pakistan. Less than two weeks later, Pakistan surrendered; the result was the creation of the state of **Bangladesh.** With Pakistan defeated, India became South Asia's key political player.

The early years of Gandhi's government were promising. The so-called **Green Revolution** introduced high-yield crops, modern farm machinery, and chemical fertilizers, but none of Indira's reforms solved the fundamental problem of insufficient production. Small farmers who could not afford modern tools couldn't compete with richer, large-scale farmers. In later years, Gandhi focused on policies designed to alleviate poverty and worked to introduce family-planning measures and self-sufficiency strategies. Her methods, however, became increasingly totalitarian.

1947-1964
Jawaharlal Nehru first prime minster of independent India

1948
Gandhi assassinated

INDIA

1961
Goa absorbed into Republic

1962
Border skirmishes with China

1965
War with Pakistan over Kashmir

1966
Indira Gandhi becomes prime minister

1971
Indo-Pakistan War. East Pakistan becomes independent nation of Bangladesh

INDIA

WHAT'S IN A NAME? No one in India has sparked as much controversy as the Gandhi family. Between the charismatic Jawaharlal Nehru, his daughter Indira Gandhi, and her son Rajiv Gandhi, the Nehru-Gandhi family has ruled over 40 out of 55 years in independent India. Rumored to have married Feroze Gandhi in order to use the Mahatma's last name (no relation), Indira Gandhi was a populist tyrant who called her rule "democracy with discipline." Sikh bodyguards assassinated her in 1984. Her son Sanjay, whom she had been grooming to take her place, died in a plane crash in 1980, so his brother Rajiv became prime minister. Rajiv too soon met an untimely death, killed by a Tamil Tiger suicide bomber while on campaign in 1991. Sanjay's widow Maneka Gandhi is a prominent animal rights activist and environmentalist, and Rajiv's widow, the Italian-born Sonia Gandhi, captured the limelight when she became president of Congress and announced her candidacy for prime minister in the October 1999 elections. She lost, but the threat of a Gandhi return still looms.

After the **oil crisis** of 1973, India faced runaway inflation and the threat of famine. Millions slipped toward starvation, but the corrupt and nepotistic government did little to help. In 1975, Mrs. Gandhi was found guilty of election fraud. Rather than step down, she declared a **National Emergency,** and suspended all civil rights: she imposed sterilization on families with more than two children, aggressively censored the press, converted India's intelligence agencies into her own private police force, and locked up her political opponents.

1975
State of emergency declared

The state of emergency ended in January 1977, by which time Mrs. Gandhi was confident that she would be re-elected legitimately. She wasn't. The **Janata Dal,** an anti-Indira coalition led by **Morarji Desai,** Mrs. Gandhi's former finance minister, came to power in March that year. Unable to hold his party together, however, Desai toppled and Mrs. Gandhi was re-elected in 1980.

1980
Indira Gandhi re-elected prime minister

Regional problems plagued her second term. In 1984 she ordered the dismissal of Kashmir's popular Chief Minister, Farooq Abdullah. Soon afterward, she gave another order to the governor of Andhra Pradesh, demanding the removal of the state's popular Chief Minister, **N.T. Rama Rao,** a former film star and leader of a major opposition party. She also confronted separatist **Sikh militants,** who had launched a terrorist campaign on behalf of a sovereign Sikh nation in **Punjab and Haryana.** In 1984, when armed Sikh militants occupied the Golden Temple in Amritsar—the Sikhs' holiest site—Mrs. Gandhi sent in troops (see p. 472). Thousands died during the ensuing four-day battle, but for Mrs. Gandhi the worst was yet to come. By desecrating the temple, Mrs. Gandhi incurred the wrath of the militants, and on October 31, 1984, two Sikh bodyguards shot her to death in her home. Her murder sparked enormous riots throughout the capital and widespread massacres of Sikhs by Hindu thugs.

1984
Occupation of Golden Temple in Amritsar; assassination of Indira Gandhi

THE RISE OF THE BJP (1984-2000). A sympathy vote in the elections that followed Indira's assassination gave an impressive majority to Rajiv Gandhi's Congress party. Many had high hopes that Rajiv's administration would help bring about the changes India so badly needed. These hopes were quickly dashed. Rajiv's term as prime minister began inauspiciously with a gas leak from the Union Carbide chemical plant that killed nearly 3000 people in **Bhopal** in December 1984. Rajiv's free-enterprise, trickle-down economic policies brought in imported luxuries for the rich, but did little for the poor.

Rajiv had mixed success with foreign policy. He improved relations with the US without moving away from the Soviet Union, but he made several ill-advised decisions in the case of **Sri Lanka,** only 35km off the south coast of India. The **Tamil Tigers,** a guerrilla group fighting for an independent Tamil state on the island, had been surreptitiously armed and trained in India during Mrs. Gandhi's administration. Rajiv sent the Indian Peace Keeping Force (IPKF) to Sri Lanka to join the fight against the Tigers, and the Sri Lankan government was only too happy to withdraw its troops from the fray. The Tigers routed the government forces—by the time the IPKF withdrew, there were 100 Indian soldiers dead for every Tiger killed.

The 1989 elections transferred power to a fragile coalition of parties led by the Hindu Nationalist **Bharatiya Janata Party (BJP),** and Prime Minister V.P. Singh of the Janata Dal. The situation in Kashmir worsened, even as Singh struggled to put an end to the crisis in Punjab. Muslim militants, trained and armed by Pakistan, attacked Indian government offices. The state capital of **Srinagar,** once a popular tourist destination, turned into a war zone. And there were other problems. A policy proposal required that 60% of university admissions and civil service jobs be reserved for lower castes and former Untouchables. The new proposal threatened to bring about the collapse of the Singh government, and higher-caste Hindus were soon marching in the streets; some even immolated themselves in protest. When L.K. Advani, the leader of the BJP, was arrested, the BJP withdrew its support, and the government fell.

The elections of 1991 reinstated Congress power, thanks largely to another sympathy vote following the assassination of Rajiv Gandhi, who was killed by a **Tamil Tiger** suicide bomber. The new prime minister, **P.V. Narasimha Rao,** won widespread support for instituting drastic economic reforms that cut government expenditure and opened India to foreign investment.

Late 1991 renewed a long-running dispute over the **Babri Masjid** in Ayodhya. In December 1992, with the BJP in power in Uttar Pradesh, Hindu nationalists called for volunteers to build a Hindu temple in place of the mosque that stood on the site of Rama's birthplace. Devotees from all over India converged on Ayodhya with bricks in hand and tore down the mosque. Hindu-Muslim violence erupted across India.

1984-1989
Rajiv Gandhi prime minister

December 1984
Gas leak at Union Carbide factory in Bhopal kills thousands

INDIA

1991
Rajiv Gandhi assassinated

1992
Destruction of Babri mosque at Ayodhya in Uttar Pradesh; thousands killed in sectarian violence

Militant Islamist campaign against Indian rule in Kashmir

1995
Nationalist Shiv Sena party takes control of Maharashtra; Bombay officially renamed Mumbai

Though considerably weakened, the Rao government clung to power and continued its economic liberalization. But by the mid-nineties, the Hindu nationalists had made a comeback. In 1995, the radical nationalist party **Shiv Sena** took control of **Maharashtra,** which includes the industrial powerhouse of Mumbai. Kashmir continued to be a problem, and the government's mishandling of the insurgency there brought international condemnation for human rights violations.

1998
Nuclear weapons tests in India and Pakistan

The BJP's bad luck in the 1996 elections enabled a coalition government of low-caste, populist, and socialist parties called the United Front to rise to power, with **H.D. Deve Gowda** as prime minister. Between 1996 and 1998, India stumbled from one teetering coalition government to another. The Hindu Nationalist BJP won elections in 1998. In May that year, a series of five nuclear weapons tests brought Prime Minister **Atal Behari Vajpayee** into the international spotlight and intensified the subcontinental arms race. Later that year, Indian and Pakistani troops exchanged heavy shelling across Kashmir's Line of Control, and more than 90 soldiers and civilians were killed. In late May 1999, Indian jets attacked Muslim guerrilla forces that had advanced beyond the Line of Control marking the disputed border with Pakistan. The battle killed hundreds and forced thousands to flee their homes.

1999
Conflict in Kargil with Pakistan over Kashmir

Cyclones rip through Orissa

In April 1999, the government collapsed after the southern **AIADMK party** withdrew its support from the ruling coalition. The opposition, headed by Congress leader **Sonia Gandhi** (widow of former PM Rajiv Gandhi) was unable to form a majority in parliament, and India went to the polls for the third time in three years. The **New Democratic Alliance,** dominated by Prime Minister Atal Bihari Vajpayee and his BJP won nearly 300 of the 536 parliamentary seats up for grabs. Their victory came on the back of success in that summer's military tussles with arch-rival Pakistan in the Kargil region of disputed Kashmir. In October 1999, a series of monster **cyclones** ripped through the eastern state of **Orissa,** killing more than 10,000 people and causing untold damage across one of the poorest parts of the country. In Kashmir, hopes of a settlement were raised briefly in July 2000, when breakaway militant group Hizbul Mojahedin agreed to a cease-fire.

January 2001
Monster earthquake hits Gujarat

These hopes were shattered when the bombings and massacres started up again soon afterward. Bill Clinton's final year as US president brought him to India in March 2000—the first visit by an American head of state for over 20 years.

A devastating **earthquake** measuring 7.9 on the Richter scale rocked the western state of Gujarat on Republic Day, January 26 2001, wreaking unprecedented damage and killing an estimated 40,000 people. Many thousands more lost their homes. The website www.tehelka.com ("News, Views, and all the Juice") made the controversial decision to broadcast footage of the BJP president Bangaru Laxman fixing a fictitious defense deal, along with images of other party members involved in similar shady dealings. The party president resigned shortly afterward.

TODAY

THIS YEAR'S NEWS

Relations with Pakistan have gone from bad to worse in the 12 months after a failed summit meeting at Agra in July 2001. In October 2001, Kashmiri separatists set off a car bomb outside the State Legislature building in Srinagar, Kashmir, leaving dozens dead and many more injured. In December, gunmen shot up the Indian Parliament in New Delhi, and a bomber killed 20 people by blowing himself up as legislators left the building. In January 2002, Pakistani President Pervez Musharraf outlawed Lashkar-e-Taiba and Jaish-e-Mohammed, two militant groups suspected of involvement in the attack, but this did little to ease tension between the two countries. In early 2002, both nations tested ballistic missiles capable of carrying nuclear warheads. **India and Pakistan amassed troops along the border throughout early 2002.** India recalled its senior diplomat from Islamabad and suspended transport links with Pakistan in January 2002. Later the same month, an attack on the American Center in Calcutta killed five policemen and left dozens injured. Pakistan denied involvement. India expelled Pakistan's high commissioner in May 2002 after an attack on an Indian army base in Jammu killed 34, many of them women and children. By June, the situation was extremely perilous. The number of troops on the border grew to the millions, and foreign embassies advised citizens to leave before the outbreak of nuclear war. Slowly, both countries backed down, and as of this writing, the nuclear danger has simmered to its customary level.

Hindu-Muslim violence broke out in Gujarat in February 2002, when a train carrying Hindu activists to a contested holy site in Ayodhya, Uttar Pradesh was set on fire, killing 50. Retaliatory violence claimed many more lives across the country, and a predominantly Muslim section of the city of Ahmedabad in Gujarat was torched later the same month, leaving dozens dead and thousands homeless. At least 1000 people died in sectarian violence already in 2002, and tensions remain high.

December 2001
Suicide bomber attacks Indian parliament building. Suspicions of Pakistani involvement high

May 2002
India expels Pakistan's high comissioner in response to repeated incursions across the Line of Control in Kashmir

June 2002
Foreign citizens urged to leave the subcontinent as fears mount of imminent outbreak of war between India and Pakistan

February 2002
Hindu-Muslim violence kills hundreds across Gujarat

INDIA

GOVERNMENT AND POLITICS

In September and October 1999, 590 million voters in India cast their ballots for over 14,000 candidates vying for 543 parliamentary seats—history's largest democratic elections. That India's frenzied politics have managed to plod along more or less successfully, despite persistent secessionist threats, extreme malnutrition and human suffering, and even a brief bout with totalitarian rule in the 1970s (see **Indira's India,** p. 79) has astonished political scientists for much of the 55 years since Independence. Somehow, the British-inspired parliamentary system has stayed afloat.

Following Hindu-Muslim violence in early 2002, the US State Department advised its citizens not to travel anywhere in **Gujarat** and to avoid the contested holy city of **Ayodhya** in Uttar Pradesh. Ongoing violence makes much of **Jammu and Kashmir** off-limits for travelers; separatists in Kashmir have kidnapped and killed several tourists. Tensions with neighboring Pakistan remain high. The presence of US troops has led to a rise in anti-Western sentiment in that country. Five people, including a US diplomat and her daughter, were killed in a church bombing in Islamabad in March 2002. In May 2002, a suicide attack on a bus in Karachi killed 15 people, including 11 French nationals. **Pakistan-based extremist groups have been blamed for several attacks on Indian soil, including a shoot-out at an American Cultural Center in Calcutta that left five dead in January 2002.**

The country's **constitution,** adopted in 1950, is the longest in the world, with 395 articles legislating, among other things, universal suffrage and fundamental rights. The Indian constitution is distinctive in combining traditional liberal rights—freedom of press, free speech, and free association—with **Directive Principles** designed to deal with the social and economic reforms essential for a poor democracy. The framers of the constitution sought to create a **federal system** that would reflect India's diversity, but they also wanted a central government strong enough to handle poverty and religious conflict. The result has been a highly centralized form of federalism, with the national government holding the power to dismiss state governments in an emergency, an option known as **"President's Rule."** President's Rule was imposed as recently as March 2002 in Uttar Pradesh.

The vice-president, a council of ministers, and the prime minister head India's government. The president (currently K.R. Narayan), appointed for a five-year term, is a figurehead. The prime minister (currently Atal Behari Vajpayee of the BJP), chosen by the majority party in the **Lok Sabha** (House of the People), the lower house, holds executive power. The Lok Sabha and the **Rajya Sabha** (Council of States), chosen by the state governments, together make up the Indian parliament.

Each of India's states has a similar government. Each state has a legislative assembly, or **Vidhan Sabha.** Although the state governments depend on the national government for financial support, they have jurisdiction over education, agriculture, welfare, and the police. India's **Supreme Court** is remarkably independent and often asserts its right to make decisions on controversial issues that others would rather avoid.

India may be a working democracy, but one family and their party, the **Congress Party,** dominated for most of the first 50 years after Independence (see **What's in a Name?,** p. 78). Despite Congress' inclusiveness, it has found it difficult to unite the conflicting interests of ideology, caste, region, and religion. As a result, politics have become highly regionalized, with parties such as the **DMK** (in Tamil Nadu), the **Communist Party of India** (in Bengal), and the **Akali Dal** (in Punjab) often earning more votes in state elections than Congress. In the 1996 national elections, no single party won a majority of seats in the Lok Sabha, leading to the formation of piecemeal left-wing coalitions such as the Janata Dal and the Communist Party of India. The party that burst the Congress bubble, the **Bharatiya Janata Party (BJP),** won a majority of the Lok Sabha seats in 1999 elections under the leadership of Atal Bihari Vajpayee, the current Prime Minister. The BJP's rise has alarmed many who fear that religious and nationalist groups pose a threat to the secularism enshrined in the Constitution.

Caste politics are increasingly influential, as lower castes begin to translate their demographic strength into political clout, particularly in Bihar and Uttar Pradesh. Corruption scandals have brought down numerous state and national governments, and groups in some regions regularly use violence and bribery to intimidate voters.

ECONOMICS

In his famous "Tryst with Destiny" speech, delivered on the eve of Independence, Prime Minister Jawaharlal Nehru promised "the ending of poverty and ignorance and disease and inequality of opportunity" in the new nation. Nehru drew inspiration from the Soviet Union and advocated heavy industrialization and state ownership of major companies. The aim of Nehruvian socialism was self-sufficiency in the tradition of the *swadeshi* movement. In a sense, this isolationist scheme worked: direct foreign investment was virtually nil throughout the 1950s and 1960s, and stringent licensing requirements, known as the **"license-permit raj,"** restricted private enterprise. The outcome was anything but self-sufficiency, however; the economy puttered along at a growth rate of 5% per annum, a figure derisively referred to as the **"Hindu rate of growth."**

In 1991, a shortfall in foreign exchange reserves resulted in a **financial crisis** that almost forced the Indian government to default on foreign debt. India made dramatic changes in its economic policies, eliminating licenses, scrapping import quotas, and disbanding a handful of state-owned companies. The immediate result of these efforts was increasing growth and investment by foreign communications, electricity, and computer companies. In recent years, high-tech industries (especially in Bangalore and Hyderabad, Microsoft's Asian headquarters) have made India a major player in international IT markets.

Economic liberalization still has a long way to go. The government has delayed the sale of money-losing public sector industries for fear of massive lay-offs, and the rise of a Hindu nationalist government has scared off some foreign investors. And rapid economic growth has yet to benefit the poorest segments of Indian society. Slums continue to proliferate in the cities, and 53% of children under five are malnourished. The national per capita is a mere US$500, half of the population is illiterate, and average life expectancy is 63 years.

MEDIA

Hundreds of newspapers are published every day in Hindi and dozens of other languages. Major English-language dailies include *The Times of India* [the largest-circulation English newspaper in the world], *The Hindu*, and *The Indian Express*. All are excellent, if a little dry and sober in style, and provide solid, up-to-date India-specific news coverage via their comprehensive Web sites (www.timesofindia.indiatimes.com; www.thehindu.com; www.indian-express.com). **www.samachar.com** provides a digest of articles, updated daily. Glossy news weeklies such as *India Today* and *Outlook* provide more in-depth analysis and coverage; both put a strong emphasis on domestic politics and economics. Slightly less cerebral (and much more popular) are specialist movie magazines like *Filmfare*, which bring the latest Bollywood gossip to hundreds of thousands of readers every month. Poverty and illiteracy mean that only one-third of the population reads the press; many more (over 50%) watch TV. Doordarshan is the national TV channel; over the past decade or so, Rupert Murdoch's Star TV network has provided a more popular alternative, bringing soap operas and live cricket broadcasts to all but the most remote and impoverished parts of the country. All India Radio is the government public station (and the only one officially allowed to broadcast the news), and often acts as a government mouthpiece. The press and other media enjoy a good degree of freedom and autonomy, although the Official Secrets Act allows government censorship "in the interests of national security," and this option is occasionally used to limit criticism, as well as to curb the influence of the often-hostile Pakistani media. India has 5.5 million Internet users; this number is expected to grow to 25 million by 2005.

INDIA

EDUCATION

The state governments control education, and policy varies greatly from one state to another. Although the Indian Constitution guarantees every citizen's right to complete primary education, in 20 of 28 states there is no compulsory education at all. Currently only around 3.8% of government spending is dedicated to education. Almost 50% of India's adult population (15 years and older) is illiterate, and less than 3% complete tertiary education. Literacy rates vary by state: in Kerala, 90% of the population is literate; in Rajasthan, only about 40% can read and write. Throughout the country, women and members of lower castes have the lowest literacy rates. Across South Asia, 20% more boys than girls are enrolled in primary education. In most states the local language is the primary language of instruction. Hindi is also compulsory in most states (Tamil Nadu is a notable exception), and English is compulsory in every state but Bihar.

PEOPLE

DEMOGRAPHICS

India is not a country; it's a world. Six major religions (see p. 85), 18 major languages, and countless racial and ethnic groups coexist (often harmoniously, sometimes not). Seventy-five percent of the population live in rural areas. The inhabitants of India's four largest cities (Mumbai, Calcutta, Delhi, and Chennai) make up only 4% of the population. The most densely packed areas are in the valley and delta of the Ganga River and in the extreme south (Tamil Nadu and Kerala). Population growth is a major concern; 20 million people are born each year, putting ever more pressure on the already depleted natural resources. UN studies project that India will top 1.5 billion within 50 years, overtaking China as the most populous country on earth.

India's ethnic make-up reflects a mixture of the light-skinned **Aryan** peoples (see p. 70), who live mostly in the north, and the darker-skinned **Dravidian** peoples of the south. Numerous smaller groups of **adivasi** (aboriginal peoples) are concentrated in Madhya Pradesh, Orissa, and Gujarat, though they also live in other parts of the subcontinent. The *adivasi* predate the arrival of the Aryans and Dravidians in India; many of them have been subject to exploitation and have been pushed off their ancestral lands.

LANGUAGE

The people of India speak 1600 dialects. North Indian languages such as **Hindi** and **Bengali** descended from Sanskrit, the language spoken by the Aryan invaders who wandered into the area around 1500 BC. These languages are part of the larger Indo-European family, and it's not unusual to find North Indian words that resemble their counterparts in English or other European languages. **Urdu,** spoken by many Muslims in India, is very similar to Hindi, but borrows heavily from Persian and Arabic. The major **South Indian languages,** Kannada, Telugu, Malayalam, and Tamil, belong to the Dravidian family and are unrelated to the North Indian languages.

The 1950s reorganization of India into new states according to linguistic boundaries recognized 18 official languages—Assamese, Bengali, Gujarati, Hindi, Kannada, Kashmiri, Konkani, Malayalam, Manipuri, Marathi, Nepali, Oriya, Punjabi, Sanskrit, Sindhi, Tamil, Telugu, and Urdu (see **Lingua Fracas,** p. 85). For basic Hindi, Bengali, Tamil, Marathi, Nepali, Gujarati, Kannada, Malayalam, and Telugu vocabularies, see the **Phrasebook,** p. 886.

LINGUA FRACAS According to the 1991 census, India counts 18 languages and 325 dialects as official. With so many tongues to choose from, it's not surprising that the average educated Indian can speak two or three languages fluently, read and write a few others moderately well, and can understand almost every other South Asian language well enough to carry on a conversation about politics, the greenhouse effect, or the latest Bollywood gossip. Nevertheless, Indian languages engage in a fierce competition for supremacy, not only with each other, but also with English. After Independence, the constitution made Hindi the national language, with English as the language of international and inter-state communication. However, a deep-rooted resentment towards the use of Hindi results in a preference for English over Hindi in the Dravidian states of the South.

RELIGION

India's politics, society, and culture are all marked by religion. India's major faiths are Hinduism, Islam, Sikhism, Buddhism, Jainism, and Zoroastrianism.

HINDUISM

Hinduism is one of the oldest of the world's religions and has approximately 800 million followers in India alone. Worship and ritual are critical to its practice; street-side shrines and temples attract constant crowds and form the centerpiece of most cities and villages. At once monotheistic and polytheistic, metaphysical and worldly, permissive and exacting, Hinduism eludes easy definition. Unlike other religions, Hinduism has no founding figure, no single central text, and no fixed regimen of formalized practice. Instead, it is a kaleidoscope of local and regional religions, all integrated into an ever-shifting whole that manages somehow to accommodate them all.

CENTRAL HINDU BELIEFS. The doctrine of Hinduism is based on an absolute, unchanging, and omnipresent reality called **Brahman.** As the universal spirit, *Brahman* is in every individual in the form of **atman,** the self or soul. The goal of life is to overcome the illusory separation between *Brahman* and *atman* (known as **maya**) and achieve supreme bliss. The individual is trapped in **samsara,** the continual cycle of birth, death, and rebirth. A person is bound to the cycle of reincarnation by **karma,** the moral law of cause and effect, where present conditions are the result of past deeds. One is reborn into the world again and again, whether as an ant or a human being or as a figment of Vishnu's imagination, until one's karmic debt has been paid. The attainment of **moksha** (liberation) for the immortal human soul is still possible, and the *Bhagavad Gita* describes four paths for making the first steps toward *moksha:* action, devotion, knowledge, and psychic exercises. Dying in the holy city of Varanasi will also grant *moksha*.

In addition to the attainment of *moksha*, there are three other aims in life. **Dharma** has several meanings, but it most commonly refers to an individual's duty to maintain social, and ultimately, cosmic order. There is also room for **kama** (sensual enjoyment) and **aartha** (wealth). Hindu thought traditionally divides life into four stages. The first 25 or so years of one's life should be devoted to the acquisition of knowledge; the second 25 to maintaining a household and fulfilling the duties to raise a family; the third stage rounds out the householder's life and is preparatory to the fourth, ascetic stage—detachment from worldly connections and complete renunciation in preparation for death.

GODS AND GODDESSES. Traditional estimates have put the number of Hindu gods and goddesses at 333 million, but no one really knows how many there are. In addition to the temples and shrines, spaces for small altars are carved out in private homes. Lately, the gods have made themselves more accessible than ever, and modern-day merchandise ranges from glossy calendar images sold by street vendors to the hologram stickers of favorite deities you'll often see on the back of cars, buses, and rickshaws.

Hindus like Shiva, Vishnu, the Devi, and their various *avatars* (incarnations) best, but there are countless others: local deities, gods described in the Vedic hymns, those from long-lost prehistoric nature cults, as well as innumerable syntheses of all these together. From the central trinity of **Brahma** (Creator), **Vishnu** (Preserver), and **Shiva** (Destroyer) emerge the countless hundreds of other gods and goddesses, each one embodying an attribute of the eternal soul. The popularity of a god can vary from region to region, village to village, and family to family.

HINDU RITUALS. Hindu ritual appeals to all five senses. Contrary to appearances, the idols and images *(murti)* worshipped in temples and household prayer rooms are merely the vessels in which the deities reside. *Puja* (loosely translated as "worship") centers on these images, and acts of reverence to a god are made through offerings of food, flowers, and incense. These offerings are normally vegetarian-friendly, though some deities accept blood or animal sacrifices. Different ritual offerings are traditionally made to different deities, depending on each god's tastes.

In the temple, the temple priests *(pujari)* pamper the gods by performing more elaborate *puja* services. Beginning at dawn, they bathe the image *(abhisheka)* in yogurt, milk, and *ghee*. After the bath, the deity is dressed in new clothes and adorned with fancy accessories behind a curtain (even the gods need their privacy). Finally, the climactic moment arrives when the curtain is drawn back and devotees clamor for a glimpse of the deity. Bells ring out through the temple, and mantras are sung as *darshan* the auspicious eye contact between deity and worshipper, communicates divine blessing. The *pujari* waves an *aarti* lamp lit by small camphor flames in front of the deity, and allows worshippers to cup their hands over the flames. He then touches their eyes and faces, symbolically transferring to them the divine light and warmth. Before leaving the temple, worshippers have their foreheads marked with ash, sandalwood paste *(sandana)*, or red turmeric powder *(kumkum)*. Priests also pour holy water and drop *prasad* (food blessed by the gods) into the hands of devotees.

In addition to temple rituals, Hindu ceremonies mark human rites of passage such as marriage and cremation. Festivals *(utsava)* punctuate the Hindu calendar (see **Festivals and Holidays,** p. 102). Hindu pilgrimages *(tirtha yatra)* to the sacred points of India are also important. People travel to these holy places, or *tirtha* (literally "ford," a liminal space between the divine and the human) to seek the fulfillment of a wish, to spread the ashes of a relative in a holy river, to boost personal health and spiritual merit, or simply for the fun of the trip. There are seven especially sacred pilgrimage destinations: Ayodhya, Mathura, Haridwar, Varanasi, Ujjain, Dwarka, and Kanchipuram.

THE CASTE SYSTEM. The practice of Hinduism relies heavily on the caste system. Ancient codes divided Hindu society into four ranks, each of which was supposed to have emerged from a different part of the primordial person, **Purusha.** The brahmin, the priestly and scholarly caste, came from his mouth; the *kshatriya*, the warrior-ruler caste, from his arms; the *vaishya*, or merchants, from his thighs; and the *shudra*, or laborers, from his feet. These four *varna* (colors), still form the basis of the Hindu caste system today. Principles of karma and reincarnation explain a person's fortune (or lack of it) in this life, and offer the consolation that things might be better the next time around. The

A HINDU WHO'S WHO (PART ONE)

Brahma: Four-faced god, often pictured sitting on a lotus growing from Vishnu's navel. Despite his role as creator of the human world, Brahma is rarely worshipped, and only a single temple in Pushkar, Rajasthan (see p. 500) is dedicated to him.

Devi: Many Hindus worship a vast array of female deities, referred to collectively as the Devi (the Great Goddess). Goddesses embody **shakti**, the female force that drives the universe. The goddess cult probably predates worship of male gods, though specific goddesses are now incorporated into the male-dominated pantheon as consorts.

Durga: This beautiful heroine was created by the combined powers of male deities too weak to destroy the demon **Mahisha.** Durga charged forth with her trusty tiger (occasionally a lion), clutching a weapon in each of her 10 hands, and emerged victorious to save the world from destruction. Most popular in Calcutta, **Durga Puja** (see p. 737) marks this cosmic event with animal sacrifices and rites of fertility.

Ganesh: Beloved by many Hindus, this chubby, elephant-headed god, also known as **Ganpati,** is revered as the "remover of obstacles." He is often the first to be worshipped in religious ceremonies, and his image adorns the thresholds of many homes and temples. He holds various weapons in his four hands, as well as a bowl of *laddoo,* his favorite sweet. And why does he have that elephant head? The story goes that Ganesh's mother Parvati once asked him to stand guard over her while she bathed. It just so happened that Shiva (Parvati's husband and Ganesh's father) chose this rather inopportune moment return from an extended romp around the world. When he tried to approach his wife, Ganesh, no longer recognizing his father, stepped in to hold him back. Incensed, Shiva chopped off the boy's head. When Parvati discovered what had happened, she demanded that Shiva bring Ganesh back to life. He did so, but in the emergency had to replace the boy's head with the head of the first living creature he could find—which happened to be an elephant. Ganesh's vehicle of choice is a mouse.

Hanuman: The flying monkey-god enjoys celebrity status in the **Ramayana** (see p. 613) as Rama's faithful sidekick. Mr. **Maruti** himself (yes, the car is named after him) is venerated for his absolute loyalty, and is often depicted tearing open his furry chest to reveal the name "Rama" etched countless times in tiny script across his heart. Hanuman is a favorite of Indian wrestlers.

Kali: Although Kali is sometimes considered a consort of Shiva, she is an independent goddess of destruction in her own right. A force to be reckoned with, Kali is easily recognized by her terrifying appearance: long, tangled hair, dark skin, protruding red tongue, serpent bracelets, and a long necklace of freshly cut heads. She takes up residence in cremation grounds, and is often depicted on the battlefield as a combatant who gets drunk on her victims' blood.

practical rules of conduct that have helped to preserve the caste system are concerned mostly with notions of purity, stipulating that indiscriminate social mingling leads to undesirable mixing of different peoples' essences. Brahmins must be exceptionally pure in order to perform religious ceremonies, and they generally will not mix with other castes at all, or even accept food that has been cooked by non-brahmins. The group of people traditionally treated as **Untouchables,** now officially referred to as **Dalits** (the Oppressed), includes those involved in occupations like toilet-cleaning, leather tanning, and other professions considered so highly polluted that they didn't even make the cut as *part* of the caste system.

In practice, the hierarchy of caste has never been as clear-cut as it sounds in theory. More important than the *varna* in daily life are the *jati,* smaller groups linked by kinship and (often) occupation. There are thousands of *jati;* some of them very

A HINDU WHO'S WHO (PART TWO)

Krishna: Mr. Popularity among the Hindu gods, Krishna is worshipped by followers in a variety of guises. He inspires affection from his earliest days as a pudgy little blue baby who can't resist stealing butter. As a young man, Krishna is adored as the flirtatious cowherder who jams on his flute and cavorts in the Yamuna river and the forests of Vrindaban with love-struck *gopi* (milkmaid) groupies, of whom Radha is his favorite. But Krishna is not all play and no work: on his days off, he is respected as the philosophical charioteer of the Bhagavad Gita.

Lakshmi: A benign, feminine goddess, Lakshmi has a reputation as a bringer of luck, wealth, fertility, and general well-being. The autumn holiday of **Diwali** is an especially auspicious time of year when Hindus look to Lakshmi to bring prosperity during the new year. She is a wife of Vishnu, and is also associated with elephants.

Saraswati: Saraswati's existence can be traced back to the *Vedas*, when she was identified with the Saraswati River. Later, Saraswati's talents brought her into her current role as goddess of speech, poetry, music, culture, and learning. This pure and transcendent goddess is often depicted seated on a lotus flower, holding various objects in her four hands: a book, a rosary, a pot, and a *veena* (a stringed instrument).

Shiva: He's terrifying. He's compassionate. He's a bad-ass. As the Destroyer, Shiva is portrayed as an uncouth ascetic who adorns himself with live cobras and leopard skins, smears ashes on his body, wields a trident, and rides his bull vehicle **Nandi.** From his dreadlocked head flows the mighty **Ganga.** But Shiva is also a family man, who lives atop Mount Kailash in the Himalayas with his wife **Parvati** and their sons **Ganesh** and the six-headed **Kartikeya.** He is worshipped through the **linga,** a simple, phallus-shaped stone shaft fixed in a circular base called the yoni. Together, they represent a symbol of divine unity between Shiva and **Shakti.** Shiva's other forms include: **Ardhinarishwara** (half-male, half-female), **Rudra** (the Howler), and **Nataraja** (the King of Dance). Most *sadhus* (Hindu ascetics and Shiva look-alikes), are devotees of Shiva.

Vishnu: Though sometimes spotted relaxing upon a serpent afloat in a sea of milk, Vishnu is on 24hr.-a-day call as ▨ Preserver of the Cosmos. Time and again he has stepped in to save the universe from calamity, in the form of one of his 11 *avatars* (manifestations), which include **Rama,** the hero of the *Ramayana* (see p. 613), **Krishna,** and the **Buddha.** Vishnu, recognizable by his blue skin and four arms, travels via a man-bird named **Garuda,** and carries a discus.

small and peculiar to a few villages, others made up of tens of millions of members spread across huge regions. Some regions of India have politically dominant *jati*, such as the *Jats* in Rajasthan and Punjab and the *Reddis* in Andhra Pradesh, whose members originally came from very low castes.

Efforts at reform and the demands of city life have done much to reduce the pernicious influence of the caste system. The notion of untouchability is on the wane, and caste in general is less likely than it once was to determine a person's social position.

Politically, caste has been an increasingly important issue in recent years. Lower castes have managed to turn their strength-in-numbers into political clout, although the sheer size of the groups involved makes internal cohesion almost impossible. Lower-caste parties have gained a following in many states; the one with real nationwide appeal is the **Janata Party.** Affirmative action programs for lower-caste Hindus have also been implemented recently, and large numbers of university places and civil service jobs are now set aside for them.

ISLAM

Around 11% of India's population is Muslim, the fourth-largest Muslim population of any country in the world. Brought to India by the Afghans in the 12th century, Islam has had a profound influence on Indian culture. Questions about the political, religious, and cultural status of India's Muslims have been some of the most emotionally charged issues in India ever since the Partition of the colonial Raj into the two separate states of India and Pakistan, and religious violence between Muslims and Hindus has been the cause of death and disruption across the nation as recently as February 2002.

HISTORY. Islam was founded by the **Prophet Mohammed,** who lived in Mecca (in what is now Saudi Arabia) during the 7th century. Between AD 610 and 622, Mohammed received a series of revelations from the angel Gabriel about the true nature of God. His teachings were received coolly in polytheistic Arabia, and he and his followers were driven from Mecca in 622; this **Hijra** (flight) to Medina marks the start of the Muslim calendar. The people of Medina were the first to embrace the new faith, and after building up an army Mohammed returned in triumph to Mecca in 630, establishing himself as the spiritual leader of a new Muslim state. After Mohammed's death, the Muslims conquered Arabia and adjacent lands at an incredible rate, and by 711, Islam had extended its rule from Spain to Sindh (in eastern Pakistan).

Islam trickled into India slowly at first; its messengers were Arabian traders, Sufi mystics from Persia, and the armies of **Mahmud of Ghazni.** Under the **Delhi Sultanate** and then the **Mughal Empire,** Islamic influence became stronger, and after 1192, India was ruled by Muslims for more than 500 years (see **The Arrival of Islam,** p. 72). Some converted to Islam to join the new elite; many low-caste Hindus converted to escape the caste system. But the vast majority of the population always remained Hindu. Only on the eastern and western frontiers of South Asia, modern-day Pakistan and Bangladesh, did large scale conversions take place. Before the British left in 1947, they carved out the nation of Pakistan, a Muslim nation with one wing on the west and one wing on the east of India. At midnight on August 15, 1947, millions of people suddenly found themselves on the "wrong" side of the border. In the violence that ensued, hundreds of thousands were killed, and millions of people fled in fear for their lives. A sizable minority of Muslims remained in India.

BELIEFS. All Muslims believe in one supreme god, **Allah,** and express their devotion to Him through the five pillars of Islam: declaration of one's faith ("there is no God but God and Mohammed is His Prophet"); praying five times daily; the giving of alms *(zakat)* to the poor; fasting during the holy month of Ramadan; and making the *Hajj* (pilgrimage to Mecca) at least once in a lifetime, barring physical or financial hardship. A single holy book, the **Qur'an,** is believed to be the direct word of God as recorded by His Prophet.

Friday is Islam's holy day, when special prayers are said at the mosque. The ninth month of the Muslim calendar marks the celebration of **Ramadan,** a holiday commemorating the Prophet's receipt of the Qur'an from God, during which all Muslims (with the exception of the very young and the very sick) abstain from food and drink during daylight hours. **Muharram** memorializes the death of the Prophet's grandson, and is of particular importance to Shi'ite community, who observe Muharram with 12 days of singing and prayer.

ISLAM IN INDIA. Unlike the Arab practice of Islam, often marked by doctrinal austerity, Islam in India tends to be much more devotionally and aesthetically oriented. While orthodox Islam frowns upon the notion of worshiping anyone but God, Indian Muslims have a tradition of *pir* (saint) worship, and both Muslims and

Hindus make pilgrimages to *pir* shrines to pray for things such as children, good grades, and safe passage. Art and architecture flourished under the Mughals, who often ignored the Islamic injunction against painting human and animal figures. Sufi mystics were responsible for the introduction of the **qawwali**, a melancholy devotional song somewhat like the Hindu *bhajan*, and the **ghazal**, poetic songs developed by Persian Muslims in India.

Islam considers all people equal and strongly prohibits any discrimination on the basis of race, but many Muslim women stay secluded in their homes according to the custom of *purdah*. Muslims are required by the Qur'an to avoid alcohol, pork, and shellfish. Unlike Hindus, however, they do eat beef, as long as the cow has been slaughtered according to religious prescription and is thus considered *halal*. At noon on Fridays, men gather for communal prayers at the *masjid;* women usually pray at home. Most Indian Muslims speak Urdu, which is linguistically similar to Hindi.

Muslims and Hindus have coexisted in a tense sort of peace for most of their time together, but this peace has been repeatedly shattered by horrible incidents of communal violence. As the British divided and conquered India, they inflamed tensions between the two groups, and since Partition there have been thousands of incidents of violence between Hindus and Muslims. Recently, relations have been marred by the rise of Hindu nationalists groups such as the BJP, who claim that India is a fundamentally Hindu country. Uneasy relations (and occasional wars) with neighboring Pakistan haven't helped. In December 1992, events came to a head when militant Hindus destroyed the **Babri Masjid**, a mosque in Ayodhya that was allegedly built on the site of the birthplace of Lord Rama. Hindu extremists have repeatedly demanded the right to build a Hindu temple on the site. In February 2002, a group of Hindu campaigners on their way to Ayodhya died when their train was set alight by Muslim protesters. Hindu retributions soon followed, and thousands lost their homes when Hindu extremists torched Muslim areas of the city of Ahmedabad in Gujarat.

SIKHISM

Guru Nanak (1469-1539), a philosopher-poet born into a *kshatriya* family in what is now Pakistan, is the venerated founder of Sikhism. After traveling to Mecca, Bengal, and many places in between, Nanak proclaimed a religious faith that fused elements of Hinduism and Islam. He followed the Islamic rejection of image-worship, borrowed Hinduism's use of music in worship, and rejected Islam's reliance on a holy book. He also discarded caste distinctions, sexual discrimination, and ancestor worship. Nanak proclaimed that the one God was **Sat** (Truth), and asserted that liberation from *samsara* was possible for those who embraced God, known to people through **gurus.** Nanak taught that bathing, the giving of alms to charity, and meditation would help to clear the way for individuals to accept God's truth.

After Nanak's death in 1539, the spiritual leadership over his *sikhs* (disciples) passed to another guru, **Angad.** Guru Angad wrote down his own, and Guru Nanak's hymns into a new script, called **Gurumukhi** (*gurmukh* means "God"), now used as the modern Punjabi script. The third guru, **Amar Das** (1509-74), encouraged Sikhs to worship publicly in temples called **gurudwaras;** the fifth guru, **Arjun Dev** (1563-1606), collected more than 5000 hymns into a book called the **Adi Granth** and founded the magnificent **Golden Temple** at Amritsar (see p. 472). During Mughal rule, there was much Mughal-Sikh tension, and the Mughal Emperor Jehangir executed Guru Arjun, issuing in an era of Mughal repression. By the time the tenth and final guru, Gobind Singh, was assassinated in 1708, raids and skirmishes had become a sad fact of life throughout Punjab, the Siwalik Hills, and other parts of northern India where large numbers of Sikhs made their homes.

Under the leadership of the tenth guru, **Guru Gobind Singh** (1666-1708), Sikhism underwent a series of radical changes that gave the faith a more cohesive identity. These changes and the military tradition they encouraged were an attempt to defend Sikhs against the persecution they had suffered. Sikh men now had to undergo a kind of "baptism;" they had to pledge not to smoke tobacco, not to eat *halal* meat, and not to have sexual relations with Muslim women. They also had to renounce their caste names; men took the name **Singh** (Lion) and women took the name **Kaur** (Princess). The Khalsa also required its members to carry with them at all times the **five kakkars:** *kangah* (wooden comb), *kirpan* (sword), *kara* (steel bracelet), *kachch* (shorts), and *kesh* (uncut hair). Sikh men are identifiable by the turbans with which they wrap their long hair. Gobind Singh added new hymns to the *Adi Granth*, re-named it the **Guru Granth Sahib,** and announced that the book would stand in as the next guru. Since Gobind Singh's death, the *Guru Granth Sahib* has been the spiritual guide and holy book of the Sikhs.

Although Sikhs have a strong military tradition (the British labeled them one of the "martial races," and there are a disproportionate number of Sikhs in the Indian Army), they also have strong traditions of equality, hospitality, and community service *(seva)*. Sikh services include *kirtan*, or hymn singing, where verses from the *Adi Granth* are sung to rhythmical clapping, after which, Sikhs gather for a meal where everybody sits at the same level and eats the same food cooked in the *gurudwara's* kitchen. Strong believers in hospitality and kindness, Sikhs offer shelter and food to anyone who comes to their *gurudwaras*. Sikh militants and members of separatist Sikh parties of Punjab, still struggle for an independent Sikh homeland, Khalistan.

JAINISM

Jainism began as one of the alternatives to established brahmin authority that came to prominence around 500 BC. The most important element in all these new developments was the doctrine of **samsara,** the cycle of death and rebirth. People are bound to go through this cycle, birth after birth, by their **karma,** or past actions. Release from the influence of karma can be gained through the practice of austerities and meditation: Jainism, Buddhism, and the Upanishads all prescribe this sort of individual effort toward liberation. Of these three, Jainism has perhaps the most radical approach. It begins with the belief that all life is sacred and that every living being (human, animal, plant, or insect) possesses an immortal soul *(jiva)*. The obligation of **ahimsa** (non-violence) toward all living beings is therefore fundamental to Jain belief. Jains have worked out the consequences of this obligation very carefully. They are strict vegetarians, and the most orthodox Jain monks wear nets over their mouths and nostrils to prevent the possibility of killing any insects that might fly in. Agriculture is avoided, since pulling a plow through the soil would murder millions of tiny creatures. Their conscientiousness is an attempt to avoid the karmic consequences of taking life (even by accident). Monks and nuns also undertake severe austerities *(tapas)*, under which death by starvation would actually be the lofty goal.

Jainism was founded by the *kshatriya* prince Vardhamana, or **Mahavira** (Great Hero). At the age of 30, he renounced the world, plucked out all his hair, and began a new life as a wandering ascetic. Mahavira's disciples were called **Jains,** meaning "followers of the *jina* (conqueror)," and Mahavira is revered as the 24th and last of a line of **tirthankaras,** or "ford-makers," those who lead the way to another side of existence. There are two sects within Jainism: the **Digambara** (Sky-Clad) and the **Shvetambara** (White-Clad). The Digambaras are more orthodox than the Shvetambaras, and more distinctively, they do not wear any clothes.

Ornate Jain temples are found throughout India, primarily in Gujarat and along the west coast. The two most famous sites are at **Palitana** in Gujarat and **Sravanabelagola** in Karnataka (see p. 293). Today there are between four and five million Jains in India, most of them in Gujarat.

BUDDHISM

Despite of its origins in the Ganga Valley, few traces of Buddhism remain in India today. **Siddhartha Gautama,** who would come to be called the Buddha (Enlightened One), was born around 560 BC in Lumbini, just within the modern borders of Nepal (see p. 834). Gautama was born a *kshatriya* (prince), but at his birth, where he emerged from between his mother's ribs, an astrologer foretold that Siddhartha would become either a *chakravartin* (universal monarch) or an enlightened sage. In response, his father denied him freedom and lavished him with comforts and luxuries in the hope that Siddhartha would learn to appreciate life in the palace. Eventually, Siddhartha persuaded his charioteer to take him on a trip out into the world beyond the palace walls. Legend tells how his travels brought him face to face with human suffering for the first time, and of his encounters with a sick man, an old man, a dead man, and a wandering ascetic. He renounced his royal lifestyle at the age of 29, leaving behind his wife, his child, and his kingdom to join a band of ascetics and wander the forests of India. He meditated, starved himself, and practiced severe austerities until he found himself on the brink of death. Realizing that neither abundant wealth nor punishing self-denial could offer release from suffering, he resolved to follow a Middle Path between the two extremes. He sat and meditated under a pipal tree in Bodh Gaya, Bihar (see p. 137), where he achieved **nirvana,** and successfully resisted the temptations offered to him by the demon **Mara.** He set off to preach the truth about suffering, and gave his first sermon in a deer park in **Sarnath** (see p. 714).

The Buddha advocated total detachment from the world. All misery stems from desire; by eliminating desire, it is possible to eliminate suffering too. Central to Buddhist doctrine is the idea of the **Four Noble Truths.** All life is suffering, and all suffering is caused by desire for physical and mental comfort. There is a way out, and that way out is the **Eightfold Path:** Right Understanding, Right Thought, Right Speech, Right Action, Right Livelihood, Right Effort, Right Mindfulness, and Right Concentration. The Buddha rejected Hinduism's gods, rituals, and its concept of an enduring soul, but he kept its doctrine of karma and rebirth. The Buddha also spoke against the caste system, and, as part of the Eightfold Path, Buddhists became advocates of **ahimsa** (non-violence).

This idea that followers should abandon all desire and worldly life put Buddhism beyond the reach of most people, and the first Buddhists tended to band together in small monastic communities. In the 3rd century BC the Mauryan Emperor **Ashoka** converted to Buddhism, and his state patronage helped to make Buddhism a major religion in India and throughout Asia. Although Buddhism had more or less died out in India by the 1st century AD, there are about 7 million Buddhists in India today, mostly in Ladakh and Sikkim, on the fringes of the Hindu world. Since the Chinese invasion of Tibet in 1959, there has been an influx of refugees, and an increased Tibetan Buddhist presence, especially in **Dharamsala** (see p. 231), home to the exiled Dalai Lama. In 1956, the champion of the Hindu Untouchables, Dr. B.R. Ambedkar, publicly converted to Buddhism as a political protest against caste discrimination; he was followed by another 200,000 Untouchables (mainly in Maharashtra). Sacred Buddhist sites like Sarnath (see p. 714) and Bodh Gaya (see p. 137) are among the most important pilgrimage centers for Buddhists, and attract millions of pilgrims every year from all over the world.

CHRISTIANITY

Since Independence, Christianity has become increasingly visible in India, attracting followers and increasing its political relevance with a speed that would have pleased the **Apostle Thomas.** In the apocryphal *Acts of Thomas*, Thomas was chosen to spread the Gospel to India. Thomas is said to have arrived on the coast of Kerala as early as AD 52, where he was able to attract a number of converts before being martyred near modern-day Chennai, where his remains were interred in the church that bears his name today (see p. 570).

In the 16th century, Portuguese missionaries led by the Jesuit St. Francis Xavier sought to spread Catholicism along the Konkan coast; their conversions left behind the strong Catholic enclave of modern-day Goa. The last years of British rule were marked by an increase in missionary activity, which concentrated on building schools and hospitals. Grand churches were built as well, mainly to serve the spiritual needs of the ruling Brits.

There are about 25 million Christians in India today, 50% more than there were in 1970. Most of India's Christians are Protestant; the largest denominations are the Church of South India and the Church of North India, both members of the worldwide Anglican church. There are also sizable Catholic populations, particularly in Goa. In recent years, Christians have fallen victim to the surge of Hindu nationalism, and killings and forced conversions have taken place across the country.

ZOROASTRIANISM

Zoroastrianism was founded in Persia between 700 and 500 BC by Zarathustra (also known as Zoroaster). The central tenet of the faith is that the world is divided between pure good (represented by the god **Ahura Mazda**) and pure evil (represented by the god **Angra Mainyu**). According to Zoroastrian belief, **Saoshyant,** an immaculately conceived messiah, will one day come to establish Ahura Mazda's reign of goodness on earth. Zoroastrians believe that burial and cremation pollute the sacred elements of earth, fire, and air, and leave their dead in specially designed **Towers of Silence,** where vultures have easy access to the bodies.

Zoroastrianism came to India in the middle of the 10th century, when Persian Zoroastrians, fleeing the advance of Islam, arrived on the Gujarati coast. Called **Parsis** because of their ancient roots in Persia, today's dwindling numbers of Indian Zoroastrians—about 95,000 are left—are concentrated in western India, especially in Mumbai. Though few in number, the Parsis are known for their great wealth. One Parsi family, the Tatas, is renowned throughout India for its manufacturing industries, and for its early support of the Independence movement.

CULTURE

CUSTOMS & ETIQUETTE

CLOTHING. Dress modestly and respectably. Only young boys wear shorts in public. Women should keep their legs covered, at least to the knee. Bare shoulders are another sign of immorality (not to mention a surefire way to get sunburned). How you dress affects the way people respond to you. In India, women will often be treated with more respect if they wear a *salwar kameez*. Men's clothing is typically more "internationalized," but men may still want to buy a thin cotton *kurta pajama*. Try to look clean and presentable. In the eyes of many Indians, foreign tourists are an affluent and privileged group, and many Indians find it hard to understand why so many Westerners choose to dress like the poorest of India's poor, who would surely dress differently if they could. (See also **Blending In,** p. 19.)

COMMUNICATION AND BODY LANGUAGE. A quick **tilt of the head,** a sort of wobbly sideways nod, means "OK," or "I understand." Many foreigners are baffled by this gesture, thinking their hosts are answering their most innocent comments and requests with a firm "no." **Indian English,** especially when written, is full of antique civilities. You will often hear people address you as "madame" or "good gentleman," and read letters asking you to "kindly do the needful" and signed "your most humble servant."

Many foreigners have trouble adjusting to the constant **stares** they receive in India. There is no taboo against staring in South Asia and no harm is intended, but be sure not to send mixed signals. Meeting someone's gaze is often tantamount to expressing a desire for further contact. Meeting new people and talking to them about their way of life is one of the things that makes travel worthwhile, but it can get hard sometimes to sustain interest and patience if you are tired and you feel you have already answered all the same questions hundreds of times already. Remember that it is sometimes both acceptable and appropriate to ignore attempts at conversation. And the more you know about cricket, the happier you will be.

FOOD. Most Indians eat with their hands, though many restaurants give cutlery to foreigners. The most important thing is to **eat with your right hand only.** The left hand is used for cleaning after defecation and is seen as polluted. You can use your left hand to hold a fork or to pass a dish, but it should never touch food or your lips directly. Any food or drink that comes into contact with one person's saliva is unclean for anyone else. Indians and Nepalis will not usually take bites of each other's food or drink from the same cup; watch how locals drink from water bottles, pouring the drink in without touching their lips. In Hindu houses, the family **hearth** is sacred. If food is cooked before you on a fire (as it frequently is in trekking lodges) never play with the fire or throw trash into it.

Almost all Jains and many Hindus (especially in South India) are **vegetarian,** and even for many non-vegetarians, meat is an expensive luxury. Because of the cow's sacred status in Hinduism, beef is scarce. Muslims do not eat pork and are supposed to shun alcohol. It is considered offensive for women to drink alcohol in public.

HYGIENE. All **bodily secretions** and products are considered polluted. The people who come into contact with them—laundrymen, barbers, latrine cleaners—have historically formed the lowest ranks of the caste system. The **head** is the most sacred part of the body, and purity decreases all the way down to the toes. To **touch something with your feet** is a grave insult; you should never touch a person with your feet, step over a seated person's outstretched legs, or point at someone with your foot. Never put your feet on a table or any other surface. Conversely, to touch somebody else's feet is an act of veneration. If you accidentally touch someone else with your foot, touch your eyes and then their knee or foot, whichever is more accessible. The **left hand** is polluted. Always use your right hand to eat, give, take, or point.

WOMEN AND MEN. Displays of physical affection between women and men are rare. Same-sex affection, on the other hand, is considered completely natural and acceptable, and you will often see men walking down the street clasping hands. Most Indian and Nepali women are meek and quiet in public, and it is considered inappropriate for strange men to talk to them. Women travelers might find it hard to meet Indian and Nepali women, though women should always try to find other women to assist in emergencies (see **Women Travelers,** p. 55).

PLACES OF WORSHIP. Be especially sensitive about etiquette in places of worship. **Dress conservatively,** keeping legs and shoulders covered, and **take off your shoes** before entering any mosque, *gurudwara,* or temple. Visitors to Sikh *gurudwaras* and women entering Muslim mosques should cover their heads as well—handkerchiefs may be provided. At the entrance to popular temples, shoe-*wallahs* will guard your shoes for a few coins. Ask before taking **photographs** in places of worship. Taking pictures of the deities in Hindu temples is normally not allowed. Many Hindu temples, especially those in Kerala, Nepal, and in pilgrimage sites such as Puri and Varanasi, ban non-Hindus from entering. In practice this rule excludes anyone who doesn't look sufficiently South Asian. Purity laws dictate that menstruating women are forbidden to enter some Hindu and Jain temples.

It is common practice in Hindu temples to partake of offerings of consecrated fruit and water called **prasad,** which is received with the right hand over the left (and no one takes seconds). It is customary to leave a small donation at the entrance to the temple sanctuary. This can cause dilemmas when temple priests aggressively force *prasad* into your hands, expecting large amounts of cash in return. Usually a donation of one or two rupees will suffice. Hinduism and Buddhism consider the right-hand side auspicious and the left-hand side inauspicious; it is customary to walk around Hindu temples and Buddhist stupas **clockwise,** with your right side toward the shrine.

FOOD AND DRINK

Once upon a time, protracted Vedic prose prescribed every dash and pinch of every spice and herb, and every plate was placed to provide the therapeutic and medicinal benefits of sustenance in just the right way. Today, the main worry for many travelers is avoiding overexposure to the intense flavors of the subcontinent's famously uncompromising cuisine. Most people in India begin the day with a small breakfast, eat lunch between noon and 2pm, enjoy sweet tea and salty snacks in the late afternoon, and eat dinner between 7 and 10pm.

Meals in India begin with the staple: usually whole wheat bread in the north, rice in the south and east. Since most Indians eat with their hands, the bread and rice replace cutlery and are used to scoop food from the plate into the mouth. In a typical North Indian meal, the bread is accompanied by one or two spicy vegetable dishes, a lentil soup called **dal,** and sometimes by rice and curd. The most basic bread, the **chappati** (or **roti**), is thin and round like a tortilla. Though flat when served, the *chappati* fills with hot air when cooked over an open fire—the more it swells, the hungrier the person waiting for it is supposed to be. Elaborate variations on the theme include: **paratha,** a two-layered bread, sometimes stuffed with vegetables such as onions, radishes, and potatoes, and usually eaten with curds at breakfast; **naan,** a thicker, chewier kind of bread made of white flour and baked in a *tandoor,* or clay oven; and **puri,** a fried version of the standard *chappati* that is generally eaten with potatoes for lunch or breakfast. Common North Indian bread dishes such as **biryani** or **pulao** come mixed with vegetables and occasionally meat. Most non-vegetarian options involve chicken or lamb, since beef is off-limits to Hindus and pork is unclean for Muslims.

South Indian cuisine uses rice and rice flour much more than northern dishes, with **dosas** (thin pancakes) and **idlis** (thick steamed cakes) taking center stage. These are accompanied by broths such as **sambar** (a thick and spicy lentil soup), **rasam** (thinner, with tomatoes and tamarind), and **kozhambu** (sour), which are poured onto the rice and mixed in with it. *Dosas* are often stuffed with spiced potatoes to make *masala dosa.* Less meat is eaten in the south, though seafood is common along the coast. A standard South Indian meal is often served on a banana leaf, or else comes in the form of a **thali,** a steel plate filled with *chappati,* rice, *sambar,* fresh yogurt, *dal,* and vegetable dishes.

Condiments like **achar** (pickles) and **papadum,** a thin, crunchy wafer that is roasted or fried serve to spice up an already spicy meal. Popular snacks include **samosa,** a spicy, fried potato turnover served with tamarind and mint sauces, and **bhel puri,** a sweet and sour mixture of fresh sprouts, potatoes, and yogurt. Desserts are often made of boiled milk, fried, and are drowned in heavy cream or whole milk flavored with pounds of sugar. For a lightweight alternative, try **paan,** the after-dinner chew that is the cause of the crimson-colored spatterings that stain every street you walk down. A *paan* leaf can be filled with everything from coconut to sweetened rose petals to flavored betel nut and tobacco.

Unfortunately, those afraid of illness often avoid many of India's delicious drinks because they contain ice cubes made of untreated water. **Lassi,** made with yogurt and sugar, salt, or fruit, and the widely sold sugarcane juice are good for cooling off. Besides the famous **chai** (tea), coffee is also popular, especially in South India.

Drinking alcohol is an accepted practice in some parts of the country, but it is frowned upon in other regions and may be hard to find (see **Drugs and Booze,** p. 21). Popular brands of beer include Taj Mahal and Kingfisher. Be careful when ordering difficult or obscure mixed drinks—what gets called Kahlua could taste a bit like fermented Ovaltine, and is probably an example of Indian-Made Foreign Liquor (IMFL). Imported brands are available in big cities, and not-so-good domestic wines are available at expensive restaurants.

THE ARTS

India is a country with a rich artistic tradition heavily influenced by cultural interaction with other civilizations, and diversified by numerous regional styles. Many Indian art forms originally served a religious function—for centuries, almost all art was used to decorate sacred buildings or to illustrate sacred stories. Today, art remains an important means of spiritual expression for Indians of all religions, but has also moved into the realm of the purely aesthetic, as well as providing a popular form of entertainment.

ARCHITECTURE

The typical **Hindu temple** is the result of thousands of years of evolution. Temples originally consisted of little more than a small, dark, square sanctum referred to as the *garbhagriha* ("womb chamber"), which housed the deity. A tall pyramid-shaped spire, or *shikhara*, was later added to symbolize the connection between heaven and earth. As temple architecture grew more elaborate, distinctive North Indian and South Indian styles began to emerge. In a typical northern temple, a series of four rooms leads to the sanctum. Each room has its own *shikhara*, though these rarely rise above the *shikhara* of the central chamber. This row of spires resembles a mountain range and perhaps symbolizes the Himalayan peaks where the gods live. Many of the greatest North Indian temples were destroyed by Islamic iconoclastic campaigns from the 12th century onward, but excellent examples remain in **Orissa** (see p. 451) and in **Khajuraho** (see p. 368). In **South India,** the sanctum was expanded, and surrounded by four rectangular entrance towers, or *gopurams*, which had *shikharas* of their own, topped by barrel-vaults. These *gopurams* eventually grew to dwarf the central *shikhara*, creating grand temple-city complexes such as those of **Madurai** (see p. 604) and **Srirangam** (see p. 603) in Tamil Nadu.

The conquest of India by Muslim forces in the 12th century brought the Islamic styles of Persia and Central Asia to India. Since Islam forbids the depiction of human and animal images, Muslim artists concentrated instead on pure mosque-building, dotting the landscape with gorgeous domes, arches, geometric patterns, and calligraphic inscriptions. The biggest and brightest of these Muslim jewels are the **Qutb Minar** complex in Mughal stronghold Delhi (see p. 163), the pink and red post-and-lintel buildings of the city of **Fatehpur Sikri** (see p. 684), and a little marble ditty in Agra called the **Taj Mahal** (see p. 672).

SCULPTURE

The people of the Indus Valley Civilization left behind them simple terra-cotta figurines and seals decorated with pictures of animals and marked with a script that has still not been deciphered. Little else remains of Indian sculpture prior to the 3rd century BC, when the Mauryan emperor **Ashoka** set up stone columns all over India as a symbol of his rule (see p. 71). These columns were often topped with elaborate animal sculptures like those found at the **Lion Capital** in **Sarnath** in Uttar Pradesh (see p. 714). With four fierce lions sitting back-to-back on a lotus platform, this sculpture has become one of India's national emblems, and appears on all national currency.

The next two centuries saw the development of two-dimensional **bas-relief sculpture,** which was often used to decorate the railings of stupas and which usually told stories from the life of the Buddha or myths about gods and goddesses. The beginnings of classical Indian sculpture can be traced to the 1st century AD, when artists in **Mathura** (Uttar Pradesh) began to carve three-dimensional images of the Buddha (see p. 686). Influenced by Greek sculpture, Gandharan artists produced ornate images of the Buddha, emphasizing intricate folds of clothing and other details.

During the Gupta period (4th-6th centuries AD), sculpture in Mathura reached its peak. Spreading throughout North India, sculptors applied principles borrowed from Buddhist imagery to depictions of Hindu gods. Distinct regional styles developed from the Mathura style, contributing to the architectural wonders at **Sarnath** (see p. 714) and in the cave temples of **Ajanta** in Maharashtra (see p. 428).

In North India, the sensuous and voluminous figures of the Mathura style of sculpture gave way to more elegant, rhythmic forms. This style climaxed in the 10th century, when it was used to adorn the exteriors of North Indian temples. A distinctively **South Indian style** produced the 7th-century bas-reliefs of **Mahabalipuram** (see p. 578), and the miniature sculptures used to decorate temples in Tamil Nadu during the 9th century. **Bronze sculpture** in South India peaked during the 9th and 10th centuries producing images like that of Shiva as **Nataraja** (Dance King) surrounded by a ring of fire. This image is common throughout Tamil Nadu, but the one at the **Brihadishwara Temple** in Thanjavur (see p. 596) is the most famous. Regional traditions developed in other areas, such as Maharashtra, where sculptors created large, stocky figures; the **Kailasa Temple** in **Ellora** (see p. 426) is a good example.

PAINTING

The history of painting in India reaches far back to the nation's ancient history, when palm leaves served as the first canvases. The only ancient paintings that have survived are those there were sheltered by rock, like the **wall paintings at Ajanta** in Maharashtra, dating from the 2nd century BC to the 5th century AD (see p. 428). The style of Indian painting best known today began in western India during the medieval period. Colorful, cluttered scenes with figures shown in profile were made to illustrate **Jain manuscripts.** This style gradually spread throughout the country, and was used for a wide variety of religious paintings.

The Delhi sultans and Mughal emperors who began to arrive in India after the 12th century brought with them a taste for Persian art and radically altered the course of Indian painting. **Emperor Akbar** (r. 1556-1605), a great patron of the arts, played a decisive part in the development of the Mughal school of painting. He supervised his painters closely as they produced beautiful miniature illustrations for written histories, myths, and fables. Among other works, his court artists illuminated a magnificent Persian edition of the *Mahabharata*, now kept in the City Palace in Jaipur. As the Mughals settled in India, some Muslim artists began to disregard the Islamic injunction against the representation of human forms, and during the reign of **Jehangir** (r. 1605-27), artistic emphasis shifted to portraiture.

INDIA

INDIAN AESTHETICS
Pink is the Navy Blue of India

Barring a few notable exceptions, the art-tourism of India has historically left few viewers looking as pleased as the serene sculpted figures upon which they gazed. While Rodin, the French sculptor, did not think twice before declaring the dancing image of Shiva, the Nataraja, as the perfect depiction of rhythmic movement, Mark Twain's reaction to Indian sculpture was far more typical. After encountering the "idols" of Varanasi while Following the Equator in 1898, he wrote: "The town is a vast museum of idols---and all of them crude, misshapen, and ugly. They flock through one's dreams at night, a wild mob of nightmares!"

Indian art, and Hindu art especially—with its panoply of multi-armed, elephant-headed, and tongue-yielding deities—invariably suffered such cultural insensitivity from the dropped jaws of Western travelers. The few brave (and greedy) 19th century aristocrats who exhibited a fondness for the stuff found beauty in the smooth limb of a carving, but did not consider a higher purpose to Indian art. These Westerners fueled their appreciation with an imported system of aesthetics. With colonial noses and arrogance at an all time high, they judged the art of India (carting "the best" off to London's sterile museums) in a way ideologically divorced from artists' intentions, an act of cultural imperialism considering India's highly developed system of aesthetics.

Indian art serves a distinct social and religious purpose; like most things characteristically Indian it defines no specific boundary between the secular and the sacred. Indian artistic practice, unlike that of its 19th century Western appraisers, is not simply art for pleasure or it's own sake. Indian sculpture, painting, architecture, dance and music together create a holistic pious experience for a devotee, engaging the senses and inviting a deep and excited worship. That said, it is important to distinguish that Indian aesthetic theory values its works as Art and not simply religion India's aesthetics revolve around the more widely applied and more emotionally varied notion of rasa. The literal meaning of rasa, is the juice or extract of a fruit or vegetable. However, rasa also means the finest part of something, its essence and sentiment. The rasa developed in any Indian artwork evokes a moving response in the viewer.

The 4th century poet, Bharata, was first to explain rasa, in his *Natyasastra*— the "Science of Dance." Attempting to describe the complete spectrum of emotions a drama could elicit from its viewers, Bharata enumerated nine varieties of rasa. The most popular rasa, especially in the plastic arts—think Krishna—-is shingara, the erotic sentiment. The other eight include: hasya, the comic; karuna, the pathetic; raudra, the furious; vira, the heroic; bhayanaka, the terrible; bibhatasa, the odious; adbhuta, the wondrous; and shanta, the peaceful. Each has a corresponding color and specific emotion, suggesting the emotion to be aroused: blue-black shingara (the erotic) evokes rasi (love), black bhayanaka (the fearful) generates bhaya (fear), yellow vira (the valiant) brings utsana (energy), and silver and jasmine shanta (peaceful) serves shana (tranquility).

The key to understanding rasa is recognizing that it privileges not the artwork, nor the artist, but the audience. An old Indian metaphor compares rasa to wine: "taste rests not in the jug that contains it, nor with the vintner that created it, but the person who tastes it." The spectator, as a connoisseur or rasika, must cultivate an awareness to be truly moved by a work of Indian art. Only then, at this heightened state of understanding and emotion, is he or she likely to smile back, fully and serenely, at the carved face of a Hindu god.

Kurt Mueller researches and writes on Indian art and cross-cultural aesthetics.

The delicate, detailed Mughal style influenced Hindu painting as well. Under the patronage of Hindu Rajput kings in the 16th and 17th centuries, the **Rajasthani School** emerged, combining the abstract forms of the western Indian style with some of the naturalism of Mughal art. Rajput paintings usually depicted religious subjects, especially myths about Krishna cavorting with his *gopis* (milkmaid consorts) or pining for Radha, his favorite.

The Mughal and Rajasthani styles had fallen into decline by the 18th and 19th centuries, when European art became influential. The first Indian attempts to copy European styles, known collectively as the **Company School,** were mostly lifeless engravings and watercolors. In the late 19th and early 20th centuries, artists of the Calcutta-based **Bengal School,** led by Rabindranath Tagore, combined older Indian styles with modern Western art. Twentieth century artists like Jamini Roy and M.F. Hussain combine eastern and western influences.

FILM

India's obsession with the movies began in 1912, when Dadasaheb Phalke produced the first Indian feature film, *Raja Harishchandra*. Jokingly referred to as "Bollywood," the Indian film industry, based in Mumbai (Bombay) is by far the most prolific in the world today (see **Bollywood Beat,** below), producing more than 800 films a year and attracting annual audiences of more than a billion people worldwide. Hindi and Tamil are the most important languages, and Chennai (Madras) in Tamil Nadu is home to its own booming movie industry and its own galaxy of stars (many of whom go on to play star roles in local politics after their retirement from the big screen). The appearance of the first talkie *(Alam Ara)* in 1931 split the movie-going audience along linguistic lines, but it wasn't long before directors hit on a solution, by incorporating into their films a language that nearly everyone could understand and enjoy—music. A tradition was born. Since then, some films have managed to squeeze in nearly 70 songs; not many can manage quite that number, but you would have to search long and hard today before you found a movie without at least one song-and-dance sequence in it somewhere. By the 1940s, the introduction of pre-recorded songs and playback singing meant that actors no longer had to be singers. The most successful playback singer, **Lata Mangeshkar,** holds the world record for most songs ever recorded, having put out more than 25,000 songs during her career. Today, a film's sound track is almost as important for its chances of success as its plot or its big-name stars. Chances are that almost all the music you hear as you travel around India will come from one of the latest blockbuster smashes; don't be surprised if you find yourself humming along by the end of your trip.

During the 1930s and 1940s, the **social film** served as a useful way of addressing the concerns of contemporary life. It also introduced the preference for loudness—gaudy costumes, flighty and capricious music, exciting choreography, and wink-wink, nudge-nudge sex—that continues to be the hallmark of Indian film to this day. The masterpieces of serious film-makers like Satyajit Ray *(Pather Panchali,* 1955) have long been acclaimed by critics around the world as some of the finest films ever made. More popular films have had to wait longer for international acceptance, but in 2002 Ashutosh Gowariker's Raj-era epic *Lagaan* was the first Indian film ever to win an Oscar nomination (for Best Foreign Film; it didn't win), and in June 2002 a major exhibit at the Victoria and Albert Museum in London brought Bollywood and its colorful history to a whole new audience. In recent years Indian pictures such as Mira Nair's *Monsoon Wedding* have shown to huge audiences around the globe. Perhaps the world is learning to dance to the Bollywood Beat at last. For all the latest Bollywood news, consult the online edition of India's favorite *filmi* magazine, *Filmfare* (www.filmfare.indiatimes.com).

BOLLYWOOD BEAT She emerges against the backdrop of a lush green Alpine landscape, singing a love song as her sari-clad hips swing in time to the beat. Hearing her voice, he rushes in to hold her in a rapturous embrace, only to be rudely interrupted by his evil nemesis and a band of thugs sent by her panicky parents to tear the two lovers apart. A brief but boisterous scuffle ensues and our hero emerges, not a hair out of place, to return to the embrace. This utopia of romance, chivalry, and cheap thrills is available to millions in the form of the ultimate modernday kitsch, the masala movie, named for the cheap-but-effective spice mixture used in Indian cooking.

No city in the world produces more action, comedy, romance, and trash than Mumbai (Bombay), playfully known as Bollywood. Playing to millions of people every day, churning out 800 formula flicks a year in 23 languages, and grossing more than US$850 million each year, Bollywood movie-making is big business. Popular film tabloids such as **Stardust, Filmfare,** and **Cineblitz** (available at any newsstand, and now on the web) sell thousands of copies throughout India and all over the world. Movie stars almost eclipse the gods with the size of their fan following—you'll probably run into more posters of Shahrukh than of Shiva. Until recently, however, movie-making was not considered a legitimate industry by government authorities, and film producers were forced to seek other sources of "informal" capital (i.e., the mob) to finance their projects. Studios' connections with Mumbai gangsters have seen many on-screen antics duplicated in real life: on January 21, 2000, filmstar hero and director Rakesh Roshan was shot when he refused to capitulate to extortion. Roshan survived the attack, and Bollywood bigwigs are now starting to form alliances with studios in Hollywood in an attempt to wriggle free of the entanglements that have come to endanger their businesses and their lives.

Frequently ridiculed for their formulaic storylines—quality typically loses out to quantity in a crushing first-round knockout—Bollywood flicks offer an easy and affordable means of escape for the average person in India, who typically wants to ignore reality or a couple of hours, not to see it re-created on the silver screen in gory technicolor. Stumble into a theater anywhere in India and you're guaranteed a good three hours or so of escapism and entertainment such as you'll find nowhere else in the world. *Let's Go* particularly recommends movies starring our lucky mascot **Hrithik Roshan,** and no traveler to Tamil Nadu should miss the opportunity to join the masses in cheering on the Tamil people's favorite action-hero, the incomparable **Rajnikanth.**

MUSIC

The art of making music is not just entertainment in India; it is a spiritual undertaking. A piece of classical Indian music is based on a *raga* and a *tala*, which form the melodic and rhythmical framework for the piece of music respectively. Derived from a Sanskrit word meaning "to color," the *raga* is the foundation of all composition and improvisation. In the Hindu tradition, each *raga* is associated with a different moment of the day or season of the year. *Ragas* differ from one another in scale and in *rasa* (mood). Unlike Western music with its fixed-pitch scales, the Indian musician is free to place the tonic note wherever he wishes. Once the musician has established the tone for the *raga*, he improvises within the constraints of the chosen *raga*, exploring its potential to be created anew with each performance. Opportunities for improvisation likewise exist between the fixed beats of the *tala* and its repeated rhythmical cycle. The *raga* and the *tala* interact, with intonation and inflection converging at regularly emphasized intervals.

Modern Indian classical music, often divided into northern **Hindustani** and southern **Carnatic** systems, has its origins in ancient chants. Musical form is first discussed in the *Bharata Natyashastra*, a textual source of music written between 2 BC and AD 4 by the sage Bharat. North Indian music was particularly influenced by the styles of Persia and Turkey, where court patronage of musicians from the Middle East encouraged the development of an elaborate and highly evolved musical culture. The song style of *qawwali*, popular during weddings, is a musical debate: singers form two groups, one boasting the accomplishments of the bride, the other singing the praises of the groom. In its romantic form, *qawwali* is a socially acceptable form of flirting, while the lilting *ghazals* are similar to a ballad.

Many Indian musicians have gained worldwide followings. **Ravi Shankar,** who introduced Hindustani music to western ears during the 1960s and attracted the attention of the Beatles, is a master of the sitar, a fretted, 20-stringed instrument with a long teak neck fixed to a seasoned gourd. **Ali Akbar Khan** has also amazed international audiences with the strains of the sarod, a fretless stringed instrument similar to a sitar. **Allah Rakha** and his son, **Zakir Hussain,** mesmerize audiences with their virtuosity on the tabla, two drums played together and capable of producing an incredible range of tones, and musicians like **"Mandolin" U. Srinivasan** and the legendary singer **M.S. Subbulakshmi** have ensured Carnatic music's place in Indian music history.

Folk music is linked closely to folk dance and varies from region to region. From Punjabi *bhangra* to Rajasthani *langa*, folk tunes remain close to the hearts of Indians, and have recently gained an even larger audience through the international releases of **Ila Arun** and *bhangra*-rap performers in the UK. Bengali musicians have produced their own unique genre, *Rabindrasangit*, in which the poetic words of Rabindranath Tagore are set to quasi-classical song.

Popular music ranges from the "filmi" love songs of **Lata Mangeshkar** to the disco-hybrid-pop of vocal diva, **Alisha,** whose album *Made in India* sold over one million copies in 1995. Popular vocalists include the playful and prolific **Kishore Kumar,** whose versatile voice has filled in the melodic blanks for more actors than anybody can remember, and Punjabi crooner **Daler Mehndi,** whose 1996 hit, "*Bolo Ta Ra Ra*," brought *bhangra* out of the North Indian countryside and onto satellite television, launching Indipop's international career.

DANCE

The Hindu god Nataraja, King of the Dance, has made his influence felt in every sphere of Indian life. Indian dance forms, both classical and folk styles, evolved as acts of worship that dramatized myths and legends. Technique and philosophy, passed down from gurus to students, have carried the "visual poetry" described in the *Natya Shastra* (dating from between the 2nd century BC and the 2nd century AD), into modern times. **Bharatnatyam,** India's most ancient dance form, originated in the temples of Tamil Nadu where dancers performed intricate, fluid combinations of eye movements, facial expressions, hand gestures, and strong, rhythmic, *ghungroo*-enhanced steps. It was originally studied as a form of worship, and performed by *devadasis*, women who lived in temples and devoted their lives to the temple's deity. **Kathak,** first performed by *nautch* (dancing courtesans) against the opulent backdrop of North India's Mughal courts, is remarkable for the dizzying speed of its characteristic footwork and hand gestures (see **Nrityagram Dance Village,** Bangalore, p. 284 and **Lucknow,** p. 690). Developed from a rigorous system of yoga, **Kathakali,** an elaborately costumed form of dance-drama unique to Kerala, presents mythological stories of heroes, lovers, gods, and battles (see **Cochin,** p. 339). The dancers, all male, must study for a minimum of 15 years before they are considered ready to come out and strut their stuff.

SPORT

Cricket isn't just a game in India—it's a national obsession. Indians turn out in their thousands to watch the big games, and an informal game or two seems to be constantly underway on every street corner in the country, often played by young boys using sticks for bats and bricks for wickets. Expect to be asked for the names of your favorite players at every turn, and be ready to give an opinion on the state of the national game if you don't want to be taken for an idiot. Like many other former colonies, India regularly beats England at its own game these days. One of the few occasions when India is able to forget its internal conflicts and come together as one nation comes whenever the Indian cricket team plays against arch-rival, Pakistan. **Test matches** are watched by millions of people across India—huge crowds gather wherever there's a game being shown on TV. Things occasionally turn nasty: the Indian team reached the semi-finals of the 1996 World Cup, only to be disqualified when fans began to throw bottles, rocks, and other missiles onto the pitch. The gentleman's game had its reputation dragged through the dirt as the new millennium began, when allegations of dodgy dealings with shady betting syndicates brought many of India's national heroes out of the dressing room and into court to answer charges of game-fixing and bribe-taking. India defeated world champion Australia in Spring 2001, and followed up with victories in Zimbabwe and against England at home before setting off to the West Indies in April 2002.

India is also a consistent Olympic medal-winner at hockey. Soccer and horse racing are especially popular in the east and in urban areas. **Kabbadi**, a breathless game of tag, is popular throughout the north.

HOLIDAYS AND FESTIVALS

Hindu, Muslim, Sikh, Buddhist, and Jain festivals correspond to the lunar calendar, so the dates vary from year to year with respect to the Gregorian calendar; the dates given are approximate. Secular holidays in India are dated according to the Gregorian calendar. The dates given here are for 2003.

DATE	HOLIDAYS AND FESTIVALS
January 1	**New Year's Day.** This traditional Indian festival culminates in drunken revelry at midnight. Held annually.
January 5	**Guru Gobind Singh's Birthday,** celebrated by Sikhs everywhere, particularly important in the Punjab.
January - February	**Kite Festival, Rajasthan**
January 26	**Republic Day,** one of India's four national public holidays; highlights include a military parade in New Delhi.
March 1	**Maha Shivaratri,** an all-day, all-night Hindu festival dedicated to Shiva, whose creation dance took place on this day.
March 4 (approx.)	**Muharram** commemorates the martyrdom of the Prophet Mohammed's grandson; especially important for Lucknow Muslims.
March 18	**Holi,** a rowdy Hindu festival of color celebrated by throwing colored water and powder at each other.
April 11	**Ramanavami** celebrates Rama's birth, with readings of the *Ramayana* in Hindu temples all over India and Nepal.
April 13	**Vaisaki,** the Sikh festival celebrating the day Guru Gobind Singh founded the Khalsa; features readings of the Guru Granth Sahib, besides major feasting.
Late April (approx.)	**Mahavira Jayanti,** Jainism's major festival, celebrates the birthday of its founder.
May 24	**Milad-un-Nabi (Eid-ul-Mulad),** the Prophet Mohammed's birthday.
May 16	**Buddha Jayanti** honors the Buddha's birthday and his attainment of *nirvana*.
June 23	**Rath Yatra,** commemorates the journey Krishna made to Mathura; Hindus throng the Jagannath's Temple in Puri and cities in the South.

DATE	HOLIDAYS AND FESTIVALS
August 12	**Raksha Bandhan** celebrates the Hindu sea god Varuna; the holiday is associated with brother and sisters.
August 15	**Independence Day,** India's biggest national holiday.
August 20	**Krishna Jayanti,** Krishna's birthday.
August 21	**Zoroastrian New Year's Day,** celebrated by Parsis in India.
August 31	**Ganesh Chaturthi** is when Hindus venerate the chubby elephant-headed god of obstacles with spectacular processions, especially in Mumbai and Rajasthan.
September 27 - October 5	**Dussehra** (also known in some parts as **Navaratri**), a 9-10-day festival, celebrates the vanquishing of demons and honors Durga, the demon-slaying goddess. Known as **Durga Puja** in West Bengal.
October 25	**Diwali (Deepavali),** a five-day festival of lights celebrating Rama and Sita's home-coming as per the *Ramayana.*
November 5-8	**Pushkar Mela (Pushkar Camel Fair),** held at the sacred lake at Pushkar, Rajasthan. Camels and pilgrims galore.
November 19	**Guru Nanak Jayanti,** the birthday of the founder of Sikhism.
November 6-December 6	**Ramadan,** a 28-day period when Muslims fast. Fasting ends with **Eid-ul-Fitr,** a three-day feast celebrating the Prophet's recording of the word of God in the Holy Koran.
November 16-19	**Pushkar Mela (Pushkar Camel Fair),** held at the sacred lake at Pushkar, Rajasthan. Camels and pilgrims galore.
November 19	**Guru Nanak Jayanti,** the birthday of the founder of Sikhism.
November 26 (approx.)	End of **Ramadan,** a 28-day period when Muslims fast. Fasting ends with **Eid-ul-Fitr,** a three-day feast.

ADDITIONAL RESOURCES

For a list of useful India-related websites, see **World Wide Web,** p. 59

GENERAL

Scoop-Wallah, by Justine Hardy (2000). Young English journalist's engaging account of a year spent working on *The Indian Express* in Delhi. Full of self-deprecating humor and minutely observed vignettes.

Travels On My Elephant, by Mark Shand (paperback reprint 1998). Hilarious and often touching memoir of a British writer's trek across India on the back of an elephant. The sequel, *The Queen of the Elephants,* is also worth a read.

Tropical Classical, by Pico Iyer (1997). Essays and articles culled from the last 10 years of the journalist's career. Always entertaining, and the history of the Raj is solid, as are the pieces set in Bombay and Nepal.

In Light of India, by Octavio Paz (1997). Nobel laureate's perceptions of India based upon his time as Mexico's man in New Delhi.

A Season in Heaven, by David Tomory (1996). Eye-opening compilation of first-person survivors' accounts from the 1960s overland hippie trail from Europe to India. An inspiration to off-beats and grungy travelers of all ages.

Culture Shock! India, by Gitanjali Kolanad (1994). A guide to Indian customs and etiquette for those planning to live and work in India, with useful advice for dealing with all sorts of social situations and bureaucratic hassles.

The Great Railway Bazaar, by Paul Theroux (1975). A classic, worth reading for descriptions of what it feels like to be a snooty Westerner jammed on a train with hundreds of others.

INDIA

HISTORY

Modern South Asia: History, Culture, and Political Economy, by Sugata Bose and Aye-sha Jalal (1998). A controversial volume by two of the most prominent historians of South Asia that questions the traditional dichotomy between India's "democracy" and Pakistan's "authoritarianism."

A Traveller's History of India, by Sinharaja Tammita-Delgoda (1995). A clear and read-able introduction to Indian history, with references to sites that can be visited today.

Sources of Indian Tradition, by Ainslie Thomas Embree and Stephen Haye (1988). This comprehensive sourcebook of Indian history follows the country's important texts from pre-historic times to the mid-eighteenth century, with valuable commentary and intro-ductions to the country's major religions.

The Discovery of India, by Jawaharlal Nehru (1946). Indian history as seen by the founder of modern India—a classic.

An Autobiography, or, the Story of My Experiments with Truth, by Mohandas K. Gandhi (1927). Gandhi's personal account of the development of his beliefs, with surprisingly little commentary on the political events of the time.

POLITICS AND ECONOMICS

India: Government and Politics in a Developing Nation, by Robert L. Hardgrave, Jr. and Stanley A. Kochanek (1996). The best summary of recent Indian political issues and the government of modern India.

India: Economic Development and Social Opportunity, by Jean Drèze and Amartya Sen (1995). Analyzes the economic development of India from a social perspective and with empathy for the underprivileged.

Operation Bluestar: The True Story, by Lt. Gen. K.S. Brar (1993). An in-depth (albeit slanted) account of the Golden Temple turmoil from an Indian commando.

No Full Stops in India, by Mark Tully (1992). Thoughtful collection of essays by former BBC correspondent, focusing on contemporary politics and current affairs.

A Million Mutinies Now, by V.S. Naipaul (1991). Nobel Prize-winner's examination of how individuals from different backgrounds cope with the tensions threatening to crack the peaceful veneer of modern India apart. Insightful, ambitious, and beauti-fully written.

RELIGION

The Sikhs: Their Religious Beliefs and Practices, by W. Owen Cole and Piara Singh Sambhi (1998). A good, succinct survey of the Sikh religious tradition.

Islam: The Straight Path, by John L. Esposito (1998). An excellent introduction. Esposito traces the development of Islam from its beginnings down to the present day.

Hinduism: A Cultural Perspective, by David R. Kinsley (1993). A comprehensive, the-matic introduction to Hindu beliefs, practices, and culture.

Karma Cola, by Gita Mehta (1979). A cynical journalistic satire about Western infatua-tion with "spiritual" India.

What The Buddha Taught, by Walpola Rahula (1959). A Sri Lankan monk's authoritative and easy-to-follow explanation of Theravada Buddhist philosophy.

GENDER ISSUES

Neither Man Nor Woman: The Hijras of India, by Serena Nanda (1998). A well-researched ethnography of India's transvestite *hijra* community.

May You Be the Mother of a Hundred Sons, by Elizabeth Bumiller (1990). A British journalist's exploration of *sati*, sex-selective abortion, and dowry deaths, this is a good introduction to Indian society and politics, with a great chapter on Hindi film actresses.

FICTION

The Vintage Book of Indian Writing, edited by Salman Rushdie and Elizabeth West. Superb anthology of Indian prose writing in English, published to celebrate 50 years of independence.

Love and Longing in Bombay, by Vikram Chandra (1997). Seven very different stories, all superbly told. Ghosts, soldiers, society ladies, and computer programmers are all brought to life in lean, perfectly chiselled prose.

The God of Small Things, by Arundhati Roy (1997). An exquisitely woven story of love, betrayal, and tragedy set against the backdrop Kerala's social and political landscape.

A Suitable Boy, by Vikram Seth (1994). If you're only going to take one book with you, it may as well be this one. Huge, sprawling, vividly imagined novel set in 1950s UP. Long enough for coast-to-coast train journeys, and heavy enough to swat rats with.

Such a Long Journey, by Rohinton Mistry (1992). A humanely written tale of Mumbai Parsis (Zoroastrians) who inadvertently become involved in Indira Gandhi's government corruption; a great read with an introduction to Parsi culture and India in the 1970s.

A Strange and Sublime Address, by Amit Chaudhuri (1991). Masterful evocation of boyhood memories of Bombay and Calcutta, marked by richly poetic language and telling attention to detail.

Malgudi Days, by R.K. Narayan (1986). One of India's first English-language writers as well as one of its best, Narayan spent most of his long career in the Indian South. No post-colonial angst here, just subtle, wry, and charming stories set in a fictional village in Tamil Nadu.

Midnight's Children, by Salman Rushdie (1980). Rushdie's masterpiece tells the magical tale of children born at midnight on the eve of Independence, and how the country's life and theirs evolve together.

A Passage to India, by E.M. Forster (1924). This classic novel tells the story of a friendship between an Englishman and an Indian during the British Raj. An honest, sensitive account whose observations about culture shock still hold true today.

POETRY

Sanskrit Poetry From Vidyakara's "Treasury", by Daniel Ingalls (paperback reprint 2000). Beautifully translated selections from an 11-century anthology of the best of classical Sanskrit verse.

Gitanjali, by Rabindranath Tagore (1913). Nobel prize-winning work of the great Bengali poet, it uses images from Indian love poetry to discuss a relationship with God.

FILMS

Monsoon Wedding, by Mira Nair (2002). Winner of the Lion d'Or at the Venice Film Festival, a poignant and dramatic look at middle-class family life in contemporary Delhi.

INDIA

Lagaan, by Ashutosh Gowariker (2001). Heroic story of a team of poor villagers who defeat their British rulers in a game of cricket and win immunity from crippling land taxes. Much more fun than it sounds.

Fire, by Deepa Mehta (1996). The story of two women bound by culture and longing for love who eventually find consolation with each other. The film was banned in India for its depiction of lesbianism and is the first of an Earth, Fire, Air trilogy by Mehta.

Muthu, by A.R. Rahman (1995). A heroic man of the people, a beautiful princess, and lots of dark family secrets ... and that's just the start of it! A light-hearted, thrill-a-minute epic that never takes itself too seriously, this is an example of the mass-market Indian blockbuster at its best. Tamil folk hero Rajnikanth shines in the title role.

Bandit Queen, by Shekhar Kapur (1994). The story of Phoolan Devi, a low-caste bandit-turned-politician. A horrifyingly graphic, true-life portrayal of caste oppression in UP.

Hello Photo, by Nina Davenport (1994). The next best thing to going there yourself, this stunning film shows one woman's experience of looking and being looked at in India.

Salaam Bombay, by Mira Nair (1988). A disturbing tale of Bombay's street children. This fictional story told in documentary style is somewhat exploitative, but it's a moving and well-acted film.

Pather Panchali, by Satyajit Ray (1955). The first film by the late master of Indian cinema. Produced on weekends with a borrowed camera and unpaid actors. Its visuals capture the beauty of the Bengali landscape and the isolation of the village where Apu and Durga, the hero and heroine, live. Musical accompaniment by Ravi Shankar.

READING WITH YOUR MOUTH FULL

In the 1970s, when Kolkata was still Calcutta, Jyoti Basu was the Chief Minister of West Bengal, and load sheddings were rampant, my father purchased a blue Lambretta scooter. The three of us, my father at the driver's seat, my sari-clad mother riding pillion in a precarious side saddle, and myself standing between my father and the handle bars, would set out for evening excursions on that scooter regularly. The destination I remember most vividly was the Victoria Memorial, perhaps the most famous monument of the British Raj in India aside from Lutyens's red sandstone buildings in New Delhi. We lived in Kolkata for twelve years and visited the Victoria Memorial innumerable times, but never stepped inside the building. The Memorial, to me, was simply a convenient spot for a variety of food hawkers selling their delicious tidbits—crunchy bhelpuri, buttery pao bhaji, crisp phuchkas filled to the brim with tamarind water, tangy alu kabli, and, of course, icy kulfis in clay saucers to combat the assault of sharp spices and sour tamarind on our tongues.

This is the sort of Kolkata street food I imagine to be the daily fare for Tridib, one of the most intriguing characters to have emerged in Indian English fiction in the twentieth century. Tridib is the unnamed narrator's uncle in Amitav Ghosh's 1988 novel *The Shadow Lines*. While his mysterious death in Dhaka may be the impetus for the narrative, it is his culinary habits that lead him to visit his relatives at unexpected moments and entertain his young nephew with visions of far-off lands. Years of greasy street delicacies and endless cups of tea have contributed to a condition known quaintly as "Tridib's gastric." He drops in on his relatives when his sudden need for a toilet leaves him no other option. Once he arrives, he is further subjected to all sorts of Bengali delicacies—all wasted no doubt on "Tridib's gastric." Every Ghosh fan should make a pilgrimage to Mouchak, the well-known sweetshop in Gol Park. Order the radhaballobhi and alur dum, and sit down with Ghosh's novel..

Leaving aside academic questions of how to read, a more pertinent question might be this: where do we read Indian English fiction? And with what accompaniment? Where should one read Salman Rushdie's *Midnight's Children?* In a pickle factory in south Mumbai under the neon sign of Mumbadevi? Of course not. On Mumbai's Juhu beach with a packet of bhel and nariyal water is a better idea. On second thought, some place like the posh Chutney Mary, Bombay Brasserie, or the newly swank Veeraswamy (oldest Indian restaurant in the city) in London might be better. Can one walk past old-money neighborhoods like Peddar Road with a Kwality choconut ice-cream cup and enjoy Saleem Sinai's boyish adventures? Better still to sit down in the air-conditioned luxury of a five-star hotel lobby at Nariman Point for that truly is the milieu of the Sinais, not the all-India, teeming-masses-type world many imagine Rushdie's novel to represent.

And what of the other novels? Will the flavors of Arundhati Roy's *The God of Small Things* be enhanced by appams and fiery red kottayam fish curry eaten at Taj resorts in places like Thekkady, Kerala? Does Anita Desai's *In Custody* come alive with the rose and kewra scented mutton biryani from the vendor outside Lucknow's Tulsi cinema hall? How best to appreciate Upamanyu Chatterjee's young college graduate stuck in a boring small town? Chatterjee's English, August, and a cup of South Indian filter coffee at New Delhi's famous student hangout, the coffeehouse in Connaught Place, are -- as the Will's Filter cigarette ads of my youth promised -- made for each other.

Harvard professor Sharmila Sen is currently writing about borders in Bollywood cinema and working on a book on consumption and representations of India in anglophone texts.

ANDAMAN ISLANDS
अंदमान द्वीपसमूह

Mobs of backpackers and Indian tourists have made the Andaman dream of secluded beaches and pristine coral little more than wishful thinking. Much of the natural splendor and marine wildlife remain as breathtaking as ever, but be prepared to see more wild Australians than wild sea turtles. During colonial times, the British built a penal colony here to imprison agitators against colonial rule. Since Independence, the Indian government has developed an anthropological interest in the indigenous inhabitants. Because the Andaman and Nicobar Islands (the latter being off-limits to foreigners) are administered directly from Delhi, the quality of the roads and infrastructure here is far above the Indian average. The population is a mishmash of ethnic groups from around the subcontinent; Telugu and Bengali speakers are the most numerous. Rising awareness of the islands' natural wealth has led to increased efforts to make sure that they survive. Temperatures are about 30°C (86°F) all year. The monsoon lasts from late May to September.

HIGHLIGHTS OF THE ANDAMAN ISLANDS

The stunning underwater scenery of **Mahatma Gandhi National Marine Park** (p. 113) will have you jumping overboard to cavort with the fish.

Ritchie's Archipelago (p. 113) is a paradise of white sand, jungle, and a few isolated villages, with abundant tropical fruit for beach picnics.

PORT BLAIR पोर्ट ब्लैअर ☎ 03192

Port Blair hasn't changed much since its days as a British penal colony, leaving nothing much to see or do in the capital. Corbyn's Cove, the one beach, is crowded, remote, and not that beautiful anyway. But, since Port Blair is the only place approaching city-status on the Andamans, it is an important place to buy a hammock and stock up on supplies for camping, snorkeling, and diving.

> **WARNING.** All government accommodations on the islands require prior booking (either in person or via phone) through the tourism offices in Port Blair.

◪ TRANSPORTATION

Flights: The **airport** is on Jungleghat Rd., south of the town center. Public buses leave from the bus stand (every 30 min. 5am-8:30pm, Rs3). Auto-rickshaws to the airport Rs20. **Indian Airlines** (☎33108). Across the street from the tourist office. Open M-Sa 9am-1pm and 2-4pm. To **Calcutta** (Sa-Tu and Th, 8am, US$195) and **Chennai** (M, W, F, Su; 8:15am; US$195). **Jet Airways** flies to **Chennai** (2hr., 9:15am, US$195).

Ships: Enhance your Andaman experience with a voyage across the Bay of Bengal. Four sailings per month connect the Islands to **Calcutta** (70hr.); three sailings head to **Chennai** (65hr.) Prices are the same for all crossings (bunk Rs1150; 2nd class cabin Rs2700; 1st class cabin Rs3420). It's worth shelling out a bit of extra cash to get a cabin since rough seas and weak stomachs make the toilet-less bunks a less-than-pleasant option. The **Directorate of Shipping Services,** in the Phoenix Bay Jetty, sells tickets for Chennai 4 days before departure. The **Shipping Corporation of India** office, in Aberdeen Bazaar,

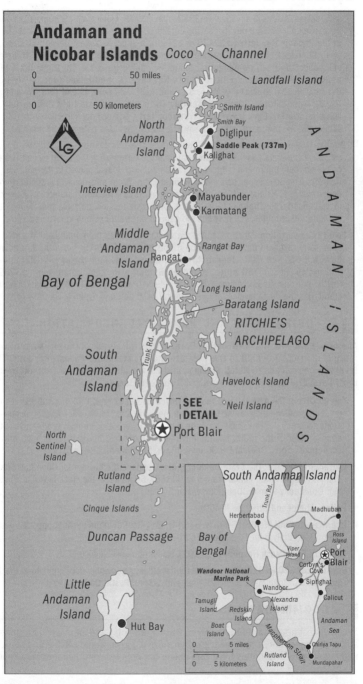

sells tickets 3 days in advance. (☎33590; fax 33778. Open 9am-12:30pm.) Oct.-Mar., tickets sell out within a day. For sailing details, consult the tourist office. The ticket booth at the **Phoenix Bay Jetty** (☎32426 or 33690), a short walk west of the bus stand, is open 9am-noon. Tickets for in-state destinations are available a day early (if there is still space) and can be bought on board for double the price. To: **Diglipur** via **Mayabunder** (14hr.; Tu 6am, F 4pm; Rs70); **Havelock** via **Neil Island** (4hr., 6 per week 6:15am, Rs15); **Rangat** (Tu, W, F, Sa 6am; Rs35) via **Long Island** (8hr., W and Sa, Rs36); **Ross Island** (20min., 4 per day Th-Tu, Rs16). Boats to **Mahatma Gandhi National Marine Park** leave from **Wandoor Jetty**, 30km from the city (24hr., Tu-Su 10am, Rs32). The tourist office's *Daily Telegrams* has up-to-date ship information.

Buses: Government bone-shakers leave from the bus station in Aberdeen Bazaar (☎32278); private coaches depart from near the bazaar. Ask the ticket-*wallahs* on the buses for route information. Prices are regular/deluxe. **Mayabunder** via **Rangat** (9hr., 5-6am, Rs70/130). Super deluxe for: **Rangat** (6hr.,11am and noon, Rs130) and **Wandoor** (1½hr.; 5:30 and 8:30am, 1:40 and 5pm; Rs10). The ferry connects with the bus in Mayabunder for **Diglipur** (2hr., Rs20). Buses are less comfortable than ferries, but on northbound routes, you may see indigenous Jarawa tribesmen in reserve territory.

Local Transportation: Most distances are walkable, though the terrain is hilly. **Autorickshaws** will take you anywhere in central Port Blair for Rs10-15, but a trip to Corbyn's Cove will cost you Rs40. **Jagganath Guest House** rents **motorbikes** (Rs120 per day) and **cycles** (Rs35). **TSG Autos,** Aberdeen Bazaar, also rents motorbikes. (☎32894. Rs120 per day, Rs500 deposit; mopeds Rs90.) **Patel Cycle Center,** behind the bus stand, has the best bicycles for hire in town (Rs35 per day). Open M-Sa 9am-7pm.

✳ 🛈 ORIENTATION AND PRACTICAL INFORMATION

Aberdeen Bazaar, at the north end of Port Blair, is the center of the city's main commercial district. Downhill to the west are the **bus stand** and **Phoenix Bay Jetty.** The level road east leads to **Netaji Stadium,** and curves along the coast for 5km to **Corbyn's Cove.** The airport is 3km south of Aberdeen Bazaar.

Tourist Office: The **A&N Islands Tourism Office** (☎32747 or 32694; fax 30933). It's the tall, spiffy-looking bldg. at the top of a hill, near the Secretariat. Bookings for all government accommodations *must* be made through this office or through the branch at the airport. Most of the major islands have government rest houses; fewer have private accommodations. Open M-F 8:30am-4:45pm, Sa 8:30am-12:30pm.

Currency Exchange: The **State Bank of India,** Opposite the bus stand. Open M-F 10am-2pm, Sa 10am-noon. **Island Travels** (☎33358), 60m east of the clock tower, is a better bet. Open daily 9am-6:30pm; off-season 3-4pm.

Police: Aberdeen Bazaar (☎32400).

Pharmacy: Devraj Medical Store (☎34344). Hospital Rd. In the bazaar opposite the stadium. Open daily 8am-1pm and 2-8pm.

Hospital: G.B. Panth Hospital (☎32102). Has ambulance service.

Post Office: GPO (☎32226). From the tourist office, go downhill and turn right at the 1st intersection. Open M-Sa 9am-12:30pm and 1-3pm. **Postal Code:** 744101.

🏠 ACCOMMODATIONS

Private guest houses around Aberdeen Bazaar are noisy and expensive. For longer stays, the government nest, near Corbyn's Cove, has a scenic setting and surprisingly good value. All hotels have 7am check-out policies. 25% discount May-Sept.

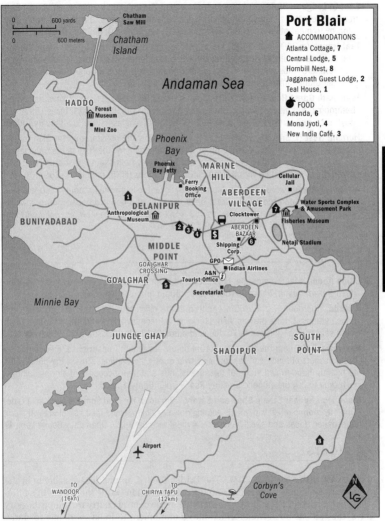

ANDAMAN ISLANDS

ENTRY REQUIREMENTS. For those arriving by air, a permit issued on arrival covers all of the Andaman Islands except the indigenous Jarawa reserve and several wildlife sanctuaries (such as Smith Island). The latter require a special permit, issued by the Forest Ranger Office in Diglipur. Almost all travelers will receive 30-day permits if they request them. Those arriving by sea should contact the **Deputy Commissioner** (☎33089), next to the ADN Tourism Office. Extensions are issued rarely. Travelers report that minor overstays go unpunished. But don't press your luck. **The Nicobar Islands are off-limits to foreigners.**

Central Lodge (☎ 33632 or 33634). In Goalghar. The ultimate budget guest house. Bare rooms offer little sensory stimulation but are clean and comfy. Even if you don't stay, stop by to meet other travelers. Camping Rs20; singles Rs60; doubles Rs90-120. ❶

Teal House (☎ 34060 or 34061). Up Moulana Azad Rd., a 15min. walk from the bus stand. Sweet-smelling, carpeted rooms with a wonderful hilltop view. Telephones, bamboo furniture, mosquito nets, and big bathrooms with hot showers. Book in advance with the tourist office. Doubles with bath Rs250-400. ❷

Jagganath Guest House (☎ 33140). Moulana Azad Rd. Well-kept rooms have balconies, bathrooms, free filtered water. Snorkeling equipment (Rs50 per day), bikes (Rs35 per day), motor bikes (Rs120 per day). Dorms Rs30-60; singles Rs200; doubles Rs300. ❶

Hornbill Nest (☎ 34006). From Netaji Stadium, follow the coastal road for 2km toward Corbyn's Cove on the east coast. All by itself amid greenery, the Nest is the only peaceful seaside place to stay in Port Blair but is 30min. from the nearest store and STD booth. Book in advance with the tourism office. Dorms Rs75; doubles Rs250-400. ❶

Atlanta Cottage (☎ 36739). On Medical Rd., over-looking Netaji stadium and the sea. Meticulously clean rooms—the front ones are light and open to ocean breezes. Multi-windowed 2nd fl. restaurant ensures you won't miss the ocean view, even if your room does. Singles Rs150; doubles Rs300-400. ❶

🍴 FOOD

▨ **China Room,** near the mosque. Fresh seafood in an intimate garden away from the Aberdeen Bazaar bustle. Shark Rs100. Open 5:30pm until you leave. ❷

Ananda, Aberdeen Bazaar. 50m uphill from the clock tower, on the left, opposite the police station. Crabs, prawns, fish, chickens, all recently killed and spiced with a thousand seasonings. Chicken Rs70, ice-cold curds Rs10. Open 6:30am-10:30pm. ❶

New India Cafe, near the bus stand, 40m before Jagganath Guest House. Frequented by Indian sailors at lunch and the foreign crowd during the evenings. This is the place to go to pick up hand-drawn maps of treasure islands and hear accounts of stormy sailings. Fish *thali* Rs20, prawn coconut curry Rs45. Open 6am-11pm.❶

Mona Jyoti Rubber Stamp Shop and Eatery, 20m down the road from the New India Cafe. One tiny room packed with locals gulping down egg curries and fried fish along with *sambar*-soaked *dosas* and *sabzi*-laden rice. A meal will cost Rs25. Open daily 6am-11pm. ❶

👁 SIGHTS

CELLULAR JAIL AND MUSEUM. The British locked up political dissidents in the Andamans Cellular Jail. If exile from the mainland didn't stifle the dissident's influence, he was led to the gallows, now visible in the central courtyard. Since its glory days, the Jail has been transformed into a monument to India's struggle for independence. The museum's ground-floor galleries chart the history of the prison and document Indian resistance to colonialism. *(From the clock tower, go down toward the ocean. Bear left and head uphill. ☎ 30117. Jail open daily 9am-5pm; museum open Tu-Su 9am-noon and 2-5pm. Sound and light show Tu-Su 7:15pm, weather permitting.)*

OTHER SIGHTS. The one-room **Zonal Anthropological Museum** displays photos and artifacts taken from the Islands' indigenous peoples. *(Open Tu-Su 9:30am-12:30pm and 1-4pm.)* A better bet for getting information about the indigenous cultures of the Andaman and Nicobar Islands would be the Tourism Department's **free documentary screenings.** *(M-F 5:30pm; M and Th at the Teal House, W and F at the Megapode Nest, and Tu at the Hornbill Nest.)* A 15min. bike ride along the coast from the Netaji Stadium leads to **Corbyn's Cove,** a beach surrounded by palms. The cove is more beautiful than any other spot in Port Blair, but packed with tourists. A visit to the **Water Sports Complex and Amusement Park** makes for a fun evening. *(Open M-Sa 4-8pm.)*

NEAR PORT BLAIR

SOUTH ANDAMAN ISLAND

On the northeast side of South Andaman island, **Ross Island** was once the center of operations for the British penal colony. The ruins are a surreal place to wander around for the day. **Ferries** leave from Phoenix Bay Jetty (2hr.; Tu-Th 8:30, 10am, 12:30, 2pm; Rs15). The last ferry back to Port Blair leaves at 5:30pm. **Viper Island** is also dominated by the haunting, overgrown ruins of the British penal project. You can reach Viper on the general **Harbour Cruise,** which leaves daily from Phoenix Bay Jetty (2hr., Th-Tu 3pm, Rs25). **Chiriya Tapu** is a fishing village at the south end of South Andaman, 30km from Port Blair. The road winds through countryside and jungle until it reaches mangroves and wooded mountains that rise from the sea. Most people come on a day trip from Port Blair to the **Mundapahar beach and wildlife area,** 2km past the village. In the **Forest Department Guest House ❶,** you can find two A/C rooms overlooking the bay; get permission from the Chief Wildlife Warden, Van Sadan, Haddo, Port Blair. (☎33549. Open M-F 8:30am-4:30pm. Rs200.) The area is excellent for snorkeling; hire a motorboat in Chiriya Tapu to take you to the coral. Be sure to bring equipment from Port Blair.

LITTLE ANDAMAN

Occasional boats from Phoenix Bay Jetty (12hr., Rs50) head to the remote Little Andaman Island. At **Hut Bay ❶,** there is a government hotel. (Doubles Rs200) The rest of the island is underdeveloped and untouristed. Bring mosquito repellent.

🏝 MAHATMA GANDHI NATIONAL MARINE PARK

The Mahatma Gandhi National Marine Park is something out of Jacques Cousteau's wildest dreams. A fantastic kaleidoscope of living coral, the marine park is also home to colorful marine life including angel fish, clown fish, starfish, butterfly fish, parrot fish, sea anemones, and sharks. From the Port Blair bus stand, the 8:30am bus to Wandoor connects with the 10am boat to either **Jolly Buoy** or **Red Skin Island** (Rs60). A park permit costs Rs15; snorkel equipment rental is Rs50, but equipment gets scarce during season—bring your own or rent it from a Port Blair hotel. For scuba diving, ask at any of the larger Port Blair hotels. Although glass-bottomed boats are available for undersea sight-seeing, you might prefer to go solo. Coral and shell collecting is forbidden. In addition to renting snorkels, **Bharat Hotel ❶,** a shack 50m from the boat dock, has small rooms for Rs50-80. The road here leads a few km past the boat dock to a beautiful beach with drift-logs perfect for setting up a tarp. (Fish curry, Rs8; *chappatis,* Rs2.) Beer (Rs65) and basic food are available at the restaurant a few yards away.

RITCHIE'S ARCHIPELAGO

Havelock Island is the most popular tourist getaway on Ritchie's Archipelago. **Neil Island, Long Island,** and **North Passage** are also open for overnight stays. Ferries from Phoenix Bay Jetty stop at Neil Island (3-4 per week 6:15am, Rs8) and Long Island (2 per week 6:15am, Rs13). Ferries from Havelock to Rangat sometimes stop at Long Island. At most ferry stops, officials check tourists' permit validity.

ANTHROPOLOGY GONE AWRY The native peoples of the Andaman Islands can smell your fear. When Trunk Rd. buses, bound from Port Blair, stop in tribal land, Jarawa tribesman sometimes approach the bus, glare at spooked tourists, and lunge at the windows, trying to provoke a flinch. The aggression is understandable. Since the days of British rule, the natives have watched their land be logged, farmed, and stolen by outside forces. Western diseases, deforestation, and armed skirmishes (spears vs. rifles) initiated a decimation of the indigenous populations that began to level off only in the 1980s. By then, the entire Andaman population, now resettled to Strait Island, had been reduced to just 28.

Since Independence, the Indian government, shifting its policy from colonize-or-bust to colonize-with-scientific-curiosity, has set aside indigenous reserves. Still, some indigenous groups have opted for zero communication with the bungling invaders. The Sentinelese of North Sentinel Island (64km southwest of Port Blair) have been a target of government anthropological excursions since 1967. Government boats pull up to the island, leave gifts of plastic buckets, roasted pigs, and sacks of coconuts in an attempt to establish contact. The Sentinelese take the gifts—and then fire arrows at the anthropologists. The Jarawas, who occupy much of the busier Middle Andaman, have been shot while trying to deter poachers and loggers (in one case by chopping off the offenders' hands). For more information on the Andaman and Nicobar indigenous peoples, see the Zonal Anthropological Museum (see p. 112).

HAVELOCK ISLAND

Havelock Island has white sand and an occasional dolphin leaping up out of the sapphire blue water. Much of the island is jungle, but the northern part has been cleared for a few villages surrounded by fruit and coconut plantations.

■ TRANSPORTATION

Ferries leaving Port Blair (4hr., Tu-Su 6:15am, Rs15) arrive at the **jetty** (also known as Govindanagar or Village #1). **Boats** leave Port Blair for Havelock Island from the Phoenix Bay Jetty (4hr., 3-4 per week 6:15am, Rs16) and return from Havelock the next day. It's a bumpy ride, so have motion sickness pills handy. Ferries from Havelock sail to **Port Blair** (10:30am) and **Rangat** (Tu, W, F, Sa 11:30am). Check with the guards on the dock for exact timings and to find out if the ship stops at Long or Neil Islands. An unpredictable **bus** chugs between the jetty and Beach #7. Your best bet is to hire a **bicycle** (Rs50 per day) or **moped** (Rs150 per day) in the jetty market. Many guest houses have mopeds, but only a few have bicycles. For gas, ask at the shops in Village #3.

■ ORIENTATION AND PRACTICAL INFORMATION

The jetty is the island's main **bazaar**. There are several restaurants and a **post office** (open M-F 10am-5pm). A road extends 3km to **Village #3**, referred to as "the capital" by islanders. This metropolis has the only **STD/ISD** booth on Havelock. In #3, the road forks 2km to the left and leads to **Beach #5**, spoiled only by a government lodge. The road to the right winds for another 11km to reach **Village** (and Beach) **#7**, Havelock's nicest but most remote beach.

ACCOMMODATIONS AND FOOD

Every inhabited area of Havelock has a few decent guest houses. The cheapest and most comfortable way to sleep at Havelock is to bring a hammock and pay a small camping fee at a beachside resort. Hidden in the jungle off Beach #7 is the **Jungle Lodge ❶,** managed by a Port Blair native who returned from Switzerland to pioneer eco-awareness in the Andamans. Forty percent of profit goes into island development projects. Jeep transportation to and from the jetty is complimentary. Reservations must be made through **Travel World** (☎37656; fax 37657), in Port Blair (Simple straw huts cost Rs200; huge luxurious huts are Rs1800.) **Eco Villa ❶,** on Beach #2, has helpful management and for Rs100 serves an excellent buffet dinner. (☎82336. Camping Rs20; huts Rs100.) A few other places are usually available on a walk-in basis. **Sea View Tourist Complex ❶,** near the jetty, is a mere 10m roll from your bed to the edge of the sea. (☎82367. Doubles with attached bath Rs150-250.) **M.S. Lodge ❶,** 100m farther along the coast, has spacious doubles. The straw huts have mattresses and mosquito nets. (☎82439. Huts Rs150 per person; rooms Rs300.) **Tent Resorts ❶,** is a government-run lodge on Beaches #5 and 7. (Singles Rs150; doubles Rs300.) **Dolphin Yatri Ninas ❷,** is another government place on Beach #5. (☎82411. Doubles with showers Rs300-800.) Both government hotels must be booked through the tourist office in Port Blair. Food is cheap and tasty at the jetty. **Anjana Restaurant ❶,** in the jetty bazaar serves ginger prawns (Rs45), garlic crabs (Rs50), and fish curry with *parathas* for Rs15. (Open 6am-1:30pm and 4:30-9pm.)

SNORKELING

The best place for snorkeling is **Elephant Beach.** Take the road toward Beach #7 until you pass a school. Leave your bike by the road, turn left onto the path through the woods, and a 45min. walk leads to the coral. To go farther afield, you will have to arrange a *dungee* with your hotel manager. An afternoon fishing trip on a local *dungee* will cost Rs800—a comfortable price when split among several people. Fishing is best in early morning. Dive shops are few, but there are some planned openings that will accommodate demand. The **Jungle Resort** will soon have its own dive outfit, and two Swiss dive-masters at the **Sea View Complex** recently started a PADI business. Many guest houses rent snorkeling equipment (Rs50).

NEIL ISLAND

Neil Island can be circumnavigated by foot in part of an afternoon. The **Shanti Guest House ❶,** has doubles with private balconies and common bathrooms (Rs150.) **Hanabill Nest ❶,** (☎82630) is a government-run accommodation. (Dorms Rs75; doubles with shower and A/C Rs400.) Some guest houses will allow you to camp for a small fee, but Long Island and Smith Island are better for the Robinson Crusoe experience.

MIDDLE ANDAMAN

RANGAT

Though Rangat and Mayabunder are transit points on the way to the wild north, a few decent beaches can be found nearby. **Ships** sail from Rangat to **Port Blair** via **Havelock** (W, Th, Sa, Su; Rs35), stopping at Neil and Long Islands (Th, Su). **Buses** run to: **Port Blair** (6hr., 7am-noon, Rs60; deluxe Rs130) and **Mayabunder** (3hr.,

5:30am-5pm, Rs16). Rangat Bay is 8km from the town itself; minibuses run back and forth. **Hotel Avis ❶**, on Church Rd., has tiny rooms with snow-white sheets. If you arrive after dark, just look for the red neon crucifix and grail-shaped beacon 100m from the main road; the tiny hotel is next to it. (☎74554. Singles Rs70; doubles Rs120.) The deserted **Hawksbill Nest ❶**, is on the beach, 15km from Rangat on the road to Mayabunder. (Dorms Rs75; doubles Rs250.)

🏞 MAYABUNDER

Mayabunder is a dull little transit town useful only for its ferry to **Kalighat** on North Andaman (2hr., 8am and 2:30pm, Rs20). From Kalighat, a bus connects to **Diglipur** (30min., Rs3) and **Aerial Bay** (40min., Rs16). Karmatang Beach is 7km from town. The **Swiflet Nest ❶**, is the local government's bid to bring you bliss. (Dorms Rs75; doubles Rs250.) **Pharmacies, STD phones,** and a **post office** are available in Mayabunder.

NORTH ANDAMAN

As you get farther from Port Blair, the tourist crowds thin out and conditions become increasingly rustic. North Island, the most remote of the major islands, is blanketed with deep jungle and has a beautiful skyline dominated by **Saddle Peak** (741m). North Andaman's main town is **Diglipur**. The main port is **Aerial Bay.**

AERIAL BAY

ENTRY REQUIREMENTS. The **Forest Range Office** (open M-Sa 6am-2pm) in Aerial Bay grants **permits** for Smith, Ross, and other islands. Just show your passport and Andaman permit. Rs10 fee. Smith Island permits are good for one day but may be updated by the ranger on Smith for several weeks.

📠 TRANSPORTATION

Ships sail for **Port Blair** (14hr.; W 6am, Sa 4pm; Rs70). Tickets can be bought from the Tehsil office in the Diglipur Bazaar (open M-F 9-11am), from the jetty ticket office, or aboard ship, for double the price. The bus from Aerial Bay to **Kalighat** (1hr., 3am, Rs6) connects with the 5am ferry to Mayabunder, which is greeted by Port Blair-bound buses. The only other ferry leaves at noon, and gets you into Mayabunder too late to catch anything going any farther than Rangat. **Buses** also run to **Diglipur** (30min., 9am-8pm, Rs3) and **Kalipur** (30min.; 6 per day 6:30am-5:30pm, last bus returning at 6pm; Rs2). Irregular boats go to **Havelock** (9½hr., Rs50).

✴ 🛈 ORIENTATION AND PRACTICAL INFORMATION

Aerial Bay, the fishing village that acts as Diglipur's port, is 12km from the town. In the **bazaar** at Aerial Bay, you will find mosquito nets, plastic sheets, strings, kerosene, pots, rice, fruit and vegetables, Beatles wigs, and a 24hr. **STD booth** to contact the outside world. The closest place to buy a hammock is Diglipur. The nearest doctor and **pharmacies** to treat your malaria and snake bites are in Diglipur.

ACCOMMODATIONS AND FOOD

To get a good night's sleep in Aerial Bay, you may need to jump through a few hoops. The rooms on the main road are bland and filled with blaring music from the street. (Doubles Rs150. ❶) A better bet is the Power and Water Department's **PWD Guest House ❶**, on a high hill overlooking the bay. The PWD's two rooms exist to house visiting employees; you'll have to get special permission from the Aerial Bay Junior Engineer to sleep there. If she isn't at the guest house, go bang on her door near the fruit market. She lives in a rickety duplex 50m from the main road. (Doubles Rs100.) Several shops on the main drag serve meals at good prices.

Twelve kilometers from Aerial Bay, in the shadow of Saddle Peak, **Kalipur** has walks along the craggy shore and a passable beach. Government-run **Turtle Resort ❶**, features hot-showers and balconies. (☎ 72553. Dorms Rs75; doubles Rs250.) A bus runs between Kalipur and Diglipur during the day. Otherwise, the 3hr. walk back to Aerial Bay goes through Bengali villages and banana and mango plantations.

ISLANDS

Smith and **Ross Islands** are as close to Robinson Crusoe as you're likely to get. Wild dogs, hermit crabs, two friendly fishing families, and one drunken forest ranger are the island's only permanent inhabitants. Waves break on beautiful coral reefs and white sand beaches, empty except for the rare skinny-dipping tourist. Free camping and the chance to live the primitive life for a few days have lured more and more travelers. For now, the numbers remain small enough to have preserved the islands' natural beauty, but the hype about the islands among backpackers on the Andamans circuit threatens to end the golden age of free camping and tropical solitude. Environmentalists worry that campfires and litter are ruining wildlife habitats, and developers have hatched plans to open a guest house. As of March 2001, campers were still pitching their hammocks free of charge.

A thin strip of sand connects Smith with its tinier sibling, Ross. A **boat** services **Aerial Bay** and **Smith** (30min., 9am and 11am, Rs50), or you can hire a local *dungee* (Rs150-200) and split the cost with as many as 12 other travelers. Bring hammocks, food, cooking supplies, and a machete with you; water is available at two wells, but you must bring containers to carry it back to your campsite. The families who live on the island might sell you some produce. If you leave food out overnight, dogs and monkeys will steal it. **Campfires are illegal,** so buy a cheap stove.

ANDHRA PRADESH

ఆంధ్ర దేశము

The state of Andhra Pradesh occupies a large chunk of southeastern India, from the dry Deccan Plateau to the coast of the Bay of Bengal. The state is named for the kingdom of the Andhras, who ruled most of the Deccan from the 2nd century BC until the 3rd century AD. As part of Emperor Ashoka's vast kingdom, the region was also a major Buddhist center. Beginning in the 16th century, Andhra Pradesh was ruled by Muslims, first under the Golconda Sultanate, then as part of the Mughal Empire, and finally under the Nizams, who ruled from Hyderabad under British protection from 1723 until 1948. In spite of the religious differences, the people of Andhra are bound together by their language, Telugu. When India gained Independence in 1947, the Nizam of Hyderabad refused to cede his lands. After a year-long standoff, the Indian government forcibly annexed the territory, which was later merged with other Telugu-speaking areas to form Andhra Pradesh. Though one of the least touristed destinations in India, the state is home to a number of superb attractions well worth visiting.

HIGHLIGHTS OF ANDHRA PRADESH

Hyderabad's bazaars and monuments (p. 125) complement the nearby spooky ruins of **Golconda Fort** (p. 123) and the gorgeous marble **Birla Mandir** (p. 125).

A visit to **Tirupati's** hilltop temple frenzy (p. 127) provides insight into contemporary Hinduism, and then thrills with a harrowing bus ride down to calmer climes.

HYDERABAD యదరాబాదు   ☎ 040

Let millions of men and women of all castes, creeds, and religions make it their abode, like fish in the ocean.
—Muhammad Quli Qutb Shah, upon laying Hyderabad's foundation

Standing as a sweet testament to the transcendent power of love, the city of Hyderabad was founded in the late 16th century by Muhammad Quli Qutb Shah, Sultan of Golconda. Though he was to ascend to the throne of one of the greatest kingdoms in India, Muhammad had fallen in love too hard and too fast to heed religious and caste barriers. His love, Bagmati, was a beautiful Hindu dancer and singer, but she was a commoner. Risking his inheritance and his neck, he made midnight journeys on horseback from Golconda to a village on the banks of the Musi River to tryst with her. Upon discovering the depths of his son's infatuation, Muhammad's father relented and allowed his son to marry her. The boy became king and planted a new city on the banks of the Musi, which he named Bhagnagar.

A legacy of tolerance has honeyed the tongues of this comfortably polyglot (and "multicuisine") metropolis quickly approaching six million. In the streets, Urdu blends with Hindi and Telugu as Muslims, settled more densely here than in any other city in the south, work and worship side by side with Hindus. The wealth of the Nizams, displayed in the city's impressive examples of Indo-Saracenic architecture, has returned in hi-tech fashion to this newly crowned capital. However, Mumbai pace comes with Mumbai tastes, and to maintain its "clean, green" image as trash collects and traffic bulges its arteries, the city is undergoing a 25-overpass surgery. Just as Hyderabad's legendary first urbanites saw its lake appear overnight, you'll watch the city change in a heartbeat. Meanwhile, women draped head-to-toe in black *burqas* will haggle away in the bazaars of the Old City, whose many Muslim monuments shine resolutely through the dust.

⌨ TRANSPORTATION

Flights: Begumpet Airport (enquiry ☎ 140, recorded flight info ☎ 142), on the north side of Husain Sagar, off Sardar Patel Rd., 8km north of Abids. Auto-rickshaws go to Abids (Rs65 fixed). Taxis cost twice as much. **Air Canada, Air France** (☎ 323 0947), **Bangladesh Biman, Gulf Air** (☎ 324 0870), **Kuwait Airways** (☎ 323 4409), **Royal Jordanian,** and **TWA** (☎ 329 8774) are all in the same bldg., Flat 202, Gupta Estate, 500m north of Basheer Bagh; **Lufthansa** (☎ 323 5537) 3-5-823 Hyderguda Rd., to the right off Basheer Bagh Circle. **Delta Airlines, Jet Airways** (☎ 3301222), **Singapore Airlines** (☎ 3311144), and **Swissair** are all in the Navbharet Chambers, Raj Bhavan Rd. **KLM Royal Dutch Airlines,** Ashok Bhopal Chambers, R.P. Rd. (☎ 772 0940). All open M-F 9:30am-5:30pm, Sa 9:30am-1:30pm. **Air India,** 5-9-193 HACA Bhavan (☎ 323 3119), opposite the Public Gardens. Open M-Sa 9:30am-1pm and 1:45-5:30pm. **Indian Airlines** (☎ 329 9333 or 141) Secretariat Rd., opposite Assembly Saifabad. Open daily 10am-1pm and 2-5:15pm. Daily flights to: **Ahmedabad** (1½hr.; US$165); **Bangalore** (1hr.; US$105); **Calcutta** (2½hr.; US$210); **Chennai** (1hr.; US$105); **Delhi** (2hr.; US$205); **Mumbai** (1hr.; US$120); **Tirupati** (1hr.; US$85).

Trains: There are tourist quotas at each of the three **stations** (centralized enquiry ☎ 131 3541): **Secunderabad, Nampally** (in Abids), and **Kachiguda** (east side of Sultan Bazaar). Secunderabad and Nampally are the most useful for tourists. Nampally (the main Hyderabad station) is convenient to budget hotels. Many trains stop at both stations. Reservations open M-Sa 8am-8pm, Su 8am-2pm. To: **Bangalore** (13½hr.; 5:40pm (Secunderabad) and 5:58pm (Kachiguda); Rs255); **Chennai** (13½hr.; 3:50 and 7pm; Rs255); **Delhi** (26hr.; 6:40am and 9:30pm; Rs200); **Mumbai** (15½hr.; 2:30 and 8:40pm; Rs255); **Tirupati** (13½hr.; 5 per day 5:30am-7pm; Rs245).

Buses: The **Imlibun Central Bus Stand** (enquiry ☎ 461 4406), across the river in Malakpet, east of the Salar Jung Museum, proclaims itself Asia's largest. You'll believe it as you wander its platforms. Open 24hr. Deluxe to: **Bangalore** (12hr.; every 30min. 4:30am-9pm; Rs294); **Chennai** (14hr.; 4:30pm; Rs344); **Hospet** (8hr.; 5:30pm; Rs230); **Mumbai** (16hr.; 10:30am and 9:30pm; Rs360); **Nagarjunakonda** (4hr.; every hr.; Rs90); **Tirupati** (14hr.; 6 per day 4:30-10pm; Rs294).

Local Transportation: Buses may not come to a full stop—you'll need turbo-*chappals* to catch one. Terminals at **Nampally, Koti, Afzalgunj,** near the **Charminar,** and **Secunderabad** Railway Station. The Nampally terminal is north of the railway station on Public Garden Rd., at the entrance to the public gardens. From Secunderabad Station to Nampally: #2 and 8A. From Nampally to Golconda Fort: #119 and 142N. **Auto-rickshaws** cost Rs6 for 1km, Rs3 per km thereafter; most drivers are (surprise, surprise) reluctant to use the meter. **Taxis** are unmetered and twice as expensive.

✦ ORIENTATION

The **Musi River** divides the **Old City**—containing the Charminar, the Mecca Masjid, and the bazaars—from the **New City,** which has government offices, glitzy downtown shops, and glimmering Birla-commissioned landmarks to the north. The

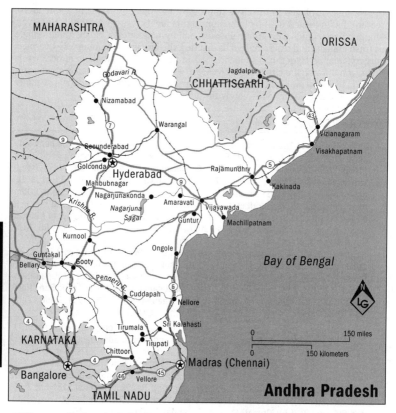

Andhra Pradesh

Abids area, the heart of the New City, is about 1½km south of the gargantuan, Gautama-guarded **Husain Sagar**, the artificial lake built back in the days of the Golconda empire. Abids adjoins **Hyderabad (Nampally) Station.** The other main transportation hub is in Hyderabad's twin city, **Secunderabad,** to the northeast of Husain Sagar, where another **railway station** sends travelers in and out of the area.

℗ PRACTICAL INFORMATION

TOURIST, LOCAL, AND FINANCIAL SERVICES

Tourist Office: Government of India Tourist Office, 3-6-140 Himayatnagar Main Rd. From Basheer Bagh, the office is 1km down the road, on the right. Free Hyderabad city map. Open M-F 9:30am-5:30pm. The **Andhra Pradesh Travel and Tourism Development Corporation Ltd. (APTTDC)** has its booking office next to Lumbini Park, Tank Bund Rd. (☎ 345 3036; apttdc@satyam.net.in). Open daily 6:30am-8:30pm. It offers local sightseeing tours (daily 8am-5:15pm, Rs130), as well as tours to Nagarjunasagar (Sa-Th 6:45am-9:45pm, Rs225), Tirupati (3 days, Rs950 includes 1night's accommodation), and other destinations in South India.

Budget Travel: Sita World Travel (☎323 3629; fax 323 4223). 3-5-874 Hyderguda Rd. next to Apollo Hospital. Turn right coming from Abids Circle to Basheer Bagh. Open M-F 9:30am-6pm, Sa 9:30am-1:30pm.

Currency Exchange: State Bank of Hyderabad (☎320 1594). MG Rd. 700m north of Abids Circle. Open M-F 10:30am-2:30pm, Sa 10am-noon. **Thomas Cook** (☎329 6521). 6-1-57 Saifabad, near the junction of Secretariat and Public Gardens Rd. Both change currency and traveler's checks. Open M-F 9:30am-5:30pm, Sa 9:30am-5pm.

Bookstore: 📕 **Walden** (☎331 3434). 6-3-871 Greenlands Rd., Begumpet, between Abids and the airport, in the Vivekananda Hospital complex. Open W-M 9am-8:30pm.

EMERGENCY AND COMMUNICATIONS

Police: Abids Circle Police Station (☎3230191). To the right as you face the GPO.

Pharmacy: Apollo Pharmacy (☎3231380). In the Apollo Hospital Complex (see below). Open 24hr. **Medwin Hospital Pharmacy** (☎3202909). Off Station Rd., on Chirag Ali Ln., in a tall bldg. visible even from the Nampally Railway Station. The pharmacy is inside the lobby to your left. Open 24hr.

Hospital: Medwin Hospital (☎3202902). **Apollo Hospital Medical Center** (☎360 7777). Jubilee Hills, 8km northwest of Abids. Open 24hr.

Internet: Yahoo Citi the Hang Out Point, 5-9-88 Fateh Maidan, 3rd fl., on your right as you turn onto Chapel Rd. from the Public Gardens Rd. Open daily 9:30am-1am. Rs32 per hr. **Netplanet** (☎3205594), 150m down Abids St. #2. Open daily 11am-11pm. Rs30 per hr. **Pragnya Infotech,** 5-4-435/1 Station Rd. (☎4732044) next to Hotel Sai Prakash. Open daily 10am-9:45pm. Rs25 per hr.

Post Office: GPO (☎474 5978). Open M-Sa 8am-8:30pm. **Postal Code:** 500001.

🏠 ACCOMMODATIONS

Budget dives are 10-paise-a-dozen in the commercial Abids area. A few lodges are around the Secunderabad Railway Station, but there's no reason to stay there unless you have a morning train to catch. Almost all hotels have 24hr. check-out.

ABIDS

Hotel Saptagiri (☎460 3601). 5-4-651 Nampally Station Rd. down a narrow dirt road opposite the CLS Bookshop. Scrubbed and polished through and through. Balconies, telephones, 24hr. hot water, some seat toilets. Singles Rs215; doubles Rs270. ❶

Hotel Jaya International (☎475 2929). 4-1-37/A&B Reddy Hostel Rd. Facing the GPO in Abids Circle, bear left along Mahipatram Rd., then take the first left at the Dhanalak-shmi Bank. The best value for its price, with huge windows, seat toilets, and showers. Singles Rs300-600; doubles Rs400-750. AmEx/MC/Visa. ❷

Taj Mahal Hotel (☎475 8221). 4-1-999 King Kothi Rd. Walk away from the GPO in Abids Circle and veer right after 200m. One of Hyderabad's most popular hotels. Large, well-kept rooms with TVs, phones, seat or squat toilets, and 24hr. hot water. Singles Rs350-500; doubles Rs500-750. AmEx/MC/Visa. ❷

Hotel Annapurna (☎473 2612). 5-4-730 Nampally Station Rd. near Hotel Saptagiri, sandwiched between electronics stores. Overwhelmingly pink (but otherwise unexciting) place has TVs, direct-dial phones, and towels. Star-shaped rooms have faux-leather couches and seat toilets. Check-out 24hr. Singles Rs220-240; doubles Rs300-530. ❶

Asian Lodge (☎650 6050). Public Garden Rd. Take a left from the station; it's one block up on the left. Cheap and dusty. Singles Rs60-100; doubles Rs100-150. ❶

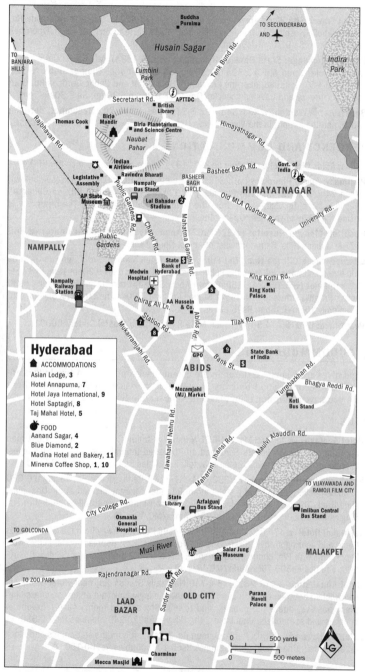

Hyderabad

🏠 ACCOMMODATIONS

Asian Lodge, **3**
Hotel Annapurna, **7**
Hotel Jaya International, **9**
Hotel Saptagiri, **8**
Taj Mahal Hotel, **5**

🍎 FOOD

Aanand Sagar, **4**
Blue Diamond, **2**
Madina Hotel and Bakery, **11**
Minerva Coffee Shop, **1**, **10**

SECUNDERABAD

Hotel Sitara (☎ 6219402). 7-1-2 SPG Church Complex. From the Secunderabad station, veer diagonally left. By far the cleanest and friendliest hotel in the area. Tiled bathrooms with squat toilets, balconies, and spacious rooms. 24hr. hot water. Singles Rs125-275; doubles Rs200-400. ❶

National Lodge (☎ 770 5572). 9-4-48 Syed Abdulla St. opposite Secunderabad station. Basic, clean rooms with narrow beds and no hot water. Dorms Rs50; singles with common bath Rs90; doubles Rs140-225. ❶

🖸 FOOD

For incendiary Andhra cuisine, gourmets make their way to the upscale terraces of Banjara Hills. The hard-working Hyderabadi plows into the *biryani* that built this town, but you can cool it down at one of the ubiquitous juice stands, bakeries, or softy joints lining the alleys.

▧ Madina Hotel & Bakery, at the 1st major intersection south of the river on Sardar Patel Rd. Topped with a hard-boiled egg, the half-order of mutton biryani (Rs42) will balloon even the billowiest *burqa* (veg. Rs30). Instant, personable service on a breezy mezzanine overlooking the action. Open Sa-Th 11am-11pm. ❶

Shalimar Icecreams & Sweets, opposite the Koti bus stand on Koti Rd. Fell right out of the dreams of every little *ladka* and *larki*. *Ragdai* and *dosa* fry on the enclosed patio, as *chaats* (Rs14) and *pav bhajis* (Rs28-35) fly off the counter. Open daily 11am-11pm. ❶

Taj Mahal, in the Taj Mahal Hotel, King Kothi Rd. off MG Rd. A family favorite, and with good reason: it's cheap, comfortable, and generous with South and North Indian favorites (Rs32-65). *Chole batura* Rs39, extensive *thali* Rs50. Tiffin 7am-9:30pm. Open daily 11am-3:30pm and 7-10:30pm. ❶

Blue Diamond, 100m south of Basheer Bagh Circle. Chinese food as authentic as possible. Wide selection includes Manchurian prawns (Rs105), Hong Kong chicken (Rs95), and sweet-and-sour pork (Rs80). Open daily 11am-3:30pm and 6-10:30pm. ❷

Minerva Coffee Shop, 22-8-290 Hamad Plaza, 1st fl. On the river, just to the left of the main bridge entering the Old City. Servers weave between the rows of potted plants as locals gossip away. *Rava dosa* Rs23, huge *puris* Rs20. "Love of California," a fluffy lime-green ice cream fantasia, only Rs20. Open daily 7am-11pm. ❶

Aanand Sagar, 50 Unity House, in Dhirag Ali Lane by Medwin Hospital. Excellent double *pav bhaji* (RS25), plus *puris*, pizzas, and juices. Open daily 9:30am-11pm. ❶

🖸 SIGHTS

GOLCONDA

8km west of the city. From the Nampally bus stand, take bus #119 or 142.

QUTB SHAHI TOMBS. Containing the remains of seven of the dynasty's patriarchs, the Qutb Shahi tombs play an undeserved second fiddle to the Golconda Fort, the latter having a steep climb and even steeper entrance fee. The tombs are magnificent buildings in amazing condition set in the midst of gardens flush with bougainvillea. Each tomb is capped with an Islamic-style onion dome and adorned with Hindu motifs. The cenotaph in the center of the tomb covers the crypt below. Though the tombs all have a similar shape, each bears the distinctive mark of its designer. The grandest tomb is that of **Sultan Muhammed Quli Qutb Shah.** It is surrounded by gardens and criss-crossed by waterways. Farthest from the entrance, the tall tomb of **Jamshid Qutb Shah** commands views of Golconda from its terrace.

Next door, a small **museum** displays artifacts from Qutb Shahi times: ceramics, weapons, handwritten texts, and portraits of the kings who have their tombs here. *(2km north of Golconda Fort. Open 9am-4:30pm. Rs2. Museum open Sa-Th 9am-1pm and 2-4:30pm. Rs2. Camera Rs5, video Rs25.)*

GOLCONDA FORT. Headquarters of the Qutb Shah kingdom from 1512 to 1687, the fort is Hyderabad's most popular attraction. The kingdom was a thriving center for the arts and learning and a bastion of religious tolerance, until it was crushed and annexed after two sieges by the Mughal emperor Aurangzeb. The 1000-step ascent to Durbar Hall takes about 30min. to climb. At the top is a panoramic view over the ramparts below, and if you squint hard enough, you should be able to make out the Birla Mandir and the Charminar to the east. If you can pass up the vista and the exercise, your Rs25 ticket to the sound and light show will get you into the fort's ground-level attractions from 5:30 onwards, after the official visiting hours.

On the way up, visitors follow the counter-clockwise path used by the common people during the fort's active days; the steep descent leads down a route once used exclusively by the king and the poor chumps who had to carry him. You first pass through the heavily studded **Balahisar Gate,** which served as the first line of defense against invaders. Ahead is the **Grand Portico,** where guides are often seen clapping to demonstrate the fort's acoustics: Golconda was engineered so that a clap at the summit of Durbar Hall would reverberate at five places along the inside perimeter of the fortress wall; a clap at the center of the Grand Portico can be heard at the summit, 1km away. This built-in communication system was used to notify the king of any visitors while they were still far away. Straight ahead are the covered **bodyguard barracks.** Ahead and to the right is the **Nagina Bagh,** a royal garden. From the gardens, a stone staircase begins the ascent to the summit. At the foot of the steps, on the right, you can see the 12m deep **water tank,** one of three within the fort. The water came from a natural spring and was transported by a complex system of limestone pipes, the stumps of which can still be seen today.

Durbar Hall commands spectacular views of Hyderabad and Secunderabad. The summit is also home to the 12th-century Hindu **Sri Jagadamba Temple.** From Durbar Hall, you have to go almost all the way down the king's staircase before you get to the next site. At the foot of the hill is a water tank; around the corner are the **Rani Mahals,** a series of buildings once occupied by the king's harem. A modest fountain is in the central courtyard, where the daily sound and light show is held. Once decorated with curtains, mirrored glass, and jewels, the main building is now occupied by bats and the gardens have been overtaken by weeds. Passing through the Rani Mahals takes you past the **Taramati Mosque** to the three-story **arsenal,** which houses dusty guns and cannon balls. *(Open daily 7am-5pm. US $5 or equivalent in rupees; video fee Rs25. 1hr. English sound and light show daily 7pm, Nov.-Feb. 6:30pm; Rs25.)*

FISHY PLACEBO
Every year in early June, thousands of asthmatics flock to the outskirts of Hyderabad to the home of the Battina Gowd brothers. The reason: they dispense an ancient Ayurvedic cure that involves ingesting a live fish wrapped in herbs. According to a loose interpretation of Vedic texts, the live fish squirms around inside the body, clearing up breathing passages. But there's an added benefit: the fish is said to be a heat-generating agent and a preventive measure for the coughs and colds that accompany the beginning of the monsoon season in early June. To accommodate the demand for this treatment, the Indian government has arranged extra trains to Hyderabad during the fish camp season and moved the carnival to the Public Gardens. It's difficult to gauge the fish's effectiveness, but many patients report a decrease in attacks and return annually to slide the slimy little suckers down their throats. The treatment is free, as is the pitch: www.fish-medicine.org.

HUSAIN SAGAR AREA

ALL THINGS BIRLA. The spectacular **Birla Mandir,** dedicated to Lord Venkatesh-wara, crowns Naubat Pahar hill. Commissioned by the industrial kings of India and built over 10 years, it has awesome views of Hyderabad and Secunderabad, especially at sunset. The pure white Rajasthani marble against the blue of Husain Sagar combine to paint quite a sublime picture. For once, the serenity is unmarred by shoe-touts or alms-driven priests. At night, the whole structure is illuminated. *(Open daily 7am-noon and 2-9pm.)* The **B.M. Birla Science Centre and Archaeological Museum** is opposite the temple. Downstairs is an archaeological section, with excavations from Vaddamanu dated between 100 BC and AD 200, sculptures, paintings, and a Dinosaurium. *(Open daily 10:30am-7:45pm, closed last Tu. Rs12.)* Exit to the right and climb the stairs to the domed **Birla Planetarium.** *(☎ 241067. 3 English shows per day. Closed last Th. Rs15; combined ticket to the planetarium and the museum Rs25.)*

HUSAIN SAGAR. Visitors to Hyderabad are drawn ineluctably to Husain Sagar, the 6½km by 800m tank whose blue waters provide a pleasant backdrop to the cityscape. Historians say that the tank was constructed during the days of the Golconda Empire. Legend says that the tank was promised hundreds of years ago by a *sadhu* who collected large sums of money from the thirsty populace. Weeks passed, and no construction had begun, prompting the people to con-front the *sadhu,* who then promised to undertake the project or return their money. The next morning, a shimmering tank was in place, and the *sadhu* had disappeared. The magic continued in the 1980s, when a monolithic **Buddha statue** was built and placed on a barge for transport across the artificial lake. It sank into the water, dragging down seven people with it. Several years ago, the statue was retrieved from the bottom intact, no damage having been inflicted by the accident. The only real park on the lake is **Lumbini Park,** which is small but nicely landscaped and well maintained. Boats are available for tours or do-it-yourself jaunts. A musical fountain chimes three times every night. *(Just off Secretariat Rd., near Public Gardens Rd. Open Tu-Sa 9am-9pm. Rs2. Boats available Tu-Su 9am-6pm; paddleboats Rs20 per person.)*

OLD CITY

The back streets of the Old City, with their distinctive Muslim flavor, are arguably the most Hyderabadi part of town. During Ramzan, the Islamic holy month (Dec.-Jan.), the action begins at sunset as *birga*-clad women flood the bazaars; fueled on cheap *haleem,* a shredded mutton delicacy, the party continues into the night. Along these streets are several pilgrimage sites sacred to Shi'a Muslims, each one housing a revered *alam,* a banner into which gold, gemstones, and precious objects are woven. If you're near the Madina Hotel, ask a local to show you the **Bibi ka alawa,** which protects a green shrine within its walls. The *alam* contains pieces of a wooden plank upon which the Prophet Muhammad's daughter is believed to have bathed. Not far away is the **Sar tauq ka alawa,** which houses an *alam* contain-ing portions of the shackles and chains which bound the fourth *imam.*

CHARMINAR. The four-minaret Charminar is Hyderabad's oldest and most recog-nizable landmark. The edifice was built by Muhammed Quli Qutb Shah in 1591 to celebrate the end of an epidemic that had been plaguing the city. An image of the four towers graces every packet of Charminar cigarettes—it's said that the last Nizam of Hyderabad refused to smoke any other brand. There's not much to see in the building, since you're no longer allowed to climb the 149 steps to the mosque on top, but a prime bazaar area surrounds the towers. The **Laad Bazaar** (see **Shop-ping,** p. 126) stretches west and south from the Charminar.

MECCA MASJID. Like the Charminar, the Mecca Masjid was built during the sultanate of Muhammad Quli Qutb Shah, but after Golconda's fall, Aurangzeb completed the mosque. It took 1400 bulls to haul the granite slabs that form the entrance. Named for the few bricks from Mecca embedded in its central arch, the mosque is the largest in Hyderabad, accommodating up to 10,000 people at Friday prayers. Before entering the Mecca Masjid, check your *chappals* at the podium on the left and walk through a pavilion containing the tombs of various Hyderabad *nizams*. *(2km south of the Musi River off Sardar Patel Rd., just southeast of Charminar.)*

SALAR JUNG MUSEUM. The impressive Salar Jung Museum is touted as one of the world's largest collections amassed by a single individual, but it is actually the work of three generations of Salar Jungs, each of whom served as the *nizam*'s *wazir* (prime minister). The huge museum is stocked with everything from Chola sculptures to mediocre European oil paintings. Room 14, the Ivory Room, displays a solid ivory chair given to Tipu Sultan by Louis XV. Room 17 has some modern paintings by premier Indian artists such as Ravi Varma and K. Hebbar. In Room 18, next door, you can trace the chronological and regional evolution of Indian miniature painting. *(CL Badari, Malakpet, south of the Musi River. Open Sa-Th 10am-5pm. Rs150.)*

🎭 🎵 NIGHTLIFE AND ENTERTAINMENT

Hyderabad is not just a political capital, but a cultural one too, hosting countless dance programs, *ghazal* sessions, and plays. **Ravindra Bharati** (☎3233672), across from the Public Gardens, stages about four events per week. **Bharatiya Vindya Bhavati** (☎3237825), off Basheer Bagh Circle, holds classical and popular dance and music concerts, often for free. Hyderabad claims to have more than 100 **cinemas.** The best English theaters are **Sangeet,** 23 Sardar Patel Rd., Secunderabad (☎770 3864), and **Skyline,** 3-6-64 Basheer Bagh Rd., Hyderabad (☎3231633). There are usually three shows per day. Balcony seats cost Rs25. The **Alliance Francaise** (☎7700734, afhyd@sol.net.in), now in Secunderabad, screens two flicks per week: one in French, the other in German or English. The **Hyderabad Film Club** (☎373265) has weekly screenings at the Sarathi Studio Preview Theatre in Ameerpet, north of Banjara Hills. Those looking for a more behind-the-scenes exposure to Telugu film should go to Ramaji Film City, 35km to the southeast; guided tours are the best ticket to get there (see graybox). *Channel 6* and *Prism*, monthly publications available at bookstores, are the best sources of information for upcoming events.

Though it's been several years since Andhra Pradesh repealed its prohibition law, the **bar scene** is still struggling to get off the ground. **One Flight Down** (☎320 4060), in the Residency on Public Garden Rd., across from the Asian Lodge, draws a fun crowd and mugs of Kingfisher for Rs45. A plusher pub (yet not too posh to offer a third-drink-free special) is the **Hare and Hound** (☎3243095) in the Hotel Amrutha Castle, the building that looks like a castle on Secretariat Rd. Other four-and five-stars in Begumpet and Banjara Hills have their own watering holes. All bars close at 11pm. For a different kind of liquid refreshment, try the **Ritz Hotel,** Hill Fort St., Basheer Bagh, where you can swim in the same **pool** as the Nizam's privileged guests. (☎233570. Open daily 3-7pm. Rs60 per hr.) If you can't handle the sultry mid-mornings, there is also a pool at the **Taj Residency,** Rd. No.1, Banjara Hills. (☎339 9999. Rs150 per hr. Open daily 7am-7pm.)

🛍 SHOPPING

Hone your bargaining skills at the bazaars around the Charminar in the Old City. The **Laad Bazaar,** extending west and south from the Charminar, is renowned for its wedding fashions, luring people from all over India for pre-nuptial purchases. Step into a shop and take a look at the heavily embroidered *kamdani* dresses for women or the sultan-esque caps for men. If you're not into buying jewelry (strands of imperfect pearls Rs100-500) and armfuls of 🅱bangles (Rs25 per set), you can always just stroll around and look into the stalls. Most of the shops in the Old City are open from 10am to 7pm; some observe Friday as a holiday. Emporiums line the roads in the Abids area. **Kalanjali Arts and Crafts,** Hill Fort Rd., opposite the Air India office, is not too expensive. (☎3231147. Open daily 9:30am-8:30pm.)

NAGARJUNAKONDA పఱఁముపూడ ☎08680

The ruins of one of the largest Buddhist monasteries and learning centers in South India lie 150km southeast of Hyderabad and about 20m underwater. Excavations in 1926 first revealed evidence of *stupas, chaityas,* and other artifacts dating back to the 2nd century BC. Much later, in the 1950s, plans to build a dam on the Krishna River adjacent to the site spurred government archaeologists to resume digging. The most important ruins were evacuated, brick by brick, to a nearby hill before the dam was finished in 1966. Today, an immense artificial lake submerges the original site, and the island of Nagarjunakonda supports the rebuilt structures and a museum. Nagarjuna, a first-century Buddhist scholar, had no problem meditating in the sleepy village of Nagarjunasagar nearby, and neither would you, but don't expect to find much else to do in this hydroelectric project.

The nearest **train station** is in Miryaiguda, about 30km from town, but Vijayawada has better service. **Buses** leave from **Nagarjunasagar** (14km from the ruins in Nagarjunakonda) and go to: **Hyderabad** (4hr.; every hr.; Rs69); **Tirupati** (13hr.; 7:30am and 1:30pm; Rs150); **Vijayawada** (4hr.; 7am and 1pm; Rs71). Buses into town will drop you off (on request) at the boat launch on the opposite end of the dam at Vijayapuri South, or an **auto-rickshaw** will cost Rs5.

The **Nagarjunasagar Dam** separates the lake to the west and the **Krishna River** to the east. To the north is **Hill Colony,** where you'll find the **bus stand** and the better hotels. The APTTDC **tourist office** is opposite the bus stand in Project House (Sagara Paryataka Vihar). They operate guided minivan tours to Nagarjunakonda, the dam, and Ethipothala Waterfall for Rs150 per person. (☎76634. Open Sa-Th 9am-6pm.) APTTDC bus tours from Hyderabad visit the same sites; they leave Hyderabad at 6:45am, returning at 9:45pm (Rs225). The **police station** (☎76533) and **post office** are on the main road from Hill Colony to the dam. **Postal Code:** 508202.

The best rooms in town are those in Hill Colony run by the APTTDC. **Project House ❷,** has an acceptable **restaurant** and large, clean doubles. (☎76540. Check-out 24hr. Rs250.) Ferries shuttle visitors to the island for an hour and back (45min.; every hr. Sa-Th 9:30am-2:30pm, subject to demand; US$5 or equivalent in rupees). The **museum** features a range of sculpture, friezes, and other artifacts, all accompanied by detailed descriptions in several languages (open Sa-Th 9am-4pm; Rs2). The rebuilt **ruins** are somewhat disappointing. The **Ethipothala Waterfall,** a popular picnic spot 16km away from the boat launch, is reachable by shared tempo (Rs200).

TIRUPATI తిరుపతి
AND TIRUMALA) తిరుమల్లు) ☎08574

Rock hills covered with greenery enfold the temple of Sri Venkateshwara, known to his devotees as Lord Balaji. The temple at Tirumala is the most popular pilgrimage site in South India. Built in the 11th century by the founder of the Sri Vaishnava sect, the temple draws in thousands of Hindu pilgrims every day. The task of housing, feeding, and moving the masses falls to Tirupati, the little boomtown 20km down the hill. Sri Venkateshwara is one of the few temples in India that allow non-Hindus into the inner sanctum, yet it is rarely visited by foreigners. Wading through the crowds for *darshan* of the image can be exhausting, but it will

ANDHRA PRADESH

give you perspective on the phenomenon of Hindu pilgrimage. The hassle that devotees will put up with for one fleeting brush with the sacred is incredible. If you're not a devout Hindu, make your trip on a weekday, preferably Tuesday, in order to escape the weekend rush; avoid early June, September, and public holidays.

TRANSPORTATION. Tirupati's **airport** is 12km from the city. **Indian Airlines** (☎25349; open daily 10am-5pm). In the Hotel Vishnupriya complex opposite the Tirumala bus stand. Flies to **Chennai** (20min.; M and F; US$40) and **Hyderabad** (1hr.; Th and Su; US$85). **Jet Airways** (☎56916) hops daily to Hyderabad (1hr.; 2:45pm; US$90). The **railway station** (enquiry ☎131) is in the heart of town, near the Govindaraja Temple. The reservations counter is opposite the station, next to the bus stand. (☎25850. Open M-Sa 8am-8pm, Su 8am-2pm.) **Trains** run to: **Chennai** (3hr.; 3 per day 6:45am-5:20pm; Rs176); **Chidambaram** (10hr.; 3:40pm; Rs148); **Hyderabad** (15hr.; 4-5 per day 5:30am-7pm; Rs245); **Mumbai** (24hr.; Th and Su 9:40pm; Rs321); **Tanjore** (2½hr.; 3:40pm; Rs175); **Trichy** (14hr.; 3:40pm; Rs194). The **APSRTC** (☎22333) is 500m from the center of Tirupati. To get there, stand with your back to the train station and follow the road that leads to your right. Bear right when you reach the Gandhi statue; the bus station will be on your left. **Buses** travel to: **Bangalore** (5½hr.; every 30min. 5:45am-2:15am; Rs258); **Chennai** (4hr.; every 30min.; Rs50); **Hyderabad** (12hr.; 5 per day; Rs248); **Nagarjunasagar** (12hr.; 6pm; Rs165); **Pondicherry** (6hr.; 11am and 9pm; Rs56); **Vijayawada** (10hr.; 4 per day; Rs150). The **Tirumala bus stand**, 250m from the railway station, sends a constant stream of buses up the hilltop along Alipiri Rd. (Rs20). Be prepared for a long wait, and buy a round-trip ticket to avoid waiting again. To dodge the crowds, you can also catch a bus to Tirumala from APSRTC station; the Tirumala terminal is in a separate building at the back corner of the complex. The bus ride to Tirumala winds for 45min. over 57 hairpin turns—you might consider taking a taxi (Rs50 per person).

ORIENTATION AND PRACTICAL INFORMATION. There are **tourist offices** near the APSRTC station (☎43306) and on the road behind the Tirumala bus stand (☎56277). Both pitch daily tours. (Tours Rs125, excluding admission fees. Open daily 10am-5pm.) The **State Bank of India** takes major traveler's checks. Follow the road opposite the Bhimas Deluxe Hotel and take the first right. (☎20699. Open M-F 10am-4pm, Sa 10am-1pm.) Gandhi Rd. fronts the **police station** (☎20352) and the **post office.** (☎22103. Open M-F 10am-5pm, Sa 10am-2pm) **Postal Code:** 517501.

ACCOMMODATIONS AND FOOD. All the decent hotels are in Tirupati. Tirumala's meager pickings include the bare-bones, but free room and board of **Devasthanam Dormitory ❶.** Trouble is, they require at least a month's advance reservation at the T.T.D. (Tirumala Tirupati Devasthanam) counter in nearby cities; Hyderabad's counter is on Himayatnagar Rd. (☎(040) 3220852) and Vellore's on Arni Rd., near the regional bus stand. All is revealed at www.tirumala.org. The **Bhimas Hotel ❶,** 42 G Car St., about a block from the railway station, is popular with Indian pilgrims because of its reasonable price and prime location. (☎25744. Singles Rs75-150; doubles Rs175-550.) One kilometer away crouch the white towers of **Hotel Bliss ❸,** Renigunta Rd., past the bus station, a three-star hotel with ambition and a swimming pool. (☎21650; fax 20657. Singles Rs475-775; doubles Rs550-925. AmEx/MC/V.) Only a few restaurants stand above the huddled crowd. **Hotel Pavithra ❶,** a block past the Bhimas on G Car, stir-fries a sizzling paneer (Rs35) and other veg. favorites (Rs20-55). You can quench your thirst with fresh juices (Rs8). (Open daily 7am-11pm.) The **Bharatmobile,** permanently parked behind the service station at Gandhi Circle, refuses to move with the masses. (Open daily 6:30am-9pm). **Hotel Bliss** and the **Bhimes Residency** nearby keep 24hr. coffee shops.

◙ **SIGHTS.** Receiving the *darshan* of Lord Venkateshwara (Balaji) at the **Sri Venkateshwara Temple** in Tirumala is something most devout Hindus hope to experience at least once during their lifetimes. It is believed that any wish made at the temple will be granted by Lord Venkateshwara, an avatar of Vishnu. Visits to the temple begin in Tirupati, where buses shuttle passengers along a mountainside road to Tirumala and deposit them at the top of the hill. From there, you can float with the crowds through broad, clean, bazaar-lined paths to the temple. Don't be surprised to see a lot of shaved heads; pilgrims here often make a sort of barber-barter deal with the gods: hair for favors. If you want to lose your locks, tonsuring stations will do the job. (Tirupati is also home to a flourishing wig industry.)

At the temple, two types of *darshan* are available. Regular *darshan* comes at no cost, but often entails a wait of 12hr. or more. The "special *darshan*" queue (Rs50) will reduce your waiting time to 2-4 hr., depending on the crowds. You can buy "special *darshan*" tickets at either the Pilgrim Amenities Center near the bus drop-off or at the counter near Rambagicha Guest House no. 3, or in Tirupati at the Tirumsala bus stand, for a fixed "reporting time." After buying a ticket, follow the "Special Entrance" signs around the right side of the temple. Do not rely on middlemen to purchase your tickets, as scams are common. Before entering the temple grounds, leave your shoes with a shop owner for a few rupees. The wait to enter the temple—even in the "special *darshan*" line—involves pressing through a network of narrow wire cages and constricted passageways with thousands of other pilgrims. Once you've entered the line, you'll have little idea of where you're going or how much farther you have to inch along. Rest assured that a few hours later, you'll round the corner to the home stretch.

The temple's interior contains some impressive sculpted columns. The *vimana* is fully covered with gold, and its dazzling brilliance is testimony to the wealth of the temple. After the long wait, *darshan* will seem exceptionally short. At the moment of truth, bare heads crane toward the holy image for one transcendent glimpse, while temple workers yank your arm to force your exit. If they recognize you as a (wealthy) foreigner, the workers may pull you aside, giving you extra *darshan* time in exchange for baksheesh. The impressive image wears a gold crown and is covered with flowers so that not much is visible, apart from the mask of Vishnu drawn clearly on its forehead. The last leg of the visit takes you to the *prasad* line, where workers dish out free *laddus* consecrated by Lord Venkateshwara. Opposite the temple is a small, unremarkable **museum.** *(Open M-F 8am-8pm; Rs3. Temple open daily 24hr.)*

BIHAR बिहार

> **⚠ WARNING.** Women should not travel alone, and **no one should travel at night in Bihar.** Physical violence against tourists is rare, but *dacoits* still terrorize Bihar's countryside.

Many of India's formative events took place in the once-lush forests of Bihar, which is today the poorest, least urbanized, and most ochlocratic state in India. The region gets its name from *vihara* (monastery), referring to the secluded centers of Buddhist learning that flourished here more than a thousand years ago. The Buddha attained enlightenment under a tree in Bodh Gaya, and the Mauryan and Gupta Empires both grew from the city of Pataliputra (modern-day Patna).

Few traces are left of Bihar's past glories. Bihari politics have seen unending controversy and periodic caste-based violence over the years. In 1997, Bihar's Chief Minister, Laloo Prasad Yadav, stepped down after a series of scandals; he appointed his illiterate wife Rabri Devi and promised to continue his rule via mobile phone from prison. In the February 2000 state elections, everything indicated that a broad anti-Laloo coalition would oust the couple from power. Defying poll predictions and common sense, the master of caste politics emerged victorious, and his party remains the strongest force in the state. In November 2000, though, Bihar was divided into two states: Bihar in the north and **Jharkhand** in the south. Jharkhand is a mineral-rich region with little to see but mines and industrial plants. Much of the Bihari countryside is ruled by *goondas* (thugs) with under-the-table connections to politicians, and *dacoits* (bandits) still roam Bihari streets.

Traveling in Bihar can be frustrating: conditions are basic, electricity cuts are frequent, and journeys of a few kilometers can take most of the day. Partly because of these inconveniences and the state's lawlessness, Bihar draws few tourists. Some, however, do find it worth putting up with Bihar's many hassles for the insight it offers into India outside the *baksheesh* cocoon of the tourist circuit.

HIGHLIGHTS OF BIHAR

The so-called **Lotus Circuit** traces the Buddha's footsteps through several of Bihar's towns: **Bodh Gaya** (p. 137), where the Buddha attained enlightenment; **Rajgir** (p. 134), where his teachings were first compiled; **Nalanda** (p. 135), a major center of learning and philosophy; and **Vaishali** (p. 142), where some of his ashes are interred.

PATNA पटना   ☎ 0612

Patna is everything you hate about India, times two. The essence of this energy-sapping sump of a city is captured in the name of one of its major streets: Boring Road. Hour-long rickshaw journeys separate Patna's unimpressive attractions, and the city streets fester with fecal grime and ditch filth of almost unimaginable foulness. The few tourists who linger more than a day before proceeding on the Buddhist pilgrimage circuit may find some interest in seeing a major Indian city almost totally unaffected by foreign tourism. For those willing to dig through the modern grit, there is plenty of historical interest in Patna. The Mauryan empire had its center here, and the Guptas also made this their capital. Pataliputra, as it was called then, was abandoned after the Guptas' decline, but it rose again during the 17th century to become a regional center for the Mughals. The birth of the last

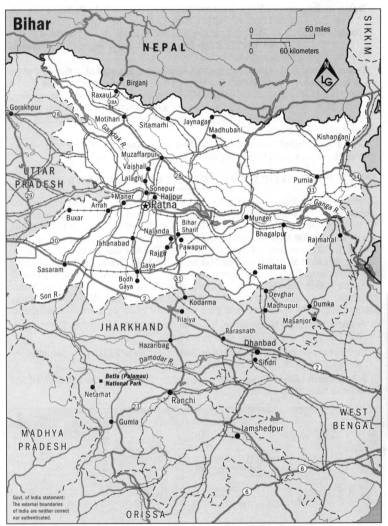

Sikh guru, Gobind Singh, turned a narrow lane in the north of the city into a major Sikh pilgrimage destination. The East India Company had its largest opium warehouses here, now converted (vice for vice) into a state government printing office.

▐ TRANSPORTATION

Flights: Patna Airport, 6km from the railway station (taxi Rs150, auto-rickshaw Rs50, cycle-rickshaw Rs25). **Indian Airlines,** Gandhi Maidan (☎ 222554). Open daily 10am-1pm and 2-4:30pm. To: **Calcutta** (1hr.; 9:25pm; US$75); **Delhi** (2hr.; 9:25am and 4:50pm; US$109); **Mumbai** (4hr.; 4:50pm; US$162). **Necon Air,** in the Ashoka Hotel, on Fraser Rd. (☎ 224511), flies to **Kathmandu** (1hr.; M, W, F; US$79).

Trains: To: **Calcutta** (7-11hr.; 6-9 per day 2:20am-9:40pm; Rs154); **Delhi** (13-25hr.; 8-11 per day 4:40am-11:55pm; Rs320); **Gaya** (2-4hr.; 4 per day 9:50am-10:40pm; Rs30); **Guwahati** (21-25hr.; 2-4 per day 5:30am-10:15pm; Rs370); **Mumbai** (33hr.; 1-3 per day 1-11:20pm; Rs409); **Rajgir** (5hr.; 7:15am and 4:30pm; Rs16); **Varanasi** (3-5hr.; 1-2 per day 6:15-11am; Rs135).

Buses: You can get anywhere in Bihar from **Harding Rd. bus station,** 500m west of the railway station. To: **Bihar Sharif** (3hr.; every 10 min. 4:30am-8pm; Rs30); **Gaya** (3hr.; 4 per day 5:30am-2:30pm; Rs40); **Rajgir** (4hr.; every 2hr. 5am-5pm; Rs40); **Raxaul** (6hr.; every 1½hr. 6am-noon and 11:30pm; Rs120); **Vaishali** (2hr.; 4 per day 5am-1:30pm; Rs25). Buses run frequently to **Hajipur,** where connections to Vaishali and Raxaul are available throughout the day.

Local Transportation: Shared **tempos** ply the main city arteries (Rs2-5 per ride) between the railway station and Gandhi Maidan.

■ ☷ ORIENTATION AND PRACTICAL INFORMATION

Patna sprawls along the south bank of the mighty Ganga. Getting from east to west across the city is a road trip in itself. Budget a minimum of two hours at peak traffic times. **Ashok Raj Path** is the main thoroughfare, sticking close to the river the whole way. **Kankar Bagh Rd. (Old Bypass Rd.)** covers the same distance on the south side of the city, just south of the railroad tracks. The east end of town is Old Patna. Most trains stop at **Patna Junction Station,** in the west. **Fraser Rd.,** where Patna's hotels, restaurants, and other conveniences are concentrated, runs straight north from the station. **Gandhi Maidan,** a large park north of Fraser Rd. (touching Ashok Raj Path), is a major landmark and local transportation hub. Next to the railway station, **Station Rd.** leads west to the **bus station** and various government buildings.

Tourist Office: Bihar Tourist Office, Fraser Rd. (☎225295). On the 2nd fl. of the Silver Oak Restaurant and Bar. Open M-Sa 10am-5pm.

Currency Exchange: State Bank of India, Gandhi Maidan (☎226134). On the left. Open M-F 10:30am-4pm, Sa 10:30am-12:30pm.

Police: Control Room, N. Gandhi Maidan (☎223131). Next to the white-domed Shri Krishna Memorial Hall.

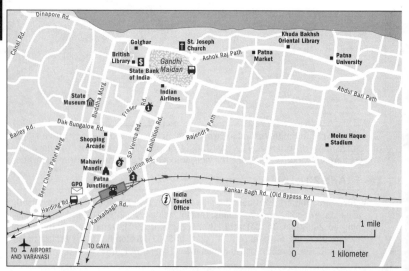

Hospital: **Raj Lakshmi Nursing Home,** Kankarbagh Rd. (☎352225 or 354320). 4km east of the Government of India Tourist Office.

Internet: **Cyberauriga,** SP Verma Rd. (☎211554). Before the intersection with Fraser Rd., Rs20 per hr. Open daily 10am-9pm.

Post Office: **GPO,** Station Rd. 500m west of the railway station. Open M-Sa 10am-4pm, Su 10am-1pm. **Postal Code:** 800001.

ACCOMMODATIONS AND FOOD

Fraser Rd. is the only place to find hotels, most of which leave much to be desired. **Hotel Anand Lok ❷,** Station Rd. (☎223960), is a large, white building towering over the railway station. A gate by the luggage office leads right to the door. The best bet for a hassle-free stay. (Singles with bath Rs214-321; doubles Rs294-428.) **Hotel Raj Laxmi ❶,** SP Verma Rd., is small but comfortable. Book in advance; rooms fill up with Indian tourists. (☎223960. Doubles Rs150-200.) **Anand Restaurant ❶,** on the 2nd fl. of the building at the intersection of Fraser and S.P. Verma Rd., serves *Kiev shashliks* (Rs65) and makes a bold attempt to be different. It works. (Open daily 10am-11pm.) **Mayfair Ice Cream Parlor and Restaurant ❶,** Fraser Rd., opposite the Bansi Vihar, 5min. north of the railway station. With the charm of a subterranean mess hall, the Mayfair overflows with people slurping ice cream (Rs12). Vegetarian and non-vegetarian fare (Rs18-60). (Open daily 8am-10:30pm.)

SIGHTS

PATNA MUSEUM. The Patna Museum contains a superb collection of stone and bronze sculpture, much of it dating from the Mauryan (3rd century BC) and Gupta (4th-6th centuries AD) periods. The most famous piece is the Chauri Bearer, in the second chamber on the left. *(Buddha Marg. Open Tu-Su 10:30am-4:40pm. Rs2.)*

HAR MANDIR. In the twisting lanes of Old Patna is Har Mandir, a Sikh *gurudwara* that marks the birthplace of the 10th and last Sikh guru, Gobind Singh (b. 1666). The second-most important throne of the Sikh religion (after the Golden Temple in Amritsar) and the only beautiful edifice in Patna, Har Mandir is a white-

BIHAR

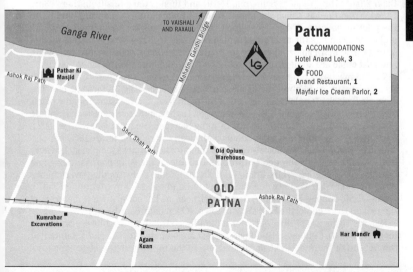

domed building set among the busy bustle of the old town's *chowk*. The present building was constructed after a 1954 earthquake destroyed the original. There is a one-room museum upstairs with exhibits on the history of Sikhism. *(Share a tempo from Sri Krishna Hall on Gandhi Maidan (Rs6). Budget 2hr. for the ride in bad traffic. Visitors need to cover their heads. Open daily 5am-9pm; museum open daily 8am-noon and 3-8pm. Free.)*

KUMRAHAR EXCAVATION PARK. You'll have to use your imagination to see Patna's historical importance. Two solitary pillars and a mound are all that is left of Ashoka's capital of Pataliputra, which once stood here. *(5km out of town. Take a tempo (Rs 4) from the railway station along Kankar Bagh Rd. Open Tu-Sa 8am-4:30pm. Rs2.)*

GOLGHAR. One of Patna's most bizarre landmarks is the Golghar, an egg-shaped grain storage bin. Built in 1786 to protect against famine, it was never used and now sits like a great stone space helmet just left of Gandhi Maidan. The two stair-cases that spiral high above the street represent the quickest way to get away from the smog and dirt; hence its otherwise inexplicable popularity

RAJGIR राजगीर ☎ 06112

Bodh Gaya will always be first in the hearts of Bihar's Buddhist pilgrims, but for the truly devoted, Rajgir is a close second. The capital of the once powerful Magadha Kingdom now lies in rubble with a few worthy sights on its mountainous outskirts. Pilgrims flock here during the winter months to climb Vulture Peak, where the Buddha delivered many of his most famous sermons. The first Buddhist Council took place in Rajgir, and the ruins of the university at Nalanda nearby show the success and scale of Buddhist learning that thrived here for nearly a thousand years. Jain influence in Rajgir was also strong; Jain temples dot the low hills around the town center, commemorating the 14 seasons that Mahavira spent in this tranquil valley. Surrounded by mountains and scattered with ruins, Rajgir is the most scenic and most relaxed of all Bihar's Buddhist towns.

Trains go to **Patna** (4hr., 5:30am and 3pm, Rs24). **Jeeps** and **buses** from Bihar Sharif pass Nalanda and arrive at the bus stand in Rajgir 15km later. From here, buses run to: **Gaya** (3hr., every 30min. 6:30am-6pm, Rs30); **Nalanda** (every 10min., Rs4); **Patna** (4hr., 3 and 6pm, Rs28). For Patna, you can also take a jeep or bus to **Bihar Sharif** (1hr., frequent 5am-7pm, Rs10) and then catch a bus from there (3hr., Rs25). From the **bus stand**, the **bypass road** continues to the hot springs and on to the pilgrimage sites. A dirt street lined with shops leads east from the bus stand, and after 200m hits the **main street** which connects with the bypass road at the hot springs. The **New Popular pharmacy** (open daily 6am-9pm), **police station** (☎ 25228), and **post office** are all next to each other on the main street. **Postal Code:** 803116.

Two monasteries offer flawless **lodging** around the ruined ramparts of an ancient fort. In January and February, Burmese travelers occasionally fill these places. The **Burmese Buddhist Temple ❶,** at the end of the main road, is a pleasant, friendly place, with views of the fields and hills. The manager, to the annoyance of visiting Burmese government officials, displays photos of Aung San and Aung San Suu Kyi. (☎ 55024. Beds in single, double, and triple rooms with clean common baths are Rs50 per person.) The **Bengali Buddhist Society Temple ❶,** next to the Burmese temple, lacks views but features geyser-equipped bathrooms capable of pleasing *bodhisattvas* and backpackers alike. (☎ 55116. Rooms Rs100-200.) There's always the government's **Hotel Gautam Vihar ❶,** between the bus stand and the railway station. (☎ 55273. Dorms Rs50; doubles Rs321-535.) **Green Hotel,** near the hot springs, a few meters past the bypass road, cooks the best *thali* in town. (Open daily 8am-10pm.)

Rajgir's **sights** are spread out over a 5km long stretch of road best covered by **tonga** (Rs35-50). Centers of Buddhist interest are on **Ratnagiri,** a scenic mountain at the far end of the road. A **chair lift** leads up to the top, where the huge Japanese-built **Vishva Shanti Stupa** (world peace *stupa*) casts its shadow over the valley below. The chair lift (Rs20) is open daily 8am-1pm and 2-5pm, but only when there are five passengers. If you don't trust this aerial contraption, there is also a 1km footpath. From the *stupa*, the small path winds around the side of the mountain back down to the road; take the first left onto a series of stony steps that leads up and down until it arrives at **Gridhrakuta,** or "Vulture's Peak." Once a favorite rainy season retreat of the Buddha, Gridhrakuta marks the site of two caves where the Buddha gave sermons. The remains of a monastery from the Gupta period are also here. At the foot of Ratnagiri are the remains of **Jivakamra Vana,** an early monastery built in the mango garden which was another of the Buddha's favorite haunts.

Near the intersection with Gaya Rd. is **King Bimbisara's jail,** where the Buddhist convert-king was imprisoned and eventually executed by his son and successor, Ajatasatru. Legend says that the king chose the site of his incarceration; from here he could look out from his cell and watch the Buddha as he meditated and taught on the mountain. Today the rubble of the prison is unimpressive. Along the dirt road that passes the *math* are two chambers carved out of the cliff-face, known as the **Swarna Bhandar,** which are said to mark the location of Bimbisara's treasury.

At the foot of Mt. Vaibhara, on the outskirts of town, is **Brahma Kunj,** where a half-dozen hot springs have been incorporated into a Hindu temple. A stone stairway past the baths leads up to **Pippala Cave,** a rectangular piece of rock that was once a hermits' refuge. The stairway continues to **Saptaparni Cave,** where 500 of the Buddha's disciples held the first Buddhist Council. The surrounding hills are home to over 40 Jain shrines, most of them connected by stone paths. Visiting the temples on the five principle mountains of the area—in clockwise direction, Vipulachal, Ratnagiri, Udaxgiri, Savrangiri, and Vaibhargiri—is an arduous but worthwhile task. Bring enough change to leave an offering with the temple keepers.

NALANDA नालन्दा

Built by the Guptas during the 5th century AD and boasting a reputation as a center of learning that dates back to the 1st millennium BC, Nalanda is the site of one of the oldest universities in the world as well as a major pilgrimage destination for Sri Lankan and Japanese Buddhists. By the time the Buddha visited Nalanda, the town was a teeming and prosperous population center. Other religious VIPs also sojourned in Nalanda: Jainism's founder Mahavira used it as a retreat from the monsoon, and Sariputra, the Buddha's earliest disciple, was born and died here. Legendary Chinese traveler Xuanzang, known for his detailed accounts of the places he visited on his sutra-collecting journeys around India, studied at the university during the 7th century along with 4000 other students studying everything from Buddhist and Vedic philosophy to logic, grammar, chemistry, and medicine. As Nalanda's fame grew during the centuries that followed, so did its size. New buildings soared to the height of nine stories, and with the aid of King Harsha of Kannauj, Nalanda amassed a library of nine million manuscripts. By the 13th century, though, successive waves of Muslim invaders had chased out all the students and reduced the library's collection to cinders.

Frequent **jeeps** and **buses** leave for **Nalanda** from the bus stand at **Rajgir** (Rs4). From Nalanda's bus stand, you can share a *tonga* (Rs5) or walk 2km to the site. The **PWD Guest House ❶,** near the park has recently begun offering Government of India hospitality at Rs70 per person.

In the tranquil, well-kept **park** run by the Archaeological Survey of India, visitors can stroll through the excavated remains of a dozen monastery buildings. There is a one-room **museum** opposite the entrance, 200m down the road, containing stone and bronze Pala sculpture. (Park open daily 7:30am-5pm. Rs230 or US$5. Museum open M-Th and Sa-Su 10am-4:40pm. Rs2.)

GAYA गया   ☎ 0631

The name "Gaya" derives from the demon Gayasura, who purified himself through a
rigorous series of yoga poses and received this sacred tract of land along the River
Phalgu as a reward. As an additional reward, Gaya also received the power to
absolve ancestral sins—it is said that one *shraddha* (funeral rite) in Gaya is equivalent to 11 *shraddhas* anywhere else. Hindu pilgrims visit each of the 45 shrines in
Gaya (including the Bodhi Tree in Bodh Gaya), offering prayers for the dead and
rupees for the *gayaval* (attending priests). The high season begins in September
when the Phalgu swells with the monsoon rains and thousands of pilgrims descend
upon the *ghats* to perform their ritual ablutions. While Gaya is slightly less important to devout Hindus than Bodh Gaya is to Buddhists, it manages to surpass its sister city in its levels of grime and poverty. Thirty-six kilometers north are the **Barabar
Caves,** a series of rock-hewn Jain temples dating from the 3rd century BC, that were
featured as the "Marabar Caves" in E.M. Forster's *A Passage to India.*

⌐ TRANSPORTATION

Trains: Trains leave from **Gaya Junction Station.** The railway **reservation office** is the
chaotic brouhaha to the right of the station. Open M-Sa 8am-8pm, Su 8am-2pm. To:
Bela (1hr., 10 per day, Rs17); **Calcutta** (6-7½hr., 4-6 per day 3:20am-11:20pm,
Rs104); **Delhi** (12-16 hr., 2-5 per day 1:30am-10pm, Rs270); **Patna** (2½hr., 2:17am in
theory, Rs31; frequent, slower "passenger" trains); **Varanasi** (4-5½hr., 4 per day 2am-
9pm, Rs61). From Bela to the **Barabar Caves,** it's a 12km *tempo* or *tonga* ride (Rs20-
25) plus a 5km walk.

Buses: Depart from the **Zila School Bus Stand** to **Bodh Gaya** (30min.-1hr., frequent,
Rs6). The **Manpur Bus Stand,** across the Phalgu River, near the bridge, has buses to
Nalanda and **Rajgir** (3hr., every hr. 6am-6pm, Rs30). Drivers congregate outside the
train station and ferry passengers directly to Bodh Gaya at slightly inflated prices.

Local Transportation: Rickshaws go to: the Zila School Bus Stand; the Vishnupad Temple; Shaktipith (Rs10). Shared **tempos** run between the railway station, Gandhi Chowk,
and the Manpur Bus Stand (Rs6).

⫶⊓ ORIENTATION AND PRACTICAL INFORMATION

Gaya is on the west bank of the Phalgu River. **Gaya Junction Station,** at the north
end of the town, connects to the main bazaar and **Gandhi Chowk** via **Station Rd.** The
southern edge of the city is marked by **Shaktipith, Brahmyoni Hill,** and **Vishnupad
Temple. Gautama Buddha (GB) Rd.** runs here from Gandhi Chowk and continues
10km south to reach **Bodh Gaya.**

Tourist Office: Inside the railway station. Has a wall map of Gaya, but nothing else of
use. Open M-Sa 8am-4pm.

Currency Exchange: The nearest banks that change currency are in Bodh Gaya. In emergencies, the **Hotel Saluja** (☎ 436243) will change major currencies and traveler's
checks. Currency exchange at the adjoining **Siddharth International Hotel** is restricted
to guests only.

Police: Control Room (☎ 223131 or 223132). **Emergency:** ☎ 20999.

Hospital: The **Magadh Medical College** (☎ 22410) is a government hospital. The state of
Bihar's government services makes Gaya an awful place to be sick.

Internet: STD/ISD stand, 50m east of the south end of South Rd. Rs1.50 per min.

Post Office: GPO, GB Rd. One block east of Zila school bus stand. Open M-Sa 10am-
4pm. There is a smaller post office on Station Rd., 150m right of the station, on the left.
Postal Code: 823001.

ACCOMMODATIONS

Pal Rest House, Station Rd. (☎436753). Turn right out of the station; the rest house is 250m down on the left-hand side, after the post office. Simple rooms around a central stairwell. Clean, cheap, and quiet. Singles Rs70-100; doubles Rs135; triples Rs250. ❶

Hotel Buddha, Laxman Sahay Ln. (☎423428). 100m east of the railway station, at the end of a road perpendicular to Station Rd. Small doubles have comfortable mattresses, TVs, and attached baths with decent showers. Singles Rs150; doubles Rs200. ❶

Ajatsatru Hotel, Station Rd. (☎434584). Opposite the railway station. One of the largest hotels along the crowded Station Rd. strip and the least spartan in terms of facilities. Check-out 24hr. Singles Rs172; doubles Rs214-321. ❶

FOOD

Haji Market, a block south of Gandhi Chowk, next to Chatta Masjid, is the place to taste the local speciality of *bakharkhani*, a crisp, round, Muslim bread. Except for some hotel restaurants and numerous roadside joints, Gaya has slim pickings for food. The **Sujata Restaurant ❶**, in the Ajatsatru Hotel, serves the best meals in town. Vegetable curry Rs25, chicken *biryani* Rs45. (Open daily 7am-10pm.)

SIGHTS

Though Gaya is one of the most sacred cities in the Hindu religion, its temples lack the splendor of those in other large pilgrimage sites. Non-Hindus may be disappointed. The shrines listed below are within walking distance of each other.

BRAHMYONI HILL. One thousand steep stones twist up to the Shiv Mandir at the top of this hill. Prepare to encounter persistent requests from Hindu priests asking for money. There is also a small goddess temple with an image of Vishnu's foot at the door. The hill is sacred to Buddhists, who associate it with Gayasirsan, the mountain where the Buddha delivered several important sermons. The summit's panorama is worth the long walk up. *(1km southwest of the Vishnupad Temple.)*

VISHNUPAD TEMPLE. Towering over the bank of the Phalgu River, this golden-spired temple contains a 2m-long footprint of Vishnu in the form of the Buddha that is enshrined in a silver basin. Non-Hindus may not enter the main shrine, but they can try to get a closer look at the sanctum (but not the footprint) by climbing the stairs of the raised area near the temple's entrance.

DURGA TEMPLE. In this rather mundane temple, non-Hindus can observe and even participate in the *shraddhas* (funeral rites). Pilgrims wishing to perform the *shraddha* at Gaya must first circumambulate their own village five times. *(1km east of the Vishnupad Temple.)*

SHAKTIPITH. Sati's breast fell here after she was cut to pieces. Images of the goddess are housed in a squat, cavernous mausoleum, inscribed on the front with the epic verse of Sati's destruction. *(Open daily 6am-noon and 1pm-midnight.)*

BODH GAYA बोध गया   ☎0631

Bodh Gaya is the holiest site in the Buddhist religion and the only Bihari pilgrimage site that attracts non-Buddhist tourism. One of the most significant events in the history of Asia took place here in the 6th century BC, when Prince Siddhartha Gautama attained enlightenment under the famous pipal tree, a descendent of which stands on the same spot today.

Buddhism in Bodh Gaya, however, is new and mostly foreign. Although Buddhist monasteries thrived here long ago, they were left to sink into the mud after Buddhism faded out of India in the 12th century. It wasn't until the 19th century

BIHAR

THE TREE OF KNOWLEDGE The Bodhi Tree at Bodh Gaya has been the subject of countless legends. Central to the mystique and holiness of this particular pipal tree is the belief that it is a direct descendent of the one under which the Buddha meditated more than 2500 years ago. Some believe that Emperor Ashoka cut down the original tree before his famous conversion to Buddhism. The tree miraculously sprang back to life, only to be hacked down again by Ashoka's wife, jealous of the attention and respect her husband had started to pay the tree since its remarkable recovery. But the tree once again sprang up from its roots. Unnerved and impressed by its hardiness, Ashoka and his wife sent a sapling from the original tree to Sri Lanka, where it is believed to still prosper today. The centuries to come witnessed a series of attacks on the tree at Bodh Gaya, which weakened it to such an extent that it finally fell to a storm in 1876. The incarnation that is the object of such veneration today grew from a seedling taken from the original tree's offspring in Sri Lanka.

---

that Bodh Gaya was reborn as an important religious center, when British-led archaeological teams persuaded monks from Sri Lanka and Burma to raise the funds necessary to restore the Mahabodhi Temple to its former glory.

The steady flow of wealthy tourists has elevated Bodh Gaya to a level of economic prosperity unmatched in Bihar. The state's usual problems of robbery and violence mostly lie within the city limits, although bandits have boarded buses at night between Gaya and Bodh Gaya. The winter (Dec.-Feb.) is the busiest time to visit, when students, pilgrims, and monks (the Dalai Lama included) congregate here. The monasteries fill up, visiting teachers offer meditation courses, tent restaurants abound, and monks from around the world intone *sutras* in monasteries and temples built in their own national styles. By April, however, the crowds thin out, many of the restaurants and hotels close down, and the streets of Bodh Gaya resume the air of meditative quietude that has reigned here for thousands of years.

▛ TRANSPORTATION

Buses leave for **Gaya** from the stand near the Burmese Temple (every 30min. 5am-6pm, Rs6), with the bus stopping every 10m for passengers to embark, disembark, and sometimes just bark. Shared *tempos* and jeeps ply the route for the same price. A bus to **Varanasi** (6am, Rs90) stops in front of the Mahabodhi Society.

◢ ℹ ORIENTATION AND PRACTICAL INFORMATION

It would require real effort to get lost in Bodh Gaya. The main road from Gaya runs through town, interrupted only by a pedestrian strip-mall in front of the **Mahabodhi Temple.** The market, Chinese Temple, museum, and Roof Institute—as well as just about every notable sight and hotel in the city—lie on this rickshaw path.

Tourist Office: (☎ 400672). Past the Thai Temple heading west on the main road out of town. Open M-Sa 10am-5pm.

Currency Exchange: State Bank of India, Bodh Gaya Rd. (☎ 400746). Next to the Chinese temple. Open M-F 10:30am-4pm, Sa 10:30am-1:30pm.

Police (☎ 400741), 200m north of the Burmese Temple.

Hospital: Conditions at the **government hospital,** on the left on the way into town, are far from ideal. Doctors at the **Japanese temple's clinic** will see tourists in an emergency.

Post Office: Gaya Rd. (☎ 400472). On the left as you enter town. Open 10:30am-5pm. **Postal Code:** 842231.

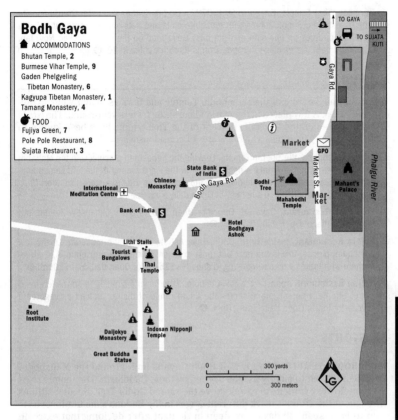

Bodh Gaya

♠ ACCOMMODATIONS
Bhutan Temple, 2
Burmese Vihar Temple, 9
Gaden Phelgyeling
  Tibetan Monastery, 6
Kagyupa Tibetan Monastery, 1
Tamang Monastery, 4

🍎 FOOD
Fujiya Green, 7
Pole Pole Restaurant, 8
Sujata Restaurant, 3

ACCOMMODATIONS

Bodh Gaya is full of hotels, but the temple- and monastery-run guest houses are the best. During the winter months, they fill up very quickly. Remember to respect the rules of the religious community—no drinking, smoking, or "improper sexual conduct" allowed.

Bhutan Temple, Temple Rd. (☎ 400710). Near the Great Buddha image. In a beautiful garden dominated by a colorful Bhutanese temple. Rooms are clean and spacious and have mosquito nets. Gates close 10pm. Fills up Nov.-Dec. Doubles Rs100-200. ❶

Gaden Phelgyeling Tibetan Monastery (☎ 400742). Next to the Mahabodhi Society. An ever-expanding universe overrun by Tibetan monks Oct.-Feb. Gates close 9:30pm. Tiny singles Rs50; larger rooms with bath Rs100. ❶

Kagyupa Tibetan Monastery, near Temple Rd. (☎ 400795). The more remote and peaceful of the two Tibetan temples, Kagyupa is less likely to be full during the packed winter months. Clean common bath with running hot water. Doubles Rs250. ❶

Tamang Monastery, Bodh Gaya Rd. (☎ 400802). On the left side of the main road, just past the museum. Minuscule rooms facing a tiny temple are filled to the brim Nov.-Jan. by Nepalese pilgrims. Rs100-200. ❶

Burmese Vihar Temple, Gaya Rd. (☎ 400721). On the right as you enter town; opposite the bus station. Simple rooms with mosquito coils and nets look out onto quiet fields and rice paddies on one side and the busy Gaya road on the other. Packed Nov.-Jan. Common bath. Gates close 9:30pm. Dorms Rs45; doubles Rs80. ❶

⌘ FOOD

Seasonal stalls in front of the Mahabodhi Temple and Burmese Vihar whip up *lassis* and cakes. A few places in the market lane sizzle fritters year-round. The *lithis* in the family-operated tea stalls in front of the Thai temple have been known to transport hungry pilgrims to higher states of consciousness.

▨ **Fujiya Green,** near the Tibetan Temple. Leaving the pedestrian precinct with the Mahabodhi Temple to your left, make a right and follow the signs around to the left. Lamps-and-shades shack serves up simple dishes to the lamas from the monastery next door. *Thukpas* Rs10, vegetable chop suey Rs25. Open daily 7am-9pm. ❶

▨ **Pole Pole Restaurant,** Gaya Rd. Opposite Deep Guest House. Exhaustive Italian and Japanese menu. Open daily 5-11pm. ❶

Sujata Restaurant, inside Hotel Bodh Gaya Ashok, next to the museum. Of the few perennial places, this is the best but most expensive. Offers an antiseptic, A/C atmosphere with Indian veg. and non-veg. dishes (Rs125-145). Open daily 8am-10pm. ❷

Kalyan Restaurant, opposite the main temple, 70m down a small lane on the left-hand side. Simple, open-air place serves the usual range of dishes as well as vegetable *gyoza* for Rs25. Open daily 7am-10pm. ❶

◉ SIGHTS

MAHABODHI TEMPLE. The town of Bodh Gaya is built around the Mahabodhi Temple, referred to simply as "the *stupa*" by most Buddhists. The temple rises up from flowery gardens to tower above the sacred Bodhi Tree. Smaller shrines throughout the grounds mark different stages in the Buddha's meditations; he is said to have spent 49 days here deep in thought after deciding that extreme asceticism was bringing him no closer to a true understanding of life's suffering than his previous life as a playboy-prince. Emperor Ashoka built the first temple on this site during the 3rd century BC, but the present temple, which has been through layers and layers of restorations, probably dates from the 6th century AD. Much of the rescue work was initiated in 1882 by Burmese monks after the temple was found neglected and overrun by squatters. Over the last 30 years, many statues have been stolen from the temple's circular niches. The oldest structure left on the site is a stone railing built in the 1st century AD to keep out wild animals; a quarter of it, however, has been whisked away to museums in London and Calcutta.

At the back of the temple is the sacred **Bodhi Tree** (see p. 138), a direct descendent of the tree under which the Buddha attained enlightenment. *(Open daily 6-8am and 6-8pm.)* Throngs of pilgrims gather around the tree during all seasons to pay respects to the enshrined plant. The **Vajrasana,** or "diamond throne," between the tree and the temple, is thought to be where the Buddha sat. A gilded image of the Buddha is behind glass in the temple, and another is on the first floor, which is open in the evenings for meditation. A part of the first floor is permanently closed due to one depraved tree surgeon's attempt to saw off a branch of the sacred tree as a souvenir. *(Temple compound open daily 5am-10pm. Free; camera fee Rs10.)*

SUJATA VILLAGE. In the winter, you can cross the dry river bed from the Mahant's palace in Bodh Gaya to the peaceful village on the other side (in summer, use the bridge 200m downstream). Here, 500m through the eastern fields, grows a descendant of the banyan tree under which the Buddha feasted on *kheer* (sweet rice milk) offered by Sujata, a local woman who has since become perhaps the most famous beverage vendor in history. This was his first meal after six years spent in ascetic solitude. The tree has been converted into a shrine. The **Matang Rishi Ashram** is the banyan's neighbor. In the middle of the village is a grass mound believed to mark the site of Sujata's house.

MAHAKALA CAVES. The Buddha undertook six years of ascetic meditation in two caves in a mountainside nearly 6.5km (2hr. walking) from Bodh Gaya. A tiny monastery marks the spot. Walk northeast from Bodh Gaya toward the mountains near Sujata village. Continue to Dungesori Mountain and Pragbodhi Village.

OTHER TEMPLES AND MONASTERIES. Throw a stone in any direction and you'll hit two temples and half a dozen monks. A 1hr. walk around Bodh Gaya will show you all the major temples. The **Thai Temple,** Bodh Gaya's second most prominent landmark, is 500m after the main road takes a sharp left. A large *wat* with classic claw-like tips on its orange roof, the temple opened in 1957 (year 2500 in the Buddhist calendar). Side-roads branch off the main road on either side of the Thai Temple. To the left are the **Bhutan Monastery** and the Japanese **Indosan Nipponji Temple.** The lane on the right side of the Thai Temple leads to the **Kagyu-pa Tibetan Monastery,** which contains brightly colored, larger-than-life murals depicting the life of the Buddha. Next door is the **Daijokyo Temple,** another Japanese construction with an oppressive concrete exterior. Just up the road is the 25m **Giant Buddha Statue,** which was built by Japanese monks and inaugurated by the Dalai Lama in 1989. The chapel walls of the **Gelug-pa Tibetan Monastery,** next to the Mahabodhi Society, are painted with *thanka*-style clouds, wheels, and *bodhisattvas*. Be sure not to neglect the **Mahant's Palace,** on the left just before you reach the center of town. Now a working Hindu temple, it offers rear views of the Niranjna Ganga River and the Mahakala Mountain beyond, making it a great spot for meditation, contemplation, or relaxation. *(Most temples open daily dawn-noon and 2pm-dusk.)* The Archaeological Survey of India has a small **museum,** just off the main road, which contains statues unearthed nearby. *(Open M-Th and Sa-Su 10am-5pm. Rs2.)*

BUDDHISM AND COMMUNITY SERVICE

During the high season, meditation courses are a major industry in Bodh Gaya. Teachers from all over the world jet (or rickshaw) in to train Buddhists and aspiring Buddhists in this temple town. A few permanent institutions in Bodh Gaya also conduct courses; though the peak season runs from October to March, a couple of places remain open and active throughout the summer. **The Root Institute for Wisdom Culture** (☎400714; fax 400548; rootinst@vsnl.com), at the edge of town down a dirt path south from the main road, offers 10-day Tibetan Buddhism courses during the winter with guest lamas and Western teachers in a quiet, intimate compound that doubles as a hospital for lepers and polio victims. (Rs2900-5300, including room and board). Daily meditation sessions which are open to outsiders on a walk-in basis are also held during the winter. Room and board is available for non-meditators, and although they don't provide instruction in the off season, visitors are welcome all year. **The International Meditation Center,** opposite the Thai monastery, offers courses in the Vipassana Method year-round. The 10-day course is free, but a donation of Rs75-100 per day will defray the costs of a dorm bed in a double or triple and three meals. Shorter courses are also available. The **Vipassana Meditation Center** (☎400437), behind the university, has 10-day courses twice every month except May and June. They will house and feed you for a donation.

BIHAR

There are a number of charitable organizations in Bodh Gaya. It may be more worthwhile to give money to these organizations than to the children begging on the streets. Locals have complained that their children are spoiled by rich pilgrims who reward undisciplined beggary with generous handouts. The **Root Institute,** which sponsors tree planting in addition to year-round leprosy and polio projects, is always looking for volunteers and donations. The **Mahabodhi Society,** set back from the road, across the street from the Mahabodhi Temple, runs a number of charitable programs including a free pharmacy, a primary school, an ambulance service, and a rehabilitation center.

VAISHALI वैशाली

Fifty-five kilometers north of Patna, Vaishali is a tiny, one-cow town, surrounded by rice paddies and home to a handful of farming families, several sites of interest to religious pilgrims, and the ruined remains of the world's first republic. As the capital of the Licchavis during the 6th century BC, Vaishali was renowned for its peace, prosperity, and elected system of government. The town is also the birthplace and hometown of Jainism's founder, Mahavir, and the site at which the Buddha preached his last sermon before announcing his approaching *parinirvana*. During the in season (Oct.-Feb.), the town occasionally attracts tourists of Bihar's Buddhist sites; off season, you will almost certainly have the place to yourself.

⌐ TRANSPORTATION

Direct **buses** go to Vaishali from the main bus stand in Patna (2 hr., 4 per day 5am-1:30pm, Rs25). Alternatively, after crossing the MG Bridge in Patna, hop on one of the frequent buses to **Hajipur** (Rs8) and get on another bus to **Lalganj** (Rs7), where many shared **taxis** (Rs10) ply the road that passes through Vaishali. Ask to be let off at the Government's Tourist Lodge. In practice, you'll just have to show up at the bus stand and repeatedly scream and holler your destination. Highly erratic direct buses from Vaishali to **Patna** (theoretically 5 per day 6:45am-3pm, Rs35) pass by the Tourist Lodge, and there are regular jeeps and trucks to Lalganj, where connections to Patna are frequent. To travel to **Raxaul** by train, take a **jeep** north from Vaishali to **Muzaffarpur** (Rs10), and then take a train (4 hr., 6 per day, Rs28) or bus straight through to **Raxaul** (4hr., Rs40).

⌂ ⌂ ACCOMMODATIONS AND FOOD

The **Tourist Lodge ❶,** on the main road, a 20min. walk from the Coronation Tank, has simple rooms with fans and attached baths. (Singles Rs62; doubles Rs108.) The luxurious **Tourist Complex ❶,** alongside the Coronation Tank is off the main road through the gateway by the tourist lodge. (Doubles Rs350.) On the north side of Coronation Tank is the **Youth Hostel ❶.** (☎ 29425. Dorms Rs40; doubles Rs150.)

⌾ SIGHTS

A large rectangular pond known as the **Coronation Tank,** once used to anoint the town's leaders during inaugural ceremonies, stands in the middle of Vaishali's tourist area. A small **museum** on the right side of the tank showcases some of the stone and terra-cotta pieces dug up from nearby sites (open M-Th and Sa-Su 10am-5pm; Rs2). Down a small lane to the back of the museum, a well-maintained garden encloses the **relics stupa,** thought to contain a portion of Buddha's ashes, which were divided up after his cremation and distributed among the leaders of the eight major kingdoms of northern India. Today, a shallow circle of stones covered by a conical green tin roof is all that remains of the *stupa*. On the other side of the tank is the **Japanese Temple** and the great crowned white dome of the new **Vishwa Shanti Peace Stupa,** consecrated here in 1996. (*Stupa* and temple open dawn-dusk.)

Fifty meters north, on the highway from the tourist lodge, is a fork which goes left through fields and villages to the walled compound containing the **Ashokan Pillar** (locally known as **Kolhua Lat**) and its lion capital, cut from a single piece of limestone. The lion faces Kushinagar, where the Buddha died (see p. 701). An age-withered **stupa** and a small tank lie in the pillar's shadow; both commemorate the spot where a monkey once presented honey to the Buddha. Some tourists, showing their solidarity with Buddhist pilgrims, are boycotting the site in protest of the shockingly exorbitant 'foreigner price' instituted in October 2000. (Open dawn-dusk. US$5.) On the other side of the main road, a 10min. walk through the village, is the ancient **Chaumukhi Mahadev Mandir**, a four-faced Shiva *linga*.

⚔ BORDER CROSSING: RAXAUL रक्सौल

Raxaul ain't pretty. Mercifully, trains are ready to whisk you away. **Trains** run from Raxaul to: **Calcutta** (19hr.; 10:10am; Rs248); **Delhi** (26-29hr.; 1-2 per day 12:45 and 8am; Rs285); **Muzafarpur** (4hr.; 5 per day 7:15-12:45am; Rs35) where more train connections are available. Erratic **buses** to **Patna** leave from the Old Bus Stand just off the main road by the railroad tracks (9hr.; every hr. 4am-6pm; Rs90). Raxaul's main street leads straight over the bridge into Birganj in Nepal, cutting through the market area and the tangle of alleyways to the east and west. **No bank changes money in Raxaul**—Birganj and Patna are the closest places. A row of money changers by the railroad tracks will do the job at emergency-only rates. The **police station** (☎ 06255 21021) is on the main street, next to the Sun Temple.

> ⚔ **BORDER PATROL.** Whether you are coming from India or Nepal, make sure you stop at *both* immigration offices. You need a Nepal departure stamp to be allowed into India and an India departure stamp to get into Nepal. The **Indian Immigration Office** is hidden below the bridge, to the left when coming from Raxaul. (Open daily 6am-8pm.) **Indian visas are not issued here.** The closest place to get one is Kathmandu. If you are leaving India and your visa has expired, you will be sent to the closest Superintendent of Police (in Motihari), who will fine and reprimand you. The Nepalese Immigration Office is next to the gate and is open daily 7am-7pm. You will need **one passport-size photo and US$30 for a single-entry 60-day visa (US$55 for double entry).** If this is your 2nd Nepalese visa within one calendar year, the cost rises to US$50 for a single entry 30-day visa (US$75 for double entry). Only US dollars are accepted; bring correct change. The cheapest way of getting across the border is to take a rickshaw from the main market in Raxaul to the Indian Immigration Office (Rs3-5), and then walk 200m across the bridge to Nepalese Immigration. From here, you can share a tonga to Birganj bus station (NRs5). Alternatively, you can hire a rickshaw to take you the whole way, but all the "waiting" causes the price to jump to IRs50. The whole border crossing ritual should be over in 30min.

DELHI दिल्ली

All of the contrasts familiar to travelers in India are in full force here in the nation's capital: rich and poor, old and new, chaos and order. Delhi maintains a dignified front as a proud metropolitan center of government and commerce, with its official-looking edifices spanning the broad green blocks that provide clean air and empty spaces to the city's south-central districts. Behind this facade of order and control are Delhi's other streets, crammed with the city's legendary slow-churning traffic and threaded by careening auto-rickshaws. It is in these streets that real life is lived, where turbaned Sikhs, dreadlocked *sadhus*, and down-and-out pavement-dwellers all rub shoulders, sharing space, if not conversation. And it is in these streets that North India's heat and humidity are refracted through layers of polluted air only worsened by the generators and air conditioners that provide electricity and cool relief for the city's wealthy elite.

The history of Delhi begins in AD 736, with the founding of Lal Kot by the Tomara clan of Rajputs. Their tumultuous and gory rule was abruptly ended in 1192 by Mohammed Gauri and his slave general Qutb-ud-din Aibak, who swept in from Central Asia and conquered great stretches of North India, introducing Islam and founding the Delhi Sultanate. For the next 300 years, Delhi was wracked by political instability, especially in 1398, when the city was sacked by another Central Asian warlord, Timur. By the early 16th century, the ruling Lodi dynasty had made its share of enemies in the region. Too meek to challenge the Sultanate on their own, they requested help from Timur's great-grandson, Babur. Babur beat the Lodis into submission and launched the Mughal Empire, which would unite much of South Asia for the next two centuries. The Mughals repeatedly shifted their capital between Delhi and Agra, leaving both cities with monumental tombs, palaces, and forts. Old Delhi's grandest edifices were built during the 17th century by the Mughal emperor Shah Jahan. Mughal strength began to wane during the 18th century, however, and the British moved in to fill the void. In 1911, the British capital was moved here from Calcutta, and the city attracted the attention of Indian nationalists, who vowed to themselves that the flag of an Indian republic would one day fly from the Red Fort. Marking the occasion with a speech by the Prime Minister delivered from the Red Fort and a tremendous parade in front of the city's most important British buildings, modern Delhi celebrates the vindication of the nationalists' predictions every year on August 15, Independence Day._

HIGHLIGHTS OF DELHI

Old Delhi is packed with bazaars and monuments, including the **Red Fort** (p. 161) and the **Jama Masjid** (p. 163), the largest mosque in India.

South of the city center are the emperor **Humayan's Tomb** (p. 166) and the phenomenal Mughal ruins at the **Qutb Minar** complex (p. 163).

Delhi's lotus shaped, garden-ringed **Baha'i Temple** (p. 164) is one of India's most beautiful modern structures.

The immensely intricate **Jantar Mantar** (p. 166) is an 18th-century astronomical observatory set in stone, complete with massive marble sundials.

▨ INTERCITY TRANSPORTATION

INTERNATIONAL FLIGHTS

Indira Gandhi International Airport (☎565 2011 or 565 2021) serves as the main entry and departure point for international flights. There is a 24hr. **State Bank of India** office in the

> **WARNING.** You may be tired from your flight, but keep your wits about you, even in the airport. If you don't understand what's going on or feel pressured or herded in a particular direction, stop to collect yourself—there's really no hurry. When paying at a counter, **count out your cash as you hand it over.** Switch-the-bill schemes are common. **Never** let a cab driver convince you that the hotel you ask for is full or closed. And remember, **the more assertive someone is with offers of help, the more likely it is that there's something in it for him.** If you need help or have a question, ask someone who hasn't approached you first.

arrivals hall, next to the **Government of India Tourism** and the **Delhi Tourism** information desks. This is the place to pay for a **pre-paid taxi,** the most hassle-free way to get into the city (Rs200-250 to the city center). Once you pay, you'll receive a receipt with your destination and a taxi number written on it—make sure that the driver takes you where *you* want to go. Delhi Transport Corporation (DTC) (☎87445) and EATS (☎331 6530) run frequent **buses** to Connaught Pl. from the airport (Rs50; Rs10 per bag). DTC buses also stop at New Delhi Railway Station and the Interstate Bus Terminal (ISBT) at Kashmiri Gate. **Auto-rickshaws** shuttle from the airport to downtown at cheaper rates (Rs100-150) than taxis but without the security of the pre-payment system. To get to the airport (international and domestic terminals), pick up the EATS bus near the Indian Airlines office on Janpath (5:30, 7, 9am, 3:30, 6, 7, 10, and 11:30pm).

INTERNATIONAL AIRLINES. Air France (☎373 8004-7) 7 Scindia House, Kg Marg; **Air India** (☎373 6446-8) Jeevan Bharati Building; **Alitalia** (☎332 9551) DCM building, 16 Barakhamba Rd.; **Bangladesh Biman** (☎341 4401-2) World Trade Centre, Babar Rd., Connaught Pl.; **British Airways/Qantas** (☎91 635 9911) Gopal Das Bhawan, 28 Barakhamba Rd.; **Cathay Pacific** (☎332 3332) 24 Barakhamba Rd.; **Delta** (☎332 7507); **El Al** (☎335 7965-7) Prakash Deep Bldg., 7 Tolstoy Marg; **Gulf Air** (☎332 4293) G-12, Connaught Pl.; **KLM/Northwest** (☎335 7747) Prakash Deep Bldg., 7 Tolstoy Marg; **Kuwait Airlines** (☎335 4373) Ansal Bhawan, 16 KG Marg; **Lufthansa** (☎332 7268) 56 Janpath; **RNAC (Royal Nepal Airlines)** (☎332 1164) 44 Janpath; **Singapore Airlines** (☎335 6283/4) Ashoka Estate Bldg., 24 Barakhamba Rd.; **Thai Airways** (☎623 9133) Park Royal Hotel, American Plaza, Nehru Palace; and **United Airlines** (☎335 3377) Ambadeep Bldg., 14 KG Marg. Indian Airlines flies to **Kathmandu, Nepal** (2hr., 1 per day US$142); for **Dhaka, Bangladesh** you must fly via Calcutta.

DOMESTIC FLIGHTS

The airport's **domestic terminal** (☎566 5125/6) is 8km from the international terminal. **Pre-paid taxis, buses,** and **rickshaws** run to and from downtown (see **Indira Gandhi International Airport,** above). Look into student fares (generally available to anyone under 30). Domestic airlines include: **Archana Airways** (☎684 2001); **Jagson** (☎372 1594); **Jet Airways** (☎685 3700); **Sahara** (☎332 6851). **Indian Airlines** (☎371 9168 or 331 0517) run flights to: **Agra** (35min.; M, W, F, and Su; US$60); **Ahmedabad** (1½hr.; 2-3 per day; US$140); **Amritsar** (1½hr.; M, Th, F, and Sa; US$105); **Aurangabad** (3½hr.; 1 per day; US$180); **Bagdogra** (2hr.; M, W, and F; US$190); **Bangalore** (2½hr.; 2 per day; US$260); **Bhopal** (1hr.; 1 per day; US$125); **Bhubaneswar** (2hr.; 1 per day; US$220); **Calcutta** (2hr.; 2-3 per day; US$205); **Chandigarh** (40min.; Th and Sa; US$80); **Chennai** (2½hr.; 2 per day; US$265); **Cochin** (4hr.; 1 per day; US$335); **Goa** (2½hr.; F-W; US$240); **Guwahati** (2½hr.; 1 per day; US$215); **Gwalior** (1hr.; T, Th, and Sa; US$75); **Hyderabad** (2hr.; 2 per day; US$210); **Jaipur** (40min.; 1 per day; US$60); **Jammu** (1hr.; 1 per day; US$110); **Khajuraho** (2hr.; M, W, F and Su; US$105); **Leh** (1½hr.; M, W, F, and Su; US$110); **Lucknow** (1hr.; 2-3 per day; US$95); **Mumbai** (2hr.; 10 per day; US$180); **Nagpur** (1½hr.; 1 per day; US$155); **Patna** (3hr.; 2 per day; US$150); **Ranchi** (1½hr.; 1 per day; US$195); **Shimla** (1hr.; M, W, and F; US$115); **Srinagar** (2½hr.; 1 per day; US$120); **Trivandrum** (4½hr.; 1 per day; US$365); **Udaipur** (3hr.; 1 per day; US$110); **Varanasi** (2hr., 1-2 per day US$130).

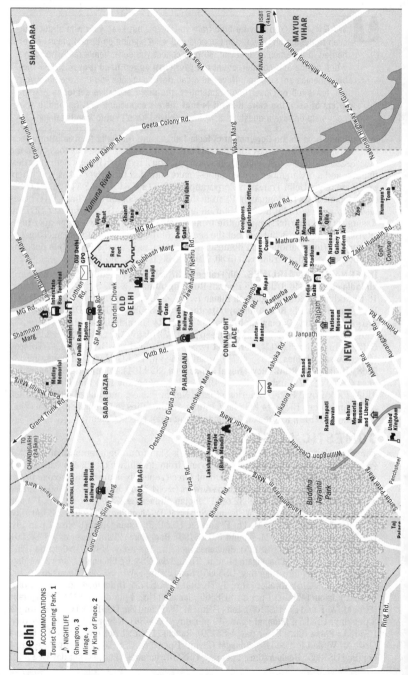

Delhi

▲ ACCOMMODATIONS
Tourist Camping Park, **1**

♪ NIGHTLIFE
Ghungroo, **3**
Mirage, **4**
My Kind of Place, **2**

SHAHDARA

MAYUR VIHAR

TO ANAND VIHAR ISBT (4km)

Vikas Marg

Geeta Colony Rd.

National Highway 24 (Guru Samrat Minihdol Marg)

Grand Trunk Rd.

Marginal Bandh Rd.

Yamuna River

Vikas Marg

Ring Rd.

Raj Ghat

Vijay Ghat

Shanti Vana

MG Rd.

Delhi Gate

Foreigners Registration Office

Crafts Museum

Purana Qila

Zoo

Humayun's Tomb

Red Fort

Netaji Subhash Marg

Jama Masjid

Jawaharlal Nehru Rd.

Supreme Court

Mathura Rd.

National Gallery of Modern Art

Dr. Zakir Hussain Rd.

Lala Hardev Sahai Marg

Interstate Bus Terminal

Old Delhi GPO

Lothian Rd.

Kashmiri Gate

SP Mukherjee Rd.

Chandni Chowk

OLD DELHI

Ajmeri Gate

New Delhi Railway Station

Nepal

Barakhamba Rd.

Kasturba Gandhi Marg

India Gate

National Stadium

Tilak Marg

Golf Course

MG Rd.

Mutiny Memorial

Shamnath Marg

Rani Jhansi Marg

Old Delhi Railway Station

Qutb Rd.

CONNAUGHT PLACE

Jantar Mantar

Janpath

Ashoka Rd.

Rajpath

National Museum

NEW DELHI

Aurangzeb Rd.

Prithviraj Rd.

Grand Trunk Rd.

SADAR BAZAR

PAHARGANJ

Deshbandhu Gupta Rd.

Panchkuin Marg

Sansad Bhavan

GPO

Talkatora Rd.

Akbar Rd.

TO CHANDIGARH (245km)

Swami Narain Marg

SEE CENTRAL DELHI MAP

KAROL BAGH

Pusa Rd.

Mandir Marg

Lakshmi Narayan Temple (Birla Mandir)

Rashtrapati Bhavan

Nehru Memorial Museum and Library

United Kingdom

Saral Rohilla Railway Station

Guru Gobind Singh Marg

Shankar Rd.

Vandemataram Marg

Willingdon Crescent

Buddha Jayanti Park

Sardar Patel Marg

Panchsheel

Patel Rd.

Taj Palace

Ring Rd.

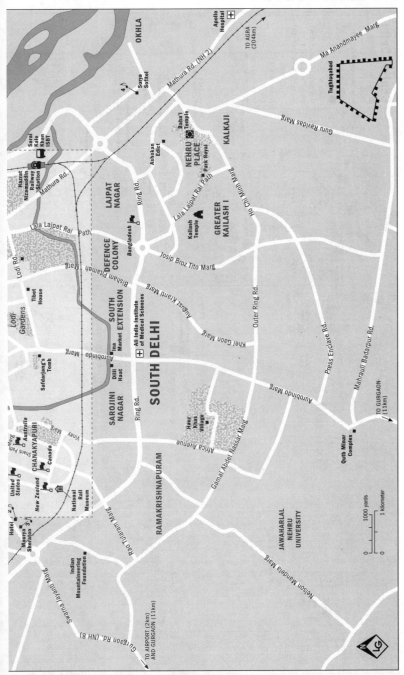

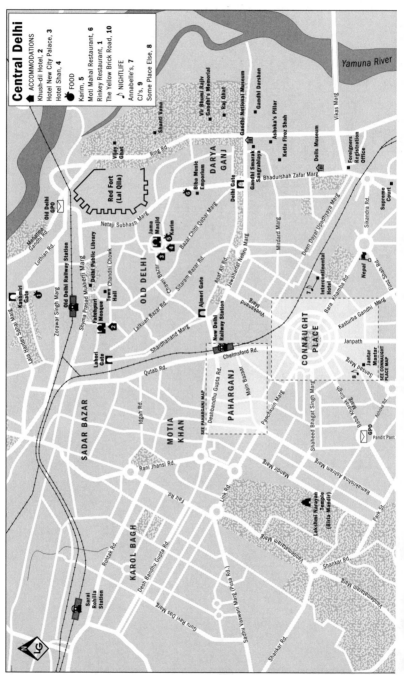

Central Delhi

ACCOMMODATIONS
Khush-dil Hotel, **2**
Hotel New City Palace, **3**
Hotel Shan, **4**

FOOD
Karim, **5**
Moti Mahal Restaurant, **6**
Rinkey Restaurant, **1**
The Yellow Brick Road, **10**

NIGHTLIFE
Annabelle's, **7**
CJ's, **9**
Some Place Else, **8**

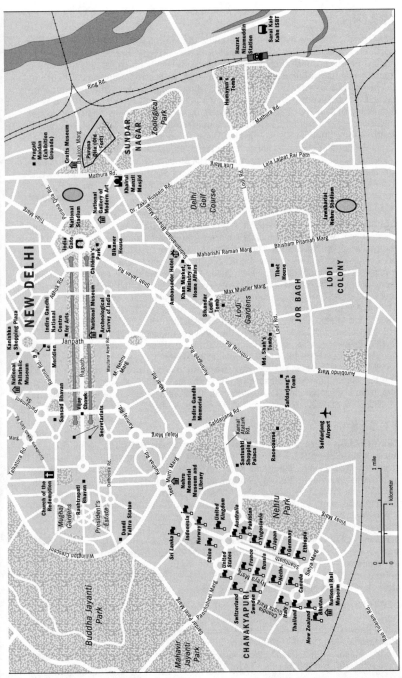

TRAINS

STATIONS. The **New Delhi Railway Station,** the main depot for trains in Delhi, is north of Connaught Pl., at the east end of Paharganj Main Bazaar. Be prepared to push your way around and beware of theft. Your best bet is to get tickets from the **International Tourist Bureau** (☎370 5156), a large, chilled room upstairs at Platform 1. The office books reservations on tourist-quota seats. Tickets from here must be bought in foreign currency or in rupees with encashment certificates. (Open M-Sa 8am-8pm; Su 8am-2pm.) You can also book train tickets at the windows in the station (for general booking) or the **Computerized Reservation Terminal,** one block south of the station on Chelmsford Rd. Book as much as a week ahead for some of the more popular trains. **Do not go to the tourist offices around the railway station.**

Delhi has three other railway stations: **Delhi Station,** in Old Delhi; **Hazrat Nizamuddin Station,** in the southeast part of the city; and **Sarai Rohilla,** in the northwest. Trains leaving from all stations can be booked at the International Tourist Bureau. Some important phone numbers are: **general enquiry** (☎131), **arrivals** and **departures** (☎1330, 1331, or 1335), and **reservations** (☎334 8686 or 334 8787).

DEPARTURES. You can make a reservation from Delhi for any train running between any two stations in India. **Timetables** for major destinations are posted in the International Tourist Bureau. The *Trains at a Glance* booklet can be bought at the book-stalls (Rs25). The air-conditioned *Shatabdi Express* and *Rajdhani Express* trains cost much more than standard 2nd-class tickets, but they get you where you're going faster and provide food and comfy seats. The listings that follow represent a tiny and fast selection from among the many trains available from **New Delhi Railway Station.** A/C chair *Shatabdi Express* trains to: **Ajmer** (#2015; 6½hr.; Tu-Su 6:10am; Rs630) via **Jaipur** (4½hr.; Rs495); **Amritsar** (#2013; 5½hr.; 4:30pm; Rs610); **Bhopal** (#2002; 8hr.; 6am; Rs850) via **Agra** (2hr.; Rs390); **Chandigarh** (#2005; 3hr.; 5:15pm; Rs435); **Chennai,** from H. Nizamuddin (#2434; 28½hr.; W and F 3:30pm; Rs2045); **Dehra Dun** (#2017; 5½hr.; 7am; Rs495); **Lucknow** (#2004; 6½hr.; 6am; Rs640) via **Kanpur** (5hr.; Rs585). A/C 3-tier *Rajdhani Express* trains to: **Ahmedabad** (#2958; 14½hr.; M, W, and F; 7:35pm; Rs1190); **Allahabad** (#2306; 2302, and 2310; 7hr.; 5pm; Rs975); **Bangalore,** from H. Nizamuddin (#2430; 34hr.; M, Tu, F, and Sa 8:50pm; Rs2205); **Calcutta** (#2302, 2306, and 2422; 17hr.; 5pm; Rs1500); **Mumbai** (#2952; 16½hr.; 4pm; Rs1485).

BUSES

TERMINALS. There are three **interstate bus terminals (ISBTs)** in Delhi: the new **Anand Vihar ISBT** (☎214 9089 or 214 8097), east of the Yamuna River about 12km from downtown Delhi; **Sarai Kale Khan ISBT** (☎469 8343 or 435 8343), two blocks east of the Nizamuddin Railway Station; and **Kashmiri Gate ISBT** (☎386 0290), north of Old Delhi Railway Station. Each ISBT serves specific cities, and there is limited overlap. Make sure to go to the correct bus station for your destination; call ahead if you don't know where to go. For information on ordinary and deluxe bus prices and schedules, call one of the bus companies: government-run **Delhi Transport Corporation** (☎386 8836 or 386 5181); **Haryana Roadways** (☎386 1262); **Himachal Roadways** (☎386 8699); **Punjab Roadways** (☎386 7842); **Rajasthan Roadways** (☎386 246); or **UP Roadways** (☎386 8709 or 323 5367). Many of the private bus companies have booths or offices in the Kashmiri Gate ISBT. Shop around for the best price and **steer clear of touts offering implausibly low rates.**

DEPARTURES. Here are just a sampling of bus destinations. **Kashmiri Gate ISBT** runs daily buses to: **Amritsar** (10hr.; Rs190), **Baijnath** (12hr.; Rs250), **Chandigarh** (5hr.; Rs109), **Dabawali** (8hr.; Rs134), **Dadari** (3hr.; Rs44), **Dehradun** (6hr.; Rs115), **Dharamsala** (11hr.; Rs235), **Haridwar** (5½hr.; Rs93), **Jammu** (14hr.; Rs242), **Kullu** (15hr.), **Manali** (17hr.; Rs250), **Mussoorie** (8hr.; Rs169), **Panipat** (2hr.; Rs38), **Rishikesh** (6hr.; Rs107), **Shimla** (9hr.; Rs180).

Anand Vihar ISBT runs daily buses to: **Allahabad** (20hr.; Rs258), **Almora** (11hr.; Rs176), **Bareilly** (7hr.; Rs109), **Basti** (22hr.; Rs290), **Deoria** (23hr.; Rs317), **Gorakhpur** (22hr.; Rs317), **Haldwani** (8hr.; Rs116), **Lucknow** (14hr.; Rs212), **Nainital** (9hr.; Rs176), **Pithoragarh** (15hr.; Rs238), **Ramnagar** (7hr.; Rs110), **Rudrapur** (8hr.; Rs104), **Ranikhet** (12hr.; Rs165), **Sunauli** (22hr.; Rs356), **Varanasi** (18hr.; Rs221).

Sarai Kale Khan ISBT runs daily buses to: **Agra** (5hr.; Rs90), **Ajmer** (8hr.; Rs165), **Chittaurgarh** (12hr.; Rs225), **Gwalior** (8hr.; Rs140), **Jaipur** (6hr.; Rs113), **Jodhpur** (14hr.; Rs230), **Mathura** (4hr.; Rs64), **Udaipur** (15hr.; Rs245), **Vrindaban** (4hr.; Rs63).

ORIENTATION

Situated west of the Yamuna River, Delhi stretches 30km from north to south and 10km from east to west. Just west of the **New Delhi Railway Station** is **Paharganj,** Delhi's backpacker ghetto, crammed with budget hotels, dreadlocked Europeans, and shops full of plastic shoes. The area north of the station is **Old Delhi.** Built by Shah Jahan (and also called Shahjahanabad), Old Delhi is a delightfully tatty tangle of streets and bazaars. The busiest road in this part of town is the **Chandni Chowk,** which runs from west to east across the old city, terminating at the red fort and **Netaji Subhash Marg,** as it runs north-south along the battlements.

South of New Delhi Station, the center of **New Delhi** radiates out from **Connaught Place,** a circular hub of two-story colonnaded buildings. Connaught Pl. is the heart (and capitalist soul) of New Delhi. Of course, with tourists come touts and tricksters—Connaught Pl.'s hustlers are aggressive and exceptionally savvy; ignore them. Off the radial roads to the south of Connaught Pl. sprout the high-rise office buildings of India's most powerful banks, airlines, and international corporations. The inner and outer circles were given new names in 1995, **Rajiv Chowk** and **Indira Chowk,** but everyone still calls it Connaught Pl.

Of the streets that radiate from Connaught Pl., **Sansad Marg** and **Janpath** are the most crowded; Sansad Marg leads to the Raj-era parliamentary buildings, on the end of Raj path, which runs 2km straight east to **India Gate,** bisected by Jan Path along the way. One kilometer southwest of the parliamentary buildings is **Chanakyapuri,** home to the embassies of many western countries. **South Delhi** begins just south of Chanakyapuri. Except for Ring Rd. and **Mehrauli Badarpur Rd.,** South Delhi's major thoroughfares run north-south. In the center is **Aurobindo Marg,** which connects Safdarjang's tomb with the **Qutb Minar Complex.** In the east is **Mathura Rd.,** which slices through **Nizamuddin** and turns into **Dr. Zakir Hussain Rd.** as it proceeds northwest back up to India Gate.

LOCAL TRANSPORTATION

RICKSHAWS

Auto-rickshaw drivers have a knack for overcharging, driving around in circles, and *then* overcharging at the end of the trip. All auto-rickshaws in Delhi have meters, but fluctuating petrol prices have made most obsolete, and even if they do work, most drivers will not use them. If you do find a meter-friendly auto-*wallah,* expect to pay three times the readout. It is usually better to set the auto-rickshaw price in advance if you don't know your way around Delhi—insisting on use of the meter can provoke the drivers into adding a few extra kilometers to the journey. **Pre-paid auto-rickshaws** are available at the airports, train stations, bus stations, and at the Delhi Traffic Police Booths on Janpath (open M-Sa, 11am-6pm) near the Government of India Tourist Office and at Palika Bazaar, along the inner circle (open M-Sa, 10am-7pm). The maximum reasonable non-pre-paid fares are: Airport to Connaught Pl. or Paharganj Rs100-150; Paharganj to Connaught Pl. Rs15-20; Paharganj to Old Delhi Rail-

DELHI

way Rs40-50; Connaught Pl. to Old Delhi Rs35-50; Connaught Pl. to Chanakyapuri Rs35-40. **Cycle-rickshaws** can't go through parts of New Delhi, but in the narrow streets of Old Delhi, they are ideal. Typical fares: Old Delhi to New Delhi Station Rs30; Paharganj to Connaught Pl. Rs5.

BUSES

City buses are extremely cheap, but using them involves a whole host of difficulties. First of all, there is the problem of over-crowding: drivers stop every five seconds to pick up passengers from the side of the road, making trips irritatingly long and uncomfortable. And then there's the problem of figuring out which bus goes where. Not even the managers of **Delhi Transport Corp (DTC)** seem to be able work out what happens to the buses once they leave the depot. The staff at the tourist office is just as clueless. Some people have been stuck on the same bus for years now. Drivers sometimes post a sign on the side of the bus with a number, the origin, and destination of the bus; more often they don't. And these signs are usually only written in Hindi anyway. For a theoretically up-to-date city bus schedule, pick up a red-cover-copy of *A Road Guide to Delhi* (Rs60). Good luck.

BICYCLES

Cycling in Delhi can be harrowing but is also the source of some adrenaline-and-leg-pumping fun. Old Delhi is congested and slow, New Delhi fast and frantic. **Mehta Cycles** (also known as Aadya Shakti Handicrafts), at the entrance to a small alley at the west end of Paharganj's Main Bazaar, just past Accente Restaurant, rents bikes (Rs40 per day, Rs6 per hr., Rs5 overnight charge; Rs600 deposit). Bell and lock are included, but the store doesn't stock helmets, claiming that they are "completely unnecessary" in Delhi. (☎354 0370. Open daily 9am-7:30pm.)

PRACTICAL INFORMATION

DELHI

TOURIST AND FINANCIAL SERVICES

WARNING. Delhi is full of "tourist offices" claiming to provide booking assistance, free maps, and other "information" and services. Several of these offices are near the railway. Their bookings are likely to be overpriced, if not fraudulent. Stick to the main government tourist office on Janpath and, for train tickets, to the tourist reservation office in the New Delhi Railway Station and government-sponsored travel bureaus. **Delhi is a haven of subversive activity.** Con-artists are as common as flies, particularly in Paharganj and other tourist hot-beds. If you realize that you've been cheated, contact the Government of India Tourist Office. They can at least put you in touch with the authorities.

Tourist Office: Government of India Tourist Office (☎332 0005 or 332 0008). 88 Janpath, just south of Connaught Circus Rd. and Scindia House, next to Kapoor Lamps and Delhi Photo Company. Great place to go for help getting around the city and in easing those first-arrival jitters. Open M-F 9am-6pm, Sa 9am-2pm. 2 other government-sponsored agencies provide information and bookings. **India Tourism Development Corporation (ITDC),** also called India Tourism or Ashok Travels, Connaught Pl. (☎332 2336), at the corner of Middle Circle and Radial Rd. 6. Open daily 7am-9pm. **Delhi Tourism (DTTDC),** Connaught Pl., N-block, Middle Circle (☎331 4229 or 331 5322). Open daily 7am-9pm. All 3 government agencies have branches in the international and domestic airport terminals. The different states of India all run offices in Delhi; many are located in the Kanishka Shopping Plaza, 19 Ashok Rd., between the Indraprastha and Kanishka

Hotels, and also around the state emporia on Baba Kharak Singh Marg. The back of the Chandralok Bldg., 36 Janpath, south of the Central Cottage Industries Emporium, houses the offices for **Uttar Pradesh** (☎371 1296 or 332 2251; open M-Sa 10am-5pm), **Himachal Pradesh** (☎332 5320; open M-Sa 10am-5pm), and **Haryana** (☎332 4911; open M-F 9am-5pm). The **Indian Mountaineering Foundation,** 6 Benito Juarez Marg, Anand Niketan (☎467 1211), provides information and services for trekkers (Open M-Sa 10am-5pm.) The **Survey of India Map Office,** 124-A Janpath (☎332 2288), sells city and trekking maps. Open M-F 9am-1pm and 1:30-5pm.

Immigration Office: Getting a visa extension is not easy, and the process brings many travelers back to Delhi again and again. For an extension (15 days max.) on a simple **tourist visa,** first head to the **Ministry of Home Affairs Foreigners Division** (☎469 3334 or 461 2543), 1st floor Lok Nayak Bhawan, behind Khan Market, off Subramaniya Bharati Marg around Lodi Estate. They're only open M-F 10am-noon, so arrive early with 4 passport photos and a letter stating your grounds for extension. If they process your application, head over to the **Foreigners Regional Registration Office** (FRRO; ☎337 9489 or 337 8179), 1st fl., Hans Bhawan, near Tilak Bridge. Open M-F 9:30am-1:30pm and 2-4pm. The FRRO is also the place to get **student visas** (with a bona fide student ID issued by a recognized school/university, bank remittance certificate, and an extension application in duplicate with 4 photos and proof of stay), as well as **permits** for restricted areas of India. If you need an **exit visa,** the FRRO can process it in 20min.

Currency Exchange: American Express, A-block, Connaught Pl. (☎371 2513 or 332 4119). Here you can buy (with rupees and encashment certificates) and change AmEx traveler's checks. Other brands cashed at 1% commission. There's a counter for lost and stolen cards, but the main office for 24hr. check replacement is at Bhasant Lok (☎614 2020). The A-block office issues and receives AmEx moneygrams and offers the usual cardmember services (see p. 15). Open M-F 9:30am-5:30pm, Sa 9:30am-2:30pm. **S.P. Securities Ltd.,** M-96, Middle Circle, Connaught Pl. (☎335 7073 or 335 7070). Open M-Sa 9:30am-8pm, Su 11:30am-2pm. **Hotel Grand Regency** (☎354 0101), Main Bazaar, 300m from the New Delhi Railway Station, changes all major currencies and traveler's checks. Open 24hr. **Bank of Baroda,** Sansad Marg (☎322 1746), in the tall, white building just beyond the Outer Circle, gives cash advances on MC and V and cashes traveler's checks. Open M-F 10am-3:45pm, Sa 10am-12:30pm. **Citibank,** in the red stone-and-mirrored, modern high-rise before the Bank of Baroda, has a 24hr. ATM (Cirrus compatible). **Standard Chartered Bank,** opposite the Bank of Baroda and in E-block, Connaught Pl., also has 24hr., Cirrus-compatible ATMs. **HSBC** has 24 ATMS dotted around Delhi; most conveniently at Ele House, on the corner of Connaught Circus and KG Marg. The main branch of **The State Bank of India** on Parliament St. (374 2290) charges currency and traveler's checks. Open M-F 10am-4pm, Sa 10am-1pm. 24hr. branch in the international terminal of the airport. In truly desperate situations, some use the **illegal money changers** along Main Bazaar in Paharganj. Don't let them go off with your money promising to return with rupees, even if they leave a "friend" with you while you wait. **Western Union and Money Transfer,** 1st fl. Sita World Travel office, F-12 Connaught Pl. (☎331 1122), charges a 5% commission to transfer money from abroad. Open M-F 9:30am-11pm, Sa 9:30am-9:30pm, and Su 10am-2pm.

EMBASSIES

Australia, 1/50-G Shantipath (☎688 8223; fax 688 5199). Open M-F 8:30am-1pm and 2-4:30pm.

Canada, 7/8 Shantipath (☎687 6500; fax 687 6579). Open M-Th 8:30am-5pm, F 8:30am-1pm.

European Commission, 65 Golf Links (☎462 9237; fax 462 9206). Open M-F 9am-5pm.

Ireland, 230 Jor Bagh (☎462 6733; fax 469 7053). Open M-F 9:30am-1:30pm and 2:30-5pm.

Israel, 3 Aurangzeb Rd. (☎301 3238; fax 301 4298). Open M-Th 9am-5pm, F 9am-3pm.

Nepal, Barakhamba Rd. (☎332 7361 or 332 9218; fax 332 6857). Open M-F 9am-1pm and 2-5pm.

New Zealand, 50-N Nyaya Marg (☎688 3170; fax 687 2317). Open M-Th 8:30am-5pm, F 8:30am-1pm.

Pakistan, 2/50-G Shantipath (☎611 0601; fax 687 2339). Open M-F 8:30am-5pm.

South Africa, B-18 Vasant Marg, Vasant Vihar (☎614 9420; fax 611 3605). Open M-F 9am-5pm.

Thailand, 56-N Nyaya Marg (☎611 8103; fax 687 2029) Open M-F 9am-5pm.

UK, Shantipath (☎687 2161; fax 687 2882). Open M-F 9am-1pm and 2-5pm.

US, Shantipath (☎419 8000; fax 419 0017). Open M-F 8:30am-1pm and 2-5:30pm.

LOCAL SERVICES

Luggage Storage: Many hotels store luggage at a nominal charge (Rs2-5), but only for guests. The railway stations also have luggage storage (Rs7-10 per day) for anyone holding a valid train ticket; just be sure to lock your bags.

Bookstore: There are several well-stocked bookstores on the Inner Circle of Connaught Pl., including **Bookworm** (☎332 2260; open May-Sept. M-Sa 10am-7:30pm; Oct-Apr. M-Sa 10am-7pm); **New Book Depot** (☎332 0020; open M-Sa 10:30am-7:30pm); **E.D. Galgotia and Sons** (☎371 3227; open M-Sa 10:30am-7:30pm). All on B-block.

Library: American Center Library, 24 Kasturba Gandhi Marg (☎331 4251; fax 332 9499). Internet and CD-ROM databases. Collection includes the embassy library. Open M-F 11am-6pm. Admission Rs10 per day. The **British Council Library,** 17 Kasturba Gandhi Marg (☎371 1401), on the opposite side of the street. Open Tu-Sa 10am-6pm. The **Ramakrishna Mission,** at the west end of Paharganj Main Bazaar, has a library with current periodicals and newspapers; most are in Hindi, but *Time, National Geographic,* and *Mad Magazine* are available. Open Tu-Su 8-11am and 4-8pm. Entrance is free.

Bi-Lesbian-Gay Organizations: Humrahi and **Sangini,** Andrews Ganj (☎685 1970). Counseling services and regular support group meetings. Call M-W or F 6-8pm.

Cultural Centers: The American Center and British Council (see above) have regular lectures and film screenings. **Max Mueller Bhavan,** 3 Kasturba Gandhi Marg (☎332 9506), has a library and shows films in Siddhartha Hall. Indian cultural centers include **Indian Council for Cultural Relations,** Azad Bhavan, I.P. Estate (☎337 9463); **India International Centre,** 40 Lodi Estate (☎461 9431); **Indira Gandhi National Centre for the Arts,** CV Mess, Janpath (☎338 9216). **Sangeet Natak Akademi,** Rabindra Bhavan (☎338 7246), has information on classical music concerts.

EMERGENCY AND COMMUNICATIONS

Police: Emergency ☎100; central control room ☎327 0000 or 328 6848. Branches all over—look for Delhi Traffic and Tourist Police kiosks at major intersections. Stations at Chandni Chowk, next to Bahrandi Mandir, and Paharganj, opposite the railway station.

Pharmacy: The multi-story **Super Bazaar** (☎341 4176), outside the M-block of Connaught Pl., has a 24hr. pharmacy. Several pharmacies along Paharganj Main Bazaar sell tampons and toilet paper as well as the usual bandages and medicine.

Hospital/Medical Services: Dr. Sharwan Kumar Gupta's **Care Clinic and Laboratory,** 1468 Sangatrashan (☎361 7841; home ☎623 3088; emergency pager ☎9632 113979). From the Paharganj Main Bazaar, take a right onto Sangatrashan before the Hotel Vivek; the clinic is 100m down on the left. English-speaking staff is used to dealing with foreign insurance companies. Recommended by IAMAT. Open M-Sa 9am-8pm,

Su 9am-1pm. The **East-West Medical Clinic**, 38 Golf Links Rd., Lodi area (☎699 229 or 623 738), is recommended by many embassies. Expensive by local standards, the clean and efficient clinic runs a 24hr. emergency room with a fully stocked, 24hr. pharmacy. Other hospitals include **Apollo**, Mathura Rd. (☎692 5858; open 24hr.), and the **All-India Institute for Medical Services**, Aurobindo Marg (☎656 1123).

Internet: In Paharganj, Internet shops are everywhere and generally cheaper than in Connaught Pl. **Hotel Gold Regency**, Main Bazaar (☎354 0101), has a "Cyber Bar-Be-Que" with full restaurant service. You might have to wait a while for one of their 60 computers, though. Rs10 per hr. Open 24hr. In Connaught Pl., **The Hub**, E-block, above Volga Restaurant, offers Internet (Rs30 per hr.) and cappuccinos (Rs10). Open daily 8am-11pm.

Post Office: Branches everywhere in Delhi. **New Delhi GPO**, Gole Dakhana on Ashoka Rd. and Baba Kharak Singh Marg (☎336 4111). Bring a passport to claim mail. Open M-F 10am-5pm, Sa 10am-4:30pm. To receive mail at **Old Delhi GPO**, Lothian Rd., near the Red Fort and ISBT, use this address: GPO, Delhi, 110006. **Overnite Express** (☎334 7423; open daily 7am-10pm) and **Blue Dart** (incorporated with FedEx; ☎336 8566; open M-Sa noon-8pm) are in Kanishka Shopping Plaza on Ashok Rd., next to the Kaniksha and Indraprastha Hotels. **Belair Travel and Cargo**, 10-B Scindia House (☎331 3440), ships bulky luggage and boxes overseas. Open M-F 9:30am-6pm, Sa 9:30am-2pm. If "every second counts," go to **DHL Express**, 11 Tolstoy Marg (☎373 7587). Open M-F 9:30am-8:30pm, Sa 9:30am-6pm. **Postal Code:** 110001.

ACCOMMODATIONS

Staying in Delhi can be frustratingly expensive. Prices have been driven up so much that it is hard to find anything acceptable for less than Rs100. There are three main budget hotel areas: Paharganj, Connaught Pl., and Old Delhi. **Paharganj** (Main Bazaar) is Delhi's main tourist enclave. Though it has adapted to travelers' needs, it still retains its legendary squalor and seediness and can be dangerous, especially for women traveling alone. Paharganj has also become the quintessential New Delhi urban legend. It is packed with STD/ISD booths, Kashmiri "travel agents," hash dealers, money changers, and people who cheat tourists for a living—be on your guard. If you've just arrived in India or are simply not into grime, head to **Connaught Pl.** for its own collection of nicer, though more expensive, guest houses and hotels. On the other hand, if you really want to put your nose in it, there's always **Old Delhi**, the purist's retreat.

PAHARGANJ

Paharganj is one long, messy line of cheap hotels and restaurants. Unless otherwise noted, check-out is at noon. Most of the better places have rooftop restaurants and generators for Delhi's all-too-frequent power outages. All of the following directions (right, left) are given as you walk west on Main Bazaar.

▨ **Hotel Rak International** (☎355 0478). Chowk Bowli, down an alley to the right off Main Bazaar. Peaceful, slightly upscale place with good views from the roof. Rooms are newly-painted and comfortable. Singles with bath Rs150-450; doubles Rs250-550. ❷

▨ **Camran Lodge** (☎352 6053). Main Bazaar, 300m on the right. Built into an old mosque, this creeping, crooked knot of rooms has more character than you'd expect. Not too sterile or modern, this is the place to dream Orientalist dreams before hitting real-life Delhi in the morning. Singles with common bath Rs80-100; doubles Rs160-300. ❶

▨ **Major's Den Guest House** (3629 599). Lakshmi Narain Street, at the west end of Main Bazaar. Turn right at metropolis, then the next right; Major's is at the end of the street on the right. The den is the perfect retreat from the tourist-bungalow-impersonality of the main bazaar. Solar panels, extra fencing, super-wide hallways, and a friendly family staff. Peaceful rooftop patio as well. Singles Rs150-250; doubles Rs250-350. ❶

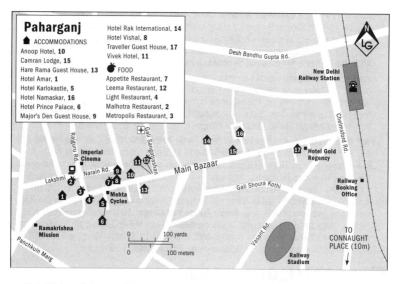

Paharganj

ACCOMMODATIONS
Anoop Hotel, **10**
Camran Lodge, **15**
Hare Rama Guest House, **13**
Hotel Amar, **1**
Hotel Karlokastle, **5**
Hotel Namaskar, **16**
Hotel Prince Palace, **6**
Major's Den Guest House, **9**

Hotel Rak International, **14**
Hotel Vishal, **8**
Traveller Guest House, **17**
Vivek Hotel, **11**

FOOD
Appetite Restaurant, **7**
Leema Restaurant, **12**
Light Restaurant, **4**
Malhotra Restaurant, **2**
Metropolis Restaurant, **3**

Hotel Prince Palace (☎351 8873/4). Gali Thanedar Wali, down an alley on the left just past Appetite Restaurant. Super-tidy rooms have attached bath and TV; some even have fridges and balconies. Singles Rs250-500; doubles Rs300-550. ❷

Hotel Karlokastle (☎351 7673). Gali Thanedar Wali, next to Hotel Prince Palace. Relaxed and clean with marble-lined hallways. Spacious rooms with attached bath and TV. The rooftop restaurant overlooks the city below. Singles Rs250-500; doubles Rs350-550. ❷

Hotel Namaskar (☎362 1234). Chanoiwalan, down an alley 300m on the right, off Main Bazaar. Turn before Camran lodge. Small, homey guest house offers cozy rooms set back from the main bazaar hubbub. Singles Rs150; doubles Rs200-450. ❶

Vivek Hotel (☎351 2900). Main Bazaar, in the heart of Paharganj. This massive, white backpacker haven is spread over several floors—try to get a room overlooking the street. Singles with attached bath Rs200-600; doubles Rs250-670. ❷

Traveller Guest House (☎354 4849). Main Bazaar, a little more than 100m on the left. Rooms are small but worth it for the TV and air-cooling. Doubles Rs260-300. ❶

Anoop Hotel (☎352 1451). Main Bazaar. Popular, multi-storied backpackers' hotel with an expansive rooftop restaurant. Spacious, well-kept rooms cooled by powerful fans. Check-out 24hr. Singles Rs150-375; doubles Rs180-425. ❷

Hare Rama Guest House (☎351 413). Main Bazaar, down an alley at the west end; look for the sign for the Ajay Guest House on the left. Normally packed and often rowdy. If you've been feeling the need for a somewhat seedy hotel complete with an "Art Shop" sporting black-lights and psychedelic nude art, this is your spot. Check-out 24hr. Singles with bath Rs180-400; doubles Rs240-495. ❷

Hotel Vishal (☎352 7629). Main Bazaar, west end, after the Hare Krishna Guest House. More mellow than other backpacker hangouts. Bathrooms cleaner than the bedrooms. Great rooftop for relaxation. Singles with attached bath Rs150; doubles Rs200-350. ❶

Hotel Amar (☎352 4642). Main Bazaar, on the west end, past Metropolis Hotel. Most with TV, air-cooling, and phone. Singles with bath Rs150-500; doubles Rs150-500. ❷

CONNAUGHT PLACE

The hotels in and around Connaught Pl. tend to be cleaner and quieter than those in Paharganj—they also tend to cost a lot more. The area is less chaotic, though some travelers might find it altogether *too* quiet, especially at night.

▨ **H.K. Choudhary Guesthouse** (☎ 332 2043). H-35/3, Middle Circle. Excellent service. Rooms are exceptionally clean and nicely decorated. Follow the tree growing through the bldg. to the rooftop terrace. Singles Rs450-550; doubles Rs550-850. ❷

Hotel Palace Heights (☎ 332 1369). Radial Rd. 6, D-block, on the top floor. High above the streets, this hotel's rooms are a bit drab but have plenty of writing surfaces in case you're in the mood to write postcards. The terrace makes a welcome break from the claustrophobic stuffiness of other cheap hotels. Singles Rs300; doubles Rs375-845. ❷

Sunny Guest House (☎ 331 2909). Scindia House, Connaught Ln., off Jan Path beyond the Outer Circle. Standard backpacker grotto. Dorm room is a rooftop shack, but more spacious than Ringo's. Dorms Rs90; singles Rs125-170; doubles Rs250-400. ❶

Ringo Guest House (☎ 331 0605). Scindia House, near Sunny Guest House. A little hideaway above the waves of cars and people. Staggeringly popular backpackers' retreat is overcrowded and overpriced but has a pleasant garden area and a relaxed, safe, and happy atmosphere. Dorms Rs90; singles Rs150; doubles Rs250-400. ❶

Royal Guest House (☎ 332 5355). 44 Janpath, above Nepal Airlines on the 2nd fl. Basic lodging with rooftop views. Rooms are clean, but bring your own furnishings. Singles with common bath Rs150; doubles with attached bath Rs400-600. ❶

OLD DELHI AND TOURIST CAMP

This is the chicken-squawking, dung-covered real thing. For better and for worse, Old Delhi doesn't aspire to impress foreign tourists. While prices are cheaper and people are less likely to try to cheat you, it can be hard to find anyone who speaks English. **Western women should exercise caution.** Stereotypes about foreigners— Western women in particular—are stronger here than elsewhere in the city. Many men will assume that solo female travelers are willing to give sexual favors; women should avoid dressing provocatively or going out alone after dark.

▨ **Hotel New City Palace** (☎ 327 9548 or 325 5820). West of the Jama Masjid. Awe-inspiring views of the mosque. The clean rooms have comfortable beds and balconies with rooftop access. Check-out 24hr. Singles with bath Rs200; doubles Rs250-650. ❶

Hotel Shan (☎ 325 3027 or 326 9615). West of the Jama Masjid. The thin walls of this homey hotel are decorated with posters of New York City, totally out-of-sync with the excellent views of the Jama Masjid from the window. Check-out 24hr. Doubles Rs150-200. ❶

Khush-Dil Hotel, Chandni Chowk (☎ 395 2110), at the west end, just south of the mosque on Fatehpuri Corner. Narrow beds, but excellent views of the busy street. Check-out 24hr. Singles with common bath Rs100; doubles Rs150-200. ❶

Tourist Camping Park (☎ 397 6458). Qudsia Garden, across the street and to the right of Kashmiri Gate ISBT. Dark and dank lodgings, common bathrooms that do not inspire confidence, but great for crashing after a bus trip. Singles Rs140; doubles Rs170. ❶

◨ FOOD

It's worth shelling out a little cash for some of Delhi's fantastic meals. There are restaurants in every price range: respectable Western-style fast-food, decent Chinese and Middle Eastern cuisine, a couple of Mexican restaurants, and, of course, excellent Indian food. For a real splurge (up to Rs300-400 per entree), head to one of the 5-star hotels, such as the Maurya Sheraton or the Ashok Frontier.

DELHI

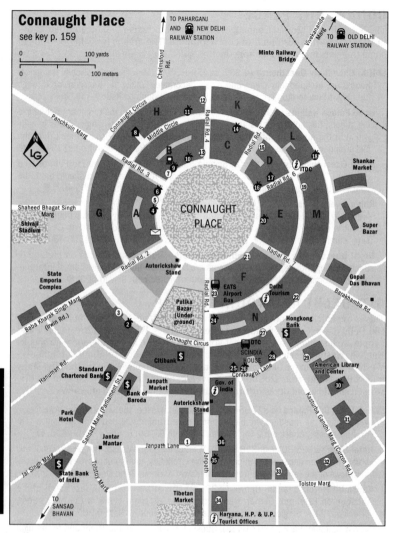

Connaught Place
see key p. 159

CONNAUGHT PLACE

PAHARGANJ

This backpackers' district has developed several hot spots for hanging out; most of them are five stories up. None of these places serves exceptional food, but the rooftops are the place to find Paharganj's backpack-rats sipping tea and slurping curd after hours. It's best to get off the Main Bazaar for food—most of the main strip's restaurants cater to the jaded palates and fragile digestive systems of backpackers. Wander the streets north of Paharganj to see where the locals are eating.

Malhotra Restaurant, 1833 Lakshmi Narain Rd. Walk west along the Main Bazaar, turn right on Rajguru Rd. at the Metropolis, then take the 1st left. An intimate place, often packed with locals. Quick, efficient service and good Indian and Chinese food (from Rs35). A/C comfort upstairs. Open daily 7:30am-11pm. ❶

Metropolis Restaurant, Main Bazaar west end, in the Metropolis Hotel. Subdued setting. Large selection of Chinese, Indian, and continental dishes. "Le Poulet Sizzling" Rs175, bean sprouts and bean curd Rs60. Open daily 8am-11pm. ❷

Appetite Restaurant and German Bakery, Main Bazaar, on the right after the Hotel Vishal. Write a postcard while munching banana cake (Rs25). Open daily 7am-11pm. ❶

Leema Restaurant, Main Bazaar, in Hotel Vivek. Perhaps the best budget-hotel restaurant in Paharganj. A/C, fresh juices, and excellent veg. sandwiches (Rs10), though the service can be painfully slow. Open daily 7am-11pm. ❶

Light Restaurant, Main Bazaar, at the west end just before Ratguru Rd. on the left. Cheap, but still yummy. Veg. *thalis* Rs20, rice pudding Rs8. Open daily 9am-10:30pm. ❶

CONNAUGHT PLACE

Catering to the elite, restaurants in Connaught Pl. serve Indian and international cuisine several times better than the muck served down the road in backpackers' paradise. Dishes are priced accordingly.

▨ **Embassy Restaurant** (☎ 332 0480). D-block. Antique setting, attentive service, and fine Indian and continental food at "oh-why-not" prices. Brain Curry Rs105, cream of asparagus soup Rs52. Open daily 10am-11pm. ❷

Rodeo, A-block, near the AmEx office. A taste of the Wild West lassoed into the New Delhi East. Cowboy-Indian waiters decked out to the spurs shoot up an array of cocktails, beer, and rather authentic Tex/Mex food. Nachos Rs95-145, entrees Rs195-250, Corona Rs105, cornbread free. Open daily noon-11pm. ❷

Nirula's (☎ 332 2419). L-block. Huge multi-restaurant the size of a multi-story car park. Head to the **ice cream bar** for smooth mango scoops and shakes, or try Indian flavors like Zafrani Badaam Pista, 21 Love, and Delhi Delight (Rs26 per scoop). Hit the **Potpourri** upstairs (open daily 7:30am-midnight) for Western fare, or sip drinks in one of two bars–the popular, pricey, **Pegasus Bar** is open 11am-midnight. The **Chinese Room** cooks up scrumptious East Asian dishes (open daily 12:30-11pm). Ice cream and fast-food branch near Wimpy on N-block. **Pastry shop** open 9am-9pm. ❶

Gaylord, Connaught Circus, to the left of the Regal Cinema. Chandeliered dining room. Top-notch food and service. Your meal here may be the most expensive and perhaps the best you'll have in India (main courses Rs100-350). Open daily 10:30am-11pm. ❸

DELHI

Zen Restaurant, B-block. If you took out the tables and chairs, the Zen would make a classy disco. Chinese food, a Japanese name, and American muzak. Veg. dishes Rs80-110, non-veg. Rs115-450. Beer Rs85. Open daily 11am-11pm. ❷

Wenger & Co. Pastry Shop, A-block, Inner Circle, next to the AmEx office. Take-out bakery and patisserie (most Rs20). Open daily 10:30am-8pm. ❶

Parikrama, 22 Kasturba Gandhi Marg. Delhi's revolving 24th fl. restaurant takes 1½hr. to go round once, and you probably won't want to finish in less. Amazing, labeled views are complimented by good but pricey Indian and Chinese dishes (entrees Rs140-410). It's a feast for your eyes and your stomach. Open daily noon-11:30pm. ❸

Mahavir Sweets, C-block, Middle Circle. Renowned for its sugary desserts, Mahavir also serves tasty and cheap Indian dishes. *Masala dosa* Rs22, *thalis* no more than Rs32, sweet *ras malai* Rs15. Open M-Sa 8am-8pm. ❶

United Coffee House, E-block. Victorian-Era flashback with high ceilings, ornately carved walls, and an incongruous background soundtrack of 1980s Euro-pop. Veg. and non-veg. dishes Rs45-170. Open daily 9am-midnight. Last orders at 11:30pm. ❷

Volga, B-block, Inner Circle. This definitely-not-Russian restaurant rolls out the red carpet for crowds of beer-drinking men who come to smoke and shout into the cold air. Good Indian dishes Rs90-150. Open daily 1-4pm and 6:30-11pm. ❷

Sona Rupa Restaurant, 46 Janpath, just before Tolstoy Marg. Indian food (Rs40-70). The most basic "vegetarian paradise" around features a great buffet for Rs95. Buffet open 12:30-3:30pm and 7:30-10:30pm. Restaurant open daily 11am-11pm. ❶

Nizam's Kami Kabab, H-block, behind Plaza Cinema. Indian fast-food joint with some of the tastiest *biryani* (Rs80-85) and kebab egg-rolls (Rs50-75) in the city. Catch forgotten music videos on the TV while waiting for your number. Open daily 12:30-11pm. ❶

Don't Pass Me By, 79 Scindia House, on Connaught Lane just past Ringo Guest House. A 3-table budget place that somehow escaped from Paharganj. Large porridge (Rs18) and veg. omelette (Rs22) for breakfast. Chinese dishes too. Open daily 7am-10pm. ❶

OLD DELHI

Old Delhi offers every everything from *dal bhat* to squawking chickens, and has a number of renowned restaurants as well.

▧ **Karim,** in a small courtyard off Matya Mahal, about eight shops down from the Jama Masjid (not visible from the road). One of the city's most popular and famous restaurants, Karim has been run by descendants of the cooks of Mughal royalty since 1913. Menu full of rich, meaty meals. Half dishes (at half-price) fit the bill for the budget traveler. Half chicken *biryani* Rs70, full mutton stew Rs76. Open daily 7am-midnight. ❶

Moti Mahal Restaurant, Netaji Subhash Marg. Delicious tandoori cuisine served in outdoor patio and chandeliered dining rooms. Kebabs from Rs105, veg. curries from Rs50. Live music W-M 8pm-midnight. Open daily 11am-midnight. ❷

Rinkey Restaurant, Bara Bazaar. From the Kashmiri Gate ISBT, turn left on Lothian Rd. and then right on Bara Bazaar. One of the few sit-down places close to the bus station. Lots of choices. Fresh pizza Rs60, onion *uttappam* Rs30. Open daily 9:30am-9:30pm. ❶

NEW DELHI

Many of Delhi's newest and best eating options are located away from the city center and beyond the usual tourist trails. Particularly in the south, at the posh arcades of Defence Colony Market and greater Kailash, hip and not always expensive restaurants are becoming the new favorites. Almost always worth the trip, these eateries make for a great night out or a well deserved break after touring.

■ **The Yellow Brick Road,** Ambassador Hotel, Sujan Singh Park, 1km south of India Gate. With pastel chairs, tables, and floor tiles, it's as if you followed the yellow brick road to a Caribbean garden party. Excellent dishes range from the mouth-tingling Bangkok vegetable curry (Rs205) to extra virgin pasta (Rs210). Leave room for the infamous "Bull's Eye" dessert (Rs120). Open 7am-midnight. ❸

■ **Sagar,** 18 Defence Colony Market. Popular eatery that has the reputation of the best South Indian food in Delhi. Lightning-quick service brings tasty *thalis* (Rs45), *dosas* (Rs26-44), *uttappams* (Rs28-42), and 30 different flavors of meal-capping ice cream. North Indian and Chinese branch a few doors down. Open 11am-11pm. ❶

◎ SIGHTS

Like any capital city, Delhi has a vast number of things to see. There are a whopping 1376 monuments, two of which are UNESCO World Heritage sites (Qutb Minar and Humayun's Tomb). If you're spending only a couple of days in Delhi, budget your time wisely. The must-sees are the Qutb Minar Complex and the sights of Old Delhi—Lal Qila (Red Fort), the Jama Masjid (Friday Mosque), and the bazaars. Round out your time by having a look at Rashtrapati Bhavan and Humayun's Tomb. If you need respite from the midday heat, head to the National Museum. You'll have most of these places to yourself in the early morning. As always, men (and occasionally women) will linger by the entrance to the various tourist attractions, flashing ID cards (often bogus) and offering their services as guides. While they often don't have their facts straight, some are quite knowledgeable. If you do hire a guide, be sure to negotiate a price in advance.

Several agencies offer **guided tours** of Delhi (about Rs210-230). These usually start in New Delhi, stopping at Jantar Mantar, the Lakshmi Narayan Temple, Humayun's Tomb, the Baha'i Temple, driving by other landmarks (such as India Gate), swinging south of the city to the Qutb Minar before heading north to the Red Fort and the sights of Old Delhi. Tours of Old Delhi might include the Red Fort, Raj Ghat, Shanti Vana, and a glimpse of the Jama Masjid (about Rs110-126). These tours are rushed, the guides are not always informed, and a full day of bus riding, even in A/C comfort, is never fun, but these tours are helpful if you've only got a short time in Delhi. Be aware that none of the tour prices includes admission to the pricey sights. Another option is to ditch the tourist bus and hire a guide and/or vehicle for 8-12hr. stints. Standard taxis cost about Rs625-650 for 8hr. Book through ITDC or Delhi Tourism (see **Tourist and Financial Services,** above).

OLD DELHI

RED FORT (LAL QILA)

Enter through Lahore Gate. Fort open Tu-Su dawn-dusk. US$5. Video camera fee Rs25. Mumtaz Mahal museum open Tu-F 10am-5pm; Naubat Khana and Sanghralaya museums open Tu-Su 10am-5pm. Museums Rs2 each. English sound and light shows Nov.-Jan. 7:30-8:30pm; Feb.-Apr. 8:30-9:30pm; May-Aug. 9-10pm; Sept.-Oct. 8:30-9:30pm. Rs30, under 12 Rs10. For reservations, call ☎ 327 4580.

Shortly after moving the capital from Agra to Delhi in 1639, Mughal emperor Shah Jahan began construction of the Red Fort. Work started on April 16 and was completed nine years later to the day. Soaring to a height of 33.5m, the fort's red sandstone ramparts form a 2km perimeter and are themselves surrounded by a moat into which the Yamuna once flowed. Military occupation now renders much of the fort inaccessible, and many of the fort's more resplendent features are gone—the famed Peacock Throne was snatched away in 1739, the gems that adorned the palaces were removed long ago, and the canals where the Stream of Paradise once gurgled now run dry. But the Red Fort remains what it has always been—an architectural marvel and an incredible monument to Mughal power.

DELHI

LAHORE GATE AND NAUBAT KHANA. The entrance to the fort is toward the middle of its west wall, at the three-story Lahore Gate, through which the Mughal emperors would leave for the Jama Masjid. Lahore Gate leads to **Chatta Chowk,** the covered passageway filled with shops that today peddle souvenirs, but which during the Mughal era provided nobles with silks, jewelry, and fine velvets. Chatta Chowk opens to the rectangular, three-storied Naubat Khana (Drum House); five times a day, music was played here in tribute to the emperor and his court. The floral carvings adorning the walls of Naubat Khana were once painted with gold.

DIWAN-I-AM. Naubat Khana leads into the palace area. Across the courtyard stands the Diwan-i-Am (Hall of Public Audience), where the early Mughal emperors used to sit (everyone else stood) for two hours a day, chatting with nobles, deciding criminal cases, and generally having a right royal time. The throne used to sit on top of the canopied, white-marble platform now on display. At the back of the platform is a series of panels adorned with flowers, birds, trees, and lions. Presiding over the entire scene is the Greek god Orpheus. Scholars speculate that the panels, returned from the British Museum in 1903, were crafted in Florence. The low marble platform in front of the emperor's platform was reserved for the prime minister, who would, within earshot of the emperor, entertain grievances.

PRIVATE PALACES. Beyond Diwan-i-Am were the private palaces of the Mughal emperor. Of the original six palaces, five remain; each was connected to its neighbor by a canal called **Nahir-i-Bihisht** (Stream of Paradise). The palaces were set in spacious, formal *charbagh* gardens. The southernmost of the palaces (the one farthest to the right when coming from Diwan-i-Am), '**Mumtaz Mahal** (Palace of Jewels) originally housed the harem. These days, it houses a museum (see below). North of Mumtaz Mahal is the **Rang Mahal** (Palace of Colors), a white marble pavilion where the emperor ate his meals. During the Mughal heyday, the ceilings were decorated with silver; other parts of the ceiling are embedded with tiny mirrors that reflected the light from the emperor's candle-lit banquet tables. Just north of the Rang Mahal is the **Khas Mahal** (Private Palace); each of the apartments was decorated in silk. The southernmost of these is the **Baithak** (Sitting Room). The emperor used to sleep in the center apartment, or **Khwabagh** (Sleeping Chamber). Attached to the outer wall of the Khwabagh is a tower called the **Muthamman Burj** (Octagonal Tower), where the emperor would greet his subjects or watch animal fights staged below. King George V and Queen Mary sat here before thousands in 1911, when the announcement was made amidst much rejoicing that the imperial capital would be moved to Delhi from Calcutta. North of the Khwabagh is the **Tasbih Khana** (Chamber for Telling Beads), where the emperor said his prayers.

DIWAN-I-KHAS AND MOTI MASJID. Just north of Khas-Mahal is the Diwan-i-Khas (Hall of Private Audience), constructed entirely of white marble. Here, the emperor would make crucial political decisions, consult privately with advisors, and speak with VIPs. Attempting to rekindle the old spark, Bahadur Shah II, the last Mughal emperor, held court here during the Mutiny of 1857; in retaliation, the British tried him in the Diwan-i-Am and then exiled him to Burma. To the north is the **Hammam** (bath), whose westernmost apartment contained a rosewater fountain. West of the Hammam is the delicate **Moti Masjid** (Pearl Mosque), built in 1662 by Emperor Aurangzeb for his personal use. The black marble outlines on the floor were designed to help with the proper placement of *musallas* (prayer mats).

MUSEUMS. There are three museums inside the Red Fort complex. **Mumtaz Mahal** is the best of the three, displaying astrolabes, royal *hookahs*, and other artifacts from the Mughal reign. The arms and weapons museum in the **Naubat Khana** concentrates on military history and displays various implements that have taken lives over the past 200 years. The **Sanghralaya Museum** traces the development of the Indian independence movement with some life-sized dioramas.

D E L H I

JAMA MASJID

1km southwest of the Red Fort. Open to tourists 30min. after dawn until 12:20pm (noon on F), 1:45pm until 20min. before prayer call, and again after prayers until 20min. before sunset. Shoes, shorts, and sleeveless shirts not allowed. Camera fee Rs20.

Built between 1650 and 1656 by Emperor Shah Jahan, the Jama Masjid is the largest active mosque in India. Set on a high platform on top of a low hill, the Jama Masjid dominates the surrounding streets with the elegant mixture of red sandstone and white marble that covers its soaring minarets. The east gate was once reserved for the emperor and his family; now it is open to all worshippers on Fridays and Muslim holidays. The huge courtyard packs in 25,000 worshippers during Friday prayers. As in most South Asian mosques, a *hauz* (tank) at the center of the courtyard is used for cleansing feet and hands before prayer, and each rectangle designates the space for one worshipper. Prayers are sung from the *imam's* platform, under the center arch at the westernmost point of the mosque. Just west of the mosque is the official residence of the *imam;* the Muslim priests have lived here since the time of Shah Jahan, and you can still see them before prayers. It's worth climbing one of the minarets for the superb views of the city (Rs10). Foreigners, however, must be in groups of two or more since the claustrophobic stairwell has attracted thieves with an eye for lone tourists.

OTHER SIGHTS

RAJ GHAT. Here, a perpetually burning flame and a simple black slab set in a grassy courtyard offer a memorial to Mahatma Gandhi, cremated at this spot after his 1948 assassination by a Hindu extremist. Gandhi's name is notably missing from the monument—the only inscription bears his last words, "Hai Ram" ("Oh God"). Hundreds of visitors come each day to cast flower petals and pray. Just south of the monument is a park full of plants bestowed by dignitaries: flowers from Eisenhower, a pine from Queen Elizabeth II, and a tree planted by Nasser. *(Off Ring Rd., 1km east of Delhi Gate and 2km southeast of the Red Fort. Open dawn-dusk. Free.)*

SHANTI VANA. North of Raj Ghat, this quiet park contains memorials to the men and women who have earned a place in India's pantheon of political heroes, including an effusive monument to slain Prime Minister Rajiv Gandhi. An adjacent memorial to his older brother Sanjay was taken down after critics reminded the government that this particular Gandhi never served in office or ever accomplished much at all. Sanjay's admirers continued to leave flowers at the spot, however, and eventually the monument returned. The grassy mound that marks the life and death of Jawaharlal Nehru mentions only his wish to have his ashes thrown in the Ganga. *(Open daily Apr.-Sept. 5am-7:30pm; Oct.-Mar. 5:30am-7pm. Free.)*

SOUTH DELHI

QUTB MINAR COMPLEX

At the intersection of Aurobindo Marg and Mehrauli Badarpur Rd., 14km southwest of Connaught Pl. Open daily dawn-dusk. US$10. Video camera Rs25.

The ruins of the **Qutb Minar** complex are beyond compare. Construction on the complex began in AD 1199 after the Turkish ex-slave Qutb-ud-din Aibak swept into North India and knocked the Rajput empire to pieces. Qutb-ud-din Aibak installed himself at Lal Kot, the site of an old Rajput city, founding what was to become India's first Muslim kingdom here in 1206, following the murder of his general, Mohammed Ghuri. The events that led to the building of the complex were epochmaking, and the Qutb Minar serves as a 72.5m high exclamation point.

The red sandstone Qutb Minar was designed as a celebration of Qutb-ud-din Aibak's triumphs in Northern India and as a milestone marking the eastern frontier of the Muslim world. As an inscription on one of the tower notes, "the tower was erected to cast the shadow of God over both East and West." Modeled on the brick victory towers of Central Asia, the Qutb Minar also served as the minaret for the Quwwat-ul-Islam Masjid (see below). Before dying, Qutb-ud-din Aibak was able to complete only the first story of the tower. His son-in-law Iltutmish added the next three stories, and Firoz Shah Tughluq tacked on some marble and a fifth story while repairing damage caused by a 1368 lightning strike. The cupola erected by Firoz was felled by an 1803 earthquake and replaced by British major Robert Smith; Smith's Mughal-style cupola now sits in the gardens, having been removed from the Qutb Minar because it was so awkward. Visitors have been forbidden to climb the minaret since 1981, when more than 30 panicked school children were trampled to death during a power outage. Most of the calligraphy carved on the minaret displays Arabic passages from the Qur'an, though a few Devanagari inscriptions prove some Indian influence in its design.

QUWWAT-UL-ISLAM MASJID. Just to the right of the Qutb Minar is the Quwwat-ul-Islam Masjid (Might of Islam Mosque), the oldest mosque in India aside from those in western Gujarat. Begun in AD 1193 and completed in AD 1197 (extensions were added over the next two centuries), the mosque was built from the remains of 21 Hindu and Jain temples destroyed by Qutb-ud-din Aibak. At the center of the courtyard is the 98% pure iron **Gupta Pillar.** According to the Sanskrit inscription, the pillar was erected in honor of Vishnu and in memory of Chandra, believed to be the Gupta emperor Chandragupta II (r. AD 375-415). Tradition holds that Anangpal, the founder of Lal Kot, brought the pillar here. It is said that those who can stand with their backs against the pillar and wrap their arms around it are blessed with superhuman strength; these days, a fence defies any attempt to do so.

ALA'I DARWAZA. Just south of Qutb Minar is the red sandstone Ala'i Darwaza, built in AD 1311 to serve as the southern entrance to the mosque. Immediately east of Ala'i Darwaza, a domed tomb with *jali* (decorative screens) holds the body of Imam Zamin, a Central Asian Sufi saint who came in the early 16th century.

ALA'I MINAR. North of the Quwwat-ul-Islam Masjid is a massive, unfinished minaret, Ala'i Minar, a monument to grandiose ambitions and plans gone awry. Expansion had doubled the size of the mosque, and Ala'i Minar was designed to be twice as tall as Qutb Minar. After its first 24.5m high story was completed around AD 1300, construction was stopped and the madly ambitious project abandoned. Just south of the Ala'i Minar is the Tomb of Iltutmish, which the sultan himself erected in 1235. Iltutmish's red sandstone tomb isn't particularly interesting from the outside, but the artfully decorated interior is well worth a look, with its mingling of Hindu and Jain themes (wheels, lotuses, and bells) and Muslim motifs (calligraphic inscriptions, geometric patterns, and alcoves facing Mecca built into the west wall). Directly south of Iltutmish's tomb are the ruins of a *madrasa*, an institution of Islamic learning. In keeping with Seljuk Turkish traditions, the tomb of the *madrasa's* founder, Ala-ud-din Khalji, has been placed within.

BAHA'I TEMPLE
4km north of Tughluqabad. Open Tu-Su Apr.-Sept. 9am-7pm; Oct.-Mar. 9:30am-5:30pm.

Over the past three decades, members of the Baha'i faith have donated millions of dollars toward the construction of seven Baha'i Temples in locations as varied as Uganda, Samoa, and the midwestern United States. The latest addition to this series was finished in 1986 and is situated in South Delhi on a 26-acre expanse of cropped grass and elegant pools. The temple, which inevitably draws comparisons to the Sydney Opera House, is built from white marble in the shape of an opening lotus flower. Silence is requested of visitors, so there's little to do but settle comfortably onto one of the wood-backed benches, listen to the dull thudding of bare feet, and gaze up at the clean lines of the temple's splendid dome.

OTHER SIGHTS

High up on top of a lonely outcropping is **Tughluqabad,** built as a fortified city by Ghiyas-ud-din Tughluq, who ruled the Delhi Sultanate from AD 1321 until his murder in 1325. Shortly after Tughluq was killed, Tughluqabad was abandoned, having been occupied for only five years. Nowadays, the still-abandoned fort has been conquered by weeds, monkeys, and a general air of desolation. Massive walls run along the 6.5km circumference of the fort and provide expansive views of the Delhi skyline. Thirteen separate gates once led through the walls, but now the only access is on the southern side. *(Mehrauli Badrapur Rd., 9km east of the Qutb Minar and 16km southeast of Connaught Pl. Open dawn-dusk. US$5.)* Across from the entrance is the red sandstone and white marble **Tomb of Ghiyas-ud-din Tughluq.**

CENTRAL NEW DELHI

SANSAD AND RASHTRAPATI BHAVANS. Of the scores of buildings built by the British when they moved their capital from Calcutta to Delhi in 1911, the Rashtrapati Bhavan (President's Residence) and the Sansad Bhavan (Parliament House) are the most impressive. Designed by the renowned architect Edwin Lutyens, the buildings possess a massive grandeur—a not-so-subtle display of the vast reserves of British power—intended to communicate the determination that India continue to be the jewel in the imperial crown. The effort backfired—the aesthetic anomaly of European-style buildings in the heart of an Indian city only helped to anger Indian nationalists, and the buildings became a lightning rod for criticism. In one memorable outburst, Gandhi described them as "architectural piles."

Sansad Bhavan, at the end of Sansad Marg, 1½km southwest of Connaught Pl., is a massive, circular, colonnaded building that vaguely resembles a flying saucer. Because India's parliament, the Lok Sabha, meets here (see **Government and Politics,** p. 81), it is often difficult to get close to the building. *(To get inside, you will have to obtain a letter from your embassy.)* To reach **Rashtrapati Bhavan,** head down to Rajpath and walk between the Secretariats to the entrance; or walk 2km due west from India Gate down Rajpath. Once the residence of the viceroy, the pinkish Rashtrapati Bhavan is now the home of India's president. *(To visit Rashtrapati Bhavan, you'll need to apply at the reception office at least 2 days in advance. Tours are offered only M, W, F. Don't forget to bring your passport.)* The 45m-high pillar between the gate and the residence was donated by the Maharaja of Jaipur and is known as the **Jaipur Column.** The pillar is capped with a bronze lotus and a six-pointed Star of India.

SECRETARIATS. Flanking Raisina Hill are the symmetrical Secretariats, which now house government ministries. The buildings are adorned with various slogans praising enlightened imperial rule. For some shade (and fresh air), pass under the slogans and into the **Great Hall,** a dark and airy room adorned with medallions and crowned by a baroque dome. Try to visit **Raisina Hill,** the area between the two Secretariats, on a Saturday, when troops march in front of Rashtrapati Bhavan. *(Ceremonial changing of the guard 8:30-9:15am in summer; 10:35-11am in winter.)* As you look east from the Secretariats, the arch in the distance is **India Gate,** a memorial to Indian soldiers killed in WWI and the Afghan War of 1919. A memorial beneath the arch commemorates those who were killed in the 1971 Indo-Pakistani War.

DELHI

HUMAYUN'S TOMB. A poem of red sandstone and black-and-white marble, Humayun's Tomb is set amid geometrical gardens and rows of palm trees. Humayun was the second Mughal emperor, ruling from 1530 until 1540, when he was vanquished by Sher Shah. He ruled again from 1555 until 1556, but an accident cut short his reign. While walking down the stairs of his library in the Old Fort, Humayun heard the *azan.* He quickly sat down on the nearest step, but, upon rising, tripped and slid down the stairs, incurring fatal injuries. His tomb, however, was not built until 1565. Later, many other prominent Mughals were buried at the site, including Dara Shikoh (Shah Jahan's favorite son) and Bahadur Shah II, the last of the Mughal emperors, who was captured here by the British during the Mutiny of 1857. Humayun's Tomb is at the center of a rectangular, quartered garden laced with channels and paths. A pioneering work of Mughal architecture and predecessor to the Taj Mahal, the octagonal tomb sits alone in a central hall, whose double dome rises to a height of 40m and is home to hordes of squealing bats, birds, and bees. *(2½km southeast of India Gate, at the end of Lodi Rd. Open dawn-dusk. US$10.)*

HAZRAT NIZAMUDDIN DARGAH. One of Sufism's greatest shrines, Hazrat Nizamuddin Dargah was originally built in AD 1325, the year its occupant, the great mystic Sheikh Nizamuddin Aulia, died. The complex was refurbished in the 16th century by Shah Jahan, one of Nizamuddin's many devotees. Its marble verandas and delicate latticework are radiant at dawn and dusk. At twilight, people gather here to sing *qawwali,* Sufi songs of spiritual ecstasy. To reach the shrine, head down the street opposite **Kataria Nursery,** through the market, and into the courtyard. On the way, you will pass the grave of the great Urdu poet, **Mirza Ghalib.** *(A short walk southwest of Humayun's tomb, across Mathura Rd., 6km from Connaught Pl.)*

JANTAR MANTAR. This Mughal astronomical observatory looks like an M.C. Escher lithograph rendered as a red-and-white, brick-and-limestone diorama, its stairs twisting around tight bends and soaring upward to the heavens. Charged by emperor Mohammed Shah with the task of revising the Indian calendar accordance to modern astronomy, Maharaja Jai Singh of Jaipur built Jantar Mantar in 1725 after studying European and Asian science and spending years observing Delhi's skies. The result is as scientifically impressive as it is visually striking: the massive instruments keep accurate time (in Delhi, London, and Japan), predict eclipses, and chart the movement of the stars. *(Connaught Pl., 200m down Sansad Marg from the outer circle, on the left. Open daily sunrise-sunset. US$5. Video camera Rs25.)*

LODI GARDENS. Though the sign at the entrance is slightly worrying—"No shooting, gambling, or cricket"—the leafy glories of the Lodi Gardens are relaxing and beautiful. A wide variety of trees and birds make their home here—spread around some crushed Magic Masala potato chips—and you're likely to attract hordes of fluorescent green, hyper-aggressive urban parrots. Along with splendid, well-maintained gardens, the park contains a jogging trail and a steamy greenhouse. A few ruined buildings rise from the closely cropped grass. Toward the center of the garden is the late-15th-century **Bara Gumbad,** a tomb of red, gray, and black stones topped by a massive dome. Scholars have no idea who is buried here. Attached to the tomb is a mosque, built in AD 1494. The interior is embellished with dense floral patterns and Qur'anic inscriptions. The square tomb just north of Bara Gumbad is the early-16th-century **Shish Gumbad** (Glazed Dome), decorated with remnants of the blue tiles that once covered it. About 200m north of Shish Gumbad is the badly weathered **Tomb of Sikandar Lodi** (1517-18). Less than 50m east of the tomb is a 16th-century bridge with seven arches. Also in the Lodi Gardens, 200m southwest of Bara Gumbad, is **Mohammed Shah's Tomb,** a high-domed octagonal building built in the mid-15th century. *(Gate 1, Lodi Rd. Gardens open dawn-dusk. Free.)*

SAFDARJANG'S TOMB. Built in 1753-54 for Safdarjang, prime minister to Mughal emperor Mohammed Shah, the tomb is the most recently built piece of great Mughal architecture in Delhi. The centerpiece of expansive *charbagh* gardens, the tall, domed edifice was constructed of marble and red sandstone stolen from another local tomb. *(West of the gardens, at the end of Lodi Rd. Open dawn-dusk. US$5.)*

PURANA QILA. The Purana Qila (Old Fort) marks a spot that has been continuously inhabited since the Mauryan period (324-184 BC). The discovery of ceramic shards dating back to 1000 BC vindicated bearers of local tradition, who have long claimed that the fort was built on the site of Indraprastha, the capital city of the Pandava heroes of the *Mahabharata* (commemorated in a nightly sound and light show). There's never been much doubt about the 16th-century function of the Purana Qila, though—the massive walls, towering gates, finely preserved mosque, and ruined library formed the centerpiece of Humayun's Delhi. Built in AD 1541 by Sher Shah, the **Qila-i-Kuhna Masjid** (Mosque of the Old Fort) is an ornate tangle of calligraphic inscriptions and red sandstone. Less impressive (and less intact) is the octagonal **Sher Mandal,** which Humayun used as a library and observatory after seizing the fort from Sher Shah. A small, free museum on the premises showcases some of the artifacts discovered in and around Purana Qila. The Shunga period (184-72 BC) plaques are particularly interesting. To get a good sense of the incredible height of the fort's ramparts, climb onto the top of the walls and admire the panoramic view of Delhi or walk the **exercise trail** below the walls. The trail winds pleasantly around a small lake where paddleboats can be rented for Rs40 per 30min. *(Off Mathura Rd., 1km east of India Gate. Open daily dawn-dusk. US$5. Sound and light show daily Nov.-Jan. 7:30pm; Feb.-Apr. and Sept.-Oct. 8:30pm; May-Aug. 9pm. Rs25.)*

Next to Purana Qila is the **National Zoological Park.** Check out the three white tigers. *(Open Su-Th Apr. 1-Oct. 15 9am-4pm; Oct. 16-Mar. 31 9:30am-4pm. Rs40.)*

BIRLA MANDIR. Built by the wealthy Birlas in honor of Lakshmi, the goddess of material well-being, the Lakshmi Narayan Temple is a marvel of Orissan-style temple architecture and opulent extravagance. The room of mirrors at the back of the temple allows you to see yourself together with infinite reflections of a flute-playing Krishna statue. The gardens contain a brightly colored fountain in the shape of a pile of cobras, gaily painted sculptures of tigers and elephants that welcome riders, and a plaster cave which can be entered through the gaping mouth of a giant plastic boar's head. *(Mandir Marg, 2km west of Connaught Pl. Open daily 4:30am-9pm.)*

🏛 MUSEUMS

NATIONAL MUSEUM. The museum's ambitious mission is to provide an overview of Indian life and culture from prehistoric times to the present. Ground-floor galleries showcase some of the museum's most popular items. Other displays trace the development of Indian scripts, iconography, and coins over the past 16 centuries. (To see the actual coins, head up to the second floor.) An A/C, room-sized vault houses the museum's jewelry collection. Highlights include gaudy gilded earrings, necklaces, and bracelets dating from the 1st century AD. Remarkable works of decorative art and a collection of Neolithic stone artifacts (3000-1500 BC) fill the remaining ground floor galleries. Upstairs, the unique maritime heritage gallery charts Indian naval progress since ancient times. On the second floor, the exhibit of weapons and armor includes a colorful, brass-reinforced Rajasthani vest, an 18th-century bejeweled rhino-hide shield of Maharana Sangram Singh II, and the curved weapons of the Pahari. More peaceful pleasures can be found in the galleries of colorful masks and clothing associated with the peoples of the northeastern states. The top-notch collection of musical instruments in the Sharan

Rani Gallery, donated in 1980 by renowned *sarod* player Sharan Rani, is remarkably comprehensive, displaying handcrafted Indian instruments including *sarangis* and sitars as well as a glass tabla. (☎ 301 9272. Janpath, just south of Rajpath. Open Tu-Su 10am-5pm. Foreigners entrance fee Rs150; camera fee Rs300. Guided tours begin at the enquiry counter at 10:30 and 11:30am, noon, 2 and 3:30pm.)

CRAFTS MUSEUM. Built in 1991, the Crafts Museum is one of the finest in South Asia. The museum is divided into three sections. Near the entrance, an open-air demonstration area provides an informative glimpse of artisans practicing their crafts: casting metal for sculptures, stringing jewelry, and weaving baskets from straw. Also outdoors is a village complex filled with life-sized reproductions of rural huts and houses brought to Delhi from their native regions. Inside, excellent displays showcase the diversity of traditional Indian crafts, including 18th-century wood carvings from Karnataka, string puppets from Rajasthan, a myriad of textiles, and a model of a Bihari wedding chamber. (Pragati Bhawan, Bharion Marg, off Mathura Rd. Open Tu-Su 10am-5pm. Outdoor displays partially closed July 1-Oct. 1. Free.)

NATIONAL GALLERY OF MODERN ART. Once the mansion of the Maharaja of Jaipur, this gallery houses a diverse collection of Indian art produced over the last 150 years. The paintings range from European landscapes to finger paintings, cubist abstractions, and even less recognizable splotches of color. Some provocative sculptures also linger precariously in the middle of the gallery halls. Highlights include the bold designs of Jamini Roy, the paintings of the turn-of-the-century Bengal School, which were inspired by South Asian folk art and East Asian high art, and Badrinath Arya's *Khoj*, a painting of subterranean stalactite-like staircases. (Jaipur House, southeast of India Gate. ☎ 338 2835. Open Tu-Su 10am-5pm. Rs150.)

NEHRU MUSEUM AND PLANETARIUM. Built inside the home of Jawaharlal Nehru, India's first prime minister, the museum has as much to say about the independence movement as a whole as it does about Nehru himself. Between voyeuristic peeks into Nehru's study, office, and living room, visitors are guided past shots of Nehru as a dour youth (with equally somber-looking relatives), as a student at Harrow and Cambridge, and as the humble, generous leader of India. Adjacent to the museum is the Nehru Planetarium. (Teen Murti Bhawan, Teen Murti Rd., 400m northeast of Chanakyapuri. Open Tu-Su 9am-5pm. Free. Planetarium exhibit open 11am-5pm. Rs1. Planetarium showings in English Tu-Su 11:30am and 3pm, in Hindi 1:30 and 4pm. Rs10.)

OTHER MUSEUMS. The **Indira Gandhi Memorial** exhibits a sentimental collection of photos and quotations honoring India's two fallen prime minsters, all arrayed in Rajiv and Indira's former residence. If the collection bores you, the macabre exhibit of Rajiv and Indira Gandhi's last outfits will surely shock you out of complacency. (1 Safdarjang. Open Tu-Su 9:30am-4:45pm.) The **National Rail Museum** has indoor and outdoor exhibits on the history of Indian Railways and a miniature "joy train" (Rs10) you can ride. (Chanakyapuri, near the NZ and Bhutan embassies. Open Apr.-Sept. Tu-Su 9:30am-7:30pm; Oct.-Mar. Tu-Su 9:30am-5:30pm. Rs10. Video fee Rs100.)

🎬 ENTERTAINMENT

To find out about weekly musical and cultural events, buy a copy of *Delhi Diary* (Rs10), which comes out every Friday. **Dances of India** is a nightly performance of Indian dance and music, including *kathak* and *manipuri*. (☎ 328 9464 or 642 9170. Parsi Anjuman Hall, opposite the Ambedkar Football Stadium, Delhi Gate. Shows 7pm.) There are many **movie theaters** in Delhi that show Hindi movies. **PVR Priya 1,** Basant Lok, Vasant Vihar (☎ 614 0048), and **PVR Anupam 4,** Saket Community Centre (☎ 686 5999), show English-language films for Rs60-130. Check daily papers for movie listings. Various cultural centers (see **Cultural Centers,** p. 154) screen foreign films and Indian "art" films not shown elsewhere.

The Red Fort's nightly **sound and light show,** focusing on the city's Mughal heritage, is unexpectedly entertaining. A Pink Floyd concert it's not, but it's as good a history lesson as you're likely to get in Delhi (see **Lal Qila,** p. 161). The Old Fort also has a nightly sound and light show on the *Mahabharata* (see **Purana Qila,** p. 167).

⌐ SHOPPING

> **⚠ WARNING.** Delhi's **touts** (men employed by shop-owners to bring customers) are the best in the business; they will go to incredible lengths to get you into their employer's office. Although few are actually out to rob or hurt you, touts often lie to tourists, using false ID and guilt trips (e.g., "Why don't you trust me? I'm trying to help you."). For more information, see **Touts, Middlemen, and Scams,** p. 17.

Like Delhi's hotels and restaurants, the options for capital-city shopping are extensive, with markets and stores ranging from the grimy and cheap to the glitzy and prohibitively expensive. Right in backpacker haven, **Paharganj's main bazaar** can satisfy all of your sticker and hippie, kitschy paraphernalia cravings. To the northwest of Paharganj, **Karol Bagh** contains shops of all sizes and kinds. If fluorescent "Om" iron-on patches aren't your style, the priciest of Delhi's boutiques are concentrated in **Connaught Pl.,** where armed guards stand in front of jewelry shops and tailors sell saris made from the finest silk. Literally under Connaught Pl. is the **Palika Bazaar,** an underground, A/C maze of stores selling anything and everything, mostly to locals. Because tourists tend not to come here, it offers better deals on clothes, fabric, and souvenirs than the stores above, provided that you have honed your bargaining skills. The quality of items here, however, is decidedly lower than above-ground, and the Palika Bazaar is not the place to search for a Rolex watch, or at least not a *real* one. (Open daily 10am-8pm.) Down Janpath from Connaught Pl. is the **Central Cottage Industries Emporium,** a multi-floored mini-mall selling high quality, pricey handicrafts from all over India—carved metal boxes, Mughal-style paintings, wooden elephants, oriental rugs, and the like. (☎332 1909. Open M-Sa 10am-7pm.) Opposite the emporium is the tourist-targeted stretch of **Tibetan Market,** which sells cheap Kashmiri crafts. (Most shops open M-F 10am-7:30pm.) Several states also have their own emporia selling unique, non-local fare on **Baba Kharak Singh Marg.** (Most open M-Sa 10am-6:30pm.) **Dilli Haat,** off Aurobindo Marg, across from Ina Market in South Delhi, features a regularly changing cast of craftsmen and a food stall from each of India's states. (Rs10 entrance fee. Open M-Sa 11am-4pm.) For more expensive souvenirs, head to the cultivated boutiques of **Hauz Khas Village** (open W-M) or the antiques market of **Sunder Nagar** (open M-Sa).

Many Delhi residents shop among the rows of name-brand and generic stores in South Delhi's markets, such as **South Extension, Sarojini Nagar, Lajpat Nagar,** and for the tragically trendy, **M and N blocks of Greater Kailash.** Alternatively, Old Delhi's **Chandni Chowk,** which runs from the Fatepuri Masjid to the Red Fort, and all of its south-leading alleys are one enormous bazaar—the road buzzes with the sound of haggling throughout the day. Many of the products sold here are of minimal interest to most tourists (plastic buckets and padlocks galore), but plenty of shops stock clothes, jewelry, and musical instruments of varying quality and price. **Netaji Subhash Marg,** which runs south from the Red Fort to Delhi Gate, has several more music stores. **Biba Music Emporium,** 500m north of Delhi Gate, has an extensive collection of sitars (Rs1800-15,000), including some beautiful antique instruments, tablas (Rs750-3800), and harmoniums for Rs1650-5000. (☎328 4558. Open M-Sa 10am-7:30pm.) **Bina Enterprises,** 200m closer to Delhi Gate from the Biba Music Emporium, also stocks tablas for Rs950-3900 and sitars for Rs2500-16,000. (☎328 9587 Open M-Sa 9:30am-7:30pm.)

■ NIGHTLIFE

Despite what the shadowy and deserted streets of Connaught Pl. might imply, Delhi's nightlife is not confined to the plastic tables and chairs of Paharganj rooftops. The clubs of the capital thump and flash with the same techno and whirling lights as the best clubs anywhere. But like the luxury hotels that house them, Delhi's discos cater to the elite, and cover charges may seem forbiddingly steep to budget travelers. If you want to get down and dirty with the jet-set of India, you'll have to cough up some serious cash and dig down deep into your pack to find the necessary clothes to fit in. On the other hand, grooving until the morning in a classy nightclub can be a welcome change from hanging out with the tokers high up on the rooftops of some budget hotel. Most of the clubs listed below are 21+, require men to be accompanied (women, however, can often get in alone), and prohibit torn clothing, sneakers, and uncool insophisticates of all kinds.

Ghungroo (☎611 2233), at the Maurya Sheraton. Bronze-plated columns enclose the dance floor and a semi-circular marble bar polished like a mirror. Ghungroo packs a mixed crowd of locals and foreigners who strut their stuff on a translucent, tiled dance floor reminiscent of Saturday Night Fever. The club pulsates with everything from techno to Middle Eastern pop music, and dancers cheer whenever a Hindi film song begins. Cover Rs300 for men; women get in free. Open M-Th 10pm-2:30am; F-Sa until 3:30am.

Mirage (☎683 5070), at the Best Western Surya Sofitel. A classy club with a subdued Egyptian theme, Mirage's flashing lights hang in profusion over the dance floor and the wrought-iron railings surrounding it. The DJ sometimes takes requests and otherwise spins techno, hip-hop, Hindi pop, and a bit of reggae. Cover W, Th, Su Rs300 per person; F Rs400 per couple; Sa Rs500 per couple. Open W-Su 9pm until the party stops.

My Kind of Place (☎611 0202), at Taj Palace. Nary a local in sight, MKOP is packed with Europeans and Africans. The club is one of Delhi's most popular with tourists. A thick haze of smoke hangs in the sweaty, hot air, but this doesn't stop anyone from dancing. The low ceiling pulses with inlaid fairy lights on a random fade and brighten cycle. Cover Su-Th Rs300 per couple, F-Sa Rs400 per couple. Open 9:30pm-2am.

CJ's (☎371 0101), at Le Meridien. From the triangular bar in the center to the dance floor on the side, everything here is in keeping with the atmosphere of the hotel: smooth and swank. The DJ plays a mix of hip-hop, techno, film songs, and anything else you might want. The sound-proof karaoke room near the entrance can be rented at Rs1000 per hr. Cover Rs500 per couple. Open 10pm-2am. Bar closes at midnight.

Annabelle's (☎370 9000), at the Intercontinental on Babar Rd., 200m from the intersection of Barakhamba Rd. and Tolstoy Marg. With a large central dance floor surrounded by silver railings, Annabelle's is clearly divided into a dancing section and a spacious sitting area complete with tables, chairs, and posters of foreign beers. The mostly Indian crowd grinds to a typical mix of techno and Hindi pop. Cover W and F Rs250 per couple, all other nights Rs500 per couple. Open daily 9:30pm-2am.

Some Place Else (☎374 3737), at the Park Hotel on Sansad Marg. Really more of a bar than a nightclub, but every Th-Sa the brick walls shake with dance music. Each night has a musical theme: M jazz night, Tu film songs, W Latino and reggae, Th hip-hop and R&B, F rock and retro, Sa techno and house, Su free-for-all. Su-W no cover, Th-Sa Rs450 per couple. Open Su-W 7pm-midnight, Th-Sa dancing 11pm-3am.

GOA गोवा

Sun-bathed white beaches, the crumbling, abandoned Portuguese manors, and an easy-going spirit have long made Goa a prime destination for travelers. Just don't expect Eden. The advancing vanguard of an invading tourist culture has splashed Goa's shores with red Coca-Cola umbrellas, burnt-to-a-crisp Germans, and hell-bent sarong peddlers. Resort complexes and pan-European and Israeli techno junkies compete for space on the beaches. Despite the development, you are never far from an unspoiled beach, where you can revel in simple splendor, drink from freshly fallen coconuts, and watch fishermen fold their nets. The parties and the the raucousness have calmed down a bit under the influence of authorities desperate to bring order to chaos, but the sweet-smelling breeze blown in off the ocean suggests that Goa is still a good place to come for a natural high.

Europeans have come to Goa since 1498, when Portuguese explorer Vasco da Gama landed on the Keralan coast in search of spices. Portugal was looking to establish a foothold in India, and in 1510, Goa became a Portuguese colony. During the 16th century, Goa developed as a trading city, where Portuguese soldiers and adventurers mixed with and married the locals, many of whom converted to Catholicism. Thanks to the "encouragement" of the Jesuit Inquisition, Goa became a stronghold of Christianity in India. The Portuguese made sure that Goa never became a part of the British Raj, and held on here until 1961, when Indian troops annexed the region. Goa thus holds the dubious distinction of being both the first piece of subcontinental soil clutched by Europeans and the last to be liberated. It first became a Union Territory, and eventually, in 1987, an official state.

After five centuries of Portuguese rule, Goa is unique among Indian states: Portuguese-speaking Roman Catholics dressed in jeans and muscle shirts live side-by-side with *lungi*-clad fishermen shouldering the day's catch. About 30% of Goa's inhabitants are Christian, and the state has literacy and income levels among the highest in India. Goa is small enough to explore thoroughly during a stay of moderate length, and locals are often eager to share their paradise with visitors.

HIGHLIGHTS OF GOA

India's most legendary (and most decadent) nightlife scene raves away all winter on the northern beaches of **Anjuna** (p. 184) and **Chapora and Vagator** (p. 188).

Time stands still in **Old Goa** (p. 178), home to Portuguese monuments, cathedrals, and the mortal remains of **St. Francis Xavier** (p. 180).

The northernmost and southernmost Goan beaches, **Arambol** (p. 190) and **Palolem** (p. 198), will do their best to seduce you into staying longer than you ever planned to.

WHEN TO GO(A)

Goa's northern beaches are hopping from early November to late March, when hot and cloudless skies draw sun-worshippers in droves. Beach fever is intense in the weeks before and after Goa's Christmas; the months of December and January are considered peak season. Almost everything closes down during the monsoon (June-Sept.), and guest house prices bottom out as tourists head north to the green fields of Manali (p. 247). The monsoon cools Goa down, but the showers often cease for long sunny stretches. Other holidays well worth the trip are the **Carnival,** Panjim's pre-Lent revelry (Feb.13, 2002), and the more solemn festivities in honor of Goa's favorite saint, Francis Xavier, held in Old Goa on December 3 every year.

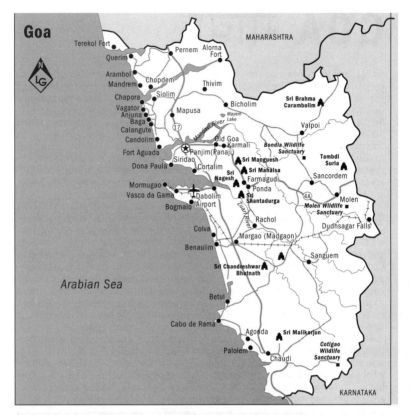

Goa

Terekol Fort
Querim
Pernem   Alorna Fort
MAHARASHTRA
Arambol
Mandrem   Chopdem
Chapora   Siolim   Thivim
Vagator
Anjuna
Baga   Mapusa
Calangute
Candolim
Fort Aguada
Dona Paula
Bicholim
Mayem Lake
Sri Brahma Carambolim
Valpoi
Old Goa
Karmali   Bondla Wildlife Sanctuary
Panjim (Panaji)   Tambdi Surla
Siridao   Sri Manguesh
Cortalim   Sri Mahalsa
Sri Nagesh   Farmagudi
Sancordem
Sri Shantadurga   Ponda
Mormugao
Vasco da Gama   Dabolim Airport
Bogmalo
Molen
Molen Wildlife Sanctuary
Rachol
Dudhsagar Falls
Colva
Margao (Madgaon)
Benaulim
Sanguem
Arabian Sea
Sri Chandreshwar Bhutnath
Betul
Cabo de Rama
Agonda   Sri Malikarjun
Cotigao Wildlife Sanctuary
Palolem   Chaudi
KARNATAKA

✈ INTERCITY TRANSPORTATION

Most travelers reach Goa from Mumbai, 600km to the north.

FLIGHTS

Dabolim Airport (info ☎ (0854) 512644), 29km south of Panjim. **Indian Airlines** and **Jet Airways** offer flights to and from: **Bangalore**, via **Mumbai** (2½hr; 3 per day; US$245-310); **Delhi** (2½hr.; 1 per day; US$167); **Mumbai** (1hr.; 4 per day; US$57-85). There is a Rs750 airport tax for all flights. During peak season, seats on the Mumbai-Goa flight can be difficult to obtain, but flights are normally available during the middle of the week; call a few days in advance.

Dabolim's prepaid **taxi** counter, outside the airport's main entrance, will ferry you just about anywhere in Goa. A board to the left of the counter lists fares (to Panjim Rs350-400). Off season (May-Sept.), *touts* clutter the main exit. **Local buses** run to Vasco da Gama (8am-8pm, Rs5), with connections to Panjim and Margao.

TRAINS

Traveling south from Mumbai on the **Konkan Railway** is efficient and comfortable. The only drawback is that the tracks were laid 15-20km outside city stations, so the railway only skirts major towns. Two trains from **Mumbai** head to Goa daily: the *Mum-*

bai-Madgaon Mandari Express 0102 (5:15am) and the *Mumbai-Madgaon Konkan Express 0111* (10:40pm). These trains stop at three stations in Goa: **Tivim,** 20km due east of Vagator beach (10¼hr.); **Karmali,** 12km due east of Panjim (10½hr.); **Margao,** in the south, 5km outside the city of Benaulim (12hr.). All Mumbai fares are Rs251 for non-A/C sleeper and Rs696 for 3rd-class 3-tier A/C with blanket and pillow. Day trains cost Rs164 for non-A/C 2nd-class, and Rs462 for the chill of A/C. The *Mandovi Express 0104* (12:30pm) and the overnight *Konkan Express 0112* (4:15pm) make the return trip for the same fares. Trains for **Delhi** leave daily from the coastal town of **Vasco da Gama,** near the airport (*Goa Exp. 2779:* 2pm, 41hr., Rs450/1750).

BUSES

Buses are the cheapest way to reach Goa from: **Bangalore** (16hr.); **Mangalore** (12hr.); **Miraj** (10hr., Rs112); **Mumbai** (15hr.); **Mysore** (15hr., Rs212); **Pune** (12hr., Rs173-250). In most cities, you can buy the tickets on the bus. **Private carriers** offer more extensive services and more comfort (except for the infamous "video coaches," see p. 51). Book private coaches through a travel agency or at one of the shacks near the bus terminals. Prices for: **Bangalore** (Rs200-330); **Mangalore** (Rs143-182); **Miraj** (Rs120-133); **Mumbai** (Rs255-366); **Mysore** (Rs222-247); **Pune** (Rs230-286). Check the individual town listings for more bus information.

▣ LOCAL TRANSPORTATION

Traveling by bus along Goa's narrow roads is not as stomach-wrenching as it often is in other parts of the country; the popular routes are generally packed but short.

BUSES

Intrastate buses go between the **Kadamba Bus Terminals** in the transport hubs of Panjim, Mapusa, and Margao. **Express buses** are the fastest; other buses stop in every village and rice paddy. There are few bus stops in the state, and most locals simply flag down non-express buses as they pass by. For more details on interstate bus travel, see listings for **Margao** (p. 193), **Mapusa** (p. 180), and **Panjim** (p. 174).

TAXIS AND RICKSHAWS

Tourist vehicles (expensive minivans) and **taxis** are available for short jaunts or longer-term rentals (Rs8 per km). **Auto-rickshaws** disinclined to set their meters zip between beaches or herd passengers in at rickshaw stands in town (Rs8 1st km, Rs5 each additional km). Their fares tend to be a little more than half of what taxis charge. During the off season and when heading to more remote areas, all require return fares. The distinctly Goan **motorcycle-rickshaws** (Rs5/Rs3 each additional km) or **pilot taxis** are the cheapest options.

MOTORCYCLES

The simplest, riskiest, and sexiest transportation method employed by many visitors is an automatic Enfield, Honda Kinetic, or Yamaha **motorcycle,** which can be rented by the day or month through most hotels and guest houses in virtually every town and beach. Prices fluctuate by season (Rs150-300 per day). Technically, you must obtain an Indian or international driver's license in order to drive one, but license enforcement on the beaches is quite lax (except in Anjuna during Wednesday's flea market). If you are pulled over by an officer and do not have a valid license, keep your cool and remember that a little *baksheesh* might go far. (Still, *Let's Go* does not recommend bribing police officers.) **Helmets** can be hard to come by, but some official bike rental places might be able to find you one. Or pick up a helmet (with a visor to block dust) in Panjim or Mumbai as a souvenir.

GOA

GOOD TO GOA Since word got out that Goa is an earthly paradise, huge resorts and small guest houses alike have been falling all over themselves to house and bathe legions of visitors. But laundering all those sweaty tourists has taken its toll, draining some village wells dry or contaminating them with salty sea water. You can help preserve Goa's glory by taking bucket baths, turning off the shower as you suds up, and having a *dhobi* wash your clothes instead of washing them in the sink. The Ghost of Tourists Past litters beaches with bottles; think about the future of tiny Goa and put your junk in a garbage can. After all, you're eating fish from just off shore. If you are considering a long stay, volunteering for one of Goa's Non-Governmental Organizations (NGOs) allow you to help on a local level. ECOFORUM in Mapusa publishes a book, *Fish Curry & Rice* (Rs200), which has a listing of Goa's activist groups.

BICYCLES

Bicycles (Rs4-6 per hr., Rs40-60 per day) can be hired from hotels and guest houses. You can pedal along the whole of Colva Beach when the tide is out; plan to get wet, and bring plastic bags for cameras and valuables. Cycling long distances is tough since rental bikes have one gear and there are many hills.

NORTH GOA

PANJIM (PANAJI)पणजी ☎0832

Red-tiled Portuguese mansions, Hindu shrines, and Catholic chapels all jostle for space in compact Panjim (pop. 100,000), Goa's capital. Many of the town's crumbling buildings date from around 1759, when the viceroy moved his residence from Old Goa to Yusuf Adil Shah's old palace in Panjim (today's Secretariat). Panjim bustles with activity and has plenty of amenities for the beach-bound traveler. The city deserves more than just a quick stocking-up stop, thanks to its proximity to lovely Old Goa and the hidden Hindu temples farther inland.

▐ TRANSPORTATION

Flights: Air India (☎431101/2/3/4). 18th June Rd., next to Hotel Fidalgo. Open M-F 9:30am-1pm and 2-5pm, Sa 9:30am-1pm. **Indian Airlines** (☎223826). DB Marg, at the northwestern edge. Open M-F 10am-1pm and 2-5pm. **Jet Airways** (☎431472). Patto Plaza, just south of the Patto Tourist Hotel. Open M-F 9:30am-1pm and 2-5pm. **Jet Air** (☎226595), 102 Rizvi Chambers, 1st fl., at the corner of Gen. Bernarado Guedes and Heliodoro Salgado Rd., is an agent for **TWA, Gulf Air,** and **Air Canada.** Open M-F 9:30am-1pm and 2-5:30pm, Sa 9:30am-1pm. **Alitalia** (☎430940). 18th June Rd. Open 9:30am-1pm and 2-5pm, Sa 9:30am-1pm. **Thakkers Travel Service** (☎436678). Mahalaxmi Chambers, on 18th June Rd. and up 4 flights of stairs, is an agent for **KLM.** Open M-F 9:30am-1pm and 2-5:30pm.

Trains: Karmali, 12km east of town, is the nearest station on the Konkan Railway (see **Getting There,** p. 172). Reservation office for **Konkan Railway** is upstairs at the **Kadamba Bust Terminal,** Patto. Open daily 8am-2pm. You can also buy tickets at Karmali Station from 8am-2pm. Buses and tourist taxis shuttle to Panjim.

Buses: Kadamba Bus Terminal, Patto. Prices listed are for regular/deluxe service. **Interstate buses** to: **Bangalore** (14hr.; 4 per day 3:30-7pm; Rs200/330); **Mangalore** (10hr.; 6 per day, 6:15am-8:30pm; Rs143/182); **Miraj** (10hr.; 3 per day 8:30-10:30am; Rs120/133); **Mumbai** (16hr.; 2 per day 3:30-5pm; Rs255/366); **Mysore**

(15hr.; 2 per day 3-5pm; Rs222/247); **Pune** (12hr.; 3 per day 6:15am-7pm; Rs230/286). Advance reservations can be made at the **booking office.** Most counters are open 9am-1pm and 2-5:30pm, but try to show up before 4pm, as some close early. **Private buses** departing for the same destinations can be booked at many hotels and travel agents, or just show up at the bus stand along the river and hunt out a bus going the right way. **Intrastate buses** zip to destinations throughout Goa 6am-7:30pm. To: **Calangute** (40min.; every 15min.; Rs7); **Mapusa** (regular 30min.; express 15min. every 5min.; Rs5-6); **Margao** (regular 45min.; express 30min. every 5-10min.; Rs15); **Ponda** (every 15min.; Rs12); **Vasco Da Gama** (every 15min.; Rs15).

Local Transportation: Taxis gather in front of the Hotel Mandovi, the Tourist Hostel, and at stands along 18th June Rd. **Auto-rickshaws** line up near the Municipal Market and the Municipal Gardens. In good weather, budding capitalists hawk **motorbikes** across the street from the GPO. It's inadvisable to rent in Panjim without an international driver's license. One-speed **bikes** are available at **Daud M. Aga** (☎ 222670). Opposite the Cinema National entrance. Open M-Sa 9am-1pm and 2-7pm, Su 9am-noon.

🔆 🔁 ORIENTATION AND PRACTICAL INFORMATION

At the intersection of the **Mandovi** and **Ourem Rivers,** Panjim is easy to get around on foot. On the east bank of the Ourem is the **Patto** area and its chaotic **bus terminal. Emidio Gracia Rd.** leads west uphill from the Ourem to **Church Sq.,** dominated by the towering white **Immaculate Conception Church.** From here, **18th June Rd.,** featuring many hotels, restaurants, and shops, leads southwest. **Dayanand Bandodkar (DB) Marg (Avenida Dom Joao Castro)** follows the bank of the Mandovi River. Most budget guest houses are in the old Portuguese quarter, **Fontainhas,** south of Emidio Garcia Rd. by the Ourem River.

Tourist Office: Government of India Tourist Office (☎ 223412). Communidade Bldg., Church Sq. Open M-F 9:30am-1pm and 2-6pm, Sa 9:30am-1pm. **Dept. of Tourism, Government of Goa** (☎ 225583; fax 228819; goatour@goa.goa.nic.in). Patto Tourist Home, between the traffic bridge and the footbridge on the bank of the Ourem River. Offers tours and the useful Goa Tourist Directory. Open 24hr. **GTDC** (☎ 226515; www.goacom.com/goatourism). Trionora Apartments, Dr. Alvares Costa Rd. Arranges accommodations, tours around Goa, and sunset cruises.

Currency Exchange: State Bank of India (☎ 224662). DB Marg, opposite the Hotel Mandovi. Open for exchange on the 2nd fl. M-F 10am-1:30pm and 3-4pm, Sa 10am-noon. **Thomas Cook,** DB Marg (☎ 221312). Exchanges cash and all traveler's checks at better-than-bank rates. Open M-Sa 9:30am-6pm; Oct.-Mar. also Su 10am-5pm.

Pharmacy: Farmacia Salcete (☎ 225959). 18th June Rd., just beyond the Municipal Gardens. Open M-Sa 9am-7:30pm.

Hospital: Dr. Bhandare Hospital (☎ 224966). Fontainhas. Go south on 31st January Rd., passing the Panjim Inn; bear left where the road forks, turn right at the People's High School, and take the 1st left.

Police: Headquarters (☎ 224488 or 223400). Malaca Rd., on the west edge of the Azad Maidan gardens.

Telephones: Panjim has recently switched from 5- to 6-digit phone numbers. Replace the leading 4 with 22, 42, or 43 in any 5-digit numbers you may stumble across (e.g. 45675 to 225675, 425675, or 435675).

Internet: Many options, like **Cosy Nook,** 18th June Rd., beyond the Municipal Garden, provide fast connections. Rs1 per min., Rs50 per hr. Open daily 8:30am-8:30pm.

Post Office: From the Patto Bridge at the Ourem River, continue along the road into Panjim. The **GPO** is on the left behind a garden. A public phone inside the GPO allows calling card calls. **Postal Code:** 403001.

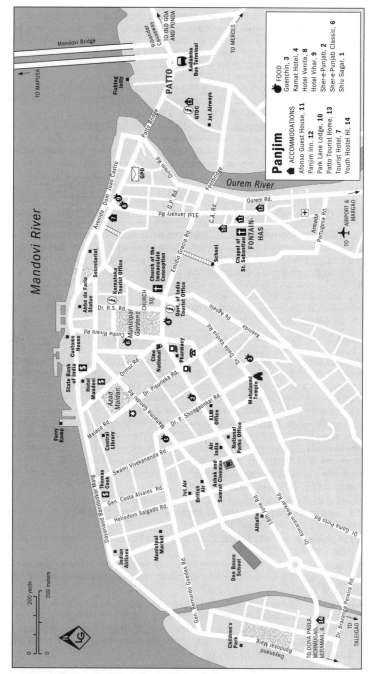

Panjim

▲ ACCOMMODATIONS
Afonso Guest House, **11**
Panjim Inn, **12**
Park Lane Lodge, **10**
Patto Tourist Home, **13**
Tourist Hotel, **7**
Youth Hostel HI, **14**

● FOOD
Goenchin, **3**
Kamat Hotel, **4**
Hotel Venite, **8**
Hotel Vihar, **9**
Sher-e-Punjab, **2**
Sher-e-Punjab Classic, **6**
Shiu Sagar, **1**

ACCOMMODATIONS

Guest houses and hotels run a brisk business, but since most people only stay a night or two before heading out to the beach, same-day accommodations are not hard to find. Standards are high; tariffs often double around Christmas. Most of the best places are in Fontainhas, south of the footbridge by the Ourem River.

Alfonso Guesthouse (☎222359). Fontainhas, on the same street as San Sebastian Chapel. This very pleasant family-run guest house has a terrace and 8 spacious rooms with attached baths. Check-out 9am. Rooms Rs450. Off season: Rs350. ❷

Patto Tourist Home (☎225715). Near the bus terminal on the road along the Ourem River. Clean rooms with bath and TV. In the bldg. with the Dept. of Tourism. 24hr. check-in. Dorms Rs80; triples Rs400. Off season: Rs260/40. ❶

Park Lane Lodge (☎227154; pklaldg@goatelecom.com). Fontainhas, near San Sebastian Chapel. From 31st January Rd., walk to San Sebastian Chapel and turn right up a flight of stairs. TV room and terrace. Rooms with common bath are roomier than those with attached bath. Check-out 8am. Internet. Singles Rs250; doubles Rs300-400. ❷

Panjim Inn (☎226523; www.panjiminn.com). On 31st January Rd., Fontainhas. On the left when heading south from Emidio Gracia Rd. This 18th-century mansion has a vine-covered veranda and gorgeous rooms. Internet service and A/C. Hot showers in all attached baths. Check-out 9am. Singles Rs585-710; doubles Rs770-990. Off season: Rs410-510. Rooms at the adjacent annex **Pousada** are 10% cheaper. ❸

Youth Hostel HI (☎22533). In suburban Miramar, a 45min. walk from the town center along DB Marg. Worth the hike if you want to pinch rupees. Buses from town head out here; ask for Miramar. Meals Rs18. Check-out 8am. Dorms Rs40, HI members Rs20. ❶

Tourist Hotel (☎227103). Dr. Alvares Costa Rd., in an institutional, multi-storied white bldg. a few blocks northwest after crossing Patto Bridge. Rooms have attached baths as well as fans, phones, clean sheets, towels, and TVs. Check-out noon. Doubles Rs500, with A/C Rs650-850. Off season: Rs400/420-630. ❷

FOOD

Panjim's restaurants are a good reason to stay in the city longer. Visitors can pick from chow mein, lasagna, South Indian snacks, Punjabi *dal*, and Goan fish curry.

Hotel Venite, on 31st January Rd., near the river. A sign will direct you up a narrow staircase to this mellow and airy space. Try the fish curry (Rs80) and nightly specials (Rs60-100). Beer Rs40, coconut or cashew *feni* Rs20. Open M-Sa 8am-3pm and 7-10pm. ❶

Shiu Sagar, MG Rd., in Shiu Sagar Hotel, opposite Centurian Bank. The most popular veg. fare in Panjim. Entrees Rs35-50. Open daily 8am-11pm. ❶

Sher-e-Punjab Classic, on the 1st fl. of Hotel Aroma, at the west edge of the Municipal Gardens. Delicacies emerge from the restaurant's well-known *tandoor* (Rs50-90). Open daily noon-3:30pm and 7pm-midnight. The cheaper and more low-key branch, **Sher-e-Punjab**, is on 18th June Rd., on the right as you walk away from the river. There's a lively bar scene at night. Beer Rs40. Entrees under Rs60. Open daily noon-11pm. ❶

Kamat Hotel, 18th June Rd., in a prime location next to the Municipal Gardens, is busy serving up *samosas* (Rs13) and generous *thalis* (Rs23). Open daily 8am-9:30pm. ❶

Hotel Vihar, MG Rd., north of Hotel Venite. This popular stainless steel and formica joint serves up meal-sized *dosas* (Rs12) and a veg. *thali* (Rs22). Open M-Sa 7am-9pm. ❶

Goenchin, Dr. Dada Vaidya Rd., on the left as you come from Church Sq. Look for a sign pointing uphill. Delicious Chinese food (only slightly Indianized) in a lush setting. Entrees Rs90-150. Veg. choices Rs60-90. Open daily 12:30-3pm and 7:30-11pm. ❷

GOA

⊙ SIGHTS

Not even tourist offices pretend that there are any real sights worth seeing in Panjim. Still, it's a pleasant enough place for idle meandering, particularly in the Fontainhas area on the west bank of the Ourem. The bright white **Chapel of San Sebastian,** dating from the 1880s, stands at the end of a short street opening off 31st January Rd. The life-sized statue of the crucified Christ that used to hang in the Palace of the Inquisition in Old Goa now hangs here, head unbowed. Towering over Church Sq. is the **Mary Immaculate Conception Church (Igreja Maria Immaculada Conceicão),** the top tier of a stack of white and blue criss-crossing staircases. The original chapel, consecrated in 1541, was the first stop for Portuguese sailors. The chapel was renovated in the 17th century. This is the main place of worship for local Christians, and its musty, dark interior is heavy with silence and prayer. *(Open Su and holy days 10:30am-1pm and 6:15-7pm, other days 9am-1pm and 3:30-6pm.)*

The **Secretariat,** constructed in the 16th century as a palace and fortress for Yusuf Adil Shah of Bijapur, sits on the banks of the River Mandovi. The Portuguese rebuilt it in 1615, and in 1759 it became the palace of the Portuguese viceroy.

🎵 🎭 ENTERTAINMENT AND NIGHTLIFE

Panjim is well set-up for the recreational pursuit of consuming alcohol. Local brews are sold in small shops, and tiny bars dot the city, especially in Fontainhas. Try Kwality Bar & Restaurant, Church Sq., a place where Chinese flavor, Stevie Wonder tunes, and Goan hipsters all come together; or the hole-in-the-wall **Sunshine Bar** at the corner of Emidio Gracia Rd. and 31st January Rd. Government-run and private companies organize **evening cruises** on the Mandovi River. The cruises feature traditional dancing—*denki, fijddi*, Portuguese, and *corredmino* styles—and stunning views of the sunset at sea. Book at any GTDC office, or just show up at the pier and look for the boat. (1hr.; daily 6, 7:15, 8:30pm).

OLD GOA ओल्ड गोवा

The cavernous Portuguese churches of Old Goa, 9km east of Panjim, prove that Europeans flocked to Goa long before Calangute's 1970 hippie blowouts. Old Goa's colonial days began in 1510, when Alfonso de Albuquerque trounced the Bijapur Sultan, Adil Shah, and seized the city on the Mandovi, then known as Ela, giving the Portuguese a virtual monopoly on regional trade. The sailors' epic debauchery attracted the Inquisition's Jesuit priests who preached and proselytized to hedonists and heathens alike with the same zeal that built Old Goa's ornate cathedrals. Old Goa declined as Portuguese power faded, the Mandovi River filled with silt, and malaria ran rampant. By the 18th century, the party was over for good, and the government seat moved to Panjim. Today the city is looked after by the Archaeological Survey of India, which plasters the churches to protect them from the monsoon. The churches are all that remain of the city's glory.

🚌 TRANSPORTATION

Auto-rickshaws (Rs50-70), **motorcycle taxis,** and **bicycles** (available for rent in Panjim) make the scenic 9km trip along the Mandovi riverbank from Panjim to Old Goa. **Buses** also shuttle from Panjim's bus terminal (20min., every 15min. 7am-7pm, Rs4). If you bike, avoid the main road; continue past the traffic circle beyond the Kadamba bus stand in Patto (the left fork goes directly to Old Goa) and go straight; take the smaller left-hand road parallel to the main road, then take the first fork to the left and follow the road through a village. Take a left at the first chapel and the road will meet up with NH4 again. Finally, turn right into Old Goa. Stands and "tourist restaurants" huddle at both ends of the Basilica de Bom Jesus.

💿 SIGHTS

As you arrive from Panjim, the **Basilica de Bom Jesus** will be on your right, the **Se Cathedral** on your left. Unofficial guides frequenting the churches in search of earthly reward expect to be tipped in return for their knowledge.

BASILICA DE BOM JESUS. Built between 1594 and 1605 to house the remains of St. Francis Xavier, the Basilica de Bom Jesus (Cathedral of the Good Jesus) is Old Goa's most legendary site. Resplendent with gold, the basilica, with its 3m statue of St. Ignatius presiding over all comings and goings, attracts sunburnt Australians, Sikh tourists, and Sisters of Charity alike. St. Francis Xavier's mausoleum is off to the right of the altar behind a curtain of stars. Inside the windowed silver casket, a lightbulb shines on St. Francis' shriveled body, "donated" by Cosimo III de Medici in exchange for a pillow on which the saint's head had rested. Though St. Francis looks sadly shrunken now, his body refused to decay for months after his death. He's still unrotted and intact (though his baptizing arm now lays in state in Rome). A doorway to the left of the mausoleum leads to a small room with historical tidbits and photographs of the relic. Stairs lead to an **art gallery.** On the way out is a lovely cloister. *(Opposite the Se Cathedral. Open M-Sa 9am-6:30pm, Su 10:30am-6:30pm. Gallery open M and W-Sa 9:30am-12:30pm and 2-5:30pm, Su 10:30am-12:30pm and 2-5:30pm.)*

AROUND THE BASILICA DE BOM JESUS. As you exit the Basilica de Bom Jesus, make a left at the first street, then take an immediate right. Up this hill are the romantic ruins of the Church of St. Augustine. The 46m tower has been standing since 1602. Gravestones pave the floor, and knobby alcoves hint at carvings that have long since eroded. Below the church is the massive Church and Convent of St. Monica Christon, built in 1636. Its "miracle cross" was once well known for its tendency to open its eyes, bleed from its wounds, and speak. *(Always open.)*

SÉ CATHEDRAL. On the left, along the main road from Panjim, the yellow Sé Cathedral complex presides over an expanse of lawn. After the Chapel of St. Catherine on your left is the **Convent and Church of St. Francis of Assisi.** The frescoed ceiling arches over a gravestone floor, paved with coats of arms from the 17th century on. Mary and Jesus are depicted with dark hair and complexions, similar to the dark-skinned cherubs in the Cathedral itself. *(Open daily 8:30am-5:30pm.)* The attached convent is now the none-too-thrilling **Archaeological Museum,** which exhibits portraits of the viceroys, currency from "India Portuguesa," Christian icons, and sculpture from Goa's Hindu temples. *(Rs5. Open Sa-Th 10am-5pm.)*

Beyond the museum is the **Sé Cathedral** dedicated to St. Catherine. Erected by the viceroy in 1564, the vast, three-naved cathedral took 80 years to build. One of the twin towers was destroyed by lightning in 1775. The other houses the mellow-toned **Sino du Ouro (Golden Bell),** said to be the largest bell in Asia. Sepulchres of expensive imported stone line the floor. Scenes from the life of St. Catherine are carved into the grand golden altar, and 14 smaller altars are set within the cavernous church. *(Open daily 8:30am-5:30pm.)*

AROUND THE SÉ CATHEDRAL. From the Cathedral's grand entrance, head straight out to the road and make a left. Signs will point you to the nearby **Church of St. Cajetan.** According to local lore, Italian friars of the Order of Theatines built the church on top of an ancient Hindu temple in the 17th century. Today, the church is known for its dome (modeled after St. Peter's in Rome) and the wood-work of its interior. *(Church open daily 8:30am-5:30pm, but may close for a 12:30-3pm siesta.)* The ruined **gate** to Yusuf Adil Shah's collapsed palace, by the entrance to the church grounds, rises in forlorn tribute to pre-Portuguese Goa. Farther up the road toward the Mandovi River is the modest **Viceroy's Arch,** whose gate bears an inscription left by Governor Francisco da Gama (r. 1597-1600) in memory of his great-grandfather, Vasco. There is a path from the arch to the Mandovi River.

🗺 DAYTRIPS FROM OLD GOA

A handful of Hindu temples near the Portuguese ruins of Old Goa are worth a look. Although far from India's finest, they remind daytrippers of the massive Hindu majority that always remained just behind the Portuguese-controlled coast.

Most of the temples hide along NH4, conveniently becoming less interesting toward drab **Ponda.** When you get tired of the temples, just hop on a bus back to **Panjim** (45min., every 15-20min. 6am-7:30pm, Rs12). Buses from Panjim are often full—tell the conductor where you want to get off, and be sure to stand near a door so you can fight your way out. The first temple is at **Mangeshi** (also called Priol) village (30min., Rs7). Head down the palm-lined path to the colorful arch that leads to the **Sri Mangesh** temple. Like most of the temples in this area, it was built in the 18th century to house deities that had been smuggled inland in the 16th century from the Inquisition-ravaged coast. Less than a 15min. walk south (1km) leads to the more sedately decorated **Sri Mahalsa,** acclaimed for the stunning wood carvings on the facades of its *mandapam* (sloping roof).

From Sri Mahalsa or the Mangeshi bus stop, get on a bus to Ponda for the 4km stretch to the Farmagudi junction. Reaching the **Sri Nagesh** temple is a 45min. uphill slog in the burning sun. At the roundabout, bear right down a narrow back road past a modern temple and through **Nageshi** village. Colorful woodcarvings in the entrance hall depict scenes from the *Ramayana* (see p. 613), though it's difficult to piece together the narrative. Ambling down the shady road for another 20min. will bring you to the red-roofed **Sri Shantadurga** temple. You'll know you've arrived when you spot the tourist taxis and the rows of stands hawking religious kitsch. Head back uphill to catch the bus back to Panjim.

MAPUSA म्हापुसा ☎ 0832

The North Goan transit hub town of Mapusa lies on a hillside, 30km north of Panjim and 10km inland from the hopping beaches at Anjuna, Calangute, and Baga. Mostly of interest to travelers for its bus terminal, beach bums from Mumbai or Bangalore jump off the bus at Mapusa and head straight for the sand. Friday's labyrinthine market lures them back to sample spices and fondle fabrics.

⌗ TRANSPORTATION. Buses shuttle frequently from the **Kadamba Bus Terminal** to a variety of sinful locations. Most intrastate buses run from 7:30am to 7:30pm and travel to: **Anjuna** (30min., every 10min., Rs5); **Arambol** (1hr., every 10min., Rs10); **Baga** and **Calangute** (30min., every 10min., Rs7); **Margao** (1½hr., every hr. 6am-8:20pm, Rs17); **Panjim** (every 5min.; local 40min., express 20min.; Rs6); **Siolim** (15min., every 15min., Rs5). If you're leaving Goa, the area around Kadamba teems with private coach operators. State-run buses also make the trip. (Long-distance booking office, opposite bus stall 8. Open daily 6am-1pm and 2-8pm.) Buses go to: **Miraj** (8hr., 10:45am, Rs115); **Mumbai** (12hr., 4:30pm, Rs250); **Pune** (12hr., 6:30am, Rs215). **Motorcycle rentals** are hard to come by, thanks to Mapusa's police crackdown on foreigners without papers.

⚞ ⁊ ORIENTATION AND PRACTICAL INFORMATION. The **State Bank of India** changes money and does cash advances (open M-F 10am-2pm, Sa 10am-noon). Head north from the bus station to the roundabout, alarmingly decorated with canons. Make a right at the roundabout and you'll see it ahead on your left. The **police station** (☎ 262231) and the **GPO** are two blocks west. **Postal Code:** 403507.

⚞ ⁊ ACCOMMODATIONS AND FOOD. Staying in Mapusa should not be necessary. It's worth taking a taxi to Calangute or Panjim rather than hanging around here. If you are forced to stay, try the well-staffed **Hotel Satya Heera ❶,** north of the bus terminal with spacious rooms, spectacular views (on the upper floors), and even an antiquated TV. (☎ 262849; satya@goa1.dot.net.in. Check-out 9am. Doubles Rs400. Off season: Rs300.) The **Tourist Hostel ❶,** at the Gandhi-statued roundabout south of the bus terminal, has adequate rooms and will make you feel like the just-off-the-bus tourist that you are. (☎ 262694. Check-out noon. Dorms Rs85; doubles Rs460. Off-season: Rs290/50.) **Ruchira ❶,** the Hotel Satyaheera's rooftop restaurant, serves Goan, Chinese, and standard Indian dishes. (Rs10-60. Open daily 7-11am and 11:30am-10:45pm.) Food stalls around the bus terminal serve the standard greasy fare, but Mapusa's **market,** southeast of the bus terminal, is for the more adventurous. Its a more authentic version of the Anjuna flea market, so if you've been craving coconuts, searching for 30cm springs, or needing a brace of live roosters, you've come to the right place. It's at its busiest every Friday (early morning-late afternoon), but there's almost always something going on.

CALANGUTE कालांगुद AND BAGA बागा ☎ 0832

The twin villages of Calangute and Baga have your name written all over them. Beachfront shacks serve up mango *lassis* while vendors from Rajasthan and Kashmir peddle carved wooden elephants, sarongs, and mirrored purses to sunburnt tourists. This former winter hang-out of the backpacker set is now the favorite stomping ground of the package tourist. Though the sugary sand and warm sea remain gorgeous, this is no longer the Goa of legend—the hedonistic heyday of free drugs and free love is long gone. Still, by late afternoon the crowds start to trickle home, and you'll be left alone with the cows to watch the sun go down.

⬛ TRANSPORTATION

Buses: Every 15min., buses from Mapusa stop at **Calangute market** and at the main roundabout en route to **Baga** (Rs3) and back to **Mapusa** (Rs7). Buses to and from **Panjim** (Rs7) stop at the market and beyond the roundabout before the beach.

Local Transportation: Tourist taxis go between Calangute and Baga for Rs40-50. **Rickshaws** and **motorbikes** make the same trip for about Rs25-30, and to Panjim (Rs70-150) and Anjuna (Rs50-100). **Motorcycle** rental is common in season (Rs150 per day). Off season, inquire near the gas station west of the market. For **bicycle** rental, ask along the main road (Rs50-60 per day).

⚞ ⁊ ORIENTATION AND PRACTICAL INFORMATION

Most buses smoke their way into **Calangute market** at the bottom of the main road that heads west to the **beach.** They also stop at the roundabout about halfway down the main east-west road before heading back to Panjim. From the market stop, continue in the same direction as the bus until you come to the roundabout and Rama Books. Turn right (north) down onto the main north-south road that runs between Calangute and Baga; the entire length of this road is lined with guest houses, restaurants, and souvenir stalls. The main east-west road leads from the **market** west to the **beach** and comprises Calangute proper.

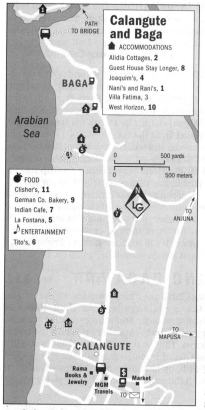

Calangute and Baga

⚓ ACCOMMODATIONS
Alidia Cottages, **2**
Guest House Stay Longer, **8**
Joaquim's, **4**
Nani's and Rani's, **1**
Villa Fatima, 3
West Horizon, **10**

Arabian Sea

🍎 FOOD
Clisher's, **11**
German Co. Bakery, **9**
Indian Cafe, **7**
La Fontana, **5**
♪ ENTERTAINMENT
Tito's, **6**

PATH TO BRIDGE

BAGA

TO ANJUNA

TO MAPUSA

CALANGUTE

Rama Books & Jewelry
MGM Travels
Market
TO ✉

Budget Travel: MGM Travels (☎/fax 276073). On the Calangute round-about. Sells plane and catamaran tickets. **STD/ISD** telephone services. Open M-Sa 7:30am-1:30pm and 2:30-5:30pm.

Currency Exchange: State Bank of India, at Calangute market. Open M-F 10am-4pm, Sa 10am-1pm. **Thomas Cook** is inside the bank. Open M-F 10am-5pm, Sa 10am-1pm. If you don't see them, ask any of the market vendors for directions.

Pharmacy: Walsons & Walsons Chemist and Druggist (☎276366). Next door to Fatima Clinic, in the same bldg. as the State Bank of India, stocks curative goodies. Open daily 8:30am-2pm and 3:30-9pm.

Post Office: In a pink bldg. south of the market. Head east from the roundabout, turn right at the market, and then take the 1st left. Open M-Sa 9am-2pm and 2:30-5pm. **Postal code:** 403516.

▛ ACCOMMODATIONS

Head north toward Baga for more pleasant surroundings, though most of the places between the villages are a fair distance from the beach. In season (Dec.-Jan.), prices can double. As usual, the taxi- and rickshaw-*wallahs* who claim a hotel is full are usually receiving commission from other places; insist on going to your first choice. Flats and houses for longer stays are usually still available in early December—the best of them are just north of Baga. Ask around.

▨ **Nani's and Rani's** (☎277014). At the northern tip of Baga, across the river. From the main road, bear right on the dirt path to the covered bridge. A bit of a haul, but worth it for a tranquil, backpacker-friendly spot. Splendid doubles with bath cluster around the popular restaurant. Doubles with bath and fan for Rs300. Off season: Rs250. ❶

Villa Fatima (☎277418; villa.fatima@sympatico.ca). On the main north-south strip, closer to Baga. Look for the sign on the left when coming from Calangute. A friendly family runs this cheerful complex, festooned with colored lights and plants. Spacious rooms with attached bath, hot water, and refrigerators surround a courtyard restaurant. Safety deposit box. Check-out 10am. Rs250-650. Off season: Rs200-450. ❷

Divine Guest House (☎279546). North of Baga. Turn in past 2 pointy-eared plaster dogs to reach this family run guest-house. Rs350-400. Off season: Rs250-300. ❷

Joaquim's (☎279696). Just off the east-west road that leads to Tito's. From the main north-south road, head east between the Sunshine Beach and Miranda Resorts and look for signs on your right to La Fantona, and continue north. Seconds from the beach. Clean rooms with attached baths. Check-out 10am. Rs300. Off season: Rs200. ❷

GOA

Guest House Stay Longer (☎277460). On the inland side of the Calangute-Baga road. Decent rooms in a wide price range. Penny-pinchers can snag the windowless ground-floor rooms with shared bath. Those who intend to stay true to the guest house's name should opt for the spacious rooms with attached baths upstairs. A pair of rooftop chairs are primed for sunset watching. Check-out 8am. Rs200-400. Off season: Rs50-150. ❷

Alidia Cottages (☎279041; alidia@rediff.com). Just beyond Villa Fatima along the road to Baga. Behind a white church on the left. Ritzy, family-run establishment with lovely rooms, all with bath. Wander through the back gate, past the tiny fishing village, and out to the beach. Safety deposit box. Check-out 11am. In Sept., rates begin to rise, reaching Rs800 by Jan. and Dec. Off season: doubles drop to Rs100-150. ❸

West Horizon (☎276489). Follow the main east-west road to the beach, and turn right just before the beach. Follow signs from the next east-west road; it's just north of Angelo's Inn. Clean rooms with attached bath. Bonus points for beach proximity. Dorms Rs500-600; doubles Rs300. Off season: rooms half-price. ❸

Tourist Dormitories, in the Calangute Resort Annex. Take the main road west toward the beach; you'll see a giant sign on your right. Cheap. Dorms Rs60. Off season: Rs40. ❶

🖪 FOOD

Numerous seafood shacks in Calangute and Baga with copycat menus offer mediocre renditions of regional delights and favorites from home. If you're just looking for a good spot to meet fellow travelers over a cold beer and a sunset, try the popular **Britto's** or **St. Anthony's,** side by side on the Baga beachfront.

German Co. Bakery, down the road to the right, opposite the Stay Longer Guest House. They swear that they use purified water in all their drinks, so linger in the shade over a fresh fruit juice (Rs10-40) and delicious homemade pastries (Rs8-35). Cinnamon rolls Rs15, omelettes Rs10-30. Open daily 8am-11pm. ❶

Indian Cafe, midway between Calangute and Baga; look for the sign on the main north-south road. This excellent, quiet lunchtime retreat serves delicious *masala dosa* (Rs20) and fruit shakes. Best and cheapest Indian food in town. Open daily 8am-6pm. ❶

Nani and Rani's Bar and Restaurant, neighboring their hotel north of Baga. Goan specialties, breezy tropical drinks, and chill card games make it worth the hike. Open daily 8am-3:30pm and 6:30-10:30pm. ❶

Clisher's, just west of the West Horizon Guest House. From the Calangute tourist complex, follow the large, fish-shaped sign. Excellent, moderately priced seafood in surroundings so quiet you can hear the waves on the shore. Indian dishes Rs30-50, seafood Rs30-60. Open daily 9am-11pm. Closed Jun. 1-Aug. 31. ❶

La Fontana, next to Joachim, across the street from Tito's. Seafood, pasta, and veggies in a friendly atmosphere allow you to transcend your belly troubles and contemplate higher things at this outpost of Tibetan, Japanese, and Chinese culinary delights. Fresh pasta Rs35-60, fish Rs65-140. Open daily 8:30am-midnight. ❶

🔺 BEACHES

It's hard to complain about the beach between Calangute and Baga. Despite all the development, the sand is still quiet in the morning, and the water always seems to be at an ideal temperature. But as the sun starts to climb higher in the sky, leather-skinned men in Speedos waddle out on to the sand. As you head north, the bodies get younger, as the backpacker crowd strives to work up a credible tan before heading off to do the North Indian circuit.

> **! WARNING.** The water on some beaches is off-limits during the monsoon season (roughly mid-June to late Aug.) because of rough waves and dangerous undertow. Ask before taking a dip, and watch for boulders and steep drop-offs.

South of Baga, a strip of beach has been set aside for water sports. **Goan Bananas** has a fleet of boats ready for just about anything (☎276362. Parasailing Rs1000). Next door, **Atlantis** will take you water-skiing (Rs650 for 15min.), set up wind-surfing lessons, rent surfboards (Rs250 per hr.), or drag you behind a boat on an inflatable banana (Rs300 for 15min.). In season, fishing boats, chartered by numerous companies, make the wet n' wild journey to the Anjuna flea market every Wednesday and offer dolphin-, crocodile-, and hippie-spotting tours for Rs200-500 per day.

■ NIGHTLIFE

Despite a raucous past, nightlife in Calangute and Baga tends to wind down early and errs on the side of resort-area hokeyness. The more upscale hotels pack their bar-restaurants with live "musicians" who'd be confined to street performing back home though there could be worse places for a night of drunken revelry.

For nightlife without the schmaltz, the **Safari: Gateway to Africa** bar—a beach shack transplanted onto the main road—pounds drums late into the night. (Happy hour 7-9pm. Open 6pm-3am). There's only one real after-hours game in town: **Tito's,** a bar-restaurant on the Baga beach that has a dance floor, boomin' hi-fi, and serves drinks (Rs60), sometimes until the break of dawn. Outside the village proper, the **West End,** a somewhat tame party venue on the road between Calangute and Panjim, hosts parties regularly in season.

■ DAYTRIPS FROM CALANGUTE

The hillside south of the Taj Holiday Village in package-touristy **Candolim** hides the impressive remains of the massive 17th-century **Aguada Fort,** which guards the mouth of the Mandovi. Follow the Candolim road south past the Taj and keep right as it winds 3km uphill. From the Calangute market, take the Mapusa bus to Sinquerim (Rs5), where the north-south road ends. Then, turn left at the bus stop and right at the chapel; a series of dirt paths winds to the top of the hill. The citadel commands an impressive view of the Mandovi and the southern coast.

ANJUNA अंजुना   ☎0832

Seaside restaurants and low, red-roofed cottages cover Anjuna's palm-fringed shoreline. For many a budget hedonist, the town remains the Goan ideal: long, lazy days on the beach, wild, raving nights, and liberal doses of cheap drugs to smooth the transition between the two. But the times they are a-changin', and while Anjuna still buzzes with beach raves, full-moon parties, jungle boogies, and other breeds of psychedelic mayhem in peak season, much of the liveliest partying these days has moved to north to Vagator or south to Gokarna. Regardless, the village's charms (or vices, for in Anjuna, they're one and the same) leave little room for complaint—each day is tagged by a beautiful sunset, each week brings free-market madness in the form of Anjuna's famous flea market (closed off-season), and each month is marked by the world-renowned full-moon rave. As Christmas approaches, the parties escalate in intensity and frequency. Though the scene isn't what it once was, Anjuna still plays host to a crazy cast of characters: from freaks to fishermen, package tourists to smacksters, and Euro-yuppies to Kashmiri handicraft hawkers, Anjuna has something for everyone.

> **WARNING.** **Theft occurs frequently in Anjuna,** particularly on party nights. Carry important documents and valuables with you or (better still) lock them somewhere safe.

TRANSPORTATION

Buses: Buses to **Mapusa** (20min., Rs5) stop at the main intersection in town and at the end of the road above the beach. Buses to **Vagator** and **Chapora** leave from the main intersection (10min., every 30-40min., Rs3). You can also flag buses down as they trundle along the road from the beach. If your bus doesn't appear, hop on one to Mapusa and make your connection there.

Local Transportation: **Motorcycles** (Rs150-250 per day) and **bicycles** (Rs100 per day) can be rented along the main road.

ORIENTATION AND PRACTICAL INFORMATION

From the main intersection (crowned by the Starco Restaurant), roads lead west to the beachfront and bus stand, east to Mapusa and most banking facilities, south to the flea market and restaurants, and north to Vagator and some of the main party venues. For a small town, Anjuna sprawls over a surprisingly large area. Most get around by motor bike; be prepared for distances to be longer than you expect. Many places listed below have abbreviated hours in the off-season.

Budget Travel: MGM Travels (☎274317). Deals with plane tickets, reconfirmations, and car rentals. Open M-Sa 9:30am-6pm.

Currency Exchange: Bank of Baroda, straight east of the main intersection. Cashes traveler's checks and gives Visa cash advances. Open daily 9:30am-1pm. **Orchard Food Stores.** From the main intersection head east, take the 1st right after Coutinho's Nest, and then the first left. Cashes Thomas Cook traveler's checks. Open daily 8am-9pm. Closed Su in the off season.

Bookstore: Walk About Books, in the Oxford Stores. Open M-Sa 9:30am-9:30pm.

Telephones: Laxmi, just south of and behind Mary's Holiday Home. Has 24hr. **STD/ISD.**

Internet: There are tons of email places in Anjuna. For the lowest rates, try **Nehal Communications,** which flanks the bus stand by the beach. Rs1 per min., minimum 10min. Open daily 8:30am-midnight. The **nameless computer shack** near Guru Bar has the same rates and an ocean view.

Post Office: 2km up the road from the beach on the right. Open M-Sa 8:30am-1pm and 3-5pm. **Postal Code:** 403509.

ACCOMMODATIONS

Anjuna has acquired a somewhat undeserved reputation as a difficult place to find a bed, particularly during the peak season. A lack of phones in some guest houses makes getting reservations tricky, but you can normally find a room somewhere just by showing up. Guest houses hug the beachfront and the main east-west road. "Room To Let" signs are everywhere. The large number of long-termers in Anjuna means that houses here aren't as prone to the insane Christmas price fluctuations of many of the places farther south. South of the flea market is a veritable colony of long-term tourists, a good place to look for bare-bones lodgings for stays ranging from a week to several months. As usual, bargain away off-season.

Mary's Holiday Home (☎273216). Next to the beachfront bus stand. Clean, quiet, and close to the beach. Simple rooms with attached bath face inland. Satisfied customers sing the praises of the showers. Check-out 10am. Doubles Rs200-400. ❶

Manali Guest House (☎273477). Just south off the main intersection. This friendly spot in a central location offers email and a convenience store. All rooms have shared bath: Rs150-200. Off-season Rs100-150. ❶

Cabin Disco's (☎273254). On the south side of the road, just east of the main intersection. Cool clientele boogie-woogie their way into comfy rooms after a mellow evening in the groovy bar-restaurant. Check-out noon. Singles Rs200; doubles Rs300-500. Off-season as low as Rs150. ❶

Coutinho's Nest (☎274386). A 15min. walk east from the main intersection. An excellent, affable place with a rooftop terrace. Check-out 10am. Doubles Rs200–500. ❷

Lolita's Guest House (☎273289). Just north of the Orchard Store, a 30min. walk from the beach. Freshly-painted bungalows and immaculate doubles with bath, fridge, cable TV, and sound systems. Call ahead Dec.-Jan. Rs400-500. Off-season Rs250. Discounts for longer stays. ❷

Guru Bar-Restaurant and Guest House (☎273319). One of the many basic cliffside options. Bare rooms are serviceable, but the outdoor common shower can get a bit muddy. Rooms Rs150-200. ❶

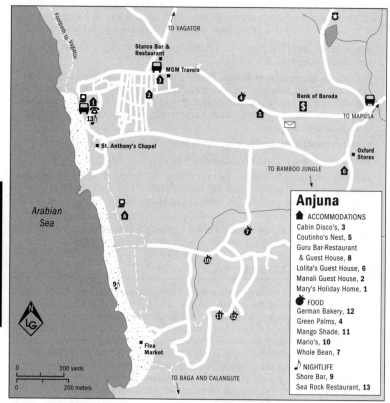

TO VAGATOR

Starco Bar & Restaurant

MGM Travels

3

2

4

Bank of Baroda

5

TO MAPUSA

St. Anthony's Chapel

13

1

Oxford Stores

TO BAMBOO JUNGLE

6

Arabian Sea

8

7

10

9

11 **12**

Flea Market

0 | 200 yards
0 | 200 meters

TO BAGA AND CALANGUTE

Anjuna

🏠 ACCOMMODATIONS
Cabin Disco's, **3**
Coutinho's Nest, **5**
Guru Bar-Restaurant & Guest House, **8**
Lolita's Guest House, **6**
Manali Guest House, **2**
Mary's Holiday Home, **1**

🍎 FOOD
German Bakery, **12**
Green Palms, **4**
Mango Shade, **11**
Mario's, **10**
Whole Bean, **7**

♪ NIGHTLIFE
Shore Bar, **9**
Sea Rock Restaurant, **13**

Footpath to Vagator

GOA

🍴 FOOD

The food served up at most of Anjuna's seaside restaurants is fast, cheap, greasy, and plentiful—perfect for snacks and sunset dinners. Those seeking variety will be better off at the restaurants that line the roads farther inland. Several vegan restaurants cater to the crunchy crowd, and falafel stands can be found anywhere. On Wednesdays, an army of food vendors materializes out of nowhere to make the **flea market**, Anjuna's premier spot for lunch or early dinner—the atmosphere is unbeatable. These places, and some of those listed below, are closed off season.

🍴 **German Bakery,** watch carefully for the sign; from the flea market road, cross the paved road and follow a worn dirt path east, or take the paved road east of Mario's. Not to be confused with the German Bakery at the Paradise Restaurant on the main road. Laid-back atmosphere comes complete with savory baked goodies every morning (Rs15-40). Veg. and North Indian food at night (Rs35-75). Open daily 7am-midnight. ❶

🍴 **Mango Shade,** Just west of the German Bakery. This often-packed spot offers cheaper food but has less atmosphere. Fresh fruit juices and *lassis* Rs20-40, sandwiches and toasts with delicious spreads (avocado, nutella) Rs30-40. Open daily 8am-5pm. ❶

Whole Bean, along the road between town and the flea market. Vegan tofu shop pours out soy milkshakes in a variety of flavors (Rs30-45). Homemade tofu and tempeh sandwiches (Rs50-60), dairy delights, and breakfast combos. Open daily 8am-5:30pm. ❶

Green Palms, on the Mapusa road, about 1.5km inland. Delicious falafel sandwiches Rs50, banana milkshakes Rs20, and melancholy Israeli pop music. Open M-Sa 10am-11pm. ❶

Mario's, from the flea market follow the road north and make a right at the end. Spacious place serves up fresh seafood (Rs60-75) and Indian rice dishes (Rs35-50). Open daily 8am-noon and 6pm-midnight. ❶

🏖 BEACHES

Not surprisingly, Anjuna's postcard-pretty shores draw crowds in season, when tanned and toned ravers in various states of tanked and stoned inebriation crash all along the strip—Wednesdays are particularly happening. The beach is plagued with annoyingly persistent hawkers every day, though; practically the only things not for sale are tranquility and solitude.

🛍 SHOPPING

"Like something?" If you've been eyeing the sarongs, *bindis*, bracelets, and magic boxes that clutter roadside stands, a trip to the **Anjuna flea market** will show you endless permutations of these tourist staples. Every Wednesday in season, the abandoned stalls and wooden poles of the market transform into a wilderness of colored fabrics and bargaining people. You'll even be able to check out those rave pants before you buy them.

🎵 NIGHTLIFE

THE RAVES. The sloping hills of Anjuna have gained international renown in recent years as a hip and happening rave venue. The monthly full moon brings out the werewolf that lurks inside many of Goa's tourists, transforming them from placid beach-chillers into wild, snarling party-animals, especially during Goa's peak season. Christmas and New Year's Eve are the biggest nights, but things are pretty wild all year round. The roads are full of people motorcycling from party to party, and huge fields are flooded by rivers of ravers. Domestic and European DJs of varying quality broadcast the rave's techno soundtrack to a core of gyrating dancers. Understandably, many locals bemoan these monthly debauches. The 24hr. party people have spurned a recent ban on all music after 10pm, though police occasionally break up a rave.

OTHER NIGHTLIFE. If there isn't any scheduled action, most of the crowd heads to the **Shore Bar,** right in the middle of the beach. The terraced steps leading down to the beach are choked with beer-guzzling sunbathers or stargazers at most hours of day and night. Upstairs, the indispensable black lights flicker and imported DJs pilot the gargantuan sound system, while techno ravers go for broke on the small, sandy dance floor. Hours vary wildly by season. The **Sea Rock Restaurant,** just south of the bus stand, is another popular hangout, especially for Westerners. Don't worry if you're not hungry—only a few of the packed restaurant's occupants are dining at any one time; the rest are having coffee, tea, or juice, scoping each other out, or sneaking a joint. Farther south, the **Guru Bar** serves tall cold ones late into the night. However, much of the busiest partying these days goes on down the road in Vagator; those with motorbikes make the commute back and forth to get the best of both worlds.

VAGATOR वागातोर ☎ 0832

Of all the northern beach towns in Goa, Vagator comes closest to striking the perfect balance between hotspot and hideaway. Popular but not over-populated, scenic but not seedy, Vagator suns all day and raves all night without losing its cheerful, down-home vibe. The town houses a large number of long-term visitors, but the regulars here seem less jaded than their southern counterparts; the rigors of the tourism boom have yet to sap Vagator's easy grace.

■ **TRANSPORTATION. Buses** stop at the crossroads about 1km inland, where the road forks for Chapora and Ozran, and run to: **Anjuna** (every hr. 7am-7pm, Rs3); **Chapora** (every 30min. 6:30am-8pm, Rs5); **Mapusa** (every 30min. 6:45am-7pm, Rs5). **Prakash Motors,** on the main road, rents and repairs **motorcycles** at good rates. (Rs150-250 per day. Open daily 8am-8:30pm.) *Touts* along the road from Ozran Beach rent motor bikes at similar rates. This area is also a good place for **bicycle rentals.** From behind Big Vagator Beach, **taxis** run to **Anjuna** (Rs50), **Arambol** (Rs250), **Chapora** (Rs30), and **Mapusa** (Rs150).

■ **ORIENTATION AND PRACTICAL INFORMATION.** Most resources for the budget traveler line the street that runs east-west from Big Vagator Beach. The **Rainbow Bookshop,** opposite the Primrose Bar, sells and swaps used **books.** A **police booth** looks out over the Big and Little Vagator beaches from atop the stairs that connect them. (Officer present M-F 9am-5pm in season.) The **Sapna Cyber Cafe,** on the dirt path beside Big Vagator, lets you check your email within the sound of the surf. (Rs50 per hr. Open daily 9am-6pm.) **Lalita Communications,** just inland, offers **currency exchange,** provides travel services, and has computers for Internet fun. (☎274481. Internet Rs50 per hr. Open daily 9:30am-10pm.) Follow the signs from the main road. The nearest **post office** is in **Anjuna.**

■ **ACCOMMODATIONS AND FOOD.** Vagator tends to cater to people here for the long haul, though in the past few years, more short-term visitors have made the trip to town. Guest houses line the main east-west road and the path to Ozran Beach, to the south. Off season, many guest houses close. ■**Reshma Guesthouse ❶,** on the south side of the road from Big Vagator Beach, is cozy and communal. (☎273568. Rooms Rs150-300. Closed Apr.-Sept.) Follow the yellow signs north of

Big Vagator Road to **Dolrina ❶**, a large and popular guest house run by a friendly family. (☎/fax 273382. Book well in advance Dec.-Mar. Doubles Rs275-350. Off-season: Rs150.) Porches surround a green garden at the tranquil **Jolly Jolly Lester ❷**, along the main road to Big Vagator. The hotel has a safe for valuables. (☎273620. Checkout 10am. Singles Rs200-400; doubles Rs350-800.)

For food, Vagator's restaurants dish up good food at low prices. Pick up a snack of pineapple or papaya from the **vendors** next to the Snackataria de World Peace. If your tolerance for beach food has diminished, try **Abu John's ❶**, Big Vagator Road. With its open kitchen, this is a popular dinner spot for tandoori and barbecue dishes. Don't miss the marvelous *naan* for Rs10-20. (Entrees Rs40-60. Open daily 8am-noon and 6pm-midnight. Closed Mar. 31-Dec. 3.) **Le Blue Bird ❶**, near the seashore along the Ozran Beach road, is particularly mellow and comfy. Patrons lounge under the thatched roof while they enjoy delicious, reasonably priced Indian and French cuisine. (Entrees Rs50-80. Open daily 9am-2pm and 6-11pm.) **Snackataria de World Peace ❶**, overlooking Big and Little Vagator beaches, at the end of the left fork of Big Vagator Road, is a great place to eat lunch. The sign says, "Shawn's Juicy Joint." The Rs30 veg. *thali* lures you in. Ice cream seals the deal. (Open daily 10am-6pm.) The **Garden Villa ❶**, next door to Abu John's, dishes up Goan, Punjabi, Chinese, and Italian food with equal flair. Bootlegged American movies aired nightly at 7:30pm. (Entrees Rs25-40. Open daily 8am-11pm.)

◨◪ **SIGHTS AND BEACHES.** The southern **Ozran Beach** reigns as Vagator's most mellow and picturesque strip of sand—coconut palms, tranquil beach-shacks, and only a minimum of vendor-fuss and daytrippers. At the southern tip of Ozran is a small bay—deep, calm, and perfect for lazy swimming. Farther north, Vagator's distinctive, gently shelving hills lead, like giant steps, to the shore at **Little Vagator Beach.** Though nothing remarkable, this rocky bit is separated from the hills by a large, grassy field—the best place in northern Goa for a seaside picnic. A white stairway leads from Little Vagator, past the Snackataria de World Peace, and down to Big Vagator Beach, the main attraction. **Big Vagator,** just north past the hills, is the longest expanse of fine, white grains around; it is occasionally cramped by crowds from Sterling Vagator Resort and the nearby bus stand. Just head toward the distant northern end of the beach if the bronzing vacationers cramp your style. To the northeast are the expansive ruins of the 17th-century **Portuguese Fort** that separates Chapora from Vagator. Today the ruins shelter only the occasional errant cow or enterprising cold drink salesman, but it's worth a quick clamber for the view, which includes a panoramic sampling of the whole Goa scene—beach-blanket bingo to the south, fishermen hauling in their nets to the east, and lush, unspoiled territory looming across the Chapora River to the north. The southern scramble from Vagator to Anjuna, along rocky beaches and a pleasant path, is another enjoyable walk.

◪ **NIGHTLIFE.** Vagator's bars bump and jive all night long in December and January; proprietors keep the beer flowing until there's no one left standing to drink it. The **Primrose Restaurant and Bar,** with black lights and techno DJs, is as good a place as any to start off the evening. Heading inland, it's the first right past the implausibly named See Green Little Tibet Cafe Brick Oven Pizza Olive Restaurant. (Entrees around Rs60, mixed drinks Rs40. Open 9am-1am.) The **Nine Bar** above Ozran Beach is another nighttime hotspot. Other places worth checking out are the **Millennium Bridge Lounge and Club,** just inland from the northern end of Ozran Beach, and **La Dolce Vita** to the south. Parties often break out between Vagator and Anjuna, with partiers commuting back and forth in search of the hippest scene. The cafes around Chapora market are usually a good source of info on where the next party will be.

GOA

NEAR VAGATOR

🔃 CHAPORA

To get to the main market area, follow the turn-off for Chapora along the main road and bear right at the fork; the teeming bazaar is just up the road on the right. On foot, follow the dirt path that continues from the end of Big Vagator Road for 5min.; when you reach another paved road, stay on the middle track. You'll end up squarely in Chapora market.

Just a few hundred meters (and one old ruined fort) away from Vagator, Chapora isn't blessed with anything remotely resembling a beach, but it more than makes up for this lack with its hippie-chic aesthetic. Tattooed and tanned back-packers suck down fresh juices in crowded cafes and muse about where to bring the party next. **Taxi drivers** huddle under the banyan tree on Chapora's main street when they're not hustling for fares to: **Anjuna** (Rs50-100); **Mapusa** (Rs150); **Panjim** (Rs250); **Vagator** (Rs50). **Buses** head to **Mapusa**, via **Vagator** (every 20min., Rs5). **Soniya Travels,** in the market area, deals with **travel arrangements** and has **email** and **phone** services. They also transfer money via Western Union. (☎273344. Open daily 9am-midnight. Off season 9am-10pm.) **Guest houses** line the main road. One good option is **Helinda's ❷,** just north of the market, which has spacious, clean rooms and a welcoming restaurant. (☎274345. Rs100-350.) **Private rooms ❶** are a good alternative (inquire at the restaurants); two can sleep well for under Rs150-200 per night. **Yak Restaurant ❶,** opposite Soniya Travel, has delicious fresh juices and gen-erous veg. and non-veg. *thalis* (Rs25-30) as well as standard Indian, Continental, Tibetan, and Chinese delights. (Open daily 6am-10pm.)

ARAMBOL (HARMAL) आरामबोल

If Arambol doesn't do it for you, then you're pretty hard to please. Pleasant and friendly, without the crowds of Calangute and Baga, the aging, drugged-out hip-pies of Anjuna, or the hipper-than-thou party-people of Vagator and Chapora, Arambol might just be the beach of your dreams. Though a bridge over the Chapora River is slowly (*very* slowly) nearing completion, the village is currently accessible only by ferry or via a not-especially-frequent bus from Mapusa. Aram-bol's pristine beaches, freshwater lake, and lines of coconut palms are therefore reserved for a select bunch of persevering travelers who come in search of some tranquility, a few rays, and a little patch of the Arabian Sea to splash around in. Which is not to say that Arambol's long and sandy stretch of whiteness is all yours and yours alone. During peak season, Arambol's seaside cafes and bars swell with daytrippers and fortnighters seeking solitude.

📠 **TRANSPORTATION.** There are several ways to reach Arambol. The simplest route to Arambol is the direct **bus** from Mapusa (1hr.; daily 8, 10am, and 1pm; Rs10). Buses arrive at **Arambol Junction** from Chopdem in the south. From the junction, backtrack south and take the first right; a sign points the way. The narrow road winds about 1km to the beach. If you miss the direct bus, you can take the bus from Mapusa (15 min., every 15 min., Rs5) to the **Siolim ferry,** which crosses to Chopdem (10min., every 15min. 6:15am-10:30pm, Rs1). From the ferry docks in Chopdem, buses run to Arambol Junction (30min., every 30min., Rs5). From the Chopdem dock, **taxis** and **auto-rickshaws** cost Rs100-150. A third option is to take the **boat** from Anjuna during the Wednesday flea market (one-way from Arjuna Rs100). **Taxis** in Vagator, Chapora, Mapusa, and Siolem run to Arambol, though outside of Dec.-Jan. you'll have to pay for a round-trip (at most Rs400) even if you're only going one-way.

Many visitors rent **motorcycles** or **mopeds** from the many vendors along the beach road (Rs100-150 per day). The region's only **petrol station** is to the north along the main road. Fill up here before heading north to Querim or Terekol.

■ ☑ **ORIENTATION AND PRACTICAL INFORMATION. Tara Travels,** at the corner where the beach road makes its final turn due west toward the beach, handles transport bookings and reconfirmations, does **currency exchange,** gives cash advances on MC and V, and has **Internet** access. (☎ 292442. Rs60 per hr. Open daily 9am-11pm.) There is a **police station** on the north side of the beach road, and a tiny **post office** at the beginning of the beach road. (Open M-Sa 10am-1pm and 2-6pm.) **Postal code:** 403524.

▐ ◨ **ACCOMMODATIONS AND FOOD.** Many visitors return here year after year and rent houses or rooms for several months. Guest houses lining the beach road are available for short-term stays, and even during peak season, accommodations can be arranged with a little legwork. Ask at restaurants and keep your eyes open for signs; the town is full of informal rooms to let, especially along the road to the beach. Expect to pay around Rs100 for a room without shower or toilet, and up to Rs200 for a spacious, toilet-endowed room. During the monsoon, most lodges and restaurants are closed. **Houses** can be rented for Rs200 per night or for Rs3000-4000 per month. Sizes and facilities vary as widely as the prices; many houses have no toilets or running water, just access to nearby bushes and wells. The most spectacular lodgings are perched at the north end of the main beach off a cliffside footpath. The cheapest beds are in rooms to let on the road to the beach. **The Ganesh Bar ❶** has beautiful rooms dramatically situated on the cliffs midway between the two beaches. (☎ 292334. Doubles Rs400.) The very basic **Relax Inn ❶,** on the beach, has few amenities, but rooms are big and the crashing of the waves will lull you to sleep. (☎ 207711. Rs150. Closed Jun. 15-Aug. 15.)

Restaurants line the road and beach front, but the cream of the crop is ▨**Fellini ❶,** an absolutely scrumptious Italian spot just inland on the beach road. Imported extra virgin olive oil and tomatoes make for a difference you can taste—*molto autentico!* Crowds of travelers pack the roof terrace for pizzas (Rs40-75), sandwiches (Rs25-60), and live music on weekend nights. (Open M-Tu and Th-Sa 10am-11pm, W 7:30-11pm, Su 2-11pm.) Lounge over a cup of tea (Rs15) and a slice of pie (Rs35) at the ▨**Double Dutch Cafe ❶;** follow the signs just past the Om Ganesh Guesthouse on the beach road. If the piled-high cacti and singing birds don't capture your attention, grab a book from their multilingual collection. (Open daily 8am-10pm.) For excellent Indian food and continental breakfasts, head to **21 Coconut Inn ❶,** on the beach, one shack south of where the road intersects with the sand. Attentive waiters serve up rice dishes (Rs20-70), Goan specialities (Rs50-60), and excellent banana pancakes (Rs25). On Saturday nights, crowds come here to hear live classical Indian music. All of these restaurants are closed off season.

◪ ◭ **BEACHES AND ENTERTAINMENT.** Arambol's gorgeous main beach stretches south as far as the eye can see. Fishing boats and a few sunbathers spread out over its wide expanse. You can walk as far south as the Chapora River on the lovely sandy expanse, though it takes a good part of the day to get there (2-3hr. walk). North of the main beach, along a rocky path negotiable only by foot, lies the smaller, more secluded **Paradise Beach.** Behind it is a picturesque **freshwater lagoon.** Next to the End of the World Restaurant at the far south end of the main beach, a shack rents body boards (Rs50) and wind-surfing equipment (Rs200, with lesson Rs250; open M-F 10am-6pm). On Wednesdays, a fun and popular daytrip can be had by catching a boat to Anjuna for the **flea market.** The **Welcome Restau-**

rant and other establishments near the beach send boats there every Wednesday morning (Rs100 1-way, Rs150 round-trip). The northernmost boat on the main beach usually makes the trip. A jazz band composed of fellow travelers plays every Friday night to a packed house at **Fellini** (see above). The dozen or so bars along the main road pour fizzies to fuzz your mind.

⚡ DAYTRIPS FROM ARAMBOL: QUERIM BEACH AND TEREKOL FORT.
North of Arambol Junction, virtually every trace of backpacker culture disappears. A couple of places stand out, though, beyond the pale of hippie settlement. The first is **Querim Beach,** a fir-backed strip of white sand where you can lounge from Noel to New Year's with hardly a Kodak or a dreadlock to disturb you. Querim (Keri) Beach is a 2hr. walk north from Paradise Beach in Arambol. Alternatively, you can head north from Arambol Junction by taxi or moped, following the signs to Keri (about 10km). Faint white writing on the road will point you to the beach.

Past Querim, you can take a ferry across the Terekol River and continue north to Terekol, at the northern tip of Goa. You'll need your own motorbike to reach this stretch of magnificent scenery. Nowadays, **Terekol Fort,** as if tired of living a lie, has given up trying to be an impressive 400-year-old fort and has recently come out as a spruced-up, overpriced hotel and restaurant. Unless you have a special thing for modestly sized, immodestly restored Portuguese forts, it's probably not worth more than a pit stop. **Buses** also make the trip from Chopdem/Arambol to Querim (20min., every hr., Rs5), stopping at the Terekol ferry. **Ferries** cross the Terekol from Querim (5min., every 30min. 6am-10pm, Rs1). From there it's just a few kilometers west—a 15min. hike or Rs50 taxi ride—to the fort (open daily 9am-6pm).

NEAR ARAMBOL

🌊 MANDREM

> *Mandrem village lies on a short stretch of road that branches off from the main thoroughfare between Arambol and Chopdem. Travel amenities are scarce. For currency exchange, buses, or even rickshaws, you basically have to schlep 5km or so up the road to Arambol. **Rickshaws** from Chopdem (Rs80) and the **bus** to Arambol will stop at Mandrem.*

Mandrem's innocence and unparalleled solitude will probably be lost someday, but for now, there are already enough other destinations nearby to keep most of the crowd away from this hidden gem. "Beach" is a bit of a misnomer for Mandrem's seaside landscape of palm trees and white sand—it's more like a desert vista. At its widest point, the vast expanses of sand stretch over 100 unspoiled meters, and it's rare to see more than a dozen beachcombers sauntering about, even on the busiest days.

Accommodations, both short- and long-term, are more plentiful in Arambol, but growing numbers of guest houses are sprouting up along the road at the Junuswaddo Junction—you'll be able to see the vast expanse of beach from the road for the first time here. At the very end of the road is the spectacular and unique **▨Villa River Cat ❷.** If you are on a bike, take the Junuswaddo Junction road to the very end. If you are walking on the beach south from Arambol, after about 40min. you'll pass a cluster of beach shacks—the last is La Brasserie—and a creek heading inland. About 3min. later, beyond the large concrete building with two towers, head inland between the tiny huts crowning the sand dunes. The sign to the Oasis Restaurant will point you in the right direction. More of a retreat than a guest house, this is a sprawling, beautiful home just off the beach. An international group of residents is encouraged to light candles and bask in the Goan paradise, cooking and eating together in the guest kitchen. Reserve in advance by email. If you arrive without a reservation and there's no room, you get a free hammock for the night. (rinoopeter7@yahoo.com. Singles Rs450; doubles Rs550-850; swanky triples with spotless shared bath Rs1200. 25% discount for "artists.") The **Miau Restaurant ❷**, is the Villa River Cat's back porch, but non-guests are welcome to join in the fantastic family-style meals. (Rs125-200. Breakfast 7-11am. Dinner served around 8pm. Book in person.) The **beach shacks ❶**, a few hundred meters north and south of the Villa, serve standard shack fare (meals Rs40-60).

SOUTH GOA

MARGAO (MADGAON) मारगाँव ☎0834

Capped with a shaking arterial highway, bounded by the glinting metal of the Konkan railway, and fed by the constant stream that oozes from the dusty maw of the gigantic KTC bus terminal, Margao is very much a transport hub. Most travelers spend only enough time here to catch their next connection, hurrying away as soon as possible. Tourist-hungry accommodations lie less than 30min. away in Colva and Benaulim. Margao doesn't exactly teem with attractions, but the bustling streets come as a reality check for anyone who has spent too many moons hopping from one other-worldly beach scene to the next.

▐▀ TRANSPORTATION

Trains: Margao Railway Station, 4km southeast of the municipal gardens and 2km east of the old railway station, along Station Rd.—a brisk 15min. walk from the gardens. The Konkan Railway's major station has service to: **Cochin** (16hr., 8pm); **Mangalore** (7hr.; 2:10, 4:10, and 11:10pm; Rs104); **Mumbai** (11hr., noon and 4pm, Rs164-251); **Trivandrum** (24hr., 6:40am and 12:05pm). Helpful info-desk (open 24hr.) and reservation desk (open M-Sa 8am-8pm, Su 8am-1pm).

Buses: KTC Bus Stand, 2km north along the road to Panjim, discharges government buses bound for: **Bangalore** (14½hr., 6:30pm, Rs246-330); **Hubli** (6hr., 5 per day 6:15am-1:45pm, Rs60); **Mangalore** (8hr., 6pm, Rs146-182); **Mumbai** (16hr., 2:30pm, Rs319-336); **Pune** (15hr., 5:15pm, Rs260-286). Travel agents around the tourist hostels book frequent **private buses** to the same destinations. **Intrastate buses** depart from KTC for **Chaudi** (30min., every 10min. 6am-7pm, Rs12) and **Panjim** (every 5min. 6am-8:40pm, Rs15). Buses to and from **Colva** via **Benaulim** (30min., every 30min. 7am-8pm, Rs5) also stop on the eastern side of the Municipal Gardens. Buses to other intrastate destinations stop on the western side of the Municipal Gardens, in front of the police station.

✖ ▐ ORIENTATION AND PRACTICAL INFORMATION

The city's center, the **Municipal Gardens,** is bounded on the west side by **National Highway 17.** The bustling **Station Rd.,** the middle of three roads heading south, originates from the southeast corner of the gardens, diagonally opposite the Bank of India. The main railway station is southeast of the gardens.

Currency Exchange: State Bank of India, west of the Municipal Gardens. Open M-F 10am-4pm, Sa 10am-1pm.

Police: Margao police station (☎705095). Just north of the State Bank of India, behind the bus depot.

Pharmacy: Raikar Medical Stores (☎732924). Station Rd. Open M-Sa 8am-8pm.

Internet: Confident Cyber Global Net, upstairs at the Golden Heart Emporium. Rs30 per hr. Open M-Sa 9:30am-9:30pm, Su 10am-2pm.

Post Office: GPO, at the northern border of the Municipal Gardens. Open M-Sa 7am-6:30pm. **Postal Code:** 403601.

ACCOMMODATIONS

Most foreigners stay one night at most in Margao; the steady influx from the trains and buses ensures that most hotels along Station Rd. fill up quickly each day.

Rukrish Hotel, Station Rd. (☎715046). In a tall, once-yellow bldg. diagonally opposite the Bank of India, just south of the Municipal Gardens. Offers decent, spacious rooms. Singles Rs100-135; doubles Rs243. ❶

Tourist Hotel (☎745528). Just south of the Municipal Garden. Overpriced but dependably institutional, and a good bet if you haven't reserved ahead. The attached bath in all the rooms will look pretty luxurious if you're coming from a spell on the beach-shack circuit. Singles Rs260; doubles Rs350-550. Off-season: Rs200/280-380. ❷

Milan Lodge, (☎722715), Station Rd. Take the 1st left after Janata Hotel. Closer to the station than Rukrish; show up early or call ahead. Singles Rs100; doubles Rs175. ❶

FOOD

Cafe Tato, one block east of the Municipal Gardens on the north-south Valaulikar Rd. in the Apna Bazaar Complex. Excellent, cheap veg. food in A/C comfort. *Thalis* Rs22. Open M-Sa 7am-9:45pm. ❶

Longuinhos, opposite the Tourist Hotel. Dishes out cheap Goan delights (Rs25-60), breakfast (Rs2-20), and copious cocktails. Open daily 8am-10:45pm. ❶

Crislene Cafe, west of the GPO. On the go snacks. Samosas Rs6. Open 7:30am-8pm. ❶

Kamat, in the Milan hotel. Makes very good veg. delights. Samosas Rs10, *thalis* Rs23. Open daily 6:30am-9:30pm. ❶

SIGHTS

Margao's "sights," more pleasant than impressive, can be seen at leisure within an hour. The central **Municipal Gardens** is a colorful public park, festooned with flowers, shrubs, and bronze busts of Portuguese dignitaries. Almost 1km north of the Gardens, at Largo de Igreja, stands the **Church of the Holy Spirit,** a classic Goan cathedral with carvings of the apostles and a history of religious conflict; it was built on the ruins of a Hindu temple sacked by Muslims and rebuilt by persistent Catholics. Open daily 6-9am. To the east is a narrow road leading up Monte Hill to **Our Lady of the Mount Chapel,** a 15min. hike or quick drive leading to expansive views of Margao's hills.

One kilometer east of the KTC bus terminal looms the largest **football arena** in Goa, with a capacity of 40,000. Consult a daily paper or ask around for upcoming games, but be prepared to fight your way to the ticket windows.

DAYTRIPS FROM MARGAO

The most interesting things to see in Margao are not really in Margao at all, but in smaller towns to the east, which are all accessible by bus. In **Rachol** *(7km from Margao; 15min. by rickshaw; 30min. by bus, every 15min., Rs5)*, the **Museum of Christian Art,** at the pretty white-washed Rachol Seminary, has an assortment of carefully labeled Christian artifacts from around Goa. The treasures include an

18th-century palanquin used to carry around ecclesiastical VIPs, a portable altar with accessories for mobile missionaries, and an enormous, kingfisher-shaped monstrance made out of silver and wood that was looted from the Sé Cathedral in Old Goa. *(Open daily 9am-1pm and 2-5pm. Rs5.)* On the kitschier side, **Ancestral Goa** (follow signs to Big Foot), in **Loutilim** *(10km east of Margao; buses 30min., every 30min., Rs5)*, offers a presentation of Goan village life as it was in the good old days, the Limca Book of World Records' longest laterite (a ferrous product of rock decay) sculpture, a garden full of fruits and spices, and a surprisingly interesting and informative tour that somehow ties these wildly disparate elements together. *(Open daily 9am-6pm. Rs20.)* You can arrange at the reception to tour **Casa Araujo Alvares**, an old, Portuguese villa. *(Open daily 10am-12:30pm and 3-6pm. Rs100.)* To get from Rachol to Loutilim without going back to Margao, take the first right past the arch leading out of the seminary and then bear left at the fork (ignore the driveway to the left); walk to a market, where you can pick up a motorcycle taxi to Loutilim *(Rs20-25)*. If the return bus from Loutilim is being shy, head from the bus stand toward Ancestral Goa, taking the right fork. In 20min., you should hit the main road where there is a constant stream of buses heading to Margao *(Rs3)*.

COLVA कोल्वा ☎ 0832

Myriad gawking Indian men, daytripping Mumbaites, English package tourists, and extortionist scarf sellers all converge at Colva's beach for a piece of resort-town action. This overdeveloped mass of concrete pavement, garish resorts, and skeletal construction sights silently urges backpackers to flee with haste. But with a cheap rented bike and a bottle of water, you can escape the beachfront mob and stake out your own private paradise a few kilometers away. Plus, Colva's cheap, airy rooms will let you snooze in low-cost luxury.

⊑ TRANSPORTATION. Buses from **Margao** stop at the crossroads and at the beachfront roundabout. Buses leave from the crossroads on their way back to **Margao,** via **Benaulim** (every 30min., Rs3). For other destinations in Goa it is necessary to travel first to Margao. From the beach and the main road, **auto-rickshaws** go to **Benaulim** (Rs50), **Margao** (Rs50), and **Palolem** (Rs300). **Taxis** charge almost twice as much. **Bicycles** (Rs50 per day) and **motorbikes** (Rs200 per day) can be rented at many shops and resorts, including **Maria Joanna Cycle Shop,** west of the crossroads (open daily 9am-6pm).

⊞ ℿ ORIENTATION AND PRACTICAL INFORMATION. Colva's main strip, **Madgaon Rd.,** begins at a beachfront restaurant **roundabout** and heads 2km east into **Colva Village.** Midway between the roundabout and the village, Madgaon Rd. intersects a major north-south street at a **crossroads.** From this fateful spot, you can head north to Vasco da Gama, south to Benaulim, or you can catch the bus to Margao. West of the church in the village, the **Bank of Baroda** gives cash advances on Visa. (Open M-Tu and Th-F 9am-1pm, Sa 9am-11am.) Any resort with an ounce of pretension will also **exchange currency,** but their rates are less than ideal. Instead, try one of the many travel agencies along Madgaon Rd.; they have slightly better rates. Just north and east of the roundabout is the **tourist police** station. (Open daily 10am-6pm.) Swap a dog-eared paperback at **Damodar's Books,** north of the roundabout. (Open daily 9:30am-9:30pm.) **Internet** services are available along the east-west road. Try **WorldLinkers,** west of the crossroads on the main road. (Rs60 per hr.) A small **post office** is right behind the church in the village. (Open M-F 9am-noon and 2-4pm). **Postal Code:** 403708.

⌐⌐ ACCOMMODATIONS AND FOOD. Transients holing up in Colva after a tour of duty in the north will be pleasantly surprised by the quality of the digs down here. Facilities vary widely, but prices are often much less than what you'd pay for comparable rooms north of Panjim. Outside Christmas week, only the most popular lodges fill up—bargain hard! The **Tourist Nest Hotel ❶,** off the road north from the crossroads (follow the signs), offers some of the softest beds and pillows in Goa. Immaculate and spacious rooms welcome those who are tired after a long day of watching the surf. (☎ 788624. Singles Rs150; doubles Rs200.) From east of the roundabout, follow signs to Louguinho's to find **Fisherman's Cottages ❶,** distinguished by a freshly whitewashed facade in view of the rolling surf. Look for a faded sign on your left. All rooms have attached bath. (☎ 788054. Doubles Rs200.) **Lucky Star ❷,** off the next paved road north of the Fisherman's Cottages, is about on par with its competitor. Fourteen attached rooms are on the second floor above the eponymous bar and restaurant. (☎ 788071. Seafood Rs80. Restaurant open daily 7am-10pm. Doubles Rs250-350. Off-season: Rs150-200.) From the crossroads, head west toward the beach and follow signs opposite William's Beach Resort to the quiet area known as the **4th Ward,** where **Vinson's Cottages ❶** has an attached Goan restaurant and pleasant, clean rooms with bath. (☎ 736481. Entrees Rs25-30. Doubles Rs200-300.) **Rennie's Cottages ❶** is a bargain; their six concrete blocks with attached baths sit beyond Vinson's—cut north past a construction site and continue 100m ahead. This place tends to attract those looking for privacy. (☎ 721926. Doubles Rs150.) **The Sea Pearl ❷,** north on the road east of the roundabout leading to Fisherman's Cottages, draws good crowds for fresh seafood specials for Rs60-175. (Open daily 8:30am-2pm.)

⌐⌐ NIGHTLIFE AND BEACHES. Colva by night is far quieter than its neighbors. The beach bars south of the roundabout host most of the action, if you can even call it that. The humdrum homogeneity of the beach pub scene has barmen wracking their brains to come up with amusements, from star-gazing to volleyball. **Splash's,** south of the roundabout, hosts a different theme party every night, but the crowd is usually in the young Indian male category. **Boomerang Bar,** also known as the **Malibu Beach House,** on the beach north of the roundabout, is another center of the so-called scene.

Colva village and its **beach** lie midway along the longest strip of sand in Goa state. Decked out with 26km of sparkling white and emerald blue, the beach is long enough to make bicycles the best way of getting about. At low tide, it's possible to bicycle on wet, packed sand along the whole length of the beach (bike rental Rs50 per day). Even when the beach gets crowded around Colva—what with Western package tourists and endless busloads of Indian tourists—solitude awaits those willing to venture 1km north or south. Between Colva and Benaulim, the relatively quiet water makes for pleasant swimming. Balmy breezes and mildly rippin' tides make **boogie boarding** and **windsurfing** popular here. Shacks south of Colva beach lease equipment (boogie board Rs30 per hr.; sailboard Rs200 per hr.).

BENAULIM बेणवलीम ☎ 0832

The miles-long glory of Colva's beach continues to Benaulim, a 20min. walk south of Colva, but none of the daytripping hordes make it this far. Still, resorts-in-training are encroaching on the buffer zone of small-scale agriculture that separates the beach and the guest houses, forcibly bending Benaulim into the shape of its northern neighbors. For now, the rooms are cheap and plentiful, and the long walk to the beach still affords pleasant encounters with local life. A rented bike will let you rattle south, down the beach, away from the sunbathers and beach shacks.

▤ TRANSPORTATION. Buses stop at the eastern (Maria Hall) crossroads. Benaulim is on both the Margao-Mobor and Margao-Colva routes (every 30min. 7:30am-8:30pm), and from Benaulim buses head to: **Colva** (15min., Rs3); **Margao** (25min., Rs4); **Varca** (10min., Rs3). **Taxis** and **auto-rickshaws** wait at the drop spot to whisk you off to the shimmering sands 2km away (Rs20 by rickshaw), to **Colva** (Rs50-75 by taxi), or to **Margao** (Rs150 by taxi). Benaulim is a 50min. taxi ride from Dabolim **airport** (Rs300). At the western crossroads, the north-south road faces the majority of guest houses and is cluttered with signs and entrepreneurs touting **bicycle** (Rs50-65) and **motorcycle** (Rs150-200) rentals.

▦ ▨ ORIENTATION AND PRACTICAL INFORMATION. Two parallel north-south roads comprise the heart of Benaulim Village; they intersect the east-west Margao Rd. as it heads west toward the beach. Travel agents, whose offices line the western crossroads, do **currency exchange. GK Tourist Centre,** at the northwest corner of the western crossroads has good rates and **Internet.** (Rs60 per hr. Open daily 9am-11pm.) The **Benaulim Medical Store,** just west of the Maria Hall crossroads on the Margao road, has medications, toiletries, and cheap film developing (☎712124. Open M-Sa 9am-1pm and 4-9pm, Su 10am-1:30pm.) To get to the **post office,** walk south from the eastern crossroads 2km and turn right (west) just past the Holy Trinity Church (open M-Sa 9am-noon and 2-4pm.) **Postal code:** 403716.

▦ ▣ ACCOMMODATIONS AND FOOD. If squatting in the half-finished beachside resort complexes isn't good enough for you, then try one of the cheap and comfortable guest houses that line Margao Rd. and the two north-south streets. Since there are so many guest houses in town, it's easy to get a room without reserving ahead. Head south from the western crossroads and watch for signs to **Diogo Con ❶,** on the dirt road 100m east of the Meridian Restaurant. One of Benaulim's best-kept secrets, here you'll find small, freshly painted rooms with baths. (☎733749. Rs100-150.) Along the east-west beach road, the pleasant **Caroline Guest House ❶** has a second-floor terrace, which provides a nice hangout. All rooms have attached bath. (☎739649. Singles Rs100-150; doubles Rs200. Off season Rs100-150.) **Casa De Caji Cottages ❶** occupies a lovely, quiet spot west of the western north-south road—watch for signs. (☎722937. Doubles Rs125-175. Off season Rs100-125.) **Cacy Rose ❶,** on the main east-west road between the two crossroads, is a brightly painted house that has rooms with shared baths. (☎721813. Singles Rs100; doubles Rs150. Off season Rs70/100.)

Palmira's Breakfast Garden ❶ is the best place in town for a morning meal. Sip your *chai* (Rs5) under bright streamers in this transplanted section of beach, west of the western crossroads on the main road. **Seaview Restaurant ❶,** on the beachfront south of the road, is particularly friendly and serves breakfast (Rs10-30) and Indian standards for Rs30-60. (Open daily 8am-midnight.) Farther inland **Amal-M ❶,** south on the western north-south road, just past the Meridian Restaurant, serves up excellent entrees (Rs50-65) and breakfasts (Rs10-25) with Elvis and Kenny Rogers in the background. (Open daily 8am-midnight.) If you have a desperate and perverse urge to be serenaded by an out-of-tune pseudo mariachi band, **Johncy's Restaurant ❶** is the place for you. Otherwise, you can just watch their *tandoor* in action. The mussels *amotik* (Rs40), with its fiery chilis, is mercilessly mouth-watering. (Open daily 8am-midnight.) **Pedro's ❶,** right next door, cooks breakfast (French toast Rs20) as well as Chinese and *tandoori* dishes for Rs35-80. (Open daily 8am-midnight.) After dark, a few beach shacks south of the road play host to people loafing around, playing cards, and chatting—Benaulim isn't a party town, but if you want to bust your moves, remember that Colva and its theme parties are just a 20min. walk north along the beach.

PALOLEM पाल्लैलेम ☎ 0832

When overworked desk jockeys daydream of quitting the rat race and starting life anew in a tropical paradise, the place they have in mind often looks a lot like this. Strolling along Palolem's kilometer-long crescent of sand, you might find it hard to shake the feeling that you've walked into a dream world. The tiny cove flanked by forested hillocks and black rocks certainly makes the outside world seem a long way away. Hammocks strung between densely packed palm trees shelter guitar-strumming hippies, and the tide recedes to connect the northern end of the beach with an island inhabited by black-faced monkeys. The only tropical beach virtue Palolem lacks is that of quiet, but the crowds are mellower, happier, and more content than most: Palolem has plenty of paradise for everybody.

■ **TRANSPORTATION.** Compared to the rest of Goa's beach towns, Palolem is fairly isolated. **Buses** run regularly to and from **Margao** (every 30-90min. 6:45am-4:30pm, Rs15). Buses pick up and drop off where the road to Chaudi turns to the beach. Fortunately, most guest house owners double as accurate bus timetables. If you miss the direct services, the bus from nearby **Chaudi** to Margao (1½hr., every hr. 8am-6:30pm, Rs10) is a viable option. If you are continuing on to **Gokarna,** take the bus toward Margao and get off in Canacona. Here you can pick up the Gokarna Express (3½hr., 2:10pm, Rs40). The Canacona **train** station is also in Chaudi. To **Margao** (40min., 7:45pm). From Chaudi to Palolem, you can take a **rickshaw** (Rs30) or **taxi** (Rs100) or take advantage of **motorcycle rental** (Rs150-200 per day).

■ ■ **ORIENTATION AND PRACTICAL INFORMATION.** The road from **Chaudi** zig-zags 4km northwest to Palolem, running parallel to the surf midway along and intersecting the beach road halfway along the half-moon of sand. There is a small **book exchange** at **Woody's Health Food** on the way to the village. (Open daily 9am-9pm.) The **Sun n' Moon** on the main road to the beach offers **currency exchange** at decent rates as well as **Internet** access. (Rs60 per hr. Open daily 7am-midnight.) The nearest **post office** is in Chaudi.

■ ■ **ACCOMMODATIONS AND FOOD.** Compared to Colva and Benaulim, Palolem's accommodations are overpriced and underkept—expect to pay Rs200 in season for the privilege of crashing in a charmless double and using a common bathroom outside. A stay in one of the **straw hut colonies ❶,** on the beachfront provides a more picturesque alternative. (On-the-ground huts Rs150-250; up-on-stilts huts Rs 250-500.) Just head south on the beach from the road, and pick among the cluster of huts. Midway down the beach, south of where the road lets out, the **Deena Bar and Restaurant ❷** rents simple huts with one lightbulb, one bed, and one chair; they do have fans and two toilets, though, and there's a safe for valuables. There's a bumpin' bar and restaurant out front. (☎643449. Restaurant open 7am-2am. Rooms Rs200-400. Off-season: Rs150.) Just south of Deena, **Island View Cottages ❷** offers similar accommodations plus bonus hammocks tied between palm trees. (☎634258. Rs200-300. Off-season: Rs150.) For the good old-fashioned four-solid-walls treatment, **Blue Jays ❶,** on the main road toward Chaudi, offers basic, clean rooms with common bath. (☎643056. Doubles Rs200. Off-season: Rs150.) There's a pleasant attached restaurant (entrees Rs20-80; open daily 8am-11pm) and beach access around the back. **Cocohuts ❷,** at the southern end of the beach, has huts on stilts, with lockers, electric fans, and a common toilet. (☎643296; ppv@goa1.dot.net.in. Doubles with great sea view Rs500; Rs200 in back.)

Restaurant fare and prices are pretty standard; look for atmosphere and a good crowd, since most serve the same food. At the far northern end of the beach, you'll find an oasis of good karma called the **Cozy Nook ❶**. People loll on reed mats as they sip drinks (Rs30-50) and play cards on tabletops made of salvaged tree trunk slabs. (Entrees Rs30-60. Open daily 8am-11pm.) **Blue Jays** and its neighbor, **Sun n' Moon ❶**, are both popular. (Seafood Rs65-95, breakfast Rs10-30. Both open daily 8am-10:30pm.) Folks can be found blowin' in the wind at **Dylan's,** circled by the sands.

▶ DAYTRIPS FROM PALOLEM. Those who tire of sharing their paradise with others can wind their way northwest from Chaudi to the as-yet-uncontaminated **Agonda Beach** (Rs3 by bus from Chaudi). A cove almost as picturesque as Palolem's (although it doesn't match it palm-for-palm), Agonda lacks everything but surf and sand. Supplies (petrol, cold snacks) are available from the garage-like complex of stores on the left as you head toward the beach (most close at 7pm). **Cocohuts** has a branch here, which is slightly cheaper than their place in Palolem.

Farther northwest (1hr. by scooter, available in Palolem for Rs150-200 per day), the immense ruins of a Portuguese fort wait for the invasion that never happened in **Cabo de Rama,** a town consisting only of a name, a fort, and a few bars scattered along the one and only road. The ruins overlook an endless seafront and exude a quiet grandeur that fits right in with a picnic. It's best to visit Agonda and Cabo de Rama by motorbike—taxis are expensive (Rs250-300 from Palolem), and the daily buses to Cabo de Rama from Margao and Agonda take 2hr.

GUJARAT ગુજરાત

One of India's richest industrial regions, Gujarat has magnificent mosques, sublime and sweet cuisine, and weird and wonderful wildlife, all of which remain for the most part unappreciated. Gujarat sees far fewer travelers than its neighbors, Rajasthan and Maharashtra, allowing you to hoard these wonders all to yourself.

Originally settled as part of the Indus Valley civilization around 2500 BC, Gujarat prospered under several empires, including the Solanki dynasty in the 11th and 12th centuries, which imbued the region with a culture influenced by a blend of Jainism and Hinduism. In AD 1299, the area was conquered by Muslims, who formed the Sultanate of Gujarat. The Portuguese stormed onto the scene in the 16th century, capturing the ports of Diu and Daman. During India's struggle for Independence, Gujarat came to prominence as the birthplace of Mahatma Gandhi, and as the home of Mohammed Ali Jinnah, architect of Pakistan.

Gujarat can be divided into three vastly different geographical regions. The eastern region, containing the capital Gandhinagar, the metropolis Ahmedabad, and the commercial cities of the mainland strip, is characterized by modern industry. The northwestern quasi-island of Kutch is a dry and isolated area renowned for its traditional villages and handicrafts. The Kathiawar Peninsula (also known as Saurashtra) features lush land, breathtaking beaches, rich temples, forts, palaces, and all things Gandhi.

> **COVERAGE LACUNAE.** Due to the recent earthquake in Gujarat, it was not possible for our researchers to cover the entire state this year. Sites that have not been updated are Sasan Gir National Park, Dwarka, and daytrips from Ahmedabad and Bhuj. The coverage for these regions was accurate as of September 2000. Problems in the state's infrastructure are likely to make travel in Gujarat unpredictable for some time to come.

On January 26, 2001, Gujarat was rocked by one of the most disastrous earthquakes ever to hit India. The 7.9-magnitude quake, whose epicenter was located in the Kutch region, created considerable tremors as far away as Chennai, Tamil Nadu. Death estimates run from 20,000 to 50,000, and up to one million people may have been made homeless by the disaster. The earthquake destroyed significant portions of the state's infrastructure and prompted groups around the globe to aid in the disaster-relief efforts. It will be years before Gujarat fully recovers from this catastrophe, and it will certainly be remembered long after that.

HIGHLIGHTS OF GUJARAT

Gandhi and gingham combine in **Ahmedabad** (below), at the Mahatma's **Sabarmati Ashram** (p. 206) and the **Calico Museum of Textiles** (p. 207).

India sets its western compass point at **Dwarka** (p. 217), where pilgrims congregate and antique lighthouses afford sublime sunset vistas.

One of India's most isolated regions, beautiful **Kutch** (p. 218) is home to unique tribal cultures and the labyrinthine port of **Mandvi** (p. 222).

Bright-colored buildings, ancient Portuguese churches, isolated beaches, and serene streets await visitors to the Union Territory of **Diu** (p. 211). However, most visitors come for the **booze** available nowhere else in the state.

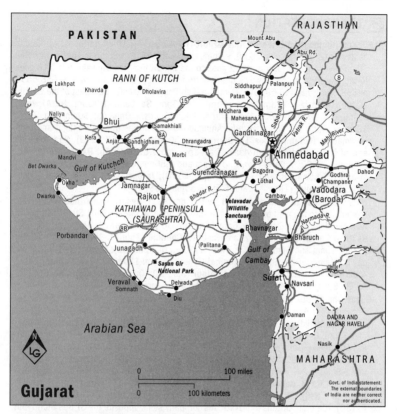

Gujarat

AHMEDABAD અમદાવાદ ☎ 079

Ahmedabad, the largest city in Gujarat, is one of Asia's most eccentric and fascinating cities, as well as one of its most polluted and congested. Founded in 1411 by Sultan Ahmed Shah, the city expanded rapidly, attracting large numbers of traders, craftsmen, and artisans. The construction of numerous mosques in the Indo-Saracenic style gave the city the Muslim character that it retains today. Ahmedabad's prosperity waxed and waned over the centuries, and its growth was periodically impeded by famines. Ahmedabad has always been known for its textiles and handicrafts, and Gandhi's *swadeshi* movement was started in an ashram here. Today, Ahmedabad has the second largest textile industry in the country.

Much of Ahmedabad's appeal is well-hidden these days, covered up by billboards and signs advertising its booming businesses. For those willing to dig a little deeper, much beauty still remains within the *pols* (self-contained neighborhoods) of the old city, where spectacular mosques, temples, and *havelis* await on nearly every corner. Wandering the streets of the old city, you can expect to see craftsmen adding the finishing touches to batiks put out to dry in the sun.

Across the river lies the new city and its expansive web of shopping arcades and cinemas, interrupted by the occasional wandering camel or stray ox cart. Though not of much interest to tourists, the new city operates at a more relaxed pace than the old city and offers all the modern conveniences available in Delhi or Mumbai.

GUJARAT

⌐ TRANSPORTATION

Flights: Ahmedabad International Airport (☎642 5633). 10km northeast of the city center. Taxis into the city Rs250, auto-rickshaws Rs125. Buses run to Lal Darwaja Bus Stand (every hr., Rs7). Bus #102 goes to the airport from Lal Darwaja; bus #18 goes to the airport from the railway station, both during flight times. **Air India** (☎658 5633 or 658 5644; fax 658 5900), behind the High Court off Ashram Rd., west of the Gandhi statue. Open M-F 10am-1:15pm and 2-5:15pm, Sa 10am-1:30pm. **Jet Airways,** Ashram Rd. (☎754 3366). 1km north of Gujarat Tourism. Open M-F 10am-7pm, Sa-Su 10am-5:30pm. The *Times of India* Ahmedabad edition has up-to-date flight and train information. **Indian Airlines,** Lal Darwaja (☎550 3061; fax 550 5599). Near the east end of Nehru Bridge. Open daily 10am-1pm and 2-5:15pm. To: **Bangalore** (1½hr., 6:50pm, US$220); **Delhi** (1½hr., 8:05am and 8:50pm, US$135); **Hyderabad** (1½hr.; M and F 7:50am, Th and Su 4:45am; US$170); **Jaipur** (1hr.; Tu, Th, Sa 6:20pm; US$75); **Mumbai** (1hr.; 7:30am, 6:50, 8:55pm; US$75).

Trains: Ahmedabad Railway Station (☎131 or 1331). **Reservation Office** (☎135). In the building to the right as you face the station. Open M-Sa 8am-8pm, Su 8am-2pm. To: **Abu Road** (4½hr., 6 per day 6am-12:30am, Rs53); **Bhopal** (14hr., 1-2 per day, Rs205); **Calcutta** (43hr., 9:20am, Rs422); **Chennai** (35hr., 6:30am, Rs390); **Delhi** (17hr., 10am and 5pm, Rs282); **Dwarka** (10hr., 6am, Rs182); **Jaipur** (12-14hr., 3 per day 8:20am-5:30pm, Rs225); **Mumbai** (7 per day 7am-11pm, Rs186); **Rajkot** (5-6hr., 4 per day 6am-2:30am, Rs117); **Udaipur** (9hr., 10:40pm, Rs134); **Varanasi** (42hr.; Tu, Th, Sa 8pm; Rs341); **Veraval** (12hr., 10 and 11pm, Rs174).

Buses: The **ST Bus Stand** (☎214 764) is near Astodia Darwaja (rickshaw Rs15 from Lal Darwaja). To: **Abu Road** (6hr., 6 per day 6:30am-2:45pm, Rs70); **Bhuj** (8hr., 12 per day 5:30am-midnight, Rs100; deluxe 8am and 9pm, Rs120); **Chittaurgarh** (9hr., 9am and 10pm, Rs135); **Diu** (10hr., 8am, Rs89); **Dwarka** (11hr., 3 per day 6:15am-11pm, Rs110; deluxe 8am and 7:30pm, Rs120); **Jaipur** (15hr., 4:30 and 9:30pm, Rs235; deluxe 6pm, Rs306); **Mt. Abu** (6hr., 3 per day 7-11am, Rs81); **Mumbai** (12hr., 5 per day 2-8pm, Rs202); **Rajkot** (5hr., every 30min., Rs68); **Udaipur** (6hr., 11 per day 5am-11:30pm, Rs93; deluxe 3 per day 11:30am-10:30pm, Rs115); **Una** (10hr., 3 per day 8am-8pm, Rs90); **Veraval** (12hr., 5 per day 6:15am-8:45pm, Rs110; deluxe 8am, Rs130). There are dozens of **private bus** company stalls opposite the ST Bus Stand, but most are ticket agents only; most private buses depart from the main company office. 2 good companies are **Punjab Travels,** Embassy Market, off Ashram Rd., north of the tourist office (☎658 9200; open daily 6am-10:30pm), and **Shrinath Travels,** Shahi Bagh, near the police commissioner's office (☎562 5351; open daily 6am-midnight).

Local Transportation: Auto-rickshaws are the most convenient local transport. Insist on the meter and ask to see the fare card. **Local buses** are cheap, and go just about everywhere. The **Lal Darwaja Bus Stand** (☎550 7739) is the local bus stand. Buses ending in 0-5 are based at Lal Darwaja; those ending in 6-9 are based near the railway station; #82 and 84 cross the river and run north up Ashram Rd.; #51, 52, 56, 57 hit Panchwati Circle; #32 runs to the ST Bus Stand and southeast to Kankaria Lake; #34 and 112 run past the Civil Hospital; #131 and 133-135 run to the railway station. Fares are never more than Rs7. A/C Ambassador **taxis** can be found at Lal Darwaja, the 2 bus stands, the airport, the railway station, and the V.S. Hospital.

⌘ ORIENTATION

Ahmedabad is divided in two by the **Sabarmati River,** which cuts a north-south path between the old and new sections of the city (the river bed is usually dry and filled with grazing water buffalo). The **Lal Darwaja (Red Gate)** opens into the old city on the east side of the river; the newer industrial and urban centers are to the west. The two parts of the city are connected by a series of five bridges.

Most of Ahmedabad's modern facilities are found in the ever-expanding **new city** to the west. **Panchwati Circle** and **CG Rd.** are bustling areas full of helpful services, but they are far away from the old city, the most interesting area to tourists. If you're taking the Nehru Bridge (that's the one from Lal Darwaja) across, keep going past the Law Gardens; this will take you right into the thick of things.

🛈 PRACTICAL INFORMATION

Tourist Office: Tourist Information Bureau (Gujarat Tourism), HK House (☎ 1364 or 658 9683). Off Ashram Rd. and down a side street opposite the South Indian Bank, between Gandhi and Nehru Bridges. Helpful English-speaking staff knows everything there is to know about the city. Free city maps, Gujarat maps Rs4. Open M-Sa 10:30am-1:30pm and 2-6pm. Closed 2nd and 4th Sa. The **tourist counter** at the airport has limited information. **City tours** depart from the tourist window at the Lal Darwaja bus stand (4hr.; 9am and 1:30pm; Rs60, A/C Rs75). Check out the **Ahmedabad city web site.** It has everything from emergency phone numbers to flight information to city tours and entertainment (www.ahmedabadcity.com).

Currency Exchange: State Bank of India (☎ 550 6116). Lal Darwaja, near Lal Darwaja bus stand. Both exchange currency and traveler's checks. **Bank of Baroda** (☎ 658 0362). Ashram Rd., south of the Gandhi statue. Gives cash advances on MC and V. Open M-F 11am-2pm, Sa 11am-noon. **Dena Bank** (☎ 658 4292). Ashram Rd., north of Nehru Bridge, 2nd fl. Open M-F 10am-2:30pm.

Market: Khas Bazaar and **Relief, Gandhi, Sardar Patel,** and **Ashram Rd.** are the main commercial areas. Most stores open daily 9am-9:30pm. There is a **handicrafts market** along the western edge of the **Law Gardens** daily 6-11pm. The main **vegetable markets** are near the railway station on **Relief** and **Kasturba Gandhi Rd.**

Police: Karanj (☎ 550 7580), in Teen Darwaja; **Shaherkotada,** opposite the railway station; and **Ellis Bridge** (☎ 657 8202,) at the intersection with Ashram Rd.

Hospital: One of the best private hospitals is **Chaturbhuj Lajpatrai Hospital,** also known as **Rajasthan Hospital** (☎ 286 6311). Dr. Tankeria Rd., south of the Police Commissioner's Office. English-speaking, modern, efficient. Well-stocked 24hr. **pharmacy.**

Internet: Interscope White House (☎ 640 4131). Panchwati Circle, Ambavadi Rd. Rs20 per hr. Open 24hr. **Cyber Valley,** Sri Krishna Shopping Centre, Mithakali (☎ 640 9200). Rs30 per hr. Open daily 8am-11pm.

Post Office: GPO, Mirzapar Rd. (☎ 550 0977). Near Lal Darwaja. Open M-Sa 10:30am-6pm, Su 10:30am-3pm. Branches at the airport, Gandhi Ashram, and opposite the railway station. Open M-Sa 10am-5pm. **Postal Code:** 380001.

🛏 ACCOMMODATIONS

The best budget hotels are conveniently scattered around the western half of the city center. Luxury hotels cluster around Khanpur Darwaja, between the Gandhi and Nehru Bridges on the east side of the river. All hotels add 10-15% luxury tax.

Hotel Sohel, Lal Darwaja (☎ 550 5465 or 550 5466). On a side street off Advance Cinema Rd. Well-kept, modern, and smack in the middle of Lal Darwaja. 24hr. hot water, TVs, and room service. Check-out 24hr. Singles Rs190-400; doubles Rs350-400. ❷

Gandhi Ashram Guest House (☎ 755 9342). Opposite Gandhi Ashram. This guest house catches some of the peaceful vibes that emanate from the ashram across the street. Grecian busts, phones, TVs, and 24hr. hot showers. Breakfast included. Good veg. restaurant. Check-out 9am. Singles Rs375-550; doubles Rs500-750. ❷

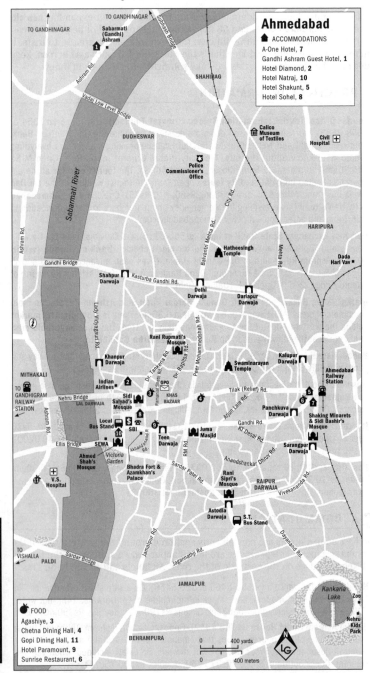

TO GANDHINAGAR

TO GANDHINAGAR

Sabarmati (Gandhi) Ashram **1**

TO GANDHINAGAR

Subhash Bridge

SHAHIBAG

Vadaj Low Level Bridge

Ashram Rd.

DUDHESWAR

Sabarmati River

Calico Museum of Textiles

Civil Hospital

Police Commissioner's Office

HARIPURA

Gandhi Bridge

Asharam Rd.

Balvantri Mehta Rd.

City Rd.

Mehta Rd.

Hatheesingh Temple

Dada Hari Vav ■

Shahpur Darwaja

Kasturba Gandhi Rd.

Delhi Darwaja

Dariapur Darwaja

Lady Vidyagauri Rd.

i

Rani Rupmati's Mosque

Khanpur Darwaja

Peer Mohammedshah Rd.

Dr. Baptisa Rd.

Dr. Tankeria Rd.

Swaminarayan Temple

Kalupur Darwaja

Ahmedabad Railway Station

MITHAKALI

Indian Airlines

2

Ramanlal Sheth Radenia R.

GPO

KHAS BAZAAR

Tilak (Relief) Rd.

5

6 **7**

TO GANDHIGRAM RAILWAY STATION

Nehru Bridge

LAL DARWAJA

Sidi Salyad's Mosque

3

4

Arjun Lala Rd.

Panchkuva Darwaja

Shaking Minarets & Sidi Bashir's Mosque

Asharam Rd.

Local Bus Stand

8

10

SBI

9

Teen Darwaja

Akhandanand Rd.

Juma Masjid

Gandhi Rd.

KT Desai Rd.

Ellis Bridge

SEWA

Ahmed Shah's Mosque

Victoria Garden

Bhadra Fort & Azamkhan's Palace

RM Rd.

Anandshankar Dhruv Rd.

Sarangpur Darwaja

11

V.S. Hospital

Sardar Patel Rd.

Rani Sipri's Mosque

RAIPUR DARWAJA

Vivekananda Rd.

Astodia Darwaja

S.T. Bus Stand

Dayanand Rd.

TO VISHALLA

PALDI

Sardar Bridge

Jamalpur Rd.

Jagannathji Rd.

JAMALPUR

Kankaria Lake

Zoo

Nehru Kids Park

BEHRAMPURA

0   400 yards

0   400 meters

N

LG

Ahmedabad

♠ ACCOMMODATIONS

A-One Hotel, **7**
Gandhi Ashram Guest Hotel, **1**
Hotel Diamond, **2**
Hotel Natraj, **10**
Hotel Shakunt, **5**
Hotel Sohel, **8**

🍴 FOOD

Agashiye, **3**
Chetna Dining Hall, **4**
Gopi Dining Hall, **11**
Hotel Paramount, **9**
Sunrise Restaurant, **6**

Hotel Shakunt (☎214 4615). Opposite the railway station. A marble staircase lined with Rajasthani art leads up to this modern hotel, featuring a pleasant terrace garden. Rooms are slightly stuffy but have TVs, phones, and baths. STD service in the lobby. Check-out 24hr. Singles Rs220-600; doubles Rs380-700. ❷

Hotel Diamond, Gujarat Samachar Rd., Khanpur (☎550 3699). A good deal for the facilities. Wall-to-wall carpeted rooms with baths, TVs, and phones, are well-insulated from the noise (and air) outside. Check-out 24hr. Singles Rs190-310; doubles Rs270-390. ❷

Hotel Natraj (☎550 6048). Next to Ahmed Shah's Mosque south of the local bus stand. Rooms with balconies overlooking the gardens of the mosque next door offer the best view in the city proper. Rooms are large but aging. All have attached baths. Check-out 24hr. Singles Rs130; doubles Rs220. ❶

A-One Hotel (☎214 9823). Opposite the railway station. The nondescript rooms are barely larger than the beds, but if you just want to crash between train rides, the inspirational posters will ease you to sleep. Check-out 24hr. Dorms (men only) Rs60; singles Rs100-175; doubles Rs150-260. ❶

⬛ FOOD

Ahmedabad has some of the best restaurants in Gujarat, and they are often very reasonably priced. Gujarati *thalis* blend several local specialties in a delightful, frequently sweet, mix. For quick and spicy stall food, **Khas Bazaar** can't be beaten.

▨ **Chetna Dining Hall,** Relief Rd., directly north of the Jama Masjid. High-quality *thali* house. South Indian dishes (*dosas* Rs20-22) downstairs noon-10pm; *thalis* (Rs60) upstairs. Every *samosa* and *sabil* spiced evocatively, and topped off with unlimited *shrikhand*. Open daily 10:30am-3pm and 6:30-10pm. ❶

▨ **Gopi Dining Hall,** off Ashram Rd. near V.S. Hospital on the west side of the river; look for the sign above the bldg. This packed little den of a place serves up excellent, enormous Gujarati and Kathiawadi *thalis* (Rs48-58). Come early, or be prepared to wait. Great service and prices. Open daily 10:30am-3pm and 6:30-10:30pm. ❶

Cona Restaurant, opposite Advance Cinema, Lal Darwaja. Superior service, massive portions and meticulous preparation distinguish this veg. restaurant from its hundred look-alike neighbors. Unbelievable "two tastes" *shahi* veg. Rs42, Punjabi dishes Rs25-42. Open daily 11am-5pm and 6-11pm. ❶

Agashiye, on the roof of the red-and-white mansion opposite the Sidi Sayid Mosque. Scented candles and flower-filled fountains welcome you to this exquisitely decorated rooftop paradise. Incredible Gujarati *thalis* (lunch Rs135, dinner Rs185). Open noon-3pm and 7-11pm. Downstairs, the **Greenhouse Restaurant** serves juices, ice cream, and *lassis* (Rs25-35) as well as a few "mini meals" (Rs45-70). Open daily 11am-11pm. ❷

Sunrise Restaurant, Reid Rd., opposite the railway stations near Hotel Shakunt. A 2m-high waterfall helps to drown out all the outside railroad noise in this busy diner where the *dosas* are salty (Rs18-30) and the cold coffee ice cream floats (Rs33) are a bittersweet end to the meal. Open daily 6am-12:30am. ❶

Hotel Paramount, near Khas Bazaar. Dim lights and A/C make this a comfortable spot. Seafood dishes under Rs50, veg. entrees under Rs45. Open daily 10am-11:15pm. ❶

Tomatoes Restaurant, CG Rd., in the new city. This diner will satisfy your food cravings. Entrees Rs78-128. Open daily noon-3pm and 7:35-11pm. Upstairs, **RGs** serves pizzas and Mexican and Thai food for Rs79-149. ❷

LET'S GO FLY A KITE For three nights in January, the skies of Ahmedabad are speckled with kites of all styles, colors, and sizes. Enthusiasts from all over the world descend upon the city for the **International Kite Festival** (Jan. 13-15, 2002) also known as **Uttarayan**, the largest kite-related event in the world. For the weeks leading up to the event, local shops and stalls sell an enormous variety of kites and kite-flying equipment, and experts roam the streets offering lessons on the finer points of the craft. In the festival itself there are competitions for kite size, originality, and beauty. At night, the skies light up with kites' illuminated tails. Dancing, singing, shows, parades, and general merriment round out the festival, which ends with a highly competitive contest in which kite strings are coated with adhesive and ground glass, turning them into razor-sharp lines. Kites are then sent flying into one another to slash at each other's lines until one kite emerges victorious.

👁 🎵 SIGHTS AND ENTERTAINMENT

HERITAGE WALK. Because Ahmedabad was built to thwart and confuse invaders the Ahmedabad Municipal Corporation decided that Ahmedabad needed a walking tour to "unveil" the city to tourists and residents alike. The guided tour takes you through the numerous *pols* (neighborhoods) and *ols* (markets) that make up the old city and explains the rationale behind Ahmedabad's design and architecture while outlining the city's history. It winds through narrow streets and secret passageways, takes you under 400-year-old, carved wooden gates, and goes past ornamented temples, community squares, and **chabutras** (bird feeders) that were once the focal point of daily life. The Heritage Walk takes you to parts of the city you would never see otherwise. *(Walk starts at the Swaminarayan Temple, up the stairs to the right of the main gate. Daily 8am, 2hr. Rs50.)*

SABARMATI (GANDHI) ASHRAM. Every year thousands of admirers and followers of Mahatma Gandhi descend upon Ahmedabad to visit this ashram, from which much of Gandhi's spiritual and political influence emanated. Gandhi founded the original ashram in the middle of the city in 1915, upon his return from South Africa. However, a city-wide plague two years later forced him to relocate to a plot of donated land on the banks of the Sabarmati River. Gandhi lived here until 1930, along with his wife, Kasturba, and 600 other residents. The Mahatma's simple living quarters, several of his personal objects, and an exhibition of his achievements are on display. The display touches not only on the political and spiritual sides of his life, but also on the role that he played in the revitalization of the Ahmedabad textile industry. Don't miss the series of moving portraits next to the ashram office. The museum library, open to visitors, holds a mammoth collection of over 36,000 of Gandhi's letters. Beyond **Vinoba/Mira Kutir,** the modest abode of two particularly fervent devotees, is a large building referred to as the "hostel," which was the first part of the ashram to be built. The room on the riverside was Gandhi's original dwelling and work room for three months. The building is now home to 2,000 orphans and children from impoverished families living in nearby slums. Also of interest is **Pasana Mandir,** a small plot of land overlooking the river where Gandhi and his fellow ashram mates recited their daily prayers. The ashram's current inhabitants hold their evening prayer sessions at the same spot *(6:30pm).* Gandhi's main residence lies to the right as you face the *mandir.* Those interested in spending time at the ashram should contact the management directly by phone. For stays of a few weeks, contact Jayesh Patel (☎755

GUJARAT

1102; safai@ad1.vsnl.net.in), next door to the ashram. The Department of Gandhian Studies of Gujarat Vidyapith offers classes structured after Gandhian principles. *(Ashram Rd., north of the Gandhi Bridge; take local bus #81, 82, 83, 84, 86, 87, 200, or 300. ☎ 755 1102. Open daily 8:30am-6:30pm. Free. Sound and light show Oct. 2-June 15 Su, W, F 8:30pm.; 1hr.; Rs5.)*

CALICO MUSEUM OF TEXTILES. Housed in the *haveli* of the city's richest family, India's premier textile museum is worth a visit simply for the building itself, which is split into two sections surrounded by peacock- and fountain-filled gardens. The first section displays non-religious textiles, and features an enormous collection of items made from every possible fabric, in every possible style, for every possible purpose, and from every part of India. The white-on-white translucent shadow work is remarkable, as are the lavish silk embroideries. Other highlights include beautiful saris (valued at Rs80,000 and up) made according to a highly complex method—one tiny mistake in the sewing ruins the entire piece—and clothes so heavily laden with gold lace that their weight exceeds 9kg. The second half of the museum displays textiles designed for religious use, and features an exquisite, 8m-long pictorial scroll, numerous old tapestries, and a series of rooms explaining the process of textile manufacture in excruciating detail—every knot, stitch, thread, and bead. *(Shahi Bagh, 3km north of Delhi Gate; take local bus #101, 102, or 106. ☎ 786 8172. Open Th-Tu. Guided tours of Foundation galleries 10:30am; of textile collection 2:45pm; both 2hr. Free. Photography permitted only in the gardens.)*

JAMA MASJID. Built in 1424 by Sultan Ahmed Shah I, the Jama Masjid centers on a large marble courtyard and a small pool that is often surrounded by devotees. The 15 domes of the mosque are supported by 256 pillars with detailed carvings, most of which are Hindu-themed. The curious black slab by the main massive archway is said to be an inverted Jain image. The twin minarets, which once towered over the main structure, collapsed in an 18th-century earthquake and the broken stubs are all that remain. The names of the prophets are written on the **north wall** so that mothers can bring their newborns here to pick a name. Through the left gate of the courtyard is the tomb of **Ahmed Shah** and the **Rani-ka-hazira**, the tomb of his queens. The cenotaphs, in vast pillared chambers, are covered with fancy gold-laced cloths. A guard can lift one for you to reveal the fine stonework underneath. *(Gandhi Rd. Women are allowed to enter the main hall, except during prayer times, but are prohibited from entering the chambers that hold tombs of male members of the family.)*

SIDI SAIYAD'S MOSQUE. Constructed in 1573 by one of Ahmed Shah's slaves, Sidi Saiyad's Mosque, in Lal Darwaja, graces at least half of Gujarat Tourism's propaganda pamphlets. The interior is impressive, with elaborately carved ceilings and domes, but the highlight is the delicate latticework on the screens of the upper walls. *(Women are not allowed to enter, but can view the screens from the gardens.)*

OTHER MOSQUES. Rani Sipri's Mosque, near the railway station, on Sardar Patel Rd., is also known as **Masjid-e-Nagira** (the "Jewel of a Mosque"). It was built in 1519, and the central grave holds Rani Sipri, who ordered the mosque to be built after her son was executed for a petty crime. The mosque is known for its exquisite latticework. Near Sarangpur Darwaja are the famous **Shaking Minarets** and **Sidi Bashir's Mosque.** A huge arch supporting two 21m-high minarets explains the name; the arches are balanced so that if one minaret shakes, the other will move to counteract the tremor, allowing the mosque to survive earthquakes and colonialist bombardments alike. *Let's Go* does not recommend shaking minarets. The **Dada Hari Vav** (step-well), in the **Dada Hari Mosque,** was built in 1501 by none other than Dada Hari. Five stories and 100 steps descend into this cavern of stones, adorned with carvings and currently inhabited by a colony of bats.

TEMPLES. The **Swaminarayan Temple,** on the north side of the city, is dedicated to Vishnu and Lakshmi. Built in 1850, this rainbow of metallic colors contrasts dramatically with the rest of Ahmedabad's stonework. The temple's fine woodwork and bright, detailed painting rival the city mosques in intricacy. *(Open daily 6am-8pm. Photography prohibited.)* The **Hatheesing Temple,** north of Delhi Lake, is one of several Jain temples in the city. Built in 1848 and dedicated to the 15th *tirthankara,* Dharamarath, this white marble temple, with detailed carvings of dancers and floral patterns, has a typical Jain design. *(Buses to the airport pass both Swaminarayan and Hatheesing Temples; be sure to let the driver know where you are going. Hatheesing Temple open to non-Jains daily 10am-noon and 4-7:30pm. Photography prohibited.)*

OTHER MUSEUMS. The **Mehta Museum of Miniatures** has a large collection of miniature paintings, most of them modern, from throughout India. *(West of the city, near the university. Open Tu-Su 10am-5:30pm. Free.)* Next door, the **L.D. Institute of Indology** offers more miniatures, as well as manuscripts, and carvings. *(Bus #52 from Lal Darwaja and bus #56 from the railway station serve both museums. Open M-Sa 10am-5:30pm. Free.)* The **Shreyas Folk Museum,** west of the city, displays indigenous costumes, handicrafts, and textiles from all over Gujarat. *(Bus #41 from Lal Darwaja. Open Tu-Su 10:30am-1:30pm and 2:30-5:30pm. Rs40.)* The **Tribal Research and Training Museum** showcases crafts from regional tribal peoples. *(North of Ashram Rd., on the campus of Gujarat Vidyapith. Open M-Sa noon-6pm. Free.)*

THE INDIAN CULTURAL CENTRE. Call in advance to watch others get their groove on at the traditional folk dance rehearsals that take place here. *(Spandan G-11 Balaji Ave., Judge's Bungalow Rd. ☎ 675 7880.)*

▶ DAYTRIPS FROM AHMEDABAD

VISHALLA. The Gujarati village mock-up of Vishalla, 4km south of Ahmedabad, offers a night of earthy village dining and rustic entertainment. Eat plentiful, spicy food from leaf plates and drink from clay cups while musicians play and attendants dressed in traditional village garb fan scented insect-repelling smoke in your face. Buffet dinner Rs188-250. *(Open daily 7-11pm. Bus #31 from Lal Darwaja and #150 from the railway station run past the Octori check-post—specify where you want to be let off. From the checkpoint, Vishalla is a 7min. walk or a short rickshaw ride for Rs5-10).*

SARKHEJ. Eight kilometers southwest of Ahmedabad is Sarkhej, formerly the summer retreat of Gujarati sultans and today a peaceful suburb that feels farther away from the city than it really is. Set on one side of an artificial lake is the tomb of Sheikh Ahmed Khattu Ganj Buksh, the spiritual mentor and unofficial advisor of Ahmed Shah. The largest **mausoleum** in the state, it has a huge central dome supported by pillars and decorated with exquisite marble, brass, and wood ornamentation. Sultan Mohammed Beghada's mausoleum and that of his wife Rajabai are also interesting. It was Sultan Beghada who transformed the solemn Sarkhej complex in the 1500s by adding palaces, gardens, fountains, and courtyards. The area has declined over the years, but it is still a good place for a quiet walk. *(Bus #31 from Lal Darwaja and #150 from the railway station make the trip here.)*

ADALAJ VAV. Nineteen kilometers north of Ahmedabad is the step-well at Adalaj Vav, one of the most impressive in the state. Built in 1499 by Rani Rudabai as a summer retreat, it now serves as a popular relaxation spot for locals. The gardens around it are pleasant, but the carvings on the well are the main attraction. Intricate lattices and detailed carvings of mythological scenes adorn the walls, pillars, and platforms of the five-story well. The best time to visit is just before noon, when sunlight illuminates the stonework all the way to the bottom. *(Buses going to Mehsama Kalol from the ST Bus Stand pass Adalaj Vav: 30min., every 30min. 6am-10pm, Rs9.)*

MODHERA. The ordinary town of Modhera, 84km northwest of Ahmedabad, is home to an extraordinary, Jain-influenced **Sun Temple.** Built in 1026 by the Solanki King Bhimdev I, the temple was constructed and positioned so that, at the time of the equinoxes, sunlight will fall directly on the image of Surya, the sun god, in the sanctuary. Many worshippers come to watch this sacred event. The main entry hall is adorned with 12 *adityas* representing the sun's phases through the year. Guides (working for tips) will eagerly point out the multitude of sexy Kama Sutra-style carvings that are all over the inner sanctum and outer walls. The step-well in front of the temple contains over 100 smaller shrines. *(Open daily sunrise to sunset. Rs2; video fee Rs25.)* Stop for a cup of *chai* (Rs5) and a *thali* (Rs45) at the GTDC-run **Torah Garden Restaurant ❶,** in front of the temple. *(Open daily 9am-6pm. Buses run frequently to Modhera from the ST Bus Stand: 3hr., 9:30am-4pm, Rs42. Connections can also be made in Mehsana, which is connected to Ahmedabad by rail.)*

LOTHAL. The discovery in 1945 of the archaeological site at Lothal ("place of the dead" in Gujarati), 90km southwest of Ahmedabad, was a major event. Lothal is all that remains of an ancient Indus Valley civilization city, dating from 2400 to 1900 BC, and the objects unearthed here have helped historians piece together a picture of what life was like in India's earliest civilizations. Lying in ruin are old roads, houses, shops, a bathhouse, and a sewer; the discovery of a dock and a cargo warehouse suggest that Lothal was a major port city. A **museum** showcases the findings of years of excavation. *(Open Sa-Th 10am-5pm. Free. To reach Lothal, take the bus to Bhavnagar: 2hr.; every 30min. 7am-1am; Rs33. Get off at Dholka, and take one of the frequent buses from there. Alternatively, catch a bus to Bagodra: 1hr.; every hr. 6am-7pm; Rs35. Take a rickshaw from there to the site for Rs150 round-trip.)*

RAJKOT રાજકોટ ☎ 0281

Rajkot is a clean, relaxed, typical Gujarati town, primarily of interest to travelers as a gateway to the Kathiawar Peninsula. Founded in the 16th century, it was the capital of the state of Saurashtra and an important administrative center for the Raj. Its recent fame is mostly due to its connection to Mahatma Gandhi, who spent his youth here. In Rajkot, Gandhi went to school, got married and received permission from his mother to go to England—the rest, as they say, is history.

▐▀ TRANSPORTATION

Flights: Rajkot Airport (☎454533). 4km northwest of town. **Indian Airlines,** Dhebar Rd. (☎234122). Near the circle. Open daily 10am-1pm and 2-5:30pm. Purchase tickets before 4:30pm. **Jet Airways,** 78 Bilkha Plaza, Kasturba Rd. (☎479623 or 479624). Opposite Lord's Banquet Restaurant. Open M-Sa 9:30am-7pm, Su 9:30am-6:30pm. Flights to **Mumbai** (50min.; 4 per week; US$75).

Trains: From **Rajkot Railway Station** to: **Ahmedabad** (5hr.; 5-7 per day 5:40pm-2:15am; Rs97); **Dwarka** (6hr.; 5 per day 6:15am-9pm; Rs61); **Junagadh** (4hr.; 3 per day 8:15am-6:20pm; Rs33); **Veraval** (6hr.; 11:15am; Rs53).

Buses: Main Bus Stand (☎235025). To: **Ahmedabad** (4hr.; every 30min.; Rs68-77); **Bhuj** (6hr.; 16 per day 4:45am-12:30pm; Rs75-79); **Diu** (6hr.; 5 per day 9:30am-2:30pm; Rs68-75); **Dwarka** (5½hr.; 8 per day 6:30am-6:15pm; Rs75-80); **Junagadh** (2hr.; frequent; Rs38-45); **Somnath** and **Veraval** (4½hr.; every hr.; Rs55-65.) **Private bus companies,** opposite the bus stand, go to cities in Gujarat and Rajasthan.

Local Transportation: Auto-rickshaws buzz to the airport (Rs15-20). **Local buses** can take you anywhere in the city (Rs5 or less), though 'anywhere' might not be where you wanted to go. **Chakka-rickshaws** (tempo-motorcycle hybrids) go most places (Rs5-10).

GUJARAT

⬛ 🚻 ORIENTATION AND PRACTICAL INFORMATION

Everything of interest in Rajkot is sandwiched between the **railway station** to the north and the **bus stand** to the south. The bus stand is on **Dhebar Rd.**, which darts north to **Trikonbaug**, a major circle that marks the city center. East of the circle is **Lakhajiraj Rd.**; west is an intersection at the eastern edge of the **Playing Fields.** To the left, **Dr. Yagnik Rd.** heads south and circles the fields; to the right, **Jawahar Rd.** runs north past Jubilee Gardens to the Civil Hospital and **Junction Rd.** A right at Junction Rd. and a left onto **Station Rd.** takes you to the railway station. From the Civil Hospital, **Kasturba Rd.** leads to the **race course,** west of the Playing Fields.

Tourist Office: Tourist Information Bureau (☎234507). Behind the State Bank of Saurashtra at the south end of Jawahar Rd.; upstairs in the yellow brick bldg. Open M-Sa 10:30am-6pm; closed 2nd and 4th Sa.

Currency Exchange: Bank of Baroda, MG Rd. (☎228396 or 225736). Changes traveler's checks. Open daily M-Sa 11am-3pm, Su 11am-1pm.

Police: Police Commissioner's Office (☎477220). Opposite the race course next to Galaxy Cinema. The **control room** (☎100) is open 24hr.

Hospital: Civil Hospital (☎440298). At the intersection of Kasturba and Jawahar Rd. Clean facilities and English-speaking staff. 24hr. pharmacy.

Internet: Dipak Cyber Cafe, Raj Talkies St., a quick right from the statue at the start of Lakhajiraj Rd. Rs30 per hr. Open daily 9:30am-midnight.

Post Office: GPO, MG Rd. (☎228611). West of Jawahar Rd., opposite Jubilee Gardens. Open M-Sa 8am-7pm, Su 10am-4pm. **Postal Code:** 360001.

🏠 ACCOMMODATIONS

Budget hotels dot the railway station area and Lakhajiraj Rd. Business hotels surround the Playing Fields. There are plenty of both behind the bus stand.

Vishram Guest House, Lakhajiraj Rd. (☎230555 or 229208). Its the blue-and-white bldg. opposite Rainbow Restaurant. The best deal in town, with spotless rooms, attached baths, and TVs to help you waste your time. Check-out 4pm. Reservations recommended. Singles Rs150-190; doubles Rs275-325. ❶

Hotel Moon Guest House (☎225522). Behind the bus stand. Don't be deterred by the betel-stained walls in the stairwell. Plain rooms with clean bathrooms and great views from the terrace. All rooms have phones. Singles and doubles Rs150-200. ❶

R.R. Hotels, Dhebar Rd. (☎236811). Between Jawahar Rd. and Para Bazaar. A better deal than the Galaxy looming above it, with 24hr. hot showers and picture windows. Singles Rs250-400; doubles Rs400-550. ❷

🍴 FOOD

Havmor Restaurant, Jawahar Rd., south of Jubilee Garden. Eat Punjabi, Chinese, and continental entrees in a mirrored A/C dining room. Veg. dishes Rs35-60, non-veg. Rs60-75, and of course, ice cream. Open daily 9am-11pm. ❶

Lord's Banquet Restaurant, Kasturba Rd. Gaudy chandeliers, cushy A/C booths, and an enormous selection of Chinese, continental, and Indian veg. specialties (Rs27-68). Open daily 11am-3pm and 7:30-11:30pm. ❶

Rainbow Restaurant, Lakhajiraj Rd., under the Himalaya Guest House. Cheap South Indian veg. snacks (Rs15-30), Punjabi and Chinese dishes, and 40 novelty ice cream confections. Dodge the flies and head upstairs (A/C). Open daily 10am-11pm. ❶

◎ SIGHTS

Flanked by stone lions, the **Watson Museum** is dedicated, strangely enough, to Col. John Watson, a 19th-century British political agent. The museum houses artifacts from the ancient Indus Valley civilization, exquisite miniature paintings, Gujarati handicrafts and metalwork, and classical Indian musical instruments. *(In the Jubilee Gardens. Open M-Sa 9am-1pm and 2-6pm; closed 2nd and 4th Sa. Rs2.)* The **Kabo Gandhi no Delo** was the Gandhi family's residence when they moved to Rajkot in 1881. It now features a small collection of photographs and memorabilia. *(Ghitaka Rd. Open M-Sa 9am-noon and 3-6pm. Small donations appreciated.)*

DIU દીવ ☎ 02875

Local life on the small island of Diu, off the southern coast of Gujarat, revolves around the pursuit of fish and alcohol. For tourists, it revolves around the pursuit of sun, sand, and, well, alcohol. A Portuguese colony until 1961, when India reclaimed it, Diu is now considered part of Union Territory rather than part of Gujarat. As a result, Gujarat's alcoholic prohibition laws don't apply here, making it prime party ground for the thousands of Gujaratis who descend upon the island every weekend. Despite this weekly migration, Diu's streets are quiet, its beaches serene, and its people accommodating.

⌐ TRANSPORTATION

Flights: Diu Airport, 5km west of Diu Town, north of Nagoa Beach (auto-rickshaw Rs30). **Gujarat Airways** (☎ 52180). Off Bunder Rd. next to the GPO. They are also an agent for **Jet Airways.** Open M-Sa 9am-1pm and 3-7pm, Su 9am-1pm and 3-6pm. Flights to **Mumbai** (50min., US$90). Departures are often delayed or canceled.

Trains: Delwada Railway Station (☎ 22226). Between Una and Goghla, 8km from Diu Town (auto-rickshaw Rs100). To **Junagadh** (7hr.; 1:30pm; Rs32) via **Sasan Gir** (5hr.; Rs18) and **Veraval** (4½hr.; 6:30am; Rs19).

Buses: ST Bus Stand, just outside the city's northern gate. Buses depart from the Main Sq. until 6am. To: **Ahmedabad** (8½hr.; 7:30 and 8am; Rs110); **Rajkot** (6½hr.; 5 per day 5:30am-2:30pm; Rs90); **Una** (40min.; every 30min. 6am-7pm; Rs7); **Veraval** (2½hr.; 7 per day 4am-2:15pm; Rs32). The **Una Bus Stand** (☎ 31600) services: **Ahmedabad** (8hr.; 9 per day 6am-10:30pm; Rs105); **Junagadh** (5hr.; 6 per day 4am-7:45pm; Rs53); **Rajkot** (6hr.; 7 per day 5am-7:45pm; Rs68); **Veraval** (2hr.; every 30min. 5:30am-8pm; Rs35). **Private bus companies** surround the Main Sq. and send buses to destinations around Gujarat and to Mumbai. **Gayatri Travels** (☎ 52346), next to the Bank of Saurashtra. Open daily 9am-noon and 3-8pm. Avoid Sunday night buses out of Diu; they're inevitably full of drunks.

Local Transportation: Auto-rickshaws travel within Diu Town (Rs5-10) and go to Nagoa Beach (Rs30) and Una (Rs80). A 3hr. tour costs about Rs150. Night travel out of Diu Town costs an extra Rs20. **Local buses,** departing from the Main Sq., service **Nagoa Beach** (departs 8:15, 10:15, 11:45am; returns 30min. later; Rs7.) **Private buses,** departing from the ST Bus Stand, go to **Delwada** (every 30min. 6:30am-7pm; Rs7). Buses from ST Bus Stand to Una (see above) also stop at Delwada (Rs5-10). Bikes, however, are your best bet for getting around the island. **Kismat Cycle Store** (☎ 52971), behind Main Sq. near the high school, rents **bikes** (Rs15 per day) and **mopeds** (Rs100 per day). Open M-Sa 9am-8pm, Su 9am-1pm.

GUJARAT

■ ▐ ORIENTATION AND PRACTICAL INFORMATION

Diu town occupies the small eastern tip of the island. **Bunder Rd.** leads past the **ST Bus Stand** into town through the northern gate, then runs along the coast to the local bus stand and the **Public Gardens** before its end at **Diu Fort,** which marks the extreme eastern tip of the town and island. The main road in the southern part of town runs east past **Sunset Point, Chakratirth Beach,** and **Jallandhar Beach,** bending past the hospital and St. Thomas' Church to Bunder Rd. **Nagoa Beach** and the **Diu Airport** are near the middle of the island, and are most easily reached by rickshaw.

Tourist Office: Tourist Information Bureau, Bunder Rd. (☎52653). Near Main Sq. Has maps and information. Open M-F 9:30am-1:30pm and 2:15-6pm, Sa 9:30am-1:30pm.

Currency Exchange: State Bank of Saurashtra (☎52135). Around the corner from the tourist office, behind the GPO. Open M-F 10am-2pm, Sa 10am-noon.

Market: Most markets and stores are closed M-Sa 1-3pm and Su. The **fish market** is behind the Main Sq.; the **vegetable market** is farther down Bunder Rd., 200m past the Main Sq. vegetable market. Open daily 8am-noon.

Police: Bunder Rd. (☎52133). Past the Public Gardens on the left. Open 24hr.

Pharmacy: Manesh Medical Store, Dr. Ragaram Kelkar Rd. Open M-Sa 8am-1pm and 2:30-7:30pm, Su 8am-12:30pm.

Hospital: Government Hospital (☎102). In St. Francis of Assisi Church, 200m north of Jallandhar Beach. English-speaking. Open 24hr. for emergencies.

Internet: Deepee Communications, Bundler Rd. Open 9am-11pm. **Gokul Cyber Cafe,** Main Bazaar, opposite Hotel Samrat. Open 9am-1am. Both charge Rs50 per hr.

Post Office: GPO, Bunder Rd. (☎52122). In Main Sq. Open M-Sa 8am-noon and 2-4pm. **Postal Code:** 362520.

▐ ▐ ACCOMMODATIONS AND FOOD

Considering that most visitors to Diu are only looking for a place to black out after a night of drinking, hotels here have no real incentive to impress. In the off season (roughly Feb.-Oct.), discounts can be substantial, but you'll need to bargain. Camping is no longer permitted on Diu's beaches. Free-standing bars are prohibited, so they parade as restaurants, providing only the minimum amount of food required by law; hotels are the best bet for decent food.

Ganga Sagar Rest House (☎52249 or 52501). Nagoa Beach. On the shore with a palm-shaded courtyard. Small rooms with green walls. Decent restaurant and bar offer limited room service. Singles Rs150-300; doubles Rs300-500. Off season Rs100-300. ❶

Jay Shankar Guest House (☎52424 or 52050). Jallandhar Beach. Caters to backpackers. Aging rooms, but peaceful location. Restaurant serves Indian and Western dishes. French toast Rs15, excellent seafood Rs50-75. Dorms Rs50; singles Rs100-200; doubles Rs150-200. Off season Rs30/60-100/80-125. ❶

Hotel Prince (☎52265). Northwest of the Main Sq. Lacks character, but makes up for it in cleanliness. Attached restaurant. Doubles Rs550-1200. Off season Rs150-600. ❸

Hotel Mozambique, Burden Rd. (☎52223). In a Portuguese building in the heart of the vegetable market. Big rooms have seaside or market views. Doubles Rs175-225. Off season Rs100-125. ❶

Rio Restaurant (☎52209). In the Kohinoor Hotel in Fudam. A little out of the way, Diu's only luxury hotel has a good restaurant serving Indian and Chinese food (Rs35-100) and beer (Rs35-50). Open daily noon-3pm and 7-11:30pm. ❶

👁 🏖 SIGHTS AND BEACHES

The massive **Diu Fort,** built between 1535 and 1541, is guarded by a tidal moat, which once made it virtually impenetrable. There is little to do here except wander through the cannons and cannonballs and catch the beautiful views over the sea and town. *(At the end of Bunder Rd. Open daily 7am-6pm.)* From the fort, you can also see the **Fortress of Panikota,** a stone structure that now floats in the middle of the sea.

Wandering through the labyrinthine streets is the best way to see the Portuguese-influenced old city. **Nagar Seth's Haveli** is the most impressive and distinctively Portuguese building in Diu Town (ask for directions once you're in the old city). **St. Paul's Church** is badly weathered but still has grand ceilings and arches, excellent paintings, and a beautiful organ. Mass is still spoken here every Sunday. *(Open daily 8am-9pm.)* Nearby, St. Thomas' Church houses the **Diu Museum,** with its Catholic paintings and statues. *(Open daily 8am-9pm.)*

Travelers sick of (or from) drinking might enjoy one of Diu's excellent beaches. The island's longest and most famous is **Nagoa Beach,** 7km west of town. On the southern side of Diu Town, **Jallandhar Beach** is rocky but great for wading. **Chakratirth Beach,** to the west of Diu Town, is better for swimming, and the nearby **Sunset Point** is a favorite local hangout. Across the bridge from Diu Town, **Goghla's** long beach is great for swimming and has fewer tourists—but also fewer palms—than Nagoa Beach. **Auto-rickshaws** shuttle people from the bazaar to Jallandhar Beach and Chakratirth (Rs20), Goghla Beach (Rs20), and Nagoa Beach (Rs30).

VERAVAL વેરાવળ AND SOMNATH સોમનાથ

☎ 02876

The busy city of Veraval is Saurashtra's most important port, home to a thriving *dhow*-building industry, and harboring over 1000 boats. The docks are an interesting (and interestingly smelly) area to stroll through, but Veraval is more important to travelers as a stepping stone to nearby Somnath, just 5km away. Somnath, known for its once-magnificent temple, is a popular vacation spot for Gujaratis.

📧 **TRANSPORTATION.** From **ST bus stand** (☎21666), **buses** go to: **Ahmedabad** (10hr.; 5 per day 7am-midnight; Rs105); **Diu** (3hr.; 4 per day 7:30am-5:30pm; Rs35); **Dwarka** (6hr.; every hr. 6:30am-midnight; Rs67); **Junagadh** (2hr.; every hr. 5am-12:30am; Rs35); **Rajkot** (4hr.; every hr. 6:30am-10:30pm; Rs65). **Local buses** run from the clocktower to **Somnath** and back (every 30min. 6am-11pm; Rs5). **Auto-rickshaws** make the same trip for Rs25. **Veraval Railway Station** (☎20444; reservation office open M-Sa 8am-8pm, Su 8am-2pm). Fares listed are for sleeper class. To: **Ahmedabad** (11hr.; 5 and 7:25pm; Rs180); **Junagadh** (2hr.; 6 per day 7:10am-3:40am; Rs104); **Rajkot** (5½hr.; 6 per day 7:10am-3:40am; Rs82).

📧 ▊ **ORIENTATION AND PRACTICAL INFORMATION.** ST Rd., Veraval's main thoroughfare, runs roughly northwest-southeast past the **ST bus stand,** through the center of town, past the **clock tower,** and to a dead-end at the port. At the clock tower, the left road heads northeast, past the **GPO** (☎21255; open M-Sa 10am-6pm). From the station, the road leads to another road that bends around Veraval Harbor, past the Temple of Somnath to the **bus stand.** The State Bank of Saurashtra, Shubash Rd., past the clock tower, toward the port, changes currency and traveler's checks. (Open M-F 11am-3pm, Sa 11am-1pm.) The **police station** is to the right of the tower. (☎20003. Open 24hr.) **Dhruv Communications,** before the tower, has Internet access. (Rs30 per hr. Open 10am-midnight.) **Postal Code:** 362265.

⌐⌐ ACCOMMODATIONS AND FOOD. Hotels line the route between the bus stand and the railway station. Although staying in Veraval is more convenient, the hotels in Somnath are cheaper and far more peaceful, if slightly spartan. ▣**Hotel Kaveri ❷**, Akar complex, 2nd floor is on the first side street to the left after you exit the Veraval bus station. Offers upscale hotel luxuries for budget hotel prices. The rooms here come with TVs and 24hr. hot water. The hotel also has laundry service and 24hr. room service. (☎20842 or 43842. Singles Rs150-500; doubles Rs200-600.) **Hotel Ajanta ❶**, on the right as you exit the Veraval bus stand, has quiet, moderately clean rooms in a central location. Laundry and 24hr. room service. (☎23202. Singles Rs150-300; doubles Rs200-350.) Most restaurants in Veraval are between the bus stand and the clock tower. Somnath has many food stalls but no real restaurants. Though Veraval is a fishing town, pious Gujarati culture relegates seafood to a handful of hotels and Muslim restaurants. Meat is nowhere to be found in Somnath. **Jill Restaurant ❶**, halfway between the bus stand and the clock tower, has an A/C dining hall with tall, cushioned booths, lively artwork on the walls, and a chef who's generous with the *ghee*. (Veg. Punjabi, South Indian, and Chinese dishes Rs30-50. Open daily 11am-3pm and 7-11pm.)

◪ SIGHTS. Somnath is renowned throughout Gujarat for the **Temple of Somnath**, a beautiful tableau cut against the sea. Also known as **Prabhas Pratan Mandir**, it holds one of India's 12 *jyotirlingas*. According to popular myth, the temple site was dedicated to *soma*, a hallucinogenic plant that appears in the *Vedas* (see **Vedic Literature**, p. 86). People say the temple was built first of pure gold by Samraj, the moon god, then of silver by Ravana, the sun god, then of wood by Krishna, and finally of stone by the Pandava brother, Bhima (of *Mahabharata* fame). Boring old historians, however, contend that the temple was built in the early 10th century AD, and that it has always been made of stone. The temple was once staffed by hundreds of dancers and musicians and was so rich that its coffers were stuffed with gold and jewelry. The notorious Mahmud of Ghazni put an end to all that when he raided and destroyed the temple in the early 11th century, starting a cycle of pillaging and rebuilding that persisted until Aurangzeb's final plundering in 1706. Sardar Patel, the philanthropist who funded the temple's reconstruction in 1950, is commemorated with a statue that stands outside the temple. The history of the temple is more interesting than the building itself; very little of the original structure remains. The stonework is quite elaborate in places, but the sea winds have worn down the carving on the ocean-side walls. (Open daily 6am-9:30pm; puja 7am, noon, 7pm. No cameras allowed inside.) The **Prabhas Pratan Museum** holds the varied remains of the temple's past glories, including paintings, latticework, stone sculptures, and pottery. (Near the temple. Open M-Sa 9am-noon and 3-6pm; closed 2nd and 4th Sa. Rs1 admission fee. Sorry, no discounts available.)

JUNAGADH જૂનાગઢ ☎ 0285

Less than 100km north of Diu, the lively town of Junagadh, also known as Junagarh, is refreshingly free of the corrupting influence of foreign tourists. From the 4th century BC until Emperor Ashoka's death, Junagadh was the capital of Mauryan Gujarat. Control of the town then passed through several hands before falling under Muslim rule, where it remained until Independence. Although its leaders wanted to unite Junagadh with Pakistan, the town's Hindu majority insisted on joining India. Situated at the base of Mount Girnar, Junagadh's wealth of temples, *havelis*, mosques, and vibrant bazaars makes it a fascinating place to get lost. Expect crowds, however, when the town hosts a wild, four-day party replete with naked sadhus during **Shivaratri** (late Feb. or early Mar.).

TRANSPORTATION. From the **ST Bus Stand** (☎630303), buses go to: **Ahmedabad** (7hr.; every hr. 6am-11pm; Rs100); **Bhuj** (6hr.; 6 per day 5:45am-4:30pm; Rs82); **Dwarka** (5hr.; 5:40 and 10am; Rs72); **Rajkot** (2hr.; every hr. 7am-11pm; Rs37); **Una**, for buses to **Diu** (5½hr.; 7 per day 6:45am-7:45pm; Rs45); **Veraval** (2hr.; every 30min. 6am-11pm; Rs27). **Private bus companies** along Dhal Rd. run comfortable minibuses and buses to **Mumbai** and to towns in Gujarat. **Junagadh Railway Station** (☎131) is on Station Rd. Reservation office open M-Sa 8am-8pm, Su 8am-2pm. Trains run to: **Ahmedabad** (9hr.; 7 and 9pm; Rs157); **Rajkot** (2½hr.; 3 per day 6:15am-1:30pm; Rs33); **Veraval** (2½hr.; 6 per day 4:40am-9pm; Rs30). You can walk just about anywhere in 15min., or **auto-rickshaws** can toot you around town for Rs5-10. **Rickshaws** to Mt. Girnar cost Rs35. **Local buses** run to **Mt. Girnar** (every hr. 6am-5pm, Rs3) from the local bus stand on MG Rd. Early morning buses are the most reliable. **Bikes** (Rs5 per hr., Rs30 per day) can be rented around Chittakhana Chowk.

ORIENTATION AND PRACTICAL INFORMATION. From the **ST Bus Stand, Dhal Rd.**, the main thoroughfare, runs east, passing through **Chittakhana Chowk** (marked by twin minarets) on its way up to **Uperkot Fort.** At Chittakhana Chowk, **Mahatma Gandhi (MG) Rd.** branches south, passing the **Government Hospital** (☎620652; open 24hr.), the **local bus stand**, the **GPO** (☎623701; open M-Sa 9:30am-5pm), the main **police station** (☎627001), and the **Bank of Baroda** (☎654684; open M-F 11am-3pm), on its way to Kalwa Chowk, another market area. Halfway between Chittakhana Chowk and Uperkot Fort, **Jhalorapa Rd.** branches south off Dhal Rd. through Diwan Chowk, near the **State Bank of India.** (☎621094. Open M-F 11am-3pm.) **Pharmacies** are in Kalwa and Chittakhana Chowk near the Government Hospital. **Shree Medical Stores,** Dhal Rd., is just west of the railway crossing. (☎631820. Open 24hr.) **Cyberpoint** (☎625635) logs on for Rs30 per hr. **Postal Code:** 362001.

ACCOMMODATIONS AND FOOD. Most hotels are on Dhal Rd. in and around Chittakhana and Kalwa Chowks, but there are also a few near the ST Bus Stand and the railway station. Reserve well in advance during Shivaratri. With a gracious and helpful staff, **Hotel Relief ❶**, Chittakhana Chowk, has unofficially assumed the role of the town's tourist information center. Above-average rooms have attached baths with hot water. The hotel has a great city map on the wall, and gives information on sights and bus and train departure times. (☎620280. Singles Rs150; doubles Rs200-500.) **Hotel Anand ❶**, Dhal Rd., between the ST Bus Stand and Chittakhana Chowk, has dimly lit, clean rooms with attached baths and TVs in a somewhat noisy area. (☎630657 and 631228. Singles Rs200; doubles Rs250-400.) **Hotel Somnath ❷**, on the right as you exit the railway station, is in the quieter outskirts of the town center. Somnath has well-furnished rooms and clean attached hot-water baths from 5-9am. (☎624644. Singles Rs200-600; doubles Rs300-700.)

Although there are food stalls and *dhabas* in Chittakhana and Kalwa Chowks, you'll find better fare at the hotel restaurants in town. **Sagar Restaurant ❶**, Riddhi Siddhi Complex, 1st floor, just past Sagar, serves excellent food in its dimly lit, A/C dining room. (☎623661. Entrees Rs20-40. Open daily 9am-3pm and 5-10:45pm.) **Swati Restaurant ❶**, Jayshree Rd., Kotecha Complex, 1st floor, is near Jayshree Cinema. Hindi pop fills the chilly air as friendly waiters serve deliciously spiced entrees (Rs25-55) in this crowded veg. restaurant. (☎625296. Open daily 9am-3pm and 5-10pm.) **Santoor Restaurant ❶**, MG Rd., before Kalwa Chowk, is a popular A/C place. Veg. dishes from Rs20. (☎625090. Open daily 9:45am-3pm and 5-11pm.)

SIGHTS. The impressive **Uperkot Fort,** on top of a mini-plateau in the middle of the town, is one of the best in the state. Built in 319 BC, it was ignored for 1,300 years until it was rediscovered in AD 976. Over the next 800 years, the fort was besieged 16 times; one ultimately unsuccessful siege lasted 12 years. A high stone *tripolia* gate marks the entrance to the fort and the start of the road that meanders to the **Jami Masjid,** built on top of a Hindu temple. Once an impressive edifice with 140 pillars supporting its high ceiling, the mosque has suffered from years of neglect. The fort also holds a 5m cannon cast in Egypt in 1531 and two step-wells: the **Adi Chadi Vav** has 170 steps, and the extraordinary **Navghan Kuva,** with its unique 11th-century circular staircase, winds down 50m into the ground. *(Fort open daily 7am-6:30pm. Rs1.)* From the fort, down the road and to the left through the double arched gate, is the **Durbar Hall Museum.** *(Open Tu-Th 9am-12:30pm and 3:30-5:30pm. Rs3.)* The **Babupyana Caves,** south of the fort, and the **Khapra Kodia Caves,** north of the fort, are also popular.

North of Chittakhana Chowk, on MG Rd., is the **Baha-ud-din-Bhar Maqbara,** with its spiraling minarets, grand arches, and numerous domes. The mausoleum's complex design and opulent interior make it unlike any other in Gujarat. Also on the way to Mt. Girnar is a granite boulder inscribed with **Ashokan edicts.** Dating from the 3rd century BC, these edicts teach moral lessons of *dharma,* tolerance, equality, love, peace, and harmony. The Sanskrit inscriptions, which refer to flooding in nearby areas, were added by later rulers. Next to it is the **Mahabat Maqbara,** which houses the remains of the nawab of Junagadh and the pastel **Jama Masjid.**

Mount Girnar, 4km east of Junagadh, is an 1100m extinct volcano that has been sacred to several religions for more than 2000 years. Nearly 5000 steps wind through forest and past outcrops of sun-scorched stone to the summit. Approximately half-way up the mountain (1½hr.), you'll come upon a cluster of intricately decorated Jain temples. The marble **Neminath Temple** is dedicated to the 22nd *tirthankara* who, according to legend, died on Mt. Girnar. Its black marble image sits amid finely carved pillars, domes, and arches. Another 2000 steps take you to the mountain's peak, where the small **Amba Mata Temple** and several other shrines offer a breathtaking view. Since a visit to the temple is said to guarantee a happy marriage, the summit sees many newlyweds. *(The hike takes approximately 5-6hr. round-trip. Begin your hike before 7am to avoid the heat. There are drink stalls along the way.)*

NEAR JUNAGADH

SASAN GIR NATIONAL PARK

The park is accessible by **train** *(Delwara Local 352, 3hr., 6:10am, Rs15) and* **bus** *(2hr., every hr. 6:30am-8pm, Rs32) from Junagadh.* **Shared jeeps** *are required to tour the park (Rs500 for up to six people; departures 7am and 3pm). Sasan Gir is open from Sept. 16 until the monsoon hits. Jeep and entry fees total about Rs215, and the camera fee is Rs40. Guides cost Rs430 for six people. An average trip through the park takes about 45min., during which you are likely to catch a glimpse of at least one of the lions.*

Sasan Gir, 65km from Junagadh, is the last stronghold of the **Asiatic lion.** These great cats once roamed forests and grasslands all the way from Greece to Bengal, but by the turn of the 20th century, there were only 239 left on the planet. In 1900, the Nawab of Junagadh invited Lord Curzon, then Viceroy of India, to a lion hunt on his land, the only place outside Africa where wild lions could still be found. The two met a barrage of criticism for further endangering the threatened species, and Lord Curzon canceled the hunt, advising the Nawab to protect the lions. The forest became a wildlife sanctuary in 1969, and it now covers over 250 square km. The lion population (today more than 300) is increasing at a healthy rate. The park's forests and grasslands are also a sanctuary for peacocks, hyenas, panthers, and several varieties of deer.

DWARKA દ્વારકા ☎ **02892**

Most Hindu legends agree on the subject of Dwarka's holiness. The *Puranas* designate it as one of the seven holy cities in which pilgrims can attain *moksha*. Krishna set up his capital here, on the westernmost point of the Kathiawar peninsula, after being forced to flee Mathura in Uttar Pradesh. Vishnu descended to Dwarka in the form of a fish to battle local demons, and the 9th-century saint Shankara established a monastery here, marking it as India's western *dham*. Few tourists come here, and Dwarka is remarkable for its sense of peace, active temple, sea breezes, and mystical remoteness.

▐ TRANSPORTATION. Trains head from the railway station (☎34044; reservations office open M-Sa 8am-8pm, Su 8am-2pm) to: **Ahmedabad** (10hr.; 12:05pm; Rs183); **Mumbai** (20hr.; 12:05pm; Rs287); **Rajkot** (5-7hr.; 3 per day 7:40am-9:40pm; Rs61). **Intercity buses** run from the main bus stand (☎34204). To: **Ahmedabad** (10hr.,;5 per day 8:45am-9pm; Rs112); **Bhuj** (9hr.; 7pm; Rs140); **Junagadh** (7hr.; 4 per day 9:30am-2:45pm; Rs90); **Mandvi** (10½hr.; 7:30am; Rs150); **Rajkot** (5hr.; 14 per day 5am-12:30am; Rs82); **Veraval** (6hr.; 7 per day 5:45am-6:45pm; Rs72). **Local buses** shuttle to **Okha** (45min.; every 10min. 6:45am-11pm; Rs10).

▧ ▐ ORIENTATION AND PRACTICAL INFORMATION. The main road into the city bends right, joining the road between the main gate into the **old city** and the **railway station.** Just before reaching the **main gate,** the road turns right, skirts an empty field, and then bends left. After the bend, there is a set of three arches—the second gate into the old city. Straight ahead is a road that runs along the coast. The main road bends left, passing the main bus stand and a small building that serves as the **GPO** (☎34529; open M-F 7:30am-12:30pm and 4-6pm, Sa 7:30am-12:30pm), and ends at **Okha,** the port for **Bet Dwarka.** The old city is a maze of tiny streets centered around the Dwarkadish Temple, with the main **police station** (☎34523) next door. Dwarka Lighthouse sits on the western outskirts of the old city. The best hospital in town, **Navajyot Hospital** (☎34419), 400m toward the coast from the main gate has a **pharmacy.** (Open daily 9am-1pm and 4:30-8:30pm. 24hr. for emergencies.) **Postal Code:** 361335.

▐ ▢ ACCOMMODATIONS AND FOOD. ▨**Hotel Rajdhani ❶,** Hospital Rd.; ask for directions. The plush rooms feature marble bed frames, color TVs, and room service. (☎34070 or 34679. Check-out 3pm. Doubles Rs250-500.) **Hotel Meera ❶,** near the main gate into the old city, has spotless, whitewashed rooms and a whole family of friendly staff. (☎34031. Check-out 24hr. Singles Rs100; doubles Rs200-575.) The **Toran Tourist Guest House ❶,** near the coast, has big, well-kept rooms with attached baths and 24hr. hot water. Mosquito coils and toilet paper provided. (☎34013. Check-out 9am. Dorms Rs50; singles Rs200-450; doubles Rs300-600.) **Shetty's Fast Food ❶,** offers cheap, tasty Punjabi and South Indian dishes (Rs15-35) and *lassis* for Rs8. (☎34512. Open daily 8am-3pm and 5:30-11pm.) **Milan Restaurant ❶,** Bhadrakali Rd., not to be confused with the Milan Dining Hall opposite the Hotel Rajdhani, serves delicious but seriously spicy entrees for Rs30-50. (☎34062. Open daily 9am-3pm and 7-11pm.) The **Meera Dining Hall ❶,** serves delicious, never-ending *thalis* for Rs25. (Open daily 10am-3pm and 7-11pm.)

◪ SIGHTS. Dwarka's principal attraction is the staggering **Dwarkadish Temple,** also known as Jagat Mandir, or "Temple of the World," which marks the center of town with its six-story main spire. The temple was allegedly constructed over 1,400 years ago, and although the spiky exterior stonework looks a bit weathered these days, the elaborate carvings of various incarnations of Vishnu are still visible on the temple's inner walls. Sixty columns support the main structure, which houses a black marble image of Krishna in a silver-plated chamber. Smaller shrines decorate the edges of the complex. *(Temple open daily 7am-1pm and 5-9:30pm. Non-Hindus must sign a release form to enter.)* The **Dwarka Lighthouse** offers spectacular views of the sunset over the Arabian Sea, though no cameras are allowed inside the lighthouse. *(Open daily 4:30pm-sunset. Rs1.)* The long, clean **beach** nearby, which is rarely crowded (except Su), is great for wading past the small beach temples.

No pilgrimage to Dwarka would be complete without a visit to the tiny island of **Bet Dwarka,** where Vishnu slayed the demon Shankasura. Right on the tip of the peninsula, Bet Dwarka has a number of Krishna temples, where devotees come for *prasad* and *puja*. The main temple, which marks the spot of Krishna's death, has a central well that is said to bring up sweet-tasting water, although it apparently draws from the surrounding ocean. Dwarka's real appeal, however, is its eery quietude. *(The island is accessible via the port at Okha, 1hr. north of Dwarka. Rickety, overloaded, pastel-colored boats make the crossing: 30min., every 20min., Rs2.)*

KUTCH 𝄞𝄞

One of the most isolated regions in India, Kutch is bordered on the south by the Gulf of Kutch and the Arabian Sea, and on the north by the Rann of Kutch, a marsh in the Thar desert that is home to pink flamingoes and wild ass. The sultans who ruled Gujarat made repeated attempts to cross into Kutch, but it managed to remain independent and developed its own customs, laws, and a thriving maritime trade with Muscat, Malabar, and the African coast. Kutch was absorbed into the Indian Union in 1948. During the monsoon season, floods in the Rann of Kutch cut the region off from its neighbors Saurashtra (Gujarat) and Sindh (Pakistan), causing varying degrees of damage every year. The Rann is a scenic place during the rest of the year. The dry northern part of Kutch is useless for agriculture, but the southern district of Banni used to be one of India's most fertile regions. Though drier today, Banni still produces cotton, castor-oil plants, sunflowers, and wheat. When the people of Kutch abandoned agriculture because of climactic changes, they turned to handicrafts.

Unfortunately, this already sensitive region was most affected by the earthquake on January 26, 2001. Thousands were crushed by the concrete rubble that alone will take years to clear; many thousands more remain displaced, living in roadside cities of tents and shipping containers. Relief efforts are directed by UNICEF.

BHUJ 𝄞𝄞 ☎ 02832

In the center of the region of Kutch, Bhuj is mainly used by tourists as a base for exploring outlying villages, but the city offers far more than just a place to leave your pack: interesting museums, varied architecture, an 18th-century palace, and an array of interesting temples. Bhuj was founded in the 16th century as the capital of Kutch by Rao Khengarji, a Jadeja Rajput, and it remained the region's center of economic activity until the establishment of the city of Gandhidam and the port of Kandla to the east. Unfortunately, Bhuj was also near the epicenter of the earthquake that hit Gujarat in January 2001, and services listed may not be running for awhile. The old city was hit especially hard.

TRANSPORTATION

Flights: Bhuj Airport (auto-rickshaw Rs40-50, taxi Rs150). **Indian Airlines,** Station Rd. (☎50204 or 21433). Open daily 10am-5:30pm. **Jet Airways,** Station Rd. (☎53671 or 53674). Open M-Sa 8am-7pm, Su 8am-4pm. **Gujarat Airways,** ST Rd. (☎52286 or 52285), is an agent for both IA and Jet. Open daily 9-11:30am and 3-7:30pm. Flights to **Mumbai** (1½hr.; 2 per day; US$100-105).

Trains: New Bhuj Railway Station (☎20950). 1km north of town (auto-rickshaw Rs20). Reservations office (☎131 or 132). Open M-Sa 8am-8pm, Su 8am-2pm. To **Ahmedabad** (8hr.; 3 per day 6:45am-6:40pm; Rs140) and **Gandhidham** (2hr.; 3 per day 7:25am-7:50pm; Rs11).

Buses: ST Bus Stand, ST Rd. (☎20002). To: **Ahmedabad** (8hr.; 10 per day 5am-11pm; Rs100; deluxe 7 per day 5am-11pm; Rs115); **Dwarka** (11hr.; 10:45am; Rs132); **Junagadh** (9hr.; 5 per day 5am-9:30pm; Rs98); **Mandvi** (1½hr.; every 30min. 5:30am-11:30pm; Rs15); **Rajkot** (every 30min. 5am-10pm; Rs79; deluxe 5 per day 7:30am-11pm; Rs86). **Private bus companies** line ST Rd. **Ashapura Travels** (☎55661). Opposite the bus stand. Open daily 6am-9pm.

Local Transportation: Auto-rickshaws around town cost Rs5-10. **Taxis** congregate around the bus stand and compete to take you to villages around Bhuj (Rs3 per km).

✈ 🛈 ORIENTATION AND PRACTICAL INFORMATION

Bhuj's main **bus stand** is in the center of **ST Rd.,** which runs roughly east-west along the southern edge of the old city. From **Mahadev Gate** at the west end of ST Rd., **Uplipad Rd.** runs along the edge of Hamirsar Lake past the Swaminarayan Temple and the walled complex of the Prag and Aina Mahals. **College Rd.** leads south from the Kutch Museum, the **police station,** and the Folk Art Museum. Near the eastern end of ST Rd., **Waniawad Rd.** leads north to **Shroff Bazaar.** From the northern edge of the old city, roads lead to the **railway station** and the **airport,** 6km away. **Station Rd.** borders the old city to the east and turns into **Hospital Rd.** as it runs south.

Tourist Office: In Aina Mahal (☎20004). Very helpful in planning rural tours. Open Su-F 9am-noon and 3-6pm.

Currency Exchange: State Bank of India, Hospital Rd. (☎56100). Open M-F 10am-2pm.

Police: The main **police station** (☎53050), on the east side of College Rd., has English-speaking officers. To get permits for the sensitive border area north of Bhuj, go to the **District Superintendent of Police** (☎53593, ext. 132), east of College Rd.'s south end, down the road opposite the Collector's Office. Bring a copy of your passport and visa. Open M-Sa 11am-2pm and 4-6pm; closed 2nd and 4th Sa of each month.

Hospital: Seth Gophandas Khetsey Hospital (☎22850). On the road to Gandhidam. Clean and modern with English-speaking doctors. Also has a 24hr. **pharmacy.**

Post Office: GPO (☎22952), off Station Rd. south of ST Rd. Open M-Sa 10am-5:45pm. Small branch on Langa Rd., opposite the City Guest House (☎22650). Open M-Sa 9am-5pm. **Postal Code:** 370001.

🏠 ACCOMMODATIONS

▨ **Hotel Annapurna,** Bhid Pol, at the top of Station Rd. (☎20831). Popular with the backpacking crowd, Annapurna offers 12 well-decorated rooms with TVs and balconies. The owner, Vinod, is knowledgeable. Outstanding restaurant downstairs. Check-out 24hr. Singles Rs90; doubles Rs150. ❶

Hotel Abha, ST Rd. (☎54451-3). While its slightly cheaper next-door neighbor is gutted, here there remain several clean rooms with attached baths, 24hr. hot water, 24hr. room service, phones, and TVs. Singles Rs200-300; doubles Rs400-1100. ❷

V.R.P. Guest House, ST Rd. (☎21388 or 22777). Since the old city falls silent at 7pm these days, you may as well just gaze at it from this rooftop. The rooms are uninspiring but functional. Singles Rs70, with attached bath Rs110; doubles Rs170-200. ❶

Hotel Gangaram, Darbargarh Chowk (☎24231), past Aina Mahal from the lake. This is a self-sufficient fortress on the fringe of the old city's rubble-desert. An alarming, life-sized clown portrait stands guard over the minty-fresh doubles (Rs300). ❶

FOOD

Most restaurants in Bhuj open only for lunch and dinner, with a hefty break between the two, making three square meals a day a virtual impossibility. Instead, take advantage of the abundance of food stalls and have a meal in the square.

Annapurna Restaurant, Bhid Pol, in Hotel Annapurna. Popular dinette allows you to custom make your own *thali*. Veg. dishes, sweets, rice, and *chappatis* are skillfully prepared. Also serves standard Punjabi fare (Rs20-40), spiced to taste. Open M-Sa 10:30am-3:30pm and 7-11:30pm, Su 10:30am-3:30pm. ❶

Hotel Noorani Palace, near the vegetable market as you walk through the main bazaar from Aina Mahal. One of the few spots in Gujarat where meat is consumed without remorse. Roasted chicken (half-order Rs55), mutton *biryani* (Rs26). Open daily 11am-3:30pm and 7:30-10pm. ❶

Rasoi Restaurant, ST Rd., in Hotel Abha. A/C dining with Punjabi, Chinese, and continental dishes (Rs35-60), or huge *thali* (Rs60). Open daily 11am-3pm and 7-11pm. ❶

Jesal, Station Rd., in Hotel Prince. If the omelette center by the bus stand doesn't do breakfast as you would like, then this place will. Lavish spreads Rs60-110, *murghi chetti nad* Rs101, prawns in garlic sauce Rs85. Open daily 12:30-3pm and 7-11pm. ❶

Joker, by the bus stand. A truly bizarre burlesque of Chinese and continental curiosities. Veg. *hakka* "nudadles" Rs40. Open 9am-3pm and 7-11pm. ❶

SIGHTS

AINA MAHAL (PALACE OF MIRRORS). Maharao Lakhad (r. 1741-60) was renowned for his love of Kutch regional art. His palace is a small, fortified structure in the old city. A raised platform here was once surrounded by a pool of water and fountains, where the maharao would sit as musicians entertained him. Inside the Aina Mahal, the beautifully designed **Maharao Madansinji Museum** is filled with artifacts and memorabilia, and the maharao's bedroom has remained untouched. His *chakri* slippers still sit by the bed; they were designed to produce an olfactory warning of his proximity—with each step a flower at the toe of the slippers opens to release scented powder. Miraculously, about 90% of the museum's collection survived the quake. *(Open Su-F 9am-noon and 3-6pm. Rs5. Photography prohibited.)*

PRAG MAHAL (NEW PALACE). Marble stairs ascend to the main hall beneath the curving arches and sandstone columns of the palace, built in 1816. The main hall is a macabre monument to death, as well as a taxidermist's nightmare—the floor is covered with the decaying heads of lions, tigers, leopards, deer, and wild cows. A spiral staircase leads to the top of the bell tower which affords fantastic views. *(Open M-Sa 9-11:45am and 3-5:45pm. Rs10; camera fee Rs15, video fee Rs50.)*

SHARAD BAGH MUSEUM. This beautifully-kept museum at the southwestern corner of Hamirsar Tank was the residence of the last maharao of Kutch until his death in 1991. Built in the mid-19th century and styled after an Italian villa, the palace is much as the maharao left it, with his TV and VCR set among his hunting trophies. *(Open Sa-Th 9am-noon and 3-6pm. Rs10; camera fee Rs10, video fee Rs50.)*

OTHER MUSEUMS. Bhuj's museums are an excellent place to learn about Kutch culture before heading out to the villages. The **Kutch Museum,** the oldest in the state, has excellent anthropological and archaeological exhibits on the region. *(College Rd. Open Th-Tu 9am-noon and 2:45-5:45pm; closed 2nd and 4th Sa. Rs0.50, camera fee Rs2 per shot.)* The **Bharatiya Sanskriti Darshan,** also called the **Folk Museum,** contains a small collection of local textiles, embroideries, paintings, and bead work, as well as a library. The highlight of the museum is its reproduction of Rabari *bhungas* (huts) with their decorated inner walls. *(Mandvi Rd., at the south end of College Rd. Open M-Sa 9am-noon and 3-6pm. Rs5; camera fee Rs50.)*

OTHER SIGHTS. On the way to Harmisar Tank from the Darbargadh complex lies the **Swaminarayan Temple.** This early 19th-century technicolor temple consists of two single-sex temples and a third for both men and women. *(Open daily 7-11am and 4-8pm.)* South of Hamirsar Tank, in the midst of a sandy, deserted plain, the eerie **Memorial Chattris** commemorate some of the previous maharaos of Kutch and their wives who committed *sati*. The red sandstone memorial to Maharao Shri Lakhpatji (1710-61) and his 15 wives is the biggest of the bunch.

▶ DAYTRIPS FROM BHUJ

VILLAGE TOURS

Tours can be made by taxi (Rs800-850 for up to four people for a full day tour to several villages) or, more slowly, by bus from Bhuj. Contact the tourist office for more information on arranging village tours.

Most tourists use Bhuj as a base from which to explore the nearby villages. These tours offer a glimpse of village life and provide opportunities for you to spend your money on local handicrafts, though the experience has been soured somewhat recently: many villages have responded to the tourist trade with aggressive merchandising and exorbitant prices. However, many of the villagers seem genuinely excited by the tourist traffic and enjoy showing visitors around, sale or no sale.

The village of **Sumrasar,** just outside of Bhuj, is home to **Kala Raksha** (☎77238), a research institute and women artists' cooperative dedicated to the "preservation of traditional arts." Founded in 1993, the center has a large collection of embroidered textiles from Kutch. A small store sells local work; the items are of excellent quality, prices are reasonable, and profits go directly to the artists. For information on research opportunities and accommodations at Kala Raksha, contact Judy Frater, Project Coordinator (☎53697; fax 55500; judyf@ad1.vsnl.net.in). From Bhuj, take a rickshaw (Rs100) or a bus (Rs6) to nearby Hajipar.

Kera, 22km south of Bhuj, is home to a Shiva temple thought to have been built in the 10th century (buses 45min., every hr. 6am-8:30pm, Rs6). Farther south is the Rabari village of **Tundawadh** (best reached by car), famed for its exquisite embroideries. **Anjar,** 40km southeast of Bhuj, is a major center for handicrafts enthusiasts and specializes in weapons, nut-crackers, jewelry, and textiles (buses 2hr., every 30min. 5am-11pm, Rs12-20). For block printing galore, head to **Dhamanka,** east of Bhuj (buses 1½hr.; every hr. 6am-9:30pm; Rs12-22). The village of **Khavda** specializes in pottery (buses 2hr.; 7 per day 8:30am-6:30pm; Rs16). **Bhirandiyari,** on the way to Khavda, is known for its embroidery, weaving, and leather work (1hr., Rs13). **Zura,** home of the copper bell, and **Nirona,** specializing in Rogan painting, are accessible by the same bus (11 per day 8am-6:30pm; Rs11-13.) The villages of Khavda and Zura were hit worst by the recent earthquake, so enquire about services before getting on the bus.

For those sick of handicrafts, head 60km northwest of Bhuj to the remote **Than Monastery** (bus 2hr.; 5pm; Rs20). The ruins of **Dholavira,** one of the largest sites uncovered in the Indus Valley, dates to 2500 BC (4½hr.; 2pm; Rs45).

MANDVI માંડવી ☎ 02834

Established by Maharao Khengarji in 1588, Mandvi rose to prominence as an important port, trading with South Africa, the Middle East, China, and Japan. The Arab and European traders who settled here in the 18th century left grand mansions behind them in the winding lanes of the old city when they left, along with a dwindling boat-building industry. Pushcarts and auto-rickshaws almost seem to be propelled by the breeze, and hand-built wooden *dhows* lean lazily against the docks and the beautifully rusted anchors beached by the tide. Shop-owners rest quietly on the steps of medieval buildings, while blacksmiths and welders send dust and sparks into the salty evening air. Bordered by vast stretches of untainted shore and surrounded by a horizon studded with palm trees, Mandvi is the ideal place to sit back and do a whole lot of nothing.

⌷ TRANSPORTATION. From the **ST Bus Stand** (☎20004), buses travel to: **Ahmedabad** (12hr.; 6:45, 8:45am, 5pm; Rs115-130); **Bhuj** (1½hr., every 30min. 5am-9pm, Rs29); **Dwarka** (11hr., 9:30am, Rs125); **Rajkot** (7hr., 5 per day 6:15am-7pm, Rs102).

◧ ◪ ORIENTATION AND PRACTICAL INFORMATION. From the **bridge** that stretches over the salt flats, a left turn takes you down **ST Rd.** past the main **police station** (☎20008; open 24hr.) and the **ST Bus Stand,** coming to a dead-end at the port. The small road straight ahead from the bridge leads to the Rukmavati Guest House. The **Shree Gokul Hospital** (☎20361), next door, is a clean, modern facility with an English-speaking staff. (Open M-F 9am-1:30pm and 4-6:30pm for consultations, 24hr. for emergencies.) There are many **pharmacies** near the hospital. (Open M-Sa 9am-9pm.) A right turn from the bridge takes you along the northern city wall and leads eventually to Vijay Vilas Palace, 8km away. At the southern end of ST Rd., near the port, **Bandar Rd.** leads off to the right past the **State Bank of India** (☎20031; open M-F 11am-3pm, Sa 11am-1pm) and several sawmills to the southern end of **Bhid Chowk,** which is the central market area. Internet is cheapest at **Sanghui Communications,** just north of the market. The **GPO** is 1km to the right away from the bridge. (☎20266. Open M-F 10am-6pm, Sa 10am-1pm.) **Postal Code:** 370465.

◪ ◪ ACCOMMODATIONS AND FOOD. The best place to stay in Mandvi is the ▧**Rukmavati Guest House ❷,** near the bridge. Enormous, well-furnished rooms open onto a plant-filled terrace with a porch swing. 24hr. hot water, laundry service, and kitchen available for guest use. (☎20557. Check-out 24hr. Dorms Rs75; singles Rs125-650; doubles Rs225-750.) The **Maitri Guest House ❶,** Kanthawalo Gate, has bright, clean rooms in the heart of the old city. (☎32583. Check-out noon. Dorms Rs70; singles Rs150-200; doubles Rs200-250.) ▧**Hotel Nayna ❶,** Azad Chowk, serves the best lunchtime *thalis* in town (Rs40). *Masala dosa* with *sambar* Rs17. (☎20183. Open daily 11am-3pm and 6-11pm.) The restaurant in the Osho Hotel, **Zorba the Buddha ❶,** dishes out unlimited *thalis* (Rs40) to a constant stream of locals. Don't let the grungy atmosphere fool you; the food is fresh and delicious. (Open daily 11:30am-2:30pm and 7:30-9:30pm.)

◧ ◪ SIGHTS AND BEACHES. Mandvi is blessed with many beautiful haunts—the old city walls, the port with its wooden ships moored on the salt flats, the canyon-like streets with their stone mansions, and the temples and mosques that crowd the eastern side of the salt flats. But the **Vijay Vilas Palace,** 9km west of town, is Mandvi's biggest draw. A domed, latticed mansion set on 692 acres, the palace was built in 1927 as a summer home for the Maharao of Kutch. Spotless marble floors, walls delicately inlaid with floral patterns, and gorgeous carved rosewood and teak furniture decorate the inside. From the third floor, a rusting spiral staircase leads to a domed terrace with a view of the Arabian Sea and the coconut trees and windmills of the flat, green Kutch. Perhaps the highlight of the palace, though, is its private **beach,** 1km away. The nearly 2km stretch of sand is litter-free and blissfully unpopulated. Follow the road past the GPO and veer left at both forks. (Open daily 9am-1pm and 2-6pm. Rs5; camera fee Rs50, video fee Rs200. Bike Rs5, rickshaw Rs15. They'll ask for Rs15 for beach access, but it's just around to the right as you leave the palace.) Mandvi's seemingly endless shoreline draws many visitors. The town's main beach, called **Windfarm** because of the numerous windmills that line it, can get a bit crowded, but the farther west you go, the more isolated it becomes. **Kashivishvanath Beach** is quieter and lies on the opposite side of the port. Cross the bridge and take your first right, following the left fork all the way to the water.

HIMACHAL PRADESH
हिमाचल प्रदेश

Travel through Himachal Pradesh is an experience of complete detachment from the urban world. You'll walk through apple orchards, cross rivers swollen with glacial run-off, and gaze in wonder at the breathless scenery of diverse worlds that exist alongside each other in Himachal Pradesh. The rain-drenched forests of Manali give way to the rock and ice of the Lahaul Valley and the vast emptiness of Spiti. From Shimla to Kaza, Hindu temples are replaced by Buddhist prayer flags and *gompas*. The road from Manali to Leh, in Kashmir, defies description.

With the unpredictable situation in Kashmir, more foreign tourists have been going to Himachal; the three main towns in HP are both backpacker retreats and gateways to the lands beyond. Dharamsala has a strong Tibetan population and is the base for treks into the Dhauladar and the Pir Panjal ranges. Manali and Shimla are favorite vacation spots with both Indian and foreign travelers. The less touristed rainshadow areas—Lahaul, Spiti, and Upper Kinnaur—can be reached from Manali via the Rohtang La or from Shimla via Kaza, but routes that should be open from June to September can close at any time due to avalanches and floods. The main tourist season in most of HP runs from May to June and from September to October, but winter—when roads to Shimla, Manali, and Dharamsala and from Shimla to Chamba remain open—is also an ideal time to visit.

HIGHLIGHTS OF HIMACHAL PRADESH

The Kullu Valley towns of **Manali** (p. 247), **Kullu** (p. 243), and **Naggar** (p. 244) are famous for green pastures, apple orchards, and great views of the Western Himalayas.

Dharamsala (p. 231) is where the mythic East meets and mixes with the equally mythic West, to the delight of hippies, pop stars, and Buddhist saints alike.

From its green forests to its icy mountain tops, HP has some of the most beautiful **trekking** in India, particularly in **Kinnaur** and **Spiti** (p. 252).

SHIMLA सिमला   ☎ 0177

With its cool air, magnificent views, and lingering spirit of the Raj, Shimla can leave visitors spellbound. A stroll along the Ridge can be a strange experience; Indian tourists, foreigners, and monkeys all vie for space along broad streets lined with Highland-esque houses. The British arrived on the scene in 1815 when local rulers asked for assistance in fending off Gorkha invaders. Over the next half century, injured soldiers and British civil servants flocked to Shimla. In 1864, imperial authorities made the summer haul to Shimla official; they declared it the seasonal capital for the Raj. Soon, Shimla became a social center. Tailors' shops lined the Mall, and Englishmen paraded along the Ridge en route to their gala balls.

Today, Shimla is a good stopover before heading to busier (or rougher) parts of the state. It is connected by a road to Kullu and Lahaul in the north, Kangra and Chamba in the west, and the Kinnaur and Spiti in the east. During May, June, September, and October, times when the town is free from both snow and monsoonal downpours, the mountain quiet disappears, and the area is flooded with Indian tourists, who drive up prices and create such a ruckus that even the monkeys hide.

TRANSPORTATION

Flights: Jubbarhatti Airport, 22km from town. Rs350 cab ride. Flights to **Delhi** (1hr.; M, W, F 10:20am; US$110) via **Kullu** (30min., US$65). Book **Indian Airlines** flights and taxis to the airport at Ambassador Travels (see p. 228).

Trains: Shimla is connected to **Kalka** via the narrow-gauge railway (5hr.; 10:45am from Town Rail Station, 2:30 and 5:30pm from Main Rail Station; Rs40). From Kalka, connections can be made to: **Ambala** (2hr.; 7am, 5:30, and 9pm; Rs40); **Amritsar** (9hr., 4pm, Rs140); **Delhi** (8hr., 4:45 and 11:30pm, Rs130).

WARNING. Foreigners planning to travel between Jangi and Sumdo, in the eastern regions of Kinnaur, must obtain an all-inclusive **inner-line permit** from the sub-divisional magistrate, as these areas are sensitive border regions. In Shimla, see the **Additional District Magistrate,** on the 2nd fl. of the left side of the green colonial building just south of The Mall, beneath the telegraph office (open M-Sa 10am-5pm, closed 1-2pm for lunch). Fill out an application and have a local travel agent sign on as a sponsor and submit the form for you—regulations require that an agency submit the form. **Band Box Heights and Valleys** (see **Budget travel**) does all this for Rs150. As of June 2001, there is no charge for the permit itself.

Buses: There are two bus stands in Shimla. **Main Station** sends buses to: **Chamba** (15hr.; 4am, 5, 6:40pm; Rs247); **Chandigarh** (4hr., every 15min. 3:30am-10:30pm, Rs71); **Delhi** (10hr.; 10 per day 6am-10:30pm, Rs182; deluxe 3 per day 8:25am-9:45pm, Rs316); **Dharamsala** (10hr., 7 per day 6:50am-10:30pm, Rs153); **Haridwar** via **Dehra Dun** (10hr., 4 per day 5am-5pm, Rs157); **Manali** via **Kullu** (10hr., 5 per day 8am-8:15pm, Rs166); **Pathankot** (12hr., 4 per day 5am-8:20pm, Rs188). **Rivoli Bus Stand** sends buses to: **Kalpa** via **Rampur, Jeuri, and Rekong-Peo** (13hr., 6am, Rs158); **Rampur** (6hr., 4 and 9am, Rs80).

ORIENTATION AND PRACTICAL INFORMATION

Shimla stretches from Himachal Pradesh University across a ridge to **Lakkar Bazaar,** where many of the town's Tibetan refugees live. Most major streets run from east to west, each at a different elevation. Trains and most buses arrive on **Cart Rd.** Above Cart Rd. is the bazaar, and above the bazaar is Shimla's main drag, **The Mall,** which is off-limits to motorized vehicles. The easiest (and laziest) way to get up and down is to take the **tourist elevator** on Cart Rd., just after the street turns south (open in summer 8am-10pm, in winter 9am-8pm. Rs5). For a workout, take any path or stairway leading up. At **Scandal Corner,** directly above the main bus stand, The Mall divides into a lower section and the upper section known as **the Ridge,** which becomes Lakkar Bazaar as it curves left beyond **Christ Church.**

Tourist Office: Himachal Tourism Marketing Office (☎252561). On the left, next to Scandal Corner. Open M-Sa 10am-6pm. Two doors down is the **Road Transport Booth,** which gives information on bus schedules and road conditions. The office also arranges helicopter tours of the Shimla area (20min.-1½hr., Rs1500-5000). Open 9am-5pm.

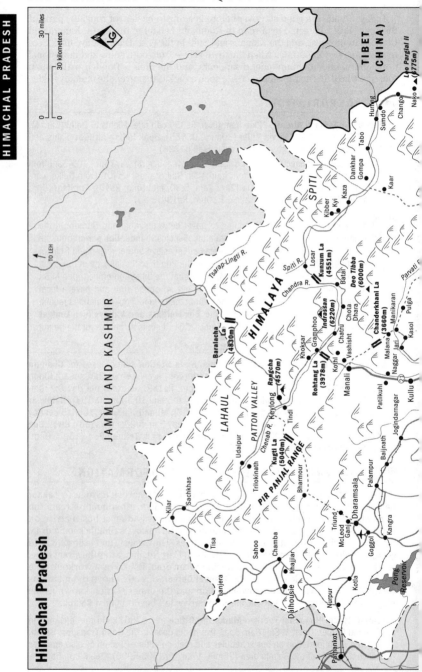

HIMACHAL PRADESH

Himachal Pradesh

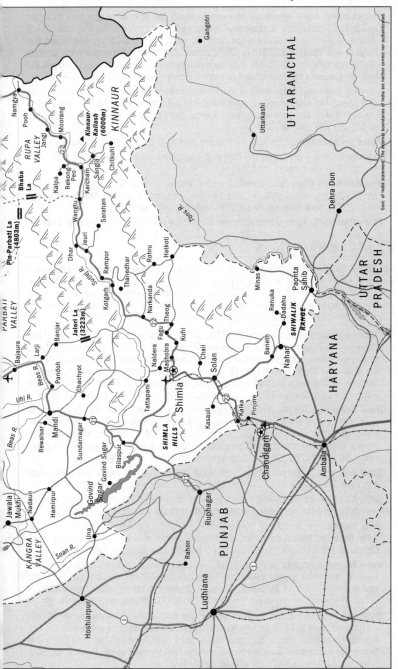

Budget Travel: Travel agents are on every corner of The Mall; most give both transport and trekking assistance. **Ambassador Travels** (☎ 258014). Below The Mall, near Gaiety Theatre. Does airline bookings quickly and efficiently. Open M-Sa 10am-6pm. **Band Box Heights and Valleys** (☎ 258157). On Scandal Corner. They arrange **inner-line permits** (Rs150 commission), 9-10 day jeep tours of Kinnaur-Spiti (Rs1600/day), and will put together groups of travelers wishing to share the cost of the jeeps. Open 9am-9pm daily.

Currency Exchange: State Bank of India, interior open M-F 10am-2pm, Sa 10am-noon; ATM open 24hr. **ANZ Grindlays,** open M-F 9:30am-2:30pm, Sa 9:30am-12:30pm. Both are on The Mall, and both change cash and traveler's checks. Grindlays gives advances on MC and Visa for a Rs100 fee.

Police: (☎ 212344). On The Mall, next to the town hall. Open M-Sa 10am-5pm.

Pharmacy: Several are along The Mall and lower Mall, including **Vohra's** (lower mall) (☎ 205530). Open daily 9am-8pm.

Hospital: Nehru Clinic (☎ 201596). The Mall. Women only. Down a side alley. Open M-Sa 10am-2pm and 4-6pm. In emergencies, call **Indira Gandhi Medical College** (☎ 203073). **Tara Hospital** (☎ 203275). Also has 24hr. service.

Post Office: GPO, above Scandal Corner. Open M-Sa 10am-6pm. **Postal Code:** 171001.

ACCOMMODATIONS

From May to June, September to October, and during Christmas season, vacancies are rare, and come only at inflated prices. Expect discounts of up to 50% off season. The really cheap places near Victory Tunnel and the bus station are crowded and tend to have only common baths (in season Rs200-250). Better hotels are up The Mall. Most levy an additional 10% tax.

YMCA (☎ 204085 or 252375; fax 211016). Up the stairs behind Christ Church. Not just for young Christian men, this is quite possibly the last affordable, truly worthwhile place to stay in Shimla. Colonial grandeur blends seamlessly with postcolonial kitsch. Rooms are clean, and the rec rooms have TV, billiards, and other diversions. Rs40 membership fee valid for one week. The staff arranges treks and jeep safaris. Breakfast included. Hot water 7pm-9am. Singles Rs200; doubles Rs250-430. Off season: singles Rs130. ❶

Hotel Uphar (☎ 257670). From the Ridge, walk up the path behind the clock, past the Dreamland Hotel; it's on your right. Rooms of varying quality and size have differing views. Hanuman's temple is close by, and the windows and balconies are all barred to protect guests from the god's curious retinue. 24hr. hot water in all rooms. Check-out noon. Doubles Rs275-325. Off season: minimum 50% discount. ❶

Hotel Ashirwad, in Lakkar Bazaar, past Hotel Auckland. Small rooms with seat toilets and color TVs. Singles Rs225; doubles Rs350-775. Off season: 50% discount. ❶

Hotel Amar Palace (☎ 204055). Right below Hotel Uphar. Good views of valley. Rooms with color TV. 24hr. hot water. Doubles Rs450-750. Off season: 50% discount. ❷

Hotel Mehman (☎ 213692 or 204390). Daisy Bank Estate. Rooms have carpets, TVs, 24hr. hot water, heat in the winter, and a doctor on call. Nice terrace restaurant on roof. Check-out noon. Doubles Rs550-1100. Off season: 25% discount. MC/V. ❷

Hotel Borovalia Resorts (☎ 252900). In the Fingask Tourist Complex. Facing the State Bank of India, walk toward the Palace Hotel; take the steps on the right and follow the narrow alley on your left for 100m. This hotel offers plush rooms hidden from the Mall's bustle. TVs and 24hr. hot water. Doubles Rs700-1200. Off season: Rs350-600. ❷

Woodville Palace (☎ 223919). 2km south of the town center, past the tourist elevator on The Mall. Built in 1938 for Raja Rana Bhagat Chandra, the prince of Jubbal, the Palace exudes colonial charm. Spacious rooms, good views, nice furniture, and baths (not to mention cable color TV) make this one of the best splurges in HP. Doubles Rs1700; suites as much as Rs6000. Off season: 1200/4500. MC/V. ❺

HIMACHAL PRADESH

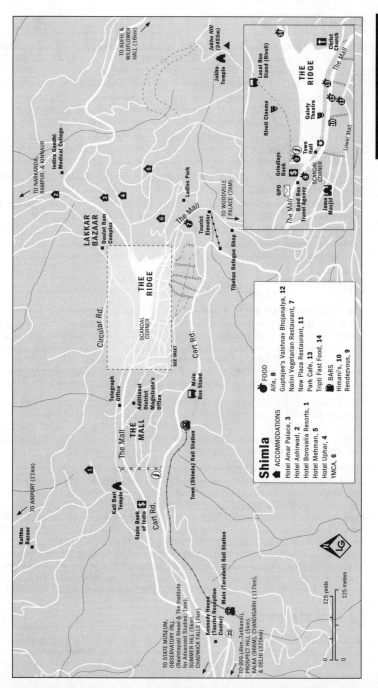

Shimla

▲ ACCOMMODATIONS
Hotel Amar Palace, 3
Hotel Ashirwad, 2
Hotel Borovalia Resorts, 1
Hotel Mehman, 5
Hotel Uphar, 4
YMCA, 6

♦ FOOD
Alfa, 8
Guptajee's Vaishnav Bhojanalya, 12
Nalini Vegetarian Restaurant, 7
New Plaza Restaurant, 11
Park Cafe, 13
Tripti Fast Food, 14

🍷 BARS
Himani's, 10
Rendezvous, 9

FOOD

Nalini Vegetarian Restaurant, on The Mall, before the elevator. Crammed into two small rooms, Nalini is well known among locals for serving the best South Indian food in town. Steeper prices than in the lower bazaar *dhabas,* but worth it. Oddly enough, the walls are covered with a mural of Olde England. *Thalis* Rs80. Open daily 9am-10:30pm. ●

Guptajee's Vaishnav Bhojanalya, on the stairway between The Mall and lower mall. Take first right after Gaiety Theatre and walk down–the restaurant will be on your right. The Special Deluxe *thali* (Rs45) is outstanding. Open daily 9am-10pm. ●

Park Cafe, on the slope between The Mall and the Ridge. Bamboo-decorated cafe enthralls regulars with American classic rock, daily papers, and foreign standards. The pizza (from Rs45) and milkshakes (Rs25-50) are excellent. Open daily 8am-10pm. ●

Alfa, on The Mall, near Scandal Corner. Has soft brown chairs and serves *Masala chai* in tin pots. The sweets are from the bakery shop in front. Open daily 11am-10pm. ●

New Plaza Restaurant, on the lower Mall, down the staircase from the Gaiety Theatre. A wide selection of Indian and not-quite-Chinese meat and veg. dishes. Excellent chicken curry Rs55. Open daily 10am-11pm. ●

Tripti Fast Food, on the right between the Ridge and Lakkar Bazaar. A wide variety of South Indian *dosas* and *utthapams.* Meals Rs25-40. Open daily 9am-10pm. ●

SIGHTS

HIMACHAL PRADESH STATE MUSEUM. It's a hike to the museum, but the collection is worth it. The first floor contains the remains of 2000-year-old sculptures and specimens of Indo-Greek coinage unearthed in HP. On the second floor are a number of Kangra Pahari miniature paintings and works by contemporary artists. If you plan to hike up to the **Jakhu Temple** (see below), the "Hanuman Adoring Rama" is worth a look. *(Walk west along The Mall until you reach a concrete ramp labeled "Museum," directly next to the Ambedkar Chowk sub-post office. Open Tu-Su 10am-1pm and 2-5pm.)*

VICEREGAL LODGE (RASHTRAPATI NIVAS). This neo-Tudor style lodge was once the summer headquarters of the Raj. In 1945, it was the site of important (but failed) negotiations between the would-be Indian and Pakistani leaders. *(Pass the entrance to the state museum and walk 10min. west along The Mall. Open daily 10am-1pm and 2-4:30pm. Rs10 admission includes a guide.)*

JAKHU TEMPLE. This red-and-yellow temple is at the top of a 2455m hill. The 20min. walk to the summit is a steep huffer and puffer, especially if you've been smoking too many *bidis.* The temple itself is fairly uninspiring, but the views are astounding. Inside the temple are the alleged footprints of the monkey god Hanuman. As tourists feed them snacks, hordes of monkeys revel in their heritage. Two networks of paths lead back to town; both cut through magnificent forests, but the sinuous paths directly to the right of the temple afford better opportunities for enjoying the scenery and taking detours. Neither set of paths is marked, but they all eventually lead down. Allow 45min.-1hr. to reach town on the way down from Jakhu; expect to emerge from the forest near Lakkar Bazaar, 15min. or so from Scandal Corner. *(At the east end of the city, with the trail beginning just left of Christ Church.)*

ENTERTAINMENT

Most visitors are content just to stroll along The Mall or the Ridge, enjoying the breezes and the architecture. Luckily, there are a few pubs. **Himani's** serves drinks at inflated prices (beer Rs75-80), and has billiard tables on the top floor. Open until

9 or 10pm. There is a bar at **Rendezvous,** just next to the statue of Lalalajpatrai (beer Rs75), and **The English Wine Shop** sells bottled spirits from a spot on the lower mall. Take the fourth right after the Gaiety Theater, and make a right onto the lower mall. For **movies,** head to **Rivoli** or **Ritz.** Rivoli, down the ramp between ANZ Grindlays Bank and Rendezvous, shows its English-language flicks at 4:30pm. The Ritz, east of Christ Church, on the ramp leading up to the YMCA Guest House, screens sexy English-language films at 5:30 and 9pm. Tickets Rs35 at both theaters. Below Rivoli is an **ice-skating rink,** which typically opens in January.

▛ SHOPPING

There are extraordinary handicrafts in Himachal: fine woodwork, engraved metalwork, patterned carpets, and traditional woolen shawls. **Kashmir Craft Emporium,** 92 The Mall, has an impressive collection of shawls (Rs150-5000) and silk saris (Rs250-4000). **Maria Brothers,** 78 The Mall, just below the church, specializes in bizarre and beautiful old books. Prices aren't cheap, but owner Rajiv Sud is equally friendly to browsers and buyers alike. (Open daily 10:30am-1pm and 3:30-8pm.)

DHARAMSALA धर्मशाला ☎ 01892

After China's occupation of Tibet began in 1959, the 14th Dalai Lama and his Buddhist government were given asylum in Dharamsala. Since then, a steady stream of Tibetan exiles has relocated here, some of them walking across the Himalayas to escape oppression and be near the man they regard as their religious and political leader. Today, Upper Dharamsala, also called McLeod Ganj—named after David McLeod, a former governor of the Punjab—attracts students, tourists, hippies, and devotees of Buddhism to its monasteries, meditation centers, and Tibetan shops, giving this refugee community the feel of an energetic international crossroads.

Embraced by the craggy Dhauladar mountains, and covered with pine and deodar forests, Dharamsala commands fantastic views of Himalayan peaks and the Kangra Valley. Several easy hikes from McLeod Ganj lead to the slopes, while more serious treks head up and over the snowy passes. In the summer, unfortunately, daily fog and rain bother even the most devout, but in July and August the flowers blossom, infusing the mountain air with a sweet-smelling freshness.

▟ TRANSPORTATION

Flights: Goggol Airport, 9km from town. Flights to **Delhi** (1hr.; M, W, F 3pm; US$150). During the summer, book in advance.

Buses: Intercity government buses usually arrive at and depart from the **New Bus Stand** in Lower Dharamsala. Booking Office (☎24903). Open daily 8am-1pm and 2-7pm. To: **Chamba** (10hr., 8:30am and 5pm, Rs115-136); **Chandigarh** (8hr., 8pm, Rs140; deluxe Rs190); **Dalhousie** (6hr., 8:30am, Rs85); **Delhi** (12hr., 9 per day 5am-8:30pm, Rs250; deluxe 7pm, Rs350); **Haridwar** (13hr., 3pm, Rs235); **Manali** (12hr., 4:45am and 6pm, Rs170); **Pathankot** (3½hr., 10 per day 4:45am-5pm, Rs55); **Shimla** (10hr., 5 per day 5am-9:30pm, Rs152). From **McLeod Ganj,** buses run to **Dehra Dun** (12hr., 8pm, Rs240). Book at any of the travel agencies. Blocked roads and mudslides mean that buses to Manali and Chamba are sporadic during the monsoon and winter.

Local Transportation: Buses run between the New Bus Stand and McLeod Ganj (every 30min. 6:30am-8:30pm, Rs4). The **shared jeeps** that run between Kotwali Bazaar and McLeod Ganj (Rs6-7) are cramped but faster. Both bus and jeep service are erratic, but you can easily hike along Jogibara Rd. (1hr. up, 45min. down). The **Taxi Union Stand** beside the bus circle has high fixed rates (Rs75 from Lower to Upper Dharamsala); they're generally only worth it if you're heading up to Dharamkot or Bhagsu at night.

◢ ORIENTATION

Dharamsala is split into two sections differing by 500m in altitude; this is a result of a massive 1905 earthquake that destroyed all of the town's buildings and killed 900 people in the Kangra Valley. Alarmed by the destruction, the British administration established **Lower Dharamsala,** which now houses mostly offices, banks, and the Indian population. The largely Tibetan enclave of **Upper Dharamsala (McLeod Ganj)** attracts the most tourists. Seven roads branch off the **main bus circle** in McLeod Ganj. The first is **Cantonment Rd.,** the route used by buses to travel to and from Lower Dharamsala. As you go clockwise, the next road is **Taxi Stand Rd.,** which leads to the Tibetan Children's Village. Next is a steep road leading to **Dharamkot,** 50min. away. The fourth spoke off the bus circle is **TIPA Rd.,** which also leads to Dharamkot, passing the Tibetan Institute of Performing Arts (TIPA) on its way. Next, **Bhagsu Rd.** leads to Bhagsu (20min.) after passing many restaurants and hotels. The sixth road is **Jogibara Rd.,** and finally, **Temple Rd.** leads to the Dalai Lama's residence, Tsuglagkhang (Main Temple), and Namgyal Monastery. As you walk along Temple Rd., you will encounter a fork; both routes lead to Namgyal, but the lower one (to your right) is quicker and has a better view. Bear left and head uphill to reach the **Himachal Tourism Office** and more expensive hotels. A steep 30min. walk down either Jogibara or Temple Rd. lands you in Gangchen Kyishong, the location of the Tibetan government-in-exile.

⚑ PRACTICAL INFORMATION

TOURIST AND FINANCIAL SERVICES

Tourist Office: Himachal Tourism Marketing Office (☎/fax 24212). 50m below Kotwali Bazaar in Lower Dharamsala, before the Bank of Baroda. Open daily 9am-1:30pm, 2-7pm. The **McLeod Ganj Office** (☎21205), off Temple Rd. behind the State Bank of India, is less helpful. Open M-Sa 10am-1:30pm and 2-5pm. Both offices are closed on official holidays and the 2nd Sa. of each month.

Budget Travel and Trekking: Most agencies in McLeod Ganj do bus and plane tickets; a few organize treks. For airline, train, and deluxe bus bookings, **Dhauladar Travel,** Temple Rd., accepts AmEx, MC, and V for charges over Rs500. Open daily 9am-1pm and 2-6pm. **Occidental Travel** (☎21938), Taxi Stand Rd., next to the bus stand, arranges treks (US$10-20 per day). Open 9am-7pm. For more info on **Trekking,** see p. 32.

Currency Exchange: Punjab National Bank, Temple Rd. In McLeod Ganj, a few steps from the bus circle. Changes currency and traveler's checks. Open M-F 10am-2pm, Sa 10-noon. **Western Union** money transfers are available at **Paul Merchants** (☎21418), in the **Surya Resorts Hotel,** a few houses after Bookworm bookshop. Open M-Sa 10am-7pm. **Bank of Baroda** (☎23175), Lower Dharamsala, opposite the Museum of Kangra Art, changes money and gives MC and V cash advances. Cash advances require 24hr. for processing. Open M-F 10am-2pm, Sa 10am-noon.

LOCAL SERVICES

Bookstore: Bookworm, on Temple Rd. At the fork, follow the sign to Hotel Bhagsu; it's 10m down on the right. Carries the standard books on Tibet and Buddhism, as well as English-language classics. Open Tu-Su 9am-6:30pm; in winter 10am-5pm. **Namgyal Bookshop,** Namgyal Monastery, next to the Tsuglaghang. All proceeds go to the government-in-exile. Open M-Sa 9am-noon and 1:30-5pm.

EMERGENCY AND COMMUNICATIONS

Police: The main police station (☎21483) is in Lower Dharamsala, below the GPO, in Forsyth Ganj, west of McLeod Ganj.

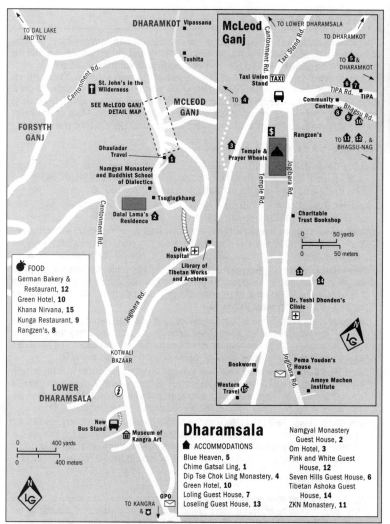

Hospital: The Tibetan **Delek Hospital,** Jogibara Rd. (☎22053, 24hr. emergency 23381). Just before Gangchen Kyishong. Has a good walk-in clinic. Open M-Sa 10am-1pm and 2-5pm. They have a branch in McLeod Ganj on Bhagsu Rd., just before the Green Cyberspace Cafe. **Dr. Yeshi Dhonden** (☎21461), off Jogibara Rd. in McLeod Ganj, practices Tibetan herbal medicine. Open Su-F 8am-1pm.

Internet: Everywhere in McLeod Ganj. The connections are fast, and the standard price is Rs30 per hr. The **Green Cyberspace Cafe,** Bhagsu Rd., in Green Hotel, has more than 10 computers. Rs30 per hr. Open daily 9am-10pm.

Post Office: **GPO,** Lower Dharamsala, 1km south of Kotwali Bazaar. Another branch is along Jogibara Rd., past the State Bank. Both open M-F 9am-2pm and 3-5pm. **Postal Code:** McLeod Ganj 176219; Lower Dharamsala 176215.

ACCOMMODATIONS

Dharamsala is usually packed in spring and autumn; even in summer it can be hard to find a room. Most tourists stay in McLeod Ganj, and guest houses continue to spring up along Jogibara, Temple, and Bhagsu Rds. If spiritual interests are what bring you here, you might want to stay in one of the monasteries. These fill up quickly, but if you put yourself on a waiting list when you arrive, you should get a room in a day or two. **Bhagsu** and **Dharamkot** are a 20min. walk from McLeod Ganj and are generally much cheaper; doubles cost as little as Rs50. Most of the guest houses are small, and many rent rooms for longer stays (Rs500-1000 per month).

MCLEOD GANJ GUEST HOUSES

Loling Guest House, (☎21072). TIPA Rd. 100m from the bus circle. One of the best deals in town. Hot showers Rs10 for guests using the common bath. Singles Rs50; doubles Rs75, with attached bath, hot water, and seat toilet Rs150. ❶

Loseling Guest House, (☎21087). Jogibara Rd. On the left, 50m from the bus circle. Loseling offers clean doubles with attached bath for Rs150-250. ❶

Tibetan Ashoka Guest House (☎21763). Off Jogibara Rd., on the left, 75m from the bus circle. With over 40 rooms, this place will have one for you. Great views help justify the high price. Gates close at 11pm. Doubles Rs60, with attached bath Rs275-330. ❶

Green Hotel, (☎21200). Bhagsu Rd. 150m from the bus circle. This open, lively place has more rooms than its neighbors but still fills up for most of the year. Good views from the back rooms. Gates shut at midnight. Singles Rs55; doubles Rs80, with attached bath Rs120, with hot water Rs250. ❶

Om Hotel (☎21313). To the right of Temple Rd., just down the paved path from the bus stand. Travelers flock to the balcony restaurant to sip *chai* and enjoy the view. The upscale rooms are large and have attached bathrooms with seat toilets and hot water. Laundry service. Rooms Rs80; doubles Rs200-275. Off season: Rs200. ❶

Seven Hills Guest House (☎21580). Next to Loling Guest House, 100m from the bus circle, on the left side of TIPA Rd. The only place in town with a front yard and beauty salon. The restaurant and Internet lab make it entirely self-sufficient. All rooms have private baths and great views. Doubles Rs150-250. Winter prices negotiable. ❶

Tara Guest House (☎21181). Next to the Chime Gatsal Ling monastery. Rooms are sparklingly new and clean, with hot showers. The rooftop balcony has the best view in McLeod Ganj of His Holiness' residence. The studios downstairs are an amazing deal if you are staying long-term. Doubles Rs165-250; studios Rs3000-3700 per month. ❶

MONASTERIES

Dip Tse Chok Ling Monastery (☎21726). A 10min. walk down the steps on the right ridge past the Om hotel. This isolated monastery is far removed from the bustle on the ridge, making it the perfect spot for meditation. Join in evening prayer with the *lamas*. Breakfast (Rs40) and dinner (Rs60) served. All rooms have 2 beds, writing tables, and most share an clean, tiled toilet. Rooms Rs125-300. Off season: Rs100-150. ❶

Zilnan Kagyeling Nyingmapa (ZKN) Monastery, 15min. walk up Bhagsu Rd.; turn left up the driveway just past Last Chance Tibetan Restaurant. Dimly lit rooms with common bath line the sides of this new monastery. Step out of your room into the transcendental, temple-style courtyard. Singles Rs60; doubles Rs80. ❶

Chime Gatsal Ling, (☎21340). Temple Rd. 75m up the driveway opposite the School of Dialectics; it's the big orange bldg. on the left. Part hotel, part housing for Nyingmapa-sect monks. Spotless, carpeted rooms are huge, and the roof is perfect for watching the sun set on the Dhauladars. Doubles Rs80-140. ❶

Namgyal Monastery Guest House (☎21492). Lets you share a courtyard with His Holiness' residence and the Tsuglagkhang (Main Temple). The unique ambience of the monks' cells complements the lavish surroundings. Doubles with bath Rs225. ●

BHAGSU AND DHARAMKOT

Pink and White Guest House (☎24527). Up the hill from the center of Bhagsu; a 15-20min. walk from McLeod. Not the cheapest, but has an array of nice rooms with private bath and 24hr. hot water. Room service 6am-11pm, meals Rs20-55. Singles Rs200; doubles Rs350-500. Off season: 40% discount. ●

Blue Heaven (☎21005). Just below Dharamkot., a 25min. walk up TIPA Rd. Turn right on the forest path. This most tranquil of places has enormous doubles with or without cushy carpet and tiled bathrooms. Doubles Rs150-200. ●

▐ FOOD

The heavy, flat noodles and hunks of mutton should remind you that you're in Tibetan culinary territory. Yet the apple pie on the dessert menu leaves no doubt that Dharamsala is, at the same time, a tourist trap and a traveler's heaven—you can find just about any national cuisine represented here.

▨ **Mt. Everest Restaurant,** Jogibara Rd. On the left, past the post office. The owners toss up authentic *Amdo* cuisine from the northeastern region of Tibet. Try the handpulled noodles *(thankthuk)* and szechuan hot sauce. Meals Rs20-45. ●

▨ **Khana Nirvana,** Temple Rd. Above Western Travels. Has possibly the best burritos this far east; guitars and drums flirt in the background as you sit on comfortably cushioned chairs. This happenin' joint features a "Sunday at Sunset" lecture series, Monday jam sessions, and an Interfaith Shabbat on Fridays. Inquire here for volunteer opportunities in Dharamsala. Entrees Rs30-60. Open Su-F 10am-10pm. ●

Kunga Restaurant and Nick's Italian Kitchen, Bhagsu Rd. Before the Green Hotel. A native New Yorker once taught his Bologna-acquired art to Tibetan chefs who have taken the skill to the requisite *bodhisattva* level of perfection. The pasta is homemade, and the parmesan is flown in fresh from the Apennines. Richard Gere comes here whenever he is in town. Open daily 6:30am-9:30pm.

Rangzen's, Bhagsu Rd. Just before Nick's Italian Kitchen. This comfortable place has great valley views and serves up Tibetan specialities. Nothing beats the *tsampa* (barley porridge), a Tibetan staple cooked here according to a *Bonpo* shaman's magic formula (see **A Bon-afide Religion,** p. 551). Most dishes Rs25-60. Open daily 8am-10pm. ●

Green Hotel and Restaurant, Bhagsu Rd. Western hangout and restaurant, this place serves carefully prepared Tibetan and Chinese dishes. Cappuccino (Rs18) makes clear why this is a traveler's favorite. Most dishes Rs25-50. Open daily 7:30am-10pm. ●

Kailash Hotel and Restaurant, Temple Rd. Near the bus circle. Owned by a Tibetan family, Kailash dishes out spicy *momos* to a mostly local crowd; wash 'em down with a cup of mild jasmine tea. Dishes Rs20-75. Open daily 8am-9pm. ●

Om Restaurant, near the bus circle. Good food and even better prices. The terrace is a delightful spot to enjoy the sunset over a cup of tea (Rs3). Most dishes Rs25-30. Open daily 8am-10pm. ●

German Bakery and Restaurant, above the Pink and White Guest House. Up the hill from central Bhagsu. This hungry hikers' haven has an array of rye breads and apple pies to complement its assortment of homemade noodle soups. Open daily 9am-10pm.

◎ SIGHTS

TSUGLAGKHANG TEMPLE. This temple, whose Tibetan name simply means "Main Temple," houses images of the Buddha, Padmasambhava, and Avalokiteshvara ("Chenresig" in Tibetan). This last image, representing the *bodhisattva* of whom the Dalai Lama is an incarnation, was rescued from the Tokhang Temple in Lhasa and brought here during the Chinese Cultural Revolution. On the days of the Buddha's birth, death, and enlightenment, hundreds of monks circumambulate the temple three times on their hands and knees, giving money to the hundreds of beggars who flock to this path during the ceremony. **Remember always to walk clockwise on this path, spin the prayer wheels clockwise, and remove footwear before entering the temple.** Monks from the School of Dialectics come to debate—snapping, clapping, and shouting at each other—in the temple's courtyard in the afternoons. Each snap, clap, and stomp corresponds to a specific point in the argument being advanced. The debates are one of the features of the Gelugpa sect's teachings and are governed by an immensely complex system of logic. *(Behind the Buddhist School of Dialectics; a 10min. walk from the bus circle in McLeod Ganj. Open daily sunrise to sunset.)*

THE BHAGSU-NAG TEMPLE. This temple rests beside several cool *kunds* (pools) where Hindus and monks bathe. According to legend, 9000 years ago, there was a drought in the kingdom of Ajmer, in present-day Rajasthan. To save his realm, King Bhagsu headed to a 5400m high peak nearby, discovered two lakes, and trapped their waters in his bowl. But as the king lay down to sleep, Nag, the cobra who owned the lakes, challenged him to a fight. Mortally wounded in the ensuing struggle, the king made a dying request for the people of Ajmer to be rid of the drought. Impressed by Bhagsu's devotion to his people, Nag granted him his wish. The fruit of his efforts is today known as the Indira Gandhi Canal, which irrigates most of Rajasthan. The **Bhagsu Waterfall** beyond the temple cascades for 10 m during the monsoon season. There are small open-air cafes around the falls. The lower cafe has cold drinks, snacks, and a crowd of Indian bathers strutting around in their underwear. The upper one, Shiva Cafe, has hot meals, chessboards, and opium-inspired paintings. Above the path to the falls, there are caves where devout monks meditate for extended periods. *(At the northern end of Bhagsu; a 25min. walk from McLeod Ganj. The waterfall is 15min. beyond the temple; follow signs to the path.)*

NORBU LINGKA. To see Tibetan art head to Norbu Lingka, a compound 10km from Dharamsala. Its bamboo groves enclose a display of Tibetan architecture designed to resemble the symmetries of a *bodhisattva*. The **Norbu Lingka Institute**, dedicated to preserving Tibetan culture, is located here and it offers an opportunity to watch *thanka* masters, woodcarvers, metal-workers, and their pupils at work. The **Losel Doll Museum** exhibits costumes from Tibet. *(Take a jeep or bus to Lower Dharamsala (Rs5). From there, take the Palampur bus, and get off at Sacred Heart High School (Rs3). From the school, it's a 20min. walk up the road to the left. ☎ 22664; open M-Sa 9am-6pm; arrive before 4pm to see the workshops or catch a guided tour. Doll Museum Rs25.)*

THE TIBETAN CHILDREN'S HANDICRAFT AND VOCATIONAL CENTER. The vocational center instructs refugees in the arts of *thanka* painting, carpet weaving, and capitalist marketing. Under the Dalai Lama's patronage, the Tibetan Children's Village School (TCV) has been housing and educating more than 2400 orphaned Tibetan children since 1960. Foreigners are welcome to visit the school. You can volunteer here for a few months or sponsor a child (US$30 per month). Donations are welcome. *(The center is a 30min. walk up the hill from the McLeod Ganj taxi stand. The TCV is a 10min. walk farther uphill, past Dal Lake on the right. School open M-F 9am-4pm.)*

SO YOU THINK YOU'RE RICHARD GERE...

To schedule a private audience with His Holiness the Dalai Lama, send your request four months in advance and start praying. Private audiences are rare but not unheard of, particularly if your reason is truly specific to the Dalai Lama. Much more common are public audiences of 300 people or so, held once or twice a month for foreigners and recent arrivals from Tibet. At a public audience, the crowd files slowly past His Holiness, who takes time to speak and laugh with each person (despite his aides' attempts to speed things up). You need to bring your passport a few days ahead to be cleared for the audience. You can contact the Office of His Holiness the Dalai Lama by mail, phone, or email. (Thekchen Choeling, McLeod Ganj, Dharamsala, HP, 176219; ☎/fax 21813; ohhdl@cta.unv.ernet.in.) Check with the security branch office near Hotel Tibet on Bhagsu Rd. to see when the Dalai Lama will next be in town.

OTHER SIGHTS. The **Dip-Tse-Chok-Ling Monastery** is home to a small (and largely young) community of monks, who built the monastery after the destruction of their own in Tibet. *(A 10min. walk from the bus circle down a stone path that begins just past Om Hotel. Open daily 7am-7pm.)* The original monastery once lay south of Lhasa, and has become functional in recent years. Some of the monks alternate between the two locations. The church of **St. John's in the Wilderness** is a functioning relic of the bygone British era. Lord Elgin, an ex-Viceroy of India, is buried in the church cemetery. *(Follow the narrow road from the Dip-Tse-Chok-Ling monastery guest house up to Cantonment Rd.; from there it's a 15min. walk downhill toward Lower Dharamsala. Open daily 9am-5pm. Sunday services in English 11:30am. Candle-light services on Christmas.)* The **Amnye Machen Institute** aims to bring Tibetan culture into the 21st century. The institute gathers contemporary writers and scholars, translates classical works into Tibetan, publishes journals on history and culture, and serves as the main cartographic center for Tibet. The institute has film festivals, lectures, and other Tibet-related events; details are on their website. *(On Jogibara Rd., just past the post office. ☎ 20173; www.amnyemachen.org.)* The **Museum of Kangra Art,** opposite the Bank of Baroda in Lower Dharamsala, has nice exhibits of old carpets, Pahari miniatures, and archaeological artifacts from the Kangra region. *(Open Tu-Su 10am-1:30pm and 2-4pm; closed on local and national holidays. Free.)* A pleasant day-hike from Dharamkot takes you to the grassy ridgetop of **Triund.** There's a small rest house here, and a second, more basic rest house 5km up the trail. Resist the urge to climb higher unless you have mountaineering experience. Be prepared for rain in the early afternoon.

GANGCHEN KYISHONG

On Jogibara Rd., halfway between McLeod Ganj and Lower Dharamsala; turn left through the archway. ☎ 22467. Monastery open M-Sa 10am-1pm and 2-5pm, closed 2nd and 4th Sa and on Buddhist holidays. Free. Tibetan center open daily 9am-1pm, 2-5pm. Library reading membership Rs50 per month. 9-month courses in Buddhist philosophy: M-Sa 9 and 11am, except 2nd and 4th Sa; Rs150 per month, plus Rs50 registration fee. Tibetan language courses: spring, summer, and fall daily 10am; Rs250 per month. Rooms available to students enrolled in two or more classes simultaneously: Rs1000-3000 per month.

The site of the administrative offices of the **Tibetan government-in-exile,** Gangchen Kyishong also houses several non-governmental organizations (NGOs), including the **Tibetan Center for Human Rights and Democracy,** on the top floor. Stop by the Ministry of Information for an update on Tibet's political situation. The **Library of Tibetan Works and Archives,** at the far end of Gangchen Kyishong, has 10,000 volumes in English and other languages on Buddhism, Tibet, and related subjects, and 70,000 texts and scrolls in Tibetan. The books and scholarly periodicals are available for general use in the reading room. Language and philosophy courses taught by renowned *lamas* are also offered. You can attend a session or two for free, although the Tibetan government would appreciate the registration fee. Arrive on time for opening prayers, behave respectfully during class hours, remove your shoes before entering the hall, and for philosophy sessions, don't stand up until the *lama* has left. The **museum** has beautiful *thankas*, Tibetan coins, and several rooms rescued from the Cultural Revolution (Rs10). The **Nechung Monastery,** next to the library, is a peaceful spot for meditation.

🎵 ENTERTAINMENT

The market section of Jogibara Rd. is home to two **movie houses** showing a random assortment of American blockbusters, cult classics, and low-grade flicks. The wooden benches are only slightly more comfortable than the seats on a bus, but the big TV screens have good reception. (Check schedule outside theaters for show times; Rs10.) **McLeo's** third-floor bar, on the bus circle, with its Hawaiian decor and haphazard mix of the Beatles, techno, and reggae, is a surreal place to swill beer (Rs75). Young Tibetans gather here to mingle with the mobs of foreigners. Occasional Godfather-infused **dance parties** last until the 95% male dance floor clears around midnight to 2am. The **Tibetan Institute of Performing Arts (TIPA)** has cultural shows, performs a Tibetan opera for the New Year, and usually has shows on Tibetan holidays. Stop in for more details. (A 10min. walk up TIPA Rd. toward Dharamkot. Call or stop by to check the schedule; if you want to see the theater, be persistent. ☎ 21748 or 21033. Open M-Sa 10am-5pm, closed 2nd and 4th Sa.)

VOLUNTEER OPPORTUNITIES

In its struggle for freedom, the Tibetan community has deemed the ability to speak English a priority; therefore, English teachers and simple conversationalists are welcome. The enthusiastic monks and Tibetan students, mostly McLeod Ganj regulars, often agree to exchange regular language lessons with foreigners. Ask around at the various monasteries to see if they would be willing to take on short- or long-term English teachers. The **Tibetan Children's Village** (☎ 21528) is always interested in committed, long-term English, math, and science teachers.

The **Earthville Institute,** Temple Rd., at the Khana Nirvana Restaurant, serves as a community center, non-profit educational society, and clearing house for info about volunteer opportunities in and around Dharamsala. (☎ 21252; www.earthville.net; dnm@earthville.net; write to Mandala, Dalai Lama Temple Rd., McLeod Ganj, Dharamsala, HP 176219. Open Su-F 10am-9pm.) The official **Community Center,** near Rangzen's on Bhagsu Rd., has postings on local events. The **Green Shop,** part of the Center, employs a squad of dedicated workers who operate the recycling unit and teach volunteers how to make paper or bind books. Contact the Tibetan Welfare Office, Environmental Desk (☎ 21059).

Those interested in short-term projects should consider the **Yong Ling Creche** (☎ 21028), opposite the nunnery on Jogibara Rd. Yong Ling also organizes home-stays (Rs200 per day including meals). Many Tibetan organizations want to put their message online, so volunteers with web-designing skills are in high demand. Try the **Amnye Machen Institute** (see **Other Sights,** above). Finally, there may be opportunities at the **Tibetan Centre for Human Rights and Democracy,** Gangchen Kyishong, northern building (☎ 23363; dsala@tchrd.org; www.tchrd.org); the **Tibetan Youth Congress,** Bhagsu Rd., opposite the Green Shop; the **Tibetan Women's Association** (☎ 21527 or 21198; fax 21528; twa@del2.vsnl.net.in); and the **Tibetan Medical Institute** (☎ 22618), in the Delek Hospital. All have English publications that need proofreading. You can contact any of the above institutions in writing: name of the institution, P.O. McLeod Ganj, Dharamsala, HP 176219. Other volunteer opportunities can be found at www.tibet.org.

MEDITATION

Everyone in Dharamsala seems to be involved in some sort of mind and body twisting activity, be it Thai massage, Reiki, yoga, or meditation. If you're interested in joining the fun, ask people who are already involved for recommendations or check the postings around in McLeod Ganj. The **Tushita Meditation Centre** offers 10-day or shorter residential courses that provide a good introduction to Tibetan Buddhism and analytical meditation. The classes are taught by a Tibetan *lama* and a Western monk. Register by phone or email two months in advance. (☎21866; tushita@ndf.vsnl.net.in. Classes Mar.-June and Sept.-Nov. Open M-Sa 10am-noon and 1-4pm; registration M-Sa 1-3pm.) The center also has a **library** with a selection of books on Buddhism, which anyone can borrow after depositing a passport. (Rs10 per book per week. Open M-Sa 10am-4pm.) Also check out the community newsletter "Contact" for info on courses. Another option is the **Vipassana Meditation Centre,** next door, which runs residential courses in single point meditation. Vipassana has centers all over the world, so you can continue your course after leaving Dharamsala. Register by mail and send a brief resume. Registrations are not accepted over the phone, so register in person M-Sa 4-5pm. Both meditation centers operate on expected donations. For professional **acupuncture** or **Thai massage,** head to the third floor of the **Mount View Hotel,** on Jogipurn Rd., past the post office. (☎/fax 21309. Open 9am-6:30pm. Reserve one or two days in advance. Massage Rs350 per hr.; acupuncture Rs250 per hr.)

DALHOUSIE डलहौज़ी   ☎01899

Built along the edge of the Dhauladar mountain range, Dalhousie was named for Lord James Ramsey, Marquis of Dalhousie, who became Governor General of India in 1848. The hill station was founded in 1854, when the British rented the land from the largely autonomous Chamba raja in order to expand vacation options for their increasingly stressed-out administrators and bureaucrats. Designed as a colonial retreat, Dalhousie also played a part in the drama that led to Indian Independence; Subhash Chandra Bose came here during the 1940s to cook up anti-British strategies for the Indian National Army. Cool air and mountainside strolls make Dalhousie a pleasant summer stop, that is, if you can stand the cooing honeymooners and frolicking families that come to town during high season (roughly Apr. 1-Jul. 15). Because of the higher prices and lack of sights and temples, many foreigners skip Dalhousie and head straight for nearby Chamba.

   Buses depart from the main bus stand to: **Chamba** (2hr., 5 per day 7am-4:30pm, Rs34); **Dharamsala** (6hr., 3 per day 7am-2pm, Rs75); **Pathankot** (4hr., 10 per day 5am-4:30pm, Rs44); **Shimla** (12hr., 12:30pm, Rs185). For more buses to Dharamsala and for buses to **Amritsar** and **Jammu,** change in Pathankot. Two buses (9:30 and 10am) go to **Khajjiar** (one way: 1hr., Rs15), **Chamba** (one way Rs50, round-trip Rs80), and back, stopping in each place for 1hr. More frequent connections run from **Banikhet,** reachable by bus (20min., 8am-5pm, Rs5) or shared jeep (Rs10).

   In Dalhousie, everything is within walking distance. From the bus stand, facing the taxi counter, the narrow road that heads to the right from the **bus stand** leads to **Subhash Chowk** (10min. walk). The steps to the left climb up to **Gandhi Chowk.** The *chowks* are connected by two horizontal roads, **Mall Rd.** on the northern side of the ridge and **Garam Sarak** to the south. Most of the hotels and restaurants are on these two streets. **Treks 'n' Travels** makes ticket reservations, and organizes treks. (☎40277; fax 40476. Open daily 9am-10pm). **Punjab National Bank,** next to the Aroma 'n' Claire on the loop road off Subhash Chowk, changes traveler's checks. (☎42190. Open M-F 10am-2pm, Sa 10am-noon.) **St. Joseph's Clinic,** just up the road from the Civil Hospital, is better than its neighbor. (Open W-Th and Sa-M 9am-4pm, F 11am-1pm.) **Dalhousie Medical Hall Pharmacy** is downhill from Subhash Chowk just before Aroma 'n' Claire. (☎42222.

Open daily 9:30am-8:30pm.) The **police station** (☎ 42126) is opposite Aroma 'n' Claire. **Richa's Cyber Sync** has Internet access and has food and drinks. (☎ 40650. Rs70 per hr.) The **post office** is at Gandhi Chowk (open M-Sa 9am-5pm). **Postal Code:** 176304.

There are plenty of hotels in Dalhousie, and during the low season you can get a sizeable room with a view and private bath for Rs200 (plus Rs100 for a heater). In-season (Apr. 15-July 1 and Sept. 15-Nov. 15), prices are usually at least double. Dalhousie has a water shortage problem, and running water is often limited or unavailable. The friendly **Hotel Crags ❸**, Garam Sarak, a 5-minute walk from Subhash Chowk, has some of the best views on the ridge. Most rooms are equipped with wood-framed beds, mirrors, and TV. (☎ 42124. Rooms Rs400-700. Off-season: 50% discount.) If you are short on cash, walk up the road opposite State Bank of India to the **Youth Hostel ❶**. The squat toilets are not exactly sparkling, but are still bearable. Check-in 7-10am and 5-9pm. Doors lock at 10pm, lights out by 11pm. (☎ 42189. Floor mats Rs30; dorms Rs50; rooms Rs100.) At Subhash Chowk, **Friends Punjabi Dhaba ❷** is well known for its good food. The service is slow, but the view makes up for it. (Entrees Rs30-150. Open daily 8:30am-10:30pm.) **Amritsari Dhaba ❶**, just beyond Friends Punjabi on loop road heading away from Sowk is a well-furnished place with quick service. *Dal mah* fried (Rs18). (Open daily 8am-11pm.)

Most people come to Dalhousie to stroll the tree-lined streets, breathe the pine-fresh air, and enjoy the mountain views. The **Garam Sarak walk** is especially pleasant, since no cars are allowed on the road. Along the road, Tibetan refugees have painted reliefs of Chenresig (of whom the Dalai Lama is an incarnation) and other Tibetan notables onto the stone cliffs. Panch Pulla Rd., off Gandhi Chowk, leads to a dried-up **water spring**, notable because Ajit Singh, a supporter of Subhash Chandra Bose, died here on Independence Day. **Khajjiar**, a pristine meadow 22km from Dalhousie, is trumpeted by the local tourist industry as "the Switzerland of the East." The scenery is beautiful, but be prepared to share it with hundreds of yodeling tourists, who arrive by the busload. **Horse riding** Rs50 per hr.

CHAMBA चम्बा   ☎ 01899

Locked in between four major mountain ranges (Shivalik, Dhauladhar, Pir Panjal, and the Greater Himalayas), the region of Chamba is often referred to as the lap of the Himalayas. At an altitude of 990m, Chamba is high enough to escape the heat that scorches Punjab, but remains warmer and drier than Dalhousie or Dharamsala. The town, filled with porticoed houses and hidden temples, stretches along the slopes that rise above the Sal and Ravi Rivers. The town was founded in AD 940 as the new capital of an older princely state administered from Bharmour. Mountain ridges, isolation, attitude, and wily diplomacy have kept the Chamba Valley pretty much independent ever since. The Mughals never managed to reach this far, and Chamba's temples were spared the miserable fate of so many Hindu shrines in other parts of the country. Improved roads have brought new residents, but Chamba has maintained its individuality. The trademark styles of cooking, handicrafts, and art that developed over the centuries can be seen in the town's restaurants, craft shops, and museum. Town spirit peaks in early August, when residents celebrate a riotous week-long harvest festival, **Minjar.**

▛ TRANSPORTATION

Buses leave for: **Bharmour** (4hr.; 7 per day; Rs38); **Dalhousie** (3hr; 9 per day; Rs34) via **Khajjiar** or **Banikhet; Dharamsala** (10hr.; 6am and 9:30pm; Rs115); **Manali** (16hr.; 11:30am; Rs265) via **Kullu; Pathankot** (5hr.; 9 per day 4:30am-4pm; Rs60). There is 24hr. luggage storage in the bus station (Rs5 per day). There are more connections from **Buniket** (2hr.; 10 per day 6am-5pm; Rs30).

ORIENTATION AND PRACTICAL INFORMATION

Most of the businesses are concentrated around **Court Rd.**, which runs from the crowded **bus stand** area in the south of town along the eastern side of the **Chaugan,** Chamba's grassy mall and cricket ground. Court Rd. becomes **Hospital Rd.** and then loops back through chicken shacks and liquor counters as **Museum Rd.** Uphill from Court Rd., past the Chaugan, is **Temple Rd.**, which leads to the **Laxmi Narayan Temple** and into alleys packed with ancient shrines. **Mani Mahesh Travels** (☎22507), next to the entrance to Laxmi Narayan Temple, is very helpful with train reservations, treks, and temple info. Farther down, on Hospital Rd., the **Punjab National Bank** changes traveler's checks. (Open M-F 10am-2pm, Sa 10am-noon.) **Pharmacies** line Hospital Rd., including **Shrikanth Chowfla and Sons,** which proudly announces that it's also "Licensed to Deal Arms and Ammunition." (☎22735. Open M-Sa 9am-8pm.) There is a **District Hospital,** Hospital Rd. (☎22223; ambulance ☎22392; open 9am-1:30pm and 2-4pm) with emergency (ambulance) 24hr. There are also a few private clinics. The **police station** is on Hospital Rd. (☎22736). There is **Internet** access at **Mani Mahesh Travels.** On the Chaugan, 20m past Hotel Inavati, is the antediluvian **post office** (open M-F 10am-5pm). **Postal Code:** 176310.

ACCOMMODATIONS AND FOOD

Chamba's budget scene ain't spectacular. The best lodging in town is **Rishi Hotel and Restaurant ❶,** up Temple Rd., on the right. Rooms are small but clean, with seat toilets and cable TV. Some rooms have views of the temple interior. (Singles Rs150; doubles Rs200-300.) **Jimmy's Inn ❶,** right across from the bus station, has small rooms with seat toilets and hot water, but with its proximity to the bus station, you may wake up to the sounds of Tata trucks. (☎24748. Check-out noon. Dorms Rs50; doubles Rs150-250.) ◪**Orchard Hut ❶** is a wood-and-clay guest house and restaurant high up on the slope away from the Sal River, 12km from Chamba in the Panj-La Valley. Everything you eat, from the plum preserves served with crisp *parathas*, to the fresh vegetables, is organically grown around the hut. Enjoy your meal amid the noise of a roaring river and a chorus of birdsong—over 50 species of birds live in the area. Call ahead or stop by Mani Mahesh Travels (see above), run by the same family. To get to the hut, take the Chamba-Sahoo bus from the Brijeshwari Temple and get off at the Chaminu stop. Walk across the river and continue 20min. uphill; ask in the Chaminu store for directions. The hut is the base for various treks into the hills. Cooking lessons are also available (Rs50). Ask about the family's small hut, a 4hr. uphill hike from town. (☎22607. Food Rs100 per day; doubles include food. Tents Rs50; doubles Rs150-300.)

Chamba is well-known for its sweet-but-fiery chili sauce, *chukh*, which the bold of palate can sample on deep-fried chicken at shops along Museum Rd. Two floors above the shops, the **Park View Restaurant and Milk Bar ❶,** serves up the local specialty, *madhara*, a dish of kidney beans and curry cooked in ghee (Rs50). (Open 9am-10pm.) Another dining option is **The Olive Green,** which has a decent menu of typical Indian fare. (Open daily 9am-9pm.)

SIGHTS

BHURI SINGH MUSEUM. To learn about Chamba's royal and military past, head north on Museum Rd. to the Bhuri Singh Museum. Named for Raja Bhuri Singh, ruler of the Chamba district from 1904-1919, the museum displays his collection of small weaponry, musical instruments, *rumals* (a form of silk embroidery native to the valley), and a collection of *pahari* miniatures. *(Open Tu-Su 10am-5pm. Free.)*

LAXMI NARAYAN TEMPLE. Chamba's collection of temples is enough to satisfy all but the most insatiable of temple freaks. The largest complex is the Laxmi Narayan Temple, up Temple Rd., opposite the Akhand Chandi Palace. The shrines in the complex date from the 9th to the 10th centuries, when Chamba's founder commissioned the main temple and the statue of Laxmi Narayan (Vishnu asleep on the cosmic ocean) inside it. The copper statue of Gauri Shankar is an excellent example of metal work in Chamba. *(Open daily 6am-1pm and 2-9pm.)* The **Hari Rai Temple,** on Museum Rd., next to the red gate, was built in the *shikhara* style during the 9th century and is covered with Kama Sutra carvings.

DURGA TEMPLES. A walk along the outskirts of town will take you past several other important holy sites. From the bus stand, a short climb south and east leads to the long staircase up to **Chamunda Devi Temple.** Chamunda Devi is a form of the goddess Durga in a wrathful temper; the brass bells are meant to clear your head of worldly scheming. At the northern edge of Chamba, above the road to Sahoo, is the ancient temple of **Vajreshwari.** Tradition has it that this is the oldest temple in Chamba, a thank-you gift from Raja Sahil Varman to the family who donated the land for the town. Although a number of stone carvings have been looted from the sides of the main shrine, finely crafted images of Durga, Undavi (the goddess of food), and other deities still grace its walls. Look for the Tibetan-style demonic faces at the back of the main shrine—their presence here remains a mystery. The stone lions out front are the gods' preferred mode of transportation (not for hire).

RANG MAHAL AND HIMACHAL EMPORIUM. When they weren't trying to keep the gods happy, Chamba's 18th-century elite retired to the Mughal-style corridors of the **Rang Mahal** ("Old Palace"). Dominating the upper center of Chamba, the palace houses the **Himachal Emporium,** a shop selling *rumals*, hand-woven shawls, candleholders, and brass plates. Ask the shopkeeper to see the workshop upstairs.

▶ DAYTRIPS FROM CHAMBA

BHARMOUR

Bharmour is a bumpy, sometimes harrowing, 3½hr. bus ride away from Chamba.

The capital of the Chamba Valley from the 6th to the early 10th centuries, Bharmour's temple square encloses 84 separate shrines, most only a few feet tall, and some dating back to the 7th century. The most famous of these is the Narsingha Temple with its half-lion, half-man statue dedicated to the incarnation of Vishnu who descended to earth to destroy an evil spirit who could not be killed. Once Narsingha tasted blood, however, he just kept on killing. Realizing his demonic powers, he went up into the mountains where there was less to kill. The temple is supposedly built on the site where he secluded himself. Aside from the temples, Bharmour is in a very peaceful spot far away from the onslaught of tourism.

Bharmour is the trailhead for **treks** over the Dhauladhar and Pir Panjal ranges. In the summer, you're likely to meet some of the nomadic shepherds who make seasonal migrations up and down the valley. It is also the starting point of the **Manimahesh Yatra,** a devotional procession that winds its way 34km up to the lake at Manimahesh, where people worship and bathe in the icy waters. The procession takes place in September, 15 days after Krishna's birthday. If you decide to stay in Bharmour, the **Chanumda Guest House ❶,** located on the lower street that runs parallel to the road, is a decent enough option. (☎25056. Singles Rs100; doubles Rs200.) There are no restaurants in town, but food stalls line the main streets.

SAHOO

A 1hr. bus ride from Chamba or a gorgeous 20min. bike ride from the Orchard Hut.

The quiet farming village of Sahoo is in the opposite direction from Bharmour, up the Sal River valley. It has an 11th-century temple and breathtaking views of the Pir Panjal range. The **Chandra Shekhar** (moon-crowned Shiva) temple houses an ancient Shiva *linga*, apparently given to spurts of rapid and inexplicable growth— a hole had to be cut into the temple's stone ceiling to accommodate the *linga's* sky-high ambitions until a visiting priest was able to bring it back down to size. The ceiling has since been removed and now stands in front of the temple, where worshippers crawl through it for luck and strength. Opposite the *linga* is a particularly fine stone sculpture of Nandi. In earlier times, when the temple bell was struck, the ball around Nandi's neck would resonate. These days, devotees coat the image with a thick layer of *ghee*, muffling the sound.

KULLU कुल्लू ☎01902

Kullu is tucked between two green mountains at the southern end of the Kullu Valley. Most tourists see Kullu only from the grimy bus stand; the town has little to offer besides bus connections to the beautiful Parbati Valley and nearby Naggar and Manali. Every year in early October, however, tourists and Indians crowd Kullu for **Dussehra,** a huge festival celebrating the 360 gods of the Himachal Valley.

Bhuntar Airport is 10km to the south of town. Most local buses heading to points south along route 21 stop at the airport (Rs12); ask before boarding to be certain. There are also 10 buses per day in each direction that connect Kullu's main bus stand to Bhuntar (Rs8). Taxis cost Rs100-125 and auto-rickshaws are around Rs75. **Ambassador Travel** has an office a short walk off the maidan on the road to Manali. They book flights from Bhuntar and for Indian Airlines in general. **Flights** go to Delhi (M, W, F 11:10am; US$130). **Buses** leave for: **Amritsar** (14hr., 3:30 and 5:30pm, Rs220); **Delhi** (16hr., 5 per day 4am-5pm, Rs250; semi-deluxe 16hr., 7pm, Rs300; deluxe 13hr., 6:30pm, Rs470); **Dharamsala** (5 per day 7am-8pm, Rs115-140); **Jammu** (14hr., 5:30pm, Rs200); **Leh** (48hr., 7am, Rs370); **Manali** (2hr., every 30min. 4am-7pm, Rs20); **Manikaran** (2½hr., 7 per day 6:30am-3pm, Rs25); **Naggar** (1hr., every 30min. 4am-7pm, Rs12); **Shimla** (9hr., 5 per day 4am-8:45pm, Rs113-152). **Deluxe buses,** booked through **HARI Travel** in the maidan, go to: **Delhi** (12hr., 6:15pm, Rs325); **Dharamsala** (8hr., 9pm, Rs250); **Shimla** (8hr., 9pm, Rs250).

The main **bus station** is at the north end of town, next to the river. Above the bus station, across the footbridge and to the left, extends the **market street,** leading to the **maidan,** Kullu's main square and cricket ground. The **State Bank of India,** 2km from the center of town, is the nearest place to exchange currency and traveler's checks. (Open M-F 10am-2pm, Sa 10am-noon.) Hotel Rohtang, one block west from the center of the maidan, has **Internet access.** (Rs100 per hr. Open M-Sa 9am-7pm) The **post office** is on the road that branches to the left of the National Hwy. as you walk north from the maidan, 20m after the split on the left. Open M-Sa 10am-5pm. **Postal Code:** 175101.

Turn right at the top of the pedestrian market, and walk 50m past the post office to reach **Baba Guest House ❶,** which rents small rooms, some with spectacular views. The place is a budget backpacker's paradise. (☎22821. Rooms Rs50-100.) Next door, **The Madhu Chandrika Guest House ❶** has balconies that look out over the town, the Beas River, and surrounding mountains. (☎24395. Dorms Rs50; doubles Rs150-300. Off season: 50% discount.) Most of the food in Kullu is of the street-stall variety. Kill your hankering for road-stall samosas and *pakoras* at the pedestrian market across the river from the bus stand. **Hotstuff ❶** dishes up excellent pizzas (Rs45 and up) and burgers (Rs40). You might find a trekking partner here too.

HIMACHAL PRADESH

🔁 DAYTRIP FROM KULLU: BIJLI MAHADEV TEMPLE. A daytrip from Kullu takes you up to the **Bijli Mahadev** (God of Electricity) **Temple** where, legend has it, lightning strikes each year and breaks the massive *linga*, which then has to be reassembled by a priest. Take a bus from town (Rs8) to the Chan Sari stop; from there, hike 3km uphill to the temple, where you can observe the pilgrimage rites.

NAGGAR नग्गर ☎ 01902

Halfway between Kullu and Manali, on the eastern side of the Beas River, rests the hillside village of Naggar, blanketed by pine forests, apple orchards, and fields of cannabis. The regional capital until the mid-1600s, Naggar is now a serene town with slate-shingled roofs, delicate temples, and perhaps the best art gallery in the Western Himalayas. While Manali has been overrun by hash-smoking tourists and Kullu is frantic and noisy, Naggar is peaceful, making it an excellent place to get a sense of life in the Kullu Valley as it once was.

◪ 🔁 ORIENTATION AND PRACTICAL INFORMATION. Buses arrive and depart by the shops on the highway 1km below the **castle.** Buses to **Kullu** (1½hr., every hr., Rs15), **Manali** (1½hr., every hr., Rs15) and other destinations such as Dharamsala and Chandigarh are more frequent at **Patilkahl,** on the other side of the river. To get to the castle from Patilkahl, walk across the bridge, and take the shortcut path along the creek in front of you; it's a 45min. walk up. Or, take a taxi or rickshaw (Rs50-80). There is a small **hospital** opposite Hotel Alliance. The **post office** is on the narrow road below the castle. (Open M-Sa 10am-5pm.) **Postal Code:** 175130.

🔁 🖸 ACCOMMODATIONS AND FOOD. Hotel Alliance ❶ is up the hill toward the Roerich Gallery. The attached restaurant offers excellent French and local cuisine. (☎ 47763. Rooms Rs80-150, with bath Rs200-250; room rates negotiable when most rooms are unoccupied.) **Poonan Mountain Lodge ❶,** 50m below the castle, blends with the traditional village architecture. Poonan also rents a fully equipped cottage, 1km above the village, and has an attached vegetarian restaurant. (☎ 47747. Doubles Rs150-250; cottage Rs300.) **Shertal Guest House ❷,** next to the castle, has rooms ranging from a dark double with common bath to a spacious room with shower and magnificent views from the balcony. (☎ 47750. Singles Rs450; doubles Rs125.) Also near the Castle, **Ragini Hotel ❷** has large rooms, 24hr. hot water, balconies in most rooms, and rooftop garden. (☎ 47855. Rooms Rs350-450. Off season: Rs250-350.) **La Purezza Hard Rock Cafe ❶,** by the bus stop, loads you with fresh pasta (Rs50-80) and other carbs before that climb up to the castle. (Open daily 10am-10pm.) **Chanchakhami Cafe ❶,** on the road above the Tripuri temple, serves hummus and tofu for Rs25-60. (Open 10:30am-10:30pm.) The patio at **Rag Cafe ❶,** before the gallery entrance, serves tea (from Rs3) as you bask.

◙ SIGHTS. Naggar's 504-year-old castle, 1km up from the highway, houses an expensive hotel and a sacred slab of stone called **Jagti Patt.** Local legend says the valley's gods were "transformed into honey bees endowed with great strength" to cut the hefty block and fly it up. On top of the hill, past the Castle Hotel, the **Tripuri Sundri Temple,** with its three-tiered pagoda roof, is the site of a local *mela* in mid-May. Farther up the pine-lined road, past the Alliance Hotel, stands the **Nikolai Roerich Art Gallery,** named for the early 20th-century Russian artist who settled there with his family. The house displays paintings which capture the spirit of the Himalayas. Roerich was also highly respected by the Indian government: letters from state authorities and a portrait of Indira Gandhi, done by Roerich's son, adorn the gallery. The Roerich-founded **Urusvati Institute,** 200m farther, once had a faculty of leading scholars of Himalayan culture. *Urusvati* means "Light of the Morning Star," and the institute was said to "radiate" the sacred knowledge revealed by the mountains. Now, it is the site of the **Himalayan Folk and Tribal Gallery,** which holds collections of traditional North Indian dress and metalwork. The gallery upstairs has some of Nikolai's earlier mystic paintings, a few works by his son Sviatoslav, and a number of paintings by local Kullu artists influenced by Roerich. *(Both galleries open Tu-Sa 9am-1pm and 2-5pm. Rs10 ticket covers both.)*

◧ TREKKING

Naggar is an ideal base for treks up the slopes of the Valley of Gods. **Himalayan Mountain Treks,** at Poonam Lodge, is a reliable trekking agency. (☎47748. Fully organized treks Rs1000 per person per day; treks with only a guide and a tent Rs500; prices are negotiable for groups of 2 or more.)

A two-day hike over the **Chandrakhani La** (3660m) takes you to **Malana,** a mountain village whose inhabitants claim to be descendants of Greek soldiers under Alexander the Great. Malana has never come under the patronage of the Government of India Tourism Department, and visitors are not allowed to touch the villagers or the holy stones; the fine for violating this law is Rs1000. There is only one guest house, with mattresses on the ground (Rs150), so you're best off bringing a tent. From here, you can continue to the **Malana glacier** or to **Manikaran,** in the Parbati Valley (see below). You can also stay in the nearby village of **Kasol** at the Raja Guest House (rooms Rs50-100). Manikaran is a base for treks over the Pin-Parbati Pass (see Treks around Kaza, p. 257). Streams in both the Kullu and Parbati Valleys have trout; many trekking agencies offer fishing trips and rent equipment.

MANIKARAN ☎01902

The town of Manikaran is situated in the beautiful Parbati Valley. With its ancient temples, famous hot springs, and plentiful supply of the valley's most renowned cash-crop, Manikaran draws trekkers, hippies, and plain old travelers looking to relax. A good alternative to Manali's tourist glut, Manikaran has convinced many a visitor to turn a short stay into a long one. The town's most famous feature, its hot springs, are a centerpiece of the modern village and a subject of legend. According to local lore, Naga, the serpent god, stole Parvati's earrings, returned to his subterranean lair, and sequestered the jewelry inside his nostrils. When Parvati's lover, Mahadeva, threatened the thief, Naga became so angry that he snorted out the earrings with such force that they tore through the earth, creating the hot springs.

Buses leave for **Kullu** and stop at the Parbati villages along the valley road (2½hr., 7 per day 5am-6pm, Rs25). **Taxis** wait near the bus stand, but they are fairly useless since the northern side of the river is closed to traffic.

Modern Manikaran straddles the Parbati River, and almost everything of interest to visitors is located on the north bank. There is a **bus/taxi stand** at the far eastern end of town where the valley road ends. A bridge crosses the river at the bus stand, and a foot-bridge straddles the river near the western end of town and leads to the **Sikh gurudwara** that contains the famous **springs.** The main road runs between these two crossing points and constitutes the 'center of town,' where most restaurants are located. Most guest houses are north of this road.

Manikaran's guest houses tend to be located off hillside paths in the north of town. A noisy but clean choice that almost always has rooms is **Hotel Amar ❶,** along the north bank road near the center of town. Some rooms have attached bath. (Doubles Rs100-400. Off season 50% discount.) Another choice is the friendly **Padha Family Guest House ❶,** near the Ram Mandir Temple. The hotel offers hot showers with spring water. (☎74228. Doubles from Rs125.) Perhaps the best of the hillside bunch is the **Parvati Guest House ❶.** (Simple singles Rs50; doubles from Rs75.)

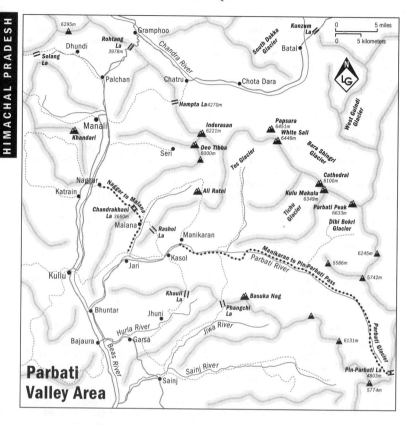

Parbati Valley Area

The **dhabas** near the center of Manikaran serve cheap eats. There are also several Indian, Western, and Israeli food places. **Parvati Ridge Restaurant ❶,** on the main northern road 75m west of the Eastern bridge, dishes out vegetarian and non-vegetarian specialties. Mutton *rogan josh* Rs70, meals Rs30-80. (Open daily 9:30am-11pm.) **Hot Spring Restaurant ❶,** near the spring, plays Western music and serves pizza (Rs30-80) and burgers. Dishes Rs25-90. (Open daily 8am-midnight.)

The **hot springs** are the highlight of the town, but to see the springs you must enter the **Guru Nanak Dev Ji Gurudwara,** at the western end of town. The people are very welcoming and will be happy to show you around. (Ask permission to enter. Remove shoes. Men should cover their heads.) You can also take a complimentary hot bath here. (Open sunrise to sunset.) The **Ram Mandir Temple,** located between the two bridges on the north bank road, is also interesting to see. Some portions are over a thousand years old, and the intricate decorations highlight the spring's importance as a site of Sikh and Hindu pilgrimage. A small donation (Rs10) is appreciated. (Open daily 8am-9pm.) The wooden **Naini Devi Temple,** located near the Ram Mandir, is not as large as its neighbor, but the temple's interior features intricate carvings of deities and religious symbols and motifs. (Open 9am-7pm.)

MANALI मनाली　　　　☎01902

Cradled among the mountains of the lesser Himalayas, Manali has long been a favorite hang-out of hashish-seeking hippies, Indian newlyweds, and travelers looking for a place to rest up before heading out on treks. Once quiet and remote, Manali's apple orchards and pine forests are now dotted with wooden guest houses and concrete hotels. The Mall and the Model Town next to it are the headquarters of the tourist invasion, but choice guest houses and restaurants make Old Manali a more mellow and inviting option. The surrounding slopes offer superb hikes, and the nearby village of Vashisht, 3km away, is well worth a daytrip.

> **❗ PARANOIA, CHAPTER XX.** Manali, where cannabis grows wild, has been touted as the cool place to hang out and smoke hash, but stories of local use have been greatly exaggerated. It is used by locals only in times of duress or during cold weather. A number of foreigners every year are searched and arrested for hash possession, resulting in hefty fines of Rs1000-10,000. Saying that you were feeling cold or under duress will get you nowhere. It might not look like it, but **hashish is illegal, even in Manali.**

▐ TRANSPORTATION

Flights: The nearest airport is in **Bhuntar**, 52km from Manali (see **Kullu**, p. 243). **Matkon Travel** (☎52838), on the intersection of Old Manali Rd. and The Mall, is the agent for Indian Airlines. To **Delhi** (M, W, F 11:10am; US$130).

Buses: The **bus stand** is right in the center of the Mall. To: **Amritsar** (15hr.; 2pm; Rs280); **Chamba** (15hr.; 2:45pm; Rs300); **Dehra Dun** (17½hr.; 5pm; Rs310); **Delhi** (16hr.; 5 per day 11:30am-5pm; Rs305; deluxe 14hr. 4:30 and 5pm; Rs492); **Dharamsala** (10hr.; 8:10 and 9:10am; Rs157; deluxe 10hr., 7:30pm, Rs250); **Haridwar** (19hr.; 10am; Rs285); **Jammu** (16hr.; 5 and 10pm; Rs260); **Keylong** (6hr.; every 45 min. 4:30am-6pm; Rs75); **Kullu** (2hr.; every 15min. 5am-6:30pm; Rs24); **Leh** (2 days; noon; Rs405); **Naggar** (1½hr.; every 30min. 5am-6:30pm; Rs15); **Shimla** (10hr.; 6am and 7am; Rs160; semi-deluxe (with fan) 9hr.; 6pm; Rs202). Government "deluxe" buses can be booked at the **Himachal Tourism Marketing Office** (☎53531), at the Mall. The deluxe bus stand is at the southern end of town, a 300m walk down along the Mall. Confirm where your bus departs from. Private deluxe buses operated by **Matkon** or **Swagatam Travel** are usually cheaper and can be booked at any travel agency around town. To: **Delhi** (15hr.; 4:30 and 5:30pm; Rs400); **Dharamsala** (10hr.; 7:30pm; Rs250); **Leh** (2 days; 10am; Rs800); **Shimla** (10hr.; 6am; Rs135). For info on the **Manali-Leh Road,** see p. 260.

✈ ℹ ORIENTATION AND PRACTICAL INFORMATION

Manali is built in a rough "Y" shape. **The Mall** makes up the trunk, where you'll find a **bus stand** and most of the other tourist services. Off to either side are alleys lined with gift shops, *dhabas*, and provision stores which are particularly common just behind and north of the bus stand. The left fork at the Nehru Statue leads uphill 1km on the **Old Manali Rd.,** separating the **Model Town** on the left from the **Great Himalayan National Park** on the right before making a sharp descent to the bridge over the Manalsu River. Across the bridge, **Old Manali** spreads out along the uphill road to your left. Taking the right fork at the statue leads you across the **Beas River bridge.** Continue 2km upstream along the road and turn right for the steep 1km ascent that leads up to the village of **Vashisht.**

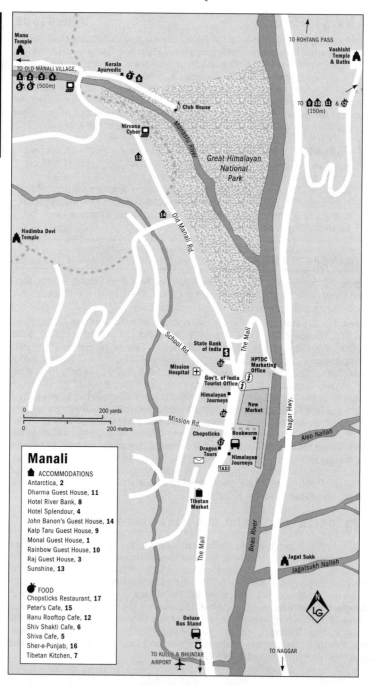

Manali

⌂ ACCOMMODATIONS
Antarctica, **2**
Dharma Guest House, **11**
Hotel River Bank, **8**
Hotel Splendour, **4**
John Banon's Guest House, **14**
Kalp Taru Guest House, **9**
Monal Guest House, **1**
Rainbow Guest House, **10**
Raj Guest House, **3**
Sunshine, **13**

🍎 FOOD
Chopsticks Restaurant, **17**
Peter's Cafe, **15**
Ranu Rooftop Cafe, **12**
Shiv Shakti Cafe, **6**
Shiva Cafe, **5**
Sher-e-Punjab, **16**
Tibetan Kitchen, **7**

Tourist Office: Government of India Tourist Office (☎52175). On the Mall, next to Hotel Kunzam. Open M-Sa 10am-5pm. **HPTDC Marketing Office** (☎52116). On the Mall, in a white bldg. on the right as you face away from the bus stand. Open M-Sa 8am-8pm; 9am-5pm during winter (Nov.-Mar.).

Budget Travel: Plenty of travel agents offer treks (US$30 per person per day, all inclusive) and rafting trips (starting at Rs900 per day). Two reliable companies are **Dragon Tours** (☎52790; fax 52769), with offices opposite the bus stand and in Old Manali, both open 10am-9pm; and **Himalayan Journeys** (☎52365; fax 53065), just past the bus stand, open 9am-9pm.

Currency Exchange: State Bank of India, Old Manali Rd., just past the Mall. Does all the usual stuff. Open M-F 10am-2pm, Sa 10am-1pm.

Police: The police station (☎52326) is next to the deluxe bus stand.

Hospital: Mission Hospital (☎52379). On School Rd. 1 block west of the mall. **Khana's Clinic,** Old Manali Rd. Open M-Sa 8am-2pm and 4-8pm, Su 10am-2pm. For holistic medicine, try **Kerala Ayurvedic Center** (☎54446), in Old Manali, next to Tibetan Kitchen. Open M-Sa 9am-6pm.

Internet: Valley of Gods, just off the road in Old Manali, 50m above Moondance. Plenty of computers. Rs30 per hr. Open daily 8am-10pm. **Cyberia,** to the left of the bridge, is email central but the wait can be long. Rs50 per hr. Open daily 9am-10pm. **Nirvana Cybercafe,** on the road between Model Town and Old Manali, has more computers. Rs40 per hr. Open daily 10am-9pm.

Post Office: Down the alley opposite the bus stand and to the right of Monal Himalayan Travels. Open M-Sa 10am-5pm. **Postal Code:** 175131.

ACCOMMODATIONS

Most travelers trek to Old Manali, where guest houses can't be told apart from village houses. The farther up the hill, the quieter the lodgings and the better the views. To avoid the crowds and enjoy a soak in some hot springs, head down to **Vashisht** (rickshaw from Manali Rs30 up, Rs20 down), where most guest houses are around the temple and have hot baths. The area between the Old Manali Rd. and the Hadimba Temple, known as the **Model Town,** is an agglomeration of large hotels inundated by Indian tourists and honeymooners.

OLD MANALI

Hotel Splendour, up the hill in Old Manali; look for signs on your right. 5min. down a side path takes you through apple orchards and cornfields. Each room has a hot water heater and seat toilet. Singles Rs150; doubles Rs250; pitch your own tent Rs75; 2-person tent rental Rs200. Off season: Rs100/200. ❶

Monal Guest House (☎53848). On the top of the hill, Monal is the last house in the village. Quiet, with beautiful views of the river and mountains. Bring a flashlight to find your way back at night. Front rooms Rs150; back Rs80. ❶

Raj Guest House (☎53570). Left of the path to Splendour. The older rooms share a clean bathroom and a porch with gorgeous views. The new rooms in the back all have tiled baths but lack the views. More lively than some of the places farther up the hill. Rooms Rs60-200. Off season: Rs50/130. ❶

Antarctica (☎53079). Above the road and to the left. All rooms have attached bath. The restaurant has a balcony. Rooms with hot showers Rs150. ❶

Hotel River Bank (☎53004 or 52968). To the right of the bridge in Old Manali. A typical concrete luxury complex. Red velvet chairs on plush blue carpets. All rooms have seat toilets and hot water. Doubles Rs450, but bargain away. Off season: Rs250. ❷

HIMACHAL PRADESH

VASHISHT

Dharma Guest House (☎52354). On a steep path 100m above the springs. Porch for reading and meditation. Wooden doubles share a common toilet; the new concrete annex has rooms with extra facilities. Rs80; new rooms Rs200. Off-season: Rs50/150. ❶

Kalp Taru Guest House (☎53443). Right next to the baths. Doubles with bath Rs150. Off-season: Rs50. ❶

Rainbow Guest House, just downhill from Dharma Guest House. Recently opened by a family, this simple guest house features clean traditional rooms and an immaculate shared bath. Hot water buckets free. Singles Rs70; doubles Rs90. ❶

MODEL TOWN

John Banon's Guest House (☎52335 or 52388; fax 52392). A 5min. walk up Old Manali Rd. from the Mall. One of the oldest hotels in Manali, with its own private apple orchard. Spacious, carpeted rooms with huge windows and working fireplaces. Doubles Rs450-550. Reservations recommended one month in advance in season.

Sunshine (☎52320). Halfway between the Mall and Old Manali. Each room has a private dressing room, bathroom, and a veranda overlooking the valley. Old-style dining room with a massive wooden table and fireplace. If you get cold, the staff will supply your fireplace with wood (Rs100 per day). Rooms Rs350. Closed Dec.-Mar.

◨ FOOD

Numerous restaurants in Old Manali have imaginative, inventive chefs. Near the bus station, there's at least one *dhaba* down every alley. Manali also boasts plenty of falafel joints and several strudel-serving "German bakeries."

▨ Tibetan Kitchen, 50m to the right of the bridge in Old Manali. With its tablecloths and well-decorated walls, this restaurant would win the prize for cleanliness and style. Extensive Tibetan offerings, as well as Japanese and Chinese food. Hong Kong chicken Rs65. Open daily 8am-midnight. ❶

Shiva Cafe, after the bend in hill-road. Has tasty Italian dishes, as well as a covered veranda and pleasant garden. Lasagna Rs45. Open daily 8am-11:30pm. ❶

Shiv Shakti Cafe, just below Monal Guest House. Has some of the best views in Manali. Serves fresh trout (Rs100) and a variety of other tasty stuff. Open daily 9am-11pm. ❷

Chopsticks Restaurant, across the Mall from the bus stand. Tries to serve authentic Tibetan/Chinese food; the not-quite-authentic result can often be quite tasty. Szechuan chicken Rs75. Open daily 8am-11pm. ❶

Peter's Cafe, down a dingy lane in a small garden, near the State Bank. Psychedelic shack serves quiche (Rs30), pie (Rs25), and cheddar omelettes (Rs30). Pete will treat you to his razor-sharp wit and collection of classical records. Open daily 8am-8pm. ❶

Sher-e-Punjab has 2 branches in the middle of the Mall. Authentic Punjabi food for those sick of Italian food and *momos*. Meals Rs30-65. Open daily 9am-11pm. ❶

Ranu Rooftop Cafe, in Vashisht, refuels hot-spring bathers with carbohydrates of both the pasta and *thukpa* variety. Most dishes Rs25-60. Open daily 8am-10pm. ❶

◉ SIGHTS

HADIMBA DEVI TEMPLE. The four-tiered Hadimba Devi Temple, with its pagoda-shaped roof, is dedicated to the demoness-turned-goddess Hadimba, wife of Bhima. Valley residents claim the king cut off the builder's hand to prevent the temple's duplication. Undaunted by the amputation, the builder trained his left hand and constructed an even more elaborate temple at Tritoknath. This time, he lost his head. *(Walk 5min. along Old Manali Rd., take a left, and follow the signs. Open to visitors between sunrise and sunset; ask permission before entering. A donation is expected.)*

MANU TEMPLE. The Manu Temple, a pleasant 30min. walk uphill from Old Manali, is reputedly where Manu first stepped onto the earth after a great flood. Manu, the first man to possess knowledge, and his wife Shatrupa, had a series of thoughtful children who developed the world's religions. The temple was rebuilt in 1992 with vaulted ceilings, elaborate woodwork, and marble floors. Dress appropriately when in the temple. *(Open 9am-6pm. Donations appreciated and expected.)*

GREAT HIMALAYAN NATIONAL PARK. The park shows visitors what the towering pine forests might have looked like before the modern architectural invasion. *(Entrance at the Wildlife Information, Education, and Awareness Center, Old Manali Rd. Open daily 10am-5pm. Rs20 for foreigners. Camera charge Rs5.)*

♫ ▢ ENTERTAINMENT AND SHOPPING

The Himachal Tourism-run **Club House,** to the right after the bridge in Old Manali, offers sundry attractions, not the least of which is a fully stocked bar (beer Rs80). Try your hand at billiards (Rs100 per hr.) or badminton (Rs60 per hr.), or just kick back in the plush lounge with one of the books from the library. (☎52141. Open daily 10am-9pm. Rs10.) **All-night raves** are frequent in Manali. Check the German Bakery and Cafe in Old Manali for notices. In addition to all the shawl shops on the Mall and Old Manali Rd., the **Tibetan Market,** at the southern end of town, provides good opportunities for good old-fashioned hard bargaining. But be forewarned— there are better deals to be had in Dharamsala. (Open daily 8am-10pm.)

▧ DAYTRIPS FROM MANALI

The temple in Vashisht has free **hot baths,** with separate rooms for men and women. (Open daily 5am-9pm.) The **Mountaineering Institute** (☎52206 or 53788; fax 53509), 2km south of the bridge over the Beas River, offers courses in mountaineering, skiing, and water sports throughout the year, with fees ranging from US$190 (skiing) to US$250 and up (for a 4-week mountaineering course). The institute can also organize expeditions for large groups. For info, write to: Mountaineering Institute, Manali, HP 175131. Farther south is **Jagat Suk** and its glorious Shiva temple. The regular bus from Manali (30min., every 15min. 5am-6:30pm, Rs3) will drop you in Jagat Suk, where you can check out the temple and drink *chai* with the locals. The **Rohtang La** (3998m), open erratically between June and September, is the only motorable way into the Lahaul-Spiti area from Manali (see **Kinnaur-Spiti Road,** below). Although it's best described as a polar dump (the place is a mess of tea tents and scattered debris), Rohtang can still make for a decent trip if you're looking for high-altitude scenery. Buses, as well as HPTDC tours (Rs150), will take you here. Check out the creative HPPWD road advice on the way up, including slogans like "Divorce speed" and "Peep, peep, don't go to sleep."

KINNAUR-SPITI

One of the most incredible routes in the world, the road from Shimla cuts through mountains of solid rock and traverses Kinnaur, Spiti, and Lahaul, eventually crossing the Rohtang La and winding down into Manali. The ride can be harrowing, but the reward for accepting the risks of travel is the chance to see some of the most awe-inspiring natural beauty in all of India. Each of the three regions that the road cuts across presents a distinct landscape. The deep Sutlej Valley connects fertile valleys inhabited by the Kinnauri, round-hut dwellers who share the name "Nogi." The Spiti River cuts through mountain deserts dotted by oases of barley fields and enclaves of Tibetan culture. After crossing the Kunzum La, it enters the Lahaul Valley, a land of glaciers and moss-covered granite that can only sustain fields of grass and nomadic shepherds and their flocks.

When the road was opened to outsiders in 1992, the only accommodations for outsiders were Public Works Department (PWD) rest houses. Today, lodges, hotels, and guest houses line the route. The road is open between June and October, but it is unlikely that you will make it through without encountering at least one road-block or delay (mudslides, stone avalanches, fallen bridges, etc.). Road conditions change in minutes, and bus drivers rely on updates from passing vehicles. If it rains, especially in the drier Spiti Valley, the roads can become treacherous. The rain-softened ground tends to loosen large boulders, and you might get stuck until the roads clear. If you're traveling by bus, you can usually get off, cross the obstacle on foot, hike to the next town, and then catch another bus from there. If you're prone to altitude sickness, it's best to start in Shimla, where the climb is more gradual. Non-Indians traveling between Jangi and Sundo must obtain an **inner-line permit** (available from the sub-divisional magistrates in Shimla, Rampur, Peo, Kaza, Chamba, Kullu, Keylong, and the home office in Delhi; for more information, see **Warning**, p. 225). The **Kaza-Manali Road** should be open from mid-June to mid-September, but weather makes it unreliable as well. **There are no facilities for currency exchange along the route.**

> **WARNING.** During July 2000, huge floods hit Himachal Pradesh. Whole villages were swept away, hundreds of people were killed, and hundreds of thousands lost their homes. The long-term implications of the floods for travel along the high-altitude roads of the state are not yet clear, but you should seek an informed second opinion before making plans to travel here. Many of the routes described below may no longer be passable; some of them might not exist at all.

THE KINNAUR-SPITI ROAD

SUTLEJ VALLEY. From Shimla, the road climbs to **Narkanda** (60km, 2½hr. by bus) and then descends to **Rampur** (120km, 3½hr. by bus). From **Jeuri** (or Jeori), 23km farther on, you can reach the Kinnauri village of **Sarahan** (see p. 253), site of the Bhima-Kali Temple. The green concrete building by the road in Jeuri has simple beds (Rs40)—an option if you get stranded. Two hours. up the road a path takes you to **Wangtu**, the trailhead for treks over the Bhaba La. Another 1hr. of prayers gets you to Karcham, where you can catch a bus to **Sangla** in the Lower Sangla Valley (see p. 253). Beds are available in one of the shacks across the bridge over the Baspa River (Rs50). From Karcham, it's 1hr. or so to **Rekong-Peo** (see p. 254), the district headquarters of Kinnaur, and **Kalpa** (see p. 254), Shiva's winter residence. From Peo, the landscape becomes drier, and military bases increase as you near the Tibetan border. You will need to show your permit and passport in Jangi. At **Khab** (or Kabo), 70km from Peo (5hr. by bus), the road climbs to the plateau above. In the middle of this brown plain is the village of **Kah**. Farther down from Yang Thang, you can take a detour to see the Tibetan village of **Nako** (see p. 255) and its green lake. Nako has the only guest houses around (a 2km uphill hike or 10km bus ride). If you get stranded in Yang Thang, there are simple beds available (Rs50). You can stay in **Chango**, 100km (3½hr.) from Peo, where there is a 13th-century temple that was supposedly hewn out of a single stone in one day.

SPITI VALLEY. The bus then proceeds through **Shalkar,** the checkpost at **Sumdo** (the Spiti boundary), and the truck-stop of **Hurling** (beds Rs50) on its way to the thousand year-old *gompa* at **Tabo** (see p. 255). The 47km Tabo-Kaza stretch passes the villages of **Poh** and **Shichling.** Near Shichling, a road branches off to **Dhankar Gompa.** One kilometer down, a bridge leads to the **Pim Valley.** Between Hurling and Tabo and between Poh and Shichling, the road passes under mountains of mud. **Do not attempt to walk this route in the rain.** From **Kaza** (see p. 256), the road gets even bumpier as it winds 50km up to the village of **Losar** (5hr.). Losar has two guest houses and is the access point for the **Kunzum La** (4500m), 18km (1½hr.) away.

LAHAUL VALLEY. After the pass, the road drops steeply to the four tents that make up **Batal,** in the Lahaul Valley (see p. 258); beds are available here. An 18km hike takes you to **Chandratal Lake.** After Batal, there is a *dhaba* in **Chota Dhara** (12km) and tented accommodations in **Chatru** (16km) before the route turns back onto a main road at **Gramphoo** (17km). From here, it's a 4hr. ride over the polar dump of Rohtang La to **Manali** (64km). The opening of the segment between Losar and Gramphoo is dependent on how long it takes the snow to melt.

SARAHAN सराहान ☎ 01782

Eight hundred meters above the Sutlej River Valley, the Kinnauri village of Sarahan is notable for its impressive wooden **Bhima-Kali Temple** complex. The temple used to be the site of human sacrifice, until the practice was banned by the British. Inside the Durga shrine, there is a council of marble Buddhas, mountain deities, and Hindu gods, showcasing the rich mingling of beliefs and traditions in the Kinnauri region. The views of the snowclad Shrimakand peak, endless fruit orchards, and groves of jacaranda pine make this a perfect setting for walks through the area. **Buses** from Jeuri go to Sarahan (1hr., every hr. 6am-5pm, Rs12). The **Temple Rest House ❶** in front of the temple, has both a dorm and private rooms. (☎74248. Dorms Rs50; rooms Rs150-300.) The huge **Shrimakand Hotel ❶** is expensive, but the 8-bed dorm is a good deal, with pleasant views and large bathrooms (beds Rs75). **Ajay Chinese Food,** next to the temple entrance, serves delicious noodles and Shanghai *momos.*

LOWER SANGLA VALLEY संगला

After a perilous 17km bus ride on a road carved out of the mountain face, the deep canyon widens, and the fertile Sangla Valley unfolds in all its splendor. For centuries, the natural barriers of the wild river and the snow-capped peaks were enough to keep this area isolated from the rest of the world, and its distinct vegetative and cultural features developed free from outside influences. The scenery between **Sangla** and the last village of **Chitkuhl** is unforgettable. The landscape and vegetation changes almost every hundred meters—the day-long hike, which takes you past villages with houses of peaked roofs, is well worth it. The valley was not open to outsiders (including Indians) until 1992, so **be very careful where you wander.**

From Sangla, the 2km road that turns left past the police station leads to the village of **Kamru,** former capital of the Baspa kingdom. On top of a rock overlooking the entrance into the valley are a Buddhist temple with rich Tibetan wall paintings and a Hindu shrine adorned with exquisite woodcarving. High above all of this is a temple dedicated to one of the mountain deities and guarded by a legion of lizards; ask permission before entering. From Chitkuhl it's another week farther up the valley and over a pass to the holy town of **Gangotri** in UP. You must be fully self-sufficient for this trek; there are no settlements of any type on the way.

The **bus** from Karcham (1hr.; 7 and 9:30am; Rs12) drops you off in **Sangla.** Buses from Sangla go to **Peo** (3hr.; 7am, 8am, 2pm; Rs25) and **Rampur** (5hr.; noon; Rs60). In the market in Sangla, there are a few restaurants, guest houses, and a **National Travelers** branch (☎42358), which organizes treks. The **Mount Kailash Guest House ❶,** just off the road in Sangla, has a clean, four-bed dorm (beds Rs75) and several doubles (Rs250-450). On the first floor, there is a restaurant and an **STD/ISD** telephone. Six kilometers along the route before you reach Rakchham village, the **Fayal Guest House ❶** has doubles (Rs150-300), a dorm, and a restaurant serving local specialties. Down the path past Fayal, in an apple orchard, is the **Ganga Gardenview Guest House ❶,** which has doubles (Rs250), and cooks local cuisine. In Chitkul, the **Chiranjan Guest House ❶** offers doubles (Rs150-300).

REKONG-PEO (PEO) पिओ ☎017852

Halfway between Shimla and Tabo, Peo serves as the district headquarters of Kinnaur. Just off the main road, the town is a small collection of concrete military barracks, *dhabas*, and market stalls, not meriting more than a few hours' visit. However, the **Lavi Fair,** during the first week of November, should not be missed. Pashmina wool, dried fruits, horses, and other goods are traded on the grounds near the District Commissioner's office. Peo is also famous for the forests nearby (10min. walk up from the bus station, toward Kalpa). Twenty minutes uphill from Peo is the *gompa* that was the site of the *kalachakra* ceremony performed by the Dalai Lama in 1992 (see p. 256). The village of Kalpa (see below) is only 3km away from Peo. Although **buses** also stop in the market, it is better to catch them at the bus stand (a 10min. uphill) since they are usually packed when they reach the market. Buses run to: **Chandigarh** (15hr.; 5:30, 7, and 10:30am; Rs190); **Kalpa** (30min., 5 per day 7:30am-5pm, Rs5); **Kaza** (13hr., 7:30am, Rs115); **Nako** (6hr.; 7:30am Kaza bus, 1pm; Rs55); **Rampur** (3hr., every hr. 4am-1:30pm, Rs30); **Sangla** (2hr., 9:30am and 4:30pm, Rs25). The **police station** is in the administrative complex near the market. The Additional District Magistrate is in the same building on the first floor and issues **inner-line permits** (see p. 225) for the road between Jangi and Sundo (open M-F 9am-5pm). To get a permit you must go through a travel agent such as **National Travellers** (☎228830), down the steps before Fairyland Guest House. Ask for Bhagwan Singh Negi. National Travellers can also help with treks. The **district hospital** is 2km uphill from town, on the road to Kalpa. The **post office** is next to the bus stand (open M-Sa 9am-1pm and 2-5pm). **Postal Code:** 172107.

The **Fairyland Hotel ❶,** above the market, has clean rooms and a restaurant. (☎22477. Doubles Rs200-300.) **Mayur Guest House ❶,** next door, is another option. (☎22771. Dorms Rs50; rooms Rs125.) The **Shivling View Guest House ❶,** past the bus stand, has a restaurant, and rooms with hot showers and TVs. (☎22421. Simple bed Rs80-120; doubles Rs200-300.)

KALPA कल्पा ☎017852

The village of Kalpa is noteworthy for its proximity to **Kimmer Kailash,** which is Shiva's winter residence, according to Hindu mythology. Aside from this, there are many festivals held here, reflecting the influences of Hinduism, Buddhism, and various mountain cults. **Fullaich,** in September, is the most famous.

The center of Kalpa is a handful of wood and stone houses and Kinnauri shrines crammed onto an outcrop overlooking the valley. The rest of the village stretches up the ridge; getting from one place to another can be a small trek in itself. There are apricots, apples, plums, and blackberries everywhere, as well as spectacular views. To reach Kalpa, walk from the bus stand along the road to the left until you reach Shivalik View Guest House. Behind the guest house begins the 3km path that takes you through woods of pine and past village houses (see below). Buses leave from the market and the bus stand to: **Peo** (5 per day, Rs5) and **Shimla** (12hr., 6am, Rs120). More connections can be made from Rekong-Peo, farther down the hill. From the market, the stone path leads to a paved road; turn right and walk 400m to reach **Aucktong Guest House ❶**, with its bright flowers out front. (☎26019. Doubles Rs200.) The family prepares meals. The **Shivalik Guest House ❶**, just to the left of where the stone path reaches the road, offers varying rooms. (☎26158. Singles Rs150; doubles Rs400.) For a real treat, head farther down to the left to **Kimmer Villa ❹**, which has luxurious rooms with a terrace. (☎26079. Rs900.) Food is available in the hotels and in the **Snow White Coffee House** in the market. The **subpost office** is next to the temple (open M-Sa 9am-5pm). **Postal Code:** 172108.

🏔 TREKS AROUND KALPA

The most popular trek within Kalpa is to **Chaka** (5-6km, a 2hr. hike one-way), a plateau above the village that makes an ideal picnic spot. Kalpa can also serve as a starting point for longer treks. The famed **Parikrama trek** begins at **Thangi** (60km from Kalpa, approachable by road) and ends 3-4 days later in Chitkul. The descent to Chitkul is extremely steep, so walk in the opposite direction only if you really want to challenge your knees. There are villages and shepherd huts on the way, making it possible to leave tents and food supplies at home. Sleeping bags and good shoes are a must, for you reach altitudes of over 5000m. The climb can be done in August and September without mountaineering equipment. **Timberline Tent Camps** (☎26006), in Kimmer Villa, can arrange guides for Rs500 per day. The most difficult route in this region—one that should only be attempted by seasoned trekkers—is the trail leading up **Kinnaur Kailash** (6050m). The base of the mountain is in **Powari**, 20km from Kalpa. The best time to do this trek is in July and August. Expect the trek to take two days each way.

NAKO नाको

Fringing a small green lake in a high-altitude bowl, this village of stone walls and mud-roof houses is one of the first fully Tibetan settlements along the way; the surrounding ridges are dotted by mud *gompas*, prayer flags, and piles of *mani* stones. The barren hills contrast sharply with the greenery of Kinnaur; the views of the deep Spiti canyon and the distant white mountains complete this region's distinctive landscape. A daily **bus** runs from Peo to Nako (6hr., 1pm, Rs55). You can also reach Nako by taking the **Kaza** (6hr.; 7:15am; Rs55) or Shalkar-bound bus and get off at **Yang Thang.** From there it is a steep 2km walk. A bus runs back from Nako to Peo at 6am (Rs60). To continue from Nako to Spiti, walk down and catch the one Kaza bus that passes through Yang Thang (anytime after 11am). **Loulan Guest House ❶**, next to the bus stand, has dorm beds (Rs50) and doubles with baths (Rs200-300). It also has the only *dhaba* in town, serving *dal*, rice, and the local barley brew (upon request). Another **guest house ❶**, 100m up the path to the left, has rooms (Rs200) and a porch where you can snooze (Rs25) if everything else is full.

TABO ताबो ☎01906

The hamlet of Tabo is home to 350 or so intensely devout people, whose mud huts cluster around the Tabo *gompa* near the river. Tabo remained in virtual isolation until the border disputes with China during the 1950s, when the geopolitical importance of this region brought it to center stage. Today the area is home to several Indian military outposts, and **foreigners must obtain a permit before visiting.**

HIMACHAL PRADESH

⌨🔢 TRANSPORTATION AND PRACTICAL INFORMATION. The **bus** to Peo arrives anytime after 10am (9hr., Rs125), and two buses go to Kaza, one after 9am and another after 4pm (2hr., Rs35). Tabo's **Primary Health Center,** at the edge of town, has treatment and medicine and operates on donations. (☎33325. Open M-Sa 9am-1pm and 3-5pm.) The closest **police** assistance is in Sumdo or Kaza. The **post office** is farther down the cow path in a barn (open M-Sa 10am-3pm). If the postmaster isn't there (most of the time he isn't), ask around; he's usually having tea in one of the nearby *dhabas*. There is one **STD/ISD** booth at the back side of the Tenzin Restaurant behind the Temple Guest House. **Postal Code: 172113.**

🔳🔲 ACCOMMODATIONS AND FOOD. The **Monastery Guest House ❶** has a number of doubles and a spacious dorm. (☎33315. Dorms Rs50; doubles Rs150-250.) Ask the receptionist to let into the library, where you can read up on Buddhism or Tibetan *thankas* (open M-Sa 1-7pm). **Ajanta Guest House ❶,** also near the temple, has carpeted doubles. (☎33312. Rs150-200.) There are two food options: the restaurant in the monastery guest house, and the Tenzin *dhaba* across the street. Their menus include Tibetan bread, *thukpa*s, and *momo*s (both open 5:30am-9:30pm).

◉ SIGHTS. According to an ancient inscription, the foundation of Tabo has been dated to the year AD 996. The **Tabo Gompa** is the largest monastic complex in the Spiti Valley, and one of the holiest Buddhist sites anywhere in the Himalayas. Following the massive cultural purges of Tibet by the Chinese government, Tabo assumed a role as treasury of Tibetan art. On the *gompa*'s 1000th birthday, the Dalai Lama came to perform the sacred **Kalachalena** ceremony, a rite of initiation, rejuvenation, and prayer offered once every four years. The monastery consists of five temples from the original settlement and four shrines that were added at a later date. At the core of the complex is the Temple of the Enlightened Gods, otherwise known as the **Assembly Hall.** At the center is a statue of the four-fold Vainocana, the Divine Being regarded by Vajnayana Buddhism as one of the spiritual sons of Adibuddha, the self-creative primordial Buddha. Vainocana is depicted turning the wheel of law. Along the wall are images of the other 33 deities of the pantheon. Hidden in darkness, the sanctum behind Vainocana is adorned with wall paintings depicting the life of the Buddha. In the ante-room, ask the lama to show you the **Bom-khang,** the Temple of Wrathful Gods. Twice a day, a lama shielded by protective meditation performs a secret ceremony to appease the fierce deities. Daily prayers are performed in the hall every morning at 6am. To the right of the Assembly Hall is the **Maitreya Temple,** with a 6m high statue of the Buddha of the Future. To the left is the **Mystic Mandala Temple,** where the initiation to monkhood takes place. On the sheer cliff face overlooking the town is a series of **caves** that once functioned as monastic dwellings. With a flashlight, you can see traces of the paintings that once adorned these walls. (*To visit the temples, ask at the reception of the monastery guest house for the temple keeper, and make sure to bring your own flashlight.*)

KAZA काज़ा ☎ 01906

Strategically situated in the middle of the valley, Kaza has traditionally been the trading center of Spiti. Half old village and half government post, Kaza has become a major base for travelers to this long-forbidden land. The millennial Kalachakra ceremony was held in the Kyi Gompa, and new hotels spring up every year.

🚍 TRANSPORTATION. Bus service to **Manali** (12hr., 4am, Rs100) begins sometime around early June and mid-August, and continues until October. Buses also go to: **Kibber** (1½hr., 2pm, Rs12) via **Kyi; Lasar** (3½hr., 9am, Rs45); **Mikim** in the Pin Valley (2hr., 8am, Rs25); **Peo** (12hr., 7am, Rs120) via **Tabo** (3hr., Rs30). Bus schedules depend on the whims of weather and drivers.

⚑⚐ ORIENTATION AND PRACTICAL INFORMATION. Both **Old Kaza** and **New Kaza** lie between the main road and the river—a small, often dry stream separates the two. New Kaza can be reached by following the road that goes up above the bus stand. The **bazaar, STD/ISD,** and restaurants are all in Old Kaza; the **hospital, police station,** and government buildings are in the new town. The **bus stand** is just off the main road in Old Kaza. The **hospital** (☎22218), in a big shed, runs an ambulance service. The Sub-divisional Magistrate's office, which grants **permits** for the journey onward to Kinnaur, is in New Kaza. The **post office** is 2 min. from the road (open M-F 10am-5pm). **Postal Code:** 172114.

⚐⚑ ACCOMMODATIONS AND FOOD. Lodging in Kaza is available from April to November. **Mahabaudha ❶,** at the top end of the market road in Old Kaza, has the cleanest rooms, common bath with hot water, and a traditional Tibetan kitchen. (☎22232. Doubles Rs150.) **Sakya's Abode ❶,** across the stream in New Kaza, has a beautiful garden area, and is where tour groups stay. (☎22254. Dorm beds Rs50; singles with bath Rs150; doubles with hot shower Rs250-450.) If you need to catch an early bus, **Art Guest House ❶,** below the bus stand, has clean rooms, all with common bath. (Doubles Rs150-250.) **Il Pomo d'Oro ❷,** left of the market, is run by a globe-trotting Italian family. The vegetarian dishes (Rs50-80) and stuffed pasta (Rs120) reveal the touch of a master chef. Try the rum-filled *tiramisu* (Rs50), and camp out in the garden if you cannot get home afterward. *Dhabas* along the market serve *dal* and noodles; the one on the second floor near the bus station frequented by bus drivers is the best source for road information.

⚐ TREKS AROUND KAZA. The most popular trek takes you through the Pin Valley National Park and over the Pin-Parbati La to **Manikaran** (6 days), where there are soothing hot springs and bus connections to Kullu and Manali. From Kaza, take a bus to **Mikim** (2hr., 8am, Rs25), where a *jula* will transport you on a rope across the river to the trailhead at Kaar village—ask for Chine Dorge, who can arrange guides for your trek. Instead of turning west over Pin-Parbati, you can continue south over the Bhaba La to **Wangtu** on the Shimla-Peo road (5 days).

⚑ DAYTRIPS FROM KAZA

KYI. The largest fort monastery in Spiti, Kyi rests on the top of a cliff 12km from Kaza. The monastery, home to 1000 lamas, has a superb collection of *thankas*. The *gompa* received a major face-lift in preparation for the **Kalachakra** ceremony: a road was cut through sand and stone to connect the new monastery guest house to the village, a large assembly hall was constructed on the hill, solar panels were installed, and repairs were made to the temples. To get to Kyi, many travelers put their faith in the erratic **bus** from Kaza (2pm), or they just walk and hope to hitch a ride with someone.

KIBBER. On a hilltop, Kibber is a Tibetan village of white mud houses surrounded by barley fields. At an altitude of 4250m, Kibber is one of the highest villages in the world reachable by motor vehicle. Kibber and the adjoining wildlife sanctuary offer amazing treks and a feeling of remoteness. A daily **bus** leaves Kaza (1½hr., 2pm, Rs12) and loops around at Kibber. If the bus driver is having a bad day, though, you might have to hike the 18km stretch or take a taxi (Rs250). The best thing to do is to start walking and hitch a ride (Rs30-50). The **Resang Hotel ❶,** at the village entrance, has doubles with baths and a kitchen (Rs150). Farther down the road, the **Pasang La Guest House ❷** charges inflated prices for its rather bleak rooms (doubles Rs300-500). **Village houses ❶** are known to provide pleasant stays to many travelers. (Rs60-100 per night; ask around.) In the village, there is a huge prayer wheel, a *gompa* for curing spiritual afflictions, and a "hospital" (i.e. local healer) for bodily ones (open M-Sa 9am-1pm and 3-5pm).

DHANKAR GOMPA. Named for its precarious location (*dhankar* means "cliff"), Dhankar Gompa was one of the first fort monasteries incorporated into Spiti's defense system. The *gompa* is an 8km hike up from the road near Shichling, about 20km from Kaza. You can either take the **Peo** bus (1hr., 7:30am, Rs15) or catch a ride along the road. The views are amazing, and the **gompa ❶** provides beds (Rs50).

LAHAUL VALLEY

With glaciers within reach, the Chandra River valley is watered by fresh water springs and melted snow, and its grassy pastures grazed upon by wild horses. Above, the **Chandrathal Lake** is the jewel of the valley.

When road conditions permit, the Kullu-Kaza **bus** runs through the valley between **Gramphoo** and **Batal.** Situated on the Manali-Keylong road, Gramphoo's two *dhabas* have beds (Rs50). Expect shepherds or family members to join you at any time. It is 17km to **Chatru,** where food and tents (Rs30) are available; bring a sleeping bag unless you want to freeze. Chatru is the trailhead for a trek over the Hamta La to Manali. The hike takes two days on the way down and three days to return. From Chatru, another 16km takes you to **Shkota Dhara,** where there is rice and *dal* and a campground. In Batal, 12km away, there are tents and bowls of *thukpa.* After the bridge in Batal, the road forks: the right branch scales the Kunzum La, while the left goes 18km until it reaches Chandrathal Lake. There is a campground nearby. Alternatively, you can descend to Chandrathal on a path that starts at the *gompa* on the Kunzum La. From Chandrathal, it is another three days of walking to the **Baralacha La** on the Manali-Leh road (p. 260). There is no accommodation available between Batal and Baralacha La, and the closest medical assistance is in Keylong.

JAMMU जम्मू AND
KASHMIR کشمیر

For centuries travelers have been drawn to Kashmir, India's northernmost state. Until a decade or so ago, it was one of the most popular tourist destinations in Asia, and many a Bollywood starlet has been filmed against the backdrop of Kashmir's stunning mountainscapes. But despite the undeniable beauty of its scenery, Jammu and Kashmir is also volatile, and since 1989 the western half of the state has been wracked by an armed insurgency. So far, the violence has been confined to the Kashmir Valley, which is predominantly Muslim, and Jammu, which has a large population of Dogra Hindus. **The lake-rimmed capital, Srinagar, is dominated by the military, and most foreign state departments advise against traveling here or anywhere in the western part of the state.** The eastern part of the state, consisting of the Tibetan Buddhist regions of Ladakh and Zanskar, is relatively safe, but travelers should check the latest information before finalizing their plans.

Kashmir's troubles began when India was partitioned along religious lines in 1947. Although the population was predominantly Muslim, the Hindu raja did not want his kingdom to become part of Pakistan *or* India, and most Kashmiri Muslim leaders agreed with him. In late 1947, however, Pathan tribesmen from what is now Pakistan crossed the border in an attempt to force Kashmir into Pakistan. Desperate, the maharaja asked India for help. The Indian government accepted the offer, and agreed to hold a plebiscite to determine whether the Kashmiri people wanted to join India. When the shooting stopped, Pakistan still held large chunks of Kashmir. India and Pakistan went to war over Kashmir again in 1965, but no territory changed hands. The 1948 cease-fire line remains the de facto India-Pakistan border, but the plebiscite promised by India has never been held.

HIGHLIGHTS OF JAMMU AND KASHMIR

The beautiful, medieval town of **Leh** (p. 261), at 3500m, is a base for treks through the surrounding mountain ranges and to the *gompas* which dot the Indus valley.

Approached by the highest motorable pass in the world, the radiant **Nubra Valley** (p. 269) features flower-filled villages, sand dunes, wild camels, and stunning views of the Karakoram.

At the end of the 1980s, many Kashmiris who had fought against the Soviet invasion of Afghanistan returned home with better guns and training. This, together with Kashmiri fears of absorption into India, led to an outbreak of violence in 1989. The violence hasn't stopped since and has claimed as many as 100,000 lives over the past 13 years. In 1995, five foreign tourists were taken hostage in Kashmir; one of them was beheaded. In July 2000, a German backpacker was kidnapped and killed in the Zanskar Valley. Hundreds of people are killed in Kashmir every year, and the continued rise of Islamist military groups makes peace and reconciliation seem increasingly unlikely in the short term. Large-scale intrusions across the line of control at Kargil in 1999 nearly escalated into another Indo-Pakistani war. Bombings and guerrilla activity are routine in many areas of the state, and Kashmir's future is uncertain. Relations between India and Pakistan reached their lowest point for more than 20 years in early 2002, when both countries tested nuclear-

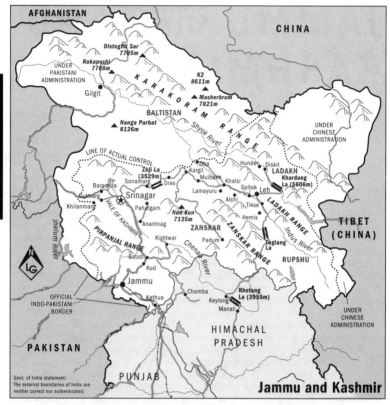

AFGHANISTAN

CHINA

Disteghil Sar
7785m

Rakaposhi
7788m

K2
8611m

UNDER
PAKISTANI
ADMINISTRATION

Gilgit

Masherbrum
7821m

BALTISTAN

Shyok River

K A R A K O R A M   R A N G E

UNDER
CHINESE
ADMINISTRATION

Nanga Parbat
8126m

LINE OF ACTUAL CONTROL

Dha

Hunder · Diskit

LADAKH

Zoji La
(3529m)

Kargil

Khardung
La (5606m)

Baramula   Sonamarg   Dras

Mulbekh

Khalsi

Spitok   Leh

Khilanmarg   Gulmarg

Srinagar

Lamayuru

Alchi

Tikse

Pahalgam

Nun Kun
7135m

Hemis

LADAKH RANGE

TIBET
(CHINA)

Anantnag

ZANSKAR

Indus River

Jhelum River

PIR PANJAL RANGE

Kishtwar

Padum

Taglang
La

RUPSHU

VALE OF KASHMIR

Batoti

Chenab River

ZANSKAR RANGE

N
LG

Kud

Jammu

OFFICIAL
INDO-PAKISTANI
BORDER

Kathua

Chamba

Rhotang
La (3955m)

Keylong

Manali

UNDER
CHINESE
ADMINISTRATION

PAKISTAN

HIMACHAL
PRADESH

Govt. of India statement:
The external boundaries of India are
neither correct nor authenticated.

PUNJAB

Jammu and Kashmir

JAMMU & KASHMIR

capable missiles and massed their troops along the border as part of open preparations for another war. **As of May 2002, most governments strongly advise their citizens to avoid all travel anywhere within the state.** Think long and hard about your priorities in life before you decide to travel anywhere in Jammu and Kashmir.

THE MANALI-LEH ROAD

Two routes connect Leh to the rest of the world: the Manali-Leh Road and the Srinagar-Leh Road. Each is a two-day-plus haul requiring you to cross several passes well over 5000m. These roads are theoretically open from mid-June to mid-September, but they can be washed out for weeks by rains and mudslides. Travel is often delayed by accidents, herds of goats, and military checkpoints. If you're on a tight schedule you might want to fly to Leh, but you'd be missing out on a lot.

! WARNING. Following the large-scale Pakistani intrusion across the Line Of Control (LOC) in spring 1999, India has cemented its position in the Dras-Kargil area, leading to increased militant activity in northern and western Kashmir. Traveling along the **Srinagar-Leh Road** can get hairy at times. Stay within the limits of the road, where a strong military presence reduces the risks.

The **Manali-Leh Road,** the second-highest motorable road in the world, is one of the most beautiful overland journeys on the planet, winding its bumpy way through green mountains, roaring streams, and across the stunning, high-altitude desert of Ladakh. The Manali-Leh road crosses the Rohtang La (3980m) and then twists through the Baralacha La (4892m) and Taglang La (5325m) passes before descending to Upshi and into Leh. **Bring warm clothes:** it can get below freezing at the high passes. And try to get a seat at the front: you'll need a crash helmet, or at least kneepads, if you get stuck in the back. Local and deluxe buses leave Manali daily (10am, Rs405/800-1000), but if you can make three friends, hire a taxi (Rs4000). This will let you stop along the way and get you to Leh quicker. It rarely rains along this road, but when it does, the road can become treacherous. You might have to get off the bus and trudge through the mud past obstructions.

Small settlements line the road from Manali to Leh, and there are places to stay all along the road. The trip can take anywhere from 30hr. to two or more days, depending on weather conditions, accidents, and the number of military checkpoints. Where you stop is determined by where you happen to be when it starts to get dark. The bus first descends into the Lahaul Valley, where it might stop in Keylong, Lahaul's administrative center, and leave the next morning (4am). At sunrise, the bus reaches **Darcha** (1hr.; tents Rs35), the trailhead for treks into the **Zanskar Valley.** Over the next two to three hours, the bus climbs the main Himalayan ridge, crossing it at **Baralacha La** (4892m). The three-day trail for **Chandratal Lake** begins here (see p. 253). The first tea stop is in **Bharatpur** (tents Rs35), 3km below Baralacha-La. A descent into a vast plain brings you to **Sarchu** (4hr.; tents Rs150), after which the road makes 27 turns, climbing 1000m to cross the Zanskar range at **Lunga-lacha La** (5059m). From here, it's "badlands" territory. You first hit the village of **Pang** (8hr.; tents Rs30-50), and after crossing a pass, the road enters the plains of **Rupshu.** At the end of the plains, below the glacier-lined **Taglang La** (5325m) pass (12hr.), there are thousands of sheep and goats, and views of the Karakoram range and the Great Himalayas. The bus then descends into the Ladakhi village of **Rumtse** (14hr.), screeching through villages and *gompas* before reaching **Upshi** (16hr.). From then on, it's smooth cruising down the main road to **Leh** (18hr.).

LEH ☎ 01982

The capital of the old kingdom of Ladakh, Leh is remarkably distinct from cities farther south in Kashmir. Its location on a 3500m desert plateau in the middle of the Indus valley, halfway between Punjab and Yarkand on the "southern" silk route, has made it a crossroads between Tibetan Buddhist culture from the east and Islamic influences from the west. While Old Leh, with its maze of narrow lanes winding up to the ruins of the Namgyal Palace, seems to be stuck in a time warp, New Leh thrives on tourism. If Kashmiri traders and the clicking of tourists' cameras get to be too much, you can seek refuge in one of the many *gompas* and deserted mountain trails near the city. Some of these follow the same routes used for centuries by traders hauling goods from Western Tibet over the Chang La (5547m) and Khardung La (5602m) into the bustling bazaars of the ancient city.

▐ TRANSPORTATION

Flights: Airport (☎52255). 4km from Leh, down Fort Rd. **Jet Airways,** main bazaar (open daily 9am-1pm and 2-4pm), has daily flights to **Delhi** (7am, US$112). Book a few weeks in advance during the summer. **Indian Airlines,** Fort Rd. (open daily 9am-1pm and 2-4pm), flies to more destinations, but you must still book ahead. Flights are often delayed or canceled due to bad weather. To: **Chandigarh** (1hr., W 7:50am, US$75); **Delhi** (1½hr., daily, US$105); **Jammu** (1hr., M and F 7:30am, US$70); **Srinagar** (1hr., Su 7:50am, US$60). Security is tight on flights to Jammu or Srinagar.

> ⚠ **WARNING.** When you make the road journey, **carry your passport with you at all times.** The routes to Leh come close to areas under Pakistani and Chinese control. When arriving by plane, remember that Leh is 3505m above sea level. **Rest for at least one day** (that means not even walking around and definitely not consuming alcohol) before undertaking anything strenuous, and **watch for any signs of Acute Mountain Sickness (AMS).** The symptoms—headaches, breathlessness, and nausea—normally develop during the first 36 hours (see **Trekking: Health and Safety,** p. 35). Leh has an emergency facility for dealing with AMS (24hr. ☎52012 or 52360). Several seats are reserved on every plane out of town for people needing to leave because of AMS.

Buses: The **Tourist Information Office,** Fort Rd., by the taxi stand, has up-to-date schedules and prices. To: **Diskit** (8hr.; Tu, Th, Sa 6am; Rs65); **Hemis** (1hr., daily 9:30am and 4:30pm, Rs25); **Kargil** (12hr., daily 5:30am, Rs143) via **Lamayuru; Matho** (2hr., 3 per day 7:30am-5pm, Rs15); **Manali** (48hr.; daily 4am; semi-deluxe Rs400, deluxe Rs525); **Panamik** (8hr., Tu 6am, Rs85); **Phyang** (30min.; daily 8am, 1:30, 5pm; Rs12); **Shey, Tikse,** and **Spituk** (every 30min., 8am-7pm, Rs15); **Srinagar** (48hr.; 5:30am; Rs220, deluxe M-Tu and Th-Sa Rs300); **Stok** (45min.; daily 8am, 2, 5pm; Rs10). **Minibuses** go to **Alchi, Saspul, Likir,** and **Bagso** (all 4pm).

Local Transportation: The **taxi union** is near the top of Fort Rd. There is a fixed rate of Rs8 per km for all destinations during the tourist season (July-Aug.).

✴ 🛈 ORIENTATION AND PRACTICAL INFORMATION

The **main bazaar** marks the western edge of the **Old City.** Running west from the center of the main bazaar is **Fort Rd.,** which is lined with restaurants, travel agents, and carpet shops. **Zangsty Rd.,** beginning at the north end of the main bazaar, connects to Fort Rd. via **Library Rd.,** and then runs north into two lanes, **Changspa** and **Karzoo,** which pass several small guest houses. Buses arrive in the south on **Airport Rd.,** a 10min. walk from the bazaar.

Tourist Office: Tourist Information Office, (☎53462). Fort Rd. .Open May-Sept. M-Sa 8am-7pm. Closed off season. Information counter at the airport open all year.

Trekking Agents: Fort Rd. is full of trekking agents. Not all are trustworthy; ask around before putting your life in the hands of a stranger. **Dreamland Trek&Tour** (☎53128, 52089, 53616; www.dreamladakh.com). Fort Rd., on the left walking away from the bazaar. An affordable agency with years of experience in putting together well-organized and worry-free treks. Credit cards accepted only for groups of several people. **Virgo Adventure** (☎52250; fax 52408; www.geocities.com/virgoadventure; virgoadventure@yahoo.com). Operated through the Two Star Guest House, this new agency has been making a name for itself, with perfectly arranged treks and great prices.

Currency Exchange: The **State Bank of India** has an exchange counter in their branch at the main bazaar just off Fort Rd. Open M-F 10am-2pm, Sa 10am-noon. Many travel agencies and shops in town will also exchange money.

Meditation Centers: Mahabodi Society, up Changspa Rd.; signs on the right. Meditation meetings (M-F 4:30pm) and yoga classes (Tu-Th 3:30pm) June 15-Sept. **Milarepa Meditation Centre** (☎44025). In Davachan, Choglamsar, on the road to Tikse.

Police: (☎52167), halfway up Zangsty Rd., on the right after the Changspa Rd. turn off.

Pharmacy: Himalaya Medical Store, opposite SNM Hospital, is the best-stocked. Open daily 9am-6pm. Pharmacies also line the main bazaar; most open daily 8am-7pm.

Hospital: SNM Hospital (☎52012, 24hr. emergency ☎52360). Below the bus stand. Well maintained and has a special ward for tourists (most of them AMS-afflicted).

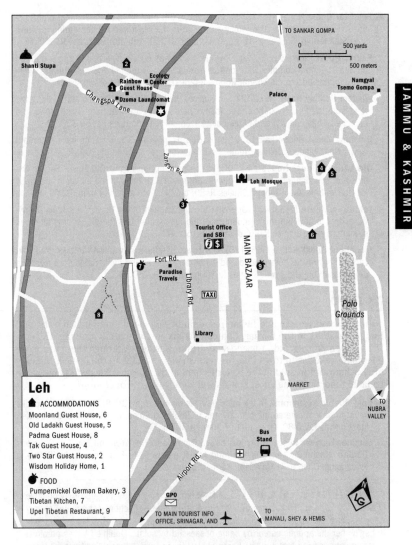

Leh

🏠 **ACCOMMODATIONS**
Moonland Guest House, 6
Old Ladakh Guest House, 5
Padma Guest House, 8
Tak Guest House, 4
Two Star Guest House, 2
Wisdom Holiday Home, 1

🍴 **FOOD**
Pumpernickel German Bakery, 3
Tibetan Kitchen, 7
Upel Tibetan Restaurant, 9

Internet: Very slow. **Gypsy's World,** Fort Rd., in the White House complex between town and the Indian Airlines office. Rs3 per min. Open daily 9am-10pm.

Post Office: GPO, 2km from town on Airport Rd. Open M-F 10am-1pm and 2-5pm. A small sub-branch is in the middle of the main bazaar. **Postal Code:** 194101.

🏠 ACCOMMODATIONS

Leh is full of small guest houses, most of them on the outskirts of town along Changspa Rd. and off Fort Rd.

JAMMU & KASHMIR

Two Star Guest House (☎ 52250). In Karzoo, 20m past the path to Wisdom and Rainbow. You will be treated like family as you sit in the windowed kitchen gazing at snow-clad Stok Kangri. Singles Rs100-150; doubles Rs250, with attached bath Rs350. ❶

Padma Guest House (☎ 52630). Down Fort Rd.; watch for a sign pointing to a path on the left. 15-room complex with rooftop restaurant, new rooms, and hot showers. Well-kept grounds add to the charm. Rooms Rs250-1200. Bargain mercilessly. ❹

Wisdom Holiday Home (☎ 52427). In Karzoo. Walk up Zangsty Rd., continue along the road from the Ecology Centre, and follow the signs. In a wheat patch, with views of a bleached-white *chorten* and rugged cliffs. Dorms Rs50; doubles Rs150-350. ❶

Rainbow Guest House (☎ 52332). In Karzoo. Family-run. Some rooms have mountain views. Near Wisdom Holiday Home. Doubles with attached bath Rs200. ❶

Old Ladakh Guest House (☎ 52951). The best option in the Old Town. Facing the mosque, turn right into a narrow alley. Continue 150m through the labyrinth. Centrally located with pleasant rooms. Singles Rs80; doubles with attached bath Rs150. ❶

Tak Guest House (☎ 53643). Opposite the Old Ladakh Guest House, Old Town. Everything here is tiny, but the friendliness of the family that runs the place turns its small size into a plus. Singles Rs80; doubles Rs150. ❶

Moonland Guest House (☎ 52175). Old Town; continue 50m down the alley from Old Ladakh toward the polo ground and watch for signs on the right. Stands out from the dinginess of the Old Town. Singles Rs150; doubles Rs250. ❶

◪ FOOD

With authentic Tibetan and Indian restaurants, not-so-authentic Italian ones, and Punjabi *dhabas* in the bazaar, Leh can satisfy just about any craving. Head to Dzomsa, on Zangsty Rd., for eco-safe drinking water. Although there are more "German" bakeries in town than you can shake a strudel at, the tastiest bread is the Kashmiri *naan* sold in the bakeries behind the mosque. No restaurants serve Ladakhi food, but some guest houses will cook you *skiw* or *chutagi*.

Upel Tibetan Restaurant, in the middle of the Main Bazaar, 3rd fl. The Darjeeling cooks seem to have mastered the culinary arts of Tibet and China. Great views of the bazaar. Most dishes Rs30-80. Open daily 7:30am-9:30pm. ❶

Summer Harvest Restaurant, just above Dreamland Trek&Tour on Fort Rd. Delicious Tibetan, Kashmiri, and Chinese food (most meals Rs45-80). The *rishta* (Rs80) is astounding. Open daily May-Sept. 7am-10:30pm. ❶

STRANGE MEDICINE Sniffly? Rheumatic? Plagued by vindictive demons? Ladakhi *lha-bas* say they can treat all of these afflictions (and more) merely by sucking the appropriate vile liquid directly through your skin! A *lha-ba* typically begins her therapeutic career by being possessed by spirits. Qualified lamas administer an initiation rite that enables her to control these spirits, channeling their influence into powers of healing. During a healing session, a *lha-ba* is first led into a trance by ritual drum-beating and singing. In that state, she is able to locate the afflicting agent, in the form of internal fluids or objects, and draw them out with her mouth without breaking the patient's skin. Reports of these nasty substances (which the *lha-ba* repeatedly spits out during the process) cover everything from "red and lumpy" or "black and tarry" to "pebble" or "small, moving, salamander thing." *Lha-bas* still practice in Ladakh; ask around, but be warned—sessions can get violent to the point of necessitating slaps on the head with a sword.

THE LION KING The mysterious circumstances surrounding King Sengge Namgyal's birth provide a fairy-tale accompaniment to his castle's splendor. In the early 1600s, Ladakhi king Vamyang Namgyal's army suffered ignominious defeat at the hands of the Balti king, Ali Min. Ladakh was looted, its king imprisoned, and doom was in the air. Legend tells of a romance between the imprisoned king and the beautiful Balti princess, resulting in an illicit pregnancy. Balti sources record a dream of King Ali Min in which he saw a lion jump out of the river and enter his daughter; at that instant, she conceived a baby, Sengge. These things happen. The Balti forces withdrew, Vamyang was subsequently restored to power, and he married one of Ali Min's daughters. A few months later, she bore a son. The greatest of Ladakhi kings, Sengge Namgyal ("Lion Victorious"), graced the region with grand castles and monasteries.

Tibetan Kitchen, 5min. down Fort Rd., just before the White House. Clean tablecloths and artistic decor. Tibetan specialties like *shaba-gleb* (meat bread Rs40) and Amdo bean stew (Rs60). Open daily 8am-3pm and 6-11pm. ❶

Pumpernickel German Bakery, between Fort Rd. and Zangsty Rd. As much an expat community center as an eatery. Board posts bulletins about taxis to Manali and ads for trekking partners. Excellent yak-cheese and tomato sandwiches Rs30, huge breakfasts Rs55-70, and a range of breads Rs45-55. Open daily 7am-9pm. ❶

🔎 SIGHTS

SENGGE NAMGYAL PALACE. Towering above the Old Town, this nine-story palace was built during the 1630s to show Leh's ascendancy over Shey as the Ladakhi capital. It is said to have inspired the Potala Palace in Lhasa. The opening of the East Gate used to be marked by the roar of a caged lion; nowadays the gate serves as the entrance. *(Open daily 8am-5pm. Rs20 for Indian nationals, US$5 for everyone else.)*

SHANTI STUPA. Referred to by locals as the **Japan Stupa,** the Shanti Stupa in Changspa village sits at the top of 560 steps. Feast your eyes on the legacy of Fujii Guraji, a Japanese Buddhist who moved to India in 1931. One of many Japanese-built *stupas* in the region, this Peace Pagoda, built in 1983, features gilt panels depicting episodes from the life of the Buddha. *(3km west of the bazaar; walk to Changspa and follow a direct line to the stupa. Open 24hr.)*

NAMGYAL TSEMO GOMPA. High above the palace, the red Namgyal Tsemo Gompa is distinguished by its *gon-khang,* which features sculptures of wrathful deities and wall-paintings of benign *Bodhisattvas.* *(Open briefly in the morning and evening when a lama climbs up from Samkar to light the butter lamps. The lama's movements are hard to predict. The inside is dark—bring a flashlight.)*

OTHER SIGHTS. The imposing **mosque** at the end of the main bazaar was built in 1666 by the Ladakhi king Deldan Namgyal as an offering to the Mughal emperor. The mosque is built in a style more Ladakhi than Islamic, but the *namaaz* prayer calls can be heard five times a day from every corner of Leh. The **polo grounds** above the Old Town see annual tournaments and occasional games between locals and soldiers. The **Sankar Gompa,** the official local residence of the reformist Gelug-pa ("Yellow Hat") sect, houses a hundred-headed, thousand-armed image of Avalokitesvara, the *Bodhisattva* of Compassion. *(Walk along the footpath across the fields from the Ecological Centre. Open daily 8-11am and 3-6pm. Rs25 donation expected.)*

JAMMU & KASHMIR

SHOPPING

There are many opportunities to shop in Leh; masks, carpets, jewelry, shawls, and so-called "antiques" fill the shops along Fort Rd., but prices are often higher than those in Delhi or Dharamsala. The **Tibetan Children's Village Handicrafts Centre,** on the road toward Choglamsar, sells crafts made at the Tibetan Children's Village. (Open M-Sa 9:30am-5pm.) The **Tibetan Handicraft Emporium,** in the main market, is approved by the Dalai Lama. (Open M-Sa 9am-1pm and 2-7pm.) The **Ecology Centre's** handicraft store sells local Ladakhi goods (open M-Sa 11am-5pm), and the **Co-operative store,** in the Galdan Hotel complex just off Fort Rd., sells similar items. These places support the local community and have fixed prices. **Cashmere Ladakh Arts,** on Zangsty Rd., is a private shop that prides itself on its fixed prices and no-hassle salesmanship. **Kpleasure Arts,** on Fort Rd., specializes in pashmina and in Ladakhi art. Shopping elsewhere is much like a sophisticated mugging.

VOLUNTEER OPPORTUNITIES

Travelers who would like to volunteer either with the **Leh Women's Alliance** or the **Ecology Centre,** or those wishing to arrange homestays at a Ladakhi farm (1 month minimum) should contact **The International Society for Ecology and Culture (ISEC),** Apple Barn, Week, Totnes, Devon TQ9 6JP, UK—preferably a year ahead. The center has ongoing projects that need volunteers, and can also refer would-be volunteers to other local organizations. (☎ (44 1803) 868 650; fax 868 651; isecuk@gov.apc.org; www.isec.org.uk. Open M-Sa 10am-4pm.) The **Student Educational and Cultural Movement of Ladakh** (SECMOL), at the Ridzong Labrang Complex in Old Leh (☎ 52421; fax 53012), between the bazaar and the polo grounds, has volunteer positions at its camp for Ladakhi youth in Choglamsar.

DAYTRIPS FROM LEH

Fifteen kilometers up the main road from Leh is the ancient Ladakhi capital of **Shey.** The hillsides are home to the famous giant twin images of Sakyamuni. The one of gilt copper is a part of a palace temple; the other is in a temple past a group of *chortens* 300m from the palace. (Open daily 8am-8pm. Rs20.) Four kilometers farther up the road, on a craggy bluff, is **Tikse,** the most photographed *gompa* in Ladakh. A few kilometers above Tikse, you can get off the bus and cross the Indus to reach the **Stakma Gompa,** which rises dramatically on a 60m high rock from the flat Indus Valley. The *gompa's* three temples are small but well maintained, and the views from their windows are superb. (Admission Rs20.)

From Stakma, you can make out the **Matho Gompa** to the southwest, set on a hill at the foot of the mountain. Separated from the Stakma *gompa* by 7km of meadows and barley fields, Matho, the only monastery in Ladakh that belongs to the Saskya-pa sect, is famous for the oracles delivered here. Lamas are chosen every three years and then spend several months fasting and praying until they are able to deliver prophecies and perform miraculous feats. The tiny *gon-khang* at the top of the *gompa* contains fierce images of deities. Unlike in most other *gon-khangs,* the ferocious faces are not covered. (Women are not allowed to enter.)

From Matho, descend to the left and follow the path at the foot of the ridge for 12km until you reach **Stok,** the residence of the Namgyal dynasty. There is a museum displaying family heirlooms; the turquoise-inlaid crown once belonged to a Chinese princess of the Tang dynasty who married a Tibetan king. Curiously enough, this is China's oldest claim to Tibet. (Open daily 8am-6pm. Rs25.)

Four kilometers from Saspol (up the Indus Valley from Leh) and across the river is Ladakh's oldest and most precious *gompa,* **Alchi,** a village founded in the 11th century. Bring a strong flashlight; the *gompa* is unlit. **Lotsava Guest House ❶,** 50m to the left of where the taxis stop, has a quiet garden (singles Rs80; doubles Rs150).

⬢ TREKKING AROUND LEH

> **⚠ WARNING.** Allow several days to acclimatize before setting out on a trek; altitude sickness is very common among visitors. Consult one of the many **trekking agents** in town (see p. 262). In case of accidents, the only available rescue is the military helicopter that operates at a cost of at least Rs40,000 per hr. and flies out only if there is a guarantee that the cost will be met. Before setting out, whether alone or with an organized group, be sure to leave the following with your guest house owner in Leh: detailed itinerary, photocopies of your passport, visa, and insurance policy, 3 filled-out forms guaranteeing payment, acceptance certificate, and indemnity bond. All are available from any travel agent in town.

Set between the world's two highest mountain ranges, Ladakh is a favorite destination for trekkers, who come for the scenery and for the (relatively) reliable weather. During the trekking season (June-Oct.), the days are hot and the nights bitterly cold. You should not attempt treks deep into the mountains with fewer than three people, and you may want to hire a guide. You can rent and buy equipment (tent Rs100 per day, stove Rs20 per day) in the **White House,** Fort Rd. (☎53048).

MARKHA VALLEY TREK

*The **Markha Valley Trek,** starting in **Spitok** and ending in **Hemis,** is one of the best routes for solo trekking and lasts 7-9 days. The landscape is varied, going through isolated villages, and the passes are high enough to brag about. There are supplies along the way and no tough river crossings, but the Stok La (4900m) is a challenge.*

DAY 1 (4-5HR.): SPITOK TO JING CHON. The trek starts in **Spitok.** The first stage is particularly barren and exposed. Turn right, and after about 1hr., follow the steep path to your left up to another jeep road. About 30min. later, you will reach a small ford. After the crossing, there is a wider stretch of river; you can either move across with the horses and guides or continue on a trail up the right bank. From the bridge, it is 20min. to camp. **Jing Chon Camping** has stream-side campsites (Rs40 per night) and a snack bar.

DAY 2 (5-6HR.): JING CHO TO YOURN TSO. After 3hr. of hiking you will arrive in **Rumbak,** where there is a tea stall and campground. After Rumbak, head upstream on the left of the river for 10-15min. Cross the bridge and continue upstream. One hour or so after Rumbak, you will reach the small village of **Yrutse** (4180m). If you continue along the trail carved into a hillside, you will reach **Yourn Tso Camping.** There are two more camping spots about 30min. up the river.

DAY 3 (6HR.): YOURN TSO TO SKIU. From Yourn Tso Camping, head up the river on the right side. A small path leaves this trail and crosses the riverbank; follow this short, steep trail up to a field where another camp is located. Follow the trail to the left and continue uphill (upstream) on the right bank of the stream. Less than 1hr. out of camp is another field. To the left (facing uphill toward the summit) is the **Ganda La** itself. Continue to the right and follow the trail uphill to the first **mountaintop.** Continue along this trail for less than 30min. to reach the pass (4900m). There will be a medium-grade descent along a narrow trail and then an easy stretch along a streambed, dry in all months but spring. Less than 1hr. down from the pass, you will reach a small **campground** with tea stalls. Continue on the trail for 30min. to reach the village of **Shingo,** after which the path climbs to a hillside on the left side of the valley. Next, the trail heads into **gorges,** which are awesome to behold. You will reach **Skiu** (and the Markha River) 4hr. later, where there is a *gompa* (usually open in

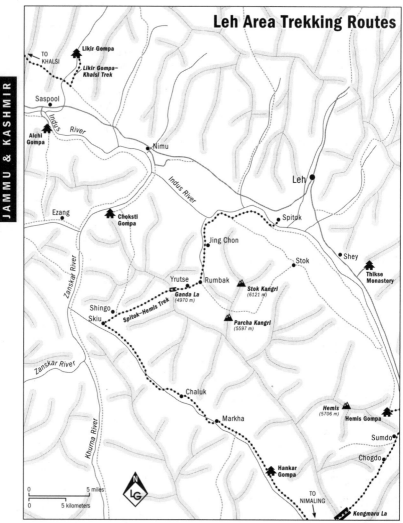

the evenings, but ask the villagers; Rs10 donation) and some tea stalls. The trail to the right (10-15min.) goes to the village itself and to the confluence of the Markha and Zanskar Rivers (3hr.). Slightly downhill, and 100m to the left, there is an excellent riverside **campground** (Rs60 per night).

DAY 4 (5-7HR.): SKIU TO MARKHA. Hike upstream along the river for 2½-3hr. to the campground at **Homurja** (Rs50 to camp). Two hours later, you will reach the village of **Chaluk** with *stupas* and green fields. After Chaluk, you can head downhill to stop early for the day (camping Rs50), or continue on for another 2hr. through boulder fields and across the river, to arrive at a campsite on the outskirts of **Markha** (Rs50 per night to camp).

DAY 5 (4-5HR.): MARKHA TO HANKAR. Cross the bridge to the left bank, going upstream; this will take you through Markha proper. Descend through the village, and after 30min. or so, ford the river. Do not attempt to take the trail carved out of the mountain face to your left; locals say it is unsafe. Ford the river again 45min. later. The trail is mainly level at this point, and after 1hr. or so, you will reach the outskirts of **Hankar.** Soon after the first tea stall, the trail leads into a gorge on the left of the Markha. Follow it up the steep switchbacks. As you come over this dry "mini-pass," the village of Hankar (2030m) comes into view.

DAY 6 (3-5HR.): HANKAR TO NIMALING. This stage is short and should be used to acclimatize for the next pass. After leaving camp, you will cross a broad stream on stepping stones. The trail becomes steep and curves left into the hillside above a small stream. After about 1hr., you'll reach a lakeside tea stall. Less than 1hr. after the stall is the camp at **Nimaling** (4850m), which costs Rs40 per day.

DAY 7 (7-8HR.): NIMALING TO SUMDO. With a pass over 5000m, a steep descent, and 7-8hr. of walking, this is the most difficult stage of the trek. Start by crossing the river on the birch-trunk bridge. The steep trail eventually becomes switchbacks until it reaches the **Kongmaru La** (5030m) after 1-1½hr. The initial descent is steep and difficult for horses and most humans. The trail soon drops into a **gorge** with walls of changing hue. This section is a challenge since it alternates between stone fields and gorge-side trails. However, the hillside sections of trail become much easier, and after about 1½hr., you will arrive in **Sumdo.** Shang Sumdo is the farthest and smallest camp, but is cheap (Rs50 per day).

DAY 8 (4-5HR.): SUMDO TO HEMIS. After leaving camp, a moderately difficult ford leads to a jeep track. Follow this for 4-5hr. to reach the Manali-Leh road at Hemis. Buses to Leh cost Rs18 and can be hailed beside the road.

OTHER TREKS
Also known as the "Baby Trek," the **Likir-Khalse** (2-4 days) leads over moderate passes to remote villages and *gompas*. The demanding **Lamayuru-Padum-Darcha** trek (19 days), which crosses both the Zanskar range and the Himalayas, is one of the most traveled in the Western Himalayas. Provisions are sold along the way. The **Karzok-Kibber** trek starts at **Tso-Morari Lake,** one day from Leh by car (you need a **permit** to reach Tso-Morari; see p. 270), and takes you through **Rupshu,** inhabited by the nomadic Changpas. On day four, you will cross the Ohirsta Phu River, which usually flows from Tibet to Tso-Morari but reverses flow seasonally. This crossing requires proper equipment. The trek climbs to the **Parang La,** where it descends to the beautiful village of **Kibber** in Spiti (see **Trekking Around Kaza,** p. 257).

THE NUBRA VALLEY
For centuries, caravans have trekked across Khardung La on the road between Punjab and Yarkand. Surrounded by the mighty mountains of Ladakh, the Nubra ("green") Valley has a varied landscape, covering long stretches of barren desert as well areas of lush greenery. Recent conflicts have reduced the passage of caravans, and only a small section of the valley (between Panamik and Hunder) is now open to the latest sources of foreign exchange: tourists. A new road has made Khardung La the highest motorable pass in the world, traveled along daily (in one direction per day) by military and tourist convoys and the occasional camel.

DISKIT
Diskit is the administrative headquarters of the Nubra Valley. The western part of Diskit is an unimpressive collection of ugly concrete buildings while the eastern half is a jumble of village houses and barley fields. There are paths on both sides of

> **WARNING.** Four newly opened areas in Ladakh–Drok-pa, Nubra Valley, Pangong Lake, and Tso-Morari Lake–require a **special permit,** issued by the Deputy Commissioner in Leh. The 7-day permit can be obtained only through a travel agent; bring a photocopy of your passport and visa. Officially, you need 5 people to get the permit, though there is nothing to stop you from traveling alone once you have the permit. Most travel agencies will have photocopies recently taken from other travelers' passports. These will be provided at a cost; expect to pay Rs100 each. The permit takes a day to arrange. You will be asked to leave a copy of your permit at every check-post; bring at least 5 photocopies with you.

the *chortens*, but you should not use the ones on the left, since the prayer-wheels should only be turned clockwise. From the prayer wheel on the main road, it's a 30min. climb up to the *gompa* along the path to the left, over a hill covered in *chortens*. There are great views from the new *du-khang* (assembly hall). You can also visit the protective deities in the *gon-khang*. Their fierce faces are unmasked on only one day of the year; their veils make it safe for women to enter (Rs20).

Buses from Leh go to Diskit (8hr.; Tu, Th, Sa 5am; Rs50), and return to Leh the next day. Guest houses line the *mani* wall, and most serve good, cheap food. When coming from the *gompa* and the main road, **Sunrise Guest House ❶** is on your right. (☎20011. Doubles Rs150.) **D. Khangsar Guest House ❶,** farther down a path to the right, is probably the best place to experience village life—you'll be shacking up with the cows. The rooms are clean, carpeted, and dirt cheap. (☎20014. Rooms Rs50. Breakfast Rs15; dinner Rs25.) Follow the road for 10min. to New Diskit, near the bus stand, where the only restaurant in town serves rice and *dal* (Rs25).

HUNDER

At the end of New Diskit, a dirt road turns off to the right, continuing along past pastures and sand dunes for 7km until it reaches Hunder. This walk is one of the most picturesque in the whole valley. Your permit allows you to go to the *gompa* near the bridge on the main road. Most sights lie outside the *gompa*; the paintings inside the biggest *chorten* are 50m below it; the temples are on the ridge above.

Once in Hunder, walk with the military barracks on your left until you see a sign for the **Snow Leopard Guest House ❶,** on the right. (Singles Rs60; doubles Rs150.) **Moon Land (Nerchungpa) Guest House ❶,** deeper inside the village, is hard to find, but the rooms (Rs75) are spacious and meals (Rs40) can be taken in the garden. There are also **campsites ❶,** in Hunder (Rs100-150), but it gets cold at night.

SUMUR

Sumur is a large village lined by *chortens* and a *mani* wall. Keeping these always on your right, walk up to **Sampan Ling Gompa.** Almost as big as Diskit Gompa, it has spectacular views and a school for young monks. A daily **bus** runs from Diskit to Sumur (2¼hr., evenings, Rs7) and returns the next morning. There are a number of guest houses along the way. **Stakrey Guest House ❶,** farther to the right, is the best—ask locals for directions. Doubles with semi-private, almost-clean bathrooms are Rs200. **Tashis Khahgsar Guest House ❶,** next to the school, 30m off the main road, has new rooms with common baths (doubles Rs150) and a shaded garden.

SRINAGAR سرینگر ☎0194

Until 12 years ago, Srinagar was one of the biggest tourist destinations in India, with over half a million people visiting every year. Things have changed. For most of the past decade, Srinagar has been a war zone. Kidnappings, bomb blasts, and random shoot-outs conspire to make this a very dangerous place indeed. **The situation in Kashmir is dangerous and unpredictable:** bring yourself up to date on recent developments before considering traveling here. **As of May 2002, most governments were advising their citizens to avoid all travel anywhere in Jammu and Kashmir state.** This is a beautiful part of the world, but until the volatile political situation improves, it must remain off-limits to all but the foolhardy.

> **WARNING.** As of May 2002, most governments were advising their citizens to avoid all travel to Jammu and Kashmir. Militant groups based in Pakistan have carried out numerous attacks on buildings in and around Srinagar over the past 12 months, and there is a constant threat that tension and mutual distrust might erupt into a full-blown war at any time. Militant activity remains widespread throughout the state. **Foreign tourists have been the targets of acts of extreme violence as recently as the summer of 2000.** Travelers who decide to come here anyway should realize that they are taking a big risk by doing so: **Kashmir is not a safe place to travel.**

TRANSPORTATION. Delhi is the best access point for Srinagar. Both **Indian Airlines** and **Jet Airways** have daily flights to Srinagar (1hr., daily, US$90-115). Jet Airways has an office near the bank (open M-Sa 10am-5pm). Several buses go to **Delhi** as well (12-15hr., daily, Rs250). You can also fly in or depart from Leh (1hr., Su) or take the bus (48hr., daily, Rs200).

ORIENTATION AND PRACTICAL INFORMATION. Sitting on the shores of both **Dal** and **Nagin Lakes,** and flush against the **Jhelum River,** Srinagar is divided into two parts: the old town and the new. **Residency Rd.,** in the new town, is where most tourist needs can be met. The **tourist registration office,** which extends visas (open M-Sa 10am-6pm) is in this area, and **ANZ Grindlay's Bank** is on Bund Residency Rd. The bank changes currency and traveler's checks and gives cash advances on MC and V. Allow one day for processing. (Open M-Sa 10am-3pm.) The offices of the **police station** are at Lal Chowk (☎452 067), Nehra Park, near Dal Lake (☎451 966), and on Nagin Lake (☎420 837). The main pharmacies are **Dar Medical Shop** (☎452 738), on Bund Residency Rd. (open daily 8am-7pm), and **Mazor Medical Store** (☎421 816), on Nagin Lake (open daily 8am-7pm). The **Institute of Medical Science (IMS)** is the best hospital in town (☎400 348 or 400 682) but is in Soura, 12km from town. **SMHS Hospital,** 3km from Residency Rd. (☎452 013 or 452 291), is more conveniently located. Internet access is available all over (Rs50-80 per hr.). The **post office** (open M-Sa 10am-5pm) is near Residency Rd. **Postal Code:** 190001.

ACCOMMODATIONS AND FOOD. A trip to Srinagar would be incomplete without a stay on a houseboat, especially since most of the hotels remain occupied by the good old boys of the Indian Army. Nagin is the quieter of the two lakes, but the quality of the houseboat and its location are more important than the lake it is on. Pre-booking in Delhi will save you some hassle, provided the travel agent does not charge you a commission. Many travel agents will also overcharge on accommodations; use the prices here as a guide. Bargain and insist on *not* pre-paying for your stay aboard, so if need be, you can find a better place. Any government tourist office can recommend a reliable booking agent (most places book for a houseboat or group of houseboats). **Houseboat Chicago ❸,** on Dal Lake, is a spacious, clean boat and is perhaps the best value on Dal. (☎477 489. Rs700 per person.) **Persian Gulf ❷,** on Dal Lake, is Chicago's more affordable cousin. (☎477 489. Rs500 per person.) **New Majestic ❹,** Nagin Lake, is clean and has a great staff. (Rs750 per person. Bargain hard. AmEx/MC/V.) **Butterfly** (☎ 420 212), on Nagin Lake, is the fanciest and most expensive houseboat. Each room has an animal theme—check out the peacock room. AmEx/MC/V. If your houseboat owner hasn't been feeding you enough curry, there are a few good restaurants on Residency Rd. **Moghul Darbar ❷**, serves Kashmiri favorites for Rs100-150. (Open daily 10am-6pm.)

SIGHTS. Many of the city's most beautiful sights are in the Old Town where most of the serious fighting took place ten years ago. The streets are poorly marked, if at all, and if you are without a guide (not a good idea), it would be wise to hire a rickshaw (Rs150-200) to take you around. The **Jhomia Mosque,** Nowhatta Rd., is the largest in Srinagar and is open to the public. Its large size, well-kept gardens, fountains, and bustling market make it a worthwhile stop. (Rs10 donation expected.) Srinagar's oldest **mosque**, built entirely from wood, is on Fatehkadal Rd. It was constructed during the 14th century by Hamdas, a Persian *shah* who brought Islam to Kashmir. Non-Muslims and women are not allowed inside, but the exterior is well worth the visit. The tomb at **Roza bal Kangar** purportedly holds the remains of Jesus, who allegedly wandered through Kashmir in his youth.

Many of Srinagar's world-renowned Mughal gardens were closed during the worst period of violence in Kashmir, but most are open now. **Shalimar Garden** is open and its central fountains have been restored to their past grandeur. The awe-inspiring **Nisha Garden** is also in full working order. Both open Tu-Su 5:30am-8pm.

⚑ SCENERY AND TREKS. Srinagar's biggest attractions are its mountains. While it is a good idea to have someone accompany you around the city, you *absolutely must* take a guide with you when you leave the city. **It is not safe to go trekking alone (or at all),** and the police will hassle you if you are found outside the city without a guide. The best way to organize a safe trek into the hills is to go through your houseboat, who can arrange for a guide, food, and horses (Rs200-300 per day). Popular treks include those to **Sonomarg** (80km from Srinagar) and to the **Gulmarg Valley,** which has the world's highest 18-hole golf course. Some of the most beautiful treks are near **Pahalgam** (97km from Srinagar), where you can go to the **Andranath Cave,** a Hindu pilgrimage site. A trip on the Jhelum River is a worthwhile non-trekking excursion. Tours cost Rs800-1000. **Exotic Adventure Travels** (☎ 421 217), in Nagin Market, arranges for English guides and is recommended by locals.

▢ SHOPPING. No one escapes Srinagar without exposure to high-intensity Kashmiri salesmanship. Prices for Kashmiri **handicrafts** are generally better here than elsewhere, and most salesmen aren't working on commission. Family-owned or collective outfits are the best sources for quality products; your houseboat owner will probably have a cousin who runs a carpet shop. If you order an item to be shipped home, make sure you pay with a credit card, so you can cancel charges if they cheat you, send you the wrong merchandise, or nothing at all.

KARNATAKA
ಕರ್ನಾಟಕ

KARNATAKA

Karnataka, with its beautiful beaches, ancient ruins, and fabulous palaces, embodies just about every romantic dream anybody ever dreamed about South India, and has yet to be discovered by the sun- and fun-seeking foreign tourists who come in such numbers to the rest of the South. The attitude here is neither stubbornly traditional nor irritatingly mellow, and Karnataka is one of India's most progressive states. The region has been dominated for centuries by the city of Mysore, which rose to political and architectural prominence during long years of Muslim rule. Karnataka first prospered under the Muslim Sultanate, and was ruled by Haider Ali and his son Tipu Sultan until the British took direct control of Mysore State in 1831. In 1956, Kannada-speaking regions in the north were added to Mysore State, creating a Kannada-speaking state, renamed Karnataka in 1973.

Karnataka's coastline is dominated by the jagged Western Ghats, which shield the Deccan Plateau from the coastal monsoons. On the plateau, orange-red earth gives way to green fields and narrow waterways. The area upland from the Ghats is covered in dense teak and sandalwood forests. The rivers produce so much hydroelectric power that Karnataka used to sell its surplus energy to neighboring states. The mines around the Ghats provided the material for some of India's architectural masterpieces: in the north, Chalukyan temples and the Vijayanagar ruins at Hampi; in the south, the temples at Belur, Halebid, and Somnathpur.

HIGHLIGHTS OF KARNATAKA

India's technology capital, **Bangalore** brims with pubs, gardens, unbelievable shopping, and all things cyber (p. 273).

The **Maharaja's Palace** is a fairy-tale vision set amid the laid-back, sweet-smelling chaos of **Mysore** (p. 284).

Hippie-tested and UNESCO-certified, **Hampi's** extensive **ruins** (p. 301) are enough to make you happy to be in the middle of nowhere.

Party hardy on **Gokarna's** gorgeous beaches (p. 310) with the holy town's hip set.

BANGALORE ಬೆಂಗಳೂರು   ☎ 080

The city of Bangalore is where the West makes its cameo on the Deccan Plateau, dressed in Indian garb—a city where American and Indian executives down *dosas* streetside, where families open cybercafes in their yards, and where rickshaws keep up with the competition by posting web addresses in their rear windows. Bangalore is ground zero for India's technological revolution. A sizable chunk of the world's software is written here, and in the conference rooms of MG and Residency Rd., India's elite drafts strategies to sell technology across the globe.

When a petty chieftain under the Vijayanagar Empire named Kempegowda founded Bangalore in 1537, his son built four watchtowers to mark the boundaries of the city. Four and a half centuries later, the towers still stand, but modern Bangalore has long since outgrown these limits. The growth of India's fifth largest city has been accelerated by the huge influx of people from rural Karnataka, Tamil

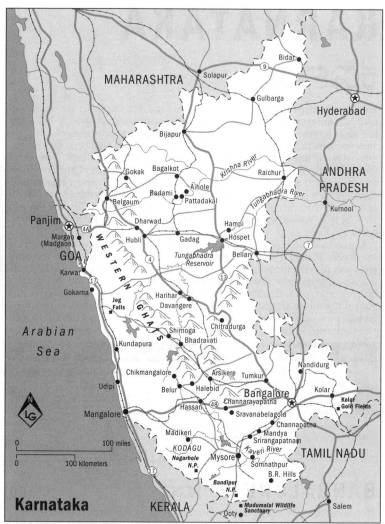

Karnataka

Nadu, Kerala, and northern India, lured here by the city's mild climate and the prospect of making it big amid its metropolitan madness. Numerous lakes, parks, gardens, and broad avenues make Bangalore one of India's most pleasant cities.

✈ INTERCITY TRANSPORTATION

FLIGHTS

The airport is 8km southeast of the city from the MG Rd. area (auto-rickshaw Rs60, or local bus #333). 24hr. pre-paid taxi booth (Rs250 to the city center).

INTERNATIONAL AIRLINES. Air India (☎227 7747; fax 227 3300). JC Rd., Unity Bldg., a block from Corporation Bldg. **Air Canada** (☎558 5394), **Air France** (☎558

9397), **Kuwait Airways** (☎ 558 9021), and **Gulf Air** (☎ 558 4702) are in Sunrise Chambers, 22 Ulsoor Rd., 1 block north of MG Rd., behind the Taj Residency. **British Airways** (☎ 227 1205; fax 224 1503). 7 St. Marks Rd. **KLM** (☎ 226 8703). Taj, Race Course Rd. **Lufthansa** (☎ 558 8791). 42-2 Dickenson Rd. near Manipal Center. **Qantas** (☎ 226 4719). 13 Westminster Cunningham Rd. near Wockhardt Hospital. **Sabena, Singapore Airlines** (☎ 286 7868), and **Swissair** (☎ 286 7868) share Park View, 17 Curve Rd., off Richmond Rd. **Thai Airways** (☎ 226 7613). Imperial Court, Cunningham Rd. **United Airlines** (☎ 224 4625). 12 Richmond Rd.

DOMESTIC AIRLINES. Indian Airlines (☎ 221 1914). Cauvery Bhavan, Kempegowda Rd. Open M-Sa 6am-5:30pm. Airport office (☎ 526 6233). Open daily 8:30am-8:30pm. **Jet Airways** (☎ 227 6617 20). 22 Ulsoor Rd., Unity Bldg., behind the Taj Residency. Open M-F 8:30am-7pm, Sa 9am-5pm. **Sahara** (☎ 558 3897 or 558 4507). 35 Church St. Open M-F 8am-8pm, Sa 10am-5pm. Airport branch (☎ 527 1286 or 527 1287). To: **Ahmedabad** (2hr., 1 per day, US$220); **Calcutta** (2½hr., 2 per day, US$265); **Chennai** (45min., 6-8 per day, US$65); **Cochin** (1hr., 2-3 per day, US$80); **Delhi** (2½hr., 7 per day, US$255); **Goa** (1hr., 2 per day, US$105); **Hyderabad** (1hr., 3 per day, US$95); **Mumbai** (1½hr., 13 per day, US$140); **Pune** (1½hr., 2 per day, US$145); **Trivandrum** (1hr., 1 per day, US$120).

TRAINS

City Railway Station (24hr. info ☎ 131 or 133), at the end of Race Course and Bhashyam Rd. The **reservations counter** (☎ 132 or 1361) is in the bldg. on your left as you face the station. Open M-Sa 8am-8pm, Su 8am-2pm. The **enquiries** counter (☎ 1361 3) is in the main bldg. Open daily 7am-10:30pm. Trains are often booked weeks in advance—there are also *tatkal* (immediate) and tourist quotas for some trains to major cities. To: **Calcutta** (37hr., W and F, Rs397); **Chennai** (5-7hr., 6-7 per day 6:30am-11:30pm, Rs87); **Coimbatore** (7-8hr., 6:15am and 11pm, Rs138); **Delhi** (42hr., 6:25pm, Rs436; *Rajdhani Exp. 2429* 35hr.; M, W, Th, Su; Rs2205); **Hospet** (15hr., 10pm, Rs163); **Mangalore** (20hr., 6:40pm, Rs235); **Mumbai** (26hr., 12:10 and 8:30pm, Rs310); **Mysore** (2-3hr., 6 per day 5:30am-11:45pm, Rs41).

BUSES

KSRTC Bus Stand (☎ 287 3377 or 287 1261). Bhashyam Rd. **Reservation counter** open 7am-11pm. To: **Badami** (9hr., 4 per day 5:30-9pm, Rs180); **Bijapur** (11hr., 10 per day 8am-10:15pm, Rs196-280); **Chennai** (7hr., 11 per day 9am-10:45pm, Rs151); **Cochin** (10hr., 4 per day 4-7:30pm, Rs190); **Hassan** (4hr., every hr. 6am-11:40pm, Rs65); **Hospet** (8hr.; 9, 10am, 8pm; Rs115); **Hyderabad** (12hr., 13 per day 6:30am-9:30pm, Rs303); **Kodaikanal** (10hr., 9:15pm, Rs160); **Mangalore** (8hr., every hour 6:30am-11:40pm, Rs150/186); **Mumbai** (24hr., 2 and 4pm, Rs475); **Mysore** (3hr., 15 per day 5am-9pm, Rs46); **Ooty** (8hr.; 8:30, 9am, 10pm; Rs145); **Panjim** (11hr.; 3:30, 4:45, 5:30pm; Rs285/308); **Trivandrum** (18hr., 1:30 and 4pm, Rs330). **Private buses** to Mumbai, Mysore, Ooty, and other destinations are near the KSRTC bus stand.

■ ORIENTATION

The hub of modern, international Bangalore is the intersection of **Mahatma Gandhi (MG)** and **Brigade Rd.** South of MG Rd. are **Church St.** and **Residency Rd.**, home to hi-tech pubs, high-class hotels, and high-price shops. North of MG Rd., the aptly named **Commercial St.** leads west toward **Shivajinagar**, a bustling market district and Bangalore's downtown. Most museums are in **Cubbon Park**, which stretches along **Kasturba (Gandhi) Rd.** from **Ambedkar Rd.** to MG Rd. The **Majestic** area, near the **City Railway Station** and **bus stand**, contains several budget hotels. South of the Majestic is the frenetic **City Market** area (also called K.R. or Krishnarajendra Market), with its unpaved narrow roads, bullock carts, temples, and mosques.

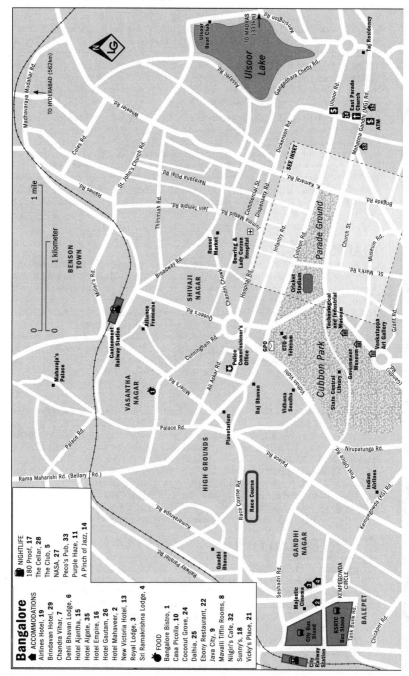

Bangalore

↟ ACCOMMODATIONS
Airlines Hotel, **19**
Brindavan Hotel, **29**
Chandra Vihar, **7**
Dehli Bhavan Lodge, **6**
Hotel Ajantha, **15**
Hotel Algate, **35**
Hotel Empire, **16**
Hotel Gautam, **26**
Hotel Mahaveer, **2**
New Victoria Hotel, **13**
Royal Lodge, **3**
Sri Ramakrishna Lodge, **4**

🍴 FOOD
Bangalore Bistro, **1**
Casa Picolla, **10**
Coconut Grove, **24**
Dalhia, **25**
Ebony Restaurant, **22**
Java City, **9**
Mavalli Tiffin Rooms, **8**
Nilgiri's Cafe, **32**
Sunny's, **18**
Vicky's Place, **21**

🍸 NIGHTLIFE
180 Proof, **17**
The Cellar, **28**
The Club, **5**
NASA, **27**
Peco's Pub, **33**
Purple Haze, **11**
A Pinch of Jazz, **14**

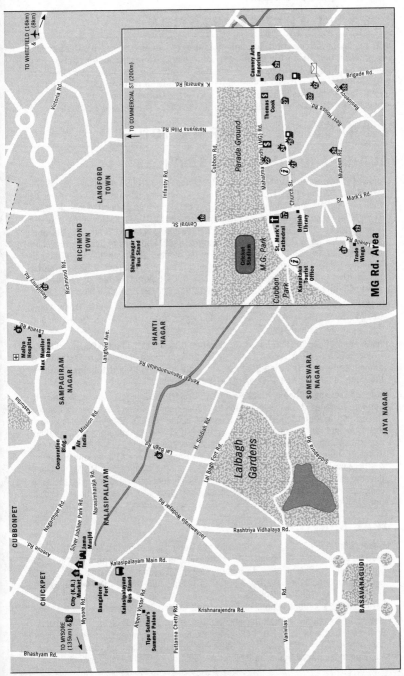

▣ LOCAL TRANSPORTATION

Don't be shy about insisting that **auto-rickshaws** use their meters—it's the law and common practice. From 10pm-6am, expect to pay 1½ times the meter charge. Two kinds of **local buses** leave from the city bus stand: ordinary buses and the more expensive Pushpak buses. Buses to MG Rd. leave from platforms 17 and 18 (frequent 6:30am-10pm, Rs3.50-5). Route #7 serves the Corporation Bldg. and MG Rd. (every 20min., Rs5). For Whitefield, take the #333E or #334 bus (1hr., Rs8).

▣ PRACTICAL INFORMATION

TOURIST AND FINANCIAL SERVICES

Tourist Offices: Government of India Tourist Office (☎ 532 1683 or ☎/fax 558 5417). KFC Bldg., 48 Church St. From Brigade Rd., turn right; the office is on the right, inside the KFC Bldg. Ask for a copy of *Bangalore This Fortnight*, a great guide to the city. Open M-F 9:30am-6pm, Sa 9am-1pm. **KSTDC** (☎ 221 2901). 104/1 Kasturba Rd. near the junction with MG Rd., opposite the Queen Victoria statue in Cubbon Park. 2 flights up in a big, off-white bldg. Daily Bangalore **bus tours** (Rs80) and tours of Belur and Halebid. Open M-Sa 10am-5:30pm; closed 2nd Sa of the month. There's another KSTDC branch in Badomi House, opposite the City Corporation Office, N.R. Sq. (☎ 227 5869). **Tourist Information Centers**: Railway Station (☎ 287 0068); airport (☎ 526 8012). **Department of Tourism** (☎ 221 5498). Kempegowda Rd., Cauvery Bhavan, F block, 1st fl.

Budget Travel: For car rental, bus, rail, air, and tour reservations, go to **Trade Wings** (☎ 221 4595). 48 Lavelle Rd., opposite the Airlines Hotel. Open M-F 9:30am-1pm and 2-5:30pm, Sa 9:30am-1pm.

Immigration Office: The **Foreigners Registration Office** is at the **Police Commissioner's Office** (☎ 225 6242 ext. 251). 1 Infantry Rd. Go north along Cubbon Park past the GPO onto Queen's Rd., then left 1 block later onto Infantry. **Visa extensions** granted brusquely at the same desk. Open M-Sa 10am-5:30pm.

Currency Exchange: Thomas Cook (☎ 558 1340). 55 MG Rd., just before the intersection with Brigade Rd. The fastest place to change foreign currency or traveler's checks. Open M-Sa 9:30am-6pm. The **Citibank ATM** inside Nilgiri's, Brigade Rd., is conveniently located but is not open 24hr. Accepts MC/V and all Citibank and Cirrus/Plus logo cards. **24hr. Citibank ATM** at the Prestige Meridian Bldg., 2 MG Rd. Toward the west end of the street, at 87, is a **24hr. Canara Bank ATM.** The ATM in Manipal Center, 47 Dickenson Rd., outside the **HSBC** bank, is also 24hr. Walk east on MG Rd., 1 block past the parade grounds. At the East Parade Church, turn left at Dickenson Rd. Accepts cards with Plus or Global Access logos; the bank gives cash advances on MC and V. Open M-F 10:30am-2:30pm and 3-4pm, Sa 10:30am-12:30pm.

LOCAL SERVICES

Market: Nilgiri's, 171 Brigade Rd., hawks fruit outdoors and the rest inside. Open M-F 9:30am-9:30pm, Sa 10:30am-1:30pm. **Russel Market,** 1.5km north of MG Rd., off Chandni Chowk, Shivajinagar. An indoor market selling fruit, flowers, veggies, meat, antiques, and bric-a-brac. Open M-Sa 9:30am-1:30pm and 4-8pm. **City Market,** 1.5km southwest of City Railway Station, near the Jama Masjid, is an enormous wholesale bazaar selling silk fabric in addition to food and flowers. Open dawn-dusk.

Bookstore: Gangaram's Book Bureau (☎ 558 6189). 72 MG Rd. Open M-Sa 10am-8pm. **Fountainhead** (☎ 221 9777). 41 Lavelle Rd. Amazing magazine selection. Open daily 10am-8:30pm. **Sidewalk vendors** (cheaper for bestsellers) are near the Cauvery Arts Emporium. **Secondhand traders** line Avenue Rd. south of Kempegowda Rd.

EMERGENCY AND COMMUNICATIONS

Police: Commissioner's Office, 1 Infantry Rd. (☎225 4501). From the intersection of MG and Kasturba Rd., walk northwest with Cubbon Park on your left; follow Queen's Rd. to Infantry Rd. and turn left. **Headquarters** (☎221 1803). Nirupatunga Rd., next to the YMCA. **Cubbon Park station** (☎556 6242). Kasturba Rd., next to the aquarium.

Pharmacy: Hosmat (☎559 3796 or 559 3797). 45 Maganath Rd. Off Richmond Rd. **Mallya Pharmacy,** in front of Mallya Hospital. Open 24hr.

Hospitals: The most respected government hospital, **Bowring and Lady Curzon Hospital** (☎559 1362), sits just off Hospital Rd., 1km north of MG Rd. **Mallya Hospital,** 2 Vittal Mallya Rd. (☎227 7991), **Manipal Hospital,** 98 Rustumbagh Airport Rd. (☎526 6646 or 526 6441), and **St. John's Medical College and Hospital,** Sarjapur Rd. (☎553 0724 or 553 0734), offer excellent private care.

Internet: Cafe Coffee Day, 13 Brigade Rd. (☎559 1602). Bangalore's first cybercafe is still the best place to grab a coffee and surf (Rs50 per hr., includes 2 coffees). Open daily 8am-10:30pm. Almost every major office or commercial bldg. has at least 1 shop; the **Brigade Gardens** bldg., 19 Church St., stands out with five (Rs10-20 per hr.).

Post Office: The **GPO** is a stone colossus on the corner of Raj Bhavan and Ambedkar Rd. in Cubbon Park. Open M-Sa 8am-7pm, Su 10:30am-1pm. There is also a branch on Brigade Rd., between Church St. and Rest House Rd. and another on Avenue Rd. south of Kempegowda Rd. Both branches open M-Sa 10am-6pm. **Postal Code: 560001.**

ᛤ ACCOMMODATIONS

Decently priced rooms in the hip, hi-tech, and happening **MG Rd.** area are always full. The area around the bus stand and railway stations has plenty of cheap places to stay—5km from the action. The lodges in **City Market** are cheap but close to traffic and noise. Prices do not include 5-12.5% taxes. Check-out is 24hr.

MG RD. AREA

▨ **Hotel Ajantha** (☎558 4321; fax 558 4780). 22-A MG Rd. 10 min. from Brigade Rd. Clean, reasonably priced rooms and a great location. Color TV and 24hr. hot water. Reserve up to a month in advance. Singles Rs210; doubles Rs350-650. ❶

▨ **Brindavan Hotel** (☎558 4000). 108 MG Rd. Pretty inexpensive rooms considering its great MG Rd. location. Reserve ahead. Singles Rs380-600; doubles Rs500-1000. ❷

▨ **Hotel Empire** (☎559 2821). 78 Central St. A 5min. walk north on St. Mark's Rd., after the cricket stadium and just past Cubbon Rd. Hotel Empire is really in Shivajinagar, but tucked away on a quiet, tree-lined block. Rooms have soft mattresses, Star TV, towels, and 24hr. hot water. Attached restaurant. Singles Rs400; doubles Rs550-750. ❷

Airlines Hotel (☎227 3783 or 227 3786). 4 Madras Bank Rd. Just east of Lavelle Rd., 5min. from MG Rd. Rooms aren't immaculate, but they're well-furnished: towels, seat toilets, and hot water until 11am. A vast complex with Internet parlor, bakery, hair salon, and drive-in diner. Singles Rs340; doubles Rs440. AmEx/MC/V. ❷

New Victoria Hotel (☎558 4076 or 558 5028). 47-48 Residency Rd. Lost in trees and wildflowers, the Victoria's cozy, quirky rooms with attached bathrooms sport canopy beds with antique furniture and Star TV. Service charge 10%. Singles Rs490; doubles Rs1360. Credit card and traveler's checks accepted. ❷

Hotel Gautam (☎558 8764 or 558 8137). 17 Museum Rd. 5 min. from Brigade Rd. Star TV and bathtubs. You'll more likely find vacancies in this behemoth than at other hotels in the area. Attached veg. restaurant. Singles Rs560; doubles Rs675. ❸

Hotel Algate (☎559 4786-89). 93 Residency Rd. At the intersection with Brigade Rd. These immaculate rooms are not cheap, but you get perks like A/C, HBO, and complimentary shampoo. Singles Rs850; doubles Rs990. AmEx/MC/V. ❹

KARNATAKA

RAILWAY STATION AND BUS STAND AREA

◪ **Sri Ramakrishna Lodge** (☎226 3041). SC Rd. Next to Kapali Theater. Rooms offer immaculate bathrooms with squat toilets. Each floor has a pleasant veranda, 24hr. hot water, laundry, room service, TVs, and phones. Two adjacent restaurants (*thalis* Rs25), travel counter, and pharmacy. Singles Rs155; doubles Rs250-300. ❶

Royal Lodge (☎226 6951). 251 SC Rd. Basic rooms with bath in a calm and welcoming atmosphere. Hot water 6:30-9am. Doubles Rs275. ❶

Hotel Pushpamala (☎287 4010). Off SC Rd. behind Sangam Theatre. Clean, bright, quiet rooms with seat toilets. Friendly staff. Singles Rs140-250; doubles Rs280-330. ❶

Hotel Mahaveer (☎287 3670). 8-1 Tankbund Rd. Near the corner of Chickpet Rd., by the south station exit. Courtyards access over 60 clean rooms with TV and attached bath. Friendly staff. Laundry service. Singles Rs285; doubles Rs390-850. MC/V. ❷

CITY MARKET

◪ **Chandra Vihar** (☎222 4146). MRR Ln. Across Avenue Rd. from K.R. Market, west of Jama Masjid. All 50 of the modern rooms have desks, Star TV, and phones. Deluxe doubles on higher floors provide spectacular views of the market. Hot showers 6-10am. Attached restaurant open 8am-9pm. Singles Rs175; doubles Rs300-320. ❶

Delhi Bhavan Lodge (☎287 5045). Avenue Rd. just north of the market area. Standard, clean rooms. Hot water 6-9am. Singles Rs70-110; doubles Rs170-205. ❶

◖ FOOD

Splurge city beckons. For those who've partied down to petty *paise*, cheap *paratha* joints at City Market stay open past midnight.

◪ **Sunny's** (☎224 3642). 35/2 Kasturba Cross, off Lavelle Rd., near Trade Wings travel agency. A multi-floor Mediterranean bistro topped with an open-air terrace. Optimal for leisurely lunch deals: bread and herb butter with a fresh mozzarella salad Rs245, assiduously *al dente* pasta Rs150-250, Shrimp Diane Rs450. Desserts Rs65-105. Bakery opens at 10am with quiche (Rs60-85) and imported cheeses (brie and feta Rs1100 per kg). 10% service charge. Open daily noon-3pm and 6-11pm. AmEx/MC/V. ❹

◪ **Mavalli Tiffin Rooms** (☎222 2022). 11 Lal Bagh Rd. MTR is a local legend. Barefoot waiters in *lungis* serve Bangalore's best *dosas* (Rs18) and never-ending "full meals" (Rs75), leaving other restaurants 10 courses in the dust. Open Tu-Su, *tiffin* 6:30-11am and 3:30-7:30pm, meals 12:30-2:45pm and 8-10pm; open M 12:30-2:45pm only. ❶

Java City, 24/1 Lavelle Rd. This popular cafe serves cappuccino (Rs20), multiple flavors of Italian sodas (Rs56), homestyle pizzas (Rs30-156), quiche (Rs35), croissant sandwiches like the "Cold American" (Rs42-54), and fresh desserts (Rs30-40). Open daily 11am-11pm. Branches at 47 Church St. and 13 Cunningham Rd. AmEx/MC/V. ❶

Casa Picolla (☎221 2907). Devatha Plaza, 131 Residency Rd., at the intersection with St. Mark's Rd. Italian in an airy setting with seaside murals. Lasagne *verde* Rs80, black forest crepes Rs45. Delivery available. Open daily 11:30am-10:30pm. AmEx/MC/V. ❶

Ebony Restaurant (☎558 9333). 84 MG Rd. On the magnificent 14th fl. balcony of the Barton Centre. Tandoori, Balti, Parsee, and French cuisine. Entrees Rs90-250, lunch buffet M-F Rs155 for men, Rs110 for women. Reservations essential. Open daily 12:30-3pm and 7:30-11:30pm. AmEx/MC/V. ❷

Coconut Grove, 86 Church St. Huge servings of culinary curiosities from Kerala and Karnataka presented beneath the palms. Try *kaikari kootu*, made from lentils and coconut (Rs60), or an unbeatable *thali* (Rs55-75). Seafood Rs110-125. Save room for pineapple-based *kaidachakka halwa* (Rs35). Open daily 12:30-4pm and 7-11pm. ❶

Dalhia (☎558 0958). G-37/38 Brigade Gardens, 19 Church St. Where else in India can you rub elbows with Japanese salarymen while slurping down a bowl of *udon* or *soba* (Rs200-250)? Sushi and sashimi (Rs120-450) M, W, F. *Tekka domburi* (Rs300) every day. Open M-Sa noon-3pm and 6:30-9:30pm. AmEx/MC/V. ❸

Bangalore Bistro (☎209 7564). 214/34 Cunningham Rd. Between Miller's and Palace Rds. *Nouvelle cuisine* arrayed on ice before your eyes. Whiz kids lunch on unlimited soup and salad (Rs125), but the intrigue of twisty squids (Rs105) and a Richmond Risotto (Rs155) draws them back. Open daily 12:30-3:30pm and 7:30-10:30pm. ❷

Vicky's Place (☎558 4717). 28 Church St. A friendly French and Italian hideaway. Spinach and mushroom casserole Rs100, chicken Kiev Rs130, and an occasional tiramisu Rs60. Open daily 11am-3pm and 7-11pm. AmEx/MC/V. ❷

Nilgiri's Cafe, 171 Brigade Rd. Hefty grilled sandwiches Rs38-60, doughy pizzas Rs65-90, hazelnut milkshakes Rs30, French toast Rs25. Open daily 9am-9pm. ❶

Karavalli, 66 Residency Rd., behind the Gateway Hotel. Bangalore's most elegant coastal Keralan cuisine and frilliest *appam*. Fish or veg. stew and coconut curries, as lush as the surrounding gardens. Lunchtime *thalis* Rs265-295, French wine Rs120-125 per glass. Open daily 12:30-3:30pm and 7:30-11:30pm. ❸

◎ SIGHTS

CUBBON PARK AND MUSEUMS. Set aside in 1864 and named for the former Viceroy of India, Lord Cubbon, the park consists of 300 acres of fresh air and greenery in the center of the city. The park extends from the corner of MG Rd. to the Corporation Bldg. and also contains several museums. The **K. Venkatappa Art Gallery** exhibits watercolor landscapes by K. Venkatappa, the court artist who painted much of the Maharaja's Palace in Mysore. The second floor displays rotating exhibitions of contemporary Karnatakan artists. The **Government Museum,** one of India's oldest, is a fine example of monumental neoclassical architecture. The first floor houses some interesting archaeological artifacts and stone Hoysalan sculptures. *(Museum and gallery open Tu-Su 10am-5pm. Rs4.)* Next door, the **Visveswaraya Industrial and Technological Museum** celebrates Bangalore's industrial progress from 1905, when City Market lit India's first light bulb, to the current boom in information technology. *(Open daily 10am-5:30pm. Rs10.)* The park also has an aquarium-cum-fish-sales-center, and a children's park, **Jawahar Bal Bhavan,** complete with boat, pony, and toy train rides, a doll museum, and a children's theater. *(Open daily 9:30am-6:30pm. Free.)* Across the park is the red **Attara Kachari,** which housed the 18 departments of the Secretariat until 1956. *(Open Tu-Su 10am-5:30pm. Rs2.)*

VIDHANA SOUDHA. One of Bangalore's most recognizable landmarks, the Vidhana Soudha houses the Secretariat. In the early 1950s, a visiting Russian delegation pointed out the abundance of European architecture in Bangalore. Spurred to action by these remarks, the Chief Minister of Mysore state decided to build this spectacular neo-Dravidian structure. The Vidhana Soudha became not only an affirmation of Indian sovereignty, but also an assertion of Bangalore's new legislative power. It was built out of pure granite by craftsmen from Andhra Pradesh (one of Bangalore's largest slums was formed by the displaced masons' families). Statues of Jawaharlal Nehru and B.R. Ambedkar stand in the front lawn, gesticulating at each other beneath the self-congratulatory inscription, "Government Work is God's Work." The building is lit up every Sunday evening. *(Across the street from Cubbon Park, to the northwest. Lights Su 7-8pm.)*

BANGALORE FORT. Built in mud and brick during the late 1600s as an extension of another of Kempegowda's forts, the Bangalore Fort was refurbished by Haider Ali and Tipu Sultan during the 18th century. It originally encompassed the area between the Corporation Offices and City Market. Most of it was destroyed during the Anglo-Mysore War, but the remains are beautifully preserved, with ornately carved, Islamic-style arches and turrets and an exquisite **Ganpati Temple** inside. *(Near City Market on Krishnarajendra Rd., opposite Vanivilas Hospital. Open daily 6am-6pm.)*

TIPU SULTAN'S SUMMER PALACE. Tipu liked to call his Summer Palace *jannat keliye jalan,* "The Envy of Heaven," but it is really just a low-budget replica of Daria Daulat in Srirangapatnam. Most of the original wall paintings have been obscured by brown paint. *(500m south of the fort. Open daily 8am-5:30pm. US$5.)*

BULL TEMPLE. The Bull Temple's massive black Nandi, over 500 years old, draws devotees from all around India. Legend has it that a raging bull used to torment local farmers by ravaging their fields at night. The frustrated farmers finally hired a night watchman to kill the bull with a crowbar. The next morning, they discovered that the carcass had transformed into a solid granite bull. Look closely, and you'll see the crowbar embedded in the poor beast's back. *(Bull Temple Rd., south of the Summer Palace. Open daily 8am-8pm.)*

LALBAGH GARDENS. Haider Ali laid out the botanical gardens in 1760. His son Tipu Sultan expanded the 16-hectare gardens to 96 hectares and added the mango grove. After Tipu's demise in 1799, the British took over. Prince Albert Victor of Wales built the Glass House in the late 1800s to resemble the Crystal Palace in London. The gardens are home to over 150 different varieties of roses, a giant floral clock, a lotus pond, a deer park, and countless walkers, joggers, and cyclists. One of Kempegowda's four watchtowers, built in 1537 to mark Bangalore's city limits, can still be seen here. *(2km south of Cubbon Park. Open daily 9am-7pm. Rs2.)*

ULSOOR LAKE. Ulsoor Lake spreads over northeastern Bangalore, its 1.5 sq. km of water speckled with tiny, picturesque islands. Enjoy a boat ride or swim at the Ulsoor Boat Club (see **Other Diversions,** p. 283). During the annual Ganesh Festival (Aug.-Sept.), devotees dunk the elephantine statue, decked out in ceremonial regalia, into the lake. *(2 blocks north of MG Rd., on Gangadhana Chetty and Kensington Rd., near the Taj Hotel and Cottage Emporium. Open daily dawn-dusk.)*

OTHER SIGHTS. The **Jawaharlal Nehru Planetarium** was built to commemorate the 100th birthday of the freedom fighter and prime minister who called Bangalore "India's city of the future." *(T. Chowdiak Rd., opposite Raj Bhavan. ☎ 220 3234. Open Tu-Su; closed 2nd Tu of the month. English shows at 4pm. Rs15.)* Just across the street and open the same days, the **Indira Gandhi Musical Dancing Fountain** puts on a kitschy little show (7 and 8pm, Rs10). The **Gandhi Picture Gallery,** on the second floor of **Gandhi Bhavan,** presents a well-organized journey through the Mahatma's life, with grainy blown-up photographs, wise old quotations, and artifacts such as Gandhi's wooden *chappals,* drinking bowls, and letters to Franklin Roosevelt, Tolstoy, Gokhale, and Nehru. Since few people visit this place, there's no permanent staff; you'll need to ask to have the door unlocked. *(From Windsor Hotel, cross the Golf Course High Grounds, and head down Kumara Krupa Rd. ☎ 226 1967. Open M-Sa noon-6pm. Free.)*

▣ NIGHTLIFE

BARS

Though plagued by water shortages, Bangalore is never dry. Its burgeoning pub culture has earned the city the title "Bar Galore." Most pubs are clustered around Brigade Rd. Pubs may serve alcohol only from 11am to 11pm. The police visit around midnight, suggesting that "good people sleep early." (Some of the sleazier establishments at City Market may hold out until 1am.) Sometimes pubs refuse admission to unaccompanied women. Most accept major credit cards.

180 Proof, 40 St. Mark's Rd., south of MG Rd. The "heppest" meeting place for Bangalore's sophisticated set, complete with black-blazered bouncers standing guard. This colonial armory-turned-loft is the place to see and be seen. Beer Rs75-180 per bottle, Rs80 per pint. Rs100 entrance fee F-Sa. Open daily noon-3pm and 6-11:30pm.

A Pinch of Jazz (☎558 4242). 47 Dickenson Rd. In The Central Park. Give the vinyl menus a spin for some Cajun standards (Rs60-140) as you kick back to Getz, Mingus, and perhaps India's only frosted margarita (Rs100). A 4-piece combo from Chennai plays live nightly 8-11pm. Happy Hour daily 12:30-3pm and 6:30-8pm.

Peco's Pub, 34 Rest House Rd., off Brigade Rd, 1 street south of Church St. Garcia, Marley, Joplin, and Zeppelin grace the walls. 3 floors packed with college-age guzzlers imbibing mugfuls (Rs30). Relaxing rooftop. Open daily 10:30am-10:30pm.

Purple Haze (☎221 3758). Residency Rd. Opposite Cache Towers. Exit light, enter nightlife. A young headbanger's ball chaperoned by the guitar greats, including a stainedglass Zappa. Pitchers Rs170, mugs Rs40. Open daily noon-11:30pm.

The Cellar, 7 Brigade Rd., Curzon Ct. Opposite the intersection with Church St. Wooden decor and cushy booths. The mellow afternoon might have been invented here, just before the swingin' evening. Chinese, continental, and *tandoori* snacks starting at Rs50, pub lunch Rs100. Pitchers Rs170, mugs Rs32. Open daily 11am-11pm.

NASA, 1/4 Church St. Like attending Space Camp with that most famous of moonwalkers, Michael Jackson. Enjoy beer (pitcher Rs200, mugs Rs45) while soaking in the laser show and other space-age exotica. Open 10:30am-10:30pm.

DISCOS

Another much-loved city ordinance, the one against the late operation of discos, prevents a proper club scene from taking root. At **The Club,** Mysore Rd., outside of town (Rs150-400 for a one-way rickshaw ride), DJs spin the latest techno, trance, and hip-hop beats, but The Club is much more than a discotheque. Site of MTV's launch into South Asia, the place draws up to 6000 revelers for its live gigs (past performers include such bright young luminaries as BoyZone, Shampoo, and Slash from Guns n' Roses) and sports a swimming pool, squash, tennis, and basketball courts, and even a 24hr. coffee shop serving snacks like "chicken 69." (☎860 0768 or 860 0769. Open M, W, F-Sa until 5am. Cover Rs350 per couple, of which Rs100 goes toward food.) Times have been far tougher on **JJ's,** Airport Rd., just before the airport, above Air India. (☎526 1929. Open F-Sa 9pm-1am. Cover Rs150.) Look for the return of Sunday **jazz night,** where patrons relax to old rock and jazz. Another spot to watch is the tiny dance floor of **Zapp's Pub,** below Purple Haze.

OTHER DIVERSIONS

A lot happens in Bangalore, so check the weekly listings in papers available at magazine stands; www.bangalorebest.com also has up-to-date information on current cultural events. Several cinemas in the MG Rd. area show English-language flicks. **The Galaxy** (☎558 2205) Residency Rd., **The Plaza** (☎558 7682) 74 MG Rd., **The Rex** (☎558 7350) Brigade Rd., and **The Symphony** (☎558 5988) 51 MG Rd., all show not-too-old American movies (show-times noon, 3:30, 6:30, 9:30pm; Rs25-60). Try to buy tickets at least an hour in advance. **Taj Residency** (☎558 4444) 41/3 MG Rd. has a sauna, jacuzzi, and health club. Go for a dip at the public **City Corporation Swimming Pool,** way up Kensington Rd., where you can also rent rowboats and paddleboats. (Rs10 per hr. for swimming. Open Th-Tu 6:30-10am and 12:30-4pm.)

▣ SHOPPING

Bangalore's arts and crafts emporiums, with handpainted or inlaid tables, saris fit for a *rani,* and life-size sandalwood Krishnas, merit a shopping expedition. The

KARNATAKA

MG Rd. area is the emporiophile's paradise, with shops selling merchandise at prices to match the superlative quality; most accept credit cards, so you can rue the purchase of that antique jade Buddha later. The government-run **Cauvery Arts Emporium,** 49 MG Rd., near Brigade Rd., has fair prices and a decent selection. (☎ 558 1118. Open daily 10am-1:30pm and 3-7:30pm.) If you'd rather bargain, shops on Cunningham Rd. will oblige. **Natesan's Antiqarts,** 76 MG Rd., sells art pieces of their own design. (☎ 558 8344. Open M-Sa 10am-7:30pm.) **Himalayan Dowry,** 72 MG Rd., sells Kashmiri and Tibetan handicrafts and donates a portion of its proceeds to anti-dowry campaigns. (☎ 559 7366. Open M-Sa 10am-9pm.) On **Commercial St.,** you'll find *salwar kameez* and saris in all permutations of style, color, and price.

⚡ DAYTRIPS FROM BANGALORE

BRINDAVAN

*City **buses** #333E and 334 run to Whitefield (1hr., Rs7). **Trains** also service the town (45 min., 7 per day 6:45am-8:15pm, Rs5).*

Sathya Sai Baba's Karnataka ashram (Brindavan) is in the town of **Whitefield,** 16km from Bangalore. Although he spends most of the year at his main ashram in Puttaparthi, Andhra Pradesh, Sai Baba often spends the summer months at Brindavan. Affectionately referred to as "Swami," Sai Baba has established free hospitals, schools, and countless public aid projects, including "The Water Project" which brought running water to several neighboring villages. He normally gives morning and afternoon *darshan*, during which he walks through the crowds of adoring, prostrating, and often fainting devotees, who have assembled here from all over the world. You can stay at Brindavan for a nominal charge. For information call the ashram office (☎ 845 2233).

NRITYAGRAM DANCE VILLAGE

***Buses** run regularly from Bangalore (#253, 253A, 253D, 253E from City Market) to Nrityagram, but the village is 5km from the bus stand, and there aren't many auto-rickshaws around. It's easier to arrange a private **taxi** (about Rs500 round-trip) or book through **KSTDC, Cosmopole Travels** (☎ 228 1591), or **Cox and Kings Travel** (☎ 223 9258).*

In Hessaraghatta, 35km from the city, on the Bangalore-Pune Highway, is the Nrityagram Dance Village (☎ 846 6313; fax 846 6312), established by the late Protima Gauri, one of the most respected *odissi* dancers of the 20th century. Dancers from all over India come to train here. Tours of the village include an hour-long lecture/demonstration of *odissi* and *kathak* dance, a lecture on Indian philosophy and culture, and an organically grown lunch. (Casual tours Rs20 per person.) During the first week of February, the dance village conducts an all-night dance and music festival. The festival is free, featuring performances by students as well as musical faves Zakir Hussain and Amjad Ali Khan. The audience usually numbers well over 25,000, so get there by 5:30pm if you want a seat. (Dance performance Rs1100, minimum 10 people; advance booking required. Village open Sept.-May Tu-Su 10am-5pm.)

MYSORE ಮೈಸೂರು   ☎ 0821

Calm, graceful, and magisterial, Mysore welcomes visitors with the easy charm of a maharaja. The Wodiyars, who ruled here from the 15th century until Independence, left behind more than just monuments lining sandalwood-scented avenues, and a palace framed in palm fronds. They left behind a pace of life not captured in the cliched brochure blurbs. Even the touts who push the innumerable incense sticks, beaded necklaces, and beauty products, seem more intent on making friends than a quick buck. It's a place of (relative) plenty, with rambling parks and *pujas* that crack open coconuts all the way up Chamundi Hill. The city explodes during the annual **Dussehra Festival,** a 10-day celebration in late October.

Mysore

🏠 ACCOMMODATIONS
Green Hotel, 8
Hotel Dasaprakash, 3
Hotel Indra Bhavan, 1
The Hotel Rajmahal Deluxe, 5
Hotel Ritz, 9
Parklane Hotel, 7

🍗 FOOD
Akshaya Vegetarian, 3
Hotel Ritz, 9
Jewel Rock Restaurant, 6

Parklane Hotel, 7
Penguin, 2

🎭 ENTERTAINMENT
Rajkamal Theatre, 4

K A R N A T A K A

▐ TRANSPORTATION

Trains: The **railway station** is at the intersection of Irwin and Jhansi Laxmi Bai Rd. The inquiry and reservations desks (☎ 131 or 422103) are open M-Sa 8am-8pm, Su 8am-2pm. To: **Bangalore** (3hr., 10-12 per day 6am-11:30pm, Rs64); **Chennai** (7-10½hr., 2:20 and 6pm, Rs166); **Hassan** (2-3hr., 7:30am and 6pm, Rs23).

Buses: Long-distance buses leave from the **Central Bus Stand** (☎ 520853). On B-N Rd., near Wesley Cathedral. Reservations desk open daily 7:30am-8pm. Buses run to: **Bangalore** (3hr., every 15min. 6:45am-10:30pm, Rs50); **Belur** (5hr., 7am and 1pm, Rs43); **Bijapur** (18hr., 1pm, Rs211); **Chennai** (12hr., 5 and 7pm, Rs173); **Coimbatore** (6hr., 11 per day 6am-11:30pm, Rs55); **Hassan** (3hr., every 30min. 5am-11pm, Rs50); **Madikeri** (3hr., every 30min. 6am-11:30pm, Rs44); **Mangalore** (7hr., every 30min. 8:45am-11:30pm, Rs93); **Ooty** (5hr., every 30min. 7am-7pm, Rs60). Buses to **Somnathpur** (Rs13) leave from Nicamebad in front of Wesley Cathedral, but you can also take a bus to **Bannur** (every hr., Rs9), 7km from Somnathpur, and catch a bus from there (every 30min., Rs3). Near the cathedral, **private bus** companies vie for space and customers. Most are open late into the night.

Local Transportation: Local buses leave from the **City Bus Stand**, off K-R Cir. Fares are Rs3-6; signs are in Kannada. To: **Brindavan Gardens** (30min., platform 6 #303, every 30min.); **Chamundi Hill** (20min., platform 7 #201, every 20min.); **Srirangapatnam** (45min., platform 7 #313 and 316, every 20min.). **Taxis** cluster in Gandhi Sq.; fares, as usual, are negotiable. Metered **auto-rickshaw** trips across town should cost Rs15.

▄ ORIENTATION

Running north-south, **Sayaji Rao Rd.** bisects Mysore into roughly equal halves, cutting through **K-R Circle,** the true center of the city. The **City Bus Stand** is in the southeast quadrant of K-R Cir., sitting like a *paan* stall before the gates of the gigantic **Maharaja's Palace.** Farther southeast looms the summit of **Chamundi Hill.** About 300m east of K-R Cir., just north of the copper-domed statue, is **Sri Harsha Rd.,** where you'll find a number of accommodations and restaurants. Sri Harsha Rd. leads east to a busy north-south thoroughfare, **Bangalore-Nilgiri (B-N) Rd.** North on B-N Rd., is the **Central Bus Stand.** Farther north is **Irwin Rd.,** which leads west past the GPO, the government hospital, the tourist office, and the domed **railway station.**

▤ PRACTICAL INFORMATION

Tourist Office: Karnataka Tourist Office (☎442096). Old Exhibition Building. At the corner of Irwin and Diwan's Rd., 1 block east of the railway station. Open M-Sa 10am-5:30pm; closed 2nd Sa of each month. There is another counter at KSRTC bus stand (☎444997). Open M-Sa 9am-8pm. The **KSTDC** (☎423652), on Jhansi Laxmi Bai Rd., adjacent to the Hotel Mayura Hoysala, will book day-tours of Mysore. Open 24hr.

Currency Exchange: The **State Bank of Mysore** (☎443866) has foreign exchange branches at the junction of Sayaji Rao and Old Bank Rd. and opposite the GPO. Open M-F 10:30am-2:30pm, Sa 10:30am-12:30pm. **Bank of Baroda,** at the northeast corner of Gandhi Sq., gives cash advances on MC and V for Rs100 plus 1% commission. Open M-F 11am-2:30pm and 3-4pm, Sa 11am-noon.

Market: Devaraja Market, tucked behind the glitzy sari shops on Sayaji Rao Rd. and the sandalwood shops on Dhanvantri Rd. Crammed with the full spectrum of brightly colored vegetables and fruit, color film, and *kum-kum* powder. Open daily dawn-dusk. **Pick 'n' Pack Mini Supermarket** (☎425445). Hotel Luciya complex, Old Bank Rd., between Gandhi Sq. and Sayaji Rao Rd. Open M-Sa 9:30am-9pm.

Police: Superintendent's Office (☎528222). On Nehru Cir. opposite the GPO.

Pharmacy: Janatha Bazaar Drug Unit (☎427678). Dhanvantri Rd. On KR Hospital grounds opposite Indra Bhavan Hotel. Open 24hr.

Hospital: Krishnarajendra (KR) Hospital (☎443300). At the corner of Sayaji Rao and Irwin Rd., opposite Cauvery Emporium. The private **Holdsworth Memorial (Mission) Hospital** (☎521650), Sawday Rd., is nicer and cleaner than the government's KR.

Internet: Take advantage of early morning connections at **Chamundi Vasathi Gruha,** on Chandraguptha Rd., between the Clock Tower and Wesley Cathedral in the lodge of the same name. Rs40 per hr. Open 24hr. **Coca-Cola Cyber Space** (☎565574). #2 Madvesha Complex, Nazarbad Rd. Rs40 per hr. Open M-Sa 10am-10:30pm, Su 10am-8pm.

Post Office: GPO (☎442165). At the intersection of Ashoka and Irwin Rd., 750m north of the Raja's statue. Open M-Sa 9am-6pm, Su 10:30am-1pm. **Postal Code:** 570001.

▟ ACCOMMODATIONS

Mysore is full of reasonably priced, centrally located hotels. Many have devoted followings, so reservations (a week ahead Nov.-Feb.) are a good idea. The state taxes rooms Rs150 and up 5-10%. Check-out is 24hr. unless otherwise noted.

Green Hotel (☎422415). 2722/2 Sri Harsha Rd. Arguably India's amplest budget rooms, with towering ceilings, big bathrooms (bucket hot water), showers, seat toilets, and desks. Some rooms even open onto a balcony. Attached restaurant and bar open daily 10:30am-2:30pm and 5:30-11pm. Singles Rs60; doubles Rs90. ❶

Parklane Hotel (☎434340 or 437370). 2720 Sri Harsha Rd. 8 small rooms, squat toilet on the 1st fl., seat toilet on the 2nd floor. Popular restaurant on the terrace. Hot water 6-10am. Singles Rs125; doubles Rs149. MC/V. ❶

The Hotel Rajmahal Deluxe (☎421196). Lakshmivilas Rd. To the right as you walk out of Jaganmohan Palace. Large, spotless rooms with huge windows; some with TVs. 24hr. room service, friendly staff, and laundry service. Singles Rs175; doubles Rs250. ❶

Hotel Ritz (☎422668). 5 B-N Rd. 100m south of the Central Bus Stand, on your right as you exit. High quality, batik-blanketed rooms with attached baths are usually booked solid. Restaurant/bar serves your private patio upstairs. Doubles Rs350. MC/V. ❶

Hotel Dasaprakash (☎442444 or 444455). On the corner of Gandhi Sq. and Old Bank Rd. Spacious and airy. Palm-fringed courtyard meets all your needs—an ice cream parlor, an astropalmist, and a travel agency. Towels and soap provided. Seat or squat toilets. Veg. restaurant. Singles Rs185-335; doubles Rs325-625. ❷

Hotel Indra Bhavan (☎423933). Dhanvantri Rd. On the SR Rd. side. Manned by cordial and sweet old men who are inflexible about three rules: no alcohol, no meat, and no dirt. Attached baths. Good restaurant. Singles Rs170; doubles Rs180-350. ❶

🍴 FOOD

Mysore's famous cornflour *pak* can be found at any of the sweet shops in the city. **Guru Sweet Mart,** Sayaji Rao Rd., at Devaraja Market, is the place to savor the best in town—still warm from the oven and dripping with *ghee* (Rs7 per 50g hunk).

▨ **Parklane Hotel,** Sri Harsha Rd., near New Statue Circle. Secluded booths are ideal for twilight wining and dining. Serves specials like Barbeque Night's *shashlik* kebab (veg. Rs65, non-veg. Rs75), and *kadai paneer* (Rs55). Beer Rs45-75. Open daily 10:30am-3:30pm and 6:30-11:30pm. Live music 7:30-9:30pm. MC/V. ❶

Penguin (☎425466), Dhanvantri Rd. Just east of Hotel Indra Bhavan. It's no mirage: this roof-top oasis shimmers with 25 varieties of *dosas* (Rs14-20), from savory set and *rava* (Mysore's specialties), to banana, *soppina,* pineapple, and . . . mother-in-law? Ice cream iterations (from Rs14). Open daily 7:30am-11pm, roof garden open after 4pm. ❶

Jewel Rock Restaurant, 2716 Sri Harsha Rd., at Hotel Maurya Palace. A chummy staff recommends delicious tandoori, *tikkas,* and *ghee*-laden *biryanis* made-to-order (Rs38-60). Dim lighting and jazz muzak. Open daily 11am-3:30pm and 6:30-11pm. ❶

Hotel Ritz, 5 B-N Rd. Candlelit dining and garden patio. Carnivores feast on the chicken dinners (from Rs60). *Rumali* rolls Rs35-60, kebab platter Rs75, veg. dishes Rs36-55. Open daily 7am-11pm. Bar open daily 11am-11pm. ❶

Akshaya Vegetarian Restaurant, in the Hotel Dasaprakash. Serves brimming *thalis* (Rs25/40) and thick Niligiri coffee (Rs6) to hordes of locals and travelers. Open daily noon-3pm and 7:45-10pm. Tiffin 6-10:30am and 4-10pm. ❶

🔵 SIGHTS

THE MAHARAJA'S PALACE. The home of the current maharaja and the jewel of the dusty Mysore plateau, the Maharaja's Palace (Amber Vilas) is impressive for its girth (it covers more than 3.5 sq. km) as well as its worth (construction cost Rs4.2 million, not a small sum 100 years ago). In 1897, during the reign of Krishnaraja Wodiyar IV, the original wooden palace burned to the ground. It was immediately rebuilt; it took a team of artisans 15 years to complete the task. Durbar Hall is plastered with murals depicting scenes from the Dussehra Festival. The museum is a must-see for those with an itch for kitsch: gold chariots, Wodiyar family portraits, a weapons room with sharpened scythes, Ganesh-stained windows, and a wax effigy of the maharaja. Visible from the palace exit, the **Maharaja's Residential Palace,** with its tarnished cutlery and shabby school uniforms, is disappointing. At 7pm sharp on Sundays and government holidays, the palace is illuminated with 80,000 light bulbs. *(Purandara Dasa Rd. Open 10am-5:30pm. Rs10; Residential Palace Rs15. Camel rides Rs10; elephant rides Rs25; horse carriage ride Rs25.)*

CHAMUNDI HILL. Even if you're not religious, a visit to Chamundi Hill can be a spiritual experience. The ride affords a divine view of the Deccan plain, with its squares of saffron and green, and of Mysore city—even at a distance, you can see the Maharaja's Palace in all its splendor. At the top of the hill, the 16m-high **Mahishasura,** the buffalo demon who plagued Mysore (and from whom the city takes its name) greets you in all his god-awful gaudiness. The **Sri Chamundeswari Temple,** with its 40m *gopuram*, derives its name from Chamundi, an incarnation of the goddess Durga who brought Mahishasura down to size. The area is a bit of a madhouse (mind your shoes!), but the rest of the hill is quite peaceful. Fridays find the hilltop swarming with devotees queueing up not only for the usual post-*darshan prasadam* of tamarind rice or sweet semolina, but for free meals—over 10,000 of which are provided each week by a private campaign. *(Temple open 7:30am-2pm and 4-8pm.)* The tiny **Godly Museum,** near the Mahishasura statue, is filled with dioramas depicting various stages of spiritual life. *(Open daily 10:30am-7pm. Free.)* Ascending or descending Chamundi Hill's 1000 steps gives you a case of Mysore feet (2hr.). If you do opt to hike, don't miss the **Shiva Temple** one-third of the way up. A granite statue of Nandi, Shiva's loyal bull, guards the temple. Nandi protects the temple, and it's rumored that he grows a bit bigger each year. It is expected that in another 300 years, Nandi will have grown so large that he'll cover the whole of Mysore. *(Southeast of town. City bus #201 and special buses, Rs5. Taxis Rs150-200 round-trip. Shiva Temple open 7:30am-2pm and 3:30-9pm.)*

OTHER SIGHTS. The **Jaganmohan Palace,** containing the **Jayachamarajendra Art Gallery,** holds a jumble of ill-exhibited *objets d'art.* There are a few gems on display: Rabindranath Tagore watercolors and Raja Ravi Varma oils, a collection of tablas, sitars, and veenas, a series of Buddhas carved onto an elephant tusk, and ancient silk game boards. *(2 blocks west of the Maharaja's Palace. Open daily 8:30am-5pm. Rs10.)* Indian tourists flock to the **Brindavan Gardens** and **Krishnarajendra Dam** on the weekends. The vast, severely tended gardens lack flowers, but the fountains are let loose at night. The dam was built across the Kaveri River at the turn of the century. *(City bus #303, Rs6. Open M-F 7am-8:30pm, Sa-Su 7am-9:30pm. Rs10, camera fee Rs20. Light show M-F 7-7:55pm, Sa-Su 7-8:55pm.)* As Indian zoos go, the **Mysore Zoo,** which spreads over 250 green acres, is rather pleasant. Plenty of tigers (including the endangered white tiger) prowl about their enclosed grounds. Efforts to house animals in their most natural habitats led to the 1994 escape of two vagrant crocodiles into rural Karnataka. *(Open W-M 8am-5pm. Rs15, camera fee Rs10, video fee Rs15.)*

■ ■ ENTERTAINMENT AND SHOPPING

Rajkamal Theatre, Vinoba Rd., screens English-language films (Rs35; show-times 11am, 3, 6:15, and 9:30pm). After the flick, switch from low light to blacklight at **Just Blues: The Blues Concept Pub,** in the Balaji Palace Hotel, a few doors back towards K-R Cir. Bask in the violet glow at the bar (mugs of beer Rs30, pitchers Rs140) as the DJ spins fresh hip-hop (open daily 11am-11:30pm). You no longer have to be the Maharaja's personal guest to use the **swimming pool** at the opulent **Lalitha Mahal Palace Hotel** at the base of Chamundi Hill. (☎571265. Rs130 per hr. Open daily 7am-7pm.) Check *The Hindu* for cultural programs at Kalamandir, 2km up JLB Rd. past the railway museum.

Mysore produces half of India's **sandal oil** as well as mass quantities of **silks** and **jewelry.** The state government's **Cauvery Emporium,** Sayaji Rao Rd., is a giant warehouse of such things. They accept AmEx, MC, Visa, and traveler's checks, and will arrange packing and export for an extra charge. (☎521258. Open daily 10am-1:30pm and 3-7:30pm.) Cauvery has an open-air annex near the palace (open M-Sa 10am-1:30pm and 3-7:30pm). Cheaper mini-emporiums crowd Dhanvantri Rd. near its intersection with Sayaji Rao Rd. Farther down Sayaji Rao Rd., near K-R Cir., silk stores sell enough saris to clothe an army of elephants. The **Government Silk**

Weaving Factory in Vidyaranyapuram allows tours. Here, you can watch your silk being woven and buy it later at mill prices. (☎481803. Open M-Sa 10am-noon and 2-4pm.) Next door is the **Government Sandal Oil Factory,** where, with permission, you can schedule a tour. (☎481803. Open M-Sa 10am-noon and 2-4pm.) Take the bus (# 9, 3, 8, 11, 13, 14, or 44; 15min., every 10 min.) to Vidyaranyapuram.

▓ DAYTRIPS FROM MYSORE

SOMNATHPUR

To get to Somnathpur, take a private bus from near Wesley Cathedral (Rs13), or hire a taxi. Temple open daily 9am-6pm. US$5; video fee Rs25.

A tiny village 38km east of Mysore, Somnathpur is the site of the beautiful **Keshava Temple,** built in 1268. The village was established and the temple commissioned by Soma, a high officer under the Hoysala King Narasimha II—hence the name Somnathpur. Legend has it that when the temple was completed, the gods deemed it too beautiful and too grand (despite its height of only 10m) for this earth and wanted to transport it to heaven. The temple quaked and began to levitate. In horror, the chief sculptor mutilated some images on the outside wall to avert such a catastrophe. The slightly disfigured temple came crashing back down to earth. These events explain why the *garudagamba* (stone pillar depicting the divine mount, the eagle Garuda) is not opposite the entrance, as is traditional, but skewed to the northeast. The Keshava Temple contains layers of carved friezes; elephants, scrolls, geese, and scenes from the *Bhagavad Gita, Mahabharata,* and the *Puranas* border the exterior, and dozens of images fill the interior.

SRIRANGAPATNAM

To reach Srirangapatnam, take a bus from the Central Bus Stand. #313 and 316, 30min., every 20 min. 6am-8pm. Last bus returns to Mysore at 9pm. Rs5.50.

Srirangapatnam, 16km from Mysore, was the site of Tipu Sultan's island fort and the seat of his vast kingdom until the fourth Anglo-Mysore war in 1799. Tipu's father, Haider Ali, defeated Mysore's Hindu maharaja in 1761. In 1782, Tipu inherited the throne, along with his father's rivalries with the Marathas, the French, and the British. He proved especially fearsome to the East India Company, to whom he dealt two sound defeats before the colonialists finally managed to turn the tide against him. Tipu met his final defeat here in 1799, ending his subcontinental conquest and opening up the path for the East India Company's expansion into South India. According to the legend, barraged by redcoat bullets, Tipu toppled off his horse into a pile of the dead and dying. A British soldier, catching a glimpse of Tipu's gold belt buckle, tried to snatch it. But the barely breathing Tipu lanced the soldier with his sword. Alas, the soldier was merely injured and was still sharp enough to lodge a bullet in Tipu's temple. It is rumored that the ghost of Tipu still wanders around his former digs in search of his stolen belt buckle.

Turn left from the bus stand to reach the **Jama Masjid,** the mosque Tipu built on the grounds of an old Hindu temple. Remnants of walls built to keep the British out surround the area. Just 500m farther on, the **Sri Ranganatha Temple,** the town's namesake, dates from the Hoysala age. *(Open daily 7:30am-1pm and 4-8pm.)*

Daria Daulat, Tipu's summer palace, is about 1km in the opposite direction from the bus stand. The manicured lawns and splendid palace still carry the whiff of that bygone era of pomp and luxury. The palace, built in 1784 in an Indo-Islamic style, is now a **museum** housing some murals, including a portrait of Tipu wearing his signature tiger stripes, which gave him the title "Tiger of Mysore." *(Rickshaw Rs15. To walk, turn right out of the bus stand platform and take an immediate left; the palace is on the left. Open Sa-Th 9am-5pm. US$5.)* Beyond Daria Daulat, another 1.5km down the road, lies **Gumbaz,** the onion-domed mausoleum where Tipu and his father rest, flanked by generals, advisors, and aunts. *(Open daily 8am-6:30pm. Free.)*

MADIKERI ☎08272

Madikeri is the capital of the tiny coffee-growing district of Kodagu (Coorg) and easily accessible, but the town sees few foreign visitors. With extensive cardamom plantations, coffee estates, and pepper vines covering the hills of the surrounding terrain, Madikeri offers unrivaled opportunities for trekking. The city is also a good base for exploring the nearby settlements and monasteries run by Tibetan exiles. Madikeri's season runs from October to May, when crisp nights follow temperate days; in the summer, the rains pound the hills.

TRANSPORTATION. The steep road to the left of the bazaar leads down to the KSRTC **bus stand.** Buses go to: **Bangalore** (6hr., every 30min. 5:30am-11pm, Rs81-105) via **Kushalnagar** (45min., Rs11) and **Mysore** (3hr., Rs37-50); **Hassan** (every 30-60min. 6am-7:30pm, Rs74); **Mangalore** (4hr.; every 30-60min. 5:30am-8:30pm, 10 night buses after 11:30pm; Rs43-56); **Ooty** (9hr., 7:30am and 8:30pm). Unmetered **auto-rickshaws** charge at least Rs15 for a trip around town.

ORIENTATION AND PRACTICAL INFORMATION. Winding along the base of a series of hills is Madikeri's main thoroughfare, **General Thimaya Rd.** (also known as Mysore Rd. or Main Rd.). It runs roughly northwest past General Thimaya (GT) Circle and the fort before reaching the town bazaar and the bus stand. At the first intersection, 200m past Thimaya Circle, **MG Rd.** heads southwest (left) toward **Raja's Seat** and several hotels. Just past the bazaar, **School Rd.** (Junior College Rd.) loops northeast (right) and back around to rejoin General Thimaya Rd. The main road continues onward to **Abbi Falls** and Mangalore. There's no tourist office in town, but you can get KSTDC-approved on **trekking** through Ganesh Aiyanna at the **Hotel Cauvery Capitol** (☎25492), or from **Coorg Travels** (☎25817) at the Hotel Vinayaka Lodge. **Canara Bank,** on the bazaar by the Bata shop, handles currency exchange and traveler's checks upstairs (open M-F 10:30am-2:30pm, Sa 10:30am-12:30pm). The **police station** (☎29333) is on the main road opposite the fort. Several **pharmacies** cluster around GT Circle; **Gautham Pharma** is the cleanest and friendliest of the bunch. (☎25768. Open daily 8:30am-8:45pm.) The **Government Headquarters Hospital** (☎23444) is 50m southeast of the General's statue. Superfast **Internet** access comes surprisingly cheap at **Netraiders.com,** a couple steps past Chowk from the main road. (Rs30 per hr. Open daily 9:30am-10:30pm.) The **Head Post Office** is on General Thimaya Rd., just up the hill from the bazaar. (☎25413. Open M-Sa 9:30am-5:30pm.) **Postal Code:** 571201.

ACCOMMODATIONS AND FOOD. The **Hotel Cauvery ❶,** hidden below its restaurant in the bazaar, is probably the best place to stay if you can stand listening to the same Hindi film songs blaring from the nearby theater all night. The lilac sheets, pink curtains, and complimentary newspaper make mornings more pleasant. (☎25492. Singles Rs200; doubles Rs350. Off-season: Rs150/Rs250.) The spectacular views at the **KSTDC Hotel Mayura Valley View ❷,** past Raja's Seat at the end of MG Rd., might get you to overlook its lackluster rooms. (☎28387. Singles Rs300; doubles from Rs400. Off season: Rs275/Rs330.) The newly built **Hotel Amrita ❸,** JC Rd., is more luxurious. The sparkling, if characterless, rooms all have TVs. (☎23607. Doubles Rs500. Off season: Rs400.) **Vinayaka Lodge ❶,** next to the bus stand, is the cheapest place in town. (☎29830. Singles Rs160; doubles Rs325.)

Compared to the crowd of stainless steel, garish "meals" hotels, **Red Fern Bar & Grill ❶,** Sudarshan Rd. (opposite MG Rd.), might as well have dropped out of the sky. This elegant roadhouse prepares chicken (Rs45-60) and stocks whisky (Rs25-90 per 60ml) in more flavors than the rest of the town combined can muster (open daily 10am-11:30pm). **Santrupti ❷,** 116/2 MG Rd., in the Hotel Rajdarshan, is still the fanciest restaurant in town. (Indian and Chinese dishes Rs38-120. Open daily 7:30am-3pm and 4:30-11pm.) **Hotel Veglands ❶,** near the police station, stands out for its small-town prices. (Meals Rs12-17. Open M-Sa 7am-9pm.)

◙ SIGHTS. A favorite of the long-gone kings, the views from **Raja's Seat,** on MG Rd., are now popular with tourists, especially at sunset. The **fort** at the center of town houses a life-sized pair of elephant statues as well as **St. Mark's Church,** now a small museum of British memorabilia and local archaeological finds. *(Open Tu-Su 9am-5pm; closed second Sa.)* Accessible from the steps leading down from the police station, the lilac **Omkareshwara Shiva Temple,** School Rd., combines Hindu, colonial British, and Islamic architectural styles. The gilded domes of the **tombs** of the Rajas glint over the town, 1km northwest of the bazaar. Note the Hindu statuettes of bulls on the Islamic-style minarets. The path, well-labeled with signposts, continues 7km through coffee plantations and cardamom estates to **Abbi Falls.** The walk is pleasant, but auto-rickshaws will take you there and back for about Rs200.

NEAR MADIKERI

BYALAKUPPE AND SERA JE

Kushalnagar is easily reached from Madikeri—all buses running between Mysore and Mangalore stop in the town. The area around Kushalnagar, 22km east of Madikeri, is dotted with **Tibetan settlements,** collectively known as **Bylakuppe,** one of the largest expatriate Tibetan communities in the world. Some 10,000 refugees were relocated here during the 1960s and early 1970s after subsisting for ten years in a former British internment camp in the jungles of Assam. Within this group were about 200 monks who had escaped when Lhasa's Sera Je Monastery was destroyed in 1959. They set about rebuilding it 6km southwest of Kushalnagar. Today the new **Sera Je Monastery** serves as a university for more than 3000 monks. The grounds are constantly abuzz with monks' praying and debating. On the road to Sera Je is the **Nyingmapa Monastery,** which houses the **Golden Temple.** The temple's three towering gilded statues and wall paneling are an amazing sight.

From Kushalnagar, **auto-rickshaws** charge Rs30 to go to Sera Je, but you can probably share one with some monks. The **Sera Je Guest House ❶,** established to raise money for the monastery, is the only place to stay in town. The manager is friendly and speaks good English. The attached restaurant is always filled. (☎54672. Doubles Rs125.) Another monkish fave is the **Norling Hotel ❶,** opposite the monastery, serving only chow mein (Rs15), *parathas*, and eggs *du jour.*

Kushalnagar has more accommodation options, but there are no gems here. **Radhakrishna Lodge ❶,** Mysore Rd., to the right as you exit the bus stand, is not the cleanest place but has attached bathrooms. (☎74822. Singles Rs75; doubles Rs100.) The nearby **Ganesh Lodge ❶,** offers minimal amenities. (☎74528. Singles Rs100; doubles Rs145.) Young monks enjoy the **Tibet Restaurant,** IB Rd., 200m across from the bus stand; look for the green sign. (Open daily 9am-9pm.)

HASSAN ಹಸನ   ☎08172

The industrial city of Hassan has little tourist appeal and no sights of its own, but its location 40km from Halebid and Belur has ensured it a place along South India's tourist trail. Hassan's railway station, bus stands, hotels, and conveniences make it a practical place to spend your nights while visiting the attractions nearby.

▛ TRANSPORTATION

Trains: The **railway station** serves **Arsikere** (1½hr.; 10:50am, 3:30 and 9pm; 2nd class Rs10) and **Mysore** (3hr., 6am and 6:30pm, Rs56). Both connect to **Bangalore,** but the Mysore connection is faster.

Buses: The **bus stand** (☎68418) is opposite Maharaja's Park. To: **Bangalore** (4hr., every 15min. 5am-9pm, Rs62) via **Channarayapatna** (1hr., Rs13); **Belur** (1½hr., every 15min. 6:15am-8:30pm, Rs13); **Halebid** (1hr., every 30min. 7am-7pm, Rs11); **Manga-**

lore (3½hr., 20 per day 6am-6:30pm, Rs50); **Mysore** (3hr., every 30min. 5am-7:30pm, Rs40). From **Channarayapatna,** connections can be made to **Sravanabelagola** (15min., every 20min., Rs4). For **Hospet/Hampi,** head to **Shimoga** (4hr., every 15min. 5am-10:45pm, Rs45) and transfer. Hordes of **private bus** companies go to Bangalore (Rs70). **Tempos** also service Belur and Halebid; from the bus stand, make a left onto Church St., take the 1st right, and proceed for a few blocks.

■ ⚡ ❷ ORIENTATION AND PRACTICAL INFORMATION

Most hotels are within 500m of the **bus stand,** which is on the southwest corner of the intersection of **Bus Stand Rd.** (north-south) and **Church Rd.** (east-west), also known as **Park Rd.** Running parallel to Bus Stand Rd., 200m to the east, is **Race Course Rd.** It intersects the second east-west thoroughfare, the **Bangalore-Mangalore (B-M) Rd.,** 300m to the south. The **railway station** is 2km farther east on B-M Rd. The city center hugs the bus stand and the intersection of Race Course and B-M Rd.

Tourist Office: Regional Tourist Office (☎ 68862). Vartha Bhavan, B-M Rd. A few blocks east of the bus stand, on the left. Open M-Sa 10am-1:30pm and 2-5:30pm.

Currency Exchange: State Bank of Mysore (☎ 68407). Bus Stand Rd., near B-M Rd. Changes US and UK currency and traveler's checks. Open M-F 10:30am-2:30pm, Sa 10:30am-12:30pm.

Police: (☎ 68000). Superintendent's Office, at the corner of Bus Stand and B-M Rds.

Pharmacy: Gopal Medicines (☎ 68678). Bus Stand Rd., opposite Karnataka Bank. Open 9am-9:30pm.

Hospital: CSI Redfern Memorial Hospital (☎ 67653). Race Course Rd., 1 block north of the intersection with Church Rd.

Internet: Cyber Park, above Vaishnavi Lodging. Rs30 per hr.

Post Office: Bus Stand Rd. Open M-Sa 10am-6pm, Su 10am-1pm. **Postal Code:** 573201.

▌ ACCOMMODATIONS

Check-out is 24hr. everywhere. Rooms costing over Rs150 get taxed.

Sri Ganesha Lodge, Devaraj Market, Subhash Sq. Exit the bus stand by the alley next to Hotel Ashraya. Friendly and family-run. The doubles have good views of the market below. Hot water 6-9am. Singles Rs125-150; doubles Rs200-225. ❶

Vaishnavi Lodging (☎ 63885-9). Harsha Mahal Rd. Take a left out of the bus stand, a right onto Church Rd., and the first left. Clean sheets, fluffy pillows, phones, and big attached baths (squat, baby, squat). Hot water 6-9am. Singles Rs110; doubles Rs170. ❶

Abhiruchi Lodge (☎ 67852). B-M Rd. From the bus stand, walk 2 blocks south on Bus Stand Rd. and take a right after the police station. Clean rooms and bathrooms. Sit or squat; shower or bucket. Hot water 6-9am. Singles Rs90-149; doubles Rs149-230. ❶

Hotel Suvarna Regency (☎ 64006 or 66774). B-M Rd. From Bus Stand Rd., turn right after the police station and follow B-M Rd. to where it turns south. Phones, showers, and travel services. Singles Rs275; doubles Rs400-550. AmEx/MC/V. ❷

◖ FOOD

Suvarna Sagar, B-M Rd., attached to Hotel Survarna. Costly *thalis* (Rs25-55) and North Indian selections (Rs24-50). The *paneer* is so fresh it melts in your mouth. Ice cream (Rs9-35). 10% surcharge to sit in the A/C section. Open daily 7am-10:30pm. ❶

Hotel GRR, Bus Stand Rd., opposite the bus stand. Excellent "Andhra-style" banana-leaf *thalis* (Rs15). Open daily 11:30am-4:30pm and 7:30-11pm. ❶

Hotel Sanman, M-O Rd. From the bus stand, head south on Bus Stand Rd. and take the last road before B-M Rd. Steam-filled *puris* (Rs10 a set, plus *sabzi*) are piled mile-high. Open daily 6am-9:45pm. *Thalis* (Rs15) served 11:30am-4pm and 7-9:45pm. ❶

Golden Gate, behind Suvarna Sagar. This pricey lounge tries hard for those who can't handle another *"meals"* joint. Spaghetti "nepolitine" Rs60, *tandoori*/Mughlai Rs60-140, Chinese Rs35-80. Drinks Rs30-120. Open noon-3pm and 7-11pm. ❷

NEAR HASSAN: SRAVANABELAGOLA
ಶ್ರವಣಬೆಳಗೊಲ ☎08176

Sravanabelagola's 17m-high statue of the Jain saint Bahubali is said to be the world's tallest monolithic statue. The beatific smile that plays across the face of the naked holy man, also called Gomateshvara, overlooks the tiny town with serenity. The streets are clean and empty, the air is suffused with calm, and the touts are less aggressive than their postcard-pushing buddies in most temple towns. While the main attraction is, of course, the towering statue, Sravanabelagola is also the site of some important and even older *bastis* (temples).

📱🔢 TRANSPORTATION AND PRACTICAL INFORMATION. The **bus stand** is on **Bangalore (CR Patna) Rd.,** opposite the hilltop *basti*. **Buses** leave for: **Bangalore** (3hr., 4 per day 6:45am-3pm, Rs49); **Channayapatna** (15min., every 15min. 6am-9pm, Rs4); **Hassan** (45min.; 6:30 and 9am, 3pm; Rs16); **Mysore** (2½hr.; 6:15 and 7:30am, 2:15pm; Rs29). Make a right from the station onto Bangalore Rd.; your first right will be **Kalyani Rd.,** which fronts many shops and leads to **Temple Rd.** Bahubali and many of the *bastis* are on a hill to the right, with the ineffectual KSTDC **tourist office** at its base. (☎57254. Open M-Sa 10am-5:30pm.)

📷📖 ACCOMMODATIONS. Most visitors make Sravanabelagola a daytrip, but the town has plenty of places to stay, in part because of the Mahamastakabhisheka ceremony, which attracts thousands of Jain pilgrims here every 12 years. Visitors should respect the Jain prohibitions on meat and alcohol. The Jain **lodging houses** ❶, which must be reserved through the central **Accommodation Office** (☎57258), have quiet, clean doubles with attached baths (seat toilet) for Rs125. Turn left from the bus stand; they're on the left. Farther down the street, **Yatri Nivas** ❶, has bigger, slightly more luxurious rooms that can also be reserved through the Accommodations Office (Dorms Rs55; doubles Rs80-160; quads Rs260).

📷 SIGHTS. Built around 980 AD, the **Bahubali statue,** on top of Indragiri Hill, is a recent fixture in Sravanabelagola. Son of the first Jain *tirthankara* and a saint in his own right, Bahubali wears an enlightened smile and not much else. Vines creep up his legs, snakes coil around his feet, and anthills fester at his ankles, all symbolizing his detachment from the world of the senses. The 620 steps leading up to the statue require about 15-20min. of dedicated climbing. Wear a pair of thick socks if your soles are not ascetically hardened to the touch of burning granite. A group of old men can carry you up in a chair for Rs85. *(The temple housing the statue is open daily sunrise-sunset. Puja 8am. Visit in the morning to avoid the crowds and the heat.)*

Every 12 years the Jain mega-*mela* of **Mahamastakabhisheka** is held here. On the eve of the ceremony, scaffolding is erected behind the monument and 1008 pots of sacred colored water are placed in front of the statue. Priests and wealthy devotees chant mantras as they anoint Bahubali with water, milk, dates, bananas, curds, sugar, almonds, and gold and silver flowers. Thousands of pilgrims attend the ceremony in pin-drop silence. The next is scheduled for 2005. Tall, naked ascetics tend to get all the attention, and Bahubali is certainly no exception. However, the hills surrounding him have been a Jain pilgrimage site since before the statue was carved. The Jain *bastis* scattered throughout the town were built over several centuries. The Mauryan emperor Chandragupta came to Sravanabelagola in 300 BC, when he abdicated his throne to become an ascetic. His guru Bhadrabahu attained enlightenment here and passed away in a cave on Chandragiri Hill. Chandragupta faithfully spent days inside the cave worshiping the footprints of his deceased teacher until he, too, died of starvation. The site still attracts pilgrims who believe that viewing the prints can cure all illness.

HALEBID ಹಳೇಬೇದು   ☎ 08177

Halebid's current name means "Destroyed City," and visitors might find it difficult to imagine Halebid during its 12th and 13th century heyday, when it was Dwarasamudram, the capital of the magnificent Hoysala Empire. Today the village of 12,000 is home to more cows and goats than kings and sculptors. But with the Western Ghats in the distance, small children playing in the road, and cows grazing along the edges of sunflower fields, Halebid can indulge all romantic stereotypes of the India of yore—until the kids start nagging you for money.

▐ TRANSPORTATION. The **bus stand** is opposite the Hoysalesvara Temple. Buses go to: **Arsikere** (3hr., 10 per day 7am-5:30pm, Rs18); **Belur** (45min., every 30min. 7am-6:30pm, Rs6); **Hassan** (1hr., 15 per day 6:30am-7:30pm, Rs8). Private **maxicabs,** found in front of the temple, go to Hassan (Rs8.50) and Belur (Rs5.50).

▮▪ ORIENTATION AND PRACTICAL INFORMATION. The **Hoysalesvara Temple,** the largest star-shaped soapstone edifice in town, is hard to miss. An energetic, safari-suited employee at the **Tourist Help Desk** will supply you with information on every conceivable subject. (Open M-Sa 10am-5:30pm.) The **Jain Temples** and the Kedareshvara Temple are 500m down the road. The **Primary Health Center** (☎73022) is directly behind the bus stand; exit to the left and take an immediate left. The **police station** (☎73201) is just beyond, on the right. The **post office** is opposite the bus stand (Open M-Sa 8:30am-4:30pm). **Postal Code:** 573121.

▮▪ ACCOMMODATIONS AND FOOD. Halebid's **Hotel Mayura Shantala ❶,** run by the Department of Tourism, is the only lodging in town. The rooms have attached baths. (☎73224. Doubles Rs150-200.) The attached **restaurant ❶,** serves the standard menu. (Veg. dishes Rs20, non-veg. Rs40-120. Open daily 7am-11pm.) The bus stand also has a **restaurant ❶.** *Thalis are* Rs15 and *dosas* are Rs9. (Open 5:30am-8:30pm.)

◪ SIGHTS. The largest of the Hoysalan temples, **Hoysalesvara Temple** overlooks the vast Dwarasamudra Lake and is surrounded by immaculately tended gardens. Construction began in 1121, but before it was completed, the armies of the Delhi Sultanate sacked the temple and ravaged the town. By the time of India's Independence, only 14 of the 84 large statues remained, and only one of the "bracket figures" (the mini-statues for which the temple is famed) was left. Those that were not destroyed were stolen—British museums display quite a few of them. The temple is actually composed of two Shiva temples on a single, star-shaped platform. The larger of the two was commissioned by the Hoysala king Vishnuvardhana, and the smaller one by his senior wife, the famed dancer Shantaladevi. Like all Hoysalan temples, the deities face east toward the sunrise. Over 20,000 elaborate figures remain in and around the temple. The funny and well-informed ASI-sanctioned **guides** will point out the best and the brightest. *(Guides Rs60 for up to 5 people.)*

ONE FOR THE ROAD The backsides of Indian motor vehicles make for interesting recreational reading. Even the most fume-filled of city drives can be brightened by a simple game of "guess-the-rickshaw-driver's-religion-from-his-bumper-stickers." Similarly, road trips offer the treat of those humorously ominous warnings painted on the backs of lumbering Tatas and Ashok-Leylands. Some carry moving (in every sense) public service announcements, marked with inverted red triangles and one of the state-sponsored family-planning slogans, "small family happy family," or "we two, our two," which has morphed into, "we two, ours one." But by far the most pervasive genre of this lorry literature is the proper-horn-use statement: "Sound-horn," "No Horn!," and the ubiquitous and inane "Horn OK Please." This last phrase has its origins in the days when many Indian goods carriers had a centered, cyclops-like brake light. The "Horn Please" directed drivers to signal if they wished to pass the larger, slower vehicle. If the truck driver saw fit to allow such a maneuver, he would tap his brake, and the center light, labeled "OK," would flash. Eventually the one tail-light became two, but by then the order had stuck. "Horn OK Please" was fixed in the mind, and the tailgate, of Indian automotive consciousness.

Six levels of **frieze work** border the base of the temple. Images include elephants, lions, geese, horsemen, scrolls, and stories from the *Puranas* and the epics. More gory engravings of gods and goddesses line the upper exterior walls: Shiva killing an elephant demon by severing his trunk and then dancing on the its stomach in celebration; Vishnu peeling off the face of a demon as you might peel a banana; and Bhima tossing elephants over his shoulders like long-nosed grenades. Leave your shoes at the entrance. *(Open dawn-dusk. Free. Rs1 for shoe storage.)*

The **Archaeological Museum**, near the temple, houses deity statues from the town's temples and nearby ruins. *(Open Sa-Th 10am-5pm. Rs2.)* The 12th-century **Jain Bastis,** built by King Vishnuvardhevna before he converted to Hinduism, are styled much like the town's Hindu temples. The most prominent of these is the **Parswanathasamy Temple,** held up by 12 columns. Their design is meant to convey the serenity of meditation and worship. *(500m south of the bus stand: past temple #1, bear left. Open 10am-5pm. Puja 9am.)* The peaceful **Kedareshvara Temple,** a smaller cousin of the Hoysalesvara, is another 300m past sunflower fields.

BELUR ಬೇಲೂರು ☎ 08177

A little town on the banks of the Yagachi River, Belur was the capital of the Hoysalan Empire, until Halebid deprived it of this honor in the 12th century. There is little trace left of the fabled Velapuri, and only the Chennakeshava Temple, set apart from the town by its tall *gopuram*, reminds visitors of Belur's glorious past. But, Belur's 200-year jump on Halebid has endowed the former with a few things the latter can't claim: a handful of hotels and restaurants and a small-town hustle.

▐ **TRANSPORTATION.** Buses run to: **Arsikere** (1½hr., every 30-45min. 6am-7pm, Rs16); **Halebid** (45min., every 30-60min. 6am-9pm, Rs7); **Hassan** (1hr., every 30min. 6am-11pm, Rs13); **Mangalore** (5hr., 6:45 and 8:15am, Rs70); **Mysore** (4hr., every 30-60min. 7:30am-11pm, Rs42). **Auto-rickshaws** to the temple (Rs5), or a 10min. walk.

▐ ▐ **ORIENTATION AND PRACTICAL INFORMATION.** There are two roads in Belur. **Main Rd.** is roughly perpendicular to **Temple Rd.,** which runs from the **bus stand** to the Chennakeshava Temple. From the bus stand, turn right out of the exit opposite the platform onto Temple Rd. Services include the brand-new **Government Hospital** (☎ 22333), just past the **Tourist Office** (☎ 22209. Open M-Sa, 10:30am-5pm), inside the Mayura Velapuri Hotel Complex; the **police station** (☎22460), on Main Rd., opposite the bus stand; and the **post office,** farther down Main Rd. (turn left out of the main entrance of the bus stand building). **Postal Code:** 573115.

▐ ▐ ACCOMMODATIONS AND FOOD. Swagath Tourist Home ❶, a few minutes' walk down Temple Rd., is cheaper and cheerier than its neighbors. Owned by the family that runs the market below, the Swagath's rooms line up along a pink arcade. (☎22159. Check-out 24hr. Doubles Rs60.) **Vishnu Regency ❶,** a quick left off Temple Rd., sits at the opposite end of the spectrum. You could imagine yourself a Hoysala ruling from this new alabaster villa. (23011-3. Doubles Rs300.) **Vishnu Sagar ❶,** downstairs, serves "chillys" (Rs30), "minimeals" (Rs25-40) and Punjabi food. Nary a roach scuffles across the clean floor of the **Hotel Mayura Velapuri ❶,** the next priciest hotel in town. (☎22209. Singles Rs160; doubles Rs190.) Its **restaurant** dishes up *thalis* for Rs25. (Open daily 6am-10:30pm.)

◙ SIGHTS. Perhaps Vishnu's fearsome eagle-mount Garuda, who guards the famous **Chennakeshava Temple,** saved it from the brutal ransacking that Halebid suffered. Along with those at Somnathpur and Halebid, this temple is considered one of the best examples of Hoysalan architecture. The Hoysala king Vishnuvardhana commissioned the temple to commemorate his conversion from Jainism to Hinduism, and even though three generations of sculptors devoted their lives to its construction, the Chennakeshava Temple was never finished. Like the temples at Halebid and Somnathpur, Chennakeshava has a base covered with astoundingly detailed horizontal friezes. To bear the weight of the temple, 644 stone elephants, each one unique, stand at the bottom. Statues of Vishnu surround the exterior. The emblem of the Hoysala empire—its first emperor smiting a half-lion, half-tiger beast—also stands outside. When he was a boy, the emperor Sala and his guru were sitting under a tree when this ferocious animal appeared. Sala stared the beast down and went on to found the great Hoysalan Empire, which ruled over Karnataka and parts of Tamil Nadu from the 10th to 14th centuries.

The temple is renowned for the 42 mini-statues, or **bracket figures,** that line the interior ceilings and exterior walls. The detail of these sculptures is incredible. Voluptuous women with jingling bangles and head pendants are carved out of a single stone. One wears an expression of longing as she holds a letter to her faraway lover while a lusty monkey tugs at the edge of her sari. The famed **Thribhanghi Nritya,** a classical dancer, contorts her body in such a way that a drop of water from her right hand grazes the tip of her nose, then her left breast, and then hits the thumb of her left hand before it lands at the arch of her right foot.

Inside the temple is a platform once used by the *devadasis* (temple dancers), a waiting area for the audience, and several four-ton columns, which were so heavy that they had to be turned by elephants while sculptors detailed them. The **Narasimha Pillar** at the center of the temple contains miniature replicas of all of the temple's other carvings. One square is left empty, to indicate that, despite the efforts of the earthly artists, God can never be truly depicted. Two images of Vishnu sit inside the **sanctum**—a large, silver-plated image that pilgrims still pray to every day, and a smaller wooden sculpture used in temple processions. Carved on the wall in front of the image is a creature with a peacock's tail, a boar's body, a lion's feet, a crocodile's mouth, a monkey's eyes, an elephant's trunk, and a cow's ears. The animal possesses the best part of each of the animals, making it fit to guard Vishnu himself. (Non-Hindus may view the images. Puja 9am and 7pm.) The Vijayanagars constructed the temple's original **gopuram,** which was destroyed by fire and rebuilt. In the bottom right-hand corner, as you exit the temple, are erotic engravings. Leave your shoes outside. (Temple open daily 8am-8:30pm. Inner sanctum closed 1-3pm and 4:30-5:30pm. Free. Rs1 for shoe storage.)

MANGALORE ಮಂಗಳೂರು   ☎ 0824

An important trading port for centuries and a major shipbuilding center during the 1700s, Mangalore today retains much of its mercantile feel but little of its former glory. Mangalore's main claim to fame today comes from its position as India's biggest cashew and coffee processor and as a major *bidi*-production center. It's little wonder that Mangalore isn't exactly a tourist magnet. As a transport node between Goa and Kerala, though, Mangalore makes a decent stopover.

⌐ TRANSPORTATION

Flights: Bajpe Airport (info ☎ 142 or ☎ 752142), 22km from town, can be reached by local buses #47B and 47C or by taxi (Rs225). **Indian Airlines** (☎ 455259) is on Hat Hill. Head west from Lalbagh Circle, and take the 1st right (rickshaw Rs12 from KS Rao Rd.). Open daily 9am-1pm and 1:45-5pm. **Jet Airways,** KS Rao Rd. (☎ 441181). Open M-Sa 8:30am-5:30pm, Su 9am-2pm. To: **Bangalore** (1hr., 1-2 per day, US$70); **Chennai** (2hr.; Tu, Th, Sa; US$95); **Mumbai** (1hr., 4 per day, US$115).

Trains: Railway station (info ☎ 131), 500m south of the intersection of KS Rao and Lighthouse Rd. From Hampankatta, take the road going south between Maidan Rd. and Falnir Rd. Reservations open 24hr. To: **Calicut** (5hr., 5-6 per day 3:15am-8:10pm, Rs95); **Chennai** (18hr., 11:15am and 8:10pm, Rs250); **Ernakulam** (10hr., 3:15am and 4:30pm, Rs148); **Margao** (5hr., 7:10am, Rs154).

Buses: KSRTC Bus Stand, in Bijai, 3km from the center of town (Rs15 by auto-rickshaw from Hampankatta). Reservations open daily 7am-9:30pm. To: **Bangalore** (8hr., 14 per day 6am-11pm, Rs109-133); **Hassan** (4hr., every 30min., Rs65); **Mysore** (7hr., 15 per day 6am-11pm, Rs79-115); **Panjim** (10hr., 9:30pm, Rs122-168). **Private buses,** at the new bus stand near the intersection of Maidan and Maidan Cross Rd., run more frequently and are closer to the city center. Many companies have offices at the old bus stand, in the alley near the intersection of Lighthouse Hill and KS Rao Rd. **Ganesh Travels** (☎ 441277; open daily 5am-10:30pm), sends buses to: **Bangalore** (8hr., 9 per day, Rs165-180); **Cochin** (10hr., 8:10pm, Rs210); **Margao** (9hr., 9 and 9:30pm, Rs170); **Mumbai** (22hr., 7:30am-3pm, Rs350-400); **Mysore** (7hr., 10pm, Rs135); **Panjim** (9hr., 4 per day, Rs170); **Udipi** (1¼hr., frequent, Rs19). Other public buses go to: **Calicut** (10am); **Ernakulum** (10am); **Hubli** (5:30am and 4pm); **Hyderabad** (noon).

Local Transportation: Most **local buses** stop on Dr. UP Maliya Rd., near Town Hall. In general, buses are numbered in front or on the side, and many stands list the buses that stop there. **Auto-rickshaws** are the easiest way to get around.

✈ ❼ ORIENTATION AND PRACTICAL INFORMATION

Mangalore's mangled street plan can make navigation tricky. The monthly *Mangalore Today* (Rs10), available at newsstands, usually includes a map. **Hampankatta,** is the central, chaotic traffic circle from which six major thoroughfares radiate. Heading northeast and sharply uphill from Hampankatta is **Lighthouse Hill Rd.** Forking east off Lighthouse Hill Rd. is **Balmatta Rd.** Just west of Lighthouse Hill Rd., **KS Rao Rd.** heads due north and is cluttered with budget hotels and restaurants. To the southwest, **Maidan Cross Rd.** passes the **Town Hall** and heads to **Shetty Circle.** Branching west off Maidan Cross Rd. is **Maidan Rd.** Due east off Hampankatta is **Falnir Rd.,** and going southeast between Falnir and Maidan Cross, is the road leading 500m south to the **railway station.**

Tourist Office: Department of Tourism Information Office, Lighthouse Hill Rd. (☎ 442926). In Hotel Indraprastha. Open M-Sa 10:30am-1:30pm and 2:30-5:30pm.

Currency Exchange: Bank of India, KS Rao Rd. Exchanges cash and traveler's checks. Open M-F 10am-2pm, Sa 10am-noon. **Travel Wings,** Lighthouse Hill Rd. (☎ 440531), also exchanges money at good rates. Open M-Sa 9:30am-1:15pm and 2-5:30pm.

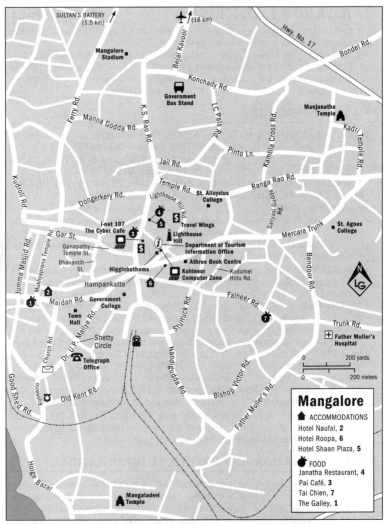

Mangalore

ACCOMMODATIONS
Hotel Naufal, **2**
Hotel Roopa, **6**
Hotel Shaan Plaza, **5**

FOOD
Janatha Restaurant, **4**
Pai Café, **3**
Tai Chien, **7**
The Galley, **1**

Police: (☎426426), by the central post office, just beyond Shetty Circle.

Pharmacy: Sharavu Medicals (☎442197). Just off KS Rao Rd. Open M-Sa 8:30am-10pm, Su 9am-9:30pm.

Hospital: City Hospital (☎217902). In Kadri, 3km from Hampankatta. **Father Muller's Hospital** (☎436301). In Kankanady (3km). Both are good and privately-run.

Internet: Check email to the beat of classic and techno rock at **I-net 107 The Cyber Cafe,** KS Rao Rd. (☎424639), in the Classique Arcade. 10 terminals. Rs40 per hr. Open daily 10:15am-11pm. **Kohinoor Computer Zone,** Lighthouse Hill Rd., close to Hotel Indraprastha. Rs50 per hr. Open M-Sa 8am-2am, Su 10am-2am.

Post Office: Dr. UP Mallya Rd. (☎423053). Southwest from Town Hall, past Shetty Circle. Open M-Sa 8:30am-6pm. **Postal Code:** 575001.

▲ ACCOMMODATIONS

Weary travelers need look no farther than KS Rao Rd., where the hotels are fairly cheap, clean, and pleasant. The places below have 24hr. check-out.

Hotel Naufal, Maidan Rd. (☎428085). Make a left out of the main exit of the bus station; it's two blocks down, on your right. The waterfront is a short walk away. Restaurant downstairs serves basic fare. Singles Rs125; doubles Rs175. ❶

Hotel Shaan Plaza, KS Rao Rd. (☎440312). Large, well-kept hotel with huge rooms and a fantastic restaurant below. Phones, seat toilets, and Star movies. Singles Rs290; doubles Rs395-430. ❷

Hotel Vasanth Mahal, KS Rao Rd. (☎441311). You'll get a cheap, big room at this sprawling hotel. Attached bath with seat toilets; some rooms have balconies. Singles Rs135; doubles Rs200. ❶

Hotel Roopa, Balmatta Rd., Hampankatta (☎421271). A good alternative to the cluster of hotels on KS Rao Rd. From the Hampankatta traffic circle, start up Lighthouse Hill Rd. and bear right at the fork. Singles Rs125; doubles Rs184-450. ❶

◖ FOOD

While in Mangalore, don't miss the town staple, **cashews,** available in countless grades and flavor permutations at dried fruit and nut shops everywhere.

▨ **Janatha Restaurant,** in the Hotel Shaan Plaza. This busy restaurant serves up marvelous North and South Indian dishes (Rs20-48) and ice cream treats (Rs8-28). Meals 11:30am-3pm and 7-10:45pm. Open daily 7am-10:30pm. ❶

Pai Cafe, in Hotel Navaratna on KS Rao Rd. An excellent veg. restaurant. Good *puri thalis* Rs20, South Indian breakfasts Rs8-14, Bengali sweets Rs7-15. Meals 7am-noon and 3-8pm. Open daily 6am-10pm. ❶

Tai Chien, in Hotel Moti Mahal, Fahir Rd. Just beyond Milagres Church. An impeccable spread of silverware, porcelain, linens, sauces, and pickles is only vaguely discernible in the dim light of Chinese lanterns, but the food is so good you won't need to see it. Szechuan pork ribs Rs75. Beer and liquor available. Open daily 7pm-midnight. ❶

The Galley, in Manjuran Hotel. Don your last clean t-shirt and head west from Shetty Circle to Mangalore's fanciest address. Pricey, but worth it for the white-glove treatment. Urdu love songs performed live Th-Su evenings. Mangalore fish curry (Rs100), frequent fixed-price specials (Rs150-200). Open daily 12:30-3pm and 7:30-11pm. ❷

◉ SIGHTS

LIGHTHOUSE HILL. The **Lighthouse** itself, orange racing stripe and all, is not worth the walk up the hill, but it is surrounded by lovely gardens with fine views of the city—a fair reward for a bit of sweat. Just beyond the lighthouse, off the road to the left, is the Jesuit **St. Aloysius College Chapel,** whose lovely painted ceilings date from 1899. *(Chapel open daily 8:30-10am, noon-2pm, and 3:30-6pm. English mass M-Sa 6:30 and 7am, Su 6:30 and 8am. Ceiling-oglers not welcome during Sa-Su services.)*

KADRI TEMPLE. Once a center for the Shiva and tantric Natha-Pantha cult, the temple is notable for its bronze figures, including a 10th-century seated Lokeshvara, considered among India's finest. A steep staircase, opposite the temple entrance, leads to several shrines and the **Shriyogishwar Math,** whose tantric sadhus are depicted contemplating Kala Bhairawa (a terrifying aspect of Shiva), Agni, and Durga. *(5km northeast of the city center, at the bottom of Kadri Hill. City buses #14 and 19; rickshaws Rs25 round-trip. Open daily 6am-1pm and 4-8pm.)*

SULTAN'S BATTERY. This fort on the headlands of the old port was constructed by Tipu Sultan. Besides the modest ruins of the tiny fortress, there's not much to see here but a peaceful river scene. *(5km northwest of the city center; take the #14, 16, or 16A bus or a rickshaw for about Rs.40.)*

HOSPET ಹೋಸಪೇಟ್   ☎08394

The Vijayanagar king Krishnadevaraya built Hospet between 1509 and 1520, and it became one of his favorite haunts. The last traces of the Vijayanagar Empire were long ago trampled into the dust, and Hospet today is typical of humdrum Karnataka, treading the line between heavy industrialization—blaring trucks transporting the products of a burgeoning steel industry—and village life—pigs, roosters, and dogs sifting through the streetside trash. Regular buses run from here to Hampi, where most of the remaining ruins are. Although food and lodging can also be found in Hampi, Hospet offers a modicum of luxury unavailable in Hampi.

◤ TRANSPORTATION

Trains: Hospet Junction Station (☎ 131). Near the bus stand, at the end of Station Rd. Reservation counter open daily 8am-8pm. To: **Bangalore** (11hr., 8:10pm, Rs88); **Gadag** for **Bijapur** (1½-2½hr., 3 per day 5:15-10:40am, Rs30); **Guntakal** for **Delhi** and **Mumbai** (1½hr., 3:25 and 8:10pm, Rs36).

Buses: Bus station (☎ 28802). Station Rd., opposite Hotel Vishwa. To: **Badami** (5hr., 1 and 4pm, Rs60); **Bangalore** (9hr., frequent, Rs107-139); **Bijapur** (5hr., 8 per day 5:30am-4pm, Rs72); **Hassan** (10hr., 7:30am, Rs90); **Hyderabad** (11hr., 6:45 and 9pm, Rs134); **Mangalore** (13hr., 7:30pm, Rs180); **Mysore** (8hr.; 6:30 and 9:30am, 5:30pm; Rs134). Deluxe **KSTDC** tourist buses to **Bangalore** (7½hr., 10pm, Rs160).

Local Transportation: Auto-rickshaws Rs60-80 to Hampi. **Cycle-rickshaws** (Rs10 to the railway station) are easily found. **Local buses** go to **Hampi** from platform 10 (30min., every 30min. 5:30am-7:30pm, Rs4). **Khizer Cycle Market,** at the circle where Station Rd. turns into the bazaar, rents **bikes** (Rs3 per hr.). Open daily 7:30am-8:30pm.

▓✳ 🛈 ORIENTATION AND PRACTICAL INFORMATION

Life in Hospet revolves around **Station Rd.** (occasionally called MG Rd.), which runs south from the **railway station,** passes the **bus station,** and grows increasingly congested as it turns into **Main Bazaar Rd.,** in Hospet's commercial area. Station Rd. bridges two canals in the process and encounters northeast-running **Hampi Rd.** and **Tungabhadra (TB) Dam Rd.,** which runs west and skirts the market area.

Tourist Office: Karnataka Dept. of Tourism and **KSTDC** share an office (☎ 28537) at the corner of College and Old Bus Stand Rd. From the bus station, turn left onto Station Rd.; take the 1st left onto College Rd. and then the 1st left onto Old Bus Stand Rd. **Tours** of Hampi and the Tungabhadra Dam (9:30am, return 5:30pm; Rs75.). Dept. of Tourism open M-Sa 10am-5:30pm. Closed 2nd Sa. KSTDC open daily 7:30am-10pm.

Currency Exchange: State Bank of India, Station Rd. (☎ 25478). A few steps north of Hotel Priyadarshini. Changes US$ and UK£ only. **Andhra Bank,** Station Rd. (☎ 24918). Just before the bazaar and above the cycle shop. Changes traveler's checks, US$, and UK£. Both open M-F 10:30am-2:30pm and 3-4pm.

Pharmacy: Several cluster around Hotel Priyadarshini.

Hospital: Medinowa (☎ 55789). 35/G-1 ISR Rd., a block west from the tourist office, is a new private hospital.

Internet: Zeal Internet, Station Rd., across from the bus stand. Rs25 per hr. Open daily 10am-10pm.

Post Office (☎28210). Station Rd., 400m south of the bus stand; take the left fork. Open M-Sa 8am-6pm. **Postal Code:** 583201.

ACCOMMODATIONS

■ **Malligi Tourist Home** (☎28101). 6/143 JN Rd., 250m south of the bus stand and east; turn left before the 2nd intersection. The luxury rooms are spectacular. Pool open Tu-Su 7am-7pm (Rs25 per hr. for non-deluxe room guests). Singles Rs140-200; doubles Rs140-250; deluxe Rs550-2250. AmEx/MC/V. ❶

■ **Hotel Vishwa** (☎27171). Station Rd., opposite the bus stand, set back from the street. The single rooms with squat toilets won't win prizes for their decor, but the double rooms have seat toilets and balconies. Singles Rs100; doubles Rs149. ❶

Hotel Karthik (☎08394 or 24938). Sardar Patel Rd. From the bus stand, turn left onto Station Rd.; take the first left onto College, then the next right. While clean, the rooms disappoint slightly after entering through the immaculate facade. Running hot water 5:30-11am and by request. Singles Rs100-300; doubles Rs225-500. ❶

Hotel Priyadarshini (☎28838). V/45 Station Rd., 500m south of the railway station. Spacious rooms with balconies and same-day laundry. Two good attached restaurants. Singles Rs140-205; doubles Rs195-250, with A/C Rs500-650. MC/V. ❶

Hotel Shalini (☎28910). Station Rd., 300m south of the railway station. This place may not be the cleanest, but with flowering trees and a pink facade, it makes up for it with character (and cheapness). Bring your own sheets. Singles Rs70; doubles Rs100. ❶

FOOD

■ **Waves Restaurant,** in Malligi. Maybe it's the mesmerizing reflections off the swimming pool, but you'll succumb to the staff's irresistible suggestions. Kashmiri *pulao* Rs50, chicken *tikka* Rs55, pancakes with honey Rs30. Open daily 6:30am-11:30pm. ❶

Manasa, in Hotel Priyadarshini. Fulfills your cravings for home with shepherd's pie (Rs80) and gazpacho (Rs25), but it also does Indian and Chinese (Rs25-60). Beer (Rs50-60), spirits (Rs17-60). Open daily noon-3pm and 7-11pm. ❶

Shanbhag Restaurant, Station Rd., next to the bus stand. Get a jump on a busy day with *idli* (Rs5), *masala dosas* (Rs10) or fruit *burfi* (Rs3). Open daily 6am-11pm. ❶

Naivedyam Restaurant, also in Hotel Priyadarshini. Dishes out huge, fresh portions. North and South Indian *thalis* Rs20, *Aloo* and *palak* (Rs18-24). Open daily 11am-3pm and 7-10:30pm (North Indian), 7am-10pm (tiffin). ❶

HAMPI ಹಂಪೆ ☎08394

It is said that gold once rained down on Hampi. The city was awash in rubies and diamonds, and wealth dripped from its rooftops, flowing into its gutters and filling its sacred tanks. The Vijayanagar king would regularly distribute his weight in precious metals to the area's needy. Five dynasties ruled from 1336, ensconcing themselves in temples, pavilions, aqueducts, and palaces, but riches eventually led to ruin. A confederacy of Muslim sultans from the north annihilated the empire in 1565 and soaked up Vijayanagar's wealth, leaving the thriving capital desolate.

After the Christmas raves in Goa, the crew packs up and heads to the Tungabhadra River and, much to the chagrin of the town's residents, drags along the acid parties. Hampi's season runs from October to March, peaking between December and February. More than a few expats have turned a week's stay into years, using the ruins for drug dens, or eloping with locals and settling down on the other side of the river to avoid the police. Isolated from urbanity, Hampi can be an alluring oasis for travelers seeking to slow down; some just decide never to leave.

📠 ⚡ TRANSPORTATION AND PRACTICAL INFORMATION

The road from **Hospet** skirts 13km of unexceptional scenery before reaching **Hampi Bazaar.** The bazaar is actually a clump of guest houses, restaurants, and bauble shops clustered around the **Virupaksha Temple** and its 53m *gopuram*. The ruins of Vijayanagar spread across 26 sq. km and are concentrated into three distinct groups. The **Virupaksha Temple,** ruins of the **Krishna Temple,** and many other shrines directly above the bazaar on Hemakuta Hill make up the **Sacred Center.** The **Royal Center** includes the **Palace Area** and the **Zenana Enclosure,** 3km southeast of Hampi, along the paved road to Kamalapuram. About 2km to the northeast of the bazaar lies the other major area of ruins, including the **Vittala Temple.**

> **⚠ WARNING.** Muggings and rapes have been reported recently in the area near Vittala Temple, on Matanga Hill, and along the foot path leading from Vittala Temple to the Royal Center (Zenana Enclosure). **Foreigners are asked to register with the police at Hampi** when they arrive in town.

Local Transportation: Buses to Hospet depart from the intersection of Hampi Bazaar and the road to **Hospet** (30min., every 30min. 6:15am-8:15pm, Rs4). **Auto-rickshaws** run between Hampi Bazaar and Kamalapuram (Rs5) and Hospet (Rs50). Prices double at night. Another way to get around is to rent a **bike** at Guru's Bicycle Shop, 25m behind the tourist office (Rs3-5 per hr., Rs25-30 per day). Open daily 6am-7pm.

Tourist Office: (☎41339), 100m toward the Virupaksha Temple from the bus stop. Detailed maps of the ruins. Approved guides (in-season Rs400-500; off-season Rs250-380). Open M-Sa 10am-5:30pm. Closed 2nd Sa of the month.

Currency Exchange: Canara Bank (☎41243). Exchanges only AmEx and Thomas Cook traveler's checks in US$, UK£, and FF. Open M-Tu, Th-F 11am-2pm, Sa 11am-12:30pm. In season, travel agencies exchange currency—try **Modi,** next to the tourist office.

Police: (☎41241). Inside the Virupaksha Temple, immediately to your right. Registering here when you get in town takes 2min. Open 24hr. There's also a branch in Kamalapuram (☎41240), 4km southeast of the bus stand.

Hospital: The nearest medical services are in Hospet.

Internet: Access in Hampi is none the quicker or cheaper for its ubiquity. Try **Net-Cafe** (☎41465), next to Shanthi Guest House. (Rs60 per hr.). Open 24hr. in season.

Post Office: (☎41242). Just outside the temple, beside the *gopuram.* Open M-Sa 9:30am-3:30pm. **Postal Code:** 583239.

🏠 ACCOMMODATIONS

To 15th-century traveler Domingo Paes, the Hampi Bazaar was "a broad and beautiful street, full of rows of fine houses and *mantapas*...[where] you will find all sorts of rubies, and diamonds, and emeralds, and pearls, and every other sort of thing there is on earth that you wish to buy." To this list, modern tourists have added pancakes, spaghetti, and hash—all of which are indulged to excess. Staying in the guest houses behind the temple, most of which are portions of homes, often requires a lack of concern for cleanliness, a fondness for squat toilets, and a tolerance for bugs, dogs, and frogs. The guest houses listed below (the best in town) are open all year; many others open only during the tourist season.

☒ **Shanthi Guest House** (☎41568). From the bus stand, walk toward the Virupaksha Temple, turn right, and go around the Sree Rama Lodge. Enclosed garden, cheerful exterior, and clean common baths make it a wellspring of tourist camaraderie. Singles Rs100; doubles Rs150. Mar.-Dec.: Rs50/70. ❶

🖾 **Gopi Guest House** (☎ 41695). Clean rooms have large windows, attached baths, and mosquito nets. Friendly proprietor ensures a pleasant atmosphere. Rooftop restaurant with good views. Singles Rs150; doubles Rs250. Off-season: Rs60/80. ❶

Laxmi Guest House (☎ 41287 or 41728). Behind the tourist office. The mattresses are thin, but the sheets are clean. Common baths. Bring your own padlock. Internet access. Doubles Rs100. Mar.-Nov.: Rs60. ❶

Vicky Guest House (☎ 41694), 200m behind the tourist office. Huge beds, fans, and attached baths. Rooms downstairs are super-modern for Hampi—a great bargain. Restaurant operates in-season. Doubles Rs125/250. Mar.-Nov.: Rs60/100. ❶

Sree Rama Tourist House (☎ 41219). The beds and rooms are decent. Attached bathrooms with squat toilets and showers. Check-out 24hr. Singles Rs100; doubles Rs120. ❶

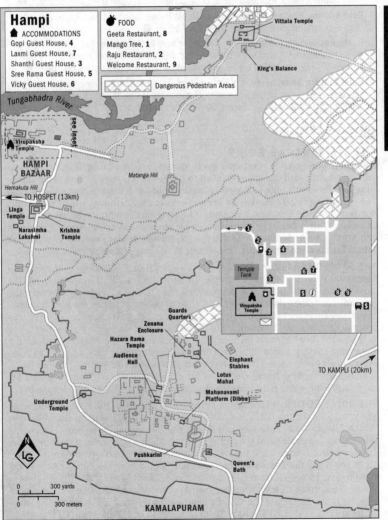

Hampi

🛏 ACCOMMODATIONS
Gopi Guest House, **4**
Laxmi Guest House, **7**
Shanthi Guest House, **3**
Sree Rama Guest House, **5**
Vicky Guest House, **6**

🍎 FOOD
Geeta Restaurant, **8**
Mango Tree, **1**
Raju Restaurant, **2**
Welcome Restaurant, **9**

Dangerous Pedestrian Areas

Vittala Temple

King's Balance

Tungabhadra River

see inset

Virupaksha Temple

HAMPI BAZAAR

Matanga Hill

Hemakuta Hill

TO HOSPET (13km)

Linga Temple

Narasimha Lakshmi

Krishna Temple

Temple Tank

Virupaksha Temple

Guards Quarters

Zenana Enclosure

Hazara Rama Temple

Audience Hall

Elephant Stables

Lotus Mahal

TO KAMPLI (20km)

Underground Temple

Mahanavami Platform (Dibba)

Pushkarini

Queen's Bath

N

0   300 yards
0   300 meters

KAMALAPURAM

KARNATAKA

🍴 FOOD

🍽 **Raju Rooftop Restaurant,** near Shanthi Guest House. Falafel *chappati* (Rs30) and tomato pasta (Rs25) combined with the spiked punch of a sangria (Rs30) capture the delightful oddity of Hampi's restaurant menus. Open daily 6am-10pm. ❶

🍽 **Mango Tree,** behind Virupaksha Temple. Follow the path around the temple past Shanthi Guest House. Set under a stand of mango trees, you can't get more sedate than this. Banana *parathas* Rs30, pancakes Rs20-25, *momos* Rs35-40, pasta Rs25. Great riverside view, but bring a flashlight if you plan on staying late. Open daily 7am-10pm. ❶

Welcome Restaurant, Hampi Bazaar. Popular for its pasta (Rs30-40) and falafel (Rs30). Rice pudding Rs20, espresso Rs35, or Caiparani Rs30. Open daily 7am-9:30pm. ❶

Gopi Rooftop Restaurant, above Gopi Guest House. Special *thalis* Rs35, *dal makhni* Rs30, coconut curry Rs30. Open daily 7am-10pm. ❶

Geeta Restaurant, Hampi Bazaar. Everything here is "Recommended in Lonely Planet." Nevertheless, the "cornflesh + banana milk" (Rs25) and the lunch and dinner options (Rs25-40) are a treat and are recommended by us, too. Open daily 6am-10pm. ❶

Hotel Mayura Bhuvaneswari, Kamalapuram. Take the road toward Kampli. The only enclosed restaurant in the whole area, it has *thalis* (Rs25-37) and veg. (Rs18-32) and chicken (Rs40-48) curries. Beer Rs55-60. Open daily 6:30am-10pm. ❶

🔭 SIGHTS

THE VIJAYANAGAR RUINS

Though it won't enable you to see every sacred cm of the 26 sq. km of ruins, you can squeeze most of the major sights into one foot-sore, back-aching, thigh-throbbing day. Renting a bike in Hospet, Kamalapuram, or Hampi Bazaar will help you see everything except the Vittala Temple area to the northeast, where the path is too rocky to ride. You can lock your bike and leave it with the tourist office or approach Vittala from the southeast, along the tour bus route. There have been reports of robbers lurking along this road. **Avoid walking along the river or behind the Vittala Temple alone.** The path to the temple from Hampi Bazaar is considered safer.

THE SACRED CENTER. At the west end of Hampi Bazaar is the imposing **Virupaksha Temple,** once the king's personal temple. To the rear is a small room where an upside-down image of the *gopuram* is projected onto the wall. Walk back toward the *gopuram* and take a right before exiting. Hike up the stony hill past the **Jain Temples** on your right. There are beautiful views of Hampi from the top. The road below eventually leads to Kamalapuram and the ruins of the Royal Center, but before you see these, you will pass the **Krishna Temple** on your right. Make a right on the dirt path to reach the **Narasimha Lakshmi statue.** When Muslim sultans sacked the city, they sliced open Narasimha's belly to see if the 7m-high monolith had eaten any gems, but they found nothing. Although the Narasimha is disfigured, he is one of Hampi's most striking figures. Beside the statue is the **Linga Temple,** containing the second-largest *linga* in India.

THE ROYAL CENTER. From the main road, continue on to the Royal Center until you see a sign for the Lotus Mahal. On your right will be the **Underground Temple,** which fills up with rainwater and fish during the monsoon season. Follow the signs to the Lotus Mahal at the end of the road. Make a left, walking away from the Hazara Rama Temple (see below), past the pink Archaeological Camp House. Here you'll see the **Zenana Enclosure,** a stone wall where the ladies of the court used to live, protected from male ogling. *(Open daily 8am-6pm. US$5.)* To the right is the pink stucco **Lotus Mahal,** a fine example of Indo-Saracenic architecture. Opposite the Lotus Mahal are the **Guard's Quarters.** To the east and through the stone walls are the 11 domed **Elephant Stables,** where 15,000 of the royal beasts, slept, rested, and ate a whole lot of elephant food back in the 15th century. Backtrack to the sign pointing to the Mahanavami Dibba and take that road south; on your right will be the **Hazara Rama Temple,** or the Temple of One Thousand Ramas. The enclosure walls are carved with scenes from the *Ramayana* on the inside and with a parade of horses, elephants, dancing girls, and soldiers on the outside. Two rare images of Vishnu incarnated as the Buddha are inside the sanctum.

Continue on the road and just as the path veers east (to your left), you will see a large platform that was once the **Audience Hall.** The **Mahanavami Platform,** also on your right, is crossed by ancient aqueducts and now-dry stone canals. This platform, where the gala Dussehra Festival was held, is one of the tallest and most ornate around. The throne inside is covered with gold and gems. South of the platform is the recently excavated **Pushkarini,** a deep, sacred water tank. On the left, just before the dirt road joins the main paved road to Kamalapuram, you will see the **Queen's Bath,** a giant stone enclosure surrounded by a moat. Inside is a huge pool where the queen used to kick back after a hard day. *(Open daily 8am-6pm. US$5.)*

Kamalapuram is another 600m down the road. There, you'll find an Archaeological Survey of India **museum,** containing all the usuals. *(Open Sa-Th 10am-5pm. Rs5.)*

VITTALA TEMPLE. Though Vittala seems small and unimpressive from the outside, the clutter of cold-drink dealers and tourist buses around the temple make it hard to miss. Construction of the temple, which was never finished or consecrated, was begun around 1513, and the work was halted when the city was destroyed in 1565. A competing bit of lore has it that Vittala, an incarnation of Vishnu, came to look at the temple, found it too grand for him, and hightailed it back to his humbler home in Maharashtra. Indeed, the carvings here are certainly the most ornate of any around the ruins. Each of the 56 musical pillars inside the temple sounds a different note when tapped, but the security guards glare sternly at tourists who try to play a tune. Just before the temple sits the fabled **King's Balance,** the arch from which the potentate's weight in gold, gems, grain, or—in leaner times—happy thoughts, would be measured and meted out to his subjects. *(US$10. From Kamalapuram, ride the paved road 5km north to the Vittala Temple, or backtrack to the Hampi Bazaar and walk 2km along the river to the temple. **It is unsafe to travel on the road from Kamapalpuram to Vittala Temple alone at night.**)*

▶ DAYTRIP FROM HAMPI: ANEGUNDI

The ancient cave temples at Anegundi are seldom visited by tourists. The Archaeological Survey of India isn't in charge here, and getting to the caves is an adventure in itself. Because there are no signs, it is best to solicit the assistance of a certified **guide** at Hampi's tourist office (see p. 302).

From the Vittala Temple, continue on the main paved road along the Tungabhadra River. Eventually the road deteriorates into a path leading to the river bank, where two boats shuttle people, bicycles, and (more perilously) motorcycles to and from Anegundi. Once you reach the other side, walk straight up a small slope and you'll see the village. A left turn at the first opportunity and then a left at the next fork will lead you past the Andhra Bank and under a small gate. After the gate, turn left onto the paved road that cuts through the rice paddies. A dirt path veers off to the left; take it and you'll be at the base of a rocky hill. Midway up the hill is the **Durga Temple,** supposedly the site where Rama killed the monkey king Vali. The temple is especially favored by soldiers who perform *puja* here to gain strength. A *bidi*-smoking *swami* offering *chai* and other treats will point you up the hill to the **Lakshmi Temple.** Here, Sita prayed for Rama's forgiveness after she had been banished, demonstrating her devotion to her husband as well as the purity of her mind, body, and soul. The nearby **Pampasarovara Pond** is believed to be the site where Parvati prayed for a husband—the reward was Shiva himself. A small 7th-century temple marks **Hanuman Hill,** the monkey-god's birthplace.

BADAMI ಬಾದಾಮಿ ☎ 08357

Badami, an unassuming little town in the middle of nowhere, was the capital of the mighty Chalukyan Empire from 543 to 757. The ancient cave temples carved into the imposing red-rock mountains surround an ancient Chalukyan tank. Badami is also the town closest to Pattadakal, 20km away, where Chalukyan kings were crowned, and Aihole, 44km away on the Malaprabha River, the first Chalukyan capital. Together, these three towns are a fascinating study, albeit an expensive one at US$20, in the development of Indian temple architecture.

▐◼ TRANSPORTATION

Buses run from Badami to: **Aihole** (2hr., 8 per day 7am-12:30pm, Rs10) via **Pattadakal; Bagalkot** (2hr., frequent 6am-10:15pm, Rs12); **Bangalore** (10hr., 8 per day 5am-8:30pm, Rs165); **Bijapur** (4hr., 12 per day 7am-6:45pm, Rs57); **Gadag** (2hr., 12 per day 5:30am-10:45pm, Rs25); **Pattadakal** (45min., 7 per day 8:35am-6:30pm, Rs6.50); **Solapur** (7hr., 6 per day 6am-8pm, Rs90) for train connections to **Mumbai.** There is **super-deluxe bus** service to **Bangalore** (9hr., 9:30pm, Rs193). Book through Hotel Mookambika Deluxe (☎ 20067). Private **maxicabs** are another way to reach Pattadakal (Rs5-8). **Trains** run north to **Bijapur** and **Solapur** for connections to Mumbai and south to **Gadag** for connections to Hospet and Bangalore.

◼ ▐ ORIENTATION AND PRACTICAL INFORMATION

Station Rd. is Badami's main road; from the **railway station** in the north, it runs 5km south to the **bus stand** and eventually to the routes to Pattadakal and Aihole. **College (Ramdurg) Rd.** runs west from Station Rd., south of the bus stand, and winds around to the KSTDC hotel and **Tourist Information Center** 1km later. (☎ 20414. Open M-Sa 10am-5:30pm; closed second Sa.) The private **hospital**, Karudagmath Nursing Home (☎ 20191), is north from the bus stand, along Station Rd., toward the railway station. Several **pharmacies** line Station Rd. between the bus stand and GPO. The **police station** (☎ 20133) is opposite the bus stand. The **GPO** (open M-Sa 7-11am and 2-5pm) is just south of the bus stand. **Postal Code:** 587201.

▐ ◖ ACCOMMODATIONS AND FOOD

Compared to Aihole and Pattadakal, Badami has plenty of places to stay; most are near the bus stand. **Hotel Mookambika Deluxe ❷**, is the cheeriest and cleanest in the area. Windows look out upon the Chalukyan hills. (☎ 20067. Singles Rs250-600; doubles Rs450-750.) The attached restaurant serves food made-to-order. Cheaper options include **Hotel Anand ❶**, opposite Hotel Mookambika (☎ 20074; singles Rs50-70; doubles Rs120-150), and the somewhat brighter **Hotel Satkar ❶**, across the street. (☎ 20417. Singles with bath Rs70-150; doubles Rs100-200.) For somewhat better quality, try **Hotel Mayura Chalukya ❶**, College Rd. Turn right from the bus stand, walk 500m, and turn right onto the first wide paved road; the hotel is 1km down on the right, next to the PWD Inspection Bungalow. The huge, relatively clean rooms look out on overgrown gardens. 24hr. hot water, and mosquito nets. Attached restaurant. (☎ 20046. Doubles Rs200.) For cheaper food, try the no-nonsense, no-chairs **Geeta Darshini ❶**, just south of the bus stand, where nothing on the menu (besides ice cream!) costs more than Rs7. (Open M-Sa 6:30am-9pm.) Next door, the **Hotel Parimal** serves cheap *dosas* and omelettes. (Open M-Sa 6:30am-9pm.)

◉ SIGHTS

SOUTH FORT TEMPLE COMPLEX. Carved out of the red sandstone cliff face and connected by steps are some of the most important cave temples in India. The first three temples are Hindu, though there has been both Jain and Buddhist influence.

Cave 1, the oldest, is dedicated to Shiva in his different guises. On the right front wall is an 18-armed dancing Shiva. There is a *linga* protected by granite cobras in the back of the cave. **Cave 2** is dedicated to Vishnu, as is **Cave 3,** the largest and best-sculpted of the group, dating from 578. The facade, pillars, and the steps leading to the foundation of Cave 3 are carved with figures of humans, gods, and dwarves. In one scene, Vishnu is depicted as Narayan, reclining on the serpent Sesa's lap at the dawn of creation. Though the caves were once painted, the only color that remains is on the ceiling of Cave 3. The path up to Cave 3 leads past a natural cave once used as a Buddhist temple; the Buddha image has since been defaced. **Cave 4,** probably the only cave here ever used as a Jain temple, overlooks the lake. The pillars appear to be held up by an assortment of creatures, including one that bears a startling resemblance to Yoda from *Star Wars*. *(From the bus stand, head right on Station Rd., past College Rd.; facing the Dr. Ambedkar statue, turn left and follow that road to the end. Temples open daily 7am-6:30pm US$5. Guides Rs250 for a 2-3hr. tour; Rs380 for a full day. Up to 4 people; French or Italian-speaking guides Rs150 extra.)*

OTHER TEMPLES. Across the lake from the caves are several other *mandirs*. The **Upper Shivalaya Temple** is one of the oldest of the group at Badami, and its carvings depict scenes from the life of Krishna. The most spectacular of the temples is the **Malegetti Shivalaya,** with its pillared hallway, flanked by both Shiva and Vishnu. The temple is on top of the hill and has spectacular views of the village and the fields below. In town, by the 6th-century **Agastyatirtha Tank,** is the **Jambulinga Temple,** built by the Vijayanagars in 699. The peaceful **Bhutanatha Temples** are on the opposite side of the tank. To reach the temples and the **Archaeological Museum,** go right from the bus stand and follow a sign. This will lead you on stone paths through a tiny neighborhood. You can also take the path from the South Fort cave temples along the tank; signs point the way. *(Museum open Sa-Th 10am-5pm. Rs2.)*

◪ DAYTRIPS FROM BADAMI

PATTADAKAL

Pattadakal makes a nice daytrip from Badami or Aihole. Buses (45 min., every 45min. 6am-7pm, Rs7) and private maxicabs (Rs5-8) make the trip to Badami. Buses also go to Aihole (1hr., 4 per day 10am-1pm, Rs6).

Pattadakal, between Badami and Aihole, was the Chalukyan capital during the 7th and 8th centuries. Its temples, the most stylistically advanced in the region, are clustered at the base of a pink sandstone hill. Pattadakal's only active temple, the **Virupaksha (Lokeshvara) Temple,** has a three-story spire with a stone Nandi sitting in front of it. Passages lead around the shrine past carvings depict episodes from the *Ramayana* (see p. 613) and *Mahabharata*, and scenes of Chalukyan martial triumphs. Other prominent temples in the compound include the **Mallikarjuna Temple,** the **Papanatha Temple,** and the **Jain Temple,** 1km south of the compound, which has an upper-story sanctuary guarded by a crocodile-carved gate. *(Temple compound open daily 6am-6pm. US$10. It's a World Heritage site. Guides Rs50.)*

AIHOLE ಐಹೊಳ

Buses run between Aihole and Badami (2hr., 5 per day 7:15am-4pm, Rs10-11), most via Pattadakal.

Aihole, 44km northeast of Badami on the banks of the Malaprabha River, is full of spectacular temples. The beautiful, half-finished temples here were once the playground of a civilization determined to build the greatest architecture around. Aihole's 100 temples combine elements of Dravidian and northern Nagar styles—there are *gopurams* of both kinds. The most impressive temple within the main compound is the **Durga Temple,** dedicated to Vishnu and named because it sits next to a *durga* (fort). The temple's Islamic-style windows are similar to those in Fatehpur Sikri and Ahmedabad,; the circular apse is evocative of Buddhist *chaitya* halls. *(Open daily 6am-6pm. US$5.)* The Jain **Meguti Temple** has a stone inscription that has been dated to AD 634, making it one of the oldest dated temples in India. Farther south in the main compound is the **Ladh Khan Temple,** named after a 19th-century Muslim who set up house in the sanctuary. This temple is believed to have been built between the late 6th and the early 8th centuries. The compound also has a less than inspiring **Archaeological Museum.** (Open Sa-Th 10am-5pm. Rs2.) Outside the compound and off the main road, but still within walking distance, is **Ravan Phadi,** a precursor to the more sophisticated cave temples of Badami.

The ⬛**KSTDC Tourist Home ❶**, (☎ (08851) 34541) is the only place for non-locals to lay their weary heads, but you're in luck. The manager is gracious, the food is cooked to order (*thalis* Rs20-25), and there are no postcard touts hanging around. Huge, clean rooms cost half of what they would in Badami. (Doubles Rs60-75.)

BIJAPUR
☎ 08352

Among its mausoleums, minarets, and museums, Bijapur has some of India's most remarkable Muslim architecture, most of which dates from the 15th to 17th centuries. Ruled from 1482 by the Adil Shahi kings, Bijapur was the capital of one of five splinter states that later reunited to sack Hampi. Unlike the Vijayanagar kings, who decorated Hampi with rubies and gold, the Adil Shahis preferred to construct more austere feats of architectural ingenuity. Today, only the Golgumbaz receives attention, but the city is peaceful and has other ruins worth visiting.

▌ TRANSPORTATION

Trains: The **railway station** serves **Gadag** (5hr., 5 per day 4:15am-6:25pm, Rs53) via **Badami** (3hr., Rs37) on slow meter-gauge lines for connections to **Bangalore** and **Solapur** (2½hr.; 3:30 and 9:45am, 4:35pm; Rs34).

Buses: The KSRTC **bus stand** is in the center of town, at the intersection of Bagalkot and Bus Stand Rd., just west of the citadel. Reservation counter open daily 7am-1:30pm and 2-8pm. To: **Aurangabad** (14hr., 6:30pm, Rs170); **Badami** (4hr.; 5:30 and 10am, 4:45pm; Rs43-47); **Bangalore** (12hr.; 9 per day mostly evening departures, Rs232); **Gadag** (5½hr.; 6:30 and 10am, 2:30pm; Rs80); **Hospet** (5hr., 5 per day 5:30am-9:30pm, Rs72); **Hyderabad** (11½hr., 5 per day 6am-9:30pm, Rs191); **Mumbai** (12hr., 4 per day 8am-9pm, Rs215) via **Pune; Mysore** (15hr., 5 and 6:15pm, Rs235); **Solapur** (3hr., every 30min., Rs40). **VRL Vijayanand Travels,** Padmashri Complex, Bagalkot Cross Rd. (☎35220), runs luxury buses. To: **Bangalore** (every 30min. 7-9:30pm, Rs220-240); **Mangalore** (4:30pm, Rs240); **Mumbai** (8 and 9pm, Rs260).

Local transportation: Bijapur's light traffic and simple layout make **biking** an ideal way to get around. Bicycles can be rented to the left of the bus stand, opposite Golgumbaz, and at Gandhi Chowk (Rs2 per hr.; all will ask for an outrageous deposit, up to Rs1500). Unmetered **auto-rickshaws** are readily available (Rs20-25 for a hop across town). Horse-drawn **tongas** are more scarce and more expensive. A local **bus** (Rs2) runs along Station Rd. from the train station to the western walls on the other side of town.

✈ ⓘ ORIENTATION AND PRACTICAL INFORMATION

The Adil Shahis built 10km of massive fortified walls around their capital, but modern Bijapur is fairly compact and easily navigated. **Station Rd.** runs the length of the town, connecting the railway station and the **Golgumbaz** mausoleum, along the eastern ramparts, to the **Ibrahim Rauza**, 6km away, beyond the western wall. **Jama Masjid Rd.** runs parallel to and south of Station Rd. The **citadel**, between Station Rd. and Jama Masjid Rd., once served as the royal enclave of the sultans. Here Jama Masjid Rd. connects to **Bagalkot Rd.,** which leads 500m farther west to the bus stand. From the bus stand, roads run north to **Gandhi Chowk,** the market center, and the GPO, which rest at opposite ends of **MG Rd.**

Tourist Office: KSTDC, Station Rd. (☎50359). Behind the KSTDC Mayura Adil Shahi Annex. Open M-Sa 10am-5:30pm; closed 2nd Sa.

Currency Exchange: Girikand Tours and Travels, 1st fl., Nishant Plaza, Ram Mandir Rd. (☎35510). Opposite the Union Bank of India. Changes 32 currencies and traveler's checks for a Rs25 fee.

Police: Gandhi Chowk Police Station (☎50033). On MG Rd, opposite Shastri Market.

Pharmacy: Pharmacies are all along Station Rd. Most close by 9pm.

Hospital: City Hospital, Hospital Rd. (☎50709). Beyond Atke Gate, 2km west of town.

Internet: Cyber Park (☎20273). Opposite the GPO on MG Rd. It's in a cloth shop, but the connection is reasonably fast. Rs40 per hr. Open daily 9:30am-11pm.

Post Office: GPO, MG Rd. (☎50224). Fifty meters west of the citadel. Open M-Sa 8am-6pm. **Postal Code**: 586101.

⌂🍴 ACCOMMODATIONS AND FOOD

Most hotels are along Station Rd. between the Golgumbaz and Gandhi Chowk. Standards tend toward the shabby side; insist on seeing rooms before booking. Dining options are not much better. Unless otherwise noted, hotels have 24hr. check-out. **Hotel Sagar Deluxe ❶**, Barakaman Rd. Near the Shivaji statue at the intersection of Station, MG, and Bus Stand Rds. Soft pillows and a central location make this the best option in town. (☎59234. Singles Rs125-200; doubles Rs150-250.) **Hotel Blue Diamond ❶**, Bus Stand Rd. (☎52941). Behind Bharat Petroleum, near Laxmi Talkies Rd. New budget alternative with small rooms and minimal amenities, but very clean. Singles Rs60-150; doubles Rs150-200. **Hotel Samrat ❶**, Station Rd. Halfway between the Golgumbaz and the stadium. Huge attached baths with squat toilets and showers. (☎51620. Singles Rs150; doubles Rs250.) The **restaurant** is popular with local families. Eat *thalis* (Rs17-40) or one of 12 kinds of *dosas* (Rs6-15) under a strange painting of Ganesh. Most dishes Rs20-45. **Hotel Madhuvan,** Station Rd. (☎55571). Down a side street 150m east of Hotel Samrat; look for the signs. The rooms are exorbitantly priced, but the **restaurant ❶**, is the best in town. The wide-ranging veg. menu includes all the standards. *Thalis* Rs20-50, north Indian and Chinese dishes Rs25-45. Open daily 8am-11pm. *Thalis* 11am-4pm. **Navar's Bar & Restaurant ❶**, Barakaman Rd. The real attraction is the atmosphere—curtained booths surround a fountain and other French Quarter fixtures. Truly bizarre. Veg. (Rs18-25) and non-veg. (Rs28-60) dishes. Open daily 10am-11pm.

👁 SIGHTS

Robust souls with resilient soles see all the sights on foot in one strenuous day; everyone else rents bicycles.

GOLGUMBAZ. As you approach it from Station Rd., the mausoleum is an awesome sight. Towering over the city's eastern fortifications, the cubic structure is reinforced by four octagonal minarets and crowned by an enormous dome, 38m across, supposed to be the second largest in the world—after St. Peter's in the Vatican. Built in 1659, the hall contains the gravestones of Mohammed Adil' Shah, several of his family members, and his favorite court dancer and mistress, Rambha. Seven stories above the hall, at the base of the dome, is the famous Whispering Gallery, where sounds are said to echo over ten times. Predictably, many visitors love to test this aspect of the acoustics; when the clapping gets to you, step outside for some stunning views of Bijapur and the Deccan plains. Also on the grounds is an **Archaeological Museum**—one of the country's finest—featuring Jain *tirthankaras*, ancient stone inscriptions, 17th-century copies of the Qur'an, and Chinese porcelain collected by the Adil Shahis. (*Open daily 6am-6pm. US$5. Video cameras Rs25; bike parking Rs1. Museum open Sa-Th 10am-5pm. Rs2.*)

KARNATAKA

IBRAHIM RAUZA. Built by Ibrahim Adil Shah II, this graceful mausoleum is the last resting place of the sultan himself, his queen, Taj Sultana, his mother, and three of his children. On the other side of a small reservoir and fountains, an equally elegant mosque lends balance to the walled compound. Together, the two structures compose one of the most graceful, least well-preserved examples of Islamic architecture in India. The walls are covered with fine stone latticework made up of elaborate inscriptions from the Qur'an. *(1km beyond the western walls, 500m south of Station Rd. Open daily 6am-6pm. US$5.)*

JAMA MASJID. One of the finest mosques in India, the Jama Masjid was built by Ali Adil Shah I to commemorate his victory over the Vijayanagars in 1565. The cavernous prayer hall is etched and painted with more than 2000 rectangular matrices for individual prayer mats. The Mughal emperor Aurangzeb added these, apparently to atone for hauling away the velvet carpet and other valuables that originally covered the hall. *(Directly opposite the Golgumbaz, Shanmukharudh Mahadwar Rd. leads under a large arch 500m to Jama Masjid Rd. Turn right (west) toward the town center, the Jama Masjid is another 500m down on the left.)*

OTHER SIGHTS. Another 500m west on Jama Masjid Rd., the ornate **Mithari Mahal** serves as a gateway to a small mosque. Today it is not much more than a beautiful facade. **Asar Mahal** can be reached by taking the wide dirt road opposite the Mithari Mahal to the end and turning left. Dating from 1646, it served as a Hall of Justice and later housed hairs from the Prophet's beard. The **citadel** is just to the west. Most of the buildings have collapsed, but the ruins of **Gagan Mahal** and **Sat Manzil,** the sultan's durbar hall and pleasure quarters respectively, still stand. Opposite the citadel, on the other side of the Shivaji statue, is the **Barakaman.** This set of arches, begun by Mohammed Adil Shah, is one story of a tower designed to match Golgumbaz in height. Along the western walls 1½km west of the citadel is a gigantic cannon, aptly named **Malik-I-Maidan,** or "Lord of the Plains." The cannon was cast around 1550. It took ten elephants, 400 oxen, and hundreds of men to haul it up to its emplacement on top of the ramparts. Visible just behind Malik-I-Maidan to the northeast, **Upli Burji** features more cannons and views of the city and plains.

GOKARNA ಗೋಕರ್ಣ ☎ 08386

Gokarna could be your typical South Indian village. The streets are filled with vendors selling kitchenware, bangles, and bright skirts (not a mirrored halter top in sight), and a Shiva temple draws pilgrims and worshipers to one of the holiest spots in India. But Gokarna has exceptional beaches. Hippies searching for that Indian coastal paradise will find what they are looking for; a string of unspoiled beaches lines the coast south of town, and—if there is no party going on—the isolated coves define tranquility. A few hipsters snooze in hammocks while *chai* shops provide them with caffeinated sustenance. Gokarna's independent town life is blissfully far removed from the tourist resort atmosphere in Goa and Kerala.

▐◼ TRANSPORTATION

From Gokarna station, 10km out of town, **trains** run north to **Goa** (2hr., 7:25am and 10:40pm, Rs30) and south to **Mangalore** (4hr., 2am, Rs46). For other train destinations take a bus to **Kumta** (see below). **Buses** from Gokarna run to: **Bangalore** (12hr., 7:30pm, Rs185); **Hospet** (12hr., 7am, Rs107); **Hubli** (3hr., 7am and 2:45pm, Rs57); **Kumta** (1hr., every 30-60min. 6am-5:15pm, Rs11); **Margao** (4hr., 8:15am, Rs50); **Mysore** (13hr., 6:45am); **Panjim** (4hr., 8:15am, Rs60) via **Hampi** (10hr., 7am and 2:45pm, Rs100). Many **buses** pass through Kumta. To: **Bangalore** (5 per day 6:45am-8:45pm); **Hyderabad** (7:30am, 8:15am, 9:45pm); **Mangalore** (every hr. around the clock); **Mumbai** (11am and 2:30pm); **Panjim** (4 per day 9am-1:30am); **Pune** (4pm). If you're heading to Gokarna from Palolem, take the local bus to Canacona to catch the **Goa-Gokarna express,** which leaves **Margao** at 1pm and hits Canacona at 2:10pm (4hr., Rs47). In Gokarna, **Vaibhav Nivas** (see below) can help book train and private bus tickets. **Minibuses** shuttle backpackers from the train station to town (Rs25). Local buses depart from in front of the bus station parking lot and head to the railway crossing, 1km from the station (15min.).

🔧 ℹ ORIENTATION AND PRACTICAL INFORMATION

Gokarna's **Main St.** runs north-south in front of the **bus station** parking lot. Main St. heads north to the post office, and, after narrowing a bit, goes south to the giant temple bathing tank. **Car St.** begins at Main St. and heads west to the **Mahabaleshwara Temple** and the **town beach.** Another road runs parallel to Main St. to the west of the bus station; it also intersects Car St. A foot path beside the temple at the bathing tank leads to Gokarna's **beaches: Kudle, Om, Half-Moon,** and **Paradise.**

It's best to **change money** before arriving, but **Om Lodging Bar,** on the road west of the bus station, has tolerable rates. (Open daily 9am-noon and 5:30-11pm.) The **police station** (☎ 56133) is up a hill on a road heading east off Main St., south of the bus station. **Hegde Medical Stores,** along the north-south stretch of Main St., can fulfill your pharmaceutical needs. (☎ 56394. Open daily 8:30am-2pm and 4-9:30pm.) Gokarna has gotten wired; the **Shivaram Internet Centre,** just south of the bus station on Main St., is just one of a bevy of online joints in town (Open daily 8am-11pm, Rs60 per hr.). The main **post office** is a 5min. walk north from the bus station along Main St.; bear right at the fork. (Open M-Sa 9am-5pm.) **Postal code:** 581326.

🏠 🍴 ACCOMMODATIONS AND FOOD

Although there are several places to stay in town, most people prefer to flop down in huts on the beach. In town, the friendly **Vaibhav Nivas ❶,** has some small but clean rooms. It's just east off the north-south Main St., north of the bus station; take a left out of the front of the bus station, and you'll see signs. (☎ 56714. Singles Rs50; doubles Rs100-125. Off-season: Rs30-40/75-100.) More snazzy lodging is available at the **Hotel Gokarna International ❶,** north of the bus station, along Main St. Immaculate rooms have balconies and hot water; for a few extra rupees you can even have a bathtub and a TV. (☎ 56622. Check-out 4pm. Singles Rs150; doubles Rs200-250.) If you are staying for a while, it makes sense to settle down in a **beach hut,** though you may want to check out how many people are on the beach before committing to a deserted strip of sand. Accommodations on Kudle Beach run the gamut—an unmarked **chai shop ❶,** just north of the German Bakery has huts in a lovely garden (Rs60). On Om Beach, people string up hammocks (Rs150 along Main St. in Gokarna) or rent thatched huts (Rs35) from a row of identical *chai* huts; Om Beach is by far the hippest address. The **Sea Shore Chai Shop ❶,** on Paradise Beach has huts from Rs25. Bring a floor mat—you'll be sleeping on a sand or clay floor. Vaibhav Nivas will store your luggage if you don't want to haul it to the beach.

On all the beaches, **chai huts ❶,** turn out snacks (Rs10-25) and the usual range of *thalis* (Rs30), eggs, and sandwiches, all often overpriced. In town, **Vaibhav Nivas ❶,** cooks nice breakfasts (Rs8-30) and snacks. (Open 8am-9:30pm.) The **Downtown Bar and Restaurant ❶,** in the Hotel Gokarna International, serves up a superior *thali* (Rs22), various curries and *tandoori* specialties (Rs35-65), and cheap beer (Rs45), but service is very slow. (Open 9am-4pm and 7pm-1am.)

👁 🏖 SIGHTS AND BEACHES

Gokarna is packed with temples. The main east-west road, Car St., leads to the **Mahabeleshwara Temple,** which houses a venerated Shiva *linga.* Two massive chariots sit outside, waiting to be dragged through Gokarna's streets for *shivaratri,*

Shiva's birthday. Foreigners are not allowed inside, but they can wander to the massive bathing **tank** and watch the washing. To get to the bathing tank, keep going south down Main St., past Car St.

The road to the temple continues straight to the **town beach,** which isn't really anything to put your flippers on and do a dance about, though it is pretty. From here you can catch a **boat taxi** to Om Beach, which is the fastest and most painless way to get there. You can also hike to the beaches—the first beach worth stripping down to your skivvies for is **Kudle Beach,** to the south. From the bathing tank, take the cowpath beside the tankside temple; it quickly climbs uphill to a rocky, barren landscape and follows a string of telephone poles before heading to the sand. When the road forks, bear right and cut left through a *chai* shop to the beach. From the wide Kudle beach, it's another 20-min. walk to the more picturesque **Om Beach,** made up of two narrow, semi-circular beaches lined with trees and *chai* shops. You can also take a **boat taxi** or **rickshaw** (Rs200) to Om; a paved road connects it to Kudle. Behind the last *chai* shop, a narrow path leads up along the ridge of the black cliffs to **Half-Moon Beach** (20min.), where there is a restaurant and not much else. If you are scared of heights, you might want to turn back at this point, but a 15-min. rocky scramble brings you to **Paradise Beach.** The views along the paths are stunning, and long strips of white beach stretch as far as the eye can see.

As the authorities toughen up and the package tourists arrive in Goa, the party scene is migrating south to Gokarna. Keep your ears open; most take place on Om Beach, and in true party fashion, the international, stoned hippie set grooves to pounding techno and trance all the live-long night while *chai* vendors serve up overpriced tea, coffee, and bottled water. If there is no party, nightlife is restricted to guitar strumming and controlled-substance smoking around bonfires.

JOG FALLS

Jog Falls are the highest waterfalls in India; the Sharavathi River falls in four separate cascades known as the Rani, Raja, Roarer, and Rocket, the tallest of which plummets 253m. The Sharavthi Dam limits the amount of water that can be released, but to please daytrippers, more water is let through on the weekends. The falls are most dramatic after the rainy season. Pleasant (if indistinct) trails twist throughout the area. The comfortable government-run **Hotel Mayura ❶,** is one of several places to stay in Jog Falls. (☎08186 44732. Doubles Rs300.)

From Gokarna, take a bus to **Kumta** (1hr., every 30-60min. 6am-6:15pm, Rs11), where buses go onward to **Jog Falls** (4hr., Rs31). Connections can also be made through the town of **Honavar** or **Talguppa** (4hr., 7 and 10:45am, Rs32). A direct bus runs from **Udipi** to **Jog Falls** (5hr., 2pm, Rs52).

UDIPI
☎ 08252

Those with an interest in Krishna temples might consider passing through small but busy Udipi, whose claim to fame is the revered Sri Krishna Temple. The temple itself isn't particularly stunning, but if you make a stopover here, the giant chariots and the constant hubbub on Car St.—drumming, chanting, and general carrying-on—might provide entertainment.

TRANSPORTATION

There are three **bus stands** in Udipi. To the northeast end of KM Marg is the local bus stand; to the southeast, behind the State Bank of India, a bus stand sends vehicles to Jog Falls. Most private and public buses go from the central bus stand at the northern end of KM Marg. **Government buses** run to: **Gokarna** (4hr., 2:45pm, Rs60); **Mangalore** (1hr., 5 per day, Rs20); **Mysore** (8hr., 7 per day, Rs130-188). **Private** companies send buses to these destinations and others. Bus companies and travel agencies cluster between the three bus stands. The **train station** is due east of the town center. If you are a glutton for pain, head east from the north end of KM Marg and hike 30min.; a sign on your right points the way to the station, 1km south of the main road. Local buses run to the junction (Rs3). Incoming trains are met by buses (Rs3) and taxis (Rs75), who will compete for the pleasure of driving you into town. **Trains** head from the station to: **Gokarna** (2hr., 8:30pm, 2nd class Rs32); **Mangalore** (1½hr., 3:30am, Rs47); **Margao** (4hr., 4 per day 6:20am-12:14am, Rs128).

ORIENTATION AND PRACTICAL INFORMATION

Udipi is slightly inland, just east of NH 17. The city's main road, **KM Marg** (occasionally called Church St.), runs south from the three bus stands. From the main stand, the second left at the Hotel Triveni will put you on **Kanakadas Rd.,** which leads west to the temple complex. The **Sri Krishna Mutt Enquiry counter,** just inside the temple complex, is run by an enthusiastic staff willing to provide info about the temple and Udipi. On Kanakadas Rd., the **Canara Bank** changes cash and traveler's checks. (Open Su-F 9:30am-12:30pm and 1:30-2:30pm, Sa 9:30-11:30am.) A **police outpost** is by the temple on Car St. On KM Marg, south of Kanakadas Rd., **Medical Emporium** has the cure for what ails you. (☎20401. Open daily 8:30am-9:30pm.) Check **email** at **Cyberdhama,** behind the Alankar Theater, on KM Marg, south of Kanakadas Rd. (☎73969. Open M-Sa 9:30am-2pm and 4-9pm, Su 10am-4:30pm. Rs40 per hr.) The head **post office** is on Kanakadas Rd., east of KM Marg. (Open 10am-1pm and 3:30-5pm.) **Postal code:** 576101.

ACCOMMODATIONS AND FOOD

Udipi's accommodations cater to business travelers, so you get a lot of bang for your buck. **Hotel Vyavahar Lodge ❶,** on Kanakadas Rd., right by the temple, is a great value, offering large rooms with bath and almost-hot water. A resident astrologer on the second floor specializes in advice on foreign travel. (☎2256. Check-out 24hr. Singles Rs85; doubles Rs150.) **Kalpana Residency ❶,** is a bit more swank; take KM Marg to its southern end and bear left. (☎20440. Check-out 24hr. Singles Rs90-140; doubles Rs195.) You'll be hard-pressed to find a banana pancake in Udipi—revel in authenticity and do a lot of pointing at unfamiliar entrees. **Sudheshna ❶,** in the Hotel Swadesh Heritage, on MV Rd., just south of Kanakadas Rd., cooks up mean veggie delights. (Veg. dishes Rs18-30; rice dishes Rs15-35. Open daily 7am-10:30pm; snacks only 3-7pm.) Right by the temple and all the action on Car St., **Davarika** makes ice cream drinks and South Indian snacks. (Open daily 9:30am-10pm.)

SIGHTS

Celebrating Krishna's incarnation as a little kid, Rama Krishna, the **Sri Krishna Temple** attracts hordes of worshippers, garland sellers, and trinket vendors to its sizable spread. There's always lots of chanting and milling about, and twice-daily temple visitors share a free meal by the thousands. *(Follow the stream of visitors down Kanakadas Rd. to reach the temple grounds.)* If you end up staying in Udipi, head to **Malpe,** which has a fairly clean beach and a thriving fishing industry that provides Karnataka with most of its seafood. **Buses** leave the Udipi local bus stand frequently for **Malpe** (15min., Rs4). From Malpe, you can take a boat to the picturesque **St. Mary's Island.** This uninhabited island is reputed to be where Vasco da Gama landed before hitting Calicut. **Anushka,** at the southern end of the beach in Malpe, sends **boats** to the island but waits until 30 people arrive before setting sail; if you show up on the weekend, you won't have to wait as long for a full boat. *(☎22844. 30min. Rs30. No service during monsoon season.)*

KERALA കേരളം

The locals call it "God's own country," and there is no denying that Kerala is a pretty spectacular part of the world. Lined with palm trees and golden beaches, the state's famous backwaters are quite stunning. Forty lazy rivers run through canals and rice paddies from the Western Ghats down to the sea, channeling their way through tiny fishing villages and islands of palm groves. Beautiful beaches have made the state second only to Goa as a coconut-oil haven for sun-worshippers and beach bums from around the world. Renowned for its unique *kathakali* dance and its age-old ayurvedic medicine, as well as for its beautiful scenery, Kerala deserves to be even more popular with tourists than it already is.

Legend tells that when Parashoram, an incarnation of Vishnu, threw his axe into the sea at Gokarna, the oceans retreated to reveal the land that is now Kerala. The foreign presence here is older than anywhere else in India. As early as the 3rd century BC, travelers from China and the Middle East had set up trade routes with Kerala, and people came here from around the ancient world in search of spices, ivory, and sandalwood. Jews fleeing Roman persecution in Palestine landed here 2000 years ago, and many believe that St. Thomas the Apostle was the first to bring the Christian gospel to Kerala, less than 20 years after the death of Jesus. Arabs dominated the spice trade for centuries, spreading Islam throughout the region, until the Portuguese landed at Calicut in 1498 and gun-boated their way to exclusive trading rights. Rivalry between the port cities of Cochin and Calicut weakened both, and Dutch and British forces ejected the Portuguese from their forts early in the 17th century. Kerala became a part of the British Raj during the 18th century.

HIGHLIGHTS OF KERALA

Through the tourist melee that has overtaken the town, **Kovalam** (p. 320) remains a haven for beach-seekers and offers all the luxuries of Indian resort-style life—boogie boarding, massage, boat cruises, and *kathakali* performances.

No troubled waters here, **backwater cruises** out of Alleppey (p. 327) run through green canals, past ancient temples and churches, through tranquil villages, and will certainly ease your mind.

The influence of foreign immigrants from St. Thomas the Apostle to Portuguese sailors has blessed **Cochin** (p. 332) with a mixture of architectural styles, spices, religions, and traditions that are to sure to fascinate any traveler.

After Independence, the princely states of Cochin and Travancore were combined to form the state of Kerala, and in 1956 Kerala's boundaries were redrawn along linguistic (Malayalam) lines to include Malabar. A year later, Kerala became the first state in the world to elect a communist government. The state's leftist tradition has brought many advantages to its citizens: reforms have given Kerala the most equitable land distribution in India, and Kerala's literacy rate—around 90%—is the highest in the country. Vestiges of ancient matrilineal, polyandrous systems, such as those still practiced by the Nayar people, have given women a somewhat higher status in Kerala than elsewhere in India, and the UN has commended the state for its exemplary women's rights record. The relative prosperity of Kerala makes it a pleasure to travel in—so crack open a coconut, grab a straw, and enjoy.

Kerala's biggest festival is Onam, held in September to celebrate the harvest, when carnivals, elephant processions, and dance performances take place all over the state. Kerala is renowned for its elephant pageants; the most famous is the Trichur Pooram in May. The Nehru Trophy Boat Race is the most popular of the many backwater boat races, and is held on the second Saturday in August.

TRIVANDRUM (THIRUVANATHAPURAM)
തിരുവനന്തപുരം ☎ 0471

While most foreign tourists consider it nothing more than a stop-off on the way to the balmy beaches of Kovalam and the backwaters of Alleppey, Kerala's state capital is worth a closer look. Speckled with parks, palaces, monuments, and museums, it is a good place to gain some insight into Kerala's culture. By the time it became the capital of Kerala in 1956, Trivandrum had already been the capital of Travancore for two centuries. It retains its trademark red-tiled, pagoda-roofed houses, winding streets, tiny cafes, and beautiful gardens. The city's Malayalam name refers to Anantha, the serpent that holds the reclining Lord Vishnu (Lord Padmanabha) in the Shree Padmanabha Swami Temple. A welcome break from beach-hopping, Trivandrum is a good place to begin or end any South Indian trip.

█ TRANSPORTATION

Flights: Trivandrum's **International airport** (☎501537 or 501542) is 6km outside town. Buses for the airport leave from the city bus station **ian Airlines**, Museum Rd. (☎531 8288). 1 block west from the intersection with MG Rd. Open M-Sa 10am-1pm and 1:35-5:35pm. **Jet Airways**, Ashkay Towers (☎321018). Sasthamamgalam Junction, about 1½km east of the museum compound along Museum Rd. Open M-Sa 9am-5:30pm, Su 9am-3pm. To: **Bangalore** (5hr.; 1:50pm; US$170); **Chennai** (1hr.; 2 per day; US$105); **Delhi** (5½hr.; 2 per day; US$360); **Mumbai** (2hr.; 3-4 per day; US$195). Also international flights to **Male** in the Maldives (1hr.; Tu-Th and Sa-Su 12:15pm; US$75) and **Colombo,** Sri Lanka (2hr.; M-Sa; Rs2560). Up-to-date schedules of trains and planes are published every Tuesday in *The Hindu.*

Trains: The **railway station,** Station Rd., a few min. east of MG Rd. Reservations open M-Sa 8am-8pm, Su 8am-2pm. Fares listed for sleeper class. To: **Alleppey** (3½hr.; 3-8 per day 9:30am-4:20am; Rs43); **Bangalore** (20hr.; 1-2 per day 9:20am-3pm; Rs245); **Chennai** (20hr.; 4-5 per day 8:40am-4:20pm; Rs260); **Cochin** (5hr.; 3-5 per day 8:40am-9:30pm; Rs90); **Kanyakumari** (2hr.; 2-3 per day 2:45pm-1:30am; Rs84); **Kollam** (1½hr.; several per day 5am-9:40pm; Rs26); **Madurai** (8hr.; 4:30am and 8:40pm; Rs80); **Mangalore** (6hr.; 5-7 per day 6am-8:30pm; Rs205); **Mumbai** (46hr.; 3-5 per day 3am-10:30pm; Rs397); **Varkala** (1hr.; several per day 5am-9:45pm; Rs21).

Buses: The **long-distance KSRTC Bus Station** is on Station Rd. (☎323886), opposite the railway station. To: **Alleppey** (4hr.; every 30min.; Rs57-70); **Cochin** (5½hr.; every 30min.; Rs100); **Kanyakumari** (2½hr.; 8 per day; Rs30); **Kollam** (2hr.; every 30min.; Rs35); **Thekkady** for Periyar (8hr.; 4, 6, 8:45am; Rs95); **Varkala** (2hr.; 10 per day 7:45am-9:30pm; Rs20). The **Tamil Nadu Transport Office** (☎327756), at the far east end of the KSRTC bus station, runs buses to cities in Tamil Nadu. Open daily 10am-6pm. To: **Chennai** (17hr.; 9 per day 11:30am-8pm; Rs237-260); **Madurai** (7hr.; 13 per day 10:30am-10:30pm; Rs102); **Pondicherry** (16hr.; 4pm; Rs204). The **local bus stand,** MG Rd., is a few min. south of the train tracks at East Fort. Buses to **Kovalam** (25min.; every 20min. 5:50am-8:30pm; Rs5.50) depart from the bus stand on Overbridge Rd., 100m south of the local stand.

Local Transportation: Auto-rickshaws should use meters; base Rs6. Rs100 to Kovalam.

█ ORIENTATION AND PRACTICAL INFORMATION

The streets tangle over 74 sq. km of coastal hills, but navigation is easy if you stick to the few main roads. The north-south **MG Rd.** dumps all its traffic onto **Museum Rd.,** at the north end of town. To the south, MG Rd. cruises downhill to a hectic intersection with the city's other main drag, **(Central) Station Rd.** One hundred meters east on Station Rd. from MG Rd., **Manjalikulam Rd.** leads north to the budget hotel district. Farther down Station Rd., the **KSRTC Long-distance Bus Station** is on the left, opposite the **railway station.** MG Rd. becomes **Overbridge Rd.** when it heads south over the railway tracks to the **East Fort** area. A great white gate marks the entrance to **Shree Padmanabha Swamy Temple,** opposite the **local bus stand.** Behind the stand, **Chalai Bazaar Rd.** leads east through the bazaar.

TOURIST, FINANCIAL, AND LOCAL SERVICES

Tourist Office: Tourist Facilitation Centre, Museum Rd. (☎321132). In the Directorate of Tourism, opposite the museum compound. Ask for the useful *Kerala Companion* and the list of festivals. Open daily 10am-5pm. Smaller branches at the **KSRTC Bus Stand**

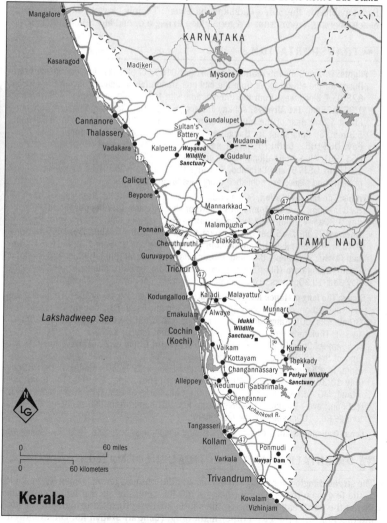

Kerala

(☎327224) and the **train station** (☎334470) also have maps. Both open M-Sa 10am-5pm. **KTDC Reception Centre,** Station Rd. (☎330031). In front of Chaitram Hotel, next to the bus stand. Promotes KTDC tours. Open M-Sa 6:30am-9:30pm.

Immigration Office: Foreigners Registration Office, Residency Rd. (☎321399). In the Office of the Commissioner of Police. Extensions for student and entry visas "with proper documents." The process should take 2 weeks, but "urgent" applications might be processed in 7 days. Open M-Sa 10:15am-1:15pm and 2-5:15pm. Closed 2nd Sa.

Currency Exchange: Central Bank of India (☎330359). In the Chaitram Hotel lobby. Exchanges foreign currency and traveler's checks. Open M-F 10am-2pm, Sa 10am-noon. **Canara Bank,** MG Rd. (☎331536), at Spencer Junction just north of the Secretariat, gives cash advances on Visa and exchanges cash and traveler's checks. Open M-F 10am-2pm and 2:30-3:30pm, Sa 10am-noon.

Market: Chalai Bazaar Rd., which intersects MG Rd. at the local bus station. The smaller and more sedate **Connemara Market** is north of Spencer Junction on MG Rd.

EMERGENCY AND COMMUNICATIONS

Police: Thampanoor Police Station, Station Rd. (☎326543). Near the KSRTC bus station, before Aristo Junction. Outpost inside the museum compound (☎315096).

Pharmacy: Darsana Medicals (☎331398). On Station Rd., just west of Manjalikalam Rd. Open daily 8am-9:30pm.

Hospital: Sree Uthradon Thirunal Hospital (☎446220). In Pattom, north of the city center (Rs25 rickshaw from Station Rd.). Considered the best private hospital here.

Internet: Orbit Cybercafe, Vasantham Chambers, SS Coil Rd., just north of Station Rd. A/C and fast. Rs60 per hr. Open daily 9:30am-10pm. **Starnet Communications,** Old Sreekanteswaram Rd. (☎464550), south of Ayurveda College Junction, is also good. Rs60 per hr. Open M-Sa 9am-9pm.

Post Office: GPO, MG Rd., south of the Secretariat. Open M-Sa 8am-8pm, Su 10am-4pm. **Postal Code:** 695001.

▟ ACCOMMODATIONS

Manjalikulam Rd. is the real budget hotel district, though MG and Station Rd. also have plenty of large hotels.

Pravin Tourist Home, Manjalikulam Rd. (☎330443). A 3min. walk north from Central Station Rd. Spacious rooms with big windows and attached bathrooms (seat and squat toilets). TV in the lobby. Check-out 24hr. Singles Rs110; doubles Rs195. ❶

Hotel Highland, Manjalikulam Rd. (☎333200 or 333421). Near Central Station Rd., on the left. Large, posh, and popular hotel has big airy rooms with TV. Seat toilets. Check-out 24hr. Singles Rs292-670; doubles Rs344-820. ❸

Hotel Regency (☎330377). Follow Manjalikulam Rd. to the first cross-street, then turn right. Big, clean rooms with TV. Several restaurants (including one on the roof). Currency exchange. Check-out 24hr. Singles Rs300-600; doubles Rs475-700. MC/V. ❸

YWCA (☎477308). 4th fl., Indian Overseas Bank Building, opposite the Secretariat. Lovely, clean rooms with attached baths. No unmarried couples allowed. Singles Rs155; doubles Rs205-355. ❶

Hotel Safari, MG Rd. (☎477202). A few min. north of Central Station Rd. Standard accommodations plus TVs. Restaurant has city views. Lone women might want to steer clear of the hotel bar. Singles Rs185-500; doubles Rs198-550. ❷

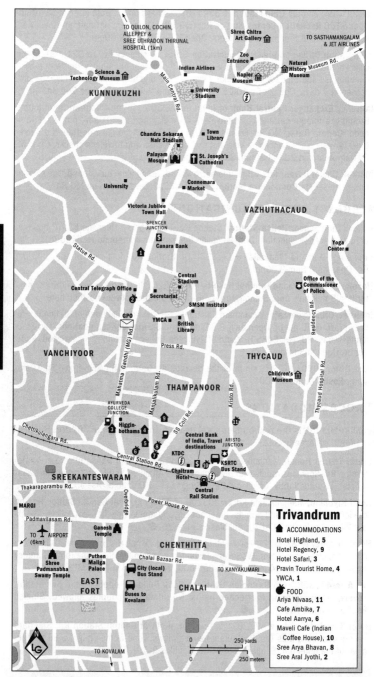

TO QUILON, COCHIN, ALLEPPEY & SREE UTHRADON THIRUNAL HOSPITAL (1km)

TO SASTHAMANGALAM & JET AIRLINES

Shree Chitra Art Gallery

Zoo Entrance

Natural History Museum Rd.

Indian Airlines

Science & Technology Museum

Napier Museum

Natural History Museum

KUNNUKUZHI

Main Central Rd.

University Stadium

Chandra Sekaran Nair Stadium

Town Library

Palayam Mosque

St. Joseph's Cathedral

University

Connemara Market

VAZHUTHACAUD

Victoria Jubilee Town Hall

SPENCER JUNCTION

Yoga Center

Statue Rd.

Canara Bank

Central Telegraph Office

Central Stadium

Office of the Commissioner of Police

Secretariat

SMSM Institute

Residency Rd.

GPO

YMCA

British Library

VANCHIYOOR

Mahatma Gandhi (MG) Rd.

Press Rd.

THYCAUD

THAMPANOOR

Manjalikulam Rd.

Aristo Rd.

Children's Museum

Thycaud Hospital Rd.

AYURVEDA COLLEGE JUNCTION

Chettukulangara Rd.

Higginbothams

SS Coil Rd.

Central Bank of India, Travel destinations

ARISTO JUNCTION

KTDC

Central Station Rd.

KSRTC Bus Stand

Chaltram Hotel

SREEKANTESWARAM

Central Rail Station

Thakaraparambu Rd.

MARGI

Padmavilasam Rd.

Power House Rd.

Overbridge

TO AIRPORT (6km)

Ganesh Temple

CHENTHITTA

Shree Padmanabha Swamy Temple

Puthen Maliga Palace

Chalai Bazaar Rd.

City (local) Bus Stand

TO KANYAKUMARI

EAST FORT

Buses to Kovalam

CHALAI

TO KOVALAM

0   250 yards
0   250 meters

Trivandrum

🏠 ACCOMMODATIONS
Hotel Highland, **5**
Hotel Regency, **9**
Hotel Safari, **3**
Pravin Tourist Home, **4**
YWCA, **1**

🍴 FOOD
Ariya Nivaas, **11**
Cafe Ambika, **7**
Hotel Aarrya, **6**
Maveli Cafe (Indian Coffee House), **10**
Sree Arya Bhavan, **8**
Sree Aral Jyothi, **2**

FOOD

It's difficult to find authentic Keralan food in Trivandrum, as most South Indian restaurants dish out a more Tamil-influenced menu. But at least it's authentic Indian—more so than banana pancakes and spaghetti.

Sree Aral Jyothi, MG Rd., opposite the Secretariat. Crowded restaurant serves authentic Keralan "raw rice meals" (Rs19) and *masala dosas* (Rs12.50). Windowless A/C space in the back, or heart-of-town street views in front. Open daily 6:30am-10pm. Meals served 11am-3pm and 7-10pm. ●

Sree Arya Bhavan, on the corner of SS Coil and Station Rd., 100m west of Hotel Chaitram. This hole-in-the-wall serves terrific North Indian veg. food. Often crowded and sometimes slow. Excellent menu changes daily. Open daily 8:30am-3pm and 7-11pm.

Hotel Aarrya, Central Station Rd., between Manjalikulam and the intersection with MG Rd. Simple but smashing South Indian meals. Good *masala dosas* (Rs12) and Keralan meals (Rs19). Open daily 6am-10pm. ●

Cafe Ambika, MG Rd., where Manjalikulam and SS Coil meet. Turns out good veg. and non-veg. meals at unbeatable prices (Rs12, *paratha* Rs2). Open daily 5:30am-1am. ●

Maveli Cafe (Indian Coffee House), facing the KSRTC long-distance bus station; it's the red, spiraling building on the left. The coolest structure in Trivandrum, it must be seen to be believed. Standard *dosas* (Rs8) and coffee. Open daily 7:30am-10pm. ●

Ariya Nivaas, around the corner from the station, toward Aristo Junction. Popular up-market veg. restaurant caters to middle-class families. Fancy *thali* served on a banana leaf (Rs45 in the A/C upstairs). Open daily 7am-10pm. ●

SIGHTS

MUSEUM COMPOUND. A big red gate marks the entrance to the lovely, 20-hectare public gardens, with its two museums, two galleries, a zoo, and crowds of moon-eyed couples. The **Natural History Museum** features dioramas of natural history, a model of a traditional upper-class house in Travancore, dolls dressed in traditional styles from all over India, and a life-sized, ivory model of a human skeleton made for Marthandavarma Maharaja in 1853. To the left as you come out of the Natural History Museum is the **K.C.S. Paniker Gallery,** which features paintings by the 20th-century Indian artist. Better maintained is the **Shree Chitra Art Gallery,** across the grounds, decked with Western-style portraits by the famed Raja Ravi Varma (1848-1906), Tibetan *thankas,* Japanese, Chinese, and Balinese paintings, 400-year-old Rajasthani miniatures, and modern Indian works.

In the center of the grounds is the **Napier Museum,** which looks suspiciously like a Walt Disney spin-off—florid gables and red, black, and pink bricks and tiles decorate the outside, while the inside is striped in yellow, pink, red, and turquoise. In fact, the building is an Indo-Saracenic experiment by Robert Fellowes Chisholm, who attempted to combine traditional Keralan and colonial architectural styles. The museum, along with the mandatory *kathakali* figures, includes Southeast Asian and Balinese art. Some choice pieces of kitsch on display, including an engraved plate to mark Kuwait Airlines' inaugural flight to Trivandrum, were gifts from foreign rulers to First Ministers of Kerala. *(Museum Rd. From Station Rd., follow MG Rd. north until it comes to a dead end, then go right (east). The complex will be on your left (2.5km total). Galleries open Tu and Th-Su 10am-4:45pm, W 1-4:45pm. Rs5 for all four museums. Purchase tickets at the Natural History Museum 10am-4pm.)*

The compound also contains a **zoo.** Though the animals probably live better than fellow-sufferers elsewhere in India, many are kept in frighteningly small cages. It might be worth a visit, however, for the impressive roost of wild fruit bats. *(Open Tu-Su 9am-5:15pm. Rs5. Camera fee Rs10, video Rs500. Tickets sold until 5pm.)*

PUTHEN MALIGA PALACE (KUTHIRAMALIKA OR HORSE PALACE). Every inch of this palace of Prince Swati Tirunal, also a famed musician and court composer, is exquisitely decorated. Its beautiful wooden carvings took four years to complete, after which the surly Swati Tirunal occupied the palace for just one year before he left in a huff. The Puthen Maliga Palace or "Horse Palace," named for the 122 horse sculptures beneath its eaves, provides some fascinating insight into how the other half once lived. The palace also functions as a museum, featuring life-size *kathakali* figures in full regalia, paintings of the rajas and ranis of Travancore, weapons, and thrones in ivory and Bohemian crystal. *(Open Tu-Su 8:30am-12:30pm and 3-5:30pm. Rs20. Camera fee Rs15. Photography prohibited inside. Official museum guides are required to accompany you.)*

SHREE PADMANABHA SWAMY TEMPLE. Marked by a large white gate, the Shree Padmanabha Swamy Temple features a 6m-high statue of a reclining Vishnu. The whole of the god's body is made visible by the opening of three doors—one at the head, one at the midsection, and one at the feet. The *gopuram* was built in 1566, but the structure was not completed until 1733. The temple itself is open only to Hindus, but non-Hindus can climb the steps and peek in at some of the less sacred images. The lane leading up to the temple, through a thicket of handicraft sellers, houses a large green **tank** used by bathing pilgrims.F

🔘 FESTIVALS

The Attukal Bhagavathy Temple, 2km south of East Fort, holds the **Festival of Attukal Pongala** in late February or early March, corresponding to the day of the Makom star. Tens of thousands of women converge on Trivandrum during this time, each one setting up a miniature kitchen on the streets in the center of town. The women offer *pongala*, a sweet rice porridge, considered the goddess's favorite food, which they cook in earthenware pots over sanctified fires from the temple. Men are not permitted in the vicinity of the temple during the festival. Trivandrum's center is closed to traffic and takes on an uncharacteristically peaceful air as the smoke from thousands of cooling fires drifts up into the heavens. The **Swati Music Festival** (late Jan.-early Feb.) presents evenings of classical music on the lawn of the Puthen Maliga Palace. The annual **Nishagandhi Dance Festival,** with outdoor classical performances, takes place during the last week of February. Contact the Tourist Facilitation Centre for a complete festival schedule.

🎭 DANCE AND THEATER

MARGI (☎478806), a school at West Fort, occasionally performs **kathakali dance drama** and **kutiyattum theater** (Keralan martial arts) in the evenings. Follow MG Rd. south over the train tracks, turn right at the corner temple, and walk 10min. into West Fort. When the street comes to a final "T," turn right. MARGI is behind Fort High School on your left—look for the big banyan tree. The sign on the door is in Malayalam, but the image of a dancer gives it away. Performances are not regularly scheduled and often take place in local temples; call for details. Trivandrum has 18 **movie theaters.** Sree Kumar and Sree Visakh (☎321222), both near the Chaitram Hotel), and New Theatre (☎323244; walk east on Central Station Rd., turn left in front of the railway station) screen English-language films.

KOVALAM കോവളം ☎0471

The pounding of hammers and the pouring of concrete have forever altered the calm landscape of Kovalam's black sands and turquoise waters. Since the arrival of the first sun-seekers back in the 1930s, Kovalam has become Kerala's most touristed beach resort and one of the most popular in India. The busy beachfront has been consumed by hotels, swallowed up by persistent touts, and spat out again by thieves dressed up as tailors and handicraft sellers. Enjoy the carnivalesque atmosphere created just for you. Beyond the tourist enclave, fishing boats still ply the bays, and life continues as it always has, amid thatched huts and rice paddies.

▐▀ TRANSPORTATION

Buses: The **bus stand**, at the top of the path from the north end of Eve's Beach, has no ticket office, but the Tourist Facilitation Centre (see below) can give bus schedules. To: **Cochin** (5½hr.; 7, 10:30, 11am; Rs82) via **Kollam** (2hr.; Rs41) and **Alleppey** (4hr.; Rs62.50); **Kanyakumari** (2½hr.; 5 per day 9:25am-6pm; Rs32) via **Nagercoil** (1½hr.; Rs25); **Trivandrum** (20min.; frequent 5am-9:30pm; Rs5.50-7.50).

Local Transportation: Rickshaws and **taxis** hover at the bottom of Lighthouse Rd., the bus stand, and Kovalam Junction. A rickshaw to Trivandrum should cost less than Rs100, one to the airport Rs150-200.

▟▐ ORIENTATION AND PRACTICAL INFORMATION

Kovalam Beach is made up of three coves divided by rocky promontories. A lighthouse marks the southernmost **Lighthouse Beach.** From here, **Lighthouse Rd.**, crawling with seafood restaurants, leads down to the water and the budget hotels favored by foreign tourists. **Eve's Beach** is north of a rocky promontory. The headland is home to the **Kovalam Ashok Beach Resort,** north of which is **Samudra Beach.** A road leads up from Eve's Beach past several travel offices, handicraft shops, and tailors to the **bus stand** at the entrance to the Ashok Beach Resort. From there, the road that leads southeast goes first to **Kovalam Junction,** 2km away, where a left turn at the fork brings you to the **post office,** and 14km later to Trivandrum. Between Lighthouse Rd. and the road to the bus stand, paths twist through the palm trees, connecting the beach to some of the quieter restaurants and hotels. The power shuts down at 8pm or 8:30pm every night for 30min. Some hotels have back-up generators, but don't count on it.

Tourist Office: Tourist Facilitation Centre (☎ 480085). Near the bus stand toward Ashok Beach Resort. Arranges tickets for the backwater cruises (see p. 323). Keeps current copies of international newspapers. Open in season daily 10am-5pm.

Budget Travel: Western Travels (☎ 481307), next to the bus stand. Organizes **sightseeing tours** in season. Currency exchange and cash advances on credit cards. Taxis for hire. Open daily 6:30am-12:30am. Off season: 7am-9pm. AmEx/MC/V.

Currency Exchange: Several shops on the beach exchange currency. The reception desk at **Wilson's Tourist Home,** behind Hotel Neelakanta, offers bank rates. Open M-Sa 9am-5pm. The **Central Bank of India** has a small branch in the Kovalam Hotel shopping complex. Open M-F 10:30am-1:30pm, Sa 10:30am-noon.

Police: (☎ 480255). Left off the road to Kovalam Junction, 10min. from the bus station on the left. In season, the **Tourist Aid Post** is on the beach. Open daily 9am-7pm.

Hospital: Upasana Hospital (☎ 480632). A right off the road to Kovalam Junction, 10min. on foot from the bus stand. **Pharmacy** open M-Sa 9:30am-1pm and 4:30-8:30pm, Su 9:30am-1pm. In an emergency, you can call Dr. Chandrasenan (☎457357) or Dr. Will (☎480270 or 480277).

Internet: There are lots of places; almost all charge Rs120 per hr. and are relatively small but fast. **Alpha Internet Services** (☎ 481926), right on Lighthouse Beach, close to the southern end, has two terminals. Rs120 per hr. Open daily 8am-9:30pm.

Post Office: Branch next to Tourist Facilitation Center. Open M-Sa 9am-3pm. The **main office** can be reached by taking a left at Kovalam Junction. Open M-Sa 9am-1pm and 1:30-5pm. **Postal Code:** 695527.

KERALA

ACCOMMODATIONS

Prices peak in December and January. Off season and during the monsoon, bargain hard—don't let persistent touts determine where you will stay. In general, the quality of rooms is high; most places don't have a separate price for singles—at best, expect to pay 25% less. All the places listed below are on Lighthouse Beach and come with attached bathrooms and (usually) hot water.

Green Valley Cottages (☎480636). From the beach, walk straight past Hotel Neptune and follow signs back to the paddies. Forsaking the beachfront has its advantages—lower prices and dreamy views of the paddies, for instance. Each immaculate room has a private balcony and chairs to loll around in. Doubles Rs450. Off season: Rs200. The same friendly folks run **Silent Valley Inn** (☎487928) right behind. Gorgeous rooms, with balconies from which you can see the sea. Doubles Rs500. Off season: Rs250. ❷

Sandy Beach Resort (☎480012; sandybeach@vsnl.com). Opposite Hotel Neptune, about 75m in from the beach. Sparkling and spacious rooms with balconies around a courtyard. Singles Rs250; doubles Rs500-600. Off season: Rs150/250. ❷

Wilson's Tourist Home (☎480051). From the beach, turn inland at the Palm Beach Restaurant and take your first right, close to Hotel Neelakanta. Rooms with massive beds and balcony. Friendly female staff is a draw for women traveling alone. Doubles Rs350-900. Off season: Rs200-600. V. ❷

Hotel Suriya (☎481012). From the beach, turn inland between the Coconut Grove Restaurant and the Coral Reef Cafe, near the Hotel Jeevan House. A little back from the beach, but the price is right, rooms are clean and spacious, and the staff is pleasant. Doubles Rs300. Off season: Rs150. ❷

Hotel Neptune (☎480222). About halfway down the beach; follow signs a little inland. Your average (clean) rooms, around a pretty greenery-filled courtyard. Singles Rs375-1100; doubles Rs450-1100. Off season: singles Rs200-600; doubles Rs250-750. ❸

Hotel Jeevan House (☎480662). On the sand midway down the cove, next to the Coral Reef Cafe. Pleasant, airy rooms with balconies, though you'll have to pay for a sea view. Doubles Rs300-1200. Off season: Rs150-1000. ❸

FOOD

Restaurants stretch in an almost uninterrupted sweep all the way along the beaches. What little Indian food there is has been de-spiced to appease Western palates. Alcohol is served at many beachfront establishments (beer Rs70).

Red Star Restaurant. This is the best place in Kovalam to get a feel for the old days. So small that you get to hang out and chat with the owner, Mani. *Masala dosa* Rs15, excellent Keralan meal Rs20, and tasty fried fish Rs34. Open daily from 6am. ❶

German Bakery, toward the south end of Lighthouse Beach. There's always a breeze at this rooftop spot. Though you're a long way from home, you wouldn't know it after a bite of that cinnamon-apple strudel (Rs25). Open daily 7:30am-11pm. ❶

Leo's Restaurant, toward the north end of Lighthouse Beach. A popular choice, and makes a mean cheese-tomato-onion-garlic omelette (Rs25). Fish and chips Rs100, spaghetti with mussels Rs60. Open 7:30am-11:30pm. ❶

Lonely Planet Restaurant. Follow directions for Green Valley cottages (above) and take a left at the fork; it's on your right, in a lovely, tranquil spot. Shame about the name. Mainly Indian veg. food. No liquor allowed. Open daily 6am-midnight.

Swiss Cafe, near the north end of Lighthouse Beach. Beautifully designed restaurant where satisfied costumers linger over sandwiches and imported Swiss cheese (Rs25). Open 7:30am-11:30pm. ❶

Garzia, on the northern end of the beach. Fresh pasta is a treat. Fresh seafood Rs100, cheese, tomato, and garlic pasta Rs77. Open daily 7am-11pm. ❶

Udaya Hotel, by the bus stop. When the beach gets too sandy, head inland to where the locals eat their meals (Rs10). Open 6am-9:30pm. ❶

🔍 🎵 SIGHTS AND ENTERTAINMENT

BEACHES. Well, you're here for the sand—no two ways about it. The most popular beach among foreign tourists is **Lighthouse Beach,** the southernmost. Here you can rent boogie boards and fend off hawkers of edibles and durables. Always swim near the lifeguard. Almost as popular is **Eve Beach.** North of the headland is **Samudra Beach,** delightful but largely ignored by the crowds.

> **⚠ WARNING.** The undertow and rip currents here can be very strong, so follow the warnings of the signs, flags, and whistle-toting lifeguards. Also, proximity to Trivandrum means there are daytrippers; though many Western women wear their bikinis with pride, some opt to swim in T-shirts to avoid unwanted attention.

MASSAGE AND YOGA. Tired of the waves? Kiss your aches and pains good-bye with an **ayurvedic massage.** Kerala is touted as an ayurvedic haven, and there are numerous establishments in Kovalam providing treatment. **Wilson's Tourist Home** has a *masseur* for men and a *masseuse* for women. (☎ 480051. Open M-Sa 9am-5pm. Rs200 per hr., Rs300 to have your head seen to as well.) **Amritha Ayurvedic Health Centre,** adjoining Hotel Neptune, does a full body massage fro Rs250. (☎ 401769. Open daily 8am-9pm.) Peak season also means that **yoga** is in full swing at many hotels and private institutions. Hotel Neptune offers classes (1hr. session Rs200).

NIGHTLIFE. During peak season, "cultural nights" featuring **kathakali dance** take place at the Hotel Ashok (☎ 480101; Tu and F, Rs150) and Hotel Neptune. (☎ 480222; M, W, and Sa; Rs125. Make-up starts at 5pm; the dance program begins at 6:45pm.) Pirated **movies,** complete with laughter from the original audience, are shown nightly at several restaurants, including the Coconut Grove Restaurant (☎ 480481) and the Hawah Beach Restaurant (☎ 484031).

BACKWATER CRUISES. The Tourist Facilitation Centre arranges **backwater cruises** around an island 5km from Kovalam. The Rs300 fee covers transportation to the boat, 3hr. of cruising time, and the return trip to Kovalam. Unlike on the Alleppey-Kollam tour, the boat used in season is a traditional, non-motorized vessel with a rattan shade; off season, an uncovered boat is used. The Tourist Facilitation Centre can book tickets for the Kollam-Alleppey backwater cruise as well. Western Travels (see p. 321) offers a 4hr. backwater cruise along some of the Alleppey-Kollam canals. (7:30am-6:30pm, Rs550.)

OTHER SIGHTS. It's worth wandering up to the landscaped grounds around the Tourist Facilitation Centre and the Kovalam Ashok Beach Resort, part of which is housed in the 250-year-old **castle** that was once the Maharaja's summer retreat. The views are gorgeous, and if you're lucky, no one will try to sell you anything. If, after spending too much time in Kovalam, you've forgotten that you're in India, take the 20min. stroll along the coastal road to the ramshackle village of **Vizhinjam** (VEER-in-yam). Only ruins of some small shrines remain in this former capital of the Ay Kings. Brightly painted fishing boats fill the harbor, crowned at the north end by a dizzying pink-and-yellow **mosque.**

FESTIVALS. Kovalam's biggest to-do is **Gramam** (Jan. 14-23) when a Keralan village is recreated on Eve's Beach, complete with the traditional *nalukettu* (square house with courtyard), where an arts and crafts fair is held.

KERALA

BILE BALANCE The predominant medical tradition in Hindu culture is associated with *ayurveda*, which translates as the "knowledge of long life." Practitioners of this are called *vaidyas*. Ayurvedic medicine takes a holistic approach to diagnosis (a broken heart is as much an ailment as a broken leg) and to treatment (a combination of herbal potions and worthy notions). The earliest known prescriptions date back to the *Atharva Veda* (c. 1000 BC), when *vaidyas* were performing surgery on wounds. Ayurvedic medicine, however, is mainly associated with maintaining balance between the three bodily essences or *doshas: vatta* (wind), *pitta* (bile), and *kapha* (phlegm). *Vatta*, associated with the nervous system and movement, represents kinetic energy. *Kapha*, potential energy, is associated with lymph and mucus, and opposes *vatta*. Finally, *pitta* mediates between these two forces, governing digestive and metabolic processes. Balance between the three *doshas* is essential to good health.

KOLLAM (QUILON) കൊല്ലം ☎0474

Kollam is one of the oldest ports on the Malabar Coast. Called "Kaulam" Mall by ancient Arabs, and "Coilum" by Marco Polo in the 13th century, the town was the center of the "heroic rebellion" against British rule led by Veluthambi Dalava. Today, however, the prosperous city is the center of the country's cashew trade, and its location on the sprawling Ashtamudi lake makes it an excellent base for exploring the backwaters. Though little remains from its glory days—shopping malls and modern storefronts have obliterated ancient palaces and most of the ancient streets—it is worth staying a night or two in the lovely Government Guest House and taking a cruise through the backwaters before heading to the coast.

⊟ TRANSPORTATION

Trains: The station is about 1km southeast of the center of town. Fares listed are sleeper class. To: **Alleppey** (1½hr.; 2-3 per day 4:50am-11:15pm; Rs30); **Bangalore** (5hr.; 1-2 per day 10:55am and 4:20pm; Rs147); **Chennai** (16hr.; 2-4 per day 5:35am-3:20pm; Rs158); **Ernakulam** (3hr.; several 4:30am-11:15pm; Rs42); **Kanyakumari** (4hr.; 2-3 per day 9:55am-9:25pm; Rs46); **Mangalore** (14hr.; 2 per day 7:15am and 7:20pm; Rs120); **Trivandrum** (1½hr.; 9 per day 6:35am-8:45pm; Rs26).

Buses: KRSTC bus station (☎752008), Jetty Rd., north toward the river and the boat jetty. To: **Alleppey** (2hr.; every 20min.; Rs32); **Ernakulam** (3½hr.; every 20min.; Rs55); **Trivandrum** (1½hr.; every 20min.; Rs26-35); **Varkala** (1½hr.; 10 per day 7:30am-8:30pm; Rs12). A Varkala bus leaves at 6:50pm, scooping up most passengers disembarking the backwater cruise from Alleppey.

✴🛈 ORIENTATION AND PRACTICAL INFORMATION

Kollam's streets follow the bends of the canals and turn at confusing angles. **National Highway (NH) 47** runs southeast to northwest through town. Beginning in the southeast end of town, NH47 passes the **railway station** before crossing the tracks to the congested center of town. At the junction of Chinnakkada, marked by the **clock tower**, it intersects with the east-west **Main Rd.** Just beyond is the large junction of NH47 with the wide north-south **Tourist Bungalow Rd.** From there NH47 twists in a northwest direction past the **post office**, the sprawling **Bishop Jerome Nagar Shopping Centre**, and the wild Shrine of Our Lady of Velankanni. The next junction is with **Jetty Rd.**, which leads to the right (north) to the **KSRTC bus station** and the **ferry jetty**, 100m away. A 10min. walk to the left (southwest) leads to the fruit and vegetable **market**.

Tourist Office: District Tourism Promotion Council (DTPC) has outposts at the railway station. Open M-Sa 9am-5:30pm. The bus station branch (☎ 745625; open M-Sa 6am-6pm) is especially helpful for backwater tour booking and hotel reservations.

Currency Exchange: State Bank of Travancore, in the Bishop Nagar Shopping Centre, changes currency. Open M-F 10am-2pm and 2:30-3:30pm, Sa 10am-12:30pm. Toward the jetty, **Bank of Baroda** does cash advances. Open M-F 10am-2pm, Sa 10am-noon.

Police Station: (☎ 742072). Right from the railway station, next to the large temple.

Pharmacy: Kochappally Medicals, Tourist Bungalow Rd. (☎ 749286). Just southwest of the main intersection with NH47 and Main Rd. Open daily 8am-9pm.

Hospital: Nair's Hospital (☎ 742413). 1½km northeast of the jetty, east off Tourist Bungalow Rd.

Internet: Net4you (☎ 741266). 2nd fl. in the Bishop Jerome Nagar Shopping Centre. Six terminals in shiny new A/C room. Rs60 per hr. Open daily 9am-9pm. **SilverNet,** on the ground floor, is not as posh but does the job. Rs60 per hr. Open M-Sa 10am-8:30pm.

Post Office: Head Post Office, NH47, northeast of the intersection with Tourist Bungalow Rd., on the left. Open M-Sa 7am-8pm. **Postal Code:** 691001.

⚑ ACCOMMODATIONS

▨ **The Tourist Bungalow (Government Guest House),** Tourist Bungalow Rd. (☎ 743620). A few km outside of town (rickshaw Rs25). This beautiful, old British mansion with its huge, echoing ballroom hung with quietly mildewing prints has rooms with 3m high ceilings and sparse antique furniture. Recently refurbished, it's more gorgeous than ever. Wonderfully romantic and often full—come for a look around even if you can't get a room. Attached bathrooms (seat toilets). Only government officials can make reservations, but call ahead to see if it's booked. Singles and doubles Rs164. ❶

Yatri Nivas (☎ 745538). Opposite the lake from the boat jetty. Phone from there for a pickup in their speedboat (Rs20); otherwise, hire a rickshaw (Rs10). Standard rooms have attached baths and great views of the water. Singles Rs110; doubles Rs165. ❶

Hotel Shah International, Tourist Bungalow Rd. (☎ 742362). 100m from NH47. A quiet and conveniently located large place with grand aspirations it doesn't quite live up to. All rooms have balconies and attached baths with seat toilets, towels, and soap. Singles Rs210-480; doubles Rs260-480. ❷

◖ FOOD

Jala Subhiksha, next to the boat jetty. A floating restaurant in a lovely traditional *kettuvallam* (boat). Delicious Chinese and Indian dishes: *saiwoo* chicken Rs55, Manchurian tofu Rs45. Open daily 6pm-10pm. ❶

Indian Coffee House, Main Rd., tucked away on the right. From the post office, turn right on NH47, then take the second right. Once a franchise, always a franchise. Banana fry Rs9. Open daily 8am-9pm. ❶

Supreme Bakers, from the post office, turn right onto NH47, then take an immediate right; it's on the left. Spic-n-span bakery serves fresh cakes, bread, and pastries for Rs4-20. Cold drinks, snacks, and A/C offer relief. Open M-Sa 9am-8pm. ❶

◉ ▮ SIGHTS AND ENTERTAINMENT

The highlight of Kollam's calender is the **Ashtamudi Craft and Art Festival** in late December and early January, when craftsmen from all over India come to demonstrate their skills. There are also demonstrations of traditional dance and music.

KERALA

BACKWATER CRUISES

Backwater cruises depart at 10:30am from the DTPC office near the KSRTC bus stand and the boat jetty, and arrive in Alleppey at 6:30pm. Report to the office by 10am. Rs150. Rs100 for ISIC holders. Village tour departures daily from KDTC 9am and 2pm; 3hr.; Rs300, Rs75 discount for students and seniors. Book online at www.dptc-quilontourism.com or by contacting the DTPC directly. Houseboat tours can be booked online at www.dptc-quilontourism.com, or by contacting the DTPC directly. Prices start at Rs2000 for two people for the 14hr. Starnight Cruise.

The backwater cruises to Alleppey are the main attraction in Kollam. The boat can take both you and your luggage, making this a convenient and beautiful mode of transport north up the Keralan coast. Many of the cruises make several stops along the way, including one at the Mata Amrithanandamayi Mission (see below). Cruises are run by the District Tourism Promotion Council (DTPC); though others offer similar service, discounts are available by booking through the DTPC. (For more information, see p. 329.) The KDTC office at the bus station organizes additional backwater tours, including a justifiably popular **village tour** that winds through barely 3m wide canals in Munroe Island in a traditional wooden boat. There is also a range of cheap **houseboat tours.**

MATA AMRITHANANDAMAYI ASHRAM

☎ (0476) 621279; mam_hq@vsnl.com. Rs125 per day in a room with attached bath and 1 or 2 roommates; meals included.

Backwater cruises frequently stop to pick up and drop off passengers at the ashram of one of India's few female gurus, Mata Amrithanandamayi, usually known as Amma, the Hugging Mother. Particularly popular with Westerners, the ashram houses hundreds of residents and visitors in pink skyscrapers that look somewhat incongruous against the surrounding backwaters. There are many amenities at the ashram including a general store, a hospital, and 24hr. STD/ISD phones. Ask in Alleppey or Kollam, or call the ashram to see if Amma is in residence and not on tour. The backwater cruise boats honor partially-used tickets—a single ticket will take you from Kollam to the ashram and, a few days later, on to Alleppey (or vice versa).

SHRINE OF OUR LADY OF VELANKANNI

NH47, near Jetty Rd. Mass W 8am and noon; 5pm mass usually in Malayalam.

This towering polygonal shrine rises above everything else in Kollam. Festooned with bright plastic flowers and tinsel, the shrine occupies a central place in Kollam's religious life. Although a mere 13 years old, the shrine has already gained a reputation for healing and performing miracles. On Wednesdays, crowds line up inside, fingering rosaries and praying for hours.

VARKALA ☎ 0472

The town of Varkala, with its quiet beach and towering cliffs, just might rescue South India's reputation for over-commercialized beaches. Though Varkala, 25km from Kollam, is slowly developing an affinity for tourist dollars, it still retains some of the beauty and tranquility for which Kovalam was once famed.

⊏ TRANSPORTATION. Buses stop at the temple junction, a short walk from the beach. To: **Kollam** (1-2hr.; every hr.; Rs15.50) and **Trivandrum** (1½hr.; 5 per day 6am-5pm; Rs16). A direct bus heads to **Kovalam** (2hr.; 4:30pm; Rs20) via **Trivandrum. Trains** are faster and more reliable, if less conveniently located; the **railway station** is a couple of kilometers from the temple junction (Rs15-20 auto-rickshaw ride). Trains run to: **Kollam** (40min.; 10 per day 7:25am-10:30pm; Rs28) and **Trivandrum** (1hr.; 9 per day 7:15am-6:30pm; Rs33).

◪ PRACTICAL INFORMATION. The **DPTC** has opened a branch at the end of Beach Rd. The office has train and bus schedules, books backwater cruises, and, in its incarnation as the private tourist office **JK Tours and Travels, exchanges currency.** (Open daily 9am-7pm.) Another **JK Tours and Travels** is at the temple junction (☎ 600713. Open daily 9am-6:30pm). A **DPTC** of Trivandrum is near the helipad. (Open daily 8am-6pm.) On Beach Rd. in Nikhil Beach Resorts, there are four terminals to check **email.** (Rs70 per hr. Open daily 7am-11pm.) Email at the Seaview Restaurant is available 24hr. (Rs80 per hr.) The tiny Janardhanapuram **post office** is at the temple junction (open M-Sa 10am-2pm). **Postal code:** 695141.

◪◪ ACCOMMODATIONS AND FOOD. The cliff-top overlooking the beach is crowded with hotels; follow Beach Rd. west and head north uphill for a sweaty 15min. Views cost money in Varkala, so wander inland if your budget is tight. Turn east from the cliff road at the Virgin Vegetarian Restaurant to find the pleasant **Greenhouse ❶.** Look for the purple walls with the name painted sporadically along several buildings. The big, clean rooms with attached baths are just in from the cliff. (☎ 604659. Doubles Rs200; off season: Rs100.) The **Clafouti Bakery ❶,** lets rooms at the north end of the cliff. Slightly inland rooms with bath are small but decent (☎ 601414. Rs200-300; off season: Rs50-75). Posher rooms are closer to the cliff and the bakery's fresh bread. (Doubles Rs500. Off season: singles Rs150; doubles Rs250.) On the cliff, the aptly named **Seaview Restaurant and Cliff House ❷,** has views of the sea. (☎ 601019. Doubles Rs400-800; off-season Rs100-200.) Varkala's restaurants, which open early and close late, have lengthy menus featuring everything from hash browns to *pad thai.* The **▨Clafouti Bakery ❶,** has delicious banana-pineapple muffins (Rs15), brownies (Rs20), and assorted fresh bagels, as well as the usual array of eggs, *dosas,* rice, and noodles. (Open daily 8:30am-11pm). At the south end of the cliff the popular **Sunset Restaurant ❶,** does breakfast by nationality. (Indian Rs30, English Rs90, French Rs75, Italian Rs40, Israeli Rs60, and just plain Special Rs40. Open daily from 8am.)

◪ SIGHTS. The town's only real **beach,** Papanasham, is at the base of a dramatic cliff, which shoulders the burden of most of Varkala's tourist infrastructure. From the cliff, steep narrow paths scramble down to the surf. There are dangerous riptides; always swim near the lifeguard and ask about conditions. The cliff-top **path** winds north for quite a distance, with superb views of the rocky coastline. Beach Rd. leads west from the **Sree Janardhana Swami Temple,** a Hindu pilgrimage site— one of the seven most important Vaishnavite shrines in India. The road passes a large **tank.** From the beach, rickety bridges lead up the cliff to the **Kerala Kathakali Centre,** which stages **kathakali dance** performances (daily; make-up 5pm, show 6:30pm; Rs100). Operations all along the beach specialize in ayurvedic treatments and assorted curative programs. Other places on the cliff-top north of the beach, including the **Scientific School of Yoga and Massage** (1¾hr. massage Rs300), promise a combination of spiritual and physical rejuvenation, and offer yoga classes.

ALLEPPEY (ALAPPUZHA) ആലപ്പുഴ ☎ 0477

The two canals that run through Alleppey were once the major arteries of a great shipping center. Today, tangles of water lilies fill the waterways, and most of the town's activity revolves around all the *coir* (woven coconut fiber) products shipped through here on small boats propelled by pole. Partly because of its fading economic importance, Alleppey is a prime example of a traditional Keralite town, complete with steeply-pitched, red-tiled roofs. The town's snake-boats (traditional Keralite battle vessels) compete several times a year, especially during the annual Nehru Trophy Boat Race (2nd Sa in Aug.). The popular backwater cruises between Alleppey and Kollam bring tourists here from all over the world.

⊡ TRANSPORTATION. The **railway station** is near the beach, 4km southwest of the town center. Trains go to **Ernakulam** (1-1½hr.; 8 per day 6am-7:20pm; Rs11) and **Trivandrum** (3hr.; 2-3 per day 7:20am-3am; Rs43). An auto-rickshaw from the train station to the boat jetty or bus station will cost you Rs25-35. Privately operated local buses leave from the street directly opposite the most eastern footbridge over the North Canal to the train station (Rs2). The **KSRTC bus station** is at the east end of **Boat Jetty Rd.,** which runs along the south bank of North Canal. Buses go to: **Cochin** (2hr.; every 20min.; Rs23); **Kollam** (2hr.; every 20 min.; Rs32); **Kottayam** (1½hr.; every hr. 5:50am-9pm; Rs19); **Periyar, Kumily,** and **Trivandrum** (4hr.; every 20min.; Rs59). Public and private **boats** leave from the **jetties** 200m west of the bus station, just before the Mullackal Rd., the large street that bridges the North Canal. Boats to **Kollam** (8hr.; daily 10:30am; Rs150).

⊞ ⊡ ORIENTATION AND PRACTICAL INFORMATION. The town is sandwiched between two east-west canals: the **North Canal** and the **South Canal,** about a 10min. walk apart. The streets between the two canals are laid out in a grid. The **bus station** is at the east end of the North Canal; boat jetties are farther west, near the **DTPC** office. **Mullackal Rd.** runs north-south, bridging the North Canal at the western edge of the boat jetties. The helpful **District Tourism Promotion Council (DTPC),** on Boat Jetty Rd. (☎251211), next to the boat jetties, sells tickets for boat rides (Rs100-200) and the Nehru Trophy Boat Race. (Open M-Sa 9am-6pm.) To get to the equally helpful **ATDC Tourist Office,** take Mullackal Rd. north, turn right immediately after crossing the canal, and then turn left; the office will be on your left. (☎243462. Open daily 8am-8pm.) **Canara Bank,** across from the DTPC on the south bank of the North Canal, gives cash advances on MC and V and cashes traveler's checks. (Open M-F 10am-2pm.) A **market** lines Mullackal Rd., both north and south of North Canal. To get to **Medical College Hospital** (☎251611), head south along the road one block west of Mullackal Rd., continue south across the Iron Bridge and the South Canal, and take the third left after the canal. **Haifa Medicals** is just south of the North Canal on Mullackal Rd. (☎251365. Open M-Sa 8:30am-9pm, Su 9am-8pm.) Take the street opposite the footbridge to **Cyber Graphix** for Internet access. (Open 8:30am-9:30pm. Rs45 per hr.) Just past Cyber Graphix, you'll spot **N&G Communications,** with three terminals. (Open 9am-11:30pm. Rs40 per hr.) Take Mullackal Rd. south until it ends at the South Canal, then turn right to reach a branch of the **post office.** (Open M-Sa 9am-5pm.) For the **Head Post Office,** continue to the west and take the second right on Exchange Rd. (Open M-Sa 9:30am-5:30pm.) **Postal Code:** 688001.

⊡ ⊡ ACCOMMODATIONS AND FOOD. Hotels line Boat Jetty Rd., the stretch of road that runs west from the bus station along the North Canal. **Hotel Raiban Annexe ❶,** just east of the boat jetty and 400m west of the bus station, is very convenient, and the price is right. (☎261017. Attached baths with seat toilets. Singles Rs86; doubles Rs172-385.) The **Arcadia Hotel ❶,** just west of the bus station, has a good location but is a bit costly. It offers comfortable rooms with seat toilets and a popular restaurant and bar. (☎251354. Singles Rs200; doubles Rs300-600.) **Mutteal Holiday Inn ❶,** Nehru Trophy Rd., on the northern side of North Canal and east of the footbridge, has double rooms and private, quiet rooms which surround a garden; each room has its own patio. (☎242955. Doubles Rs300.) The **Karthika Tourist Home ❶,** 50m north over the North Canal traffic bridge, has great prices for plain rooms. Attached baths with squat toilets. (☎245524. Singles Rs60; doubles Rs100.)

Hotel Annapoorna ❶, Boat Jetty Rd., across from the boat jetty, next to Hotel Raiban Annexe, serves standard South Indian veg. fare for Rs14-18. (Open daily 7am-9pm. Meals 12:30-2pm.) **Cafe Venice ❶,** next to the DPTC, is named for its location overlooking the picturesque, fetid canal. For a giant, tasty lunch, ask for

the Kerala meal (Rs25). Cafe Venice is also a convenient breakfast stop for departing backwater trippers. (Open daily 8am-10pm.) Ruffle-clad waiters at the **Indian
Coffee House,** Mullackal Rd., a few blocks south of the North Canal, serve the standard snacks and coffee. (Open daily 8am-9pm.) **Bakeries** line Boat Jetty Rd. Most of
Alleppey's hotels also have restaurants.

📷 📺 **SIGHTS AND ENTERTAINMENT.** The highlight of Alleppey's tourist calendar is the annual **Nehru Trophy Boat Race,** which finds hundreds of oarsmen
rowing 65m-long snake-boats. The first race was held in honor of Prime Minister
Jawaharlal Nehru during his visit here in 1952. Nehru was so flattered and fasci-
nated by the race that he awarded the winners a trophy; the event soon developed into an Alleppey institution. (Tickets are available from the ATDC and DTPC
and may be purchased up to one week in advance or on the day. Rs 10-500.) Other
races are held throughout the year, including the **Moolam Boat Race** at Champa-
kulam in July. The ATDC runs boat rides to the race (Rs100 round-trip).

🛶 **BACKWATER TRIPS.** Daily **backwater cruises** run the 80km of green canals
that separate Alleppey from Kollam. From the boat, you can see an 11th-century
statue of the Buddha, temples, churches, *coir*-producing villages, and an ashram.
A traditional Keralite meal is served on a banana leaf for lunch (Rs40-50) and
drinks are sold aboard the boats. The ATDC and DTPC both operate cruises.
(10:30am departure, 6:30pm arrival; tours operate in both directions. Make reservations one day in advance or on the day, before 10am. During June and July, trips with
fewer than 10 people will be canceled. Both the ATDC and DTPC charge Rs150 and
give a Rs50 discount to ISIC cardholders and children under 12. If you decide to stop
for a few days at the ashram, your ticket will be honored whenever you resume your
journey.) The ATDC, DTPC, and private agencies along Boat Jetty Rd., including
Penguin Tourist Service (☎261522. Open daily 8am-6pm.), north of Mullackal Rd.,
arrange shorter trips around Alleppey's rice fields and Kuttanad.

Private agencies, including Penguin Tourist Service, also arrange stays on traditional cargo boats—converted **houseboats** with tiny bedrooms, bathrooms, dining areas, and two fellows to pilot the boat. (Rs5000 for 2 people for 24hr.; Rs7500
for 4 people.) The DPTC and ATDC can also arrange **village stays** for Rs300-500.
The budget backwater cruise is the public **ferry ride** to and from Kottayam (3hr., 7
per day 7am-5:30pm, Rs9). Most Kottayam ferries stick to the wide canals, but
those going to Nedumudi (11am and 2:25pm) and Changansherry (1pm), besides
being cheaper, also cruise along the narrow canals and capture more local flavor.
(From Kottayam a 2:30pm ferry goes to Mannar; get off at Nedumudi and catch a local
bus for the 15min. ride to Alleppey.)

PERIYAR TIGER RESERVE AND KUMILY ☎0486

The wooded, misty highlands of Periyar Tiger Reserve shelter wild boar and elephants, 140 species of orchid, a turtle-friendly lake, and a few predatory tigers. Set
aside as reserved forests in 1899, these woods on the edge of Tamil Nadu became
the Nellikkampatty Sanctuary in 1934 and were incorporated into Project Tiger in
1979 (see p. 367). Tigers are elusive, but a twilight boat cruise usually turns up
herds of wild elephant munching grass or taking a dip in the lake. Surrounded by
spice plantations, Kumily, where most tourists stay, is suffused with the sweet
smells of cardamom, cinnamon, cloves, and nutmeg. Kumily's religious fervor
makes it a lively contrast to **Thekkady,** the cluster of hotels within the park; the
mosque and temple keep up a steady stream of chanting, singing, and bell-tolling,
which is blasted all over town by a network of loudspeakers.

KERALA

▄ TRANSPORTATION

Buses: Both private and state buses operate out of **Kumily Bus Stand** at the northern edge of town. From Kumily to: **Ernakulam** (6hr.; every hr. 5:30am-10:30pm; Rs70); **Kottayam** (4hr.; every 30min. 2am-11pm; Rs43); **Munnar** (5hr.; 4 per day 6am-1:30pm; Rs39). A **Tamil Nadu Bus Stand** a bit farther north sends buses to **Madurai** (4hr., every 30min., Rs30). A few buses service Thekkady and its pricey hotels, stopping in Kumily 15min. later. From Thekkady to: **Theni,** for transferring to other Tamil Nadu destinations (every 30min. 6am-7pm; Rs50); **Ernakulam** (6:30am and 2:30pm; Rs70); **Trivandrum** (8hr.; 4 per day 8am-8:30pm; Rs92).

Local Transportation: Taxis, jeeps, and **auto-rickshaws** to the boat jetty in Periyar are available from the Kumily bus stand. A **park bus** runs between the bus stand in Kumily and the Periyar boat landing about every 30min., but waits for a full bus (first bus from Kumily 8:30am; last bus to Kumily waits for the boat tour at 6pm; Rs4). Any bus to Kottayam can drop you at the Spring Valley Spice Garden for a truly budget tour (Rs50).

▞ ORIENTATION AND PRACTICAL INFORMATION

Periyar's borders contain the reserve, a boat dock, information office, and a few expensive hotels that form the hamlet of **Thekkady.** Most tourists stay in **Kumily,** the town that lies on the northwest border of the park. The cheap hotels are along **Thekkady Rd.,** which runs from the Kumily bus station on the border of Tamil Nadu to the Thekkady boat jetty. The entrance to the reserve is about 1½km from the bus stand; it's another 3km to the boat jetty. Walking through the park is permitted as long as you stay on the road, but you may not enter the forest without a guide. **Unless otherwise noted, the following listings are for Kumily.**

Tourist Office: When you step off the bus in town, grab a map and some friendly advice from the **tourist police** booth at the station. Open daily 8am-7pm. For more detailed info, visit the larger **Idukki District Tourism Information Office, Dept. of Tourism Govt. of Kerala** (☎322620), 10min. from the bus station toward the reserve. It's on the left, away from the road, up the stairs in a yellow bldg. Arranges private tours of local spice plantations (2hr., Rs550 for 2 people). Open M-Sa 10am-5pm. **Rickshaw drivers** also offer tours of spice plantations; it should cost Rs250 for 3hr. For information on activities in Periyar, see the **Wildlife Information Centre** (☎322028) at the boat jetty in Thekkady. Open daily 6:30am-5pm.

Currency Exchange: The State Bank of Travancore, behind the bus station, exchanges foreign currency and traveler's checks. Open M-F 10am-2pm, Sa 10am-noon.

Bookstore: DC Books, a bit beyond the tourist office. Open daily 9:30am-9:30pm.

Police: (☎322049). Past the bus station toward the border. **Tourist Police Office,** at the bus station and also on Thekkady Rd. Open daily 8am-7pm.

Pharmacy: High Range Drug House (☎322043). About 5min. away from the bus stand toward the reserve. Open M-Sa 8:30am-8:30pm.

Hospital: St. Augustine Hospital, Spring Valley (☎322042). 3km from the town center. Take a rickshaw (Rs25) or any bus toward Kottayam. The smaller **Kumily Central Hospital** (☎322045) is on the road to the reserve.

Internet: Rissas Communication (☎322103). Opposite the Lake Queen Tourist Home on Thekkady Rd. Open 8am-11:30pm. Rs60 per hr.

Post Office: Next to the Kerala bus stand. Open M-Sa 9am-5pm. There is also a branch at the park entrance. Open M-Sa 9am-5pm. **Postal Code:** 685509.

ACCOMMODATIONS

There are only three hotels inside the reserve, all run by the KTDC. Expect to pay high prices and be locked in at 6pm every night. Stay in Kumily for cheaper accommodations.

Lake Queen Tourist Home (☎322084). Five hundred meters down the main road from the bus stand. Run by a charitable foundation and managed by a retired military man. "Special" doubles feature mosquito nets, towels, and soap. All rooms have attached baths. 24hr. checkout. Singles Rs130; doubles Rs320. Student discounts. ●

Hotel Regent Tower (☎322570). Fifty meters from the bus stand on the main road. Big rooms with access to balconies overlooking the bus station, the music-broadcasting temple, and the mountains. Attached baths with seat toilets. Buckets of hot water. Soap and towels included. Singles Rs150; doubles Rs250-350. ●

Coffee Inn (coffeeinn@satyam.net.in). Five hundred meters before the park entrance. Six cottages and two bamboo shacks with attached baths. The inn also has a book exchange and an excellent tea house. Singles Rs150; doubles Rs200-250. ●

Hotel Ambadi (☎322193). One kilometer from the bus stand. Carved wooden doors open into well-furnished, dim rooms with ceiling mirrors. Attached baths with towels and toilet paper. Check-out noon. Cottages Rs425; rooms Rs690-990. MC/V. ❷

Periyar House (☎322026). Two kilometers inside the reserve. The cheapest option within the park. High-ceilinged rooms with attached baths and seat toilets. Breakfast and dinner included. No check-in (or leaving the bldg.) after 6pm. Singles Rs700; doubles Rs900-1100. MC/V. ❸

FOOD

Stalls opposite the bus stand cook up stacks of delicious, piping hot *parathas* (Rs2) every night.

Coffee Inn, 500m before the park entrance. Try teas from cardamom to hibiscus (Rs10) in this mural-painted domain of tribal and space-age music. Fantastic view of the surrounding hills. The meals don't match the high-quality tea, but try the homemade brown bread (Rs10). Live *tabla* performances M-F 6:15-7:15pm. Open 7am-9:30pm. ●

Cafe Periyarenis, near the Thekkady jetty. Run by the park staff cooperative society, Periyarenis is the only non-hotel food option in the reserve. Snacks, drinks in biodegradable containers, and *dosas* (Rs10) served beside the Periyar River. Open daily 8am-6pm. ●

Hotel Maharani, on the 1st fl. of the Regent Tower Hotel, packs them in for the midday Keralite meal (Rs20; with an excellent fish curry Rs32). Watch Indian soap operas while you eat. Egg breakfasts Rs15-25. Open daily 7am-10pm. ●

Hotel Ambadi Restaurant, in the hotel of the same name. Offers all the standards. Check out the stained glass and multi-religious wall decor. The "Kerala meal" (Rs25) is delicious. Open daily 6:30am-10:30pm. ●

Cafe Machan, by the turn-off for the tourist police. Coffee and tea in a chic setting. Full English breakfast Rs60; sandwiches Rs25; lunch Rs30. Open daily 8:30am-8:30pm. ●

THE RESERVE

Open daily 6am-6pm. Rs50 per multiple-entry day. **KDTC Boat Tours** *(7, 9:30, 11:30am, 2, and 4pm; Rs100 top deck, Rs50 lower deck).* **Park boats** *(9:30, 11:30am, 2, and 4pm; Rs15). Boat rides last 2hr. Purchase tickets at Wildlife Information Centre for their smaller, cheaper boats, or at the KTDC ticket booth at the boat jetty, just up the stairs toward Aranya Nivas. Only same-day advance bookings. If a boat cruise is sold out,*

KERALA

*enquire about left-over tickets at the reception desk of the Aranya Nivas Hotel, up the steps behind the jetty. **Jungle walks** (7am and 2pm, 3hr., Rs60); **elephant rides** (30min., every 30min. 11am-12:30pm and 2-4:30pm, Rs30). Book jungle walks and elephant rides at the Wildlife Information Center.*

The reserve is home to a wide variety of animals, including wild boar, monkeys, the Nilgiri Langur, Malabar giant squirrels, barking deer, and gaur. Most people, however, come to Periyar to see its main attractions: wild elephants and rarely spotted tigers. Periyar claims to be home to at least 49 of the world's 3700 remaining wild tigers, but you would have to be very lucky to see a tiger. At a cool and breezy 900m above sea level, Periyar is a good place to relax, take a leisurely boat cruise, and watch herds of wild elephants bathe. September to March is the best time to visit; January through April are the dry months, when animals come down to the lake to drink. During the monsoon, come prepared to encounter leeches.

> ▌ **WARNING.** So-called "official" guides often approach tourists with offers of jungle walks and jeep tours. Contracting them is illegal, and you may be fined.

The two main ways of exploring the reserve are by **boat tour** and ▌**trekking.** Early morning and evening are the best times to see the animals. Jungle-walking groups are limited to six and allow you the closest look you'll get at the park's flora and fauna. During the morning trek you might startle herds of wild boar or catch elephants eating their breakfasts. To get the most out of your Rs50 daily entrance fee, take the morning jungle walk and the tranquil afternoon cruise. If you want more variety, some of the fancier hotels—including the KTDC hotels in the park and Hotel Ambadi—have government permission to lead jungle treks. The Wildlife Information Center can also organize additional walks for small groups. On both the walk and the boat rides, you are likely to see wild elephants, herds of boar, and tons of birds.

Elephant rides are purely for entertainment, so you probably won't see very much. One of the best ways to see the wildlife is to spend a night in one of two **observation towers.** The Wildlife Information Centre handles the necessary reservations. The tower houses a maximum of two people, who must provide their own food, water, and bedding. The center will arrange transportation by boat (Rs50 per person, park boat fee Rs15). Try to reserve in advance, as demand can be high for these coveted spots.

COCHIN (KOCHI) കൊсоമ്പി   ☎ 0484

The pungent scent of fresh pepper has lured spice fiends to Cochin from as far away as King Solomon's Israel, ancient Rome, Kublai Khan's pleasure dome, and colony-hungry Portugal, Holland, and England. Cochin's magnificent eclecticism is legendary: Chinese fishing nets line the harbor's mouth, Dutch-style houses cram narrow streets, and sacks of spices fill the air with the same evocative smells that drew merchants and explorers. Across the water from Fort Cochin, Ernakulam plays the part of modern alter-ego; its frantic, brash, and polluted streets contrast with the archaic, vaguely European quality of Cochin.

Foreign visitors have flocked to Cochin for thousands of years. St. Thomas the Apostle stopped by in AD 54, and Jews fleeing Jerusalem landed nearby in AD 70. Chinese and Arab traders were making regular visits at least 2000 years ago. In 1341, torrential floods from the Western Ghats hollowed out Lake Vembanad, giving Cochin a perfect harbor—the "Queen of the Arabian Sea." Vasco da Gama arrived in the late 15th century, launching an international scramble for the lucrative Malabar spice trade. The Portuguese were followed by the Dutch and then the British, who briefly ruled the Chennai Presidency from here.

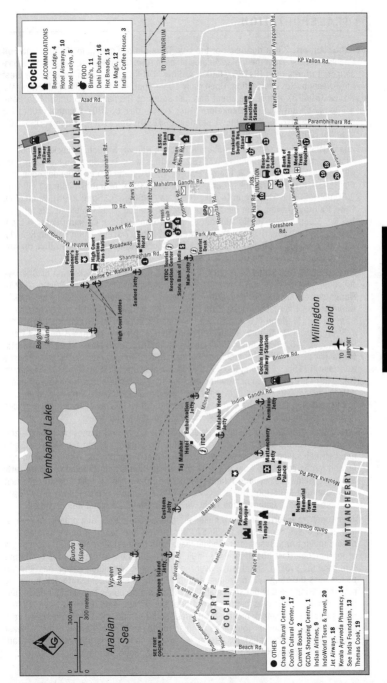

Cochin

▲ ACCOMMODATIONS
Basato Lodge, 4
Hotel Aiswarya, 10
Hotel Luciya, 5

● FOOD
Bimbi's, 11
Delhi Durbar, 16
Hot Breads, 15
Ice Magic, 12
Indian Coffee House, 3

● OTHER
Charara Cultural Center, 6
Cochin Cultural Center, 17
Current Books, 2
GCDA Shopping Centre, 1
Indian Airlines, 9
IndoWorld Tours & Travel, 20
Jet Airways, 18
Kerala Ayurveda Pharmacy, 14
See India Foundation, 13
Thomas Cook, 19

KERALA

▢ TRANSPORTATION

Flights: Airport, 25km northeast of the city. Taxis run to Ernakulam (Rs300) and Fort Cochin (Rs400). From the Indian Airlines office in town, a private shuttle transports passengers to the airport (Rs125). **Indian Airlines,** DH Rd., Ernakulam (☎371141), near the Foreshore Rd. intersection. Open daily 10am-1pm and 1:45-5pm. **Jet Airways,** MG Rd. (☎369423), across the street and just south of Thomas Cook. Open M-Sa 9am-5:30pm, Su 9am-4pm. To: **Bangalore** (1hr.; 2-3 per day; US$80); **Chennai** (10hr.; 1-2 per day; US$110); **Delhi** (40hr.; 1 per day; US$330); **Goa** (10hr.; M and F; US$110); **Mumbai** (2hr.; 4-5 per day; US$150).

Trains: Cochin has 3 stations. **Ernakulam Junction Railway Station,** 2 blocks east of Jos Junction, handles most traffic. (☎371132, inquiries M-Sa 8am-8pm, Su 8am-2pm). To: **Alleppey** (1½hr.; 7 per day 6:15am-11:50pm; Rs39); **Delhi** (59hr.; 4 per day noon-midnight; Rs450); **Hyderabad** (26hr.; 10:10am; Rs385); **Mumbai** (26hr.; 1:30 and 2:50pm; Rs337); **Trivandrum** (4½hr.; 6 per day 5:50am-5:15pm; Rs95). **Ernakulam Town Railway Station,** 4km north of the Junction Station along Banerji Rd., is far from MG Rd. Sleeper class to: **Bangalore** (13hr.; 2:35pm; Rs193); **Calicut** (4½hr.; 4-5 per day 10:55am-2:10am, 11pm; Rs83); **Chennai** (13hr.; 7:10pm and midnight; Rs211); **Kanyakumari** (15hr.; 6 and 9:15am; Rs179). **Cochin Harbour Railway Station,** on Willingdon Island, is serviced by few trains.

Buses: KSRTC Bus Stand (☎372033), central Ernakulam, 2 blocks east of Shenoys Junction. Reservations 9am-1pm and 2-5pm. To: **Alleppey** (1½hr.; every 30min.; Rs25); **Bangalore** (14hr.; 14 per day 6am-9:30pm; Rs240); **Calicut** (5hr.; every hr.; Rs95); **Coimbatore** (4½hr.; 12 per day 6am-3am; Rs73); **Kollam** (3½hr.; 5 per day 6:30am-9pm; Rs55); **Madurai** (10hr.; 8:15am, 7:45 and 8:30pm; Rs130); **Mangalore** (10hr.; 7:30pm; Rs150); **Munnar** (5hr.; 6:30am; Rs52); **Mysore** (10hr.; 8 per day 6am-9:30pm; Rs190); **Trivandrum** (5hr.; frequent; Rs100). **Tamil Nadu State Transportation** services, around the corner from the main KSRTC enquiry desk services, has buses to **Chennai** (15hr.; 3:30pm; Rs248) and **Madurai** (10hr.; 8:15am; Rs133) via **Kumily** (6hr.; Rs77). **Private bus companies** also run long-distance buses from several terminals in Cochin: Ernakulam South, opposite the Ernakulam Junction Railway Station, and High Court Junction, at the end of Shanmugham Rd. Several agencies have offices around Jos Junction, Ernakulam. *Hello Cochin* lists departure times.

Ferries: Water transport is the most scenic—and often only—way to move from one island to another. Ferries are cheap (usually around Rs2), generally run 6am-9:40pm, and hop between islands along a variety of routes. Vypeen Island is the center of water traffic and ferries go to and from this jetty frequently. Routes from **Ernakulam: Main Jetty** are listed below. To: **Vypeen Island** (frequent 5:50am-10pm); **Fort Cochin** (frequent 6am-noon and 1-9:50pm; buy tickets at the SWTD counter); **Mattancherry Jetty** (6 per day 6am-9:10pm); **Embarkation Jetty,** Willingdon Island (frequent 6am-9:50pm).

Other Local Transportation: Local buses are cheap (under Rs5) and orderly. In Ernakulam, local buses depart from the KRSTC bus station and can also be nabbed as they pass through town. Buses to Ft. Cochin leave from the east side of MG Rd., just south of Jos Junction (last bus 9pm, Rs4). In Ft. Cochin, local buses run from the bus stand (opposite the Vypeen Island jetty), over the bridge onto Willingdon Island, past the airport, across the bridge to Ernakulam, and up MG Rd. In Ernakulam, **auto-rickshaws** are plentiful during the day but scarce at night. There are no buses through Ft. Cochin, but taxis and auto-rickshaws can be found near the jetties. Auto-rickshaw-*wallahs* often refuse to use their meters; most in-town fares should be under Rs15. For rickshaws from Ernakulam to Fort Cochin you will be charged round-trip fare for a one-way trip (at least Rs80; twice that after dark). It's easy to get around on foot, and **bike** rentals are available from the **Vasco Hospitality Center** (Rs5 per hr., Rs35 per day).

ORIENTATION

Wider Cochin consists of a bunch of islands around **Lake Vembanad** and the mainland city of **Ernakulam**. **Fort Cochin** and **Mattancherry** occupy a peninsula that juts into the Arabian Sea; nearby islands include **Vypeen Island** and the smaller islands of Willingdon, Vallarpadam, Gundy, and Bolghatty. The central railway, bus stations, and many of the hotels are in Ernakulam, but tourists generally devote their waking hours to Fort Cochin and the peninsula with its many attractions.

Ernakulam's three main streets, **Shanmugham, Mahatma Gandhi (MG),** and **Chittoor Rd.,** run north-south, parallel to the shore. Three major cross-streets intersect MG Rd. and lead to the lake shore: **Convent Rd.** intersects at **Shenoys Junction,** a couple of blocks west of the **central bus station;** three blocks south of Shenoys Junction, **Hospital Rd.** runs to the lake-front; farther south, **Jos Junction** marks the intersection with **Durbar Hall (DH) Rd.** The **Main Jetty** is midway between **Press Club Rd.** (the western extension of Convent Rd.) and Hospital Rd.

The north-south **Princess St.** is Fort Cochin's main drag. It begins at **Calvathy Rd.** (called River Rd. in the west and Bazaar Rd. in the east), which curves along the shoreline. **Jew Town,** Mattancherry, and the Dutch Palace, are south of Fort Cochin, on the eastern side of the peninsula. In the early 20th century, a mammoth dredging project created **Willingdon Island,** sandwiched between Ernakulam and the peninsula. Willingdon is home to the **Cochin Harbour Railway Station.** With a 270° view of the harbor, the Taj Malabar Hotel is at the northern tip of the island.

PRACTICAL INFORMATION

Tourist Office: There is a privately run **Tourist Desk** in Ernakulam (☎371761), at the dock-side ticket office of the Main Jetty. For information on their **Backwater Cruises,** see p. 342. Open daily 9am-6pm. **KTDC Tourist Reception Centre,** Shanmugham Rd., Ernakulam (☎353234), next to the State Bank of India, just northwest of the end of Press Club Rd., offers backwater tours. Open daily 8am-7pm. There are a number of private tourist offices in and around Princess St., Ft. Cochin, including the helpful **Vasco Information Centre** (☎229877), which distributes the informative map and brochure *Walking Through Ft. Cochin.* Open daily 9:30am-11pm.

Budget Travel: Indwelled Tours and Travels, MG Rd. (☎370127). At the intersection with Ravipuram Rd in Ernakulam. Arranges backwater tours (Rs300-800), trips throughout Kerala, and wildlife tours. Open M-Sa 8am-6:30pm, Su 8am-2:30pm.

Currency Exchange: Thomas Cook, MG Rd., Ernakulam (☎369729). Near the Air India bldg. There's also a branch at the **airport** (☎610052). Both open M-Sa 9:30am-6pm. **Bank of Baroda,** MG Rd. (☎351205). A few blocks south of Jos Junction in Ernakulam, on the west side of the street. Gives cash advances. Open M-F 10am-2pm and 2:30-3:30pm, Sa 10am-12:30pm. In Ft. Cochin, **Canara Bank,** TM Mohammed Rd. (☎224812). At Kunnumpuram Junction, one block east of where Bastian and KB Jacob Rd. meet. Gives cash advances and changes traveler's checks. Open M-F 10am-2pm, Sa 10am-noon.

Bookstore: Current Books, Press Club Rd., Ernakulam. Has a wide selection. Open M-Sa 9:30am-7:30pm. **Idiom Books** has two locations—one at Bastian and Quirose St. in Ft. Cochin (open M-Sa noon-9pm), and one in Mattancherry, opposite the Pardesi Synagogue (open daily 10am-6pm). Idiom has a good selection of Keralan authors.

Market: In Ernakulam there are many different shops in Jos Junction and around Broadway, where spices and clothes abound. In the area near the jetty, roadside hawkers set up shop, and there are used-book kiosks (especially great on MG Rd.) and fruit stands. In Ft. Cochin, beach shacks near the bus stand sell fresh fish and fruit. If you're looking to buy trinkets, lanterns, or *salwar kameez,* visit Jew Town in Mattancherry.

KERALA

Police: For the Ernakulam central **police station** (☎394500), head inland from Shanmugham Rd. and take the first left onto Erg Rd. Then, turn right onto Banerji Rd. **Fort Cochin Police** (☎224055) is behind the bus station, opposite the Vypeen Island Jetty.

Hospital: Medical Trust Hospital, MG Rd., Ernakulam (☎371852). 3 blocks south of Jos Junction. Newly renovated. The **pharmacy** inside is open 24hr. **Gautham Hospital** (☎223055) is 3km from Ft. Cochin, to the southeast, in Chullickal.

Pharmacy: In Ft. Cochin, **Jeny Medicals,** Kunnumpuram Junction (☎224253), at the intersection of TM Mohammed and Bastian Rd. Open daily 8:15am-10pm.

Telephones: Central Telegraph Office (☎355601). At the north edge of Jos Junction in Ernakulam. Allows 24hr. collect calls.

Internet: In Ernakulam, **Times,** DD Angadi Bldg. (☎381892), at the corner of Press Club and Market Rd. Rs40 per hr. Open M-Sa 9am-9pm, Su 10am-9pm. **Campus Web,** Press Club Rd., is only Rs30 per hr. but has fewer terminals. Open M-Sa 9:30am-10pm. In Ft. Cochin, email is ubiquitous but costs more. **Call'n'Fax/Shop'n'Save,** Princess St. (☎223438), next to Elite Hotel, is relatively fast and is Ft. Cochin's cheapest option. Rs60 per hr. Open M-Sa 8am-11pm; in-season Su 5-11pm.

Post Office: Kochi Head Post Office, Ft. Cochin. Open M-Sa 9am-5pm. Ernakulam's **GPO,** Hospital Rd., between Foreshore and MG Rd. Open M-F 8:30am-8pm, Sa 9:30am-8pm, Su 10am-5pm. **Postal Code:** 682011 (Ernakulam) and 682001 (Cochin).

⌐ ACCOMMODATIONS

FORT COCHIN

The tranquility of Ft. Cochin is preferable to craziness of Ernakulam; plus, you'll get more quality for your rupees. In season (Dec.-Jan.), accommodations can fill up fast, though it would be unusual not to find somewhere to stay. Most hotels double as tourist offices, offering backwater cruises, ayurvedic massages, and tickets for dance shows. Things are cheaper off season (roughly late-Mar.-Nov.).

▨ **Spencer's Tourist Home,** Parade St. (☎225049). Spencer's is the handsome, rambling old house on the left, at Paradise Rd. and Lily St. Big common room with cable TV, couch, and reading materials. Large, clean rooms with huge soft beds. Hang out in the backyard garden. Dorms Rs75; singles Rs100-150; doubles with bath Rs200. ❶

▨ **Chiramel Residency,** Lily St. (☎227310; chiramel@rediff.com). Close to the intersection with Parade St. A small, attractive, family-run guest house. Mosquito-proof, shoe-free, and beautifully furnished; if you request in advance, you can get home-cooked meals. Check-out noon. Rooms Rs200-600. Off-season: 25% off. ❷

Delight Tourist Resort, Rose St. (☎217658; www.delightfulhomestay.com). South from St. Francis Church; on the left, just before the end of the field. Hardly qualifies as a resort, but it's certainly a delightful place to stay. Large rooms with attached baths set in a lovely house with a large library. Internet. Check-out noon. Rooms Rs250-700. Off-season: 50% discount. ❷

Vasco Hospitality Centre (☎229877), on the corner of Bastian and Rose St. Offers 7 basic rooms in a tired old house. Local legend has it that Vasco da Gama expired here on Christmas Eve, 1524. Provides tourist information, bike rentals (Rs5 per hr., Rs35 per day), and Internet access (Rs75 per hr.). Singles Rs75; doubles with bath Rs125-200. Off-season: Rs60-100. ❶

Tharavadu Tourist Home, Quirose St. (☎226897). From the south end of Princess St., turn right, then left. Well-maintained, 400-year-old house with eight clean rooms, two with common bath (seat toilet and shower). Rooms Rs135-205. ❶

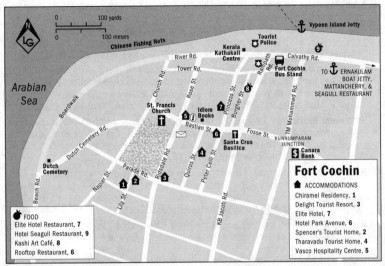

Fort Cochin

▲ ACCOMMODATIONS
Chiramel Residency, 1
Delight Tourist Resort, 3
Elite Hotel, 7
Hotel Park Avenue, 6
Spencer's Tourist Home, 2
Tharavadu Tourist Home, 4
Vasco Hospitality Centre, 5

🍴 FOOD
Elite Hotel Restaurant, 7
Hotel Seagull Restaurant, 9
Kashi Art Café, 8
Rooftop Restaurant, 6

KERALA

Elite Hotel, Princess St. (☎ 225733). Has 15 rooms ranging from basic to spacious with tiled floors. Most rooms have attached bath. Check-out noon. Singles Rs150; doubles with bath Rs300. ❶

Hotel Park Avenue (☎ 222671). At the intersection of Princess and Bastian St. A marble-faced monstrosity that is nevertheless a great place to stay. Modest-sized rooms have attached baths, and everything works. Rooftop restaurant. Check-out noon. Add 7-15% tax. Singles Rs200-500; doubles Rs300-800. Off-season: 30% discount. ❷

ERNAKULAM

Ernakulam's rooms tend to be characterless and overpriced, but they're convenient if you arrive late at night.

Hotel Luciya (☎ 381177). Behind the KRSTC bus station on Stadium Rd. Well-run. Its enormous size almost guarantees room availability. Check-out 24hr. Singles (squat toilet) Rs130-300; doubles (seat toilet and balcony) Rs260-425. ❷

Basoto Lodge, Press Club Rd. (☎ 352140). Close to Market Rd. Comfortable and popular with foreigners, Basoto has basic facilities and high ceilings. Check-out 24hr. Singles Rs60; doubles with bath (squat toilets) Rs120. ❶

Hotel Aiswarya, Warriam Rd. (☎ 364454). Near Jos Junction, where Warriam meets DH Rd. Cool marble floors and decent furnishings. All rooms have TV and bath with hot water and seat toilets. Check-out 24hr. Prices do not include 7.5% tax. Singles Rs300-650; doubles Rs400-650. MC/V. ❸

🖪 FOOD

FORT COCHIN

Ft. Cochin has few restaurants, but there are shacks on the sea-front that grill fish to order and serve the usual fried snacks. The restaurants here tend to be expensive and prefer to serve Western, rather than Indian food. Bakeries and vegetable stores cluster at the intersection of Bastian St. and TM Mohammed (one block east and parallel to KB Jacob), and fruit is sold near the bus stand. There are also some bakeries along Fosse and Pullupalam Rd., the eastern extensions of Bastian Rd.

Kashi Art Cafe, Burgher St. One block from Princess St. A little pretentious and over-priced perhaps—all that art on the walls—but you can reacquaint yourself with *real* coffee (Rs30) and make lots of tourist friends. A menu of Euro meals changes daily (Rs45-55). For Rs5, fill up your water bottle with boiled and purified water and spare the street another piece of plastic. Open M-Sa 8:30am-6:30pm, Su 8:30am-2:30pm. ❶

Bojana Shala, Peter Ceili St. Near the end of Princess St. Tired of criticism that their menu was too touristy, the owners of the Kashi Art Cafe opened this Kerala-cuisine restaurant. A helpful waitstaff will guide you through a daily Muslim-influenced menu. Lunch Rs50. Entrees Rs70-80. Open daily 12:30-2:30pm and 6:30-9:30pm. ❶

Elite Hotel Restaurant, Princess St. On the ground floor of the hotel. Locals hang out while tourists catch up on the latest news from Goa and try the seafood of the day with finger chips (Rs50). *Dosas* (Rs15) served after 5pm. Egg breakfasts Rs10-20. Open daily from 8am until the crowd trickles out (10 or 11pm). ❶

Hotel Seagull Restaurant, Calvathy Rd. On the waterfront. Enter through the east entrance to the Family Garden Restaurant, where you'll be served fresh seafood and cold beer (Rs60) to wash it all down on an open air patio overhanging the sea. Excellent ginger fish Rs80, crab fry Rs60, vegetable curry Rs30. Open daily 7am-10:30pm. ❶

Rooftop Restaurant, perched above the Hotel Park Avenue. Quiet and calm. Serves affordable Keralite seafood dishes (fish masala Rs35). Open daily 7am-10:30pm. ❶

ERNAKULAM

Ernakulam's eateries serve both international foodstuffs and Indian food (so rare in Fort Cochin). Try local foods like *appam* (a thick *dosa* served with fish stew), and dishes prepared with coconut. Excellent bakeries and tempting juice bars (no water, no ice) line the streets.

Bimbi's, Jos Junction. The chaotic ambience of this local landmark is mesmerizing, and its food is good and cheap. Pay at the register, claim your food at the counter, then sit down and watch the world whiz by. Excellent *masala dosa* Rs15. Huge selection of sweets at the front. Open daily 8am-9:30pm. ❶

Delhi Durbar, MG Rd. A few blocks south of Jos Junction. Here you'll find Ernakulam's best slice of North Indian cuisine: succulent chicken *tikka masala* (Rs50) and great garlic *naan* (Rs15) in A/C comfort. Open daily noon-3:30pm and 6pm-1am. ❶

Ice Magic, South Railway Station Rd. Toward MG Rd. from the station—one in a row of enticing juice bars. Select the fruit of your choice to be blended up (Rs10-15) or go for the mean mango milkshake (Rs20). Open daily 10am-11:30pm. ❶

Indian Coffee House, one is opposite Main Boat Jetty, the other is in Jos Junction, opposite Bimbi's. Beloved by purists and tourists alike, ICH is convenient and fast. Veg. *biryani* Rs15; banana fry Rs3; and *dosas* Rs8. Open daily 7:30am-9pm. ❶

Hot Breads, Warriam Rd. Follow MG Rd. south from Jos Junction and turn right; it's on the right. Fresh pastries and cakes, including chocolate croissants (Rs10) and brownies (Rs10). Pizza, burgers, and sandwiches, too. Open daily 9am-9pm. ❶

👁 SIGHTS

FORT COCHIN

As the heavy orange sun sinks down into the Arabian sea, fishermen haul up Chinese fishing nets while ancient church bells toll; all the romantic fantasies of old come true in Fort Cochin. The brochure *Walking Through Fort Cochin,* available at tourist offices, offers informative details about the area in a walking-tour format.

DON'T MAKE THAT FACE OR IT'LL STAY

THAT WAY **Kathakali,** which means "story play," is one of India's four major schools of classical dance. Transformed into gods and demons with wildly colored make-up, massive golden headdresses, and skirts bright and full enough to put any ballerina to shame, the performers blink, bound, and flap expressively to tell their tale. Usually male, the actors study scripture, Kalaripayatu, ayurvedic massage, and music for eight years, beginning at age 10 or 12. They then train in dance for four years. Emphasis is given to proper lifestyle and the deep understanding of archetypes portrayed in the *Vedas.* The dancers communicate ideas and feelings through 24 *mudras,* hand gestures combined with convulsive eye and face movements and the pounding of *ghungroo*-laden feet. By using combinations of these *mudras*—signifying things like "love," "sarcasm," "bee drinking from a lotus flower," etc.—the dancers depict stories from the *Ramayana* and *Mahabharata* while piercing drums and classical vocals provide narration. Although traditional *kathakali* was—and still is on special holy days— performed as part of a temple ritual, modern-day shows last only an hour or so and are performed for tourists who come to "watch the Gods dance."

ST. FRANCIS CHURCH. Believed to be the first church built by Europeans in India, St. Francis Church (locally called the Vasco da Gama Church), was built around 1500 by Franciscan friars from Portugal. The stone version, constructed a few years later, still stands among the houses built by British traders and Dutch farmers. When **Vasco da Gama** died in Cochin in 1524, he was buried beneath the church floor. Fourteen years later, his relatives moved his body to Lisbon, leaving behind his worn, empty tomb. Cochin fell to the Dutch in 1663, and the church was Protestantized in 1779. Although the British occupied Cochin in 1795, the church remained a Dutch stronghold, and Dutch gravestones cover the walls. The church became Anglican in 1864; the Church of South India has since dedicated it to St. Francis. Pre-electricity fans hang from the ceilings; a very sweaty crew had to pull constantly at the cords to keep the flaps flapping and a breeze blowing down on the worshipers below. Behind the church, local kids play cricket on the wide **Parade Ground,** which was once the site of colonial era demonstrations. *(Open M-F 9:30am-1pm and 2:30-5:30pm.)*

CHINESE FISHING NETS. Like giant spiders, Cochin's Chinese fishing nets surround the northern edge of the peninsula. The first of these nets was set up between 1350 and 1450 when Kublai Khan's traders brought the design to Kerala. As massive cargo ships pull into the harbor, fishermen in their canoe-like boats return from the sea with the day's catch. Stick around to watch teams of men pull up the nets; high tide is the time to see them in action. Keep an eye out for dolphins, who feast on the fish near the nets.

MATTANCHERRY AND JEW TOWN

A 45min. stroll from Ft. Cochin brings you to the heart of Mattancherry, one of the historic centers of the international spice trade. Follow Calvathy Rd. to the Customs Jetty and keep going as it turns into Bazaar Rd.—it's a pleasant walk past rows of export warehouses, where rich smells of tea, pepper, and spices waft out from every alley. The shops are most lively M-F 9am-5pm. If you want to add exhaust fumes to this olfactory kaleidoscope, you can also take an auto-rickshaw from Ft. Cochin (Rs25).

PARDESI SYNAGOGUE. Originally built in 1568 (though the current structure dates from 1664), the synagogue is lit by 19th-century oil-burning chandeliers suspended over a floor of blue-and-white Cantonese tiles given in 1762. The 1100 handpainted tiles vary subtly from each other, using three main scenes (a river landscape, a rosebush, and a willow tree) to create endless variations. The synagogue's Torah is written on sheepskin scrolls and stored in ornate metal canisters, one of them a gift from the Raja of Cochin. A Helnas-inscribed stone set into the outside wall of the synagogue comes from a now-defunct synagogue built in 1344 in Kochangadi. Gravestones with Hebrew inscriptions are propped around the outside of the synagogue. The synagogue in **Jew Town** is tucked in an alleyway parallel to Bazaar Rd. The area is teeming with stores selling curios and antiques—bargain hard. (5min. from the Dutch Palace. Walk away from Ft. Cochin until the road makes a right turn and make a sharp right there; the synagogue is at the end of the street on the right. Open M-F and Su 10am-noon and 3-5pm. Rs2. Services held F 6:30pm and Sa 8:30am if enough people arrive.)

THE DUTCH PALACE. The **Mattancherry Palace** (a.k.a. the Dutch Palace) was built by the Portuguese in 1555 for Raja Virakerala Varma; its construction was a "goodwill gesture," probably made in exchange for trading rights. During their occupation in 1663, the Dutch renovated and renamed the palace. Two **temples,** one dedicated to Krishna and the other to Shiva, were built on the palace grounds by the Portuguese, but today only Hindus may enter. Beautiful, detailed **murals** depicting scenes from the *Ramayana*, the *Mahabharata*, and the *Puranas* in distinct Keralite style cover nearly 300 sq. m of the palace walls. In one, Krishna uses six hands and two feet to pleasure a group of admiring *gopis* (milkmaids) and two more hands to play the flute. Downstairs, a number of less detailed paintings show divine sexual scenes set in a beautiful forest. Rooms without murals make up a **museum** and house oil portraits of Cochin rajas with their palanquins, robes, weapons, Dutch drawings, and umbrellas. (Palace open Sa-Th 10am-5pm. Rs2. No photography permitted.)

VYPEEN ISLAND

Miles of ignored **beaches** roll along the Arabian Sea on Vypeen Island, passing a **Lighthouse** at Ochanthuruth (1.5km west of the main road; open daily 3-5pm) and the early 16th-century **Pallipuran Fort** (open Th 10am-5pm). The beaches are empty, except for herds of sunbathing cows and a few fishing boats, until the in-season, when scattered foreigners arrive. Men come from the nearby villages to see the show—women are advised to swim in a t-shirt and shorts or pants. **Cherai Beach,** just a few kilometers shy of the northern tip of the island, is frequented by more foreigners and is probably safer for women than the others. From Vypeen Island, catch one of the frequent buses (50min., Rs5.75) to Cherai Junction. From there, continue away from Vypeen and bear left (west) onto Cherai Beach Rd. for a scenic walk to the beach (15min.; Rs20 by rickshaw). Sprinkled along the main road are bakeries and produce stands; just before Cherai Beach, the tranquil **Kadaloram** serves the usual snacks for Rs10-20 and Chinese and Indian cuisine for Rs20-60. (Open daily 8am-9:30pm.) **Ferries** run between Vypeen Island and Ernakulam's Main Jetty (every 20min. 5:30am-10:30pm). Ferries from Ft. Cochin to Vypeen (6:30am-9pm) depart from the launch opposite the bus stand.

■ ENTERTAINMENT

KATHAKALI DANCE

Cochin offers spectacular nightly performances of ▨**kathakali dance,** Kerala's startling and gorgeous brand of traditional music and movement (see p. 339). Frequently geared toward tourists, these performances are usually prefaced by elaborate make-up demonstrations, an explanation of the music and hand-symbols, and a synopsis of the tale to be enacted. Performances last from one hour to 90min., or, in true authenticity, a whopping eight hours.

ANY MATZOH WITH THAT PALAK PANEER?

Jews probably first came to Kerala during the 10th century BC as traders from King Solomon's Israel; 1000 years later, the Romans destroyed the Temple in Jerusalem, dispersing Jews throughout Europe. A few landed in Shingly (30km north of Cochin, now known as Cranganore) a few years later. Their descendants still live in Cochin today. In AD 379, Joseph Rabban, was made a prince of Anjuvanam and established a Jewish Kingdom. Around AD 500, another large group of Jews immigrated here from Iraq and Iran. During the Portuguese Inquisition in the 16th century, the Jews were expelled from Shingly. Legend has it that Joseph Azar, the last surviving Jewish prince, swam to Cochin with his wife on his shoulders. The Jewish Keralans placed themselves under the protection of the Raja of Cochin, who gave them a parcel of land for a synagogue next to his palace (see p. 339).

Emigration to Mumbai and Israel has pared Cochin's Jewish population down to a geriatric group of 14, but you'll still see menorahs in some of the windows. There has been no rabbi here for several years, so the elders of the synagogue conduct ceremonies and make decisions regarding Jewish law. Happy to discuss their future with visitors, the remaining Jews seem unconcerned about the survival of their community. Sixty or seventy Jews remain in Kerala, along with some four to five thousand in India as a whole, most of whom live in Mumbai.

Kerala Kathakali Centre (☎221827). Near the Ft. Cochin bus stand and the Chinese fishing nets, has a young troupe of artists who perform in a dockside version of a black-box theater. Lively and fun. Make-up 5pm, performance 6:30pm; Rs100.

See India Foundation (☎369471). From MG Rd. in Ernakulam, head east on Warriam Rd. for 2 blocks; the Foundation is on the right under the painted face. Director Devan has been performing here for 30 years. Make-up 5:45pm, performance 6:45pm; Rs100.

Kerala Kathakali Kendra, Bolghatty Island (☎355003). In the Bolghatty Palace Hotel near the jetty. A good pretext for visiting this palace built by the Dutch in 1744. Make-up 6pm, performance 7pm; Rs100.

Cochin Cultural Centre (☎380366). From Jos Junction in Ernakulam, head south on MG Rd., turn left on Sahodaran Ayappan Rd., right on Chittoor Rd., and finally, left onto Manikath Rd. Make-up 5:30pm, performance 6:30pm; Rs125.

AYURVEDIC BLISS

The **Kerala Ayurveda Pharmacy,** on Warriam Rd. in Ernakulam, just east of MG Rd., is one of many places in Cochin that offers **ayurvedic massage.** (☎361202. Open M-Sa 8am-7pm, Su 8am-4pm; men only M-Sa 4-7pm. Rs350, with steam wash Rs450.) The **Sree Narayana Holistic Clinic,** on Vypeen Island, offers a full body ayurvedic massage and steam bath as well as an excellent home-cooked Keralite meal for Rs600. (☎502362. Open for appointments daily 9:30am-5pm. The doctor will pick you up from the Vypeen ferry jetty. Many guest houses also set up appointments.) Since it's an important component of *kathakali*, several dance centers also offer ayurvedic massage by appointment: **Cochin Cultural Centre** (☎380366), **Chavara Cultural Centre** (☎368443), and **Kerala Kathakali Kendra** (☎740030).

■ BACKWATER CRUISES

Beyond the city lie magical green fields, towering palms, and lazy backwaters—some of India's most remarkably green and pleasant landscapes. Kerala's tourist industry has capitalized on all this, offering ▓**backwater tours** on non-motorized boats through the maze of lagoons, lakes, canals, and streams. A guide paddles the vessel, which can hold four to eight people, for several enchanting hours, stopping for a fresh coconut break and a stroll through paddy fields. The whole scene is enthralling, especially for bird-watchers. The tours also offer a unique opportunity to see Keralite village life up close without the feeling of being an invasive tourist. Some tours provide a traditional lunch on banana leaves. **Moonlight cruises** on full-moon nights are offered in season. The **Tourist Desk,** Main Jetty, Ernakulam, charters daily tours. In season, reserve at least one day in advance; off season, show up 30min. before departure. (☎371761. Tours 9am-1:30pm and 2-6:30pm; Rs300, save Rs50 by booking directly at the Tourist Office.) The **KTDC** also provides backwater tours on country boats (8:30am and 2:30pm; Rs315, minimum two people), and water tours of Cochin from the Sealord Jetty (day cruise 9am-12:30pm and 2-5pm, Rs70; sunset cruise 5:30 and 7:30pm, Rs40). Most hotels also arrange backwater cruises and offer an additional 6hr. cruise that includes a tasty traditional lunch (Rs800; inquire at any hotel).

MUNNAR വുന്നാർ ☎0486

A scruffy little town surrounded by soaring mountain peaks and miles of rolling tea plantations, Munnar is an invigorating antidote to the steamy heat of the plains. Towered over by Mt. Anaimudi (2694m), it is also the highest point in India south of the Himalayas. It was a Scot, J.D. Munro, who kicked off the town's development during the 1870s, creating a fiefdom for generations of Scottish tea-planters. When Munro and friends finally left in the 1970s, they left their rolling oceans of tea to Tata Tea Ltd., an offshoot of the same Parsi-owned mega-company that built the bus that brought you here. Tea dominates every aspect of life in Munnar today, though the burgeoning tourist industry contributes more and more to the local economy every year. Munnar is trying to reinvent itself as a hill station, and its unique mix of climate, wildlife, and scenery will not go unnoticed for long.

⌂ TRANSPORTATION. Buses depart from the KSRTC bus station, 2km south of town; most buses also stop by the main bazaar in the center of town. To: **Cochin** (5hr.; 8 per day 5:30am-1:50pm; Rs45); **Coimbatore** (6hr.; 6:30am and 3:30pm; Rs50); **Madurai** (6hr.; 2:30pm; Rs48); **Theni** (4hr.; 13 per day 4:30am-7:30pm). **Jeeps** and **rickshaws** (Rs20 from "New" to "Old" Munnar) are hard to miss; bargain hard.

▊▊ ORIENTATION AND PRACTICAL INFORMATION. In Tamil, Munnar means "Three Rivers," and the heart of the town centers on the point where the three rivers meet. The road from Cochin enters the relatively flat valley alongside the main river 3km south of Munnar's town center. Several budget hotels, restaurants, tourist offices, and local bus stands are compacted into the bazaar here, overlooked by the **Tata Tea Regional Headquarters** on Cochin Rd. Joseph Iype, in his tiny **tourist information shop** in the main bazaar, is Munnar's local action hero. Keen to share the delights of the region, he can provide bus times, tours, and hiking maps. He also offers lodging in his cottage and will find you a doctor if you need one. Batteries sold separately. (☎531136, or at home 530349. Open daily 9am-1pm and 3-6pm.) You can change money at the **Federal Bank,** a short walk from the main bazaar with the temple on your right. (Open M-F 10am-2pm, Sa 10am-noon.) Farther along the same road is the town **hospital.** The only place in Munnar with Internet access is **Ramm Communications,** close to Krishna Lodge and the Chicken Corner restaurant in the bazaar. (Rs60 per hr. Open daily 8am-9:30pm.) The **post office** is across the river from Tata Tea. (Open M-Sa 8am-5pm.) **Postal Code:** 685612.

ⁿℂ ACCOMMODATIONS AND FOOD. Most of the cheap eating and sleeping options are in the center of town. **Hilltop Lodge ❶**, is the best of Munnar's basic lodges. Clean, compact rooms come with attached squat toilets. (☎530655. Singles Rs150; doubles Rs215.) **Krishna Lodge ❶**, on the opposite side of the river, has singles with shared bath or doubles with clean, attached bath and seat toilets. (☎530669. Singles Rs100; doubles Rs250.) **Iype's Cottage ❶**, a snug cottage up in the hills owned by Joe Iype, is a short ride through the tea plantations. Comfortable rooms with hot water and seat toilets. (☎530349 or 531136. Rs400-500.)

The snazziest place to eat in the center of town is the **Silver Spoon Restaurant ❶**, in the Munnar Inn next to the bus stand—a brand new shiny place serving a wide range of Indian and Western dishes such as chicken 65 (Rs90), beef pepper fry (Rs45), and mutton *vindaloo* (Rs55). (Open daily 8:30am-9:30pm.) Another good mid-range option is **Greens ❶**, in the East End Hotel, a short walk from the main bazaar. It's a big, wide, airy place with an extensive menu that ranges from fish curry (Rs45) to fried chicken (Rs75), plus *aloo mutter* (Rs40) and *navratan korma* (Rs40). (Open daily 7:30am-9:30pm.) In the bazaar itself, **Rapsy Restaurant ❶**, (aka **Chicken Corner**) is a nifty little place deservedly popular for its efficient service and excellent spicy chicken dishes. They offer chicken 65 (Rs50), egg roast (Rs10), and veg. *biryani* (Rs25). (Open daily 9am-8pm.) For "meals" and all other fall-back favorites, the **Hotel Plaza ❶**, attached to the Hill Top Lodge, tempts with egg *biryani* (Rs28) and fish curry (Rs15). (Open daily 7am-9pm.)

◐◪ SIGHTS AND HIKING. The best way to experience Munnar is to stroll through the tea fields and splash around in the waterfalls. Large cascades can be found just off Cochin Rd. They are accessible by foot with the option of returning by local bus. Fifteen kilometers away is a lake with boating and (land-bound) elephants. For more information on these places and other scenic walks around Munnar, see Joseph Iype in his tourist information shop in the bazaar.

Munnar's biggest attraction is the **◪Eravikulam National Park**, 15km away, established in 1978 to protect the spectacular Mt. Anaimundi (2694m), the highest Indian peak south of the Himalayas. The mountain and its surroundings are home to the endangered Nilgiri tahr (only 2500 are left), a mountain goat that's a lot more interesting than it sounds. The park's ecosystem also supports gaur, wild dogs, jungle cats, mongoose, and barking deer. Surrounded by beautiful tea fields, visitors can stroll past waterfalls and through fields of grass along the mountainside to where the wild goats are. Take an auto-rickshaw from town to the second forest check-point (one-way Rs100, with 1hr. wait Rs150), the farthest a rickshaw can go. From there, it is a 2km walk up to Rajamalai Gap on the mountain's shoulder and then another 4km down to a tea factory. Unless you have a rickshaw waiting for you, walk 4km back down the hill from the check-point to catch a local bus on Munnar Rd. *(Park admission Rs50 for foreigners, Rs10 for Indians, rickshaw fee Rs5.)*

Lockhart Mountain offers another superb mountain ridge hike. Take a bus (Rs3) or a rickshaw (Rs120) to Lockhart Gap. The round-trip hike takes about 3hr. and offers some spectacular views. A lazier way to soak in the scenery is to bus it to **Top Station.** The first bus of the day (1½hr., 7:15am) should get you there before the clouds come down and the haze comes up.

◖◪ ENTERTAINMENT AND NIGHTLIFE. Tata Tea isn't exactly keen on conducting **tours** of its factories, but a little polite persistence or a word with Joe Iype may prove fruitful. If you have extra reserves of patience left over, you might also try to get yourself admitted to the exclusive members-only **High Range Club,** where the old world atmosphere of the planters' social world still lives on in the gentlemen's bar, lined with hunting trophies and a collection of venerable headwear. Call first to speak to the club secretary (☎530253) and be prepared to dig around at the bottom of your pack for clean clothes and evidence of Scottish ancestry.

COCO-LOCO The coconut tree, or *kalpa vrishka*, "the heaven-gifted tree" as Malayalees call it, and its products are everywhere in Kerala, from the rug beneath your feet to the bed you sleep in at night. Coconut trees mature in 7-8 years. Every 40 days, a flower bud pops out among the leaves, containing a sticky liquid which ferments into toddy, the sweet local booze that gets stronger as the day goes on. Each bud blossoms into 10-12 tender coconuts within three months; the sweet water inside will mellow even the meanest toddy hangover. In a year, the water inside dries and condenses into white coconut meat, which is grated and used in cooking. The drying coconuts you see along the roadside are squashed for coconut oil, which is used in cooking, ayurvedic massages, and Kathakali make-up. The fibrous husks of the coconut shells are spun into *coir* ropes and woven into mats. The shells are used to make spoons, cups, bowls, and vases, and as charcoal for cooking sweets. Dried palm fronds thatch roofs and are woven into hut walls and fences; stems are used as brooms. After 80 years this hard-working tree is felled and sculpted into furniture.

TRICHUR (THRISSUR) തൃശ്ശൂർ ☎ 0487

Though Trichur bills itself as the "cultural capital of Kerala," its only real draw is the annual **Puram Festival,** held in early May. During Puram, deity-bearing revelers from neighboring villages descend on the town, heralded by musicians and brightly decorated elephants. Trichur isn't worth a detour during the rest of the year, though its temple and park make it a fine stopover.

▐▀ TRANSPORTATION

Trains: The **railway station** (☎ 423150) is on Railway Station Rd. Fares listed are 2nd class. To: **Bangalore** (12hr.; 4:30 and 9:25pm; Rs113); **Calicut** (3hr.; 6 per day 4am-6pm; Rs56); **Chennai** (12hr.; 5 per day; Rs204); **Delhi** (43hr.; 5:20 and 7:30pm; Rs495); **Ernakulam** (1½hr.; frequent; Rs44); **Kanyakumari** (11hr.; 4:25am and 4pm; Rs195); **Mangalore** (10hr.; 12:45am and 12:30pm; Rs247); **Margao** (12hr.; 2-3 per day 11:35am-7:55pm; Rs235); **Mumbai** (26hr.; 1-2 per day 9:30am and 2:10pm; Rs369); **Trivandrum** (6hr.; 8 per day; Rs111).

Buses: The **KSRTC bus stand,** Masjid Rd. (☎ 421150), is near the railway station, south of Railway Station Rd. To: **Alleppey** (3½hr.; frequent; Rs70); **Calicut** (3hr.; frequent; Rs45); **Chennai** (14hr.; 2:50 and 5:30pm; Rs186); **Coimbatore** (2½hr.; frequent; Rs43); **Ernakulam** (2hr.; frequent; Rs30); **Kottayam** (3hr.; frequent; Rs50); **Mangalore** (12hr.; 7:30am and 9pm; Rs147); **Trivandrum** (7hr.; frequent; Rs105). **Sakthan Thampuran Bus Stand,** TB Rd., 1.5km south of the Round (follow MO Rd. south), has frequent private buses to **Guruvayur.**

Local Transportation: Most of Trichur's sights and accommodations are within walking distance. **Auto-rickshaws** are plentiful. Rs6 first km, Rs3 per km thereafter.

◤▐ ORIENTATION AND PRACTICAL INFORMATION

Trichur is laid out like a wheel. The hubcap is the vast, green **Swaraj Round,** the site of the **Vadakkunathan Temple.** The major roads are the spokes: moving clockwise from the western edge, these are **Mahatma Gandhi (MG), Shornur, Palace, College, High, Municipal Office (MO), Chembottil, Kurrapam,** and **Marar Rd.** Most hotels and restaurants are on these thoroughfares, near the Round. **Railway Station Rd.** runs east-west, 500m south of the Round; to get to the KSRTC **bus stand** and **railway station,** head south down Kurrapam Rd. from the Round to Railway Station Rd. and follow the signs.

Tourist Office: KTDC, near the corner of Palace and Museum Rd., across from the Town Hall, provides advice about Trichur and travel throughout Kerala. Open daily 9am-5pm.

Currency Exchange: State Bank of Travancore, Town Hall Rd. (☎331302). Just off Round East. Changes cash and AmEx traveler's checks. Open M-F 10am-2pm and 2:30-3:30pm, Sa 10am-12:30pm.

Pharmacy: Girija Medical Stores, Round South (☎421571). Open daily 8:45am-8:45pm.

Hospital: Jubilee Mission Hospital (☎420361), East Fort. Northeast of the city center. The best private hospital. Auto-rickshaw from city center Rs10.

Police: East Police Station (☎421400), off MO Rd. Just south of Railway Station Rd.

Internet: Bhavana Systems and Communications, MO Rd. (☎424708). 3rd fl. of the bldg. opposite the Municipal Office. Rs60 per hr. Open M-Sa 9am-6pm.

Post Office: Trichur City Post Office, Railway Station Rd. at MO Rd. Open M-Sa 9am-5pm. **Postal Code:** 680001.

ACCOMMODATIONS

During Puram, the room rates listed below often quadruple. Check-out 24hr. Backpackers are scarce in Trichur; get ready to meet lots of middle-aged businessmen.

Alukkas Tourist Home, Railway Station Rd. (☎424067). Opposite the bus station. The best option for those arriving on late-night buses, this hotel welcomes you with a barrage of newspapers and blaring Keralite TV. Soap, towels, and seat toilets. Singles Rs215-325; doubles Rs275-400. ❷

Chandy's Tourist Hotel, Railway Station Rd. (☎421167). Between the bus and train stations. Simple rooms with attached bath at this cheap and convenient place. Singles Rs95; doubles Rs170. ❶

Hotel Elite International, Chembottil Ln. (☎421033). Off the Round South, between Kurrappam and Municipal Office Rd. Comfortable place with 24hr. hot water, phones, seat toilets, and balconies with city and parking lot views. Attached restaurant. Singles Rs260-500; doubles Rs370-650. ❷

FOOD

▨ **Delite Sweet Parlour,** on Round South at the corner of Chembottil Ln., turns out excellent sweet and savory snacks (Rs3-10) with a crumbly Mysore *pak* (Rs8) to write home about. Open daily 9am-8:30pm. ❶

Hotel Bharath Restaurant, Chembottil Ln. Between Round South and Railway Station Rd. Cheap South (*thali* Rs18) and North Indian veg. fare (*aloo gobhi* Rs19). Frenetic at mealtimes and justly popular. Open daily 6:30am-10:30pm. ❶

Ming Palace, opposite the Hotel Elite, on the 2nd fl. of the Pathans bldg. Chinese and Thai dishes (Rs25-50) served by a courteous staff. Open daily 11am-10pm. ❶

SIGHTS AND ENTERTAINMENT

Most tourists know Trichur only by its association with the annual **Puram Festival** in early May. Featuring a multitude of elephants, onlookers, and noisy bands, the festival is Indian pageantry at its very best. Hotels fill up fast and charge exorbitant rates during the festival, so plan well in advance, or better yet, just make a daytrip from Cochin. It is held on the grounds of the **Vadakkunathan Temple,** the oldest and largest temple complex in the state, which lies at the center of the Swaraj Round in the heart of town. Dedicated to Shiva, the temple sits on the site where Nandi, Shiva's bull, is said to have rested. The temple is closed to non-Hindus.

KERALA

Outside of Puram, you'll be hard pressed to have a rip-roaring good time in Trichur. Check out the exterior of the **Vadakkumnathan Temple** at the center of the Round, since you probably won't be allowed inside. In the northeast corner of Trichur, 2km from the Round, you'll find a zoo and museum complex. Though the **zoo** is full of school kids gawking at depressed animals in tiny cages, the **art museum** on the same grounds has some decent sculptures and carvings. There is also a "multipurpose" museum that contains plenty of dusty *kathakali* dance costumes, dried leaves, and what are presumably the stuffed remains of erstwhile zoo occupants. (Open Tu-Su 10am-5pm. Free.) You'll find more carvings at the **Archaeological Museum,** 100m farther along Museum Rd. (Open Tu-Su 9:30am-5pm. Free.)

The **market area** behind Municipal Office Rd. is worth exploring; colorful vegetable and spice stands pack the narrow streets. The pretty **Puttanpalli Church,** just off High Rd., is also worth a look-see. (Open M-Sa 9am-5:30pm, Su 2-4pm.)

CALICUT (KOZHIKODE) കോഴിക്കോട ☎0495

Calicut was the harbor of choice for Chinese and Middle Eastern spice traders as early as the 7th century, and this mercantile mayhem expanded to Europe in 1498 when Vasco da Gama trod his first subcontinental steps just north of here. Eventually Tipu Sultan trashed the region in 1789, but the British took over three years later and immortalized Calicut by dubbing the locally produced fabric "calico." Those who imagine a city of ruined forts, wharfside temples, and cartloads of black pepper have probably been reading too much Salman Rushdie (part of his *The Moor's Last Sigh* is set here). Still, the heaping piles of mangos and brimming sacks of dried chili peppers add charm to this small city, which serves mainly as a stopover for tourists between Cochin and Mysore.

▐ TRANSPORTATION

Flights: The **airport** is in Karipur, 28km from Calicut. Taxis cost Rs150-200. **Air India,** Eroh Centre, Bank Rd., 1st fl. (☎766669). Open M-Sa 9:30am-5:30pm. To **Mumbai** (1½hr., 5 per week, US$100). **Indian Airlines** (☎766243), is next door. Open M-Sa 10am-5:35pm. To: **Chennai** (1½-2hr., 4 per week, US$90); **Coimbatore** (30min., 1 per day, US$40); **Mumbai** (1½hr., 2 per day, US$140).

Trains: The **railway station** (☎703822), is 1km south of the park; follow Town Hall Rd. To: **Chennai** (18hr., 1:30am and 4:35pm); **Delhi** (36hr., 1-2 per day 3:15am and 5pm, Rs489); **Ernakulam** (5hr., 3-4 per day 6:40am-11:45pm, Rs83); **Mangalore** (5hr., 5-6 per day 12:55am-6pm, Rs95); **Trivandrum** (9hr., 3 per day 8:50am-11:40pm).

Buses: There are several bus stands in town. **KSRTC Bus Stand,** Mavoor Rd. (☎723796), is not far from the intersection with Bank Rd. To: **Bangalore** (8½hr., 9 per day 7am-11:45pm, Rs130); **Cochin** (5½hr., 30 per day, Rs95); **Mangalore** (7hr., 4 per day, Rs97); **Mysore** (5½-6½hr., 19 per day 6am-11:30pm, Rs81); **Trivandrum** (10½hr., 15 per day 12:30pm-midnight, Rs195). Cleaner and cheaper **private buses** run from the bus stand farther down Mavoor Rd., at the intersection with Stadium Rd. To: **Cochin** (6hr., 6 per day, Rs73); **Devala,** near Ooty (10hr., 2:15pm, Rs56); **Mangalore** (6hr., 5 per day, Rs73); **Mysore** (6hr., 6 and 8:30am, Rs73).

Local Transportation: Auto-rickshaws are your best bet (Rs6 per km). **Taxis** are unmetered and everywhere. **Local buses** run around town, to Beypore and to the beach.

⚐ ▐ ORIENTATION AND PRACTICAL INFORMATION

Calicut's layout is a confused mess; it's easiest to get around by the cheap and omnipresent auto-rickshaws. At the center of town is **Ansari Park,** which is flanked to the west by **Town Hall Rd.,** and to the east by **Bank Rd.,** which turns into **GH Rd.**

SM Rd. begins at the south end of the park and runs between Town Hall Rd. and GH Rd. **Mavoor Rd. (Indira Gandhi Rd.)** veers east off Bank Rd., leading to the KSRTC and private **bus stations.** To the south, GH Rd. intersects with east-west **MM Ali Rd.,** which leads east to an older part of the city, and west to the beach as **Palayam Rd.** The **railway station** is on Town Hall Rd., south of the park. The **beach,** 2km west of the town center, is unsafe at night.

Tourist Office: The **KTDC** office (☎ 722392) is at the reception desk of the Malabar Mansion, on the south side of the park. Open 24hr. The **Kerala Tourism Information Booth** (☎ 702606) at the railway station can also help. Open M-Sa 10am-1pm and 2-5pm.

Budget Travel: PL Worldways, Lakhotia Computer Centre, 3rd fl. (☎ 722564). At the intersection of Mavoor and Bank Rd. Books airline reservations and processes foreign visas. Open M-F 9:30am-1pm and 2-5:30pm, Sa 9:30am-1:30pm.

Currency Exchange: State Bank of India, Bank Rd. (☎ 721321). Changes currency and traveler's checks. Open M-F 10am-2pm, Sa 10am-noon. **PL Worldways** (see above) also cashes traveler's checks.

Police: Manachira (☎ 722673). On the east edge of the park.

Hospital: National Hospital, Mavoor Rd. (☎ 723061 or 723062). Near the intersection with Bank Rd. The best in town. Its **pharmacy** is open daily 8am-midnight.

Internet: Metropolitan Internet Point, Bank Rd. (☎ 310904). On the 2nd fl., above the Cochin Bakery. Rs50 per hr. Open M-Sa 10am-10pm.

Post Office: (☎ 722663). On the west edge of the park. Open M-Sa 10am-7:45pm, Su 2-4:45pm. **Postal Code:** 673001.

ACCOMMODATIONS

A legion of (mostly) high-quality tourist homes vies for your business in Calicut.

Sasthapuri Tourist Home (☎ 723281). Down MM Ali Rd. from GH Rd., on the left. Good value in a lively part of town, convenient to the train and bus stations. Attached bath. Don't miss the fern-filled rooftop and its lovely restaurant (open 5-10pm). Check-out 24hr. Singles Rs75-120; doubles Rs150-250. ●

Malabar Mansion (☎ 722391). On the south side of the park. KTDC-run, with a tourist reception desk, snack-bar, restaurant, and beer parlor. All rooms have TV, phone, and attached bath. Check-out 24hr. Singles Rs185-360; doubles Rs225-400. ❷

Kalpaka Tourist Home, Town Hall Rd. (☎ 720222). Just south of the park. The decor is spartan, but the owners run the place efficiently. Big beds, in big rooms. Hot water 24hr. Check-out 24hr. Singles Rs250; doubles Rs322. MC/V. ●

Metro Tourist Home (☎ 766029). At the junction of Mavoor and Bank Rd. In the frenetic heart of town. All rooms have seat toilets and A/C. Doubles Rs200-500. ●

FOOD

Woodlands Restaurant, in the Hotel Whitelines on GH Rd., not far from the intersection with MM Ali Rd. Feels more like a diner than a *dhaba,* but its excellent all-veg. food is the real thing. *Thalis* Rs25-40. Open daily 8am-10pm. ●

Dakshin-The Veg, Mavoor Rd. Near the intersection with Bank Rd. Good food, great name. Self-service downstairs; A/C and non-A/C restaurants upstairs. North Indian veg. dishes Rs35; South Indian *thali* Rs25. Open daily 6am-11pm. ●

Cochin Bakery, opposite the State Bank of India. Spicy snacks, cold drinks, and pastries from Rs4. Open daily 7am-10pm. ●

Malabar Mansion Restaurant, in KTDC hotel, 1st fl., serves up the usual assortment of dishes (Rs25-35), and has eggs for breakfast (Rs12-15). Open daily 7am-10pm. ●

KERALA

⬤ 🎭 SIGHTS AND ENTERTAINMENT

ANSARI PARK. Ansari Park, also known as **Manchira Maidan,** gives a splash of well-maintained green to Calicut's center. The **tank** on the western edge of the park is all that remains of a palace built by one of the local rulers, the Zamorin king Manavikrama. The public **library** on the south edge of the park is a good example of traditional Keralite architecture. Every evening at the park, a little guy in a box madly flips switches to manipulate a **Music Fountain** choreographed to Hindi pop. *(30min.; show at 7:15pm; Rs3.)* The art deco **Crown Theatre,** Town Hall Rd., at the southwest corner of the park, screens Western films.

BEACH. The city's long, sandy **beach,** just 2km from the city center, is worth a visit. Head north on the beach; farther from town, fishermen and their colorful boats take over the scene.

MUSEUMS. The **Pazhassiraja Museum** is one of those all-purpose Indian museums that contain everything anyone ever thought of putting in a museum and lots of other stuff too. Most of it is junk, but downstairs there are a number of well displayed stone carvings. *(East Hill, 5km from Calicut; rickshaw Rs35. Or take a bus from in front of the Hotel Malabar Mansion to West Hill—15min.; Rs2—get off at the stop opposite St. Michael's Church, take the first right, then left where the street ends, and right at that street's end. Head uphill on the left fork to the museum. Open Tu-Su 10am-1pm and 2-4:30pm. Free.)* Around the back, the **Krishna Menon Museum** houses the personal belongings of the late Indian president (b. Calicut 1896, d. Delhi 1974), including his Seiko watch and a couple of portraits of Lenin. The **Art Gallery** upstairs contains a collection of paintings by Raja Ravi Varma and Raja Raja Varma. *(Museums and gallery open Tu-Su 10am-5pm.)*

SHOPPING. Calicut has always been a trading city; indulging in a bit of bartering and haggling can provide plenty of entertainment. For giant quantities of spices, veggies, and fruits, visit the **market** around the old bus station on MM Ali Rd. east of GH Rd. The **Comtrust Store,** south of the park and just off Town Hall Rd. produces the hand-loomed fabrics that made Calicut famous. *(Open M-Sa 10am-1pm and 2:30-7pm.)*

MADHYA PRADESH
मध्य प्रदेश

True to its name, Madhya Pradesh (the "Middle State") stretches right across the center of India. Outside the fertile and heavily populated Narmada River Valley, the land is dominated by dense forests, scrubby hills, and ravines, which provide an unravaged homeland for the region's indigenous groups and a refuge for *dacoits* (bandits) and tigers. Also hidden and protected by the forests are the ruined cities of Mandu and Orchha, as well as the erotic temple carvings of Khajuraho.

During the 3rd century BC, the great Buddhist convert-king Ashoka founded Sanchi as a religious center. Mughal emperors ruled the region from the north until they lost control to the Marathas, who ruled until Independence. Today, 93% of the population is Hindu, and state politics are dominated by the BJP, but the landscape of Madhya Pradesh—from its ancient Buddhist pilgrimage sites to its timeless national parks—preserves vivid reminders of a rich and varied past. In November 2000, Madhya Pradesh was divided into two states, Madhya Pradesh in the north and **Chattisgarh** in the south. Our coverage includes no destinations in Chattisgarh, a region with few claims to fame except its natural resources.

HIGHLIGHTS OF MADHYA PRADESH

Madhya Pradesh has the largest tiger population of any Indian state, and **Kanha National Park** (p. 367), the *Jungle Book's* inspiration, is the best place to see them.

The middle-of-nowhere temple town of **Khajuraho** (p. 368), with its titillating erotic sculpture, is one of the great architectural marvels of the world.

The 3rd century BC Buddhist *stupas* at **Sanchi** (p. 354), perched atop a lush green hill and pleasantly devoid of touts, are easily accessible and well worth any detour.

The ruins of the town of **Mandu** (p. 360) open a window onto the Muslim Malwa culture of the 14th century.

The fort in **Gwalior** (p. 384) is one of the most impressive in India.

BHOPAL भोपाल   ☎ 0755

The capital of Madhya Pradesh, Bhopal (pop. 1.2 million) is one of those cities that should be great to visit but just falls short. Its good range of hotels, great restaurants, two lakes, and several mosques are not sufficient to warrant a visit to Bhopal, save as a transit point to the nearby Buddhist retreat at Sanchi, or elsewhere. The program of civic improvements begun during the 19th century left the city with lakes and parks; however, the 20th century transformed Bhopal into an industrial metropolis that proved lethal when, in December 1984, thousands of people died in a toxic gas leak from a Union Carbide factory in northern Bhopal.

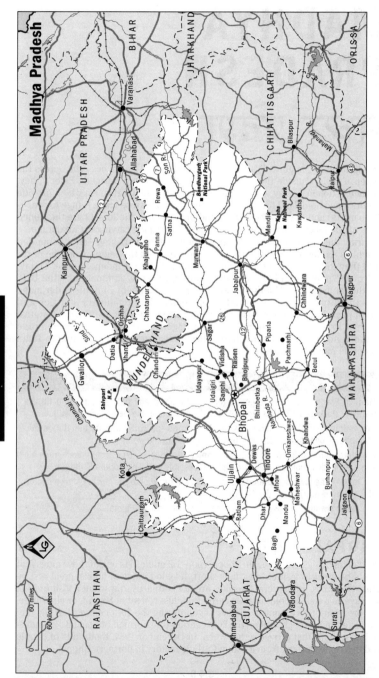

TRANSPORTATION

Flights: The **airport** is on Agra Rd. (☎521277), 12km from the city center (taxis Rs100-150; rickshaws Rs80-100). **Indian Airlines** (☎770480), next door to the Gangotri Building in TT Nagar, past the Rang Mahal cinema 100m on the left. Open daily 10am-1pm and 2-5pm. To **Delhi** (2hr., daily noon, US$125) and **Mumbai** (2hr., daily 4pm, US$135) via **Indore** (30min., $55).

Trains: Railway station (☎131). Down the street and off the bend in Hamidia Rd., 1km east of the bus station, exit through platform #5. Reservation office outside platform #1, on the far right as you face the station. Open M-Sa 8am-8pm, Su 8am-2pm. Prices listed are for 2nd class sleeper. To: **Delhi** (8-12hr., 16-20 per day 12:40am-10:40pm, Rs221) via **Agra** (6-8hr., Rs174); **Gwalior** (4½-6hr., Rs138); **Hyderabad** (15-22hr., 2-4 per day 3:43am-11:35pm, Rs267) via **Indore** (4-6hr., 4 per day 7:50am-9:40pm, Rs67) via **Ujjain** (3hr., Rs52); **Jabalpur** (7½hr., 1-2 per day 4 and 11pm, Rs81-126); **Jhansi** (3-4½hr., Rs112); **Mumbai** (16hr., 2 per day 6am and 4:50pm, Rs245).

Buses: Nadra Bus Stand (☎540841). Hamidia Rd., west of the train station, 1km down on the right. Frequent departures for **Indore** (5hr., every 10min. 6am-6:30pm, Rs60) and other cities around the state. Private operators outside the bus stand run to **Sanchi** (1½hr., frequent 6am-6pm, Rs19).

Local Transportation: Auto-rickshaws overcharge madly: Rs5.50 to start, and the metered rate is Rs3.75 per km. **Minibuses** will take you almost as far for much less. Minibus #9 goes from the railway station to TT Nagar; #7 and 11 go by Sultania Rd.; #2 goes from Hamidia Rd. to New Market and MP Nagar.

ORIENTATION AND PRACTICAL INFORMATION

The huge **Upper Lake** and smaller **Lower Lake** separate Old Bhopal in the northwest from the **New Town** in the southeast. **Hamidia Rd.** runs near the Taj-ul-Masjid (the city's largest mosque) on the western fringes of the old town, past the **bus stand** to the **railway station** in the east. If arriving by train, exit via platform #5 for Hamidia Rd. From the station area, with its many cheap hotels and restaurants, Hamidia Rd. turns right and runs south toward the new town and government center. The MPSTDC, Indian Airlines office, and the banks are all in **TT Nagar. MPSTDC main office,** 4th fl., Gangotri Building, TT Nagar, New Town, offers tourist services and additional branches in the airport and railway station. (☎774340. Open M-F and 1st and 4th Sa 10:30am-5pm.) In TT Nagar are the **State Bank of India,** Parcharad Building (☎564118; open M-F 10:30am-2:30pm) and **IDBI Bank,** in TT Nagar (open M-F 10am-4pm and Sa 10am-2pm). The **police station** is on Sultania Rd. (☎540880) and **Hamidia Hospital** is on Royal Market Rd. (☎540222) and has a **24hr. pharmacy. Loveknot Photo State & Net Cafe,** at 1 Hamidia Rd. (☎255712), has fast connections for Rs30 per hr. (Open daily 7:30am-11pm.) Good luck retrieving your *Poste Restante* from the **Post Office** on Sultania Rd., opposite the Taj-ul-Masjid. Open M-Sa 7am-6pm. **Postal Code:** 462001.

ACCOMMODATIONS

Hotels in Bhopal cater largely to business travelers. There are not many good budget places around, and every place in town levies taxes and service charges of up to 20%. This does mean, though, that "luxuries" like TVs, telephones, and attached bathrooms are pretty standard. **Hotel Sonali ❸,** on Radha Talkies Rd., has luxurious clean rooms with hot-water showers, TVs, 24hr. room service and check-out. (☎533880. Singles Rs210-700; doubles Rs285-800.) **Hotel Meghdoot ❶,** is left from the train station on Hamidia Rd. (☎713407 or 710131. Singles Rs126; doubles Rs250-350.) **Hotel Banjara ❷,** though pricey, is complete with balconies and sparkling, spacious rooms. (☎544585. Singles Rs300-500; doubles Rs400-900.)

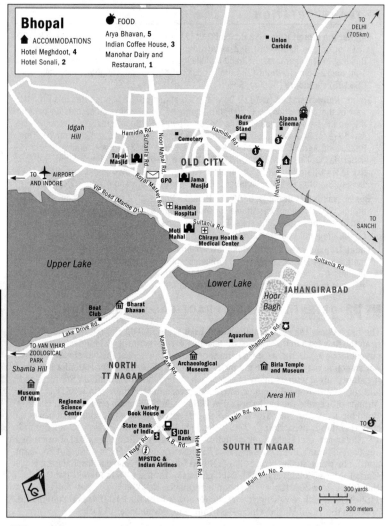

Bhopal

🏠 ACCOMMODATIONS
Hotel Meghdoot, **4**
Hotel Sonali, **2**

🍎 FOOD
Arya Bhavan, **5**
Indian Coffee House, **3**
Manohar Dairy and
Restaurant, **1**

FOOD

Restaurants in Bhopal offer a wide selection of surprisingly good fare. **Indian Coffee House ❶,** on Hamidia Rd., opposite Hotel Ranjit, is the friendliest restaurant in town with great snacks for Rs10-30 and superb coffee for Rs6-10. (Open daily 7am-10pm.) Equally pleasant is **Manohar Dairy and Restaurant ❶,** 6 Hamidia Rd., which offers good, cheap South Indian fare and lively service. South Indian snacks Rs10-40, fresh juices Rs12-20, pizza Rs30-40, a wide variety of desserts Rs12-45. (Open daily 6am-midnight.) **Arya Bhavan ❶,** in MP Nagar, Zone II., offers excellent vegetarian food and delicious desserts at reasonable prices around Rs24-50. (Open daily 11am-3pm and 7-10:30pm.)

🎵 👁 ENTERTAINMENT AND SIGHTS

BHARAT BHAVAN. A cultural center that produces exhibitions of theater, music, poetry, and the fine arts, the Bharat Bhavan is one of India's finest museums. Architect Charles Correa crafted it into a charming public space with multi-layered courtyards overlooking the scenic Upper Lake. Check at the ticket office for scheduled performances. A library and cafe complete this culture vulture's oasis. *(Lake Drive Rd., in the new town. ☎ 540353. Auto-rickshaw from the old town Rs25-30. Open Tu-Su 1-7pm; Feb. 1-Oct. 31 Tu-Su 2-8pm. Rs10.)*

OLD TOWN. Bhopal's status as an independent, Muslim-ruled princely state until 1952 endowed the city with a strong Muslim character and a wealth of mosques. The old Muslim bazaar quarter, or **Chowk,** wedged in the crook of a turn in Hamidia Rd., has the strongest Islamic flavor. The **Taj-ul-Masjid,** Bhopal's biggest mosque, is a spectacular illustration of Bhopal's Islamic tradition. The plans of the original builder, Nawab Shajehar Begum, were so grandiose that they have still not been completed. The 18-story minarets, the three huge domes over the prayer hall filled with students of the Qur'an, the vast courtyard, and the nearby river create a grand impression. The mosque can only be approached from Royal Market Rd. *(Open dawn-dusk. Free.)* The **Jama Masjid,** built by Kudsia Begum in 1837, has impressive gold-spiked minarets. The **Moti Mahal,** constructed in 1860 by Kudsia Begum's daughter, continues the Mughal tradition of small-scale, elegant, more "personal" mosques. Although less opulent than its big city counterparts, this mosque imitates many features (including the striped domes) of the Jama Masjid in Delhi.

TRIBAL HABITAT (MUSEUM OF MAN). The Tribal Habitat reconstructs the dwellings of various indigenous Indian tribes and attempts to provide a glimpse of actual tribal life. The open-air exhibition matches the natural surroundings of the tribal villages. *(Shamla Hill, close to Bharat Bhavan. 2km auto-rickshaw ride to exhibition area Rs15. Open Tu-Su 10am-6pm. Free.)*

OTHER MUSEUMS. The **Regional Science Center** is a science museum containing nearly 300 participatory exhibits in the "Invention" and "Fun in Science" galleries and planetarium. *(Shamla Hill. Open Tu-Su 10:30am-6:30pm. Rs2.)* The **government archaeological museum** has a small collection, including several noteworthy sculptures from around Madhya Pradesh, tribal art, and paintings from the Bagh Caves near Mandu. *(Banganga Rd. Open Tu-Su 10am-6pm. Free.)* The **Birla Museum** features a collection of 9th- and 10th-century sculptures from the Raisen, Sehore, Mandsaur, and Shahdol districts of MP. *(Arera Hill. Open Tu-Su 10am-5pm. Rs3.)* Next door, the **Birla Temple** has yet another scenic view of the city, especially at night. *(Open daily 6-11:30am and 4-9pm; in winter 6:30-noon and 4-8:30pm. Free.)*

SANCHI सांची   ☎ 07482

In the 3rd century BC, the emperor Ashoka founded the Buddhist retreat at Sanchi as a haven for meditation, and 22 centuries have done little to undermine his purpose. Sanchi re-entered the limelight when a British officer stumbled across its ruins in 1818. The huge white *stupas*, with additions of exquisite sculpture, were named a UNESCO World Heritage site in 1989. Despite increased visibility, Sanchi remains a tiny village, rewarding visitors with a nearly complete compendium of Buddhist architectural history. Sanchi is best visited as a day trip from Bhopal.

TRANSPORTATION

Frequent **buses** ply the roads between Bhopal's bus stand and Sanchi (1½hr., Rs19). Some take the long route via Raisen (2½hr.), so be sure to ask which is which. Sanchi is on the main line from Bhopal to Delhi, but only two express **trains** from Bhopal stop at Sanchi (1hr., 8am and 2:40pm, Rs19). Other trains from Bhopal are slow (2½-3hr.) and not worth taking.

ORIENTATION

The two main roads in Sanchi intersect one another. One leads southwest from the **railway station,** past the few budget hotels and the **police station,** and up a hill to the **main gate** of the ruins. The road to Bhopal crosses this street at a right angle, continuing on to Vidisha, 10km to the northeast. The **small market** and **bus stand** occupy the quadrant on the station side of the main road and the Bhopal side of the crossroads. An **STD/ISD** booth is at the bus stand.

ACCOMMODATIONS AND FOOD

Though many visitors see the sights in a couple of hours, accommodations are plentiful—most convenient is the (one) **railway retiring room ❶,** complete with dressing room, shower-less bathroom, and mosquito nets (Rs120). The **Tourist Cafeteria ❶,** just before the museum, has bright, airy, spotless rooms. (☎62743. Singles Rs220; doubles Rs319.) The cafeteria serves the standard MPSTDC fare. (Snacks Rs12-25, soups Rs25-30, entrees Rs20-45. Open daily 7am-10pm.) Near the railway station, the **Pathak** and **Rohit** restaurants serve basic Indian meals.

SIGHTS

(Archaeological ruins and hilltop ruins both US$10 or equivalent.)

The main road from the railway station leads past a kiosk on the left that sells tickets for both the archaeological museum and the hilltop ruins. The useful *Sanchi* guide, published by the Archaeological Survey of India, is sometimes available here (Rs15). Past the museum, a road winds its way up the hill; if you're on foot, the steep staircase leading off to the right is the more direct route to the ruins. There are several *stupas* scattered on the hill, as well as a number of columns, temples, and monasteries. The most important (and best preserved) of these structures is **Stupa 1,** known as the **Great Stupa.** It is encircled by a wall and flanked by four *toranas,* or gateways. If you come up from the staircase, you will approach the Great Stupa from the North Gateway.

Even though the Enlightened One never visited Sanchi (as far as is known), the complex of temples and monasteries here chronicles the entire ancient history of Indian Buddhism. Mauryan Emperor Ashoka himself erected a pillar at the Great Stupa, and sculptures dating from the end of the Buddhist period resemble deities from the Hindu pantheon. Surprisingly, though Sanchi was an active Buddhist site for over 1000 years, only scattered references to it have been identified in the vast corpus of Buddhist literature. Archaeology provides the only hints about the history behind the hilltop ruins here.

THE GREAT STUPA

The oldest structure at Sanchi, the Great Stupa was erected by Emperor Ashoka in the 3rd century BC. When the ruins were unearthed, archaeologists nearly destroyed the massive 16m *stupa* in their rush to find valuable artifacts before discovering that there was no treasure inside—the *stupa* was solid throughout.

In the 1st century BC, the Satavahanas tacked on Sanchi's richest addition: the four monumental gateways facing the cardinal directions. Archaeologists attribute the intricate sculpture to ivory carvers accustomed to making maximum use of minimum surface; the theory is borne out by a Pali inscription on the south gate. Since all the sculpture, except the four **seated Buddhas** inside each gate, dates from the Theravada period, no direct depictions of the Buddha appear on the gates. He is referred to only obliquely, with symbols such as the lotus flower (for his birth), the pipal tree (for his enlightenment), and the wheel (for his sermons). Figures commonly depicted include six *manushis*, the Buddha's predecessors who appear as *stupas* or trees. *Jatakas* (tales from the Buddha's previous lives), are also illustrated on the pillars of the temples. One of these is the **Chhadanta Jataka,** where, as an elephant, the Buddha helps a hunter saw off his own tusks. There are also stories detailing the distribution of the Buddha's relics.

NORTH GATEWAY. The north gateway, less scarred by the ravages of time than its counterparts, is adorned on top by a partially preserved wheel of law. It shows the **Vessarkara Jataka** around both sides of the bottom rung. In the tale, the Buddha successively gives up a magic elephant, his horse and chariot, and his wife and children before being reinstated to his princedom.

EAST GATEWAY. While the upper registers of the east gateway repeat earlier scenes, the south pillar depicts the Buddha walking on water (on the outside) and facing a fearsome cobra (on the inside). Below this scene is a depiction of villagers trying to make a sacrificial fire which won't light without the Buddha's permission. Hanging off the bottom right architrave is a *yakshi* (maiden).

SOUTH GATEWAY. The south gate, opposite the path to the ruins, was once the main entrance, as evidenced by the stump of a pillar erected by Ashoka to the right of it. A local *zamindar* (landlord) broke off the rest of the pillar to use in a sugar-cane press. The middle architrave of the south gate shows Ashoka's army arriving at the last of the eight original *stupas* containing the Buddha's relics at Rama-grama, but Ashoka is prevented from carting off the loot (as he had at the other seven) by the army of snake people to the left. On the inside, the middle rung depicts the *Chhadanta Jataka;* above this scene are the trees and *stupas* of the *manushis.* The bottom rung shows the siege of Kushinagar (see p. 701), the archetypical story of Buddhist non-violence.

WEST GATEWAY. This gateway is best recognized by the funny dwarves that support its architraves. The front face of the west gateway features (from top to bottom) more *manushis*, the Buddha's first sermon (note the wheel), and more scenes of the *Chhadanta Jataka.* Inside, the top two architraves show more wrangling over relics, and the bottom reveals the Buddha attaining enlightenment despite the distracting demons sent by Mara. On the southern pillar of this gate, the **Mahakapi Jataka** depicts the Buddha as a monkey turning himself into a bridge so that his brethren can escape to safety over a river.

OTHER RUINS

There are four other *stupas* at Sanchi, all of them younger than the Great Stupa. **Stupa 3,** on the way to the Great Stupa, is marked by one gateway. **Stupa 2,** down the hill on the way back to the village, has no gateways but is decorated by interesting frescoes. Past the south gateway of the Great Stupa stand several *chaityas* (temples) whose style resembles that of ancient Greek temples. The largest of the remaining monasteries is **Monastery 51,** to the right of the Great Stupa and back toward the village. The **Great Bowl,** now broken, is positioned just past the monastery and once served as a depository for the monks' food and offerings.

MUSEUM. The small museum holds a modest collection of statues unearthed at Sanchi, including some impressive, lion-headed Ashokan pillar capitals and a buxom *yakshi* swinging down from a mango tree. *(Closed F.)*

INDORE इंदौर ☎ 0731

Indore (pop. 1.2 million) has not been blessed with any spectacular sights to attract visitors, but it is a friendly, pleasant city of parks and broad avenues. As the commercial heart of Madhya Pradesh, Indore has solid infrastructure and the smog-choked air of modernity. Its markets are great for gift-shopping and cluttered with everything from saris and silver to carpets. Well-connected via rail and road, Indore is an ideal base from which to go into the ancient cities of Mandu and Ujjain, as well as Maheshwar and Omkareshwar.

⌐ TRANSPORTATION

Flights: The airport (☎ 410452 and 413747) is 8km west of the city center, along Mahatma Ghandi Rd. Auto-rickshaw Rs60-70. **Indian Airlines** (☎ 431595 or 431596) on RS Bandari Marg. From Gandhi's statue, head away from the center, turn left, then right, and walk for 5min.; IA will be on the right. Daily flights to **Delhi** (2hr., 11am, US$140) via **Bhopal** (30min., US$60) and **Mumbai** (1hr., 5pm, US$95). **Jet Airways,** G-2 Vidyapati Bhawan, 17 Racecourse Rd. (☎ 544592 or 433211). Open M-Sa 9:30am-6pm, Su 9:30am-1pm. To **Delhi** and **Mumbai** (1 hr., 1 per day, US$95-100). **Sahara Airlines,** G-6 Industry House, Agra-Bombay Rd. (☎ 266399 or 432637) also has a flight to **Mumbai**. Open daily 10am-6pm.

Trains: The **railway station** is on Station Rd. (☎ 131 or 521685). The **reservation office** is on the street directly across from the main entrance, in a pink bldg. on the right. Open M-Sa 8am-8pm, Su 8am-2pm. To: **Ahmedabad** (*Capital Express* 10hr., 10:30pm, Rs220); **Bhopal** (6hr.; 4 per day Tu-F 6am-4:40pm, M and Sa-Su 6am-8:35pm; Rs125); **Calcutta** (36hr.; Tu, Th, Sa 8:45pm; Rs394); **Delhi** (21hr., 1 and 4pm, Rs284) via **Gwalior** and **Agra; Jaipur** (16hr., daily 9:50pm, Rs225); **Mumbai** (16hr., 3:50pm, Rs284); **Udaipur** (15hr., daily 5:55pm, Rs155); **Ujjain** (2hr., frequent 6am-8pm, Rs32).

Buses: Sarwate bus stand (☎ 465688). At the intersection of Nasia Rd. and Kibe Compound Rd., 500m south of the train station. Turn right and go under the Patel flyover as you exit the railway station. To: **Aurangabad** (5am and 9pm, Rs197); **Bhopal** (4½hr., every 30min. 4:30am-12:30am, Rs86-130); **Mandu** (6, 7, 8am); **Omkareshwar** (3½hr., frequent 6am-4pm, Rs34); **Ujjain** (2hr., every 15min. 6am-10pm, Rs27). **Gangwal bus stand,** about 3km west of the train station, serves **Mandu,** but you need to change buses in **Dhar** (4hr., frequent, Rs52). For a more comfortable ride to these and other destinations, including **Maheshwar,** try the private operators on the street opposite the train station, near the reservation office.

Local Transportation: English street signs are rare, and the old part of town is a labyrinth. Take advantage of the ubiquitous **auto-rickshaws.** Prices range from Rs10 for short rides to Rs25 to go across town. The meters are actually accurate in Indore, so make sure that your driver uses his. Or jump aboard one of the **tempos** that ply the main thoroughfares (Rs3).

◼ ⌐ ORIENTATION AND PRACTICAL INFORMATION

The **train station** is in the center of Indore, and the railway lines bisect the city down the middle into eastern and western halves. To the east, workshops and business hotels are built on top of each other; to the west is the older part of town, containing most of the city's sights and endless bazaars. Two bridges link the two halves of the city. Shastri Bridge is 250m north from the railway station along **Station Rd.** From Shastri Bridge, Mahatma Gandhi (MG) Rd. leads to the sights in the west and to the **Gandhi statue,** at the intersection with **RN Tagore Rd.,** in the east. A 500m walk south (right) from the railway station takes you under the Patel Bridge to **Sarwate bus stand.** A 5min. walk away from the railway lines from either the Patel Bridge or the bus stand takes you to the **Nehru statue** and to **Maharaja Yeshwantrao (MY) Hospital Rd.,** which leads southeast to the bank, GPO, and Central Museum. From the railway station, exit through platform #1 for the east side of the city and platform #4 for the west side.

Tourist Office: MPSTDC (☎528653 or 521818), RN Tagore Rd. From MG Rd., turn right onto RNT Rd. at the Gandhi statue; it's in a park on the left. Open M-Sa 10am-5pm.

Currency Exchange: State Bank of India, Main Branch, Agra-Bombay Rd., on the left before the GPO and Central Museum. At least a 20min. walk from the train or bus station. Head east, past the Nehru statue, turn right at the Indian Coffee House, then make another right. **IDBI Bank,** Agra-Bombay Rd. Follow directions to the State Bank of India, and take another left at the big intersection; it's on the left, 5min. down the road. AmEx **ATM** outside. Open M-F 10am-4pm, Sa 10am-2pm.

Police: (☎464488 or 100 for emergencies), under the Patel flyover, between the railway station and Sarwate. Police Commissioner's Office (☎513026).

Pharmacy: MY Hospital Pharmacy, MY Hospital Rd., between the Nehru statue and State Bank of India. Open 24hr.

Hospital: Choithrom Hospital, Monik Barg Rd. (☎362491-8).

Internet: There are many internet cafes on RN Tagore Rd. with slow connections. **Cyber Dream,** 166 RN Tagore Rd., just past the Woodlands Restaurant, has fast ones in A/C booths. Rs30 per hr. Open daily 8:30am-11:30pm.

Post Office: GPO, Agra-Bombay Rd. (☎700244). Between the State Bank of India and the museum; turn right off MY Hospital Rd. Open M-Sa 8am-7:30pm, Su 10:30am-3:30pm. **Postal Code:** 452001.

▎ ACCOMMODATIONS

Hotels in Indore fill up with itinerant businessmen, especially at the beginning of the month. The cheaper places, which are between the Sarwate bus stand and the Nehru statue, cater to middle-class Indians, and usually offer 24hr. check-out, TVs, phones, and *dhobi* service. Prices quoted do not include state taxes of 10%.

Hotel Ashoka, 14 Nasia Rd. (☎465991 or 475496). Opposite the Sarwate bus stand. The hallways smell funky - but don't be deceived—even the most ordinary rooms on the top floor are very clean and modern. Singles Rs150-310; doubles Rs200-360. ❶

Hotel Neelam, 33/2 Patel Bridge Corner (☎466001-03 or 464616-17). From the Sarwate bus stand, take the alley that leads alongside the fly-over; it's on the side street on the right. The higher up you climb the endless staircase, the brighter and airier the rooms get. All the usual amenities. Singles Rs150-320; doubles Rs200-370. ❷

Hotel Royal Residency, 225 RN Tagore Rd. (☎705633; fax 405677). From the train or bus station, walk east to the Nehru statue, then turn right. This gorgeous, modern hotel is pure luxury, but the cheapest rooms are not too far from standard budget price-wise. Check-out 9am. Singles Rs450-850; doubles Rs650-1050. AmEx/MC/Visa. ❸

▎ FOOD

Indore is not a city of culinary delights, and most restaurants are in the better hotels near RN Tagore Rd. Fortunately, prices tend to be reasonable. There are bar-restaurants, fruit stands, and sweets-stalls to the left of the Sarwate bus stand.

MADHYA PRADESH

Woodlands Restaurant, Hotel President, 163 RN Tagore Rd., near the Nehru statue. A respite from the frantic frenzy of outdoor Indore, Woodlands serves breakfasts (Rs65-85), typical veg. dinners (Rs70-100), and South Indian snacks (Rs30-50). Open daily 7am-11pm; meals 7-11am, noon-3pm, and 7-11pm. ❶

Landmark Restaurant, 163 RN Tagore Rd., between Woodlands Restaurant and the Nehru statue. This is *the* place to satisfy your salad cravings (Rs15-50). Landmark's menu proudly proclaims that it will take *at least* 20min. to prepare its French-inspired continental, Indian, and Chinese meals from fresh ingredients. Soups Rs30-35, most entrees Rs50-70, chicken dishes Rs90-100. Open daily 11am-11pm. ❶

Indian Coffee House, MG Rd., 250m past Gandhi Hall, on the left inside a courtyard heading west toward Rajwada. As always, this stylish, wanna-be traditional cafe serves the best coffee and cheap snacks. No item on the menu is more than Rs28. A 2nd location, opposite the MY Hospital (continue east past the Nehru statue), has superb outdoor tables in a small park. Both open daily 8am-10pm. ❶

◉ SIGHTS

CENTRAL MUSEUM. Presenting religious sculptures, stone inscriptions, and Sanskrit copper plates from western MP, among other things, the Central Museum has a collection that is both beautiful and unique. Unfortunately, poor presentation does little to illuminate cultural context. Unlike in many other museums, however, it is OK to touch the sculpture, and the pieces scattered outside in the grass make the art accessible to all. Ask one of the attendants for a tour. *(On the Agra-Bombay Rd. beyond the GPO. Open Tu-Su 10:30am-5:50pm. Free.)*

LAL BAGH PALACE. This British-style manor was built by the Holkar Maharajas between 1886 and 1921. Along with the usual stuffed wildcats, the house features an underground tunnel connecting the main house with the kitchens on the other side of the river, as well as imposing gates that are replicas of the ones at Buckingham Palace. Don't jump out of your *chappals* when a statue of a certainly-not-amused Queen Victoria pops up at the exit to see you off the premises. *(Between the train station and Gangwal Bus Stand. Open Tu-Su 10am-5pm. Rs2. Guidebooks Rs3.)*

OTHER SIGHTS. On the western side of town, off MG Rd., **Rajwada** pays homage to the faded splendor of the Holkars. This 18th-century palace was built in a style that blended Mughal, French, and Maratha influences. The mostly wooden structure did not prove very resistant to fires, so only the front facade survives today. Wander the streets of the lively **Khajuri Bazaar** on your way to the nearby **Kanch Mandir,** a Jain temple made entirely of mirrored tiles. The 1875 **Bada Ganapati,** otherwise uninteresting, houses the largest Ganesh statue in the world (8m). Finally, those interested in Raj-era architecture might want to visit **Gandhi Hall,** now a Town Hall, on MG Rd. just west of Shastri Bridge.

NEAR INDORE

◉ MAHESHWAR

Maheshwar is not connected directly with any major cities, but if you don't mind transferring, it's quite easy to reach. Frequent buses run to Dhamnod (30min., Rs5), from which there are connections to Mandu (2hr., Rs27) and Indore (3hr., Rs30). Four buses per day go to Omkareshwar (3hr., Rs30).

Both the *Ramayana* and the *Mahabharata* mention **Mahishmati** (Maheshwar's previous incarnation), once a glorious city and the capital of King Arjuna Kartavirya's realm around 200 BC. The city fell into oblivion until the late 18th century, when the Holkar queen, Ahilyabai, made it her capital, building a fortified palace and two richly decorated temples along the Narmada River. The queen also established a center for producing fine, handloomed saris, and legend has it that she created the simple but distinctive geometric border design that makes Maheshwari saris famous throughout India today.

To reach the sights, clustered inside the **fort,** turn left out of the bus station and head straight across the main road. The right fork in the village road leads up to the fort. Past the main gate, a smaller gate leads into the palace grounds, where a two-room **museum** contains a jumble of broken statuary and Holkar dynasty paraphernalia. Through the gate to the left of the museum are steps down to the **sari workshop** and the temples and *ghats* below. The workshop at the top of the stairs, run by the Rehwa Society (established in 1978 to preserve Maheshwar's silk-cotton sari-weaving tradition), is set up for the benefit of tourists. In a dark, low, historic building lit by fluorescent tubes, workers, most of them women, spin and weave material in a stunning array of colors and designs. The manager, who sits just inside the door, will call somebody up to show you around. Though saris are most definitely *not* sold on the premises (abandon the thought), they are available in town for Rs400-2500. (Open W-M 10am-5pm. Free.) Past the sari workshop, at the bottom of the stairs, Maheshwar's **temples** are pressed into small courtyards that make them seem larger than they are.

Ajanta Lodge ❶, on the main road 100m to the right of the bus stand, provides clean rooms. (☎07283 73226. Singles Rs40-50; doubles Rs55-70.) For food, **VIP Cottage ❶,** on the main road 400m to the left of the bus stand, just over the bridge, has all the usual stuff (Rs15-150).

◉ OMKARESHWAR

Buses run directly from Omkareshwar to Indore (3hr., frequent 5am-4:15pm, Rs34). Four buses per day also make it to Maheshwar (3hr., last one 3:30pm, Rs30) on what long ago used to qualify as "roads." Buses run to Ujjain (5hr., 1 per day, Rs56).

For centuries, Omkareshwar, an island shaped like the holiest of all Hindu symbols, the "Om" (ॐ), has drawn pilgrims to its temples and *ghats*. With its endless night-and-day chants, repeated *Hare Om* greetings, and the buzz of flies, Omkareshwar is like a miniature Varanasi. Its temples rise up over jagged cliffs, while the *ghats* climb serenely from the banks of the Narmada and Kaveri rivers.

To reach the temples, follow the crowds through the village until you reach the footbridge that spans the deep gully dividing the island. Otherwise, descend to the *ghats* and take a ferry across (Rs5). From the river you can see the town's major temples. The remarkably detailed five-story **Shri Omkar Mandhata,** home to one of only 12 *jyotirlingas* (naturally occurring phallic symbols that are a sign of Shiva) in India, is the reason why most people come to Omkareshwar. Compared to the *jyotirlinga* in Ujjain (see p. 362), this one seems embarrassingly small. The **Siddhnath Temple,** also worth visiting, is an early medieval brahmin temple.

The **police station** (☎344015; open daily 9am-5pm) and the **post office** (☎02780 71222; open M-Sa 9am-5pm) are near the bus station. There is no place in the village to change currency or have a decent meal. From the bus station, a 3min. walk through the village takes you past the **Government Hospital** on the right (open daily 8am-noon and 5-6pm) and the **pharmacy** on the left (open daily 7:30am-9:30pm). **Yatrika Guest House ❶,** is behind the bus station. (☎02780 71308. Singles Rs150; doubles Rs200.) For nicer rooms and more scenic views, try the **Hotel Aishwarya ❷,** where prices are open to negotiation. Take the small side street directly across from the bus station, and follow the signs for 20min. (☎02780 71325 or 71326. Singles Rs250-300; doubles Rs350-450. 10% luxury tax.)

MANDU माण्डव ☎ 02792

Mandu, the so-called "City of Joy," is the kind of agricultural idyll that India likes to promote in its tourist brochures. Goats munch on the grass surrounding the ruins, while women walk by with pots on their head, and children run over to say "hello." Stretched out on top of a narrow plateau in the Vindhya mountain range, the city was fortified as long ago as the 6th century. Mandu's golden age lasted from 1401 to 1526, when the Muslim rulers of the kingdom of Malwa called it their home, building walls, mosques, palaces, and pleasure domes in stone and marble across the length of the plateau. Five centuries later, their monuments still stand in a tranquil, underpopulated mountain region set against a backdrop of great natural beauty. The main tourist season is between October and March, but the monsoon season is perhaps the best time to visit, when the life-giving rains paint the surrounding countryside a lush green.

⊏ TRANSPORTATION

Buses depart from the village sq. to: **Dhar** (1½hr., 14 per day 7am-6:15pm, Rs15); **Indore** (3hr., 5-6 per day 6am-4:45pm, Rs52); **Maheshwar** (3hr., frequent, Rs32) via **Dhamnod.** Bus service is often less frequent during monsoon season. The easiest and most pleasant way of getting around is on **bikes,** which you can rent from several villagers living on the main road or from **Ajay's Bicycle Shop,** also on the main road, just south of the square (Rs3 per hr., Rs25 per day). Alternatively, Nitin Traders will wheel out the one village **auto-rickshaw** (Rs100 per hr.) or call up private **taxis** to Indore (Rs725, book 1½hr. before departure). They're just south of the square opposite the Jain temple; look for the sign. (Open daily 8am-8pm.)

✈ 🛈 ORIENTATION AND PRACTICAL INFORMATION

The only way out of the village is from the north. The **main road** runs north/south, past the **village square** and **Jama Masjid,** ending at the **Rewa Kund** ruins 6km south of the village. **Jahaz Mahal Rd.** shoots out of the village square and leads to the **Royal Enclave** ruins. The sights around town are well-marked, and there are signs in English to direct visitors to the ruins. All the hotels and restaurants, as well as the **post office** (☎63222; open M-Sa 9am-5pm), **police station** (☎63223), and **pharmacy** (open daily 9am-7pm), are on the main road. There are several doctors' offices in Mandu, but the closest hospital is in Indore. There is no tourist office in Mandu, but the **MPSTDC** in Indore can help with hotel reservations (recommended in winter). **STD/ISD** calls can be placed from a market square stall (open daily 8:30am-9pm) or from the Rupmati Hospital. Power outages are frequent, and phone lines are often down during the monsoon. **Postal Code:** 454010.

🛏 🍴 ACCOMMODATIONS AND FOOD

All accommodations in Mandu are over priced given the quality (or lack thereof) of lodging they provide. Despite this, it is worth staying here overnight. Ask the bus driver to drop you off at one of them. **Hotel Maharaja ❶,** on Jahaz Mahal Rd., has small but clean rooms with attached baths, and is probably the best deal in town. (☎63288. Singles Rs100; doubles 200. Off-season 75/100.) The Nepalese kitchen staff whip up Indian, Chinese, Continental, and, yes, Nepalese cuisine. SADA's **Tourist Rest House ❶,** at the corner of the village square and Jahaz Mahal Rd., has dark, dingy cells with squat toilets (☎63234. Doubles Rs125.). MPSTDC has two comfortable but pricey hotels in Mandu. The **Travelers' Lodge ❷,** 1km north of the square on the main road, has scenic views over the eastern ravine. (☎63221. Singles Rs290; doubles Rs390.)

The **MPSTDC Tourist Cottages** ❸, on the main road 2km south of the square, has better rooms in small cottages with lake views. (☎ 63235. Singles Rs350-750; doubles Rs450-850.) Both places charge 10% luxury tax but offer 25% discounts in May and June. Reservations can be made in any MPSTDC office (recommended in season). Both have **restaurants** ❶, with the standard menu of snacks (Rs5-40), continental dishes (Rs30-100), and veg. (Rs20-45) and non-veg. (Rs30-100) options. (MPSTDC restaurants open daily 6-10am, noon-3pm, and 7-11pm; snacks available between meal times.) The **Rupmati Hotel** ❷, the best in town, has large rooms and magnificent terraces overlooking the ravine. (☎ 63270, or in Indore 702055. Doubles Rs400-750; 10% luxury tax.) The **restaurant** ❷, is more affordable than the rooms. The open-air pavilion overlooking a landscaped lawn, complete with swings and slides, serves veg. (Rs30-55) and non-veg. (Rs50-250) dishes. The restaurant also holds the only liquor license in town. (Beer Rs50-75. Open daily 7am-11pm.) The **Relax Point Restaurant** ❶, in the main square, offers veg. *thalis* for only Rs30 (open daily 8am-10:30pm).

🔆 SIGHTS

Ruins are everywhere in Mandu, dominating the landscape, from the gateways you pass on the way into town to the mosque and tomb in the market square; from the crumbling houses along the sides of the main street to the palace at the tip of the plateau. The attractions are in three main areas: the **central group** in the village center, the **Royal Enclave** in the north, and the **Rewa Kund complex** in the south. The last group is 6km away from the village, and a bike is strongly recommended. All sights are open from sunrise to sunset and only some charge an entrance fee (see below).

THE CENTRAL GROUP. In the middle of both the plateau and the village, the central group includes the beautiful **Jama Masjid,** one of India's largest mosques. Like the other monuments here, it typifies the austere architectural style imported from Afghanistan by Hoshang Shah. Reputedly modeled on the mosque in Damascus, and completed in 1454, the Jama Masjid is remarkable for both its sheer scale and the simplicity of its design. Hoshang Shah's son built a white marble **mausoleum** behind the Jama Masjid for his father. The structure so inspired Shah Jahan that he sent his architects to study it before they began work on the Taj Mahal. *(Mausoleum US$5 or equivalent; not worth it.)*

THE ROYAL ENCLAVE. Sultan Ghiyas Shah constructed the huge 15th-century **Jahaz Mahal** (or "ship palace"), inside the gateway, to house his huge harem. The long, narrow design and the two artificial lakes on either side are what give the building its name, especially apt during the rainy season, when water comes cascading through the palace's complex system of pools and conduits. Behind the Jahaz Mahal stands the **Hindola Mahal,** an audience hall nicknamed the "Swinging Palace" due to its sloping buttresses, which look as if they're swinging out at an angle. Ghiyas Shah had a ramp built so that he could ride to the upper floor without the hassle of getting down from his elephant. Many other ruins, including **Dilwar Khan's Mosque** and **Gada Shah's Shop,** are also in this enclave. *(Jahaz Mahal Rd., next to Hoshang Shah's tomb, continues to the Royal Enclave. US$5; definitely worth it.)*

REWA KUND. The main road ends 6km from the sq., at the **Rewa Kund** complex, named after the tank that used to supply water to the nearby palaces. Baz Bahadur, the last independent ruler of Mandu, built his **palace,** the **Baz Bahadur,** in the 16th century to serve as a quiet retreat, with views of the surrounding greenery. But even this tranquil spot could not satisfy the stunning Rupmati, the sultan's favorite dancer. She was from the plains, and dreary luxuries of the high-life up on the plateau made her homesick. According to legend, Rupmati demanded that Baz Bahadur build her a pavilion on the crest of a hill, from which she could see her former village in the Narmada Valley far below. No sooner had the dutiful sultan completed **Rupmati's Pavilion** than the jealous Akbar stormed Mandu to seize the renowned dancer. Baz Bahadur fled, Rupmati swallowed poison, and Akbar, after a brief stay, let his testosterone guide him to the next desirable dancing girl (see **Orchha, p. 378**), leaving Mandu desolate. The views from the palace are superb. *(Entrance to the complex US$5 or equivalent.)*

NIL KANTH TEMPLE. Originally a Mughal pleasure pavilion, complete with running water that flowed over ribbed stones in front of candles, the temple today has been taken over by the Shaivites. From this inspirational spot on the valley slopes, just below the clifftop, people worship an incarnation of Shiva whose throat turned blue when he drank poison. *(At the southern end of the village, a fork leads right, or west, from the main road to the Nil Kanth Temple, 3km away.)*

UJJAIN उज्जैन ☎ 0734

Ujjain's long and varied history stretches back to the 3rd century BC, when the city was the imperial seat of Ashoka, Buddhism's first patron. Later, Ujjain served as a major center of Indian astronomy. Long before the days of the prime meridian, Hindu stargazers made Ujjain India's Greenwich. An 18th-century observatory on the southwestern side of town is still in use today. Ujjain is also among the holiest of holy Hindu cities; legend has it that when Hindu gods scrambled with demons for the nectar that grants immortality, one of the four drops of the nectar that fell to Earth landed smack dab in the middle of Ujjayini (Ujjain's ancient name, meaning "one who conquers with pride"). Ujjain is thus one of the four cities that hosts the **Kumbh Mela** festival every 12 years. The town attracts millions of people every year with the promise of a hard-earned space along the city *ghats* for a dip in the sacred river Shipra. While Ujjain's temples are not the most inspiring in the world, its hectic religious atmosphere makes it a worthwhile day stop.

▮ TRANSPORTATION

Trains: The **railway station** is on Subhash Rd., 150m west of the bus station. A **reservation office** is on the left after exiting the main station building. Open M-Sa 8am-8pm, Su 8am-2pm. Use platform #1 to exit to town, platform #7 to the MPSTDC and Hotel Shipra. To: **Ahmedabad** (10hr., 9:05pm, Rs159); **Bhopal** (3-4hr., 6-8 per day 1am-10:15pm, Rs52); **Delhi** (17hr., 2:45 and 6:25pm, Rs268); **Gwalior** (10½hr., daily 2:45pm, Rs190); **Indore** (2-3hr., 14 per day 2am-8:40pm, Rs23); **Jaipur** (9hr., about 1 per day, Rs196); **Mumbai** (13hr., 5:35pm, Rs268).

Buses: Mahakal Bus Stand, on the corner to the right (northeast) as you leave the train station. To **Bhopal** (5hr., 4 per day 6am-9:30pm, Rs78) and **Indore** (2hr., frequent 4:30am-9:30pm, Rs27). Buses to Indore are faster than trains. Other connections are through Indore.

Local Transportation: Things are spread out, and most **auto-rickshaw** drivers refuse to use meters. Bargain—the longest ride should cost no more than Rs30-35. **Tempos #2** and 9 go to the Mahakaleshwar Mandir; #4 and 10 go to the Gopal Mandir.

▮▮ ORIENTATION AND PRACTICAL INFORMATION

Hemmed in by the **Shipra River** to the west and the **railroad tracks** to the south, Ujjain's **old city** charms visitors with many small shops and drives them crazy with frustratingly narrow lanes. There are no street signs, few landmarks, and countless little roads to nowhere. Most of the temples and *ghats* are within walking distance, but other places require a rickshaw ride. The railway station, bus stand, GPO, and most hotels are all clustered around one intersection.

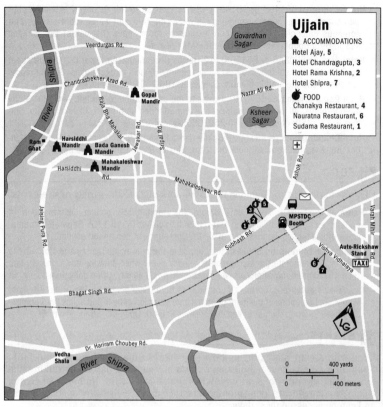

Ujjain

🏠 ACCOMMODATIONS
Hotel Ajay, **5**
Hotel Chandragupta, **3**
Hotel Rama Krishna, **2**
Hotel Shipra, **7**

🍅 FOOD
Chanakya Restaurant, **4**
Nauratna Restaurant, **6**
Sudama Restaurant, **1**

Tourist Office: MPSTDC has a booth in the railway station that provides great maps of the city. Open daily 8am-3pm. The staff at the reception desk of the **MPSTDC Hotel Shipra** (☎ 551495 or 551496), Vishva Vidhyalaya Rd., will also provide information. Exit the railway station through platform #7. Go left and turn right on the wide avenue; the hotel is 200m down on the right. Open 24hr. Ask here for Raju Pawar, the only government-licensed guide in Ujjain (Rs300-600 for a tour of the city).

Currency Exchange: The closest place to exchange currency is in Indore.

Police Superintendent: ☎ 513300.

Hospital: Civil Hospital, Ashok Rd. From the train station, it's 200m beyond Mahakal bus stand on the opposite side of the street. **24hr. pharmacy.** For private medical assistance, the MPSTDC recommends Dr. Rita Shinde or Dr. Bishi (☎ 555067).

Post Office: GPO (☎ 551023). Behind the bus stand at the 2nd gate on the left. Open M-Sa 10am-10pm, Su 10am-2pm. **Postal Code:** 456001.

🏠 ACCOMMODATIONS

The only "luxurious" place to stay is MPTDC's Hotel Shipra (see below). All other budget hotels are pretty basic and grubby, with hot water in buckets and no showers. They cluster around the railway station. Prices listed do not include state taxes of 5% on rooms Rs60-149 and 10% on rooms Rs150 and above.

Hotel Shipra (☎551495 or 551496). Vishva Vidhyalaya Rd. Relatively expensive, but with spacious, airy rooms, sparkling showers with 24hr. hot water, room service, and gorgeous balconies. Only the more expensive rooms have (big cable) TVs. Singles Rs350-690; doubles Rs390-790. AmEx/MC/Visa. ❷

Hotel Ajay (☎550856 or 551354). 12 Dewas Gate, Mahakaleshwar Rd. On the street opposite the bus station. The best choice among Ujjain's budget hotels. Sizable rooms are clean, and the staff is friendly. Singles Rs100-200; doubles Rs200-300. ❶

Hotel Rama Krishna (☎557012). Opposite the train station to the left. Avoid the stuffy interior rooms. All rooms have air-cooling and attached bathrooms. Checkout 24hr. Singles Rs130-450; doubles Rs170-250/550. ❶

Hotel Chandragupta (☎561600). By the Rama Krishna. Slightly cheaper than its neighbor. Attached bathrooms. Check-out 24hr. Singles Rs80-130; doubles Rs160-220. ❶

🍴 FOOD

Ujjain's charm won't be found in its restaurants; stick to the variety of street eats.

Nauratna Restaurant, inside Hotel Shipra. The standard MP Tourism menu made up of an uninspiring range of veg. and non-veg. Indian dishes (Rs15-175). Separate bar area. Open officially daily noon-3pm and 7-10:30pm, but can serve food anytime. ❷

Sudama Restaurant, on Subhash Rd., opposite the railway station, next to Hotel Rama Krishna. Contemplate the fascinating cut-mirror decor while chowing down on veg. fare (Rs6-45). Dinner only after 7pm, but snacks (Rs6-32) all day. Open daily 9am-11pm. ❶

Chanakya Restaurant, on the ground floor of Hotel Chandragupta. The whole extended family can fit into one of the giant booths. Large selection of beer and spirits, and unmissable pseudo-erotic sculpture. Veg.-only dishes Rs6-40. Open daily 8am-11pm. ❶

👁 SIGHTS

Even with a map, start praying now—it's hard to find anything without faith. Thankfully, the largest temples and *ghats* are within a half-hour walking distance from the railway station down Mahakaleshwar Rd. Rather than sights, Ujjain's landmarks are living monuments; they don't really have "opening hours" and can be accessed most days.

THE TEMPLES. The rosy *shikhara* of the **Mahakaleshwar Mandir** caps a series of long, narrow tunnels that eventually lead to an underground room containing one of the twelve *jyotirlingas*. These are believed to derive their power from within themselves; other *lingas* must have their power renewed from time to time by ritual. Amitabh Bachchan, the godfather of Bollywood cinema, was miraculously cured here after an accident in the movie *Sholay. (From the bus stand, Mahakaleshwar Rd. leads 1½km directly to the temple.)*

As its name suggests, the **Bada Ganesh Mandir** enshrines a sculpture of Ganesh. *(100m down the road that goes around behind the Mahakaleshwar Mandir to the right.)* The **Harsiddhi Mandir,** the large temple complex behind high white walls, is the focal point of Devi worship. It marks the spot where Parvati's arm was severed when Shiva pulled her from her *sati* pyre. A famous image of the goddess Annapurna is kept in the temple shrine. *(From the Mahakaleshwar Mandir, continue on the road past the Bada Ganesh Mandir into and over the marsh beyond; when you hit dry land, turn right.)*

Gopal Mandir (Ganesh Temple) sits behind a high, whitewashed, onion-domed fortification in the midst of a busy market square, where vendors display the season's most sought-after devotional paraphernalia. Inside, pilgrims lounge under the arched platforms that encircle the complex's perimeter, while in the sumptuous main hall, a figure of Ganesh sits obediently between figures of his parents, Shiva and Parvati. *(In the center of town, head north 300m on Spiral Rd.)*

THE VEDHA SHALA. The instruments of the Vedha Shala (Veda School) sit in a compound behind a gate with a sign reading "Shree Jiwagi Observatory." The mathematically inclined will wonder at the precision of gadgets like the parallel sundials on either end of a meter-high cylinder. Each side tells the time for exactly half the year. Located on top of a hill with a view of the river and fields beyond, the observatory would be a pleasant place to sit and admire the view, if it weren't for the truck traffic just outside the gate. *(On a road leading southwest from the back of the railway station, on top of the hill. Approximately Rs25 by rickshaw.)*

OTHER SIGHTS. Many holy sights are scattered throughout the city. If you have the fortitude to see them all, consult the enyclopedic MPSTDC map-guide. The **Ram Ghat** is the largest, although not always busiest, of the long row of *ghats* that line both sides of the river. *(Take the road between the Harsiddhi Mandir back down the slope toward the river.)* Toward the northern end of the row, the **Bhartirihari Caves** are home to the hoop-earringed Kanpatha yogis. Three kilometers north of town, worshippers still make offerings of sweets and alcohol at the Kal Bhairava Mandir.

JABALPUR जबलपुर ☎0761

The Madhya Pradesh tourism office touts a series of scenic white cliffs as the main attraction to Jabalpur, a city of just over a million people. Besides the dazzling Marble Rocks however, the city itself is rather anti-climactic, and is important only as a staging point for trips to Kanha and Bandhavgarh National Parks.

▐ TRANSPORTATION

Flights: To **Delhi** (3hr.; Tu, Th, Sa; US$200) via **Gwalior** (1½hr., US$135). Buy tickets at **3a Travels,** opposite the museum.

Trains: The **railway station** (☎1311132) is a Rs15 rickshaw ride to the east of Russel Chowk. Reservation office open M-Sa 8am-8pm, Su 8am-2pm. Window #3 serves tourists. To: **Bhopal** (7½hr., 4:25am and 10:15pm, Rs133); **Calcutta** (23hr., 11:40am and 2pm, Rs300); **Delhi** (23hr., 5 and 5:40pm, Rs299); **Jalgaon** for Ajanta (11hr.; 5 per day 4:45-9:45am, 3:20-11pm; Rs190); **Patna** (16hr., 1-3 per day 4pm-1am, Rs289); **Satna** for Khajuraho (3hr., frequent, Rs60); **Umaria** for Bandhavgarh N.P. (*Narmada Exp.* 8233, 1hr., 6:20am, Rs31); **Varanasi** (10hr.; 2-4 per day 10am-5pm, 10pm-1:30am; Rs182, 1st class Rs546).

Buses: The chaotic **bus stand,** near the museum, has both public (MPSRTC) and private sections. To: **Bhopal** (9hr., every 30min. 5:30am-midnight, Rs130); **Kanha National Park** (7hr., 7 and 11am, Rs85); **Khajuraho** (10hr., 8:30pm, Rs68). For Khajuraho, it is much quicker and easier to take the train to Satna first. For **Bandhavgarh,** take the train to **Umaria** and change to the Bandhavgarh bus there.

Local Transportation: Tempos run from the museum to the White Rocks for Rs10.

✦ ⓘ ORIENTATION AND PRACTICAL INFORMATION

Collectorate Rd. curves north from behind the **railway station,** past the hospital and Gothic High Court to the **clock tower,** which marks the beginning of the **bazaar area.** Russel Chowk, the center of town, where the accommodations and bus stands are, is 200m to the left through the bazaar streets. **Station Rd.** is south of the station.

Tourist Office: MPTDC (☎322111). Inside the railway station. Makes reservations for MPTDC facilities at Kanha and Bandhavgarh. In season (Dec.-Mar.) bookings for accommodations in parks should be made at least 72hr. in advance from this or any other MPTDC office; full payment required. Open M-Sa 6am-8pm.

Currency Exchange: State Bank of India (☎322259). Opposite Hotel Rishi Regency, near the railway underpass. Open M-F 10:30am-4pm.

Police: Collectorate Rd., Civil Lines (☎320352). In front of the clock tower.

Hospital: Medical College (☎322117). Nagpur Rd. 8 km south of the bus stand. Has a **24hr. pharmacy.**

Telephones: 24hr. **STD/ISD** booth at the railway station.

Internet: Honey's Cyber World, opposite Hotel Shivalaya on Russel Chowk. Rs20 per hr. Open 10am-10pm. Other cybercafes are sprouting up around the city.

Post Office: GPO, Residency Rd. From the station, turn left on Station Rd. and then right on the next main road. The GPO is 500m down on the left. Open M-Sa 10am-6pm. **Postal Code:** 482002.

ACCOMMODATIONS AND FOOD

Most hotels are around Russel Chowk. Many have 24hr. check-out and slap a 15-20% tax on top of already exorbitant charges for their miserable rooms.

Lodge Shivalaya (☎325188). Opposite Jyoti Cinema on Russel Chowk. Clean rooms with attached bath and intermittently functional color TVs lead to enormous balconies overlooking the center of town. Singles Rs90-110; doubles Rs150-175. ❶

Hotel Natraj (☎310931). Near Karamchand Chowk. Heading north (away from Russel Chowk), cross the Navdra Bridge and then take the right fork. Turn right after 100m or so; it's on the left, opposite the Indian Coffee House. Best budget place, but hopelessly booked most of the time. Rooms with attached baths have TV, air-cooling, and hand-held showers. Singles Rs50-70; doubles Rs110-130. ❶

Hotel Adargh Bhedeghat (☎83502). Near the rocks. Comfortable, quiet doubles in a peaceful setting. Doubles Rs250. ❶

Indian Coffee House, Malaviya Marg, near Karamchand Chowk, opposite Hotel Natraj. The mother ship of everybody's favorite chain. Sky-high ceilings, rock-solid tables, wicker chairs, and vintage advertisements make this a classic. *Dosas, uttappams* (Rs13), and other snacks. Great unsweetened coffee Rs4. Open daily 7am-9:30pm. ❶

Hotel Republic Bar, just over Navdra Bridge (from Russel Chowk); it's on the right. Rows of tall, straight-backed chairs and the no-nonsense Sikh owner behind the bar give the Republic a wild west feel. Butter chicken (Rs75) is their specialty. They also serve vegetarian dishes (from Rs15) and a full range of booze. Open daily 10am-11:30pm. ❶

SIGHTS

On the road from Russel Chowk to the bus stand is a small **museum,** which contains temple sculptures. *(Open Tu-Su 10am-5pm. Free.)* The star attraction in all MPTDC brochures are the **Marble Rocks,** 15km away from Jabalpur, which is where the Narmada River passes through a spectacular white-cliffed gorge and then drops 100 feet down a huge waterfall. The Marble Rocks are fully illuminated at night to maximize tourist viewing hours. Local men in swimsuits offer to dive into the rapids for Rs10; it's worth every rupee. Day and night, rowboats bob up and down in the river, allowing you an unadulterated view of the cliffs. *(Tempos go to Marble Rocks from in front of the museum for Rs100. Rowboats Rs10.)* On the way to the Rocks is the old grand fortress of **Madan Mahal,** testimony to Jabalpur's status as capital of the Gond kingdom from the 12th century on.

PROJECT TIGER At the turn of the 20th century, there were more than 100,000 tigers in the wild; today, fewer than 6,000 survive worldwide, more than half of them in India. Faced with this shocking drop in the tiger population, caused by rapid industrialization and persistent hunting, Indira Gandhi inaugurated a drastic initiative to save the tiger in 1973. **Project Tiger** set aside nine areas of tiger territory as national parks and hired a staff of armed guards to patrol the areas and protect the animals from poachers. Initially successful, the plan boosted the tiger population from just a few hundred to several thousand. Ten more national parks were eventually set aside. Lately, however, poaching has increased as the forces protecting the sanctuaries have become less formidable. Tiger products—many believed to have healing and aphrodisiacal properties—fetch high prices on domestic and international markets. The tiger remains an endangered species and some fear it could soon face extinction again. The best places in India to see tigers are at **Corbett** and **Kanha National Parks** (see below).

🐾 NATIONAL PARKS

KANHA NATIONAL PARK

*The park is open sunrise to sunset November 1-June 30; it closes down during the monsoon. Peak season is March to April. There is a one-time permit fee (Rs200) plus a camera fee (Rs25 for still 35mm), payable at Kisli and Mukki gates. The park has two main gates, one at **Kisli**, in the northwest, and another at **Mukki**, on the west side. **Buses** depart from Jabalpur to **Kisli** (6hr., 7 and 11am, Rs85), stopping on the way at Khatia gate near the **Visitor Centre**, where most non-MPTDC accommodations and food can be found. All accommodations and tourist infrastructure is at Khatia and Kisli. Beyond the Khatia Gate Visitor Centre, it is necessary to take a **jeep** (Rs10 per km); walking is out of the question as it's 4km from the Khatia to Kisli.*

Beautiful Kanha and the animals that live here have had an up-and-down history. The same Brits who cantered across the continent with their rifles, driving game to the brink of extinction, also set aside Kanha as a hunting preserve, saving it from the encroachment of the local population. Kanha became a wildlife reserve in 1933, and the result of these preservation efforts is nearly 2000 square kilometers of untainted jungle that served as the setting for Rudyard Kipling's *Jungle Book* and other stories. With 114 tigers in the park, sightings are frequent, and the tiger population only keeps increasing (though not too quickly, as the males display a predilection to eat their own children). Once a tiger is spotted, it is held at bay by elephants until everyone gets a look. Besides the well-fed tigers, you can also see their friends (and food): leopards, deer, sambar, wild boar, bears, pythons, porcupines, and over 300 species of birds. Your chances of seeing a tiger here are better than anywhere in India.

Two MPTDC-run accommodations exist in and around the park. The **Baghira Log Huts ❸**, in the park, have posh singles for Rs590 and doubles with private baths for Rs690. The **Tourist Hostel ❷**, in Kisli, offers dorms for an exorbitant Rs250 and also contains a depressing canteen with bland snacks. For information or reservations, contact one of the MPTDC offices in major Madhya Pradesh cities or in Mumbai, Delhi, and Calcutta; the head office is in Bhopal (☎ (0755) 764397). It's a good idea to book MPTDC hotel rooms in advance during the in-season. The MPTDC requires pre-payment in full for their accommodations, leaving last-minute visitors at a loss. Risk-takers will delight in the range of budget accommodations at nearby **Khatia ❶**, most of which double as restaurants (*thalis* Rs25-30) and jeep stops.

◪**Van Vihar ❶**, 400m from the road, on the right as you walk away from the gate, has simple doubles with bucket showers. Surrounded by thatched huts and jungle, Van Vihar's village atmosphere and delicious home-cooked food have conspired to make many stay here much longer than they ever planned. (Rs50 per person; Feb.-Mar. Rs40.) Scattered around the woods by the gate are the huts of the forest department **Jungle Camp ❶**, which has doubles with attached baths (and running water!) for Rs100 and an impersonal central dining hall. Set back from the road is the comfortable and friendly **Mogli Guest House ❸**. The rooms are a little more expensive, but still a fabulous deal. Call for reservations. (☎ 77228. Rs350-1100.) The only **STD/ISD** booth in Khatia operates from here. (Open 8am-10pm.) New tea stalls sprout up along the road like mushrooms after a thunder storm, allowing you to ignore more institutional options like the **restaurant ❶**, in Baghira, whose choices are at least better than the canteen (Rs50-100).

Although you might catch one of the nightly man-eater films (7pm in English, at the Khatia Gate Visitor Centre) or take the somewhat disorienting 1.5km **jungle walk** from Khatia gate, you're really here to see the law of the jungle at work. Jeep trips, the only way to go, run through Sher Jahan-land for around Rs400-600 plus nominal sundry fees (Rs200 per trip), which can be split between a maximum of six passengers. Consult the manager of your hotel for a berth. Trips run in the morning (4-5hr., 6am) and afternoon (2-3hr., around 3pm). The morning trip, which makes a breakfast stop (fritters and *chai* Rs9) in Kanha village at the heart of the park, is usually a better time for sightings. If there are tigers about, your jeep will take you to an **elephant** (an outrageous Rs300 for a 10min. ride) for closer, more silent viewing. Bring warm clothing and a blanket in winter, as the mornings are very cold and the evening chill sets in quickly.

BANDHAVGARH NATIONAL PARK

*To reach the park from Jabalpur, take a train to **Umaria** (6:20am, 4½hr., Rs60) and then a connecting bus (1hr., Rs15). If you are coming from the north, you can catch the train to Umaria from **Katni Junction,** 18km south of Satna. The bus returns to Umaria at 3pm, in time to catch the 5:30pm train to Katni and Jabalpur. **Jeeps** depart at sunrise and three hours before sunset for 3-4 hr. tours of the park (Rs400). Pay the relevant fees beforehand at the park office: Rs200 per person per day; Rs100 vehicle fee; Rs80 guide fee.*

Although often overshadowed by the nearby Kanha Park, the small Bandhavgarh (170km northeast of Jabalpur) has the highest-density tiger population anywhere in India. In 1952, the last white tiger in India was sighted here. Given its easier accessibility from places like Varanasi and Khajuraho, the park has been attracting an increasing number of tiger-seekers in recent years. The park is made up of two distinct habitats: one of jungle and one of sandy desert hills dotted with the ancient ruins of the maharajas of Rewa. When a tiger is spotted, everybody leaps from the jeep and climbs on top of elephants (Rs300 a ride), which will take you within a safe shooting (by camera, that is) range. Accommodations are available close to the park entrance at the **Gitanjali Guest House ❶** (doubles Rs150-200). MPTDC operates the overpriced **White Tiger Forest Lodge,** which must be booked and paid for several days (or, even better, years) in advance.

KHAJURAHO खजुराहो ☎ 07686

This dusty hamlet (pop. 4680), stuck in the middle of nowhere in northern Madhya Pradesh, nonetheless plays host to one of India's major tourist attractions: the extraordinary temples of Khajuraho. These sites of worship, collectively designated a UNESCO World Heritage Site, are legacies of the Chandela dynasty, whose mighty capital rose and fell here a thousand years ago. The temples are (in)famous for the pulse-quickening, erotic sculptures adorning their walls; couples are shown prominently copulating in any and every position imaginable, with each explicit detail meticulously rendered in the sandstone facades. Surrounding the main temple area, the unavoidable souvenir stands are full of pocket paperback editions of the *Kama Sutra* translated into all of the world's major languages, and late-night conversation in the town's restaurants and cafes seems to focus on the advisability—indeed, even the possibility—of performing the feats of flexibility and ingenuity depicted here. But there is much more to Khajuraho's temples than a few exquisitely executed sex scenes. For all the attention they are given, the scenes represent only a small part of the cultural insight offered by these holy sites. From war to love, from joy to sorrow, the carvings cover the breadth of human experience.

⊏ TRANSPORTATION

Khajuraho isn't really en route to anywhere, but it is most easily slotted between Varanasi and Agra. Buses are the only form of ground transport to Khajuraho and connect regularly to the nearest railheads at Jhansi (175km away; convenient from Delhi or Mumbai) and Satna (117km; convenient from Varanasi or Allahabad). Among those who can afford it, flying is a popular alternative.

Flights: Khajuraho Civil Aerodrome, 6km south of town. Make reservations at least one day in advance at **Indian Airlines** (☎ 74035, airport office 74036), 2km south of town on Main Rd. Open daily 10am-1:15pm and 2-5pm. Daily flights to: **Agra** (45min., US$85); **Delhi** (1½hr., US$105); **Varanasi** (45min., US$85).

Buses: The station, a 10min. walk south of Main Sq. on Link Rd. No. 2, posts English bus schedules and also hosts a computerized **train reservation office** from which you can reserve onward connections from Jhansi, Satna, or any other rail station. (Open M-Sa 8-11am and 2-5pm.) Buses go to: **Agra** (12hr., 9am, Rs190); **Bhopal** (12hr., 6 and 7pm, Rs200); **Gwalior** (6½hr.; 9am, 11:15am, and 4pm; Rs130); **Jabalpur** (12hr., 6am, Rs130); **Jhansi** (4-5hr., 7 per day 5:30am-4:15pm, Rs90); **Mahoba** (3hr., every 45min. 7:30am-4:30pm, Rs35) for trains to **Varanasi; Satna** (4hr., 4 per day 9:30am-4pm, Rs50) for trains to **Varanasi.** There is one direct bus to **Varanasi** (13hr., 4pm, Rs175). The last buses to Khajuraho leave Satna at 2:30pm, Jhansi at 1:15pm, and Mahoba at 5pm.

Local Transportation: Bicycles, the most practical mode of transport, can be rented at hotels or stands in the square for Rs15-30 per day. The few **auto-rickshaws** are over-priced. A **cycle-rickshaw** trip should cost Rs5-10. It is a 20-25min. walk from the Western to the Eastern Group.

⊞ ⏊ ORIENTATION AND PRACTICAL INFORMATION

Khajuraho is tiny, but unmarked roads can make directions confusing. There is only one main road, which leads up from the airport in the south to the **Western Group** (the main temple complex) and the mess of hotels, restaurants, and post-card shops that comprise the "new village." **Jain Temple Rd.** leads east from here to the **Eastern Group** of temples (the second main group), scattered around the old village. The bus stand is on **Link Rd. No. Two,** south of Jain Temple Rd., a 10min. walk from the main group of temples and most accommodations.

Tourist Office: (☎ 72348). Main Rd. Opposite the Western Group. Distributes free copies of a hand-drawn Khajuraho map. Open M-F 9:30am-1:30pm and 2-6pm.

Currency Exchange: State Bank of India (☎ 72373). Main Sq. Opposite the Western Group, cashes traveler's checks and changes many currencies. Open M-F 10:30am-2:30pm and 3-4pm, Sa 10:30am-1pm.

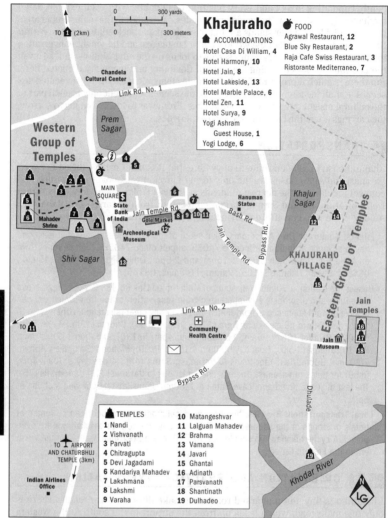

Khajuraho

FOOD
Agrawal Restaurant, **12**
Blue Sky Restaurant, **2**
Raja Cafe Swiss Restaurant, **3**
Ristorante Mediterraneo, **7**

ACCOMMODATIONS
Hotel Casa Di William, **4**
Hotel Harmony, **10**
Hotel Jain, **8**
Hotel Lakeside, **13**
Hotel Marble Palace, **6**
Hotel Zen, **11**
Hotel Surya, **9**
Yogi Ashram Guest House, **1**
Yogi Lodge, **6**

TEMPLES
1 Nandi
2 Vishvanath
3 Parvati
4 Chitragupta
5 Devi Jagadami
6 Kandariya Mahadev
7 Lakshmana
8 Lakshmi
9 Varaha
10 Matangeshvar
11 Lalguan Mahadev
12 Brahma
13 Vamana
14 Javari
15 Ghantai
16 Adinath
17 Parsvanath
18 Shantinath
19 Dulhadeo

Police: (☎ 74032). Just beyond the bus stand on Link Rd. No. 2; second booth more centrally located in Main Sq.

Hospital: Dr. R.K. Khare (☎ 74177, residence 72374). Recommended by local luxury hotels. His **clinic** is in the strip mall beside the bus station. Open M-Sa 10am-2pm and 6-9pm. There is a **24hr. pharmacy** (☎ 74453) to the right of Dr. Khare's clinic.

Post Office: Opposite the bus stand. Open M-Sa 9am-5pm. **Postal Code:** 471606.

ACCOMMODATIONS

Competition between guest houses in Khajuraho is intense, meaning you typically don't have to worry about finding a bed, even if you arrive late in the day in high season. Most places are also good bargains. All incoming buses are met by hordes of rickshaw-*wallahs* and hotel agents; as usual, you'll be in a much better bargaining position if you hoof it instead of agreeing to go with one of them.

The cheapest guest houses in town are all centrally located near the Western Group, with a string of similar places lined up side-by-side along Jain Temple Rd. The prices below apply to high season; in low season (Apr.-June), prices typically plummet. All accommodations below offer hot water unless otherwise noted.

Hotel Jain (☎ 72352; jainbanglesh@yahoomail.com). Jain Temple Rd. Next to Hotel Surya. Cheap, clean, friendly—what more do you want? The owner's family home, rooftop restaurant, and 20 guest rooms are arranged around a central courtyard. Dorms Rs40; singles Rs60-80, with bath Rs150-170; doubles with bath Rs100-250. 25% off-season discount. ❶

Yogi Lodge (☎ 74158). Down an alley on the left side of Main Sq. (with your back to the Western Group). Simple rooms in this popular guest house don't sparkle, but they suffice for simple lodging. Most have hot water and air cooling. Singles Rs50-70; doubles Rs80-150. The owner also runs the quaint, smaller, and more secluded **Yogi Ashram Guest House** 1.5km north of town on Main Rd. (on the left), where he gives free morning meditation lessons. Guests are welcome to use the communal kitchen and TV and enjoy fruit from the garden. Dorms/singles Rs50; doubles Rs100-150. ❶

Hotel Zen (☎ 74228; oshozen@hotmail.com). Jain Temple Rd. The last in the chain of guest houses, all the way down on the right. A classy place offering well-furnished rooms with attached bath, marble floors, and a courtyard. Higher-end rooms have bathtub and A/C. Singles Rs200-450; doubles Rs250-650. 50% off-season discount. ❷

Hotel Harmony (☎ 74135). Jain Temple Rd. On the right from Main Sq. Air-cooled rooms all with wood furnishings, TV, and attached bath. Doubles Rs250-350, with A/C Rs750; single occupants pay Rs100 less. 50% off-season discount. ❶

Hotel Surya (☎ 74145). Jain Temple Rd. On the right from Main Sq. Spacious, spotless rooms with bath, marble floors, and air-cooler; some with balconies. Singles Rs200-350; doubles Rs250-550. 30-40% discount May 1-July 15. ❷

Hotel Marble Palace (☎ 74353). Jain Temple Rd. On the left, set back from the street, opposite Gole Market. Designed by a Japanese architect with marble floors and fixtures, sleek black beds, and maharaja-inspired arched doorways. The Marble Palace earns its name with class, though you'll pay for it. Sheets changed daily. All rooms have bathtubs. Singles Rs350; doubles Rs450, with A/C Rs650. 20% off-season discount. ❷

Hotel Casa Di William (☎ 74244; hotelcasadiwilliam@123india.com). Prem Sagar Lake Rd. Take the 1st right north of the Western Group. Clean rooms with tasteful furniture, writing desk, and phone. Singles Rs300-500; doubles Rs400-600. 15% *Let's Go* discount; 25% off-season discount. ❷

Hotel Lakeside (☎ 74120). Main Rd. Opposite Shiv Sagar Lake, south of Main Sq. Popular but spartan budget place with good rooftop views of the lake and busy street below. Crowded dorms Rs40; singles Rs150-500; doubles Rs250-500, with A/C Rs800-1400. 40% off-season discount. ❶

▸ FOOD

Agrawal Restaurant, Gole Market. Just back from Jain Temple Rd. This modest joint serves up delicious *shudh shakahari* (pure veg.) South Indian dishes at wallet-friendly prices that put the tourist restaurants in town to shame. Indian *thalis, masalas,* and *paneers* Rs25-60. Open daily 8am-11pm. ❶

Blue Sky Restaurant, Main Rd. Just north of Main Sq. The restaurant's two-story terrace offers unparalleled views of the Western Group temples. Chef cooks a wide range of tasty Indian, continental, and Japanese dishes. Full breakfast Rs40-60; soups Rs25-40; main courses Rs30-60. Open daily 8am-10:30pm. ❶

Raja Cafe Swiss Restaurant, Main Rd. Directly opposite the Western Group. Run by a gregarious Swiss woman, the cafe dishes out full breakfasts (Rs80), Chinese and Indian food (Rs50-90), *au gratin* dishes (Rs80), and spot-on Western desserts, like only an expat could make 'em. Open daily 8am-10pm. ❶

Ristorante Mediterraneo, Jain Temple Rd. 200m from Main Rd., on the left, opposite Hotel Surya. 1000km from the nearest source of mozzarella, the Mediterraneo serves up good (for India) pizza, pasta, and wine-sized bottles of well-chilled beer to a European crowd that chatters the night away on the rooftop terrace. Pastas Rs50-130; pizzas from Rs130; crepes Rs40-75. Open daily 7:30am-10:30pm. ❷

🔘 SIGHTS

Construction of the temples at Khajuraho, which took place between AD 900 and 1100, was sponsored by the Chandela dynasty, a Rajput clan descended from Central Asian tribes that ruled over Central India from the 9th to the 13th centuries. When Chandela power waned, the temples were forgotten and lay hidden deep in the jungle for 700 years before the outside world—represented by British officer T.S. Burt—stumbled across them in 1838 (see **Sex in Khajuraho,** p. 373). Of the original 85 temples, only 25 still stand today.

Khajuraho's temples are conventionally divided into three groups; the Western Group contains the most famous and impressive of the temples, although all of them are stunning. You could see all three groups in one day, but it would be a very busy day. Splitting the Western and Eastern/Southern Groups between two mornings allows a more leisurely tour, and since almost all the temples face east, it brings the added benefit of enjoying the early morning light that highlights many intricate carvings that are difficult to see later on. For the biggest event in town, the annual **Khajuraho Dance Festival** (Feb. 14-20 each year through 2005), the government brings in India's best classical dancers to perform in front of the temples.

THE WESTERN GROUP

Open daily sunrise-sunset. Tour groups roll in by 9 or 10am; to save both your photos and your sanity, show up by 8am at the latest. US$10, or the equivalent in rupees. Audio guide Rs50.

The Western Group of temples, most of which are contained in a grassy, fenced-in compound maintained by the Archaeological Survey of India, holds many of the best examples of Khajuraho's magnificent architecture, including the Lakshmana and Kandariya Mahadev Temples. The custom of *pradakshina* dictates that visitors walk around the whole group clockwise and circle each temple the same way.

LAKSHMI AND VARAHA TEMPLES. The first stop on your *pradakshina* is the least impressive: the **Lakshmi Temple,** a small shrine that 19th-century repairs left with a jagged cement roof. Next door, the open-air, 10th-century **Varaha Mandap,** built for Vishnu's avatar as a boar ("Varaha"), offers a more promising beginning. The huge, solid-sandstone boar is so well polished that it shines like glazed porcelain. It is covered with rows of tiny gods and goddesses that total over 764 figures, including the deities of the sacred rivers Ganga, Yamuna, and Saraswati.

LAKSHMANA TEMPLE. Dating from around AD 941, the magnificent Lakshmana Temple, opposite the Lakshmi and Varaha temples and dedicated to Vishnu, is one of the largest, oldest, and best-wrought in Khajuraho. Its plan features two pairs of transepts and reflects the classic, five-component design that characterizes Khajuraho's great temples: an **ardhamandapa,** or entrance platform; a **mandapa,** or hallway, directly behind the entrance; a **mahamandapa,** or central hall, encircled by a small passageway and stone columns; a **garbagriha,** or inner shrine, which houses

SEX IN KHAJURAHO

The sculptor had at times allowed his subject to grow rather warmer than there was any absolute necessity for his doing; indeed, some of the sculptures here were extremely indecent and offensive.
——T. S. Burt, on Khajuraho, 1838

Ever since the temples were rediscovered by hapless, unprepared Mr. Burt, art historians and religious scholars have been trying to figure out why so much sex was carved into their walls. Some have suggested that the sculptures were offerings to the gods, especially Indra, the lord of lightning, who wouldn't dare destroy something that satiated his voyeuristic urges. Others maintain that they were used as sex education for privileged but isolated young boys. Yet another theory argues that tantric cults, which hold that spiritual development and physical pleasure are equally valid paths to *moksha* (salvation), used the temples for ritualized sex. Other Hindus read the sculpture as part of the wedding myth of Shiva and Parvati: the posing women, caught admiring themselves in the mirror, have stopped to watch the wedding procession; all the other gods are here as guests. When the marriage is consummated, the great lovemaking session lasts 1000 god-years.

Evidence in support of perhaps the most plausible theory, however, is carved right into the temples. Alongside the women prancing, preening, and panting are other women doing everyday things—applying makeup, caring for babies, writing letters, drying their hair, and removing thorns from their feet. And the pairs of lovers really make up only a small percentage of the participants in Khajuraho's pageant of life—hunters, acrobats, warriors, kings, dancers, and devotees, just to name a few, are there too. All this points to the conclusion that the erotic scenes at Khajuraho simply commemorated one aspect of daily life in a society in which sex was not considered taboo.

a representation of the deity to which the temple is consecrated (for instance, a *linga* for Shiva or a monkey statue for Hanuman); and a **pradakshina,** or closed passageway, around this sanctuary. The abbreviated, three-part Khajuraho temples lack the *mandapa* and *pradakshina* (see p. 96 for more info on Hindu temple architecture). Secondary shrines are arranged at the four corners of the main Lakshmana platform; all five temples are oriented such that a devotee ascending the terrace steps faces each door simultaneously. The Lakshmana Temple's carvings are exceptionally intricate, from the *mandapa* ceiling inside to the two bands of sculptures (instead of the usual three) lining the outer walls and the panoramic friezes that wind around the base. These fantastic sculptures showcase an endless procession of elephants, horses, and soldiers marching together in riotous disorder. The hunting and battle scenes intermittently devolve into orgiastic celebrations of the parts that God gave us (and the various ways in which they fit together)—the kinds of erotic scenes that put Khajuraho on the map and which continue to elicit giggles and blushes from visitors. Keep an eye out for the rather dismayed-looking elephant in the bottom-most frieze, just around to the left as you face the entrance. The frieze depicts the unfortunate way in which one hard-up soldier found that *their* parts fit together.

KANDARIYA MAHADEV TEMPLE. Straight ahead at the far end of the park, three temples stand together on the same platform. Built between 1025 and 1050 and dedicated to Shiva, the Kandariya Mahadev Temple, on the left, is the tallest temple in Khajuraho. It is considered the culmination of the Khajuraho school of architecture. The subordinate shrines that once graced the temple's four corners

MADHYA PRADESH

have long since disappeared, but the main shrine is extremely well preserved. An incredible wealth of sculptures adorns the walls, each exquisite specimen vying for the observer's attention. By one count, at least 226 statues line the interior, while 646 grace the exterior—872 in total, most nearly 3 ft. tall. A sex scene on the southern walls delights gaggles of gawkers, but the famous erotic scenes are really just one part of a wide variety of superlative sculpture here. A recent chemical treatment to remove the black mold that mars some other temples has enhanced the intricacy of the Kandariya Temple's adornments.

MAHADEV SHRINE AND DEVI JAGADAMI TEMPLE. On the same platform, next to the Kandariya Temple, is the **Mahadev Shrine,** which houses one of the finest sculptures at Khajuraho depicting a human figure grappling with a lion. It is thought that what remains here is merely the entrance portico of what was once a temple to Shiva. On the other side of the Mahadev Shrine is the **Devi Jagadami Temple.** Though smaller than the Lakshmana and Kandariya temples, it has some superb sculptures, most notably its directional guardians, who are stationed between boldly flirting women and delicate, sensual scenes. The image of Vishnu positioned over the doorway indicates that the temple was originally dedicated to him, though it now enshrines an image of Kali (Parvati painted black).

CHITRAGUPTA TEMPLE. Set apart from the other three temples along the back wall of the enclosure, this is Khajuraho's only temple to Surya (the sun god). Built circa AD 1000-1025, its plan is identical to Devi Jagadami's, though it is slightly more ornate and developed. Small processions run around the lower portion of the temple wall; higher up are many amorous couples. The damaged wall and roof were repaired with concrete. Most of the statues inside the temple have been decapitated, but the main image of Surya, driving his chariot across the sky, is missing only the arms.

PARVATI, VISHVANATH, AND NANDI TEMPLES. Continuing around the circuit, the next temple is the small and damaged **Parvati Temple,** overshadowed by the more spectacular **Vishvanath Temple** next to it, a large Shiva temple dated to AD 1002 from an inscription inside. The stairs on the northern side are flanked by a pair of lions; the stairs on the southern side, by a pair of elephants. The bawdy sculptures on the Vishvanath Temple are some of the best and depict whole scenes in which the couples' attendants also get caught up in the action. There are also some fascinating sculptures of posing women (called *apsaras* if they are dancing and *surasundaris* if performing other daily tasks)—look for the one on the south side twisting her hair to dry and the one on the ceiling inside holding a tiny baby. Some of the figures are sculpted in astonishing detail down to the very cuticles of their fingernails. The Vishvanath Temple originally had a shrine at each corner of its foundation as the Lakshmana Temple does, but only two remain. In front of the temple is the **Nandi Mandap,** an open square pavilion from which Shiva's bull, Nandi, gazes into the temple.

MATANGESHVAR TEMPLE. The three members of the Western Group that stray outside the fence are older and noticeably different from the others. Just over the fence from the Lakshmana Temple is the first, the Matangeshvar Temple. Built around AD 900, it is the only temple in this group that is still in use—more people come here to worship than to view the architecture. It is a relatively plain temple with only thin stripes of carving. Inside, a *linga* sits on top of a huge, stone platform. The temple's upper-level terrace has good views of the Lakshmana Temple.

CHAUSAT YOGINIS. Along the south side of Shiv Sagar Lake, a narrow, tree-lined path leads off to the right to the temple of Chausat Yoginis ("Sixty-Four Goddesses"). Built during the 9th century, Chausat Yoginis distinguishes itself as the oldest temple in Khajuraho and is made of crudely cut blocks of granite piled together like sandbags. Scarcely more than a large stone platform, the top is ringed by a gallery of empty shrines—only 35 of the original 64 remain.

LALGUAN MAHADEV TEMPLE. A further 500m west from Chausat Yoginis lies this small, ruined Shiva temple. It is part granite, part sandstone and is similar in design to the Brahma Temple.

ARCHAEOLOGICAL MUSEUM. Across the street from the Western Group enclosure, the Archaeological Museum houses sculptures separated from their temples. A wonderful Ganesh dances in the entrance hall. In the center of the Miscellaneous Gallery on the right, a king and queen—possibly the sculptor's Chandela patron—sit together making an offering. Also note the unfinished couple whose noses have been left stuck together, making them look like a pair of kissing Pinocchios. There are few pieces here to compare with the best sculpture still on the temples—the museum's main virtue is that it offers close-up views of sculptures otherwise hidden high up on the temple walls. *(Open M-Th and Sa-Su 10am-5pm. US$10, or the equivalent in rupees.)*

EASTERN AND SOUTHERN GROUPS

*To get to the Eastern Group from Main Sq., head down Jain Temple Rd. past Hotel Zen and bear left at the fork onto Basti Rd.; follow the sign to the old village. The temples are scattered throughout the village, with a few clustered in the Jain temple complex. The Southern Group is comprised of only three temples. Dulhadeo Temple is 600m down the paved road to your left as you walk out of the Jain temple complex. To get to the other two—Chaturbhuj and Bijamandal Temples—cruise 3km south of town on Main Rd., take the first left after the bridge, and head down this paved road to the temples. The easiest way to tour these groups is by bike; see **Local Transportation,** p. 369. Both groups open daily sunrise-sunset. Free.*

Located in and around Khajuraho village, the temples of the Eastern Group are not as stunning as those of the Western Group. But since they are visited by fewer people, they have an atmosphere of relative quiet and seclusion often missing from the temples of the main group. The Southern Group's three temples are farther apart from one another than from either of the other two groups.

The text below is organized as a biking (or walking) tour that first visits the Eastern Group temples in the old village, then the Eastern Group Jain temples clumped together beyond the village, and finally the Southern Group temples. By bike, you should be able to complete the tour leisurely in three to five hours.

EASTERN GROUP. On your left heading to the old village, you'll pass a **Hanuman Shrine** containing one of the oldest sculptures in Khajuraho, a large *sindur-*smeared Hanuman (monkey god) image that dates from AD 922. Crossing Bypass Rd. and entering Khajuraho village, the path veers to the left along the side of a seasonal pond called the **Khajur Sagar.** Not far along it on the left is the small **Brahma Temple,** misnamed by 19th-century art historians. A four-faced Shiva *linga* sits in the sanctuary, and Vishnu is carved on the lintel above the door. Continuing north and following the small path to the right brings you to the **Javari Temple,** which features a number of interesting pieces despite its small size and relatively simple design. The women dancing around the temple walls manage to look remarkably life-like and sprightly, though most of them had their heads knocked off centuries ago by Mughals. Continuing north on the main path leads to the **Vamana Temple.** As large as some of the temples in the Western Group, but simpler in design, it has slightly less impressive sculpture and decoration. Backtrack down the lakeside path and ask locals to point out the path to **Ghantai Temple,** or at least what remains of it—an entrance porch and tall pillars supporting a flat, ornate roof. The frieze illustrates the 16 dreams of Mahavira's mother.

Heading south and turning left on Jain Temple Rd. (follow the sign to the Jain temples) will bring you to the second subgroup of the Eastern Group, which consists of three Jain temples walled into a monastery complex on the far side of Khajuraho village. The old temples here are interspersed with newer ones. This mixture is embodied in the **Shantinath Temple,** the first temple as you enter the complex, which was built recently but has heavy pillars and doorways taken from older temples. Inside the temple is a collection of photographs, posters of Jain pilgrimage sites, plenty of sculptures, and paintings of naked monks.

To the left of the Shantinath Temple is an enclosure housing the two adjacent remaining temples. The most impressive Eastern Group temple, the **Parsvanath Temple,** is notable for its simple design and the small shrine at the back. In addition to Jain *tirthankaras* (saints), the sculptures on the outside depict just about every major Hindu deity, suggesting that this was once a Hindu temple. Some of the most famous sculptures in Khajuraho are here, including one of a woman putting on ankle-bells and another of a woman applying her makeup. The **Adinath Temple,** whose porch has been reconstructed in concrete, features limber women climbing up the walls. Shiny black *tirthankara* images sit inside both temples.

Just outside the Jain temple complex, the small but worthwhile **Jain Museum** houses a gallery of Jain sculptures and architecture. *(Open daily 7am-6pm. Rs52.)*

SOUTHERN GROUP. The **Dulhadeo Temple** dates from around AD 1100, by which time standards had started to slip in Khajuraho—the sculpture here is generally held to be inferior to that of the other temples. There are still plenty of interesting little scenes, though, including numerous dragon-like mythical beasts and people shown going about their daily lives. At the southern end of the temple is a pair of dioramas showing first a man and then a woman unsuccessfully imitating some of the other sex-in-stone scenes so prevalent in Khajuraho. The *linga* inside the temple is overlaid with dozens of tiny replicas of itself, giving it a curiously scaly appearance. The *mahamandapa*, with its great rotunda ceiling, is carved in an elaborate star shape. By the time this temple was built, sculptors were getting so carried away with the ornaments and jewelry on their human figures that the quality of the sculptures themselves had begun to decline.

The trip to **Chaturbhuj Temple** is best made in the late afternoon, since Chaturbhuj is the only big temple in Khajuraho that faces west. The evening light shines warmly on its 2.7m *dakshinamurti* statue of three deities carved from one stone. This huge image is a combination of Shiva, Vishnu, and Krishna. The sculptures around the outside feature another interesting hybrid: on the southern side, an image of Ardhanarishvara (half-Shiva, half-Parvati) is split down the middle, illustrating the motif of male and female union that was so significant to those who produced the marvelous sculptures at Khajuraho. Chaturbhuj is well-worth the trip, despite the fact that it is the only temple at Khajuraho without any erotic sculptures.

From Chaturbhuj, you'll be able to catch a glimpse (to the northeast) of what looks like not too much more than a pile of rubble, but is actually the fascinating remains of **Bijamandal Temple.** To get there, follow the marked dirt path that forked left as you followed the paved path right to Chaturbhuj. This newest member of the Southern Group (it was just opened to visitors in 1999) is still under excavation, but the lowest portions are clear and some tantalizing carvings (as well as the remains of a Shiva *linga*) poke out from the rock piles above. The temple is quite large, and will be a fantastic sight to behold once restoration is complete.

JHANSI झांसी   ☎ 0517

Travelers would be well advised to take a good, long look at the timetables before coming to Jhansi—this is not the kind of town you want to be stranded in. Jhansi (pop. 379,000), though technically in Uttar Pradesh, draws tourists because of its proximity to Orchha and its function as a railhead for Khajuraho, both in Madhya Pradesh. If schedules conspire to keep you here, you can while away the hours lamenting the recent price increases that have made two of the city's three time-killers, the Jhansi Fort and the Rani Mahal, prohibitively expensive.

▐ TRANSPORTATION. Buses for Khajuraho leave from the railway station (4 per day 5:30-11am) and the bus stand (11:45am and 1:15pm, Rs75-85). Frequent Delhi-bound **trains** leave throughout the day, of which the fastest is the A/C *Shatabdi Exp. 2001*, which goes to **Delhi** (5hr., 5:55pm, Rs565) via **Agra** (2¼hr., Rs390) and **Gwalior** (1¼hr., Rs495). Frequent trains also run to **Bhopal** (*Shatabdi Exp. 2002*, 4 hr., 10:32am, Rs480) and **Jabalpur** (*Mahakoshal Exp. 1450*, 11½hr., 11:05pm, sleeper Rs166). **Tempos** for Orchha (Rs6) leave from the bus stand.

▐▌ ▐▌ ORIENTATION AND PRACTICAL INFORMATION. Downtown Jhansi covers a 5km span from the **railway station** in the west to the **bus stand** in the east. Heading left out of the railway station and turning right at Chitra Crossing (1km from the station) brings you to **Shivpuri Rd.**, which leads toward the town's central crossing and the fort. As the town is quite spread out, you'll need auto-rickshaws to get around—they should take you anywhere local for Rs10. The **Madhya Pradesh Tourism** booth on platform #1 of the railway station provides transit info and maps of the city. (☎ 442622. Open daily 10am-6pm.) The **State Bank of India,** at the center of town, near Elite Crossing, changes only American Express traveler's checks. (☎ 443919. Open M-F 10am-4pm, Sa 10am-1pm.) The **GPO,** Sadarj Marg, Civil Lines, is across the street from the Jhansi Hotel. (Open M-Sa 10am-6pm.) The government **hospital** (☎ 440572) is on Manik Chowk, the market at the base of the fort. The **police station** is on the Main Rd. (☎ 440538). **Postal Code:** 284001.

▐▌ ▐▌ ACCOMMODATIONS AND FOOD. Hotel Samrat ❷, Chitra Sq., Shivpuri Rd., 1km from the train station, provides the best value in town. All rooms come with attached (cold-water) bath, TVs, and phones. (☎ 444943. Singles Rs200-500; doubles Rs250-550.) **The Prakash Regency Guest House ❷,** Sardari Lal Market, Civil Lines, just north of Elite Crossing (the center of town) on the right, offers pleasant mid-range lodgings, all with air-cooling and attached bath. The Prakash Regency also boasts—wonder-of-all-wonders for a budget hotel—a swimming pool. (☎ 330133. Singles Rs250-600; doubles Rs350-600.) **Hotel Veerangana ❶,** 10min. past Hotel Samrat on Shivpuri Rd., is a U.P. Tourism-run place with clean dorms (men-only) and large, clean rooms. (☎ 442402. Dorms Rs60; singles Rs200-525; doubles Rs275-600.) The **restaurant ❶,** in the █Hotel Sita, Shivpuri Rd., serves first-rate food in a plush, climate-controlled environment. (Main courses from Rs45. Open daily 6:30-10:30am, noon-3pm, 7-11pm.)

◪ SIGHTS. The **Jhansi Fort** is dedicated to Maharani Lakshmi Bai, a celebrated revolutionary who joined the anti-British sepoys in the Mutiny of 1857. As the British recaptured the region, Jhansi was one of the last rebel holdouts. Dressed as a man, her guns blazing, the maharani rode out into battle to meet her demise 180km from Jhansi. Today the fort serves primarily as an empty and decrepit home to bands of monkeys and bats, though the maze of archways, stairwells, turrets, and abandoned rooms can provide for some interesting exploration. However, for most, the view isn't worth the exorbitant admission fee. *(Open daily sunrise-sunset. US$5, or the equivalent in rupees.)* You can get a few jollies for free just outside the fort, along the southern wall as you approach the main entrance, from the bizarre life-sized model depicting a battle between heroic Indian freedom-fighters and their dastardly redcoat oppressors during the Mutiny of 1857. "Who cannot remain unimpressed by this life-like picturisation?" asks a nearby sign—a pertinent question, indeed.

The colorful **Rani Mahal** palace, down the other side of the hill from the fort and a few minutes to the left, was constructed in the late 18th century and today houses sculptures from the late Pratihar and Chandela periods. *(Open daily 9:30am-5:30pm. US$5, or the equivalent in rupees. Same ticket covers fort and Rani Mahal.)* The only reasonably priced way to kill time in Jhansi is the **U.P. Government Museum,** at the base of the road leading up to the fort, which houses more archaeological finds from the area, though to call the largely empty museum worthwhile might be a stretch. *(Open July-Apr. 15 10:30am-4:30pm; Apr. 16-June 7:30am-12:30pm. Rs2.)*

ORCHHA ओरछा ☎ 07680

On a loop in the Betwa river, 16km from Jhansi, the wistful little town of Orchha sits in the shadows of an abandoned 17th-century city that once served as the capital of the Bundela kingdom. Raja Rudra Pratap Bundela founded the capital here in 1531, and Orchha continued to grow and prosper up through its golden age in the early 17th century. Throughout this period, the Bundelas managed to keep the neighboring Mughal Empire at bay. Raja Bir Singh Deo (r. 1605-27), the greatest Bundela king, befriended the emperor Jehangir and even welcomed him as a visitor in 1606. Under Bir Singh Deo, the Bundelas controlled the whole region of Bundelkhand, which still bears their name. Later rulers were less successful at appeasing the Mughals, and the kingdom's long, slow decline began as soon as the emperor Shah Jahan attacked Orchha. The city was abandoned in 1783, when the onslaught of Mughal and Maratha attacks became too much for the residents to withstand.

The Bundelas left a landscape filled with palaces and temples, and nothing but the forces of nature (and now tourists) have disturbed them in the two centuries since. Orchha, meaning "hidden," lives up to its name—when human rulers gave up the attempt to conceal the city from invaders, nature took up the challenge. The ruins are overgrown with trees and weeds, cracked walls are shrouded with vines, and empty palace courtyards echo the screeching songs of squeaking bats.

▐▌▐▌ TRANSPORTATION AND PRACTICAL INFORMATION

Tempos (Rs6) and **auto-rickshaws** (Rs60) make the quick trip from Jhansi to Orchha. **Buses** between Jhansi and Khajuraho also stop just north of town; you can catch a tempo or walk the 1km to Orchha. The town itself is tiny, with only one **crossroads.** If you're coming from Jhansi or Khajuraho, the road straight through the crossroads leads south to the chhattris and the Betwa River; to the left and east, a bridge crosses over to the palaces on Orchha Island; to the right and west are most of the accommodations in town, as well as the temples. Just north of the crossroads on the righthand side is **Canara Bank,** which exchanges traveler's checks and US dollars. (Open M-F 10:30am-2:30pm, Sa 10:30am-12:30pm.) Just east of the crossroads is the **post office. Postal code: 472245.**

▐▌▐▌ ACCOMMODATIONS AND FOOD

The best value in town is the new, brightly painted **Sharma Guest House ❶,** which offers clean rooms and a nice rooftop view. It's on the right as you head south from the crossroads. (Rooms with common bath Rs125, with bath Rs150.) Of the string of budget places lined up just west of the crossroads, the best is the **Shri Mahant Guest House ❶**. (☎52715. Doubles with attached bath Rs200-250.) The nearby **Hotel Mansarovar ❶**, is much more basic. (☎52623. Doubles with bath Rs150.) The cheapest beds in town are buried inside the **Palki Mahal ❶**, the run-down palace to the right of Ram Raja Temple as you face it; the manager's office is opposite the entrance. (☎52633. Dorms Rs25; doubles with common bath Rs90.) The MPSTDC has converted an 18th-century palace in the middle of the ruins into the moderately priced **Sheesh Mahal Hotel ❷**, where only the most expensive suites are really palatial. The best rooms are decked out with rugs, marble baths, decorative hookahs, and TVs. (Singles Rs190-490; doubles Rs590; suites Rs1990-2990. Email reservations at least 10-15 days in advance to mail@mptourism.com.)

Betwa Tarang Restaurant ❶, near the bridge on the crossroads side, serves Indian food and the usual traveler fare (Rs20-50) on a rooftop with palace views. (Open daily 7:30am-10:30pm.) The **Orchha Resort's ❶**, shiny, A/C, all-vegetarian restaurant serves excellent meals for Rs85 and up. (Open daily 7am-9:30pm.)

◎ SIGHTS

ORCHHA RUINS

All locations open daily 9am-5pm. Rs30 for a ticket that covers all the main sights, including the Lakshmi Narayan Temple and the chhattris. Photography Rs20. Walkman tour 2hr.; Rs50, Rs500 deposit.

The ruins of Orchha are scattered along a bend in the Betwa, and they spill across from the main island to the present-day village and beyond. Nothing much has happened in Orchha over the past 200 years to clear them away, and nothing of consequence has been built here since the Bundelas shut up shop and left the place to the winds. The old buildings still dominate the landscape, and abandoned palaces and temples stand undisturbed amid the grasses and trees. Slumping towers and overgrown archways are everywhere, most of them unnamed and unmarked. MP Tourism offers a **walkman tour,** available at Sheesh Mahal Hotel, built into a wing of the Jehangir Mahal, that covers the three main palaces. This is well worth taking for the historical background, though you'll probably find your finger twitching over the fast-forward button from time to time as the breathless narrator launches into yet another dramatic "picture-the-scene" sequence. If any of the ruins are closed and locked as you make the tour, a complaint at the ticket office can often prompt someone to find the keys to the gate.

RAJ MAHAL. The Raj Mahal was the king's residence, with a room for his private audiences and several chambers for his harem. Constructed in the 16th century and one of the oldest buildings in Orchha, the palace lacks any notable ornamental features, though the walls and ceilings of many of the rooms are painted with intricate botanical patterns and murals depicting religious and mythical scenes. The top windows offer a good view of the town. *(On the right as you approach the Sheesh Mahal Hotel.)*

RAI PRAVEEN MAHAL. Built and named for Raja Indramani's favorite dancing concubine, the smallest of the three main palaces was intended to be level with the treetops in the Anand Mandal Bagh gardens behind it. These can still be seen from the 2nd floor, and though neither the palace nor its gardens have exactly improved with age, it is still possible to imagine (as your audio-guide will constantly remind you) that this must once have been quite a nice place to kick back and relax after a long hard day spent wielding supreme executive power. *(Follow the road around to the left instead of heading up the stairs toward the hotel and the Raj Mahal.)*

JEHANGIR MAHAL. Built for Emperor Jehangir when he visited Orchha in 1606, the Jehangir Mahal palace surpasses anything else the Bundelas ever built in Orchha. Two elephants nod in welcome on both sides of the entrance, and inside, the Jehangir Mahal is filled with balconies, walkways, and railings. Traces of Islamic style can be seen in the stone screens and decorated domes. The views from the third-floor balconies are some of Orchha's best: the Betwa river curls through the countryside and into the village, winding its way past the ruins. Throughout the palace are fine carvings of peacocks, parrots, snakes, and other animals. There is also a tiny **museum** (closed M) on the ground floor, whose most interesting piece is a tremendous metal pot. *(Continue along the path to the right, past the camel stables, to the main entrance.)*

TEMPLES

The three most important Bundela temples lie across the bridge from the ruins and to the right of the crossroads as you approach from Jhansi and Khajuraho.

RAM RAJA TEMPLE. The devout Raja Madhukar Shah had a dream in which Lord Rama appeared to him and ordered him to bring an image of the Lord to Orchha from Rama's holy hometown of Ayodhya. The king did as he was told, but arriving back in Orchha before his workmen had completed the temple designed to house the image, he decided to keep the holy image in his own palace until the temple could be completed. When the time came to relocate him, though, Lord Rama refused to budge. The palace had to be given up, and it became the Ram Raja Temple, where Rama has been worshipped in his role as a king ever since. Painted pink and yellow and overlooking a cobbled square, Ram Raja is now a popular temple. You'll have to leave your machine-gun and jackboots at home, though—no firearms or leather goods are allowed inside. *(Open daily 8am-12:30pm and 8-10:30pm.)*

CHHATURBHUJ TEMPLE. The massive but defunct Chhaturbhuj Temple is only marked by the remaining great arching assembly hall and several large spires. Spiral staircases at each corner of the cross-shaped floorplan lead to high lookout points that offer fantastic views of the palace complex across the river. *(To the left of the Ram Raja Temple.)*

LAKSHMI NARAYAN TEMPLE. Isolated from the rest of Orchha and positioned at the crest of a hill, the Lakshmi Narayan temple's location seems fit for a fort, and it is built like one with four high walls, turrets at the corners, and two mighty stone lions standing guard at the entrance. Inside the temple are the best paintings to be found anywhere in Orchha, dating from the 17th to 19th centuries, including one fabulous post-Mutiny scene of British soldiers swarming around an Indian fort. Other scenes depict the Ramayana and Krishna stories and the marriage of Shiva. The breathtaking view from the top surveys all of Orchha, from the temples and palaces all the way down to the chhattris and beyond. *(Follow the westward path from behind Ram Raja Temple for 1km. Open daily 10am-5pm.)*

OTHER SIGHTS

On the island, turning left after passing through the **Royal Gate** and then walking through another archway in a wall brings you to the north end of the island, which is a good place to fight back the thornbushes and explore. The area is dotted with **old temples** that have been neglected and are now surrounded by small wheat farms. People still dip into the ancient wells for their water here, and in some cases, the temples have become makeshift tool sheds, kitchens, and cow barns.

In town, to the right of the Palki Mahal palace, the **Phool Bagh Gardens** contain a formally laid out garden featuring a row of fountains and a small palace-pavilion. The Orchha kings retreated to a cool underground structure here to seek refuge from the summer heat.

Clustered along the peaceful, tree-lined banks of the Betwa river south of town is a series of 14 royal chhattris (cenotaphs). The Hindu Bundelas cremated their dead, but this did not stop them from borrowing the Mughal custom of mauso-leum-building in order to commemorate the departed. Admission to the impressive complex is included in the same ticket that covers the rest of the sights in town. *(On foot, 10min. south of town and just past the Betwa Cottages and Orchha Resort.)*

GWALIOR ग्वालियर   ☎ 0751

Currently boasting a population of almost one million, Gwalior has long been legendary for its massive fort, dubbed "the pearl amongst the fortresses of Hind" by Emperor Babur. Generations of conquerors have gazed down on the world from its mighty walls. During the Raj, the British granted the Maharaja of Gwalior one of only five 21-gun salutes ever bestowed upon Indian potentates in recognition of his loyalty during the Mutiny. This stands in stark contrast to the fate of Maharani Lakshmi Bai, who resisted the British from nearby Jhansi (see p. 377). The Scindia royal family is still the focus of Gwalior's civic pride— their palace, a 19th-century shrine to conspicuous consumption, offers a glimpse into a fairy-tale world of kitschy chaos and conforms to every preconceived notion of what a maharaja's house should look like.

▛ TRANSPORTATION

Flights: The **airport,** Bhind Rd. (☎470272), is 10km northeast of the city. **Indian Airlines,** MLB Rd. (☎326872, airport office ☎368124). Open M-Sa 10am-1:15pm and 2-4:45pm. To **Delhi** (45min.; M and F 1:15pm, Tu, Th, and Sa noon; US$75) and **Jabalpur** (1½hr.; Tu, Th, and Sa 8:25am; US$135).

Trains: Railway Station, MLB Rd., Morar (☎341344). **Computerized reservation office** open M-Sa 8am-8pm, Su 8am-2pm. *Shatabdi Exp.* fares are for A/C chair-car; others are for sleeper class. To: **Agra** (2-3hr., frequent 4:15am-2:35am, Rs56; **Bhopal** (6-8hr., 15-20 per day 9:15am-3am, Rs140; *Shatabdi Exp. 2002,* 4½hr., 9:15am, Rs545); **Delhi** (5½-7hr., frequent 3:45am-2am, Rs123; *Shatabdi Exp. 2001,* 4hr., 7pm, Rs495); **Jhansi** (1½-2hr., frequent 3:45am-2am, Rs50); **Lucknow** (9hr.; daily 11:15am; also Tu 4:15am; Rs83); **Mumbai** (22 hr., daily 10:25am, Rs310) via **Kanpur** (7hr.); **Mathura** (3hr., frequent 3:45am-1am, Rs80).

Buses: State bus stand (☎340192), near the railway station, off MLB Rd. To: **Agra** (3hr., frequent 5am-9:30pm, Rs56-62); **Bhopal** (11hr., 7:30am, Rs174); **Delhi** (8hr., 18 per day 5am-9:30pm, Rs156); **Jhansi** (3hr., every 30min. 4am-10pm, Rs46-51); **Khajuraho** (8½hr., 7:25 and 8:30am, Rs129).

▓▐ ORIENTATION AND PRACTICAL INFORMATION

Gwalior is quite spread out, wrapped in an irregular "U" shape around the **fort.** The **Old Town,** containing the **railway station** and the **state bus stand,** lies to the east of the fort. The **Morar** area, dominated by the gaudy **palace,** is to the southeast, and the **Lashkar** area (the heart of modern Gwalior and home to **Bada Chowk**) is in the southwest. **Maharani Lakshmi Bai (MLB) Rd.** runs across town from the northeast, near the station, to Lashkar. Tuesday is Gwalior's **business holiday.**

Tourist Office: MPSTDC (☎540777). Platform #1 of the railway station. Open M-Sa 9am-8pm. The **main regional tourist office,** Gandhi Rd. (☎340370), is inside the Hotel Tansen. Map guide Rs10. Open M-Sa 11am-5pm; if closed, ask at reception.

Currency Exchange: State Bank of India, Bada Chowk (☎336291). Changes traveler's checks and foreign currency. Open M-F 10:30am-4pm, Sa 10:30am-1:30pm.

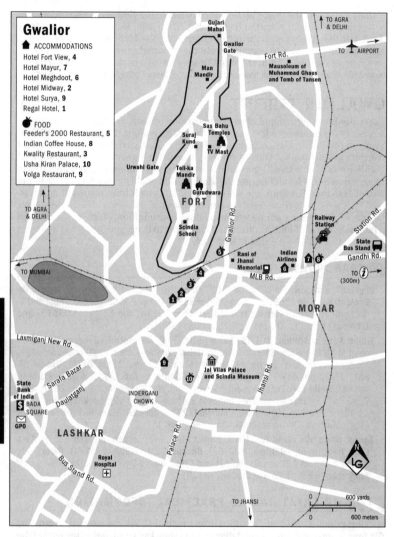

Gwalior

⌂ ACCOMMODATIONS
Hotel Fort View, **4**
Hotel Mayur, **7**
Hotel Meghdoot, **6**
Hotel Midway, **2**
Hotel Surya, **9**
Regal Hotel, **1**

● FOOD
Feeder's 2000 Restaurant, **5**
Indian Coffee House, **8**
Kwality Restaurant, **3**
Usha Kiran Palace, **10**
Volga Restaurant, **9**

Police: Jayendra Ganj (emergency ☎ 100).

Hospital: Royal Hospital, Kampoo (☎ 332711). Near Roxy Cinema. A recommended private hospital, with doctors available 24hr. **Pharmacy** open 24hr. **Kasturba Medical Stores,** 6 Kasturba Market (☎ 310953), is open 24hr.

Internet: Several places have sprung up along MLB Rd. and around town; most charge Rs25-35 per hr. **Bhargava Computers,** opposite the Miss Hill School, Lakshmi Bai Colony (☎ 428946). A short distance west of the Indian Airlines office, turn through the eastern gate to the colony; the store is 100m down on the left. Web access Rs35 per hr.; after 5pm Rs25 per hr. Open daily 9:30am-9:30pm.

Post Office: GPO, Bada Chowk. Open M-Sa 8am-8pm, Su 10am-6pm. **Postal Code:** 474001.

ACCOMMODATIONS

Accommodations in Gwalior are frustratingly expensive, and most hotels (including all those listed below) will slap a **20% luxury tax/service charge** onto your bill to boot, but in most cases you get what you pay for (i.e. hot water bath and cable TV). Those really traveling on a shoestring can check out the budget hotels lining the market in front of the railway station, but in general, these are overpriced (from Rs135) for what you get (musty, very unappealing rooms).

Hotel Mayur, Padav (☎325559). Turn right out of the railway station and go over the fly-over; double back down the small road to the right, and look for the sign down an alley on the left. Clean, well-furnished, mid-range rooms with cold-water bath (bucket hot water available) and cable TV. Dorms (men-only) Rs55; singles Rs120-500; doubles Rs150-600. ❷

Hotel Fort View, MLB Rd. (☎423409). One of a string of places along the main road in the shadow of the fort. Decent rooms all come with attached (hot-water) bath and TV. Check-out noon. Singles Rs250-425; doubles Rs300-500. Off season: 10-15% discount. ❷

Hotel Midway, MLB Rd. (☎424392). 2km from the railway station. A complex with clean sheets and towels, satellite TVs, phones that work, attached hot-water baths, and complimentary (for guests) email facilities. Singles Rs250-450; doubles Rs300-550. 10% discount for Let's Go readers. ❷

Regal Hotel, Shinde Ki Chhawanii, MLB Rd. (☎334469). Another decent place facing the main road, with slightly worn but fairly spacious rooms with TV and hot-water bath. Breezy garden terrace upstairs and airless beer bar downstairs. Singles Rs200-300; doubles Rs250-400. ❷

Hotel Meghdoot, Padav (☎326148). In the back of a commercial plaza next to the Indian Airlines office, just after the fly-over from the railway station. Well-furnished rooms with wall-to-wall carpets. Good location for rail access. Singles Rs200-350; doubles Rs350-450. ❷

Hotel Surya, Jayendra Ganj, Lashkar (☎331183). A bit removed from the tourist scene—you'll need a rickshaw to find it. Wood furniture, hot water, color TVs, and balconies with scenic views of the brick buildings next door. Singles Rs275-375; doubles Rs350-550. ❷

FOOD

Feeder's 2000 Restaurant, Gwalior Rd. On the left, just north of the intersection with MLB Rd. It may look a little shady from the outside, but this underground lair serves up tasty Indian dishes (entrees Rs28-50) in a clean and tasteful environment. Open daily 9am-11:30pm. ❶

Indian Coffee House, Station Rd. Under Hotel India. In the strip of shops between the two exits of the railway station. Same old reliable veg. snacks and a good cup of coffee. The old waiters-in-white-caps routine never fails. Open daily 7am-10:30pm.

Volga Restaurant, Tayendra Ganj. Inside Hotel Surya. No Russian food at this chandeliered, A/C bastion of the *bourzhaozya*, but good Indian food and even a few Chinese dishes to bridge the Sino-Soviet split. Entrees Rs28-50. Open daily 9:30am-11pm. ❶

Kwality Restaurant, Deendayal Market, MLB Rd. Chalk up another one for the dim, nondescript, A/C chain with a spelling problem. Standard range of north Indian veg. (Rs28-50), chicken (Rs40-130), and *biryani* (Rs20-40) dishes. Open daily 10am-11pm. ❶

Usha Kiran Palace, Jayendraganj, Lashkar. Next to the Jai Vilas Palace. This tasteful restaurant inside Gwalior's most beautiful hotel is the place to come to if the luxury at nearby Jai Vilas Palace has whet your appetite for the finer things in life. *Haute cuisine* from around the world (main courses Rs110-200). Open daily 6-10:30am, noon-3pm, and 7-11pm. ❷

🔘 SIGHTS

GWALIOR FORT

Open daily 8am-6pm. Admission to complex Rs0.20; additional joint ticket good for entry into Man Mandir Palace, Teli-ka Mandir, and Sas Bahu temples US$5 or rupee equivalent. English-language sound and light show (at Man Mandir Palace) daily 7:30pm; Rs100.

Gwalior's amazing fort, almost 3km long and at points 1km wide, dominates the city from 90m above, behind hulking 10m high walls. It has been the center of the region's power for all of recorded history. According to legend, King Suraj built the fort in the first century AD and named it after a holy hermit, Gwalipa, who cured Suraj's leprosy. Since then, the fort has been ruled by all of the region's succeeding dynasties: Rajputs, Delhi Sultans, Mughals, Marathas, and eventually the British. Since 1886, the fort has belonged to the Scindias, Gwalior's royal family. Through the ages, the fort has accumulated palaces and temples and more recently, a prestigious boys' school, a TV relay station, and two post offices.

There are two entrances to the fort: **Gwalior Gate** on the northeast side next to the Old Town, and **Urwahi Gate** on the southwest, which can be entered through a long gorge. Both have long, steep ramps that must be climbed on foot, although cars and taxis (but not auto-rickshaws) can enter through Urwahi Gate. The following sights are listed from northeast (Gwalior Gate) to southwest (Urwahi Gate); seeing them in this order is recommended as the view of Man Mandir's Palace above from Gwalior Gate yields a powerful first impression. *(An auto-rickshaw ride here from town should run about Rs20.)*

GUJARI MAHAL AND ARCHAEOLOGICAL MUSEUM. At the base of the hill, just inside Gwalior Gate, is the well-preserved **Gujari Mahal Palace,** built by Man Singh Tomar for his favorite queen. Inside the palace courtyard is a charming **archaeological museum** with a melange of Hindu and Jain sculptures and paintings from the region. The curator keeps a miniature sculpture of the tree-goddess Gyraspur—a priceless piece of art history—under lock and key, but you might be able to coax him into letting you see it. *(Museum open Tu-Su 10am-5pm. Rs2; photography Rs2.)*

NORTHEASTERN RAMP. The northeastern ramp continues up through a series of arched gateways past Jain and Hindu shrines. The first gate, **Alamgiri Gate,** was built in 1660. The third (the second did not survive), **Badalgarh,** was named after Man Singh's uncle, Badal Singh. The 15th-century **Ganesh Gate** is a small temple dedicated to Gwalipa. After a string of small but interesting Jain and Hindu shrines cut into the rock face is the 9th-century **Chaturbhuj Mandir,** a temple dedicated to Vishnu. At the top of the incline is the **Elephant Gate,** which is the fifth and final gate in the series, as well as the entrance to the palace.

MAN MANDIR PALACE AND ARCHAEOLOGICAL MUSEUM. The Man Mandir, marked by its distinctive blue-splotched towers, is the most interesting and best-preserved of Gwalior's palaces. Inside the palace, built by Raja Man Singh in the 15th century, are many small rooms split by lattices carved into the shape of animals and dancers. These elaborate, perforated screens bear witness to the system of *purdah*, or veiling, that is customary among certain groups of Hindus and Muslims. Women would spend much of their time sitting behind these screens, peering through them at the world outside. A flashlight will show the way down to the two-level subterranean dungeon complex where, in the 17th century, the Mughal emperor Aurangzeb had his brother Murad chained up and slowly killed by starvation and intoxication, feeding him nothing but boiled, mashed-up poppies. Near the Man Mandir Palace is a **museum,** run by the Archaeological Survey of India. *(Open M-Th and Sa-Su 10am-5pm. Rs2.)*

OTHER PALACES. Passing through the gate on your right as you exit Man Mandir will bring you to the north end of the fort. This area is a barren landscape where ruined palaces and dried-up tanks cling to the edge of the hill. Several points along the northeastern wall here offer spectacular views of the Man Mandir towering over the Gujari Mahal and modern Gwalior below. The ruins of the **Jehangir Mahal, Shah Jahan Mahal,** and **Vikram Mahal** beg for exploration. The huge **Jauhar Tank** nearby is remembered for the *jauhar* (self-immolation) of Rajput queens here in 1232, when Sultan Iltutmish of Delhi was on the verge of capturing the fort.

SAS BAHU TEMPLES. About halfway along the eastern edge of the hilltop are the Sas Bahu, or Mother-in-Law and Daughter-in-Law temples, built from the 9th to 11th centuries. The edge of the fort here offers a drab view of the city; the most interesting thing visible is the big, brown dome of Mohammed Ghaus' tomb. The west side of the fort has better views of the huge city and its craggy landscape.

TELI-KA MANDIR AND GURUDWARA. Toward the southern end of the fort, past the massive TV tower, stands the **Teli-ka Mandir** (Oilman's Temple), a tall chunk of carved stone dating from the 9th century. It was once a Vishnu temple, but when the British occupied the fort in the 19th century, they turned it into a soda-water factory. There is nothing inside now but a fetid stink. The outside is pretty enough, though, with a Dravidian (southern Indian) roof and Indo-Aryan (northern Indian) decoration.

Just east of the temple is the **Bandi Chhor Gurudwara,** a Sikh pilgrimage site that marks the spot where the sixth Sikh Guru, Hargobind, was imprisoned for two years by Emperor Jehangir. Ritual cleansing is required, and cloths are provided for you to cover your head before entering the *gurudwara.* Inside, men sit and chant Sikh scriptures above a sunken, silver chamber marking the guru's jail.

SOUTHWESTERN RAMP. Backtracking a bit north from the Teli-ka Mandir and passing through part of the grounds of the Scindia School brings you to the other main road connecting the fort with town. It snakes down through the long Urwahi Gorge, a natural rift in the hillside. Its walls are decorated with rows of **Jain sculptures** dating from between the 7th and 15th centuries. These figures of *tirthankaras* still stand impassively above the road, despite the best efforts of Mughal conqueror Babur, who damaged many of the statues by smashing their faces and genitals to pieces. One statue, an image of Adhinath, is 19m tall. More of these carvings are on the southeastern side of the fort, including one still used as a Jain shrine.

COME ON BABY, FIGHT MY FIRE

Legend has it that Akbar's greatest court singer, Miyan Tansen, learned the powerful *raga dipak* after seeing a twig spontaneously catch fire in a songbird's beak. The *raga,* when performed at full intensity, supposedly turns the performer's vocal chords into ashes. When Tansen's jealous rivals challenged him to sing *dipak* for the emperor, he welcomed the opportunity. Little did they know that the savvy musician had trained his wife in the rain-inducing *raga mahar* to counter *dipak's* fiery impact. When the crooner began to ignite, his wife was called in, and the subsequent duet of fire and water so impressed Akbar that he aided Tansen's ascendancy in the imperial court.

OUTSIDE THE FORT

JAI VILAS PALACE AND MUSEUM. Maharaja Jiyaji Rao Scindia commissioned a British architect to build this great white whale of a complex for him in an attempt to impress the Prince of Wales (later Edward VII) on his state visit here in 1875. Generations of Scindias have since filled it with the most outrageous *objets d'art* and kitsch imaginable. Today, part of it is open as the **Scindia Museum** (the rest is still the family's residence). Chairs, dressers, and tables from Versailles, a set of shimmering crystal furniture, and a dining table with tracks for a silver toy train that once wheeled around after-dinner brandy and cigars are only a few of the palace's notable features. From the gilded ceiling of Durbar Hall hang two enormous Belgian chandeliers, each weighing 3.5 tons; below them is the largest handmade carpet in Asia. To test the strength of the hall's ceiling, ten elephants were led up ramps onto the roof. *(Tell the rickshaw-wallah "Jai Vilas Museum,"; a different entrance is used for the palace. Open daily M-Tu and Th-Su 9:30am-5pm. Rs175 for foreigners. Keep your ticket stub for entry to both wings.)*

MAUSOLEUM OF MUHAMMAD GHAUS AND TOMB OF TANSEN. On a beautiful grassy expanse 10min. east of the fort's northeastern gate is the **Mausoleum of Sheik Muhammad Ghaus,** named for the Afghan prince and Muslim saint who helped the emperor Babur capture Gwalior Fort. The walls of this fine early Mughal monument are made up of a series of cut-stone screens carved into beautiful geometric patterns. The **Tomb of Tansen** is in the same graveyard; this 16th-century raga-singer was one of the greatest musicians in Indian history (see **Come on Baby, Fight My Fire,** above). Chewing the leaves of the tamarind tree near the tomb is supposed to make your voice as sweet as Tansen's. A classical music festival takes place here in Nov. or Dec.

MAHARASHTRA

महाराष्ट्र

Maharashtra, the "Great Country," straddles the Indian Peninsula, from the tropical coast to the arid Deccan Plateau, from the fringes of the hot and hectic Ganga Plain to the balmier, palmier, more easy-going South, and from isolated villages to metropolitan Mumbai. From the sacred Godavari at Nasik and the giddy, red-robed, Birkenstock-clad acolytes of the Osho Commune to the businessmen and billboards of Mumbai, Maharashtra has more than enough to keep you happy. More than half of India's foreign trade and nearly 40% of its tax revenue flow from here, but two-thirds of Maharashtra's population still practices subsistence agriculture. Many people here are proud of the the bold martial traditions of their state, and are quick to embrace the fierce regional independence of their forbears, the Marathas, hardy fighters bred in the rocky hinterland. This heritage is embodied in the warrior-king and folk-hero Shivaji (1627-80) and is currently exploited by the ruling Shiv Sena ("Shiva's Army") Party, a Hindu nationalist ally of the BJP.

HIGHLIGHTS OF MAHARASHTRA

The intricately carved **cave temples** at **Ajanta** (p. 428) and **Ellora** (p. 426), both UNESCO World Heritage Sites, are architectural wonders par excellence.

A hissing, buzzing helter-skelter of a city, **Mumbai** (below) will make your head spin, with its sights, sounds, nightlife, and inexhaustible energy.

MUMBAI (BOMBAY) मुंबई ☎ 022

India's largest city, in attitude if not in population, Mumbai unites all the country's languages, religions, ethnicities, castes, and classes in one heaving, seething sizzler of a metropolis. The city blends traditions and innovations from every region, city, and village in India and beyond, offering everything from *bhel puri* to bell-bottoms. Trade through the city accounts for 50% of India's imports and exports, its densest concentration of industry, and its largest stock exchange. Rupee and dollar billionaires, film stars, models, and politicians flock to frolic to the city's hotels, discos, and restaurants. But Mumbai is by no means a "Western" city. It also harbors more of the desperately poor than any other Indian city; the shanty-town at Dharavi has become Asia's (and perhaps the world's) largest slum. As many as half of Mumbai's 16 million residents live in shacks or on the street, and an estimated 10,000 people flood into Mumbai every day in hopes of making their homes and fortunes in the country's commercial heart known as Gold City.

The huge population, combined with arcane rent control provisions, has driven real estate prices in Mumbai sky-high. A decent-sized, three-bedroom flat on the southern cusp of the city can cost up to US$2 million—this in a country where the yearly per capita income is just US$350. The city's crowding, pollution, and religious tension have often made it the arena for India's social struggles (witness a 1999 scheme by the Shiv Sena to deport all of the bazaar district's Bengali-speaking Muslims to Bangladesh). It is also the lair of the nation's only urban crime syndicate. Yet none of the recent upheavals seem to be slowing Mumbai down very much, and the decade-long bull run on Dalal St. means that the Mumbai Stock Exchange and its millions face the new millennium from uncharted heights.

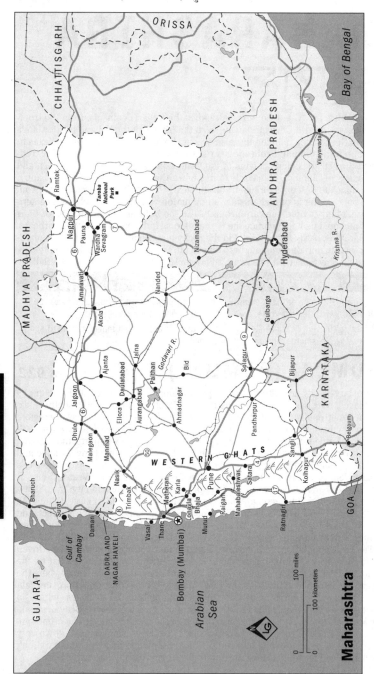

Maharashtra

Mumbai sprang from modest roots. Artifacts found in the suburb of Kandivli prove that the original seven islands that make up the city have been inhabited since the Stone Age. Successive dynasties ignored Mumbai's potential as a port, but when the Portuguese acquired the islands in 1534, they called them Bom Bahia ("Good Port"). The British made good on the name after the dowry of Catherine of Braganza brought the islands to Charles II of England. The fourth East India Company Governor of Bombay, Gerald Aungier, set his dreams in motion by ordering a construction spree in 1672. In 1675, Zoroastrians fleeing Persia built their first fire temple in the city and initiated a flow of affluent refugees. Twelve years later, Mumbai became the capital of the Company's regional holdings.

The cotton shortage in Britain during the American Civil War prompted a boom in Bombay, resulting in an array of late Victorian public works, including a land reclamation project that consolidated the city's seven islands into one. In 1885, an organization called the Indian National Congress held its inaugural meeting in Bombay. It was at another Bombay session in 1942 that the group first voiced its demand for full independence. After India's independence, disputes between the Marathi- and Gujarati-speaking populations ended in the partition of Bombay State into Maharashtra and Gujarat in 1960. Even during the conflict, the economy boomed, as it continues to do today. In 1995, politicians gave the city a new official name—Mumbai, from Mumbadevi, the local version of the goddess Durga.

Despite all these changes, Mumbai remains irrepressible. Today, the city makes the most movies in India, and India makes far more movies than any other place on earth—a fact that earned the local film industry its nickname, "Bollywood."

The tourists who come to gawk at the city's insane extremes make hardly a ripple. The manic mix of London double-deckers and bullock carts, *sadhus* and stockbrokers, and the perpetual motion of it all is enough to floor first-time visitors. Mumbai defies expectations of an India filled only with pot-bellied cows and ramshackle temples, although it has plenty of both. Instead, the city forces travelers to come face to face with an explosive fusion of development and despair. Whether it delights or disgusts, it cannot be denied that this ebullient city is leading the pack as India charges into the new century. *Salaam Bombay,* indeed.

◪ TRANSPORTATION

INTERNATIONAL FLIGHTS

Sahar International Airport, Vile Parle (☎836 6700; Air India flight information 836 6767), 20km north of downtown Mumbai. This chaotic, mosquito-ridden complex prepares arriving travelers for the continent beyond. The **State Bank of India** and **Govt. of India Tourist Office** operate counters in the arrival hall for currency exchange and info (24hr.). The easiest way to get downtown from the airport is by **pre-paid taxi** (1½hr.; Rs 300, Rs 370 for a car with A/C). Pay for a taxi at the counter in the arrival hall, and then go outside to the line of taxis and find the one whose number matches the number on your receipt. The non-pre-paid drivers at the airport are not to be trusted, but from Mumbai to the airport, any metered cab will do. Allow 2hr. during rush hour (to the city 8-11am, from the city 5-8pm).

 There is a Rs500 **departure tax,** which all travelers must pay before going through customs and leaving India (Rs250 if you're headed to another South Asian country). Most airlines do not include this tax in their ticket prices. Set aside enough cash for the tax before exchanging your last rupees.

INTERNATIONAL AIRLINES. Air India, Marine Dr., Nariman Point (☎202 4142). Open M-F 9:15am-6:30pm, Sa-Su 9:15am-5:15pm. **Air Lanka,** Mittal Tower, C Wing, Nariman Point (☎282 3288). Open M-Sa 9am-5:30pm, Sa 9am-4pm. **Bangladesh Biman,** Airline Hotel Building, 199 J. Tata Rd., #32, Churchgate (☎282 4580). Open M-F 9am-

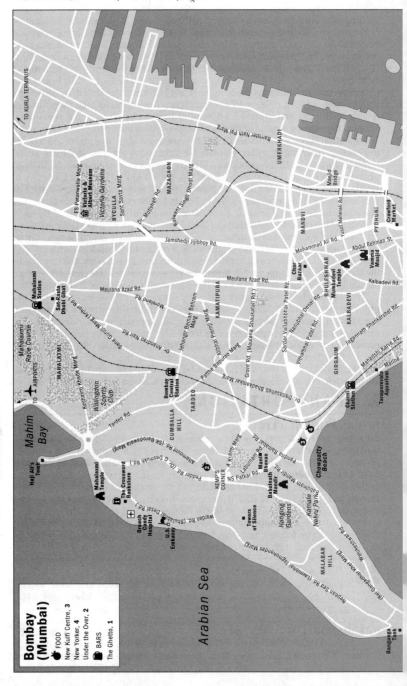

Bombay (Mumbai)

🍴 FOOD
New Kulfi Centre, **3**
New Yorker, **4**
Under the Over, **2**

🍸 BARS
The Ghetto, **1**

Arabian Sea

Mahim Bay

TO KURLA TERMINUS

Bamster Nath Pai Marg

UMERKHADI

Masjid Bridge

MAZAGAON

BYCULLA

ES Patanwalla Marg
Victoria & Albert Museum
Victoria Gardens
Sant-Savta Marg

Dr. Morshed Rd.

Balwant Singh Dhodi Marg

Jamshedji Jijibhoy Rd.

MANDVI

Mohammad Ali Rd.

Yusof Meherali Rd.

PYDHUNI

Crawford Market

Abdul Rehman St.

Vanta Masjid

Chor Bazaar

BHULESHWAR

Mumbadevi Temple

KALBADEVI

Kalbadevi Rd.

Maulana Azad Rd.

Mahalaxmi Station

Sat-Rasta Dhobi Ghat

Maulana Azad Rd.

Moreland Rd.

KAMATIPURA

Jehangir Boman Behram Marg

Pattne Alibhai Premji Marg

Sardar Vallabhbhai Patel Rd.

Nanubhai Desai Rd.

Vithalbhai Patel Rd.

GIRGAUM

Jagannath Shankarshet Rd.

Maharishi Karve Rd.

Marine

Charni Station

Taraporevala Aquarium

Grant Rd. (Maulana Shaukatali Rd.)

Pandita Ramabai Rd.

Chowpatty Beach

Sane Guruji Marg (Arthur Rd.)

Dr. Anandrao Nair Rd.

Dr. Dadasaheb Bhadkamkar Marg

Bombay Central Station

TARDEO

Tardeo Rd.

CUMBALLA HILL

Mahalaxmi Race Course

MAHALAXMI

Willingdon Sports Club

Keshavrao Khade Marg

TO AIRPORTS

Altamount Rd. (SK Barodawala Marg)

Pedder Rd. (Dr. G Deshmukh Rd.)

KEMP'S CORNER

A K Saini Marg

Labumam Rd.

NS Patkar Rd.

Mani Bhavan

Babulnath Mandir Rd.

Babulnath Mandir

Kamala Nehru Park

Hanging Gardens

Haji Ali's Tomb

Mahalaxmi Temple

The Crossword Bookstore

Warden Rd. (Bhulabhai Desai Rd.)

Breach Candy Hospital

U.S. Embassy

Towers of Silence

MALABAR HILL

Nepean Sea Rd. (Laxmibai Jagmohandas Marg)

BG Kher Marg (Ridge Rd.)

Walkeshwar Rd.

Banganga Tank

Arabian Sea

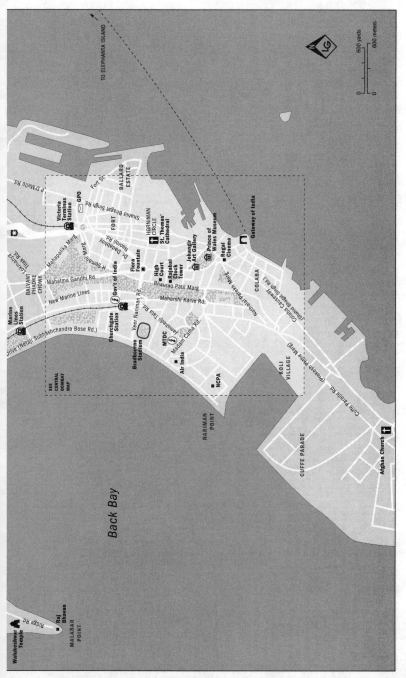

TO ELEPHANTA ISLAND

Victoria Terminus Station
GPO
Fort St.
BALLARD ESTATE
Shahid Bhagat Singh Rd.
FORT
Naoroji Rd.
HORNIMAN CIRCLE
St. Thomas' Cathedral
Prince of Wales Museum
Dr. Dadabhoy Naoroji Rd.
Flora Fountain
High Court
Rajabai Clock Tower
Jehangir Art Gallery
Regal Cinema
Gateway of India
Govt. of India
New Marine Lines
Mahatma Gandhi Rd.
Mahapalika Marg
Lokmanya Tilak Rd.
H. Somani Marg
BALVANT PHADKE CHOWK
Marine Lines Station
Bhaurao Patil Marg
Maharshi Karve Rd.
COLABA
Colaba Causeway (Shahid Bhagat Singh Rd.)
Nathalal Parekh Marg
Veer Nariman Rd.
Churchgate Station
Jamshedji Tata Rd.
MTDC
Madam Cama Rd.
Air India
Bradbourne Stadium
NCPA
KOLI VILLAGE
NARIMAN POINT
Prive (Netaji Subhashchandra Bose Rd.)
SEE CENTRAL BOMBAY MAP
Cuffe Parade Rd. (Pratesh Pethe Marg)
CUFFE PARADE
Afghan Church
Back Bay
Walukeshwar Temple
Raj Bhavan
Ridge Rd.
MALABAR POINT
P. D'Mello Rd.

N

0   600 yards
0   600 meters

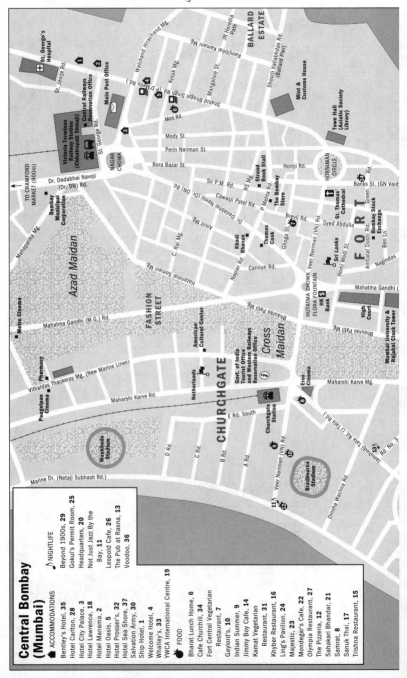

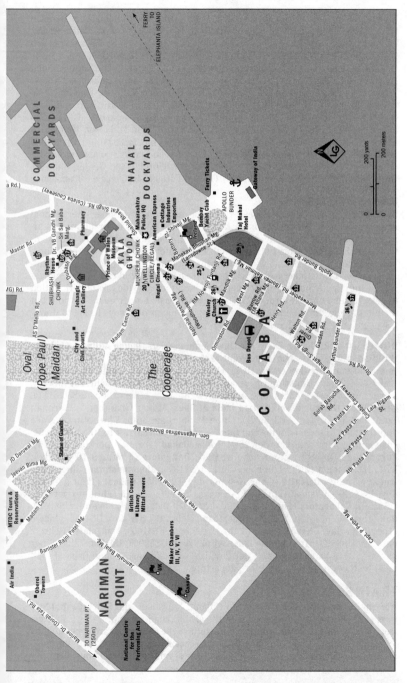

5:30pm, Sa 9am-3pm. **British Airways,** 202-B Vulcan Insurance Building, Veer Nariman Rd., Churchgate (☎282 0888). Open M-Sa 9:30am-1pm and 2:45-5:30pm. **Cathay Pacific,** Taj Mahal Hotel, Apollo Bunder, Colaba (☎202 9113). Open M-Sa 9:30am-1pm and 1:45-5:30pm. **Delta,** Taj Mahal Hotel, Apollo Bunder, Colaba (☎288 3274 or 288 5652). Open M-Sa 9am-1pm and 1:30-5:30pm. **Emirates,** Mittal Chambers, 288 Nariman Point (☎287 1649 or 287 1650). Open M-Sa 9am-5:30pm, Su 9am-4pm. **Lufthansa,** Express Towers, Nariman Point (☎202 3430 or 287 5264). Open M-F 9am-1pm and 1:45-5:45pm, Sa 9am-1pm. **Pakistan International Airlines,** Mittal Towers, Nariman Point (☎202 1598). Open M-Sa 9:30am-1pm and 2-5:30pm. **Royal Jordanian,** 403 Dalamal Towers, B-Wing, 4th fl., Nariman Point (☎202 2779). Open M-Sa 9am-1pm and 2-5:30pm. **Royal Nepal,** 222 Maker Chamber SV, Nariman Point (☎283 6197). Open M-Sa 10am-5:30pm. **Singapore Airlines,** Taj Mahal Hotel, Apollo Bunder, Colaba (☎202 3316 or 202 2747). Open M-Sa 9:15am-5:30pm. **Thai Air,** World Trade Center, Shop 15, Ground floor, Cuffe Parade (☎218 5426). Open M-F 9:30am-5:30pm, Sa 9:30am-2pm.

DOMESTIC FLIGHTS

Santa Cruz Airport is 20km northeast of downtown, 3km from Sahar International Airport. The new Terminal 1A is for Indian Airlines, and 1B is for all private carriers; **free shuttle buses** connect the two (every 15min.; 4am-midnight). Free shuttle buses also depart from both terminals to the international airport (every hr.). Take a metered auto-rickshaw (about Rs40) from the airport to the Andheri Railway Station, buy a ticket for any **city-bound train** (45min.; 2nd class Rs5), and get off at Churchgate Station, or vice versa. Exit on the east side of Andheri Station to get a rickshaw to the airports. There are **no pre-paid taxis** from this airport, but the ones at the stand outside should follow the meter one-way (Rs200 to downtown; under Rs75 to Sahar International Airport).

DOMESTIC AIRLINES. There are three main carriers: **Indian Airlines,** Air India Building, Marine Dr., Nariman Point (24hr. enquiry ☎140 or 141 for reservations and confirmation ☎287 6161). Open M-Sa 8:30am-7:30pm, Su 10am-1pm and 1:45-5:30pm; ticketing office at domestic airport open 24hr. **Jet Airways,** Amarchand Mansion, Madam Cama Rd. (☎285 5788, reservations ☎836 6111). Open M-Sa 10am-5:30pm. **Sahara India Airlines,** Maker Chamber V, Nariman Point (☎283 5671 or 283 5672). Open M-Sa 10am-6pm. The following are approximate flight schedules and rates. Contact each carrier for the best deals. Discounts for travelers under 26. To: **Ahmedabad** (1hr., 6-7 per day, US$75); **Aurangabad** (45min., 2 per day, US$92); **Bangalore** (1½hr., 9-10 per day, US$168); **Bhopal** (2hr., 1 per day Su-F, US$130); **Bhubaneshwar** (3hr., 3 per week, US$250); **Calcutta** (2½hr., 5-6 per day, US$235); **Calicut** (1½hr., 3-4 per day, US$145); **Chennai** (2hr., 8-9 per day, US$160); **Cochin** (2hr., 4-5 per day, US$150); **Coimbatore** (2hr., 2 per day, US$180); **Delhi** (2hr., several, US$208); **Goa** (1hr., 4-5 per day, US$98); **Hyderabad** (1½hr., 6-7 per day, US$125); **Indore** (1hr., 2 per day, US$95); **Jaipur** (3½hr., 2 per day, US$160); **Mangalore** (1½hr., 2 per day, US$120); **Trivandrum** (2hr., 3-4 per day, US$200); **Udaipur** (2hr., 2 per day, US$130); **Varanasi** (5hr., 1 per day, US$235). Flights booked from abroad must be reconfirmed 72hr. before departure.

TRAINS

Western Railways connects Mumbai to Gujarat, Rajasthan, and Delhi. **Central Railways** serves Delhi and destinations to the east. Some long-haul trains also leave from **Dadar, Kurla,** 15km northeast of downtown, or **Bandra;** all are accessible by local train from Victoria Terminus. For train **schedules,** arm yourself with the indispensable *Trains at a Glance* (Rs25), available at railway station bookstalls.

CENTRAL RAILWAYS. Central Reservation Office, **Victoria Terminus (VT)**, officially known as **Chhatrapati Shivaji Terminus** (enquiry ☎ 135 or 269 5959; automated info 265 6565). In the right wing of the complex as you face it. Go to the train station at Churchgate for all west-bound trains (see **Western Railways,** below). Head for **Window 7,** the Foreign Tourist Guide (open M-Sa 9am-1pm and 1:30-4pm). They sell tickets for US$ or UK£, or for rupees with an encashment certificate. They release tourist quota seats on a first-come, first-served basis on the day *before* departure for trains leaving before 2pm, or on the day *of* departure for trains leaving after 2pm. The following trains, which leave from VT, are just a select few of the many available. To: **Agra** (22hr.; 7:10pm, Rs326; 1-2 trains per day from Dadar Station 7:55am and 10:40pm); **Aurangabad** (7½hr.; 6:10am and 9:20pm; Rs137); **Bangalore** (24hr.; 1-2 per day 7:55am and 10:40pm; Rs310); **Bhopal** (14hr.; 8am and 7pm; Rs244; 1-2 per day from Dadar Station 7:55am and 10:40pm); **Calcutta** (33hr.; 3 per day 6am-9pm; Rs393); **Chennai** (24hr.; 2 and 11:20pm; Rs314; daily from Dadar 7:50pm); **Ernakulam** (28hr.; 1-2 per day 12:15 and 3:30pm; Rs207); **Hyderabad** (15-17½hr.; 12:35 and 9:55pm; Rs151); **Margao** (11hr.; 5:15am and 10:30pm; Rs225); **Pune** (4hr.; 16 per day; Rs53); **Trivandrum** (44hr.; 12:15 and 3:35pm; Rs256).

WESTERN RAILWAYS. Western Railways, Churchgate Reservation Office, Maharishi Karve Rd., Churchgate (enquiry ☎ 131, booking info 209 5959; arrivals from Delhi 132, from Gujarat 133). Across the street from Churchgate Station, in the same building as the Government of India Tourist Office. To get to the **Foreign Tourist Counter,** ignore the first reservation office and walk past the tourist office; it's the next door on your left, upstairs. Tourist quota procedures are the same as at VT (see above), but here an agent is specially assigned to help you. Open M-F 9:30am-1:30pm and 2-4:30pm, Sa 9:30am-2:30pm. The following trains leave from **Mumbai Central** (see **Local Trains,** p. 397). To: **Ahmedabad** (7-8½hr., 5-7 per day 5:45am-9:50pm, Rs107; 4 per day from Bandra 3-8:50pm); **Delhi** (17-22hr., 5-6 per day 7:25am-10:40pm, Rs212; A/C 3-tier sleeper Rs1485; daily from Dadar station 10:40pm; daily from Bandra 10:25pm); **Jaipur** (18hr., 7:05pm, Rs184).

MUMBAI SAPPHIRE

Most tourists spin or stroll down Nataji Subhas Chandra Bose Rd. in Mumbai without even realizing it. They, like all the city's residents, know this street by its colonial name, Marine Drive. The new street names may be patriotic, but people continue to rebel against today's authorities by refusing to relinquish the street names of past oppressors. Nepean Sea Rd. is never Laxmibhai Jagmohandas Marg; even the bus conductors say Ridge Rd. for Bal Gangadhar Kher Marg; Shahid Bhagat Singh Marg evinces blank stares from taxi drivers—but everyone recognizes Colaba Causeway. On the rare occasions when Mumbai's citizens accept the new names, they inevitably abbreviate them beyond recognition: Sir Pherozeshah Mehta Rd. becomes PM Rd.; Doctor Dadabhoy Naoroji barely escapes as Dr. DN.

Mumbai's name game developed from small-scale civil disobedience to big-time politics. The Hindu nationalist Shiv Sena party, senior partners in the state's coalition government at the time, decided that streets by any other name would smell more sweet. In 1995, the Sena dropped their biggest bomb when they renamed the whole city Mumbai, in line with its "traditional" Marathi name. Madras followed suit in 1996, switching its name to the hardly homophonic Chennai. The struggle for naming continues, and urbanites now wryly refer to the city as "Slumbai."

MAHARASHTRA

BUSES

State Transport Terminal, JB Behran Marg (☎307 4272 or 307 6622), opposite Central Railway Station, next to the Maratha Mandir Cinema. **Maharashtra State Road Transport Corporation** runs quiet, comfortable, and expensive buses to the major tourist destinations in the state; services are cut back during monsoon. To **Aurangabad** (10hr., 2 per day, Rs 204) and **Mahabaleshwar** (7hr., 2 per day, Rs150). For other destinations in Maharashtra, you have to book at the ASIAD office (☎413 6835) in Dadar, or at an MTDC luxury service office, although trains are likely to be quicker and more convenient. **Goa State Transport** (Kadamba) runs a daily luxury bus to **Panjim** (15hr., 5pm, Rs280). **Gujarat State Transport** has at least 2 daily buses to **Ahmedabad** (12hr., 3 and 7pm, Rs168). **MTDC,** CDO Hutments, Madam Cama Rd. (☎202 6713), runs buses Oct.-May. To: **Ganpatipule** (8-10hr., 1 per day, Rs250); **Mahabaleshwar** (7hr., 7am, Rs230); **Shirdi** (7hr., 1 per day, Rs300; Off season 1 per week). Services change frequently, so check for up-to-date route info.

▛ LOCAL TRANSPORTATION

LOCAL BUSES

Trains are easier to deal with than buses, but if you're going to be in town for a while, it's worth the (Herculean) effort required to come to terms with the city's chaotic bus system. For a complete guide to stops and routes, pick up a city bus map (Rs20) from the bus terminal office on Colaba Causeway (open M-F 9am-5pm). Try to learn the Marathi numerals so that you can recognize the bus as it approaches (the Roman numeral and English destination are only written on the side—often visible too late to allow you to clamber on board before the bus roars off again). Red numbers indicate "limited" services, which supposedly stop less frequently and cost marginally less. No fare within the city should exceed Rs3, limited or otherwise.

MAHARASHTRA

BUS #	MARATHI	ROUTE AND DESTINATION
1 ltd.	१	Colaba-Regal-Flora-VT-Crawford Market-Mahim
3	३	Afghan Church-Colaba-Regal-Flora-VT-Jijanatra Velyan
6	६	Colaba-Regal-VT-Crawford-Byculla-Chesbus Colony
62	६२	Flora-Metro-Marine Lines-Mumbai Central-Dadar Station
61	६१	Mantulaya-Regal-Metro-Opera House-Mumbai Central-Dadar Station
81 ltd.	८१	VT-Kemp's Corner-Breach Candy and Haji Ali-Nehru Planetarium-Santa Cruz
91	९१	Mumbai Central-Dadar-Kurla
106	१०६	Afghan Church-Colaba-Regal-Chowpatty-Kamala Nehru Park
108	१०८	VT-Regal-Chowpatty-Kamala Nehru Park
125	१२५	Colaba-Crawford Market-Haji Ali-Worli Village
132	१३२	Regal-Churchgate-Breach Candy and Haji Ali
188 ltd.	१८८	Borivli (E)-Sanjay Gandhi NP-Kanheri Caves
231	२३१	Santa Cruz (W)-Juhu Beach
321 ltd.	३२१	Worti-Airport-Vile Parle (E)
343	३४३	Goregaon (E)-Film City

LOCAL TRAINS

Mumbai's commuter rail system runs along two lines. **Western Railways** runs one line, from **Churchgate** through Mumbai Central, Mahalaxmi, Dadar, Bandra, Santa Cruz (for Juhu), Andheri (for the airports), and a dozen other stations before Borivli (Sanjay Gandhi NP) and beyond. The **Central Railways** line runs to and from **VT** (check the final destination; be sure you're on the right line) and tends to be of less use to the tourist. Most trains out of VT stop at Dadar, where you can cross the platform and change onto a Western train. One-way tickets (2nd class Rs3-10, 1st class Rs8-32) are sold at windows in each station. When boarding a train, check the illuminated display—the first letter code is the first letter of the final destination, the second code is the time, and the "F" or "S" indicates whether the train is (relatively) fast or (especially) slow. Fast trains skip the stations whose names are illuminated on the board below. That's right, the names that are lit up brightly are the **places it does not go.** There are special, less crowded cars exclusively for women on all trains.

TAXIS

Taxis rule in Mumbai, since auto-rickshaws aren't allowed in the downtown area and public transport is so crowded. Set the meter and go—this shouldn't be too much of a struggle unless it's very late or the weather's very bad. You pay roughly Rs13 per km—for the precise figure, consult the chart that the driver should carry. **Auto-rickshaws** only roam the suburbs; you pay about seven times the meter.

⊞ ORIENTATION

The city of Mumbai reaches into the Arabian Sea like a cupped hand, the fingers and thumb forming a backward letter "c" off the western coast of India. For purposes of orientation, it is more important to familiarize yourself with the names of the city's different areas than specific street addresses, as most locals (and taxi drivers) navigate and give directions according to the names of neighborhoods and well-known landmarks. At the fingertip of **Colaba,** toward the southern end of the city, is the tourist ghetto. The area's main thoroughfare, **Colaba Causeway** (also known as SBS Marg, see **Mumbai Sapphire** graybox), is where you'll find most of the budget accommodations and lost-looking backpackers. The Causeway ends in the north at a huge, circular intersection universally known as **Regal** because of the movie theater that presides over it. Directly west of Regal, jutting into the bay, are **Cuffe Parade,** an elite residential area, and **Nariman Point,** Mumbai's most prestigious corporate address, housing the offices of many international banks, airlines, and a few consulates. North of Regal, past the Prince of Wales Museum, stretches **Fort,** Mumbai's oldest neighborhood and its main financial district. Banks cluster near its most prominent landmark, **Flora Fountain (Hutatma Chowk).**

West of Fort and north of Nariman Point is the **Churchgate** neighborhood, where you'll find the Churchgate railway station and several trendy restaurants. **Marine Dr.** (Nataji Subhash Rd.) runs along the western edge of the city, curving from Nariman Point in the south to Churchgate in the north, and farther still to **Chowpatty Beach.** North of Chowpatty are the upmarket **Malabar Hill** community and the northern suburbs.

Most travelers arriving by train will enter Mumbai at **Victoria Terminus (VT),** now officially called **Chhatrapati Shivaji Terminus (CST),** just north of the Fort. From VT, a taxi ride to Colaba costs Rs25, though taxi drivers will try to charge more; stick to your guns. North of VT, **Crawford Market** (Phule) marks the beginning of the **bazaar district.**

MAHARASHTRA

◢ PRACTICAL INFORMATION

TOURIST AND FINANCIAL SERVICES

Tourist Office: Government of India Tourist Office, 123 Maharishi Karve Rd. (☎203 3144), across the street from the Churchgate Station. Dispenses maps of Mumbai (free) and some useful info. Open M-F 8:30am-6pm, Sa 8:30am-2pm. Also at Sahar International Airport (☎832 5331; open 24hr.) and at Santa Cruz Domestic Airport (☎615 9200; open during flight arrival times). **Maharashtra Tourism Development Corporation (MTDC),** CDO Hutments, Madam Cama Rd. (☎202 6713). From the Air India Bldg., walk away from Marine Dr. along Madam Cama Rd.; it's on the left, just past the giant Nehru statue. Open M-Sa 9:30am-6:30pm. Other offices at Santa Cruz airport, Sahar International Airport, Churchgate Station, and the Gateway of India.

Consulates: Australia, Maker Towers E., 16th fl., Cuffe Parade (☎218 1071). Open M-F 9am-5pm. **Canada,** 41/42 Maker Chambers VI, Nariman Point (☎287 6027). Open M-Th 9am-5:30pm, F 9am-3pm. **Ireland,** Bombay Yacht Club, Apollo Bunder, Colaba (☎202 4607). Open M-F 9am-5pm. **South Africa,** Gandhi Mansion, Altamount Rd. (☎389 3725). Near Kemp's Corner. Open M-F 9am-5pm. **Sri Lanka,** Jehangir Wadhwa, 1st fl., 34 Homi Modi St., Fort (☎204 5861 or 204 8303). Most visas obtainable upon arrival in Sri Lanka. Open for visas M-F 9:30-11:30am. **Thailand,** Malabar View Bldg., Chowpatty Beach (☎363 1404). Near Purandevi Hospital. Two-month visa Rs400; many nationalities can enter for up to 2 months without a visa. Open for visas M-F 9am-noon. **UK,** Maker Chambers IV, 1st and 2nd fl., J.B. Marg, 521 Nariman Point (☎283 3602 or 283 0517). Open M-F 8am-4pm. **US,** Lincoln House, 78 Bhulabhai Desai Rd., Breach Candy (☎363 3611 or 363 3617). Open M-F 8:30am-1pm and 2-3:45pm.

Currency Exchange: Hong Kong Bank, 52/60 MG Rd., Flora Fountain (☎267 4921). Cash advances on MC and V. On-site **ATM** is connected to the Plus network. Open M-F 10am-6pm, Sa 10am-2pm. **Grindlays,** 90 MG Rd. (☎267 0162). Next to Hong Kong Bank. Charges Rs200 for cashing traveler's checks and has a **24hr. ATM** connected to the Cirrus and Plus systems. Open M-Sa 10am-7pm. **Thomas Cook,** Dr. DN Rd., Fort (☎204 8556). On the left, 2 blocks up from Flora, with the bright red sign. Cashes Thomas Cook traveler's checks for free; Rs30 per transaction for other brands. Open M-Sa 9:30am-6pm. **American Express,** Regal Cinema Bldg., Shivaji Marg (☎204 8291), on Wellington Circle. Cashes AmEx traveler's checks for free; 1% fee on other brands. Open M-F 9:30am-6:30pm, Sa 9:30am-2:30pm.

LOCAL SERVICES

Luggage Storage: Cloak Room at VT, inside the station bldg., near platform 13. Rs7-10 per day, 31-day max. Similar facilities at all big stations. Bags must be locked. Don't lose the receipt. Limited space. Open 24hr. except 7:30-8am, 3-3:30pm, and 11:30pm-midnight.

Bookstore: ◼ **Crossword Bookstore,** Mahalaxmi Chambers, 1st fl., 22 Bhulabhai Desai Rd., Breach Candy (☎492 4882). Look up for the yellow sign in the window. Open M-F 10am-8pm, Sa-Su 10am-9pm. Outdoor booksellers pack the sidewalk on VN Rd., between Flora and the Churchgate Station. **The Strand Book Stall,** Sir PM Rd., Fort (☎266 1994). Just above Horniman Cir. Favorite of the Mumbai intelligentsia, the Strand's crowded collection is hand-picked. Search carefully for discounts. Open M-Sa 10am-7pm. **Nalanda,** Taj Mahal Hotel, 1st fl. (☎202 2514). A fine selection of fiction, travel, and ethnographic literature. Open daily 8am-midnight.

Library and Cultural Center: The Asiatic Society Library, SBS Marg, Fort (☎266 0956), Horniman Cir. A beautiful old cavern of a reading room in the old town hall; a great place to read and browse a wide selection of daily press. Open M-Sa 10am-7:30pm. **American Center (USIS) Library,** 4 New Marine Lines, Churchgate (☎262 4590). The barricaded bldg. on the right-hand side as you walk from Churchgate Station. For Rs10 per day, non-members may lounge in the A/C calm and read dated US papers. Open M-F noon-6pm. **British Council**, A Wing, Mittal Towers, 1st fl., Nariman Point (☎282 3560). Open Tu-Sa 10am-9pm.

Market: M Phule Market, north end of Dr. DN Rd. Universally known as **Crawford Market.** Anything from kitchen supplies and vegetables to birds and European chocolates. See also **Shopping,** p. 408. Open M-Sa 6am-6pm.

EMERGENCY AND COMMUNICATIONS

Pharmacy: Apollo Pharmacy, 18/20 K. Dubash Marg, Kala Ghoda (☎285 1873 or 282 9707), behind Prince of Wales Museum, under the arcade. Open 24hr. New Marine Lines is lined with late-night chemists, such as **New Bombay Chemists,** Churchgate (☎200 1173), opposite the cinema and next to the hospital. Open daily 8am-11pm.

Hospital: Breach Candy Hospital, 60 Warden Rd., Breach Candy (☎363 3651, 367 1888, or 367 2888), just past the American Consulate and the Breach Candy Swimming Club. Not near Colaba, but one of the most modern hospitals in Mumbai and accustomed to dealing with foreigners. Open 24hr. **Bombay Hospital,** 12 New Marine Lines (☎206 7676). Modern, established, and centrally located. Open 24hr. **Ambulance** ☎102.

Police: Police Commissioner's Office, Dr. DN Rd., Crawford Market (☎100), opposite the market building, behind an iron fence. You can report thefts at this head office; expect a bureaucratic nightmare, but miracles might happen. Open M-F 9am-4pm.

Internet: ▓**Waghela,** 23-B Nowroji Furdunji Rd., Colaba (☎204 8718), around the corner from Leopold Cafe, off Colaba Causeway. Rs30 per hr. Open daily 8:30am-midnight. **Nikhil,** 268-270 SBS Rd. (☎270 1513), directly across from the Welcome Hotel. Rs40 per hr. Open daily 6-1am. Both the American Cultural Council (Rs40 per hr.) and the British Council (Rs60 per hr.) also have Internet access.

Post Office: GPO, W. Hirachand Marg (☎262 0956). The huge stone building next door to VT, off Nagar Chowk. *Poste Restante* at counter #92. Open M-Sa 9am-8pm, Su 10am-5pm. **Postal Code:** 400001.

▐ ACCOMMODATIONS

Most foreign tourists gravitate toward the peaceful, crumbling mansions of Colaba despite the area's proximity to Gateway of India touts and the (decidedly non-budget) Taj Mahal Hotel. Mumbai real estate being what it is, "budget" means something entirely different in this city from what it means elsewhere in India. Even bottom-of-the-barrel digs charge rates that would mortify any self-respecting budget dive in a smaller Indian city. Reservations are a good idea at any time, especially in season Nov.-Feb. Check-out is noon unless otherwise noted. Most hotels have a variety of rooms ranging from windowless cells to comfortable, airy rooms; prices are marginally different.

COLABA

Hotel Lawrence, 3rd fl., ITTS House, 33 Sri Sai Baba Marg, Rope Walk Ln. (☎284 3618). First left off K. Dubash Marg when coming from B.G. Rd., just past the Sanuk Thai restaurant. Nine clean, airy rooms with shared bath and friendly, helpful staff. Breakfast included. Hot water upon request. Reserve 2 weeks in advance. Singles Rs300; doubles Rs400; triples Rs450. ❷

Hotel Carlton, Florence House, 12 Mereweather Rd., Boman Behram Marg. (☎202 0642 or 202 0259). One block away from the Salvation Army, behind the Taj. The lively veranda, equipped with chairs and tables, allows residents to escape their cramped quarters for a glimpse of cathouse life across the street. Singles Rs350; doubles Rs550-600; triples with A/C and bath Rs1200; quads Rs900. ❷

Salvation Army, 30 Mereweather Rd., Boman Behram Marg (☎284 1824). Behind the Taj Mahal Hotel, under the arcade. Pistachio-green walls make it as drab and institutional as you'd expect, but nothing beats it on a budget. Passable dorms and large, nondescript doubles. Breakfast included. No hot water. Lockers Rs50 per day. Max. 1-week stay. Check-in 10am. Check-out 9am. Dorms Rs130 (Rs190 if full); doubles with bath Rs460-660. ❶

YWCA International Centre, 18 Madam Cama Rd. (☎202 5053 or 202 0598; fax 202 0445; ywcaic@bom8.vsnl.net.in). 4min. walk from Regal, on the left. Although it's more expensive than most budget hotels, you get your money's worth at the Y. Rates include all-you-can-eat buffet breakfast and dinner, TV lounge, daily room cleaning, telephones, and towels in spotless, spacious rooms with balconies. All have attached bath. Reserve 15 days in advance. Rs100 membership fee (good for 6 months). Dorms Rs660; singles Rs762-850; doubles Rs1429-1550. ❸

Bentley's Hotel, 17 Oliver Rd. (☎284 1474 or 284 1733; fax 287 1846; email bentleyshotel@hotmail.com). A real treat—vintage rooms with hardwood floors, whitewashed balconies, and mosaic tiling. Individual baths, TVs, and breakfast included in price. 70 beds total. Doubles Rs680-1095. A/C Rs200 extra. MC/V. ❸

Whalley's, Jaiji Mansion, 41 Mereweather Rd. (☎282 1802). Tiny, ordinary rooms in a big, breezy villa surrounded by greenery. The birds make more noise than the traffic. Breakfast included. Singles Rs900; doubles Rs1000-1200. ❹

Hotel Sea Shore, 1-49 Kamal Mansion, 4th fl., Arthur Bunder Rd. (☎287 4237 or 287 4238). From Regal, follow the Causeway to Arthur Bunder, 9 blocks down on the left. The entrance to Kamal Mansion is on the right, down an alley before Arthur Bunder hits the ocean. The rooms range from claustrophobic cubicles to large, airy, ocean-view suites. Sparkling common bath. Singles Rs320; doubles with TV Rs450-500. ❷

Hotel Prosser's, Curzon House, 2-4 Henry Rd., Apollo Bunder Rd. (☎284 1715 or 283 4937). Where Henry Rd. (the 6th left off the Causeway, south of Regal) meets the sea. High ceilings and spacious rooms. Common bath. Singles or doubles, Rs400-600. Off-season: Rs350/Rs550. ❷

BEYOND COLABA

Ship Hotel, Bharati Bhavari, 3rd floor, 219 P D'Mello Rd. Right next to Hotel Manama (see below). Newly renovated, with clean rooms and baths and very friendly staff. Meals at on-site canteen Rs25. TVs in every room. Check-out 9am. Dorms Rs120 (with built-in lockers!); singles Rs175; doubles Rs300. ❶

Hotel Manama, P D'Mello Rd. (☎261 3412; fax 261 3860). Close to St. George Hospital. With your back to the GPO, head left on Hirachand Marg, then turn left on P D'Mello; it's on the right. Good-value, crowded, middle-class hotel. Doubles Rs600-800. ❸

Hotel Oasis, 276 Shahid Bhagat Singh Rd. (☎269 7886; fax 262 6498). With your back to the GPO, head left on W. Hirachand Marg, then right onto Sahid Bhagat Singh; it's on the right. Decent-sized rooms with phones and TVs. No advance booking for singles. Singles Rs490; doubles Rs640-980. ❷

Welcome Hotel, 257 Shahid Bhagat Singh Rd. (☎261 2196 or 261 7474; fax 262 2715; welcome_hotel@vsnl.com), near the Hotel Oasis. Glamorous and clean, with TVs and phones. Breakfast, morning, and evening tea included. Singles Rs550-800; doubles Rs800-1100; rooms with bath Rs850-2000. ❸

Hotel City Palace, 121 City Terrace, W. Hirachand Marg (☎261 5515 or 261 4759; fax 267 6890). Opposite VT. Most rooms cost more than they're worth, but the ground-floor A/C cubicles with common bath are cheap. Prices include morning tea or coffee. Singles Rs750-1100; doubles Rs650-1550. ❹

◘ FOOD

Eating in Mumbai can result in anything from gastronomical delight to gastrointestinal distress. The distinctive street food is a constant temptation, and the city's restaurants brim with the best international food in India, as well as every conceivable type of Indian cuisine, including a few (Parsi, Malvani) not to be found anywhere else. Not surprisingly, the Good Port of Mumbai is also renowned for its seafood. There is no better place to splurge on your meals. Serious eaters should refer to the *Mid-Day Good Food Guide* (Rs50). Some Mumbai specialties are **pao bhaji**, batter-fried balls of potato and chilies served on white bread, and **puri**, innocent-looking fried pastry shells, which come in two varieties—flat and disc-like or hollow and spherical—and can be filled with anything from green chutney, tamarind sauce, chili paste, fried vermicelli and puffed rice to potato, tomato, onion, green mango, and coriander.

COLABA

▓ **Fort Central Vegetarian Restaurant,** Cawasji Patel Rd., Fort (☎ 287 0080). From Flora, take VN Rd. away from Churchgate and turn left onto C. Patel. Punjabi food at its best. Great service. Open daily 8:30am-11:30pm. Delectable *masala dosa* Rs13, main dishes Rs24-50. ❶

▓ **Kamat Vegetarian Resaurant,** Colaba Causeway (☎ 287 4734), opposite Electric House. The self-proclaimed specialists in South Indian delicacies and North Indian dishes serve a wide variety of *dosas* (Rs20-48), great *thalis* Rs35, Kashmiri *dum aloo* (Rs55). Open daily 8:30am-9pm. ❶

▓ **Trishna Restaurant,** 7 Sri Sai Baba Marg (☎ 267 2176 or 265 9644). Follow Dr. VB Gandhi Marg past Rhythm House, turn left at the first intersection and walk 2 blocks; it's on the right. Trishna started out as a food stall, and by word of mouth became Mumbai's trendiest seafood restaurant. Freakishly-sized shellfish at rock-bottom prices. Medium prawns with butter, pepper, and garlic are worth every *paise* of the Rs160. Pomfret (enough for two) Rs270; crisp calamari Rs130. Reservations essential for dinner. Open M-Sa noon-4pm and 6pm-midnight, Su noon-4pm and 7pm-midnight. ❷

Sahakari Bhandar, to the right as you face the Regal Cinema. Fast and friendly snack joint. A convenient and dependable place for *bhel puri* (Rs13-15) and *pao bhaji* (Rs22). Don't miss the Chicu Milkshake (Rs25). Great, cheap South Indian tiffin (*dosas* Rs15). Open M-Sa 8am-9pm. ❶

Cafe Churchill, Colaba Causeway, between Walton and Garden Rd. This tiny, brightly colored cafe serves American snacks that taste better and cost less than those at the big tourist hangouts in the area. All-day breakfast skillets Rs40-60; sandwiches Rs40-60; brownies and cakes Rs25-50. Open daily 10am-11:30pm. ❶

Olympia Restaurant and Coffee House, Rahim Mansion, opposite Mondegar's, Colaba Causeway. Time stands still in this 2-tiered, turn-of-the-century, Iranian-style cafe. Today's owners are Bengali Muslims, but they've preserved the ancient carved chairs, marble-topped tables, and affordable Iranian cuisine that characterize one of Mumbai's most distinctive genres of food. Brain *masala* fry (Rs27) is their most famous dish, but no-brainers will also be satisfied. Mutton *biryani* Rs14. Open daily 11am-11pm. ❶

Majestic, Colaba Causeway, opposite Mondegar's, up a few stairs. Proves that there is such a thing as budget in Mumbai. Simple dishes (Rs18-40) and basic *thalis* (Rs25) served in a huge hall with low tables under whirring fans. Open daily 7am-11pm. ❶

Mondegar's Cafe, Metro House, Colaba Causeway. The first corner on the left after Regal. Bond with fellow backpackers grooving to the CD jukebox. Breakfast Rs50-65; dinner Rs45-80. Beer Rs120 per bottle. Open daily 8am-midnight. ❶

MAHARASHTRA

Ling's Pavilion, Mahakavi Bhushan Mg. (☎ 285 0023). Head north up the Causeway; it's the last street on the right before Regal. Ling's serves Chinese food free of mutation *a la masala* in an ultra-swanky, multi-colored fantasyland where iridescent fish frolic in a purple pond. Cantonese dishes include *dim sum* for two (Rs100) and a variety of tasty meat, seafood, and veg. options (entrees Rs100-200). Open M noon-3pm and 7-11pm and Tu-Su noon-11pm. ❷

Khyber Restaurant, 145 MG Rd. (☎ 267 3227). Where MG Rd. meets K. Dubash Marg. The finest Mughlai cuisine in all the city served in a setting of lavish antiques-and-mirrors decoration. This expensive hotspot is Mumbai's most popular restaurant. Chicken *makhanwala* (Rs225) swims in thick, tangy tomato sauce; chicken *badami* (Rs225) is superb. Reservations essential. Open daily 12:30-3:45pm and 7:30-11:45pm. ❸

Sanuk Thai, 30 K. Dubash Marg (☎ 204 4233). Classy, authentic Thai food. Meat and veg. curries Rs180-280. *Pad thai* Rs120-220. Reservations recommended. Open daily 12:30-3:30pm and 7:30-11:30pm. ❸

BEYOND COLABA

▨ **Indian Summer,** 80 Veer Nariman Rd., Churchgate (☎ 283 5445). You won't need to eat again for days after one of Indian Summer's upscale, sumptuous, all-you-can-eat Mughlai lunch buffets, which include appetizers, bread, meat, dessert, and a pint of beer (Rs270 plus 20% tax). Epic seafood buffet M night (Rs300 plus tax), and a large *a la carte* menu, too. Chicken and lamb dishes Rs175, veg. Rs150-160. Live music Sa nights. Open daily noon-4pm and 7pm-midnight. ❸

Bharat Lunch Home (the Excellensea), 317 Mint Rd., Fort (☎ 261 8991), 3 blocks south of the GPO. Two restaurants in one. At Bharat, the budget option on the ground floor, tubfuls of live crabs await their cruel, creamy end (Rs150). Draft beer Rs40; fried squid *kolwada* Rs80. The A/C Excellensea offers longer menus, giant lobsters, and bigger bills. Open daily 11:30am-4pm and 7pm-midnight. ❷

The Pizzeria, 143 Marine Dr., Churchgate (☎ 285 6115). Where VN Rd. meets Marine Dr. A cool bay breeze and pizza as authentic as anything Mumbai can bake. Choices include margherita (8in.) and the stuffed-crust Meat Ultimo (Rs270). Pasta dishes Rs165-185. Open daily noon-12:45am. ❸

Samrat, Prem Court, J. Tata Rd., Churchgate. From Churchgate, it's on the left side of the road that leads to the right of Eros. Fancy, pure-veg. restaurant specializes in slightly sweet Gujarati *thalis* (Rs100-130). You can wash down the all-you-can-eat *chappatis, dal,* and vegetables with a bottle of beer (Rs90). Open daily noon-10:30pm. ❷

Gaylord's, VN Rd., Churchgate (☎ 282 1259). On the left as you walk from Churchgate to Marine Dr. The sidewalk cafe, barricaded by potted plants, offers a pleasant compromise between indoor and out. Skip the overpriced menu (grilled sandwiches Rs80-95) in favor of the European pastries (Rs40-80) and freshly baked breads from the adjoining bakery as you linger over a cappuccino. Open daily 10am-midnight. ❶

Jimmy Boy Cafe, 11 Bank St., Fort (☎ 270 0880), 1 block south of Horniman Cir., at Green Rd. A sleek Anglo-US fast-food conceit hides very Parsi roots. Burgers and sandwiches (Rs40-75) are good, but even better are the sweet-and-sour spiced Parsi veg. or non-veg. meals served on a banana leaf (Rs80-100), the *saas-ni-machhi* (a spicy fish curry, Rs90), and the *kid gosht,* served in a bed of saffron rice (Rs80). Open M-Sa 11am-11pm. ❶

New Yorker, 25 Chowpatty Seaface (☎ 363 2923). America gets class in this A/C eatery opposite Chowpatty Beach. Trendsters down well-prepared plates of everything from pizza and sandwiches to nachos and falafel (Rs35-115). Open daily 11:30am-11:30pm. ❶

Rajdhani, Sheikh Memon St. (☎ 342 6919), opposite Mangaldas Market, near Crawford Market. From Crawford, look down the crowded lanes opposite Dr. DN Rd.; it's on the right of the lane with the white turret at the far end. Mumbai's best, richest Gujarati lunchtime *thalis* (Rs85). Open daily 11:30am-3:30pm and 7-11pm. ❶

New Kulfi Centre, opposite Chowpatty. Near the pedestrian overpass where SVP Rd. meets Marine Dr. Locals stand on the sidewalk to wolf down creamy *kulfi* desserts in every possible flavor at this legendary street-side stall (Rs20-40). Ask for *mutka kulfi,* served in small, earthen pots that you can take home. Open daily 10am-12:30am. ❶

Under the Over, 36 Altamount Rd., Kemp's Corner (☎386 1393). Just beyond (and "under") the flyover at Kemp's Corner. Deep South shrimp gumbo Rs255; pasta Rs150-200; chimichangas Rs165; brownies or cheesecake Rs110. Open daily noon-3:30pm and 7-11:30pm. ❷

◉ SIGHTS

The Raj might have ended over half a century ago, but the mostly British-influenced area continues to dominate the sight-seeing scene in modern Mumbai.

COLABA

THE GATEWAY OF INDIA. The quintessential starting point from which to lose yourself in the endless metropolis is the Gateway of India. Built to commemorate the visit of King George V and Queen Mary in 1911, this Indianized triumphal arch stands guard over the harbor next to the Taj Mahal Hotel. With a cosmopolitan nonchalance typical of Mumbai, the gateway combines carved brackets derived from Gujarati temple architecture with Islamic motifs such as the minaret-like finials in a purely European building type. By day, the area is a sea of relentless tour touts. In the evening, however, the gateway is a favorite haunt of strolling couples, camera-happy tourists, peanut vendors, and snake charmers. In the small park nearby stands an imposing equestrian statue of the great 17th-century Maratha leader **Shivaji Bhonsle** (see p. 418). The reputation of this historical king and legendary hero has been hijacked by the right-wing Maharashtrian party, Shiv Sena, which decks out the unwitting image in marigold garlands and saffron flags.

TAJ MAHAL HOTEL. While the modern tower of the Taj Mahal Hotel dwarfs Shivaji, the building's older wing is the real eye-catcher. Jamshedji Tata, one of India's first industrialists, built this Mumbai landmark in 1899 in retaliation against the Europeans-only policies of other Raj-era hotels. Like all the other Tata enterprises which dominate today's Indian economy, the Taj soared to success, monopolizing both the hotel industry and the city's early skyline. A self-assured expression wins even grubby backpackers access to the corridors inside.

AFGHAN CHURCH. Down at the southernmost end of the Causeway stands the 19th-century Afghan Church, built to commemorate the soldiers who died to keep the Khyber Pass British. This area also houses an old colonial cemetery and the now-defunct Colaba **lighthouse.**

KALA GHODA

PRINCE OF WALES MUSEUM. Opposite the Regal Cinema is the Prince of Wales Museum. The intervening gardens provide a buffer between the newly restored domed gallery and the relentless traffic outside. The most impressive exhibit is the collection of miniature paintings from the 16th to 18th centuries. These painstakingly detailed works showcase the various Rajasthani, Deccani, and Mughali schools of painting through scenes of palace life and Hindu mythology. Other areas of the museum feature cluttered displays of everything from Mughal miniatures to stuffed animals and fourth-rate oil paintings. The first hall contains a trove of archaeological treasures dating back to the Indus Valley civilization. They include well-preserved stone tools and burial urns from both Harappa and Mohenjo-Daro. Another highlight is the collection of metal deities. (☎284 4484. *Open Tu-Su 10:15am-6pm. Rs150, students with ISIC Rs6.)*

M
A
H
A
R
A
S
H
T
R
A

◪ THE JEHANGIR ART GALLERY. The building next to the Prince of Wales Museum consists of several rooms, each hosting an exhibit by a different contemporary Indian artist. Even better, artists are on-site and happy to chat with you about their work and the meaning of life. New shows every week. A posterboard outside lists exhibits at other galleries around Mumbai. *(☎ 284 3989. Open daily 11am-7pm. Free)* Inside the museum, Cafe Samovar, opening onto a garden, provides a peaceful escape, where you can have a light meal or munch on snacks. *(Open M-Sa 10:30am-7:30pm.)*

NEAR MUMBAI UNIVERSITY. The buildings of Mumbai University and the **High Court** line the left side of MG Rd. from the Prince of Wales Museum to Flora Fountain. These Victorian-Gothic extravaganzas, centering on the 85m **Rajabai Clock Tower,** occupied the seafront until the Art Deco neighborhood opposite was built on reclaimed land in the 20s and 30s. Today, their finest facades face the Oval Maidan, one block to the west. The wide, grassy maidans, which now support enthusiastic cricket matches, used to separate the British residential communities in Fort from the Indian areas on the other side. *(Open daily 11am-5pm.)*

THE FORT AREA

Another group of sights stretches north from **Flora Fountain,** now renamed **Hutatma Chowk (Martyrs' Sq.)** in honor of the protesters who died agitating for a separate Marathi-speaking state in 1959-1960. Flora is lined by still more Raj-era Gothic buildings, now inhabited by foreign banks.

HORNIMAN CIRCLE. Horniman Circle strikes a calm, dignified note in the midst of the surrounding commercial hubbub. The elegant neoclassical colonnade faces the early-19th-century **Asiatic Society Library** (originally the Town Hall) across a small park complete with fountain. The neighboring **Mint and Customs House** also dates from the early 1800s. Mumbai's oldest English building is **St. Thomas's Cathedral,** at the southwest corner of the circle. Although begun by East India Company Governor Gerald Aungier in 1672, when Surat was still the capital of the Mumbai Presidency, St. Thomas's remained incomplete until 1718. The interior reveals a fascinating slice of colonial life with its *punkahs* and endless marble memorials to long-gone English types. *(Open daily 6:30am-6pm.)*

NORTH FORT. At the northern edge of the Fort area stand the grand colonial edifices of the GPO (post office) and **Victoria Terminus (VT).** Opposite VT, the **Mumbai Municipal Corporation Building** comes as close to scraping the sky as any Victorian building could. The rotunda of the **Crawford Market** sends a lesser, yet equally improbable spire into the sky. Lockwood Kipling, Rudyard's father, designed the sculptures on the exterior during his tenure at the nearby art school. *(MJ Phule Market. A quick stroll up Dr. DN Rd. from VT, past the huge Times of India building and the Mumbai School of Art.)*

CHURCHGATE AND BACK BAY COAST

NEAR CHURCHGATE STATION. The pink-and-white wedding cake of the **Eros Cinema** in the middle of this period-piece area exemplifies Mumbai's unparalleled wealth of interwar architecture. A functioning cinema, Eros shows Bollywood's latest hits. *(Advance booking open daily 9:30am-2pm and 4-7pm. Tickets Rs40-100. Buy tickets at least 3 days in advance.)* Some of the surrounding buildings, on the same sq. as Churchgate Station, have been restored to their original waxy, zig-zag glory, but most have suffered from the damp, salty air and landlords constrained by rent control. Visitors strolling down the side of the maidan from Churchgate will find it hard to believe that these dilapidated apartments fetch millions of dollars on the rare occasions when they come up for sale.

KOLI VILLAGE. From the maidan, Maharishi Karve Rd. merges with Cuffe Parade Rd., where an abrupt gap in the land reclamation schemes has left a small bay between the towers of Nariman Point and the Cuffe Parade Extension. A fishing village, still populated by the original inhabitants of Mumbai, the Kolis, lines the shore here.

MARINE DRIVE. In the opposite direction from Churchgate, Marine Dr. runs along the rim of the Arabian Sea, stretching all the way from Nariman Point to Chowpatty Beach at the foot of Malabar Hill. Near the beach, the Drive is lined with backstock from the supply of massive, gray "tetrapods" that keep downtown Mumbai from the waves below. At sunset, people come to stroll, power-walk, and jog along the sea front, chatting, buying snacks, and treating their children to rides on toy cars and merry-go-rounds. Meanwhile, Chowpatty Beach comes alive with vendors, locals, and Kolis mending their nets. During the monsoons, tremendous waves crash down on the street, but its roasted-corn hawkers, buses, and cars seem unperturbed. At night, neon ads and a long string of streetlights transform the seaside strip into what is still popularly known as the **Queen's Necklace.**

MALABAR HILL

Beyond the beach rises Malabar Hill, Mumbai's wealthiest residential district.

BANGANGA TANK. The **Walukeshwar Temple** hides in one of the many old back streets that wind through Malabar, lined with bright flower stalls and renegade chickens. In local legend, the area harbored the banished hero of the *Ramayana*, Rama, and his brother Lakshmana, as they traveled south to free Rama's wife from captivity in Lanka. In order for Rama to perform his daily worship, Lakshmana had to bring a *linga* from far-off Varanasi. He was late one day, prompting Rama to make one from the only material he had, sand *(waluk)*, thus creating a *walukeshwar* ("sand god"). The temple's massive gray *shikhara* sits at the head of Banganga Tank, a huge rectangular pool of greenish water surrounded by jagged lines of rundown settlements and as full of legend as it is of bathers and *dhobis*. The thirsty Rama created the tank by shooting his arrow into the ground, and water began to gush forth to quench his thirst. What was once a celestial drinking fountain is now a glorified sink. Just behind the temple, the maze of *dhobi ghats* along the shore is crowded with row upon row of half-dressed washermen crouched low on the rocks and beating to smithereens the washables of everyone else in the city. The city has even more impressive *dhobi ghats* near the Mahalaxmi race course, but these are less accessible to most tourists.

THE GARDENS. The city's two most famous gardens are spread over the top of Malabar Hill. Sir Pherozeshah Mehta Garden, locally known as the **Hanging Garden,** is at the terminus of buses #106 and 108. Although its tree sculptures of various animals border on kitsch, the garden offers a welcome break from the bustling city. *(Open daily 5am-9pm. Free.)* The **Kamala Nehru Children's Park** across the street features a replica of the shoe that the old lady and all her children used to live in. *(Open daily 5am-8pm. Free.)* Old people, families, and young lovebirds come to the park to relax, walk among topiary and penguin-shaped trash cans, lounge on lawns and benches, and take in the views of the city. Crowning Malabar Hill are the seven massive **Parsi Towers of Silence,** where Zoroastrians set out their dead for vultures to eat. The whole complex is screened from sight by artful landscaping. The funerary customs of the Parsis nonetheless caused a stir a few years ago when the vultures threatened to contaminate the city's water supply by dropping leftover morsels in nearby reservoirs.

MAHARASHTRA

■**BABULNATH MANDIR.** The entrance to Babulnath Mandir on Babulnath Mandir Rd. is an unassuming set of three small stone arches, seemingly held up by the throngs of flower sellers, holy men, and worshipers around their base. The gates open up to a world far removed from the jams of Marutis below, where a concert of blaring bells and chanting voices blankets the path up the stone-stepped hill, lined with the living quarters of worshippers. The temple itself is loudly alive during worship. As you head back down, your ears still ringing, don't be surprised to find lines of women squatting beside baskets of coiled cobras asking for money to feed their serpents milk—feeding them on certain days of the week is considered an auspicious tribute to Shiva.

■**MANI BHAVAN.** As the site of the first meeting of the Indian National Congress, Mumbai pays tribute to the Father of the Nation and one-time citizen of the city, Mahatma Gandhi. The Mahatma stayed at Mani Bhavan during his frequent visits to Mumbai. The building now houses a **museum** dedicated to the great man, with a huge research library on Indian history, Gandhi, and independence. Along with a film archive, the museum includes a small collection of old photos and a "look-and-see" diorama version of the great moments in Gandhi's life and the struggle for independence. *(19 Laburnum Rd. Walk up Babulnath Mandir Rd. and turn right at its end, then take the first left onto Pandita Ramabai Rd. Open daily 9:30am-6pm. Free.)*

MAHALAXMI AREA

MAHALAXMI TEMPLE. The Mahalaxmi Temple's patron goddess (like Mumbai itself) devotes herself to wealth and beauty, making this *mandir* the city's most popular. In addition to a depiction of Lakshmi riding a tiger, the temple contains images of Kali and Saraswati, two other major goddesses of the Hindu pantheon. *(North past the flyover-covered shopping hub of Kemp's Corner, near the sea on Warden Rd., also called Bhulabhai Desai Rd.)*

TOMB OF HAJI ALI. Just beyond Mahalaxmi, on an island in the middle of the Arabian Sea, the shrine of the Sufi saint Haji Ali battles the waves daily. The bright white building stands out against the blue or gray of the sea like a beacon to all camera owners. The narrow causeway to the island disappears at high tide and during the monsoon storms, but at other times even non-Muslims can stride past the expectant rows of beggars as far as the outer chambers. On dry ground next to Haji Ali, the **Mahalaxmi Racecourse** cuts a green gash through the gray cityscape. The races run on weekends from December to May.

NEAR WORLI. Farther north still, on the edges of the upscale neighborhood of Worli, the **Nehru Centre** showcases Indian history, culture, and science. The theater offers both Indian and Western performing arts (see **Entertainment**, p. 407). The **Nehru Science Museum,** whose park is dotted with animal rides and old train cars, is mostly geared to children, but it also offers an exhibit on Indian contributions to science, from ancient ayurvedic medicine and the dawn of mathematics to current genetic discoveries by H.G. Khorana. *(☎493 2667. Open Tu-Su 11am-5pm.)*

CENTRAL AND NORTHERN MUMBAI

West of Crawford stretches an endless string of bazaars: first **Zaveri (Silversmiths) Bazaar,** then **Bhuleshwar Market** near the Mumbadevi Temple, and finally **Chor (Thieves) Bazaar,** northward by Johar Chowk.

BYCULLA. North from Johar Chowk along Sir JJ Rd., in the neighborhood of Byculla, the **Victoria and Albert Museum** (now Veermata Jijabhai) sees relatively few foreign tourists. The exhibits on Mumbai's history include the carved stone elephant that gave Elephanta Island its name. *(Open Th-Tu 9:30am-5pm. Rs2.)* For the real thing, head next door to Mumbai's **zoo,** where mangy animals subsist in depressing surroundings. The adjacent **Botanical Gardens** are a more salubrious setting for a stroll. *(Open Th-Tu 10:30am-4:30pm. Rs2.)* The architecture in Byculla, in contrast to the examples farther south, is dominated by congested housing complexes known as *chawls,* which flourished during the first half of the 20th century when Mumbai was enjoying its status as the country's premier cotton manufacturer and textile producer. The center of the city, where most of the factories were located, became the center of working class life, and the *chawls* served as a cauldron for labor unions to brew in. By the 1950s, however, rapid industrialization in other areas brought about a decline in textiles and with it a degeneration of Mumbai's *chawls.* Today, 20% of Mumbai's population lives in this tenement-style housing, where 10 families might share one room, a kitchen, and a toilet.

JUHU BEACH. Scruffy palm trees and litter make this a less-than-idyllic sunbathing spot, but that doesn't stop crowds of city-dwellers from flocking here as the sun sinks down into the Arabian Sea. In a carnivalesque atmosphere, you can bounce along in horse-drawn carriages, ride rickety ferris wheels, chow down at *chaat* stands, join in pick-up volleyball games, or simply stroll and wade along the water's edge. One of the best-known spots in the city, the Juhu area is also home to many a Bollywood star. The bungalow of the country's most famous actor, Amitabh Bachchan, is constantly surrounded by a small pack of curious crowds hoping to catch a glimpse of their hero. *(Take a local train from Churchgate to Santa Cruz station. (45min., Rs5.) Exit station on the west side, and take a rickshaw to Juhu Beach. Rs15.)*

SANJAY GANDHI NATIONAL PARK. The Sanjay Gandhi National Park features over 100 rock-cut caves, although only a few amount to much more than holes in the wall. Nonetheless, those planning to hit Ajanta, Ellora, or Karla and Bhaja can come here for a quick prep course, while others can treat this as a kind of consolation prize. Cave 3, a *chaitya* hall guarded by two huge standing Buddhas, is the most interesting place to explore. *(In the northern suburb of Borivili. Take the train to the Borivili stop. Open daily 9am-5:30pm. Rs2.)*

🎵 ENTERTAINMENT

Check *This Fortnight* or the *Bombay Times* section of the *Times of India* for the weekly bulletin of the latest concerts and plays at the **Tata Theatre,** the **Nehru Centre,** and a host of smaller venues.

Nehru Centre, Dr. Annie Besant Rd., Worli (☎492 0510). In the same complex as the Nehru Planetarium, on the right just past the Mahalaxmi race course. Indian and Western classical music and theater. The **Planetarium** within has English shows Tu-Su at 3 and 6pm, Rs10.

National Centre for the Performing Arts, Marine Drive (☎283 3737). At the very tip of Nariman Pt., just beyond the Oberoi. The compound houses a main theater, an experimental theater, and a third venue scheduled to open soon. More European and American offerings than at the Nehru, but good Indian music and theater, too.

Prithvi Theatre, Janki-Kutir, Juhu-Church Rd. (☎614 9546). Along a lane that juts off the main road leading to the Juhu bus station. The theater hall here is a city legend and one of Mumbai's most popular, with performances in many languages. Tickets Rs100. Call for dates and times of English shows.

□ SHOPPING

Like some enormous, quasi-tropical Mall of India, Mumbai can fulfill material needs and wanton consumer desire in every price range. A two-minute walk north from Flora Fountain leads to a part of MG Rd. known as **Fashion St.**, an endless chain of street stalls selling cheap and disorientingly similar merchandise. The hawkers of Western designer cast-offs can spot naive tourists a mile off, so bargain without shame. (Open daily roughly 10am-8pm.) For those who need a hiatus from haggling, **Cottage Industries Emporium,** Shivaji Marg, near Wellington Circle, offers a government **fixed-price** alternative. Though it's unabashedly geared toward tourists, and, compared to the chaos of the streets outside, rather sterile, you're guaranteed good quality and reasonably fair prices. The emporium is an almost-too-convenient, one-stop souvenir shop, proffering such wares as batik fabrics, silk Nehru jackets and scarves, and all things sandalwood. (Open M-Sa 10am-7pm. Accepts major credit cards and exchanges money.)

The **Khadi Bhavan Village Industries Emporium,** at the corner of Dr. DN Rd. and Sir P.M. Rd. in Fort, offers hand-woven cotton cloth, *kurtas,* and traditional knick-knacks at reasonable prices. (☎207 3280. Open M-Sa 10:30am-6:30pm.) The more upscale **Bombay Store,** formerly known as the Mumbai Swadeshi Store, is along Sir P.M. Rd. in Fort. The store's gleaming glass cases and polished hardwood shelves bear little resemblance to the *swadeshi* movement's spinning wheels and simple, homemade cloth. Like a department store specializing in "ethnic" merchandise, this is sterile, spoon-fed shopping, but the quality and selection is hard to grumble about. (☎288 5048. Open M-Sa 10am-7:30pm, Su 10:30am-6:30pm. Major credit cards accepted.) Travelers with particularly fat wallets should head over to **Warden Rd. (Bhulabai Desai Rd.)** near Kemp's Corner. This line of stores is the place to go if you want to match, thread for thread, the clothing worn by Mumbai's hipsters.

■ NIGHTLIFE

Unlike most cities in India, Mumbai knows how to party. International Bright Young Things pack the city's pubs and discos in search of the next "in" thing. Beware of the pervasive "couples only" policies on busy nights, and the occasional refusal of dirty-looking T-shirted or sandal-clad travelers. Bars and clubs in Mumbai tend to close by 1-2am, causing a mass exodus to the 24hr. coffee shops at luxury hotels. If you're looking to splurge, try the **Taj Mahal Hotel,** Apollo Bunder (☎202 3366), in Colaba; the **Ambassador Hotel,** VN Rd. (☎204 1131) in Churchgate; the **President Hotel** in Cuffe Parade; or **The Oberoi,** Marine Drive (☎202 5757), in Nariman Point.

The Ghetto, 30 Bhulabhai Desai Rd., Breach Candy (☎492 1556). In an alley on the seaward side of the road, just before Mahalaxmi. Photos of the Edge and Jim Morrison, and loads of graffiti adorn the walls of this popular, yuppie-filled bar. Great atmosphere and music make this worth the Rs70 taxi ride from Colaba. Beer Rs100, spirits Rs70 and up. Open daily 7pm-1:30am.

Leopold Cafe, Colaba Causeway, Colaba (☎202 0131), 3blocks down from Regal, on the left. The ultimate tourist hangout. The dimly lit A/C bar upstairs hosts the serious drinkers. Beer Rs130; pitchers Rs200. Open daily 1pm-1am. Downstairs open daily 8am-11pm.

Not Just Jazz By the Bay, 143 Marine Dr. (☎ 285 1876 or 282 0957), right next to the Pizzeria, at the corner with Veer Narimar Rd. Caters to expats and the local elite, although it might as well be in London or New York. The "Jazz"'s great food, A/C, and live music every night compensate for the steep prices. Beer Rs130; spirits Rs150-250. Cover Rs150. Reservations necessary on F and Sa nights. Open daily 11am-2pm and 6pm-1:30am.

Headquarters, Colaba Causeway (☎288 3982). Upstairs from Cafe Royal, across the intersection from Regal Cinema. HQ is the hotspot for a teenage crowd that drinks and dances the night away, especially on packed W, F, and Sa nights. W, F Rs400 cover per couple; Sa Rs500 per couple; other nights no cover. Draft beer Rs70; pitchers Rs200. Open daily 8:30pm-1am.

Beyond 1900s, in the Taj Mahal Hotel, Colaba (☎202 3366). Ushering in the new millennium with a major renovation and a new name, the disco formerly known as 1900s is priced to maintain its status as Mumbai's most glamorous pretty-person nightspot. Cover Rs330 per head; Su-Th Rs300 goes toward drinks. Open daily 10pm-2am.

Gokul's Permit Room, Tullock Rd., parallel to the Taj Hotel, one street behind Colaba, next to Gokul's Communication Centre. This working man's beer-and-scotch joint is as authentic an Indian watering hole as can be. Escape the glitz and have a bottle of beer (0.33L Rs45-50) and a plate of fried Mumbai duck (Rs45). Open daily 11am-11pm.

Voodoo, Arthur Bunder Rd., Colaba. 4doors up on the left from the sea front. A dive for desperate straight men during the week, Voodoo transforms into Mumbai's only aboveground gay disco on Saturday nights. India's most famous gay rights activist, Ashok Rao Kavi, is a regular. Beer Rs65. Cover Rs180. Open daily 7pm-1:30am.

The Pub at Rasna, J. Tata Rd., Churchgate (☎282 0995), on the left side of the road that leads to the right of Eros from Churchgate, just after the small circle. Futuristic—if the future hinges on tall metal chairs, neon lights, streamlined decor, and a confusing floor plan. The children of Mumbai's jet-set jam up against the aerodynamic bar, leaving breathing space only on the small dance floor. Beer Rs120. Open M-Sa 7pm-1am.

⚡ DAYTRIP FROM MUMBAI

ELEPHANTA ISLAND

Elephanta is a 1hr. ferry ride from the Gateway of India. It is not unheard of for the slow-moving ferries to ram into each other. Only luxury boats run during the monsoon months (roughly June-Sept.), and then only when waters are navigable. Enquiry ☎202 6364. Every hr. 9am-2pm, return 11am-6:30pm. Round-trip Rs65-85. Open Tu-Su 9am-5:30pm. US$10. Admission includes a group tour of the caves with government-approved guide, provided one is available.

About 10km northeast of the Gateway of India, Elephanta Island, in Mumbai Harbor, offers travelers a fleeting glimpse of an Indian fishing village in its heyday. Well, almost—Elephanta is what happens to a quaint village when more tourists than fish are dragged in from the water. The island's cave temples of unknown origin (estimated 2BC-AD12) have lured in thousands of visitors, and locals haven't hesitated to capitalize. Point your Nikon at fisherwomen draped in emerald, magenta, and lime saris, and risk the repercussions—they will chase you, squawking demands for baksheesh (without upsetting the silver *mutkas* balanced on their heads). Also be prepared for the free-roaming monkeys ready to strip you of chips, Frooties, and bananas. Overall, the over-commercialized sight is a disappointing experience, worth the US$10 admission fee only if you're desperate to leave Mumbai and see some green, or if this is your one shot at seeing a cave.

In spite of its hassles (the ferry ride itself is an adventure), Elephanta remains renowned for its UNESCO-protected **cave temples.** The cave, at the end of a 125-step climb up the mountainside, covers over 5000 sq. m, much of which is filled with moss and bats. The main chamber has a cross-like arrangement of massive pillars with no functional purpose. The image of Shiva as the cosmic dancer Nataraja, is carved in detail near the entrance; the damage is due to the Portuguese, who reportedly used it for target practice when they occupied the island in the

1800s. A weathered and beaten-up panel of Lakulisha, a saint considered to be an incarnation of Shiva, stands opposite. The main **Linga Shrine** in the center of the cave is accessed by entrances on all four sides, each flanked by a pair of *dwarapalas*, guardians at least as vicious as the fisherwomen. The other attractions in the cave are the elaborate **wall panels** depicting scenes from Shiva mythology in remarkable detail. On the north side is a lively panel of Shiva as Bhairava killing the demon Andhaka, who was attempting to steal a divine tree. The 6m-tall bust of Shiva as the three-faced Trimurti, creator, protector, and destroyer of the Universe, is the main attraction. On the sides, the descent of Ganga and Shiva as Ardhanarishvara (half male, half female) is shown. Near another entrance is a detailed panel showing Ravana's attempt to uproot Mount Kailasa.

MATHERAN मथेरान ☎ 02148

Once an exclusive retreat for Raj-era sahibs, the hill station of Matheran (95km east of Mumbai) now swarms with Indian weekend vacationers. The village shuts down from mid-June to August, when the monsoon rains arrive in full. For frazzled Mumbaites and city-weary travelers alike, the high-class, full-board resorts found here may be a welcome relief. Filled with open public spaces, red clay paths leading through leafy forests, and magnificent views, Matheran can be a good spot for a few days of relaxation.

▐ TRANSPORTATION. The access point for Matheran is the small town of **Neral**, which lies at the base of the hill station. From Mumbai's VT Station, local trains to **Karjat** stop at Neral Junction (2hr., approximately every hr. 6am-1am, Rs16). Only a few of the Mumbai-Pune express trains stop at Neral (2½hr.; *Deccan Exp.*, 6:40am; *Koyana Exp.*, 8:45am; Rs30). From Neral, Matheran is 21km up the hill. It's a toss-up as to which ascent is more nerve-wracking—a **taxi** hired at the station (Rs45 per person shared; Rs225 solo ride) or the **miniature train** (2½hr;, 8:40, 11am, 5pm; return 5:45am, 1:10, 2:35pm; Rs24). Tickets for the train can be reserved 3 days in advance, but not on the day of departure, at Pune and Mumbai VT stations. During the monsoon, mini-train service is sporadic and may be cancelled entirely. Since motor vehicles are prohibited in Matheran, taxis cannot take you all the way into town. The taxi stand/drop-off is 2.5km north of the railway station; to complete the trip, you're left with a 40min. hike (a porter will carry your bags for Rs40), a rocky but fun horse ride (Rs80), or a hand-pulled rickshaw (Rs120). Matheran levies an entry tax on all visitors (adults Rs10, children Rs5).

▐▐ ORIENTATION AND PRACTICAL INFORMATION. The miniature train pulls into the **Matheran Railway Station,** on the main road, **Mahatma Gandhi Marg (MG Marg),** at the center of town. The **tourist office** is opposite the railway station and has town maps. (Open M-Sa 9:30am-5:30pm; closed during the off-season) **Currency exchange** is available at **Union Bank of India,** on the right side of MG Marg as you walk south from the station. (☎30282. Open M-F 10am-2pm, Sa 10am-noon.) The **police station** is on the right fork off MG Marg as you walk south from the railway station. There is a separate **phone code** when calling from Mumbai: ☎952148. The **GPO** is across from Union Bank of India on MG Marg.

▐▐ ACCOMMODATIONS AND FOOD. Matheran is a resort town, and prices can be high, especially in season, when reservations are required. In the off-season, many hotels close down or offer substantial discounts. Mid-week prices are generally open to a bit of haggling. Single rates are rare, and many family resorts will turn away solo travelers. Check-out times are distressingly early (7am is standard), and hotels will gleefully charge you for another half-day if you sleep in. The **Hotel Prasanna ❷**, with all-Hindi signs, is opposite the train station. It contains tidier-than-usual bath and warm showers. (☎30258. Doubles Rs600. Closed in the off season.) North of the train station, on the opposite side of the tracks from MG Marg, the family-run **Hunjer House ❷**, offers one of the more pleasant budget options, with balconies on some of its basic-but-clean rooms and hot water in the mornings. (☎30536. Doubles Rs600. Off season: Rs250.) The best room-and-board deal is the **Janata Happy Home ❸**, on Kasturba Rd. Heading south from the station, take the first right, and then turn left onto Kasturba. (☎30229; booking in Mumbai 022 619 3899. Two-night min. stay. Doubles Rs800-1000. Off season: 30-50% discount.) For a more resorty option, with room service, a pool (with waterslide!), and a playground, try the **Gujarat Bhavan Hotel ❸**, Maulana Azad Rd. Walk south on MG Rd., and then follow the signs. (☎30278; in Mumbai (022) 203 0876. Two night min. stay. Five types of rooms range from Rs650-1500, meals included. Off season: 40% discount)

There are several simple restaurants on MG Marg, south of the railway station. The amiable **Kwality Restaurant ❶** has *bhel puri* for Rs18 and *dosas* for Rs18-22. (Open daily 9am-9:30pm; closed June 15-Aug. 15.) Many hotels offer full board—a good choice in the heavily discounted off-season, when non-hotel meals are few and far between. **Divadkar Hotel ❶**, opposite the train station, serves non-guests. (Chinese and Indian dishes Rs40-80, beer Rs65. Open daily noon-2:30pm and 7-10:30pm.) Local specialties include *chikki*—a sweet, sticky, crunchy peanut brittle—and mango fudge, which tastes much better than it sounds (or looks, for that matter).

◙ **VIEWS.** The borders of the hill station are marked by numerous sheer cliff outcrops. Many of these have been set up as viewpoints. On the western side, **Porcupine and Louisa Points** provide a glimpse of Neral in the distance. Also popular are **Monkey Point** to the north and **Alexandra Point** to the south. **Panorama Point** sits to the far north. The viewpoints are very romantic at sunset and sunrise: expect to feel left out if you're not here on honeymoon. Women are advised not to explore the more remote locales alone at night.

NASIK नाशिक ☎ 0253

Smaller than Mumbai or Pune but no less frantic, Nasik (NA-shik; pop. 1 million) is best known for the sacred Godavari River that runs through it. The city is believed to be the site where *Ramayana* bad-guy Ravana abducted Rama's wife Sita, igniting one of the greatest match-ups in Hindu lore (see **The Ramayana**, p. 613). Today, Nasik's purity as a religious haven seems threatened by the growth of industry. The jingle-jangle of temple bells and the hypnotic humming of the meditative syllable *om* clash with the chug and spit of smokestacks and exhaust pipes. Nevertheless, every year thousands of devotees head to Nasik to walk along the same pathways their gods and goddesses once trod. Nasik plays host to the **Kumbh Mela** festival (see p. 720) every 12 years (the next one will occur in July and August 2003). During the Mela, one of the most auspicious moments in the Hindu calendar, millions come here to take a purifying dip in the waters of the Godavari.

▐▀ **TRANSPORTATION**

Trains: Railway Station (☎561274 or 563625), Nasik Rd., 8km from the city center. As you leave the platforms, the booking office is on the left. To **Mumbai** (4hr.; 10 per day; Rs53) and **Nagpur** (12hr.; 4 per day 12:20am-11:45pm; Rs225). For most other destinations around Maharashtra, it is easier to take a bus.

Buses: Central Bus Stand (universally known as CBS; ☎572854). Sharanpur Rd. To: **Ahmedabad** (12hr.; 5 per day noon-1am; Rs90); **Aurangabad** (4½hr.; every hr. 5:30am-2am; Rs97); **Mumbai** (5hr.; every hr.; Rs90); **Nagpur** (15hr.; 10pm; Rs350); **Pune** (5hr.; every hr.; Rs110).

Local Transportation: Auto-rickshaws rule the road and are grudgingly subject to meters. Fare is approximately Rs12 per unit on the meter.

✈ 🛈 ORIENTATION AND PRACTICAL INFORMATION

Nasik's spiritual life centers on the banks of the **Godavari River.** Its commercial heart is a couple of kilometers away, near the **Central Bus Stand (CBS),** at the intersection of **Sharanpur** and **Old Agra Rd.** Going up Old Agra Rd. from the CBS will lead to **MG Rd.** (the first road on the right), Nasik's main street, which provides access to the Godavari River. Going down leads to **Trimbak Rd.** and the tourist office, post office, police station, and hospital. The **Nasik Road Railway Station** is 8km southeast of the CBS. Nearby is chaotic **Dwarka Circle** (bus to CBS Rs4; auto-rickshaw Rs40).

Tourist Office: MTDC (☎570059), T-1, Golf Club, Old Agra Rd. From the CBS, head down Old Agra Rd., past the State Bank. Turn right at the 2nd major intersection; the MTDC is 5min. down on the right. Unlike other MTDC branches, this one is very resourceful and gives free maps of the city. Open M-F and 1st and 3rd Sa 10am-5:45pm.

Currency Exchange: State Bank of India (☎599935), Old Agra Rd. Go right from the CBS; it's 200m after the intersection on the left. Open M-F 11am-5pm, Sa 11am-2pm.

Police: Police Commissioner's Office (☎570183 or 352122), off Sharanpur Rd.

Hospital: General Hospital (☎576268), Trimbak Rd. Same directions as to the MTDC (see above), but turn right at the 1st intersection.

Internet: Matrix Cyber Cafe, straight across from Hotel Basera (see below). Faster than elsewhere. Rs30 per hr. Open daily 9am-midnight. Several cybercafes are in **United Arcade,** on College Rd., opposite B.Y.K. College's main gate. Rs20-35 per hr. Open daily 9am-midnight.

Post Office: GPO (☎500141). Trimbak Rd. Go down Old Agra Rd. from the CBS and turn left at the first major intersection. The GPO is on the right, beyond the next intersection. Open M-Sa 10am-6pm, Su 10am-1pm. **Postal Code: 42001.**

🏠 ACCOMMODATIONS

Budget hotels cluster near the CBS on Shivaji and Old Agra Rd., and along Dwarka Circle. Most have noon check-out. Good luck finding a room during the Mela.

Raj Mahal Lodge (☎580501; fax 571096; rajmahallodge@vsnl.com). Sharanpur Rd. opposite the CBS. Basic rooms, unbeatable location, and relatively cheap rates conspire to fill the Raj's rooms early, so act fast. 24hr. STD/ISD in the lobby, TVs and telephones in all rooms. Singles Rs190-500; doubles Rs260-600. ❷

Hotel Pathik (☎596884-5 or 598784-5), 1370 Q Pathik Complex, Nehru Garden. From the CBS, cross the intersection and walk down Sharanpur Rd. (it will merge with another street), then take the 1st left; it's on the right at the end of the street. Pleasant, newly renovated rooms with attractive bath, cable TV, and phone. Great restaurant downstairs. Singles Rs250-400; doubles Rs300-490. ❷

Hotel Basera (☎575616 or 575618), Shivaji Rd. Cross the intersection from the CBS and head down the small alley on the left. Comfortable rooms in slight disrepair all have TV and phone. Singles Rs230-400; doubles Rs350-500. Tax Rs9. ❷

Hotel Padma (☎576837), Sharanpur Rd. Opposite CBS. Simple, clean, cheap, and central. Singles Rs250-300; doubles Rs325-400. ❷

Hotel Vaishali (☎579910 or 573311; fax 575909), Gole Colony. At its end farthest from the river, MG Rd. turns into a dirt alley; Vaishali is on this alley. Tidy, passable pink rooms in a location just close enough (and just far enough) from the chaos of the Godavari. TV and phone in all rooms. Singles Rs290-550; doubles Rs425-725. ❷

◖ FOOD

The **Samrat Restaurant** ❶, in the Hotel Samrat, Old Agra Rd., opposite the State Bank, serves up pure veg. Gujarati *thalis* (Rs70) that are popular with locals. The canteen-like ambience mixes well with the bus stand hullabaloo nearby. (Open daily 8am-11:30pm.) **Suruchi Vegetarian Restaurant,** around the corner from Hotel Basera, dishes out cheap Indian fare all day long. (Open daily 6:30am-10:30pm.)

◉ SIGHTS

GODAVARI RIVER. The easiest way to get to the sacred Godavari River is via the narrow, meandering alleys that shoot off from MG Rd. You don't have to walk far down the sloping pathways before you leave the thick traffic fumes behind you and are surrounded by the clatter of candy, *kurta,* and cloth vendors. Just beyond the Old Quarter, shallow squares of murky water can be seen next to the **Santar Gardhi Mahara Bridge.** Most mornings they are merely a gathering place for hundreds of *dhobi-wallahs* scrubbing clothes on the Godavari's stone steps, while huge groups of baksheesh babies tenaciously follow more moneyed visitors. Every 12 years, however, these *ghats* experience the onslaught of thousands of devotees who flood Nasik during the **Kumbh Mela.** Nasik's next Mela will take place during July and August 2003, but it's not impossible to imagine the frenzied cacophony that ensues at festival time—one glance at the sprawling **market** directly behind the *ghats* will give you an idea. Rickety stalls sell row upon cluttered row of religious paraphernalia as well as fruits, vegetables, nuts, lentils, steel jewelry, carved statuettes, and bronze vessels.

OTHER SIGHTS. Among the market stalls around the *ghats* are several sites steeped in mythology. Nasik's religious focal point, several meters to the left of the **Ram Sita footbridge,** is the **Ram Kund.** Thousands of people immerse themselves here in order to purify themselves of sin. The waters here are also supposed to have the unusual power to dissolve bones; the remains of several celebrities and top politicians (from members of the Nehru-Gandhi dynasty to Rama's father, King Dasharatha) languish here in the **Astivilaya Tirth** ("Bone Immersion Tank"). Up the hill from Ram Kund is **Kala Rama Mandir,** a temple at the site where, according to the *Ramayana,* Rama's brother Lakshman sliced off the nose (in Sanskrit, *nasika,* and hence the town's name) of Ravana's monstrous sister, Shurparnakha. The *mandir* houses ebony images of the myth's protagonists. Sita's cave, or **Gumpha,** marks the site where Sita was abducted by the demon Ravana.

PUNE पुणे ☎020

As Mumbai has become increasingly congested and cosmopolitan, the steady trickle of daily commuters between Mumbai and Pune (POO-nuh) has turned into a flood. In recent years there has been a mini-exodus to the cooler, more relaxed Pune, a four-hour climb up the Deccan Plateau. Birthplace of the Maratha hero Shivaji, capital of his successors, and an almost purely Marathi-speaking city, Pune lays a much more credible claim to son-of-the-soil status than its upstart cousin on the coast. Though much of the urban chaos (and accompanying pollution) that characterizes Mumbai also rules in Pune, the city has plenty of greenery,

MAHARASHTRA

fresh air, and pleasant strolling grounds. The city's biggest dose of internationalism springs from Pune's famous ashram, the Osho Commune International, established by the late "export guru" Rajneesh. The Birkenstock-clad crowd in their maroon robes (called *sannyasins*) come from all over the world to converge on Pune and undergo Osho's various meditation therapies. Pune's other attractions may not be as renowned as its ashram, but its hospitable residents and laid-back atmosphere make it a great place to rest for a few days.

▐ TRANSPORTATION

Flights: Airport (☎ 6685591), Pune Nagar Rd., 10km from the city. An Ex-Servicemen's bus leaves every hr. from outside the GPO (Rs25). **Indian Airlines** (☎ 632140). Ambedkar Rd., near the Sangam Bridge, in Camp. **Jet Airways** (☎ 6137181). To: **Bangalore** (Indian Airlines: 1½hr.; 1 per day; US$150); **Chennai** (Jet Airways: 3hr.; daily; US$175); **Delhi** (Indian Airlines and Jet Airways: 2hr.; 1 per day; US$210); **Mumbai** (Jet Airways: 35min.; 2 per day; US$85).

Trains: Railway Station, MPL Rd. The booking office, on your left as you face the station, deals with local tickets, reservations, and Mumbai trains. Reservations office upstairs. To: **Bangalore** (20hr., 2:35am and noon, Rs284); **Hyderabad** (13hr., 4:45pm, Rs194); **Miraj** for **Goa** (9½hr., 5:30pm, Rs109); **Mumbai** (4hr., 5 per day 6am-6:20pm, Rs89); **Neral** for **Matheran** (2hr., 2 per day 6am and 3pm, Rs104).

Buses: Pune has three main state stations and many private carriers. The most convenient station for tourists is right next to the railway station. To: **Mahabaleshwar** (4hr., 10 per day 5:30am-6:30pm, Rs65-84); **Mumbai** (4½hr., every 15min. 5am-10pm, Rs110); **Panjim** (11hr., 4 per day, Rs230-290). Buses from **Shivajinagar Station** in Deccan head for: **Aurangabad** (6hr., 12 per day 5am-6pm, Rs115); **Lonavla** (1½hr., every hr., Rs35); **Nasik** (5hr., every hr., Rs110). Go to **Swargate Station** for buses to **Bangalore** (20hr., 2:30pm, Rs300). It's worth shelling out the extra rupees for a private "deluxe" bus instead of the rickety old state machines. One reliable private carrier is **Prasanna** (☎ 6123137 or 6129721), Connaught Rd., just around the corner from MPL Rd. Open daily 6am-11pm.

Local Transportation: Auto-rickshaws are the best means of getting around Pune. The conversion rate is roughly 4-5 times the meter reading; ask to see a chart. **Local bus #4** goes to Deccan; **#5, 6,** and **31** go south toward Swargate bus station and the old town.

✴ ORIENTATION

Although it's relatively quiet, Pune is still a huge city, with a population of three million. The city is divided into two vaguely defined sections: the **Camp** and the **Old Town.** The railway station and one of the major bus stands rub shoulders in Camp, between **Sassoon Rd.** (formerly part of Connaught Rd.) to the east and **MPL Rd.** to the south. Camp's upscale shops and restaurants cluster around **MG Rd.** A 10min. rickshaw ride west of here is the Old Town, where traditional *wadas* (mansions) surround the Swargate Bus Terminal, Raja Kelkar Museum, Phule Market, and the ruined Shaniwar Wada Palace. Farther west across the Mutha River is the middle-class neighborhood of **Deccan,** which stretches to Fergusson College Rd., where Pune's students hobnob in a string of restaurants and cafes. The Koregaon Park suburb to the northeast of Camp, home to the **Osho Commune,** occupies its own distinctive physical (and psychological) space.

Street names can be confusing in Pune. The old Connaught Rd. is now called Sassoon Rd. north of its intersection with Byramji, and Sadhu Vaswani to the south, even though it is essentially one street. Sassoon Rd. and Bund Garden Rd. flow into each other in a similar fashion, as do Ambedkar and Moledina Rd. To make matters worse, street signs are only in Hindi.

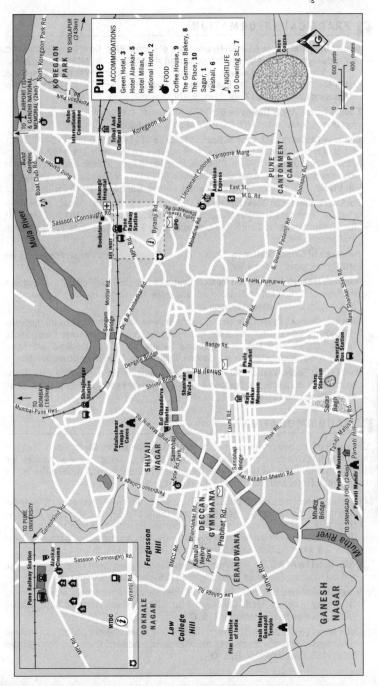

Pune

▲ ACCOMMODATIONS
Green Hotel, 3
Hotel Alankar, 5
Hotel Milan, 4
National Hotel, 2

♣ FOOD
Coffee House, 9
The German Bakery, 8
The Place, 10
Sagar, 1
Vaishali, 6

♪ NIGHTLIFE
10 Downing St., 7

MAHARASHTRA

ⓘ PRACTICAL INFORMATION

Tourist Office: MTDC (☎6126867), one block of Central Bldg. Complex on Byramji Rd. Enter through the main gate and follow the road straight back. The MTDC is the 1st bldg. on the left after the road curves. Not worth the walk, unless you're really desperate. Open M-F 10am-5:30pm. The **Bus Station Branch Office** (☎6125342) offers 15-point sightseeing tours of Pune (7½hr., 9am, Rs100).

Budget Travel: Apple Travels (☎628185), Amir Hotel, Connaught Rd., in Camp, at the junction of Sassoon and MPL Rd. Open M-Sa 9:30am-6pm.

Currency Exchange: AXE Central Bank of India (☎6131413), MG Rd., in Camp, 5min. south of Moledina Rd. Up to US$500 cash advance on MC and V. Open M-F 10:30am-2:50pm, Sa 10:30am-1:30pm. **Citibank,** East Rd., in Camp, 10min. south of Moledina Rd., has a **24hr. ATM. American Express** (☎6055337), 9 Moledina Rd., 2nd branch on MG Rd., just past the intersection with Moledina. Open M-Sa 10am-5:30pm.

Bookstore: Crossword Bookstore (☎6111603), Sohrab Mall, 1st fl., across from Jehangir Hospital. Open daily 10:30am-8:30pm. **Manney's Bookstore** (☎6131683), 7 Moledina Rd., Clover Centre, in Camp. The best source for Pune maps. Open M-Sa 9:30am-1:30pm and 4-8pm.

Police: Bund Garden Station (☎62202), Byramji Rd, at the giant intersection next to the MTDC (see above). Open 24hr.

Hospital: Jehangir Hospital and Medical Centre (☎6122551 or 6050550), 32 Sassoon Rd. From MPL, turn left on Sassoon Rd. and cross the railroad tracks; it's immediately on the right. On-site **pharmacy** open 24hr.

Internet: Connect Cyber Cafe (☎6051918), Ashoka Mall, Bund Garden Rd. opposite Holiday Inn. Cheap, but very slow. Rs12 per hr. Open 24hr. **Internet Cafe,** Sadhu Yaswani Chowk. From MPL, turn right onto Sassoon Rd. It's on the block with many stores, immediately before the intersection. Rs30 per hr. Open daily 8am-midnight.

Post Office: Sadhu Vaswani Rd. A domed, stone bldg. in the park on the right, 5min. south of the intersection of Sassoon and MPL Rd. *Poste Restante* at window #8. Open M-Sa 10am-6pm. **Postal Code:** 411001.

⌂ ACCOMMODATIONS

Almost all of the budget hotels in Pune are within the **Wilson Garden** area. Many of these buildings were once opulent personal *wadas*, though quite a number are starting to crumble a bit these days. To get here, take the small lane to the left of the National Hotel and turn right at the corner.

◪ **National Hotel** (☎6125054 or 6127780), opposite the railway station. Vast verandas sprout from the well-tended gardens of this 150-year old palace-turned-hotel. Large, clean rooms with high ceilings and big windows. Friendly staff who cook breakfast (Rs10-20) and serve tea or coffee (Rs5-10). Doubles have attached bath. Check-out noon. Hot water 7-11am. Singles Rs180; doubles Rs300-350. ❶

Green Hotel (☎6125229), 16 Wilson Garden. Stained glass, wood finish, wrought iron, and old furniture. Check-out 5pm. Singles Rs175; doubles Rs300-350. ❶

Hotel Alankar (☎6120484), 14 Wilson Circle. Simple rooms (some with balconies) along long, quiet corridors. Check-out 24hr. All rooms with attached bath. Singles Rs280; doubles Rs325; triples Rs375. ❷

Hotel Milan (☎6122024), 19 Wilson Garden. One of the cheaper places with TVs and telephones. The rooms themselves are nothing extraordinary. Check-out 5pm. Singles Rs260-450; doubles Rs260-525. ❷

⚑ FOOD

Lieutenant Colonel Tarapore Marg, which crosses Sadhu Vaswani Rd. a block before Moledina Rd., becomes a huge open-air cafe in the afternoons and evenings. Countless drink and *chaat* stalls lure revelers into street-side seats (or squats) to gossip and people-watch (closed Su). The area between the bus stand and the railway booking office is full of fruit carts. There's a western-style **supermarket** at 1 Moledina Rd. (Open daily 8am-9pm.)

🔳 **Sagar,** Hotel Dreamland Bldg., MPL Rd. Just before the intersection with Sasson Rd. Look for the yellow Marathi sign. Superb Indian, Chinese, and continental dishes in a comfortable, well-lit interior. Delicious club sandwich Rs25. Entrees Rs40-55. Open daily 10am-11pm. ❶

The Place: Touché the Sizzler, 7 Moledina Rd., Camp. The snappy, two-tier Tudor interior packs in Pune's yuppies for "sizzlers"—iron skillets filled with vegetables, fries, and a choice of entree (veg. Rs100-120, non-veg. Rs150-200). *Tandoori* dishes also available (Rs70-200). A hotspot, indeed. Open daily 11:30am-3:30pm and 7-11pm. ❷

Woodland Restaurant, Woodland Hotel, Byramji Rd., Camp. Go south along Sassoon Rd. and turn right at the first intersection. Punjabi and Chinese dishes Rs50-75. The Mysore *dosa* is magnificent. Buffet breakfast Rs75. Open daily 7am-11pm. ❶

Coffee House, 2 Moledina Rd., Camp. Decent coffee and the standard array of Chinese and Indian dishes (Rs30-60). Tables are jammed with locals at peak times. Open daily for snacks 8am-11:30pm; meals 11am-3pm and 7-11:30pm. ❶

Vaishali, Fergusson College Rd., Deccan. Opposite Saraswat Bank. Tree-canopied backyard overflows during the day with students, and at night with families, who all flock here for the *bhel puri* and South Indian snacks (Rs15-30), ice cream and shakes (Rs20-40), and the lively scene. Open daily 7am-11pm. ❶

The German Bakery, North Koregaon Park Rd. From the Osho ashram, take a right at the gate, walk to the end of the road, and turn left; it's on the right. Homesick *sannyasins* spill *Apfelstrudel* (Rs25) crumbs onto their maroon robes in this popular, open-air, chill-out spot. More upbeat devotees can chat over cappuccino (Rs20) or "sterilized" pineapple juice, all the while pondering the merits of the acupuncture, *tai chi,* and Tao healing lessons advertised colorfully around them. Open daily 7am-midnight. ❶

🎵 🎭 ENTERTAINMENT AND NIGHTLIFE

One of the few disco-pubs around to cater to postcolonial partygoers is **10 Downing St.,** Boat Club Rd., off Bund Garden Rd., at the northern edge of town. Legions of students grind away on the strobe-lit upstairs dance floor, while a more mixed crowd throws back beers (Rs50) on the chill, ultraswank first floor. Dance floor is couples and single women only. (☎6128343. Cover Rs150. W ladies free, Sa Rs250. Open daily 7pm-12:30am.) Huge crowds take in Bollywood flicks, afternoon and night, at Pune's theaters, including **Alankar Cinema** (☎6123333; Rs15-50), Sassoon Rd., and **West End Cinema,** next to Touché the Sizzler on Moledina Rd., which also shows big Western releases. **The Film Institute of India,** Law College Rd., offers more high-brow stuff, but (in theory) you have to be a member to get in. **Nehru Memorial Hall,** Moledina Rd. (☎6128560), and **Bal Gandharva Theater,** Jangli Maharaj Rd. (☎5532959), stage performances of Indian drama, music, and dance. For more detailed listings and schedules, see the "Pune Plus" section of the *Times of India.*

SLIPPERY SOLDIER Pune is justly proud of its status as the birthplace of one of India's great national heroes, Shivaji Bhonsle. By the time of his birth in 1630, Muslims had dominated the subcontinent for 400 years, and persecution of Hindu subjects was widespread. Against this backdrop of oppression, the 16-year-old nobleman from the landholding Hindu Bhonsle family of the Maratha region declared his divine mission: the violent restoration of religious tolerance.

Shivaji's cunning and courage kept him one step ahead of his nemesis, the ardently Muslim Mughal emperor Aurangzeb. In 1659, Shivaji lured the Bijapur Sultan's Muslim general, Afzal Khan, into a "discussion" and ripped out his innards with his *wagh nakh*, or metal "tiger claws." Meanwhile, his troops annihilated the Bijapuri army. In 1666, Shivaji gave himself up at Agra, only to smuggle himself out of house arrest in a basket of sweets. On another occasion, he supposedly captured the sheer-walled fort of Sinhagad (see p. 419) by training lizards to carry ropes up the cliff face.

Shivaji ruled his Maratha Confederacy with religious impartiality, recruiting both Hindu and Muslim officers. Even after his death in 1680, the Confederacy continued to prosper until the British arrived. In the 1950s, Balasahek (Bal) Thackeray, a Mumbai-based cartoonist, revived Shivaji's status as a folk hero and founded a political party called the Shiv Sena in his honor. The party, however, does not share Shivaji's tolerance, opting for a doctrine of rigid Hindu nationalism and hostility toward Muslims.

👁 SIGHTS

OSHO COMMUNE INTERNATIONAL. Upwardly mobile meditators worldwide flock to Pune's famous ashram, a weird synthesis of health-club luxury and Eastern spirituality. Here, followers of the late, great, and intercontinentally controversial guru, Osho (also known as Bhagwan Shree Rajneesh), gather to practice his New Age meditation techniques among lush tropical plants. As the guru himself said: "The very air has a different vibe." Though most nirvana-seekers come on a journey of self-transformation, the classy facilities—including an open-air meditation hall, swimming pool, library, bookstore, vegetarian canteen, jacuzzi, and "*zen*nis courts"—don't hurt, either. However, these are only vaguely visible from the tour; to be a real part of the Osho Commune requires an HIV test (Rs125), two passport photographs, three robes, and Rs150 per day (Rs40 for Indians). Apart from six daily meditations—which encourage you to "become an empty vessel" or engage in the cathartic explosion of "shouting wildly the mantra 'Hoo!'"—all courses, food, and other services cost extra. (*17 Koregaon Park, in the northwest part of Camp. ☎ 628562; commune@osho.com; www.osho.com. Visitors Center open daily 9:30am-1pm and 2-4pm. Daily 1hr. guided tours: 10:30am and 2:30pm, Rs10. Try to reserve 1 day in advance.*)

SHANIWAR WADA. Amid the narrow, winding streets of Old Town, the remains of the massive Shaniwar Palace, built in 1736, are Pune's most celebrated and decrepit landmark. At the height of its glory, it enclosed the multi-story home of the Peshwa rulers, the opulent bureaucratic center of the powerful Maratha empire that governed all of central India. Sadly, the inner structures burned down in 1828, leaving only the foundation and the palace's outer walls and gates for tourists and picnickers to explore. (*Shivaji Rd. Open daily 8am-6pm. US$5 or equivalent.*)

RAJA KELKAR MUSEUM. The pack-rat passion of the late Dr. D.G. Kelkar, the museum's founder, has resulted in a vast collection that is as eclectic as it is eccentric. Enthusiastic guides lead groups through three floors of galleries, highlighting unique exhibits and their peculiarities: an elephant-shaped foot scrubber, eight images of Ganesh carved on a bean, and a painstakingly relocated and reconstructed 18th-century royal palace room from Madhya Pradesh. More than just a mish-mash of kitschy bric-a-brac, the exhibits here take obvious delight in the diversity of India's cultures in a light-hearted style often missing from more high-minded exhibits. *(Baji Rao Rd., Deccan Gymkhana. Open M-Sa 8:30am-6pm. Rs120.)*

TRIBAL AND CULTURAL MUSEUM. India has over 600 tribal communities, incorporating 67.7 million people—9% of the nation's population. This obscure gem of a museum celebrates those cultures and their craftwork with over 2000 artifacts, taken primarily from the 47 Maharashtrian groups. *(Koregaon Park Rd., just south of the railroad tracks. Open M-F 10am-5pm. Free.)*

PATALESHWAR TEMPLE CAVES. Almost overshadowed by the modern temple next door, the 8th-century Pataleshwar Caves exude spirituality. A circular stone gazebo (a Nandi *mandapam*) stands by the entrance to the small underground temple, a marvelous escape from the bustle of modern Pune. *(On Jangali Maharaj Rd., near the intersection with Shivaji Rd. Free and open to the public.)*

OTHER SIGHTS. The **Gandhi National Memorial** is sadly neglected. The elegant architecture of the Aga Khan Palace, where Gandhi was once imprisoned, fades behind the crumbling paint and stained floors you see as you approach. A timeline of Gandhi's life, in similar condition, leads you through a few rooms and, outside, to the *samadhis* containing the ashes of Gandhi's wife. *(Aga Khan Palace, Pune-Nagar Rd., on the way to the airport. Open daily 9am-5:45pm. Requested donation Rs5.)* **Parvati Hill,** at the far southwest corner of Pune, has a pleasant view of the city and surroundings. A sloping staircase leads from a side street off Tanaji Malusane Rd. up to two temples, several outlooks, and the **Peshwa Museum.** *(Open daily 7:30am-8pm. Rs5.)*

◆ DAYTRIP FROM PUNE: SINHAGAD FORT

Spread high atop the rugged green hills 24km southwest of Pune, Sinhagad Fort makes for a pleasant day's ramble away from the city. The fort is one of the most important historical sites in the area; its conquest by the great Maratha king, Shivaji, was an important step in the fierce drive to reclaim the area from the Mughals. Though not much is left of the fort today, it is still possible to enjoy the awesome, sweeping views across the plateaus and to get a sense of the power and grandeur of the 17th-century warring empires. Locals make the weekend pilgrimage to their hero's mountaintop, wandering about the massive ruins, drinking the revered "sweet water" from the well, and snacking at the many ramshackle huts at the top of the fort area.

To reach Sinhagad from Pune, take public **bus #50** (Rs12) from the Nehru Stadium bus stop. If you have enough fellow travelers, it's worth taking a **tempo** (about Rs15 per person). From the bus drop-off, it's a 1½-2hr. uphill **hike** to the fort—bring plenty of food and water—or a Rs25 per person **jeep** ride.

LONAVLA लोनावला ☎ 02114

Lonavla is a popular destination for both foreign and Indian tourists, thanks to its proximity to the **Buddhist caves** at Karla and Bhaja. It is also easily accessible by train and bus on the Mumbai-Pune routes.

⌐ TRANSPORTATION. The **train station** divides Lonavla in half. Facing the same direction as Pune-bound trains, turning right leads to nothing much but shops. A left takes you to the bus station and to hotels. Lonavla's **bus station** is at the intersection of **Shivaji Rd.** and **National Hwy. 4.** Buses head to: **Mumbai** (3hr.; every hr.; Rs60); **Pune** (1½hr.; every hr.; Rs35); the Karla and Bhaja caves (see below). **Trains** to **Mumbai** (3hr.; Rs39) and **Pune** (1hr.; Rs28) depart frequently.

⌐⌐ ACCOMMODATIONS AND FOOD. Most of the tourists in Lonavla are families from Mumbai and Pune looking to splurge on resort-style, hill station living. Budget travelers have few accommodation options, especially in high season (Apr.-June). About 100m to the left of the bus station on Shivaji Rd., the **Hotel Chandralok ❷**, with its clean baths and friendly staff, is the best choice. (☎ 72294 or 72921. Singles Rs290; doubles Rs390-890.) A less tidy budget option is the **Adarsh Hotel ❷**, across Shivaji Rd. from the Chandralok. (☎ 72353. Doubles Rs600.) The **Hotel Swiss Cottage ❷**, is neither Swiss nor a cottage, though it does have a vaguely homey, lodge-like feel. From the train station, walk straight toward town, take the first paved right, and follow the signs up the driveway on the left. (☎ 71320. Singles Rs300; doubles Rs600.) The area around the bus station has the best selection of restaurants, whereas the railway station neighborhood is dominated by shops and the market. **Hotel Chandralok ❶** (see above) serves big, bottomless Gujarati *thalis* (Rs90). The **Udipi Restaurant ❶**, on the Mumbai-Pune Rd., is popular with locals and has both South and North Indian food for Rs20-40. Open daily 9am-11pm.

◙ SIGHTS. Tourists come here not for the town itself (which is eminently forgettable), but for the exquisite first-century BC Buddhist caves chiseled into the high, basalt cliffs at nearby **Karla** and **Bhaja**. Several **buses** per day cover the 12km from Lonavla's bus station to Karla (Rs6). At Karla, a steep staircase leads up from the small bazaar to the outcrop high above the plain, where the main cave is located. Several religions have claimed this outcrop as their holy space. The main *chaitya* (temple) hall—the largest in India—was carved out by Hinayana Buddhists. Mahayana Buddhists added sculptures of elephants and people, and a modern Hindu shrine obscures the entrance to the *chaitya*. The pipal-shaped window, which signifies learning, illuminates the Buddhist *stupa*. (Karla caves open daily 8am-6pm. US$5.) It's a 5km walk or rickshaw ride (Rs60 one-way) from the Karla staircase to the Bhaja steps. To walk, go back along the Karla road, cross over the main road, and keep going straight. Turn right immediately after you cross the Malouvil Station tracks, and follow the road to the Bhaja steps. A serene atmosphere prevails at these 18 cleaner, calmer, less-touristed, and better-preserved caves, which were carved in the 2nd century BC. *Viharas* surround the main *chaitya* and include a celebrated relief of a war elephant tearing up trees in its path. Past the main area, there is a cave containing 14 identical *stupas*, and a room with sculptured reliefs of the Buddha and Vishnu side-by-side. Farther still, down a narrow path, a lone *stupa* is tucked away behind a trickling waterfall. (Bhaja caves open dawn-dusk. Free.) If you have time after the caves, check out the Maratha-era **Lohagad** and **Visapur Forts,** visible in the hills behind Bhaja.

About 5km south of town is Lonavla's most popular attraction during the monsoons, the **Bhushi Dam.** The dam has rock steps along part of its face, and at the peak of the rainy season, it overflows, allowing foamy water to spill down these stairs, where tourists and locals delight in the bubbles.

MAHABALESHWAR महाबलेश्वर ☎ 02168

Mahabaleshwar is Indian hill station life at its finest. Thirty viewpoints, several waterfalls, a lake, and numerous old temples call out to those eager to escape the hustle of Pune or Mumbai. Like older hill stations, though, Mahabaleshwar shuts down during the monsoon. In the peak season (Apr.-May), on the contrary, make hotel reservations well in advance.

⧉ TRANSPORTATION. Buses run to: **Mumbai** (7hr., 5 per day 9:15am-9pm, Rs100-200); **Pune** (4hr., every hr. 6:30am-7:30pm, Rs65-84); **Satara,** for train connections (2hr., 11 per day 5:30am-3pm, Rs28). **Taxis** loiter at the stand opposite the bus station; they offer tours (2½hr., Rs250-280) of Mahabaleshwar and nearby Panchgari.

⧉⚈ ORIENTATION AND PRACTICAL INFORMATION. All visitors to Mahabaleshwar are charged a Rs5 entry tax. The main part of the town is south of Old Mahabaleshwar. **Dr. Sabane Rd. (Main St.)** runs east-west. On this road is the town's bazaar, the heart of Mahabaleshwar. The **bus station** is at the far western end of Main St. **Masjid Rd.** runs parallel to Main St. to the north, and **Murray Peth Rd.** is parallel to the south. **Exchange currency** or cash traveler's checks at the State Bank of India, Masjid Rd., a 5min. walk east and one block north from the bus stand. (Open M-F 11am-2:30pm, Sa 11am-1pm.) The **police station** is on the right, farther east on Main St. (☎60333. Open 24hr.) **Morarji Gokuldas Rural Hospital** (☎60247) Shivaji Circle, is farther north, and has a **24hr. pharmacy. Bicycle rental** is available at the east end of the bazaar (Rs5 per hr.). The **GPO/Telephone Office,** FG Rd., is north of the bus station. **Postal Code:** 6061.

⧉⧉ ACCOMMODATIONS AND FOOD. During the wet season, even the best hotels go for next to nothing; in season, however, rates can more than triple. The closest thing to a budget option, especially in season, is the **MTDC Holiday Resort ❶,** 2km south of the bus stand, which has clean doubles with 24hr. hot water. (☎60318. Dorms Rs80; doubles Rs500. Off season: 30% discount. A taxi to the MTDC should cost around Rs40.) **Hotel Nells ❸,** Main St., offers the best cheap beds in town with spare but neat rooms with TVs. (☎60323. Doubles Rs550. Off-season: Rs150.) At the newly restored **Kalpana Excellency ❺,** Murray Peth Rd., small rooms with TVs surround a stone and marble courtyard. (☎60419. Doubles Rs1200. Off season: Rs400.) **Hotel Aman ❹,** Masjid Rd., has clean rooms with 24hr. hot water (in-season), phones, and TVs. (☎61087 or 60417. Rs800. Off season: Rs200.) Mahabaleshwar is famous for its ▨berries, which can be found in season all over town.

SIGHTS. In the dry season, you can see the ocean from **Arthur's Seat.** Other lookouts such as **Mumbai Port** and **Kate's Port** provide good views out over the surrounding countryside. **Venna Lake** in the north offers boating and fishing, and nearby **Old Mahabaleshwar** enchants with its endless historic cobblestone streets and two ancient temples—**Panchaganga Mandir,** which is purported to contain the springs of five rivers, and **Mahabaleshwar Mandir,** which encloses a natural rock *linga.* The historic **Pratapghad** and **Kamalghad Forts** are also nearby. During the particularly rainy monsoon season (mid-June to mid-Sept.), however, thick fogs make it hard to see anything more than the ground beneath your feet.

AURANGABAD औरंगाबाद ☎0240

Cradled by the crags of the Deccan Plateau, Aurangabad (pop. 830,000) is a pleasant, mid-sized city with enough sights to put its larger neighbors in its pocket. The city's proximity to the celebrated caves at Ellora and Ajanta, plus its remarkable tourist infrastructure, make it a must-see destination in Maharashtra. The boulevards are broad and clean, and run under 52 huge, 17th-century gates built by ultra-orthodox Aurangzeb, the last of the Mughal bigshots to rule India. Right-wing Shiv Sena councillors recently renamed the city in honor of Sambhaji, Shivaji's son and Maratha Hindu hero. To most, the city is still named for Aurangzeb, and the old square, the stone houses, the sizable Muslim population, and the silky *himroo* fabric (patterned after the paintings in Ajanta) give the city a distinctly Islamic air. These days, Aurangabad enjoys the economic boom typical of Mumbai's hinterland. The brewing capital of India, Aurangabad is a mellow place to throw back a few locally made "Australian" lagers after a long day touring the nearby ruins.

▐ TRANSPORTATION

Flights: The **airport**, in Chikalthana, Jalna Rd., is 10km from the city center. Buses run to and from the city bus office at the railway station (Rs5), but are inconvenient as they don't run all the way to the terminal. A much better option are taxis (to town Rs50). **Indian Airlines (IA)** (☎485421 or 483392). Jalna Rd., 150m west of Rama International Hotel. Open daily 10am-1pm and 1:30-5pm. **Jet Airways** (☎441770 or 441392). Opposite Indian Airlines. Open daily 10am-1pm and 1:30-5pm. Under 40 25% discount. Both IA and Jet fly to **Mumbai** (45min.; 1 per day; US$75). IA also has service to **Delhi** (3½hr.; 1 per day; US$175).

Trains: Railway Station (☎331015, reservations and inquiry ☎131 and ☎132), Station Rd. Fares listed are 2nd-class. Five days a week, the Sachkhand Express from **Nanded** to **Amritsar** arrives in Aurangabad at 12:30pm, and continues on to **Bhopal** (12hr.; Rs251), **Agra** (20hr., Rs357), and **Delhi** (25hr.; Rs369). Trains also run to **Mumbai** (8½hr.; Tapovan Express 2:40pm, Deogiri Express 9:20pm; Rs157).

Buses: Central Bus Stand (☎331647), Dr. Ambedkar Rd., 2km north of the railway station, west along the continuation of Station Rd. Schedules and fares are for regular buses. The "semi-deluxe" buses cost about 30% more; full-on "deluxe" buses are 60% more. To: **Ahmedabad** (14hr.; 9pm; Rs175); **Ajanta** (3hr.; every hr.; Rs47); **Daulatabad** (20min.; frequent; Rs7); **Ellora** (45min.; every 20 min.; Rs15); **Hyderabad** (12hr.; 3pm; Rs200); **Jalgaon** (4hr.; 10 per day 6am-6pm; Rs50); **Mumbai** (10hr.; 15 per day 8am-10pm; Rs170-250); **Pune** (6hr.; every 30min. 5am-midnight; Rs101-120).

Local Transportation: Auto-rickshaws are convenient, but make sure that they use the meters. By 2002, all rickshaws should have new meters that show the correct fare (Rs7.50 per 1.8km). Cost-effective **tempos** function as mini-buses, scooting up and down major city routes. **Bicycles** are for rent just outside the railway station, on your left as you face the station. Rs3 per hr.; Rs20 per day.

■✴ 🛈 ORIENTATION AND PRACTICAL INFORMATION

Tourist facilities are along **Station Rd.**, which has two branches: the western half runs north from the railway station to the bus stand; the eastern branch runs northeast past several hotels and restaurants to **Kranti Chowk**, a major business area. From Kranti Chowk, **Jalna Rd.** runs east to the airline offices and the airport. **Dr. Rajendra Prasad Marg** cuts back west to intersect Station Rd. North of this intersection, near the bus stand, Station Rd. becomes **Dr. Ambedkar Marg.** It ends at the north end of town near the Bibi-Ka-Maqbara and the Aurangabad Caves.

Tourist Office: Government of India Tourist Office (☎331217), Krishna Vilas, Station Rd. On right side of the main (western) branch of Station Rd., about 250m from the station. The amazing Mr. Yadav brims with answers. Open M-F 8:30am-6pm, Sa 8:30am-1:30pm. **Maharashtra Tourism Development Corporation** (MTDC), MTDC Holiday Resort, Station Rd. East (☎331513 or 331198), has tours. Open M-F 10:30am-6pm.

Budget Travel: Classic Travel (☎335598 or 337788), MTDC Holiday Resort, Station Rd. East, inside the lobby to the right. This friendly office provides tours. A branch is also at the airport. Both open daily 7am-10:30pm. AmEx/MC/V.

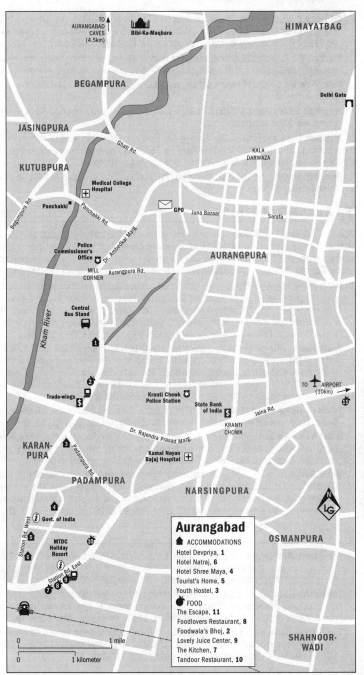

TO
AURANGABAD
CAVES
(4.5km)

Bibi-Ka-Maqbara

HIMAYATBAG

BEGAMPURA

Delhi Gate

JASINGPURA

Ghati Rd.

KALA
DARWAZA

KUTUBPURA

Begampura Rd.

Medical College
Hospital

Panchakki

Panchakki Rd.

GPO

Juna Bazaar

Sarafa

Dr. Ambedkar Marg

Police
Commissioner's
Office

AURANGPURA

MILL
CORNER

Aurangpura Rd.

Central
Bus Stand

Kham River

Trade-wings

TO ✈ AIRPORT
(10km)

Kranti Chowk
Police Station

State Bank
of India

Jalna Rd.

Dr. Rajendra Prasad Marg.

KRANTI
CHOWK

KARAN-
PURA

Padampura Rd.

Kamal Nayan
Bajaj Hospital

PADAMPURA

NARSINGPURA

Govt. of India

Station Rd. West

MTDC
Holiday
Resort

OSMANPURA

Station Rd. East

SHAHNOOR-
WADI

Aurangabad

🛏 ACCOMMODATIONS
Hotel Devpriya, 1
Hotel Natraj, 6
Hotel Shree Maya, 4
Tourist's Home, 5
Youth Hostel, 3

🍗 FOOD
The Escape, 11
Foodlovers Restaurant, 8
Foodwala's Bhoj, 2
Lovely Juice Center, 9
The Kitchen, 7
Tandoor Restaurant, 10

0   1 mile
0   1 kilometer

MAHARASHTRA

Currency Exchange: State Bank of India (☎351126 or 331872), Dr. Rajendra Prasad Marg, Kranti Chowk. Open M-F 10:30am-2pm, Sa 10:30am-noon. **Trade-wings** (☎332677). Dr. Ambedkar Marg, opposite Hotel Printravel. Open daily 9am-7:30pm.

Market: The Aurangpura area is one giant market, selling everything from chandeliers to pomegranates—a much better shopping spot than the tourist bazaars near the caves.

Police: Police Commissioner's Office (☎334333, 321100, and 334675), Mill Corner, north of the bus station.

Hospital: Government Medical College Hospital (☎331402 through 331410), Panchakki Rd. **24hr. pharmacy.**

Internet: Many cyber cafes line Station Rd. East and West, but tend to cost more than elsewhere in India. **Uma Internet Cafe** (☎358303), Dr. Ambedkar Marg, a few doors down from Trade-wings. Rs50 per hr. Open daily 10am-midnight.

Post Office: GPO (☎331420), Juna Bazaar, Bazaar District. Open M-Sa 10am-8pm. **Postal Code:** 431005.

⚑ ACCOMMODATIONS

Most of Aurangabad's budget hotels cluster around the railway station and the bus stand. Those around the railway station are nicer; but the budget hotel ghetto across from the bus will always have a cheap room ready. The Government of India Tourist Office also arranges homestays with local residents (Rs200-400).

▨ **Hotel Shree Maya** (☎333093; fax 331043; shrimaya@bom4.vsnl.net.in), Bharuka Complex, Padampura Rd. Walk north on Station Rd. from Government Tourist Office, take first two right turns; 100m on right. Upscale and worth it. Attractive rooms with cable TVs, telephones, attached baths, and A/C. Great staff, room service, Internet (Rs60 per hr), and meals. Check-out 24hr. Singles Rs175-395; doubles Rs245-395. ❷

Youth Hostel (HI) (☎334892), Station Rd. West, 1km from the station, on the right just south of the intersection with Dr. Rajendra Prasad Marg. Well-run and spotless. Cheap, mosquito-netted dorms, warm-water bathrs, and cafeteria (breakfast Rs12, lunch and dinner Rs22). Check-in 7-11am and 4-8pm. Check-out 9am. Curfew 10pm. Unbeatable prices: dorms Rs25, non-members Rs45; doubles Rs100. ❶

Tourist's Home (☎337212), Station Rd. West, a 5min. walk from the railway station. Basic, solid ,and clean with attached bath. Singles Rs100; doubles Rs150. ❶

Hotel Natraj (☎324260), Station Rd. West, just before the Tourist Home when walking from the railway station. This family-run house is cheap, clean, and well located. All rooms have attached bath. Singles Rs80; doubles Rs100; triples Rs150. ❶

Hotel Devpriya (☎332344), Dr. Ambedkar Marg, just south of the Central Bus Stand. Despite the bus station cacophony, this giant place has plenty of flavor. The impressive hallway is its best feature, but the rooms are fine, too, and the staff is friendly. Attached baths and morning hot water. Check-out 24hr. Singles Rs150; doubles Rs250. ❶

◖ FOOD

Foodlovers Restaurant, Station Rd. East, on the right, 150m from the station. Garden seating, candles, and music do more for the atmosphere than the food. Chinese definitely beats Indian items here. Dishes Rs30-120. Beer Rs55-60. ❶

The Kitchen, Station Rd. East, by the train station. The budget trinity of good, cheap, and clean converge in Kitchen's South Indian snacks, bacon 'n' eggs breakfasts, and Bengali dishes. Entrees Rs15-50. Open daily 6am-11pm; off season 7am-11pm. ❶

The Escape, Jalna Rd., in Hotel Rajdoot. Good Chinese food, amid framed American vintage rock posters. Savory noodles, veg., chicken, lamb, and seafood entrees (Rs50-100). Large Indian selection, too. Open daily 11am-11:30pm. ❶

Foodwala's Bhoj, Dr. Ambedkar Marg, in a big building 200m south of the bus stand, on the right, one floor up. A hideaway for Aurangabad's elite, with a small but classy central fountain. Tremendous *thalis* (Rs50) compensate for a limited menu. Punjabi dishes Rs20-30; *dosas* and *uttappams* Rs12-20. Open daily 11am-3pm and 7-11pm. ❶

Tandoor Restaurant, Shyam Chambers, Barsilal Nagar, Station Rd. East. Classy, civilized carnivores feast on tandoori specialities (Rs80-150). Mughlai (Rs80) and veg. (Rs35-65) dishes are also excellent. Open daily 11am-4pm and 6:30-11pm. ❷

Lovely Juice Center, Station Rd. East, in the complex right across from the MTDC. Excellent shakes Rs15-30. Open daily 10am-11pm. ❶

🌀 SIGHTS

If you're pressed for time or just want some comfort, try one of the MTDC or Classic Travels tours that cover both Ellora and sights in Aurangabad.

AURANGABAD CAVES. Aurangabad's cave temples are often eclipsed by the glamor that surrounds the caves at Ellora and Ajanta. But blissfully free of tour groups and touts, they remain a wonderful introduction to the breathtaking sculpture to be found all along Maharashtra's cave-trail. Split into western and eastern sections, these distinctive examples of Buddhist art and architecture were created by two great dynasties during the 6th, 7th, and 8th centuries. The western caves, numbers 1 through 5, are off the dirt road at the top of a treacherous climb up winding stone steps. The third and most beautiful cave was once a *vihara* (residence hall) for the wandering Buddhist monks *(bikshus)* of the time, who gathered in monastic communities in caves like these around the state. Some fragments of the original paintings depict stories about the Buddha's previous incarnations. The fourth cave is a *chaitya* hall, used for congregation and prayer. The eastern caves at the end of the right fork, numbers 6 through 9, afford incredible views of the surrounding landscape, including the silhouette of Bibi-Ka-Maqbara against the city in the distance. The seventh cave greets visitors with lotus-framed *apsaras* (celestial dancing nymphs) at the entrance to the crypt. A shadowed Buddha sits inside the sanctuary, his feet surrounded by the frozen faces of the disciples. Outside the final cave is a giant (broken) sculpture of the Buddha after his death. Visit the caves early in the morning when few tourists are there. *(In the hills behind the Bibi-Ka-Maqbara, up the dirt road that leads past the tomb; 10min. by auto-rickshaw or a 1hr. walk. Open daily dawn-dusk. US$5 or equivalent. Bring a flashlight.)*

BIBI-KA-MAQBARA. Aurangzeb's son's milk-white monument to his mother, Begum Rabi'a Durani, has been the object of scorn as an inferior Taj Mahal knock-off. The Bibi-Ka-Maqbara was important to the tradition of Mughal mausolea, but this rather small tomb could never have challenged the Taj, even if cash shortages had not forced ungainly corner-cutting, such as the abandonment of marble for plaster a meter up the wall. *(Open daily dawn-10pm. US$5, or peek from the gates for free.)*

PANCHAKKI. The Mughal water mill at Panchakki is a good stopover on the return trip from the caves or Bibi-Ka-Maqbara. The mill was built in 1624 in honor of the Muslim saint Baba Shah Musafir to help feed the hundreds of orphans, paupers, and fakirs who were his devotees. From a well in the hills 11km away, water gushes through earthen pipes, is raised by a siphon, and then drops with intense force upon the blades of the water wheel. In the Panchakki's heyday, the output was almost four tons of finely ground grain. Today, Panchakki has been reduced to a breeding ground for hawkers and crafts shops specializing in the city's unique *himroo* fabric. *(Panchakki Rd. Open daily 7am-8:30pm. Rs5.)*

⚡ DAYTRIPS FROM AURANGABAD

DAULATABAD दौलताबाद AND KHULDABAD खुल्दबाद

Most buses from Aurangabad to Ellora stop at Daulatabad, Rs6. Open daily 6am-6pm. US$5.

Several important sights lie along the road between Aurangabad and Ellora. The most impressive is the **Daulatabad fortress,** on top of a hill 13km from Aurangabad. Originally erected in the 9th century, the fortress gained "fame" in the 14th century when Muhammad Tughlaq, the whimsical Sultan of Delhi, decided this was the spot for a capital. Rather than leave the development of a thriving city to chance, the not-so-savvy sultan marched the entire population of Delhi 1000km across India to people it. The small proportion of the deportees who did not die on the way greeted life in the Deccan with a resentment not conducive to prosperity. The Sultan abandoned his project after only eight years and marched the few survivors back home. Nevertheless, Daulatabad did grow to be an important city, and the fort itself is considered India's second most impregnable, after the Amber Fort in Rajasthan. Today, the ruins of the fort are inhabited only by monkeys and lizards.

Behind the first gate, spiked as usual to prevent elephant attacks, is a series of labyrinthine streets, designed to confuse the potential invader. A left turn after the first gate leads to a wall, but a right turn provides access to the ruined walled city. The pink **Chand Minar** victory tower, built in 1435, rises over a water tank. Across the water tank is the **Bharatmata Temple** (Mother India), a 10th-century Hindu structure that resisted several attemps to convert it into a mosque. A series of steps leads up the hill past ruined palaces to the blue-tiled **Chini Mahal,** where the last king of Golconda met his end. On top of the small tower next door, a re-creation of a cannon called Qila Shikan (Fort Breaker) points menacingly out at the horizon. From here, the defenses begin in earnest; you have to cross a moat to get into the sheer-walled citadel. Inside the fort's walls is a night-dark passage designed as an ambush path for intruders. A guide will save you from attack and lead you through it with a kerosene lamp, in anticipation, of course, of a little *baksheesh.* Endless stairs lead upward, reemerging into daylight and to a farther series of palaces lining the slope to the fort's summit. From the top, there are magnificent views of Aurangabad and the surrounding countryside.

Back toward Aurangabad lies **Khuldabad,** or Rauza, a small, strongly Muslim town where the Emperor Aurangzeb finally found rest from the struggle to subjugate Maharashtra. In a departure from the grandiose mausolea of his Mughal forbears, not to mention his wife, Aurangzeb asked for a modest grave funded by the proceeds from his own transcription of the Qur'an. At Aurangzeb's own request, the only thing decorating his grave is a mint plant. The nicer tomb in the same courtyard belongs to the emperor's guru.

ELLORA इलोरा ☎ 02437

The UNESCO-protected "caves" at Ellora and Ajanta make up Maharashtra's most celebrated tourist attractions. Though still referred to as caves, they are actually man-made architectural and sculptural wonders. A total of 34 caves were carved out of the volcanic basalt rock by several generations of artisans between AD 600 and 1000. Unlike the earlier, Buddhist-only structures at Ajanta, Ellora's Buddhist, Hindu, and Jain caves reflect the rise and fall of religions in India. Also in Ellora is the **Ghrashneshwar Temple,** one of the *jyotirlingas,* where Shiva is said to have burst from the earth. The same square also houses three ancient temple-like structures said to be the tombs of Shivaji's father and grandfathers—locals maintain that this village, not Pune, is Shivaji's birthplace. A mere 29km from Aurangabad, Ellora makes for an ideal daytrip from the city.

TRANSPORTATION

The main road runs west from the bus stand by the entrance site, concealing one budget hotel amid stalls of trinkets and cold drinks. Frequent **buses** run to Ellora via Daulatabad (45min., 6am-6pm, Rs15). **Shared taxis** run from the stand opposite Aurangabad's Central Bus Station (Rs15). The jam-packed **jeeps** that cruise the Ellora-Aurangabad road cost about the same as the bus, and allow you to see both Ellora and Daulatabad in a day. MTDC's and Classic Travel's more expensive and comfortable tours do the same (see p. 398).

ACCOMMODATIONS AND FOOD

The MTDC's **Kailas Hotel ❶** is clean and well-run. (☎44543 or 44468. Dorms Rs100; singles Rs500; doubles Rs200-1000.) Food options in Ellora involve sodas and *pakoras* and a few minimalist restaurants. The **Kailas Hotel Restaurant ❶** serves *thalis* for Rs50. (Open daily 7am-9:30pm.) Ellora's best restaurant, **Hotel Milan ❶** has veg. dishes for Rs15-50. (Open daily 8am-5pm and 8-11pm.)

THE CAVES

Caves open Tu-Su sunrise to sunset. Cave 16 open Tu-Su 6am-6pm. US$10 or equivalent; video fee Rs25, exterior only. All other caves free.

Of Ellora's 34 caves, the oldest ones are Buddhist (built AD 600-800) and are numbered 1 through 12. The slightly more recent Hindu caves (AD 700-900) bear numbers 13-29, and include Ellora's greatest attraction, the **Kailasa Temple** (Cave 16). The youngest Jain caves (numbers 30-34; AD 800-1000) are a 10min. walk uphill or a short ride from the other caves.

BUDDHIST CAVES. With the exception of Cave 10, all Buddhist caves at Ellora are *viharas* (monasteries). They are quite simple in design and decoration and do not compare to the caves at Ajanta. **Cave 5** stands out among the first ten. The flat, low ridges in its floor are believed to have served as benches to make a community dining hall. The stern Vajrapani (the *bodhisattva* holding a thunderbolt) and the more forgiving Padmapani (flower-power in the form of a lotus-totin' *bodhisattva*) presided over the meals from the sides of the central shrine. **Cave 10,** the only *chaitya* (temple), is called Carpenter's Cave after the ribbed ceiling designed to look like wood. It is the most interesting Buddhist cave at Ellora, with strong tantric influences. The 3-floor **Cave 12,** with a courtyard and balconies, is the most recent and most ornate of the group, probably in order to compete with the elaborate Hindu caves. The top floor houses beautiful sculpture: *bodhisattvas* line the side walls, and the seven previous incarnations of the Buddha flank the main shrine. A different type of tree shades each Buddha, a symbolic technique developed at Sanchi (see p. 353) and other early Buddhist monuments. Traces of paint in the sanctum and chamber hint at the once colorful painting inside the caves.

HINDU CAVES. The densely sculptured temples share many repeating motifs, most often depicting the Hindu trinity: Brahma (creator), Vishnu (protector), and Shiva (destroyer, also known as Manesh). Shiva appears most often on Mount Kailasa playing dice with wife Parvati while a demon tries frantically, in vain, to dislodge him; at other times he dances "Nataraja", the dance of the gods. Vishnu crops up as Narasimha (the man-lion), Varaha (the boar), and, most commonly, as Narayan asleep in the coils of a serpent floating on the cosmic sea. From his navel grows a lotus, out of which Brahma emerges to create the world. The image of the Seven Mothers, buxom goddesses with children, flanked by Kala and Kali (goddesses of death), also appears regularly. **Cave 14** was originally a Buddhist monastery, converted into a Hindu temple and dedicated to Shiva. **Cave 15** depicts Shiva emerging from a *linga*, among other things, while Brahma and Vishnu kneel before him—(yet another) testimony to Shiva-worship among Ellora's patrons.

Cave 16, the **Kailasa Temple,** is the highlight of Ellora and the climax of Hindu sculpting mastery. A replica of Shiva's home in the Himalayas, the Kailasa Temple is the largest monolithic sculpture in the world, and was sculpted from the top down over the course of 150 years during the 8th and 9th centuries. The sheer scale of this structure defies belief, and this is even before you consider the technical challenge of slicing it all out from one solid rock. Traces of white plaster (imitation of snow in the Himalayas) and paint bear witness to further decorative complexity. The central courtyard (80m deep) is surrounded by galleries and contains a massive shrine, flanked by a statue of an elephant on each side. Apart from countless other elephants, the temple contains images from Hindu mythology. Of these, the most impressive are the panels depicting scenes from the *Mahabharata* on the left of the temple, and from the *Ramayana* on the right sides. The temple itself now serves tourists only, so you don't have to take off your shoes. If you don't want to shell out the US$10 fee for Cave 16 (though you should), you can climb up the stairs on the right of the cave for a view of the structure from above. The remaining 12 Hindu caves may be reached by the paved road left of the temple, but they pale in comparison to Kailasa.

Cave 29, with its view of a rainy-season waterfall, is Ellora's second-largest cave contains perhaps the only mooner protected under UNESCO world heritage provisions: in another panel of Shiva ignoring Ravana's ruckus, you'll notice a dwarf baring his ass. The cave is also among the most structurally impressive, with three lion-guarded entrances protecting it.

JAIN CAVES. Ellora's latest structures, the Jain Caves, date back to the 9th and 10th centuries, and reflect the temporary resurgence of Jainism in the region. Though some sections remain unfinished, others hold some of the most intricately detailed carvings anywhere in Ellora. Both **Cave 30** and **Cave 32** are smaller imitations of the Kailasa Temple. Cave 32 depicts the *tirthankara* Gomatesvara so deep in meditation that he has not noticed the vines growing on his limbs or the animals surrounding him. This temple is dedicated to Indra, king of the gods, the pot-bellied god chilling under a banyan tree.

AJANTA अजन्ता ☎ 02438

Ajanta is almost as remote today as it was in the 1st century BC, when it was a Buddhist retreat. Its architects chose a sheer cliff face above a horseshoe-shaped canyon along the Waghora River to render their contemplative spiritual visions in painting and sculpture. The 29 caves were carved out between the first century BC and the 6th century AD in two separate phases. Caves from the early period are much less sophisticated than the later ones and depict Buddha solely in the form of images, such as the wheel of law. Their construction was halted when Hinduism became dominant in the first century AD. It wasn't until emperor Harisena of the Vakataka Dynasty, a Buddhist, came to power in the 5th century AD, that excavation of Ajanta's caves resumed. During this later, *Mahayana* Buddhist phase, Buddha was worshiped in his physical form—a fact reflected in the countless elaborate statues of Buddha found in the caves from this period. In contrast to the communal funding of the earlier caves, excavations were sponsored by private donors and the scale of decorations became a measure of the donor's wealth. After Harisena's death, the region descended into chaos; both artists and monks abandoned the site. Only the locals knew that these masterpieces even existed, until British army officer John Smith spied Cave 10 from the opposite ridge in 1819 while tiger hunting. Two thousand years might have chipped the paint, but Ajanta's colorful, meticulously detailed wall paintings continue to tell stories of the Buddha's incarnations as *bodhisattva*—known as the *Jataka* tales—and other legends. The UNESCO-protected caves should make it onto every traveler's itinerary. It's best to visit the more ancient Ajanta prior to Ellora.

⊫ TRANSPORTATION

Visitors have to suffer through a hot, jolting **bus** ride to get here. Many buses stop at Ajanta between Aurangabad (3½hr., 108km south, Rs47) and Jalgaon (1hr., 58km north, Rs10), arriving at 5:30pm from Aurangabad and 6:30pm from Jalgaon. The best way to see the caves is to come from one town, leave your bags to be guarded in the cloak room at the base of the caves (theoretically free), and go to the next town the same evening. The MDTC organizes convenient tours from Aurangabad (Rs180; see p. 399).

⌂⌂ ACCOMMODATIONS AND FOOD

The MTDC runs the **hotel and restaurant ❶** at the caves themselves. Their rooms are clean but spare, with balconies and common baths. (☎4226. Singles Rs200; doubles Rs250. Attached restaurant: entrees Rs22-50; open daily 9am-5pm.) For reservations, call the regional MTDC manager in Aurangabad (☎331198 or 331513). A better but pricier option is the **Forest Rest House ❷**, 500m back down the road. It has two air-cooled doubles with hot water, a cook, mosquito nets, and a veranda. Book in advance with the Divisional Forest Officer, Osmanpura, Aurangabad. (☎334203. Rs400 per person.)

◉ THE CAVES

Open Tu-Su 9am-5:30pm. US$10 or equivalent; video fee Rs25, exterior-only guide Rs100. The caves are up the steps behind the drink stands and over the rise.

The guided tours often rely on gimmicks but also illuminate some of the murals' convoluted story lines. If possible, try to get Mr. Al Mohammedi Abdul Nasir as your guide. As in Ellora, two types of caves are found here: *chaitya* halls (9, 10, 19, 26, and 29), where locals came to worship Buddha, and *viharas* (monasteries), where monks meditated away in their stone cells. Caves not described below are unfinished (3, 5, 8, 23-25, 28, 29); while they are heaven for archaeologists, as they reveal various stages of carving, they are of less interest to tourists.

CAVE 1. This 5th-century cave was sponsored by Emperor Harisena himself and contains some of the most delicate paintings at Ajanta. The paintings are also among the best preserved, as the cave was never used for worship and was thus spared charring by smoke. With the exception of Persian blue, which was imported from present-day Iran, all colors used in the paintings are natural local colors. All paintings show the use of perspective, a technique not discovered in Europe until the Renaissance. On the left-hand wall, a king, newly converted to Buddhism, abandons earthly pleasures for a life of meditation. Just to the left of the rear shrine, a painting depicts the elegant Padmapani (the lotus-holding *bodhi-*

sattva). Vajrapani stands guard to his right with his thunderbolt. The statue of Buddha (notice the lotus position, symbolizing meditation, and the teaching position of his hands) changes expressions (from meditative to serious to happy) when illuminated at different angles.

CAVE 2. Paintings on the left wall of this 6th-century cave show Buddha's mother's dream of a six-tusked elephant, foretelling his conception and miraculous birth. Farther on the same wall is the unfinished mural of a Thousand Buddhas. In the right-hand rear corner, a sculptural frieze of a classroom of 500 children depicts a student pulling the hair of the girl in front. Above to the right, the demon Hariti dances furiously. The ceiling at the back resembles a Persian rug, testifying to the influence of Persian culture at the time.

CAVE 4. Due to a ceiling collapse, the largest *vihara* at Ajanta is unfinished.

CAVE 6. The unusually high number of columns (16) in this cave is probably due to the presence of a second floor, a unique occurrence at Ajanta.

CAVE 9. This *chaitya* hall dates back to the first century BC. There are oblique references to the Enlightened One, including the pipal-tree-shaped window in the facade, signifying learning, and the huge *stupa* in the apse, symbolizing the relics of the Buddha.

CAVE 10. The oldest Hinayana *chaitya* at Ajanta, dating back to the 2nd century BC, was also the first one sighted by the British officers in 1819. Sadly, the majority of the cave was destroyed by vandals, including its "discoverer" John Smith, who inscribed his name on a rear column on the right.

CAVE 12. One of the oldest *viharas*, Cave 12 contains 12 cells, each with two rockbeds for Buddhist monks.

CAVE 16. Sponsored by the prime minister of Emperor Harisena, Varhadeva, this cave carries the inscription of his name on the left side wall. The columns at the front are supported by *ganas*, miserable Japanese sumo wrestlers, and shiny happy couples. The front left corner, the most celebrated fresco of all, shows a princess swooning in distress as her husband throws in the worldly towel. At the back sits the 5m tall Buddha in teaching position, the largest statue in Ajanta.

CAVE 17. This cave showcases the greatest number of surviving murals, mostly *Jataka*, and a number of confusing tales of seductive beauties and bloodthirsty demons, depicted in remarkably accurate anatomical detail. The most significant *Jataka* tale, on the rear wall on the right, shows Buddha as a six-tusked elephant who breaks off his own tusks in order not to get killed by hunters. Also worth noticing is the Wheel of Life on the left side wall.

CAVE 19. Believed to be the latest carved cave at Ajanta, this *chaitya* represents the culmination of Buddhist art in the region. Inside is a statue of Buddha with his palm pointing down, a so-called "giving" position.

CAVE 26. The most splendid example reclines along the left-hand wall of Cave 26: the Buddha on the verge of leaving this world, and entering nirvana. The procession of people below him is mourning his departure from earth, but in the heavens, everyone is rejoicing. Farther back along the same wall sits Buddha in meditation so deep that he fails to notice the flirtatious Mara. The path in front of Cave 16 leads down the hill to a bridge. From here, a path to the right leads to views of a rainy-season waterfall that surges over the cliffs. Visitors can head left and then climb to a **viewpoint** to relive the astonishment of the Brits who stumbled across the caves back in 1819. The river made its own contribution to local sculpture with gorges carved by its seven waterfalls. Backtracking down to the river bank opposite the caves will bring you to the parking lot.

NAGPUR नागपुर   ☎0712

Smack dab in the center of India, Nagpur is the hub where virtually every major road and rail route meets. But it certainly doesn't *feel* as though an entire subcontinent revolves around this city of two million. The streets are filled with tattered *tongas* and auto-rickshaws rather than taxis and aggressive Tata two-tonners. The seat of the state legislature alternates between Nagpur and Mumbai, but Nagpur lacks the skyscrapers and concrete that characterize many other cities of its size. In fact, with all its parks and playgrounds, Nagpur is one of the greenest cities in India. Most visitors are corporate types attending conferences, and for tourists, there is little to no reason to come here, unless you're heading for Sevagram or one of the national parks nearby.

TRANSPORTATION. The **airport** (☎260348 or 260433) is 9km from the city center; a taxi should not cost more than Rs250. The **Indian Airlines office** is on Palm Rd., in Civil Lines. (☎523069, at airport ☎532025. Open daily 10am-5pm.) **Flights** go to: **Bhopal** (45min., Tu and Sa 1:05pm, US$80); **Calcutta** (1½hr.; W, F, Su 7:30am; US$150); **Delhi** (1½hr., 10:30pm, US$135); **Hyderabad** (1hr.; M, W, F 8pm; US$135); **Mumbai** (1¼hr., 7:30am and 8:45pm, US$120). **Gujarat Airways,** c/o Handling Agents, Globe Travels (☎560141), operates a flight to **Pune** (1hr., 3 per week, $85). **Trains** go to: **Calcutta** (19-20hr., 5-7 per day 6:40am-8:15pm, Rs297); **Chennai** (15-21hr., 4-5 per day 6:05am-1:25pm, Rs290); **Delhi** (14-22hr., 7-10 per day 2:05am-11:05pm, Rs290); **Hyderabad** (2-4 per day, 5:20am-6pm, Rs190); **Mumbai** (14-18hr., 5-7 per day, Rs244); **Sevagram** (1hr., 8 per day 4:20am-3:55pm, Rs29). The **local bus stand,** 2km south of the railway station, has buses to: **Indore** (16hr., 5:30am, Rs224); **Jabalpur** (6 per day 9:45am-11pm, Rs120); **Wardha** (2hr., 28 per day 7:15am-8:30pm, Rs33). It isn't advisable to travel by bus to Madhya Pradesh, as the road is in a sorry state. **Taxis** around Nagpur cost 10-15Rs per km.

ORIENTATION AND PRACTICAL INFORMATION. Nagpur's **railway station** is on **Central Avenue;** the tracks split the city into eastern and western halves. Central Avenue becomes **Kingsway Rd.** after the station. South of and parallel to Kingsway Rd. is **Palm Rd.** Farther south is the tourist center, **Sitabuldi,** with shops and hotels. North and west of Sitabuldi is **Civil Lines.** Wardha Rd. (NH7) runs parallel to the train tracks. The **MTDC tourist office,** Sanskrutik Bachat Bhavan, Dr. Munje Rd., opposite the Laxmi theater in Sitabuldi, provides information on area parks and lakes. (☎533325. Open M-F and 1st and 3rd Sa 10am-6pm.) The **State Bank of India,** Kingsway Rd., near the railway station, exchanges currency and cashes traveler's checks at the **foreign exchange office** in the center of the building on the left. (☎521196, ext. 416. Open M-F 10:30am-2pm.) **Trade Wings,** Lokmat Bhavan 4th fl., also exchanges currency. (☎538437. Open M-F 9:30am-5pm, Sa 9:30am-1pm.) **Mayo Hospital** (☎728621), on Central Ave., near the railway station, has a 24hr. **pharmacy. Cyber Nook,** opposite the Liberty Cinema, Residency Rd., in Sardar, has good **Internet** connections. (Open 24hr. Rs25 per hr.) The **GPO** is on Palm Rd. (Open M-Sa 8am-10pm, Su 9am-1pm.) **Postal Code:** 440001.

MAHARASHTRA

⌐⌐⌐ **ACCOMMODATIONS, FOOD, AND ENTERTAINMENT.** The large number of business travelers passing through has given the city an abundance of accommodations. A luxury tax of 14% is often added to basic room rates. The thickest tangle of disorientingly similar budget hotels is on Central Avenue and its arteries. **Hotel Blue Diamond ❶**, 113 Central Ave., Dosar Chowk, is a good bet if you think you can handle the huge psychedelic honeycomb. The cheap rooms share a common bath. (☎727461. Singles Rs100-150; doubles Rs150-300.) Nearby, **Hotel Midland ❷** has tidy rooms and baths. (☎726131. Singles Rs230-300; doubles Rs400-600, A/C rooms from Rs650.) Another cluster of cheapies is in **Sitabuldi**, in the heart of Nagpur's market district. Head east along Mahatma Gandhi Rd. away from his statue and take the third left to reach **Hotel Amrta ❷**, Modi No. 3. Even the "regular rooms" in this aqua oasis put most other places to shame. (☎543762; fax 553123. Check-out 24hr. Singles Rs400; doubles Rs450. AmEx/MC/V.)

Nanking ❷, Mount Rd., Sardar, is the best-known, best-value Chinese place in town. (Chicken Rs65-100; seafood Rs75-150; veggies Rs35-90. Open Tu-Su noon-3pm and 6-10pm.) **The Zodiac**, 24 Central Bazaar Rd., in the Hotel Centre Point, a popular spot among locals, is the most happening pub-cum-discotheque in town. (☎520910. Open for "jam sessions" W 2-6pm, Rs150 per couple; discotheque Sa 10pm-1am, Rs300 per couple.) **Ambajhari Lake and Garden,** on the western outskirts of Nagpur, is ideal for early morning or evening strolls. (Open daily sunrise-sunset).

NEAR NAGPUR: SEVAGRAM

Trains from Nagpur to Mumbai and Chennai will stop at Sevagram (1hr., 8 per day 4:20am-3:55pm, Rs29) or at Wardha (1hr., 12 per day 11:50am-8:40pm, Rs29), 8km away. Frequent MSRTC buses also run from Nagpur to Sevagram and Wardha (2hr., 28 per day, Rs33). Shared auto-rickshaws travel between Wardha and Sevagram (Rs5). Buses also travel from Wardha to the ashram (15min., every 10min. 7:30am-8pm, Rs2). Ashram open daily sunrise-sunset.

Mahatma Gandhi founded an ashram in Sevagram (literally the "Village of Service") after he left his Sabarmati retreat in Ahmedabad, Gujarat (see p. 201) in 1936. From Sevagram, Gandhi directed the Independence movement, leading India to victory against the British in 1947 with his policy of non-violence. The community continues to thrive and is a paragon of simple living and self-sufficiency. The town is also the site of the **Nai Talimi Sangh,** the university founded by Gandhi to ensure that the town could meet its own aesthetic, spiritual, and intellectual needs. Far from the bustle of the rest of urban India, Sevagram is clean, serene, and spiritual. Even people with little interest in Gandhi will find Sevagram a delightful place to relax for a few days.

Sevagram Ashram has kept all of its original buildings and Gandhi's personal belongings intact, complete with explanatory English signposts. Ashramites will also gladly answer questions. (Open daily sunrise to sunset.) A shop near the entrance sells Gandhi's books and *khadi*, the hand-spun cloth that played an important role in the freedom movement, signifying *swaraj* (self-sufficiency) and a rejection of the reliance upon imported textiles. The *chakra* (wheel) that Gandhi used to spin the cloth now figures as the central motif on India's flag. Opposite the ashram, the **Gandhi Picture Exhibition** displays a photographic timeline of the Mahatma's life. (Open Sa-Th 10am-6pm. Free.) In the neighboring town of Wardha, **Magan Nadi,** the home of Gandhi's nephew, a history of *khadi* is on display.

The Center of Science for Villagers, 4km away, devotes itself to explaining Gandhi's philosophy of village-based economics. (Open daily 9am-1pm and 2-5pm. Free.) Adjoining the center is the **Leprosy Home,** where sufferers engage in a variety of tasks including agriculture, shoe-making, weaving, and spinning.

The women who run **Vinobaji's Ashram** in Paunar, 3km away, provide a living testament to the success of the self-sufficient community that Gandhi envisioned. A fervent disciple of Gandhi, Vinoba Bhave was a social activist and reformer who advocated land reform and the eradication of caste hierarchy. **Vinobaji's Museum** has exhibits explaining Gandhi's and his efforts to get landlords to give land to the destitute. (Open daily 9am-1pm and 2-5pm. Free.)

The **MTDC ❶** in Wardha offers basic accommodations. (☎ 07152 43872. Rs150-220.) However, the **Sevagram Ashram ❶** is cheaper and nicer. (Dorms Rs30; doubles Rs80. Meals Rs7-80 per day.) **Yatri Nivas ❶,** opposite the ashram, has rooms and meals for the same price. **Vinobaji's Ashram** (☎ 07152 43518), in Paunar (3km away), prefers to house only women and requires advance notification by mail (Vinobaji's Ashram, Paunar, District Wardha, Maharashtra, 442111) or by telephone. For food, **Goras Bhandar Wardha ❶,** in the main square of Sevagram near the Central Bank (look for the cow on the sign), sells delicious bread and milk. Try the hot milk with cardamom for Rs5. (Open daily 10am-5pm.) Unless you're staying in a guest house or ashram, you'll have to make the trip to Wardha for a fuller meal.

MAHARASHTRA

NORTHEAST INDIA

According to legend, a son of Kublai Khan traveled to Northeast India and sired scores of children, thereby giving Northeast India's people a distinct Asiatic look that is still visible today. At the heart of the region lies the Brahmaputra Valley state of Assam, which once encompassed the entire region. The Northeast is inhabited in part by *adivasis* (indigenous peoples) who have had little exposure to the industrial civilization that has overrun other regions of the subcontinent. In 1963, these peoples' struggles for autonomy led to the splintering of Assam into six states: Arunachal Pradesh, Nagaland, Manipur, Mizoram, Tripura, and Meghalaya, which together constitute the mountainous area bordering China, Myanmar, and Bangladesh. Much turmoil accompanied the changes, and instability threatens the region still today. Assam's capital moved from Shillong to Guwahati in 1974, two years after Meghalaya became a separate state.

The tradition of armed insurrection in Tripura, Mizoram, Nagaland, and Assam has only partially abated, and political violence is common in the Northeast. Dissidents claim that India plunders the region's rich natural resources, especially Assam's oil, and neglects its social problems and decaying infrastructure. Political instability, coupled with fears of a Chinese invasion (China still claims Arunachal Pradesh), kept the region closed to foreigners until 1995. Assam, Meghalaya, and Tripura are now open to tourism. The other states require **permits,** which can in theory be obtained in Delhi, but which are practically impossible to get. Your best bet is to apply as a group (of four or more) and to find an organization or travel agent willing to recommend you for a permit. Miracles happen, but the limited-time, place-specific permits are not worth the effort unless you are looking for long-lost relatives or writing a dissertation on Naga culture. Talk is in the air about opening Manipur and Mizoram; ask around for the most current information.

Visiting the parks and villages of Assam and Meghalaya doesn't involve jumping through hoops, and they offer ample natural beauty and cultural attraction. Tripura has a proud cultural legacy and is a good gateway into rarely-visited Bangladesh. The Northeast's lack of tourists—a traveler can go weeks without seeing a foreigner—makes exploration that much more exciting and creates a sense of remoteness rarely encountered elsewhere in India.

HIGHLIGHTS OF NORTHEAST INDIA

Assam's **Kaziranga National Park** (p. 441) teems with wildlife, including a large population of protected rhinos.

One of the wettest places on earth, **Meghalaya** (p. 445) welcomes visitors with hospitality, sublime scenery, and well-watered greenery.

ASSAM অসম

Stretching 800km through the Brahmaputra Valley, Assam is the largest of the seven northeast states. Despite appearances in both the *Mahabharata* and the *Puranas*, Assam didn't really enter recorded history until the 13th century, when a group of Thai Buddhists called the Ahom conquered the area and established

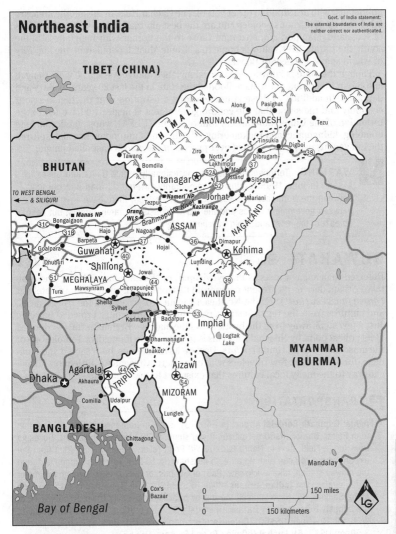

Northeast India

Govt. of India statement:
The external boundaries of India are
neither correct nor authenticated.

TIBET (CHINA)

HIMALAYA

ARUNACHAL PRADESH

Along   Pasighat

Tezu

Tawang   Ziro   North   Tinsukia   Digboi
Bomdila   Lakhimpur   Dibrugarh   38
BHUTAN   Itanagar   52A   Majuli   37
                              Island   Sibsagar
TO WEST BENGAL   52
& SILIGURI   Nameri NP   Jorhat   Mariani
              Tezpur   Brahmaputra River   Kaziranga
        Orang   NP
■ Manas NP   WLS   ASSAM
Bongaigaon   31C   Nagaon   NAGALAND
    31B   Hajo   36   Dimapur
    Barpeta   Kohima
Goalpara   Guwahati   37   Hojai
Dhuburi   40   Lumding   39
    Shillong   Jowai
51   MEGHALAYA   44
Tura   Mawsynram   Cherrapunjee   Dawki   MANIPUR
        Shella   Pawki
        Sylhet   Silchar   Imphal
    Karimganj   Badarpur   53
                    Logtak
    Dharmanagar   Lake   MYANMAR
    Unakoti   (BURMA)
Agartala   44   Aizawl
Dhaka   Akhaura   TRIPURA
    Comilla   Udaipur   54
        MIZORAM
BANGLADESH   Lungleh

    Chittagong   Mandalay

                    0   150 miles
    Cox's   0   150 kilometers   N
    Bazaar   LG
Bay of Bengal

their capital in Sibsagar. The cultural victory, however, belonged to the Hindus, who quickly converted their conquerors. Even today, East-Asian-looking Assamese speakers perform *puja* alongside Aryan Indian pilgrims. In the 19th century, the Burmese took over Assam, but they soon deferred to the British, who built Asia's first oil refinery and took advantage of the hilly terrain and seasonal rains to establish plantations that today produce over half of India's tea.

Geographically as well as culturally, Assam is divided into three regions. In the north, the Brahmaputra Valley combines alluvial lands and islands, hilly tea estates and pristine jungle and wilderness. Unfortunately, in the last three years, forests have been slashed and burnt at an alarming rate, without a squeak from politicians, who are afraid to upset voters. The Cachar Hills, in the middle area, are inhabited by indigenous peoples and are the best alternative to a visit to the states of Nagaland, Manipur, and Mizoram. Close to the border with Bangladesh in the south, the Barak River Valley is home to a sizable Muslim population, the majority of whom speak a dialect of Bengali.

Though the state is known for its racial melange, native Assamese view Bengali and Bihari immigrants, who have flooded the state in the last 20 years, as dirty and depraved. In addition to these ethnic tensions, frustration over the region's poor economy and the sense that the central government is neglectful have led to the formation of the United Liberation Front of Assam (ULFA), whose tactics include bombing, kidnapping, and racketeering. The dream of autonomy has also spurred the indigenous people into taking over parcels of the state's unspoiled jungle.

> **! WARNING.** Terrorists and bandits occasionally attack trains and buses in Assam. In June 1998, explosions temporarily severed all road and rail links between the Northeast and West Bengal. Since then, there have been clashes between government forces and the ULFA. Tourists are rarely targets, but keep abreast of the news and avoid traveling at night.

GUWAHATI গুয়াহাটি ☎ 0361

Referred to in ancient texts as Pragjyoyishpur, or "Eastern Ray of Light," the capital of Assam derives its present name from its more earthly function as a betel-nut (*guwa*) market (*hatt*). As the Northeast's main crossroads, all the tribes, races, and cultures from the region's states pass through Guwahati's crowded bazaars. Just a few steps away from the bustle flows the majestic Brahmaputra, overlooked at its holiest point by Nilachal Hill. This is the site of the Kamakhya Temple, one of the most sacred of all Hindu *tirthas*. Despite its attractions, both sacred and mundane, for most of the few travelers who come here, Guwahati is little more than a gateway to the many local cultures that exist just to the south and east.

▐ TRANSPORTATION

Flights: Gopinath Bordelai Airport (☎ 840279), is 24km from town in Borjhar. Taxis run from Paltan Bazaar (Rs60 per person if you share, Rs300 for the whole car). Buses go from Judge Field, next to Nehru Park, to VIP Point (every 30min., Rs3), 2km from the airport, where you can pick up an auto-rickshaw (Rs10-20). To get to Judge Field from the railway station, take a rickshaw (Rs5) or city bus, or walk straight through two major traffic circles. The **Indian Airlines** office (☎ 564425) is in Ganeshguri, a 15min. ride along Shillong Rd. Save yourself the trip by booking at Dynasty Travel (☎ 511872), at the Dynasty Hotel in Fancy Bazaar. Open daily 9:30am-6:30pm. To: **Agartala** (45min.; W, F, Su 12:15pm; US$50); **Calcutta** (1hr.; noon; US$75); **Delhi** (2½hr.; daily 2:10-3:50pm; US$215); **Imphal** (50min.; Th and Su 1pm; US$55).

Trains: The main railway station in the Northeast, **Guwahati Junction,** is next to Paltan Bazaar. To book sleeper tickets, go to the **North Eastern Railways Reservation Bldg.** (☎ 541799), 200m in front of the railway station. To: **Calcutta** (20-23hr.; 2-4 per day; Rs270); **Delhi** (36hr.; 3-4 per day; Rs402); **Dimapur,** for buses to **Kohima** and **Imphal** (5-6hr.; 4-5 per day 2:30pm-1am; Rs100); **Jorhat** (13hr.; 7:30pm; Rs126).

Buses: Throughout the Northeast, private buses, which depart from **Paltan Bazaar,** are more frequent, more reliable, and better than state transport. For booking inquiries, go to **Royal Tour and Travel** (☎ 635621), which has buses to: **Agartala** (24hr.; 4 and 5pm; Rs330); **Dimapur** (10hr.; 8pm; Rs210); **Imphal** (15hr.; 4 and 7:30pm; Rs400); **Jorhat**

(6hr.; 4 per day; Rs140); **Shillong** (4hr.; frequent; Rs70); **Silchar** (12hr.; 5:30pm and 6pm; Rs215); **Siliguri** (15hr.; 7am and 5:30pm; Rs290); **Tezpur** (5hr.; frequent, Rs85). **Assam and Meghalaya State Transport** buses depart from the depot between the railway station and Paltan Bazaar. To: **Agartala** (24hr.; 3:30pm; Rs300); **Jorhat** (9hr., frequent 6:30am-8pm, Rs100); **Shillong** (4hr.; every hr. 6am-4pm; Rs50); **Silchar** (12hr.; 6am and 5pm; Rs180); **Tezpur** (5hr.; every hr. 7:30am-4pm; Rs66). For **Kaziranga,** take the Jorhat bus to **Kohora** (6hr.; Rs80).

Local Transportation: Cycle-rickshaws and **auto-rickshaws** park on either side of the railway station. City **buses** run on MG, AT, Shillong, and GS Rd. (Rs1-3 within the city). You can catch a bus going west along MG Rd. to the base of Nilachal Hill and the Kamakhya Temple. **Ferries** run to Umananda (Rs10 per person), unless the river is too high. **River cruises** also leave from the Al Fresco Restaurant landing (1hr.; 5, 6, 7pm; Rs45).

> **WARNING.** Sniff your driver's breath for booze before getting into his vehicle. Alcoholism is a serious problem all over Assam, and though it is unlikely that you'll find a 100% sober rickshaw-*wallah*, you can still pick one who is more or less in control of his bodily functions. It is not unknown for travelers to end up pedaling themselves to their destination while the driver sleeps off his hangover.

ORIENTATION AND PRACTICAL INFORMATION

The **Guwahati Junction Railway Station** is the heart of the town. South of it lies **Paltan Bazaar,** the departure point for buses. A 10min. bus ride along **Shillong Rd.** brings you to **Dispur,** where you will find the government offices of Assam and other Northeastern states. Northwest of the station are the **Pan** and **Fancy Bazaars** (Rs5 rickshaw ride or a 10min. walk), the liveliest areas of town. **Mahatma Gandhi (MG) Rd.** runs behind Pan Bazaar along the river's edge; government buses ply this route to the Kamakhya Temple, 8km west, and the Navagraha Temple, 1km east.

Tourist Office: Government of India Tourist Office (☎547407). In G.L. Publication Complex, off Shillong Rd. From Paltan Bazaar, take a bus to Lachit Nagar; the office is in the tall building on the left. Open M-F 9:30am-5:30pm, Sa 10am-1pm.

Currency Exchange: Grindlays Bank (☎540445). Near the Assam State Museum. Cashes traveler's checks and gives credit card advances. Open for exchange M-F 10am-3pm, Sa 10am-12:30pm.

Police: Stations in Pan Bazaar (☎540106) and Paltan Bazaar (☎540126). The **Superintendent of Police** (☎540278) is near the District Court. Open M-Sa 10am-4:30pm.

Hospital: Down Town Hospital, GS Rd., Dispur (☎560824 or 562741). Near Capitol Complex. Has fluent English speakers on staff and is the best place for extended stays.

Post Office: GPO, Meghdoot Bhawan (☎543588). Near Pan Bazaar. Open M-F 10am-5pm, Sa 10am-3pm. **Postal Code:** 781001.

ACCOMMODATIONS

There are decent places in Paltan Bazaar if you're just passing through. To groove with the locals, you'd be better off in one of the pricier lodges in Pan Bazaar.

 Mayur Hotel (☎548809). Behind the bus station on AT Rd., in Paltan Bazaar. Very cheap, modern rooms. Good veg. dishes. Singles Rs121-154; doubles Rs198-242. ❶

Assam Tourist Lodge (☎544475). In front of the railway station. Spacious doubles with bathroom, balcony, and dressing room. Singles Rs175; doubles Rs261. ❶

Hotel Suradevi, M.N. Rd. (☎545050). 100m from MG Rd. Cheap, comfortable rooms make this the best value near Pan Bazaar. Singles Rs85-95; doubles Rs120-150. ❶

Hotel Gajraj, SS Rd. (☎525070). Near Pan Bazaar. Rooms have attached bath. Strict no meat policy. Singles Rs154; doubles Rs230; triples Rs342. ❶

🍴 FOOD

Assamese cuisine is heavy on fish, rice, and mustard.

▨ **Paradise,** GN Bandoloi Rd., Silpukuri. Excellent Assamese dishes in a soothing environ- ment. The *thali* (Rs55) has 11 different varieties, including fried fish and chili chicken. Beer Rs55. Open daily 10am-3:30pm and 6-9:30pm. ❶

▨ **Chopsticks Restaurant,** on SS Rd., in the Dynasty Hotel. The *nilgiri korma* (Rs95) will carry you to the hills of Kerala in a matter of minutes. Open daily 7am-11pm. ❷

Seven Sisters, on Kacheria Ghat, next to the Umananda Ferry. The food isn't great, but the peaceful river is a good reason to pass a few hours here. Open daily 9am-8pm.

Madras Cabin, Paltan Bazaar, near Mayur Hotel. A shot of southern comfort to comple- ment the northern grit of the surrounding *dhabas*. Open daily 5am-10pm.

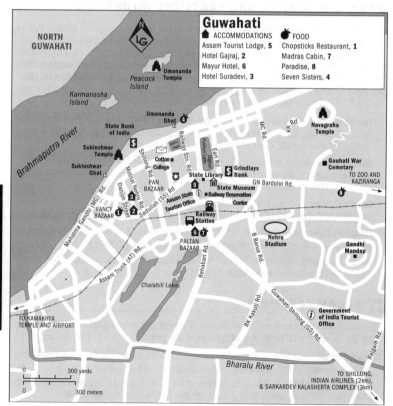

Guwahati

ACCOMMODATIONS
Assam Tourist Lodge, 5
Hotel Gajraj, 2
Mayur Hotel, 6
Hotel Suradevi, 3

FOOD
Chopsticks Restaurant, 1
Madras Cabin, 7
Paradise, 8
Seven Sisters, 4

NORTH GUWAHATI

Peacock Island
Umananda Temple
Karmanasha Island

Brahmaputra River

State Bank of India
Sukleshwar Temple
Sukleshwar Ghat

Umananda Ghat

Navagraha Temple

Gauhati War Cemetary
TO ZOO AND KAZIRANGA

Cotton College
State Library
Grindlays Bank
GN Bardoloi Rd.
State Museum
Assam State Tourism Office
Railway Reservation Center

PAN BAZAAR
FANCY BAZAAR

Railway Station

PALTAN BAZAAR

Nehru Stadium

Gandhi Mandap

Chalabill Lakes

Government of India Tourist Office

TO KAMAKHYA TEMPLE AND AIRPORT

Bharalu River

TO SHILLONG, INDIAN AIRLINES (2km), & SARKARDEV KALASHERTA COMPLEX (3km)

0   300 yards
0   300 meters

🌀 SIGHTS

NILICHAL AND KAMAKHYA TEMPLE. The Blue Hill is the highest peak in the area and is crisscrossed by paths leading up to 10 shrines, each dedicated to a different form of Kali, the bloodthirsty goddess. By far the most important site is the Kamakhya Temple, the principle *shakti pitha* for Hindus. It is said that the goddess Sati's vulva fell here when she was cut into pieces by Vishnu (see **Divine Dismemberment**, p. 440). After it was torched by a brahmin priest who converted to Islam, the temple, with its beehive-shaped spire, was rebuilt in 1665 by King Naranarayana. The king is said to have inaugurated his new temple by offering 140 human heads to the goddess Kamakhya. Inside, the Mother-Goddess is worshipped in the form of a crack in a rock, rather than as a sculpted image. The ancient stone bleachers that rise from the base of the temple provide seating to spectators eager to see sacrifices. Goats tied to the posts at the main temple gate each morning are decapitated by the evening. The shrine inside the temple is open to non-Hindus, but you will need to have a good deal of change on you to satisfy all the guardian priests. *(The bus from Guwahati, which you can catch anywhere on MG Rd. or near the Tourist Lodge, will drop you on MG Rd. From here, you can walk up the path to the temple in 30min., or catch a taxi up the winding road. From Kamakhya, a 20min. scenic walk leads up to the peaceful Bhubaneshwari Temple, under a pipal tree at the top of the hill. Last bus from Kamakhya leaves 6pm. Rs15.)*

BRAHMAPUTRA RIVER. The mighty Brahmaputra ("Son of Brahma") surges past the city's north edge. Though the river might look serene, during the rainy season, it often overflows and washes away riverside settlements. The river's vast hydro-electric potential has not yet been exploited, but engineers claim that the Brahmaputra could satisfy 30% of India's energy needs. Ferries run between 7am and 4pm (Rs10) from Umananda Ghat, next to Seven Sisters restaurant, to the Umananda Temple, on a small island in the middle of the river. Along the way to the temple is the **Urbashi Kharti,** a yardstick that measures the water level during the monsoon; according to legend, it's a beautiful woman, transformed into a rock.

NAVAGRAHA TEMPLE. The Navagraha ("nine planets") Temple overlooks Guwahati from a hill and gives stargazers the best local view. An echo chamber holds nine *lingas*, dedicated to the nine heavenly bodies that ancient Indians identified: the sun, the moon, the ascending and descending nodes of the moon, Mercury, Venus, Mars, Jupiter, and Saturn. The dark, dank temple now seems more abandoned than mysterious. A family of wild, territorial monkeys terrorizes visitors. *(On Citrachaila Hill in east Guwahati. Open daily 10am-6pm.)*

OTHER SIGHTS. The Assam State Museum, across from the **Dighali Pukhi pond,** has Assamese cultural artifacts, Japanese weaponry from WWII, and an exhibit of photographs, and documents from the Indian independence movement. The library next door is stocked with literature on regional cultures. *(Both open Tu-Sa 10am-5pm; in winter 10am-4:15pm; closed 2nd and 4th Sa. Rs2.)* A cultural center, the **Sarkardev Kalashetra Complex,** opened recently on the 6th mile of GS Rd. Named for an Assamese artisan who devoted his life to the promotion of regional culture, the center is a theme park of all things Assamese, complete with temples, an open air amphitheater, and a beautifully landscaped "Heritage Park," which contains sculptures, paintings, and mosaics depicting scenes from rural Assamese life. *(Take a bus along GS Rd., or hire an auto-rickshaw from the Paltan Bazaar (Rs60). Open daily 10am-7pm. Rs5.)* The **Guwahati War Cemetery,** on a side street south of Navagraha Temple, is a quiet, flower-filled resting place for those Guwahati's who perished in WWII.

DIVINE DISMEMBERMENT Shiva, a stinky ascetic, fell in love with the beautiful, high-bred goddess Sati, and she was unfortunate enough to love him back. Her father, Daksha, disapproved. He snubbed Shiva, and at his grand sacrifice celebration, he invited every god but the vagabond groom. Furious, Sati flung herself weeping on the sacrificial pyre, where her tears boiled away and she burned alive. When Shiva learned of his wife's demise, he lifted her blackened body and sobbed so convulsively that the universe shook. To save the cosmos from being shaken into a pile of rubble, the god Vishnu stepped in and hacked at the charred corpse with his *chakra* (discus). With the corpse gone, Shiva was consoled, and the universe was saved. The spots on earth where bits of Sati's body landed became *shakti pithas*. These sacred sites, which number 4, 51, or 108, depending on who's counting, began as independent goddess shrines, but the myth of Sati's dismemberment provides a unifying thread. The most important *shakti pithas* are those from the most potent parts of Sati; the Kamakhya Temple in Guwahati is the greatest of them all.

TEZPUR ☎03712

Tezpur, the "town of blood," is a pleasant little place with a grim mythological past. According to legend, Hari (Krishna) and Hara (Shiva, in the form of Banasura) fought their battle here and drenched the town with their blood. Today, the red stains on the street are from betel-chewers. At **Da-Parbatia**, an astonishingly small gate is all that remains of one of the oldest temples in Assam. In **Agnigargh**, 5km out of town, on a hillside facing the river, are the ruins of a rampart. The main reason to come to Tezpur, though, is its location on the north bank of the Brahmaputra, close to Orang, Nameri, and Kaziranga National Parks. Nearby is the breathtaking Bomdila road, which ends at the **Tawang Gompa**. Tezpur is also the gateway to the western part of Arunachal Pradesh. **Permits** are required, and foreigners can obtain them only from the Home Ministry in Delhi (extremely difficult and frustrating) or through a local travel agent. Permits are issued to groups of four or more, and the cost is US$150 per person per day (US$50 to the state government, US$100 to the tour operator). Tsering Wange of **Himalayan Holidays** in Bomdila is one of the savvier tour operators. Call ahead. (☎(03782) 22017).

Buses arrive at **Kekarapul** bus station, near Cole Lake, a 10min. walk from the town center. Buses run to: **Guwahati** (every hr. 7am-4pm, Rs70); **Jorhat** (frequent, Rs70); **Siliguri** (1 per day, Rs320). The town centers on the **Main Rd.**, which ends at a market near the mosque. Travel companies cluster on **Kabarkhana Rd.**, which runs parallel to the Main Rd. from the state transport bus stand. **Shambala Tour/ Himalayan Holidays** runs Tata Sumos to Bomdila. (☎52108. 6hr., two per day 5:30am and 1pm, Rs120.) To get to Kaziranga, take a Jorhat bus and alert the driver to your destination (Rs30). **No currency exchange** is available in town. The **police station** is in the middle of the main road. **Internet** cafes are on the main road. The **post office** is three blocks southeast. (☎20183. Open M-Sa 7am-5pm. **Postal code** 754001.)

Hotel Green View Lodge ❶, on the main road 200m from the police station, has big, clean, quiet rooms. (☎30667. Singles Rs70; doubles Rs100.) **Basant Hotel ❶**, on the main road, 100m from the police station, is more expensive but has posher rooms. (☎30831. Singles Rs165-95; doubles Rs220.) The **Tourist Lodge❶**, on Kabarkhana Rd., dispenses travel advice about local parks. (☎21026. Dorms Rs30; doubles Rs207.) **Flora Restaurant and Bar ❶**, on Jonaki Cinema Rd., near the police station, is the local favorite for beer and food. Mood lighting is in effect at all hours of the day; bring a flashlight to see what you're eating. (Rs45 per bottle. Open daily 10am-10pm.)

NATIONAL PARKS

⚄ NAMERI NATIONAL PARK

To reach the park from Tezpur, take a bus to Hathiket on Bhalukpung Rd. (2hr., Rs16). From the road it is a 2.3km walk to the Forest Ranger Office and the ECO Camp, on the southern bank of the Bhoroli river. The camp is run by the Bhoroli Angling Association and sometimes fills up, so book in advance.

Together with the Pakhui Wildlife Sanctuary in Arunachal, Nameri comprises 1000 sq. km of evergreen forest from the northern bank of the Jia Bhoroli River to the Himalayas. Ideal elephant country, it is also known for orchids, a steadily increasing tiger population, and the endangered White Winged Wood Duck. The best way to visit the park is on a 2hr. walk at sunrise or sunset, the only times you will see any wildlife. A ranger, armed with an anti-tiger cannon, will accompany you and point out ducks, flowers, and footprints of fierce creatures. Only 29 tigers live in the park, though, so you probably won't spot a live one. Pay the Rs175 daily fee at the Forest Ranger Office (open daily 8am-5pm), and the ranger will arrange a ferry across the river. There are "luxury tents" (Rs720-880) and a few beds in double rooms with common bath (Rs120). Meals are served here. Call ahead to reserve a place (☎ (03714) 44246) or to get permission to camp. Managers **Mr. Phukan** and **Mr. Agarwal** are knowledgeable and can arrange rafting trips (Rs750). If you want to fish, bring your own equipment and secure a permit in Tezpur.

⚄ ORANG WILDLIFE SANCTUARY

*From Tezpur, take the Guwahati bus to **Orang** (1hr., Rs10). From here, another bus goes to Silbari, a 2km walk from the park. Alternatively, a car can be hired in Tezpur (Rs200). Before you go, contact the BFO office in Tezpur (☎ (03712) 20803) to get permission to stay in the park.*

This "mini-Kaziranga" packs rhinos, elephants, a small population of tigers, and rare birds (including the Bengal Florican) into just 76 sq. km. At the edge of a village of Bangledeshi Muslims—150km from Guwahati and 32km from Tezpur, on the northern bank of the Brahmaputra—remote, quiet Orang makes a great one-night getaway. Accommodations consist of two basic **forest bungalows ❶**, the better of which is within the confines of the park. (For booking call ☎ (03713) 22065. Doubles Rs120.) Bring your own food; the ranger might help you cook.

⚄ MANAS NATIONAL PARK

One of the most beautiful wildlife parks in the whole of Asia, Manas National Park is a UNESCO World Heritage Site and home to rhinos, elephants, and tigers. It is also home to violent Bodo (National Democratic Front of Bodoland) rebels. Even the poachers are afraid to enter the park these days. The park is closed to visitors, unless they have a heavy-duty police escort.

⚄ KAZIRANGA NATIONAL PARK

*Kaziranga is 217km from Guwahati and 96km from Jorhat, the closest airport. From Guwahati take a Jorhat bus to **Kohora,** the gate of the park (6hr., several per day, Rs80). From Tezpur, take the Jorhat bus to Kohora (2hr., 7am-8pm, Rs30). From Jorhat, it takes 3hr. and costs Rs40. Park entrance fee Rs175 per person per day. Rs175 daily camera fee, as well as Rs575 for the elephant ride. Forest Range Office open 7:30-9:30am, 2-3:30pm, and 8-9pm to reserve elephant seats for the next morning. The sanctuary is open from November to late April; during the monsoon, animals flee the flooded marshland for the muddy roads, making passage dangerous or impossible.*

The Kaziranga National Park (☎ 03776), in tea-country 217km from Guwahati, is Assam's top tourist attraction and the most scenic of wildlife parks in the Northeast. Most visitors come here to see the Indian **one-horned rhinoceros**—Kaziranga is home to 65% of the world's population of this endangered species. Since 1966, the park's rhino population has tripled, despite the best efforts of horny horn hunters (the phallic proboscis is a much-coveted aphrodisiac). There is no doubt that the rhinos are the stars of the show, but Kaziranga's cast of supporting characters is also impressive. Your chances of seeing a tiger are close to nil (the park has only 80), but Asiatic wild buffalo (or *gaur*), equipped with mammoth horns, are all over the place. The park is also home to four kinds of deer and packs of wild elephants. For bird-lovers and twitchers, there are Fish Eagles, Gray-headed Pelicans, and even the rare and much sought-after megatick, the Bengal Florican.

The 430 sq. km sanctuary is a hodgepodge of habitats. Swampland gives way to jungle, which rises up to deciduous forests and eventually to the evergreen slopes of the Karbi Anglong Hills. The Karbi hill people are engaged in a blood feud with the plains folks. This does not ordinarily affect travelers, but visitors should exercise caution nonetheless. The best view of the animals is from the back of an elephant—each seats up to four people—since they are able to get much closer to the animals than jeeps.

The bus from Jorhat drops you off on the main road by the Park View Restaurant, the cheapest restaurant in Kaziranga. (Open daily 6am-10pm.) Take the road behind the restaurant and past the **police station** (☎ 62426). After 10min., you will find the Kohora village, the **Park Office,** and all the accommodations. Assam Tourism runs four lodges. To the left is the **Bonani Lodge ❷,** with spacious rooms and enormous bathrooms. (☎ 62423. Singles Rs250; doubles Rs380.) The reception at Bonani also deals with bookings for **Bonoshree ❷,** which has basic doubles (Rs260) and **Kunjaban ❶,** which has dorms (Rs50). To the right of the road is **Aranya ❷,** which has the most expensive but not the best rooms. (☎ 62429. Doubles Rs555.) Another 15min. walk along the road takes you to the **Soil Conservation Guest House ❶,** facing a tea plantation and protected by a muzzle gun. (☎ 62409. Dorms Rs25; doubles Rs200-300.)

◪ VISITING THE PARK. There are two ways to visit the park—by jeep and by elephant. Either way, you will start your trip from the Forest Range Office in Kohora. Jeeps depart from the office at 5:30 and 6:30am to the elephant-mounting point in the center of the park. The elephant ride lasts 1hr. and gets you within sniffing range of buffalo and rhino. Jeep safaris depart from the office at 8:30-9:30am and at 2:30pm. There are three routes. Each jeep holds eight people, so latch on to a larger group to save money. Diganta Borah is a guide who speaks good English and will help you find the safari that best suits your interest. (☎ 62428.) The **Central Region route** is the shortest and most popular (3hr., Rs680). There are normally enough people around to split the cost for this route, but it is harder to find people for the western and eastern routes. Sightings of elephants and eagles are guaranteed, both from the jeep and from the look-out towers. The **Western Range route** has good chances to see elephants and rhinos (4hr., Rs750). The **Eastern Range route** leads through a pelican colony and other major bird habitats (7hr., Rs1150). Spotting one of them big cats on these routes is possible, though your chances are slim. Bring your binoculars and keep your eyes peeled.

JORHAT ☎ 0376

Though it's not much of a destination itself, you might have to spend a night in Jorhat on your way somewhere else. Buses stop here on their way to Sibsagar, to the Gibbon Wildlife Sanctuary, and to Majuli, a huge island and the site of several prominent *satras* (Vaishnava monasteries).

E TRANSPORTATION. Rowriah Airport (☎340881) 5km from Jorhat, has flights to **Calcutta** (2hr., 2 per week, US$95) and **Dimapur** (30min., 2 per week, US$50). **Trains** run to **Guwahati**, but you are not allowed to take them because tourists aren't allowed in Nagaland, where the train passes for a fraction of its journey. The **bus stand** is on MG Rd., near AT Rd. Buses run to: **Guwahati** via **Kohora** (9hr., every hr. 6am-9pm, Rs120); **Mariani**, for the **Gibbon Wildlife Sanctuary** (1hr., every hr. 7am-4pm, Rs10); **Nimati Ghat**, for the ferry to **Majuli** (1hr.; 9am for the 10:30 ferry, 2pm for 3:30pm ferry; Rs5); **Sibsagar** (2hr., every 30min. 6:45am-4:30pm, Rs20).

🖬 🔃 ORIENTATION AND PRACTICAL INFORMATION. Jorhat is 80km east of Kaziranga, on the southern banks of the Brahmaputra. The town centers on a quadrant defined by **AT Rd.** and **KB Rd.**, running east-west, and **MG Rd.** and **Gar Ali**, running north-south. The **tourist office** is on MG Rd., close to the bus stand (☎321579). The **Police station** is next door (☎320022). **Pelican Travels** on MG Rd., opposite the police station, books flights. (☎321128. Open M-Sa, 10am-5pm.) The **State Bank of India** exchanges foreign currency. (Open M-F 10am-4pm.) The **post office** is near the bus stand. (☎320045. Open M-Sa 10am-5pm.) **Postal Code:** 785001.

🔃🔃 ACCOMMODATIONS AND FOOD. A growing number of hotels cluster on AT Rd. **Arbees Guest House ❶**, next to the Plurabelle Restaurant on A.T Rd. 500m west of the bus stand, has the cheapest and most pleasant rooms. (☎320562. Singles Rs85; doubles Rs175.) The **Assam Tourist Lodge ❶**, in the same building as the Tourist Office, has spacious doubles with mosquito nets. (☎321579. Singles Rs100; doubles Rs170.) The **Food Hut ❶**, near the Tourist Office on MG Rd., serves good Indian, Chinese, and continental food. (Dishes Rs25-50. Open daily 9:30am-9:30pm.)

NEAR JORHAT ☎0376

🔃 MAJULI

*Buses leave Jorhat for **Nimiti Ghat** at 9am (for the 10:30am ferry) and 2pm (for the 3:30pm ferry). The ferry lands at **Kamalabasi Ghat** (1½hr., Rs10), from which buses cross the burning sands to **Kamalabari**, the largest town on the island (30min., Rs7). The bus continues to **Garamur** (6km) and then onto another ferry to **Lahkimpur** in northern Assam. To get back, buses depart from Kamalabari for the Kamalabari-Nimiti ferry at 8am (for the 9am ferry) and at 1pm (for the 2pm ferry).*

The world's largest river island, Majuli is populated by indigenous groups isolated from the mainland by the Brahmaputra. The peaceful remoteness of the island was perhaps what attracted Shankardeva, the 16th-century Vaishnava saint, who established *satras* (Vaishnava monasteries) here. Today, the largest of them, **Auniati Satra**, has 300 residents and gives insight into the song-and-dance-oriented Vaishnava cult. While the Shaivite *sadhus* who hang out along the Ganga worship Shiva, the Vasihnavas worship Vishnu. Walking between the *satras* takes you through backwoods villages, where a cup of *chai* with the locals might prove to be more fun than a *bhajan* sing-along with the priests.

At Kamalabari, you are required to report to the **police station** (☎73429) by the bridge, perhaps because the officer is fond of chatting with the rare foreign visitor. There is a **post office** in Kamalabari. **Postal Code:** 785106.

There are two guest houses on the island. To reach the **Kamalabari Satra Guest House ❶**, take the dirt road opposite the police station and walk 15min. along the river. Contact *Ensign Swami* (the head priest) for reservations. The monks are friendly and fond of dancing. (☎73302. Rs60 per person.)

444 ■ ASSAM অসম

One kilometer from the Circuit House is the **Garamur Satra,** the most famous of the island's *satras* because of the patronage of Sibsagar's Ahom kings. Today, however, only fallen stone pillars, a hidden Boxtop gun, and a richly adorned Vishnu altar sheltered in a shack testify to the glorious past. The community (one of the few non-celibate ones on the island) is undergoing a major transition, and debates continue about the future of the once great *satra.* At the **Auniati Satra,** the compounds are clean, and the monastic community is flourishing. Ask for the head priest, who speaks excellent English and enlightens visitors with tales from local history. Auniati Satra is a 5km walk from the town of Kamalabari. The other large monastery, **Dakhimpat Satra,** is a long 18km walk from Kamalabari, but the route is worth the effort, as it leads through some interesting villages. Trucks and motorcycles motor along this stretch and will usually give you a ride.

GIBBON WILDLIFE SANCTUARY

Twenty kilometers south of Jorhat, the Gibbon Wildlife Sanctuary is home to the largest number of primate species in India. Seven kinds of monkeys swing from the jungle branches here, making this the best spot to catch a glimpse of rare macaques and capped languors. To reach the sanctuary from Jorhat, take a **bus** to Mariami (1hr., Rs10) and then hire a rickshaw or walk the remaining 5km to the ranger's office, following the signs for the Indo-US Primate Project. There is a two-room **Forest Department Bungalow** on the premises, but you need a permit from the District Forest Official in Jorhat to stay there. It's worth the hassle; wildlife is best observed at sunrise and sunset, and you'll miss it if you're just daytripping.

SILCHAR   ☎ 03482

In the middle of the Barak River valley, Silchar, the biggest town in southern Assam, is a transit point for the lucky Manipur and Mizoram inner-line permit-holders, as well as for anyone bound for Tripura from Assam or Meghalaya. Silchar itself has nothing to distinguish it from any other small, rural, goats-on-the-sidewalk town of the Northeast. Travelers may want to take the 4hr. train ride north to the Cachar Hills, the best place to experience the indigenous groups of the northeastern hills. Foreigners need a **permit** before they can travel to Imphal from Silchar or have any hope of getting near the restricted area of Mizoram. Contact the Home Ministry in Delhi. The check posts are heavily guarded.

TRANSPORTATION. Given the inaccessibility of Nagaland to foreign visitors and the precarious condition of the Silchar-Imphal road, flying is the only practical way to get into Manipur. The **Indian Airlines** office is on Club Rd., by the police circle. (☎45649. Open M-Sa 10am-4:30pm.) **Flights** connect Silchar to **Calcutta** (1hr., M-Sa, US$80) and **Imphal** (30min.; Tu, Th, Sa; US$30). **Trains** go via **Haflong** to **Lumding,** where connections can be made to **Guwahati** (11hr.; *Barak Valley Exp. 5812,* 7:30am; *Cachar Exp. 5802,* 6:30pm; Rs59). Private **buses** leave from Club Rd. for: **Agartala** (14hr., 6:30am and 6:30pm, Rs180); **Aizwal** (9hr., 7:30pm, Rs165); **Guwahati** (13hr., 7am and 5:30pm, Rs215) via **Shillong** (10hr., Rs165); and **Imphal** (12hr., 3:30am, Rs195). **Sumos** are a much better option if you want to get to **Aizwal;** they leave from Club Rd. Many bus companies operate around Club Rd. **Capital Travels** (☎36566) has a branch near the railway station.

ORIENTATION AND PRACTICAL INFORMATION. The Railway Station is an extension of Park Rd.; most buses arrive near Club Rd. The **State Bank of India** on Park Rd., next to Borail View Hotel, exchanges foreign currency. (Open M-F 10am-2pm, Sa 10am-1pm.) The **Superintendent of Police** (☎45866) lives on Park Rd., and he should be able to answer permit-related questions. **Postal code:** 788001.

⌐⌐ ACCOMMODATIONS AND FOOD. Assam Tourist Lodge ❶, a Rs5 rickshaw ride from Club Rd. or the train station, has rooms with mosquito nets and bathroom. (☎32376. Dorms Rs50; singles Rs210; doubles Rs260.) **Hotel Ellora ❶,** near the police circle on Club Rd., has a remarkable variety of rooming options. (☎47412. Bare dorms Rs50; passable singles Rs90; luxury doubles Rs260.) **Bholanath Bakery ❶,** near the train station, sells fresh, crisp pastries and breads. (Open daily 7am-10pm.) **Restaurant Sreyashi ❶,** next to Hotel Ellora, serves good Chinese and Indian food. Egg *masala* Rs40. (Open daily 10am-10pm.)

MEGHALAYA

Travelers who take the hilly roads to Meghalaya discover why the region is called the "Abode of Clouds." The cool mists that envelop the hilly state of Meghalaya burst into violent rains, dousing the valley and swelling the Brahmaputra River. The rain makes Cherrapunjee and Mawsyn two of the wettest places on earth and supports a wealth of vegetation, from pine forests to steaming jungles.

Two indigenous groups inhabit Meghalaya: the Hynniewtrep people who live in the Khasi Hills to the east and the Achiks (or Garos) in the Garo Hills to the west. In the 19th century, Welsh and Italian missionaries and the officers of the British Raj were added to the melting pot. The missionaries created a strong Christian foundation (75% of Meghalayans remain Christian today) and stressed education, now demonstrated by Meghalaya's claim to the second-highest literacy rates in India. In contrast, the British were more keen on using the hills as an escape from the torturous heat of the Brahmaputra plains. Having defeated (and beheaded) the local independence hero, Raja of Nongkhlaw, during the 1830s, they established a hill station in Cherrapunjee, only to be driven out by the rains. They decamped to Shillong, which they converted into the capital of Assam, and they furnished it with essential modern amenities, including a golf course and tennis club. To this day the missionaries are remembered with fondness, while the British are resented, particularly for their discouragement of human sacrifice.

In 1972, Meghalaya gained independence from Assam and became India's 21st state. Despite the various outside influences, Meghalayans have managed to hold on to their unique traditional institutions such as matrilineal descent and property inheritance. Offices, families, and bazaars are run primarily by women. Democratic values are supported by regional *syiem* (kings) who have long allowed and pushed for self-government through public discourse and referenda.

Opened to unrestricted tourism only in 1995, Meghalaya has just begun attracting foreign travelers. Most people come to enjoy the cool weather of Shillong and the Khasi Hills and to visit the wildlife sanctuaries of West Meghalaya. The bumpy road that cuts west from Shillong to Phulbari gives the more adventurous an opportunity to explore the hill cultures in greater depth.

SHILLONG ☎0364

From a distance, the lovely hill station of Shillong looks much like any Scottish highland town, being blessed with a cool climate and surrounded by green hills. A visit to the Iewduh Market (Bara Bazaar), alive with the local cultures of Meghalaya, may convince you otherwise. The city, named for an incarnation of the Khasi creator god Shillong, is still marked by its British past, visible in the churches, botanical gardens, and colonial cottages that still dominate the old European center of town. Shillong's excellent schools, its cool climate, and cultural scene draw people from all over the Northeast and Bengal. The area glows with a prosperity that has yet to attract the throngs of tourists that flock to Darjeeling and Shimla. The city's solid infrastructure, unmatched in the Northeast, makes it an excellent spot for relaxation and a good base for walking expeditions in the hills.

TRANSPORTATION

Flights: The closest **airport** is in Guwahati. **Jais Travels**, MG Rd. (☎222777), 100m from the State Bank of India, connected to the Indian Airlines and Jet Airways reservation terminals. Open daily 10am-5pm. **Arrow Tours** (☎501240). In Police Bazaar. Runs a bus to Guwahati airport (3hr., 6:40am, Rs170). Open M-Sa 10am-5pm, Su 10am-noon.

Buses: Government buses depart from the **MTC bus stand** in Police Bazaar; tickets can be bought at the MTC bldg. To **Guwahati** (4hr., every hr. 6:30am-5pm, Rs46) and **Tura** and **Williamnagar Wildlife Preserve** (12hr., 5pm, Rs180). For **Aizwal** and **Imphal**, go to **Silchar** to make a connection (8hr., 7am and 7pm, Rs134). Government buses also go to **Ranikor;** you can jump off on the way and walk 2km to **Mawsyn.** Frequent **private buses** for **Guwahati** and **Silchar** depart from the Polo Ground; make reservations at any travel agency in Police Bazaar. **Sumos** and buses for **Cherrapunjee** depart from Bara Bazaar (2hr., 6am-4:30pm, Rs25). **Capital Travels** (☎225674) near the cathedral on Jowai Rd., runs a direct bus to **Agartala** (23hr., 6pm, Rs275).

Local Transportation: Shared taxis, Rs5 per head, barrel through the city streets without even coming to a complete stop to pick up passengers. Taxis can be hired for trips to more remote tourist spots for about twice the local rate.

ORIENTATION AND PRACTICAL INFORMATION

Shillong is a hilly mess. Tiny roads snake out from around the MTC bus stand in **Police Bazaar. Guwahati-Shillong (GS) Rd.,** lined with budget hotels, bends westward and leads to **Bara Bazaar. MG Rd. (Kacheri Rd.)** winds southeast away from Police Bazaar and fronts many government offices. Along this wide boulevard are the Shillong Club, the State Bank of India, and at its southern tip, the State Museum. Apart from **Ward Lake,** most of Shillong's natural wonders are out of town.

Tourist Office: Government of India Tourist Office, GS Rd. (☎225632). Near Police Bazaar. Open M-F 9:30am-5:30pm, Sa 9:30am-2pm. **Meghalaya Tourist Information** (☎226220). At the bus stand, Police Bazaar, opposite the MTC bldg. Open M-Sa 7:30am-4:30pm, Su 7:30-11am.

Currency Exchange: State Bank of India, MG Rd. (☎223520). Accepts AmEx and MC travelers checks in US$ only. Open M-F 10am-4pm, Sa 10am-1pm.

Market: The **Bara Bazaar** is an endless maze of market lanes strewn with pineapple tops and animal fat. Sells everything from star fruit to cow hooves to electronic equipment.

Police: Superintendent of Police, MG Rd. (☎224150). Next to the Secretariat. Empowered to deal with foreigners. Open M-F 10am-4pm.

Pharmacy: Economic Medical Hall (☎224237). Open 24hr. for emergencies; regular hours 8am-8pm.

Hospital: Nazareth Hospital, Arbuthnot Rd. (☎210188). Offers the best care in town.

Post Office: GPO (☎222302). Opposite Raj Bhavan. Open M-Sa 10am-7pm. **Postal Code:** 793001.

ACCOMMODATIONS

Rooms in the hotels between GS Rd. and Police Bazaar are uniformly cramped and dark. For space, light, and peace, you are better off hopping into one of the black-yellow cabs (Rs5) and heading out of the jostling heart of the city.

KJP Synod Guest House, MG Rd. (☎228611). Opposite the State Museum. Run by a tiny Khasi woman and an army of her nieces. Breakfast, heater, and buckets of hot water are standard issue. Hearty Khasi lunches also available. Beds Rs75. ❶

Assembly Guest House, MG Rd. (☎226828). Behind KJP Guest House. The Presbyterian Church offers a few cheap, well maintained rooms. Doubles Rs100. ❶

Shillong Club, MG Rd. (☎227497). Recent renovations have returned some of the Club's British-era polish. Each room has a throne-style toilet, TV, a fireplace, and a balcony overlooking Ward Lake. For Rs25, guests get access to billiard tables and the red clay "lawn tennis" court. Doubles Rs478-565; triples Rs730; cottage Rs830. MC. ❷

🍴 FOOD

Decent Chinese food is available in Police Bazaar. The stalls along the Bara Bazaar serve the meat- and fish-loaded cuisine particular to the Khasi Hills.

🍴 **Abba Restaurant,** GS Rd., by the Monsoon Hotel. There is another branch on Jowai Rd., just below the Anchorage Guest House. Authentically Chinese dishes include fabulous noodles (Rs40). The Jowai Rd. location has a pleasant watering hole next door, the Liza Bar, where locals shout at each other over whiskey. Open daily 10am-7pm. ❶

New World Chinese Restaurant, at the end of the Police Bazaar. New World has invented some amazing Szechuan/Korean noodle mixtures (Rs70-90). Enjoy these dishes while watching the town stroll by. Open daily 10am-8:30pm. ❶

Pizza (Fast Food), Jail Rd., Police Bazaar. Near the bus stand. American food with an Indian twist. Veggie burger (Rs20) is fat and flavorful. Open daily 9am-7:30pm. ❶

Broadway Restaurant, GS Rd., in the Broadway Hotel. Delicate curry and tandoori flavors. Mutton curry Rs60; vegetable shish kebab Rs50. Open daily 10am-8:30pm. ❶

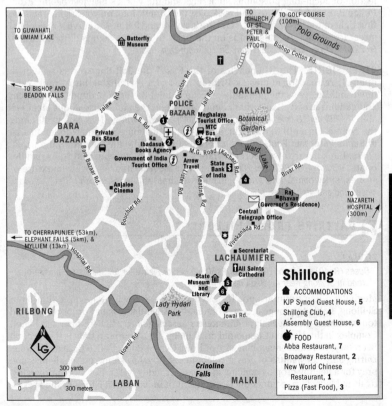

Shillong

🏠 ACCOMMODATIONS
KJP Synod Guest House, 5
Shillong Club, 4
Assembly Guest House, 6

🍴 FOOD
Abba Restaurant, 7
Broadway Restaurant, 2
New World Chinese
  Restaurant, 1
Pizza (Fast Food), 3

NORTHEAST INDIA

🔒 SIGHTS

Shillong's wooden colonial houses are scattered over crooked hills and ridges; each hill has its own church and its own identity. Several sights on the outskirts of town make decent half-day excursions.

SHILLONG PEAK. Although hard to reach, Shillong Peak is the most spectacular of the sights near the city. Follow Howell Rd. up through Laban, where it turns into a stone path as it enters a pine wood. The path takes you to the **Shillong Observation Point** (1hr.). From here, follow the road right through the Northeastern Air Command military installation, past a heavily guarded gate, and through potato fields. **Bara Peak,** the highest point in Meghalaya, is off the road to the left, about 1km after the gate (1-2hr. from Shillong). To get back to town, follow the same road for another 3km through the woods until you hit the Shillong-Cherrapunjee road. Turn left and walk for 600m to **Elephant Falls,** recently cleaned and renovated as a business venture by local teenagers. *(Open daily 8:30am-5pm. Rs2.)* Buses and jeeps running along this road will give you a lift down to Shillong *(30min., 6am-7pm, Rs10).*

THE BUTTERFLY MUSEUM. Started by a Mr. Wankhar in the 1930s, the Butterfly Museum, now looked after by his grandson, includes such priceless items as a collection of 30cm-long poisonous stick bugs and the world's heaviest beetle. From Police Bazaar, take GS Rd. and walk past the Grand Hotel on your right. Take the first right onto Umsohsun Rd.; at the fork, go left and follow the curving residential street for 500m. The museum is on the right, though the sign is difficult to see. *(☎ 223411. Open M-F 10:30am-4pm, Sa 10:30am-1pm. Rs5.)*

OTHER SIGHTS. The "Gleneagles of the East," the **Golf Course** was a favorite open-air retreat for homesick Brits in need of a revitalizing bit of rain. Walk down Jail Rd., pass the jail, and continue behind the Polo Grounds. Equipment and caddies are available year-round; inquire in the clubhouse about membership *(Rs250 per 18 holes, caddy and club rental included).* Non-golfers can stroll along the course. On a hill to the right, at the end of the course, is the wooden **Church of Saints Peter and Paul,** run by a Venetian priest who has been in India for 52 years. Back in the town center is **Ward's Lake,** where you can rent rusty paddleboats *(9:30am-4pm, Rs15 per 20min.)* The **State Museum** houses a weird mixture of stones, silkworms, and wax figurines of Khasi villagers. *(Open M-Sa 10am-4pm, closed 2nd and 4th Sa. Free.)*

🔒 DAYTRIPS FROM SHILLONG

JOWAI

Buses (Rs40) and jeeps (Rs350, or Rs50 per person) leave for Jowai from the private bus stand in Shillong near Anjalee Cinema Hall.

Meghalaya is a popular spot for caving, and the town of Jowai, 64km from Shillong, holds the longest cave in India, the **Krem Um Lawan.** For more info and tours, contact the **Meghalaya Adventurers Association** (☎ 243059), near the Synod Complex in the Mission Compound, in Shillong. B.O. Kharpran Daly is the General Secretary; you can contact him care of Hotel Centre Point, Police Bazaar, Shillong. During July, the Jaintas of Jowai celebrate a festival to stomp out epidemics and pray for a healthy crop by dancing in a pool of muddy water. For more info on festivals in Meghalaya, contact the Government of India Tourist Office or the MTDC.

CHERRAPUNJEE

Buses and sumos leave from Bara Bazaar in Shillong for Cherrapunjee (2hr., 7am-5pm, Rs25). The bus arrives next to the Ramakrishna Mission in Cherrapunjee. The last bus from Cherrapunjee to Shillong leaves around 4:30pm. Guided tours depart from the MTDC office in Shillong daily at 8am, as long as at least 15 people sign up; tours return at 4:30pm. Rs125.

Until recently, the town of Cherrapunjee, 56km south of Shillong, held the world record for the most rainfall within a 24hr. period; an unbelievable 104cm (40in.) of rain fell here on June 16, 1876. The southern ridges of the Khasi Hills are so wet that trees cannot grow on them. In winter, Cherapunjee is relatively dry, with blue skies and calm mountain winds. The road that runs up to the left of the Mission High School leads to **Nohkalikai Falls** 4km away. The path down from the bus stand takes you to the **Welsh Mission**—Cherrapunjee was the site of their first church in the area. The **Circuit House ❶**, 500m farther down to the left off the main road, is meant primarily for government guests, but they do sometimes take tourists. Contact the Sub-Divisional Officer next door for reservations. (☎ (0927) 35222 or 35326. Rs35 per person in mosquito-netted rooms.)

Five kilometers past the Circuit House, along the main road, is the **Mawsmai Village,** known for its cave and waterfalls. Souvenir hounds have broken off most of the stalactites, but the cave is still dramatic. The 50m slippery limestone passageway leads to a lush, bright jungle on the other side. Stay with your guide, or they might turn off the generator, thinking you've left the cave, in which case you'll be left in the dark underground. The **Nohsngi Thiang (Seven Sisters) Falls,** the second highest in India, are a few meters off the main road past Mawsmai Village. Although the falls are amazing for most of the year, they dry up during the winter. Another 10km from here is the **Trop U Rambah,** an enormous rock that Hindus regard as the world's largest Shiva *linga*. Close by, **Thangkhang Park** is a popular picnic spot. The town of Mylliem, 13km from Shillong on the way to Cherapunjee, can be seen separately or as part of a daytrip to Cherrapunjee. About 150 Khasi households live here, and the families welcome the occasional foreigner.

TRIPURA ☎ 0381

The tiny state of Tripura is a narrow finger of land poking into Bangladesh. At the southwestern corner of Northeast India, the state is distinct from its neighbors, both historically and ethnically. The Manikya, the traditional rulers of Tripura, submitted to Mughal authority but regained and retained control of the state during the Raj. Tripura was a princely state until 1949, when it joined the Indian Union. Several ethnic groups continue to inhabit the state, but the majority of the population today is Bengali, and speaks Bengali (and, on occasion, Hindi). Tripura has several beautiful forests and wildlife sanctuaries, but development is threatening these precious ecological preserves. Most of the few tourists who visit Tripura are drawn by its cultural attractions, which are all close to one another.

Agartala, Tripura's capital, has few attractions of its own, but it is a good hub from which to see outlying sights. **Buses** connect Agartala with **Silchar** (12hr., Rs180) and continue to **Shillong** (18hr., Rs320) and **Guwahati** (24hr., Rs360). Buses leave at 6am and 12pm from Sagar Travels on Laximinarayan Rd. near the Palace. You can also **fly** out of the city to **Calcutta** (1hr.; M, W, Th, F, Su; US$55) and **Guwahati** (45min.; W, F, Su; US$50). The town is dominated by the **Ujjayanta Palace** at its center. This sprawling white structure was built in 1901 by Radhakishore Manikya and now houses the State Legislature. In the evening, the palace is lit by floodlights and features a "musical fountain," which is a regular fountain accompanied by a cassette player. (Open daily 5-7pm. Rs3.) At other times, the palace and its well-kept flower gardens are closed. Go to the back for the **Tripura Tourist Office.** (☎ 225930 or 223893. Open M-F 10am-4pm, Sa 3-5pm.) The staff can direct you to the **currency exchange** bureau and the **Bangladesh visa office,** near Circuit House and the Palace (☎ 224807; open M-F 10am-5pm). The fee is US$5-50 and is processed within a day. Agartala seems to have more hotels than tourists. Among the cheapest and best is **Hotel Sausastra ❶,** on HGB Rd. (☎ 225573. Singles Rs58; doubles with attached bath Rs116.) The nearby **Hotel Ambar ❶,** has a television and telephone in every room. (☎ 223587. Singles Rs88; doubles Rs165.) **Hotel Moonlight ❶,** serves a set vegetarian lunch (Rs22) and hosts a lively back-slapping crowd. A short rickshaw ride will take you to the Bangladeshi town of Akhaura. Frequent buses and two trains a day (2½hr., 12:20 and 6:30pm, taka130) leave for **Dhaka.** From Dhaka there are frequent buses to **Calcutta** (taka500).

The famed **Water Palace** at Neermahal is 53km south of Agartala. Built in 1930 as a summer resort for Bir Bikram Kishore Manikya, the palace is an exquisite example of Indo-Saracenic architecture. The red-and-white structure lies in the middle of a large lake. A **tourist lodge** and a few restaurants dot the shore, but the area is left blissfully deserted at night. Neermahal is 1km from Melaghar. Buses leave for **Melaghar** from Agartala's Battala bus stop on HGB Rd. (2hr., every 40min., Rs20). Temple aficionados might enjoy Matabari temple, near Udaipur. Buses, jeeps, and taxis leave the Battala stop for **Matabari** (1½hr., every 30min., Rs18).

OTHER NORTHEAST STATES. Manipur, Mizoram, Nagaland, and **Arunachal Pradesh** are unstable regions with little tourism. For those who wish to travel in these states, **permits must be obtained in Delhi.** These permits are obtainable from the **Ministry of Home Affairs** in Khan Market. (☎ 469 3334 or 461 2543. Open M-F 10:00am-noon). The officers, here, though, like to direct foreigners to the **Foreigners Registration Office,** 1st Fl., Hansa Bhavan, Tilak Marg, where after making you wait for a couple hours they are likely to laugh at the absurd suggestion that they might be able to issue a permit.

ORISSA ଓଡ଼ିଶା

In October 1999, the state of Orissa was ravaged by one of the worst cyclones ever to hit India. Over 10,000 people were killed. The people of Orissa have been rebuilding their lives, but the devastation was frightening, and the path to recovery will be a long and painful one.

The state's coastline stretches for almost 500km, and nearly all of Orissa's urban residents live within a stone's throw of the Mahanadi River Delta. Most of the rural population work in rice paddies; the rest can be found manning wooden fishing boats—a far cry from the maritime prowess of the Kalingas and other dynasties that once sent colonists as far away as Java. The thick forest cover of the Eastern Ghats has allowed the indigenous *adivasis* to survive relatively undisturbed.

Orissa has defended its independence for thousands of years. The Kalingas held out against the Mauryan Empire in the 3rd century BC, capitulating only after a battle so bloody that it convinced Emperor Ashoka to convert to Buddhism. Orissa withstood Muslim rule until 1568, long after surrounding regions had been conquered. The state's cultural autonomy has led to the development of distinctive art forms, including its glorious temple architecture and the *odissi* form of dance.

HIGHLIGHTS OF ORISSA

On the coast of the Bay of Bengal, **Puri** (p. 460) juggles dual roles as religious center and beach-side resort.

Temple-packed **Bhubaneswar** (below) showcases the unique beauty of the region's varied and intricate Hindu architecture.

Konark (p. 458), the third point of Orissa's "Golden Triangle" of tourism, is the site of the spectacular **Sun Temple** and a wonderfully tranquil beach.

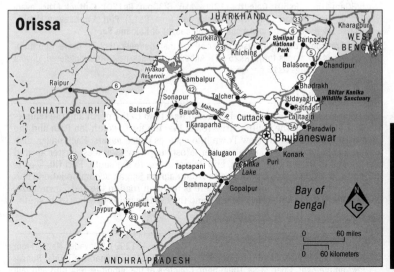

ORISSA

BHUBANESWAR ଭୁବନେଶ୍ୱର ☎ 0674

Bhubaneswar has one of the finest collection of Hindu temples in India, and its mighty *lingaraj* spire forms the apex of Orissa's "Golden Triangle." The city also has a Buddhist Peace Pagoda and a Jain temple, reflecting its other influences.

As the capital of the powerful maritime dynasties that ruled the Bay of Bengal, Bhubaneswar was the center of trade and commerce in the area now known as Orissa. Members of the Hindu ruling classes erected the finest devotional structures, and under their patronage, temple architecture grew into an art form. Under Muslim and British rule, however, neglect reduced many of the monuments to rubble. When Bhubaneswar became the capital of Orissa in 1950, it received a makeover; urban planners built monumental warrens along wide avenues. The preservation of the remaining temples became a religious and civic imperative. Today, the city exhibits both the outward characteristics of a modern state capital and the enduring spirit of the majestic kingdom that was classical Orissa.

▄ TRANSPORTATION

Flights: Bhubaneswar Airport (☎ 534472 or 534084). Southwest of the New Town. **Indian Airlines** (☎ 530533 or 530544). Gaputi Nagar. Off Raj Path just before the intersection with Sachivalaya Marg. Open daily 10am-1:15pm and 2-4:45pm. To: **Calcutta** (1hr.; 1 per day; US$90); **Chennai** (2½hr.; M, W, F, Su; US$205) via **Visakhapatnam** (1hr., US$125); **Delhi** (2hr., 1 per day, US$220); **Hyderabad** (1½hr.; Tu, Th, Sa; US$165); **Mumbai** (2hr.; Tu, Th, Sa; US$255).

Trains: Bhubaneswar Railway Station, Station Sq. (reservations ☎ 502042). To: **Calcutta** (8-13hr., 10-14 per day 4:20am-11pm, Rs154); **Chennai** (21-23hr., 2-4 per day 3:28am-10:53pm, Rs312); **Cuttack** (30min.-1hr., 12-14 per day 4:20am-10:15pm, Rs19); **Delhi** (31-42hr., 3-4 per day 8:15am-9:47pm, Rs374; *Rajdhani Express*, 25hr., W and Su 9:10am, Rs1725); **Hyderabad/Secunderabad** (21-24hr., 4 per day 7:25am-7:18pm, Rs286); **Puri** (2-3hr., 6-8 per day, Rs26).

Buses: Baramunda New Bus Station (☎ 526977). On NH5 5km west of the city center. To: **Balasore** (4hr., every 10min. 4:30am-10pm, Rs70); **Berhampur** (4hr., every 10min. 5:30am-10pm, Rs50); **Calcutta** (13hr.; 4, 6, 6:30pm; Rs120); **Cuttack** (1hr., every 10min.; Rs7); **Konark** (2hr., every 30min. 6am-5pm, Rs12); **Puri** (1½hr.; every 15min.; Rs18). Buses to nearby towns can also be caught at **Kalpana Sq.**

Local Transportation: Minibuses cover all the major streets (Rs2-3). **Cycle-** and **auto-rickshaws** zip across town (Rs25-50). Although auto-rickshaws are unmetered, drivers will usually charge Rs10 per km.

▄ ORIENTATION

Bhubaneswar consists of the well-planned **New Town** to the north and the temple-packed **Old Town** to the south. Large roads like the north-south **Jan Path** and the east-west **Raj Path** cut the New Town into squares called **nagars.** Each nagar, also called a **unit,** has a name and a number. Most shops and services cluster around **Station Sq.,** in front of the station, and **Rajmahal Sq.,** to the south. Puri Rd. (Lewis Rd.) and Vivekananda Marg run south from **Kalpana Sq.,** an accommodations hub in the southeast, to the Old Town. There is no main road in the Old Town maze, but the **Bindu Sagar** tank is at its center and the tall **Lingaraj Temple** lies to its south.

▄ PRACTICAL INFORMATION

Tourist Office: Government of Orissa Tourist Office (☎ 431299). 5 Jayadev Nagar. From Kalinga Sq., head south down Lewis Rd.; it's just past the Panthanivas Tourist Bungalow, on the right. Open M-Sa 10am-5pm. Counters at the airport (☎ 534006) and railway station (☎530715) are open 24hr. **OTDC** (☎432282), behind the Panthanivas, arranges cheap tours of Bhubaneswar, Puri, and Konark. **Government of India Tourist Office** (☎432203). B-21 BJB Nagar. From the railway station, take the last left before the fork that leads to Puri Rd.; it's on a side road 750m down on the right. Open M-F 9am-6pm, Sa 9am-1pm.

Currency Exchange: State Bank of India (☎533671). Main Branch, Raj Path. Near Raj Mahal Sq., opposite Capital Market. Open M-F 11am-3:30pm, Sa 10:30am-12:30pm.

Pharmacy: Rabindra Medical Hall (☎531028). Raj Mahal Bldg., Gautam Nagar. In the complex at the southeast corner of Raj Mahal Sq., on the side facing Raj Path. Open daily 8:30am-10:30pm. **Capital Hospital's** pharmacy is open 24hr.

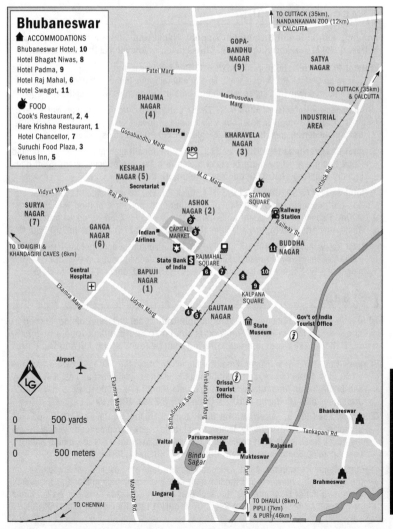

Bhubaneswar

▲ ACCOMMODATIONS
Bhubaneswar Hotel, **10**
Hotel Bhagat Niwas, **8**
Hotel Padma, **9**
Hotel Raj Mahal, **6**
Hotel Swagat, **11**

🍴 FOOD
Cook's Restaurant, **2, 4**
Hare Krishna Restaurant, **1**
Hotel Chancellor, **7**
Suruchi Food Plaza, **3**
Venus Inn, **5**

TO CUTTACK (35km),
NANDANKANAN ZOO (12km)
& CALCUTTA

GOPA-BANDHU NAGAR (9)

SATYA NAGAR

Patel Marg

BHAUMA NAGAR (4)

Madhusudan Marg

TO CUTTACK (35km)
& CALCUTTA

INDUSTRIAL AREA

Gopabandhu Marg

Library

KHARAVELA NAGAR (3)

GPO

KESHARI NAGAR (5)

M.G. Marg

Secretariat

Vidyut Marg

Raj Path

ASHOK NAGAR (2)

STATION SQUARE

Cuttack Rd.

SURYA NAGAR (7)

GANGA NAGAR (6)

Indian Airlines

CAPITAL MARKET

Railway Station

Railway St.

TO UDAIGIRI &
KHANDAGIRI CAVES (6km)

State Bank of India

RAJMAHAL SQUARE

BUDDHA NAGAR

Central Hospital

BAPUJI NAGAR (1)

Ekamra Marg

Udyan Marg

KALPANA SQUARE

GAUTAM NAGAR

State Museum

Gov't of India Tourist Office

Airport

Ekamra Marg

Vivekananda Marg

Orissa Tourist Office

Lewis Rd.

Bhaskareswar

0   500 yards

0   500 meters

Barhabanda Sahi

Tankapani Rd.

Vaital

Parsurameswar

Rajarani

Bindu Sagar

Mukteswar

Brahmeswar

Lingaraj

Mahatab Rd.

Puri Rd.

TO DHAULI (8km),
PIPLI (7km)
& PURI (46km)

TO CHENNAI

Hospital: Capital Hospital (☎ 400688 or 401983). Unit 6, Ganga Nagar. From Raj Mahal Sq., go south on Jan Path; after 1 block, turn right (west) on Udyan Marg and continue past Sachivalaya Marg; to the left is the 24hr. government hospital. **Ayurvedic Hospital** (☎ 432347). Malisha Sq. Opposite the Rameswar Temple, 200m east of Vivekananda Marg, on the left.

Internet: Hi-Tech Cyber Café (☎ 539777). 137-6 Ashok Nagar. Head north up Jan Path from Raj Mahal Sq.; it's 100m on the right, upstairs. Internet (Rs15 per hr.) with A/C, ice cream, and cold drinks. Open daily 8am-11pm.

Post Office: GPO (☎ 402132). PMG Sq. From Station Sq., go northwest on MG Marg. It's at the intersection with Sachivalay Marg. Open daily 10am-6pm. **Postal Code:** 751001.

ACCOMMODATIONS

Lodging can be found throughout Buddha Nagar and Gautam Nagar, especially between Raj Mahal and Kalpana Sq. Those listed below have 24hr. check-out.

▨ **Hotel Padma** (☎ 416626 or 416628). 67 Buddha Nagar, Kalpana Sq. On your left as you go up Cuttack Rd. A long, white ship of a hotel with a friendly staff, spacious rooms, and a rooftop garden. Singles with shared bath Rs70; doubles with bath Rs200-250. ❶

Bhubaneswar Hotel (☎ 313245 or 313246). Cuttack Rd. Just past Swagat. Not as fancy as it looks, this popular hotel has well-appointed rooms served by friendly bell-hops. Restaurant serves great breakfasts. Singles Rs150-300; doubles Rs200-400. ❶

Hotel Bhagat Niwas (☎ 311345 or 313708). 9 Buddha Nagar. In Kalpana Sq., behind Hotel Padma. A yellow maze of small rooms with TVs and attached bath. Staff does laundry. Singles Rs120-160; doubles Rs250-650. ❶

Hotel Swagat (☎ 312686 or 311934). Cuttack Rd. Exit the east side of the railway station (not the main exit facing Station Sq.), turn right, and look for it on your right after 200m. Decent rooms, decent prices and room service that brings drinks until 10pm. Restaurant attached (open daily 8am-10pm). Singles Rs175; doubles Rs200-550. ❶

Hotel Raj Mahal (☎ 532448). Raj Mahal Sq. At the southeast corner of Jan Path and Raj Path. Airy hallways lead to large, cool rooms with attached bath and the sound of your neighbor's TV. Some have balconies. Singles Rs150-200; doubles Rs250-600. ❶

FOOD

Bhubaneswar is the perfect place to sample traditional Orissan cuisine, served in small *ginas* on large *thalis*. The food is similar to South Indian food, but toned-down. Delicious veg. and non-veg. offerings can be found along Jan and Raj Paths.

▨ **Venus Inn,** 217 Bapuj, Nagar. From Raj Mahal Sq., take the 2nd right before the train tracks; it is 400m further, on the left. One of Bhubaneswar's oldest and its best for veg. and South Indian food. Classy decor, A/C, and Hindi beats. Butter cheese *kofta* Rs30, *uttappams* Rs9-16, *dosas* Rs10-25. Open daily 6:30am-10pm. ❶

▨ **Suruchi Food Plaza,** Eastern Market Bldg., Capital Market, off Raj Path. Dark and cool but full of hot, mouth-watering dishes, the plaza is highly recommended by locals; even the house *lassi*, a blend of berries and nuts, is a culinary treat (Rs20). Indian and Chinese upstairs, South Indian below. Open daily 7:30am-11:30pm. ❶

Hare Krishna Restaurant, 1st fl., Lalchand Market, Jan Path, just north of Station Sq., on the right. Posh, shiny, low-lit establishment with a very serious atmosphere. The menu, though, is full of tasty interpretations of Braj country "delights" and the playful lord's "favorites." All veg. Entrees from Rs45. Open daily 11am-3pm and 7-10pm. ❶

Cook's Kitchen/Restaurant, 260 Bapuji Nagar. Head south on Jan Path from Station Sq. and take the third left past Raj Mahal Sq. Street-side kitchen has curries (from Rs18). The "culinary people" of the A/C restaurant (1st fl. of Blue Heaven Hotel) serve a variety of dishes. Open daily 10:30am-10:30pm. ❶

Hotel Chancellor, Buddha Nagar, down off Raj Path between Raj Mahal Sq. and the railway crossing. Basic, open-air restaurant always packed with locals. Wall-mounted menu has the usual Indian fare in half and full plates. Open daily noon-4pm and 7-11pm.

🔘 SIGHTS

It is said that there are more ancient temples in Orissa than in the rest of North India put together. Puri and Konark have more famous and monumental temples, but for sheer numbers, Bhubaneswar is the place to be. Carved between the 7th and 12th centuries AD, the sculptures tell the story of Hinduism's resurgence—the frequent depiction of a lion pouncing on an elephant represents Hinduism's triumph over Buddhism. Lakulisa, a 5th-century Shaivite saint who converted many Orissans, also appears on temple walls. Most of Bhubaneswar's temples are dedicated to Shiva, whose cult remains an important part of the lives of many of the region's inhabitants. The temples, in the middle of the Old Town around Bindu Sagar, can be explored in a few hours. Guides prowl the temples soliciting customers; ignore them. Certified guides can be hired from the state tourism office. Be wary of the men with a "temple register" listing foreign contributions—it's a scam. The temples are all are open from dawn to dusk, with the exception of the Lingaraj temple (see below).

LINGARAJ TEMPLE. The Lingaraj is one of Orissa's great temples, notable for the balanced placement of sculpture on its 45m spire. Completed around 1100, it has a four-chambered temple structure: a sanctuary (under the spire), a porch, a dance hall, and an offering hall. Shiva is worshiped here in the form of Tribhubaneswar (Lord of Three Worlds), hence the city's name. Devotional songs have been sung here since the temple was built. The compound contains ornate stonework as well—more than 50 smaller temples surround the main one. The second-largest temple in the compound, to the right in front of the main temple, is devoted to Shiva's consort, Parvati. The compound is closed to non-Hindus, but the British built a viewing platform right next to the North wall. *(Open 6am-3pm and 6-9:30pm.)*

PARSURAMESWAR TEMPLE. The oldest and one of the best-preserved of Bhubaneswar's temples, the 7th-century Parsurameswar Temple exhibits many of the features characteristic of earlier Orissan temples, including a small, squat *shikhara* and an uncarved roof over the porch. Standing sentinel on the left side of the rear entrance, is a *linga* with 1000 other tiny *lingas* carved into it. *(From the New Town, turn down the road to the left just before the Bindu Sagar; the temple is on the left not far from here. Photography is not permitted.)*

MUKTESWAR TEMPLE. In contrast to its elder neighbor Parsurameswar, the Mukteswar Temple is a series of small monuments. The complex features a U-shaped archway, an evolutionary link between the first and second phases of Orissan temples, and plenty of intricate sculpture. On the exterior, monkeys are shown doing monkey things—riding crocodiles, picking lice, and falling into the clutches of crabs. Ornate and well-preserved, Mukteswar is considered "The Gem of Orissan Architecture." *(On the left, near the Parsurameswar Temple.)*

KEDARESWAR TEMPLE. Opposite the Mukteswar Temple, the white-washed **Kedareswar** is the most active temple in Bhubaneswar after the Lingaraj.

RAJARANI TEMPLE. Originally named for the *raja* (red) and *rani* (yellow) stones from which it was built, this now-defunct 11th-century temple is looked after by the Archaeological Survey of India. The temple is famous for its *shikhara*, built with miniature temple spires clustered around the main tower. Though common in other parts of India, this style is rare in Orissa. Even stranger, the temple lacks a presiding deity. For those who brave the high entrance fee, *nayikas* show women looking in the mirror, playing instruments, and, of course, engaging in amorous play. *(Up Puri Rd. behind the Mukteswar Temple, then a right on Tankapani Rd.; after 100m you'll see the temple on the right, at the back of a rectangular park. Foreigner entrance fee US$5.)*

BHASKARESWAR AND BRAHMESWAR TEMPLES. The chunky **Bhaskareswar Temple** is no artistic triumph, but it does contain a 3m high *linga* encased in what is thought to be an Ashokan column from the 3rd century BC. Wander down a lane to the right after the Bhaskareswar Temple to the 9th-century **Brahmeswar Temple.** The temple walls are carved in standard Orissan fashion and proportions, making it seem like a miniature version of the Lingaraj Temple. The temple has smaller Shiva shrines at the four corners of its compound. *(A short rickshaw ride down Tankapani Rd., 1km past the pretty sewage canal.)*

VAITAL TEMPLE. The Vaital Temple, sunk in the ground at a crossroads on the western side of the Bindu Sagar, has unique style. Its oblong, barrel-shaped *shikhara* betrays a Buddhist influence, although local priests will insist that Vaital resembles a ship. Take a light with you inside to illuminate scenes of human sacrifice and gory tantric carvings, depicting the skull-clad goddess Chamunda with her attendant owl and jackal. Beside the Vaital Temple is the **Sisireswar Temple,** a near-duplicate of the nearby **Markandeswar Temple.** In both temples, images were carved directly into the walls, a technique that was later discontinued.

BINDU SAGAR. Central to the city's religious life is this Old Town landmark, a large green tank at the foot of Vivekananda Marg. The waters of the Bindu Sagar (Ocean-Drop Tank) are believed to contain droplets from all of India's holy pools and streams. Early-morning bathers come here to take advantage of the blessings the waters bestow. Every April during Bhubaneswar's Car Festival, the Lingaraj's image of Lord Tribhubaneswar comes to the tank for his own ritual washing.

MUSEUM. The **State Museum** contains a collection of palm leaf manuscripts and Orissan musical instruments, as well as ethnographic exhibits on Orissa's indigenous peoples. *(Puri Rd., close to Kalpana Sq. Open Tu-Su 10am-1pm and 2-4pm. Rs2.)*

▶ DAYTRIPS FROM BHUBANESWAR

UDAIGIRI AND KHANDAGIRI CAVES
Auto-rickshaws from Bhubaneswar Rs70. Caves open daily 8am-6pm. US$5.

More vestiges of antiquity can be found at the Udaigiri and Khandagiri Caves, 6km west of Bhubaneswar, less than 1km off NH5 past Baramunda Bus Station. Cut into the hillside are 33 niches that functioned as retreats for Jain ascetics during the 1st and 2nd centuries BC. King Kharavela of the Kalinga Dynasty also took refuge here after the Kalinga War at Dhauli. A road now divides the Udaigiri caves (on the right) from the Khandagiri caves (on the left). An explanation of the carvings and paintings is in the "Inscription of Kharavela" at Udaigiri, near Cave 12.

The best sculptures are found in and around Cave 1 at Udaigiri, otherwise known as **Rani Gumpha** (Queen's Cave). Originally 10 stories high, the cave now has only 2 stories; the rest were wiped out by earthquakes. The central area of the first floor contains hiding places once used by the king and his ministers. Large holes in the ceiling served as communication channels, air tunnels, and water drains. Intricate carvings inside the caves depict the marriage of the gods. Cave 12 is carved as the gaping mouth of a tiger, and a triple-hooded snake decorates the facade of Cave 13. Cave 14, the **Hathi Gumpha** (Elephant Cave), has a ceiling inscription from the reign of King Kharavela of the Chedi Dynasty, the greatest of Kalinga kings and patron of the caves. Images from Jain legends, mythology, and iconography decorate **Rani Nur** and **Ganesh Gumpha** (Cave 10).

Though the caves of Khandagiri are not as well-carved, nor as well-maintained, they do house an old temple with 26 *sadhus* and 26 goddesses carved in two rows. This temple is still an active religious center; the *pundits* are friendly, but beware of their fanatical pursuit of donations. An active **Jain temple** at the top of the hill offers fantastic views over Bhubaneswar. On a clear day, you can spot the Lingaraj Temple and Dhauli Hill. The best-preserved carvings at Khandagiri are in **Cave 3.** Only a few of the caves are fenced, so climb inside for some monkish meditation. Just make sure your niche of choice is not already occupied by the caves' more regular visitors: hungry, all-too-common langorous and romancing Bhubaneswar teenagers. If you're interested in the caves' history, hire a certified guide (Rs60).

DHAULI
You can visit Dhauli as part of an ODTC guided bus tour. Auto-rickshaws cost Rs100 round-trip; buses (Rs4) drop you off 3km from the hill. Open daily 5am-8pm. Free.

The hill of Dhauli (also known as Dhauligiri), 8km south of Bhubaneswar on the Puri road, is Orissa's greatest historical claim to fame. In a horrific battle here in 261 BC, the Mauryan emperor Ashoka the Terrible defeated his foes and claimed victory in the Great Kalinga War. But profoundly appalled by the bloodshed—the Daya River was running red—he renounced violence forever, converted to Buddhism, and changed his surname to "the Righteous." A long-winded rock edict in Brahmi script at the foot of Dhauli Hill explains Ashoka's new theory of governance according to the principle of *dharma* (an English translation is posted near these inscriptions). In the rock above is one of India's earliest rock cuts–a simple head of an elephant commemorating the emperor's conversion. On the summit of Dhauli hill, affording fantastic views of Bhubaneswar and the sandy River Durga, is the **Shanti Stupa** (Peace Pagoda), built in 1974 by the same team of Japanese Buddhists who created the almost identical *stupas* in Vaishali and Lumbini.

NANDANKAN ZOOLOGICAL PARK
Buses from Bhubaneswar cost Rs5 for the 1hr. trip; auto-rickshaws Rs120 each way. Open daily 7:30am-5pm. Rs40, vehicles Rs30.

This zoo and wildlife park, in a vast expanse of the Chandaka forest, has a huge collection of animals from all over the world. But the gardens are best known for their successful breeding of rare local specifics such as white tigers, gharials, and white peacocks. Fame turned to shame in July 2000, when several of its prized Bengal white tigers died under mysterious circumstances. Most animals are squeezed into cages and artificial ponds, although several of the larger animals roam the attached preserve. A single, bored lion thrills the locales on the **bus safari** (Rs6), paddleboats take you around the large, artificial lake (Rs15), a toy train (Rs22) makes a loop through the park, and a ropeway (Rs22) rides above it. Guides are neither necessary nor helpful.

ORISSA

KONARK ଚକାଶାର୍କ   ☎ 06758

On this isolated stretch of Orissan coastline, life revolves completely around its glorious temple to the sun god Surya. Beginning at first light, tourists stream off buses to catch a glimpse of the temple, only rediscovered in the early 20th century. Even in its present dilapidated state, the chariot-shaped shrine still stands as one of India's greatest architectural and sculptural marvels. The adjacent "village" is a tiny collection of hotels and *dhabas*, but it is well worth an overnight stay here, for it becomes quiet once the daytrippers leave. The town is also very popular for its annual **Odissi Dance Festival,** held around early December.

➍ ▨ ORIENTATION AND PRACTICAL INFORMATION

Curiously, Konark's street plan resembles a setting sun on the horizon. The semi-circular arch is the main street, which contains the temple entrance and the town's few shops; the left horizon line is the road to Bhubaneswar; the right is the tree-lined Marine Rd. to Puri, which passes beautiful, deserted beaches along the way; the Sun Temple sits in the middle of the semi-circle. **Buses** depart from the inter-section halfway between Yatri Nivas and the temple entrance. To **Bhubaneswar** (3hr., every 30min. 5am-5:30pm, Rs18) and **Puri** (1hr., every 15min. 7am-8pm, Rs9). Labanya Lodge rents **bikes** (Rs25), and the **Orissa State Tourism Office,** inside the Yatri Nivas, can arrange for **taxis.** (☎ 36821. Open M-Sa 10am-5pm.) **Richa Cyber Dhaba** has Internet (Rs60 per hr.) as well as STD/ISD phones. (☎ 36745. Open 6am-11pm.) **Canara Bank,** just past Sun Temple Hotel, changes traveler's checks. (☎ 36825. Open M-F 10am-2pm, Sa 10am-noon.) **Police:** ☎ 35825. The **post office** is next to Geetanjali Restaurant. (Open M-Sa 9am-5pm.) **Postal Code:** 75211.

▨ ▢ ACCOMMODATIONS AND FOOD

The laid-back **Labanya Lodge ❶,** just out of town on the road to Puri, is a pink and teal palm-tree-filled bungalow popular with backpackers. (☎ 36824 or 36860. Singles Rs50; doubles with bath Rs75-150.) Orissa Tourism's **Yatri Nivas ❶,** next to the museum, has immaculate rooms, well-trimmed garden-court-yards, and a stern institutional atmosphere. (☎ 36820. Doubles Rs150-325.) **Bijaya Lodge ❶,** on the junction with the road to Puri, has dark rooms. It's cheap, and you get little more than you pay for. (☎ 36478. Doubles with bath Rs50-100.) A decent meal can be found at the "ancient" **Sun Temple Hotel ❶,** just past the bank, on the right. (Entrees under Rs55. Open daily 7am-10pm.) **Sharma Mawadi Hotel ❶,** a little farther down towards the temple entrance, is an all-veg. eatery with a variety of slow-cooked but tasty *thalis* for Rs23-51. (Open daily 7am-10pm.) The pyramid-capped **Geetanjali Restaurant,** next to the Panthanivas, has cheap breakfasts. (Open daily 6am-10pm.)

◔ SIGHTS

THE SUN TEMPLE

The ticket booth is up to the left of the gated entrance. Another entrance to the grounds, the next left after the Archaeological Museum, brings you to the outer wall of the complex, but you still have to walk around to the booth to pay. Open dawn-dusk. US$10.

Konark's Sun Temple, dedicated to the sun god Surya, is built in the form of a huge chariot, Surya's heavenly vehicle. With its intricate carvings, erotic imag-ery, and grand design, it is possibly the most impressive example of Orissan temple architecture anywhere. Originally sitting on the shoreline (it is now more than 3km from the sea), the temple was used as a navigational aid by European sailors, who called it the "Black Pagoda" to distinguish it from Puri's similar but white Jaggannath Temple (see p. 463). There has been a Surya temple in Konark as far back as the 9th century AD, but most of the existing structure dates from 400 years later, the time of Narasimha Deva I. Victim to centuries of pillagers and the weathering effects of nature, the crumbling temple is now preserved as an archaeological site and remains the central feature in the geographic—and economic—landscape of the area. Every year the ruins serve as backdrop to the **Konark Festival** (Dec. 1-5, 2002), an open-air celebration featuring renowned Odissi dances. Half the town, it seems, freelances as "guides" to the temple's racy iconography, while the other half hawks trinkets from the street-side stalls surrounding the temple's entrance.

NATAMANDIRA AND JAGAMOHAN. Upon entering the walled compound, the first visible structure is the *natamandira* (dance or festival hall), a pillared platform decorated with carvings of Odissi dance poses and flanked by two *gajasimhas*, the motif of a Hindu lion mounting a Buddhist elephant and trampling the desires of men. Beyond rises the staggering step-pyramid of the *jagamohan* (porch or assembly hall), the temple's most prominent feature at over 50m high. The porch's east-facing door was designed to catch the light of the rising sun and to reflect it into the sanctuary. To prevent the porch from collapsing, it was filled with concrete and sand in 1904, thus blocking the sanctuary's usual entrance.

PLATFORM AND PORCH. The *jagamohan* and the sanctuary are mounted on a heavily ornamented platform. Carved as a mythical chariot, the platform contains 24 giant wheels (representing the fortnights of the year) and is driven by seven horses (symbolic of the light spectrum) on the sides of the eastern staircases. (This chariot-wheel motif is regularly incorporated into the facades of contemporary Orissan buildings.) Images decorating the clock-like spokes of the wheels follow the progress of a typical day. Looking at the fourth wheel on the southern side, the first four spokes depict a woman bathing and performing housework, while the last four spokes—the nighttime hours—show her making love to her husband.

The carvings on the *jagamohan*, conceived to reflect the entirety of the world, are divided into three levels whose heights correspond to the age of their intended audience: G-rated animal parades line the platform's bottom edge, erotic images above entice the imaginations of young men and women, and slightly more pious, mature images fill the highest tier. Close inspection of the masterful friezes reveals a depiction of a giraffe, a naughty priest, and some new ideas for bedtime.

SANCTUARY. Behind the porch, steps lead up to the exterior of the sanctuary and three beautiful images of Surya on the southern, western, and northern sides, showing his increasing fatigue as he makes his daily run. Two modern staircases lead from the statues down to the remains of the sanctuary itself. Considering the breathtaking appearance of the sun temple as a whole, the sanctuary is rather plain. The Surya statue that once presided here no longer exists, and archaeologists can only speculate about its design. Some tour guides claim that the statue floated in the air, suspended by powerful magnets. It seems more likely that it rested on the chlorite pedestal that still exists. The frieze on the eastern side of the pedestal shows King Narasimha and his queen. The northern and southern faces portray the retinues of the king and queen respectively.

MAYADEVI TEMPLE. Behind the sanctuary of the Sun Temple are the remains of a **Mayadevi Temple.** Now considered to be an earlier Surya temple, the small sanctuary and porch may have housed an image of one of Surya's wives once the main temple was built. More intricate, racy sculpture decorates the exterior.

OTHER SIGHTS

NINE PLANETS SHRINE (NAVAGRAHA). A six-meter-long, black marble mono-lith, exquisitely carved with the faces of the nine planets, used to rest above the eastern entrance to the *jagamohana*. The British cut it in half in an unsuccessful attempt to move it to a museum. Now the slab sits in a shed near the northeastern corner of the compound and is a center of local worship.

ARCHAEOLOGICAL MUSEUM. Sculptures from the temple were scattered about the site by successive waves of plunderers and collectors. Some of the finest fragments—cleaned, polished, and reconstructed—are now on display in the Archaeological Museum. (Other fragments from the temple's sculptures are kept in the Indian Museum in Calcutta and the Victoria and Albert Museum in London.) The museum also sells the Archaeological Survey's informative guide to the Sun Temple for Rs50. *(Just past the Yatri Nivas. Open Sa-Th 10am-5pm. Rs5.)*

🌊 BEACHES

Three kilometers down the road to Puri, the legendary Chandrabhaga (a water-hole where the original Surya image for the first Sun Temple was found) and a small fishing village give way to vacant expanses of white sand and endless sea. Beautiful and unspoiled, the beaches stretch for miles—however, gaping at the scenery is all you can really do, as **the fast currents and uneven sea bed make it dangerous for swimmers.**

PURI ପୁରୀ   ☎ 06752

Despite the multitudes who have descended upon its shores throughout the ages, the small, quiet beach town of Puri still remains very much a pilgrim's paradise. As one of the four holy *dhams* of India, Puri and its skyline are dominated by the immense Jaggannath temple, dedicated to the Lord of the Universe as his "place of eating." Under the temple's shadow, miles of white beach lure small armies of vacationers from landlocked cities all over India. Moreover, in the 1960s and 1970s, Puri's permissive attitudes (and plentiful supply of drugs) made it a popular stop along India's well-established hippie trail. Today, three distinct varieties of visitors haunt Puri, each claiming a section of town as their hangout and rarely intermingling. Hindu pilgrims tend to occupy the moral high ground up by the Jagganath Temple (closed to non-Hindus) and the eight *dharamsalas* that line the Baba Danda (Grand Rd.); Indians on holiday or honeymoon overpopulate the busy downtown boardwalk area; and middle-aged men, youthful Japanese, and other international characters mellow out in the emptier, wallet-friendly eastern portion. Besides the local deities, the city's most regular residents are probably the friendly, hardworking fishermen, still farming the seas in boats from a bygone era.

🚌 TRANSPORTATION

Trains: Puri Railway Station, Station Rd. and Hospital Rd. To **Calcutta** (11½hr.; 7 and 9:15pm; Rs145) and **Delhi** (32-43½hr.; 3 per day 9:05am-8:15pm; Rs380). There are regular trains to **Bhubaneswar** (2hr.; Rs26), but the bus is more convenient.

Buses: New Bus Stand, at the east end of Grand Rd., next to the Guchinda temple. To: **Bhubaneswar** (2hr.; every 30min. 5am-5pm; Rs18); **Calcutta** (16hr.; 6am; Rs180); **Cuttack** (3½hr.; every 30min. 5am-5pm; Rs25); **Konark** (1hr.; every 15min. 7am-7pm; Rs10). Numerous **private companies** operate interstate buses; tour agencies and hotel desks make arrangements.

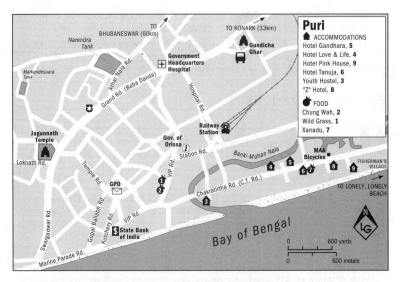

Puri

🏠 ACCOMMODATIONS
Hotel Gandhara, **5**
Hotel Love & Life, **4**
Hotel Pink House, **9**
Hotel Tanuja, **6**
Youth Hostel, **3**
"Z" Hotel, **8**

🍎 FOOD
Chung Wah, **2**
Wild Grass, **1**
Xanadu, **7**

Local Transportation: Unrushed **cycle-** and **auto-rickshaws** pedal and hoot their way from one corner of Puri to another for less than Rs20—the going rate is Rs5 per km; expect to be charged more. **Local buses** (under Rs5) are often in poor condition. One useful route runs from the New Bus Stand to the Jaggannath Temple, to the beach, and back (Rs3). **Maa Unique,** just past "2" hotel on the inland side of Ct Rd., rents bicycles (Rs15 per day), mopeds (Rs150 per day), and a variety of motorcycles (Rs150-250 per day). Deposit, payment, and license required. Open daily 7:30am-9pm.

✈ 🛈 ORIENTATION AND PRACTICAL INFORMATION

Puri's extra-wide main drag, **Grand Avenue**, runs east-west through the northern (inland) part of town, arching southwest near the **Jaggannath Temple** to become **Swargardwar Rd.** The Bay of Bengal forms the town's southern border. Along the shore, **Chakratirtha (CT) Rd.** has a number of budget hotels and restaurants catering to foreigners. As it heads west, CT Rd. intersects with **VIP Rd.** and eventually becomes **Marine Parade Rd.**, a seaside strip most popular with vacationing Indians.

Tourist Office: Government of Orissa Tourist Office (☎22664). Station Rd. From the railway station, follow Station Rd. west for 200m. The office is on the right just before VIP Rd. Open M-Sa 10am-5pm. They run a more helpful counter in the station as well (☎23536). Open daily 8am-8pm.

Currency Exchange: State Bank of India (☎23995 or 23682). VIP Rd. From the station, head west on Station Rd., turn left onto VIP Rd., then right at the Chandra Bose statue; it is 400m down on the left, just before Kutchery Rd. Open M-F 10am-2pm and 2:30-3:30pm, Sa 10am-12:30pm. **Hotel Gandhara** changes traveler's checks for a fee. Open M-Sa 8am-8pm, Su 8am-2pm.

Police: Town Police Station (☎24059). Grand Rd., near Jaggannath Temple. Control room open 24hr. **City Beach Police** (☎22025, emergency 100).

Hospital: Government Headquarters Hospital (☎23742). Grand Rd. Most hotels have doctors on call. **Emergency:** ☎22094.

ORISSA

Internet: Nanako Tour and Travels (☎29696). CT Rd. Internet Rs50 per hr. Open daily 8:30am-11:30pm. Many other Ct. Rd. establishments also have connections.

Post Office: GPO (☎22051). Kutchery Rd. From CT Rd., walk west past the Bose statue and turn right after the State Bank of India. Go north on Kutchery Rd.; the GPO is on the first street to the left. Open M-Sa 9am-6pm, Su 3-5:30pm. **Postal Code:** 752001.

ACCOMMODATIONS

> **! WARNING.** Rickshaw-*wallahs* play a commission game with some hotel owners, who kick back up to 50% of the rent—ignore their claims that the hotel you are looking for is closed, full, very expensive, or has changed its name.

Budget accommodations (including those listed below) are all located along the length of CT. Rd., becoming more concentrated at its eastern end. Most have early morning checkouts, no-guest policies, and loosely enforced curfews. Most hotels on Marine Parade Dr. cater exclusively to Indian tourists.

"Z" Hotel (☎22554). East of Hotel Gandhara, diagonally across from Mickey Mouse. Large and airy, "Z' (pronounced "zed") was once the home of the Maharaja of Puri. Hints of luxury are still found with the sea-view rooms and sprawling courtyard. Staff managed by a former chief minister of Orissa. Excellent cook and 24hr. room service. Beach access. Dorms (women only) Rs60; singles Rs150; doubles Rs200-400. ●

Hotel Gandhara (☎24117). 700m down CT Rd., just beyond Hotel Love & Life, opposite a path to the beach. The 19th-century bungalow in front contains a dorm and some budget rooms; the 5-story bldg. behind is pricier. Smart and well-run, with a travel agency, garden and restaurant serving Japanese food for Rs100. Check-out 9am. Dorms Rs40-50; singles Rs110; doubles Rs150-750. AmEx/V. ●

Hotel Pink House (☎22253). At the end of the beach access alley, 50m past "Z." With a location and prices that can't be beat, this ultra-budget cottage offers cheap views of the Bay of Bengal. Slightly run down rooms open onto the beach, making for beautiful sunrises, sedate evenings, and sandy floors. Constant sea breeze means mosquito defense is "unnecessary." Transportation and dining options. Doubles Rs80-150. ●

Hotel Love & Life (☎24433; fax 26093). Next to Hotel Gandhara. A long-time favorite with travelers. Less romantic—but just as relaxed—as the name suggests. Dorms Rs30; singles Rs80-125; doubles Rs100-250; cottages (double occupancy) Rs200-250. ●

Hotel Tanuja (☎20717). Just down the road from Gandhara, on the beach side of CT Rd. Alcohol, smoking, and visitors are allowed in the rooms—what more could you want? How about mosquito nets, a TV room, laundry service, in-house postal service, and a tribal tour agency? Rooms Rs60-70, with attached bath Rs100-350. ●

Youth Hostel (☎22424). On the right, 100m past the sewage stream. A large concrete block rising out of the sands, the hostel has all the usual institutional comforts, cleanliness, and conduct codes. Check-out 8am. Dorms Rs40, members Rs20. ●

FOOD

Food in Puri is cheap and tailor-made for foreign tourists, with a wide array of non-Indian options on CT Rd. Fish (and lobster) is as fresh as you'd expect it to be.

"Z" Hotel Restaurant. The kitchen staff does a superlative job of cooking up a spicy fish curry (Rs40). The *navaratan* (Rs30) and *aloo dum* (Rs15) are outstanding, and the beer (Rs70) always chilled. Bring insect repellent. Open daily 7am-3pm and 6-10:30pm. ❶

Hotel Pink House Restaurant, next to the hotel. Open-air thatched hut with a Hindu Bob Marley mural, a superb stereo system, and a sea-breezin', wave-crashin' ocean just outside. International menu includes *thalis* (Rs24-40) and seafood. Open 7am-11pm. ❶

Xanadu, CT Rd., about 75m past Hotel Gandhara. This little shack-and-garden makes pretty much anything you could want. Polite service, mosquito coils, and Madonna tunes included. Breakfast with baked beans Rs65. Open daily 7am-11pm. ❶

Chung Wah, VIP Rd. Head west on CT Rd. then right on VIP Rd., about 150m down on the left. Clean, cool, and the most authentic Chinese grub in Orissa. Veg. dishes Rs25-50, garlic fish Rs85. Open daily 11:30am-3pm and 6:30-10:30pm. ❶

Wild Grass, VIP Rd., around the corner from Chung Wah. Orissan sculpture and plenty of jungle all around—kind of hokey, but fun. Slightly pricey Chinese, Indian, and seafood (Rs50-120). Eat in your choice of tree-house or hut. Open daily 11:30am-11:30pm. ❷

◎ SIGHTS

JAGGANNATH TEMPLE. Constructed in the early 12th century by the Ganga king Anantavaram Chodaganga, the Jaggannath Temple is one of the most stunning examples of Kalinga-style temple architecture and one of the holiest sites in Orissa. With its central *viman* rising to a height of 65m, it is the main feature of Puri's skyline, the visible destination of many a pilgrim's journey, and a symbol of the power Jaggannath, Lord of the Universe, continues to wield over the town below. Also observable from many miles out at sea, the white, sandstone temple is sometimes referred to as the "white pagoda," a name given by British sailors who used it as a navigational point.

Inside the tower, the mighty lord (a form of Krishna), his brother Balabhadra, and his sister Subhadra reside in roughly-hewn, abstract, wooden bodies. Tiny arms extend from stumpy, legless abdomens; enormous eyes glare out from the disproportionately large faces. It is said that Lord Jaggannath has no eyelids, so that he can continually look after the well-being of the world; his small arms stretch outward in a gesture of love. Temple priests cite ancient myths to explain the peculiarly shaped forms—the peeking eyes of a king's wife prevented the architect from finishing his work—while academics suggest that the deities have their origins in the cults of Orissa's indigenous people. Some 6000 priests attend to the divine trinity, performing an elaborate set of daily activities that include bathing, feeding, dressing (five different changes), and brushing teeth. Every 12-19 years the pampered images are carved anew from specially chosen trees.

Patterned on the same architectural principles as the older Lingaraj Temple in Bhubaneswar, Jaggannath's abode is strictly aligned from east to west and completely surrounded by a 20m high wall. There is an entrance at each compass point, but the eastern **simbhadwara** (lion gate), off Grand Rd., sees most of the temple's traffic. The *bhog mandap* (offering hall) and *nritya mandap* (dance hall) nearest to the entrance were 15th- and 16th-century additions to the original *jagamohana* (assembly hall). These halls and their white, pyramidal roofs lead up to the flag-and-wheel-crowned *deul* (inner sanctuary), the divine trio's resting-place. Protected by a second wall and raised on a platform, the centermost structures were originally surrounded by water and accessible only by boat. Over the years, the moat was filled in to make the structure more stable and better protected from the cyclones that sweep in from the Bay of Bengal.

ORISSA

A TOUR OF THE UNIVERSE
Sweating, singing, shouting, and praying, exuberant crowds move en masse to enact an event of cosmic proportions. Though the **Rath Yatra** (Cart Festival) of Puri is celebrated two days after the new moon in the month of Ashadha (June-July), preparations begin a month beforehand. New *raths* (chariots) are built every year. On the full moon of the previous month, Jyeshtha (May-June), the deities are bathed and retired from public view for 14 days of treatment and rest. They reappear, refreshed, invigorated, and ready to roll three days before the festival day kicks off. The grand day begins with the divine procession **(Pahandi Bije),** during which the gods are carried from the temple to their chariots in a rhythmical march called *pahandi*, accompanied by beating cymbals and drums and thousands of devotees chanting prayers. This is followed by the **Gajapati's** (the King of Puri) gesture of *chhera paharna*, ritually "sweeping" the chariots to symbolize humanity humbling itself in preparation for the mercy and goodwill of the gods. As the mesmerizing chants and ecstatic shouts of "Jai Jagganath" fill the air, some 4000 people pull the three chariots from the main gate of the temple east along Grand Ave. As if propelled by divine force, the *ratha* carriers proceed slowly forward on a 3km journey, usually lasting late into the night. The three gods spend seven days at **Gundicha Ghar** (Garden House), where they are dressed anew each day and eat specially prepared rice cakes. Their symbolic tour of the universe, as erratic and intensely delirious as the trip to Gundicha Ghar, is completed with a processional performance back to the Jagannath Temple on the 10th day of the new moon during Ashadha. The deities are dressed in golden clothes the following day, before taking up their places in the temple again. Nineteenth-century British observers reported that people would sometimes throw themselves under the wheels of the carts to obtain instant *moksha*. The word "juggernaut" (an object that crushes everything in its path) comes from Jagannath's name.

The massive temple compound hosts action-packed days of *darshan* and treats worshipers to devotionals and sacred dances at night. Over 20,000 people earn their livelihood in the complex: entire communities of artists and cooks work to produce the ritual materials, which include 56 different food offerings. Besides feeding the gods, the massive kitchen serves *mahaprasad* to 10,000 devotees every day (and up to 25,000 during festival time) in the adjacent **Ananda Bazaar.** The temple does not allow cameras, leather, or non-Hindus—even former Prime Minister Indira Gandhi was denied access because of her marriage to a Parsi.

To get a gander at the action beyond the temple walls, follow the monkeys and climb to the top of the **Raghunandan Library,** opposite the eastern gate. *(Open daily 7am-noon and 4-8pm.)* Other views may be obtained from the roofs of the buildings to the west of the compound; the landlord will request some *baksheesh* (Rs30).

OTHER SIGHTS. The **Gundicha Mandir,** 3km west of the Jagannath at the other end of Grand Rd., is the vacation home of Puri's idols for the nine days during the yearly Rama Yatra. Filled with palm trees, the temple is closed to non-Hindus. Above the tourist office on Station Rd., a small branch of the **state museum** displays local handicrafts and examples of the deities' *veshas* (dressings). Open Tu-Su 10am-5pm. Some of Puri's sacred **tanks** can be found north of Grand Rd.

◪ BEACHES

Puri's beaches have a reputation as the most beautiful in eastern India, although too-regular visits by foreigners, nationals, and toiletless locals mean they are far from any image of a pristine paradise. Still, the sun, sand, and surf are all too inviting and all the entertainment many travelers need. At the main strip, **Sea Beach,** near the town center, Indian tourists wade in their customary fully-clothed style; farther east by CT Rd., **Golden Beach** has fewer coral-salesmen and oily massage-*wallahs* offering their services. Beyond the fishing village, you only have to share the white sands with a few pieces of driftwood. The lifeguards offer inner tubes, and the local fishermen can be talked into providing a 3hr. tour (Rs150), though rough waters and tricky tides can make this a risky business.

WARNING! The beaches here are generally free of violent crime, but locals advise against going alone at night. Always leave your valuables in your hotel.

FESTIVALS AND ENTERTAINMENT

In a pilgrim city like Puri, festivals are common throughout the year, although locals don't always make them well-known. The granddaddy of them all is the **Rath Yatra Festival,** when Lord Jaggannath, his brother Balabhadra, and his sister Subhadra are paraded through the city on large wooden chariots (see **Gods on Wheels,** p. 464). Puri's **Beach Festival** (February 5th-9th), showcases the best of Orissan folk dancing, music, and handicrafts. The Government of Orissa Tourist Office also arranges **dance and theatrical programs** (check their bulletin board for current information). You can always take an evening stroll along Marine Parade through the Swargadwar area and the **night market** of western Puri. Alternatively, the younger fishermen like to throw beach parties. You supply the beer (Rs50 a pop) and they will bring the fish and fire, but be careful not to get scammed.

NEAR PURI

LALITAGIRI, UDAYAGIRI, AND RATNAGIRI

Orissa's "Golden Triangle" of tourist points might be shaped by the Hindu shrines of Bhubaneswar, Konark, and Puri, but the state has a rich Buddhist heritage as well. Forming their own "mini golden triangle," Udayagiri, Lalitagiri, and Ratnagiri stand as remarkable ancient monuments to a religious culture steeped in art and learning. Excavations of the ruins, only discovered in 1984, are ongoing and provide great opportunities to view the holy and historic relics before they get bundled away to museums. The site at **Lalitagiri,** dating from the 1st century AD, is the oldest in the region and also the most easily accessed. A large brick monastery, a ceremonial hall, and plenty of votive *stupas* lead up to a museum and, at the crest of the hill, a reconstructed *stupa*. **Ratnagiri,** the largest of Orissa's Buddhist sites, features two monasteries, a gorgeous green chlorite doorway, an impressive *stupa*, and several other shrines and sculptures over its extensive, fenced grounds. An Archaeological Survey of India **Museum** displays artifacts from the three sites, including two giant Buddha heads. (Open Sa-Th 10am-5pm. Rs2.) The remains of 7th-century **Udayagiri**—a square platform *stupa*, a stone well, two monasteries, and a variety of *bodhisvatta* sculptures—are the most unspoiled, having been only recently unearthed.

All three towns can be visited on a long daytrip from **Cuttack,** with lots of gorgeous natural scenery to feast your eyes on along the way. Buses from Puri to Cuttack leave daily every 30min. 5am-5pm (3½hr. Rs25). From the bus stand in Cuttack, take the 60km (1hr.) ride to **Chandikol** (Rs13). *Tempos* from the bus stop make the journey to Ratnagiri and stop at Udayagiri on the way back (Rs350 round-trip, add Rs100 for Lalitagiri). You can also climb aboard a *tempo* ferrying locals to villages near the sites; Balichandrapur and Patharajpur are the convenient turn-offs. It's possible to complete the entire circuit in this way for less than Rs40, but you will need very good karma to find *tempos* when you need them. Bring plenty of water—*dhabas* are ubiquitous in Chandikol, but bottled water is scarce. (All sites open daily dawn-dusk. Ratnagiri and Lalitagiri each have a US$5 foreigner entrance fee. Udayagiri free.)

PUNJAB ਪੰਜਾਬ AND
HARYANA हरियाणा

In 1947, when Partition divided the Punjab between India and Pakistan, only two of the five rivers to which the Persian *punj aab* refers were left inside India's new borders. Nineteen years later, the Indian state was divided again, this time along linguistic lines, to form the states of Punjab and Haryana. These states share a capital (Chandigarh), a fertile geography, and the pride of overcoming a long and turbulent history to become India's most prosperous region.

Punjab has long been the foyer through which aggressive guests have entered the subcontinent. The arrival of the Aryans here in 1500 BC led to the writing of the *Vedas* and the *Mahabharata*. With the AD 1526 Battle of Panipat came the Mughals, who dominated the region until the advent of the British viceroyalty in the mid-18th century. Punjab has wielded great influence on India, largely through the Sikh religion, founded during the 15th century by Guru Nanak. The majority of Sikhs, and their holy city of Amritsar, are in Punjab (see **Sikhism**, p. 90).

Although Punjab is India's "bread basket," peace has not always come with prosperity. More died in Punjab than anywhere else during the massacres that followed the Partition of 1947. More recently, there has been friction in Punjab between moderates and Sikh militants of the Shiromani Akali Dal party, who demand an independent Sikh nation, Khalistan ("Land of the Pure.") Things came to a head in 1983-84; Sikh-militants massacred Hindus and the Indian army raided the militants' headquarters in Amritsar's Golden Temple. The siege of the temple led to Sikh army desertions, mutinies, and, eventually, the murder of Indira Gandhi by her Sikh bodyguards. Thousands of Sikhs were killed in the ensuing Hindu rioting. Support for the Khalistan movement has only recently begun to wane.

HIGHLIGHTS OF PUNJAB AND HARYANA

Amritsar's **Golden Temple** (p. 476), the most sacred site of the Sikh religion, is one of the most astoundingly beautiful places in the whole of India.

Weird and wonderful **Chandigarh's** (p. 467) pre-planned sectors and structures represent a dead Frenchman's dream of the future, set in pre-poured concrete.

CHANDIGARH चंडीगढ़ ਚੰਡੀਗੜ੍ਹ ☎ 0172

Chandigarh was born of the optimism of India's newly independent government. When Punjab (including present-day Haryana) was partitioned, its original capital, Lahore, lay across the border in Pakistan. A new capital was needed, and the Nehru government decided on the present site of Chandigarh. Nehru employed a team of Western architects, the most prominent being, Le Corbusier, who seized this opportunity to mobilize his plans for a revolution in urban landscape. The result is a huge grid of broad, park-filled avenues and "sectors." Today, Le Corbusier's dream of "sun, space, and silence" has become crowded and polluted, but it still has some refreshing spots. Indians love Chandigarh for its cleanliness, orderliness, and relative lack of animals in the streets; foreigners are often disappointed for the same reasons.

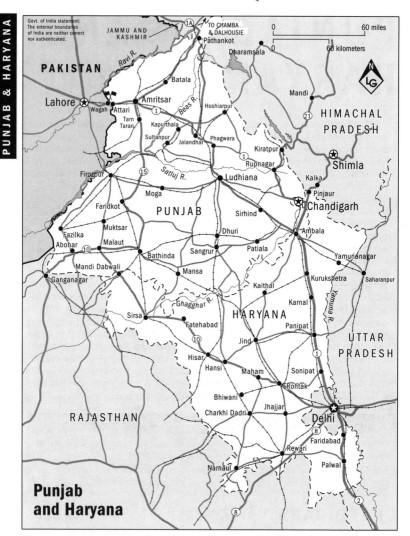

Govt. of India statement:
The external boundaries of India are neither correct nor authenticated.

Punjab and Haryana

TRANSPORTATION

Flights: Airport, 11km out of town (auto-rickshaw Rs80-120). **Indian Airlines** (☎ 703510) flies to: **Amritsar** (30min., W and F, US$65); **Delhi** (40min., W and F 1:15pm, US$75); **Leh** (1hr., W 9:20am, US$70). Book well in advance for Leh. **Jet Airlines** (☎ 741465) offers daily flights to Delhi (1hr., 2:40pm, US$75).

Trains: The **railway station** is 8km southeast of town. Local bus #37 connects the station to the bus stand (20min., Rs5). Auto-rickshaws will go there for Rs20-30. **Train Reservation Enquiry** (☎ 653131), on the 3rd fl. of the bus stand. Open M-Sa 8am-8pm,

Su 8am-2pm. To **Amritsar** (7hr., 5pm, Rs100) and **Delhi** (3½hr., 4 per day 1am-5:30pm, 2nd class reserved Rs82; *Shatabdi Exp.* 2006, 6:50am; *Shatabdi Exp.* 2012, 12:30pm; A/C chair Rs450). For **Jammu** and **Rishikesh**, go to **Ambala** (1hr., several per day, Rs45) and connect there. Tickets for trains from Ambala can be bought in Chandigarh if you book a day in advance. For **Shimla**, change in **Kalka** (30min., several per day, Rs30) for the narrow-gauge rail. Tickets sold only in Kalka.

Buses: Inter-State Bus Terminal, on the southwest side of Sector 17, opposite the hotels in Sector 22. Buses depart for **Dehra Dun** (5½hr., 6 per day 7:30am-3pm, Rs96; 5hr., deluxe 9am, Rs190); **Delhi** (5½hr., every 30min. 7am-12:30am, Rs109; deluxe 3 per day, Rs 165); **Dharamsala** (8hr., 10 per day 5am-1am, Rs110; deluxe 3am and 11pm, Rs220); **Jaipur** (12hr., 6 per day 4am-2:50pm, Rs185; deluxe 8:30am, Rs380); **Jammu** (8hr.; 7, 10am, 1pm; Rs135); **Manali** (12hr., 7 per day 5am-3:30pm, Rs165); **Rishikesh** (8hr., 10:30am and 8:30pm, Rs108); **Shimla** (4:30am-7pm; deluxe 9:30, 11:30am, 1pm, Rs140). **Dalhousie** or **Chamba** can be reached via **Pathankot** (8hr., Rs110). Pathankot to Dalhousie (3½hr., 10 per day 6:40am-5pm, Rs40). For many Punjab destinations, you must catch your ride from the I.S.B.T. No. 2 bus station in Sector 43. Among other places, this bus station services **Amritsar** (5½hr., every 30min., Rs99).

Local Transportation: Cycle-rickshaws charge Rs10 for a 2-sector trip. **Auto-rickshaws** charge about double. Local **buses** leave from the main bus station, Sector 17. Bus #13 goes to the Rock Garden (15min., Rs5), bus #37 to the train station (20min., Rs5).

PUNJAB & HARYANA

ORIENTATION

No one could accuse Chandigarh of being illogical—the city was plotted on a massive grid—but it can be confusing, nonetheless, as all the roads look identical. The streets run northwest to southeast and northeast to southwest, dividing the town into 50 sectors. Each sector is a self-sufficient unit with its own market places and shopping centers. **Sector 1** is to the north, where the main government buildings, **Sukhna Lake,** and the **Rock Garden** are situated. The rest are numbered from west to east, then east to west, in rows proceeding to the south. **Sector 17** is the heart of the city and most services, including the **bus station,** are located here. **Sector 22** has its share of cheap restaurants and hotels as well as several interesting temples.

PRACTICAL INFORMATION

Tourist Office: Chandigarh Industrial and Tourism Development Corp. (CITCO) (☎704614, railway station 658005). Has offices upstairs in the bus stand (open M-Sa 9am-5pm) and at the railway station (open during train arrivals). At the bus stand, there are also **Punjab** (☎781138), **UP** (☎707649), and **HP** (☎708569) **Tourist Information Centres.** Open M-F 9am-5pm.

Currency Exchange: Banks cluster around the "Bank Sq." in Sector 17B. **Bank of Baroda** (☎709692) changes traveler's checks and gives cash advances on MC/V. Open M-F 10am-2pm, Sa 10am-noon.

Market: Sectors 17, 22, and 23 are said to have the best markets.

Police: (☎742655), in Police Headquarters, opposite Sector 9. Open M-Sa 10am-6pm.

Pharmacy: All around the medical center in Sector 17. Several late-night pharmacies in Sector 22-C, like **Anil and Co.,** Bayshop #42 (☎777565). Open daily 8am-9:30pm.

Hospital/Medical Services: Post Graduate Institute (PGI), Sector 12 (☎543823-27). The best hospital in Chandigarh and one of the most reputable in India. 24hr. emergency services. **Government Medical College and Hospital,** Sector 32, Dakshin Marg (☎665253-59, emergency ext. 1200). Has an ambulance service.

Internet: Connections are unreliable. **Cyber Cafe,** Sector 17B (☎ 712209). Opposite KC Mezbaam's. Rs35 per hr. Open M-Sa 9am-10pm.

Post Office: GPO, Sector 17A. Open M-Sa 10am-5pm. **DHL** and other express couriers are in Sector 17. **Postal Code:** 160017.

▐ ACCOMMODATIONS

Staying in Chandigarh is easy on the wallet and can be an experience in itself. Treat yourself to simplicity in a **gurudwara.** Stubborn persistence in the face of glowering, spear-wielding guardians will eventually win you the privilege of bedding down for the night in a large room with floor mats open to everyone, usually for free. Unless you plan to stay in one in Amritsar, don't pass up this chance. No cigarettes, alcohol, or other intoxicants are allowed inside the compound. If this isn't quite your cup of tea, trot across the street from the bus station into the hotel jungle of Sector 22 or try the government *bhawan,* which fills up quickly.

Gurudwaras. The Sikh owners of Sector 19's *gurudwara* are friendly and eager to instruct you about their faith, once you persuade them to let you stay. Large communal room (free.) Max. stay of 3 days. Sector 22 and Sector 9 *gurudwaras* have large communal rooms (free) or doubles with fan and shared bathroom (Rs50). ❶

Hotel Divyadeep, 1090-91, Sector 22B (☎ 705191 or 721169). On the southeast side of Sector 22, 250m from the bus station. Clean rooms with seat toilets. Some rooms have A/C, TV, and a balcony. Check-out 24hr. Singles Rs250-500; doubles Rs300-600.

Panchayat Bhawan, Sector 18 (☎ 780701). On the northeast side. Large rooms around a courtyard. Reservations recommended. Doubles with bath Rs200-500. ❷

Shivalik Lodge, Sector 22B (☎ 774540). Just behind the restaurant/hotel, opposite the bus station. Not to be confused with the large, pricey Shivalikview Hotel in Sector 17. Clean bathrooms with squat toilets and hot water. Check-out noon. Doubles with air-cooling and TV Rs350. ❷

Jullundur Hotel, Sector 22 (☎ 706777 or 701121). Opposite the bus station, next to Sunbeam. Rooms are a bit pricey but all have A/C, fan, color TV, and hot water. Check-out noon. Singles Rs300-550; doubles Rs750. ❷

▐ FOOD

There's no restaurant shortage in Chandigarh. Sector 17 offers a combination of pricey restaurants and American-style fast-food joints, as well as cheap *dhabas. Thalis, samosas,* and local food, can best be found outside sectors 17 or 22.

▨ **KC's Mezbaam,** Sector 17. On the north side, behind KC Cinema. Muslim-influenced culinary styles—from the nawab of Avadh's favorite *gushtaba* (Kashmiri meatballs in yogurt sauce, Rs125) to the nizam of Hyderabad's beloved *mung malai tikka* (Rs125). Flowers, fountains, and beer on tap (Rs25). Open daily 11am-11:30pm. ❷

Shangri-La, SCO 96, Sector 17C. Nepali-run, Chinese restaurant decorated with red paneling, dragon paintings, silk lanterns, and a picture of the Dalai Lama. Szechuan-style sliced lamb Rs90, jasmine tea Rs12. Open daily 11am-10pm. ❶

Bhoj Vegetarian Restaurant, Sector 22B, directly below Hotel Divyadeep. Serves delicious enormous veg. *thalis* (Rs 65) and a full Indian dessert menu (Rs7-15) in a clean, comfortable environment. Open daily 11am-10pm. ❶

Indian Coffee House, has 4 locations in Sector 17, all offering the same fare. Some of the best dressed waiters in town serve you your choice of 6 types of coffee (Rs7-15), 6 types of *dosas* (Rs11-25), and 6 types of eggs (Rs15-30). Open daily 9am-10pm. ❶

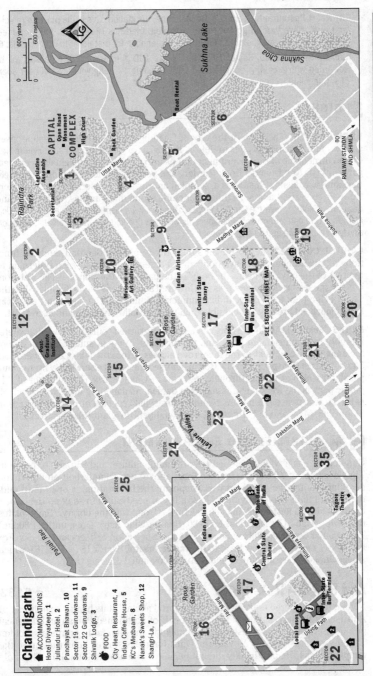

Chandigarh

▲ ACCOMMODATIONS
Hotel Divyadeep, 1
Jullundur Hotel, 2
Panchayat Bhawan, 10
Sector 19 Gurudwaras, 11
Sector 22 Gurudwaras, 9
Shivalik Lodge, 3

● FOOD
City Heart Restaurant, 4
Indian Coffee House, 5
KC's Mezbaam, 8
Nanak's Sweets Shop, 12
Shangri-La, 7

City Heart Restaurant, Sector 22. Opposite the bus station. This is the place to refuel if you don't have time to go far. Helpings of veg. fried rice (Rs25) and *mutter paneer* (Rs20) are huge, but the prices leave you with enough for that ticket to Dharamsala. ❶

Nanak's Sweets Shop, Sector 19D. Next to the 19D *gurudwara.* Brave palates will be rewarded with a chalky, dough-based taste-sensation. Strong whiskey-and-beer aperitifs. Chocolate, coconut, and pistachio *barfi* Rs80.❶

◉ SIGHTS

ROCK GARDEN. The birth of the city of Chandigarh as a government-supervised golden child gave rise to piles of debris. In 1985, road construction supervisor Nek Chand turned one of the government dumps into an almost unimaginable concrete garden. Visit Nek Chand's Rock Garden, and you'll never look at Indian concrete the same way again. Chand has assembled an escapist wonderland that meanders through 40 surreal acres. Highlights include stone duck armies, waterfalls, and dancers. *(Sector 1, near the Capital Complex. Open daily Apr.-Sept. 9am-1pm and 3-7pm; Oct.-Mar. 9am-1pm and 2-6pm. Rs5. Appointments with Nek Chand, the garden's creator, occasionally available; inquire at the ticket window.)*

CAPITOL COMPLEX. Le Corbusier's built the Capitol in Sector 1, and the functions of government are in symbolic and geometric relation to each other and to the rest of the city (as "head" to "body"—the parks are the "lungs.") The slab concrete, exposed brick, and *bris-soleil* (lowered sun-screens) style distinguishes the Capitol Complex from other Indian municipal buildings. The **High Court** and **Open Hand Monument** are more accessible than the **Legislative Assembly** and **Secretariat.**

PARKS. Sukhna Lake, in the north, is a reservoir-turned-tourist-trap with a cafeteria, pub, mini-amusement park, and paddleboats. Come at sunset, hop in one of the **swan boats,** and float to the mangrove **alcoves** across the lake. *(2-seater Rs30 per 30min., 4-seater Rs60 per 30min.)* Le Corbusier used the term **Leisure Valley** for the long parkland which stretches through the heart of Chandigarh. The highlight of this public park is the Dr. Zakir Hussain **Rose Garden,** off Jan Marg in Sector 16, which is the largest rose garden in Asia and features 4000 species of roses. They are in bloom Jan.-Mar., and in February, the garden hosts the giant Rose Festival.

▣ ♫ NIGHTLIFE AND ENTERTAINMENT

Chandigarh has a well-developed beer-drinking culture, and 25 pubs to prove it. The basement of **KC's Mezbaam** (see **Food,** above) has Thunderbolt on tap. If you need later hours, **Pub 22,** Sector 22, opposite the bus station, is open until midnight. Both pubs serve only beer (Rs25). If you need cakes to soak up the booze, try the **Ambrozia Restaurant and Pub,** Sector 17C, opposite the library. (Small plates of *tandoori* and Chinese food Rs35-80, Riviera wine Rs65. Open until 11:30pm.) The popular **Gymkhana Pub,** in Sector 17D, has a selection of beers and snacks. For a more refined experience, head to the **Tagore Theatre,** Sector 18 (☎ 774278), which stages Shakespeare in Punjabi and features costumed dancing troupes.

AMRITSAR ਅਮ੍ਰਿਤਸਰ ☎ 0183

Named for the sacred tank or "pool of immortal nectar" at its heart, the holy city of Amritsar is the largest city in the Indian half of partitioned Punjab and the focal point of Sikhism. An awe-inspiring monument to the Sikh faith, Amritsar's Golden Temple is a must-see for all visitors. Guru Ram Das started construction of the temple in AD 1579, but the city did not begin to form around it until the Sikh holy

Amritsar

🛏 ACCOMMODATIONS

Chinar Hotel, **1**
Grand Hotel, **2**
Hotel Shiraz, **3**
Hotel Sita Niwas, **15**
Sharma Guest House, **10**
Gujurati Lodge and Guest
    House, **11**
Sri Guru Ram
    Das Niwas Gurudwara, **13**
Sri Guru Hargobind Niwas, **14**
Tourist Guest House, **6**

🍎 FOOD
Bharawanda Dhaba, **8**
Bubby Dhaba, **12**
Neelam's, **9**
Sindhi Coffee House, **4**
Subhash Juice Bar, **7**
Surjit Chicken House, **5**

book, the Guru Granth Sahib, was enshrined here by the fifth Guru, Arjun. Centuries of Mughal invasions kicked off a cycle of destruction and reconstruction, and the calamities continued into the 1980s. Early in the 20th century, Amritsar played an important role in the formation of the Indian nationalist movement. In 1919, British Brigadier General Dyer shot dead 400 unarmed Indians in the closed compound of Jallianwala Bagh, sparking waves of protest all over India. Tanks bulldozed through the city gates in 1984, as the government put down an uprising of Sikh extremists. Amritsar today is a thriving industrial center that stretches far beyond the labyrinth of narrow streets that winds between the 20 gates of the old city. The proximity to the Pakistani border is itself an attraction; every evening an elaborate military ceremony accompanies the closing of the border gates.

█ TRANSPORTATION

Flights: Raja Sanhsi Airport, 12km northwest of town. To **Delhi** (2hr.; M and F 9am; W and F 2:30pm; US$100). Book at the **Indian Airlines** office, Court Rd. (☎213392), halfway between Albert and Mall Rd. Open M-Sa 10am-5pm.

Trains: The **computer reservation** complex (☎562811 or 562812) is in the south end of the railway station. Open M-Sa 8am-1:30pm and 2-8pm, Su 8am-2pm. To: **Agra** (11hr.; 5:30, 8:15am, 4:10pm; Rs232); **Delhi** (5½-8hr., 12 per day 5:15am-9:30pm, Rs194);

Haridwar (12hr., 8:55pm, Rs104); **Jaipur** (19hr., W and Su 4pm, Rs270); **Lahore, Mumbai** (33hr., 3 per day 7:55am-9:30pm, Rs420); **Pakistan** (*Lahore Exp.* 4607,4hr., M and Th 7am, Rs50; no reservations—purchase ticket at the platform); **Lucknow** (18hr., 5 per day 5:45-9:15pm, Rs282); **Patna** (34hr., 5:30 and 6:30pm, Rs346).

Buses: Enquiry Office (☎ 551734). Departure times change frequently. To: **Attari** (1hr., every 30min. 6:40am-5:30pm, Rs12); **Chandigarh** (5hr., every 30min. 4:20am-4pm, Rs100; deluxe 9am, noon, 3pm; Rs200); **Dalhousie** (6hr., 9:15am, Rs89); **Dehra Dun** (7hr., 7am, Rs177); **Delhi** (9hr., frequent 5:45am-9pm, Rs180; deluxe 8hr., every hr. 6:10-8:10pm, Rs320); **Dharamsala** (7hr., 11:50am, Rs98); **Jammu** (7hr., every 30min. 5am-4:30pm, Rs100); **Shimla** (11hr., 5:30am and 7:20pm, Rs177; or go to Chandigarh and change there). For connections at friendlier hours, go to **Pathankot** (3hr., 4:30am-8pm, Rs45).

Local Transportation: Bicycle rental is available at **Raja Cycles**, across the street north of the bus stand, next to the Janta Store's signs. Rs25 per day plus Rs1000 deposit. Open M-Sa 10am-6pm. **Cycle-rickshaws** will run anywhere in town for Rs10-20. In the "new sections," **auto-rickshaws** can speed things up; in the old parts, they have to move at the snail's pace of the cycle-rickshaw-dominated narrow streets.

🛪 ORIENTATION

Amritsar's **railway tracks** divide the city into northern and southern sections. The older, livelier section of the city is beyond the gates, to the south of the railway. **Bhandari Bridge** is the major vehicle conduit connecting north and south. North of the bridge is **Ram Bagh** park and the modern parts of the city. The old town is farther south, enclosed by **Circular Rd.**, which runs where the wall once stood. The Golden Temple is at the center of the circle. Most tourists visit only the temple compound and the area immediately north of it, but the maze of alleys and bazaars south and west of the temple also capture the feel of old Amritsar. The **bus stand** is northeast of the center, on the road from Delhi to the **railway station.**

🛂 PRACTICAL INFORMATION

Tourist Office: Punjab Government Tourist Office (☎ 402452). In the Palace Hotel, opposite the railway station. Open M-F 9am-5pm. There is also a helpful Information Center at the Golden Temple.

Currency Exchange: Grindlays Bank (☎ 224626). At the intersection of Lawrence and Mall Rd. Accepts traveler's checks. Cash advances on MC/V. The railway area also has several offices that change **Pakistani rupees.** There are a number of licensed money changers in the Golden Temple area. **Satija Trading Co.** (☎ 293517), located behind the Hargobind Niwas Gurudwara on Gail Sangal Wali Rs., is an official Western Union branch office. Open 24hr.

Market: The **bazaar** immediately in front of the main entrance to the Golden Temple carries a wide selection of merchandise, from Rajasthani shoes to Sikh daggers and swords. The steel bracelets *(kara)* worn by all Sikhs to symbolize strength of will and determination, are sold here. Be discriminating—*kara* that are not made of stainless steel will erode after a few months of wear. Each narrow lane south and west of the shrine specializes in a particular product or craft. The Hall Bazaar area between Town Hall and Gandhi Gate is where the locals go, and features a wider, cheaper range of pretty much everything.

Police: ☎ 211864 or 220043.

Pharmacy: Chemists cluster on Cooper Rd., around the corner from Crystal Restaurant, several blocks northeast of the railway station. Among these, **Sham Medicine** (☎ 228905) carries tampons and is otherwise well-stocked. Open daily 8:30am-10pm.

Hospital: Kakkar Hospital, Green Ave. (☎210964). Near the intersection of Mall and Albert Rd. The most reputable in town; enough people know the name to point the way. **24hr. emergency room** on Mahna Singh Rd., in the Golden Temple area.

Internet: Cyber City (☎210706). Off Lawrence Rd., near the intersection of Queens and Lawrence Rd. Rs60 per hr. Open daily 7:30am-11pm. **Sharma Guest House** and **Hotel Sita Niwas** each have a computer hooked up to the web at decent speeds, and both charge between Rs40-50 per hr.

Post Office: Court Rd. (☎566032). Northwest of the railway station. Open M-Sa 9am-5pm. The **Golden Temple Post Office** is open M-Sa 9am-5pm. **Postal Code:** 143001.

ACCOMMODATIONS

Amritsar's hotels are in three parts of the city: by the bus stand, near the railway station, and around the Golden Temple. The cheapest places are near the bus stand, but many of these are neither clean nor safe—over the years the area has become a red-light district where rooms are rented out by the hour. A number of decent hotels near the railway station are good if you're anxious to keep the heart of the city at a safe distance. Hotels near the temple are more scarce, but this is the most vibrant part of the city. Perhaps the best place to stay is in the temple compound itself, although all the rules can get pretty tiresome after a few days.

INSIDE THE GOLDEN TEMPLE

▨ **Sri Guru Ram Das Niwas Gurudwara,** on the east side of the temple compound past the community kitchen. Foreign guests sleep on beds or floor mats within the packed confines of an open-ceiling bunker. No reservations accepted; get there in the afternoon and place some of your belongings (nothing valuable!) on a bed to increase your chances of getting it for the night. No smoking or drinking allowed. Prayers broadcast periodically through the courtyard, adding to the atmosphere. Foreign compound is guarded 24hr. In-house closets provided. Donations at the charity box are appreciated. Max. stay 3 days. ❶

Sri Guru Hargobind Niwas (temple manager ☎553953, Hargobind Niwas ext. 323), 100m south of Ram Das Niwas Gurudwara. If the free digs are a bit too free for your taste, pay a token tariff for a sparkling new, marble-covered double with attached bath. The place is nearly always full, but if you are persistent, or if you keep coming back, you may get in eventually. No drinking or smoking. Doubles with bath Rs60. ❶

GOLDEN TEMPLE AREA

Sharma Guest House, Mahna Singh Rd. (☎551757). On the street between the main and the eastern entrances to the temple. Great location, familial atmosphere, and excellent room service. Clean doubles including some sparkling new rooms with seat toilets, cable TV, and phones. A few rooms look into Jallianwalla Bagh. Check-out 24hr. Reservations recommended. Doubles Rs200-500. ❷

Shri Gujrati Lodge and Guest House (☎557870). A block in front of the main temple entrance, next to the passage to Jallianwala Bagh. The 8-bed dormitory overlooks the memorial park; cramped doubles with tiny bathrooms open onto Amritsar's chaotic central market. The 3rd floor balcony is so huge that you could probably play a game of cricket out there on the cooler days, or fry a giant *dosa* on the warmer ones. No reservations accepted. Dorms Rs70-80; doubles with seat toilets Rs165-300. ❷

Hotel Sita Niwas (☎543092). Near the eastern temple entrance—you can't miss it. Spartan singles are fairly cheap, but the price skyrockets as you add amenities like toilets, hot water, air coolers, TV, or A/C. Gurudwaras are cleaner and more luxurious than many of these rooms. STD/ISD. Singles Rs150; doubles Rs250-800. ❶

RAILWAY AREA

▧ **Tourist Guest House,** GT Rd. (☎553830). Near Bhandari Bridge, on the road from the bus stand to the railway station. 50 years ago, a British colonel turned his mansion into this guest house; since then, tourists have flocked here for a taste of the Raj lifestyle. Some rooms have high ceilings, air cooling, and TVs. Dorms Rs85; doubles with fans and bath Rs100-250. ❶

Grand Hotel (☎562424). As you leave the railway station, just to the right on Queens Rd. Small, but well-kept rooms surround a pleasant courtyard with a garden and lawn chairs. Attached baths with seat toilets, running hot water, and color TV. Room service 7am-10pm. Check-out noon. Excellent restaurant and bar downstairs. Singles Rs395-775; doubles Rs500-900. ❸

Hotel Shiraz (☎220886). Off Queen's Rd., a 10min. walk from the station. Large rooms with color TVs, seat toilets, and hot water. Room service 7am-11pm. Check-out noon. Singles Rs300-400; doubles Rs350-450, with A/C add Rs150. ❷

Chinar Hotel, Railway Links Rd. (☎564655). A half-block up from the railway station. Moderately clean, with huge front-side rooms. Rooms come with TV and air coolers. Check-out noon. Singles Rs300-500; doubles Rs400-600. ❷

◗ FOOD

You should try to eat at least one meal in the Golden Temple itself—the *dal* might leave you yearning for more.

▧ **Neelam's,** a few doors down from the entrance to Jallianwala Bagh. A/C and cushy booths make it the most comfortable *dhaba* in the temple area. Enormous and tasty portions. *Malai kofta* Rs40; excellent *masala dosa* Rs25. Open daily 10am-10pm. ❶

Bubby Dhaba, directly in front of the main temple entrance, provides a standard menu. Relax in the A/C room in the back, and watch all the action in the front of the Golden Temple, or stay up front to chat with the cooks. Open daily 6:30am-11pm.

Bharawanda Dhaba, opposite the Town Hall and next door to Punjab National Bank. Well-known, well-stocked, well-lit cafeteria with superb *thalis* (Rs29-39). Great *paneer* dishes Rs32. Speedy service and foreigner-friendly. Open daily 8:30am-11:30pm. ❶

Surjit Chicken House, right below Cyber City, off Lawrence Rd. The best grilled chicken in town (Rs65) according to locals. Open daily 10am-9pm. ❶

Subhash Juice Bar, 1 block southwest of Gandhi Gate. Black, mirrored booths, livened up by a colorful selection of juices and shakes. Mango shake with *pista badam* Rs15. Excellent *anar* (pomegranate) juice (Rs15). Open daily 7am-11pm. ❶

Sindhi Coffee House, Lawrence Rd. Opposite Ram Bagh Gardens. Comfy chairs and palatable coffee (Rs20). A good place to bring a date for some "tooti fruitty" ice cream (Rs 40). Open daily 9am-9pm. ❶

◉ SIGHTS

THE GOLDEN TEMPLE

Golden Temple Information Centre (☎553954) *is on the northeast side of the complex. No tobacco, alcohol, or stimulants of any kind are allowed. Visitors must deposit cigarettes a block away from the temple's entrance. Shoes, socks, and umbrellas must be left at free depositories at each of the main entrances or at the Tourist Information Centre. Visitors must rinse their feet in the tanks in front of the entrances. Photography is allowed inside the temple complex, but not inside the temple itself. Head-coverings are required at all times inside the temple. They are available for free at the Information Centre and for sale (Rs10) outside the temple, but any scarf, hat, or towel will do. Information Centre open daily Apr.-Aug. 8am-8pm, Sept.-Mar. 8am-7pm. Complex open daily 24hr. Free.*

No matter what you choose to call it—the Golden Temple, Hari Mandir, or Darbar Sahib (as it's known in Punjabi)—Amritsar's focal monument is inspiringly beautiful, hauntingly serene, and oblivious to the grind and grime just a few feet outside its walls. The Golden Temple's tranquility is especially impressive, given the tumultuous history of the Sikhs and of the temple itself. Ever since it was built nearly 400 years ago, the temple has been plagued by almost incessant destruction and desecration from outsiders. All Sikhs try to make a pilgrimage here at least once in their lifetime. The best time to visit is at night when the lights sparkling in the blackened tank and the lanterns illuminating the causeway impart a soft, ethereal glow to this awe-inspiring place of worship.

Although Guru Nanak, the founder of Sikhism, once lived near the site of the modern tank, it was **Guru Ram Das** who ignited the growth of a religious center here when he began work on the pool in 1574. That project was completed under Guru Arjun 15 years later, when the area was named Amritsar. Guru Arjun built the **Hari Mandir** at the center of the tank and placed the Guru Granth Sahib, the Sikh holy book, inside it. A series of destructive Mughal invasions followed the completion of the temple in 1601. The temple alternated between Mughal and Sikh control until Ahmad Shah Abdali captured it, and taking no chances, blew it to smithereens. The Sikhs regained control of the site under the leadership of Punjab ruler Maharaja Ranjit Singh. The one-eyed maharaja rebuilt the complex, decorated parts of it with marble and copper, and coated the newly built Hari Mandir in gold leaf. The British assumed a less-than-reverent management of the temple during the 19th century, and it wasn't until the 1920s that the practice of pure Sikhism was restored within the temple's walls.

The temple has continued to be a site of frequent violence. The 1980s saw the rise of a vocal Sikh militant group that called for the creation of an independent Sikh nation. Tensions came to a head in 1983, when the movement's leader, Sant Bhindranwale, sequestered himself in the Golden Temple and incited acts of violence against Hindus. With over 350 Hindus killed by the summer of 1984, Indira Gandhi ordered the national army to storm the temple, a plan dubbed **Operation Bluestar.** What was intended as a commando raid became a three-day siege. When the smoke had cleared, more the 750 people were dead, including Bhindranwale and 83 soldiers. The Sikhs retaliated with the assassination of Indira Gandhi. Tour guides and brochures tend to be hush-hush about this latter-day violence, emphasizing instead historically distant bloodbaths and the site's current state of peace.

PARIKRAMA. The main entrance to the Golden Temple is on the north side of the complex, beneath the **clock tower.** Here also is the main shoe depository and the **Tourist Information Centre,** which provides informative brochures about the temple and the Sikh religion and conducts tours in English every hour. The clock tower leads to the Parikrama, the 12m-wide marble promenade that encircles the tank. The four entrances to the temple complex symbolize an openness to friendly visitors from all sides—both geographically and metaphorically in terms of caste and creed. Guru Arjun once exclaimed, "My faith is for people of all castes and all creeds from whichever direction they come and to whichever direction they bow." Traffic moves clockwise around the Parikrama. Here, the **68 Holy Places** represent the 68 holiest Hindu sites in India—just to walk along this northern edge, Guru Arjun declared, is to attain the holiness a Hindu takes a lifetime to acquire. Some of the holy sites have been converted into the **Central Sikh Museum,** or Gallery of Martyrs, housed in the northern part of the temple complex; the entrance is to the right of the main gate. Along the walls are portraits of renowned Sikhs, including Baba Deep Singh and Sevapanthi Bhai Mansha Singh, who swam across the tank through gunfire to keep the temple lit. The display of heavy-duty arms includes everything from spears to blunderbusses. Paintings of martyred bodies sawed to pieces at Chandni Chowk in Delhi and photographs of slain Sikh martyrs with pop-eyed, bloody faces are not for the faint of heart. *(Open daily 8am-6pm. Free.)* The small tree at the northeast corner of the tank is said to have been the site of the miraculous healing of a cripple; today the healthy, wealthy, crippled, and destitute alike seek the benefits of the tank's curative powers at the adjoining **bathing ghats.** Just next to the *ghats* is one of four booths where priests read from the Guru Granth Sahib. Ongoing readings are meant to ensure the survival of Sikh beliefs. Each priest recites for three hours; a complete reading takes 50 hours.

On the east side of the Parikrama are the **Ramgarhia Minars,** two brick towers that were damaged when tanks rumbled through this entrance in 1984. This access leads to the Guru-ka-Langar, the communal kitchen, and the *gurudwaras*. The south side of the tank has a shrine to **Baba Deep Singh,** whose struggles made him a Sikh hero. When the Mughal Ahmad Shah Abdali blew up the Golden Temple in 1761 and filled the sacred tank with trash, Baba Deep Singh began a defense of the desecrated temple. On his way, however, his head was cut off by a Muslim soldier. Disembodied and with head in hand, the Sikh leader trudged on, eventually crossing the temple's gates and plopping his head in the water before dying. The west end of the tank has several notable structures. The first window is where devotees collect *prasad*, the sweet lumps of cornmeal used as an offering inside the Hari Mandir. Moving clockwise, opposite the entrance to the Hari Mandir, is the **Akal Takhat,** the second-holiest place of the temple. Guru Hargobind, the sixth Sikh guru, built the Akal Takhat in 1609 as a decision-making center. Many weapons, fine pieces of jewelry, and other Sikh artifacts are stored here. The two towering flagstaffs next to the Akal Takhat represent the religious and political facets of Sikhism; the two are joined by the **double swords of Hargobind,** demonstrating how intertwined these aspects of Sikhism are. Illuminated at the very top, the poles are intended as beacons for pilgrims heading into Amritsar. Near the flagstaffs is the shrine to the last and most militant guru, Gobind Singh. The last noteworthy spot along the Parikrama, other than the Hari Mandir itself, is the 450-year old **jujube** tree under which the Baba Buddhaja, the temple's first priest, used to spend his time. The tree is thought to bring fertility to anyone who touches it.

HARI MANDIR. Seemingly afloat in the middle of the tank, the Hari Mandir is the holiest part of the entire complex. Photography is not allowed past the gate to the temple walkway. The architecture of the Golden Temple fuses Hindu and Muslim styles—this is particularly noticeable in the synthesis of the Hindu temple's rectangular form with the domes and minarets of the Muslim mosque. The three stories of the Hari Mandir, capped by an inverted lotus dome, are made of marble, copper, and about 100 kilograms of pure gold leaf. Inside the temple on the ground floor, the chief priest and his musicians recite *gurbani* (hymns) from the Guru Granth Sahib. People sit around the center and toss flowers and money toward the jewel-studded canopy, where the silk-enshrouded Guru Granth Sahib lies.

The **Guru Granth Sahib** (considered by the Sikhs to be a living teacher, not just a book) is brought to the temple from the Akal Takhat each day and returned at night. The morning ceremony takes place at around 3:30am, the procession at 10pm. Arrive about an hour early to observe the ceremony from the second floor of the Hari Mandir. Hymns echo through the building before the book is revealed and the priest takes over the prayers; he chants, folds the book in gold leaf and more silk, and finally places it on the golden palanquin. Head downstairs at this point, and you might end up in the line of devotees pushing each other for the privilege of bearing the holy burden. Finally, a blaring serpentine horn and communal drum signal a final prayer that puts the book to bed, near the flagstaff. The entire ceremony lasts about an hour and a half.

GATAKA: THE ART OF WAR The Sikhs' success in resisting centuries of oppression is partly due to their skill as warriors. Through countless battles, they developed a martial art known as *gataka*. Today, young would-be warriors practice *gataka* on the roof of the Guru-ka-Langar (daily 8:30-11pm). They enjoy having visitors watch as they wield their *neja* (spears), swords, bamboo sticks, and other ancient weapons and practice *talwar baji* (fencing), or as it's more bluntly known, *kirpan* (the art of stabbing). The most impressive weapon is the *chakkar*, a wooden ring with stone spheres dangling from it by 4 ft. strings. The warrior stands in the middle and spins the ring, as the whirling balls form a barrier around him, and then tosses it up into the air (still spinning) for someone to catch. Watching the spectacle is exciting, but participating is even better, which the warriors will often let you do. To really indulge in *gataka*, they recommend heading out to Raia, 50km outside of Amritsar, where you can visit Baba Bakala, the training center for the most hard-core students.

AROUND THE TEMPLE. Step outside to the left (north) side onto the *pradakhina*, the marble path leading around the temple. On this side is a stairwell leading to the second floor, where flowers, animals, and hymns ornament the walls. From here, you can catch a good look at the procession and Adi Granth below. A small *shish mahal* (hall of mirrors) fills the east side of this floor. Once occupied by the gurus, the halls now reverberate with the voices of priests engaged in the *akhand path*, the ongoing reading of the holy book. The **Har-ki-Pari** (Steps of God), on the ground floor of the temple's east (back) side, allows visitors easy access to the most sacred section of the tank's waters.

No visit to the Golden Temple would be complete without a meal at the **Guru-ka-Langar,** the enormous community kitchen characteristic of all Sikh temples. Sikh founder Guru Nanak instituted the custom of *pangat* (dining together) to reinforce the idea of equality. *Pangat* continues in the dining hall, where basic meals are dished out daily to rows of thousands who sit together, regardless of wealth or caste. As one row eats, the next gathers, in an ongoing cycle. The meal consists of all-you-can-eat *dal* and chappatis; simply hold out cupped hands as the chappati chappie walks by, and he'll toss you more. Afterwards, leave a donation in one of the charity boxes—these meals are largely funded by such contributions.

Just south of the Hargobind *gurudwara* is the nine-story **Tower of Baba Atal Rai,** named after the son of Guru Hargobind. According to legend, he performed a miracle at age nine, which annoyed his father to no end. In shame, the young *baba* came here and died. On the first floor are some detailed miniatures depicting episodes from Guru Nanak's life and a *nagarah* (drum). The other floors are empty, but you can climb to the top for unsurpassed views of Amritsar, the Golden Temple, and the tank of Kamalsar to the south.

OTHER SIGHTS

JALLIANWALA BAGH. About two blocks north of the temple's main entrance is Jallianwala Bagh, the site of one of the most horrific moments in the history of colonial India. On April 13, 1919, crowds filled Jallianwala Bagh to peacefully protest a law allowing the British to imprison Indians without trial. British Brigadier-General Reginald E.H. Dyer was brought in to quell the disturbance. Dyer stood behind 150 troops in front of the main alley, the only entrance and exit to the compound and ordered his men to open fire without warning on the 10,000 men, women, and children who had gathered here. The shooting continued for 15min. People were shot as they perched to jump over walls; others drowned after diving into wells. Dyer's troops had fired 1650 rounds, and nearly all of them found their mark. In all, about 400 people died, and 1500 were left wounded. The massacre sparked a rallying cry for Indian insurgence. The Bengali poet Rabindranath Tagore, who had been knighted after winning the Nobel Prize for Literature in 1913, returned his knighthood after the massacre. Dyer was reprimanded and relieved of his duties but never charged with any crime. In 1997, Queen Elizabeth II visited Jallianwala Bagh. Although no official apology was made during her controversial visit, the British Monarch remarked on the regrettability of the massacre and laid a wreath at the memorial to the victims. Today, Jallianwala Bagh is a calm garden, frequented by college kids and picnicking families. The stone well is a monument to the drowned Indians who jumped to their deaths in an attempt to flee. The Martyr's Gallery features portraits of some of those involved in the massacre. *(Open daily in summer 9am-5pm, in winter 10am-1pm and 3-7pm.)*

RAM BAGH. Northeast of the railway station is Ram Bagh, the park between The Mall and Queens Rd. At the south edge of the park, the impressive Darshani Deorhi gate is all that is left of the solid ramparts and moat that once surrounded the area. At the northwest corner stands a menacing statue of Maharaja Ranjit Singh, the Sikh leader who was responsible for the early 19th-century restoration of the Golden Temple. Ram Bagh served as his summer residence between 1818 and 1837, and the central building now houses the Ranjit Singh Museum, which contains oil paintings, weapons, manuscripts, and miniatures from the maharaja's era. The tourist office's pamphlet, *Amritsar: Spiritual Centre of Punjab*, is a good guide to the museum. *(Museum open Tu-Su 10am-4:45pm. Rs5.)*

DURGIANA MANDIR. The high profile of the Golden Temple overshadows the tiny Hindu shrines tucked into the alleyways all around it, as well as the impressive Durgiana Mandir. This temple, set back from the busy street four blocks northwest of the Golden Temple, honors the goddess Durga.

INDIAN ACADEMY OF FINE ARTS. Opposite Ram Bagh on Lawrence Rd., east of the Sindhi Coffee House, the Indian Academy of Fine Arts puts on periodic exhibitions of modern Indian art. *(Open daily 9am-7pm. Free.)*

🔾 DAYTRIP FROM AMRITSAR: TARN TARAN ਟਰਨ ਟਾਰਨ

Once the Hari Mandir has whetted your appetite for shiny, golden Sikh temples, head 22km south to the town of Tarn Taran. Buses leave every 30min. from the main bus stand (1hr., Rs10). From the Tarn Taran bus stand, it's a 15min. walk along the main road and through the narrow alley of the bazaar up to the local *gurudwara*. Its founder, Guru Arjun Dev, built the temple in 1768 to commemorate Guru Ram Das, who slept side-by-side with a leper to show his compassion. Though local doctors can't provide any evidence for the common belief that the water here cures leprosy, they do attest to its curative effects on several minor skin conditions. The architectural style here resembles that of the Amritsar complex; the *parikrama* encircling the still waters is actually larger than its counterpart in the Golden Temple. The *gurudwara* provides decent rooms (free) in the large yellow building just outsides the west (not the main) entrance.

> **WARNING.** As of May 2002, most foreign governments were advising their nationals to avoid all travel to Pakistan. Nearly one million troops are massed along the India-Pakistan border, and many areas around the Wagah crossing have been extensively mined. If you do decide to go, **make sure you have a Pakistani visa and that your Indian visa allows multiple entries.** For more information, see **Surrounding Countries**, p. 11, **Border Crossings**, p. 46, and **This Year's News**, p. 81.

ᗡ BORDER WITH PAKISTAN: WAGAH

The *only* border crossing between India and Pakistan is at **Wagah,** 32km from Amritsar. Take a **bus** to **Attari** (1hr., every 15min. 7am-6pm, Rs12), and look for the impressive Khalsa College on the right. From Attari, it is a 2km rickshaw ride to the border (Rs10-20). Taxis will go the entire distance for Rs150 each way. The border is open daily from 10am to 4pm. If you only wish to visit, wait until after 4pm, or better still, arrive even later for the flag-lowering ceremony (see **Border Ballet,** below). The ceremony's start time varies by season—it begins at 7pm in the middle of summer, and around 6pm in the dead of winter. Arrive at least 30min. early (1hr. early on Sundays) to get a good seat. The last bus to **Amritsar** leaves Attari at 6pm. If you are here for the flag ceremony, you will have to take a taxi back. If you are crossing over, pass through customs on the left and walk the remaining 200m to the actual line. The **train** from Amritsar to **Lahore** was suspended effective January 1, 2002. The direct **bus** service between Delhi and Lahore has also been suspended indefinitely.

At Wagah, **Punjab Tourism,** just behind the checkpoint, supplies the standard outdated brochures and maps (open M-Sa 10am-4pm). Next door, the **State Bank of India** changes traveler's checks but not Pakistani rupees (open 11am-4pm). The money-changers do change Pakistani rupees. There is a **post office** for last minute send-offs. If you are stranded overnight, the **Niagara Falls Guest House ❷,** provides both spacious and cramped rooms. (☎382646. Rs 300-450.)

BORDER BALLET A few people go to Wagah to *cross* the border, but a huge crowd always shows up to *watch* the border. A half-hour before sunset, an elaborate nightly ritual accompanies the closing of the border and the lowering of the flags. Three to six thousand visitors clamor around the spiked gate on either side and jostle for the best views. More or less on schedule, the ceremony unfolds. As one officer barks an order and another follows with furious stomping and wild high-stepping, the audiences on both sides break into raucous applause and scream out patriotic chants. The scene is more like a cricket match than a solemn ritual. The military police shove the roaring throngs back behind an imaginary line, only for the masses to retake their turf the moment the officers push on. After some more machismo-packed face-offs and lengthy siren-like yells, the respective flags are lowered, the lights go bright, the bugles blare, and the visitors mob the gate for a glimpse of the faces on the other side—or for a chance to toe one of the world's most famous white lines.

RAJASTHAN
राजस्थान

The northwestern desert state of Rajasthan is India's "Land of Kings," ruled for more than a millennium by the legendary Rajput warrior clans. The days of bloodshed and mass immolation are long gone now, but the vivid memories of Rajasthan's gory and colorful past continue to ooze out of the state's crumbling forts and romantic palaces. Life in Rajasthan is the stuff that tourist-brochure dreams are made of: camels and elephants mosey alongside cars and oblivious locals, turbanned men twirl their foot-long moustaches, and women in brightly colored saris balance water jugs on their heads. Few people leave Rajasthan without some fantastic pictures and a new set of travel tales for a rainy day back home.

In the 6th and 7th centuries, the Rajputs emerged as the rulers of the area now known as Rajasthan. Much of the history of Rajasthan is comprised of struggles between these abutting feudal states of the warrior Rajput clans and a long saga of encroachments as the Mughals extended their power across northern India. Most of the Rajput royal houses, too individually weak to resist the burgeoning Mughal empire, kowtowed to its mighty rulers. The threat from the Mughals receded after the death of the last great Mughal emperor, Aurangzeb, in 1707, but then the Rajputs had to contend with the Marathas. When the British came, the Rajput royal houses leapt at the chance to exchange their support of the Raj for British protection. After Independence in 1947, the single state of Rajasthan was pieced together from the various Rajput kingdoms, and Jaipur emerged as the capital.

Rajasthan is made up of three geographical regions. The flat lands of the east are studded with rich national parks and cosmopolitan centers like Jaipur, the state's capital and the western corner of India's "Golden Triangle" of tourism. In the western Marwar region, the plains yield to the vast barrenness of the Thar Desert and its formidable forts. In the south, the majestic Aravalli Mountains of the Mewar region contrast with the rest of the state's sand-duned landscape, with lush valleys and mountain-top lakes. However, Rajasthan is certainly not as idyllic as it might seem; its picture-perfect exterior belies a state ridden with poverty, India's lowest literacy rate, and immense caste and gender inequalities. And the tourist boom has brought not only money and a much-needed infrastructure to Rajasthan, but also a fiercely competitive clamor for dollars, pounds, and yen. An over-abundance of tourist traffic threatens to obscure the local culture in many cities, yet traces of the old storybook India still survive—in the colored *bandhani* cloth of Jaipur's marketplaces, on the back of a camel in sacred Pushkar, or out on the serene waters of exotic Lake Pichhola in Udaipur.

JAIPUR जयपुर

Rajasthan's most popular tourist destination, Jaipur hugs the southwest corner of India's "Golden Triangle," joining ranks with Delhi and Agra. On the one hand, Jaipur is a tourist's dream, brimming with extraordinary bazaars, forts, and elegant architecture, and its cosmopolitan spirit lends the city an unmistakably regal air. On the other hand, Jaipur has proved unable to escape the effects of industrialization, which has catapulted it into the ranks of India's most polluted and heavily-trafficked cities. Jaipur characterizes India at its hectic best and worst.

HIGHLIGHTS OF RAJASTHAN

Jaipur is Rajasthan's most popular destination. Its **City Palace** (p. 492), bustling bazaars (p. 491), and **Amber Fort** (p. 493) are worth all the hype.

The **Lake Palace** of **Udaipur** (p. 512) has long been the ultimate romantic draw for honeymooners and secret agents alike—one glimpse of the sunrise city and you'll see why.

Jaisalmer's illuminated fort (p. 528) satiates most tourists' cravings for a taste of life in the middle ages—the restful journey into the desert on the hump of a camel.

Peaceful **Pushkar** (p. 500) is a quiet oasis, soothing weary pilgrims and travelers 361 days a year. The four-day **Pushkar Camel Fair** (p. 504) is another story entirely.

The **Jain temples** at **Ranakpur** (p. 516) and **Mt. Abu** (p. 517) showcase poems carved in marble.

The city was born out of the vision and prudent urban planning of the 18th-century Rajput leader Maharaja Sawai Jai Singh II, who ruled the region from 1699 to 1744. Though his kingdom was threatened by both the Marathas and the Mughals, the maharaja's intelligence won him the respect and alliance of the Mughal emperor **Aurangzeb** (see **History,** p. 70), and his military savvy led the Rajput forces to decisive victories against the Marathas. Having established political stability in his territories by the mid-1720s, Jai Singh decided to move the capital from its hillside fort in Amber to a city of his design. With help from the renowned Bengali architect Vidyadhar Chakravarti, the maharaja built the walled city of Jaipur. Carefully laying out Jaipur according to the mathematical grid model of the ancient Hindu map of the universe, Jai Singh and Chakravarti made their city both beautiful and functional. High walls were constructed for defense, and the entrances to stores and homes were placed on side streets so that the maharaja's royal processions could pass without disrupting daily life. Wide pavements and streets were designed to facilitate the flow of pedestrian traffic, and a complex system of underground aqueducts brought drinking water into the fortified city.

The British presence during the 19th century brought about a drastic cosmetic transformation; to celebrate Prince Albert's visit in 1856, the city painted itself pink. The city was dubbed Jaipur the "Pink City," and both the name and the color-wash stuck. Over time, a fusion of old and new has forged a city as unforgettable as Jai Singh's Jaipur ever was—from the rosy hues of the bazaars at sunset, to the sea of monkeys and worshippers lining the temple-studded gorge at Galta.

▇ TRANSPORTATION

Flights: Sanganer Airport, 15km south of the city, currently serves only **domestic** flights but is expected to commence international service soon. Very crowded local buses (every 30min., Rs4-5) leave Ajmeri Gate for the airport. Rickshaws Rs100, taxis Rs200. A number of international airlines also maintain representation in Jaipur. Many airline and airline agent offices are centrally located in Jaipur Towers, on MI Rd. **Domestic carriers: Indian Airlines,** Nehru Place, Tonk Rd. (☎743324; airport 721333 or 721519). Open daily 10am-1pm and 2-5pm. To: **Ahmedabad** (1hr.; M, W, F 6:10pm; US$110); **Calcutta** (2½-3½hr.; M-Sa; US$225); **Delhi** (40min.; daily 8:30pm; US$60); **Jodhpur** (40min.; daily 7:20am; US$85); **Mumbai** (1hr.; daily 7:20am; US$160); **Udaipur** (2hr.; daily 7:20am; US$85). The more centrally located **Satyam Travels and Tours,** Jaipur Towers, ground fl. (☎378794; fax 200133), is much more conveniently located, has a computerized link with IA, and can book and deliver tickets at no extra fee. Open M-Sa 9:30am-7:30pm. **Jet Airways,** Jaipur Towers, 1st fl. (☎360763 or 370594, airport 546230 or 551953; fax 374242). To: **Delhi** (1hr.; daily 9:45am and 5:40pm; US$60); **Mumbai** (1½hr.; daily 7:30pm; US$160); **Udaipur** (1hr.; daily 7:35am;

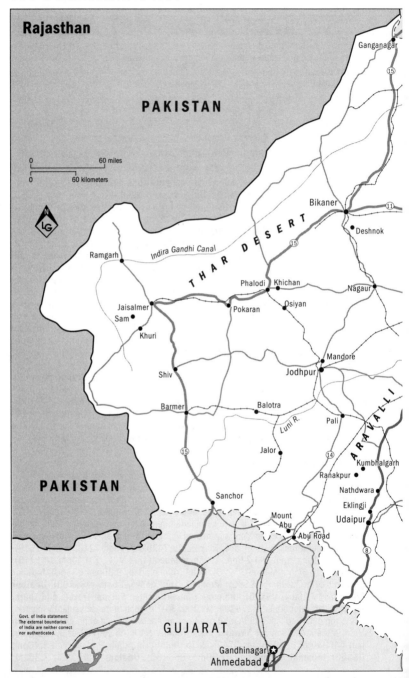

Rajasthan

Ganganagar

PAKISTAN

0   60 miles
0   60 kilometers

N
LG

Ramgarh

Indira Gandhi Canal

T H A R   D E S E R T

Bikaner

Deshnok

15

11

Phalodi Khichan

Nagaur

Jaisalmer
Sam

Pokaran

Osiyan

Khuri

Shiv

Mandore

Jodhpur

A R A V A L L I

Barmer

Balotra

Luni R.

Pali

15

Jalor

14

Kumbhalgarh

Ranakpur

Nathdwara

Sanchor

Eklingji

Mount
Abu

Udaipur

8

Abu Road

PAKISTAN

Govt. of India statement:
The external boundaries
of India are neither correct
nor authenticated.

GUJARAT

Gandhinagar
Ahmedabad

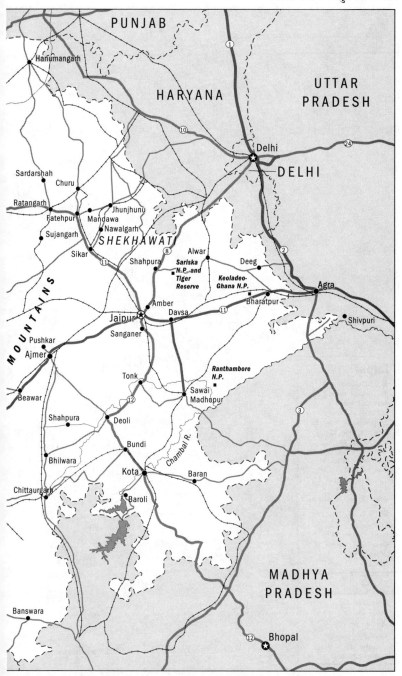

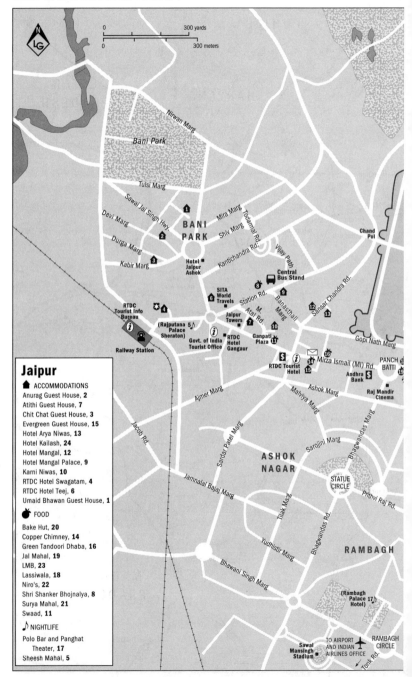

Jaipur

🏠 ACCOMMODATIONS

Anurag Guest House, **2**
Atithi Guest House, **7**
Chit Chat Guest House, **3**
Evergreen Guest House, **15**
Hotel Arya Niwas, **13**
Hotel Kailash, **24**
Hotel Mangal, **12**
Hotel Mangal Palace, **9**
Karni Niwas, **10**
RTDC Hotel Swagatam, **4**
RTDC Hotel Teej, **6**
Umaid Bhawan Guest House, **1**

🍖 FOOD

Bake Hut, **20**
Copper Chimney, **14**
Green Tandoori Dhaba, **16**
Jal Mahal, **19**
LMB, **23**
Lassiwala, **18**
Niro's, **22**
Shri Shanker Bhojnalya, **8**
Surya Mahal, **21**
Swaad, **11**

♪ NIGHTLIFE

Polo Bar and Panghat
  Theater, **17**
Sheesh Mahal, **5**

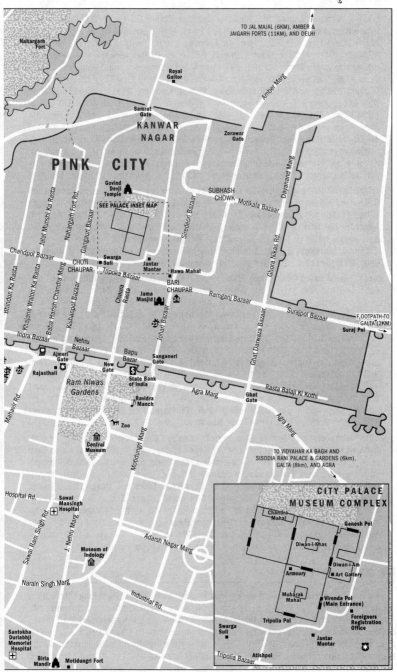

To Jal Majal (6km), Amber & Jaigarh Forts (11km), and Delhi

Nahargarh Fort

Royal Gaitor

Samrat Gate

Amber Marg

KANWAR NAGAR

Zorawar Gate

PINK CITY

Govind Devji Temple

SUBHASH CHOWK

Motikala Bazaar

Dayanand Marg

SEE PALACE INSET MAP

Jalaf Munshi Ka Rasta

Nahargarh Fort Rd.

Siredeori Bazaar

Gangauri Bazaar

Ghora Nikas Rd.

Chandpol Bazaar

Swarga Suli

CHOTI CHAUPAR

Tripolia Bazaar

Jantar Mantar

Hawa Mahal

BARI CHAUPAR

Bhindon Ka Rasta

Khajane Walon Ka Rasta

Baba Harsh Chandra Marg

Kishanpol Bazaar

Chaura Rasta

Jama Masjid

Johari Bazaar

Ramganj Bazaar

Surajpol Bazaar

Ghat Darwaza Bazaar

FOOTPATH TO GALTA (2KM)

Suraj Pol

Indra Bazaar

Nehru Bazaar

Ajmeri Gate

Bapu Bazar

Sanganeri Gate

Rajasthali

New Gate

State Bank of India

Ram Niwas Gardens

Ravidra Manch

Agra Marg

Ghat Gate

Rasta Balaji Ki Kothi

Mahavir Rd.

Zoo

Central Museum

Motidungri Marg

Agra Marg

TO VIDYAHAR KA BAGH AND SISODIA RANI PALACE & GARDENS (6km), GALTA (8km), AND AGRA

Hospital Rd.

Sawal Mansingh Hospital

Sawai Ram Singh Rd.

J. Nehru Marg

Adarsh Nagar Marg

Museum of Indology

Narain Singh Marg

Industrial Rd.

Santokba Durlabhji Memorial Hospital

Birla Mandir

Motidungri Fort

Tripolia Bazaar

CITY PALACE MUSEUM COMPLEX

Chandra Mahal

Ganesh Pol

Diwan-I-Khas

Diwan-I-Am

Armoury

Art Gallery

Mubarak Mahal

Virenda Pol (Main Entrance)

Foreigners Registration Office

Swarga Suli

Tripolia Pol

Jantar Mantar

Atishpol

US$85). **Sahara Airlines,** 203 Shalimar Complex, Church Rd. (☎377637 or 365741). **International carriers: Air India,** Ganpati Plaza, MI Rd. (☎368047 or 36821). Open M-F 9:30am-1pm and 2-5:30pm. **Air France,** Jaipur Towers, 2nd fl. (☎377051 or 370509). Open M-Sa 9:30am-1pm and 2-5:30pm. **British Airways,** Usha Plaza, MI Rd., next to Jaipur Towers (☎361065). Open M-F 9:30am-1pm and 2-6pm, Sa 9:30am-2pm. **KLM/Northwest Airlines,** Jaipur Towers, 2nd fl., MI Rd. (☎367772). Open M-Sa 9:30am-1:30pm and 2-6pm. **Lufthansa,** Saraogi Mansion, MI Rd. (☎561360). Near New Gate. Open M-F 9:30am-6pm, Sa 9:30am-2pm. **Jet Air Limited** (☎375430 or 367409; fax 374242), in the same office as Jet Airways, is an agent for American Airlines, Austrian Airlines, Bangladesh Biman, Gulf Air, Royal Jordanian, and TWA. **Global Air Travel Service,** Jaipur Towers, ground fl. (☎373495), represents Air Lanka, All Nippon Airways, Cathay Pacific, Kuwait Air, Kenya Airways, Korean Air, Malaysia Airlines, Royal Nepal Airlines, SAS, Saudi, Singapore Air, Swissair, Syrian Air, United, and others. **Delhi Express Travels,** Jaipur Towers (☎361519 or 360188), represents Thai.

Trains: Jaipur Railway Station (☎131). To book early, go to the **Advance Reservation Office** (☎135), to the left of the station. Open M-Sa 8am-8pm, Su 8am-2pm. To: **Agra** (7hr., 11:15pm); **Ahmedabad** (10-13hr., 3-7 per day 4:40am-12:45am, Rs205); **Ajmer** for **Pushkar** (2-3hr., 5-7 per day 4:40am-12:45am, Rs62); **Bikaner** (7hr., 4am and 3pm); **Delhi** (5-8hr., 5-10 per day, Rs120); **Jodhpur** (6hr., 4 per day 4pm-2:45am); **Mumbai** (18½hr., 1:30pm; numerous other slower routes go via Ahmedabad); **Udaipur** (12hr., 10:10pm, Rs154); **Varanasi** (20hr., 1:25pm, Rs270).

Buses: Sindhi Camp Central Bus Stand, Station Rd. Platforms serving different destinations have different enquiry and ticket counters. All deluxe buses depart from platform 3, in the back. **Platform 1** to **Sariska** (counter #8, 3hr., every 30min. 5am-10pm, Rs49). **Platform 2** (☎206055) to **Sawai Madhopur** (5hr., 5:15pm, Rs71). **Platform 3,** for deluxe buses (☎205621). To: **Abu Road** (10hr., 8pm, Rs227); **Agra** (5hr., 14 per day 6am-midnight, Rs117); **Ahmedabad** (14hr., 6pm, Rs310); **Ajmer** for **Pushkar** (2½hr., 6 per day 8:30am-8pm, Rs66); **Bikaner** (7hr., 1pm, Rs169); **Chittaurgarh** (7hr., 4 per day 10am-midnight, Rs151); **Delhi** (5½hr., every 30min-1hr. 5:30am-1am, Rs206); **Jaisalmer** (13hr., 10:15pm, Rs200); **Jodhpur** (7hr.; 4, 8:30am, 11:30pm; Rs109-161); **Udaipur** (9hr., 6 per day 9:15am-midnight, Rs200). **Private buses** depart from the same stand. Private bus companies line Station Rd. and Motilal Atal Rd., off MI Rd.; most hotels can make reservations. **Platform 4** to: **Jhunjhunu** (4hr., every 30min.-1hr. 3:45am-11pm, Rs87) via **Nawalgarh** (3hr., Rs71).

Local Transportation: Unmetered **auto-rickshaws** are the quickest way to get around. **Cycle-rickshaws** are cheaper (bus or train station to Bani Park Rs10; GPO to Ajmeri Gate Rs10). **Local buses** leave from the Central Bus Stand, all sights, and most major intersections every 5-15min. **Taxi stands** are opposite the RTDC Tourist Hotel and outside Sanganeri Gate. **Cars** can be rented (with driver) from **RTDC Tours and Travels,** RTDC Tourist Hotel (☎375466; open daily 7am-8am) or **Sita World Travels,** Station Rd. (☎204688). Roughly Rs7 per km for A/C, plus an additional Rs75-150 per night for the driver's lodgings. **Bicycle rental** is available at **Kishanpol Bazaar,** near Ajmeri Gate (Rs35-50 per day; open daily 8am-10pm) and **Mohan Cycle Works,** MI Rd., between Ajmeri and New Gates (☎372335; Rs25 per day, 5-day minimum; open M-Sa 10:30am-8pm).

◢ ORIENTATION

Jaipur's wide, straight roads make getting around easy. The walled **Pink City,** which contains most of Jaipur's tourist attractions, is in the northeast; the **new city** sprawls south and west. From **Jaipur Railway Station,** on the western edge of town, **Station Rd.** leads past the **Central Bus Stand** on its way to **Chand Pol,** the western gate into the Pink City. The Pink City's main thoroughfare changes names four times—**Chandpol, Tripolia, Ramganj,** and **Surajpol Bazaars**—before exiting the walled city under **Suraj Pol**, the eastern gate. The **City Palace complex** is just north of Tripolia Bazaar. **Johari Bazaar** is the principal shopping street in the old city. **Mirza Ismail (MI) Rd.**, the new city's main thoroughfare, is lined with shops, restaurants, and tourist services. Just south of New Gate and beyond the Ram Niwas Gardens, **Jawaharlal Nehru Marg** runs south past several hospitals and the Birla Mandir.

⚇ PRACTICAL INFORMATION

TOURIST AND FINANCIAL SERVICES

Tourist Office: The Government of India Tourist Office (☎ 1363 or 372200). In Hotel Khasa Kothi, south of the MI Rd. and Station Rd. intersection. Open M-F 9am-6pm, Sa 9am-1:30pm. Other offices include the **Rajasthan Department of Tourism Office** (☎ 365256), in the RTDC Tourist Hotel bldg. (through the "TRC Information Counter" door), and the conveniently located **RTDC Tourist Information Bureau** (☎ 315714), platform 1 of the railway station. Next door to the RTDC are sister offices for **Uttar Pradesh** and **Gujarat Tourism**. The **RTDC Central Reservations Office** (☎ 202581), RTDC Hotel Swagatam Campus, Jaipur 302006, makes bookings for 46 RTDC hotels throughout Rajasthan as well as the Pushkar Fair and RTDC Tourist Village. Payment for Pushkar tents must be received in full 60 days prior to commencement of the fair.

Tours: RTDC runs bilingual **city tours.** (Usually daily in high season, 10 person minimum.) The half-day tour (8am-1pm and 1:30-6pm; Rs90, excluding entrance fees) includes stops at Amber, the City Palace, and Jantar Mantar and drive-by glimpses of a few other sights; the full-day tour (9am-6pm; Rs135, excluding entrance fees) stops at Nahargarh and Jaigarh Forts as well. Book the day before by phone (☎ 375466) or at any RTDC hotel. Both the RTDC and the Government of India Tourist Office can arrange government-approved private **guides** (half-day Rs250 for up to four people).

Currency Exchange: The following institutions all change cash and traveler's checks, in addition to offering other services listed below. **State Bank of India** (☎ 561163), MI Rd., near Sanganeri Gate. Open M-F 10am-2pm and 2:30-5pm, Sa 10am-2pm. **Andhra Bank,** MI Rd. (☎ 374529), near Panch Batti. Gives cash advances on MC and V (1% commission). Open M-F 10am-2pm and 2:30-3:30pm, Sa 10am-noon. **Thomas Cook,** Jaipur Towers, ground fl. (☎ 360940). Moneygram services. Open M-Sa 9:30am-6pm. **CitiBank,** on MI Rd. near Ganpati Plaza., has a 24hr. **ATM** (MC/V/Cirrus/Plus).

EMERGENCY AND COMMUNICATIONS

Police: Rajasthan Police Headquarters (☎ 606111 or 606122). Inside the City Palace complex, behind the Hawa Mahal. **Police Control Room** (☎ 565555), in King Edward Memorial Bldg., near Ajmeri Gate.

Hospital/Medical Services: Ambulance (☎ 102). **Sawai Mansingh Hospital,** Sawai Ram Singh Rd. (☎ 560291). Government-run, large, and efficient. Of the many private hospitals, the best are **Santokba Durlabhji Memorial Hospital,** Bhawani Singh Marg (☎ 566251), and **Soni Hospital, Kahota Bagh** (☎ 562028), off J. Nehru Marg.

Pharmacy: Pharmacies line Station Rd. and surround the hospitals. One is also on Shiv Marg, opposite Jaipur Inn. Most open daily 8am-10pm.

Internet: Cybarea, Ganpati Plaza (☎ 379644), has 12 machines. Rs40 per hr. **Net Point Cyber Cafe,** MI Rd. (☎ 214824), between Panch Batti and Ajmeri Gate. Rs30 per hr. Open daily 7am-11pm. **Communicator,** Jaipur Towers, ground fl. (☎ 368061). Rs40 per hr. Open M-Sa 9am-9pm, Su 11am-4pm.

Post Office: GPO, MI Rd. (☎ 368740). Open M-Sa 8am-7:45pm, Su 10am-7:45pm. Parcels heavier than 2kg must be inspected and sent from the **Foreign Post Office,** around the back (bring a box). Open M-Sa 10am-5pm. Branches near the Govt. of India Tourist Office and at the Central Bus Stand. Open M-Sa 9am-5pm. **Postal Code:** 302001.

ACCOMMODATIONS

The budget hotel scene in Jaipur is frustratingly competitive. As soon as you arrive, you will be mobbed by rickshaw drivers prodding you to a particular hotel. It's a win-win situation for them: either they'll receive a commission or charge you three times the usual price. Your cheapest bet is to pay the triple fare and go where you want to go. Or just walk down a block and find slightly less ruthless local transportation. Hotels around MI Rd., near the bus and railway stations, offer easy access to the services of the new city but are noisier. Those in the residential area of Bani Park provide a more peaceful environment. Few hotels are within the Pink City itself. Hotels offer discounts of 25-40% off season (Apr.-Aug.). Home-stays can be arranged through the tourist office at the railway station (Rs200-1500 per night). Though more expensive, the last three hotels listed are worth the money.

◙ **Evergreen Guest House** (☎363446 or 362415; fax 204234; evergreen34@hotmail.com). Off MI Rd. A huge, staggeringly popular cheapie, set around a lush green courtyard. Very centrally located and a good place to meet other travelers, but rooms (all with attached bath) are rather bare and service can be brusque. Internet Rs1.50 per min. Singles Rs150/175-250; doubles Rs175/200-300, with A/C Rs500. ❶

◙ **Atithi Guest House,** 1 Park House Scheme. MI Rd. (☎378679; fax 379496; tanmay@jp1.dot.net.in). Near All India Radio. Sparklingly-clean, airy rooms with marble floors, attached baths, and phones. Garden and plant-filled rooftop terrace provides a getaway from the bustle and noise. Great veg. cooking. Internet Rs70 per hr. Reservations recommended. Singles Rs300-550; doubles Rs350-600, with A/C Rs750-800. ❷

Chit Chat Guest House, D-160 Kabir Marg, Bani Park (☎201899). An intimate place with six simple rooms set far away from the hustle and bustle. Excellent value. Huge, chill restaurant serves good food. Rooms Rs80, with attached bath Rs100-150. ❶

Anurag Guest House, D-249 Devi Marg (☎201679 or 205016). Bani Park. Six spacious, more-or-less clean rooms and a lovely lawn area. All rooms have hot-water baths and air coolers. Check-out 24hr. Doubles Rs250. ❶

Hotel Kailash, Johari Bazaar (☎565372). Between stalls 209 and 210, nearly opposite Jama Masjid. One of the few in the heart of the Pink City. It's noisy, but action-packed. Rooms that get cheaper the higher you climb, all with air cooling and TVs and most with attached bath. Check-out 24hr. Singles Rs160-360; doubles Rs180-410. ❷

RTDC Hotel Swagatam, MI Rd. (☎200595), near the train station, and **RTDC Hotel Teej,** Collectorate Rd. (☎205482), are as uninspiring as any other RTDC hotel, but if you're on a tight budget, their dorms (Rs50 per bed) are the best deal in town. Teej's is the nicer of the two, very clean and with hot-water shower facilities. Swagatam also has decent doubles—convenient if you arrive late at night by train (Rs350-550). ❷

Hotel Arya Niwas, Sansar Chandra Rd. (☎372456 or 371773; fax 364376; tarvn@aryaniwas.com). A popular, well-run hotel in a light and airy bldg. brimming with potted plants. Rooms are simple but modern and pleasant, with clean attached baths. All room with coolers, most with TVs. Nice garden sitting area out front. Restaurant. Singles Rs350-450, with A/C Rs550; doubles Rs450-600/Rs700-740. ❷

Karni Niwas, Motilal Atal Rd. (☎365433 or 216947; fax 375034; karniniwas@hotmail.com), behind Hotel Neelam. Run by four brothers, Niwas has 13 clean, comfortable rooms, most with private terraces, in a residential area. Free pickup at train or bus station. Singles Rs275-500, with A/C Rs700; doubles Rs325-550/Rs800. ❷

Hotel Mangal, Sansar Chandra Marg (☎375126), and **Hotel Mangal Palace,** Station Rd. (☎378901), opposite the Central Bus Stand, are typical Indian budget hotels (big and impersonal, though amazingly clean for their ilk) but make good fallback options if you arrive late or if more backpacker-friendly places are full. Check-out 24hr. Both places: singles Rs325-425, with A/C Rs700; doubles Rs375-475/Rs740. ❷

Umaid Bhawan Guest House, D-1/2-A Via Bank Rd., Bani Park (☎316184; fax 207445; umaid_bhawan@yahoo.com). Behind Collectorate. Elegantly furnished rooms with spotless baths and TVs, most with balconies, are worth a splurge. Non-A/C budget rooms go for Rs400, but the more expensive rooms are better value. Pool, Internet, restaurant. Rooms with A/C Rs500-750; beautiful suites Rs800-1050. ❸

⌂ FOOD

For cheap quickies, the *bhojnalyas* (diners) on Station Rd. are local favorites, while more expensive restaurants are on MI Rd. For those with a sweet tooth, the *mishri, mawas,* and *ghevars* of Jaipur are the best in the state; **Lassiwala,** on MI Rd., also whips up a delicious sweet *lassi.* **Dominoes Pizza, Pizza Hut,** and **Baskin Robbins** are all in Ganpati Plaza if you're yearning for international *haute cuisine.*

Swaad, Ganpati Plaza, MI Rd. (☎360749). Sit back in the comfy chairs while the classical Indian music and delicious food lull you to sleep. Most dishes Rs65-130. Live music daily 8pm. Open daily 11am-11pm. ❷

Niro's, MI Rd., near Panch Batti. A Jaipur institution, very popular with both locals and tourists. All your old Indian, Chinese and Continental favorites are here, and yours for only Rs80-150. Open daily 10am-11pm. ❷

Copper Chimney, MI Rd., opposite the GPO. Huge portions of yummy Indian food (Rs60-135). Free home delivery (☎372275). Open daily 11:30am-3:30pm and 6-11pm. ❷

Surya Mahal, MI Rd. Next to Niro's. Popular among businessmen, families, teens, and tourists alike. Specializes in South Indian, Chinese, and pizza. *Dosas* Rs40-56, veg. dishes Rs45-80. Open daily 8am-11pm. Its affiliated bakery, **Bake Hut,** around the back, is full of Westerners with pastries in hand. Open daily 9am-10:30pm. ❶

LMB, Johari Bazaar in the old city. Incredible veg. food in a quirky A/C environment. Try not to fill up first at the attached sweet shop. Open daily 8am-11:30pm.

Green Tandoori Dhaba, off MI Rd., down the street opposite Hotel Shaan. When you get tired of all the yuppie (and pricey) places listed above, join locals at this unpretentious joint for lip-smacking non-veg. food at great prices. Full *tandoori* chicken Rs90, chicken curry or chicken *muglas* Rs42-50. Open daily 11am-11pm. ❶

Shri Shanker Bhojnalya, Station Rd., west of the bus stand. The sign's in Hindi; it's just to the left of Santosh Bhojnalya. Not flashy but one of the most popular *bhojnalyas* in town. Excellent *thalis* (Rs30) and *tandoori.* Open daily 9am-11pm. ❶

Jal Mahal, MI Rd., next to Surya Mahal. Perfect for dessert after a meal at any of the MI restaurants. Tasty ice cream cones, floats, shakes, and sundaes go for Rs18-45. ❶

◎ SIGHTS

THE PINK CITY

The avenues of the Pink City are broad and meticulously planned. At the heart of the Pink City lies the **City Palace Complex,** which contains the City Palace Museum, the Hawa Mahal, and the Jantar Mantar observatory. Tourists must access the complex via **Atishpol** (Stable Gate), to the west of **Tripolia Pol,** or from the east via **Siredeori Bazaar.** The **bazaars** surrounding the complex are as interesting as the palace itself and provide lots of shopping opportunities (see **Shopping,** p. 478).

CHILLIN'—MAHARAJA-STYLE
The current maharaja of Jaipur, Sawai Bhawani Singh, is a man of refinement and verve. Paying him a visit is about the coolest thing you can do in Jaipur. An old military man, the maharaja is an avid polo player who enjoys driving fancy cars and talks with excitement about computers and ham radio. The maharaja typically grants **private audiences** to visitors on weekdays. To make an appointment, ask at the main entrance of the City Palace for the ADC (Aide de Camp) Office. There you can speak with the PPS (Principal Private Secretary), who organizes the maharaja's schedule. It's best to give the PPS a couple of days' advance notice. Be persistent in confirming the date and time of the appointment. Throughout the process, modest, respectful clothing and behavior are expected.

CITY PALACE AND MUSEUM. Built between 1729 and 1732 by Jai Singh II, founder of Jaipur, the City Palace encompasses nearly 15% of the Pink City's total area. Early maharajas filled the palace with scientific and artistic treasures. Others cultivated a lively palace harem, which reputedly held over 1000 women. In recent decades, the palace has taken on a new public role in the life of the city. It opened to tourists in the 1950s, and scenes from over 400 films—including *North by Northwest* and the Errol Flynn version of Rudyard Kipling's *Kim*—have been shot within its walls. As the home of the current maharaja, Sawai Bhawani Singh, much of the palace is off-limits, but what you can see is delightful.

There are two entrances to the **museum** once you've entered the City Palace complex; the main one is via **Virendra Pol,** near the Jantar Mantar. The building directly ahead as you enter through Virendra Pol is the **Mubarak Mahal,** carved out of white marble. The ground floor is occupied by the offices of the palace's director, a museum complex, and a library that is accessible only with the permission of the director. The second floor of the building houses a **Textile Museum,** with collections of cloth and costumes, including the big robes of the Notorious "Fat Maharaja," Sawai Madho Singh I, who reportedly weighed over 250kg. Behind the Mubarak Mahal and to the right, in the northwest corner of the same courtyard, is the **Arms and Weapons Museum.** Apart from some amusing greetings on the walls, spelled out in English using various instruments of death, the armory is more memorable for the exquisite mirror-work and gold-leaf paintings on the ceilings.

Adjacent to the armory is the elaborate **Rajendra Gate,** whose massive brass doors, flanked by two marble elephants, lead to a second courtyard. At the center is the **Diwan-i-Khas,** or Hall of Private Audience, which contains two huge silver urns. With the Guinness-certified distinction as the largest pieces of silver in the world, these urns were used to store a reserve of holy Ganges water for Maharaja Madho Singh, who refused to drink, bathe in, or use any other water.

Through the door on the right (on the eastern side of the courtyard) is the **Diwan-i-Am** (Hall of Public Audience), which houses the **Art Gallery,** whose hodge-podge of objects includes an extensive collection of manuscripts, miniature paintings, works on astronomy, and a 16th-century edition of Aristotle. As you exit the AA Gallery, **Peacock Gate,** on the opposite side of the courtyard leads into a third courtyard. On an adjacent wall of the courtyard is the **Chandra Mahal,** the maharaja's residence. Parts of the first floor are open to the public. *(Open daily 9:30am-5pm.* ☎ *608055. Rs150; video fee Rs150. No photography in the galleries. Government-authorized guides Rs150.)*

HAWA MAHAL (PALACE OF WINDS). Jaipur's most recognizable landmark, the Hawa Mahal's five-story pink sandstone edifice was built in 1799 as a comfortable retreat for Maharaja Sawai Pratap Singh. Designed to catch the breeze, the Hawa Mahal was named for the many brass wind vanes that adorned it until the 1960s. Underground tunnels connected the palace to the harem. A small **government**

museum displays some sculptures on the ground floor. *(To reach the entrance from the front of the facade, head south down Sireedeon Bazaar, turn right on Tripolia Bazaar, and take your 1st right. ☎ 668862. Open M-Th and Sa-Su 9am-4:30pm. Rs2. Camera fee Rs30, video Rs70.)*

JANTAR MANTAR. The largest stone observatory in the world, Jantar Mantar ("instrument of calculation") is one of the Maharaja Jai Singh's most conspicuous contributions to Jaipur. Before building it in 1728-34, Jai Singh sent emissaries east and west for cutting-edge technical manuals, including a copy of La Hire's "Tables." After building the Jantar Mantar, Jai Singh found that it produced readings 20 seconds more accurate than La Hire's. The observatory features 18 instruments, including a 30m sundial—impressive, but incomprehensible without a guide or a solid knowledge of astronomy. *(South of the City Palace. ☎ 660494. Open daily 9am-4:30pm. Rs4, free M. Camera fee Rs50, video Rs100. Guides Rs150.)*

GOVIND DEVJI TEMPLE. Surrounded by sprawling gardens, Govind Devji Temple contains an image of Lord Krishna as Govind Devji, the patron deity of the royal family, and his mate, Radha. *(North of the City Palace, off Sireedeori Bazaar. Darshan times change every two months but are always clearly posted outside the temple. The following may have been changed; be sure to get updated hours before visiting: 4:45-5, 7:70-8:30, 9:30-9:45, 11:15-11:30am, 6:15-6:30, 7-8, 9-9:15pm. Free.)*

SWARGA SULI. This towering minaret lies southwest of the City Palace and is the highest structure within the walls of the Pink City. The maharaja would sometimes bring criminals to the top of the tower and throw them to their deaths below.

NORTH OF THE PINK CITY

The sights north of the Pink City are all approached via turnoffs from the same road and, thus, are most conveniently visited in the same trip. A round-trip rickshaw to all of the following sights should cost Rs230-250. Alternatively, if you're just interested in visiting Amber and Jaigarh, you can take a bus to Amber and hike the shortcut path up to Jaigarh instead of driving the long way around to Jaigarh.

AMBER FORT. Standing guard over the Pink City, the three Garland Forts dominate the northern horizon. Foremost among these is the Amber, the ancient capital of Jaipur State. Built in 1592 by Raja Man Singh, Amber synthesizes both Hindu and Islamic architectural styles. While Jaigarh Fort was built primarily for defensive purposes, Amber was intended mainly as a residential fort, and its elaborate palace complex features decorative artwork and many other creature comforts.

Buses and rickshaws will drop you off at the base of the mountain; you can either walk the 15min. up to the fort or hop on an elephant (Rs400 round-trip for up to 4 people) or jeep (Rs120 round-trip per person). From the main courtyard, a flight of stairs leads to **Diwan-i-Am** (Hall of Public Audience). To the right is the mosaic-tiled **Ganesh Pol,** the main gate into the palace. Just inside are the maharaja's former apartments, with their labyrinthine corridors, balconies, terraces, and rooms built for the maharaja, his 12 wives, and his 350 women on the side. Parts are in poor repair, but some, like the famous **Jai Mandir** (Hall of Victory), are in better condition, exhibiting blinding mirror-work and beautifully preserved coloring. Other attractions include the **Sheesh Mahal,** the original private chambers of the maharaja, and the **Sukh Mahal** (Pleasure Palace), opposite the Jai Mandir. Back down off the main courtyard is the **Shri Sila Devi Temple** whose majestic silver doors lead to a black marble sculpture of the goddess of strength. The government-approved **guides** (Rs100 for two people) are extremely well-informed and armed with stories that make the palace come alive. *(11km north of Jaipur. Amber-bound buses leave regularly from the Central Bus Stand and from the front of the Hawa Mahal; Rs5. Open daily 9am-4:30pm. Rs50. Camera fee Rs25, video fee Rs100.)*

JAIGARH FORT. Stocky Jaigarh, the second in the Garland trio, is perched on an even higher hill with a breathtaking view of Amber Fort. It once served as the royal treasury, and some people still think there's some royal treasure hidden somewhere on the grounds; even the Indian government ransacked it in 1976 in the hopes of finding it. Inside is a moderately interesting **museum;** an **armory,** with the usual instruments of death; and the gigantic **Jaivana,** the largest wheeled cannon in the world. *(The fort can be reached by a 20min. climb, by jeep (Rs100-150), or by rickshaw. Open daily 9am-4:30pm. Rs20, free with City Palace ticket stub; camera fee Rs20; video Rs100.)*

JAL MAHAL (WATER PALACE). About 6km north of Jaipur along the road to Amber is the Jal Mahal (Water Palace), which appears to float on a lake and resembles the Lake Palace in Udaipur. Unfortunately, you can't go inside.

NAHARGARH FORT. The third Garland Fort, the Nahargarh, is also known as the Tiger Fort. Painted floral patterns brighten the walls of the many chambers, which are strung together in a maze-like floorplan. Because of Nahargarh's isolated locale, be wary of bringing valuables or traveling here alone. *(Vehicle-accessible via a windy 15km road from Jaipur, or take a steep 2km hike from the northwest corner of the old city. Open daily 10am-5:30pm. Rs5. Camera fee Rs30, video fee Rs70. Guides available.)*

ROYAL GAITOR. Just north of the old city, set against a backdrop of hills are the cenotaphs of the maharajas of Jaipur. The older ones are toward the back of the complex, including the beautifully carved cenotaph of Jai Singh. On the hill to the left, you can see Nahargarh Fort; to the right, steps lead uphill (20min.) to a **Ganesh temple.** *(North of Samrat Gate. Open daily 9am-4:30pm. Free. Camera Rs10; video Rs20.)*

SOUTH OF THE PINK CITY

BIRLA MANDIR. Officially called the Lakshmi Narayan Mandir, this blindingly white and industrially sponsored temple is rapidly becoming one of Jaipur's most beloved buildings. Built by the wealthy Birla family, the temple was styled with the family's multi-denominational approach to religion in mind: the three domes have each been styled according to a different type of religious architecture. The theme of pluralism is further evident in the artwork of the *parikrama*—done by a Muslim—and the pillars flanking the temple, which include carvings of Hindu deities as well as depictions of Moses, Jesus, Zarathustra, and Socrates. Near the entrance to Birla Mandir are a variety of small temples. On the hill overlooking the Birla Mandir are the remains of **Motidungri Fort,** owned by the maharaja. The fort complex contains a **Shiva temple** that is open to the public only on Shivaratri, during the first week of March. *(Jawaharlal Nehru Marg, where it intersects Bhawani Sing Marg. Open daily Nov.-Feb. 6:30am-noon and 3-9:30pm; Mar.-Oct. 6am-noon and 3-10pm.)*

CENTRAL MUSEUM AND RAM NIWAS GARDENS. Ram Niwas Gardens shelters Jaipur's Central Museum, often called **Albert Hall.** The building itself, a mixture of pillars, arches, and courtyards adorned with murals, is more interesting than the museum. The halls contain exhibits on traditional Rajasthani dance, musical instruments, and decorative arts. *(In the Ram Niwas Gardens, south of the old city. Open Sa-Th 10am-5pm. Rs30, M free. Photography prohibited inside.)*

MUSEUM OF INDOLOGY. The eccentric, privately funded Museum of Indology features the encyclopedic treasure troves of Vyakul (recently deceased poet, painter, and pack-rat)—ancient manuscripts, curio pieces, and some real treasures. In one room, the marriage contract of the last Mughal emperor competes with a grain of rice with a full-color map of India drawn on it. *(About 500m south of the Central Museum, just off Nehru Marg. Open daily 9am-6pm. Admission with guide Rs40.)*

EAST OF THE PINK CITY

GALTA (MONKEY TEMPLE). This series of beautifully frescoed temples and pavilions lines a rocky valley 3km east of Jaipur. The temples are grouped around a sacred pool in which worshippers bathe and swim while monkeys scamper and splash nearby. The best time to visit is before noon, when the tide of worshippers is at its fullest. The most direct route to Galta is a steep 2.5km foot path that begins just outside Suraj Pol and takes about 30min.; this route takes you past the **Surya Mandir,** with exquisite views, before leading you down into the gorge. The lazier route is a 10km drive via Agra Marg (auto-rickshaw Rs150 round-trip).

SISODIA RANI KA BAGH & PALACE AND VIDHYADHAR KA BAGH. The **Sisodia Rani Palace and Gardens,** 8km east of Jaipur on Agra Marg, was built by Jai Singh in 1710 for his princess. The delicately painted palace and pavilions are washed in a pale yellow—the original color of the Pink City. Nearby, the **Vidhyadhar Gardens** provide a pocket of green wedged between two sheer rock faces. If you're driving to Galta, both make a pleasant stop right on the way. *(Both open daily 8am-6pm. Rs5.)*

▣ ♫ ENTERTAINMENT AND NIGHTLIFE

THE ARTS. Most regularly scheduled performances take place only during the high season. For authentic Rajasthani dance and music, the **Panghat Theater** (☎381919), in Rambagh Palace, off Bhawani Singh Rd., has in-season nightly performances in high-class surroundings for Rs300 per person. Shows are generally 7-9pm. Call in advance. Many of the high-end hotels put on a dance, music, or puppet show every night. Try the Rajputana Palace Sheraton, the Man Singh Palace, or the Rambagh Palace. **Ravindra Manch** (☎609061), in Ram Niwas Gardens, offers occasional evening performances of Rajasthani dance, music, and plays. The Modern Art Gallery upstairs is free (☎618531; open M-Sa 10am-5pm). **Jawahar Kala Kendra,** Jawaharlal Nehru Marg (☎510501), run by the Dept. of Art and Culture, shows regular in-season Rajasthani plays and performance.

FESTIVALS. The **Gangauri Fair** celebrates the union of Shiva ("Gan") and Parvati ("Gauri") and lasts for 18 days after *Holi* (Apr. 4-5, 2003). In addition to performances and parades, the **Elephant Festival** features elephant polo and a man versus beast tug-of-war (Mar. 17, 2003). The **Teej Fair** (Festival of Swings) celebrates the monsoon (Aug. 1-2, 2003).

CINEMA. Jaipur's 16 cinemas are packed with people at every Hindi film showing. The world-renowned **Raj Mandir Cinema,** just south of Panch Batti, is an experience in itself. The showings are *always* sold out; arrive *at least* 1hr. in advance to get tickets. Look for the tourist/student queue. (☎374694. Movie screenings daily 11:45am, 3, 6:15, 9:30pm. Advance booking for next-day shows 1-2 and 4-5pm.)

CHOWKI DHANI. This exhibition of village life, 20km south of the city, is surprisingly well done. The admission fee includes a traditional (spicy and very heavy) Rajasthani dinner, served on leaf plates in a large mud hut, after which you can roam freely about the "village" to watch performances of traditional palmistry, snake charming, *mehendi* hand-art, puppet shows, acrobatics, and a (man-powered!) ferris wheel. (Dinner Rs50. *Baksheesh* expected at some performances. Open daily 6-11pm. Auto-rickshaw 45min. one-way; Rs250 round-trip.)

BARS. Only hotels can legally serve anything stronger than beer. For classy, A/C boozing, try the **Polo Bar** in Rambagh Palace, off Bhawani Singh Rd. (open daily 11am-11:30pm; cocktails Rs235-265), or the **Sheesh Mahal,** in the Rajputana Palace Sheraton near the railway station (open daily 11am to 11pm; cocktails Rs200). For budget sloshing, try **Talab Bar,** in Swagatam Tourist Bungalow (open daily noon-3pm and 6-11pm), or any of the other budget hotel bars near the railway station.

RAJASTHAN

☐ SHOPPING

Jaipur is the shopping capital of Rajasthan—you'll find a huge assortment of handicrafts, pottery, silk, textiles, jewelry, and perfumes. Shopping here can be draining because you have to haggle incessantly, but the effort is worth it. Rajasthan is known for its colorful, unbeatable selection of tie-dyed fabrics called *bandhani.* The jewelry and gem work of Jaipur are world-famous and remarkably inexpensive, but be on the lookout for scams. The fixed-price emporium **Rajasthali**, opposite Ajmeri Gate, carries a variety of goods from throughout Rajasthan. (Open M-Sa 11am-7:30pm.) In front is the **Rajasthan Handloom House,** the government emporium for textiles. More high-quality crafts can be found at the award-winning showroom in the **City Palace museum,** but beware of the insanely inflated prices. The **bazaars** of the palace complex also offer great shopping. The Johari Bazaar and two lanes off it—Gopal ka Rasta and Haldiyon ka Rasta—are the prime spots for **jewelry;** Nehru Bazaar and Bapu Bazaar specialize in **textiles, perfumes,** and **shoes.** Tripolia Bazaar and Chaura Rasta sell a variety of items and **trinkets.** Watch master **carpet-makers** at work in Siredeori Bazaar, find exquisite **marble sculpture** on Khajane Walon Ka Rasta, which crosses bustling Chandpol Bazaar and behold **shoemakers** at work on Ramganj Bazaar. (Most stores open M-Sa 10am-8pm.)

☑ DAYTRIP FROM JAIPUR: SANGANER

The small village of Sanganer, 16km south of Jaipur, is the largest producer of **handmade paper** in the country and is also known for **block printing.** On a half-day visit, you can visit a handmade paper-production factory and see textile printers laying out brightly-colored fabrics to dry in the sun. Buses run regularly to Sanganer from the Central Bus Stand (30min., Rs6); tempos also leave from Ajmeri Gate.

BHARATPUR भरतपुर ☎ 05644

A convenient stop on the tourist route between Agra (56km) and Jaipur (172km), Bharatpur's spectacular Keoladeo Ghana National Park, one of the best bird sanctuaries in the world, is well worth a visit. During the winter, the beautifully maintained park draws millions of migrating birds. Founded by Badan Singh in 1733 as a princely state, Bharatpur soon became known for the fierce armies of Suraj Mal. The state of Bharatpur was recognized as autonomous by the Mughals and successfully resisted two attacks by the British before it was finally captured by Lord Combermere in 1826. It became part of Rajasthan after Independence.

⬚ TRANSPORTATION. The **train station** is several kilometers north of town. To: **Delhi** (3½-5hr.; 5 per day 6:30am-2:45am; Rs80) via **Mathura** (1hr.); **Mumbai** (19-22hr.; daily 10:50am, 6:25, and 7:55pm; Rs304). No trains run from Bharatpur to Jaipur; you must change trains in Mathura. The **bus station,** on the western edge of town, sends buses to: **Agra** (1½hr.; every 30min. 5am-1am; Rs28) via **Fatehpur Sikri** (30min.); **Alwar** (3½hr.; every 1½hr. 6am-5pm; Rs45); **Bikaner** (12hr.; 12:30pm; Rs211); **Delhi** (5hr.; every hr. 4:30am-11:30pm; Rs81); **Jaipur** (4hr.; every 30min. 5am-12:30am; Rs71); **Udaipur** (14hr.; 7:45am, 2:30 and 7:45pm; Rs236). **Rickshaws** cost Rs15-20 to the hotel area. **Tempos** (Rs4) run between the train and bus terminals. You can rent **bicycles** at several hotels near the sanctuary (Rs20-30 per day).

⬚ ⬚ ORIENTATION AND PRACTICAL INFORMATION. The bird sanctuary and the hotels are a few kilometers south of the center of town, along the road to Agra and Fatehpur Sikri. If you arrive by train or by bus from Jaipur, you'll need to take a rickshaw to get there (Rs15-20); if coming by bus from Agra or Fatehpur Sikri, hop off the bus early (look for guest house signs) and head down the main drag. The town center sprawls around the ruins of an ancient fort and is best avoided unless you need to change money or mail a postcard. The **RTDC Tourist Reception Centre,** in the middle of the strip opposite government-run Hotel Saras (a local landmark), has free brochures and maps. (☎22542. Open M-Sa 10am-5pm.) The **State Bank,** near B. Narayan Gate, a 15min. walk northwest of Birdland, changes currency and traveler's checks. (☎22441. Open M-Sa 10am-2pm.) Other services include: **General Hospital,** Station Rd. (emergency ☎23633); **Police** (☎23116); **Post Office,** near Gandhi Park. (Open M-Sa 6:30am-6pm.) **Postal Code:** 321001.

⌐◘ ACCOMMODATIONS AND FOOD. All the hotels below are out of town, along one main strip leading to the park entrance. Most establishments rent bicycles, binoculars, and field guides. Prices listed are for the winter; off season (Apr.-Aug.) discounts often run as high as 50%. Reserve ahead Nov.-Feb.

The ◪**Jungle Lodge ❷,** at the end of the strip, is set in a peaceful garden and run by a couple who will wow you with their spotless rooms and encyclopedic knowledge of local birdlife. (☎25622. Doubles with attached bath Rs200-300.) Right next door, **Falcon Guesthouse ❷,** also has clean rooms and a pleasant garden courtyard. (☎23815. Doubles with attached bath Rs200-450.) Between the park entrance and Hotel Saras is backpacker favorite **Hotel Pelican ❷,** good value with a decent restaurant to boot. (☎24221. Doubles with attached bath Rs200-350.) Just behind Hotel Saras is budget staple **Hotel Spoonbill ❶,** not quite as shiny as some of its competitors, but eager to please and offering some cheaper rooms with common bath. (☎23571. Doubles Rs100-500.) In addition to these standard guest houses along the main road, there are several cozy family-run places on nearby Rajendra Nagar, parallel to the highway. Two of these are particularly friendly, and offer rooms of extremely good value: ◪**Kiran Guest House ❶,** also serves up painstakingly prepared home-style dinners (☎23845; doubles with attached bath Rs100-150). **Green Valley Guesthouse ❶,** is just up the road (☎29576; doubles with attached bath Rs150-200). To reach Rajendra Nagar from Hotel Saras, turn left (as you face the hotel) down the main road to Bharatpur and turn left after 150m when you see the signs.

The restaurants attached to the guest houses in Bharatpur serve mediocre food at inflated prices, but it's so far to the town center that few travelers put up a fight. If you've got a bike, a good compromise is **Jeet Restaurant ❶,** 5min. down the road to Bharatpur from Hotel Saras. This local favorite serves up rich Punjabi food by the plateful (Rs15 per plate)—after a burning *masala channa,* the ice-cold Kingfisher might just be the best bird you have seen all day.

◙ SIGHTS. The main reason foreigners flock to Bharatpur is to go cuckoo over the hordes of birds at the Keoladeo Ghana National Park (see below). If you're in town and sick of binoculars, you could check out the 18th-century **Lohagarh** (Iron Fort), on an artificial island surrounded by a wide moat in the center of town. Built by Maharaja Suraj Mal, the fort has a reputation of being notoriously resistant to attack; British weapons are said to have bounced off the walls. Inside are two towers, **Jawahar Burg** and **Fateh Burg,** built by Suraj to commemorate his victories over the Mughals and the British, as well as the decaying remains of three former palaces. One of them contains a **museum** that features three large galleries of Jain sculpture and fort artifacts. *(Open M-Th and Sa-Su 10am-4:30pm. Rs3.)*

◪ KEOLADEO GHANA NATIONAL PARK. Today one of the best birdwatching spots in the world, Keoladeo Ghana National Park started out as a 29 sq. km, anything-goes play zone for the maharaja of Bharatpur and his buddies to indulge their passion for hunting in the late 19th century. Originally a protected deer shooting site, it was flooded at the turn of the century to create an artificial duck shooting reserve. A sandstone plaque in the park bears testimony to a bag of 4276 duck and geese shot down in one long, record-breaking day in 1938. Since then, the area has been declared a national park and a World Heritage Natural Site.

The park has plenty to offer, even if your interest in birds doesn't normally go much beyond backyard birdfeeders. Renowned in birding circles as the finest wetland reserve in northern India, it is home to such waterfowl as storks, cormorants, egrets, herons, and spoonbills. These locals nest during the monsoon season (starting mid-Aug.), populating the park with eager, young chirpers by early winter. Starting in September, the park also plays host to species (from places as far as Siberia and Tibet) which migrate south for the winter. At its peak bird population in the winter (Nov.-Jan. is the best time to visit), the park houses nearly 430 species, 375 of which are year-round residents. Additionally, the dry-land sections of the park, comprising about two-thirds of the total area, are also rich with life.

As motor vehicles are not allowed past Keoladeo's only entrance, and the park is too expansive to be traversed on foot, you'll need to hire transportation. Going solo on a rented **bike** (Rs20-30 per day, available at the entrance gate and local hotels) allows you to explore at your own pace; this is especially recommended if you intend to venture beyond the central marsh area (where the birds are located) and check out the dry-land scenery, but be forewarned that many paths in the park are extremely rocky. If you're planning to visit just the main bird area, you can hire a **tonga** (horsecart; Rs60 per hr.) or authorized **cycle-rickshaw** (look for the yellow ID tag and number; Rs30 per hr.). Either way, a **guide** will eagerly accompany you for Rs35 per hr. The best way to see the birds is on an early-morning boat trip, which allows you to float up to hundreds of nesting herons, egrets, cranes, storks, and spoonbills. You can hire a **boat** for up to four people in season *(1hr., Rs80)*.

Just past the ticket counter, a small **Orientation Center** features nests, eggs, and stuffed specimens, as well as a color map of the park. A stall at the second checkpost, 1km past the entrance gate, sells bird-books and postcards. *(Open daily 8:15am-5:30pm.)* A small **canteen** near Keoladeo Temple sells beverages, but no food is available within the park, so plan to bring food. Most guest houses happily pack lunches for birdwatchers. *(Park Office ☎ 22777. Park open daily sunrise-sunset. Rs200 per entry; with video camera additional Rs200.)*

AJMER अजमेर ☎ 0145

The bustling town of Ajmer (pop. 401,930), 132km west of Jaipur in the heart of the Aravalli Mountains, is significant to Muslims as the final resting place of Khwaja Muin-ud-din Chishti, founder of India's most important Sufi order. Hundreds of thousands of Muslims and Hindus make a pilgrimage to Ajmer during the annual Urs Ajmer Sharif (Aug. 31-Sept. 1, 2003), during which the town bursts with people and festivities. The rest of the year, most travelers chug straight through to the nearby backpacker mecca of Pushkar, and with good reason—Ajmer has a relatively poor selection of hotels and restaurants. Ajmer's few worthwhile sights are easily visited on a half-day excursion from Pushkar.

◰ **TRANSPORTATION.** Ajmer sends trains along the major Delhi-Ahmedabad broad-gauge line. The railway reservation office is on the second floor above the main entrance to the station. (Enquiries ☎ 131, reservations ☎ 431965. Open M-Sa 8am-8pm, Su 8am-2pm.) To: **Ahmedabad** (10hr;, 3-5 per day 7:20am-2:40am; Rs166) via **Abu Road** (5hr.; Rs120); **Delhi** (7-9hr.; 3-5 per day 5:30am-1:50am; Rs154); **Jaipur** (2-3hr.; 5-7 per day 5:30am-2:25am; Rs50). Meter-gauge trains also head to **Udaipur** (9-10hr.; 1:50 and 7:50am; Rs112) via **Chittaurgarh** (5hr.; Rs81). Buses run from the

main bus stand (☎429398) to: **Abu Road** (9hr.; 3 per day 5:45am-midnight; Rs138); **Ahmedabad** (13½hr.; 5 per day 5:45am-midnight; Rs211-245); **Bikaner** (7hr.; 11 per day 5am-1am; Rs111); **Chittaurgarh** (5hr.; every hr. 6am-1am; Rs73); **Jaipur** (3¼hr.; every 20min. 7:30am-10:30pm; Rs51-62); **Jodhpur** (5hr.; every hr. 4:30am-2:30am; Rs81-96); **Udaipur** (7hr.; every hr. 5:15am-1:15am; Rs114-145). **Private bus** companies line Kutchery Rd. and send deluxe buses to most destinations. Buses to **Pushkar** leave regularly from both the main bus stand and the Station-Kutchery Rd. intersection (100m to the right as you exit the train station). For Rs10-25, cycle- and auto-**rickshaws** will get you anywhere. Crowded **tempos** charge Rs3-5.

■ ⊠ **ORIENTATION AND PRACTICAL INFORMATION.** Ajmer is a small town, only about 3km long. Heading right (north) out of the train station along **Station Rd.** leads to the **Pushkar Bus Stand** and the town's main intersection, where Station Rd. meets **Kutchery Rd.** Following Kutchery Rd. 1.5km northeast brings you to the **Main Bus Stand.** The main **tourist office** is nearby, inside the Hotel Khadim. (☎627426. Open M-Sa 8am-noon and 3-6pm.) A small branch is also at the train station. The **Bank of Baroda,** Prithviraj Marg, opposite the GPO, changes traveler's checks and issues cash advances on AmEx, MC, and V. (☎422575. Open M-F 10am-3pm, Sa 10am-12:30pm.) The **police** (☎425080) are opposite the railway station. Dr. Yadava's **Pratap Memorial Hospital,** Kutchery Rd. (☎626406), the best private hospital, has a 24hr. **pharmacy** in front. The **GPO** is near the Station-Kutchery Rd. intersection. (☎432145. Open M-Sa 10am-6pm.) **Postal Code:** 305001.

⌐ ☐ ACCOMMODATIONS AND FOOD. Ajmer has a disappointing selection of hotels and independent restaurants, but if you haven't booked something ahead in Pushkar for the Mela, they may provide a cheaper alternative. Numerous dirt-cheap, no-frills hotels catering to Muslim pilgrims lie opposite the railway station and are scattered throughout the bazaar area. The most appealing budget option is **Nagpal Tourist Hotel ❶,** Station Rd. (visible to the left as you exit the train station), where the cheapest rooms have TVs and attached baths. (☎627427. Check-out 24hr. Singles Rs150-800; doubles Rs300-1000.) The best of the cheapies is **Bhola Hotel ❶,** Prithviraj Marg, near Agra Gate, which has well-decorated rooms with tiled bathrooms and a tiny terrace. (☎432844. Singles Rs125; doubles Rs200.) Through the gate 100m to the left as you face Bhola is **Hotel Poonam ❶,** near Sadar Kotwali, which has dingier rooms but boasts attached hot-water baths. (☎621711. Singles Rs150; doubles Rs200.) The **Bhola Hotel ❶,** has an excellent and inexpensive restaurant that serves up pure veg. dishes for Rs25-40. (Open daily 9am-11pm.) The **Honeydew Restaurant ❶,** Station Rd., to the left of Nagpal Tourist Hotel, serves Indian and Chinese dishes and ice cream galore in a clean, calm environment with two pool tables. (Main courses Rs30-60. Pool Rs50 per hr. Open daily 9am-11pm.) Nearby, in an alley, by the clock tower opposite the station, **Jai Hind Restaurant,** also serves very good pure veg. food. (Open daily 8:30am-10:30pm.)

◙ **SIGHTS.** Thousands of people flock to Ajmer during the Urs Ajmer Sharif to see **Dargah,** the tomb of the Sufi saint **Khwaja Muin-ud-din Chishti** (who died here in 1236). On the west side of town, in the old city, the tomb looms high above the surrounding bazaars. The elaborate marble complex constitutes one of the most important destinations for Muslim pilgrims in South Asia; Emperor Akbar himself used to pay regular homage to Dargah and even walked here twice all the way from Agra. Originally a simple brick cenotaph completed by Humayun, Dargah has been expanded and improved upon as subsequent rulers have paid tribute. A tall, elaborate gateway, added by the Nizam of Hyderabad, leads to the first courtyard, where two massive cauldrons called *degs* are filled with rice that is sold to devotees as *tabarukh,* a sanctified food. Akbar's mosque is to the right, and Shah

RAJASTHAN

Jahan's grand mosque is farther inside. The actual tomb of the saint is in the central domed marble mosque, encircled by silver railings and overflowing with flower offerings and legions of devotees. Just outside the tomb, *qawwali* singers perform the same hypnotic tunes that have been sung here for the past 700 years. You will inevitably be approached by "guides" when you enter Dargah, but they are not necessary; be firm. Similarly, decline any offers to sign a "visitor's book," which only serves as a slippery slope to demands for large donations. A head scarf is required to enter certain parts of the complex; pick one up from the bazaar that leads up to the tomb. Be sure to keep a close eye on your personal belongings when you enter. Respectful behavior and a small donation are expected.

On the same road, about 500m east of Dargah, is the **Adhai-Din-ka-Jhonpra** (Mosque of Two-and-a-Half Days), named for the remarkably short time Muhammad of Ghur took to add the massive arched screen that converted the former Sanskrit college into a mosque in 1193. The breathtaking screen consists of seven arches carved with Persian calligraphy. The pillared hall behind it is also a beautiful architectural specimen. The magnificently red **Nasiyan Temple,** in the bazaars near Agra Gate, houses a museum, where the Jain conception of the universe is illustrated using a two-floor golden model. A local Jain family used over 1000kg of gold to construct the exhibit in 1865, and the project—with its kaleidoscope of mirrors, colored glass, and gilded figures—took 20 artisans 40 years to complete. (Open daily 8:30am-5:30pm. Rs3.) Not too far away, just beyond the Hotel Poonam, is **Akbar's Palace** (Daulat Khona), an uninspiring palace built by the emperor in 1570. A small **government museum** exhibits ancient tablets, sculptures, and weaponry. (Open M-Th and Sa-Su 10am-4:30pm. Rs3; M free.) The **Dault Bagh** gardens are on the northwest side of town by the banks of **Ana Sagar Lake.** They contain marble pavilions built by Shah Jahan in 1637. (Paddleboats Rs40 per 30min.)

PUSHKAR पुष्कर ☎ 0145

Tiny Pushkar (pop. 13,000) is a major pilgrimage center; devout Hindus are expected to take a dip in the waters here at least once in their lifetime, and for many, this is the final stop on a tour of India's sacred sites. A staggering number of devotees converge upon Pushkar during the full moon of the Hindu lunar month of Kartika (Oct.-Nov.), which coincides with the world-famous Pushkar *oont mela* (camel fair), the largest fair of its kind in the world. At these times, the tiny town is transformed into a swarming beehive of activity—don't miss it.

Given its sacred atmosphere, picturesque surroundings, and *mela*-induced fame, Pushkar probably had no chance of escaping its fate as a backpacker mecca. The main street—a jumble of Internet cafes, shops, and rooftop restaurants—feels more like a traveler's fantasy land than it does like India. Should you be able to tear yourself away from the mesmerizing array of tie-dye gear, you'll find that a quick walk to the other side of the lake or up into the surrounding hills will instantly rekindle the magic that drew people to Pushkar in the first place.

▐ TRANSPORTATION

Ajmer, 11km south of Pushkar, is the usual gateway to Pushkar.

Buses: Ajmer Bus Stand, Ajmer Rd. To: **Ajmer's Pushkar Bus Stand** (30min.; every 15min. 5:30am-9pm; Rs7). **Marwar Bus Stand** serves: **Bikaner** (7hr.; 12 per day 5:30am-11pm; Rs104); **Jaipur** (3½hr.; 6 per day 8am-6:45pm; Rs50); **Jodhpur** (5hr.; 9:45am; Rs77). All other destinations can be reached via the **Main Bus Stand** (☎429398) in Ajmer. **Private bus** companies line Sadar Bazaar and the area around Marwar Bus Stand. Most private buses depart from Ajmer, though free transport from Pushkar to Ajmer and Ajmer's Main Bus Stand is typically included. **Ekta Travels** (see below) has daily buses from Pushkar to major cities in Rajasthan.

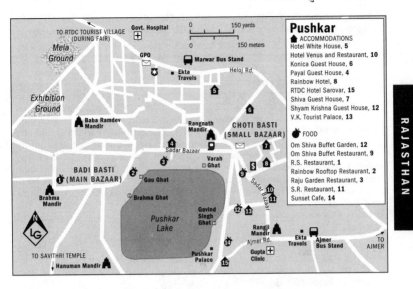

Pushkar

▲ ACCOMMODATIONS
Hotel White House, **5**
Hotel Venus and Restaurant, **10**
Konica Guest House, **6**
Payal Guest House, **4**
Rainbow Hotel, **8**
RTDC Hotel Sarovar, **15**
Shiva Guest House, **7**
Shyam Krishna Guest House, **12**
V.K. Tourist Palace, **13**

◆ FOOD
Om Shiva Buffet Garden, **12**
Om Shiva Buffet Restaurant, **9**
R.S. Restaurant, **1**
Rainbow Rooftop Restaurant, **2**
Raju Garden Restaurant, **3**
S.R. Restaurant, **11**
Sunset Cafe, **14**

RAJASTHAN

✳ 🛈 ORIENTATION AND PRACTICAL INFORMATION

Pushkar is a small town, and a very tourist-friendly one at that, so getting lost is hardly an issue. Most travelers arrive at **Ajmer Bus Stand**, on Ajmer Rd., in the southeast of town. As it winds into town, Ajmer Rd. becomes **Sadar Bazaar,** the main thoroughfare, which follows the northern shore of **Pushkar Lake** and ends on the west side of town, near the **Brahma Mandir.** Roughly speaking, the eastern half of the town is referred to as **Choti Basti (Small Bazaar),** while the western half is known as **Badi Basti (Main Bazaar).** A right turn on any one of the twisting side streets off Sadar Bazaar leads to the road that marks the northern boundary of the town, where you'll find **Marwar Bus Stand.**

Tourist Office: There is no official tourist office in Pushkar, though Ekta Travels (see below) has maps. The **Ajmer Tourist Office** (☎ 627426) has information about Pushkar. During the Pushkar Fair, the RTDC-run **Tourist Village** (☎ 772074) provides information.

Budget Travel: Ekta Travels (☎ 772131). Near Marwar Bus Stand. A smaller branch (☎ 772931) is near Ajmer Bus Stand. This sole government-approved agency in Pushkar issues Indian Airlines, train, and private bus tickets. Both open daily 9am-10pm.

Currency Exchange: State Bank of Bikaner and Jaipur (☎ 772006). Sadar Bazaar. Changes only traveler's checks. Open M-F 10am-2pm, Sa 10am-noon. Money-changers along Sadar Bazaar change cash at good rates, but count your rupees carefully.

Police: Main Police Station (☎ 772046). On the northern side of town. Tourist-friendly and English-speaking. Open 24hr.

Pharmacy: Most pharmacies line the northern side of town near the hospital and Marwar Bus Stand, but there are several in Sadar Bazaar as well. Most open daily 8am-8pm.

Hospital/Medical Services: Dr. Sanjay Gupta (☎ 772672). Between the Hotels Om and Sarovar. Runs an excellent clinic for medical assistance to travelers. Open daily 10am-8pm; on call after-hours. **Government Community Health Centre** (☎ 772029). Near Marwar Bus Stand. English-speaking staff. Open 24hr. for emergencies.

Internet: Myriad, depressingly slow connections. Most places charge Rs1 per min., Rs50 per hr. **Cyber Space,** Sadar Bazaar, blows away the competition with 15 computers.

Post Office: GPO (☎ 720222). On the north side of town. There is a branch on the eastern side of Sadar Bazaar. Open M-Sa 9am-5pm. **Postal Code:** 305022.

ACCOMMODATIONS

Pushkar is a shoestring traveler's dream when it comes to accommodations. Competition is so intense that you shouldn't have to pay more than Rs80-150 for a double with attached bath and running hot water. And Pushkar is so small that you can proceed on foot from the bus station and check out several hotels before choosing one. During the Pushkar Fair, reserve at least a month in advance and expect to pay 10 times as much for every square inch of space. Alternative lodgings (temporary tents) are also available during the *mela*, but many are quite luxurious and expensive. The cheapest, the RTDC's **Tourist Village ❷,** has dorm tents (☎ 772074. US$7). Book through the reservation office (☎ (0141) 202586; fax 201045). Otherwise, you may find it cheaper to stay in Ajmer and commute to Pushkar.

Hotel White House (☎ 772147). Near Marwar Bus Stand. Spotless, marble-floored rooms around an airy courtyard, a rooftop restaurant starring fresh veggies from the garden below. Free welcome mango tea. Internet. Singles Rs60-80, with bath Rs100-250; doubles Rs100-450. ❶

Rainbow Hotel (☎ 772167). Near the bank. Rooms are small but bright and clean. 24hr. room service, washing machine, and a particularly nice restaurant. Most rooms with attached bath. Singles Rs70-100; doubles Rs100-150. ❶

V.K. Tourist Palace (☎ 772174). Near Hotel Pushkar Palace. Spacious, breezy rooms and marble floors. A good value. Singles with attached bath Rs120; doubles Rs150.

Shyam Krishna Guest House (☎ 772461). Sadar Bazaar, Choti Basti. Sizable rooms set around a central garden, most outfitted with a sitting area. Singles with common/attached bath Rs110/180; doubles Rs125/200. ❶

Payal Guest House (☎ 772163). Sadar Bazaar. Centrally located and popular with travelers. Also has a garden and small bakery. Cramped singles with common/attached bath Rs50/100; doubles Rs100/150. ❶

Hotel Venus (☎ 772323). Sadar Bazaar, Choti Basti. Standard rooms with common bath. Helpful owner. Popular restaurant. Singles Rs100-175; doubles Rs150-200. ❶

Konica Guest House (☎ 772728). Choti Basti. Small, family-run place with plain rooms and home-style meals. Singles with attached bath Rs100; doubles Rs120-200. ❶

Shiva Guest House (☎ 772120). Choti Basti. Ten modest rooms around a blue courtyard. Charged with "Shiva power." Rooms with common/attached bath Rs50/100. ❶

RTDC Hotel Sarovar (☎ 772040). Ajmer Rd. Wow, a government hotel with character! Nice, large, but overpriced (for Pushkar) rooms and a (small) pool with mountain views. Singles with common/attached bath Rs100/300-700; doubles Rs200/400-800. ❶

FOOD

Impostors are everywhere—don't be fooled by restaurants bearing remarkably similar names to more popular places.

S.R. Restaurant, Gau Ghat, Sadar Bazaar. Don't be deterred by the food-stall set-up. Whips up delicious food in enormous helpings at great prices. Speedy service. Main courses Rs10-45, massive special *thali* Rs50. Open daily 7am-10:30pm. ❶

Rainbow Rooftop Restaurant, near Brahma Mandir. Well-prepared Indian and Western cuisine from a menu almost as stunning as the lakeside view. Falafel Rs40-90, home-made pasta Rs30-70, chocolate truffles Rs10. Extensive desserts. Open 8am-11pm. ❶

Venus Restaurant, Sadar Bazaar, Choti Basti. A popular multi-cuisine restaurant with particularly tasty Indian dishes (Rs15-40), fresh juice (Rs12), and a prime people-watching spot perched above the street below. Absurdly cheap prices relative to the competition. Open daily 7am-11pm. ❶

Sunset Cafe, near Hotel Pushkar Palace, right on the lake. *The* place to be at sunset, though the view is superb at any time of day. Standard Indian dishes and an extensive Italian menu (foccacia Rs30, pasta Rs90-110). Open daily 7am-midnight. ❷

Raju Garden Restaurant, Sadar Bazaar, Badi Basti. International cuisine, "all cooked with love by Raju." Lakeside view. Indian dishes Rs25-60. Open daily 8am-10:30pm. ❶

R.S. Restaurant, opposite Brahma Mandir. Quite possibly the only restaurant on tourist-dominated Sadar Bazaar where you will see Indians eating. Tasty Indian dishes Rs24-45, spaghetti Rs50, fresh juices Rs12-15. Open daily 7am-10:30pm. ❶

Om Shiva Buffet Garden Restaurant, near Hotel Pushkar Palace. **Om Shiva Buffet Restaurant,** opposite the bank. Both offer extensive, similar buffets (Rs45). Breakfast 7am-12:30pm, lunch 1-4pm, dinner 5-10pm. ❶

◉ SIGHTS

PUSHKAR LAKE. Legend has it that at the beginning of time, Lord Brahma dropped a *pushkara*, or lotus flower, into the desert. A holy lake sprang up where the flower fell and became a place where pilgrims could be cleaned of all their sins. This lake is still the central attraction in Pushkar. Fifty-two broad *ghats* (one for each of Rajasthan's maharajas) line its shores, of which the most important are: **Gau Ghat,** where an assortment of politicians, ministers, and VIPs have paid their respects; **Brahma Ghat,** which Brahma himself is said to have used; and the central **Varaha Ghat,** where Vishnu once appeared in the form of a boar. Signs in hotels instruct visitors to remove their shoes and to refrain from smoking and taking photographs. Pilgrims and tourists at the *ghats* are frequently accosted by local priests (some carry a small "certified brahmin" photo ID card) to perform a Pushkar *puja*, a ceremony of scripture-reading and flower-scattering. Do not feel pressured into donating the exorbitant amounts that the priests insist are "standard." After the *puja*, your patronage is officially recognized with a red wristband—the "Pushkar Passport"—theoretically giving you the freedom to visit *ghats* and stroll around town without priestly harassment.

TEMPLES. Most of Pushkar's 540 temples were rebuilt after pillaging raids by the Mughal emperor Aurangzeb in the 17th century. Several are open only to Hindus. The most popular is the **Brahma Mandir,** the only temple in India dedicated to Brahma, the Hindu creator-god. Note the status of the *hans* (goose; Brahma's vehicle of choice) over the entrance. Other temples of interest include the **Rangji Mandir,** with its white stone facade, the **Hanuman Mandir,** a colorful tower depicting Hanuman's exploits, the turquoise-green **Baba Ramdev Mandir,** and the 800 year-old **Ragnath Mandir.** Two major hillside temples in Pushkar command superb views of the town and valley, especially at sunset and sunrise. Named for two of Brahma's wives, **Savithri Mandir** and **Gayatri Mandir,** each 1½hr. from the center of Pushkar, crown hills on the eastern and western sides of town, respectively.

CAMELS. Camel safaris into the desert are becoming increasingly popular in Pushkar, along with camel treks across the desert to Jaisalmer, Jodhpur, or Bikaner. Most hotels and travel agents can arrange these for you; expect to pay around Rs350-450 per day for a good camel safari. If you don't have enough time for a safari or trek but want get close to a dromedary, go for a camel ride—loops around the city cost Rs40 per hr.

THE PUSHKAR MELA (CAMEL FAIR)

The annual *mela* (Oct. 31-Nov. 8, 2003) is an event that crowds 200,000 people from all over the world into one sq. km. Thousands of pilgrims bathe in the lake's holy waters to seek redemption for their sins. Beyond the lake, the dry desert landscape teems with more than 50,000 camels that alternately race, parade, primp, and participate in auctions, besides carrying tourists on desert safaris. Stalls selling handicrafts from all over India fill the streets, while street performers jump and juggle on every corner. Contributing to the mayhem of the festival are carnival rides set up next to the camel campgrounds. The first half of the *mela* sees the peak amount of camel trading, while the second half is more of a religious jamboree that attracts legions of devotees, so plan accordingly.

CHITTAURGARH चित्तौड़गढ़ ☎ 01472

Rajasthan boasts many impressive forts, but none can rival the rich history or air of tragic nostalgia surrounding Chittaurgarh's. Chittaurgarh (or "Chittaur"; pop. 71,600) epitomizes the community's concept of Rajput valor, particularly the traditional insistence upon death-before-dishonor. Three times has the fort fallen under siege: in 1303, when the Delhi Sultan Ala-ud-din Khilji decided he couldn't live without the Maharaja's wife; in 1535, when the Gujarati Sultan Bahadur Shah attacked the city by surprise; and in 1568, when Mughal emperor Akbar attempted a similar takeover. All three times the residents of Chittaurgarh responded according to the legendary Rajput code of honor: the men slapped on their saffron robes of martyrdom and rode out of the fort, despite the overwhelming odds; and the women, unwilling to live with military defeat, immolated themselves in a huge funeral pyre. The stories have been told and retold with much relish and gusto over the years, and by now the estimates of total Rajput lives lost to *jauhar* has grown to 30,000 women and 40,000 warriors. The fort today, the largest in Asia, is a 5km stretch of awe-inspiring views, the last vestiges of the city's past glory. The only invaders these days are tourists pursuing their photographic plunder. Chittaurgarh may be off the beaten path, but its fort is well worth the day-long detour.

TRANSPORTATION

As Chittaurgarh's rail lines are still undergoing conversion from meter- to broadgauge, most destinations remain most easily reached by bus.

> **Trains: Railway Station** (enquiries ☎ 40131). Station Rd. Reservation office open daily 10am-5pm. To: **Ahmedabad** (17hr.; 1:45pm; Rs148); **Jaipur** (8hr.; 5:50am and 10pm; Rs123) via **Ajmer** (4½hr.; Rs83); **Udaipur** (4hr.; 6:50am and 1:45pm; Rs56).

> **Buses: Roadways Bus Stand** (☎ 41177). To: **Abu Road** (10hr.; 7am; Rs125); **Ahmedabad** (10hr.; 7:30am; Rs147); **Bundi** (6hr.; 8:30, 10:30, 11:15am; Rs68); **Jaipur** (8hr.; every hr. 5am-1am; Rs125-148) via **Ajmer** (5hr.; Rs75); **Jodhpur** (8hr.; 6, 7:30, and 9:30pm; Rs125); **Kota** (6hr.; 6 per day 7:30am-10pm; Rs68-85); **Udaipur** (2½hr.; every hr. 5am-7:45pm; Rs45). **Private buses** on Station Rd. go to most places.

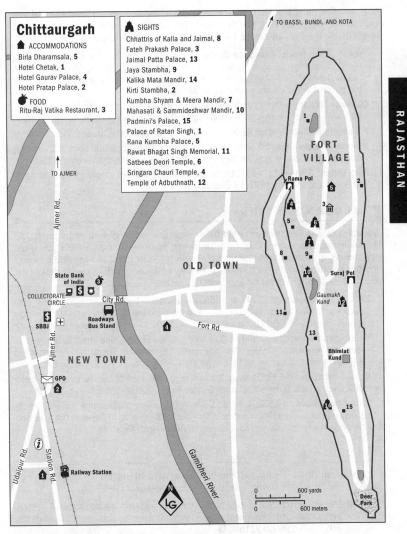

Chittaurgarh

ACCOMMODATIONS
Birla Dharamsala, **5**
Hotel Chetak, **1**
Hotel Gaurav Palace, **4**
Hotel Pratap Palace, **2**

FOOD
Ritu-Raj Vatika Restaurant, **3**

SIGHTS
Chhattris of Kalla and Jaimal, **8**
Fateh Prakash Palace, **3**
Jaimal Patta Palace, **13**
Jaya Stambha, **9**
Kalika Mata Mandir, **14**
Kirti Stambha, **2**
Kumbha Shyam & Meera Mandir, **7**
Mahasati & Sammideshwar Mandir, **10**
Padmini's Palace, **15**
Palace of Ratan Singh, **1**
Rana Kumbha Palace, **5**
Rawat Bhagat Singh Memorial, **11**
Satbees Deori Temple, **6**
Sringara Chauri Temple, **4**
Temple of Adbuthnath, **12**

TO BASSI, BUNDI, AND KOTA

RAJASTHAN

TO AJMER

Ajmer Rd.

FORT VILLAGE

Rama Pol

State Bank of India
COLLECTORATE CIRCLE
City Rd.
SBBJ
Roadways Bus Stand

OLD TOWN

Suraj Pol

Gaumukh Kund

Fort Rd.

NEW TOWN

GPO

13

Bhimlat Kund

Gambheri River

Railway Station

Deer Park

0   600 yards
0   600 meters

Local Transportation: Shared **auto-rickshaws** are the most common mode of transport (within town Rs3-5, to the fort Rs15-20). **Bicycles** can be rented (Rs25 per day) from shops near the railway station.

ORIENTATION AND PRACTICAL INFORMATION

Chittaurgarh is too spread out to get around on foot. The **railway station** is on the southwest side of town. **Station Rd.** heads north, becoming **Ajmer Rd.** on its way to **Collectorate Circle.** From here, **City Rd.** heads east, passing the **Roadways Bus Stand** before crossing the **Gambheri River** and proceeding to the base of the Fort, where it becomes **Fort Rd.** The main commercial area and the **new city** are here. Fort Rd. zig-zags steeply up to the **Fort,** which sprawls 5km across the plateau. One main road loops inside the Fort and leads to Chittaurgarh's major sights.

Tourist Office: Tourist Reception Centre (☎41089). Station Rd. Maps Rs2. Open M-Sa 10am-1:30pm and 2-5pm. **Tours:** of the nine licensed guides in Chittaurgarh, **Mr. Sudhir Sukhwal** (☎43245) is particularly recommended. He speaks excellent English and makes the fort's history come alive (half-day Rs340).

Currency Exchange: Due to problems with phony traveler's checks, no banks in Chittaurgarh will exchange money now. **Hotel Pratap Palace** offers private exchange services.

Police: Main Police Station (☎40006). Opposite the bus stand. Open 24hr.

Hospital: General Hospital (☎41102). Ajmer Rd. English-speaking. Consultations daily in winter 9am-1pm; in summer 8am-noon. **Pharmacy** and emergency open 24hr.

Post Office: GPO (☎41159). Station Rd. Near the railroad crossing. Open M-Sa 7-10:30am and 2:30-6pm. **Postal Code:** 312001.

ACCOMMODATIONS

Budget hotels in Chittaurgarh tend to be basic and not very well maintained, and the acceptable ones are overpriced. However, huge discounts (30-60%) are often negotiable at Chittaurgarh's nicer hotels, so try your hand at bargaining before resigning yourself to one of its more unsavory options (which, if you're desperate, are clustered around the train and bus stations).

Hotel Pratap Palace (☎40099 or 43563). Station Rd. Opposite the GPO. Clean, spacious rooms with wicker furniture, TVs, and attached baths. 24hr. hot water. Laundry service. Singles Rs600-1150; doubles Rs650-1200. 50% discounts even in season. ❸

Hotel Gaurav Palace (☎46904). Off Fort Rd., on the first big side street to the right as you move away from City Rd. Decently sized, well-furnished rooms, all with attached hot-water bath and some with TV. Singles Rs200-325; doubles Rs270-425. ❷

Hotel Chetak (☎41588). Opposite the railway station. Best of the cheapies, with clean rooms and attached hot-water baths. Singles Rs150-300; doubles Rs275-400. ❶

Birla Dharamsala (☎45386). Inside the fort. Offers very basic rooms (catering to pilgrims) with common toilet (no shower facilities). Prime location between the ruins and the present-day fort village. *Thalis* available. Rooms from Rs50. ❶

FOOD

For cheap eats in Chittaurgarh, your best bet is to head toward the Roadways Bus Stand, where roadside *bhojnalyas* serve steaming *thalis* (Rs25-30).

Ritu-Raj Vatika Restaurant, set back from the road just past the bus stand. A popular place with garden and indoor seating specializing in *tandoori* and South Indian dishes (Rs20-50). Open daily 8am-11pm. ❶

Shakti Restaurant, inside Hotel Pratap Palace. Offers quiet, comfortable dining and a range of cuisines. Most dishes Rs25-50. Open daily 7am-3:30pm and 7-10pm. ❶

SIGHTS

THE FORT

*Open daily sunrise-sunset. Admission and most sights free; US$5 to climb Tower of Victory only. As the area inside the fort spans 13 sq. km, most visitors hire an auto-rickshaw for a half-day tour (Rs120, off season Rs100). In winter, walking between the sights is a pleasant alternative, provided that you have the time. Guides are available (see **Tourist Office,** above).*

RAJASTHAN

Jutting out abruptly from the plateau below, the Chittaurgarh Fort is one of the most historically significant in all of Rajasthan. Believed to have been constructed by the Pandava brother Bhima, of *Mahabharata* fame, the fort contains 113 temples, in various stages of decay, as well as 84 tanks, 20 of which still contain water.

ASCENT AND ENTRANCE. **Padan Pol** is the first gate *(pol)* in a series of seven that punctuate the steep, kilometer-long climb to the top. Near the second *pol* are the **chhattris** (cenotaphs) of the heroic martyrs Kalla and Jaimal, who died in the third sacking of Chittaurgarh in 1568. The seventh and final gate, **Rama Pol**, was originally the back entrance to the fort but is now the main one.

SRINGARA CHAURI MANDIR. The first stop on a counterclockwise tour of the fort's sights, this 15th-century Jain temple shows Hindu influences in its elaborate decoration. It also shows Muslim influence in its top level—after the Mughals conquered Chittaurgarh, they knocked off the Hindu *shikhara* (spire) and replaced it with a dome to make the temple look more like a mosque. The thick stone wall that now stops just short of the temple is also of interest, for it was part of a conspiratorial plot against Prince Udai Singh. Banvir Singh, the royal cousin, tried to seize power and have the prince killed. The prince's nurse, Pannadhai, discovered Banvir's dastardly scheme and sacrificed her own son, switching him with the prince, whom she whisked away to safety. When he learned that the prince was still alive, Banvir partitioned the fort, hoping that this would allow him to share power with the young prince. He conveniently constructed the wall so that his section of the fort included the treasury and the tax-paying residential area.

RANA KUMBHA PALACE. The impressive remains of the 8th-century Rana Kumbha Palace are believed to be where Chittaurgarh's first *jauhar* (self-immolation) took place in 1303, in an underground tunnel leading to Gaumukh Kund. All that remained after the siege of the city were stables (including a stable said to house Genda Hathi, a sword-wielding military elephant) and a Shiva temple. In the back on the right is the nurse's palace, where Pannadhai's son was slain in the place of the young prince. Also nearby are the elegant **Meera Mandir**, which honors the Jodhpuri mystic poet Mirabai (see **Mirabai**, p. 517), the towering **Kumbha Shyam Mandir**, built in 1448, and the notable **Jatashankar Mahadev.**

FATEH PRAKASH PALACE AND SATBEES DEORI TEMPLE. The incongruous **Fateh Prakash Palace** (built within the last century) today houses an unexciting **museum** of archaeological finds from Chittaurgarh and surrounding areas. Just south lies the elaborate 11th-century Jain **Satbees Deori Temple,** consisting of three main shrines and 24 subsidiary ones (one for each *tirthankara*).

JAYA STAMBHA. The subject of every Chittaurgarh brochure and postcard, the Jaya Stambha (Tower of Victory) is an imposing gray limestone tower whose 37m high exterior walls tell the story of the city's gory past. The tower's construction began in 1458 to commemorate a victory over the Muslim rulers of Malwa and Gujarat and took 10 years to complete. The view from the top is breathtaking, not that most travelers are willing to pay to find out. *(Open daily 8am-5:30pm. Free to gawk at from outside; US$5 to climb.)* The 11th-century **Sammidheshwar Mandir** is down the hill from the Jaya Stambha. Nearby is **Mahasti,** a series of cenotaphs (memorials) marking the supposed spot of the second *jauhar* in 1537, committed by Queen Karnawati and 16,000 Rajput women. The **Gaumukh Kund** (Cow's Mouth Tank), farther south, features a carved cow who fills the tank with water.

PADMINI'S PALACE. According to legend, it was here that Ala-Ud-Din Khilji caught a glimpse of the beautiful Padmini (seated on the pavilion steps below) in a palace mirror, prompting him to set his sights on her (and his army on Chittaurgarh). After the siege proved successful, Padmini and 13,000 Rajput women committed *jauhar* rather than face the humiliation of capture. The palace is set in a shallow pool and houses a lush garden. The **Kalika Mata Mandir,** directly opposite, was dedicated during the 8th century to the sun god Surya but now pays tribute to Kali. Still the most active temple in the Mewar region, it comes alive on Sundays when devotees from all over the countryside flock to pay their respects.

BHIMLAT KUND. The road loops south past the often-empty **Deer Park** to the quiet Bhimlat Kund. This legendary tank was created by the Pandava brother Bhima to satiate his mother's thirst. The giant Bhima, who was said to have the strength of 1000 elephants, stomped his foot down in this spot, and the lake was formed by the imprint it left. Much later, this was also the supposed site of the third *jauhar* in 1567, in which 'only' a few hundred Rajput women threw themselves upon that well-used Chittaurgarh pyre. The road then turns north again past **Suraj Pol,** the eastern gate of the fort, originally the main entrance.

KIRTI STAMBHA (TOWER OF FAME). Built by the *Digamber* (nudist) Jain sect, the 12th-century, 23m Tower of Fame is covered with images of the Jain pantheon, particularly that of Adinath, the first *tirthankara*, to whom the tower is dedicated. Like the Tower of Victory, it's also scalable (provided you can locate the attendant to unlock the door and negotiate the narrow entrance and staircase), but unlike its more photographed sister, it's free.

UDAIPUR उदयपुर ☎ 0294

Udaipur, City of Sunrise, reinforces the romantic stereotype of Rajasthan and serves as one of the state's biggest tourist draws. Its cobblestoned old city hugs the shore of green Lake Pichhola, whose serene waters harbor two exotic island palaces. On shore, its whitewashed *havelis*, lush gardens, and massive City Palace complex inspire hours of awe and contemplation. Although this longtime capital of the Mewar kingdom hasn't altogether managed to fend off the chaos and pollution of industry, the old city has nevertheless somehow managed to retain a number of fairy-tale qualities. A city of monumental architectural and aesthetic importance, Udaipur should certainly take up several days in tourists' itinerary.

Maharaja Udai Singh II moved the Mewari capital to Udaipur after the final siege of Chittaurgarh in 1568. Upon his death four years later, he was succeeded by his son, Pratap, who remains the most revered of the Mewari Rulers for his legendary heroism during the repeated Mughal attacks that followed. As the city thrived, the Udaipuri school of miniature painting developed and many of the city's majestic palaces were built. In 1736, the city was crippled by the mighty Marathas, but it bounced back again with British aid, somehow managing to remain firmly independent. Since then, the city's arts have continued to flourish, James Bond films notwithstanding (yes, Roger Moore's *Octopussy* was filmed here).

▐▇ TRANSPORTATION

Flights: Dabok Airport (☎655453). 25km east of Udaipur (taxi Rs220). **Indian Airlines,** Delhi Pol (☎410999). Open daily 10am-1:15pm and 2-5pm. To: **Delhi** (3hr.; daily 6:10pm; US$110); **Jaipur** (2hr.; daily 6:10pm; US$80); **Jodhpur** (40min.; daily 6:10pm; US$65); **Mumbai** (1hr.; daily 9:40am; US$125). **Jet Airways,** Blue Circle Business Centre (☎561105). Near the GPO. To: **Delhi** (2½hr.; daily 8:10am; US$110) via **Jaipur** (1hr.; US$80); **Mumbai** (1½hr.; daily 9:20am and 9:25pm M-F and Su 7:15pm; US$125). **Gangaur Tour 'n' Travels,** 28 Gangaur Ghat (☎411476), is the only authorized IA and Jet agent in the Jagdish Temple Area. Open daily 9am-9pm.

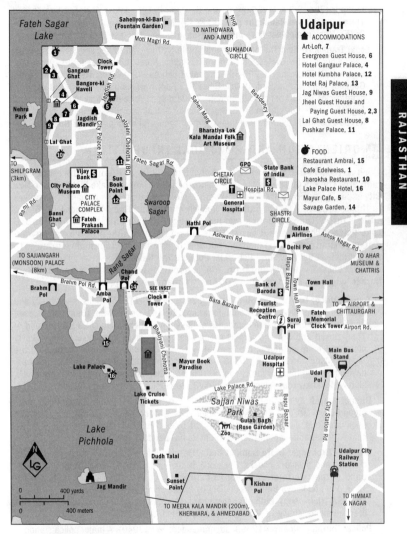

Fateh Sagar Lake

Saheliyon-ki-Bari (Fountain Garden) ■

Moti Magri Rd.

TO NATHDWARA AND AJMER

SUKHADIA CIRCLE

Clock Tower

Gangaur Ghat

Bangore-ki Haveli

Nehru Park ■

Jagdish Mandir

Lal Ghat

Bhatiyani Chohatta Rd.

City Palace Rd.

Sahelí Marg

Residency Rd.

Bharatiya Lok Kala Mandal Folk Art Museum

TO SHILPGRAM (3km)

Vijay Bank

City Palace Museum

Sun Book Point

CITY PALACE COMPLEX

Fateh Prakash Palace

Fateh Sagar Rd.

Swaroop Sagar

Bansi Ghat

Rami Rd.

GPO

CHETAK CIRCLE

State Bank of India

Hospital Rd.

General Hospital

SHASTRI CIRCLE

Hathi Pol

Ashwani Rd.

Indian Airlines

Delhi Pol

Ashok Nagar Rd.

TO AHAR MUSEUM & CHATTRIS

TO SAJJANGARH (MONSOON) PALACE (8km)

Rang Sagar

Brahm Pol Rd.

Chand Pol

Amba Pol

Brahm Pol

SEE INSET

Clock Tower

Bhatiyani Chohatta

Bara Bazaar

Bapu Bazaar

Bank of Baroda

Tourist Reception Centre

Suraj Pol

Town Hall Rd.

Town Hall

Fateh Memorial Clock Tower

TO AIRPORT & CHITTAURGARH

Airport Rd.

Main Bus Stand

Udai Pol

Mayur Book Paradise

Udaipur Hospital

Lake Palace

Lake Palace Rd.

Lake Cruise Tickets

Sajjan Niwas Park

Gulab Bagh (Rose Garden) Zoo

Bapu Bazaar

City Station Rd.

Lake Pichhola

Dudh Talai

Jag Mandir

Sunset Point

Kishan Pol

Udaipur City Railway Station

TO HIMMAT & NAGAR

400 yards

400 meters

TO MEERA KALA MANDIR (200m), KHERWARA, & AHMEDABAD

Udaipur

🏠 **ACCOMMODATIONS**
Art-Loft, **7**
Evergreen Guest House, **6**
Hotel Gangaur Palace, **4**
Hotel Kumbha Palace, **12**
Hotel Raj Palace, **13**
Jag Niwas Guest House, **9**
Jheel Guest House and
  Paying Guest House, **2,3**
Lal Ghat Guest House, **8**
Pushkar Palace, **11**

🍴 **FOOD**
Restaurant Ambrai, **15**
Cafe Edelweiss, **1**
Jharokha Restaurant, **10**
Lake Palace Hotel, **16**
Mayur Cafe, **5**
Savage Garden, **14**

Trains: Udaipur City Station (enquiries ☎ 131; reservations ☎ 483979). It's several kilometers southeast of the old city; **don't get off at Udaipur Station,** much farther north. To: **Ahmedabad** (9½hr.; 9:15pm; Rs114); **Delhi** (19-23hr.; 8am and 6:10pm; Rs225) via **Chittaurgarh** (4hr.; Rs55) and **Ajmer** (8-12hr.; Rs120); **Jaipur** (1½hr.; 6:10pm; Rs154).

Buses: Main Bus Stand (☎ 484191). To: **Ahmedabad** (6hr.; every 30min. 5am-10pm; Rs100); **Bikaner** (14hr.; 4:30pm; Rs216); **Chittaurgarh** (3hr.; every 30min. 6am-10:30pm; Rs38; deluxe 2½hr.; 8:30, 10:15am, 12:30pm; Rs54); **Delhi** (14hr.; 1:15, 4, 6pm; Rs270; deluxe 11am and 3:45pm; Rs404); **Jaipur** (9hr.; every hr. 4am-9:30pm; Rs170; deluxe 9hr.; 6 per day 8:30am-10:30pm; Rs200) via **Ajmer** (7hr.; Rs110-143);

Jodhpur (7hr.; 9:30, 10:30am, 6, and 8:30pm; Rs106; deluxe 7hr.; 5:30am, 3, and 10pm; Rs128) via **Ranakpur** (2½ hr.; Rs35); **Mt. Abu** (6hr.; every hr. 5am-10:30pm; Rs75). Many companies have **private buses** to major cities (see **Budget Travel,** below).

Local Transportation: The old city is navigable on foot, but to get anywhere else you'll need wheels. **Vijay Cycles,** BC, next to Raj Palace Hotel, rents bikes for Rs20 per day. Scooters Rs50 per hr., Rs200-300 per day. Open daily 9am-8pm. **Heera Cycle Store,** Gangaur Marg, inside Badi Haveli. Bikes Rs25 per day; scooters Rs150-200 per day; motorcycles Rs300 per day. Open daily 7:30am-9pm. **Auto-rickshaw** typical fares from Jagdish Mandir: bus station Rs15; Bansi Ghat or Dhetak Circle Rs20. Full-day sightseeing Rs150-200. **Taxis** can be hired through travel agents for daytrips around Udaipur.

❋ ORIENTATION AND PRACTICAL INFORMATION

Udaipur rests in the shadows of the Aravalli mountains, 113km southwest of Chittaurgarh. The **Old City** curves along the northeastern bank of **Lake Pichhola**; the **New City** expands to the north, east, and south. Most budget travelers base themselves in the area of the Old City around **Jagdish Mandir** and **Bhatiyani Chohotta (BC),** a stone's throw from Udaipur's two most famous monuments, the **City Palace** and **Lake Palace.** The **train** and **bus stations** are on the east side of town, far beyond walking distance from the main accommodations area. The four main entrances to the old city—**Udai Pol, Suraj Pol, Delhi Pol,** and the **Hathi Pol**—serve as major landmarks. **Chetak Circle,** beyond Hathi Pol, is home to the **GPO. Bapu Bazaar** and **Bara Bazaar,** which intersect at Suraj Pol, are two major shopping streets.

Tourist Office: Tourist Reception Centre, Suraj Pol (☎411535). Sells maps (Rs2) and arranges home stays (see **Accommodations,** below). Open M-Sa 10am-5pm, closed 2nd Sa. There are also small branches at the **train station** (open M-Sa 8-11am and 4-7pm, closed 2nd Sa) and **airport** (open when flights arrive and depart). More convenient and more helpful is the bi-monthly *Out and About,* available throughout the Jagdish Mandir area (Rs10). **RTDC Hotel Kajri,** Shastri Circle (☎410501) offers half-day sightseeing tours of the city for Rs105, excluding admission fees. A do-it-yourself, all day **rickshaw tour** will cost about Rs200 (excluding the Monsoon Palace).

Budget Travel: Agents line City Station Rd. and the Jagdish Mandir area, with more around Delhi Pol and Chetak Circle. Most hotels double as travel agencies and can book train, bus, and plane tickets; city tours by car (Rs350-450); airport taxis (Rs200); camel, horse, and elephant safaris (from Rs400 per day); and bus tours.

Currency Exchange: State Bank of India, Hospital Rd. (☎528857). Exchanges foreign currency and traveler's checks. Open M-F 10am-4pm, Sa 10am-1pm. **Bank of Baroda,** Bapu Bazaar, north of Suraj Pol (☎420671; open M-F 10am-2:30pm, Sa 10am-12:30pm) and **Vijaya Bank,** inside the City Palace complex (☎411381; open M-F 10am-2pm, Sa 10am-noon). Both offer credit card advances for a 1% commission. Numerous licensed money changers populate the area around Jagdish Mandir.

Police: Tourist police (☎412693; superintendent, ☎413949). A major police station is at every gate. The biggest are at **Delhi Pol** and **Udai Pol.**

Pharmacy: Hospital Rd. and Udai Pol have several pharmacies. Most open daily 7am-9:30pm. **Udaipur Hospital** has a well-stocked 24hr. pharmacy (☎421900).

Hospital: Maharana Bhopal General Hospital, Hospital Rd. (☎528811 to 528817). Government-run. **Udaipur Hospital** (☎420322). Gulab Bagh Rd., near Udai Pol. Has excellent facilities. Both hospitals are English-speaking and open 24hr.

Internet: The usual rate in the Jagdish Mandir area is Rs1 per min., Rs50 per hr. The biggest banks of computers are at **Mayur Cafe** (open daily 8am-10pm) and **One Stop Shop,** 35 Lal Ghat (☎419810; open daily 9am-11pm).

Post Office: GPO (☎528622). Chetak Circle. Parcels sent M-F 10am-4pm, Sa 10am-1pm. Open M-Sa 10am-7pm, Su 10am-3pm. *Poste Restante* mail is held at the **City Post Office**, Shastri Circle. Open M-Sa 8am-4pm. **Postal Code** (both offices): 313001.

ACCOMMODATIONS

The hotels in the Jagdish Mandir (temple) area on the beautiful east bank of Lake Pichhola are far better than any others in the city. To avoid touts, it's easiest to ask your rickshaw driver to drop you off at Jagdish Temple and then walk to your hotel of choice. Next best are those along **Lake Palace Rd.** and **BC.** Hotels in the **new city** are cheap and noisy. There are over 70 **paying guest houses ❷,** in Udaipur, but only 10 to 20 offer genuine homestay experiences (Rs100-500 per night, depending on amenities and location); contact the tourist office for more info. Most hotels listed below have laundry, travel agencies, attached restaurants, and 24hr. hot water.

Hotel Gangaur Palace (☎422303; fax 561121). Gangaur Ghat. In the 250-year-old Ashoka *haveli*. Soft mattresses and spotless bathrooms in spacious rooms surrounding a central courtyard. Helpful staff and excellent attached restaurant (see below). Singles Rs80, with attached bath Rs150; doubles Rs100/250-500. ❶

Hotel Raj Palace, 103 BC (☎410364 or 527092; fax 410395). Beautiful rooms all have stained-glass windows, marble floors, and cushioned window seats. The deluxe rooms have bathtubs and A/C. Good service. It's a little pricey, but a steal relative to the *haveli* competition. Singles Rs150-1100; doubles Rs250-1200. ❸

Pushkar Palace, 93 BC (☎417685). Eight huge, well-kept rooms above courtyards and a family home in the gorgeous converted *haveli*. The most expensive rooms are fantastic value. Breakfast only. Rooms Rs60, with attached bath Rs80-150. ❶

Art-Loft (☎420304 or 420163). Lal Ghat. Breezy rooms with marble floors and attached baths. Run by a chef and artist family, this intimate guest house (six rooms) offers art and cookery lessons and serves delcious food. Singles Rs300-400; doubles Rs400-500. ❷

Jag Niwas Guest House, 21 Gangaur Ghat Marg (☎416022). No longer owned by the Maharaja, but still has style. Spacious rooms with attached baths and air-cooling. Good restaurant upstairs; free cooking lessons. Singles Rs100-350; doubles Rs150-400. ❶

Hotel Kumbha Palace, 104 BC (☎422702). Distinctive rooms have colorful stained-glass windows, Jaisalmeri desert decorations, as well as attached baths and air coolers. Lovely garden area borders the walls of the City Palace. Run by an Indian-Dutch couple. Singles Rs50, with attached bath Rs100-150; doubles with bath Rs150-200. ❶

Jheel Guest House and **Paying Guest House,** 56/52 Gangaur Ghat (☎421352). Affiliated guest houses with a single reception at Jheel GH. The Paying GH, in a newer bldg., has rooms with marble floors and attached baths (Rs300-500; deluxe with balcony Rs600); those at Jheel GH are more basic (Rs100, with attached bath Rs200-250). ❶

Lal Ghat Guest House, 22 Lal Ghat. Popular with budget travelers. Dorms Rs50; rooms Rs75-150, with attached bath Rs200-300. If the self-serve kitchen doesn't suit you, head next door to the lake-view restaurant at **Evergreen Guest House,** which also has simple rooms. Singles Rs100, with attached bath Rs 150; doubles Rs150/200-250. ❶

FOOD

Udaipur has a good range of restaurants to choose from, many of which are graced with round-the-clock screenings of *Octopussy*.

RAJASTHAN

🏨 **Lake Palace Hotel** (☎527961). Floating in the middle of Lake Pichhola. The ultimate Udaipur dining experience: unbelievably delectable food, amazing views, and unparalleled ambience. It's the ultimate splurge. Reserve ahead, wear your least-grubby outfit, and bring your own water—the food's worth paying for, but the water (Rs50) is not. Buffet Rs500 for lunch, Rs750 for dinner; includes boat transport from Bansi Ghat. ❺

🏨 **Restaurant Ambrai,** Panch Devri Marg. In Amet-ki-Haveli, beyond Chand Pol. Clinches the romantic dining cliche. Recommended for dinner, when palaces are lit and music is played. Veg. dishes Rs45-65, non-veg. Rs75-100. Open daily 8am-11pm. ❶

Natural City View Restaurant, inside Hotel Gangaur Palace. When you've had your fill of Udaipuri romance and are ready to re-embrace banana pancakes and free movies, head to this 3-tier rooftop restaurant. Most popular at dinner time, when unobstructed views of the sunset are followed by two movies (both 7pm), only one of which is *Octopussy*. Veg. dishes Rs25-40, tasty baked goods Rs10-30. Open daily 8am-10:30pm. ❶

Jharokha Restaurant, Lal Ghat. Inside the Jagat Niwas Pvt. Ltd. Hotel. Affordable, lakeview dining luxury inside a gorgeous renovated *haveli*. The rooms are expensive, but dinner is not. Veg. dishes Rs35-50, non-veg. Rs45-75. If you're lucky, you'll be able to snag the ultra-cool window-seat alcove. Open daily 7:30am-11pm. ❶

Savage Garden, near Chand Pol. Breaks the mold with its offbeat decor, small but thoughtful menu (meals Rs75-80), and tasty food. Open daily 9am-10pm. ❶

Mayur Cafe, opposite Jagdish Mandir. Quality food, quick service, and an A/C dining hall make the Mayur a popular backpacker haunt. Leafy garden dining in back. A good, cheap place for breakfast. Indian veg. dishes Rs28-40. Open daily 8am-10:30pm. ❶

Cafe Edelweiss, 36 Gadiya Devra, Chandpol Rd., and **Coffee.com,** Lal Ghat, serve tasty baked goods. Open daily 8:30am-9pm.

🔵 SIGHTS

LAKE PICHHOLA

Lake Pichhola is not as stunning nowadays as it usually is; a string of poor monsoons over the last few years has left it pretty dry, such that you can practically walk to the Lake Palace. That said, it's still the undeniable centerpiece of Udaipur.

JAG NIWAS (LAKE PALACE). The Lake Palace occupies the entirety of Jag Niwas island, giving the impression that the one-time summer residence of the royal family is floating in the middle of the lake. Converted into a luxury hotel in the 1960s, the palace still houses stunning garden courtyards and an exquisite interior, but it's hard to get a look at them if you're not a guest (you can try swimming up to the island in an alligator suit like James Bond). The best (non-life-threatening) way to get onto the palace grounds is to treat yourself to a meal at the hotel's restaurant (see **Food** listings, above). Trust us, it's worth every penny.

JAG MANDIR ISLAND AND LAKE CRUISES. The slightly smaller Jag Mandir island, just south of the Lake Palace, is home to **Jag Mandir,** the palace that sheltered the Mughal Emperor-to-be Shah Jahan in 1623-24 as he led a revolt against his father, Jehangir. Several centuries later, Jag Mandir also served as a refuge for British women and children during the Mutiny of 1857. The palace today isn't in as good condition as some of its counterparts in Udaipur, but a few rooms are open for exploration, and there's a very nice garden in back. Some beautiful stone carvings, including a mighty row of huge elephants encircling the island, also make the trip worthwhile. The only way to see Jag Mandir up close is to take a boat cruise from Bansi Ghat (the City Palace jetty); the half-hour cruise gets you only a glimpse of the elephants, while the hour-long cruise earns you a 25min. stopover (boats depart every hr. 10am-5pm; Rs125 per 30min., Rs225 per 1hr.).

A HELLUVA HORSE The cow might be a more common object of worship for Hindus, but the Rajputs of Rajasthan have a special place in their hearts for a certain white stallion named Chetak. Indeed, his name lives on in Udaipur's main circle and is emblazoned across the carriages of Rajasthan's main express trains. Chetak, whose statues are a common sight in Udaipur, was the loyal battle companion of Rana Pratap. At the famous bloodbath of Haldighati in 1532, Chetak's leg was cut by an enemy elephant wielding a machete in its trunk; Pratap was also wounded. Though hobbled, Chetak carried his master from the battlefield through a narrow passage, leaping a 3m crevice before coming to rest under a tree 6km away. Having saved his master's life, poor Chetak breathed his last. Many tours of the Udaipur area stop at Haldighati to pay respects at Chetak's tomb and hear the tale of his valiant death.

CITY PALACE COMPLEX

The jewel of Udaipur is its grand palace complex, the largest in Rajasthan, begun in 1559 by **Udai Singh,** the proud Mewar migrant who founded the city. An architectural amalgam reflecting the efforts of more than 20 kings, today the City Palace is part museum, part royal residence (inhabited by the 76th Maharaja of Mewar, who lacks political power but still plays a role in civil life), and part luxury hotel.

CITY PALACE MUSEUM. The two sections of the City Palace of interest to visitors are the **Mardana Mahal** (men's quarters) and **Zenana Mahal** (women's quarters), which have been reincarnated as the City Museum. Before entering the palace, note the two large stone indentations—they were once elephant beds. Inside, **Ganesh Deoti Gate** marks the point past which commoners were not allowed and at which the museum begins. The museum is a maze of rooms and courtyards interconnected by narrow passages; colored glass mosaics, detailed miniature paintings, and beautiful mirror-work can be seen throughout. The most notable areas of the palace include: **Mor Chowk,** with inlaid glass peacocks and convex mirrors; **Krishna Vilas,** a small room bathed in miniature paintings (dedicated to Krishna Kumari, a 16-year-old princess who committed suicide before war could break out between vying suitors from Jaipur and Jodhpur); and the **Bari Mahal,** which encloses a beautiful garden courtyard. The Zenana Mahal (women's quarters) next door, is ill-maintained and consists of only a courtyard (today used for social functions) and a few miniature paintings upstairs. (*The museum is accessible via the main entrance to the City Palace, just down City Palace Rd. from Jagdish Mandir. Open daily 9:30am-4:30pm. Rs35; camera fee Rs75; video fee Rs300. Tours for up to 5 people Rs95 per hr.*)

OTHER SIGHTS. The back side of the City Palace complex provides access to the Maharaja's private residence as well as the two palaces-cum-luxury-hotels inside the complex, the Shiv Niwas Palace and Fateh Prakash Palace. All are closed to the public except for the section of Fateh Prakash housing the Crystal Gallery, which exhibits the outrageously extensive collection of crystal ordered from England by Maharaja Sajgan Singh in 1877. Besides the usual dishware and chandeliers, there are also hookahs, entire sets of furniture, not to mention a dazzling carpet and peacock throne studded with jewels. It's good to be the Maharaja. The gallery overlooks the massive and lavishly decorated **Durbar Hall** (audience hall). (*The entrance to Fateh Prakash Palace is just above the City Palace Jetty, around the back side of the complex. Crystal Gallery open daily 10am-8pm; Rs200, includes tea or coffee.*)

ELSEWHERE IN UDAIPUR

JAGDISH MANDIR. Built by Maharaja Jagat Singh, this 17th-century temple in the center of the old city is dedicated to Vishnu's avatar Jagannath, whose black marble image resides in the sanctum. The outer structure is a pyramid-like *shikhara* decorated with elephants, *apsaras*, and figures from Mewari mythology. A bronze Garuda, Vishnu's mount, guards the entrance. The cornerstone at the left base of the stairs supposedly brings good luck to those who rub it seven times. The central dome teems with mythological figures and houses a huge silver bed meant for the gods. *(Open daily 5am-2pm and 4-10:30pm; Oct.-Feb. 5:30am-2pm and 4-10pm. Free.)*

SHILPIGRAM. Another link in the government-sponsored chain of "rural arts and crafts complexes," Shilpigram seeks to educate foreign and Indian tourists about the rural and indigenous communities of Rajasthan, Gujarat, Maharashtra, and Goa through life-size models of their traditional homes, complete with imported traditional families. At any given time, four or five "habitats" feature cultural performances from the areas they represent (puppetry, singing, dancing, etc.) and offer live demonstrations of their crafts (e.g. pottery). Tips and purchases help to sustain the "village." The complex has an undeniably artificial feel—it strikes some as little more than a human zoo—but even those who feel uncomfortable patronizing the village should find the uninhabited model homes interesting. The complex is at its liveliest during the **Shilpigram Festival** (annually Dec. 24-Jan. 2).

BHARATIYA LOK KALA MANDAL FOLK ART MUSEUM. Intended as a center for the preservation and promotion of indigenous arts, this museum exhibits a variety of items ranging from colorfully painted masks to clay figure dioramas of local festivals. The museum's highlight is its collection of traditional Rajasthani **puppets** called *kathpurli*—wide-eyed wooden string puppets dressed in bright, traditional costumes. Don't miss the free and excellent 10min. **puppet show,** repeated every 20 minutes. *(Saheli Marg, just past Chetak Circle. Museum open daily 9am-6pm. Rs25; camera fee Rs25. Longer puppet-and-traditional-dance shows performed nightly; see **Entertainment**, below.)*

CHHATTRIS AND AHAR MUSEUM. More than 200 *chhattris* (cenotaphs) of Mewari maharajas and their families are in a plot northeast of the city. These were overgrown and inaccessible to the public until a recent project unearthed them. Most are simple in design (that of Sangram Singh is a notable exception) and haphazardly arranged, but their isolation from the city makes them a great addition to Udaipur's sights. *(Open 24hr. Free.)* The nearby **Ahar Museum** exhibits 4000-year-old relics from the civilization of the same name, unearthed from an excavation behind the museum. *(Open M-Th and Sa-Su 10am-4:30pm. Rs3; M free.)*

SAHELIYON-KI-BARI. The 18th-century Saheliyon-ki-Bari (Garden of the Maids of Honor), built by Maharaja Sangram Singh for his wife and her friends and servants, lies 2km to the north of town. These days the garden, with its palm trees and lotus pool, is more of a tourist site than a refuge. Note that the fountains and irrigation system are both powered by water pressure from the lake, so the garden is spectacular during and after the monsoon. *(Open daily 10am-4pm. Rs5.)*

FATAH SAGAR LAKE. Lake Pichhola's less celebrated sister lies not too far west of Saheliyon-ki-Bari. As of spring 2001, the lake was almost completely dried up; a good monsoon should revitalize it. On an island in the middle of the lake, **Nehru Park** is spread over fountain-sprinkled grounds, with domed cupolas, swaying palm trees, and bubbles of bougainvillea. Small boats leave from the east side of the lake every 20min. in season. *(Open daily in winter 8am-6pm; in summer 8am-7pm. Rs10 includes admission and shuttle boat.)* You can also cruise around the lake in a **paddleboat** (Rs100 per hr.). A few minutes from the jetty is **Moti Magri** (Pearl Hill), whose gardens and statue memorialize the legendary Mewar hero Maharaja Pratap Singh.

SAJJANGARH (MONSOON) PALACE. Perched on a steep, barren hill 5km from Udaipur, the royal family's third palace (City Palace for winter, Lake Palace for summer, Monsoon Palace for—duh—the Monsoon) looks menacing from afar. These days, even non-agents brave the ascent for the mind-blowing view of the city and valley from the top. The Palace is officially closed to the public, but a little *baksheesh* to the guards can never hurt your chances. *(Rs100 round-trip. Entrance fee Rs80 per person, Rs20 per rickshaw. Agent 007 free.)*

OTHER SIGHTS. Sunset Point is well known for its views at sunset. They're almost as impressive as those from the Monsoon Palace, but they're free. *(Ask a rickshaw driver to drop you off at Dudh Talai water tank, then climb 10-15min. uphill.)* Just south of Lake Palace Rd., the sprawling **Sajjan Niwas Park** contains the **Gulab Bagh** (Rose Garden) as well as a zoo and a notable *bhawan*, but it is less maintained than Udaipur's other gardens. The **Bangore-ki-Haveli,** built by the prime minister of Mewar in the 18th century, has been converted into a museum of Mewar aristocratic life. The mansion's architecture and glass inlay work are more captivating than the exhibits. *(Gangaur Ghat. Open daily 10am-5pm. Rs5.)*

🎵 🎭 ENTERTAINMENT AND FESTIVALS

Traditional **Rajasthani folk dances** and music performances, involving a blend of local trance dances and circus-like balancing stunts, take place at **Meera Kala Mandir,** near the Pars Theater in Sector 11, a Rs25-30 rickshaw ride from the old city. (☎583176. Shows held M-Sa 7-8pm. Tickets Rs60. Book at Heera Cycle Store, Gangaur Marg, across the road leading to Lal Ghat.) Right in the heart of the tourist ghetto, the government-run **West Zone Cultural Center** hosts cultural performances; these aren't as professional but feel perhaps more authentic. (In Bangore-ki Haveli, Gangaur Ghat. Daily 7pm. Rs25.) **Bharatiya Lok Kala Folk Art Museum** offers a nightly show that consists of half-folk-dancing, half-puppetry (see **Elsewhere in Udaipur,** above; shows daily 6pm, Rs50). The **Mewar Festival** (Apr. 4-5, 2003), dedicated to Parvati, celebrates the arrival of spring with music, fireworks, and a colorful procession down to the lake.

🛍 SHOPPING

Clothing, jewelry, textile, and handicraft shops are crowded into the areas around Jagdish Mandir, Lake Palace Rd., and Bara and Bapu Bazaars. They sell wares from all over Rajasthan at inflated but negotiable prices. Don't *ever* accept an invitation into a shop by a rickshaw-*wallah* or tout. That is, unless you're feeling generous enough to pay their 30% commission. The shopping areas are easily navigable on foot, so you should have no problem on your own. **Miniature painting** is an Udaipuri speciality, and in many shops you can watch skilled artists work without any obligation to buy. It's best to shop in stores that are run by the artist himself. Prices depend on the intricacy and level of detail rather than the size of the painting. Three dealers who sell high-quality paintings at reasonable prices are: **Artisan,** 117 BC; **Ashok Art,** inside Hotel Gangaur Palace; and **Hare Krishna Arts,** City Palace Rd. Tailors are also particularly abundant and cheap in Udaipur.

🏞 DAYTRIPS FROM UDAIPUR

Nagda, Eklingji, and Nathdwara are easily visited together in a half-day excursion from Udaipur. Most convenient is to rent a **motorbike** or hire a **car** and driver through a travel agency (about Rs500). **Rickshaws** can take you to Nagda and Eklingji (Rs250 round-trip) but are not permitted as far as Nathdwara. Frequent

local buses go between Udaipur and Nathdwara via Eklingji (2.5km from Nagda).
RTDC Hotel Kajri, Shastri Circle, offers a rushed tour to Eklingji and Nathdwara
(☎410501; daily 2-7pm depending on demand; Rs105). You can visit the Jain temple at **Ranakpur** as a (long) daytrip from Udaipur.

EKLINGJI AND NAGDA

> *Buses run to Eklingji from Udaipur (45min., frequent 4am-9:30pm, Rs13). Eklingi temple
> open daily 4-7am, 10:30am-1:30pm, 5-7pm. Nagda temples open daily 5am-6pm.*

Twenty-two kilometers north of Udaipur, is the village of **Eklingji,** home to a magnificent Shiva temple. The marble temple encloses a four-faced, solid black image
of Shiva and is adorned with silver doors, lamps, parcels, and a solid silver bull.
According to legend, this marks the spot where a hermit (depicted above the
entrance) bestowed a blessing upon Bappa Rawal (the first Mewar suzerain, rendered in statue form opposite the entrance) to found a great dynasty. The original
temple was erected in AD 734, but the 107 other temples in the complex, added
over the next 750 years by Bappa Rawal's royal descendants, proves the hermit's
prophecy. Two kilometers down a path that turns left off the main road just before
Eklingji is **Nagda,** legendary birthplace of Bappa Rawal and the first capital of the
Mewar kingdom (preceeding the capital at Chittaurgarh). Today Nagda remains
the home of the **Sas Bahu** (Mother and Daughter-in-Law) Temples, which were rendered inactive by Mughal attack. Even though the central icons were destroyed,
these 10th-century temples have retained their beautiful carvings.

NATHDWARA

> *Buses run to Nathdwara from Udaipur (1½hr., every 15min. 4am-9:30pm, Rs19-22). Tem-
> ple hours are highly variable but are approximately 4:45-6am, 7-7:15am, 9-9:30am, 11:15-
> 11:45am, 3:45-4pm, 4:30-4:45pm, 5-5:15pm. Free.*

Forty-eight kilometers north of Udaipur is the Vaishnava pilgrimage site of **Nathdwara,** built entirely around its incredible **Sri Nathji Mandir,** a temple dedicated to
Krishna's *avatar* as the baby Sri Nathji. Legend maintains that, during the 17th
century, a chariot carrying Krishna's image from Mathura to Udaipur became
trapped inexplicably in the mud; the bearers interpreted the situation as a divine
signal and built a temple on the spot. The image of Sri Nathji, with blazing dia-
mond-studded eyes and Mughal dress, is found on decorative items in households
all over India. The stalls outside the temple have commercialized the image, and
there is Krishna paraphernalia everywhere. Although the temple's architecture is a
visual feast, the evening ceremonies (5pm ceremonies following the ritual feeding,
bathing, and putting-to-bed of the image) are far more interesting. For each *darshan* (viewing window), a different backdrop is displayed behind the statue in
order to depict various scenes from Krishna's life.

RANAKPUR रनकपुर   ☎02934

Eighty kilometers northwest of Udaipur stand Ranakpur's superb Jain temples,
which comprise a complex that rivals Dilwara on Mt. Abu. The main white-marble
Chaumukha Temple, built in 1439, is dedicated to Adinath, the first *tirthankara*
(Jain teacher). Inside, there are 29 halls, 80 domes, and 1444 pillars (no two of
them alike), all intricately carved and sculpted. The temple's most intricate carvings surround a four-faced image of Adinath in the innermost sanctum. In addition
to this Adinath temple, the complex contains three other shrines: the smaller but
equally superb **Parsavath Temple,** straight ahead to the left as you enter the complex, and the less notable **Neminath Temple** and Hindu **Sun Temple** farther back to
the right. *(Open to non-Jain tourists daily 11:30am-5pm; to Jains and Indians 7am-8pm. Menstruating women are not supposed to enter. Camera fee Rs40.)*

A WIFE FOR KRISHNA Visitors from far and wide come to Chittaurgarh to visit Meera Mandir, a tribute to the mystic poetess Mirabai, whose *bhajans* (devotional songs) grace the airwaves nationwide. Born in the 15th century to a Rajput family in the village of Kurki, outside of Jodhpur, Mirabai displayed an early affection for the Lord Krishna—she claimed him as her husband at a tender age. When she was matched with a mortal spouse, Raltan Singh of Chittaurgarh, Mirabai persisted in her devotion. She defied her new family (staunch devotees of Shiva) and Rajput customs by leaving the fort to worship Krishna. The final straw for the royal family was her refusal to commit *sati* upon her husband's death. She claimed her true spouse was Krishna, citing his immortality as a reason for not mourning. Members of the enraged royal family plotted to take her life, first by sending her poison to drink and then by releasing a black cobra to kill her. Mira consumed the poison as if it were a *lassi*, and the cobra became a garland of flowers around her neck. After the attempts on her life, Mirabai took her statue of Krishna and fled to Dwarka in Gujarat. When Udai Singh came to power, he attempted to redress his family's transgressions and invited Mirabai back to Chittaurgarh. Legend has it that, after a visit to the Krishna temple that housed her statue, she dissolved into the statue. Mirabai's cherished Krishna icon is now the personal property of the royal family of Udaipur. The songs Mirabai composed out of her devotional love *(bhakti)* remain a popular means of Krishna worship.

Ranakpur is a good breaking point for the long bus journey between Udaipur (2½-3hr.) and Jodhpur (4½hr.). Make sure the driver knows you want to get off at Ranakpur. Buses stop by the *chai* stand on the main road en route to: **Abu Road** (5hr., 6am, Rs75); **Jodhpur** (4½hr.; 8am, noon, 6pm; Rs85); **Udaipur** (3hr.; every hr. 7am-7pm, Rs35; deluxe 2½hr.; 10am, 4, 7:30pm; Rs42). As there's nothing to see in "town" besides the temples, you could conceivably move onto your next destination the same night or even do a daytrip to Ranakpur from Udaipur, but Ranakpur is a pleasant enough place to stay. The friendly **RTDC Hotel Shilpi ❷**, 150m up the road (toward Jodhpur) from the bus stand and temples, has spacious, pleasant rooms with bath and serves reasonably priced meals. (☎85074. Singles Rs200-600; doubles Rs300-700.) The **dharamsala ❶**, inside the temple complex offers very basic lodgings and plentiful meals. (☎85019. Meals Rs15. Rooms Rs20-50.)

MOUNT ABU माऊंट आबू ☎02974

Situated on a plateau near the Gujarati border, Mt. Abu (pop. 16,000; elev. 1220m) is unique among Rajasthan's tourist destinations. Besides being Rajasthan's only hill station, it's far more popular with Indian tourists than with foreigners. While some come to worship at the breathtaking Dilwara temples, to take a dip in the holy waters of Nakki Lake, or to honor Vashishta, the sage who gave rise to the five Rajput clans, most tourists are thinking more along physical rather than spiritual lines. Families come here to seek refuge from the heat at lower altitudes, and honeymooners come to frolic among the ice-cream shops and endless parade of pony rides. With so many wordily delights, the few foreign visitors to the city are unlikely to leave disappointed—the Dilwara temples are nothing less than spectacular, and the cool temperatures and abundant greenery make the town a fantastic place to relax for a few days before heading back into the thick of things.

▣ TRANSPORTATION

A Rs5 tourist tax is levied on all visitors at the end of the long climb up the mountain, so keep some small change handy.

Trains: Abu Road Railway Station (☎22222). 27km from town; it's on the main broad-gauge line between Delhi and Mumbai via Ahmedabad. **Western Railway Out Agency,** Nakki Lake Rd. (☎38697), next to the bus stand, handles reservations to Delhi and Mumbai. Open M-Sa 9am-1pm and 2-3pm, Su 9am-noon. To: **Ahmedabad** (4-5½hr., 5 per day 11:10am-4:23am, Rs83); **Jodhpur** (5-6hr.; 1:50, 4:40am, 1:20pm; Rs120); **Jaipur** (7-8hr., 3-5 per day 11:10am-9:23pm, Rs154) via **Ajmer** (4½-6hr., Rs120).

Buses: Main Bus Stand (☎43434). To: **Ahmedabad** (6½hr., 11 per day 6am-9pm, Rs87); **Jaipur** (12hr., 9:45am and 1:30pm, Rs202; deluxe 6:30pm, Rs247); **Jaisalmer** (11hr., 6:15am, Rs176); **Jodhpur** (7½hr., 6:45am, Rs121; deluxe 3:30pm, Rs355); **Udaipur** (6½hr., 4 per day 8:45am-4pm, Rs75; deluxe 7pm, Rs140). **Private bus companies** line Nakki Lake Rd. **Shobha Travels** (☎38302) is next door to Hotel Samrat. Open daily 7am-10:30pm. All bus transportation arranged in Mt. Abu departs from Mt. Abu proper, but arrangements made in other cities for service to Mt. Abu may only come as far as Abu Road, 1hr. away—be sure to check in advance.

Local Transportation: Buses to **Abu Road** depart frequently from the Main Bus Stand (1hr., every 30min. 6am-9pm, Rs13-15). Jeeps and vans serving as local **taxis** leave from the taxi stand at the southern end of the Polo Grounds. A shared **jeep** to Abu Road costs Rs15 per person; private taxis are Rs200 one-way. To the Dilwara Temples, private taxis cost Rs30; shared jeeps, leaving from Cha Cha Circle, are Rs5 per person.

✴ ? ORIENTATION AND PRACTICAL INFORMATION

The small town can be crossed from one side to the other in 25min. The main drag, **Nakki Lake Rd.,** leads into town from Abu Road, passing the Tourist Reception Center and Main Bus Stand before following the eastern edge of the **Polo Grounds** to **Cha Cha Circle.** From there, bearing right brings you down **Sadar Bazaar** (the main market) toward the **GPO,** while heading left takes you to **Nakki Lake.** The **Dilwara Jain Temples** are 3km northeast of town on Raj Bhavan Rd.

Tourist Office: Tourist Reception Centre (☎43151). Opposite the bus stand. Maps Rs2. Open M-Sa 10am-5pm. Closed 2nd Sa. of each month.

Currency Exchange: Bank of Baroda (☎43166). Near the taxi stand, changes cash and traveler's checks and gives advances on MC and V for a 1% commission. Open M-F 10am-3pm, Sa 10am-12:30pm.

Police: Main Police Station (☎38333). Near the Main Bus Stand. Open 24hr.

Hospital: J. Watumull Global Hospital and Research Centre (☎38347 or 38348). 1km out of town on the road to the Dilwara Temples. An ultra-clean, ultra-modern private facility. Open M-Sa 9am-1pm and 3-5pm. Open for emergencies 24hr.

Post Office: GPO (☎43170). Open M-F 9am-3pm, Sa 9am-2pm. **Postal Code:** 307501.

▐ ACCOMMODATIONS

The majority of hotels in town cater to Indian families and honeymooners rather than backpackers, and the dozens of "youth hostels" around town are intended principally for students attending Mt. Abu's private schools. Room rates skyrocket during high season (May-June and Oct.-Nov.), particularly at the time of **Diwali** (see p. 88), when tariffs can jump to Rs1000 for a shabby double. During low season (Dec.-Apr. and July-Sept.), prices are more reasonable. Buses will drop you off within walking distance of several hotels that are far from the lake. Though your first instinct will be to avoid touts, they can be very helpful in finding you a room during peak season. Unless otherwise noted, all hotels listed have 9am check-out.

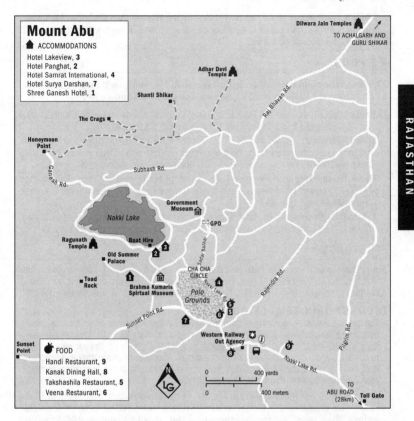

Mount Abu

▲ ACCOMMODATIONS

Hotel Lakeview, **3**
Hotel Panghat, **2**
Hotel Samrat International, **4**
Hotel Surya Darshan, **7**
Shree Ganesh Hotel, **1**

Dilwara Jain Temples
TO ACHALGARH AND
GURU SHIKAR

Adhar Devi
Temple

Shanti Shikar

Raj Bhavan Rd.

The Crags

Honeymoon
Point

Ganesh Rd.

Subhash Rd.

Government
Museum

GPO

Nakki Lake

Boat Hire

Ragunath
Temple

Old Summer
Palace

Sadar Bazaar

Toad
Rock

Brahma Kumaris
Spirtual Museum

CHA CHA
CIRCLE

Polo
Grounds

Nakki Lake Rd.

Rajendra Rd.

Sunset Point Rd.

Sunset
Point

Western Railway
Out Agency

Pilgrim Rd.

Nakki Lake Rd.

TO
ABU ROAD
(28km)

Toll Gate

N

0   400 yards
0   400 meters

🍎 FOOD

Handi Restaurant, **9**
Kanak Dining Hall, **8**
Takshashila Restaurant, **5**
Veena Restaurant, **6**

Shree Ganesh Hotel (☎43591 or 37292). On the road to the Old Summer Palace. The rooms, are comfy, but what sets this place apart is the hospitality and range of facilities. The only hotel in Mt. Abu that caters primarily to foreigners, Shree Ganesh keeps a foreign-tourist quota until 10pm and offers free pickup/drop-off at the station. Internet (Rs1 per min.). Jeep tours to Achalgarh and the Dilwara temples (Rs60 per person). Singles Rs150-175; doubles Rs200-250. Low season: Rs50 less. ❶

Hotel Samrat International (☎43173 or 43153). Nakki Lake Rd. Beautiful, clean, modern rooms, all with TVs, sitting areas, and attached baths (hot water 6am-noon). A great choice if it's in your price range. Good restaurant too (see below). Check-out noon. Rooms Rs500-850. Low season: Rs200-580. ❸

Hotel Panghat (☎38886). Nakki Lake. Unexciting but adequate rooms, all with attached baths and TVs. Good values considering their lakeside location, though the carnival vibes from the streets below might test your patience after a while. Rooms Rs350-450. Low season: Rs125-150. ❷

Hotel Lakeview (☎38659). Nakki Lake. Another lakeside hotel with good views. Geared toward honeymooners—reams of red velvet give the rooms a Vegas touch. Deluxe rooms have lakeside swings for two. All rooms with attached baths (hot water 7-11am). Rooftop restaurant. Rooms Rs500-600. Low season: Rs250-300. ❸

Hotel Surya Darshan (☎ 43165 or 37149). By the Western Polo Grounds. Rooms vary dramatically—ask to see a few before deciding on one. Rooms with hot-water bath Rs150-250. Low season: Rs80-15. ❶

🍴 FOOD

Thanks to the abundance of Gujarati tourists in Mt. Abu, you'll find Gujarati food as often as you will the typical Rajasthani, Punjabi, and Chinese items.

Kanak Dining Hall, near the Main Bus Stand. Come at lunchtime to see stainless steel fly. Gujarati *thalis* Rs45. Open daily 11am-3pm and 7-11pm. ❶

Veena Restaurant, Nakki Lake Rd., opposite the Bank of Baroda. Quick food joint specializing in South Indian food. Twist your hips to Hindi pop as you munch on a tasty *dosa* (Rs20-40) or a veg. meal (Rs25-50). Open daily 7am-midnight. ❶

Handi Restaurant, in the Hilltone Hotel, south of the Main Bus Stand. Superb food (Rs50-80) served in an upscale environment. Indoor or garden seating. Attached bar. Open daily 7am-11pm. ❶

Takshashila Restaurant, in Hotel Samrat. Tasty veg. food in a central location. Indian, Chinese, and continental options Rs40-60. Open daily 8am-3pm and 7-11pm. ❶

👁 SIGHTS

Many travel agencies offer half- and full-day tours of Mt. Abu and its environs, but these tend to be very rushed (e.g. less than 1hr. at the Dilwara complex) and cater to Indian tourists (most are in Hindi), so it's more advisable to wander by yourself.

DILWARA JAIN TEMPLE COMPLEX

The temples are 3km northeast of town, along Raj Bhavan Rd. Jeeps from Cha Cha Circle head to the temples every 15min. for Rs3; chartering a taxi costs Rs30-40. The walk between town and Dilwara is most pleasant on the way back, when it's downhill. The complex is open to non-Jains noon-6pm; Jains can visit sunrise-sunset. Photography and leather items prohibited; don't bring anything you wouldn't feel comfortable leaving at the mandatory storage area. Menstruating women are not supposed to enter.

The Jain temple complex at Dilwara is one of the architectural highlights of India. The temples are famed for the incredible intricacy and detail of their white-marble carvings. Even more impressive, though, is the amazing variation of figures and ornamentation; from the pillars to ceiling reliefs, no two designs are identical.

The first temple is the small, modest **Temple of Mahaveer Swami,** built in 1582 and dedicated to the 24th *tirthankara.* Next up, on the right, is the **Hasti Shala** (elephant cell), which contains three rows of huge, beautifully carved pachyderms.

Opposite the Hasti Shala sits the original and most famous temple at Dilwara, the **Vimal Vasahi,** built during the 11th century by Vimal Shah, Chief Minister to the Solanki King of Gujarat, and dedicated to the first *tirthankara,* Adinath. Construction took 1200 laborers, 1500 artists, and 14 years to complete. The "dancing dome" just inside the entrance features statues of the 16 *Vidhyadevus* (goddesses of education), and magnificent carvings line the pillars supporting the dome and the main sanctuary just behind it. Surrounding the sanctum itself is a circumambulatory corridor with 57 cells, each of which contains a *tirthankara* statue and is embellished by a unique lintel. As you make the rounds, look up for the best artwork—it's carved into the ceiling panels in front of the cells. The subject matter of the panels encompasses ornamental lotus flowers, birds, and scenes from the lives of the Jain *tirthankaras,* and sculptures of many-limbed goddesses. The statue of Adinath at the center of the temple is modeled on a 3500-year-old granite statue housed in the temple. According to legend, Vimal Shah discovered the statue on this spot under a sweet-smelling *champa* tree. The dome and walls of the sanctuary were left undecorated to avoid distracting meditators.

The next temple, the **Luna Vasahi,** known as the Tejpal Temple, was built two centuries after the Vimal, and although smaller than Vimal, its marble carvings are more intricate and delicate. Workers carved the tiered lotus dome from a single block of marble. The Tejpal is dedicated to Neminath, the 22nd *tirthankara*, and the 52 cells along the corridor contain images of the *tirthankaras*.

The last two temples, the **Pittahar** (c. 1315-1433) and **Parshwanath** (c. 1458), pale in comparison to the Vimal and Tejpal. The story goes that the artisans and laborers working on the main temples used leftover scraps of materials from the other temples to build the three-story Parshwanath Temple. Unfortunately, logic undermines the romance of the tale: the Parshwanath was built much later from gray sandstone rather than white marble.

🚶 HIKING AND OUTDOOR ACTIVITIES

NAKKI LAKE. Visiting Nakki Lake, where most of Mt. Abu's activity is focused, is like attending a carnival—popcorn sellers, photo stalls, and brightly decorated **ponies** *(rides Rs100 per hr.)* crowd the streets, and mobs constantly clamor for **paddleboats** and **rowboats** available at the dock *(Rs50 per 30min.).* The festive atmosphere tends to obscure the religious significance of the lake, thought to contain holy waters because it was dug out by the nails *(nakh)* of a god. Taking a scenic walk along the left bank, from which you can see **Toad Rock,** leads past the small **Ragunath Temple** to a quiet side of the lake lined with huge estates and stately homes.

VIEWPOINTS AND HIKES. Sunset Point lies 500m west of the Polo Grounds along Sunset Pt. Rd. (a short but very nice nature trail runs parallel to the main road). Though it offers a beautiful view of the setting sun, the crowd of tourists has made it a much better people-watching spot. A similar fate has befallen **Honeymoon Point,** off the road leading northwest behind Nakki Lake. The view from here is also superb, and the name draws newlyweds by the dozen. From here you can see the **Crags** or hike up a little farther to the **Shanti Shikhar** for dazzling panoramic views. A left off the northeast road to Dilwara leads to the base of a 30min., heart-pumping trek up 360 steps to the mountain-top **Adhar Devi Temple.** Dedicated to the patron goddess of Mt. Abu, the "temple" is a natural cleft in the rock that can only be entered by crawling on all fours. It commands a spectacular view of the valleys below. Numerous other hiking possibilities exist for those looking to take advantage of Mt. Abu's fantastic scenery, uniquely green for Rajasthan. For suggested hikes, see the sign near Sunset Point. Friendly 🏔**Lalit** at the Shree Ganesh Hotel leads hikes through less-trampled places; non-guests might be able to tag along along after eating at the restaurant or utilizing the hotel's travel services.

🏔 DAYTRIPS FROM MOUNT ABU

Buses head to Achalgarh from the main bus stand in Mt. Abu. 30min.; 10am, 12:15, 4pm; Rs6; return 10:30am, 12:45, 4:30pm. Shree Ganesh Hotel organizes jeep tours to the Dilwara temples and Achalgarh: Rs60.

Eight kilometers past Dilwara at **Achalgarh,** there stands a small 9th-century temple to Achaleshwar Mahadev, an incarnation of Shiva. The temple marks a small, supposedly bottomless crater that was created by Shiva's big toe. The temple also contains a Nandi statue made of over 4000kg of silver, brass, gold, copper, and tin. A path leads up the steep hillside from Achaleshwar Mahadev to the less visited, even more impressive **Adhaswer** Jain temple complex that looms above. The main temple in the complex is 500 years old and features 3D murals (new additions) depicting Jain temples and their environs throughout India. The smaller Adinath and Kuntinath temples house painted columns and figures. The view from the top is breathtaking. Just past Achalgarh on the main road is the turnoff to **Guru Shikar** (1721m), the highest point in Rajasthan. Although it's marked by a Vishnu temple, it is mainly a scenic viewpoint. It takes about 30min. to drive to the top.

JODHPUR जोधपुर ☎ 0291

Once the capital of the state of Marwar ("Land of Death"), founded by the warrior clans of Rathore, Jodhpur (pop. 1,000,000) borders on the Thar Desert and is the second largest city in Rajasthan. Despite its size and bustle, Jodhpur has yet to emerge as a tourist destination in its own right, though it's a pleasant enough place to spend a few days before continuing on to more exotic destinations like Jaisalmer and Udaipur. Jodhpur's highlights include its formidable and lavishly decorated fort, which looms over the city; its bustling bazaar area; and the old town's winding streets and sea of color-washed homes, which have earned Jodhpur its nickname, "The Blue City." These sights can be seen in a day or two, after which many travelers tack on a daytrip to the nearby desert villages of the Bishnoi.

Jodhpur was founded in AD 1459 by Rao Jodha, the chief of the Rathore Rajput clan, originally from the Kanauj area to the east. The Marwar state grew and prospered and eventually became one of the most peaceful in the region. During the 18th century, however, Mughals overran the city and exiled Maharaja Ajit Singh to Afghanistan, where he was murdered. Thirty years later, his son rode back to Jodhpur with his army and drove out the Mughals, who never returned.

▐ TRANSPORTATION

Flights: Jodhpur Airport (flight info ☎ 142), 6km from the city center, down Airport Rd. 25min. from town by auto-rickshaw (Rs50) or taxi (Rs100). **Indian Airlines** (☎ 510757 or 510758, airport office 512617). Airport Rd. Open daily 10am-1:15pm and 2-4:30pm. To: **Delhi** (2hr., daily 7:20pm, US$110) via **Jaipur** (40min., US$85); **Mumbai** (2½hr., daily 8:30am, US$155) via **Udaipur** (40min., US$70).

Trains: Jodhpur Railway Station, Railway Station Rd. (☎ 131 or 132). Most trains also stop at **Raika Bagh Railway Station,** on the east side of town. Reserve at the **Advance Reservation Office,** Station Rd. (☎ 636407). Next to the GPO. Open M-Sa 8am-8pm, Su 8am-2pm. To: **Ahmedabad** (10hr.; 2, 3:15, 6:55pm; Rs159) via **Abu Road** (5hr.); **Bikaner** (5-6hr.; 10:30, 10:45am, 7:50pm; Rs109); **Delhi** (11-12hr., 7:30 and 11pm); **Jaipur** (4-7hr.; 5:45am, 5:15, 7:30, 11pm); **Jaisalmer** (6½hr., 11:15pm).

Buses: Main Bus Station (☎ 544686 or 544989). High Court Rd. To: **Ahmedabad** (12hr., 6 per day 6am-7:30pm, Rs173; deluxe 6 and 9pm, Rs208); **Ajmer** (4½hr., every 30min. 5:15am-midnight, Rs82); **Bikaner** (6hr., 12 per day 5:30am-7:45pm, Rs102); **Delhi** (14hr.; 9, 10am, 3:30, 4pm; Rs243; deluxe 4pm, Rs365); **Jaipur** (7½hr., 11 per day 5:15am-midnight, Rs131; deluxe 11am, 4, 10pm; Rs260); **Jaisalmer** (5hr., 9 per day 5am-5:30pm, Rs92); **Mount Abu** (7hr., noon, Rs120; deluxe 5:30am, Rs360); **Udaipur** (8hr., 4 per day 7:15am-10pm, Rs108; deluxe 7hr.; 5:30, 11:45am, 3, 10:30pm; Rs108). There are dozens of **private bus companies** around; most are along High Court Rd., near the main railway station.

Local Transportation: Local **buses** (Rs2-7) and **tempos** (Rs1-5) are the cheapest option, provided you can figure out their routes. **Auto-rickshaws,** the best way to maneuver through the streets of the old city, congregate around the major sights and stations (Rs10-30 to most destinations). **Bicycles** are available for rent at Prem Cycle Store, opposite the railway station. **Taxis,** available in front of the tourist office (Rs3 per km, Rs60 minimum charge), are good for longer hauls.

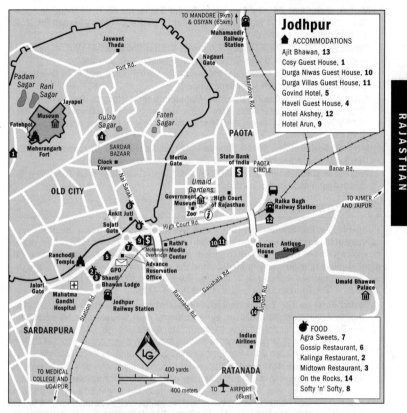

ORIENTATION AND PRACTICAL INFORMATION

Much of modern Jodhpur lies beyond the old city walls. **Jodhpur Railway Station** is in the southwestern part of town, along **Station Rd.** Nearby are the two most important gates to the old city and Jodhpur's modern-day commercial centers—**Jalori Gate,** at the end of the road running perpendicular to the station, and **Sojati Gate,** to the right as you exit the station, along Station Rd. **High Court Rd.** continues east from Sojati Gate past the **Umaid Gardens** and the **Tourist Reception Center** to **Raika Bagh Railway Station** and the bus stand. The main artery of the old city, **Nai Sarak,** leads north from the old city walls to **Sardar Bazaar** (the main market area), punctuated by the **Clock Tower.** Looming over the tangled web of old-city streets are **Meherangarh Fort** and the memorial **Jaswant Thada.** The old city is almost impossible to navigate—take a rickshaw, or be prepared to ask for lots of directions.

Tourist Office: Tourist Reception Centre, High Court Rd. (☎545083). In RTDC Hotel Ghoomar. Maps Rs2. Open M-Sa 8am-8pm. Daily tours take in the fort, the Umaid Bhawan Palace and Garden, Jaswant Thada, and Mandore Gardens (9am-1pm or 2-6pm, 6-person minimum, Rs85 without entrance fees). For info on **village safaris,** see p. 527).

Currency Exchange: Bank of Baroda, Sojati Gate (☎439746). Under Hotel Arun. Changes traveler's checks and gives cash advances on MC and V (1% commission). Open M-F 10am-3pm, Sa 10am-12:30pm.

Market: High Court Rd., Nai Sarak, and **Sardar Bazaar** are the main shopping areas. There are fresh fruit and vegetable stalls in Sardar Bazaar and along **Station Rd.** Most stores open daily 10am-9pm.

Police: (☎633700). The Ratanada Rd. **Police Control Room** (☎547180), at the intersection of Nai Sarak and High Court Rd., is also helpful in an emergency.

Pharmacy: Most of the stores near the hospitals, around Sojati and Jalori Gates, and along Nai Sarak are open M-Sa 8am-10pm.

Hospital: Mahatma Gandhi Hospital, Mahatma Gandhi Hospital Rd. (☎636437). Between Sojati and Jalori Gates. Also accessible from Station Rd. **Goyal Hospital,** Residency Rd. (☎432144). Near the Medical College. One of the best private hospitals. Both open 24hr.

Internet: Govind Hotel, Shanti Bhawan Lodge, and a few small STD places along the Nai Sarak offer email services for Rs1 per min. Most open 8am-11pm.

Post Office: GPO, Station Rd. (☎636695). Near Sojati Gate. Open M-Sa 10am-6pm, Su 10am-4pm. **Postal Code:** 342001.

🎒 ACCOMMODATIONS

Budget hotels line Station and High Court Rd. Accommodations on the other side of the railroad tracks are more peaceful but necessitate heavy reliance on autorickshaws to see the rest of town (about Rs20 to Sojati Gate/Nai Sarak). Several smaller guest houses are sprinkled around the clock tower (tout city) and throughout the old city—these can be charming, though hard to find and lacking modern amenities. The tourist office also arranges home-stays.

Govind Hotel (☎622758; govindhotel2000@yahoo.com). Opposite the GPO, a 5min. walk from railway station. Modern, well-kept rooms, most with attached hot-water bath and TV. Govind's central location, its very helpful owner, Jagdish, and its good rooftop veg. restaurant (with fantastic views of the fort) make this a very popular budget choice. Narrow but clean 6-bed dorm Rs70; singles Rs200-300; doubles Rs250-350. ❶

Haveli Guest House, Makrana Mohalla (☎614615; havelight@sify.com). 5min. on foot from the clock tower in the old city. Another popular refuge for travelers, housed in a beautiful 250-year-old *haveli*. Rooms are smallish but bright and clean, all with attached hot-water bath. Amazing views from the rooftop veg. restaurant look up to the fort and out over a sea of blue old-city homes. Pricey-but-worth-it, older 1st fl. rooms without a view Rs150; rooms with A/C, tub, and a view Rs800. ❶

Durga Niwas Guest House, 1st Old Public Park (☎639092; duragniwas@usa.net). Family-run guest house with spotless, beautifully decorated rooms. Fantastic value. Reputable camel and village safaris. Rooms with attached (hot) bath Rs200-500. ❷

Durga Villas (☎312298; durgavillas@usa.net). Next door to the Durga Niwas. More ornate rooms than its similarly-named neighbor, all with attached (hot) bath (Rs150-550). Call for free pickup from the station or airport. ❷

Hotel Akshey (☎510327 or 510181). Behind Raika Bagh Railway Station. Conveniently accessible via a door behind Platform 2. Quiet (except when trains are passing by), well-scrubbed rooms (all with TV and attached hot-water bath) and a pleasant garden area. Room service. Check-out 24hr. Dorms Rs60; singles Rs200-275; doubles Rs250-350, with A/C Rs450-550. 10% service charge. Next door, **Hotel Anand** (☎510483) has big, clean nice rooms with TVs and attached baths. Check-out 24hr. Singles Rs500-600. 10% service charge. ❶

Cosy Guest House, Novechokiya Rd., Bhram Puri, Chuna Ki Choki (☎612066). Buried deep in the old city, a 5min. walk from the fort's back gate. Formerly known as Joshi's Blue House, this intimate lodge has cramped but quaint rooms in the oldest part of the old city. Rooftop restaurant serves home-cooked food. Dorm Rs60; small doubles with clean common bath Rs150, with attached hot-water bath and TV Rs250. ❶

Hotel Arun (☎ 620238 or 621824; fax 634228). Opposite Sojati Gate. Small, plain, but clean rooms off a busy intersection. Bucket hot water only. Room service. Singles with common/attached bath Rs150-210; doubles Rs220/310. ❶

Ajit Bhawan, Airport Rd. (☎ 511410 or 510410). This delightful Heritage Hotel is made up of 54 round, individually-decorated luxury cottages, most with terraces, set amidst lush gardens far from the commotion of the city. All this beauty will cost you dearly, though. The hotel also houses a fantastic restaurant, a weight room, and an incredible pool complete with a huge water-wheel and waterfalls. Singles Rs1895; doubles Rs2295; deluxe cottages Rs2900-3500. 10% luxury tax. ❺

FOOD

Local specialties include *mawa* sweets, available at shops at the intersection of Nai Sarak and High Court Rd., *chakki-ka-sagh*, wheat sponge cooked in rich gravy, and the *makhania lassi*, a thick, sweet *lassi* flavored with saffron.

On the Rocks, adjacent to Ajit Bhawan Hotel, on Airport Rd. Excellent Indian, Chinese, and continental food served in a relaxing outdoor courtyard that's illuminated in the evenings. Popular with locals and tourists alike. Live Indian classical music Sa and Su. Veg. dishes Rs50-80, non-veg. Rs100-195. Open daily 12:30-3pm and 7-11pm. ❶

Midtown Restaurant, in the Shanti Bhawan Lodge, opposite the railway station on Station Rd. A great introduction to Rajasthani cuisine, this veg. restaurant has a range of local specialties (Rs35-55). Sample everything with a *Rajasthani Maharaja Thali* (Rs80). Open daily 7am-11pm. ❶

Kalinga Restaurant, in the Kalinga Hotel, on the road straight ahead of the railway station. Indian, Chinese, and Italian food in an upscale setting. Veg. dishes Rs40-65, "hunter's paradise" items Rs50-110. Open daily 7am-10:30pm. ❶

Gossip Restaurant, 32 Nai Sarak, in the mid-range City Palace Hotel. Tasty Rajasthani veg. dishes for Rs35-65. Open daily 7am-10:30pm (dinner served after 7:30pm). ❶

Agra Sweets, opposite Sojati Gate. The oldest shop in Jodhpur serves up a wide range of sweets and Rajasthani snacks, including an almost sickly sweet *makhania lassi* (Rs12)—*Gourmet Magazine* once wanted the recipe. Open daily 8:30am-10:30pm. ❶

Softy 'n' Softy, Nai Sarak. Just around the corner from Agra Sweets. Perfect if you're craving sweet relief from the heat. Soft-serve cones Rs15, excellent shakes Rs20-35. Open daily 10am-11:30pm. ❶

SIGHTS

MEHERANGARH FORT

The main entrance to the fort, in the northeast corner, is most easily reached by rickshaw; the 5km climb will cost you about Rs40. Most people exit the same way; Fatehpol gate, an alternate exit, dumps you out to the southwest. Open daily 9am-5pm. Rs50; camera fee Rs50; video fee Rs100.

Rising magnificently above Jodhpur, Meherangarh is one of the best-preserved forts in Rajasthan. It may be quite small compared with some of its sprawling counterparts, but the interior has been beautifully restored and now houses a fascinating collection of artifacts. The fort was originally built in AD 1459, by Rao Jodha, but has been expanded over the years by subsequent maharajas. Seven *pols* (gates) mark the various entrances. The **Jayapol,** the main entrance, commemorates the military achievements of Maharaja Man Singh. The impressive **Fatehpol** (Victory Gate), created by Maharaja Ajit Singh after his return from exile, marks the original entrance into the fort. The **Lohapol** (Iron Gate) features 15 handprints that honor the *sati* sacrifice of Maharaja Man Singh's widows in 1843. Beyond the final gigantic **Surajpol** is the centerpiece of the modern fort, the **Meherangarh Museum,** housed in a red sandstone palace. Filling its halls are extravagant silver *howdahs* (elephant seats), exquisite wood and ivory artifacts, a weapons room, the royal dumbbells of the maharani, a beautiful 250-year-old tent canopy (a prized acquisition seized during a raid on the Mughals in Delhi), 150 types of cannons, fancy baby cradles, musical instruments, miniature paintings, and a 300-piece turban collection. Of particular interest are the **Phool Mahal** (Flower Palace), an elaborate, mirrored dance hall embellished with gold, and the **Moti Mahal** (Pearl Palace), a conference room with a glass and gold ceiling.

After exiting the museum, you can stroll along the ramparts to the southern end of the fort, which commands a breathtaking view out over the wash of blue, old-city homes. Some claim that the distinctive color was intended to denote brahmin residences, while others hold that the copper sulfate was added primarily because of its protective powers against termites and mosquitoes. The **Chamunda Temple** is also at this end of the fort.

UMAID BHAWAN PALACE. The Umaid Bhawan Palace is a majestic marble and sandstone palace that dominates the eastern part of the city. Built just before Independence, the palace is impressive enough but lacks some of the charm of Rajasthan's older palaces. The current maharaja, Gaj Singh II, and a luxury hotel occupy most of the palace, but six rooms have been converted into a **museum** and are thus open to the public. The eccentric collection includes antique clocks, opulent furniture, Chinese vases, stuffed animals, and miscellaneous relics—all property of the Maharaja. *(Open daily 9am-5pm. Rs40. Cameras strictly prohibited.)*

JASWANT THADA. This impressive white-marble memorial to the beloved Maharaja Jaswant Singh II was erected by his wife in 1899. Adjoining the memorial are four smaller cenotaphs of rulers who followed Jaswant; those who came before him are memorialized at Mandore. The view of the fort is spectacular. *(10min. downhill from the main fort entrance. Open daily 9am-1pm and 2-5pm. Rs10.)*

OTHER SITES. The **Clock Tower** is an important landmark in the old city and a great place to start exploring—the colorful market of **Sardar Bazaar** is right here, and various bazaars (with different areas dedicated to different trades) radiate out from the area (see **Shopping,** below). Back outside the old city walls, the **Umaid Gardens** are a good place for the aimless wanderer. *(Gardens open M-Th and Sa-Su 10am-4:30pm. Rs3. Zoo open M and W-Su 10am-6pm. Rs1.)*

ENTERTAINMENT

The **Ajit Bhawan** hotel organizes performances of Rajasthani folk singing and dancing to accompany a delicious buffet dinner (nightly in season 7:30pm, Rs350; check with reception for off-season times). For those with a less cultural form of entertainment in mind, **On the Rocks** and **Gossip** have well-stocked bars, though nothing in Jodhpur is open after 11:30pm. The annual **Marwar Festival** (Oct. 8-9, 2003) showcases local history, dance, art, and most of all, food.

SHOPPING

The **Sojati Gate** and **Nai Sarak** areas, especially **Sardar Bazaar** by the Clock Tower, are crammed full of shops peddling everything imaginable. Along with handicrafts of the bedspread-and-pillowcase variety (most of which actually come from nearby Barmer and environs), aromatic **spices** are very popular purchases among visitors. There are numerous spice shops around the clock tower, but everybody's favorite spice shop is **Mohanlal Verhomal,** stall 209B at the *sabzi* (vegetable) market. Mohan Gehani, the owner, might charge a little more than some of his competitors, but he's very knowledgeable, and his mail-order service is reliable.

Another major Jodhpur specialty is **antiques.** The area leading to Umaid Bhawan Palace is filled with huge treasure troves of Rajasthani paraphernalia (both genuine and "instant" antiques). Most, however, are not for popular tourist consumption—items run on the large and expensive side (e.g. elaborately painted wooden furniture) and are geared toward Western art and antique dealers and overseas exporters. Still, their collections are fun to peruse, and most of them also offer modest selections of smaller (and more affordable) items in wood, brass, marble, iron, clay, *papier mâché*, and textiles—all handmade in Rajasthan. Two good places to start are **Lalji Handicrafts** (☎744868; open daily 9:30am-7:30pm) and **Ajay Art Emporium** (☎510269; open daily 9am-8pm), both on Umaid Bhawan Palace Rd.

RAJASTHAN

🔛 DAYTRIPS FROM JODHPUR

Almost as strong a draw to Jodhpur as the fort and bazaars are the daytrip possibilities in the surrounding area. During a half- or full-day trip, it's possible to visit the desert villages of the Bishnoi people; in another day it's possible to see the exquisitely sculpted Jain temples at Osiyan and the *chhattris* at Mandore.

BISHNOI VILLAGES

The only practical way to see these villages is with an organized tour, since they're spread out far from each other and a translator-guide is necessary for any meaningful communication. Many hotels in Jodhpur offer village safaris (a 5hr. visit to four villages costs Rs350-450 per person), as does the tourist office (Rs750 per jeep). Take care when selecting an operator, as a poor choice can mean the difference between a fulfilling cultural experience and a tacky, intervillage shopping expedition. The tourist office, Hotel Govind, Durga Niwas Guest House, and Cosy Guest House run reputable operations.

The Bishnoi people, who established themselves as a group in the 15th century, are well-known for their devotion to environmental protection. They regard all fauna as sacred (they're pure vegetarians), as well as some flora (e.g., acacia trees), and live their lives according to 29 conservative principles (*"bishnoi"* means "29"). Bishnoi villages are scattered throughout northwest India, including the area southeast of Jodhpur (along the road to Pali), and "village safaris" from Jodhpur are a popular way for tourists to view a bit of rural Rajasthani life. In traditional desert homes, typically cow-dung complexes or thatched huts, visitors can learn about herbal medicines, taste desert cuisine, and watch local craftspeople spinning, making pottery, and weaving carpets.

OSIYAN

*65km north of Jodhpur. **Buses** run to Osiyan from Jodhpur: 1½-2hr., every 30min. 5:30am-9pm, Rs6. Alternatively, get together with other travelers and rent a **jeep** from the tourist office for Rs750; the trip takes an hour by car. Mahavira Jain Temple Rs5; camera fee Rs30.*

The desert town of Osiyan is home to the largest group of early Jain and Hindu temples in Rajasthan. From the 8th to the 12th centuries, this was a prosperous trading town, and its primarily Jain merchants poured their wealth into these beautifully sculpted, fairly well-preserved temples. You can visit them on a daytrip from Jodhpur, or if you're pressed for time and can't go to Jaisalmer or Bikaner, stay longer and organize a camel trek from here.

Right near the bus stand is the oldest group of temples, consisting of the red 8th-and 9th-century **Vishnu** and **Harihara** temples. Follow the main road from Jodhpur to Phalodi, then continue straight ahead (toward the town center) as the road bends right. In the middle of town is the massive and very busy **Sachiya Mata** temple, perched atop a large staircase. Women and men line up separately and are admitted in alternating waves, but no matter what your sex, be prepared to push and shove when it comes time for you and your fellow pilgrims to enter the main temple. The principal worshipping area dates from the 12th century, though the mirror-work in the main hall is modern. The central idol is Sachiya, the ninth (and last) incarnation of Durga. As you promenade down the exit ramp from the temple, continue straight ahead down the path directly opposite the exit to reach the third group of temples. The **Mahavira Jain Temple,** built in the 8th century and renovated in the 10th, is arguably the most impressive at Osiyan. It's much more peaceful than Sadhiya Mata, and much more spacious as well. The dome of the *mandapa*, lined with beautiful *apsara* sculptures, is supported by 20 intricately-carved pillars. Inside, the sanctum features a colorful, restored frieze and a stunning gold-coated icon of Mahavira, the last of the Jain *tirthankaras.* A few minutes' walk beyond the Mahavira temple are two more temples dedicated to Surya.

For those who want to stay in Osiyan, English-speaking priest Bhanu Sharma runs a small **guest house ❶,** opposite the Mahavira temples (☎02922, 74296. Rs200). Mr. Sharma also organizes short camel rides and trips to Bishnoi villages.

JAISALMER जैसलमेर ☎ 02992

In the heart of the Thar Desert, 285km west of Jodhpur and 100km from the Pakistan border, is the "Golden City" of Jaisalmer (pop. 40,000), named for the color diffused through its sandstone skyline by the setting sun. The maze-like streets of the old city are filled with scores of breathtakingly carved *havelis* (royal mansions), and a surprise is behind every corner; getting lost here is half the fun. And then of course there's the heart and soul, the bread and butter of the Jaisalmer tourist industry: the camel safari.

After a dark medieval period characterized by Mughal sieges and dramatic *jauhars*, the city enjoyed a "golden age" (16-18th c.) during which art and architecture flourished. Under the British, maritime trade eclipsed the desert trade routes, and Partition in 1947 cut them off altogether, diminishing Jaisalmer's wealth and importance. With the Indo-Pakistan tensions of the 1960s, Jaisalmer became a military outpost once again, and today, the heavy army presence is a source of income second only to the booming tourism industry.

▐ TRANSPORTATION

Flights: Jaisalmer Airport (☎50048 or 52960). 5km from the city center down Sam Rd., 15min. by auto-rickshaw (Rs30-40). **Crown Tours Limited,** Sam Rd. (☎/fax 51912), near Hanuman Circle, is an agent for **Indian Airlines.** Open daily 9:30am-8:30pm. Flights operate in season only (Oct.-Mar.). To: **Delhi** (3½hr.; Tu, Th, and Sa); **Jaipur** (2hr.); **Udaipur** (55min).

Trains: Jaisalmer Railway Station (☎52354, enquiry 51301). A Rs10 rickshaw ride from Gopa Chowk. Connected by meter-gauge line to **Jodhpur** (7hr.; 10:25pm). Connecting reservations can be made at the **computerized reservation counter** (open M-Sa 8am-1:45pm and 2-8pm, Su 8am-2pm).

Buses: Main Bus Stand (☎51541). Near the railway station, but most government buses originate at a **second bus stand** near the Hotel Neeraj (south of Hanuman Circle). **Private buses** arranged through hotels or agencies on Hanuman Circle; some

RAJASTHAN

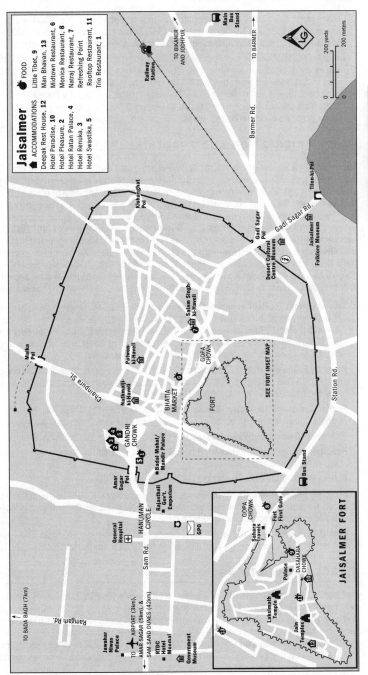

Jaisalmer

▲ ACCOMMODATIONS
Deepak Rest House, 12
Hotel Paradise, 10
Hotel Pleasure, 2
Hotel Ratan Palace, 4
Hotel Renuka, 3
Hotel Swastika, 5

🍴 FOOD
Little Tibet, 9
Man Bhavan, 13
Midtown Restaurant, 6
Monica Restaurant, 8
Natraj Restaurant, 7
Refreshing Point
Rooftop Restaurant, 11
Trio Restaurant, 1

JAISALMER FORT

buses leave here; others leave from the station near Hotel Neeraj. To: **Bikaner** (7hr., 6 per day 6am-9pm, Rs113; deluxe 5pm, Rs134); **Jaipur** (12hr.; deluxe 5pm; Rs201) via **Jodhpur** (5hr.; Rs92) and **Ajmer** (8hr.; Rs160); **Mt. Abu** (12hr.; 6am; Rs176).

Local Transportation: On foot, it takes 15-20min. to cross the city. Unmetered **auto-rickshaws** are everywhere, except in the fort during peak tourist hours (8am-noon and 4-7pm in high season), when they are not permitted to enter. From the train or bus station to Gopa Chowk is Rs10. **Bicycles** are available for rental at Gandhi Chowk (Rs15 per day). More serious vehicles are needed to venture beyond the city; agencies at Hanuman Circle and many hotels rent **jeeps** (Rs3 per km) and **cars** (Rs4 per km).

■✴🛈 ORIENTATION AND PRACTICAL INFORMATION

Hanuman Circle is just outside **Amar Sagar Pol,** the main entrance to the old city. Littered with jeeps, buses, and taxis for hire, Hanuman Circle is easily identified by a stationed jet fighter, a relic from a war with Pakistan. Just inside Amar Sagar Pol is **Gandhi Chowk,** the main commercial square, which hosts money changers, shops, and tour operators. Narrow, shop-lined **Bhatia Market** (the main commercial artery) connects Gandhi Chowk to **Gopa Chowk,** at the base of the **Fort** (the entrance to the fort here is also known as **Fort First Gate**). Heading north from anywhere along here will lead you into the tangled web of Jaisalmer's old-city streets, with their exquisitely carved golden *havelis*. **Gadi Sagar Rd.** leads from Gopa Chowk to **Lake Gadi Sagar** and Jaisalmer's twin culture museums via **Gadi Sagar Rd.** A 10min. walk outside Gadi Sagar Pol will lead you to the **railway** and **bus stations.**

Tourist Office: Tourist Reception Centre (☎52406). Exit Gadi Sagar Pol and turn right at the first intersection. Open Sept.-Mar. M-Sa 7am-8pm; Apr.-Aug. M-Sa 10am-5pm. The **RTDC Hotel Moomal** (☎52392). Off Sam Rd., across town. **Hotel Fort View** (☎50740), operates a central and very well-established travel counter that arranges excursions (1-day camel safari Rs325), books train tickets, etc.

Currency Exchange: Bank of Baroda (☎52402). Just inside Amar Sagar Pol. Cashes currency (US$ and UK£) and traveler's checks and grants cash advances on MC and V. (1% commission plus Rs100). Open M-F 10am-2pm, Sa 10-11am.

English-Language Bookstore: Bhatia News Agency (☎52671). Court Rd., just east of Gandhi Chowk. Decent selection of fiction. Buys used books. Open daily 9am-9pm.

Pharmacy: Government Pharmacy, outside the Government Hospital. Open 24hr.

Hospital: Sri Jawahar Government Hospital (☎52343). Sam Rd. Open daily for consultations 8am-noon and 5:30-7pm.

Police: Main Police Office (☎52233). South of Hanuman Circle.

Internet: Joshi Cyber Cafe, Gopa Chowk. The biggest and most convenient, at Rs30 per hour. Open daily 8am-midnight. Scattered shops throughout the fort and Bhatia Market also offer internet access for Rs30-50 per hr.

Post Office: GPO (☎52407 or 51377). South of the police station, 5min. from Amar Sagar Pol. Offices around the city. All open M-Sa 10am-5pm. **Postal Code:** 345001.

▟ ACCOMMODATIONS

Ordinarily, the amazing depth of budget accommodations in Jaisalmer (the competition is stiffer than Mr. Desert's mustache) would spell backpacker heaven, if it weren't for one dastardly snag–the camel safari. Camel safaris are much more lucrative than budget rooms, and hotels (and the touts they employ) will hassle you from the moment you arrive, offering you incredible room rates (Rs10), provided you go on their camel safari. The tourist office, recognizing these headaches, has set up a **Tourist Protection Force** to keep the touts at bay; though this is reasonably effective at the train station, the bus station and airport are much harder to police. To bypass the touting situation, some hotels send their own vehicles to pick up travelers free of charge—look for hotel banners, not business cards.

Budget hotels in town (most are on the two parallel streets off Gandhi Chowk) tend to be basic but cheap. The slightly pricier hotels in the fort tend to be charming, but are reportedly going to be closed down within the next two or three years. Most hotels in Jaisalmer have an ungenerous 9am checkout time. During high season (Oct.-Mar.), the pressure to validate the hotel space you take up by going on safari is at its most intense; things relax a bit during shoulder season (July-Sept. and Apr.). Huge discounts are available in May and June. During the **Desert Festival** (Feb. 14-16, 2003), expect rates to double (at least).

Hotel Renuka (☎52757; hotelrenuka@rediffmail.com). Chainpura St. Family atmosphere and clean, basic rooms. Rooftop restaurant and spectacular view. Look for their jeep at the station. Hot water 8am-noon and 6-9pm. Singles Rs30-60, with attached bath Rs80-170; doubles Rs40-80, with attached bath Rs100-200. Just down the street is **Hotel Ratan Palace** (☎51119). Run by the same family, it boasts spacious, more upscale rooms that are good value. Rooms with attached bath Rs200-300. ❶

Hotel Paradise (☎52674; hotelparadisejsm@yahoo.com). In the fort. This beautiful *haveli* is built around a pleasant garden. Bright, tasteful, clean rooms make for a very popular choice. Great rooftop views. Breakfast only. Hot water 7am-noon, 5-10pm, and on request. Call for free pick-up. Rooftop budget digs Rs50; singles Rs100-200; with attached bath Rs300-700; doubles Rs150-300, with attached bath Rs400-1050. ❶

Hotel Swastika (☎52483). Chainpura St. Very well-maintained rooms (most with common bath); a popular budget choice. Free pick-up. Breakfast only. Free morning tea. Internet Rs40 per hr. Singles Rs70-80, with attached bath Rs120; doubles Rs150-200, with attached bath Rs200-250. May-Oct. 40% discount. ❶

Hotel Shri Giriraj Palace (☎52268). Manak Chowk. Near Fort First Gate. Housed in a 350-year-old merchant's palace and decorated with pastel pinks and greens, this is the most atmospheric budget accommodation outside the fort. Nine rooms, most with attached bath. Restaurant. Free morning tea. Singles Rs50-70, with attached bath (free bucket hot water) Rs60-100, with hot water Rs150-200. ❶

Hotel Pleasure (☎52323). Off Gandhi Chowk. Clean, simple rooms managed by a friendly family. Breakfast-time room service, free storage while on camel safari, free call-backs, refrigerator/freezer, and free washing machine. Singles Rs50-60; doubles Rs80, with attached bath Rs100-150. ❶

Deepak Rest House (☎52665 or 52070). In the fort, behind the Jain temples. A veritable backpacker's institution, with 25 clean, modest rooms (most with attached hot bath), a chill rooftop restaurant, and sitting area set into the fort wall. For the most part, very well established. Internet Rs40 per hour. Dorms Rs30; singles Rs60, with attached bath Rs120; doubles Rs80-120, with attached bath Rs200-500. ❶

🍴 FOOD

The main reason to eat in Jaisalmer is the rooftop view, but the desert cuisine found here is unique. Be sure to experience *ker sangri*, a mix of capers and beans (it looks like a bundle of gravied twigs); *gatta*, *dal*–flour dumplings; and *kadhai pakoras*, a yogurt-based appetizer.

Monica Restaurant, Gopa Chowk. A betel-spit left of the fort gate. Tasty Indian and Chinese food; a great place to try authentic Rajasthani specialties (*thali* Rs70). Local musicians play here nightly. Veg. Rs35-45, non-veg. Rs60-75. Open daily 7am-11pm. ❶

Trio Restaurant (☎ 52733). Amar Sagar Pol. Considered by many to be the best restaurant in Jaisalmer, Trio features great views, 1st-class service, well-prepared specialties (Royal Safari soup Rs45), and traditional Rajasthani music from 6:30pm. A tad pricey (veg. dishes Rs40-75, non-veg. Rs85-130) but worth it. Open daily 7am-10:30pm. ❷

Natraj Restaurant, near the Salam Singh-ki-Haveli. Well-prepared dishes (Rs40-60) and a rooftop view of the Salam Singh-ki-Haveli. A/C dining room. Open daily 8am-11pm. ❶

Midtown Restaurant, Gopa Chowk. Standard traveler's cafe, with the usual Indian and Chinese dishes as well as pizza and some Western desserts. Good breakfast place. Rajasthani *thalis* Rs50. Open daily 7am-11pm. ❶

Man Bhavan, to the right (as you face Fort First Gate) around the base of the fort from Gopa Chawla. Serves delicious South Indian, Bengali, Gujarati, and Rajasthani food for under Rs40. Popular with the locals and tourists alike. Open daily 7am-11pm. ❶

Little Tibet, in the fort, just off the Main Chowk. Serves the best food in the fort. Huge menu ranges from Tibetan *momos* to burgers to enchiladas. Good Indian food as well. Main courses Rs35-60. Open daily 7:30am-10:30pm. ❶

Refreshing Point Rooftop Restaurant, in the fort, Main Chowk. Very popular, central backpacker staple. Main courses Rs35-50. Open daily 8am-11pm. ❶

👁 SIGHTS

JAISALMER FORT

Jaisalmer's fort was founded in 1156 by Maharaja Jaisal, a king of the Bhati clan of Rajputs. Surrounded by 99 circular bastions, the fort is Rajasthan's second oldest (after Chittaurgarh), and like Chittaurgarh, is exceptional in that it remains today a "living" fort with current inhabitants. The fort is entered through **Akhaipol** (a.k.a. **Fort First Gate**) from Gopa Chowk. A paved ramp winds its way to the last gate, **Hawapol,** which opens up onto the **Main Chowk.**

RAJ MAHAL (FORT PALACE MUSEUM). The Royal Palace, which dominates the fort's Main Chowk, consists of five smaller palaces built by various Maharawals. There is some tile and mirror-work still intact, as well as some wall paintings and stained glass, but the main attraction is the fine architecture of the building itself. The view from the top over the fort and old city is fantastic. *(Open daily in winter 9am-5pm; in summer 8am-5pm Rs10; camera Rs20; video Rs50.)*

WELCOME TO MR. DESERT COUNTRY Moustaches twisted to follicular perfection, camels dripping with shells, mirrors, and buttons, and turban-tying pros await those willing to brave the onslaught of tourists at the annual **Desert Festival of Jaisalmer** (Feb. 14-16, 2003). The event kicks off with a procession of "ships of the desert" and local bands followed by an odd assortment of competitions: tug-of-war, turban tying, a battle of the moustaches, camel racing, camel decoration, and, the high point of the festival, the "crowning of Mr. Desert." The prestigious and lucrative title is bestowed upon the man who best epitomizes Rajasthan—the one who exudes masculinity in his traditional dress, bushy beard, and gravity-defying moustache. Mr. Shri Laxmi Narain Bissa captured the crown for four consecutive years before being forcibly removed from the competition and bestowed with the lifelong title "Mr. Desert Emeritus." His face can now be seen staring out of *haveli* windows on posters promoting Rajasthan and gracing advertisements for Jaisalmer brand cigarettes, a stint that has earned him the title "The Indian Marlboro Man."

JAIN TEMPLES. Along the southern wall of the fort lies a string of eight Jain temples, all of which exhibit extraordinary workmanship. Unfortunately, six of them (including the main temple) are closed to non-Jains. *(The first two temples on the right-hand side as you approach from the Main Chowk are open to tourists; follow the alley past Hotel Paradise. Open daily 7am-noon. Rs10; camera Rs50; video Rs100. No leather or menstruating women permitted inside.)*

OTHER TEMPLES. There are also many Hindu temples inside the fort, the most famous of which is the **Laxminath Temple.** Built in 1495, the temple is simpler than its Jain counterparts, but boasts a heavily decorated, white marble central icon.

HAVELIS

Any walk through the old city will bring you past numerous beautiful *havelis*, or open-air mansions (after the Persian for "air-house"), but there are three particularly impressive ones open to the public.

PATWON-KI-HAVELI. The most celebrated of Jaisalmer's *havelis* is actually a complex containing five different homes, one for each of the five prosperous merchant Patwa brothers (constructed 1800-1860). Today their common golden facade soars four dramatic stories, each fitted with stone balconies topped by arched stone umbrellas and exquisite latticed windows. Counting from the main gate, the first *haveli*, privately owned, is open to the public. *(Entrance to 1st haveli on the right, open 9am-7pm; Rs10, camera fee Rs10. Entrances to the 2nd and 5th havelis are on the left; both open daily 10am-5pm; Rs2.)*

SALAM SINGH-KI-HAVELI. This *haveli*, with peacock buttresses adorning its exterior, was built by the notorious prime minister Salam Singh Mohta around 1800. Considered a tyrant for his crippling taxes, he tried to add two additional levels to his own *haveli* to make it taller than the maharaja's. But the maharaja had the offending appendages torn down (and had him assassinated). On the top floor is the Moti Mahal, an elaborately decorated dancing ball surrounded by an exquisitely carved balcony. *(Open daily in winter 8am-6pm; in summer 7am-5:30pm. Rs 15.)*

NATHMALJI-KI-HAVELI. Once a Prime Minister's home, this *haveli* has only one room open to the public at present, but it features some very nice paintings. The two artisan brothers who built the *haveli*, Lalu and Hathi, split it right down the middle. *(Open daily 9am-8pm. Donation requested.)*

OTHER SIGHTS

LAKE GADI SAGAR. A reservoir constructed in 1367, Lake Gadi Sagar was once Jaisalmer's only source of water. Today, it is frequented by bathers, *dhobi-wal-lahs*, and visitors who come to view the nearby museums. The other attraction is a yellow sandstone gateway, the **Tilon-ki-Pol.** With its grand arched windows, this gateway once held beautifully carved rooms where the royal family stayed during the monsoon. Built by the king's chief courtesan, the gate was once a source of great controversy for the town's citizens, who refused to allow their womenfolk to walk beneath the "tainted" creation. As a compromise, a smaller entrance to the lake was built to the right. The lake is now decorated with royal stone *chhattris*.

MUSEUMS. Both museums between Gadi Sagar Pol and the lake promote local desert culture through collections of traditional instruments, clothing, and the like. The **Folklore Museum** is near the lake, and the **Desert Cultural Centre Museum** is next to the tourist office. Besides the usual ancient fossils, coins, and sculptures, the government museum exhibits Jaisalmeri textiles and puppets. It is south of the tourist office, west of Hanuman Chowk. *(Folklore Museum open daily Aug.-Mar. 8am-6:30pm; Apr.-July 4:30-7:30pm; Rs10. Desert Museum open daily 10am-5pm; free with stub from Folklore Museum. Government Museum open M-Th and Sa-Su 10am-4:30pm; Rs3; M free.)*

CAMEL SAFARIS

By far the best and most popular way to get a glimpse of desert life is to go on a camel safari. By day you'll cross paths with women picking berries and boys tending herds of goats; by night you'll sleep under some of the starriest skies you've ever seen. As for the mode of transportation, the strange smells and noises that come from both ends are sure to provide you with hours of entertainment.

Though longer cross-desert safaris (e.g. to Bikaner) are also possible, the most popular safari routes are two-to-four-day loops around Jaisalmer. Due to Jaisalmer's proximity to the Pakistan border, the government has laid down heavy restrictions on safari routes; most safaris are concentrated in a small, easily accessible area to the north and west of town and tend to take in a pretty standard set of well-trampled sights (Lodurva, Amar Sagar, Bada Bagh, Sam Dand dunes, etc.). Between sunrise and sunset you can expect anywhere from 3-6hr. of a camel riding, punctuated by meals, sightseeing stops, and at least one extended break. The following, well-respected agencies, all headquartered in Gandhi Chowk, specialize in deluxe safaris (Rs750-6000) per day, but arrange basic safaris (Rs450-1000 per day) as well, provided that you already have a group of sufficient size.

> **WARNING.** The #1 rule of going on safari in Jaisalmer is to choose your safari operator carefully. A good operator can be the difference between an amazing experience and a completely miserable one. When you choose a safari, beware of scams and hidden charges, such as charging Rs50 for a bottle of water. A realistic minimum for a safari is Rs350 per day, but simply agreeing to pay isn't equivalent to clinching a satisfactory safari experience. Reputation is *key*. The most reliable safaris are those booked through independent agencies, whose sole concern is building up good reputations for their safaris.

Thar Safari (☎54296; tharsafari@hotmail.com), in Nachana *haveli.*

Royal Safari (☎52538; royalsafari@satyam.net.in), in Nachana *haveli.*

Sahara Travels (☎52609; safari_tours@yahoo.com), near Fort First Gate, is quite popular and run by Mr. Desert himself (see p. 532); he can easily form groups. Basic safaris Rs500 per day; deluxe Rs800 per day.

Hotel Paradise (from Rs400 per day) and **Hotel Renuka** (1½ days Rs750, plus Rs150 per additional day) also offer well-reviewed safaris.

ENTERTAINMENT

For the wildest time in Jaisalmer, come to the annual **Desert Festival** (Feb. 14-16, 2003; see **Welcome to Mr. Desert Country,** p. 532). Prices double (at least) and tourists mob the place, but you'll still be able to enjoy traditional music and folk dance, camel races, camel polo, camel dances, puppeteers, **moustache contests,** and more. RTDC sets up a tourist tent-village for accommodations.

Other diversions include **swimming** in Lake Gadi Sagar or at Narayan Niwas Palace's indoor pool (near Patwon-ki-Haveli, Rs100). Film fans can indulge at Hindi **cinemas,** including **Ramesh Talkies** (☎52242), near Patwon-ki-Haveli.

SHOPPING

Jaisalmer is a haven for **handicrafts,** including embroidery, patchwork, leather goods, and mirror-work, as well as stone carving, silver, and pottery. Bargain hard, and don't even think about shopping during the Desert Festival. **Gandhi**

Chowk and the main road connecting it to Gadi Sagar Pol are the primary commercial areas. The **Rajasthali Government Emporium,** just outside Amar Sagar Pol, sells a vast selection of Rajasthani desert handicrafts in brass, silver, wood, and textiles, as well as carpets and paintings, all at fixed prices. (☎52461. Open daily 10am-8pm.) **Parmar Jewelers Emporium** has a good selection of silver and semi-precious jewelry. (☎51373. Open daily 9am-8pm.)

🔲 DAYTRIPS FROM JAISALMER

*The sights below are most easily visited while on camel safari (often you'll visit some or all of them by jeep before commencing the actual camel riding portion of the safari). Of all the places below, only Khuri is accessible by public bus, so if you don't go on safari here you'll need a jeep to visit them. Access to the area 45km west of Jaisalmer is restricted because of border disputes, and special permission (forget it) is required from the **District Magistrate Office,** near the police station.*

BADA BAGH, AMAR SAGAR, AND MOOL SAGAR
Gardens open daily 8am-8pm. Admission Rs10. Temple entrance fee Rs10; camera fee Rs50, video fee Rs100. Menstruating women are not supposed to enter. Garden Palace entrance fee Rs5.

About 7km north of Jaisalmer is **Bada Bagh,** where 500-year-old sandstone cenotaphs stand next to the 300-year-old mango trees of the royal garden. To the far left is the most recent tomb, constructed in 1991 for the grandfather of the current maharaja. The gardens, which used to supply food to all of Jaisalmer, are a popular picnic spot in wet season. Another well-known spot for tea and tiffin is **Amar Sagar,** 5km northwest of Jaisalmer, where a beautifully carved Jain temple, constructed under the orders of Maharaja Amar Singh, guards a lake and fertile gardens. The green oasis of **Mool Sagar Garden Palace,** 7km to the southwest of Jaisalmer, was once the picnic palace of the Maharaja.

LODURVA
Open daily 7am-8pm. Admission Rs10. Camera fee Rs50, video fee Rs100.

Once the capital of the region, Lodurva now lies in ruins 15km north of Jaisalmer. Restored Jain temples are all that remain of the town's former splendor. An amazing 1000-year-old archway from the original temple still stands in the courtyard. A cobra occasionally makes an appearance out of a small hole in the temple; glimpsing the snake is deemed auspicious.

SAM SAND DUNES
*The tourist office runs sunset **jeep tours** to Sam for Rs125 per person.*

The Sam Sand Dunes are within striking distance of Jaisalmer (42km west), but unfortunately they're far from undiscovered. The scene here at sunset is nothing less than a circus, with legions of Indian and foreign tourists and an almost comical number of camels and camel drivers chasing after them. This is not the place to come for solitude, but it is nevertheless a stunning place to be at sunrise or sunset, and if you're in the market for a camel ride, you couldn't pick a better locale (Rs5-20 for a sunset stroll). Those who want to stay the night but aren't satisfied sleeping under the stars can stay at the clean but pricey **RTDC Sam Dhani ❸,** right next to the dunes. (Rooms with attached bath Rs500. Book through the tourist office.)

KHURI
*Four **buses** per day run to and from Jaisalmer (2hr., Rs25).*

Forty-five kilometers southwest of Jaisalmer is the small village of Khuri (pop. 2100) which boasts its own set of sand dunes (sunset ride Rs150-200) and is growing increasingly popular with travelers who enjoy desert solitude.

KHICHAN

Khichan is difficult to reach by public transport. However, if you are travelling between Jodhpur and Jaisalmer by car (as many opt to do), it's a sight that should not be missed.

Khichan, a slight detour off the dusty road from Jodhpur to Jaisalmer (about midway near Phalodi) is unremarkable as a town but quite remarkable as the site where thousands of **demoiselle cranes** *(Anthropoides virgo)* feed upon grain spread by villagers each morning and evening from September to March.

BIKANER बीकानेर ☎ 0151

The fourth largest city in Rajasthan (pop. 420,000), Bikaner has been trying to draw tourists, but its remoteness and competition from its desert neighbors have proved formidable. However, those who make the trek out here are rewarded with Jain temples, an amazing fort, *havelis*, and lots of camels. Bikaner, much lower-key than Jaisalmer, is a good place to arrange a camel safari. It's also near the moderately terrifying but indisputably fascinating "Rat Temple" at Deshnok.

Founded in 1488 by Rao Bika, a Rathore prince descended from the founder of Jodhpur, Bikaner was originally a stop on the Silk Route, as well as an important center for camel breeding. In the 16th century, its Maharaja, Rei Singh, became one of the most successful generals in Emperor Akbar's all-but-invincible army. By the 18th century, Bikaner was a power to be reckoned with, a deadly enemy of Jodhpur, and the home of the legendary Bikaner Camel Corps. Since Independence, the city has been almost exclusively concerned with its own economic advancement, leading to increased industrialization. Only recently has Bikaner looked to tourism as an avenue for economic development, an interest apparent in the grand show it puts on for the annual tourist magnet, the **Camel Festival** (Jan. 17-18, 2003), a celebration of food, music, and all things camel.

☞ TRANSPORTATION

Trains: Bikaner Railway Station (☎ 131 or 132, computerized inquiry ☎ 1330), a Rs20-30 auto-rickshaw ride from anywhere in the city. The computerized **Advance Reservation Office** (☎ 523132) is next to the railway station. Open M-Sa 8am-2pm, 2:15-8pm, Su 8am-2pm. To: **Delhi** (10½-12hr; 8:30am-5:55pm, 7:45pm.); **Jaipur** (5-10½hr.; 5am, 3:40 and 8:30pm; Rs176); **Jodhpur** (5hr.; 1, 9:35am, 12:30pm; Rs109).

Buses: Central Bus Stand (☎ 523800). 3 km north of the city, opposite Lalgarh Palace. To: **Ahmedabad** (10hr., 1:30pm, Rs273); **Ajmer** (7hr., every hr. 5:15am-11:30pm, Rs108; deluxe 5pm); **Delhi** (12hr.; 6 per day 5:30am-7:15pm; Rs189); **Fatehpur** (4hr.; catch any Jaipur-bound bus; Rs73); **Jaipur** (7hr.; every hr. 5am-10pm; Rs138; deluxe 7:45am and 9:45pm); **Jaisalmer** (7hr.; 5 per day 5am-9pm; Rs135); **Jhunjhunu** (5hr.; 4 per day 8:15-6:30pm; Rs89) **Jodhpur** (6½hr.; every hour 4:45am-12:30am; Rs102); **Udaipur** (14hr.; Rs216). **Private buses** can be arranged behind the fort, and through hotels, excursion agents, and the bus agencies that congregate around Goga Gate, south of Kote Gate.

Local Transportation: Auto-rickshaws are unmetered and take you anywhere in the city for Rs15-30. **Bicycles** can be rented from cycle stores opposite the police station on Station Rd. (Rs3 per hr., Rs15 per day. Open daily 8:30am-10pm). **Jeeps** can be rented near the railway station and opposite the fort's front entrance for Rs3-5 per km.

✳ ☞ ORIENTATION AND PRACTICAL INFORMATION

Station Rd., the main budget hotel strip, runs parallel to the tracks in front of the **railway station.** To the right of the station, it intersects the main commercial thoroughfare, **KEM Rd.,** and then continues to the **Junagarh Fort** and the GPO. A left turn on KEM Rd. leads to **Kote Gate,** the main entrance to the **old city.** A left on Station

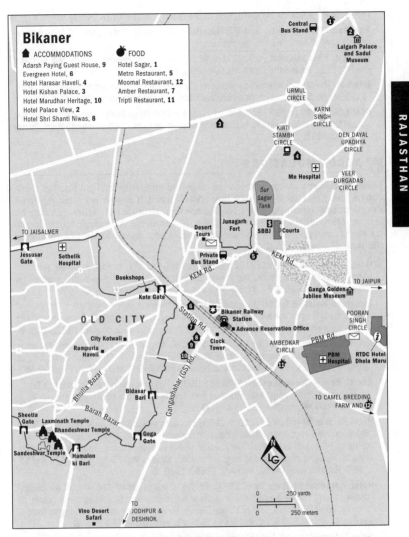

Bikaner

🏠 ACCOMMODATIONS

Adarsh Paying Guest House, 9
Evergreen Hotel, 6
Hotel Harasar Haveli, 4
Hotel Kishan Palace, 3
Hotel Marudhar Heritage, 10
Hotel Palace View, 2
Hotel Shri Shanti Niwas, 8

🍴 FOOD

Hotel Sagar, 1
Metro Restaurant, 5
Moomal Restaurant, 12
Amber Restaurant, 7
Tripti Restaurant, 11

Rd. from the station leads past the **Clock Tower** through two intersections; a left at the second intersection will lead you to **Ambedkar Circle.** Because of the distances involved, the city is best traversed by rickshaw.

Tourist Office: Tourist Reception Centre, on the RTDC Hotel Dhola Mayu campus (☎544125). Near Pooran Singh Circle. Maps Rs2. Open M-Sa 10am-5pm. For helpful information on Bikaner, cruise www.realbikaner.com.

Currency Exchange: Bank of Baroda (☎545053). Opposite the railway station. Changes traveler's checks only. Open M-F 10am-3pm, Sa 10am-12:30pm. **State Bank of Bikaner and Jaipur** (☎544034). Near the fort entrance. Changes cash and traveler's checks. Open M-F 8am-noon and 1-5pm, Sa 9-11am and 1-3pm.

Police: Main office (☎ 200840). Next to the railway station. Open 24hr.

Pharmacy: PBM Hospital and MN Hospital (☎ 544423). Both operate 24hr. pharmacies. Other pharmacies line Hospital Rd.

Hospital: PBM Hospital (☎ 61931). PBM Rd. Large and government-run. **MN Hospital** (☎ 544122). Near Karni Singh Stadium. Privately run.

Internet: The fastest internet connections are available at shops at Kirti Stambh Circle. Rs25 per hr. Slower connections are available at STD shops along Station Rd.

Post Office: GPO (☎ 524185). Behind Junagarh Fort. Open M-Sa 10am-6pm. Branches near PBM Hospital, inside Kote Gate, and near State Bank of Bikaner and Jaipur. **Postal Code:** 334001.

ACCOMMODATIONS

Most of Bikaner's budget options are clustered on Station and GS Rd., but these can be pretty lackluster. The last three hotels listed, if in your price range, are all excellent and worth the extra fee. **Home-stays,** with local families can also be arranged through the tourist office (Rs80-750 per night). A lethargic tourist industry keeps hotel prices steady year-round, but expect drastic jumps in fares during the annual Camel Festival.

Hotel Kishan Palace (☎ 527762). 8B Gajner Rd. Friendly, family-run place, removed from the Station Rd. bustle. Big rooms, all with attached hot-water baths; a bit better than any of the Station Rd. hotels. Free pickup. Rooms Rs100-250. ❶

Evergreen Hotel (☎ 542061). Station Rd. Better than average for a Station Rd. budget hotel, though some rooms are cell-like. Clean enough (for the price). Some rooms with TV. Restaurant downstairs. Check-out 24hr. Singles Rs80-125; doubles Rs125-175. ❶

Hotel Shri Shanti Niwas (☎ 521925 or 542320). GS Rd. Pretty basic rooms; the more expensive ones are cleaner and have Western toilets and TV. Check-out 24hr. Singles Rs80/115-125, with A/C Rs450; doubles with bath Rs165-350, with A/C Rs600. ❶

Adarsh Paying Guest House (☎ 548716). GS Rd. Tiny place with basic rooms in a family environment. Most rooms with attached bath (hot water by the bucket). Check-out 24hr. Singles Rs60-80; doubles Rs100-175. ❶

Hotel Harasar Haveli (☎ 527318 or 209891). North of Sur Sagar Tank, near Karni Singh Stadium. New (but *haveli*-style) bldg. with decorated rooms and glistening bathrooms (all with hot water and tubs). Great value and a popular choice. Rooftop terrace with view of fort and palace. Good veg. restaurant. Singles Rs175-350, with A/C Rs750-1100; doubles Rs250-450, with A/C Rs650-1200. ❶

Hotel Marudhar Heritage (☎ 522524). GS Rd. If you're unsatisfied with all the budget options along Station and GS Rd., this place will please you. Spacious, clean rooms, all with TV, cooler, bathtub, and hot water. Room service. Check-out 24hr. Singles Rs250-375, with A/C Rs500-900; doubles Rs350-475, with A/C Rs650-999. ❷

Hotel Palace View (☎ 543625; opnanin@jpl.dot.net.in). In the Palace. Clean, well-decorated rooms with sitting areas and spotless bathrooms. Good restaurant. Rooms Rs300-450, with A/C Rs500-700. ❷

FOOD

Moomal Restaurant, Panch Sebi Circle, 2km from the city center, on the way to the Camel Breeding Farm. A large, air-cooled veg. restaurant serves everybody's favorite Indian dishes: well worth the 20min. walk. Fast service. Main courses Rs40-60, *dosas* Rs20-33. Open daily 11am-3pm and 6:30-10:30pm. ❶

Hotel Sagar, near Lalgarh Palace. Opposite the bus station. Quiet restaurant in an upscale hotel. A tad expensive, but the food and service make it worth it. Veg dishes Rs35-80. Open daily 6am-10:30pm. ❶

Tripti Restaurant, Hospital Rd., Ambedkar Circle. A popular local haunt with a bizarre thatched-hut-meets-chandeliers decor. Meals Rs30-50, South Indian snacks Rs20-40. Open daily 8am-3:30pm and 7:30-10:30pm. ❶

Metro Restaurant, at the front of the fort near Sadul Singh Circle. Air-cooled, 3-level restaurant. Veg. dishes Rs30-70, non-veg. Rs40-150. Open daily 8am-10:30pm. ❷

Amber Restaurant, Station Rd. Very conveniently located and popular with tourists. Decent food. *Dosas* Rs20-38, veg. dishes Rs35-58. Open daily 8am-10pm. ❶

👁 SIGHTS

A stroll through the **old city** is an essential part of any visit to Bikaner. The wealth brought in by camel caravans is reflected in over 200 towering *havelis;* those of the **Ramapuria Estate,** on Jail Rd., near Kotwali police station, are of particular interest. The only portion of the complex that is open to the public is the part that has been converted into the Hotel Bhanwar Niwas. You might be able to sneak a peek by feigning interest in (and the ability to pay for) a room, but you'll have to admire the rest of the estate from outside.

JUNAGARH FORT. Rajasthan certainly has no shortage of forts, but Bikaner truly has some of the most magnificent. Along with Meherangarh at Jodhpur, **Junagarh** is one of Rajasthan's two forts to have undergone significant restoration. Built in 1589 by Rai Singh, it is one of the few in the country that has never been conquered, despite the fact that (unlike many of its conquered counterparts) it does not command a hilltop position. The fort is a solid structure whose 986m long wall is capped with 37 bastions and surrounded by a 9m-wide moat. The fort entrance is on the east side through a succession of gates. Near the second gate, **Daulat Pol,** are 24 handprints, left behind by the women who performed *sati* here after their husbands perished in an attempt to hold off a siege. The fort's main entrance is the **Suraj Pol** (Sun Gate), a large iron-spiked door flanked by two stone elephants.

TURBAN LEGENDS Once upon a time, no one wore turbans in India; the idea of wrapping cotton cloth around the head had simply never entered the popular imagination. This changed forever when the turbanned Mughals poured into northern India in 1526, an invasion that sent shockwaves through the world of South Asian fashion. Originally worn as a sign of respect when one appeared before a Mughal official, turbans soon became a symbol of the Sikh religion and an indicator of status among high-caste Hindus. In Rajasthan today, turban colors and styles vary according to region. In Bikaner, brahmins wear a yellow turban except when mourning, when they cut their hair off and switch to white headwear. Bikaner Rajputs, a *kshatriya* caste, wear brightly colored, striped, or *bandhani* (tie-dyed) turbans wrapped around one ear with a long tail in the back. Jats and Bishnois, the farming castes, wear enormous white turbans (called *safas*), and *vaishya* castes wear small turbans known as *pagoris*. Untouchables and *shudras* are not allowed to wrap their heads at all. Turbans can be deeply symbolic; exchanging turbans signifies deep friendship; placing one's turban at another's feet is a request for mercy; and having one's turban forcibly removed in public (as is often done with debtors and criminals) brings great shame. In earlier times, the value of a turban was sometimes literal as well as symbolic; earlier moneylenders often made loans only after mortgaging the borrower's turban!

The fort is an intricate complex of palaces, courtyards, pavilions, and temples (37 in all), added over time by successive rulers. The **Karan Mahal,** built after an important victory over the Mughal army of Emperor Aurangzeb, features gold-leaf paintings and the silver throne of Lord Karan Singh. The breathtaking **Anup Mahal,** decorated by the same artist, boasts Italian tiles, inlaid mirrors, and more intricate gold-leaf paintings. The **Phool Mahal** (Flower Palace) was constructed under Gaj Singh a hundred years later. The **Chandra Mahal** (Moon Palace) is a beautifully painted *puja* room adorned with Hindu gods and goddesses. To the side is the **Sheesh Mahal** (Mirror Palace), the maharaja's glittering bedroom. **Hanuman Temple** is filled with an array of swords, saws, spears, and nails, which are danced upon every January by *fakirs* from neighboring villages. The **Ganga Singh Hall,** the last portion of the fort, houses a **museum** whose collection of weapons and various relics includes a World War I biplane. *(Open daily 10am-5pm. Rs50; camera fee Rs30; video fee Rs100. Guides may barrage you as you approach the entrance but are by no means necessary, as a guided tour is included in the price of admission.)*

Also in the fort complex is the **Prachina Museum,** which displays, among other things, portraits of the Bikaneri royal family and a beautiful array of traditional embroidered dresses. *(Open daily 9am-6pm. Rs25.)*

LALGARH PALACE. This red-sandstone palace was designed in 1902 for Maharaja Ganga Singh, in commemoration of his late father, Lal Singh. The royal family of Bikaner still lives in part of the palace, a luxury hotel takes up some more space, and the **Sri Sadul Museum** occupies the rest. The museum is essentially a shrine to the House of Bikaner's two greatest and most beloved rulers, Maharaja Ganga Singh (r.1887-1943) and grandson Maharaja Karini Singh (r.1950-88). Its corridors and halls are filled with everything from a picture of Ganga Singh signing the Treaty of Versailles to his grandson's personal effects, including his electric toothbrush, sunglasses, and a rifle from the 1960 Olympics, where he was a silver medalist. *(3km north of the city, near the Central Bus Stand. Museum open M-Sa 10am-5pm. Rs20.)*

TEMPLES

Bhandeshwar and Sandeshwar temples open daily 7am-1pm and 4-8pm. Free. Camera fee Rs20; video fee Rs30. Laxminath temple open daily 6am-1pm and 5:30-10:30pm. Free. No socks, shorts, umbrellas, watches, cameras, or leather goods.

In the southern end of the old city, past a spice market, stand two extraordinary 16th-century Jain temples, unusual in their employment of paintings. The two temples are accessible through the same entrance. The first, the stunning **Bhandeshwar Temple,** is decorated with gilded floral motifs painted by Persian artists from Emperor Akbar's court. Fifty years, 500 laborers, and 40,000kg of *ghee* went into its construction. The *ghee* was used in place of water to make the temple's cement foundation; on hot days, the temple's base supposedly oozes. Each of the temple's three floors houses different *tirthankara* idols, for a total of 12; the other 12 (the Jain religion features 24 prophets in total) are housed in the neighboring **Sandeshwar Temple.** This smaller temple isn't nearly as amazing as the main one, but has some nice carvings and painted pillars. Next to the Jain complex is the Hindu **Laxminath Temple,** a carved stone temple with superb views of the desert and city.

SRI GANGA GOLDEN JUBILEE MUSEUM. This museum (also known as Ganga Government Museum) pays homage, once again, to Bikaner's most accomplished maharaja, Ganga Singh. In addition to the usual stuffed tigers, old coins, and armory exhibits, the museum boasts some interesting glimpses back into history, including a painting depicting the signing of the Treaty of Versailles (with Ganga Singh present) and an original letter from Crown Prince (soon-to-be-Mughal-Emperor) Jehangir urging the maharajas of Bikaner to proceed with haste to Delhi, as "Emperor Akbar is dying." The collection also includes some terra-cotta ware from the Gupta Period (AD 300-500). *(Open M-Th and Sa–Su 9:30am-4:30pm. Rs3.)*

SAFARIS

Although nowhere near the colossal proportions of Jaisalmer, camel safaris have grown increasingly popular in Bikaner. The safari experience is both more laid-back and more expensive. Border-induced government restrictions, similar to those in Jaisalmer, limit most safaris to the area south and southeast of Bikaner. Three-day loops around Deshnok (of Rat Temple fame) are most popular; also common (and more so than in Jaisalmer) are longer inter-city safaris to Phaladi (6 days) and Jaisalmer (13-14 days). This latter, one-way type typically involves the usage of a camel cart, which accommodates heavy luggage and weary bums. The lower-end safaris (including those operated by the agencies below) do not include any jeep transport (travel is by local bus) or mineral water (boiled well-water is promised free of charge)–be sure to ask. A few hotels organize safaris, but usually they are run through independent agencies; to eliminate commission headaches for the agencies, it's best to book directly. The most popular safari operator in town is **Vino Desert Safari,** run by the friendly Vinod Bhojak, who organizes safaris for two to thirteen days for Rs400-800 per day. Vinod operates out of his home, near Gopeshwar Temple, a 15min. walk south of the old city. It can be a bit hard to find; look for signs along the road leading south from Goga Gate, or call for free pickup. (☎270445; www.vinodesertsafari.com; vino_desertsafari@yahoo.com. Open daily 8am-5pm.) **Desert Tours** (☎521967; bikanermail@rediffmail.com), behind the GPO, has a wide range of safaris for Rs500-5000 per day.

SHOPPING

Bikaner is a good place to shop for **handicrafts.** The main commercial areas are **KEM Rd.** and the **old city.** Just inside Kote Gate on the left are cloth and textile stores. The government-approved **Abhivyakti,** recently relocated to outside the camel breeding farm (see below), sells high-quality handicrafts from villages around the city. The proceeds go to artisans and projects that promote health care, literacy, and women's rights. (Open same hours as camel-breeding farm.)

DAYTRIPS FROM BIKANER

DEVIKUND SAGAR
8km west of Bikaner.

This area contains the marble and red sandstone *chhattris* (cenotaphs) of Bikaner rulers and their wives and mistresses, whose handprints commemorate their self-sacrifice. There is a *sati* temple where the spirits of the women are worshipped. It all surrounds a tranquil lake inhabited by pigeons and peacocks.

CAMEL RESEARCH AND BREEDING FARM
10km south of the city (☎230070). Round-trip auto-rickshaw Rs80, including 45min. wait. Open M-Sa 3-5pm. Free. Cameras Rs10. Government-authorized guides Rs50 per person.

The largest in Asia, with an average population of 280 camels, the camel breeding farm produces 50% of India's bred camels. Visitors are allowed in the afternoon to watch the camels' mass procession back to the farm. The trip is most worthwhile during breeding season (Dec.-Mar.), when baby camels populate the farm. A walk around the grounds includes a tour of the stud quarters, where overeager male camels fidget and froth at the mouth in anticipation. In season they bear the responsibility of inseminating up to six or seven female camels per day.

KARNI MATA TEMPLE (RAT TEMPLE)

The temple is accessible by taxi (about Rs200 round-trip) and by bus from Bikaner (45min., every 30min. 4:45am-12:30am, Rs11-13). Open daily 4am-10pm. Camera fee Rs20, video fee Rs50.

At the Karni Mata Temple in Deshnok, 30km from Bikaner, thousands of holy rats run rampant at the feet of worshippers, who bask in their footsteps. According to local legend, the patron deity of Bikaner, Karni Mata, was asked to resurrect her favorite nephew. She called up Yama, the god of death, who told her that the boy had been reborn as a rat and that all her male descendants would be born as rats in her temple at Deshnok. The best time to visit is during the Navratri festival in March, when the temple swarms with people (and rats). It also boasts a magnificent solid silver gate, donated by Maharaja Ganga Singh.

SIKKIM सिक्किम

Shambala, Tazik, Shangri-La—whatever you want to call it, most people agree that Sikkim is heaven. Its natural beauty is without compare. The tropical valleys, sheltered and watered by the surrounding peaks, support rice, mustard, papaya, wheat, and millet farming, while vertical ridges hide small villages and monasteries. Bordered by Nepal, Tibet, and Bhutan, the state's cultural bounty is just as appealing; the native Lepchas peacefully coexist with Tibetan Bonpos and Bhutanese. Sikkim is so peaceful, in fact, that it once appeared in the *Guinness Book of World Records* for going 10 years without a single criminal case. Perhaps the most charming aspect of the state, however, is its seclusion. Because foreigners are only allowed to visit for a limited period of time (see **Sikkim Permits,** p. 545), the state has thus far escaped the crushing tourist influx of neighboring Nepal.

Hindu Nepalese currently represent 75% of the population, although Sikkim, which is home to over 250 monasteries, is historically a Buddhist kingdom with close ties to Tibet. The earliest known inhabitants of Sikkim were the Lepchas, who arrived from the north sometime around the 8th century. A second wave of immigration 500 years later brought the Bhutia people from Tibet, who set themselves up as rulers and appointed the first *chogyul* (king) of Sikkim in 1641. The British protectorate, begun in 1861, brought Hindu Nepalese to Sikkim to work on tea plantations, and they soon outnumbered the Lepchas and Tibetans. This ethnic diversity has resulted in a friendly confluence of cultures. People from the flatlands to the south are "Indian," while those who grew up in the mountains identify themselves by their ancestry: Nepalese, Bhutanese, Tibetan, or Lepcha.

When India became independent in 1947, Sikkim was made a semi-independent Indian protectorate. Strife between the traditional monarchy the middle class led the *chogyal* to ask the Indian government to intervene. The result was a 1975 referendum, in which 97% of Sikkim's electorate voted to become India's 22nd province. Many Sikkimese resent Indian dominion, and there is some question as to how democratic the referendum really was. There is still a *chogyal* of Sikkim, but he has retired to a monastery and holds no official power. Sikkim has only recently opened its borders to tourists, and it still remains largely undiscovered. The government has carefully fostered an eco-friendly tourism industry that also respects and preserves Sikkimese cultural traditions; a visit to Sikkim is refreshingly hassle-free and tranquil. The best times to visit are from late March to May, when the flowers are in bloom, and October to November, when clear views are guaranteed. **Visitors to Sikkim must obtain permits first** (see **Special Permits,** p. 10).

HIGHLIGHTS OF SIKKIM

Peaceful **Pelling** (p. 550) is a good place to relax and soak up the views, or to begin the scenic, four-day **Local Trek** (p. 552).

Headquarters of the *karma-pa* sect of Tibetan Buddhism, the beautiful hilltop village of **Rumtek** (p. 549) is a getaway from the world where you can sit back and watch the vegetables grow.

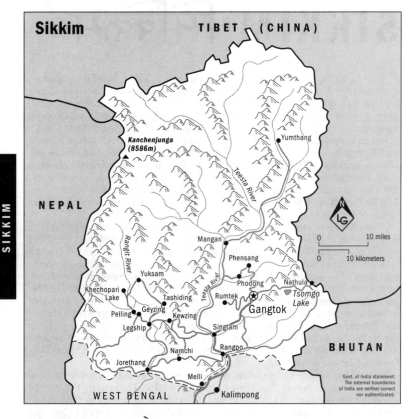

Sikkim

TIBET (CHINA)

NEPAL

Kanchenjunga
(8586m)

Yumthang

Teesta River

Rangit River

Mangan

Phensang

Yuksam

Phodong

Nathula

Khechopari
Lake

Tashiding

Teesta River

Rumtek

Tsomgo
Lake

Pelling

Gёyzing

Kewzing

Gangtok

Legship

Singtam

BHUTAN

Namchi

Rangpo

Jorethang

Govt. of India statement:
The external boundaries
of India are neither correct
nor authenticated.

Melli

WEST BENGAL

Kalimpong

0 — 10 miles
0 — 10 kilometers

SIKKIM

GANGTOK गातोक ☎ 03592

Carved out of the hillside, Sikkim's capital is dwarfed by its spectacular surroundings, but has its own appeal, with its friendly people and relatively clean streets. The tourist infrastructure dominates the town's activity, making it the best place to find store-bought goods and supplies. This is also the place to organize treks, extend Sikkim permits, stock up on equipment, and send off a batch of emails. Perhaps the most charming aspect of the city, though, is its intermittent power supply—Gangtok blinks into and out of the modern era many times a day, and shops and hotels are all prepared with candles, flashlights. The refusal to electrify is a pleasant reminder that technological progress has yet to tame Gangtok entirely.

▣ TRANSPORTATION

Flights: The nearest airport is **Bagdogra,** near Siliguri. **Josse and Josse,** MG Rd. (☎24682), next to Raj Enterprise, are authorized agents for Jet Airways, Sahara, and Skyline NEPC. Open daily M-Sa 9am-7pm, Su 9am-2pm. The proprietor of the **Green Hotel,** MG Rd. (☎25057), is a sub-agent for Indian Airlines and Jet Airways.

Trains: The **railway reservations window,** at the south end of the SNT Bus Terminal, has quota tickets on major trains leaving New Jalpaiguri. Open M-Sa 8am-2pm, Su 8-11am.

Buses: Sikkim Nation Transport (SNT) Bus Terminal (☎ 22016). Down from the National Hwy., at the north end of town. Book tickets early (the previous day for morning departure) at the far left window. Open daily 5:30am-4pm. The crowded **buses** are the cheapest and slowest mode of transport. To: **Darjeeling** (5hr., 7am, Rs78); **Geyzing** (5hr., 7am, Rs78); **Jorethang** (3hr., 2pm, Rs55); **Kalimpong** (3hr., 7:15am, Rs55); **Mangan** (5hr., 8am and 3pm, Rs55); **Namchi** (4hr., 7:30am and 2pm, Rs50); **Rumtek** (1½hr., 4pm, Rs20); **Siliguri** (4hr., 7 per day 6am-12:15pm, Rs70). **Shared jeeps,** available below Lal Bazaar, above the highway, and near the SNT Terminal, run to the same destinations as the SNT throughout the day, and are faster and costlier. To: **Darjeeling** (Rs105); **Kalimpong** (Rs69); **Siliguri** (Rs95); **Rumtek** (Rs24). Make sure you are sharing a jeep; solo rides cost over Rs1000.

Local Transportation: Mini-van taxis run up and down the National Highway and idle along the north end of MG Rd. Negotiate first; it shouldn't cost more than Rs25 to traverse the city. Shared taxis run from Gangtok to Deorali, 2km down the road, for Rs7.

> **SIKKIM PERMITS.** The Sikkim permit process can seem endlessly bureaucratic, but in fact, its pretty simple. Most people only need the basic permit, called an ILP (Inner Line Permit). This permit is free, and you can obtain one instantly if you bring a passport photo to the Sikkim Tourist Office in New Delhi, Calcutta, or Siliguri. You can get a similar permit in Darjeeling with more hassle but no passport photo. The easiest option is to apply for it along with your Indian visa so that it's stamped onto the visa and starts whenever you arrive in Sikkim. Regardless of where you obtain the permit, it's valid for 15 days and allows you free range to travel in the southern half of Sikkim: Gangtok, Mangan, Geyzing, Namchi, Soveng, Ravangla, Pakyong, Rongli, Singhik, Yuksam, and Tashiding, as well as other towns inside this boundary. Permit Extensions are available from the tourist office in Gangtok and the District Administrative Office in Tikjuk, near Pelling. You are allowed up to two extensions, allowing a total stay of 45 days. Apply for an extension a few days before the last has run out. Permits, as well as passports and visas, are checked at the Sikkim border. However, if you're reading this for the first time on a Sikkim-bound bus and are permit-less, don't panic. The border post at Rangpo is authorized to issue a two-day permit, allowing absent-minded travelers to continue on to Gangtok and apply for an extension. Beyond a basic area permit, all special permits *must* be handled through a tourist agency. There are two sorts—a PAP (Protected Area Permit) and a Trekking Permit. Both are only available in Gangtok and require a minimum of four people. The PAP covers destinations like Tsomgo Lake (one-day) and Yumthang (five-day). Finally, it's important to remember that *all* Sikkim permits are issued for tourism only, so even if you're here for something else (religious pilgrimage, studying the flowers), it's best to just lump it all under "tourism."

■★ 🛈 ORIENTATION AND PRACTICAL INFORMATION

The **National Hwy.** cuts northeast, diagonally up the hill, with roads branching off horizontally above and below. The **SNT Bus Terminal** is 100m off the highway at the northern end of town. **Mahatma Gandhi (MG) Rd.,** which serves as the center of town, branches south off the highway, 50m downhill from the intersection that leads to the SNT Bus Terminal. The large, hard-to-miss **tourist centre** sits at the intersection of MG Rd. and the highway. A road which leads up from the tourist office passes the police station to join **Tibet Rd.,** which has most of the backpacker-friendly hotels. Farther south on MG Rd., **Lal Bazaar Rd.** branches off to the right and leads down to the bazaar as well as to waiting taxis and jeeps. Other taxis and jeeps depart from the lot on the National Hwy. just above Hungry Jack Restaurant.

S I K K I M

Tourist Office: National Tourist Centre (☎23425 or 22064). On the corner of MG Rd. and the highway. Issues Sikkim permit extensions, trekking permits, and protected area permits (see **Sikkim Permits,** p. 545), and provides helpful information and brochures. The office also organizes 20min. helicopter tours of Kanchenjunga (8am departures daily, weather permitting; Rs1200). Office open in season daily 9am-7pm; off season closed on Su and every second Sa. Permit extensions M-Sa 10am-4pm.

Tours: Tour companies provide comprehensive trek services, including permits, guides, and equipment. Tours cost around US$25 per day. One professional operation is **Modern Tours and Treks,** MG Rd. (☎27319), in the same bldg. as the Gangtok Lodge, opposite the tourist office. Run by the proprietors of the Modern Central Hotel, the tours are mid-range in price and well-equipped. Open daily 7am-8:30pm. **River rafting** in the Teesta river is popular; tour agencies, including several along MG Rd., organize trips. **Brothers Tours and Treks** (☎24220), 50m along the road that climbs up from MG Rd. opposite the tourist office, on the west side of the jeep lot, runs trips on the Teesta and Rangit from Sept.-May. Four person minimum. Daytrips Rs550 per person; Rs750 with food and transport. 2-day trips Rs1850; equipment, food, and transport included.

Currency Exchange: State Bank of India, MG Rd. (☎26091). Opposite the tourist office. Changes AmEx traveler's checks (Rs25 commission) and cash (Rs135 commission) on the 3rd fl. Open M-F 10am-2pm and 2:30-4pm, Sa 10am-1pm.

Police: (☎22033; 100 for emergencies). 60m up the road that climbs up from MG Rd. opposite the tourist office, on the left side of the road.

Pharmacy: Many along MG Rd. and Naya Bazaar. Locals like **Chiranjilal Lalchand Pharmacy,** MG Rd., opposite the Green Hotel. Open daily 8:30am-8:30pm.

Hospital: Sir Thutab Namgyal Memorial (STNM) Hospital, National Hwy. (☎22944). Fifty meters north of the tourist office. Enter via the footbridge overpass.

Internet: Somani Cyber-Cafe, MG Marg (☎23813), on your right 50m south of the road leading down to Lel Bazaar, has the cheapest. Rs60 per hr. Open daily 8:30am-8pm.

Post Office: (☎23085). Halfway between the SNT Terminal and the National Hwy. Open M-F 9am-3pm, Sa 9am-2pm. **Postal Code:** 737101

▐ ACCOMMODATIONS

Many of Gangtok's hotels cater toward wealthier Indian tourists, and the few budget places are usually crowded. Always ask for a discount—many managers take pity on travelers. Consider staying near the **Rumtek Monastery** (see p. 549), 24km away. During peak season (Sept.-Dec. and Mar.-May), prices rise and hotels fill up.

▨ **Kewzing Home,** Helipad Bye Pass Rd. (☎23702). Go downhill past the SNT Bus Terminal and take the upper fork with the sign to "Holiday Hill" near the stadium. Kewzing Home is 100m down the road on your right up a short flight of steps; it's a 4-story yellow bldg. with prayer flags. Kewzing gives you unfeigned hospitality. The 4 rooms have attached baths, hot water, and TVs. More important is the family atmosphere—guests are invited to eat with the family and then relax in the living room with mug of millet *chang.* Breakfast included. Dinner Rs50. Singles Rs350-400; doubles Rs500-600. ❷

▨ **Modern Central Lodge,** Tibet Rd. (☎24670). Go up the road that climbs up from MG Rd. opposite the tourist office. At its end, turn left on Tibet Rd. and walk 100m up. Very popular with backpackers, and for good reason. The front rooms have nice views of the valley, there's a TV room upstairs, and the restaurant serves tasty meals. Dorms Rs40; singles Rs80; doubles Rs150, with bath Rs250. Bargain, particularly off season. ❶

Hotel Mig-Tin, Tibet Rd. (☎24101). 200m south of the Modern Central. Less popular with backpackers than Modern Central, Mig-Tin is still a great budget option. Clean and roomy doubles have attached bathrooms with seat toilets and hot water. The upstairs rooms have terrific views. Dorms Rs50; doubles Rs200. Off season: Rs150. ❶

Gangtok Lodge, MG Marg (☎26562). Right near the State Bank of India. A slightly more upscale offering than the Modern Central Lodge. Centrally located, with comfortable rooms, all with attached bath. Doubles Rs250, with satellite color TV Rs300. ❶

Green Hotel, MG Marg (☎24439 or 25057). In the dead center of town, Green is a convenient and popular spot with tourists. Has STD, fax, travel agency, money changer, restaurant, TV, and a generator for those rare power outages. Singles Rs150-200; doubles Rs350-475; triples Rs450. Off season: up to 50% discount. MC/V. ❶

Travel Lodge, Tibet Rd. (☎23858). 50m south of the Modern Central. Huge rooms have balconies, and some have TV. Breakfast, lunch, tea, and dinner Rs350 per person per day. Doubles Rs450; triples Rs700; quads Rs900. Off season: Rs250/500/750. ❷

▐ FOOD

Food can be expensive in Gangtok. Bulk foods for hiking are available along **Naya Bazaar,** which has the best selection in Sikkim.

Crispy Cuisine, MG Rd., 10m south of the Tibet Rd. intersection, on the 1st fl. A pleasant place overlooking a busy corner of MG Marg. Serves Indian and Tibetan, and a particularly strong and varied selection of Chinese dishes (Rs30-65). Open daily 8am-7pm. ❶

Parivar Restaurant, MG Rd. In the basement of the Yama bldg., 100m south of the tourist office. This all-veg. restaurant is popular with Indians, and it serves standard favorites at reasonable prices. *Paneer kofta* Rs30, *dosas* Rs20. Open daily 8am-9pm. ❶

Hungry Jack Restaurant, National Hwy. South of the lower taxi/private bus stand, beyond the gas pumps. Clean, spacious, western-style restaurant and bar. North Indian entrees Rs25-60, sandwiches Rs25-50. Open daily 8am-8:30pm. ❶

Blue Sheep Restaurant, MG Marg. Next door to the tourist office. While the food isn't particularly fast, this is a convenient place to grab a familiar bite. There is Internet on the premises. Chicken burger Rs30, fish n' chips Rs35. Open daily 8am-8pm. ❶

Sagar, Durga, and **Laxmi Sweets,** MG Rd. Across and a bit south from the Green Hotel. A popular trio of adjacent snack shops. Pastries Rs5-10 each. Open daily 6am-8pm. ❶

CHANG-TASTIC Cheaper, tastier, and more potent than beer, Sikkimese millet chang is traditionally served in a bamboo (now usually stainless steel) jug called a tomba. Pour hot water on the fermented millet, let it settle for two or three minutes, then suck the juicy mixture up through a special filtered straw. Chang is easy to make: stock up on a few simple supplies (all easily purchased at Gangtok's Lal Bazaar), and you can relive your most blurred memories of Sikkim once you return home. All you need is some millet (mincha in Bhutia, kodo in Nepali) and pho—Sikkimese yeast—and you're ready to brew. First, wash and soak the millet; then, carefully sort through it to remove stray sand and pebbles. Cook the millet as you would rice, and let it cool for a couple of hours. Next, grind the pho (5-10g per 1kg of millet) into powder and mix it into the millet. Wrap this mixture in cloth, let it sit for two nights, and then let it ferment for a week or two (depending on how potent you want it) in a well-sealed plastic bag. After the fermentation period, you're ready to kick-back and enjoy your homemade brew.

SIKKIM

◎ SIGHTS

Many of the sights can be visited on foot or by cab, and many tour agencies also operate whirlwind tour-of-attractions daytrips (Rs300-600). Contact the Tourist Department (see p. 546) for more info. Also, look for the helpful *Gangtok in a Nutshell* (Rs30), a map guide available in some stationery stores around the city.

SIKKIM INSTITUTE OF TIBETOLOGY AND DO DRUL CHORTEN. The nearby town of Deorali is home to a hilltop complex containing the enormous **Do Drul Chorten,** the **Sikkim Institute of Tibetology,** and a flower garden that has orchids and giant ferns. The Institute, founded by the Dalai Lama in 1957, contains one of the largest collections of Tibetan documents in the world. The upper-floor library houses roughly 30,000 volumes of Tibetan documents (mostly wooden boards called xylographs). Of greater interest to non-scholars is the ground-floor collection of *thankas*, but there is also some gruesome ritual items, such as *kanglings* (trumpets made from human thighbones) and a *kapala* (bowl made from a human skull). Further up the hill, the Do Drul Chorten, surrounded by 108 prayer wheels, is one of the most important *stupas* in Sikkim. Below the institute is a flower garden, with a number of benches. *(Deorali is 2km south and downhill from Gangtok on the National Hwy. Institute ☎ 22525. Open M-Sa 10am-4pm. Rs5. Chorten and Garden free.)*

ENCHEY MONASTERY. The **Enchey Monastery** is on the landing spot of Lama Druptob Karpo, who is said to have flown over from Maenam Hill over 200 years ago. The building itself dates from 1909 and has beautiful views of Kanchenjunga, and Gangtok. *(Next to the TV Tower, a 30min. walk from downtown Gangtok. Head uphill to Ridge Rd., and walk north past the White Hall. Make a right at the intersection before the arch for Raj Bhawan, and follow the winding road to the monastery. Open to the public M-Sa 6am-4pm.)*

TSUGLA KHANG. The murals of the **Tsugla Khang,** or Royal Chapel, enclose collections of scriptures. Officially, the monastery and chapel are closed to tourists, but you may be able to charm your way in as long as you're not toting a camera. *(At the south end of Ridge Rd., overlooking Bhanu Path and the government offices of Tashiling.)*

FLOWER SHOW VENUE. The best time to visit this venue is in March, during the annual flower show, when orchids and other blooming beauties vie for top honors. The flowers remain on display until June and are brought out again Oct.-Dec. *(On ridge Rd., just south of the White Hall. Open daily 8am-5pm. Entrance Rs5; camera fee Rs5.)*

▐ SHOPPING

The Government Institute of Cottage Industries serves as a "factory" for handicrafts and furniture. Follow the National Hwy. 20min. north of the tourist office. Showroom open M-Sa 10am-4pm. The best local market for everything from prayer flags to potatoes is Lal Market, below MG Rd., beyond the taxi lot.

KEEPING SIKKIM GREEN With the central government preoccupied by pervasive poverty, disputed borders, and inter-ethnic conflict, it is little wonder that India's environmental health is often overlooked. Token clean-up efforts such as the "Keep India Green" postering campaign in India's urban centers have proven unsuccessful as the mounds of refuse keep growing. In Sikkim, however, environmental action is no joke. In 1999, the state's Chief Minister Pawan Kumar Chamling was honored by environmentalists as India's most green-friendly state head by instituting a complete ban on the use of plastic bags. In recognizing Chamling, the Centre for Science and Environment expressed hope that the rest of India might soon follow suit.

▨ DAYTRIPS FROM GANGTOK

RUMTEK

*The SNT **bus** (1½hr., 4pm, Rs20) is the cheapest option, although you can take a **shared jeep** (45min., Rs24) or a **taxi** (round-trip Rs400, including 1hr. wait; Rs250 one-way).*

Rumtek is a tranquil village only 24km away, on the opposite side of the valley from Gangtok. The centerpiece of the town is the **Rumtek Monastery,** the headquarters of the Karma-pa (Black Hat) sect of the Kagyu-pa order of Tibetan Buddhism. Built in the 1960s, the monastery is modeled on the main Kagyu-pa monastery in Tsorpu, Tibet. In a back room is an impressive collection of golden statues of the 16th Gwalpa, who fled Tibet when China invaded. A monk might let you take a peek. The building, directly behind the main monastery, houses the **Golden Stupa** protected by a glass window and surrounded by elaborate *thankas.* Step outside and you can grab a cup of tea (Rs3) and challenge the monks to a game of carom.

Behind the monastery is the **Karmae Shri Nalanda Institute for Higher Buddhist Studies,** opened in 1981 and affiliated with the Sanskrit University of Varanasi. There is a shrine room on the 4th floor, and a small **Buddha Shrine** in the courtyard.

Following the path up and past the monastery to the left will lead you on a wood hike that affords views of the monastery complex and surrounding countryside.

The Rumtek Monastery is also the site of a number of important Buddhist **pujas** and **chaam** mask dances. The best times to visit are around *Losar* (in February) and on the 10th day of the fifth month of the Tibetan calendar (sometime in July). Check with the tourist office in Gangtok for events. A 20min. walk along the main road past the police check-post is the impressive **Old Monastery.** The main sight here is the collection of sometimes uplifting, sometimes horrifying wall paintings.

Accommodations around Rumtek are cheaper and more peaceful than those in Gangtok, but they are also less convenient for those with business in the capital. The best is the **Sun-gay Guest House ❶,** with large rooms with balconies, attached baths with hot showers, and a lively staff who serves up great food. (☎52221. Singles Rs100; doubles Rs150). Another good option is the **Sangay Hotel ❶,** up the hill beyond the checkpoint for the monastery, run by a friendly family who serves up good food. (☎52238. Singles Rs60; doubles Rs100.) The best value in town is the **Hotel 93 ❶,** tucked away (without any sign) behind the Kunga Delek, just south of the courtyard in front of the monastery. Pristine attached baths, hardwood floors, hot water showers, and majestic views grace every room. It is mainly intended for visiting monks, and is almost always full during festivals. (☎52221. Doubles Rs100.)

▨ TSOMGO LAKE

A 2hr. jeep ride east of Gangtok (round-trip US$10; 4 person min.). Book with any local travel agent.

Cradled at the top of some of Eastern Sikkim's highest peaks, the sacred **Tsomgo Lake** (3700m), also known as Tsonga Lake or Changu Lake, has something to offer year-round. The lake is frozen from December to January, ringed with snow until April, and surrounded by wildflowers in the warmer seasons. The jeep tour is well worth the price. For the energetic, a short, steep hike up to the ridge overlooking the lake gives a spectacular, 360° panorama which includes (in clockwise order) the lake, the Kanchenjunga range, and the mountains of Tibet and Bhutan (4000m, 1hr. ascent, 20min. descent). Garishly decorated yaks can trot you about the lake for Rs10-100. Tsomgo lake may be above the treeline, but it's not above the snackbar line (*momos* Rs15 at any of the cafeterias). A special permit is required for Tsomgo (see **Sikkim Permits,** p. 545), but your tour company should take care of it.

WESTERN SIKKIM

Rich in history and blessed with attractions like the Pemayangtse Monastery and Khechopalri Lake, there is plenty to see in western Sikkim. Its true appeal, though, is its relaxing atmosphere and its scenery, exceptional even by Sikkimese standards. The easiest way to enter Western Sikkim is by bus from Gangtok or Darjeeling. Transportation to the region will usually stop in Geyzing or Pelling, transit points for treks or rides to the rest of Western Sikkim. Most towns are 5-6hr. walk apart; the trip is only slightly shorter if you travel over the roads by bus or jeep.

GEYZING गेज़िन्ग   ☎ 03595

Geyzing is the district headquarters of Western Sikkim and it is the departure or termination point for many of the local buses and jeeps. It also has a number of facilities (e.g. a hospital) unavailable elsewhere. The town has no tourist appeal (aside, perhaps, from its **Sunday markets**), and new arrivals would do better to head up the hill to Pelling for a bed. Geyzing's **SNT Bus Terminal** (ticket office open daily 6:30am-4pm) is down the main road from the central sq. at the bend in the road. **Buses** run to: **Gangtok** (5hr., 7:30am, Rs70); **Jorethang** (2hr., 9:30am, Rs28); **Pelling** (30min., 5pm, Rs10); **Siliguri** (5hr., 7:30am, Rs78). **Jeeps** leave from the lot uphill from the SNT Terminal; the ticket offices (open daily 6:30am-4pm) are above the lot. They depart for: **Khechopalri Lake** (1½hr., noon, Rs50); **Pelling** (30min., frequent, Rs10); **Tashiding** (2hr., noon, Rs50); **Yuksam** (3hr., noon, Rs60).

The **Tourist Office** in Pelling, just up the street from the Hotel Garuda, has free booklets about the area and current transportation information (open daily 6:30am-9pm). **Currency exchange is not available anywhere in Western Sikkim.** Geyzing's **hospital** (☎ 50634), 100m up the road that curves left past Kanchanjanga Hotel, is a pretty dismal. **Gupta Medical Store** (☎50298), 30m north of the main sq. along the same road, has a doctor on call 24hr. The **police** (☎50833) in Geyzing are 25m up the steepest hill leading uphill from Hotel Kanchanjanga. The **post office** is 10m off the main square (open M-F 9am-4pm, Sa 9am-2pm). **Postal Code:** 737111.

Accommodations in Geyzing are limited. Unless you're catching an early bus or jeep, there's no reason to stay the night. Most hotels are in the central sq. area. Your best bet is **Hotel Chopstick ❶**, whose friendly environment makes up for the cramped, dingy quarters. Two rooms, four beds, and a common bath. (☎50225. Rs40 per person.) Slightly more upscale, but not worth the extra expense, is the **Kanchanjanga Hotel ❶**, 20m up the main road from the central sq. The big rooms all have common bath. (☎50489. Doubles Rs120). **Hotel No Name ❶**, is not worth a night's stay but does have a decent attached restaurant. Curry chicken Rs35.

PELLING पेल्लिगं   ☎ 03595

An 8km drive uphill from Geyzing, Pelling is Western Sikkim's tourism center. Since it is the starting point for paths to Yuksam, Tashiding, and Khechopalri Lake, the town caters to trekkers, and its accommodations are excellent sources of hiking information. There are also monasteries, waterfalls, archaeological ruins and Lepcha villages all within a day's hike of the town.

◼◼ ORIENTATION AND PRACTICAL INFORMATION. Upper Pelling is on the top of a ridge. Everything you'll need is in Upper Pelling; you won't have to descend the ridge unless you're setting out for Khechopalri Lake. The best point of orientation is the town's single crossroads at the top of the ridge: roads follow the ridge east (toward Pemayangtse and Geyzing) and west (toward Sarga Choeling Monastery), and descend the ridge to the north (toward Middle Pelling) and south (toward smaller villages). Most **buses** leave from Geyzing, but a bus to **Siliguri**

A BON-AFIDE RELIGION Among its many wonders, Sikkim is home to Bon, one of the oldest and least understood religions in Asia, which predates Buddhism by hundreds if not thousands of years. Followers of Bon (known as Bonpo) adhere to the teachings of their own enlightened one, **Tonpa Shenrab.** Bon was the original religion of Tibet, but the arrival of Buddhism in the 8th century did not bode well for the future, and Bonpos were forced to convert or were driven from the country. Time, however, has mended the wound, and today the two religions are so remarkably similar that Bon is often considered the "Fifth Sect" of Mahayana Buddhism. Many of the rituals are similar to, if not the same as, their Buddhist counterparts; both sides claim that they invented them. But there is one obvious difference in the direction of ritual motion: Bonpos do everything counter-clockwise, opposite from the Buddhists.

Over the years, the number of Bonpos has dwindled, and the number of contemporary adherents outside of Tibet is small. Sikkim, though, harbors a sizable population and is home to one of the three Bon monasteries in India. The **Yungdrung Kundrakling Bon Monastery,** just outside the town of Kewzing, has a small community of monks and struggles to preserve its traditions. While the monastery is small and its facilities modest, the monks leap at the chance to show visitors around. They'll even let you sit in on their morning and evening rituals (daily 6am and 6pm), which last about 30min. At the monastery, ask for **Kalsang Nyima,** the resident painter, who speaks English.

Kewzing sits on the front road between Gangtok and Legship. From Gangtok, any Kewzing-, Legship-, Geyzing-, Pelling-, or Jorethang-bound bus or jeep will pass by the monastery, about 5km before town. While in Gangtok, you can meet with the monastery's head Lama, **Yungdrung Lama,** at his photo store opposite the tourist office, on MG Rd.

S I K K I M

(5½hr., 7am, Rs58) via **Geyzing** departs daily from the SNT office in Middle Pelling. **Jeeps** to **Geyzing** (30min., Rs10) pass through Pelling's main intersection throughout the day. For **police** or **medical** assistance, you have to head to Geyzing. **STD/ISD** services are available at **Sister Guest House** and at **Hotel Window Park,** next to Hotel Garuda. The only **Internet access** in Western Sikkim is available at the **Phamrong Hotel,** next to Hotel Garuda, but service is sporadic and unreliable. (Open daily 8am-9pm, Rs1.50 per min.) **Sikkim Permit extensions** are available at the District Administrative Office in Tikjuk, a 45min. walk from Pelling on the road to Geyzing (open M-Sa 10am-4pm). Pelling's **post office** is aside the Sikkim Tourist Centre building (open M-F 9am-4pm, Sa 9am-2pm). **Postal Code**: 737113.

▐▌ ACCOMMODATIONS AND FOOD. Upper Pelling has a number of good accommodations, but the prices are high. The most popular choice is **Hotel Garuda ❶**, just below the town's central intersection. They give out a helpful area map, have a detailed trekking logbook, and have a book exchange. The attached restaurant serves Sikkimese, Chinese, and continental food (dishes Rs20-40). You can store your gear here and grab a packed lunch before you go traipsing about. (☎58319. Dorms Rs50; doubles with common bath Rs100-120, with attached bath Rs200-350.) Another excellent choice is the **Sister Guest House ❶**, farther down the hill. Bucket showers only, but the rooms are attractive and the attached restaurant serves the best food in town. (☎50569. Dorm Rs50; singles Rs80; doubles Rs100.) **Hotel Kabur ❶**, 50m uphill from the main intersection on the road toward Geyzing, has great views, attached baths in every room, and good advice for trekkers. (☎50685. Dorms Rs100; doubles Rs250-350. Off-season: 50% discount.) If these prices seem steep, try the **Ladakh Guest House ❶**, 20m from the main intersection on the road toward Sanga Choeling Monastery. Rooms are basic but clean; common baths are outside. (Dorms Rs40; doubles Rs100.) For a change from hotel fare, try the **Alpine Restaurant ❶**, next door to the Sister Guest House. It serves outstanding food in a private setting. (Chow mein Rs25-35, *momos* Rs20-40. Open daily 6:30am-9pm.)

VOLUNTEER OPPORTUNITIES

Up the hill from Pelling, toward Pemayangtse Monastery (see below) on the main road, is the **Denjong Padma Choeling Academy**, a school for disadvantaged Sikkimese children, many of whom are orphans. The school needs English-speaking volunteers to teach the children everything from math to art, as well as anyone willing to help with tasks from carpentry to computers. The school provides food and housing for its volunteers, as well as optional instruction in the Bhutia language and Sikkimese Buddhism. For this, you can extend your stay in Sikkim beyond 45 days. To find out more, drop by the school, or contact the school's director (the *lama* at the Pemanyangtse Monastery), Yapo S. Yongda. *(DPC Academy, Yongda Hill, Drakchong Dzong 737113, West Sikkim, India. ☎ 50760; fax 24802; netuk@sikkim.org.)*

NEAR PELLING

PEMAYANGTSE पमयान्नाटसे

The monastery is a 30min. walk from Pelling along the road to Geyzing. A sign will direct you uphill toward the monastery. Open to the public daily 7am-4pm.

Founded in 1705 by Lhatsun Chenpo, one of the three "Great Lamas" of Yuksam, the **Pemayangtse Monastery** (Monastery of the Sublime Perfect Lotus), is the third-oldest monastery in Sikkim. Currently the key *Nyingma-pa* (Red Hat) monastery, it is also one of the most artistically stunning in the region. Intricate wall paintings incorporate everything from wrathful deities to serene and detached *bodhisattvas*. An enormous pair of terrifying Dorje Taras guard the main room, while an enlightened Guru Padma Sambhava looks on from the top of a lotus. The monastery's centerpiece, though, is the **Sang Thog Palri;** a detailed, seven- meter-high wooden rendering of the Maha Guru's paradise. The Sang Thog Palri is encased in glass and occupies the monastery's top room. A meditation center, where students can study Buddhist philosophy and meditation, and the Bhutia language, is in the works for October 2001. Contact Yapo S. Yongda (see **Volunteer Opportunities,** above) for more info.

RABDENTSE PALACE RUINS

Slightly beyond the turnoff for Pemyangtse along the road toward Geyzing, a sign points the way toward the palace. Follow the path into a meadow, and then a cobblestone path for 10min.; signs mark the way.

The second king of Sikkim, Tenzung Namgyal, moved the capital from Yuksam to this spot in 1670, and it served as the seat of royal power until 1814. On the right as you climb through the ruins is the remains of the stable and military headquarters; on the left is the site of the main throne. The view from here takes in the holiest areas of Western Sikkim, including Yuksam and Tashiding. At the top of the hill, on the right, you can see the remains of a public temple.

SANGA CHOELING MONASTERY

The monastery is about a 45min. hike from town, in the opposite direction from Pemayngtse. The road soon reaches a football field; bear left around the small hill and take the lower road when it splits in two. This path leads all the way to the monastery. The same trail continues past Sanga Choeling—it's easy to miss; watch for the faded wooden sign. The forested ridge behind it is a popular destination for day hikes.

The **Sanga Choeling Monastery** is older than Pemayangtse, but is not as flashy or popular. It is just more peaceful and sedate. Ancient pine forests surround the hilltop complex, and the (literally) breathtaking climb alone is worth the trip. Inside the main building are three central statues—the Buddha on the left, Dorje Sempa in the middle, and Guru Padma Sambhava on the right. On the far side of the main building, behind the row of white *stupas*, is a pair of rocks covering a hole. Local legend has it that this hole leads all the way to a cave near Legship, and that this cave is the source of the eerie wind that emanates from the hole. Whatever its actual source, the gusts are real. Drop a few blades of grass in and watch them blow back out.

◪ TREKKING IN WESTERN SIKKIM

The best way to take in the lakes, monasteries, jungles, and villages of Western Sikkim is by foot. Though the most popular sites are connected by road, the most enjoyable (and most challenging) routes are the unmarked "shortcuts." It's easy to get lost since these trails have many branches, but there are plenty of farmers around who will help you find your way. Keep in mind that while finding dinner and a place to sleep is rarely a problem, lunch or bottled water is generally unavailable along the trail. Many hotels will provide a packed lunch for Rs20-30.

THE LOCAL TREK

The Local Trek is very popular, and with good reason. More of a walk than a trek, it is relatively easy, does not require much advance planning, and takes you past some of the most impressive sights and scenery in Western Sikkim. The trek is a four-day loop, which starts and ends in Pelling going through villages along the way. Food and accommodations are available on the route, and the towns are connected by jeep service. The route described is the longest and proceeds in the more popular (and more auspicious) clockwise direction.

DAY 1 (4½-6½HR.): PELLING TO KHECHOPALRI LAKE. From the tourist office in Pelling, the road bends sharply and heads down the ridge past the Alpine Restaurant. Follow this road into lower Pelling until you see the sign for Mondol Lodge. In front of this sign, a concrete path descends to the right and heads down to the river. The concrete disappears, and the path begins to fork regularly. Almost all of the forks will take you where you want to go, but when in doubt, favor the more downhill option. The descent to the Rimbi river takes 45min. to 1½hr. At the river, there's a rickety bamboo bridge, and then the trail climbs quickly to the road. Follow the road east for about 20min., where a clearly-marked road leads toward Khechopalri, 10km away. Numerous shortcuts traverse the initial switchbacks, and locals point them out. The road eventually levels, winds up the valley, crosses a stream, and then spins back out and around the next ridge before reaching the lake. Snacks and bottled water are available at some of the roadside villages.

Khechopalri Lake is considered the holiest lake in Sikkim, and legend says that if even a single leaf falls on its surface, a bird will pluck it up. Local tradition says that it can grant wishes, so wish wisely! **Swimming is not allowed.** The main shrine is on the eastern side of the lake; a small platform extends from it to the lake's edge. A "trail" of sorts continues on and circles the lake, but it's hard to follow in some places. Also accessible from the lake are the **Chubuk and Dupuk caves,** where local monks perform religious ceremonies, and the **"footprint rock"** a rock that a monk stepped on in legend, hence the footprint. Ask at the trekkers' hut (see below) for directions. A small monastery above the lake commands excellent views.

The best accommodation at the lake is the privatized **trekkers' hut ❶,** on the road 200m before the lake. The serene ambience and friendly staff are complemented by huge communal dinners for Rs25. (Double rooms Rs40 per bed). The **pilgrims' hut ❶,** by the entrance to the lake, has a grander exterior, but a drabber interior (dorms Rs40). A jeep runs from Geyzing to Khechopalri Lake at noon (Rs50), and an SNT bus makes the trip at 2pm (Rs20).

DAY 2 (3-5HR.): KHECHOPALRI LAKE TO YUKSAM. From the lake, a short-cut trail descends off the main road just opposite the trail leading up to the monastery. The trail drops past a few houses and some rows of white prayer flags, and after 45min. to 1hr., it crosses a stream. From there, you can follow the downhill

road or take the much steeper path over the ridge. Either way, you will have to join the path that crosses the crystal-clear Rathong River on a suspension bridge. The steep shortcut to Yuksam climbs up from the road just a few hundred meters past the bridge. This trail zig-zags through terraced fields all the way up to an unused stretch of road 1hr. away. Follow this road to the right all the way to **Yuksam.** Before the village, the road snakes around to the left and passes by a school before arriving at Yuksam proper five minutes later.

Yuksam itself is relatively built-up, for it is the starting point for the popular **Dzongri Trek.** Yuksam (Lepcha for "three *lamas*") became the first capital of Sikkim in 1641 when three *lamas*, Lhatsun Chenpo, Rigdzin Chenpo, and Nadak

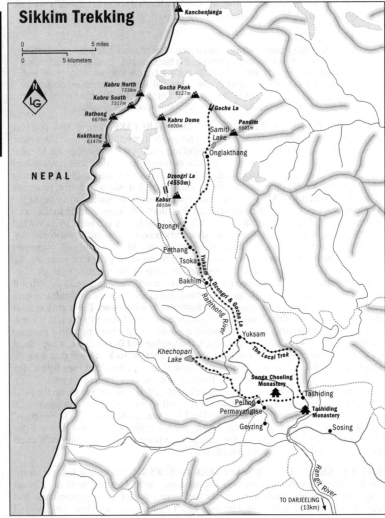

Sikkim Trekking

0 ————— 5 miles
0 ————— 5 kilometers

Kanchenjunga

NEPAL

Kabru North 7338m
Kabru South 7317m
Rathong 6679m
Kokthang 6147m

Gocha Peak 6127m
Gocha La
Kabru Dome 6600m
Pandim 6691m
Samiti Lake
Onglakthang

Dzongri La (4550m)
Kabur 4810m

Dzongri
Pethang
Tsoka
Bakhim

Rathong River
Yuksam to Dzongri & Gocha La

Yuksam

Khechopari Lake

The Local Trek

Sanga Choeling Monastery
Tashiding
Pelling
Permayangtse
Tashiding Monastery
Geyzing
Sosing

Rangit River

TO DARJEELING (13km)

Sempa Chenpo, met here to consecrate the first king of Sikkim, Phontsog Namgyal. The spot of the ceremony, a white stone throne, is still intact, and is known as the **Norbugang Chorten.** This dignified monument rests in a wooded glade 10min. down the road past Hotel Tashi Gang. The capital has long since moved, but Yuksam still has some basic services. There is a **police outpost** on the main road, 150m north of the Wild Orchid Hotel, and a **hospital** another 100m north on the road that curves to the right. If you take a left up the road that diverges from the main road between the police outpost and the hospital, you will reach the luxurious **Hotel Tashi Gang,** which has STD/ISD service.

The best place to stay is the **Hotel Yangrigang ❶,** at the bend in the main road, just south of the bazaar. The rooms are clean, the lobby has comfy couches, and the restaurant dishes out veg. chow mein for Rs25. (Dorm Rs50; doubles with bath Rs150. Off-season: Rs40/100.) Though not quite the seductive paradise its name suggests, **Wild Orchid Hotel ❶,** just south of the main bazaar, is another reliable option. All rooms have a common bath and hot water is available at Rs10 per bucket. (Singles Rs50; doubles Rs100.) For a good meal outside the hotels, try the **Gupta Restaurant ❶,** just north of the Wild Orchid Hotel. (Veg. *momos* Rs10, beer Rs35. Open daily 5:30am-8pm.) The nearby **Dubdi Monastery,** built in 1701, is the oldest in Sikkim. A well-maintained trail below the hospital leads to the hilltop monastery 45min. away. **Jeeps** for this leg of the trip (Khechopalri Lake to Yuksam) depart from in front of the trekkers' hut in Khechopalri (6:30am, Rs30).

DAY 3 (4-6HR.): YUKSAM TO TASHIDING. The walk from Yuksam to Tashiding is long, but not strenuous; most of it is downhill, and much of it is along the road. The only shortcut worth taking comes at the very beginning. From Yuksam, a trail descends off the main road, beginning just before the Hotel Yangrigang. This trail cuts diagonally downhill for about 2km; at every fork, opt for the more downhill path. Eventually, the trail intersects the road. From this point on, the hike follows the road, and while the route is lovely and there is not much traffic, many trekkers choose to hop on a jeep for this leg. A half hour after joining the main road, you'll pass **Phamrong Falls;** farther along the path passes through the village of **Gerethang,** where bottled water and snacks are available. You will be able to see **Tashiding** about an hour before you arrive. Tashiding is on top of a ridge, looking down on the Rathong River to the west and the Rangeet River to the east.

The **Tashiding Monastery,** the real attraction of the day, is a 45min. hike from town up the *stupa*-dotted hill to the south. (You have to walk this stretch, even if you come by jeep.) The monastery dates from 1716 and houses about 50 monks and the **Bhumchu,** a sacred water vase that is the center of a local festival on the first full moon after Losar, the Tibetan New Year in February or March. Each year, the vase is filled with 21 jugs of water and sealed for a year. At the following year's festival, the water is measured out; if there are still 21 jugs of water, it is a good omen, but any evaporation portends bad times. The water is then diluted with regular water and given to everyone to sample. The **Thong Wa Rang To Chorten,** considered the holiest *chorten* in Sikkim, is also on the premises. Simply beholding its glory is said to wash away all sin.

If you are looking for a place to stay in Tashiding, keep your eyes peeled for the **Hotel Blue Bird ❶,** just north up the hill from the main intersection. Rooms are simple, and all share a common bath. There's a comfortable sitting area upstairs, and free buckets of hot water are provided. (Dorm Rs25; singles Rs40; doubles Rs50.) The restaurant serves cheap meals (veg. rice Rs20, chicken rice Rs40).

Jeep service for this part of the trek runs mostly in the early morning (1hr., departure before 6:30am, Rs30); it is possible to visit Tashiding early and then continue on to either Legship or Pelling in the evening.

DAY 4 (5-7HR. OR 3-5HR.): TASHIDING TO PELLING OR LEGSHIP. You have two options from Tashiding: one is to take the shortcut trail directly down to the river and up to the other side to **Pelling;** the other is to follow the road down to **Legship,** where buses and jeeps run up to Pelling, Gangtok, Jorethang, and Siliguri.

Heading straight to Pelling requires more energy. The shortcut trail departs directly from the town of Tashiding (ask at the Hotel Blue Bird, see above) and and after 1½-2½hr. reaches a suspension bridge. Across the river, the trail begins to ascend; at the few forks in the trail, veer toward the more uphill path. This eventually leads to **Naku Chumbong Village** (2½-3hr.), where a number of paths converge. Take the most uphill trail, which will take you to Pelling in 1-1½ hr.

The other option is to follow the descending path to Legship, a better choice for those headed to other parts of Sikkim or West Bengal, since most buses and jeeps pass through Legship. Navigation is easy, just follow the road, but keep in mind that there is no food or water available along the way. The road crosses the Rangeet River (1½-2½hr.), winds downstream, and crosses the river again at Legship (1½-2½hr.) It's a long walk, but the path is mostly downhill. **Jeeps** run from Tashiding to Legship in the morning (45 min., departure before 8am, Rs20).Trucks on the route will often stop for trekkers (Rs10). **Let's Go does not recommend hitchhiking.**

In Legship, **buses** run to **Gangtok** (4hr., 8:30am, Rs65) and **Siliguri** (4hr.; 6:30, 8:30, 9am; Rs65). **Jeeps** head to: **Geyzing** (45min., frequent 7:30am-5pm, Rs20); **Jorethang** (1hr., frequent 7:30am-5pm, Rs25), for connections to Gangtok; **Siliguri** (4hr., frequent 8:30am-4pm, Rs70). The only real accommodation in town is the **Hotel Trishna ❶,** up the street from the bus terminal, at the main intersection. Their rooms are clean, and they'll wake you up for early buses and jeeps. (☎50887. Free buckets of hot water for common bath. Doubles Rs100 per person.) Ask the hotel for directions to the **hot springs,** a half-hour walk from town.

OTHER TREKS

For serious trekkers, the more challenging (and more costly) **Dzongri Trek** (6-10 days) leaves from Yuksam and ascends well above 4000m. It must be booked ahead of time in Gangtok, and the cost of US$20-25 per person per day will cover food, tents, a guide, and porters. The trek goes from **Yuksam** (1780m) to **Dzongri** (4024m) over a period of three days. Some trips continue for three more days to **Goeche La** (4940m) before returning to the "lowlands." The newly-opened **Singalelah Trek** (14-21 days) has the same final destination as the Dzongri Trek, but follows a circuitous, less traveled, more spectacular route along the Sikkim-Nepal border. The trek crosses into Nepal at several points, but no visa is necessary. Although most of these treks are guided and relatively safe, read up on Acute Mountain Sickness (AMS) before you go (see p. 36).

TAMIL NADU
தமிழ் நாடு

The southernmost state in mainland India, Tamil Nadu is the heartland of Dravidian culture and a stronghold of Hindu practice, making it one of the most conservative and traditional regions in the whole country. Travelers here can lose themselves in the local culture without worrying about falling victim to overzealous trinket-dealers, mudslides, or undercooked vegetable chowmein. Some of the finest temples in India are in Tamil Nadu: vividly colored towers and gateways soaring over huge temple-city complexes and dusty streets are sent spiraling around shrines abuzz with worshippers. The state moves to the pulsing rhythms of *bharatnatyam*, India's most popular classical dance form. Most of the population is Dravidian, the descendents of the earliest inhabitants of the subcontinent. Since the 1st century, the state has nurtured South India's oldest literary tradition in its mother tongue, Tamil. The refusal to welcome Hindi into its schools and administration has tinged the state's recent history with separatism and linguistic pride.

During the last few centuries BC, Tamil Nadu was ruled by three rival dynasties: the Cholas, the Pandyas, and the Cheras. By the 4th century AD, the Pallava kingdom had risen to power and ruled until the 9th century, when it was toppled by the Cholas, who eventually came to rule the whole of South India. Under the British, Tamil Nadu was part of the Chennai Presidency, which included parts of present-day Andhra Pradesh, Kerala, and Karnataka.

Tamil Nadu is a patchwork of terrains and cultures, ranging from green paddy-fields and red tilled earth on the coast to foggy hill stations and bustling cities catering to the needs of any traveler.

HIGHLIGHTS OF TAMIL NADU

A unique cultural mix distinguishes **Pondicherry** (p. 583), the former capital of French India, now home to the famously surreal **Aurobindo Ashram** (p. 587).

Thousands flock to the **Meenakshi Amman Temple** in **Madurai** (p. 604), perhaps the most impressive of all the holy sites in South India.

Kodaikanal (p. 617), in the Western Ghats, has all the standard hill station amusements, set against some of India's finest film-grade scenery.

CHENNAI (MADRAS) சென்னை   ☎ 044

Dubbed the "Gateway to the South" by its champions, Chennai is India's fourth largest city and most travelers' first stop in Tamil Nadu. The capital of the state, Chennai is a bastion of South Indian culture, and its dance and music festivals attract bigger crowds than the few sights sprinkled within the city limits. Nonetheless, Chennai has never been much of a tourist destination, and most travelers get out of town as soon as they can. But, if you're arriving from a big city elsewhere in India, you may be pleasantly surprised by the relative calm that manages to survive here, underneath the traffic fumes and mad wheeling thrum present in all subcontinental cities. Lending to the more relaxed feel of Chennai are large patches of greenery, which provide welcome relief from the burning heat and complement the city's long, lazy stretches of sand along the Bay of Bengal.

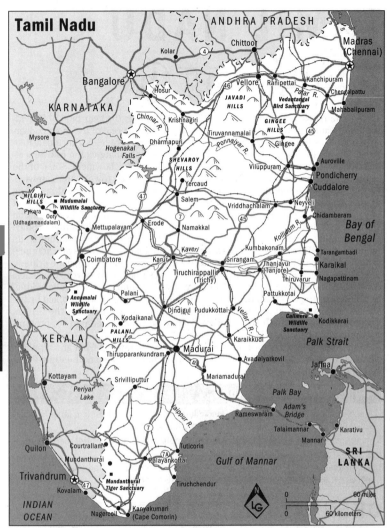

Tamil Nadu

ANDHRA PRADESH

Madras (Chennai)

Chittoor

Kolar

KARNATAKA

Bangalore

Vellore · Ranipettai · Kanchipuram

Hosur · JAVADI HILLS · Chengalpattu

Palar R. · Vedantangal Bird Sanctuary · Mahabalipuram

Chinnar R. · Krishnagiri

Mysore · Dharmapuri · Tiruvannamalai · GINGEE HILLS

Hogenakal Falls · Ponnaiyar R. · Gingee

SHEVAROY HILLS · Viluppuram · Auroville

NILGIRI HILLS · Yercaud · Pondicherry

Mudumalai Wildlife Sanctuary · Salem · Vriddhachalam · Cuddalore

Pykara · Ooty (Udhagamandalam) · Neyveli

Mettupalayam · Erode · Namakkal · Chidambaram

Kaveri · Kollidam R. · Bay of Bengal

Coimbatore · Karur · Kumbakonam · Tarangambadi

Srirangam · Thanjavur (Tanjore) · Karaikal

Tiruchirappalli (Trichy) · Thiruvarur · Nagapattinam

Palani · Pattukkottai

Annamalai Wildlife Sanctuary · Kodaikanal · Dindigul · Pudukkottai · Velar R. · Calimere Wildlife Sanctuary · Kodikkarai

PALANI HILLS · Karaikkudi · Palk Strait

KERALA · Thirupparankundram · Madurai

Avadaiyarkovil

Kottayam · Srivilliputtur · Manamadurai · Jaffna

Periyar Lake · Palk Bay

Adam's Bridge · SRI LANKA

Vaipajur R. · Rameswaram · Talaimannar · Karativu

Mannar

Quilon · Courtrallam · Tuticorin · Gulf of Mannar

Mundanthurai · Palayankottai

Trivandrum · Mundanthurai Tiger Sanctuary · Tiruchchendur

Kovalam · INDIAN OCEAN · Nagercoil · Kanyakumari (Cape Comorin)

0   60 miles
0   60 kilometers

Chennai's climb from humble fishing village to horn-honking metropolis began in 1639, when East India Company worker Francis Day founded a trading outpost. French forces stormed, seized, and sacked the city in 1746, but Madras (as it was known then) continued to develop as a thriving economic center. By the late 19th century, its factories were spinning out thousands of bales of cotton clothing for export throughout the Empire.

Recently, Chennai has been swept up in India's wave of politically motivated name changes, and many of the town's major thoroughfares have been stripped of their colonial names and renamed in honor of Tamil leaders. In 1996, the city's old name, "Madras," was officially replaced by "Chennai," a Tamil name that evokes the original Indian settlement of Chennaipatnam.

■ INTERCITY TRANSPORTATION

FLIGHTS

Chennai Meenambakkam is not as heavily used as the airports in Delhi and Mumbai, making Chennai a relatively peaceful port of entry and exit. The city center is 16km north of the airport, and there are a number of ways of getting there. **Local buses** (#52, 52A, 52B, 52D, 52E, 52G, 60E, 60G; Rs15) are too crowded to be useful unless you are carrying all your luggage in your pockets. The **minibus service** running between the airport and the major hotels (Rs100) is a tedious and time-consuming way of making it into the city. Tickets are sold at a counter in the international terminal. The **pre-paid taxi booth** inside the international terminal will fix you up with a taxi downtown for about Rs250; regular taxis are likely to cost substantially more. **Auto-rickshaws** are not allowed inside the airport compound, so you will have to hike to the main road before you can start haggling over a fare, which should be Rs150-200. Another option is the urban **train** system; it runs from Tirusulam Station (a short walk from the terminals) to Egmore Station, the site of a number of cheap hotels (Rs5, last train at around midnight).

INTERNATIONAL AIRLINES. Most airline offices are open M-F 9:30am-5:30pm and Sa 9:30am-1:30pm. **American Airlines** and **TWA** share an office at 43-44 Thaper House, Montieth Rd. (☎ 859 2564). **Air France** (☎ 855 4894) is on White's Rd. **Air India** (☎ 855 4488 or 855 4477). 19 Marshalls Rd. **British Airways** (☎ 855 4680). Alsa Mall Khaleeli Centre, Montieth Rd. **Delta Airlines** (☎ 852 5655 or 852 5755). 47 White's Rd., Royapettah. Open M-F 9:30am-5:30pm, Sa 9:30am-1:30pm. **Gulf Air** (☎ 855 4417 or 855 3101). 52 Montieth Rd. **Lufthansa** (☎ 852 3272). 167 Anna Salai. **Malaysia Airlines** (☎ 434 9651). 498 Anna Salai. **Singapore Airlines** (☎ 852 2871). 108 Dr. Radhakrishnan Salai. **Sri Lankan Airlines** (☎ 826 1535). 76 Cathedral Rd., opposite Chola Hotel. **Swiss Air** (☎ 852 2541). 191 Anna Salai. **Thai Airways, United Airlines, SAS, Air New Zealand,** and **Varig Airlines** (☎ 822 6150 or 822 6149) share an office at the Malavikas Centre, 144 Kodambakkam Rd. Sri Lankan Airlines and Air India both fly to **Colombo, Sri Lanka** (1½hr., 4-5 per day, US$90).

DOMESTIC AIRLINES. **Jet Airways** (☎ 841 4141). Thaper House, 43-44 Montieth Rd. Open M-Sa 8:30am-8:30pm. **Indian Airlines** (☎ 855 5200). 19 Marshalls Rd. Daily fights to: **Bangalore** (7-8 per day, US$70); **Calcutta** (2-3 per day, US$225); **Cochin** (1-3 per day, US$125); **Coimbatore** (2-3 per day, US$95); **Delhi** (6-7 per day, US$265); **Hyderabad** (3-4 per day, US$110); **Mumbai** (7-9 per day, US$165); **Trivandrum** (2 per day, US$110).

TRAINS

Chennai has two main train stations: **Egmore,** for travel within Tamil Nadu, and **Chennai Central,** for trains to other parts of the country. Both are in the north of town on Periyar EVR Rd. (Poonamallee High Rd.). For **arrival and departure information,** call ☎ 1361 and dial the train number after the beep. Southern Railways maintains an extremely useful and up-to-date website of schedules and route maps that finally relegates *Trains At A Glance* to the status of an ancient abacus. Ride the rails at www.srailway.com or www.southernrailway.org.

CHENNAI CENTRAL. Long-distance trains arrive at and depart from Chennai Central, in Georgetown, near the Buckingham Canal, not far from the hotels of Gandhi Irwin Rd. The reservation counter is upstairs in the administrative building, the 10-story concrete structure to the left of the huge red station. The helpful "Foreigners Assistance Cell" is upstairs on the first floor. (General inquiries ☎ 132. Open M-Sa 8am-8pm, Su 8am-2pm.) To: **Ahmedabad** (35hr., 9:30am, Rs390); **Bangalore** (7hr., 6-7 per day 5am-10:45pm, Rs135); **Calcutta** (33hr., 2-3 per day 7:35am-10:45pm, Rs366);

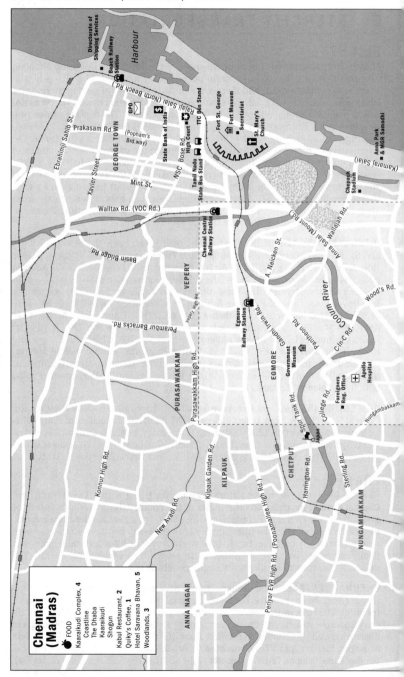

Chennai (Madras)

FOOD

Kaaraikudi Complex, **4**
Coastline
The Dhaba
Kaaraikudi
Shōgun
Kabul Restaurant, **2**
Quiky's Coffee, **1**
Hotel Saravana Bhavan, **5**
Woodlands, **3**

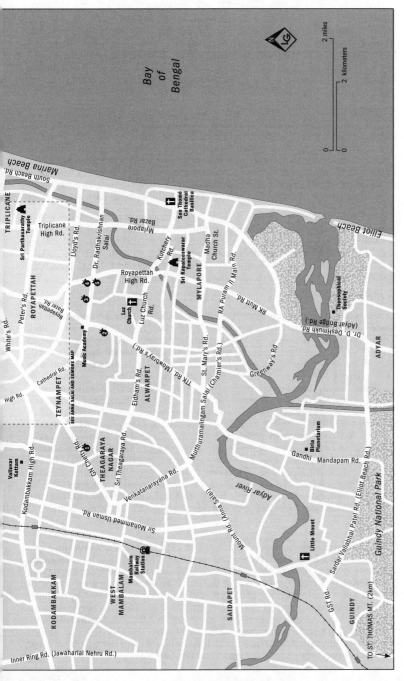

Coimbatore (8½hr., 7-8 per day 6:15am-4:40am, Rs166); **Delhi** (35hr.; M, Th, F 5:30am; Rs410); **Ernakulam** and/or **Cochin** (13½hr., 3-4 per day noon-4:40am, Rs214); **Hyderabad** (14½hr., 4 and 6:10pm, Rs236); **Kanyakumari** (16hr., 7pm, Rs228); **Mangalore** (19hr., 11am and 7:15pm, Rs259); **Mumbai** (30hr.; 6:50, 11:45am, 9:30pm; Rs315); **Mysore** (12hr., 10:45pm, Rs166; *Shatabdi Express* 7hr., Th-Tu 6am, Rs630); **Tirupati** (3hr.; 6:25am, 1:50, 4:15pm; Rs75); **Trivandrum** (17hr.; daily 7pm, 1-2 other trains per day Su-F noon-4:40am; Rs259); **Varanasi** (39hr., Tu and Su 5:30pm, Rs407).

EGMORE RAILWAY STATION. Most trains to destinations within Tamil Nadu depart from the Egmore Railway Station, though some trains now run from Tambaram, an hour away (see below). Egmore Station is north of Gandhi Irwin Rd. The reservation counter is to your left as you enter. The tourist cell at Chennai Central deals with bookings for trains out of both stations. (☎ 135. Open M-Sa 8am-2pm and 2:15-6pm, Su 8am-2pm.) To: **Chidambaram** (6hr., 7:30pm, Rs97); **Kodaikanal** (9½hr., 4 per day 6:15-9pm, Rs159); **Madurai** (5 per day 12:15-9pm, Rs166); **Tanjore** (9hr., 10pm, Rs138); **Trichy** (7½hr., 7-8 per day 12:25-10:30pm, Rs126).

TAMBARAM. Schedule changes made in July 2000 mean that some trains within Tamil Nadu now run from Tambaram, an hour from Chennai. Suburban trains run between Tambaran and Egmore (every 15min. 4am-midnight, Rs5). Destinations served from Tambaram include: **Chidambaram** (5½hr., 4 per day 2:10pm-2:20am, Rs97); **Kumbakonam** (7hr.; 8:45am, 1, 4pm; Rs111); **Rameswaram** (17½hr., 1 and 9pm, Rs205); **Tanjore** (8½hr., 4 per day 8:45am-10:45pm, Rs138).

BUSES

Buses to most tourist sights leave from the **State Express Transport Corporation Bus Stand** (☎ 534 1835), on the south side of Georgetown, in an area known as Park Town. Open daily 7am-9pm. To take any inter-city bus, you'll need a reservation form (Rs0.25) from the counter upstairs. SETC runs buses to: **Bangalore** (#831, 8hr., 17 buses per day 5:30am-9:45pm, Rs122) via **Kanchi** or **Vellore; Chidambaram** (#300; 6hr.; 1:30, 3:30, 5, 10pm; Rs65); **Coimbatore** (#460, 12hr., 7 per day 5:30-10:15pm, Rs173); **Kanyakumari** (#282, 19hr., 6 per day, Rs239); **Kodaikanal** (#461, 14hr., 5:45pm, Rs178); **Kumbakonam** (#303, 308, 332S, 336S; 7hr.; 22 per day 7:45am-11:05pm; Rs76-99); **Madurai** (#137, 10hr., 15 per day 9am-10:30pm, Rs118-154); **Mysore** (#863, 10hr., 5 and 8pm, Rs191); **Ooty** (#465S, 14hr., 5pm, Rs201; #468S, 7:15pm, Rs176); **Pondicherry** (#803 and 803E, 4hr., 5 per day 5:15am-9pm, Rs47); **Rameswaram** (#466S, 13hr., 5pm, Rs176); **Tanjore** (#323, 8hr., 9 per day 5:30am-10pm, Rs87); **Trichy** (#123, 6hr., 24 per day 7am-11pm, Rs86); **Tirupati** (#911, 4hr., 19 per day 5:40am-10:45pm, Rs52). **Broadway Terminal,** opposite the State Express stand, is more chaotic and necessary only for travelers headed to: **Kanchi** (#76, 79, 130; 3hr.; frequent 4:40am-10:30pm; Rs20); **Mahabalipuram** (#19C, 119, 188, 189; 2½hr.; frequent 5am-10pm; Rs25); **Vellore** (4hr., frequent 4am-12:30am, Rs36).

BOATS

There are weekly sailings from Chennai to Port Blair in the **Andaman Islands.** Fares are Rs1100 for a bunk, Rs2700 for a 2nd class cabin, Rs3400 for a 1st class cabin, and Rs4150 for a "deluxe" cabin. To purchase tickets, foreigners need two passport photos (get them done at one of the shops on Anna Salai), a photocopy of their passport and Indian visa, and a "proof of residence form" issued by the hotel at which they are staying. Contact the Deputy Director of Shipping Services, Andaman & Nicobar Administration, NSC Bose Rd. (☎ 522 6873. Open daily 8am-4:30pm. For more information, see p. 108.) Don't forget the special permit needed for travel to this restricted area, for which you will need two more ID photos and yet another photocopy of your passport and visa (see p. 565).

⚑ ORIENTATION

Chennai is a massive, sprawling city, extending more than 15km along the western shores of the **Bay of Bengal**. The city can be divided into three distinct sections. Northernmost is **Georgetown**, an area of long, straight streets running south to **Fort Saint George** and the **Central Railway Station.** George Town's major east-west artery is **NSC Bose Rd.**, which runs across town, parallel to **Prakasam Rd. (Broadway),** to the shoreline, where it meets **Rajaji Rd. (North Beach Rd.),** which leads south to Marina Beach. **Parry's Corner,** at the intersection of NSC Bose and Rajaji Rd., is the wheeling, dealing market area. The city's major **bus terminals** are here.

The southernmost part of town is 10km south of Georgetown and stretches from **Mylapore** in the north to the residential areas south of the **Adyar River.** To the west are the **Guindy National Park** and **St. Thomas Mt.**

Between Georgetown and Mylapore is the real center of the city, including **Egmore** and **Anna Salai (Mount Rd.),** the longest and busiest street in Chennai. Many of the city's tourist services are along Anna Salai, which runs northeast to southwest. North of Anna Salai is the congested Egmore area, full of cheap hotels. Egmore's northern boundary is **Egmore Railway Station,** just off hotel-rich **Gandhi Irwin Rd. Pantheon Rd.** runs parallel to and south of Gandhi Irwin Rd. **Periyar EVR Road (Poonamallee High Rd.)** is to the north. Perpendicular to both are **Commander-in-Chief Rd. (C-in-C Rd.)** and, farther southwest, **Nungambakkam High Rd. (NH Rd.),** two busy streets where many of Chennai's businesses are. **Triplicane** is a mix of hotels, residences, and businesses in a central location near the coast and just south of Anna Salai. Nungambakkam, T. Nagar, and Dr. Radhakrishnan Salai are good areas for coffee shops, stores, and restaurants.

⚏ LOCAL TRANSPORTATION

AUTO-RICKSHAWS

The streets of Chennai are infested with swarms of auto-rickshaws, probably the easiest (though not cheapest) way of getting around. It is sometimes easier just to agree on a price before getting in, though the first price you're offered will almost always be about double the going rate. Rs20-30 is a typical fare between two downtown destinations. Most rickshaw-*wallahs* will meet you at your hotel in the morning or will take you around town for the day—simply discuss your plans beforehand and agree on a lump sum in advance (Rs80-200). If you have serious trouble with a driver, threaten to take down his number (on the back of the vehicle or on a black pin worn on his shirt) and report him to the police.

TAXIS

Taxis are much less common and about twice as expensive as auto-rickshaws. Most have meters, but again, it's often best to fix a price beforehand. Expect to pay at least Rs100 from the railway stations to Anna Salai or to Triplicane.

LOCAL BUSES

The very thought of getting onto an Indian city bus is enough to make some people ill. Chennia's bus system is efficient and reliable when compared with others though. Also, it is (marginally) less crowded than those in Calcutta, Delhi, and Mumbai. Most public buses are green and have their destination displayed at the front and on the side. There is a bus stand every few blocks throughout the city. Rush hour (7:30-10:30am and 5:30-7pm) is for masochistic crowd-lovers only.

TAMIL NADU

Buses are boarded from behind. The conductor will soon amble along and extract payment (usually Rs2-3). Many buses are unofficially segregated by sex—women on one side, men on the other. Regular bus service runs 5am-10pm. Night buses are less frequent and run only along select routes.

BUS #	ROUTE
22, 27, 27B, 29A	Egmore-Triplicane
23C	Egmore-Anna Salai-Adyar Depot
9, 10, 17, 17E	Egmore-Central
9, 10	Parry's Corner-Central-Egmore-T. Nagar
9A, 17D	Parry's Corner-Central-Egmore
18A, A18, 52B	Broadway-Anna Salai-Airport
21G	High Court-Adyar-Guindy National Park-Airport
21	Parry's Corner-Central-Mylapore
17A, 17G, 25B, 25E	Anna Salai-Nungambakkan
25B, 27, 40	Anna Salai-Triplicane-Egmore
23A, 23B, 23C, PP23C	Adyar Bus Depot-Anna Salai-Egmore
25, 25A	Anna Salai-Triplicane
40, 40A	Triplicane-Egmore

MOPEDS

You need an international license to rent a moped (Rs150 per day). For your own wheels, check out **U-Rent Services Ltd.,** 36 II Main Rd., in the Gandhi Nagar district, south of the Adyar River. (☎491 0838. Open daily 8:30am-8pm.)

SUBURBAN TRAINS

Two suburban train lines run along the eastern and western extremities of Chennai. These trains—cheap, frequent, and only packed during morning and evening rush-hours—are the best means of reaching places south of the city center. From Beach Railway Station near the Head Post Office in Georgetown in the north of the city, trains run south to Egmore, Park (close to Chennai Central), Nungambakkam, Mambalam (for T. Nagar), Guindy, St. Thomas Mt., and then on to the airport and Tambaram. The eastern line runs south from Beach Railway Station to Triplicane, Luz, and Gandhi Nagar. Trains run every 10-15min. between 4am and midnight, and fares for most journeys are Rs5 or less.

🔃 PRACTICAL INFORMATION

For up-to-date information, tourists should pick up a copy of **Hallo! Madras,** a monthly listings pamphlet detailing everything from practical information to sights and shopping. Copies are available from the tourist information center and from bookshops around town.

TOURIST AND FINANCIAL SERVICES

Tourist Office: Government of India Tourist Office, 154 Anna Salai (☎846 0285 or 846 1459; fax 846 0193; goirto@vsnl.com). At the corner of Clubhouse Rd. The best place to start collecting informational pamphlets on Chennai, Tamil Nadu, and the country beyond. Open M-F 9:15am-5:45pm, Sa 9am-1pm. There are also smaller **information counters** in the domestic and international airports, and at Egmore and Central railway stations. Open daily 6am-9:30pm. **Tamil Tourism Development Corporation (TTDC) Office** (☎535 3351), near Chennai Central RW Station, books TTDC tours. Open daily "around the clock." Many **regional tourist agencies** (including those for Kerala, Rajasthan, Uttar Pradesh, and Himachal Pradesh) share an office at 28 C-in-C Rd. (☎827 9862). Open M-Sa 10am-5pm (closed 2nd Sa of the month).

Consulates: Australia (☎827 6036). 115 Mahatma Gandhi Rd. **France** (☎826 6561). 202 Prestige Point Bldg., 16 Haddows Rd. **Germany** (☎827 1747). 22 Ethiraj Salai. **Netherlands** (☎538 5829). Catholic Center, 64 Armenian St. **Sri Lanka** (☎827 0831). 9D Nawab Habibullah Ave. Open M-F 9am-5:15pm. **UK** (☎827 3136, 24hr. coverage). 24 Anderson Rd. **US** (☎811 2060). 220 Anna Salai, at Cathedral Rd. Open M-F 1:30-4:30pm. 24hr. emergency.

Immigration Office: Foreigners Registration Office (☎827 5424). Sastri Bhavan Annex, 26 Haddows Rd., off NH Rd. Applications dropped off in the morning are usually available later the same day. Bring 2 passport photos and copies of your passport and visa. Issues special permits for restricted areas such as the Andaman Islands. Open M-F 9:30am-6pm.

Currency Exchange: Dozens of banks and money changers all over town exchange most major currencies and traveler's checks. The **State Bank of India** and many of the other big national and international banks are on Anna Salai. **CitiBank,** 766 Anna Salai (☎852 2151), 500m past the tourist office, on the left as you head south, has 24hr. ATM machines that accept international cards. Open M-F 10am-2pm, Sa 10am-noon. **Thomas Cook** (☎827 2610). Eldorado Bldg., 112 NH Rd., and Ceebros Centre, 45 Montieth Rd. Open M-F 9am-6:30pm, Sa 9am-6pm. **American Express** (☎852 3628). Anna Salai, ground floor of Spencer Plaza Mall. Open M-F 9:30am-6:30pm, Sa 9:30am-2:30pm.

LOCAL SERVICES

Bookstore: Landmark, Apex Plaza, 3 NH Rd., is a huge store with a wide selection. Open M-Sa 9am-9pm, Su noon-9pm. **Higginbothams,** 814 Anna Salai. Open M-Sa 9am-7pm. **Giggles,** attached to the Taj Connemara hotel on Binny Rd., just off Anna Salai. The cramped, narrow premises are covered in towering piles of serious reading. In the back sits the most knowledgeable bookseller in all of Chennai. Open M-Sa 11am-8pm.

Libraries: American Library, US consulate bldg. (see **Consulates,** above). A/C library with all the latest magazines. Open M-F noon-6pm. **British Council,** 737 Anna Salai. Open Tu-Sa 11am-7pm.

Cultural Centers: Alliance Française, 40 College Rd., Nungambakkam (☎827 9803). Open M-Sa 9am-1pm and 3:30-6:30pm. **Max Mueller Bhavan,** 13 KN Khan Rd. (☎826 1314).

Markets: You can find everything from carnations to computers at **Parry's Corner,** NSC Bose Rd., in Georgetown, northeast of the city center. The nearby **Burma Bazaar** hawks imported goods. **Spencer Plaza Mall** on Anna Salai is a huge, modern, A/C shopping mall, with several good bookstores and ice cream parlors. Open daily 9:30am-9:30pm.

EMERGENCY AND COMMUNICATIONS

Police: Stations are all over town. Those closest to major tourist enclaves include: **Anna Salai** (☎852 1720), **Egmore** (☎825 0952), **Triplicane** (☎536 5610).

Hospital and Pharmacy: Apollo Hospital, 21 Greams Ln., off Greams Rd. (☎829 3333 or 829 0200, emergency 829 0792). The best hospital in Chennai. Hospital and attached pharmacy both open 24hr.

Internet: You will have no difficulty getting on line in Chennai; Internet facilities are everywhere. Particularly convenient for travelers are: **BPM Exports,** Shop No. 119, 1st fl., Spencer Plaza, Anna Salai. Rs30 per hr.; open daily 9:30am-9:30pm. **Internet Station,** on the left at the end of Kennet Lane as you walk toward Egmore railway station. Rs30 per hr.; open daily 7am-midnight. **Gee Gee Internet Centre,** just before Broadlands on Vallabha Agraharem St., Triplicane. Rs20 per hr.; open daily 24hr.

Post Office: The **GPO** is in Parry's Corner in Georgetown, in the northeast of the city. **Postal Code:** 600001. More convenient is the **Head Post Office** on Anna Salai. Open daily 10am-8:30pm. **Postal Code:** 600002. There is also a branch office in Egmore, on Kennet Ln. Open M-Sa 10am-4pm. **Postal Code:** 600008.

⚓ ACCOMMODATIONS

Hotels in Chennai cater to virtually every budget, but this is a big city, and if you've been on the road a while, you'll find Chennai pricey. Budget hotels are concentrated in Triplicane and on or around Gandhi Irwin Rd. and Kennet Ln. in Egmore. Reservations are always a good idea, especially during peak times (Oct.-Apr.). Check-out is 24hr., unless otherwise noted.

Broadlands, 16 Vallabha Agraharam, Triplicane (☎854 8131 or 854 5573). Opposite Star Theaters. This labyrinthine villa has been around for nearly 50 years. Lots of crumbling walls, plenty of old-world atmosphere, and several Bangladesh-bound busloads of bearded backpackers. Singles Rs150-160; doubles Rs200-350. ❶

Dayal-De Lodge, 486 Pantheon Rd. (☎822 7328; fax 825 1159). Just west of the intersection with Kennet Ln. Driveway leads to a villa removed from the hectic rush and push of the main road. High-ceilinged, pastel rooms with attached (seat) toilets. Singles Rs185; doubles Rs300. ❶

Salvation Army Red Shield Guest House, 31 Ritherdon Rd. Just north of Egmore Station off EUR Periyar High Rd. Very clean and welcoming hostel. The best rock-bottom budget deals in town. "French-style" windows, with typical British colonial shutters. Dorms Rs70; doubles with attached (seat) bath Rs250-500. ❶

YWCA International Guest House, 1086 EVR Periyar Salai (☎532 4234; fax 532 4263). Removed from the noisy streets by a tree-filled courtyard, the YWCA has beautiful lilac-scented rooms and bathrooms (seat toilets). Comfy wicker chairs and large TVs in common areas. Attached restaurant. If you're not a member, you can buy a month's YMCA membership (Rs20). Breakfast included. Very popular with middle-class family groups. Advance bookings recommended. Singles Rs500-680; doubles Rs630-800. ❸

Cristal Guest House, 34 CNK Rd., Triplicane (☎857 2721 or 858 5605). Down a small lane opposite Maharaja's restaurant, this modern, multi-storied hotel has clean, white-tiled doubles with attached (squat) bathrooms for Rs150. ❶

Hotel Regal, 15 Kennet Ln. (☎823 1766; fax 825 1261). Slightly run-down, standard-issue budget hotel. Rooms come complete with satellite TV and attached (squat) bathrooms. Attached restaurant. Singles Rs258-408; doubles Rs330-480. ❷

Hotel Pandian, 9 Kennet Ln. (☎825 2901 or 822 6558; fax 825 8459; hotelpandian@vsnl.com). The luxuries offered here—satellite TV, complimentary towels and soap, round-the-clock money-changers, and room service—all help you to deal with those jet-lagged, culture-shocked, first-night blues. Singles Rs450-800; doubles Rs700-1200. ❸

Paradise Guest House (☎854 7542). Next to Broadlands. Bright rooms with sparkling bathrooms. Phone and TV. Singles Rs200; doubles Rs250. ❶

Hotel Dasaprakash, 100 EVR Periyar Salai (☎825 5111). North of Egmore Station. This creaky old place has huge rooms with sitting areas and plenty of wooden furniture. A good mid-range option with atmosphere and decrepit charm. Attached restaurant and ice cream parlor. Singles Rs300-575; doubles Rs575-720. ❷

▊ FOOD

EGMORE

There are plenty of cheap places to eat in and around the budget hotels close to Egmore railway station, many of them all-but-identical "meal" joints serving up banana leaf *thalis* and other simple South Indian snacks.

Vasanta Bhavan, at the corner of Gandhi Irwin Rd. and Kennet Ln. The South Indian restaurant that follows you wherever you go. Excellent selection of food and extremely cheap prices ensure constant crowds. "Meals" Rs24-45. Open daily 6am-11:30pm. ❶

TAMIL NADU

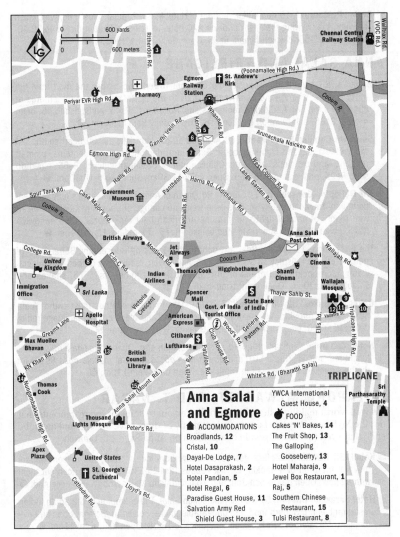

Jewel Box Restaurant, 934 EVR Periyar Salai, next to Hotel Blue Diamond. Chic and tidy multi-cuisine restaurant with lots of windows and a huge photo poster of the Manhattan skyline. Mutton *masala* Rs55, fish steak Rs105. Open daily 7:30am-11pm. ●

Raj, 9 Kennet Ln., attached to Hotel Pandian. Good mid-range hotel restaurant with ice-box A/C and excitable sound system. Tandoori and Chinese dishes as well as all the usual stuff. Most main courses Rs30-75. Open daily 6:30am-11pm. ●

Tulsi Restaurant, 6 College Rd. Versatile fast-food restaurant popular with students for its cheap and filling meals and its mind-numbing soundtrack of drum-machine-driven American "music." *Idlis* Rs15, burritos Rs40, chopsuey Rs70. Open daily 11am-11pm. ●

Ceylon Restaurant, 15 Kennet Ln., in front of Hotel Mass. Popular, mostly non-veg. cross between the whirring *thali*-joint and the A/C hotel restaurant. Mutton dishes Rs26-40, chicken Rs25-50, chicken *biryani* Rs35. Open daily 7am-11:30pm. ❶

ANNA SALAI AND TRIPLICANE

Buhari's, 83 Anna Salai, opposite the Tarapore Towers and across the road from the mosque, near where Anna Salai veers slightly to the right. Large, airy canteen area at street level, and an A/C dining room upstairs. *Rogan josh* Rs45, garlic fish Rs45, brain *masala* Rs35, half *tandoori* chicken Rs60. Open daily 8am-midnight. ❶

Southern Chinese Restaurant, 683 Anna Salai, on your right as you head south, just before the Thousand Lights mosque. Small and romantic, with red lanterns, painted dragons, and delicious, authentic Chinese meals. Szechuan chicken Rs65, egg-drop soup Rs25, pork dishes Rs55-65. Open daily 11:30am-3pm and 6-10:30pm. ❶

The Galloping Gooseberry, 11 Greams Rd., north of Anna Salai. Chennai's only "authentic Italian American eatery" comes as a welcome change of pace. Immaculately clean with plenty of natural light and genuine American light rock muzak. Club sandwich Rs75, pasta Rs75-95, American fried chicken Rs75. Open daily 11am-11pm. ❶

The Fruit Shop, 11 Greams Rd., next door to the Galloping Gooseberry. Barrel-loads of fruit are on open display all over this small, A/C haven, ready to be pulped into mineral water juice cocktails. Dozens of different fresh fruit juices Rs20-75, shakes and smoothies Rs20-70. Open daily 10am-midnight. ❶

Cakes 'N' Bakes, 32 NH Rd. (☎827 7075). 1km from the southernmost end of Anna Salai. Small, popular, A/C bakery sells ice creams and plays English language radio. Cakes Rs10-20, chili chicken roll Rs35. Open daily 10am-10pm. ❶

Hotel Maharaja, Triplicane High Rd., at the Wallajah end. Quality breakfast *idlis* (Rs6), lunchtime "meals" (Rs30-50), and dinner time *dosas* (special *masala dosa* Rs13) for the backpackers camped out in Triplicane. Open daily 7am-11pm. ❶

MYLAPORE, ALWARPET, AND T. NAGAR

It's well worth making a short dinner-time trek out to some of the restaurants that dot the Mylapore/Alwarpet area of town; many of them have a menu and an ambience that even the more upscale competition on Anna Salai can't match.

▧ **Kabul,** 35 TKK Rd. This place gets rave reviews from locals, with good reason: waiters move at the drop of a napkin, serving kebabs (Rs125-135) so soft you can cut them with a straw. Open daily noon-3pm and 7pm-midnight. Major credit cards accepted. ❷

Hotel Saravana Bhavan, 57 Dr. Radhakrishnan Salai. The champion of the South Indian restaurant world. Superb food and unbeatable prices, served in a clean, open-air environment. *Masala dosa* Rs17, fresh fruit juices Rs18-28. Open daily 6am-11pm. ❶

Coastline, Kaaraikudi, The Dhaba, and **Shogun,** at the Kaaraikudi Complex, 84 Dr. Radhakrishna Salai. 4 different restaurants in one complex: seafood, kebabs, Far Eastern, and South Indian food. Open daily 11am-4pm and 7-11:30pm.

Quiky's Coffee Pub, 93 GN Chetty Rd. next to the Residency Hotel, T. Nagar. Suspiciously like the American Starbucks. Quiky's has coffee (Rs30-40) and good sandwiches too (Rs30-60). Don't forget to ring the cowbell on your way out. Open daily 7am-11pm. ❶

Woodlands, 72/75 Dr. Radhakrishnan Salai, attached to the New Woodlands Hotel. Good-value hotel restaurant; efficient, prompt service in cool surroundings. South Indian *thali* Rs45, *idli* Rs10, *dosas* Rs18.50. Open daily 6:30am-10pm. ❶

⊙ SIGHTS

For a city of six million, Chennai is not big on sight-seeing. However, the city is a proud center of Carnatic culture, and the performances of traditional music and dance at one of its many *sabhas* are well worth a visit. (Free admission.)

FORT ST. GEORGE. Foremost among the city's traditional attractions, the huge Fort St. George was the first fort built by the British in India and a major enclave of colonial power for more than 300 years. This is where the modern city, not Chennai, began, when East India Company official Francis Day won permission from a local ruler to begin work on fortifications here in 1639. Work on the first buildings was completed (appropriately enough) on St. George's Day, 1640, and the fort continued to be the center of local administration until Independence and beyond. Many of the original buildings were damaged or destroyed during mid-18th-century French attacks, though several remain. These days, the fort complex is home to Tamil Nadu's state government, which has closed much of it to tourists.

Amid the everyday workings of the Tamil Nadu Legislative Assembly and Council, the ghost of the fort's colonial past lingers in the **Fort Museum,** which displays an impressive assortment of items from colonial times, including uniforms, weapons, coins, lithographs, and a collection of manuscripts written by Robert Clive. *(Open Sa-Th 10am-5pm. US$5 or equivalent in rupees.)*

South of the museum, the fascinating **St. Mary's Church,** consecrated in 1679, is the oldest Anglican church east of the Suez. The walls are covered with plaques dedicated to the immortal memory of various long-forgotten Englishmen and their wives. The church was built with a bomb-proof ceiling to withstand the frequent attacks on the fort. *(Open daily 9:30am-5pm. Services Su 9am.)*

Not far from Fort St. George rise the minarets of the **High Court** and the **Law College,** constructed in an Indo-Saracenic style in the mid-19th century and still in use.

MARINA BEACH. The 12km of the Marina Beach, one of the world's largest city beaches, are spectacular at dusk, when the setting sun casts an iridescent glow as peddlers hawk roasted peanuts and balloons. Palm readers lure customers, telling fortunes with the aid of seashells and tarot parrots. Few people swim here, in part because of the dangerously strong tides, in part because of the social current—wearing a swimsuit in public is frowned upon. Near the beach are **Anna Park** and the antenna-like **MGR Samadhi,** memorials to former Tamil Nadu Chief Ministers C.N. Annadurai and M.G. Ramachandran. There are also several decrepit swimming pools and a slimy aquarium. Deserted areas of the beach are often unsafe, especially at night.

GOVERNMENT MUSEUM. A string of six buildings, the Government Museum covers everything from archaeology and zoology to modern art. The main highlights are the excellent collection of stone sculpture in the main building, and the free-standing **bronze gallery,** whose unparalleled collection of Chola bronzes includes a complete set of characters from the *Ramayana* and a succession of excellent dancing Shivas. West of the bronze gallery is the less-than-thrilling **Children's Museum** with its large plastic dinosaurs. Next door is the **National Art Gallery,** housed in a splendid Indo-Saracenic edifice, built in 1906, that is more impressive than most of the stuff inside. *(Pantheon Rd., south of Egmore Station. Open Sa-Th 9:30am-5pm; ticket booth closes at 4:30pm. Rs3. Camera fee Rs10. Free tours at 10am, noon, 2, 4pm.)*

SRI KAPALEESWARAR TEMPLE. The Vijayanagar kings built the present structure in the 16th century and the majestic 37m *gopuram* (gateway) at its entrance after a much older temple on the shoreline was destroyed by the Portuguese. The great saint Ugnanasambandar sang a hymn here to Lord Kapaleeswarar in order to resurrect a girl who had died of a snake bite; a shrine and statue in front of the temple commemorate the event. Another explanation for the temple's name is derived from a mythical meeting of Brahma and Shiva on top of Mount Kailas. When Brahma failed to show Shiva the respect and courtesy due to him, an angry Shiva plucked off one of his *kapalams* (heads). In an act of regretful penance, Brahma came to Mylapore and installed Shiva's *linga* himself. Non-Hindus are allowed only as far as the outer courtyard, which houses a shrine to Parvati in peacock form. *(Mylapore, off Kutchery Rd. Open daily 5:30am-noon and 4-9:30pm.)*

About a ten-minute walk west from the Sri Kapaleeswarar Temple is the Portuguese-built **Luz Church,** the oldest in the city. The white-washed church has an altar in good condition and still retains a good deal of old-world atmosphere.

SANTHOME CATHEDRAL BASILICA. Built over the tomb of Thomas the Apostle, the basilica is an important pilgrimage site. It is believed that Thomas arrived in Kerala from Palestine in AD 52, and that he was killed in what is now Chennai in AD 72. About 1000 years later, Thomas's remains were moved inland, and a church was built close to the site of the present cathedral. In 1606, the church was refurbished and made into a cathedral by the Portuguese, who carted off most of the relics to Rome. All that is left here of Thomas now is a small piece of his little toe. In 1896, the church was rebuilt again, as a basilica. San Thome is more interesting for its historical and religious significance than for its aesthetic appeal, although the peaceful church sanctuary bears a large stained glass window depicting the apostle's life. A **museum** on the premises contains the cathedral's most prized relics: a small piece of the apostle's bone and a fragment of the spear that killed him. *(Eastern Mylapore, 6km south of Egmore. Open daily 6am-6pm. Museum open M-Sa 9:30am-12:30pm and 2-5:30pm.)*

SRI PARTHASARATHY TEMPLE. Originally built by the Pallavas in the 8th century and renovated by the Cholas and Vijayanagar kings, this temple is dedicated to Krishna. Its distinguishing feature is that it contains the images of four of Vishnu's avatars: Varaha (boar incarnation), Narasimha (lion incarnation), Rama, and Lord Venkatakrishna. *(Triplicane, west of South Beach Rd. Open daily 7am-noon and 4-8pm.)*

LITTLE MOUNT AND ST. THOMAS MOUNT. Just south of the Adyar River is **Little Mount,** a complex of mildly interesting caves where St. Thomas led the life of an ascetic, occasionally offering sermons from his rocky pulpit. According to local lore, the impressions in the caves are St. Thomas's handprints. Little Mount has two churches, both of which attract plenty of pilgrims. The older church was built over the caves in 1551 by the Portuguese. The newer one, Sacred to Our Lady of Health, was consecrated in 1971. *(Little Mount is about 8km south of the city center. Auto-rickshaws from downtown Rs40-50.)* About 5km southwest of Little Mount, 134 steep steps lead up to **Saint Thomas Mount (Great Mount),** where St. Thomas is said to have been killed after fleeing his home at Little Mount. The Portuguese church at the top was put up in 1523 on the site of a church built by Armenian traders nearly 1000 years earlier. The altar is supposed to stand on the very spot where St. Thomas died, and legend holds that the paintings over the altar were done by St. Luke. The "bleeding cross" that hangs above the altar was discovered while digging the foundations for a new church here in 1547. It is believed to have been shaped by the hands of the saint himself, and legend has it that the cross was seen to sweat blood on several occasions during the 16th century. The cool, stone church is a very mellow and atmospheric place, and there are fantastic views of the city and the airport from the hilltop. To get there, take a suburban train south from Egmore to St. Thomas Mt. station (Rs5). It is a 20min. walk or short auto-rickshaw ride from the station to the bottom of the steps leading up to the church. Those with an interest in Chennai's present-day Christian community can visit the largest church in India—the 15,000 member congregation of New Life Assembly of God. *(Near Little Mount. English services Su 8am and 4pm.)*

OTHER SIGHTS. Guindy National Park is a peaceful, though increasingly scruffy, place where herds of deer, antelope, and mongoose are supposed to run wild, but your chances of seeing anything more exciting than an occasional monkey are slim indeed. Before you can enter the National Park, you will need to get official permission from the wildlife warden, who can normally be found drinking tea with his cronies inside the Children's Park within the same grounds, in front of the entrance to the National Park itself. *(Open W-M 9am-5pm. Rs5.)* Also on the premises is an uninspiring **Snake Park.** *(Open W-M 8:30am-5:30pm. Rs3; camera fee Rs10.)* Eastern Adyar harbors the headquarters of the **Theosophical Society,** a spiritual movement founded by a pair of Americans in 1875. The mansion is surrounded by elaborate gardens, containing "The Great Banyan Tree," one of the largest in the world. *(☎ 491 7198. Open M-Sa 8:30-10am and 2-4pm.)*

ENTERTAINMENT

Chennai is home to India's second-largest film industry; taking in a Tamil talkie is a fun way to spend a couple of hours. You don't need to know much Tamil to figure out the plot, and you'll probably leave the theater having learned *something*. A cinema is on nearly every corner; many screen English-language movies. Two of the best movie theaters in Chennai are on Anna Salai, opposite the Head Post Office: **Devi** (☎ 855 5660) has four showings daily, at 11:45am, 2:45, 6:15, 9:45pm; **Shanti** cinema, almost next door, has showings at 1, 4, 7, 10pm. Tickets cost Rs6-40. Women should be careful—dark cinemas are popular hang-outs for dirty old men. *The Hindu* has listings of screenings and cultural events.

Performances are often given at the city's various music and dance academies *(sabhas)*. The **Carnatic Music and Dance Festival** takes place every year from early December to mid-January. **The Music Academy** (☎811 2231 or 811 5162), 115 E. Mowbray's Rd., often gives away free tickets for shows.

SEX, LIES, AND VIDEOTAPE While many of India's politicians involuntarily participate in the entertainment industry, Tamil Nadu's current Chief Minister, Jayalalitha Jayaram, can actually claim to have been a star of the silver screen. In 1990, the former actress and dancer and now leader of the regional AIADMK party came to power in the first installment of an up-and-down political saga that ran throughout the rest of the decade. JJ, or "Amma," as she is affectionately called by her groupies, quickly became embroiled in corruption charges that forced her to make a hasty exit in 1995. However, JJ made a sensational comeback in early 2001, when she managed to have herself re-elected, despite the charges against her. Doubts about the legitimacy (and even the legality) of JJ's re-election were not about to cramp her style, however, and one of her first acts after moving back into the Chief Minister's residence was to have several of her biggest rivals rounded up and arrested on charges of—you guessed it—corruption.

As if her political career weren't melodramatic enough, JJ's personal life has also been substantial tabloid material, including past romances with playboy-politician M.G. Ramachandran. In any event, JJ's biggest fan is herself. The city of Chennai is peppered with huge "cutout" images of Amma, sometimes 10-15 times larger than life.

☐ SHOPPING

Before you bust your wallet, take a moment to reflect on your itinerary. Many crafts and silks can be had for considerably less in smaller towns, where you can purchase handicrafts directly from the people who make them. Dozens of make-shift shops line the streets in **Luz** (directly south of city center in **Alwarpet**) and **Ranganathan St.** in **T. Nagar,** which is a bazaar of the South Indian variety: "cut-piece junctions" jockey for space with bangle and bindi sellers. **Radha Silk House (RASI),** 1 Sannadhi St., Mylapore, next to the Kapaleeswarar Temple, is a hot favorite, with silk fabrics and saris of all kinds in a profusion of colors. The base-ment has a decent selection of gift items, wooden carved boxes, brassware, and paintings. (☎494 1906. Open daily 9am-9pm. MC/V.) Also of interest are more glitzy shopping plazas, such as **Alsa Mall,** 149 Montieth Rd., Egmore, where you can buy beautiful *salwaar kameez.*

☐ NIGHTLIFE

Tamil Nadu only recently repealed its prohibition laws, and there is still a stigma attached to alcohol consumption. Most bars have heavily tinted win-dows and doors, as if to obscure the shameful goings-on inside. The situation is slightly better in Chennai than in most other places in Tamil Nadu, and nearly every three-to-five-star hotel has its own permit room. Most permit rooms are stocked with whatever liquor the owners can get their hands on. In a few of them, there is almost enough light for you to see what you're drinking. The bars in the **Pandian** and **New Victoria** hotels, both on Kennet Ln., are both reasonably pleasant by local standards. Around the corner in the Hotel Chan-dra Towers, **Bon Sante** has a good selection of the day's papers, which you can just about read by the flickering half-light of the (relatively restrained) TV in the corner. A good place for a pre-dinner drink if you're eating at one of the restaurants on Dr. Radhakrishnan Salai is the bar in the **Hotel Savera,** next to the New Woodlands Hotel. It's well-lit, with comfortable bamboo chairs and well-behaved TVs, and your beer comes with a tasty selection of munchies and snacks. Most bars are open daily 11am-11pm.

If you're looking for more serious kinds of nightlife, you've come to the wrong place. For glitzy discos and other forms of stroboscopy, the five-star hotels are the venues to look into, though many of these places seem to come and go with the seasons. At press time, the **G2 (Gatsby's)** disco, in the Park Sheraton at the bottom of TTK (Mowbray's) Rd., was one of the few places open for late-night dancing.

KANCHIPURAM காஞ்சிபுரம்   ☎04112

A huge, smoky city still dominated by the towering *gopurams* of its ancient tem-ples, Kanchipuram is a major center of pilgrimage and one of Hinduism's seven most sacred cities. The city's name comes from the words *Ka* (another name for Brahma, the creator) and *anchi* ("worship")—Brahma worshiped Vishnu and the goddess Kamakshi here. Some magnificent temples were built in the city between the 4th and 8th centuries, when Kanchi was the capital of the Pallava kings. Kanchi was also the seat of the guru Shankara (AD 780-820) and has been a center of phi-losophy and learning ever since. Today, Kanchipuram is famous as the producer of some of the finest saris in India, and silk emporiums are everywhere along the city's major thoroughfares. Impressive as the temples are, unless you're a serious pilgrim, Kanchipuram is best seen as a daytrip from Chennai. The modern city is a dusty, smoky, fume-filled wreck of a place, with little to offer the traveler.

TRANSPORTATION

Trains: Railway station, Station Rd. (☎23149). East of the Vaikuntha Perumal Temple. Take E. Raja Veethi north, and follow the signs. This is not a busy place; there are only five passenger trains a day, which run to **Anakkonam** (3hr., 9:05am and 6:40pm, Rs16) and **Chennai** (3hr.; 8:30am and 6pm, direct 7:05am; Rs16) via **Chengalpattu.**

Buses: The chaotic **bus stand,** hidden behind storefronts, is at the intersection of Kamarajar and Nellukkara St. To: **Chennai** (#76B and 76C, 2½hr., every 30min., Rs18); **Chengalpattu** (#212H and 212B, 1½hr., frequent 4:15am-10pm, Rs8.50); **Mahabalipuram** (2hr., 10 per day 4:15am-8:30pm, Rs25); **Vellore** (2½hr., every 30min. 5am-10:30pm, Rs15.25). Frequent buses to **Pondicherry** depart from Chengalpattu.

Local Transportation: Auto-rickshaws can be flagged down on Kamarajar St. or Gandhi Rd. or picked up next to the bus stand. A ride from the bus stand to the outskirts of town should cost no more than Rs25.

ORIENTATION AND PRACTICAL INFORMATION

The **bus stand** has one main entrance on **Kamarajar St.** (formerly known as Kossa St.), which runs north-south through the center of town, where many shops and eating places are located. You can also find food and lodging on **Nellukkara St.,** which runs perpendicular to Kamarajar St. at its northern end. **Gandhi Rd.** runs parallel to Nellukkara St., about 500m down from the bus stand, turning into **T. Nambi Koil St.** Most of Kanchi's famous silk emporiums are along these roads.

Tourist Office: There is no official tourist office, but you can get basic info and maps at the TTDC-sponsored **Hotel Tamil Nadu,** Railway Station Rd. (☎22553 or 22554). Near the railway station.

Currency Exchange: None of the banks in Kanchipuram deals with foreign exchange. In an emergency, try one of the big hotels, such as the Baboo Soorya (see below).

Market: Rajaji Market, at the intersection of Railway and Gandhi Rd. Sells all the fruit, vegetables, and mutton you could want. Open daily 7am-7pm.

Police: Police Control Room, Kamarajar St. (☎22000 or 22805).

Pharmacy: Tamil Nadu Medicals, 25 Nellukkara St. (☎22285). West of the intersection with Kamarajar St. Open M-Sa 8am-11:30pm.

Hospital: Manohar General Hospital, Railway Rd. (☎22102). A private facility.

Internet: Dishnet DSL HUB Internet Browsing Center, Kamarajar Rd. Turn left out of the bus station, and it will be on your right after 250m. Dozens of lightning-quick computers in icy A/C cold. Rs30 per hr. Open daily till midnight.

Post Office: GPO, Railway Rd. Open M-F 9am-5pm. **Postal Code:** 631502.

ACCOMMODATIONS

Most of Kanchi's budget hotels are along the busy, noisy streets around the bus station. All are fine for a short, one-night stay, but if fresh air and clean bathrooms are a priority, then this is a good place to upgrade to a mid-range accommodation.

Hotel Jaybala International (☎24348). 504 Gandhi Rd. Almost luxurious, mid-range hotel under the same management as Kanchipuram's most popular restaurant and one of its most successful silk emporiums. Satellite TV, snappy service, and soap. Singles Rs125; doubles Rs340. AmEx/MC/V. ❶

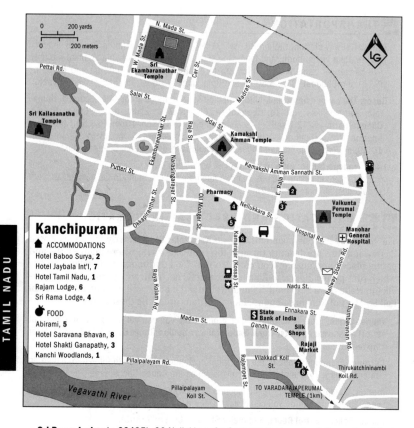

Kanchipuram

▲ ACCOMMODATIONS
Hotel Baboo Surya, 2
Hotel Jaybala Int'l, 7
Hotel Tamil Nadu, 1
Rajam Lodge, 6
Sri Rama Lodge, 4

● FOOD
Abirami, 5
Hotel Saravana Bhavan, 8
Hotel Shakti Ganapathy, 3
Kanchi Woodlands, 1

Sri Rama Lodge (☎ 22435). 20 Nellukkara St. Opposite the bus stand. Rumor has it that this is where Leonardo DiCaprio comes to escape the paparazzi. Rumor is probably wrong, but this is about as good as it gets budget-wise in Kanchipuram. Simple and sometimes-clean rooms with attached (squat) bath. Singles Rs85; doubles Rs160. ❶

Hotel Tamil Nadu (☎ 23428, fax 22552). Two minute walk from the station on Railway Station Rd. Dark and deserted government-run hotel. It might just be worth putting up with the inflated prices and curt service for the peace that comes with the out-of-the-way location; this is one of the few hotels where you won't be disturbed by the noise of buzzing buses all through the night. Doubles with attached (seat) bath Rs350-650. ❶

Rajam Lodge (☎ 22519). 9 Kamarajar St. Near the bus stand entrance. Ask for a double on the 2nd floor, where most of the rooms have windows (a scarce commodity in this town). Squat toilets. Singles Rs70; doubles Rs110. ❶

Hotel Baboo Surya (☎ 22555, fax 22556). 85 E. Raja Veethi. Near the Perumal Temple, a 5min. walk from the bus stand. If you want glitz and polish, you've come to the right place. One of the best hotels in town, and you get what you pay for: immaculate rooms, seat toilets, and the morning paper. All rooms have Star TV. Excellent attached restaurant. Singles Rs300-450; doubles Rs575-525. 20% luxury tax. AmEx/MC. ❷

🍴 FOOD

🍽 **Hotel Saravana Bhavan,** 504 Gandhi Rd. Next to Hotel Jaybala International. The most popular spot in town—with good reason. Dozens of open-air tables and a cool A/C room inside. Splendid "rice meals" (Rs28) 10am-4pm and 7-10pm. Ghee-roasted *masala dosa* Rs63. Open daily 7am-10pm. ❶

Hotel Shakti Ganapathy, E. Raja Veethi St. About 2min. north from the bus stand. Typical South Indian "meals" joint, Shakti serves all your old favorites. An always-crowded cross between a Salvation Army soup kitchen and a summer camp cafeteria. Onion *uttappam* Rs13, "meals" Rs18, *idli* Rs5 per piece. Open daily 5:30am-8:30pm. ❶

Kanchi Woodlands, inside Hotel Baboo Surya. Igloo-like restaurant with white ceilings, white walls, white floors, and A/C cold enough to make a polar bear shiver. Excellent North and South Indian food. South Indian *thali* Rs35, continental breakfast Rs50. Open daily 7am-10:30pm. ❶

Abirami, 109B Kamaraj St. Underneath the hotel of the same name. Lively and popular "meals" place set far enough back from the street to be out of the fumes without losing the hustle-and-bustle views. Meals Rs18, *tiffin* Rs5-15. Open daily 6am-11pm. ❶

👁 SIGHTS

The temples here are among India's most sacred for Hindus. They are also fairly spread out. Auto-rickshaw drivers will ask for Rs150-200 for a tour, including "waiting charges." An alternative is to rent a bicycle for the day. Below, the temples are arranged in a roughly clockwise order.

SRI KAILASANATHA TEMPLE. Built by Rajasimba Pallava in the first quarter of the 8th century, this temple is the oldest building in Kanchi. Its relatively modest size and soft amber sandstone are both characteristic of Pallava temples; the famous shore temple at Mahabalipuram was built by the same team at about the same time. The interior of the wall surrounding the shrine is marked by a row of 58 small meditation chambers. In some, traces of the temple's frescoes can still be seen. On the rear wall of the sanctum are carvings of Shiva performing the Urdhwa Tandava dance of destruction. The inner sanctum houses a *linga* to which it is believed Vishnu prayed for help in defeating the demon Tripurantaka. The temple is often relatively empty since most visitors opt for either the Kamakshi Amman or Sri Ekambaranathar temples in the center of town. (*1½km out of town. Follow Nellukkara St. westward until it becomes Putteri St. Sri Kailasanatha is on the right past a small lake. Open daily 8:30am-noon and 4-6pm. To make the most of your visit, arrive before sunset.*)

SRI EKAMBARANATHAR TEMPLE. The magnificent white *gopuram* of the Sri Ekambaranathar Temple dominates the skyline all across the northern part of town. The origins of the temple are recorded in the *sthalapurana*, which recounts Parvati's mischief when she jokingly covered the eyes of her soon-to-be husband Shiva and upset the process of creation and destruction. Shiva was so angry that he ordered Parvati down to earth, where she came to a mango tree on the banks of the river Kampa in Kanchi and fashioned a *linga* of sand. To test her devotion, Shiva placed before her numerous obstacles, all of which Parvati overcame. Finally, Shiva let the Ganga flow from his hair, hoping to inundate Kanchi and wash the *linga* away. But Parvati's devotion was so great that she held tight, protecting the *linga* through the torrent. Duly impressed, Shiva took her back.

Shiva and Parvati were married under the same mango tree that now stands inside the temple grounds. It is from this tree that the temple derives its name—the root "Eka" means "mango tree." Each of its four branches—they represent the four books of the Vedas and are supposedly 3500 years old—is said to produce a different type of leaf, as well as fruit of a different taste. Locals believe that eating the fruit cures women of infertility, and many women hang brightly colored ribbons and offerings from the branches. Also within the inner sanctum is the *linga* fashioned by Parvati. A cavernous hallway surrounding the sanctum houses many *lingas* and statues of the 63 Alvar poet-saints. These colorful works are displayed during the temple's festivals in April and July. Shiva and Parvati's wedding anniversary is celebrated during the full moon in March. *(Puthupalayam St. leads directly north to the temple. Open daily 6am-12:30pm and 4-8pm. Puja 6, 7am, noon, 4, 5, 9pm.)*

KAMAKSHI AMMAN TEMPLE. *Gopurams* cast in soft shades of yellow, green, and pink and capped with tiny wooden spires adorn this temple, dedicated to Kamakshi, an incarnation of the goddess Devi and the town's resident deity. The temple is one of India's sacred *shakti pithas*, sites devoted to the worship of the female element in creation (*shakti*). The inner sanctum (inaccessible to non-Hindus) is a squarish chamber with inscriptions on all sides. Outside, a golden tower gleams in the sunlight. The sacred tank in the back is also steeped in legend—Vishnu supposedly sent two servants-turned-demons to bathe here to cleanse them of their evil ways. *(From W. Raja St., turn right onto Amman Koli St. Photography not permitted. Open daily 5am-12:30pm and 4-8:30pm.)*

VAIKUNTA PERUMAL TEMPLE. This temple, dedicated to Vishnu, is one of the oldest in Kanchipuram. Ancient texts proclaim that those who worship devotedly on the holiday of *Maha Shivaratri* will have sons who will be followers of Vishnu. The courtyard surrounding the inner sanctum is lined with granite pillars and carvings depicting the Pallava kings, battle scenes, and musicians. The back left corner has a panel showing Xuanzang, the Chinese Buddhist pilgrim who traveled all over India during the 7th century.

The inner sanctum (with its images of Vishnu) is usually locked, but a bit of baksheesh to the key-wielding guard can work wonders. The central spire contains three images of Vishnu, one on top of the other. On the ground floor he is seen sitting; on the second floor, reclining on the serpent *ananta;* on the top, standing in an ascetic pose. A small walkway around the *vimana* is filled with well-preserved panels of Vishnu and his consort Lakshmi. *(From E. Raja St., turn right; the temple is several hundred meters ahead. Open daily 8am-noon and 4-8pm.)*

☎ SHOPPING

Each Kanchi sari is woven by hand and takes between 15 days and one month to complete. Kanchi silks start around Rs1000 and skyrocket into the tens of thousands for elaborate wedding saris. Expect to pay at least Rs3000 for a good quality sari with a fair amount of *zari* (pure gold thread) and an intricately woven *pallu* (the part that drapes over the shoulder). Store owners should give you at least a Rs1200 "discount" off the first price named. Most owners will gladly take you to the back of the stores to show you silk yarn and demonstrate the process of adding *zari* designs onto saris. Turn right onto the road perpendicular to Sannadhi St. (outside Varadaraja Perumal Temple), and take a left at **Ammangar St.,** which is full of silk weavers who are eager to demonstrate their craft. Weavers' cooperatives cluster near temple entrances, where you'll probably be accosted by salesmen wielding business cards.

VELLORE வெல்லூர்   ☎ 0416

Vellore, 145km southwest of Chennai, is not for the claustrophobic. Vendors choke every inch of the narrow streets, and masses of pedestrians and bicycles scramble toward the famous hospital in the city center, to which hundreds of people come every day in hope of a cure. For the traveler, Vellore's well-preserved relics provide insight into its past as a medieval city of the Vijayanagar kingdom.

TRANSPORTATION. Buses run from the bus stand on PTC Road to **Chennai** (3½hr., every 10min., Rs28) and **Trichy** (5hr., 5 per day, Rs60). PATC goes to: **Bangalore** (6hr., 11 per day 5:30am-10pm, Rs57); **Chennai** (4hr., every 15min., Rs31.50); **Kanchi** (2hr., every 30min., Rs14); **Tirupati** (3hr., every hr. 7am-11pm, Rs18).

ORIENTATION AND PRACTICAL INFORMATION. Everything you need is in the immediate vicinity of the **CMC Hospital,** in the center of town. (☎222102. Open 24hr.) Most restaurants are on **Ida Scudder Rd.,** which runs directly parallel to the hospital. **Babu Rao St.,** parallel to and south of Ida Scudder Rd., and **KVS Chetty St.,** running south from the mouth of Babu Rao, front most of Vellore's hotels and lodges. The **Main Bazaar,** two streets south, and parallel to KVS St., leads straight to the fort and temple entrances. The temple's major cross street is **PTC Rd.;** turning right onto it from the Main Bazaar will lead you to the **public bus stand,** which is mostly useless; turning left, walking about1km, and crossing the street will get you to the **private bus stand,** which services major destinations. **Currency exchange** is just opposite the hospital at the Tamil Nadu Mercantile Bank on Mundy St. The **North Vellore Police Station** (☎200021), on the corner of PTC Rd. by the bus station, and the **pharmacy** (☎222121), attached to the hospital, are both open 24hr. The **post office** is on Katpadi Rd. (Open M-F 10am-6pm, Sa 10am-4pm.) **Postal Code:** 632004.

ACCOMMODATIONS AND FOOD. Hotel vacancies increase the farther you get from the hospital. **VDM Lodge ❶,** on Beri Bakkali St., has small but clean rooms. (☎224008. Check-out 24hr. Singles Rs70; doubles Rs100.) **Srinivasa Lodge ❶,** opposite VDM Lodge, has slightly bigger, well-lit rooms, all with attached bath and free hot water from 5 to 8am. (☎226389. Singles Rs135; doubles Rs160.) Vellore's grimy diners are not to be trifled with. At **Chinatown ❶,** on Arcott Rd. above Hotel Susil Classic, bow-tied waiters serve fried rice (Rs35), wonton soup (Rs30), and *naan* (Rs18) in a small, cool dining room. (Open daily noon-3pm and 6-11pm.)

SIGHTS. Legend has it that the **Vellore Fort** was built in an attempt to lift a curse placed on the temple that previously stood on this site. The town of Vellore sprouted from this huge granite fortress and its beautiful moat, constructed in the 13th century under the rule of the Vijayanagar kings. For several turbulent centuries, control of the fort changed hands regularly, beginning in the 1600s when the Bhamini Sultans occupied it. The Sultans were ousted by the Marathas, who held power until they were booted out by the Mughals. In the 18th century, the British took over. The fort was the scene of the short-lived **Vellore Mutiny,** in which South Indian troops in the British Army protested changes in headgear and uniform by storming the fort. Several British officers were killed before the mutiny was put down by the no-nonsense Colonel Robert Gillespie, who had the mutineers blown to pieces. Today, there are picnics outside and several government offices, schools, and businesses inside, as well as a **museum** containing some interesting stone carvings. (On PTC Rd. Fort open daily 6am-8pm. Free. Museum open Sa-Th 9:30am-5pm. Free.) The beautiful limestone **Jalakanteshwara Temple** was built just before the fort, and its white statues and carvings remain in superb condition. On top of the *gopuram* above the main entrance is a small carving of the fort's builder and his wife. To the left of the entrance, a series of spectacularly carved outer pillars, all carved from one stone, supports a great hall. (The temple is inside the fort.)

NEAR VELLORE

👁 TIRUVANNAMALAI

> **Buses** go to and from: **Bangalore** (5½hr., every 30min., Rs52); **Vellore** (2hr., every 15min., Rs19); **Villapuram** (3hr., every 15min., Rs18).

Tiruvannamalai's main attraction is the **Siva-Parvati Temple of Arunachaleswar** (open daily 6am-8pm), a truly awe-inspiring monument, though the town's tranquility also comes as a welcome relief from the bustle of other South Indian cities. A peaceful morning can be had watching the sun rise over the ivory-colored *gopurams* and exploring the five gigantic courtyards. Opposite the eastern temple wall—the one you'll hit coming from the bus stand—the **Sri Kalaimagal Lodge ❶**, N. Othavadai St., has large rooms with floors as clean as *thali* plates. (☎24215. Singles Rs100; doubles Rs150.) The sparkling **Hotel Aryas ❶**, lights the way to and from the bus stand but doesn't have many bright ideas beyond *idli* and *dosa* (Rs12). Okay, two: *puri* or *pongal* (Rs9). Open daily 6:30am-10:30pm.

MAHABALIPURAM மஹாபலீஷ்புரம் ☎ 04114

Until about 20 years ago, Mahabalipuram was a quiet little fishing village on the Bay of Bengal. And then came the tourists, drawn here in their thousands by the prospect of sun, sand, and sea, and by the unique collection of stone sculpture left behind from Mahabalipuram's glory days over 1000 years ago, when it was the major sea port of the Pallava dynasty. Today, Mahabalipuram is dominated by the tourist trade, and there seems to be a hotel, restaurant, or overzealous tour operator lurking behind almost every door. There is even a festival devoted to all the foreign visitors: the Tourist Dance Festival, which takes place from late December to late January every year, when the tourist madness really hits its peak. With sunset, calm descends on Mahabalipuram, and the incessant pushes of tourists and touts are softened by the beauty of the evening sea. Fresh fish and cool breezes keep cafes and rooftop restaurants pleasant and popular until the early hours.

▐▆ TRANSPORTATION

Buses: The **bus stand** is on E. Raja St. To: **Chennai** (2hr., every 30min. 5:15am-11:15pm, Rs27); **Chengalpattu** (#212H and 108B; 1hr.; every 30min. 7:40am-3pm, 4 evening buses 4-9:30pm; Rs12); **Kanchi** (#157M and 212H, 4 per day 5am-9pm, Rs25.50); **Kovalam** (#117, 118, 188V; 30min.; 13 per day 5:45am-8pm; Rs6); **Tirupati** (2½hr.; 5:20am, 1:30, 3pm; Rs25); **Pondicherry** (2½hr., every 30min. 6:30am-10:15pm, Rs25.50).

Local Transportation: Auto-rickshaws and **tourist taxis** wait outside the bus stand, but you won't need them unless you stay at one of the beach resorts outside town. Several places rent **bikes,** including Moonraker's, on Othavadai St. (Rs 25 per day).

> **❗ WARNING.** The Bay of Bengal can be very dangerous, and many people drown every year. Ask at the tourist office and at your hotel about the advisability of swimming. Even if you are an experienced swimmer, don't underestimate the force of the undertow. And don't even *look* at the water if you've been drinking.

ORIENTATION AND PRACTICAL INFORMATION

Finding your way around in Mahabalipuram is a cinch. From the **inter-city bus stand**, it's a 5min. walk north (left) along **East Raja St.** to the **tourist office.** On the way, you'll cross three east-west streets. The first, unmarked, small street to the right (look for Baskin Robbins) leads to the hospital and several lodges and restaurants on Thirikula St., which runs parallel to E. Raja St. The second, larger, unmarked street is **Othavadai Rd.,** which leads east to more lodges and restaurants. A bit farther north, **TKM Rd.** cuts across E. Raja St. on its left-hand side, leading to the **bank.** At the tourist office, E. Raja St. becomes **Kovalam Rd.,** which stretches out of town to the beach resorts and Tiger Cave. To get to the **Shore Temple** and the beach, take a right from the bus stand onto E. Raja St., and then take a left onto **Shore Temple Rd.** To get to the **mandapams** and Arjuna's Penance, turn right on Shore Temple Rd. and then right again onto W. Raja St., parallel to E. Raja St.

Tourist Office: TTDC (☎ 42232). E. Raja St. Open daily 7:30am-5:30pm.

Currency Exchange: Indian Overseas Bank, TKM Rd. Walk north on E. Raja St., and turn left onto TKM. Changes cash and AmEx and Thomas Cook traveler's checks. Open M-F 10am-2pm, Sa 10am-noon. **Prithvi Exchange,** 69E. Raja St. Right out of the bus stand. Changes most currencies and traveler's checks. Open M-Sa 10am-6:30pm.

Mahabalipuram (Mamallapuram)

ACCOMMODATIONS
Hotel Sea Breeze, **3**
Hotel Tamil Nadu II: Camping, **10**
Lakshmi Lodge, **2**
Mamalla Bhavan Annexe, **6**
Ramakrishna Lodge, **5**

FOOD
Golden Palate Restaurant, **6**
La Vie en Rose, **9**
Mamalla Bhavan, **8**
Moonrakers, **4**
New Papillon Restaurant, **7**
Santana Beach Restaurant, **1**

TAMIL NADU

Police: Police Station (☎ 42221). E. Raja St. Next to the tourist office. Open 24hr.

Hospital: Suradeep Hospital (☎ 42099 or 42448). Thirukula St. Next to Baskin Robbins, has a **24hr. pharmacy.** If you're seriously ill, your best bet is to go to Chennai.

Internet: VAT Telecom Center (☎ 42711). E. Raja St. Just north of Othavadai St. Open 5:30am-10:30pm.

Post Office: On a small lane off E. Raja St., near the tourist office. Open M-Sa 9am-4pm. **Postal Code:** 603104.

ACCOMMODATIONS

You won't struggle to find a place to stay in Mahabalipuram. Dozens of cheap hotels have sprung up to cater to the tourists who came here during high season. Most of the cheapest places are on or near E. Raja, Othavadai, and Thirakua St.

Ramakrishna Lodge (☎ 42331 or 42431). 8 Othavadai St. One of the largest of the budget places, as well as one of the best. Wide rooms with big beds and mosquito screens, arranged around a large courtyard filled with potted plants. Attached bath, seat toilets, and fresh hot water. Singles Rs75; doubles Rs125. ❶

Lakshmi Lodge (☎ 42463). 5 Othavadai St. Down the dirt road to the right after Moonrakers Restaurant. Sea-side lodge full of foreigners. Bright, well-kept rooms, many overlooking the sea. Most bathrooms have seat toilets. Staff will arrange practically anything for guests, including bikes, massage, and astrology readings. Attached rooftop restaurant. Checkout noon. Rooms Rs100-250. ❶

Hotel Tamil Nadu II: Camping Site (☎ 42287). Off Shore Temple Rd. You can't miss the billboard. Government-run hotel, with the cheapest dorms in town. You can pitch a tent out back, but they'll charge you Rs100 for the privilege. Dorms Rs50; cottages Rs300-450. ❶

Hotel Sea Breeze (☎ 43035, fax 43065). Down the dirt road to the right, off Othavadai St., past Moonrakers. Marble floors, wooden furniture, and breezy balconies. Pool can be used by non-guests for Rs75. Singles Rs300; doubles Rs450-950. ❶

Mamalla Bhavan Annexe (☎ 42060, fax 42160). 104 E. Raja St. The swankiest and most luxurious budget spot in town. Spacious rooms have marble-tiled floors with double beds and cable TVs. Attached restaurant. Doubles Rs350-700. ❷

FOOD

Mahabalipuram is full of restaurants offering backpackers' favorites like *muesli*, banana pancakes, and seafood, but you'll have a difficult time finding straightforward Indian food. Beer is available, though it's not on most menus; just ask. Many places close down off season; most of the restaurants listed below should be open throughout the year.

Moonrakers, Othavadai St. European breakfasts are popular (*muesli* and yogurt Rs40), but the mellow vibes keep travelers here throughout the day. The most-visited backpacker hangout in town. Fish and chips Rs100, calamari Rs100, honey crepes Rs25. Open daily 7am-1am. ❷

Santana Beach Resort, at the end of Othavadai St. A simple little place on the beach, with tables set in the sand overlooking the sea. Fish Rs75-150, calamari Rs100. Open 11am-11pm. ❷

New Papillon Restaurant, Shore Temple Rd. Opposite the turnoff for the Hotel Tamil Nadu. Cute little pastel-painted place with clean white tablecloths and a small selection of Western music. Grilled snapper Rs70, jumbo prawns Rs100, fresh fruit juices Rs25. Open daily 8am-10pm. ❶

La Vie En Rose, E. Raja St. Near the bus stand, 150m down the left-hand side. Small and quiet upstairs balcony, away from the heat and hassles of the street. Despite the French name, the menu here is pretty much the same one you will see in every other restaurant in town. Grilled fish Rs70, beer Rs70. Open daily 7am-10:30pm. ●

Golden Palate Restaurant, 104 E. Raja St. Inside Mamalla Bhavan Annexe. Good, classy A/C joint with professional service and a good range of North and South Indian food. *Tandoori gobi* Rs55, *malai kofta* Rs45, South Indian *thali* Rs50. Open daily 7am-10:30pm. ●

Mamalla Bhavan, off E. Raja St. Opposite the bus stand. The most popular "meals hotel" around. If you can't take the tourists any more, come here for your daily dose of *dosas*. Special "meals" Rs27. Open daily 5am-9:30pm. ●

👁 SIGHTS

Mahabalipuram has an incredible collection of well-preserved sculpture, weathered by hundreds of years' worth of sun, sand, and surf. Scholars agree that most of these masterpieces were sculpted under the patronage of the 7th-century Pallava leader Narasimhavarman I, who went by the fearsome name Mamalla, which means "Great Wrestler"—hence the town's (official) name. The sights are all in the southern part of town, within easy walking distance of most of the hotels.

SHORE TEMPLE. Dedicated to Shiva and Vishnu, Mahabalipuram's famous shore temple was built during the 8th century and was probably the first South Indian temple built entirely of stone. The Pallavas' maritime exploits helped spread their culture far and wide, and echoes of the Shore Temple's lion carvings and stocky spires can be seen throughout South Asian temple architecture from the period. Inside the temple are a flower-strewn image of Vishnu reclining on the serpent Sesa and a broken, fluted-granite Shiva *linga*. Outside the temple, carved panels depict scenes from the lives of its Pallava creators. There has been speculation that the Shore Temple once served as a lighthouse, which would explain its oddly elongated *vimana*. It is now protected and kept litter-free by the Archaeological Society of India, which for the past 12 months or so has also ensured that most foreign visitors get no closer to the temple than the well-guarded perimeter fence, thanks to the US$10 charge that non-Indians are now expected to pay. *(On Shore Temple Rd., jutting into the Bay of Bengal, 1km to the right of the bus stand. Open daily 6am-5:30pm. US$10 or equivalent in rupees includes admission to the five Rathas.)*

ARJUNA'S PENANCE AND KRISHNA MANDAPAM. One of the largest bas-relief sculptures in the world, Arjuna's Penance is the most impressive sight in town. Particularly engaging are the elegant, humorous depictions of animals and birds which include whimsical renderings of an elephant family and an ascetic, meditating cat surrounded by dancing rats. The spectacle itself is easy enough to admire, but scholars are still scratching their heads trying to figure out what it's all supposed to mean. According to one widely accepted theory, Arjuna's Penance depicts a story from the *Mahabharata*—the scrawny man standing on one leg is the penitent archer Arjuna, who is gazing through a prism and imploring Shiva to give him the *pashupatashastra*, a powerful magic arrow. Other historians believe that the images represent Rama's ancestor, Bhagiratha, begging the gods to give the Ganga River to the people of the world. The gods have agreed to comply with Bhagiratha's request, and the whole of creation has turned out to watch the miracle of Ganga gushing down from the Himalayas. *(In town, just behind the bus stand on W. Raja St.)* **Krishna Mandapam,** a large mid-7th-century bas-relief, shows Krishna holding up Mount Govardhana to protect his relatives and their cows from the floods brought on by the god Indra. Other panels illustrate scenes from Krishna's life, including his flirtatious play *(lila)* with the milkmaids *(gopis)*. *(Just meters away from Arjuna's Penance; to the left as you face the monument.)*

TAMIL NADU

RATHAS. This collection of worn yet stunning monoliths known as the **Pancha Pandava Rathas,** was carved during the reign of Narasimhavarman I, and they are thought to be scale models of temples known to the Dravidian builders of the 7th century. The five temples were clearly influenced by Buddhist temple architecture and are named for the five Pandava brothers, the heroes of the *Mahabharata.* The largest, the **Dharmaraja Ratha,** is adorned with various carvings of demi-gods and Narasimhavarman. The complex also includes life-size animals carved out of stone. (*About 1½km south of town along E. Raja St. US$10 or the equivalent in rupees, includes admission to the Shore Temple.*)

MANDAPAMS AND SURROUNDING MONUMENTS. The hilly area behind the bus stand and Arjuna's Penance is strewn with massive boulders and 10 small **mandapams** (cave temples), which depict tales from Hindu mythology. Finding your way from one *mandapam* to the next is not difficult; a well-marked path links most of the main monuments. Just around the corner to the right from Arjuna's Penance is the **Ganesha Ratha,** containing an image of the elephant-headed son of Shiva and Parvati. North of the *ratha* and off to the left is **Krishna's Butterball,** a massive boulder balanced on the side of a hill. The name comes from popular stories of Krishna's youth, which recount an incident when the baby Krishna was caught stealing *ghee* from an urn. North of the Butterball and next to a Pallavan water tank is the **Trimurti Cave,** which contains shrines to Shiva, Vishnu, and Brahma; all are depicted with their right hands in the *abhya* or blessing pose. The **Kotikal Mandapam,** dating from the turn of the 7th century, is down the hill to the left. A small cell in the back is guarded by stone carvings of female attendants.

Heading south back toward Arjuna's Penance, you'll first pass the 7th-century **Varaha Mandapam.** Its four panels represent the goddess Varaha raising the earth from the ocean. Most impressive is the one on the left, which depicts Vishnu in the form of a boar with the goddess Bhumidevi (Earth) seated in his lap. Another panel depicts the goddess of wealth, Lakshmi, accompanied by elephants.

Up the steep hill directly west of the Krishna Mandapam is the decaying **Rayala Gopuram.** This uncompleted structure bears slender vertical panels that portray the 10 incarnations of Vishnu. From the Krishna Mandapam, it's a short walk south to the **Ramanuja Mandapam,** built in the mid-7th-century and almost completely ruined by vandals who chiseled away at many of the temple's elaborate panels. From here, you can see the 100-year-old **New Lighthouse.** Next to the lighthouse is a Shiva temple at an especially high elevation which was used as a lighthouse until the turn of the last century.

TIGER CAVE. The so-called Tiger Cave is actually the remains of an 8th-century Pallava temple sacred to the mighty goddess Durga. A large rock-hewn monument survives and is decorated with a dozen or so carvings of snarling tigers, Durga's constant companions. Several meters away, down a small flights of steps, is a small, wind-worn Shiva temple. (*About 3km north of Mahabalipuram on the beach just off the main road to Chennai.*)

GOVERNMENT COLLEGE OF SCULPTURE AND ARCHITECTURE. Hundreds of artists-in-training learn their craft at this lively seaside complex. Contact the tourist office or college directly to make an appointment to have a look around. (☎ *42261. About 3km north of Central Mahabalipuram along Kovalam Rd.*)

CROCODILE TANK. The crocodile tank in Vodanammali, a small town about 15km north of Mahabalipuram on the main road to Chennai, was set up about 30 years ago in an attempt to breed endangered species of alligators and crocodiles in captivity. The project has been a big success, and the park now contains thousands of crocodiles, including many very rare breeds. Next door is the government-run **Snake Venom Extraction** facility. (*15km north of Mahabalipuram. Open daily Tu-Su 8am-5:30pm. Rs20.*)

PONDICHERRY பா டிகிசெழ்   ☎ 0413

Many visitors to Pondicherry expect the one-time capital of French India to be an unadulterated enclave of European culture, but this coastal town's claim to fame is somewhat tinged with hyperbole. Pondicherry isn't Paris. It's a town with a split personality and is divided geographically and culturally by a narrow canal. To the west is plain old Pondy, your basic, bustling, medium-sized South Indian city. To the east of the canal is *Pondichérie*, where bougainvillea bursts over white-washed walls, the streets are well-kept, the *flics* sport red *képis*, restaurants serve French food, and the architecture is European.

Most of the city's elaborate buildings were built during the French occupation, begun in 1673 by François Martin, who hoped to gain a commercial advantage for his country over the Dutch and English. For the next two centuries, the French ruled their South Asian colonial enclaves from here. In 1954, they handed over their scattered territories to the Indian government. With Pondicherry as their capital, these became a semi-autonomous Union Territory. Today, the overwhelming influence on the city is the Sri Aurobindo Ashram, established in 1926. The French artist Mirra Alfassa (later known as "the Mother") helped the Bengali poet and philosopher Sri Aurobindo Ghose popularize his spiritual teachings among thousands of devotees worldwide. The fruits of their efforts are readily apparent today: the ashram owns huge chunks of real estate in Pondy, and followers from around the world still live in the Mother's experimental utopian community at **Auroville,** 12km north of the city. For these devotees, Auroville is a meaningful, alternative lifestyle. For everybody else, it's just a good place to come and giggle. Lingering French influence has rendered Pondy a relaxing, chic, and decidedly pricey city.

▐ TRANSPORTATION

Trains: The **railway station** (☎ 36684), on South Blvd., serves **Villupuram** for connections to the Chennai-Rameswaram line (1hr., 4 per day 5am-7:20pm, Rs8).

Buses: The massive bus station is on Lal Bahadur Shastri. There are several reservation and inquiry counters, including **SETC (State Express Transport Corp.), TNSTC (Tamil Nadu State Transport Corp.),** Pondicherry, and "local." All have timetables posted in English. Compare departure and journey times before boarding a bus. **Bangalore** (7hr., 4 per day 7:20am-10:15pm, Rs79-105; TNSTC 7:20am and 11:15pm); **Chennai** (4hr., every 30min., Rs47); **Chidambaram** (2hr., every 15min.); **Coimbatore** (4 per day 7:45-10:05pm, Rs112); **Kanchi** (4hr., 4 per day 7:30am-8:10pm, Rs25-75); **Mahabalipuram** (2hr., every 30min., Rs26-50); **Trichy** (4 per day 4:45am-10pm, Rs 44-50); **Trivandrum** (16hr., 4pm, Rs204); **Vellore** (7am, 5, 9:15pm; Rs136).

Local Transportation: Auto-rickshaws are everywhere, as usual. Pay no more than Rs25 for a trip between the bus stands and the French side of town. **Bicycles** are available for hire from Le Cafe for Rs70 per day, or from Park Guest House (if you're staying there) for Rs20 per day.

✦ ORIENTATION

Pondy is a well-planned city, bordered on the east by the **Bay of Bengal** and divided into eastern and western sections by a covered canal. Streets are laid out in a simple grid. Three major commercial thoroughfares (from north to south), **Jawaharlal Nehru (JN), Ranga Pillai,** and **Lal Bahadur Shastri St.,** run east-west. Lal Bahadur Shastri leads past the **bus stand.** West of the canal, the major north-south avenue is **Mahatma Gandhi (MG) Rd.** East of the canal, the major roads are **rue Suffren** and **rue Romain Roland,** both of which run north to **Government Place,** a small park at the center of the old French part of town. **Goubert Salai** (Beach Road) runs along the shore as it heads south, becoming **South Blvd.** (Subbaiyah Salai). The **railway station** is off Subbaiyah Salai. As Subbaiyah Salai heads north, it passes the Botanical Gardens and becomes **West Blvd.** (Anna Salai). To the north, **North Blvd.** (Sardar Vallabhai Patel Salai) links West Blvd. and Goubert Salai.

🛈 PRACTICAL INFORMATION

Tourist Office: Pondicherry Tourism and Transport Development Corporation (PTTDC) (☎334978). 40 Goubert Salai. **Tours** of the city (including Auroville) depart from the office (2pm, Rs52.50). Make reservations by 1pm. Open daily 8:45am-1pm and 2-5pm.

Currency Exchange: State Bank of India (☎336151). Rue Surcouf. At the intersection with rue Suffren. Foreign exchange desk open M-F 10am-2pm, Sa 10am-noon. On the west side of town, **Mutthu Enterprises,** 173 Mission St., changes cash and traveler's checks. Open daily 9am-9pm.

Cultural Centers: Alliance Française (☎334351). 38 rue Suffren. Has a French library, cultural events and art displays. Open M-Sa 8:30am-12:30pm and 4-7pm.

Bookstore: Higginbothams, Gingy St. Just north of Rangapillai St. Open M-Sa 9am-1pm and 3:30-7:30pm. **French Bookshop,** rue Suffren. Just south of the Alliance Française. Open M-Sa 9am-12:30pm and 3:30-7:30pm.

Pharmacy: New Ananda Emporium, 160 JN St. Just west of the intersection with GMG Rd.

Police: (☎337243). Rue Dumas. Just south of rue Mahe de Labourdonnais; turn left off Goubert Salai at Le Cafe.

Hospital/Medical Services: The best place to go is **Jawaharlal Institute of Medical and Educational Research** (☎372380). A few kilometers north of town; take NH 45 straight. **St. Joseph's Hospital,** 16 rue Romain Roland (☎339513), is also good. Emergency ward open 24hr. Consultations 8-11am and 4-6pm.

Internet: Sree Annai Netcorner, Mission St. Quickest connections in town. Open 24hr. Rs30 per hr. **Netsurf,** Goubert Salai. Open daily 9:30am-10:30pm. Rs35 per hr.

Post Office: GPO, Ranga Pillai St. Open M-Sa 10am-7:30pm. **Postal Code:** 605001.

🛏 ACCOMMODATIONS

Apart from a couple of overpriced "luxury" hotels, accommodations in Pondy fall into two basic categories: standard Indian lodges and ashram guest houses. Most of the cheap budget places are just west of the canal, in the real center of the city. The ashram-run guest houses, all on the French side of town, offer some great deals and include extremely cheap meals at the ashram dining hall as long as you don't mind a few rules (no drinking, no smoking, and no fun after lights-out) and a lot of overbearing Philosophy of Life propaganda. All ashram guest houses close their gates at 10:30pm. The ashram guest houses were originally set up to accommodate devotees of Sri Aurobindo and the Mother. Unrepentant materialists in search of nothing more than a good time may feel slightly out of place.

Park Guest House (☎344412). Goubert Salai. The best setting in all of Pondicherry— right at the Southern end of Goubert Salai, with balconies looking out over manicured lawns to the Bay of Bengal beyond. Cleaned daily, rooms have couch, desk, comfy bed, mosquito net, and bureau. Attached baths with seat toilet, towels, soap, and showers. Bike rental Rs20 per day. Attached restaurant. Check-out noon. Rs200 per person. ❶

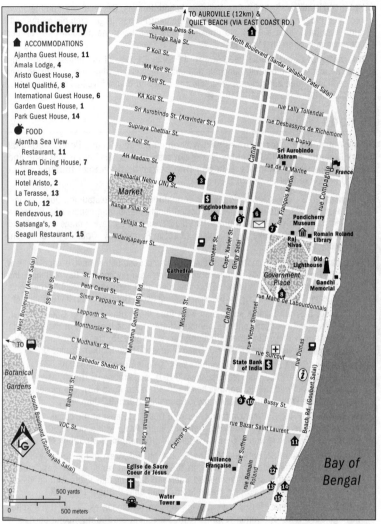

Amala Lodge (☎338910). 92 Ranga Pillai St. Just west of the canal. Popular place with tidy rooms and plenty of plants. Check-out 24hr. Singles Rs85; doubles Rs150-175. ❶

Aristo Guest House (☎336728). 12A Mission St. Just north of JN St. Mellow management. Cool, clean rooms. Check-out 24hr. Singles Rs150; doubles Rs250. ❶

Garden Guest House (☎20797). Akkasamy Madam St. Extremely cheap and clean ashram guest house in a leafy neighborhood in the north end of town. Rooms with attached bath (squat toilets) Rs40. ❶

Ajantha Guest House (☎338898). 22 Goubert Salai. South of the tourist office. Slightly stuffy rooms could use some light, but the location (right on the ocean front) compensates. Attached baths with seat toilets. Check-out 24hr. Doubles Rs300. ❶

Hotel Qualithé (☎334325). Rue Mahe de Labourdonnais. Decrepit, old, tumble-down colonial bldg. at the southern end of Government Pl. has large, crumbly rooms with attached bath (seat toilets). No drinking restrictions here; the popular open-air bar downstairs is open till 11pm. ❶

International Guest House (☎336699). 47 Gingy St. One of the largest ashram-run guest houses, but often full. Spacious and sparklingly clean, white rooms watched over by serious-minded ashram devotees. Idle chit-chat and tourist frivolity not encouraged. Singles Rs80; doubles Rs100-400. ❶

▣ FOOD

Eating out in Pondicherry comes as a welcome change of pace. Pondy's colonial legacy includes a handful of glitzy European restaurants serving French food and cheapish beer and cocktails. You can find better-than-average Indian food at inflated prices on both sides of the canal.

▨ **Satsanga's,** 13 Bussy St. Around the corner from Rendezvous Restaurant. Quite the lovers' nest at night, with its high arches, potted jungle plants, and candlelight. Perfectly-cooked pasta (Rs85-105) and pizza (Rs 95-120) as well as a wide range of meat and fish dishes (Rs120) make this *the* place to eat in Pondicherry. Open Tu-Su 8am-2pm (breakfast till noon) and 5-10pm. ❷

▨ **Seagulls Restaurant,** 19 rue Dumas. At the southernmost end of the street, overlooking Park Guest House. Surrounded by palm trees and just meters away from the Bay of Bengal, the open-air dining area upstairs is the perfect spot for a quiet evening beer (Rs42). The food's not bad either. *Paneer masala* Rs45, chicken *korma* Rs60. Open daily 11am-10:30pm. ❶

La Terasse, 5 South Blvd. A short jaunt west from the southern end of Goubert Salai. Relax in a small courtyard under a bamboo-slatted roof as the scent of the wood-fire oven wafts into the dining area. Thin-crust pizza Rs60-125, fresh fruit juices Rs20, Indian veg./non-veg. dishes Rs40-60. Open M-Tu and Th-Su 8:30am-10pm. ❶

Hot Breads, Gingy St. Next to Higginbothams. Air-conditioned cafe-patisserie selling fresh-baked bread (Rs11 per loaf), scones (Rs10), and croissants (Rs10) as well as a range of snacks and meals (sandwiches Rs25-35, pizza Rs35-65). The closest thing you'll find to a French cafe in Pondicherry. Open daily 10am-9:30pm. ❶

Rendezvous, 30 Rue Suffren. On the corner with Bussy St., east of the canal. Tuxedoed waiters and elegantly folded napkins. *Très chic,* man. Pasta with sauce Rs60-100, rich mousse Rs25. Open M and W-Su 8-10:30am, 11:30am-3pm, 6-10:30pm. ❶

Hotel Aristo, 714 JN St. Between Mission St. and MG Rd., west of the canal. Multi-storied mega-restaurant deservedly popular for its excellent range of non-veg. meals. Lovely open-air rooftop area with trellised vines and dangling fairy lights. Mutton *keems* Rs71, chicken *kashmir* Rs75, ice cream Rs25. Open daily 9:30am-10pm. ❶

Le Club, 33 rue Dumas. This is a great place to come for dinner, especially if you're not paying. Open-terraced French restaurant with excellent food and graceful service in English or French. Club sandwich Rs90, pepper steak Rs95. Open daily 7:30am-10:30pm. AmEx/V. ❷

Ajantha Sea View Restaurant, 22 Goubert Salai. Upstairs from the hotel of the same name. Good views out over Goubert Salai to the sea; very popular place to sit and chill in the evenings. Good range of seafood, chicken, and mutton dishes (Rs60), as well as all the veg. standards (Rs35) and beer (Rs40). Open daily 10am-11pm. ❶

Ashram Dining House, on Ranga Pillai St. Just east of the post office. Lodgers at the ashram guest houses can purchase Rs20 vouchers in advance that entitle them to three meals here. Piles of *basmati* rice and fresh fruits will be heaped upon your metal platter. Daily serving times: 6:40-7:45am, 11:15am-12:30pm; dinner as posted. ❶

◎ SIGHTS

SRI AUROBINDO ASHRAM

Rue de la Marine. Children under 3 not permitted. Photography allowed only with prior permission. Open daily 8am-noon and 2-6pm. Free.

The "integral yoga" of Bengali mystic **Sri Aurobindo Ghose** was an attempt to combine the principles of yoga with the findings of modern science. The eventual aim was the calling down to earth of a "supramental consciousness" that would enable Aurobindo and his disciples to evolve to a "level beyond the human." Whether he succeeded or not depends on your point of view. Born in Calcutta in 1872 and educated in England, Aurobindo returned to India to head an Indian nationalist newspaper; in 1908, his opposition to British rule led to his imprisonment. From inside his prison cell, he underwent a series of profound spiritual experiences, and in 1910 he gave up politics and headed for French-ruled Pondicherry. Here, Sri Aurobindo met **Mirra Alfassa,** an artist and ascetic who had come to India to further her spiritual development. Later known as "the Mother," she would eventually become Aurobindo's constant companion.

The ashram was founded in 1926, as Sri Aurobindo writes, "not for the renunciation of the world but as a center and field of practice for the evolution of another kind and form of life which would in the final end be moved by a higher spiritual consciousness." To this end, the ashram includes businesses, educational centers, farms, and all kinds of other money-spinning ventures among its many facilities.

It was largely the charisma and energy of the Mother that brought these projects to life, as she oversaw the growth of the ashram during Aurobindo's later life and after his death in 1950. When the Mother died in 1973, the ashram faced tumultuous times, and internal struggles developed over the direction the ashram should take; tensions were especially high with regard to the fate of Auroville, the ashram's experimental community (see **Auroville,** below). These days, the ashram houses the flower-strewn **samadhis** (mausolea) of Sri Aurobindo and the Mother. At any time of the day, devotees mill around the perimeter of the *samadhis*, bowing their heads in silent prayer and prostrating themselves on the grass. The ashram is full of people from all over the world who have chosen to follow the teachings of Sri Aurobindo. You can get a good map and brochure at any ashram shop, guest house, or from the Bureau Central, on the western side of the canal, around the corner from Telecom Complex. **Autocare,** 3 blocks north, just over the canal, conducts morning tours of ashram industries and afternoon tours of the Matrimandir (see **Auroville,** below) in Auroville (Rs42).

OTHER SIGHTS

Aside from the ashram, most of Pondicherry's attractions are clustered around **Goubert Salai,** the promenade where locals go to see and be seen in the evening hours. During the day, the street is peaceful and deserted, disturbed only by tourists and the occasional ice cream vendor. The 1500m-long rocky beach is pretty to look at but not safe for swimming. Along the beach is a 4m-high statue of Mahatma Gandhi, surrounded by eight elaborately sculpted monoliths, as well as some splendid French architecture that includes a monument built in memory of Indians who died fighting on the French side during WWI.

The French side of town is a scenic walk full of pristine villas and crumbling old colonial relics that give this part of Pondicherry an atmosphere quite different from anywhere else in India.

Just west of Goubert Salai is the **Government Place,** a grassy quadrangle framing a solemn, neo-classical monument dating from the time of Napoleon III. On the northern edge of the park is the elegant, French-built **Raj Nivas,** now the plush residence of Pondicherry's Lieutenant Governor. Next door is the **Pondicherry Museum,** which displays dusty 19th-century French furniture, a small collection of Chola bronze sculpture, and an assortment of pottery and other objects dug up at the nearby site of Arikamedu. *(Museum open Tu-Su 10am-5pm. Rs1.)*

Follow Goubert Salai to South Blvd. to reach the **Botanical Gardens.** Planted in 1826, the gardens contain species from around the world. *(Open daily 9am-5:30pm.)* On your way to the gardens, have a look at the **Eglise du Sacré Coeur de Jésus,** where the altar is flanked by three stained-glass panels depicting the life of Christ.

⬛ ENTERTAINMENT

By Tamil Nadu's conservative standards, alcohol flows quite freely in Pondicherry, and bars are relatively common on the French side. Two of the best places for an evening beer are the open-air seafront terrace at the **Seagulls Restaurant** (see p. 586), and for a slightly more seedy atmosphere, the bar in the **Hotel Qualithé** (see p. 586), a dusty old time capsule of a place that hasn't seen a speck of paint since the French left town nearly 50 years ago.

Chunnamber Boat House, 10km out of town on the backwaters of the Bay of Bengal, offers boat rentals (kayak, paddle, sail, water scooter Rs10-75). It is also possible to go deep-sea fishing or take a dolphin-watching **sea cruise.** Contact the tourist office (☎339497) for more information.

⬛ DAYTRIPS FROM PONDICHERRY

AUROVILLE ஆரோவில்

*For a brief visit to Auroville, **tours** are sponsored by the tourist office in Pondicherry (Rs52.50) or by Autocare (2pm, Rs50). Another option is to get a **rickshaw** in Pondy (Rs100 plus waiting charges) or go solo down East Coast Rd. by **bike.** Look out for the "To Auroville" sign about 6km out of Pondy; this leads you left off the main road onto a smaller dirt track that runs (uphill!) for 8km or so to the Information Center.*

The utopian New Age community of Auroville, about 12km north of Pondicherry, was an attempt to realize the Mother's dream of a place where seekers from all over the world could come together to live a progressive life in the service of Divine Truth. Auroville was designed to be a peaceful international city of the future, arranged in the shape of a galaxy around the huge golf-ball shaped **Matrimandir** (Mother Temple) at its center.

At the community's inauguration in 1968, children from 124 countries gathered to place handfuls of their native soil in a large urn. Today, there are around 1500 people living here, more than two-thirds of them foreigners, including some of the original settlers. The town covers an area of over 50 hectares. Citizens are grouped into small rural settlements around the urn and the **Matrimandir.** A geodesic dome housing a huge crystalline meditation chamber, the solar-powered Matrimandir symbolizes the goals of the Mother by integrating science and meditation within a peaceful, industrious international community. The temple has been a source of some tension within the community, however, as some residents feel the considerable amount of money and energy funneled into the project has been misdirected.

For now, the real center of the community is the **Solar Kitchen,** where many residents gather for lunch or an afternoon cappuccino and email in the rooftop cafe. Residents live in small settlements named after development goals such as Utility, Certitude, and Revelation. Entrepreneurial and research institutions include a

Building Research Center dedicated to new, low-cost housing technologies, and Aurelec, the town's computer company. There are also innovative agricultural and environmental projects, schools, and a village development program.

◎ **VISITING AUROVILLE.** Understandably, residents are unappreciative of tourists who lack sincere interest in their way of life and come to gawk at them as a relic of the 1960s. As part of a **tour** group, you'll avoid the hassles of transportation and the bureaucracy of getting to see the Matrimandir, though you may feel rather herded. The tour goes first to the Visitors' Information Center, which sells brochures and displays photos and exhibits detailing Auroville's mission and development, including a model of the proposed town. A 20min. video about the community is shown regularly between 10am and 3:30pm every day except Sunday. Just across from the exhibits is a boutique, selling all things New Age. (Open M-Sa 9am-1pm and 2-5:30pm.) A small **cafeteria ❶**, opposite the Information Center sells drinks and snacks (chocolate cake Rs15) throughout the day and serves dinner at 6:30pm every day except Sunday. (Open M-Sa 8:30am-9:30pm, Su 8:30am-6pm.) The Matrimandir is open for viewing from 4-5pm, and for meditation from 5-6pm. Passes must be obtained from the Information Center (free, last pass issued at 4pm). A strict code of silence is enforced as visitors are ushered down a gravel path and up a ramp past construction work to glance inside the otherworldly meditation chamber, which houses a large crystal ball surrounded by a ring of slender white columns. The crystal is illuminated by sunlight reflected from a mirror on top of the dome; when the sky is overcast, solar-powered lamps provide the necessary light. Stepping into the Matrimandir is a bit like entering another dimension—don't be surprised if even this quick peek leaves you dazed; but to go where you've never gone before, you need a separate ticket for the meditation hour. The gardens next to the Matrimandir are open daily 8:30am-3pm.

To go solo, you can take a **rickshaw** or even a **bike.** One advantage of visiting the community on your own is that you'll have a better chance of actually meeting Auroville settlers, though it is a good idea to proceed to the Visitors' Center first to gain a bit of background on the community and obtain a map and newspaper. It is also possible to eat lunch at the Solar Kitchen (12:15pm) if invited by a resident, or sometimes by contacting Guest Services above the kitchen at around 9:30am.

ⴲ STAYING ON. If you are intrigued by Auroville, you might consider a longer stay in one of the **guest houses ❶**, for Rs150-750 per day. Many of the accommodations include kitchen facilities, bath, laundry services, and breakfast. The Visitors' Information Center will provide a list and make arrangements. For more information, contact **La Boutique d'Auroville**, 12 JN St. (☎622150), Pondicherry. Alternatively, you can contact the **Visitors' Information Center** in Auroville directly. (☎622239; fax 622704. Open daily M-Sa 9am-1pm and 1:30-5:30pm, Su 9am-1pm and 2-4 pm.) If you'd like to plan your trip before you leave for India, contact **Auroville Guest Service,** Solar Kitchen building, Auroville 605101 (avguests@auroville.org.in).

CHIDAMBARAM / தயபராயு ☎ 04144

The awe-inspiring temple complex at Chidambaram, 70km south of Pondicherry, is one of the architectural highlights of Tamil Nadu. It was here that Shiva descended from the divine firmament as Nataraja ("King of Dance") and performed the *ananda tandavam* ("Cosmic Dance"). The forested clearing where Nataraja danced became sacred ground; the town that grew around it was dubbed "Chit Ambaram," the "Hall of Wisdom." Construction on the temple here began under the Cholas, who made Chidambaram their capital in AD 907.

During the **"car festivals"** in mid-December and mid-June, thousands come to watch ritual chariots glide through the four streets bearing their names. The Tamil New Year (April 14th every year) is also a time of huge celebration. Every February, prominent dancers from throughout the country converge in Chidambaram to present dance-offerings to Nataraja in the Natyanjali Festival. The town itself, despite its prominent university, is small and quiet, and well worth a trip from Pondicherry or Tanjore.

▐ TRANSPORTATION

Trains: The sleepy railway station is little more than a rural outpost. Most travelers stick to the buses, which are normally quicker. To: **Chennai** (6hr., 4 per day noon-3:30am, Rs220); **Rameswaram** (11hr., 2am and 6:30pm, Rs149); **Tirupati** (11hr., 6:15pm, Rs128); **Trichy** (5hr., 5 per day 2:10pm-2:20am, Rs157) via **Kumbakonam** and **Tanjore.**

Buses: The **bus stand,** just off the eastern end of S. Car St., services all parts of Tamil Nadu. To: **Chennai** (5-6hr., every hr., Rs53); **Kumbakonam** (2hr., frequent, Rs19); **Madurai** (8hr., 5 per day 7:30am-5:30pm, Rs63); **Pondicherry** (2hr., every 30min., Rs16); **Tanjore** (3hr., every hr., Rs28); **Trichy** (5½hr., every 1-2hr., Rs40).

▐ ▐ ORIENTATION AND PRACTICAL INFORMATION

Chidambaram is small and easy to navigate. **North, South, East,** and **West Car St.** form a rectangular border around the temple. To reach them from the bus stand, turn right out of the bus stand and then take your first right onto Venugopal, a.k.a **VGP St.** After three major intersections, VGP St. turns into S. Car St. To get to the **Tourist Office** from the bus stand, take a left and then another left about 200m later onto **Pillaiyar Koil St.** Cross over the **Khan Sahib Canal** before making your first right onto **Railway Feeder Rd.** The railway station is at the end of this street.

Tourist Office: TTDC (☎38739). At the beginning of Railway Feeder Rd., next to Hotel Tamil Nadu, on the way to the railway station. Open M-F 10am-5:45pm.

Currency Exchange: The nearest place to change money is in Pondicherry.

Police Station: Chidambaram Police Station, W. Car St. (☎22201). Open 24hr.

Pharmacy: There are many in town, and most are open until 10 or 11pm.

Hospital: Raja Muthandi Medical College and Hospital (☎38147). On Bazaar Street., off W. Car St.

Internet: Pick Up Internet Browsing Centre, 100m up W. Car St., on the right as you head north. One floor up inside the Saba Lodge bldg. Rs30 per hr. Open 24hr.

Post Office: A tall, cream-colored bldg. covered by a patchwork of orange squares at the western end of N. Car St. Open M-Sa 10am-6pm. **Postal Code:** 608001.

▐ ACCOMMODATIONS

Star Lodging (☎22742). At the easternmost end of S. Car St. Large, clean rooms with attached bath (squat toilets) in a friendly, well-run establishment. The best budget option in town. Singles Rs50; doubles Rs75. ❶

Hotel Akshaya, 17-18 E. Car St. (☎20192). On the left hand side heading north, toward the end of the street. Good value mid-range hotel, offering standard rooms with attached bath (seat toilet). Rooftop terrace offers a spectacular aerial view of the temple. Excellent attached restaurant. Singles Rs175; doubles Rs199-499. ❶

⊡ FOOD

Hotel Saradharam, opposite the bus stand. Three different restaurants, each with its own flavor. **Pallavi ❶,** in front, serves the best veg. food in town and is always crowded. South Indian "special" dishes Rs 15-30. Open 6am-10:30pm. **Annu Pallavi,** in back, cooks up spicy, non-veg. dishes. Open daily 11am-11pm. **The Pizza Shop ❶,** serves pizza and burgers (Rs30) and has Internet access (Rs40 per hr.). Open 11am-11pm.

Aswini Restaurant ❶, 17-18 E. Car St., in the Hotel Akshaya. Menu features all the standard items, served in a cool, quiet A/C dining room. Veg. curry Rs20; *aloo gobhi* Rs22. Open daily 7-10am, 11am-3pm, and 6-10pm.

Bombay Sweets ❶, halfway down W. Car St. on the right hand side. Sells a wide range of sweets and savories. Rs4 per piece.

⊙ SIGHTS: SABHANAYAKA NATARAJA TEMPLE

Open daily 6am-noon and 4-10pm. Puja at 7, 9, 11am, noon, 6, 8, 10pm.

Distinctive as one of the few temples where Shiva and Vishnu are enshrined together, the Sabhanayaka Nataraja Temple draws crowds of thousands daily. It was here that the dance duel took place between Kali and Shiva, the Lord of the Dance (Nataraja). The temple is also one of the five Shiva temples in South India dedicated to the five Vedic elements (earth, air, water, fire, and ether); Chidambaram is dedicated to the "Ether of Consciousness."

Covering more than 54 hectares, the temple dominates central Chidambaram. Scholars believe that work on the temple began during the 10th century, but local tradition holds that there has been a temple on this site for thousands of years. The present Nataraja Temple, according to legend, was built in the 6th century when the Kashmiri monarch Simhavarman II (r. 550-575) made a pilgrimage to Chidambaram, hoping that bathing in the tank of the ancient Nataraja Temple would cure his leprosy. When he recovered soon after his bath, the king—thereafter known as Hiranyavarman, or the "golden-bodied one"—gave orders for the temple to be enlarged. In addition, Hiranyavarman decreed that the holy entourage of 3000 brahmin priests *(Dikshitars)* who had accompanied him from Kashmir should remain behind at Chidambaram to serve the temple. Lepers still come to the temple for its holy healing powers, and descendants of the *Dikshitars* still live in Chidambaram. You'll recognize them by the knot of hair on top of their heads.

THE OUTERMOST EDGE. Most visitors enter through the eastern or western *gopuram* (gateway), where **guides** immediately accost any foreign-looking person. Also beware of English-speaking individuals trying to usher you to a priest who will anoint you with *kumkum* for a "voluntary" donation. To avoid most of the general hassle, use the northernmost gate instead.

The temple's four massive, pyramidal *gopuram* are painted every 50 years in a rainbow of pastel tones, and each has a distinctive character. The eastern *gopuram* is supposed to invoke a feeling of love, with the worshipper approaching the Nataraja as he would approach his beloved. From the south, the soul approaches as a child, and from the west, as a friend. One enters the northern *gopuram* in a position of subservience. The 42m-high northern *gopuram*, erected in the 14th century, bears an inscription claiming that it was built by a 16th-century Vijayanagar king. Its interior is embellished with carvings of the 108 dance poses associated with *bharatnatyam*. The southern *gopuram*, put up in the 12th century, contains a set of impressive carvings of the goddess Lakshmi. Each of the four *gopurams* still has its original granite base, although the brick towers have been replaced numerous times, often falling victim to the winter monsoon. Across the front of each base are carvings of Shiva and Parvati.

On the eastern side of the temple is a depiction of Ganesh taken from a story in which Lord Shiva held a contest between his two sons, Ganesh and Kartikkeya. The deal was that a delicious mango would be given to the son who could go around the universe and back first. Kartikkeya leapt onto his peacock and set off, confident of victory. The short, plump Ganesh had only a little mouse for a mount. He thought for a while and then rode around his parents, Shiva and Parvati. When Shiva asked his son what he was up to, Ganesh replied: "Going around the supreme Lord Shiva and Goddess Parvati who create and contain the universe is equivalent to going around the universe." Shiva smiled in satisfaction and presented the mango to his slow-footed but quick-witted son.

The **Shivaganga Tank** is to the left as you come in through the northern gate. This is where King Simhavarman bathed, emerging with golden-hued skin. Opposite the tank is the **Shivakumarasundari Temple,** dedicated to Shiva's consort Parvati. On the other side of the tank, in the northeast corner of the temple grounds, stands the 103m-long **Raja Sabha,** the temple's "1000-pillared corridor" where the victory processions of the Pandavas, Cholas, and other local powers were held. The corridor has only 999 pillars; Shiva's leg serves as the 1000th.

THE INNER CHAMBERS. The inner chambers are accessible from the north and south. On the eastern side of the enclosure, the **Devasabha,** or "Hall of the Gods," is where images of deities are stored when they are not being used; this is also where temple meetings are held. In the southwest corner of the second enclosure, the **Nritya Sabha** (Dance Hall) marks the spot where Shiva and Kali had their famous dance duel. The hall is adorned with 56 pillars representing various dance poses.

Inside the innermost shrine, accessible from the southern side of the second enclosure, it is possible to get a glimpse of the gold-roofed **Chit Sabha** and **Kanaka Sabha,** the holiest points in the entire complex. The atmosphere here is often highly charged, particularly during evening *puja*, when crowds pray here to the raucous accompaniment of horns, drums, and temple bells. Five silver-plated stone steps lead to the Chit Sabha; they represent the five Sanskrit letters that spell out the famous Hindu Panchakshara mantra, "Nama Shivaya." The Chit Sabha contains images of Nataraja and Parvati. To the right, behind a string of leaves, are the **Chidambara Rahasyam** ("Secret of Chidambaram") and the **Akasa Linga,** representing the elusive and invisible element *akasa* (ether). In the passageway to the sanctum is a hallway that leads to the **Govindaraja Temple,** dedicated to Vishnu.

K U M B A K O N A M குடிகோணயு ☎ 0435

A slow-paced temple town that sees very few foreign tourists, Kumbakonam has a history that stretches back more than 2000 years. Millions of people from all over India flock to Kumbakonam every twelve years, when the waters of the nine sacred rivers are supposed to flow into the Mahamakham Tank in the center of town. The rest of the time, Kumbakonam is a quiet and relaxing place to spend a few days. In addition to the five major temples within the town itself, Kumbakonam is also a good base for daytrips out to the Chola-era sites at Darasuram and Gangaikondacholapuram.

▨ TRANSPORTATION

Trains: The **railway reservations counter** (☎ 433134) is open M-Sa 8am-noon and 2-5pm, Su 8am-2pm. To: **Chennai** (10hr.; 10:10am, 9:15, 11:35pm; Rs151); **Rameswaram** (10hr., 4:05am and 8:15pm, Rs131); **Tanjore** (1½hr., 4 per day 3:55pm-4:05am, Rs31); **Trichy** (3hr., 4 per day 3:55pm-4:15am, Rs65); **Villupuram** (5hr., 4 per day 10am-11:40pm, Rs72).

Buses: The bus stand is at the eastern end of the city, not far from the railway station, a 1km walk out of town from Mahamalkham Tank along Kamaraj Rd. To: **Bangalore** (11hr., 6:30pm, Rs132); **Chennai** (6hr., every hr. 8am-11:45pm, Rs71-94); **Chidambaram** (frequent, Rs29); **Karaikal** (2hr., every 30min., Rs13); **Tanjore** (1½hr., every 30min., Rs10); **Tirupati** (10hr., 9pm, Rs114); **Trichy** (2½hr., every 20min., Rs23).

ORIENTATION AND PRACTICAL INFORMATION

Kumbakonam is not a hard place to find your way around; most things are within easy walking distance, and there is always someone to point you in the right direction if you get lost. To get from the train station to the center of town, turn right out of the station, take your first left on **Kamaraj Rd.**, and walk straight for 1km. From the bus stand, exit left and then take a right onto Kamaraj Rd., which runs into **Head Post Office (HPO) Rd.** near the large **Mahamakham Tank.** Turn right on HPO Rd., and head past Hotel Raya's to Kumbakonam's main east-west street. **TSR Big St.,** marked by VPR Hotel Siva and many banks, runs parallel and to the north of the main street.

Currency Exchange: City Union bank Ltd., 140 TSR Big St. (☎ 420088). **State Bank of India,** also on TRS Big St. Both open M-Sa 10am-2pm, Su 10am-noon.

Police: West Police Station, Ayikulam Rd. (☎ 421450). Opposite the Sarangapani Temple, near the Athityaa hotel.

Hospital: ST Hospital, HPO Rd. (☎ 430839). Between Ayikulam Rd. and Hotel Raya's. Attached **pharmacy.** Open 24hr.

Internet: Universal Computer Ed., 7 TSR Big St. (☎ 421163). Two blocks east of City Union Bank. Rs40 per hr. Open 8am-10pm.

Post Office: The **Head Post Office,** HPO Rd., next to Hotel Rayas. Open M-Sa 8am-6pm. **Postal code:** 612001.

ACCOMMODATIONS

All the following have 24hr. check-out policies. Prices do not include tax.

VPR Lodge, 102/3 TSR Big St. (☎ 421949). At the very end of the road. Bare, basic, time-capsule-like hotel offering simple well-kept rooms with attached bath (squat toilets). Singles Rs60-90; doubles Rs100-140. ❶

Femina Lodge (☎ 420369). Up two flights of stairs in the red-tiled bldg. opposite Hotel Raya's. Central location, just a minute's walk from the Mahamalkham Tank. Large beds in modest rooms, all with attached bath (squat or seat toilets). Doubles Rs150. ❶

Pandiyan Hotel, 52 Sarangapani East Rd. (☎ 430397). Across from the main entrance to the Sarangapani Temple. Clean, well-run place with decent-sized doubles with attached bath. Rs150. ❶

Hotel ARR, TSR Big St. (☎ 421234). Opposite City Union Bank Ltd. Rooms have color TVs, sofas, and seat or squat toilets. Doubles Rs375-660. ❷

Hotel Athityaa (☎ 421794). Across the road from the Potramai Tank at the back of the Sarangapani Temple on Ayikulam Rd. Friendly management and well-furnished rooms with towels and TVs. Both seat and squat toilets. Restaurant and bar. Singles Rs350-500; doubles Rs375-625. ❷

FOOD

Sathars, inside Hotel Raya's, on HPO Rd. Excellent non-veg. restaurant serves a wide range of chicken, mutton, and seafood dishes from around India. Entrees Rs30-60. Open daily 11am-11:30pm. ❶

Arul, near the Sarangapani Temple, opposite Pandiyar Hotel. Whirring floor fans and dim lighting create a relaxed setting for excellent *thalis* (Rs25-30, 10am-4pm only). Open daily 10am-11pm. ❶

Pandiyar Hotel, opposite the main entrance to the Sarangapani Temple. Banana leaf *thali* (Rs15) is constructed one heaped spoonful at a time. Other items around Rs20 each. Open daily 11:30am-2pm and 4-10pm. ❶

Arogya, in the Hotel Athityaa (see above). Standard mid-range hotel restaurant popular for its never-ending "meals" (Rs20) and other snacks. Open daily 11am-11pm. ❶

◎ SIGHTS

KUMBESHWARA TEMPLE. Facing east, the Kumbeshwara Temple is the largest and most important Shiva temple in Kumbakonam; the *linga* enshrined here is believed to have been shaped by Shiva himself. According to legend, Brahma anticipated the Great Deluge, "Mahapralaya," and entreated Shiva to save creation from destruction. Shiva instructed him to place a pot, or *kumbh*, containing sacred nectar and the seed of creation on top of Mt. Meru in the Himalayas. The Great Deluge carried the sacred *kumbh* south to rest at Kumbakonam, where Lord Shiva, in the guise of a hunter, shattered the pot with an arrow and spilled the nectar. He then gathered the broken shards and shaped the **Mahalinga** that now stands inside the temple. Nectar from the broken pot trickled to five other places within a 16km radius of Kumbakonam, as well as to the Mahamakham Tank itself. Traditionally, pilgrims visit these shrines before coming to Kumbeshwara. *(At the western end of Ayikulam Rd. Open daily 7am-1pm and 4-9pm. Puja 7, 8:30am, noon, 5, 7, 8:30pm.)*

SARANGAPANI TEMPLE. Sarangapani is one of the three most sacred Vishnu shrines in India, along with Srirangam near Trichy (see p. 603) and Tirupati in Andhra Pradesh (see p. 127). On the left of the main sanctum is a golden shrine to Lakshmi, the goddess of prosperity, which depicts her seated on a thousand-petal lotus, worshipping Vishnu; legend holds that she was discovered in this position in the temple's tank. It was only later that Vishnu came to Kumbakonam to marry her. Around the inner sanctum are fine carvings of Vishnu's 10 avatars. Within the sanctum is a huge reclining Vishnu, ornamented with silver and watched over by his two wives, Lakshmi and Saraswati. *(Take your first left and then walk down Ayikulam Rd. for approx. 200m. Take the first major road to the left; the temple will be on your right. Open daily 7am-noon and 4:30-9pm. Puja at 9, 10am, noon, 6, 8, 9pm.)*

NAGESHWARA TEMPLE. Built during the 10th century, the Nageshwara Temple, dedicated to Shiva, is thought to be the oldest temple in Kumbakonam. The sculpted figures adorning the *gopurams* are some of the best examples of early Chola workmanship. Many of the temple's finest sculptures are within the sanctum itself; all around are niches containing carvings of Shiva and Parvati. The temple has been constructed so that sunlight passes through the opening in the *gopuram* three times a year and illuminates the shrine's image. It is believed that Surya (the sun god) worships Shiva at these times. *(From the bottom of HPO Rd., take your first left and then your first right. Open daily 6am-noon and 4:30-8pm. Puja on the hr.)*

MAHAMAKHAM TANK. The Mahamakham Tank is believed by Hindus to be the place where the sacred nectar from Brahma's *kumbh* was collected when the pot was shattered by an arrow from Shiva. A multi-functional pond where people go to swim, do laundry, or worship, the Mahamakham Tank is especially pleasant in the evening, when you can rent paddle-boats (Rs10 per 30min.). Every 12 years, the tank's tranquility is disrupted by the **Kumbh Mela** (see p. 720), a huge festival where hundreds of thousands of pilgrims come to Kumbakonam to bathe in the waters here. When Jupiter passes Leo, the waters of the Ganga and eight other sacred Indian rivers—the Yamuna, Kaveri, Godavari, Narmada, Krishna, Saraswati, Sarayu, and Tungabhadra—are believed to flow into the tank. The last festival, in 1992, brought well over one million devotees to Kumbakonam. When controversial political leader and current Chief Minister of Tamil Nadu, Jayalalitha Jayaram, went to take her purifying dip, a stampede ensued that killed 60 pilgrims. *(At HPO Rd. and Kamarajar Rd. Open 24hr.)*

◪ DAYTRIPS FROM KUMBAKONAM

DARASURAM

There are frequent local buses from Kumbakonam to Darasuram (20min.). An auto-rickshaw should cost about Rs30.

Just 3km from Kumbakonam, Darasuram is famous for its **Airavateshwara Temple,** a superb example of 12th-century Chola architecture. The granite temple gets its name from Airavata, the white elephant mount of Indra. An angry god turned its skin color from white to black, and Airavata worshipped Shiva here in the hope of changing its skin color back. Near the base of the inner wall are some remarkably well-preserved carvings, depicting gymnasts, *bharatnatyam* dancers, and a woman giving birth. The Archaeological Survey of India has done a fair bit of work here, and the temple and its carvings are in an excellent state of affairs.

GANGAIKONDACHOLAPURAM

Buses pass through every hr. from Kumbakonam (1hr., Rs8).

Situated in exquisitely maintained grounds in a rural village 37km from Kumbakonam, the beautifully restored temple complex at Gangaikondacholapuram is perhaps the most appealing of all the Chola sites in Tamil Nadu. Gangaikondacholapuram, whose name means "the city of the Chola who conquered the Ganga," was built by King Rajendra I (r.1012-1044), son of Raja Raja of Tanjore Temple fame, when he defeated the kingdoms to the north and brought lands north of the Ganga under the control of a southern dynasty for the first time. To commemorate his victory, the king had water from the Ganga transported to the temple's tank. The temple is dedicated to Shiva—a large Nandi guards the entrance—and among the most impressive carvings is a frieze that depicts Shiva and Parvati crowning King Rajendra. Worship still goes on inside the temple's candle-lit interior. The upper stories, which served as a fortress, are accessible to visitors (and bats!).

KARAIKAL AND VELANKANNI

*Buses from Kumbakonam head to **Karaikal** (2hr., every 30min., Rs13). From Karaikal, take a bus to **Nagapattinam** (45min., frequent., Rs2) and switch to a bus going to **Velankanni** (20min., frequent., Rs3).*

A French possession until the 1950's, the coastal town of **Karaikal** is still ruled as a a part of the Union Territory of Pondicherry. There's not much evidence left of French influence today, though there are a few more churches (and a lot more bars) here than elsewhere in Tamil Nadu. This is not a big tourist destination by any means, but the constant stream of pilgrims ensures that Karaikal is well set-up to deal with visitors. Hindu pilgrims come here to worship at the **Darbanyeswar** and **Ammaiyar** temples, on Bharathiar Rd, and people of all religions stop off here on their way to pray for miracles at the Roman Catholic Church of our Lady of Good Health at Velankanni, 36km away.

TAMIL NADU

The bus stand in Karaikal, on Bharathiar Rd., services: **Chennai** (8hr., 10pm, Rs75); **Chidambaram** (2hr., frequent 4:30am-10pm, Rs15); **Kumbakonam** (2hr., every 30min. 4am-10:30pm, Rs13); **Mylar** (1hr., every 30min., Rs20); **Pondicherry** (4hr., every 2hr., Rs30). The main **Tourist Office** is inconveniently located on Nehru St., about 1.5km along Bharathiar Rd. from the bus stand. (Open daily 9am-1pm and 2-5:30pm). The **State Bank of India,** 58 Bharathiar Rd., on the right, about 1km left out of the bus stand, changes money. (☎ (04368) 22407. Open M-F 10am-4pm, Sa 10am-noon.) **Mano Computers,** opposite the State Bank of India, on the left hand side of Bharathiar Rd. as you walk left out of the bus station, has Internet access for Rs 40 per hr. (☎ (04368) 21028. Open 24hr.) For lodging, the best option, by far, is the **Government Tourist Home ❶.** Turn left out of the bus stand and the hotel is on your right. Huge, clean, government-subsidized rooms with attached bath (singles Rs12; doubles Rs20, with A/C Rs80). For more upscale lodging, the **Hotel Paris International ❶,** further down Bharathiyar Rd., is a good bet. (☎ (04368) 20304. Singles Rs175; doubles Rs300-475.) There are a number of simple restaurants and bars on Bharathiyar Rd. The **Tasty Restaurant,** inside the Hotel Paris International, is clean, cool, and cheap (open daily 6-9pm).

According to local belief, the Virgin Mary appeared to a boy selling buttermilk in **Velankanni** nearly 400 years ago. She cured him of his lameness and instructed him to build a church to her in return. Thousands of pilgrims visit this church, the **Roman Catholic Church of our Lady of Good Health,** every day, drawn by the site's legendary healing powers. The **Museum of Offerings,** at the back of the church, houses a bizarre array gifts donated by the miraculously cured, including several hearts and lungs made out of solid silver. If your appetite for Christian kitsch demands an overnight visit, there are dozens of places to stay around the church and bus stand. *(Church open daily 5am-9pm. English mass daily 10am and Sa 5:45pm with car procession. Museum of Offerings open 6:30am-8pm.)*

TANJORE (THANJAVUR) தஞ்சா/ஸி ☎ 04362

Less than two hours by bus from Trichy or Kumbakonam, Tanjore is a prosperous commercial city of 250,000. For more than 400 years, until the end of the 13th century, it was the most important city in the Chola empire, which at its height encompassed most of southern India and stretched as far south as Java. Not many foreign tourists make it here, but Tanjore is well worth a visit to see the Chola's greatest monuments: the Brihadishwara Temple, which still dominates the city skyline, and the old palace compound, which houses an impressive collection of Chola-era bronzes.

▣ TRANSPORTATION. The **railway station** is on the aptly-named Railway Station Rd., 600m south of the canal. The easiest way to get to the center of town is to take any of the buses (Rs2) that pass in front of the station to the Old Bus Stand, a 5min. walk from the temple. Auto rickshaws cover the same route for under Rs20. To: **Chennai** (*Cholan Express 6154,* 9hr., 9:20am, Rs84; 3 night trains, 10hr.); **Chidambaram** (2hr., 4 per day 9:15am-10:40pm, Rs53); **Rameswaram** (9hr., 5:20am and 9:50pm, Rs123); **Trichy** (all trains from Chennai or to Madurai go through Trichy; 2hr., 6 per day 11:45am-10pm, Rs35). The **Old Bus Stand** is in the city center, where Gandhiji Rd. turns into East Main Rd. The **New Bus Stand** is 7km from the city center. Buses to and from **Chennai** and **Kumbakonam** and most local destinations use the old bus stand; buses to most other places leave from the new stand. Local buses # 74, 74A, 74B, and 74D travel between the two stands (Rs2). Auto-rickshaws between the two bus stands cost around Rs40. Frequent buses run to: **Chennai** (9hr., Rs87); **Chidambaram** (4hr., Rs30); **Kumbakonam** (1½hr., Rs10); **Pondicherry** (6hr., 3:40am-9:30pm, Rs44); **Trichy** (1½hr., Rs15).

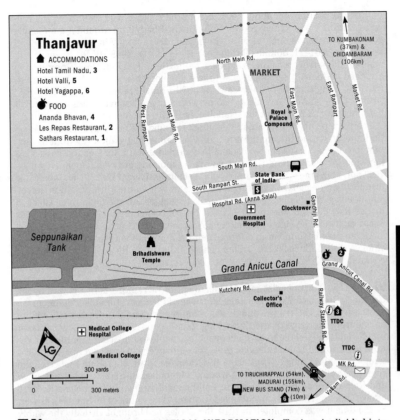

Thanjavur

♠ ACCOMMODATIONS
Hotel Tamil Nadu, **3**
Hotel Valli, **5**
Hotel Yagappa, **6**

🍎 FOOD
Ananda Bhavan, **4**
Les Repas Restaurant, **2**
Sathars Restaurant, **1**

TAMIL NADU

◪ ⁊ ORIENTATION AND PRACTICAL INFORMATION. Tanjore is divided into northern and southern sections by the **Grand Anicut Canal.** From the station, **Railway Station Rd.** curves slightly as it heads north, passing a branch of the **tourist office** (☎30984. Open daily 10am-5:45pm) and several hotels before reaching the canal. As it crosses the canal, Railway Station Rd. becomes **Gandhiji Rd.,** where every second building seems to be selling silk saris. The busiest part of town is the area around the bus stands, immediately north of the intersection of Gandhiji Rd. and **Hospital Rd.,** where the **Raja Merusudad Government Hospital** (☎31023) is situated. The **State Bank of India,** opposite the government hospital, changes currency and traveler's checks. (☎30698. Open M-F 10am-4pm, Sa 10am-1pm.) **Thanjavur Medical College Hospital,** Medical College Rd. (☎40124), a 15min. rickshaw ride from the station toward Tamil Nadu University. The superintendent of **police** (☎31313) is on Collector Office Road. The best place for Internet is the **Netclub Internet Zone,** one of the shops just after the Hotel Tamil Nadu. (Open 24hr. Rs35 per hr.) The head **post office,** MK Rd., is off Railway Station Rd. in the southern part of town. (☎31022. Open M-Sa 7am-7pm, Su noon-4pm.) **Postal Code:** 613001.

◪ ◩ ACCOMMODATIONS AND FOOD. Places south of the canal tend to be quieter than those overlooking the bus stand. All hotels have a 24hr. check-out policy. Perhaps the best of the lot is **Hotel Tamil Nadu ❷,** a large, white complex on Railway Station Rd. about 100m before the canal as you walk from the railways station. Comfortable rooms with attached bath built around a mini-jungle courtyard are big enough to settle down and raise a family in. Attached bar and restaurant (☎31421; doubles Rs330-600). **Hotel Valli ❶**, 2948 MK Rd., is on a well-shaded side-street a 5min. walk east from the railway station. Rooms have attached baths with squat and seat toilets; the hotel has an attached restaurant. (☎31580. Singles Rs185; doubles Rs200-300.) **Hotel Yagappa ❶**, #1 Trichy Rd., south of the station, has clean rooms with attached squat toilets and bucket bath. Sheets and hot water are available. (☎30421. Rooms Rs250.)

There are plenty of vegetarian restaurants around the bus stand. **Ananda Bhavan ❶**, Railway Station Rd., up the street on your left as you walk away from the station into town, serves simple banana leaf meals for Rs15. Its location makes it a key stop for locals going to work, so expect morning crowds. (Open daily 6:30-10:30am, 11:00am-10:30pm.) The popular **Sathars Restaurant ❶**, 167 Gandhiji Rd., is just north of the canal on your right heading away from the railway station. Excellent non-veg. meals in a dark, fan-flapped setting just off the main road. Chicken dishes Rs30-60, mutton *rogan josh* Rs26-105. (Open daily noon-11:30pm.) **Les Repas ❷**, inside the Hotel Parisutham, 55 Grand Anicut Canal Road, showcases a large, multi-cuisine menu in a formal setting, complete with a waterfall. Various chicken dishes for Rs90-140, grilled cheese Rs100, soup Rs40-60. Bar downstairs; cocktails Rs100-140, beer Rs100. (Open 6am-11pm.)

🔲 **SIGHTS.** The **Brihadishwara Temple,** the pride of Tanjore, is recognized by the United Nations as a World Heritage Site. One of the most stunning monuments in southern India, the temple stands as an impressive reminder of the city's glory days during the reign of the Chola king Raja Raja I (r. 985-1014). Legend has it that he built the temple to save his own life. Unable to find a cure for his leprosy, Raja Raja turned to his religious tutor for guidance, who advised him to build a temple to Shiva using a *linga* from the Narmada River. Raja Raja rushed to the river and pulled a *linga* from the water; as he pulled, the *linga* grew and grew, and Raja Raja had no choice but to build a massive temple to enclose it. More likely the temple was simply intended to stand as a symbol of its builder's power; by the time it was completed in 1010, the Cholas had brought virtually the whole of southern India under their control.

Above the *linga* rises the stepped superstructure, called a *vimana*, which represents Mt. Meru, the cosmic mountain around at the center of the Hindu universe. In an inversion of traditional South Indian architectural order, the *vimana* soars over the *gopurams*, or entry gates. The set of exquisite carvings on the frontal face, depicting Shiva, Parvati, and other gods on top of Mt. Meru, has earned the temple the local nickname "Himalaya of the South." The monolithic *stupa* that caps the *vimana* was raised via a ramp more than 6km long. Also within the temple's courtyard walls are a 16th-century temple to Krishna, famed for its intricate miniature carvings, and another to Ganesh and Parvati. The temple complex is guarded by a giant sculpture of Nandi (Shiva's bull). This massive sculpture weighs over 25 tons, making it one of the largest in India. Over 1000 smaller Nandis and 252 *linga* also keep careful watch from the walls.

Awe-inspiring by day, the temple acquires an added aura of magic at sunset as couples stroll and families picnic in its park-like atmosphere. When night falls, artfully placed lights bring the sculptures into sharp relief. A pathway to the left as you leave the temple leads 100m down a small lane to the **Shivaganga Gardens,** where couples and families throw picnic leftovers at caged monkeys and peacocks. *(Temple complex open daily roughly 6am-noon and 4-9pm.)*

The large **Royal Palace** was built as a residence by the Nayaks in the 16th century and was subsequently refurbished by the Marathas. These days, the palace has been colonized by a number of incongruous outfits, including a secondary school, an agricultural office, and a martial arts academy. The only real reason to come here is the excellent collection of Chola bronzes and stone sculptures in the **Durbar Hall Art Museum.** *(Once inside the palace, follow signs for the art gallery. Open daily 9am-1pm and 3-6pm. Rs10, Rs30 camera fee.)* The **Saraswati Mahal Library,** also in the palace, houses thousands of palm-leafed manuscripts. With 33,433 holdings, the collection is one of the world's finest. Most of the collection is closed to the public, but a small selection of weird and wonderful pieces is on display in a room by the entrance. *(Open Tu-Th 10am-1:30pm and 2:30-5:30pm. Free.)*

TIRUCHIRAPPALLI (TRICHY) ரு௫ிராடழின் ☎ 0431

For a growing industrial center of over a million people, Tiruchirappalli (commonly referred to by *Let's Go* as Trichy or Tiruchi) is a relatively sane and manageable city. The city has been occupied for over 2000 years and controlled at various times by the Cholas, Pandyas, Pallavas, and Nayaks, whose prosperous reign brought about the creation of the imposing Rock Fort, still the city's dominant landmark. Since the late 19th century, when the railways brought industry to South India, Trichy has been ruled by manufacturing—today, the city produces staggering quantities of *bindis* and costume jewelry. Trichy's biggest attraction is the temple town of Srirangam, 4km north of the city center. Trichy is also a convenient transportation hub to destinations farther south, including the railway station, bus stand, and a wide range of hotels all within comfortable walking distance of one another.

TAMIL NADU

▐ TRANSPORTATION

Flights: The **airport** is 8km south of the city, 25min. by bus #59 or K1 (frequent until 10pm, Rs2) or taxi (Rs100). **Indian Airlines** (☎ 480233 or 481433), on Dindigul Rd., about 1.5km southwest of the intersection with Junction Rd. has flights to **Chennai** (Tu, W, Th, Sa, Su; US$70-90) and **Cochin** (M, W, F; US$90). **Sri Lankan Airlines** (☎ 460844 or 462381). Williams Rd. Hotel Femina Complex. Open M-Sa 9am-5:30pm. To **Colombo, Sri Lanka** (1hr.; M, W, F, Sa; Rs3325).

Trains: The **Trichy Junction Railway Station** in the south of town, off the intersection of Junction and Madurai Rd. The **Reservations Bldg.** (☎ 461362) is the small white structure to your left as you approach the main station complex. Open M-Sa 8am-8pm, Su 8am-2pm. Fares listed are for sleeper class. To: **Chidambaram** (5hr., 5 per day 8am-9:30pm, Rs104); **Chennai** (5½-7hr., 11-13 per day 6:30am-11:45pm, Rs146); **Madurai** (3hr., 5-7 per day 5:40pm-3:40am, Rs104; *Madurai Exp.* Sa 8:30am); **Rameswaram** (7½hr.; 12:05 and 7:35am, 9:30pm; Rs124); **Tanjore** (2hr., 8 per day 5am-9:30pm, Rs164); **Tirupati** (15hr., Th 2pm and Sa 12:40pm, Rs169).

Buses: The **State Bus Stand** at the intersection of Rockins and Royal Rd. To: **Bangalore** (10hr., 8:30am and 9:10pm, Rs100); **Chennai** (7hr., 42 per day 5:30am-11:30pm, Rs82-107); **Coimbatore** (6hr., frequent around the clock, Rs50); **Dindigul** (3½hr., frequent around the clock, Rs22); **Kodaikanal** (6hr.; 6:15 and 9:15am, 3:15pm; Rs50); **Madurai** (3½hr., frequent around the clock, Rs38); **Pondicherry** (5hr., 11:30am and 5:15pm, Rs55); **Tanjore** (2½hr., frequent around the clock, Rs14). Private buses to Bangalore (Rs200), Chennai (Rs185), and Madurai (Rs50) are also easy to find.

Local Transportation: Trichy's **local bus** system is probably the most efficient in all of Tamil Nadu. A fleet of shiny silver buses, most equipped with deafening sound systems, shuttles passengers around the city. The **#1 bus** is every tourist's best friend; it passes the railway station, the State Bank of India, and the Head Post Office on its way to the Rock Fort (Rs2) and the Srirangam Temple (Rs2.75). Buses depart every few min. from the State Bus Stand. As a result, Trichy has hordes of hardly used **rickshaws**, which congregate in the bus stand/tourist office area. They aren't really necessary, unless you need to get to the airport (Rs50).

ORIENTATION AND PRACTICAL INFORMATION

With the **Kaveri River** forming its northern border, Trichy is split into two segments by the **Woyakondan Channel.** The northernmost portion (nearest to the Kaveri River) is Trichy's industrial area, full of textile shops and dominated by the majestic **Rock Fort** and the town's **railway station.** To the south of the channel is the busy **Trichy Junction** area, where you'll find the city's main **railway station.** The streets around the railway station are full of hotels and banks. This area also contains the GPO, the tourist office, and the **bus stands.**

Tourist Office: Government of Tamil Nadu Tourist Office (☎ 460136). On the corner of McDonald's Rd. and Williams Rd. Diagonally opposite the central bus stand. Open M-F 10am-5:45pm. Info counters also at the airport and railway junction.

Currency Exchange: State Bank of India. Turn left at the end of McDonald's Rd., after Jenney's Residency. The bank will be on your left. Changes cash and the following traveler's checks only: AmEx checks in US$ and Thomas Cook in US$ and UK£. Open M-F 10am-2pm, Sa 10am-noon.

Swimming Pools: Jenney's Residency (see below). Rs100. Open daily 6am-7pm.

Police: Cantonment station on Municipal Office Rd. Open 24hr.

Pharmacy and Hospital: The private **Sea Horse Hospital** (☎ 415660). 6 Royal Rd. Has a well-stocked pharmacy. Open 24hr.

Telephones: 24hr. **STD/ISD** booths opposite the bus stand next to the Hotel Tamil Nadu on McDonald's Rd.

Internet: MasNet Vision, Royal Rd. Opposite the bus stand. Open 24hr. Rs20 per hr.

Post Office: Head Post Office, on Bird's Rd., 500m walk up from the State Bank of India. Open M-Sa 8am-6pm. Speedpost (in adjacent bldg.) 10am-7pm. **Postal Code:** 620001.

ACCOMMODATIONS

The Trichy Junction area has plenty of places to stay, all with 24hr. check-out. Many of the larger hotels have huge flashing neon signs that light up the night sky.

Ashby Hotel (☎ 460652 or 460653). 17-A Rockins Rd. Close to both the bus stand and the railway station. This is a good old-fashioned Raj-era place that has been well-kept without losing its character. Large rooms come with attached bath (seat toilets) and TVs, and you can have your morning coffee in the leafy courtyard restaurant. Attached bar is better than average. Singles Rs175, with A/C 552; doubles Rs290-720. ❶

Hotel Arun (☎ 415021). 24 State Bank Rd. (Dinidigul Rd.) From the railway station take the second road to the right, and the hotel will be on your right-hand side. Clean and welcoming place with TVs and attached bathrooms (squat toilets). Singles Rs160-350; doubles Rs185-400. ❶

Hotel Gajapria (☎ 414411). 5&6 Royal Rd. With the bus stand behind you (facing the Vasanta Bhavan Restaurant), turn left onto Royal Rd. The hotel is 500m ahead on the right. Spacious rooms have modern furniture, TVs, and attached bathrooms with seat toilets and hot water. The best value of the mid-range hotels in the area. Attached Chinese restaurant/bar. Singles Rs190-450; doubles Rs330-600. DC/MC/V. ❷

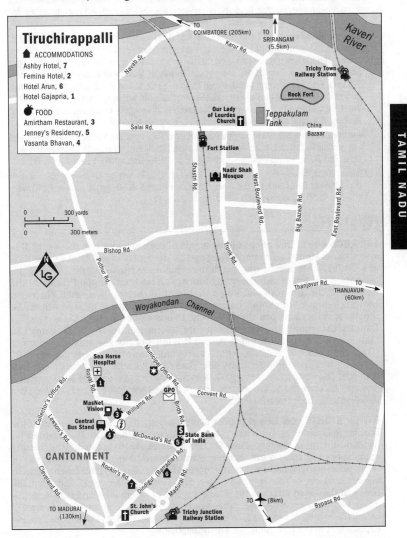

Tiruchirappalli

🏠 ACCOMMODATIONS
Ashby Hotel, **7**
Femina Hotel, **2**
Hotel Arun, **6**
Hotel Gajapria, **1**

🍴 FOOD
Amirtham Restaurant, **3**
Jenney's Residency, **5**
Vasanta Bhavan, **4**

TO COIMBATORE (205km)
TO SRIRANGAM (5.5km)
Kaveri River
Karur Rd.
Navab St.
Trichy Town Railway Station
Rock Fort
Our Lady of Lourdes Church
Teppakulam Tank
China Bazaar
Salai Rd.
Fort Station
Nadir Shah Mosque
Shastri Rd.
West Boulevard Rd.
Big Bazaar Rd.
East Boulevard Rd.

0   300 yards
0   300 meters

Bishop Rd.
Puthur Rd.
Trunk Rd.
Thanjavur Rd.
TO THANJAVUR (60km)

Woyakondan Channel

Sea Horse Hospital
Municipal Office Rd.
Royal Rd.
MasNet Vision
Williams Rd.
GPO
Birds Rd.
Convent Rd.
Central Bus Stand
McDonald's Rd.
State Bank of India
Collector's Office Rd.
Lawson's Rd.
CANTONMENT
Rockin's Rd.
Dindigul (Bazadiar) Rd.
Madurai Rd.
Cleveland Rd.
TO MADURAI (130km)
St. John's Church
Trichy Junction Railway Station
TO ✈ (8km)
Bypass Rd.

TAMIL NADU

Femina Hotel (☎ 414501 or 414274; femina@md3.vsnl.net.in). 14-C Williams Rd. The cavernous lobby sparkles with the polish of a businessman's welcome. Even if you're not here for the vacuum cleaners sales conference, this is a good place to stay if you're ready to leave the real world behind for a while and retreat into the A/C wonderland of satellite TV, 24hr. room service, and seat toilets specially "disinfected for your protection." Singles Rs300-1050; doubles Rs500-1400. DC/MC/V. ❹

◐ 🎵 FOOD AND ENTERTAINMENT

Vasanta Bhavan, on the ground fl. of Hotel Abhirami, opposite the bus stand. If it's good, cheap south Indian food you're craving, then look no further. Lunch-time "meals" Rs20, *dosa* Rs12, *uttappam* Rs12. Open daily 6am-11pm. ❶

Jenney's Residency, 3/14 McDonald's Rd. Operated by the Park Sheraton Chain, Trichy's top 5-star hotel has 2 excellent restaurants, both serving the same multi-cuisine menu. Chandeliers, tablecloths, and marble floors make for a swish and shiny setting at **Suvia,** open daily 7am-11pm. The popular **Peaks of Kunlun** ❶ is open for dinner only 7-11pm. Fish Manchurian Rs90, sliced lamb in garlic sauce Rs80, chili pork Rs70, fish and chips Rs120. Jenney's also has the most original watering hole in town, the **Wild West Bar,** an old-fashioned saloon complete with swinging doors and a well-watered cowboy clutching an economy-size bottle of liquor. Open daily 11am-11pm.

Amirthan Restaurant, Ramyas Hotel on Williams Rd., near the tourist office. Small and tidy well-lit A/C place, ideal for a quick lunch. Small and quiet, with excellent service. *Dosa* Rs12-15, "meals" Rs25-40, chili *gobi* fry Rs35. Open daily 11am-11pm. ❶

Golden Rock, inside the Femina Hotel. Small, A/C cafe serving all the standard Indian and Chinese items around the clock. *Navratan Korma* Rs50, *palak paneer* Rs40, veg. noodles Rs55, Chennai meals Rs50. Open 24hr. ❶

◉ SIGHTS

THE ROCK FORT. One of the oldest lumps of rock anywhere in the world, this site was developed as a citadel long ago by the Pallavas and later by the Nayaks. Today, most people who reach the summit are Hindu pilgrims visiting the temples at the top or camera-happy tourists on the hunt for good views. At the bottom of the 400 rock-cut steps that lead to the top is a small shrine to Ganesh; remove your shoes before you start your climb. The views from the top are spectacular—you should be able to make out the *gopurams* of the Sri Ranganathaswamy and Sri Jambukeshwara temples in nearby Srirangam. The main Shiva temple is off-limits to non-Hindus, but not the smaller Vinayaka (Ganesh) shrine at the top, where a viewing platform affords superb 360° views of the surrounding countryside. *(Take bus #1 (Rs2) and get off at the huge Lady of Lourdes Church; from here, turn right, walk through the arch, and continue along the bazaar road until you come to a temple entrance on the left. Steps from here lead up to the fort. Open daily 6am-8pm. Rs1; camera fee Rs10.)*

OTHER SIGHTS. Our Lady of Lourdes Church, a Catholic church modeled after the Basilica in Lourdes, is worth a stop on your way to the Rock Fort. Back in town on Dindigul Rd., near the bus stand, **St. John's Church** (1816) is a mildly-interesting colonial-era Anglican Church, complete with louvered doors and the usual array of florid plaques to the faithful departed, most of whom seem to have fallen victim to cholera, malaria, or enemy bullets. Open daily 6am-6pm. Between 7 and 11am, the banks of the **Kaveri River** are the site of a series of ceremonies and rituals, as pilgrims bathe for good fortune, priests pray for childbirth, and mourners scatter ashes. *(Take the #1 bus and ask to be let off at Amma Mandapam, Rs4.)* For a more detailed explanation of the goings-on, see **Srirangam,** below.

NEAR TRICHY

SRIRANGAM பூர்ரங்கப்

Five kilometers north of Trichy, on a peninsula formed by the Kaveri River and its tributary, is **Srirangam,** home of the **Sri Ranganathaswamy Temple.** The sheer size of the temple, dedicated to Vishnu in his role as "Director of the Universe," makes it unique—over the centuries, the seven concentric walls have come to absorb an entire town. Work on most of the biggest buildings was begun by the Vijayanagar and Nayak dynasties. Construction has continued into the modern era; the largest of the temple's 21 *gopurams* was completed as recently as 1987.

Unusually, the entrance to the temple complex faces south rather than east; the reason, like so many things in India, is the stuff that legends are made of. Vibishana, the good brother of the demon Ravana (see **Ramayana,** p. 613), was awarded a reclining statue of Vishnu in recognition of his valor in war, under the stipulation that the *murti* should never be allowed to touch the ground. When Vibishana stopped by the Kaveri River to bathe, he gave the statue to a young klutz of a boy who dropped it. Infuriated, Vibishana chased the boy to the spot where the Rock Fort stands today and struck him on the head, at which point the boy was instantly transformed into a statue of Ganesh. The fallen Vishnu image was stuck forever to the place where it had fallen and bade Vibishana to rule Sri Lanka wisely with the words, "I will watch over you to the South."

You don't need to remove your shoes until you reach the fourth wall, beyond which are the elaborate sculptures that make this temple a rewarding masterpiece even for non-Hindus denied access to the sanctum itself. The fantastical *yalis* (face of lion, body of horse, legs of tiger, trunk of elephant, tail of cow) that greet you are a Nayak invention perhaps representing Hinduism's victory over Buddhism, symbolized by the elephant crouched under the *yali*. A little farther along is access to the roof, with its fantastic views and large statue of Garuda, Vishnu's vehicle. On the eastern side of the fourth enclosure of the complex is the "1000-pillared hall," containing 936 columns carved in the shape of horsemen riding rearing steeds. The 16th century Vijayanagara horse pillars portray the battle between the forces of good (horses) and evil (tigers). Behind them are the 10 avatars of Vishnu.

The **Amma Mandapam,** by the banks of the Kaveri, is on the way to the **Sri Ranganathaswamy Temple.** Pilgrims come here to purify themselves before offering further *puja* at the temple. Many of the ceremonies take place on the 10th day after birth or death; you may also see a plantain ceremony aimed at preventing second marriages, or small bags that have been tied to trees in hopes of pregnancy. This site has been sacred since ancient times, and the older gods and goddesses of the earth are remembered in the worship of snake sculptures placed under a spreading tree. *(Take the #1 bus from Trichy Bus Stand and get off at Amma Mandapam. Rs4.)*

The **Vaikunta Ekadasi Festival** (Dec.-Jan.) draws thousands of pilgrims to the site; during the festival, a procession enters through a doorway called the "Gateway of Heaven" to ensure everlasting afterlife. *(Bus #1 leaves from Trichy's bus stand. Temple open daily 6am-9pm.)*

The **Sri Jambukeshwara Temple,** shrine of the submerged *linga,* lies 2km east of Srirangam. One of the oldest and largest Shiva temples in Tamil Nadu, it is one of five Shaivite temples in southern India dedicated to the five elements; this one is dedicated to water. The temple, with five enclosures, contains an 800-pillar *mandapam* and a tank fed by a natural spring. At around noon every morning, a priest, clad in sari and crown representing Parvati, proceeds with an elephant from the sanctuary of the goddess to that of her husband, Shiva, and back again. *(Regular #1 bus service is currently interrupted by construction, making it easier to take a rickshaw for Rs30* *from the Vishnu temple to the Sri Jambukeshwara. Then, from the main street near the Sri Jambukeshwara, take any one of a number of buses going back to Rock Fort or to Trichy's Central Bus Stand. Temple open 6am-noon and 4-9pm. Free. Camera fee Rs10; video Rs125.)*

MADURAI மதுரை   ☎ 0452

According to legend, Shiva himself once stood over Madurai to dry his matted hair; the nectar that fell from his holy locks soaked the city and gave it its name, derived from the Tamil word *madhuram* (sweetness). The sugar buzz is still going strong in modern Madurai, a small but turbulent temple town that energizes the thousands who visit it every day. Madurai has thrived as a cultural center since it was founded as the capital of the Pandya kingdom that ruled much of South India in the 4th century BC. The powerful Vijayanagar Kingdom reigned from here throughout the 15th and early 16th centuries, when the city's famous Meenakshi Amman Temple was built. From 1559 onward, Madurai was ruled by the Nayak dynasty, which built what are the city's other main attractions today—the Teppakkulam and the Raya Gopuram. The Nayaks lost power in 1736, when the East India Company bought and defortified the city, tearing down its walls and filling in the moat that once stood where the Veli streets run today.

Madurai has survived to become an important commercial hub, with a population of well over a million. Huge electronic signboards illuminate the night sky, and large volumes of traffic (cars and cows) surge through the streets. For all its vibrant clamor, Madurai still moves to the rhythm of the temple's activities, and the towering *gopurams* of the Meenakshi temple can be seen from almost everywhere in the city. Huge crowds descend on Madurai during the city's many **festivals,** the most important being the **Chittrai Festival,** taking place in April-May. This celebrates the marriage of Meenakshi (Parvati) to Lord Sundareswarar (Shiva).

▐▀ TRANSPORTATION-

Flights: The **airport** (☎ 671333) is 15km south of the city center. A taxi into town costs around Rs200. City buses also run between the airport and the city center, but don't count on one being around waiting for you when you arrive. **Indian Airlines** (☎ 741236; airport 670133). 7A W. Veli St., opposite the railway station. Open M-Sa 10am-5pm. To **Chennai** (daily, US$95) and **Mumbai** (daily, US$190).

Trains: Madurai Junction Railway Station (☎ 743131). W. Veli St. Reservations open M-Sa 8am-1:30pm and 2-8pm, Su 8am-2pm. To: **Bangalore** (12hr., daily 3:40pm, Rs180); **Chennai** (10hr., 6-7 per day 6:45am-10pm, Rs166); **Coimbatore** (5hr., daily 6:40am and 11:20pm, Rs95); **Kanyakumari** (6hr.; daily 4:25am, W 7:10am; Rs97); Rs166); **Rameswaram** (5-5½hr., daily 4:45 and 6:15am, Rs84); **Tirupati** (12hr.; Th, Sa 9:30am; Rs193); **Trichy** (3hr., 6-8 per day 6:45am-10pm, Rs84). For trains to **Chidambaram, Tanjore,** and **Tirupati,** change at Trichy.

Buses: There are 2 interstate bus stands. Buses (Rs2-3) or auto-rickshaws (Rs40) connect the two. **Mattu Thavani Bus Stand** serves: **Bangalore** (10hr., 7 per day 6am-9pm, Rs145); **Chennai** (10hr., every 30min. Rs113-203); **Cochin** (11hr., 9am and 9pm, Rs117); **Kanyakumari** (6hr., 13 per day 6:15am-4:30am, Rs60); **Pondicherry** (8hr., 8:45 and 10pm, Rs90); **Rameswaram** (4hr., every 30min., Rs33-44); **Tanjore** (4hr., 4 per day 12:30pm-3:30am, Rs43); **Trichy** (4hr., frequent around the clock, Rs32-38); **Trivandrum** (8hr., 15 per day 6am-4:30am, Rs96). **Arapalayam Bus Stand** serves the north. To: **Coimbatore** (5hr., frequent around the clock, Rs46-51); **Kodaikanal** (4hr., 11 per day 6am-4:45pm, Rs26); **Munnar** (6hr., 8am).

TAMIL NADU

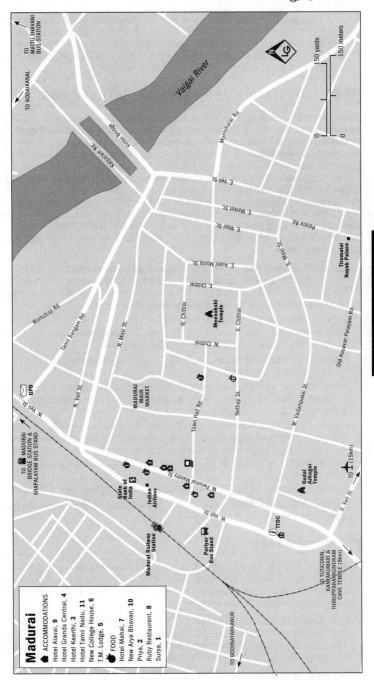

Madurai

▲ ACCOMMODATIONS
Hotel Alavai, **9**
Hotel Grands Central, **4**
Hotel Keerthi, **3**
Hotel Tamil Nadu, **11**
New College House, **6**
T.M. Lodge, **5**

● FOOD
Hotel Mahal, **7**
New Arya Bhavan, **10**
Priya, **2**
Ruby Restaurant, **8**
Surya, **1**

Local Transportation: Local buses leave from the **Periyar Bus Stand** on W. Veli St., a 2min. walk right out of the railway station. The stand is so congested that a small overflow lot has been set up east of the bus stand between W. Veli and W. Perumal Maistry St. Auto- and cycle-**rickshaws** are everywhere; the main stand is right outside the railway station. A pre-paid rickshaw booth opens when trains arrive.

■ ▮ ORIENTATION AND PRACTICAL INFORMATION

Madurai stretches north and south of the **Vaigai River.** The city is bordered on the south and west by railway tracks and is dominated by the **Meenakshi Temple.** The **Periyar Bus Stand** and **Madurai Junction Railway Station** are off **W. Veli St.,** 1km west of the temple. To reach the city center and the budget hotels from the railway station, turn right onto W. Veli St., and then left again on Town Hall Rd., which leads east toward the temple; from **Periyar bus stand,** follow the wider **Nethaji (Dindigul) Rd.,** marked by the Hotel Empee. Streets are arranged concentrically around the temple, forming an irregular grid. Closest to the temple are North, East, South, and West **Chittrai St.** Farther from the temple are North, East, South, and West **Avani Moola St.** North, East, South, and West **Masi St.** are encircled by North, East, South, and West **Veli St.** To cross the Vaigai River, head 1km northeast of the temple and across **Victor Bridge.**

Tourist Office: Tamil Nadu Tourism Development Corporation (TTDC) (☎ 734757). W. Veli St. Next to the Hotel Tamil Nadu. Turn right out of the railway station and walk straight down W. Veli St.; it's on the left after 5min. or so. Open M-F 10am-5:30pm. There are also offices at the airport and railway station.

Currency Exchange: State Bank of India (☎ 742127). 6 W. Veli St. Sangam Towers, north of the railway station and across the street. Changes a wide range of currencies and traveler's checks. Open M-F 10am-4pm, Sa 10am-1pm.

Bookstore: Malligai Book Centre, 11 W. Veli St. Opposite the railway station. Open M-Sa 9am-1pm and 3:30-9pm.

Police: The main station (☎ 538015) is on the north bank, on the road to Natham. The B-7 station, on W. Veli St. (☎ 73665) just past the tourist office, is the closest to the hotel area.

Pharmacy & Hospital: There are plenty of pharmacies along Town Hall Rd. and around the budget hotel area, most of them open 8am-10pm. The private **Jawahar Hospital** (☎ 580022, 23, 24). 14 Main Rd., KK Nagar, on the northern bank of Vaigai, and the **Apollo Hospital** (☎ 580892 or 581148), Lake View Rd., also in KK Nagar, both have 24hr. pharmacies.

Internet: Global Net, Nethaji St. Near W. Perumal Maistry St. Rs20 per hr. Open 24hr.

Post Office: Head Post Office, on N. Veli St. Open M-Sa 9am-7pm, Su 8am-5pm. **Postal Code:** 625001.

▮ ACCOMMODATIONS

Nearly all of Madurai's hotels are within walking distance of the Meenakshi Temple and the city's transportation hubs. Many of the budget places are on West Perumal Maistry St., which runs parallel to W. Veli St., a 1min. walk from the railway station. 24hr. check-out is standard.

Hotel Keerthi (☎ 741501; fax 741510). 40 W. Perumal Maistry St. 2 blocks north of Town Hall Rd. Polite staff and whitewashed rooms with spotless sheets, ample lighting, TVs, and phones. Clean attached baths with 24hr. hot water. A/C rooms have seat toilets. Singles Rs175; doubles Rs220-300. ❶

New College House (☎ 742971). 2 Town Hall Rd. Huge, labyrinthine eel's-nest of a place, with over 100 large, clean rooms and attached (squat toilets) baths and TVs—your best bet during peak season, when other hotels fill up. Self-contained mini-village offers relief from the congestion of the area. Single Rs150-250; doubles Rs199-500. ❶

Hotel Grands Central (☎ 743940). 47 W. Perumal Maistry St. Good-sized rooms with clean sheets and TVs. Attached bath with seat toilet and hot water. Singles Rs175; doubles Rs195-300. ❶

Hotel Alavai (☎ 740551 or 741550). 86 W. Perumal Maistry St. Clean and large rooms containing the usual budget combo: rickety bed, plastic chair, and attached bathroom with squat toilet. A good rock-bottom option. Singles Rs75; doubles Rs120. ❶

Hotel Tamil Nadu (☎ 737471). W. Veli St. Turn right out of the station and walk straight for 5min.; it's on the left. Singles Rs150; doubles Rs195-575. ❶

T.M. Lodge (☎ 741651). W. Perumal Maisty St. A touch above most other places in this range. Rooms come with TV, towel, soap, and hot water. Attached bathroom (seat toilets). Singles Rs195; doubles Rs260-420. ❶

🍴 FOOD

The best restaurants in Madurai are in and around the hotels on W. Perumal Maistry St. and Town Hall Rd. Many of the hotels have rooftop dining, which usually means quiet surroundings, cool breezes, and great temple views.

🍴 **New Arya Bhavan,** 241-A W. Masi St., at Nethaji Rd., on a corner on your left as you head from N. Perumal Maistry toward the temple. A large, calm oasis on a busy street, this local favorite serves up delicious *masala dosas* (Rs12), *uttappam* (Rs11), and all the rest. A/C banquet booths available upstairs for heat-hassled tourists in need of a quick cool-down. Attached sweet shop. Open daily 6:30-10:30pm. ❶

Surya, 110 W. Perumal Maistry St., on the roof of Hotel Supreme. Relax with a few beers (Rs80) in a pleasant open-air setting 10 floors up from all the noise and fumes of the street. *Dosas* Rs25, *Malai kofta* Rs40, veg. sizzler Rs90. Rooftop restaurant open daily 4-11pm; A/C restaurant on ground fl. open daily 6am-11pm. If you're in the mood for surreal basement noise, try the **Apollo 96 Bar** downstairs. Once upon a time, this is what people thought the world would look like in AD 2001. Open daily 11am-11pm. ❶

Priya, 102 W. Perumal Maistry St., in Hotel Prem Nivas. Typical mid-range hotel restaurant, with good Indian food and foreigner-friendly luxury items like cornflakes (Rs20). *Aloo gobi* Rs25, *malai kofta* Rs25, veg. sandwich Rs20. Open daily 7am-10:30pm. ❶

Hotel Mahal, 21 Town Hall Rd., on the left as you head toward the temple. Long narrow room filled with whirling fans and lined with private dining booths full of potted plants. The menu here is the most varied in town: *madura* chicken Rs45, roast leg of lamb Rs80, beer Rs70. Popular with foreign tourists. Open daily 7am-11pm. ❶

Ruby Restaurant, W. Perumal Maistry St., next to Ruby Lodge. One of Madurai's main foreigner hubs. Best visited at night. Egg fried rice Rs40, chicken balls Rs60, *mutter* dishes Rs50-75, fish and prawns Rs30-60. Open daily 10am-late. ❶

👁 SIGHTS

MEENAKSHI AMMAN TEMPLE

The temple complex is accessible via any of the 4 gopurams. Open daily 6:30am-12:30pm and 4-9pm. Free. Camera fee Rs30.

The Meenakshi Amman Temple, drawing more than 10,000 people every day, is one of the most splendid in all of Tamil Nadu. Besides dazzling visitors with the 30 million sculptures that adorn the complex, the temple is also impressive for its sheer size—it covers an incredible 65,000 sq. meters, and the tallest of the temple's twelve *gopurams* is nearly 50m high.

Dedicated to Shiva (Sundareswarar) as well as to his consort Parvati (Meenakshi), the temple was originally a humble shrine built by the Pandyas, later enriched and expanded by the patronage of the Vijayanagar kings. The complex grew further when the Nayaks came to power in the 16th century and began work on the temple's famous towering *gopurams*. The temple was opened to Untouchables after Gandhi's visit here in 1946.

Legend has it that Pandya King Malayadwaja was childless and desperate for a male heir, so the king appealed to the gods for help and set about performing a series of *yagnas*, or fire sacrifices. Much to the king's surprise, a three-year-old girl emerged from the flames to stand before him one day—a beautiful girl with fish-like eyes ("Meenakshi" means fish-eyed), three breasts, and a whole lot of divine attitude. The king was a trifle troubled by his daughter's unconventional appearance, but a voice from above assured him that her third breast would disappear once she found the man who would one day become her husband. Meenakshi eventually grew up to become a beautiful princess, and eventually set out to conquer the world. One after another the gods fell before her, powerless in the face of her beauty and power, until only Shiva was left. When she confronted Shiva, Meenakshi's heart turned to *ghee*. Her third breast disappeared, and her wild ways were soon a thing of the past. Meenakshi and Sundareswar (aka Shiva) were married in Madurai and ruled the Pandya kingdom together from here. The **Meenakshi Kalyanam** festival commemorating the wedding takes place in April-May.

ASHTA SHAKTI AND MEENAKSHI NAYAKKAR MANDAPAMS. In the southeastern corner is the brightly painted Ashta Shakti Mandapam (Eight Shakti Corridor), where hawkers peddle postcards, curios, and *puja* offerings. The passage was named for the eight *avatars* of the goddess Shakti carved on its pillars. Other sculptures and paintings depict the miracles *(tiruvilayadal)* of Shiva. The Meenakshi Nayakkar Mandapam has two rows of pillars carved with images of the *yali*, a mythological beast with the body of a lion and the head of an elephant, commonly used as a symbol of Nayak power.

POLLY WANT A TAROT In these modern times of high-tech gizmos and Internet heart-break, the hand-cast horoscope looks set to go the ill-starred way of the wind-up automobile and the beehive hairdo. Thanks to computers, you can now have your horoscope *(jadagam)* plotted just by specifying your date of birth, which will be checked against a database of planetary positions and star migrations. The result is spooled out unceremoniously in barely legible dot matrix. In some parts of India, though, you can still get your fortune told the good old-fashioned way: by *kili josyam* (parrot astrology). The human astrologer (merely the hands and mouth of the parrot) has a number of cards placed face down in front of him, marked with pictures of deities. To determine a client's fortune, he releases a highly trained parrot from its cage, and the bird grabs one of the cards in its beak. Each deity corresponds to a chapter in the *Agastya Arudal,* an ancient fortune-telling treatise written by the sage Agastya. The astrologer then divines the client's fortune from the designated chapter. The prognosticating polly is re-caged, but the game continues, as the same astrologer is usually also a palmist and has a million ways to clarify or elaborate upon the parrot's prediction.

POTRAMARAI KULAM. The corridors around the Potramarai Kulam (Golden Lotus Tank) are often crowded by devotees relaxing in the shade or taking in the spectacular view of the temple's southern *gopuram*. The tank itself is frequented by pilgrims seeking a purifying bath in its light green waters, following the tradition of Indra, who is said to have bathed here. In ancient times, the Tamil Sangam (Academy of Poets) used to meet in the area around the tank. Locals claim that the Sangam judged the merit of literary works by tossing submissions into the tank. If a work sank, the aspiring writer's hopes went along with it. Only works that floated were deemed worthy of the Sangam's attention.

KILIKOOTU MANDAPAM. The northwest corner of the tank leads directly to the Meenakshi Shrine, which is closed to non-Hindus; the corridor surrounding the shrine, however, is open to all. Called the Kilikootu Mandapam, or Parrot Cage Corridor, the space was once used to keep green parrots, lucky birds who were trained to repeat Meenakshi's name in offerings to the goddess.

OONJAL MANDAPAM. The golden images of Meenakshi and Sundareswar are carried into the neighboring 16th-century Oonjal Mandapam (Swing Corridor) to be placed on a swing and sung to every Friday at 5:30pm. The shrine has a three-story *gopuram* guarded by two stern *dwarapalakas* (watchmen) and is supported by golden, rectangular columns that bear the mark of a lotus. Along the perimeter of the chamber, granite panels of the divine couple overlook the crowds.

KAMBATHADI MANDAPAM. North of the Oonjal Mandapam is the **Sundareswar Shrine,** with its eight-foot image of Ganesh (Mukkuruni Vinayakar). The idol was discovered in the 17th century when King Tirumalai Nayak began digging the Mariamman Teppakulam in the southeastern corner of the city. To the right, in the northeast corner of the enclosure, is the Kambathadi Mandapam, adorned with elegant pillars, each of which bears a sculpture of Meenakshi or Shiva. Sculptures of Shiva and Kali trying to out-dance one another are pelted with balls of *ghee* by devotees. On the left are two sculptures of Shiva killing the demon child. A golden flagstaff with 32 sections symbolizes the human backbone and is surrounded by various gods, including Durga and Siddhar. The inner chamber contains the image of Sundareswar and an image of Nataraja, unique for having his right foot raised.

AYIRAKKAL MANDAPAM. East of the Kambathadi Mandapam is a lively market, where vendors sell postcards and religious trinkets. These stands surround the Ayirakkal Mandapam (Thousand Pillar Hall), which contains 985 carved pillars (no word on the other 15). It has been converted into a quiet **museum** with a substantial collection of sculptures. *(Open daily 7am-7:30pm. Rs2; camera fee Rs10.)*

OTHER SIGHTS

GANDHI MUSEUM. The Mahatma visited Madurai several times, but this museum does much more than merely chronicle his stops. One section presents a fiery version of the events leading up to Independence; the other focuses on samples of Gandhi's correspondence and houses relics such as the loincloth he was wearing when he was killed. *(Bus #3 from Periyar to Anna Bus stand. Auto-rickshaw Rs20. Open 10am-1pm and 2-5:30pm. Free. Camera fee Rs10; video Rs50.)*

TIRUMALAI NAYAK PALACE. All that remains of Tirumalai's grand 17th-century palace is the cavernous **Swargavilasam** (Celestial Pavilion), a stretching courtyard lined with pillars and arcades. Nayak rulers held their public audiences under the domed ceiling of the pavilion. A passage at the back of the audience chamber leads to the former dance hall, large parts of which have been fully restored. This is the

TAMIL NADU

most impressive part of the palace—carvings of gargoyle-like dragons and elephants line the rich crimson and cream walls, and give a hint of the palace's former grandeur. The palace houses a small collection of stone carvings and early terracottas. *(1.5km southeast of the Meenakshi Temple. Open daily 9am-1pm and 2-5pm. Rs1.)*

VANDIYUR MARIAMMAN TEPPAKULAM. This square water tank has a tree-surrounded **shrine** in the center. The tank was built in 1646 by Tirumalai Nayak, who retired with his harem to the central shrine. These days the tank is usually dry, and the only activity in the area is boys playing cricket. Every year, a colorful float festival (Jan.-Feb.) commemorates the birth of its builder. *(Kamarajar Rd., 5km southeast of the railway station. Bus #4 or 4A.)*

THIRUPPARANKUNDRAM. Though not as awe-inspiring as Meenakshi Amman, Thirupparankundram is an impressive cave-temple dedicated to Lord Subramanya guarded by sculptures of prancing horses. The **inner sanctum** is carved right out of the rock in the side of a mountain and is accessible to non-Hindus. *(8km south of town from Periyar Bus Stand. Bus #5, 15min., Rs2.50. Open 5am-12:30pm and 4-9:30pm.)*

🎵 🛍 ENTERTAINMENT AND SHOPPING

There are several **cinemas** near the Periyar Bus Stand. *The Hindu* has the latest listings for English-language films. Check with the tourist office for **cultural programs** such as classical dancing and music in Lakshmi Sundaram Hall, Tallakulam (☎530858). Madurai is full of **textile shops** and sari showrooms. You will be accosted wherever you go by tailors keen to make you an exact copy of whatever you're wearing for a nominal cost. As always, beware of auto-rickshaw drivers who steer you toward a particular handicraft store—they're just after the commission. Even if you don't plan on buying anything, you may find yourself slurping down yet another free 7-Up as a smooth-talking salesman tries to talk you into buying that Rs500 parakeet-embroidered pillowcase you never knew you wanted. **Parameswari Stores,** 21 East Chittrai St., just outside the southern *gopuram* of the Meenakshi Temple, is well-known for its silk-cotton blends (☎747988. Open daily 9am-10pm). **Khadi Emporium,** Town Hall Rd., is a good place to buy gifts and wooden carvings. For the full Kashmiri-carpet experience, try the large multi-story **Madurai Gallery,** Cottage Expo Crafts, 19 N. Chittrai St. (☎627851. Open daily 9am-9pm.) **Meenakshi Treasures,** also on N. Chittrai St., has a beautiful but expensive jewelry collection upstairs, as well as an extensive range of silks, sandalwood, and silverware. (☎630240. Open daily 9am-8:30pm.)

RAMESWARAM இராமேசுவரயு ☎04573

The setting of some of the most important scenes in the *Ramayana* (see p. 613), Rameswaram is the venerated spot from which Rama, the epic's hero, launched an attack on Ravana's fortress on the island of Lanka. According to a later myth, Rama made a *linga* of sand here after defeating Ravana, to honor Shiva and expiate the sin of murder. Situated on a remote island off the country's southeastern coast, Rameswaram is a tiny town dominated by one huge monument, the Ramanathaswamy Temple, which draws thousands of Hindu pilgrims from all over India. Rameswaram is also significant as the southern holy *dham* (abode), one of India's four sacred places marking the cardinal directions. (The others are Dwarka in the west, Badrinath in the north, and Puri in the east.) A number of major festivals take place in Rameswaram, including **Thai Amavasai** (Jan.), **Masi Sivarathiri** (Feb.-Mar.), and **Adiammavasai** (Jul.-Aug.). For the rest of the year, Rameswaram is a quiet, slow-paced little town that sees relatively few foreign tourists, and a pleasant place to kick back and watch the waves for a few days.

TRANSPORTATION

Trains: Rameswaram Station (☎21226). 1 km. southwest of the temple. To: **Chennai (Tambaram)** (17hr., noon and 3:10pm, Rs240); **Coimbatore** (12hr., 5pm, Rs140); **Madurai** (5hr., 4pm, 2nd class Rs27; 7hr., 7pm, sleeper Rs48); **Trichy** (7½hr., 9:30pm, Rs125).

Buses: The **bus stand** is on Bazaar Rd., 2km west of the temple. Frequent buses run between the temple and the bus stand 24hr. (10min., Rs1.50). Buses to: **Chennai** (12hr., 5pm, Rs240); **Kanyakumari** (12hr.; 7:30am, 7:30 and 8pm; Rs170); **Madurai** (4hr., every 20min. around the clock, Rs38); **Tanjore** (6hr., 4 per day 6:55am-4pm, Rs52); **Trichy** (6hr., 20 per day 4am-9:20pm, Rs52).

Local Transportation: Unmetered **cycle-** and **auto-rickshaws** go all over town, and silver-and-red **local buses** shuttle between the bus stand and E. Car St. **Bikes** can be hired (Rs3 per hr.) from a stall opposite the Tourist Information Centre on East Car St.

ORIENTATION AND PRACTICAL INFORMATION

Getting around Rameswaram involves wandering the four **Car Streets**—North, East, South, and West—surrounding the **Ramanathaswamy Temple.** Most of the hotels and restaurants are on these four streets and on **Sannadhi St.,** which runs east from the middle of E. Car St. to the Bay of Bengal. To reach the temple from the railway station, walk out of the main entrance and follow the road for about 300m as it curves slightly, then turn left (north) when you hit the principal north-south thoroughfare. Walk north for 500m until you reach **Middle St.,** which leads east (right) to the middle of W. Car St. and the western entrance to the temple.

Tourist Office: (☎21371). 14 E. Car St. Has rudimentary maps of Rameswaram. Open M-F 10am-5:45pm. The Tourist Information Centre, inside the train station, and the Temple Information Center, inside the temple, are less useful and often closed.

Police station: (☎21246). In a red brick bldg. at the junction of E. and N. Car St.

Pharmacy: Sekar Medicals, on the corner of Middle St. and Bazaar St., 200m up the road from Hotel Maharaja's. Open daily 7:30am-10:30pm.

Hospital: There is a **government hospital** near the railway station, but you might find better medical resources in Madurai.

Post office: (☎21230). On Middle St., 500m down on the left-hand side as you head away from the temple toward the bus stand. Open M-Sa 9am-3:30pm.

ACCOMMODATIONS

Except for the TTDC Rest House, most hotels are in the immediate vicinity of the Ramanathaswamy Temple. Accommodations are very basic, catering to pilgrims looking for a cheap place to crash for the night. Rameswaram's tap water can be salty, and showers are extremely rare, so test the plumbing before checking in. Reserve ahead during the pilgrimage season (July-Aug.).

Hotel Maharaja's (☎21271or 21721; fax 21161). 32 Middle St. Pleasant rooms with cable TV and a view of the temple's *gopurams*. Attached squat toilets are the cleanest you'll find; hot water available. Check-out 24hr. Singles Rs150; doubles Rs265-510. ❶

TAMIL NADU

Hotel Tamil Nadu (☎21277 or 21064; fax 21070). On the beachfront, just past the holy bathing spot. More expensive, but farther from the temple noise. The rooms here are clean and blessed with more air, light, and life than those in most TTDC-run hotels. All rooms have attached baths (seat toilets) and hot water showers. Good attached restaurant and bar from which you can see the sea. Doubles Rs400-600. ❷

Hotel Guru (☎21134 or 21531). 12 E. Car St., at the northernmost end of the street. Very basic rooms with attached (squat) bath. Singles Rs100; doubles Rs175-650. ❶

🍴 FOOD

For the most part, dining options in the town are restricted to a choice between all-but-identical "meals" joints serving up the familiar *idlis*, *dosas*, and *sambar* rice. The better hotels in town often have decent attached restaurants.

Vasanta Bhavan, at the southern end of E. Car St. As always, the quality of the food here is very good, and the prices are unbeatable. "Meals" Rs15. Open daily 6am-10pm. ❶

Ganesh Mess, near Hotel Maharaja's and the western gate. Another very popular "meals" place serving all your South Indian favorites. Onion *uttappam* Rs10, special *dosa* Rs10, "meals" Rs17. Open daily 7am-3:30pm and 7-10pm. ❶

👁 SIGHTS

THE RAMANATHASWAMY TEMPLE. The Bay of Bengal and the 22 tanks of the Ramanasthawamy Temple form part of one of the most sacred pilgrimages a Hindu can make; its spiritual power is akin to jumping in the waters of the Ganga at Varanasi (see p. 703). Before taking *darshan* at the temple's resident deities, pilgrims first bathe in the sea at **Agni Theetum** ("Holy Fire Water") and then proceed to the wet temple where they are led from wet holy tank to wet holy tank. To expedite the process, temple employees are on hand to dump buckets of salty water on devotees. The best time to visit is at dawn, when water-splashing is at its peak and thousands of dripping-wet pilgrims scurry from one wet washing place to the next. If you're so inclined, an aggressive squad of guides and friendly touts will compete to help get your hair wet as well. Taking part in the ritual without their help may be tricky, as certain parts of the temple complex are off-limits to non-Hindus.

The inner sanctum houses two *lingas*, one of which was fashioned out of sand by Rama himself. According to a later version of the *Ramayana*, Rama returned to Rameswaram after he had killed Ravana in Lanka, only to discover that Ravana had been a brahmin and that his murder was therefore a grave sin. Rama sent Hanuman to bring back a *linga* with which Rama could worship Shiva and expiate his guilt, but the monkey was slow in returning, and Rama had to make do with a *linga* of sand. When Hanuman finally returned and tried to replace the makeshift *linga*, it would not budge; the new *linga* was installed to the left of it.

Construction of the temple, famous for its sculpted pillars and long wet corridors, began in the 12th century under the Chola empire; the last major alterations to the temple were made in the mid-18th century by the Raja of Ramnathapuram, Muthuramalinga Sethupathi. The eastern *gopuram* was completed during the 20th century, and this, along with recent renovation work, has led to the presence of a number of incongruous-looking concrete pillars within this centuries-old complex. *(Wet temple open daily 4am-8pm. Rs2. Bathing at dawn. Inner sanctum closed noon-4pm.)*

THE RAMAYANA Arguably the most culturally influential work of literature in India, the *Ramayana* (literally, "the romance of Rama") has inspired thousands
of dances, paintings, shadow puppet shows, inter-religious riots, and even its own TV
mini-series. The epic's main characters, Rama and Sita, are revered as archetypes of
those who unwaveringly follow their *dharma* (duty or fate). The Sanskrit poet Valmiki is
thought to have composed the *Ramayana* around 400 BC, basing it on events that
took place between 1000 and 700 BC. Here's our take two:

   Act I, Scene 1: Rama is born to King Dasaratha's wife Kausalya in Ayodhya, capital
of Kosala. Dasaratha's other wives, Kaikeyi and Sumithra, bear him Bharata and the
twins Lakshman and Shatrugna, respectively. **Scene 2:** Rama journeys with his guru
Viswamitra to the kingdom of Mithila, where he falls in love at first sight with King Janaka's beautiful daughter, Sita. But winning her hand is not an easy task. Fearing he will
lose his daughter to an unworthy man, Janaka declares that only he who is able to
break Shiva's divine bow can have her hand in marriage. **Scene 3:** Rama successfully
breaks the bow, and the two kingdoms delight in the wedding of Rama and Sita. **Scene
4:** The aging Dasaratha names Rama as his successor, but his wife Kaikeyi refuses to
accept Rama as king, forcing Dasaratha to banish Rama to the forest for 14 years.
Kaikeyi's son Bharata is crowned king instead.

   Act II, Scene 1: Rama, Sita, and Rama's faithful brother Lakshman leave Ayodhya for
the forest. The sorrowful Dasaratha soon dies, and Bharata rushes to the forest, begging Rama to return to claim the throne. Unwilling to break his promise to his father,
Rama stays in the forest for the next 14 years. **Scene 2:** Ravana, chief of the *asuras*
(demons), abducts Sita to his island kingdom of Lanka. **Scene 3:** Rama and Lakshman
journey in search of Sita, encountering, en route, the clever monkey Hanuman, son of
the wind god. Rama sends Hanuman to Lanka to assess the situation and deliver a
token to his beloved wife. Hanuman, with a classic arsonist move, sets fire to the entire
capital of Lanka before he leaves. **Scene 4:** With the help of a Lankan spy, Rama and
his army of monkeys advance on Lanka. The valiant monkeys build a bridge to Lanka,
and a celestial battle ensues. Rama emerges victorious, vanquishing Ravana and winning back Sita. **Scene 5:** 14 years are up, and Rama, Lakshman, Sita, and Hanuman
return to Kosala. Rama is crowned king, and Ayodhya erupts in celebration upon the
revelation that Rama is an avatar of Vishnu. **Scene 6:** Sita's fidelity during Rama's
absence is questioned. Subordinating his trust in Sita to his princely duty, Rama subjects her to an ordeal of fire, from which she emerges unscathed and vindicated. However, mortified by her husband's lack of faith, she prefers to be swallowed up by
mother Earth than to be his queen. S'long mate. **The end.**

OTHER SIGHTS. The Gandamadana Paravtham, a simple, white-washed temple on
top of the highest hill in town, houses an imprint of Lord Rama's feet and commands
splendid views of the sandy island terrain. *(3km north of the Ramanathaswamy Temple.
Head away from Ramanathaswamy Temple along Middle St., and turn right at the first crossroads. Follow the road straight uphill to the temple.)* The southeastern end of the island
forms a great finger of sand pointing toward Sri Lanka. The railway line to Dhanushkodi was destroyed by a cyclone that roared through in 1964, but it is accessible today
by bus. *(Take bus #3 from E. Car St. (30min., Rs3.50) to the "new" Dhanushkodi; from there it's
3km of sand, seashells, and surf to the village itself.)* The Kothandaramar Temple, 20km
along the road to Dhanushkodi, dedicated to Rama, is said to mark the site where
Ravana's brother, Vibhishana, was crowned king of Lanka after Ravana's death.
Painted scenes from the *Ramayana* line the walls of the interior. *(Accessible by the #3
bus to Dhanushkodi. Open daily 8am-5pm.)* Touts and tour guides near the temple and holy

bathing spot will compete to take you out snorkeling over the beautiful coral reefs that lie a few km offshore. Prices vary enormously according to supply and demand; bargain hard, and aim to pay around Rs200-300 for an afternoon's float. For a genuinely friendly guide, it is worth seeking out **A. "Vijay" Kulanthaiswamy,** a young fisherman who lives in the village of Olaikuda, a couple of km north along the coast. He speaks good English and likes to invite his new-found friends back home for meals of rice and freshly caught fish. He can also arrange cheap snorkeling and fishing excursions. His friends at the STD booth in Hotel Maharaja's can help find him.

KANYAKUMARI கஇந் யாகுமாஸ் ☎ 04652

Kanyakumari (Cape Comorin), the southernmost tip of the Indian subcontinent, is particularly auspicious for Hindus because it is the meeting place of three major bodies of water—the Arabian Ocean, the Bay of Bengal, and the Indian Ocean. Hindu pilgrims come by the thousands to sacred Kanyakumari to watch the sun set into one ocean and rise out of another. Just as South India's beach resorts provide sun, sand, and tropical fruits in one easy-to-swallow package for consumption by Western tourists, so Kanyakumari provides an equally irresistible dose of patriotism, spirituality, and tacky shell art for Indian tourists. As well as monuments to Gandhi and Swami Vivekandanda, Kanyakumari is also the site of the Kumari Amman Temple, dedicated to Devi Kanya, a virginal incarnation of Parvati. The holiness that Kanyakumari's monuments impart to the town is hard to spot by day, however, as tour buses parked along the seafront disgorge masses of pilgrims into the waiting arms of beach vendors hawking cheap souvenirs. Screeching families, scores of scantily clad men, and children shooting their plastic guns all push and shove their way through the monuments. But when the sun goes down and the hyperactive pilgrims slow down to munch on deep-fried peppers and bananas at lit-up street stalls, the carnivalesque air just about manages to mitigate the town's grimness. Weekends are a peak of activity; avoid them if at all possible.

▄ TRANSPORTATION

Trains: Railway station, on Main Rd., a 15min. walk from the sea. Reservations open M-Sa 8am-noon and 2-4pm, Su 8am-2pm. To: **Bangalore** (20hr., 6:30am, Rs252); **Chennai** (17hr., 5:45am and 3:40pm, Rs228); **Ernakulam** (10hr., 2-3 per day 12:45pm-6:30am, Rs405); **Trivandrum** (2½hr., 2-3 per day 12:45pm-6:30am, Rs84).

Buses: The **bus stand** posts schedules in English. All buses also stop on Main Rd.; save yourself the walk and get off opposite the Government Hospital. **Tamil Nadu State Express Transport** (☎ 46019) runs buses to: **Chennai** (16hr., 8 per day 9:30am-8:30pm, Rs217-238); **Coimbatore** (11hr., 5:45pm, Rs146); **Kodai** (10hr., 8:45pm, Rs101); **Madurai** (6hr., frequent 9:30am-8:45pm, Rs82); **Ooty** (14hr., 5:45 and 6:30pm, Rs152). Buses also go to **Nagercoil** (30min., every 5min., Rs4.50), where there are frequent connections to many other cities. **Kerala's state buses,** KRSTC, leave from platform #4 of the bus station and go to: **Ernakulam** (8hr., 7:15 and 9am, Rs89); **Kovalam** (3hr., 6:30am and 1pm, Rs35); **Trivandrum** (2½hr., 11 per day 5:45am-9:15pm, Rs20). The Kovalam schedule is particularly variable; it may be easiest to go to Trivandrum and take a local bus from there.

▄ ▄ ORIENTATION AND PRACTICAL INFORMATION

Buses from Trivandrum and Madurai head south down **Main Rd.** past the **railway station.** Buses stop on Main Rd., just north of S. Car St. and then turn west onto **Bus Stand Rd.,** past the **lighthouse,** to the **bus stand.** Main Rd. continues south past the junction to the **tourist office** and peters out at the seafront by the **Gandhi Memorial.** Running east from Main Rd. Junction, Bus Stand Rd. crosses **Sannadhi St.** before ending at the **ferry service station.** Sannadhi St. heads south through the stalls to the **Kumari Amman Temple,** at the very tip of the subcontinent.

Tourist Office: Main Rd. (☎46276). On the right, in a circular building north of the Gandhi Memorial. Open M-F 10am-5:45pm. Open for shorter hours some weekends.

Currency Exchange: Canara Bank, Main Rd., a 5-10min. walk north of Main Rd. Junction, on the left. Changes AmEx and Thomas Cook traveler's checks. Gives cash advances on AmEx/MC/V. Allow at least 1hr. Open M-F 10am-2pm, Sa 10am-noon.

Police: Main Rd. (☎46224). Next to the GPO.

Pharmacy: Sastha Pharmacy, Main Rd. (☎46455). Halfway between the railway station and the tourist office, just beyond Hotel Sangam. Open daily 8:30am-9:30pm.

Hospital: Dr. Arumugam's clinic, E. Car St. (☎46349). Between Hotels Manickham and Maadhini.

Internet: LS Computers, Middle St., in Hotel Ashoka, parallel to E. Car St. Rs90 per hr. Open M-Sa 9:30am-11pm, Su 10:30am-11pm.

Post Office: GPO, Main Rd., just south of Canara Bank. Open M-Sa 8am-noon and 1:30-4:30pm. **Postal Code:** 629702.

ACCOMMODATIONS

Every second building in Kanyakumari provides lodging of some kind. Prices begin to soar in August and peak between October and February. There is no such thing as tranquility here—families wake up noisily at 5:30am to catch the sunrise. All hotels listed have attached restaurants.

Manickam Tourist House, N. Car St. (☎46387). Near Hotel Maadhini. Decent amenities and views of the sea. Facilities are a little tired, but cheap. Clean rooms with attached bathrooms and balconies. Check-out 24hr. Singles Rs160-250; doubles Rs250-350. ❶

Hotel Maadhini, E. Car St. (☎46787). On the shore, 200m north of the temple. Carpeted rooms with bright lighting and large disinfected baths with soap and towels. Balcony views of the ocean and fishing villages. 24hr. hot water. Doubles Rs350-900. ❸

Hotel Sangam, Main Rd. (☎46351). Opposite the GPO. Less-than-tranquil location. Clean, well-lit rooms have sea views and spotless baths with seat toilets and towels. Rooftop views of the sunrise. 24hr. room service. Singles and doubles Rs380-900. ❸

Kerala House (☎46229). On the seaward side of Bus Stand Rd., between the bus stand and Main Rd.; look for signs. Upscale government place, with dining room tables, dressing rooms, and ocean views. Faded, but still an elegant option. Doubles Rs500-750. ❷

Hotel Narmadha, Bus Stand Rd. (☎71365). Close to Main Rd. Junction. Clean, spacious doubles. Attached baths have squat toilets. Rooms Rs150-250. ❶

FOOD

Since people come to attend to spiritual affairs and buy souvenirs, it's perhaps not surprising that material matters, like food, lean toward simple and uninspiring. The stalls, which set up at night at the junction of Main and Bus Station Rd., will slap down a banana leaf in front of you and serve excellent fast meals (chicken or fish fry with a veg. curry and *parathas*) for less than Rs25.

Hotel Saravana has two very popular branches: one on Sannadhi St., 50m in front of the temple, and another around the corner toward Main Rd. Junction. South Indian breakfasts (excellent *masala dosa* Rs16), and Gujarati, Rajasthani, Punjabi, and South Indian veg. *thalis* (Rs25). *Thalis* served 11am-3pm. Both open daily 6am-10pm. ❶

Hotel Sangam, Main Rd., opposite the GPO. One of the few places with Chinese and non-veg. fare. A wide range of slightly misspelled tasties. Most dishes Rs25-70, eggs and sandwiches Rs15-25. Open daily 6:30am-11:30pm. ❶

Sree Bhagavath Amman Canteen, right next to the temple entrance. Serves up basic food to hungry pilgrims. *Masala dosa* Rs12, veg. meal Rs15. Open daily 6am-9pm. ❶

Anila Restaurant (or Hotel Alana depending on the sign), Bus Stand Rd., next to Hotel Narmadha, close to Main Rd. Junction. Decent, if basic, source for North Indian veg. dishes. *Aloo gobhi* Rs12, meals Rs20. Open daily 7am-10:30pm. ❶

🗗 SIGHTS

KUMARI AMMAN TEMPLE. The seaside Kumari Amman Temple, with its unmistakable red-and-white vertical temple stripes, is at the very tip of India. Dedicated to Kanya Devi, an incarnation of Parvati, the temple celebrates the penance she did in the hope of winning Shiva's hand in marriage. Shiva consented and set off for the midnight wedding ceremony. The other gods, wanting Kanya Devi to retain her divine *shakti* by remaining a virgin, hatched a plot to spoil the wedding. The sage Narada, assuming the form of a rooster, crowed for dawn long before sunrise to make Shiva think he was late for the ceremony. Shiva fell for the trick and went home, leaving poor, heartbroken Kanya Devi an eternal virgin.

Foreigners should expect to pay an entrance fee and will find it difficult to shake amateur guides. All visitors must remove their shoes to enter, and men must go shirtless. *(Open daily 4:30am-noon and 4-8:15pm. Rs10. Camera Rs2.)*

GANDHI MANDAPAM. This unusual rendition of Orissan-style architecture overlooks the southernmost tip of India. A black marble box marks the spot where the ashes of Mahatma Gandhi were stored before being scattered seaward. The *mandapam* rises 23m (79 ft.), one foot for each year of Gandhi's life. It was designed so that it is hit by rays of sunlight at noon every year on October 2, his birthday. *(At the seaward end of Main Rd. Open daily 7am-7pm.)*

VIVEKANANDA MEMORIAL. Accessible only by ferry, the two rocks marking the Vivekananda Memorial sit in the Bay of Bengal east of Kanyakumari. The Hindu reformer Swami Vivekananda swam here and meditated on top of the rocks for several days in 1892 before heading to Chicago for the 1893 World Religions Conference. The glossy Vivekananda Memorial temple commemorates the event. Arrows mark a path around the island, which also houses a temple built around one of **Parvati's footprints.** The notice board at the ferry terminal on the mainland gives information on sunrise times. Expect a wait for the ferry on weekends. *(Ferries daily 7:45am-4pm. Rs10. Memorial entrance fee Rs10.)*

WANDERING MONK EXHIBITION. Infinitely more tranquil, if a little less picturesque than the other monuments, this small museum is devoted to the life of Swami Vivekananda. Panels chronicle his life, his wanderings, and his goals. For those with little prior knowledge of the Swami, it is well worth a wander. *(At the junction of Bus Stand and Main Rd. Open daily 8am-noon and 4-8pm. Rs2.)*

FISHING VILLAGE. The village on the east coast north of the hotel district has many charms—bright yellow and lavender houses, small church-shrines, and a thriving catamaran fishing business. The elegant and imposing **Holy Land of Ransom Church,** with its impressive facade, towers over the southern edge of the village.

THIRUVALLUVAR STATUE. Impossible to miss, this impressive stone statue rises from a rocky island next to the Vivekananda Rock Memorial and commemorates the Tamil poet who lived over 2000 years ago. His *Thirukkural* consists of 1330 couplets on ethical and moral themes. Accordingly, the statue stands 133 ft. high.

FESTIVALS

Kanyakumari's **Pongal Festival** (Jan. 10-15) marks the end of the rice harvest with the ritual cooking and offering of South India's beloved sweet (sticky rice in earthen pots) to the goddess. The tourist office runs trips to nearby villages to watch the festivities. The tourist office also organizes the **Cape Festival**, a celebration of Tamil culture, especially *bharatnatyam* dance. Finally, **World Tourism Day** (Sept. 27) is a party of free cultural shows, free food, and free garlands for foreigners.

DAYTRIPS FROM KANYAKUMARI

Both Suchindram and Padmanabhapuram can be visited by taking bus #303 from Kanyakumari.

SUCHINDRAM TEMPLE. The beautifully carved Suchindram Temple, 13km from Kanyakumari, is dedicated to the holy trinity of Hinduism—Shiva, Vishnu, and Brahma—and contains large numbers of sculptural odds and ends, including India's only depiction of a female Ganesh. Also of note are several hollow pillars, each sounding a different musical note when hit, and a huge Hanuman statue. *(Open daily 4:30am-noon and 4:30-8:45pm.)*

PADMANABHAPURAM. Located 45km from Kanyakumari on the way to Trivandrum, Padmanabhapuram was the capital of Travancore until 1790. Padmanabhapuram's grand **palace** spans more than half of the 6½ acre grounds of the town. The original palace dates from 1550; the other buildings date from the 17th century. The mostly wooden palace has exquisitely carved teak ceilings designed by Chinese architects and a smooth black floor that has stood the test of time remarkably well considering that it is made out of charcoal, egg, coconut oil, river sand, lime, and sugar. The famous murals in the meditation room are being restored, but the beautiful grounds and building are definitely worth the trek. *(Bus #303 from Kanyakumari goes to Thuckalai: every 15min., 1¼hr. From Thuckalai bus station, backtrack, head left downhill at the fork, turn right at the next fork, and then right again to the palace; or take a rickshaw or local bus #13D. Frequent buses head back to Kanyakumari. Palace open Tu-Su 9am-4:30pm. Ticket counter closed 1-2pm. Rs6. Camera fee Rs16. Knowledgeable guides accompany you through the palace; circumvent the large groups and have a small English tour—guides expect baksheesh.)*

KODAIKANAL கொடை · கானடு ☎04542

Hours away from the nearest major city and surrounded by towering cliffs and protected forests, Kodaikanal is one of the most popular (and most beautiful) hill stations in southern India. The heady scent of eucalyptus mingles with the fresh breezes that blow across Kodai's mountainside, covered in blue-gums and *kurinji* blossoms. During the hottest months of the year (Apr.-June), the town swarms with tourists, who descend en masse to stroll along the gentle slopes and breathe in the crisp country air—a trend that's been popular ever since the Brits set up shop here in the 1840s to escape the sweltering, malaria-infested plains. Today, the town itself is a somewhat scarred jumble of tour buses and cheap hotels, but Kodai's setting is arguably the most stunning of any hill station, and it doesn't take much effort to get away from the crowds and to the majestic scenery of Kodai's unspoilt surroundings. Temperatures are 10-20°C cooler than in Chennai, and nights are often nippy enough for warm shawls and fireplaces.

Kodaikanal

♠ ACCOMMODATIONS
Greenland's Youth Hostel, **8**
Hotel Astoria, **3**
International Tourist Lodge, **6**
Snooze Inn, **4**
Sri Guru Lodge, **5**
Taj Villa, **7**

🍎 FOOD
Green Manor Restaurant, **1**
New Hotel Punjab, **2**
Tibetan Brothers, **2**

🗺 TRANSPORTATION

Trains: Kodaikanal Road Station (☎ 4543 38226) is a 3hr. bus ride from town. From Kodaikanal Rd. to **Chennai** (4 per day 12:30-1pm, Rs159).

Buses: The **bus stand** is a dirt lot just off Anna Salai, on Wood Will Rd. A reservation and inquiry booth is open daily 9am-1pm and 2-4pm. To: **Bangalore** (12hr., 6pm, Rs160); **Chennai** (12hr., 6:30pm, Rs173); **Coimbatore** (6hr., 8:30am and 4:30pm, Rs139); **Dindigul** (7 per day 7:15am-6:20pm); **Kanyakumari** (9hr., 9am, Rs96); **Madurai** (4hr., 13 per day 6:45am-4:40pm, Rs26); **Palani** (3hr., 11 per day 6am-6pm., Rs15); **Trichy** (6hr., 12:20 and 2:30pm, Rs46). A number of **private bus** operators on Anna Salai offer minibus service to Bangalore, Chennai, Coimbatore, Madurai, Ooty (Rs100-700).

Local Transportation: The best way to get around is on foot or by bike. **Bikes** are available for hire from stalls along the lakeside (Rs10 per hr.). **Taxis** are also available outside the bus stand to help you deal with Kodai's hilly roads (minimum charge Rs60).

✴🛈 ORIENTATION AND PRACTICAL INFORMATION

Buses pull into a lot on the corner of **Anna Salai Rd.** and **Wood Will Rd.,** by the Hotel Astoria. Going uphill on Wood Will Rd. (toward the bus reservation booth) leads to

Coaker's Walk, the Youth Hostel, and then on to **Pillar Rocks** and other scenic spots and viewpoints. Downhill from the bus stand on Anna Salai are most of the budget hotels and the post office. Flat along Anna Salai in the other direction is a large intersection with **PT Rd.**, home to many of the town's most popular restaurants. From here, the lake is down the hill to the left.

Tourist Office: (☎41675). On the northern side of Anna Salai, a 2min. walk downhill from the bus stand; on the left. Open M-F 10am-5:45pm. For more information on hikes around Kodaikanal, visit the **District Forestry Office** (☎40287) to get a brochure and an application for the (free) trekking permit. Turn left off Anna Salai after the police station and follow the road downhill for about 5min. Open M-F 10:30am-6pm.

Budget Travel: For bus, train, and airline bookings, try the **Almond Travel Agency** (☎43376) or **Kurinji Tours and Travels** (☎40008), near Hilltop Towers Hotel, Club Rd. Open M-Sa 9am-9pm.

Currency Exchange: Indian Bank, Anna Salai, on the left as you head toward the lake from the bus stand, changes cash and traveler's checks in most major currencies. Open M-F 10am-2pm, Sa 10am-noon.

Internet: Alpha Net, next to EcoNet and the Royal Tibet restaurant on PT Rd. Rs60 per hr. Open daily 9am-10pm.

Supermarket: Spencer's, downhill from Hilltop towers on Club Rd., heading toward the lake, is a well-stocked supermarket selling donuts, CDs, and apple-scented shampoo. Open daily 7:30am-7:30pm.

Hospital: Van Allen (☎41273 or 41254). A reputable private hospital near Coaker's Walk. Regular surgery hours M-Sa 10am-1pm and 3-5pm; open 24hr. for emergencies.

Pharmacy: Valliappa Medicals, on PT Rd., next to the Royal Tibet restaurant. Open daily 9am-9pm.

Police: (☎40262). On Anna Salai, on the left, past Snooze Inn as you head downhill.

Post Office: on Anna Salai, opposite Snooze Inn. Open M-Sa 9am-5pm. **Postal Code:** 624101.

▐ ACCOMMODATIONS

Every other building in Kodai seems to have rooms for rent. Most of the cheapest places are along Anna Salai. As you move away from the town center, quality and prices increase exponentially. The high season runs from April to mid-June.

Greenland's Youth Hostel (☎40899). St. Mary's Rd. From the bus stand, go uphill on Wood Will Rd. and past Coaker's Walk on St. Mary's Rd. for 10min. In a secluded spot near a cliff, the grassy terraces command stunning views of the plains and ridges in the distance. Private rooms have attached toilets and fireplaces. Hot water available 7-9am. Dorms Rs75; doubles Rs240-340. Off season Rs55/200-290. ❶

Taj Villa (☎43556 or 43557; fax 40940; tajvilla@yahoo.com, tajvilla@vsnl.com). St. Mary's Rd., at the start of Coaker's Walk from the bus stand. The views here rival those from the Youth Hostel. Tastefully furnished, spotless rooms with 24hr. hot water, telephone, and TV. Check-out 11am. Doubles Rs590-790. Off season Rs290-4900. ❸

Snooze Inn (☎40837; fax 660657). Anna Salai, downhill from the bus stand, on the left. Slightly stuffy rooms (with or without faded tatty carpet) with clean sheets, towels, and tiny TVs. Attached bathrooms with seat toilets and 24hr. hot water. Check-out 24hr. Doubles Rs295-450. Off season Rs250-425. ❷

Hotel Astoria (☎40524; astoria1@vsnl.com). At the intersection of Wood Will Rd. and Anna Salai. Classy mid-range hotel popular with the imported suitcase crowd. Large beds, seat toilets, and satellite TV. Hot water all day. Check-out 9am. Off season 24hr. check-out. Doubles Rs700. Off-season: Rs350. ❸

International Tourist Lodge (☎40542). Anna Salai, on the right as you head downhill from the bus stand. One of the better rock-bottom places. Simple rooms with attached (squat) bath. Check-out 24hr. Doubles Rs300. Off season Rs150. ❶

Sri Guru Lodge (☎40234). On Anna Salai, on the right as you head downhill from the bus stand. No thrills, no frills; just simple, unadorned rooms with rickety beds and (optional) attached squat bath. Doubles Rs120-150. Off season Rs75-125. ❶

🖸 FOOD

🔳 **New Hotel Punjab,** PT Rd. Excellent North Indian non-veg. restaurant with an extensive menu. Mutton *keema* Rs80, chicken *tandoori* Rs50. Open daily 11am-10:30pm. ❶

Green Manor Restaurant, Lake Rd. near Convent Rd. Beautiful garden setting overlooking the lake and excellent food—from chicken sizzlers (Rs80) to Kerala-style fish curries (Rs50). Indian and Chinese entrees Rs45-60. Beer Rs90. Open daily 7am-10pm. ❶

Tibetan Brothers Restaurant, PT Rd., 2nd fl., on the left. Crisp vegetable *momos* (Rs30), Tibetan bread (Rs10), and lemon tea (Rs25) are perfect for a cool day in Kodai. Open daily noon-4pm and 5:30-10pm. ❶

Hotel Astoria. See **Accommodations,** above. Join the crowds and sit back to enjoy some quality people-watching as you demolish yet another mountain range of rice and *sambar*. Meals (Rs23). Open daily 7am-9:30pm. ❶

Kavi Bala Café, opposite the bus stand. Good veg.-only dishes served in this dim, classy hotel restaurant. South Indian *thali* Rs45, *malai kofta* Rs35. Open daily 7am-10:30pm. ❶

👁 🖎 SIGHTS AND SCENERY

THE LAKE AND ENVIRONS. Tourist activity centers around the man-made lake; the 5km path that leads around it is a pleasant bike ride. **Bike rental** places and **horseback riding** are between the boat club and Bryant Park on Lake Rd. *(Bike rental Rs10 per hr.; horses negotiable at around Rs100 per hr.)* Hire those cute little paddleboats from the **Boathouse** *(2 seat paddleboat Rs20 per 30min. plus Rs20 deposit; rowboat and four-seat paddleboat Rs80 per 30min. plus Rs80 deposit. Open 9am-5:30pm.)* Just south of the lake is **Bryant's Park,** with a **botanical garden** founded in 1902. *(Open daily 8:30am-6:30pm. Rs5; camera fee Rs25.)*

COAKER'S WALK. Kodai's most famous scenic promenade is Coaker's Walk, a 10min. stroll along a paved precipice that traces an arc from Taj Villa to Greenland's Youth Hostel. On clear mornings, the views of the surrounding hills and plains are amazing—you can see as far as Madurai. A small **telescope house** near the far end gives you a closer look at the surrounding countryside. *(Open daily dawn-dusk Rs2; camera fee Rs5; telescope house Rs1.)*

PILLAR ROCKS, GREEN VALLEY VIEW, AND BERIJAM LAKE. For some of the best views around, follow the crowds out to **Pillar Rocks,** a popular viewpoint about 8km from town, overlooking soaring cliffs and miles of green-carpeted valleys. The road is well-signed from Coaker's Walk and Greenland's Youth Hostel and is relatively flat and easy to cycle along. *(From town, bike 8km up Upper Shola Rd. past Fairy Falls and the Golf Club. Garden park open 8am-8pm.)* Expect to share the road with a convoy of noisy tour buses on their way out to **Green Valley View** and Pillar Rocks. Three kilometers farther on up the road is another lookout spot—**Moir's**

Point. From here, the road splits to continue downhill to town via Observatory Rd. (9km), or to **Berijam Lake** (15km). *(Permission from the District Forest Officer in Kodai is required for travel to the lake by car or to Silent Valley or Cap Play View. Get a permit at least 1 day in advance. ☎ 40287. Open M-F 10am-6pm. Free.)*

DOLPHIN'S NOSE AND VELLAGAVI VILLAGE. A pleasant stroll through a hillside village and shimmering eucalyptus leads to the breathtaking promontory known as **Dolphin's Nose.** The views continue as the rocky path winds downhill, eventually reaching the terraced farms of Vellagavi, a small village you can almost make out from Dolphin's Nose. *(From Coaker's Walk, follow the signs past the Youth Hostel to La Salette shrine; walk past the radio tower and the thermometer factory, and then continue down the cobbled road to the right of the Salette Church. When the road dips, take the small dirt path to the left. Cross the bridge when you come to it and stay left, following the winding path downhill. Make another left at the sign for Voyce, down the steep, root-rutted path that leads through a village of turquoise houses. 90 min. down to Dolphin's Nose. For Vellagavi, allow a whole day's hike.)*

CHETTIAR PARK. The secluded Chettiar Park is the center of attention every 12 years, when the chronically shy *kurinji* plant springs into bloom. The next scheduled blossoms are not due until 2006, though there are a few plants whose biological clocks are off-kilter. The gardens here attract few daytrippers, making them a peaceful place to visit. *(Walk straight down Anna Salai, and then continue down along the leftmost of the 2 roads at the bottom. Walk uphill past the Zion School, and then take the steep steps to the right as the road curves left and winds its way slowly uphill. The park is at the very top of the steps.)* Just past Chettiar Park is the **Kurinji Andavar Temple** (dedicated to Murugan), with a viewing platform. *(3 km northeast of the bus stand.)*

COIMBATORE ☎ 0422

Perhaps it is the protective ring of the surrounding mountains, but somehow, Coimbatore manages to maintain an air of organized calm even as its bus stands and railway stations overflow with travelers, most going to or from Ooty, Kerala, or Karnataka. Most travelers stop here just long enough to check email and grab a few hours of sleep, leaving most of this pulsating industrial city unexplored.

Coimbatore's **airport** is 10km northeast of the city center. Indian Airlines (☎ 399833) has daily flights to: **Bangalore** (US$85); **Chennai** (US$90); **Mumbai** (US$150); and two flights a week to **Cochin** (M, F; US$45). **Jet Airways** (☎ 212034) flies daily to: **Bangalore, Chennai,** and **Mumbai.**

Coimbatore Junction Railway Station is on Bank Rd., in the southern part of the city. (Reservations office upstairs ☎ 131. Open M-Sa 8am-8pm, Su 8am-2pm). To: **Bangalore** (7hr., 4 per day 5:15am-8pm, Rs138); **Chennai** (8hr., 6-8 per day 6:30am-11:10pm, Rs166); **Cochin** (5hr., 11-14 per day 6am-2:50am, Rs89); **Delhi** (20hr., 1-2 per day, Rs472); **Kanyakumari** (12hr.; 1:20 and 4:55am, Th 1:15pm; Rs176); **Madurai** (6hr., 12:45 and 10:10pm, Rs95); **Mettupalayam** for the "toy train" to **Ooty** (1hr., 5:25am, Rs84); **Mumbai** (23hr.; 3:05 and 11:20am, Th 11:30pm; Rs343).

Three of the city's four **bus stands** are at the northern end of Dr. Nanjappa Rd., 1½km from the railway station. The **Town Bus Stand** (known as **Gandhipuram**), marked by the pedestrian flyover on Dr. Nanjappa Rd., provides efficient local service, including buses to the railway station (take any bus except #3, 5, or 15). Behind Gandhipuram, on Cross Cut Rd., is the main **Interstate Station** with reservation desks for Tamil Nadu, Kerala, and Karnataka State Buses. (Desks open daily 7am-10pm.) From the interstate station buses go to **Bangalore** (11hr., 4 per day 8:15am-10pm, Rs102-122). The **State (Central) Bus Stand** is across the road, servicing: **Chennai** (11hr., 6 per day 6am-10pm, Rs153-168); **Cochin** (6hr., 13 per day 4am-10:30pm, Rs73-88); **Mysore** (6hr., 14 per day 4:30am-11pm, Rs58); **Ooty** (3hr., every 20min. 4am-8:30pm, Rs21). A fourth stand, **Ukkadam,** 3km south of the other three, services mostly smaller towns to the south. Buses to: **Kodaikanal** (6hr., 10am, Rs39); **Madurai** (5½hr., 6 per day 6am-5:30pm, Rs48); **Munnar** (6½hr., 8:15am and 2:25pm, Rs48); **Palani** (3hr., frequent, Rs23). From Gandhipuram, **local buses** #3, 15, 24 run to Ukkadam bus stand. Bus #38B runs from Ukkadam to the railway station.

Home to a number of tourist services, the north-south thoroughfare of **Bank Rd.** heads north from the bank; it forks 200m before it hits **Mill Rd.** (called **Avinashi Rd.** farther east). The right fork feeds into Avinashi Rd. The left fork hits Mill Rd. and continues north as **Dr. Nanjappa Rd.** Walk left out of the railway station on Bank Rd. to get to the **State Bank of India**, which changes most currencies and traveler's checks. (☎301932. Open M-F 10am-4pm, Sa 10am-1pm.) Just past the bank on the left is the **police station** (☎300300). Turn right at the end of Bank Rd. to get to **KG Hospital** (☎212121), near the railway station on Art College Rd. (open 24hr). The **Head Post Office** is on Railway Feeder Rd.; from Bank Rd. walk straight through the railway station and turn right; it's on the left after 600m. (Open M-Sa 9am-7pm, Su 10am-4pm.) Access the **Internet** at **Netsea** in Raj Rajeswara Tower, opposite Gandhipuram bus stand. (Rs30 per hr. Open daily 7am-9pm.) **Postal Code:** 641001.

Most of Coimbatore's budget hotels and restaurants are close to the railway station or the bus stands. The best option if you need to catch an early train is the **railway retiring rooms ❷**, upstairs in the station building, opposite the computerized reservation area. However, these are often full, and advance bookings are not possible. (Rooms Rs300, with A/C Rs350-400.) A small path across the street from the railway station entrance leads to several good budget options, including **Hotel Anand Vihar ❶**, which has basic rooms with baths and squat toilets. (☎300580 or 300435. Singles Rs60-120; doubles Rs110-180.) Probably the best of the hotels near the bus station is the **Hotel Blue Star ❶**, 369S Nehru St., a polished mid-range hotel with attached restaurant and bar. Look for the sign near the bus stand. (☎231636 or 230635. Singles Rs150-195; doubles Rs260-550.) For cheap food, head to **Sree Annapoorna ❶**, at the State Bus Stand on Dr. Nanjappa Rd., where you will find many travelers slurping *sambar* by the bucketful. (Meals Rs20. Open daily 6:30am-10:30pm.) **Hotel Gayathri (Chat Corner) ❶**, opposite the Hotel Blue Star on Nehru St., is a pleasant restaurant with outside dining and features fresh-squeezed fruit juices and *aloo dum kashmiri* (Rs35). (Open daily 6am-11pm.)

OOTY (UDHAGAMANDALAM) உண்டு ☎0423

Shrouded in mist and movie mystique, the verdant hill station of Ooty is a favorite backdrop for Indian filmmakers as well as a promised land for many of the country's holiday-makers. Established in 1821 by John Sullivan, an enterprising collector with the East India Company, Ooty quickly earned a reputation as a high-class getaway. No longer the exclusive retreat of the gin-and-tonic-at-sundown crowd, Ooty is often overrun by tourists: exhaust fumes sully the crisp mountain air, sewage clogs the once-pristine lake, and the booming hotel and package-tour industries noisily exploit Ooty's quiet charm.

It's not hard, however, to escape the crowds, and just a few kilometers off the beaten path you'll find yourself face-to-face with what made Ooty special in the first place: the laid-back locals, the tea, potato, and carrot plantations, and the mighty Mt. Doddabetta, which, at 2638m, is about as close as you can get to heaven in South India. Ooty's season runs from April to mid-June and from September to October, when temperatures hover around a dry 25°C during the day, and the nights can be chilly. Monsoon season runs from July to August. Ooty's cold, relatively dry winter stretches from November to March.

TRANSPORTATION

Trains: Railway Station, North Lake Rd. Reservations counter open daily 10am-noon and 3:30-4:30pm. The Blue Mountain Railway (the "toy train") chugs through tea and potato plantations and past waterfalls; like Ooty, it's often crowded. To **Coonoor** (1hr.; 9:15am, 12:15, 3, 6pm; return 7:45, 10:45am, 1:35, 4:30pm; Rs5) and **Mettupalayam** (3½hr.; 9:15am and 3pm; return 7:10am and 1:15pm; Rs10).

Buses: The **bus stand** is 100m south of the railway station. Regular and private buses operate out of 1 dusty lot. The departure bays are labeled in English (wow!), and the buses actually use them, most of the time. The **TSTC** reservations counter (☎494 969) is open daily 9:30am-1pm and 1:30-5pm. Make reservations for long-distance buses 2 days in advance. To: **Bangalore** (8hr., every 30-90min. 9:30am-2pm and 8:30-10:30pm, Rs109-151); **Calicut** (6hr., 4 per day 6:30am-3:15pm, Rs54); **Chennai** (8hr., 5:45pm, Rs133); **Coimbatore** (3hr., every 10min. 6:45am-5:20pm, Rs20); **Hassan** (8hr., 10am, Rs91); **Kodaikanal** (8hr., 6:30am, Rs70); **Madikeri** (8hr., 11:30am and 5:30pm, Rs82); **Mysore** (5hr., 8am and 3:30pm, Rs45/74). **Karnataka State Road Transport Corporation (KSRTC)** has a reservations counter open daily 6:30am-10:30pm. To: **Bangalore** (8:30, 10, 11:15am; Rs131); **Hassan** (11:30am and 3pm, Rs90); **Mysore** (9am and 1:30pm, Rs50). Local **TTRC** buses go to: **Coonoor** (30min., frequent 5:30am-11pm, Rs5); **Doddabetta Junction** (20min., every 30min., Rs4); **Doddabetta Peak** (30min., 11:30am, Rs5); **Mettupalayam** (every 15min. 5:30am-8:30pm, Rs14); **Mudumalai** (3hr., every 30min., Rs31); **Pykara** (30min., every 30 min. 6:30am-4:30pm, Rs6).

Local Transportation: Unmetered **auto-rickshaws** charge at least Rs15 for a ride from the railway station to Charing Cross.

ORIENTATION AND PRACTICAL INFORMATION

Getting around Ooty can be tricky because its streets skirt the valley and snake up the surrounding mountainsides. Not to worry—the town itself is fairly small, and locals are used to directing tourists. Ooty's expansive **lake** is in the southwest of town, a 200m walk west from the **railway station** and **bus stand** along **North Lake Rd.** From the railway station, walk northeast for 1½km along **Upper Bazaar Rd.** to get to **Charing Cross,** the town center. From the bus stand, you can reach Charing Cross via **Lower Bazaar Rd.,** with the fruit market and the **race course** below; it then becomes **Commercial Rd.** 750m before it hits Charing Cross. Climb the steps 500m behind Charing Cross to reach **Town West Circle.** From there, **Hospital Rd.** makes a steep and lengthy westward descent to the railway station area. Past Charing Cross, Commercial Rd. splits again. Follow **Garden Rd.** 1km north to reach the **Botanical Gardens** or **Ettines Rd.** around the south edge of the race course loop back to the bus stand; two more roads lead to Mt. Dodabetta and Coonoor.

Tourist Office: The new **Government of Tamil Nadu Tourist Office** (☎443 977). Wenlock Rd., 200m above Charing Cross. Open M-F 10am-5:45pm. Trekking requires a permit, obtainable 3-4 days in advance. Open M-F 10am-5:45pm. The Udhagamandalam Forest Department, behind the tourist office, supervises trekking outside the park; the Deputy Forest Officer (north: ☎443 968) issues permits for the northern and eastern Nilgiris, and the DFO (south: ☎444 083) handles the southern Nilgiris. Brief 4-seat elephant excursions are Rs125.

Currency Exchange: State Bank of India (☎444 099). Town West Circle. The pleasant foreign exchange desk changes AmEx and Thomas Cook traveler's checks in US$ and UK£. Open M-F 10am-2pm and 3-5:50pm, Sa 10am-noon. **Canara Bank** (☎432 408). Commercial Rd., to your left as you look up the steps to Town West Circle. Also gives cash advances on MC and V. Open M-F 10am-2pm, Sa 10am-noon.

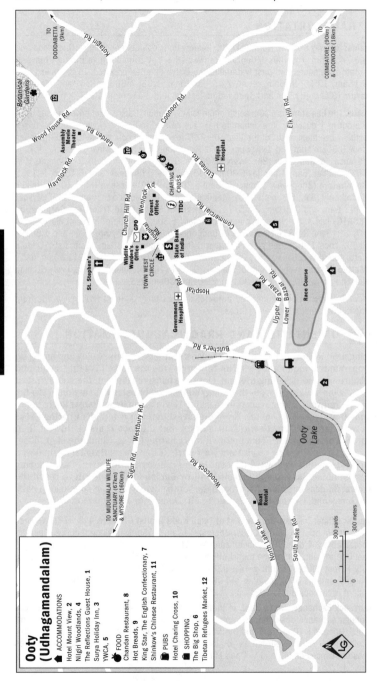

TAMIL NADU

Ooty
(Udhagamandalam)

🏠 ACCOMMODATIONS
Hotel Mount View, **2**
Nilgiri Woodlands, **4**
The Reflections Guest House, **1**
Surya Holiday Inn, **3**
YWCA, **5**

🍴 FOOD
Chandan Restaurant, **8**
Hot Breads, **9**
King Star, The English Confectionary, **7**
Shinkow's Chinese Restaurant, **11**

🍺 PUBS
Hotel Charing Cross, **10**

🛍 SHOPPING
The Big Shop, **6**
Tibetan Refugees Market, **12**

Bookstore: Higginbothams (☎ 443 736). Commercial Rd. between the co-op supermarkets. Open Th-Tu 9:30am-1pm and 3:30-7:30pm.

Police: (☎ 443 973). Town West Circle, near the collector's office.

Hospital: Government Hospital (☎ 442 212). Jail Hill, Hospital Rd. **Vijaya Hospital** (☎ 442 058). Ettines Rd. Behind Alankar Theatres.

Internet: Globalnet, Commercial Rd., 50m past Tandoor Mahal, on the opposite side of the street. Open daily 8:30am-10:30pm. **SatCom,** Garden Rd., 50m from Charing Cross on the right. Open daily 10am-10pm. Both charge Rs40 per hr.

Post Office: GPO (☎ 443 791). Town West Circle. Head northwest up the staircase on the side of the hill. Open M-Sa 9am-5pm. Another at Charing Cross, south of Coonoor Rd. **Postal Code:** 643001.

ACCOMMODATIONS

Seeing that this *is* a resort town, it should come as no surprise that most of Ooty's buildings are hotels. The lake area has more spacious and quieter lodging options.

🏨 **Hotel Mount View** (☎ 443 307 or 444 182). Ettines Rd. House-turned-hotel with spacious rooms and pine-wood floors—worth the hike up. Raj-reminiscent. Seat toilet, hot water 5:30pm-10am. Doubles Rs400-900. Off season: Rs300-500. 15% luxury tax. ❸

🏨 **The Reflections Guest House** (☎ 443 834; reflectionsin@yahoo.com). North Lake Rd. 500m west of the bus stand. The proprietress, Mrs. Dique, is legendary in backpacker circles for her home-cooked meals and maternal disposition. Wildflowers and a lake view. Clean bathrooms, heat in the winter, hot water 6-11am. Reserve 14 days ahead in season. Rooms Rs400-500. Off season: Rs250-350. ❷

Nilgiri Woodlands (☎ 442 551 or 442 451). Ettines Rd. Up a forking garden path. Spacious rooms with high ceilings, antique furniture, and carpets. Attached baths with tubs, seat toilets, and 24hr. hot water. Rooms Rs550-1200; cottages Rs1200. Off season: Rs400-1000. AmEx/MC/V. ❹

YWCA (☎ 442 218). Ettines Rd. 500m from the racetrack. Sparkling cottages with wicker chairs and seat toilets. Sunlit sitting room in the main bldg. with TV and piano. Bare dormitory lacks the same charm. Attached restaurant. Dorms Rs77; cottages Rs300-1040. Off season: Rs66/195-655. ❶

Surya Holiday Inn (☎ 442 567). Upper Bazaar. Rooms aren't large, but you won't have to share them with any dust. Hot water 7:30-8:30am. Singles Rs250; doubles Rs300. ❶

FOOD

Hotel New Tamilaagham, Main Bazaar Rd. A white sliver on the hill at the crossing before Commercial Rd. Cleanest and tastiest of the *dosa* dives, its clientele come for Rs5 *idli,* Rs10 *puri-sabzi* sets, and an eye-popping Rs20 chili mushroom. Plus, there's ice cream. Open daily 7:30am-10pm. ❶

Chandan Restaurant, Commercial Rd. In Hotel Nahar 100m from Charing Cross. Carefully spiced vegetarian selections (Rs55-70) served in heated *kadhais* in a wood-paneled room. Popular with Indian families. Open daily noon-3:30pm and 7-10:30pm. ❶

Hot Breads (☎ 445 333). Charing Cross. Near the international school. Warm, fresh baked breads, pizzas (Rs38-48), and pastries. Chicken dizzy dogs Rs19, exquisite slices of chocolate truffle cake Rs17. Open daily 10am-8:30pm. ❶

Shinkow's Chinese Restaurant (☎ 442811). 38-42 Commissioners Rd. Opposite the State Bank of India, Town West Circle. Serving mouth-watering but overpriced stir-fry to locals and tourists since 1954. Varied menu includes sliced beef with broccoli (Rs50/70) and cashew chicken (Rs80-100). Open daily 12:30-9:45pm. ❶

King Star, The English Confectionery (☎445742). Commercial Rd. A few hundred meters from Charing Cross. Chocolate in many forms: covering walnuts or ginger, flavored like mango or coconut, Rs 30-45 per 100g. Open F-W 11:30am-8:30pm. ❶

🔍 SIGHTS

BOTANICAL GARDENS. Ooty's Botanical Gardens were originally established in 1847 and spruced up again in 1995. A century and a half after they were opened, they are as green as ever. With more than 2000 species on display, the gardens have come a long way from their original purpose of producing "English vegetables at reasonable cost." From the vivid colors of the rose garden to the quiet, well-sculpted knolls that surround the park, the whole area is gorgeous. *(Open daily 8am-6:30pm. Rs5; camera fee Rs25, video Rs500.)*

CENTENARY ROSE GARDEN. Another floral fantasia awaits 1km south of Charing Cross, up Rose Garden Rd. Over 2000 species of roses fill this terraced hillside with a panoramic view of the town. *(Open daily 9am-6:30pm. Rs5; camera fee Rs25.)*

LAKE. Just west of the railway station and bus stand is Ooty's lily-filled, sewage-stopped **lake**, constructed in the 1820s by good old John Sullivan. Near the boat house is a **miniature train.** *(Rs 5 a whirl.)* **Horse rentals** near the lake are officially Rs150 per hr., though you will be able to bargain. *(Rowboats and pedal boats Rs50 per 30min.; boat house 1km down North Lake Rd.: admission Rs3; camera fee Rs10.)*

🎵 🎭 ENTERTAINMENT AND SHOPPING

If occupied at all, **bars** in Ooty usually have just a few sorry-looking men mumbling to each other in a darkened corner. A slightly more cheerful watering hole is the bar at **Hotel Charing Cross.** (☎444 387. Kingfisher Rs40. Open daily 11am-11pm.)

Atari-nostalgics can satisfy their urges at one of several **arcades** along Commercial Rd. **Moodmaker's** is near the Hotel Charing Cross, beyond the brandy shop. (Open daily 10am-9:30pm.) Farther down the street is the underground **Missing Link,** 49 Commercial Rd., where bug-eyed boys feed Rs2 tokens into bad knockoffs of Spy Hunter and Street Fighter. (Open daily 10am-11pm.) About 750m up from Moodmaker's on Garden Rd. is the **Assembly Rooms Theater,** which screens dated American flicks. (Su-F 2:30 and 6:30pm, Sa 2:30, 6, 8:30pm. Rs2-12.) The **Race Course,** near the bus stand, is a 1¼mi. loop where jodhpured jockeys run their horses to the delight of riotous but low-betting crowds. Races are held April-June.

Shopping in Ooty revolves around locally made body oils and textiles. **The Big Shop,** halfway between Charing Cross and the Lower Bazaar on Commercial Rd., sells Toda tribal shawls (Rs200-300), silver jewelry, and handicrafts. (☎444 136. Open daily 9:30am-8:30pm. Traveler's checks, AmEx/MC/V accepted.) A **Tibetan Refugees' Market,** along Garden Rd., near the Botanical Gardens, has stands selling mohair sweaters and colorful wool blankets. (Open daily 8:30am-8pm.) Charing Cross also fronts a Hindustan Photofilms (HPF) Showroom, with a slim selection of Hindi and Tamil videotapes. (Open daily 8am-8pm.)

🏞 DAYTRIPS FROM OOTY: PYKARA

Twenty kilometers west of Ooty is the tranquil village of **Pykara,** the perfect place for anybody longing for the hills. A small boathouse on Pykara's lake rents out boats and sells snacks for visitors to munch on as they float around. (Boats Rs50-100 per 30min.) Near the lake is **Pykara Dam,** 2½km downstream, with an attractive series of rocky **waterfalls,** especially impressive during July and August. (All buses to Gudalur from Ooty pass through Pykara. 30min., every 30min. 6:30am-9pm, Rs6.) If you're up for the climb, the 9km hike up **Mt. Doddabetta** gives you views you won't get from an aisle seat of a tour bus. (Trail open daily 8:30am-5:30pm.) No visit to Ooty's environs would be complete without a **Filmy Chakkar** ("Film Trip"), a tour of scenic spots where romantic pairs have frolicked before Bollywood's cameras.

NEAR OOTY

▄ COONOOR

*Trains creak along narrow-gauge tracks to **Mettupalayam** (2hr., 10:35am and 4:15pm, Rs8) and **Ooty** (1 hr., 4 per day 7:45am-4:30pm, Rs5). **Buses** go to: **Coimbatore** (2hr., frequent 6:30am-8pm, Rs16) via **Mettupalayam** (1hr., Rs9); **Dolphin's Nose** and **Lamb's Rock** (30min., every 2hr. 7:30am-6:30pm, Rs4); **Ooty** (45min., frequent 5:30am-10:30pm, Rs5). It is probably easier to hire a **taxi** (Rs250-400) for the sights, so that you can take your time and not be at the mercy of mass transport. **Auto-rickshaws** run between Lower and Upper Coonoor (Rs20-25); the **local buses** along Mount Rd. follow the same route for less (Rs2).*

Deep in the tea-growing region of the Nilgiris, the quiet and calm of upper Coonoor come as a welcome break from the commercial bustle of Ooty, only 18km away. Coonoor is easily accessible (see **Ooty: Transportation,** p. 623); it's getting out to the spectacular panoramic views that takes a bit of effort. The town is separated into two parts: the railway station and bus stand are in the town center of Lower Coonoor, down in the valley; most of the attractions are in Upper Coonoor, around **Bedford Circle.** The **railway station** and **bus stand** are on the Ooty-Mettupalayam Rd., near **Mount Rd.,** which winds 2km up to **Upper Coonoor.** The **police station** (☎30100), **post office** (open M-Sa 9am-5pm), and **Sagayamatha Hospital** (☎31919) are all on Balaclava Hill.

From the bus stand, go straight across the railway tracks past the Gandhi statue, 200m up the road, and take the steps up the steep slope to the left. Most of the places to stay are in Upper Coonoor. The **YWCA "Wyoming" Guest House ❶,** off Upasi Rd., between Church of the Sacred Heart and Nankem Hospital, is one of the most congenial places in the whole of South India. Rooms overlook tea and flower gardens from a bluff above the bazaar. Home-cooked meals (Rs40-60) and 24hr. hot water are provided. (☎34426. Singles Rs200; doubles Rs400. Off season: Rs150/300.) The **Quality Restaurant ❶,** Mount Rd., near Bedford Circle, serves decent Indian and Chinese food. (Most dishes Rs35-70. Open daily 8am-10:30pm.)

Coonoor's response to Ooty's Botanical Gardens is **Sim's Park,** high on **Gray's Hill** on the road to Kotagiri, 3km from the Coonoor bus stand. Set in a small ravine, the park displays varieties of flowers and plants not found in Ooty. (Open daily 8am-6:30pm. Rs5, children Rs2; camera fee Rs5, video Rs25.) Travel around Coonoor invariably involves tramping across tea plantations. For those with piqued pekoe passions, the **Highfield Tea Estate** will let you frolic in the fields and tour the factory. (☎30023. Open daily 8am-7pm.) From Sim's Park, the estate is 2km up Kotagiri Rd., but it is accessible from the park via a shortcut along the park's eastern edge; take a sharp left as you exit the east gate. In January, there's a week-long Tea and Tourism Festival. **Lamb's Rock,** 12km from Lower Coonoor, overlooks the Coimbatore plains far below. Four kilometers farther is Dolphin's Nose, a rock formation with views of a gaping, waterfall-filled gorge.

UTTARANCHAL
उत्तरांचल

In November 2000, after 10 years of struggle, the hilly northern regions of Uttar Pradesh won the right to form a new state. Uttaranchal, which means "Northern Mountains," embodies the holy, the hilly, and (at times) the downright helly. Comprising the regions of Garhwal and Kumaon, with their 7000m peaks and deodar forests, frenetic hill stations, Maruti-packed roads, ashrams, and sacred rivers, the state encompasses enough to enthrall, enlighten, amuse, and annoy any visitor.

The South Indian saint Shankara came to Garhwal during the 9th century, bringing the local population into the Hindu fold and establishing several important temples. Long before that, however, parts of the *Mahabharata* and *Ramayana* had already occurred here, enshrouding the hills of Uttarakhand with the religious mystique that the region has held for centuries. Today, these hills are still a major sanctuary of Hinduism.

In the early 19th century, Garhwal and Kumaon were overrun by the Nepali commander Amar Singh Thapa. He was bumped out in 1816 by the Brits, who set up regimental headquarters here and made Garhwal and Kumaon part of the United Provinces. When India obtained independence, the mountainous area of Uttarakhand was lumped together with the plains to form Uttar Pradesh. Currently, although Uttar Pradesh and Uttaranchal (or UA for short) still remain bound by the Ganga and Yamuna Rivers, the two states have little else in common. UA's Himalayan setting affords majestic mountain vistas from almost every town, village, and truck-stop in the state, and because it's in the mountains, temperatures in UA are usually more pleasant. But Uttaranchal's most significant distinguishing characteristic is its culture. People flock here from all over the globe to take part in or merely observe the religious rituals enacted here, as well as to absorb the small town charm that pervades the state.

HIGHLIGHTS OF UTTARANCHAL

Ashram towns such as **Rishikesh** (p. 644) and **Haridwar** (p. 639), pilgrimage centers like **Gangotri** (p. 651) and **Yamnotri** (p. 651), and national reserves such as **Corbett National Park** (p. 655) and the **Valley of Flowers** (p. 654) beckon lovers of the natural and the supernatural alike to Uttaranchal's hills.

DEHRA DUN देहरादून   ☎ 0135

Dehra Dun is not exactly a tourist town. As Uttaranchal's thriving capital city, it has most of the advantages, and many of the drawbacks, of big-city life in India. But there is another, more gentle side to Dehra Dun that comes with the relaxed, life-loving atmosphere of the nearby mountain villages. Bus-drivers and rickshaw-*wallahs* jockey for room on the congested roadways here just as they do everywhere else on the subcontinent, but at least they do it with a smile. Residents take pride in their reputation for honesty and are fond of pointing out how kind and good-natured Dehra Dun's people are relative to the big city nasties down in Delhi. Most travelers stop in Dehra Dun for a day or two before going to the Shivalik foothills to the north or to the hill station of Mussoorie, whose lights are visible from the city at night. There is plenty to do here—temples, parks, and sulfur springs—but in the end, there's too much "city" and not enough "town" to keep visitors here for more than a couple of days.

Govt. of India statement: The external boundaries of India are neither correct nor authenticated.

▛ TRANSPORTATION

Trains: As a terminus of the **Northern Railway,** Dehra Dun sends trains all over India. The enquiry office is in the main terminal, the booking office is next door, and the computerized reservation complex is across the way. Open M-Sa 8am-1:30pm and 2:30-8pm, Su 8am-2pm. To: **Delhi** (7hr., 4 per day 6am-9:15pm, Rs143); **Haridwar** (1½hr., 8 per day 6am-9:15pm, Rs104); **Lucknow** (12hr., 2-3 per day 7:30-8:30pm, Rs202).

Buses: Several companies operate from the **Delhi Bus Stand,** next to Hotel Drona. **UP Roadways** (☎653797) runs buses to: **Delhi** (every 30min. 5am-10:15pm, Rs90-140); **Haldwani** (9hr., 4 per day, Rs120); **Haridwar** (every 30min., 5am-7pm, Rs20); **Rishikesh** (1½hr., 14 per day 5am-7pm, Rs16). **Himachal Bus Lines** (☎623435) sends buses to **Shimla** (10hr., 6 per day, Rs110). **Punjab Roadways** (☎624410) goes to **Amritsar** (14hr., 5:30 and 7:30am, Rs141). UP Roadways also leaves from the **Mussoorie Bus Stand.** To: **Almora** (12hr., 6am, Rs150); **Mussoorie** (1½hr., every 30min. 6am-8pm, Rs22); **Nainital** (11hr., 8am, Rs130); **Uttarkashi** (9hr; 6, 8:30, and 10:30am; Rs89). **Highway Motors,** 69 Gandhi Rd. (☎624211), next to the railway station, serves **Hanuman Chatti** (8½hr.; Apr.-Aug. 6am, Sept.-Mar. 6:30am; Rs78). Daily deluxe buses run from Hotel Shivalik on Rajpur Rd. to **Delhi** (6hr., 11am, Rs250). **Shared taxis,** opposite the bus stands, run as far as **Mussoorie** (Rs50 per person).

Local Transportation: Local **buses** go to nearby destinations from the City Bus Stand, north of the clock tower. **Tempos,** known locally as *vikrants*, are common, clean, and cheap and run along fixed routes from the clock tower (Rs3-4). **Auto-rickshaws** from the Delhi Bus Stand to the Botanical Gardens cost around Rs50.

■ ORIENTATION

Dehra Dun can be broken down into three main areas: the **railway station** area, the **Paltan Bazaar** area, and the **Astley Hall** area. The railway station is to the south; the **Mussoorie Bus Stand** is right next to the station, and the **Delhi Bus Stand** (servicing most destinations *not* in the hills) is a 5min. walk north along **Gandhi Rd.,** just past the hard-to-miss **Hotel Drona.** Following Gandhi Rd. north leads to the second main focus of the city, the area around the tall **clock tower.** The **city bus stand** and Gandhi Park are just north of the clock tower along **Rajpur Rd.,** where many visitor services, high-end hotels, and restaurants lie. This strip is referred to as **Astley Hall** or **Dilaram Bazaar** farther north. Continuing on Gandhi Rd. from the clock tower will bring you back to Rajpur Rd. The web of streets just south of the clock tower is known as **Paltan Bazaar;** the part of the bazaar nearest to the railway station is called **Darshani Gate.**

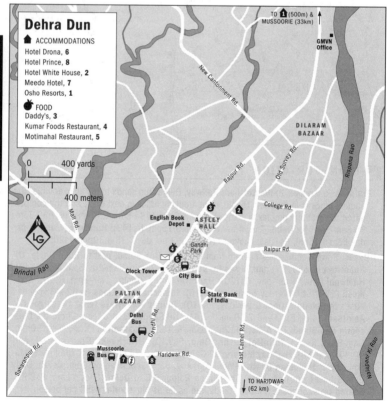

Dehra Dun

ACCOMMODATIONS
Hotel Drona, **6**
Hotel Prince, **8**
Hotel White House, **2**
Meedo Hotel, **7**
Osho Resorts, **1**

FOOD
Daddy's, **3**
Kumar Foods Restaurant, **4**
Motimahal Restaurant, **5**

🛈 PRACTICAL INFORMATION

Tourist Office: UA Tourist Office (☎ 653217). Attached to the Hotel Drona, next to the Delhi Bus Stand. Open M-Sa 10am-5pm. For trekking tips and other info about the Garhwal region, try the government-run **GMVN Headquarters,** 71/1 Rajpur Rd. (☎ 746817). Open M-Sa 10am-5pm.

Trekking Agency: There are many private agents in town who arrange treks, such as **Garhwal Tours and Trekking** (☎ 654774). In Rohini Plaza near Hotel Ambassador. Open M-Sa 9:15am-1:30pm.

Currency Exchange: The main branch of the **State Bank of India** (☎ 653240). One block east of the clock tower. Changes currency and traveler's checks. Open M-F 9am-1pm and 3:30-6:30pm, Sa 10am-noon. **Punjab National Bank,** Astley Hall (☎ 656012). Gandhi Park. Also changes currency and traveler's checks. Open M-F 10am-2pm.

Bookstore: English bookstores line Rajpur Rd. in the Astley Hall area. Try **English Book Depot** (☎ 655192). Next to Kumar Restaurant. Founded in 1923. Open M-Sa 10am-1:30pm and 2:30-8pm. **The Green Bookshop,** 17 Rajpur Rd. (☎ 653382). Has maps of the Garhwal region. Open M-Sa 10am-1:30pm and 3-8pm.

Market: Paltan Bazaar, between the clock tower and railway station. Has hundreds of shops, selling everything from sitars to saris. Open daily 9am-9pm.

Police: Dhara Chowki Station, Rajpur Rd. (☎ 653648). South of Hotel Ambassador.

Hospital: Jain Hospital (☎ 627766 or 621727). Open 24hr. **Dr. Diwan,** Kacheri Rd. (☎ 657660), is available 9:30am-2pm and 6-8pm.

Pharmacy: Fair Deal Chemists, 14 Darshani Gate (☎ 625252). Open M-Sa 8:30am-9pm, Su 8:30am-2pm.

Internet: A number of cyber-cafes line Rajpur Rd. near Astley Hall. Most charge Rs30-40 per hr.

Post Office: Head Post Office, by the clock tower. Open M-Sa 10am-6pm. **Postal Code:** 248001.

🛏 ACCOMMODATIONS

Hotels around the bus stands and the clock tower tend to be either bland high-end boxes or dingy budget dives, but the noise and stink are tolerable if you're only staying a night. Nicer (and sometimes cheaper) hotels line Rajpur Rd., along Astley Hall and beyond.

Hotel White House, Astley Hall (☎ 652765). One block east of Rajpur Rd. Near enough to Astley Hall for great shopping and good eats, but far enough from downtown to avoid most of the grime and congestion. Amazing mountain views. Huge rooms, pleasant gardens, and a friendly manager. Singles Rs215-260; doubles Rs315-395. AmEx. ❶

Hotel Prince, Gandhi Rd. (☎ 627070). Two blocks south of the Delhi Bus Stand and two blocks east of the Mussoorie Bus Stand. A multi-story business hotel without the high prices and pretension. Great top-floor views. Basic rooms with fans, desks, and hot water (but no showers). Some rooms have seat toilets. A friendly staff adds to the value. Singles Rs250; doubles Rs300-600. ❶

Meedo Hotel, 71 Gandhi Rd. (☎ 627088). One block from the railway station. Not to be confused with the expensive Meedo Grand out on Rajpur Rd. Bucket showers, seat toilets, clean rooms. Attached restaurant. Check-out 24hr. Singles Rs250-300; doubles Rs300-400. ❷

Osho Resorts, 111 Rajpur Rd. (☎ 749544). One kilometer beyond the GMVN Tourist Office. Well-kept rooms, TVs, hot water, and super-guru Osho himself (see p. 418). Read Osho books, watch Osho TV, or seek enlightenment in the lush meditation center. All rooms have a shower. The attached restaurant, **Heaven's Gate,** serves excellent food. Singles Rs490-1090; doubles Rs590-1290. Nov.-Mar. rates are Rs100 less. ❸

Hotel Drona (☎ 654371 or 652794). Next to Delhi Bus Stand, on Gandhi Rd. GMVN-run hotel has a tourist office, garden, STD booth, and large rooms with attached bath. Doubles Rs350-700. ❸

🍴 FOOD

Restaurants near Astley Hall and on Rajpur Rd. are a bit more up-market than the ones in the grime of the bus stand. The Paltan Bazaar area has good bakers and sweets vendors, plus a row of fruit stands near the clock tower. The **Venus** and **Ahuja restaurants** (opposite the explosives plant on Gandhi Rd., just east of the railway gate) are open throughout the day.

Kumar Foods Restaurant, 15B Rajpur Rd. Between the post office and Motel Himshri. Magically delicious renditions of Indian specialties. The *rogan josh* (Rs65) and chicken *tikka masala* (Rs130) are superb. Great service in a quiet and classy atmosphere. Open daily noon-4pm and 7-10:30pm; closed last Tu of the month. ❷

Motimahal Restaurant, Rajpur Rd. Opposite the Hotel Ambassador, in the coolest duckaway spot in town. Quality non-veg. food from a large menu. Chicken curry Rs65, mutton *shahi korma* Rs60, *dal makhani* Rs40. Open daily 9am-10:30pm. ❶

Daddy's, Rajpur Rd. Next to the Hotel President. A western-style burger joint in a surreal atmosphere complete with early 80s easy listening, blasted over a speaker system. A varied menu of pizza (Rs 30-50), "thirst aids," fries (Rs18), and theme burgers (Rs18-40) including the "Great Daddy's Twin" (Rs40). Open daily 9:30am-8pm. ❶

👁 SIGHTS

Most of the sights are outside the city. Buses and tempos will take you where you want to go from the city bus stand; taxis and auto-rickshaws charge Rs40-100 for trips to any of the sights and Rs400-500 for a full day. If you really want to take your time, pick a destination and make it a full day's excursion. The GMVN's daylong bus tour, **Doon Darshan,** covers the FRI, Tapkeshwar Temple, Malsi Deer Park, and Sahastra Dhara (Rs100). The bus stops for 45-90min. at each place (daily at 10:30am, returns at 5pm). Contact **Drona Travel,** 45 Gandhi Rd., by the Hotel Drona. (☎ 654371. Open daily 7am-10pm.)

ROBBER'S CAVE. A 200m-long, 15m-high gorge, the so-called Robber's Cave or **Guchu Pani,** is a popular picnic spot where you can swim in a calm pool beneath a waterfall. Wear sandals, as some of the rocks in the stream can be sharp. *(8km north of town. Take a bus from the city bus stand to Supply, Rs3. From there, a* vikrant *(Rs3) will take you to the trailhead at Anarwala, 2km from the cave's entrance.)*

FOREST RESEARCH INSTITUTE (FRI). Established under British auspices in 1906, the FRI works toward a better understanding of the uses and abuses of forestry, botany, and biodiversity conservation. Even if you're not into forestry, there's still quite a bit to do here: six museums focus on different aspects of forest life, from the chemicals in the leaves to the bugs in the bark. The green lawn of the institute's **Botanical Gardens** is a wonderful picnic spot. There is a canteen for afternoon tea or snacks and an information desk at the far corner of the institute. *(Visitors gate on Trevor Rd. Open M-F 9am-5:30pm. Museums open M-F 10am-5:30pm, Su 10am-2pm. Botanical Gardens Rs10.)*

TAPKESHWAR TEMPLE. Built into the mountain beside a running stream, this Shiva temple is the most important temple in the area. There are several shrines around the temple's entrance, and the nearby stream also serves as a popular swimming hole. Tapkeshwar Temple hosts the **Shivaratri celebration** during the last week of March and the first week of April. *(6km northwest of town. One-way auto-rickshaw Rs60; city bus or tempo from the clock tower Rs3. Open daily 5:30am-9pm.)*

MUSSOORIE मसूरी ☎ 0135

The mountain hill station of Mussoorie, a convenient access point to the forests nearby, certainly isn't for everyone. Travelers looking to shun commercialism in favor of spirituality should stay in nearby Haridwar or Rishikesh to avoid Mussoorie's high prices and overcrowding, and those hoping for mountain tranquility might be better off in Kumaon. But anyone with an interest in the bizarre subculture of Indian tourism could hope for no better point of observation. A trip to Mussoorie will take you back to an era where big hair, clunky roller skates, and the original Nintendo ruled the entertainment scene.

A favorite destination of heat-fleeing tourists from Delhi (it's the closest hill station to the capital), the town was settled in 1827 by an Englishman, Captain Young. British officials developed Mussoorie into a Victorian home-away-from-home, complete with an exclusive club, several libraries, and an Anglican Church. The central promenade, The Mall, was made for afternoon strolls and chit-chat, all in full view of the snow-peaked Himalayas to the northeast and the Doon Valley to the south.

Where once the British rulers ascended 11km carried by porters, Indian throngs now pack their Marutis and cruise up the scenic drive from the plains. Peak season is between May and July. Mid-season extends from July to October (the foggy monsoon months) and from March to May. The off season, November through March, brings solitude and snowfall.

> **WARNING.** There is an Indian Army encampment at **Chakrata**, 82km northwest of Mussoorie. No foreigners are allowed north of the east-west road between Yamuna Bridge and Kalsi without a permit from the army. Foreign tourists heading by road for Shimla or eastern Himachal Pradesh must do so via Herbertpur. Foreign tourists have been arrested for traveling north of Kalsi.

▣ TRANSPORTATION

Trains: No tracks run to Mussoorie, but computerized reservations for trains from Dehra Dun can be made at the **Northern Railways Out Agency,** on The Mall, below the post office. Open M-F 9am-1pm and 3-5pm, Sa 9-11am and noon-4pm, Su 9am-2pm.

Buses: UP Roadways buses leave from **Kulri** (☎ 632259) or **Library Bus Stand** (☎ 632258), both below The Mall, and service only **Dehra Dun** (1½hr., every 30min. 6am-7pm, Rs22). Several signs around town advertise direct Dehra Dun-Delhi deluxe service, but you have to get to Dehra Dun yourself. Try **Mussoorie Novelty Store** (☎ 632795). Opposite the railway booking office. Non-A/C buses (11am and 10pm, Rs150) and A/C buses (8, 11am, and 10pm; Rs250) depart from the clock tower in Dehra Dun.

Taxis: Booking stands are next to both bus stands. To **Dehra Dun** (Rs50 per seat, Rs200 per car) and **Haridwar** (Rs650 per car).

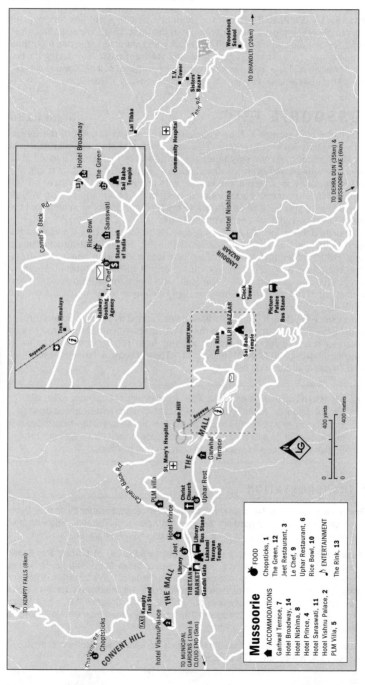

UTTARANCHAL

Mussoorie

▲ ACCOMMODATIONS
Garhwal Terrace, 7
Hotel Broadway, 14
Hotel Nishima, 8
Hotel Prince, 4
Hotel Saraswati, 11
Hotel Vishnu Palace, 2
PLM Villa, 5

🍴 FOOD
Chopsticks, 1
The Green, 12
Jeet Restaurant, 3
Le Chef, 9
Uphar Restaurant, 6
Rice Bowl, 10

♪ ENTERTAINMENT
The Rink, 13

ORIENTATION

Mussoorie is 15km long, stretching around the mountain overlooking Dehra Dun. The town has two centers, the **Library Bazaar** and **Kulri Bazaar** areas, connected by a 20min. walk along The Mall, which is lined with murals and shops of all kinds. Buses from the valley stop near both bazaars. The plaza in front of the library, with a statue of the Mahatma, is called **Gandhi Chowk**; the gate by the library is **Gandhi Gate. Camel's Back Rd.** runs along the back side of the mountain and connects the two bazaars. **Landour Bazaar,** with its large clock tower, is a 10min. walk east of Kulri. The **Tibetan Colony** is to the left of **Convent Hill** on **Kempty Falls Rd.**

PRACTICAL INFORMATION

Tourist Office: (☎632863). Near the ropeway, halfway between Kulri and Library Bazaars. Open May-June daily 9am-7pm; July-Apr. M-Sa 10am-5pm.

Budget Travel: GMVN (☎631281). At the Library Bus Stand. Runs tours of the northern pilgrimage sites departing from Delhi and Rishikesh. Trips range from a 4-day excursion to Badrinath (Rs2000) to 12-day trips to Yamnotri, Gangotri, Kedarnath, and Badrinath (Rs5000). Open daily May-July 9am-7pm; Aug.-Apr. 9am-5pm. For travel into the hills, try **Trek Himalaya** (☎30491). On The Mall, above the ropeway. Provides assistance for organized trips and drop-in consultations. Guides available. Tent rental Rs80-100 per day. Fully planned excursions US$50-70 per person for groups of 4 or more. Open daily Mar.-Oct. 10am-8:30pm.

Currency Exchange: State Bank of India, Kulri Bazaar (☎632533). Changes currency and traveler's checks. Open M-F 10am-4pm, Sa 10am-2pm.

Bookstore: There are several good bookstores along The Mall in Kulri. Most are open daily 8am-8pm. Try the **Prabhu Book Depot,** near Banares House Sarees in Kulri.

Market: Tibetan Market, along and below The Mall, near the library. Along **Kulri Bazaar** are many stores specializing in curios, woolens, and tourist trifles. Bazaars generally open 9am-9pm. The smaller **Five Sisters Bazaar** is on the road behind Tehri Rd., near the TV tower. **Prakash Stores,** a favorite with students at the Language School, stocks foreign food products. Open M-Sa 10am-8:30pm.

Police: (☎632083). Above The Mall, just west of the Hotel Mall Queen. Open 24hr.

Pharmacies: P.B. Hamers & Co. (☎632502). Up from the Rialto Cinema, by President's Restaurant. Has a wide selection. Open daily 10am-9pm.

Hospital/Medical Services: The **Community Hospital** (☎632541). In Landour, 1½km east of the clock tower. Offers 24hr. emergency care. For private treatment, try the **clinic** of Dr. Nautiyal (☎632014), on Camel's Back Road, 3min. from Library Bazaar. Open daily 10am-1pm and 4-7pm.

Internet: Cyber Corner, Camel's Back Rd. (☎630230). Three minutes from the library. Rs60 per hr. Open daily 9am-9pm. In Kulri Bazaar, try **Cyber Zone.** Across from the Four Seasons Restaurant. Rs80 per hr.

Post Office: (☎632806). Near State Bank of India, above The Mall in Kulri. Open M-F 9am-1pm and 1:30-5pm, Sa 9am-noon. **Postal Code:** 248179.

ACCOMMODATIONS

Most low-end options are in the **Kulri Bazaar** area. It's a good idea to book ahead of time in peak season (May-June), when rates are higher. Expect discounts mid-season (Mar.-May and July-Oct.) and much lower prices Nov.-Mar. Rates vary from day to day and may be flexible, so try your hand at a little haggling. Unless otherwise noted, check-out is 10am.

KULRI AND LANDOUR

Hotel Nishima, Landour Bazaar (☎ 632227). Five minutes walk past the clock tower. Popular among language school students, Nimisha has bright rooms and huge buckets of hot water. Rest easy on thick mattresses behind heavy metal doors. TV in the lobby. Food is available, and there are seat toilets for the lucky few. May-July: doubles Rs250-550, Aug.-Apr.: Rs125-250. ❷

Hotel Broadway, Camel's Back Rd. (☎ 632243). Close to the rink near Kulri Bazaar. This converted English guest house retains its charm in a peaceful setting away from most of the noise. Rooms with balconies have breathtaking valley views; some have seat toilets. May-July: doubles Rs400-800. Off-season: 30% discount. ❸

Garhwal Terrace (☎ 632682 or 632683). On The Mall, between Kulri and Library Bazaars. This GMVN-run hotel has dormitories that open up to a lovely veranda with valley views. Pricey doubles aren't worth it. Reserve in advance during peak season. Dorms Rs300; rooms Rs1300. July 16-Apr. 15: Rs100/Rs800. ❷

Hotel Saraswati (☎ 631005). Up the ramp from the more visible Hotel Amar, past Hotel Mansarovar. Because of its somewhat hidden location, it's likely to have rooms when all else is full. Immaculate rooms with mirrors, TVs, seat toilets, and hot water. The surroundings are peaceful in comparison to the activity on Mall Rd. Doubles Rs600-1000. Off-season: 50% discount. ❸

LIBRARY AREA

🖼 **Hotel Prince** (☎ 632674). Off The Mall, up the ramp from the horse stand—look for the alley access 30m toward Kulri from the library. Once a British hotel, this magnificent site is high above The Mall in a century-old summer getaway. Regal halls, huge rooms, and high ceilings; have tea in the drawing room or on the patio. One of the few hotels that offer both mountain and valley views. May 15-July 15: doubles Rs300-1500. Off-season: 50% discount. ❸

Hotel Vishnu Palace (☎ 632932 or 631732). 100m toward Kempty Falls when coming from the library. Clean rooms with views and attached baths. Low-end rooms are a good value. Doubles Rs550-1500. Off-season: 40% discount. ❸

PLM Villa (☎ 631090). Off Camel's Back Rd., a 5min. walk from the library. Small garden-fronted place popular with Indian families. Small rooms with spectacular views. Food 7am-10pm. Check-out noon. Doubles Rs400-900. Off-season: 50% discount. ❸

OUTSIDE MUSSOORIE

Cloud End Forest Resort (☎ 632242; fax 625657; cloudend@nde.vsnl.net.in). West of the library, on the road to the municipal gardens; 7km by jeep. Set in 2000 acres of forest on a ridge overlooking Mussoorie. Built in 1838, this is one of the oldest buildings in Mussoorie. The period ambience has been scrupulously preserved, with old photographs, plush armchairs, and dark wooden beds. At night, guests enjoy tea and snacks beside bonfires. The restaurant serves unusually fresh and flavorful food. The doubles are pricey, but spartan dorm bunks get you in cheaply. There are some beautiful walks from here to the George Everest House and Kempty Falls. Camping is also an option (Rs400 per person, Rs200 if you have your own tent). Reserve a day ahead to have a jeep pick you up from the library. Dorm bunks Rs450; doubles Rs1400. Off-season: 50% discount. Closed Jan. to mid-Mar. AmEx/MC/V. ❷

🎨 FOOD

Roasted and boiled *masala* corn (Rs5-15) is sold along The Mall, and sweets are scooped up at **Krishna's** in Kulri. For Tibetan food, head to Convent Hill.

■ **The Green,** Kulri Bazaar. Serves delicious veg. food at reasonable prices, though a long stream of late-night customers can make it impossible to take your time. For breakfast, try the "Green Special Paratha," stuffed with peas, *paneer*, cashews, and raisins (Rs20). Also serves delightful Punjabi (Rs40-55) and Chinese (Rs30-70) dishes. Open daily 7am-3:30pm and 7-10pm. Off-season: 8am-3:30pm and 7:30-10:30pm. ❶

Jeet Restaurant, Gandhi Chowk. Next to the library and Jeet Hotel. The ideal place to plan your trek or your next move—some of the tables have maps built into them. Veg. fare Rs30-55, chicken curry Rs45, cocoa Rs15. Open daily 8am-11pm. ❶

Uphar Restaurant, Mall Rd. In Library Bazaar. Much like the Green, offers great veg. fare at reasonable rates. Great cheese *kofta* (Rs50). Open daily 8:30am-10:30pm. ❶

Chopsticks, Convent Hill. Before the IAS Academy. Very far from town, but a good place to take a break during a forest trek. The food is remarkably fresh. The chow mein (Rs20-35) and Talumein soup (Rs35) are delicious. ❶

Le Chef, near the State Bank of India in Kulri. French fries (Rs20), pizza (Rs50-90), hot dogs (Rs35), "gravy items," and fountain drinks. A popular hang-out for roller-skating teens. Open daily 10am-11pm. ❶

Rice Bowl, Kulri Bazaar. Opposite the President restaurant. Cubicles with street view. Chinese and Tibetan food. Garlic chicken Rs60, mutton *momos* Rs30, huge portions of noodles and rice Rs50-80. Open daily 11am-11:30pm. Off-season: 11am-9:30pm. ❶

⊙ SIGHTS

GUN HILL. Directly over the town is an extinct volcano known as Gun Hill, whose name comes from a Raj-era ritual in which guns were fired from the top at midday—the townspeople used to set their watches by it. You can walk for 20min. or ride rented horses *(15min., Rs70)* up the path, which starts at the main police station. The best way to go is via Mussoorie's **ropeway**—come early or get stuck waiting for hours. *(Open daily 8am-10pm; last car up at 8pm. Off-season: 10am-7pm. Rs25 round-trip.)* The top of Gun Hill has several lookout points, food vendors, a surreal **Laugh House** *(Rs10),* and photo stands that will capture you in glittery local costume.

LAL TIBBA. On the far side of the mountain with the TV Tower is Lal Tibba, a glorious **lookout point** for the distant Himalayas. It's a steep 1hr. walk from Kulri; a taxi *(Rs120 round trip)* is another option. The 30min. walk from here to the TV Tower and Sisters' Bazaar around the backside of the mountain affords an even more serene retreat.

CAMEL'S BACK ROAD. Several good **walks** start from Mussoorie and pass through fragrant pine and deodar forests. Camel's Back Rd., which winds behind the town *(3km total),* has great views of the Himalayas. Points of interest include the **cemetery** (if the main gate is closed, try the side gate), studded with interesting British tombstones, **Camel's Back Rock** (guess at its shape), and **Chatra (Umbrella) Point,** where you can buy *chai* and snacks and look through a telescope, if it isn't broken. The entire walk takes 30min. On a clear day, the sunset view from the road is spectacular.

MUSSOORIE LAKE. The town's newest attraction is an artificially constructed lake 6km from town on the road to Dehra Dun. Catch a breeze and gaze at the hills while gliding around the lake in a paddle boat *(Rs80 per 30min.).* There's not much here apart from a few small shops, though this might be just what you're seeking.

STRANGE BREW Though an Englishman founded Mussoorie, it took an unruly Scot to set the tone for the revelry that has outlasted the Brits in the hill station. In the 1880s, a fellow named Mackinnon discovered limestone springs near present-day Gandhi Chowk. Mackinnon thought that the waters here might be good for brewing, and he built a brewery on the land, which soon began producing Garhwal's first beer. From the beginning, Mussoorie was a fun-loving town, and the beer-brewing led to a level of bacchanalian debauchery that wrinkled more than a few official brows. Local lore has it that one English lass, well progressed in the appreciation of the Scotch-Indian brew, stood on a chair on Mall Rd. and sold kisses for Rs5. That spelled trouble for Mackinnon. Since an outright ban on Mackinnon's operation would have been illegal, the authorities shrewdly crippled him by refusing him the right to import barley on the government road. Shut down but not broken in spirit, Mackinnon would not be snubbed—especially by the English. In a daring scheme, he built his own road, 20km long, fitting it with carts to transport his barley. He even set up a watchtower and tollbooth and ran it as a private highway. Aside from barley, much of the heavy European furniture in Mussoorie was brought up on "Mr. Buckles' Bullock-Cart Train," as the venture was called. And so, Mussoorie had its beer.

To thank his consumers, Mackinnon threw a massive bash, where he cracked a huge wooden cask of new brew. The rollicking horde polished off most of the barrel, noting repeatedly that it tasted better than any beer in brewing history. But a scream of horror suddenly broke up the festivities, and the party collapsed into pandemonium—in the dregs of the cask lay a rotting human body. Apparently, an impatient imbiber had slipped into the cellar, packed down a few too many, and fallen in with the hops. The brew was through. Mackinnon's ruined brewery looms on the Lynndale Estate 3km west of Mussoorie, but his bullock-cart road now forms 20km of the present road to Rajpur.

🎵 ENTERTAINMENT

The **Vasu Cinema,** in the Library area, and the **Rialto Cinema,** in Kulri, opposite the President's restaurant, show Hindi movies (4 per day). There is an abundance of **arcade games** (some date to the pre-Pac-Man era) in the parlors of Kulri (Rs3 per game). There are a few discos in the Mussoorie area. **Moovers,** at Kulri Bazaar, rocks every night, but only local men seem to go. (☎632850. Cover Rs375 per couple. Open daily 8-11pm.) Outside town, **Residency Manor,** Hotel Jaypee, has dancing on the weekends. (☎631800. Cover Rs250-375, dinner included.)

Mussoorie's true hotspot, **The Rink,** in Kulri, is India's largest roller-skating rink. It dates back 100 years to when British couples experimented with what was then all the rage back home. (Open daily 8:30am-9:30pm. Admission with rental Rs40.)

📷 DAYTRIPS FROM MUSSOORIE

To the west of Mussoorie lie **Happy Valley** and the nearby **Municipal Garden** *(3km from Mussoorie),* which has a tiny pool for paddle-boats. Two kilometers from the garden are the ruins of the old Mackinnon brewery (see **Strange Brew,** p. 638). A more distant destination to the northwest of town is **Kempty Falls,** a popular "retreat" that has sadly degenerated from an idyllic spot overlooking pristine, rushing falls and peaceful pools to the same old glitz that pervades the rest of town. GMVN runs a 3hr. bus trip to Kempty falls. *(Times vary; check at the GMVN office at the Library Bus Stand. Rs50.)* Taxis leave from the Kempty Taxi Stand, a 10min. walk up Kempty Rd. from the library (Rs105 per person round-trip.) Keen hikers can spend a morning walking through the untouched forests from Cloud's End to the source of Kempty and then to the falls (12km). You can also make daytrips out to the orchards and dense deodar forest of **Dhanolti** *(25km away)*, the artificial lake and boating facilities at **Jheel,** and **Surkanda Devi** *(35km from Mussoorie, Rs120).* This temple, at the top of the highest mountain in the area (3300m), provides great views of snow-covered peaks. It's a strenuous 2km walk to the temple from the road head. **Cloud's End** (see Mussoorie **Accommodations,** above), 7km away, is a fairly untouched hiking spot. A 1hr. walk through apple orchards brings you to the **George Everest House,** the home of the First Surveyor General of India. Famous British-Indian author Ruskin Bond lives near the Masonic Lodge Bus Stand and always welcomes friendly visitors.

LANDOUR LANGUAGE SCHOOL. At the top of the mountain, above Landour Bazaar, is the Landour Language School. Founded in 1870 by British missionaries and grammarians, it launched the international academic study of modern Indian languages and now offers programs in tandem with the University of Chicago and UC Berkeley, among others. Classes are small, with plenty of individual instruction for the school's 80 or so students. Courses offered range from introductory to advanced-level classes. A 12-week introductory Hindi class costs Rs18,000. Private lessons are Rs75 per hr. Students usually stay in private houses (Rs5000 per month) or in one of the two guest houses near the school (Rs300 per day including food). Contact Principal Chitranjan Datt, Landour Language School, Landour, Mussoorie, UP, 248179 (☎631487; fax 631917).

HARIDWAR हरिद्वार ☎ 0133

Steeped in legend, cloaked in forests, and bordered by the Ganga as it emerges from the mountains to carve its winding way across India, Haridwar (Gateway to Lord Shiva) or Haridwar (Gateway to the gods) is one of Hinduism's sacred sites. The city's spiritual pre-eminence is rooted in the belief that the Ganga flows here in its purest form at the Har-ki-Pairi (Footstep of God), the main *ghat* to the Ganga. Today, tens of thousands of Hindus bathe in, drink from, and pray to the Ganga. At sundown, *arati* is performed at Har-ki-Pairi; pilgrims float candle-lit flower boats down the Ganga to the sound of *bhajans*. A major pilgrimage destination, Haridwar hosts the Kumbh Mela every 12 years when millions of people rush the Har-ki-Pairi *ghat* at a precisely calculated moment; 14 people were trampled to death at the last Mela held here in 1998.

▐ TRANSPORTATION

Trains: Northern Railway Station, next to the bus stand on Railway Rd. Enquiries office on the right-hand side; reservation counter on the left. Tickets can be bought at the **Northern Railway Booking Office,** Railway Rd. (☎427724), north of Lalita Rao Bridge. To: **Dehra Dun** (2hr., 11 per day 5:35am-4:51pm, Rs104); **Delhi** (7-8hr.; 5 per day 7am-8:40pm; Rs131, A/C chair Rs460); **Lucknow** (11hr., 3 per day 11am-10:15pm, Rs186); **Rishikesh** (1hr., 8:45am, Rs65.); **Varanasi** (20hr., 11am and 10:15pm, Rs262).

Buses: The **bus stand** is opposite the train station, at the southwest end of Railway Rd. **UP Roadways** (☎427037) runs buses to: **Agra** (11hr.; 7 per day 5:40am-9pm, Rs149); **Dehra Dun** (1½hr., every 30min. 6am-7:30pm, Rs26); **Delhi** (5hr., every 15min. 4am-11pm, Rs98); **Lucknow** (14hr., 10am and 7:30pm, Rs210); **Rishikesh** (45min.; every 20min. 6am-9pm, every 30min. 9pm-5am; Rs14); **Shimla** (12hr., 11am, Rs165). Deluxe buses cost 70% more and are available to every place listed above except Lucknow and Shimla.

Local Transportation: Auto-rickshaws and tempos are not allowed in the northern half of town (past the post office). For this reason, **cycle-rickshaws** are your best bet for transport to Har-ki-Pairi and the surrounding area. They'll go anywhere in the city for Rs10.

✈ ❓ ORIENTATION AND PRACTICAL INFORMATION

Haridwar runs along the banks of the Ganga, which flows from northeast to southwest. The **bus stand** and **railway station** face each other at the southwest end of **Railway Rd.**, the town's main thoroughfare. Walking northeast on Railway Rd., you'll cross a bridge over a small stream before reaching the post office. Just south of the post office is a barricade that prohibits four-wheeled traffic from continuing up Railway Rd. North of this barricade, Railway Rd. becomes **Upper Rd.**; the **Har-ki-Pairi** is at the northeast end of Upper Rd. The main bazaar, **Moti Bazaar,** runs parallel to the river along the streets shooting out from Upper Rd. near Har-ki-Pairi. Beyond that is the **Broken Bridge.** On the other side of the river are most of the accommodations and the **taxi stand.**

Tourist Office: GMVN, Railway Rd. (☎ 424240). Two blocks south of the Post Office. Provides good maps and has information on local treks. Open M-Sa 10am-5pm. **UA Tourism** (☎ 427370). In Rahi Motel, opposite the railway station. Open M-Sa 10am-5pm. They also operate a desk inside the railway station. Open during train arrivals.

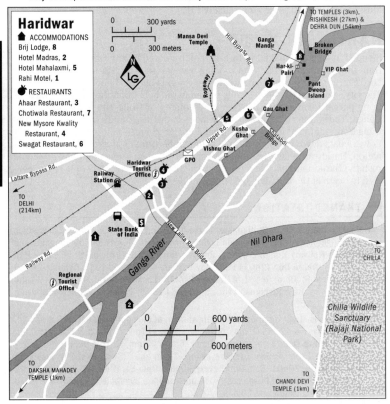

Haridwar

🏠 ACCOMMODATIONS
Brij Lodge, **8**
Hotel Madras, **2**
Hotel Mahalaxmi, **5**
Rahi Motel, **1**

🍴 RESTAURANTS
Ahaar Restaurant, **3**
Chotiwala Restaurant, **7**
New Mysore Kwality
  Restaurant, **4**
Swagat Restaurant, **6**

Budget Travel: Ashwani Travels, Railway Rd. (☎424581). Just south of Laltarao Bridge. Open daily 8am-10pm. **Shivalik Travels,** Upper Rd. (☎426855). Opposite Gorakh Nath Ashram. Specializes in transportation to northern pilgrimage sites. Open daily 7am-3pm and 5-10pm. Pilgrimage destinations open May-Oct.

Currency Exchange: State Bank of India, Sharwan Nath Nagar. Changes US currency. Open M-F 10am-2pm, Sa 10am-noon.

Market: Moti Bazaar, on the narrow streets just south of Har-ki-pairi. Features a wide selection of brass and wooden goods.

Police: Main station, Upper Rd. (☎426200 or 425200).

Pharmacy: Milap Medical Hall, Railway Rd. (☎427193). South of the post office, on the opposite side of the road. Open M-Sa 8am-10pm. **Dr. B.C. Hasaram & Sons,** Railway Rd. (☎427860). Opposite the police station. Specializes in ayurvedic medicines. Open daily 8am-9pm.

Hospital/Medical Services: There are several private clinics on Railway Rd. **Dr. Kailash Pande's clinic** (☎426023, emergency ☎424343). Just south of the Post Office. Provides 24hr. emergency care. Open 11:30am-2:30pm and 6:30-9:30pm.

Internet: Balkrishan Dinesh Kumar's self-titled phone booth, Railway Rd. (☎427615). Just south of the post office. Offers Internet access for Rs2 per min.

Post Office: Railway Rd. (☎427025). North of Laltarao Bridge. Open M-Sa 10am-4pm. **Postal Code:** 249401.

▚ ACCOMMODATIONS

Except for a few diamonds in the rough, most hotels in Haridwar are old and run-down. The closer you get to Har-ki-Pairi, the more you pay for location. Though the *dharamsalas* may look inviting, most are not open to foreigners. From Nov.-Mar. prices are significantly lower. The prices listed below are for high (pilgrimage) season.

Hotel Mahalaxmi (☎427238). Upper Rd. Next to the path to Mansa Nevi. Brand-spanking new, marble-tiled rooms come with seat toilets, TVs, and running hot water 6hr. per day. Doubles Rs550, with A/C Rs850-900. Off-season: Rs100 discount. ❷

Hotel Madras (☎426356). Off Railway Rd., 2 blocks north of the railway station. Turn right after the Kailash Hotel. An old, low-end lodge conveniently close to transport. Highly attentive staff. Singles Rs80; doubles Rs150. ❶

Hotel Aldenanda (☎426379). Cross Laltarao Bridge, turn right, and walk 1km. Buses pass by on the way into town. Though pricey and far from most of the sights, it's the best place for peace and quiet, with a little lawn, flower garden, and a strip of riverbank on the holy Ganga. All rooms have air-cooling and attached bath with hot water and seat toilets. Restaurant open 6:30am-10:30pm. Check-out noon. Dorms Rs100; air-cooled rooms Rs750; A/C rooms Rs1500. Off-season: 20% discount. ❶

Rahi Motel (☎426430). Railway Rd. One block south of the bus stand. Good location for late arrivals. UA Tourism Office is in an attached bldg. Decent-sized rooms with seat toilets and hot showers. Singles Rs500-1000; doubles Rs600-1100. ❸

Brij Lodge (☎426872). The first bldg. north of Har-ki-Pairi on the right, near the Broken Bridge (the name of the hotel is not visible from the road—walk down the steps to the lobby). Watch the nightly *arati* ritual from the expansive balcony overlooking the Ganga. All rooms have attached bath with seat toilets but no showers. Doubles Rs600. Off-season: 50% discount. ❷

◹ FOOD

Purity of diet follows purity of spirit in Haridwar, so alcohol and meat are not available. Most major restaurants are on Railway Rd., midway between the bus stand and Har-ki-Pairi. Street vendors in the Moti Bazaar near Har-ki-Pairi offer delicious *saag puris*, as well as sugar-filled *jalebis* that look like clogged arteries even *before* you eat them. But be sure to find a relatively clean place: the Ganga can cleanse your soul, but not your digestive tract.

Ahaar Restaurant, Railway Rd. Two blocks south of the Post Office. South Indian, Chinese, and Punjabi food in a dark, tranquil, subterranean wooden chamber. *Thalis* Rs35-50, *dosas* Rs18-30. Open daily 9am-12pm. ❶

New Mysore Kwality Restaurant, on the west side of Railway Rd. One block south of the Post Office. Unassuming atmosphere, cool air, and great prices. *Thalis* Rs30, *dosas* Rs18. Open daily 7am-10:30pm, in winter 7am-9pm. ❶

Swagat Restaurant, Upper Rd. Next to Hotel Mansarovar. If you can deal with the dingy atmosphere, you'll find some great *paneer* dishes (Rs40). Veg. chow mein Rs30. Open daily 6am-11pm. ❶

Chotiwala Restaurant, Upper Rd. Near Har-ki-Pairi. There are about a dozen (unrelated) restaurants named Chotiwala in town; this one is particularly good. Veg. *thalis* (Rs25-60) and a wide variety of other Indian and Chinese dishes. Open daily 8am-10pm. ❶

◎ SIGHTS

HAR-KI-PAIRI GHAT. The most important spot in Haridwar is the holy *ghat* of Har-ki-Pairi, site of Vishnu's footprint and the place where the sacred Ganga flows out into the plains. Many pilgrims fill a bottle or two to take home for use in religious ceremonies. The **Ganga Mandir** marks the spot where the drop of sacred nectar fell during the mythical match-up between the demon *asuras* and the good-guy gods that is now celebrated during the Kumbh Mela. Most people bathe here at sunrise, though you'll see people here throughout the day; there are chains to keep bathers from getting swept off to Varanasi by the strong undertow. The area is constantly crowded with pilgrims, beggars, lepers, sadhus, and several uniformed men who wander the area asking for donations for various "trusts." Many of these individuals pocket their earnings—donate via the charity boxes around the area or at the office of Ganga Sabha, above the temple at the *ghat*. Every evening at sundown, the sublime and spectacular **arati** ceremony takes place. Thousands gather to pay tribute to the gods with *diyas* (colorful lamps made of cupped leaves filled with flower petals and a lit candle) that float on the river. Arrive early (around 6:45pm) in high season. The best view is from the bridge on the south end of Har-ki-Pairi and the strip by the clock tower. You can check your shoes at the stand if you want to go down to the *ghat*, but avoid the 8pm shoe-return stampede.

MANSA DEVI AND CHANDI DEVI TEMPLE. Haridwar is dotted with temples, but the two most important and beautiful ones can only be reached by ropeway or trek. Just above the city, on top of Bilwa Parvat, is the **Mansa Devi Temple,** dedicated to the goddess by the same name who can make the wishes of faithful and holy people come true. Mansa is believed to have bathed at Har-ki-Pairi every morning. The temple houses two intricately carved statues of the goddess—one with five arms and three mouths, the other with eight arms. To get to the shrine, stand in line for one of the ropeway trolleys that whisk you up and over a garden to the hilltop, where views, vendors, and the temple await. You can avoid the long wait in line by making the 30min. hike up the hill yourself. The **Chandi Devi Temple**

is across the river a few kilometers from town, but the ropeway operator offers a package deal including a bus to the base of Chandi Devi's longer, 750m ropeway. The temple itself is smaller than Mansa Devi, but the breathtaking views of the Himalayas, Haridwar, and the Ganga make it well worth the journey. *(Mansa Devi ropeway trolley open daily 6:30am-8pm; Rs25 round-trip. Chandi Devi ropeway trolley open daily 8:30am-6pm; Rs50 roundtrip. Package tour Rs95; includes A/C bus between ropeways, as well as ropeway fare.)*

OTHER TEMPLES. En route to **Kankhal,** south of Haridwar, are two other temples. The **Pareshwar Mahadev Temple,** 4km down the road, is famous for a *linga* made of mercury. One kilometer farther is the **Dakseshwara Temple** (also called the Daksha Mahadev) and **Sati Kund,** where King Daksha Prajaputi, Brahma's son and Sati's father, held a public sacrifice. Sati was invited but her husband-to-be, Shiva, didn't make the guest list. Sati was so insulted that she threw herself on the sacrificial pyre.

BHARAT MATA MANDIR AND ENVIRONS. North of Haridwar, on the road to Rishikesh, is a group of unusual temples that are either opulent and justly grand or just chintzy and overdone. The temples can be visited by tempo (Rs200-250 for a 3hr. tour). They're all within easy walking distance of each other, though, and it may be better to use your own two feet for transport between them. One kilometer from Har-ki-Pairi is the **Bhimgoda Tank,** where Bhima, one of the strongest of the five Pandavas, took a bath. A little farther is the **Jai Ram Ashram,** whose bone-white sculptures, depicting the battles between gods and demons, are a departure from the colorful deities that characterize most Hindu temples.

The **Pawan Dham Temple,** along Swami Sukhdevanand Rd. from Haridwar, is most representative of the local houses of worship. Its many shrines are made almost entirely of mirrors and stained glass. Shiva and Arjuna ride on mirror-covered horses while Krishna eyes his 100 lovers. The road then proceeds to the **Bharat Mata Mandir,** an eight-story shrine to Mother India and its leaders that resembles a modern apartment building capped by colorful temple domes. The top story houses the Hindu gods while the floor below hosts the goddesses, including Ganga and Saraswati, goddess of knowledge. The lower floors honor the saints of India's various religions (from Guru Nanak of the Sikhs to the Buddha and Swami Vivekenanda), saintly sisters (including Gandhi's devotees Annie Besant and Sister Nivedita), and freedom fighters. The second floor has paintings highlighting characteristic features of India's states, and the ground floor has a giant relief model of the country. Near the Bharat Mata Mandir, **Maa Vaishnodevi Mandir** attempts to simulate the experience of visiting a cave in Kashmir, complete with artificial, fruit-bearing mango trees, a giant Ganga Mata with a crocodile, and a tunnel with knee-deep water through which visitors duck and wade. **Bhuma Niketan,** south of Maa Vaishnodevi Mandir, has the added bonus of automation; pay Rs1 to enter a room to watch robotic representations of Hindu heroes cavort with a giant devil. Venture off to the **Sapta Rishi Ashram,** at the north end of the cluster, to pay homage to the seven saints in the ashram's seven temples. It's believed that when Ganga arrived, the seven sages were involved in deep *tapasya* (austerities). To please all seven by touching their feet, she divided herself at this spot into seven streams which were distinctly visible as recently as 10 years ago.

▟ ASHRAMS

Hindu pilgrims and sadhus flock to Haridwar for spiritual enrichment and often stay at one of the numerous ashrams within or near the city. Western spiritual seekers, on the other hand, often find themselves more at home in **Rishikesh** (see p. 644), where the yoga centers and ashrams are more likely to accept foreigners. In Haridwar, if you're not Indian, you'll have to do something special to impress the gurus and gain residence in their ashrams. However, the famous **Shantikunj** (☎424309; fax 423866; shantikunj.hardwar@sml.sprintrpg.ems.vsnl.net.in) is open to foreigners and offers 9-, 30-, and 90-day courses that use meditation, music, and chanting as means of attaining higher spiritual states. The nine-day courses begin on the 1st, 11th, and 21st of every month—reserve one month in advance. Single or two-day stays are also possible. (Payment by donation.)

RISHIKESH ऋषिकेश   ☎0135

Most travelers come to Rishikesh to find *something*—a cure to some deep-rooted ailment, a spiritual leader, or, most often, themselves. Something about Rishikesh has the power to transform—sages first arrived here to find spirituality in the crashing of the Ganga before heading north through the forests to the region's pilgrimage sites. Every year, thousands turn up for the **International Yoga Week** (Feb. 2-7) on the banks of the Ganga. Even the Beatles sought a new path here in 1968 under the guidance of the Maharishi Mahesh Yogi (see **Instant Karma**, p. 649). There are fewer temples in Rishikesh than in Haridwar, but more Westerners, more ashrams, more peace, and more sadhus. Summer is the yoga off season; winter has fewer Indian tourists.

Rishikesh

FOOD
Amrita, **7**
Chotiwala & Chotiwala, **12**
Ganga Darshan, **14**
Ganga View Restaurant, **13**
Madras Café, **5**

TO GANGOTRI
TO DEVPRAYAG (64km)
Badrinath Rd.
Lakshmanjhula Bridge
Lakshman Temple
Dhalwala Bypass Rd.
Sivananda Ramesh Music School
Ganga River
Shivpuri Reserved Forest
Tehri Rd.
Ramjhula Bridge
Gohri Reserved Forest
Clock Tower
SWARGASHRAM
TO NEELKANTH MAHADEV (30km)
Chandrabhaga
Lakshmanjhula Rd.
GMVN ℹ
Garhwal Himalayan Explorations
Dehradun Rd.
Yatra Bus Stand
River
Step Himalaya Adventures
Gov't. Hospital
Baba Massage Center
State Bank of India
Station Rd.
Bengali Rd.
Yatra Tourist Office
Bharat Mandir
Main Bus Stand
RISHIKESH
Hanuman Mandir
Agrawal Rd.
Haridwar Rd.
Triveni Ghat
TO HARIDWAR (24km)

Rishikesh

ACCOMMODATIONS
Bhandari Swiss Cottage, **1**
Brijwasi Palace, **10**
Green Hotel, **11**
High Bank Peasant's Cottage, **2**
Yoga Niketan Guest House, **4**

ASHRAMS
Omkarananda Ganga Sadan, **6**
Vanprastha Ashram, **8**
Ved Niketan, **9**
Yoga Niketan, **3**
Yoga Study Centre, **15**

TRANSPORTATION

Trains: Railway Station, at the west end of Rishikesh on (surprise!) Railway Rd. Reservations office open daily 8am-2pm. Most connections to major destinations start in Haridwar. To **Haridwar** (1½hr., 6 per day, Rs35) and **Delhi** (10hr., 6:40am, Rs67).

Buses: Rishikesh has 2 bus stands. Smog-belchers heading for the plains leave from the **UP Roadways Main Bus Stand,** Agarwal and Bengali Rd. (☎430066), on the south side of central Rishikesh. To: **Agra** (12hr., 8am and 6pm, Rs210); **Almora** (12hr., 9am, Rs180); **Chandigarh** (6hr., 9am, Rs110); **Dehra Dun** (1hr., every 30min. 5:30am-8pm, Rs22); **Delhi** (6½hr., every hr. 4am-10:30pm, Rs165); **Haldwani** (10hr., 9am, Rs100); **Haridwar** (every 30min. 4am-10:30pm, Rs18); **Nainital** (12hr., 8am, Rs145). For buses to the northern pilgrimage sites, go to the **Yatra Bus Stand** (☎430344), on Dehra Dun Rd., at the northwest end of Rishikesh. A rickshaw from the UP stand to the Yatra Bus Stand costs Rs10-15. Tickets for Yamnotri, Gangotri, Kedarnath, and Badrinath can be bought 1 day in advance. To: **Badrinath** (5 per day 3:30-6am, Rs170); **Chamoli** (7hr., Rs90); **Gangotri** (12hr., 5:30am, Rs130); **Hanuman Chatti** (12hr., 7am, Rs80); **Joshimath** (11hr., 5 per day 3:30-6am, Rs152); **Kedarnath** (12hr., 5am, Rs95); **Srinagar, UP** (4hr., every 30min. 4am-3pm, Rs50); **Tehri** (3½hr., every 30min. 3:15am-5:15pm, Rs40); **Uttarkashi** (7hr., 10 per day 3:15am-1pm, Rs72). Tehri and Uttarkashi serve as launch points for Yamnotri and Gangotri, Srinagar for Kedarnath and Badrinath. **Shared taxis** to **Uttarkashi** (5hr.; Rs1200 per cab, up to 5 seats) leave from outside the bus stand.

Local Transportation: Getting to Ramjhula and Lakshmanjhula from Rishikesh is best done via one of the **tempos** that run along Lakshmanjhula Rd. (Rs3-5). Both bridges must be traversed on foot—no cross-river traffic. Both sides of the river teem with **autorickshaws** and **taxis.** A seat in a taxi to Rishikesh from the Ramjhula Bridge costs Rs20; the rickshaw fare from the UP bus stand to Lakshmanjhula is Rs45.

ORIENTATION

Rishikesh is divided into three parts by the **Ganga** and the **Chandrabhaga Rivers.** Northeast of the dry bed of the Chandrabagha River is **Ramjhula,** and farther northeast is **Lakshmanjhula.** Both straddle the Ganga and are connected by footbridges. For better accommodations, most travelers head toward the bridges. It's a 5km hike into Rishikesh if you're staying in Lakshmanjhula, but the distance from the noise and clutter of the station makes the walk well worth it. The trek from Lakshmanjhula Bridge to the road and taxi stand is beautiful but arduous.

The very small business center of Rishikesh is on the triangular land mass between the Chandrabhaga and the Ganga Rivers. The river banks are lined with temples, and a grid of streets covers the rest of the land. The **railway station** and **main bus stand** are in the northwestern corner of Rishikesh. The tourist office, banks, and post office are in the small city center. **Dehradun Rd.** runs along the Chandrabhaga at the northwestern end of Rishikesh, intersecting at its eastern end with Laksmanjhula Rd. The eastern part of Ramjhula is known as **Swargashram** and its western part is called **Muni-ki-Reti** (named for the nearby hill where Lord Hanuman brought herbs to cure Lord Rama's illness). **Kailash Gate,** 1km south of Ramjhula taxi stand in the city center, is a major landmark.

PRACTICAL INFORMATION

Tourist Office: CUA Tourism, Railway Rd. (☎430209). Three blocks west of the State Bank of India, up the outdoor flight of stairs by the white statue. Open M-Sa 10am-5pm, closed 2nd Sa. **GMVN Trekking and Mountaineering Office** (☎430799). Kailash Gate. Offers info on treks and rents equipment at great prices. Open daily May-June and Sept.-Oct. 10am-5pm. Off-season: closed Su. The **Yatra Tourist Office,** Haridwar Rd., past the post office. An authority on trips to the northern pilgrimage sites. Open M-Sa 10am-5pm.

Budget Travel: Several agencies line Lakshmanjhula Rd., north of the dry river bed, on the way to Ramjhula. **Step Himalayan Adventures** (☎432581). Organizes treks and rafting trips, rents equipment, and offers free advice for those planning their own trips. Open M-Sa 8am-5pm. **Garhwal Himalayan Explorations Pvt. Ltd.** (☎433478; fax 431654). Kailash Gate, opposite Union Bank of India. They are a group of trained adventure sports buffs offering the most professional and reliable service in the area.

Currency Exchange: State Bank of India (☎430114). Changes currency at its main Rishikesh office, on the north side of Railway Rd., a 5min. walk from Lakshmanjhula Rd. Open M-F 10am-4pm, Sa 10am-1pm. **Bank of Baroda,** 74 Dehradun Rd. (☎430653). Changes traveler's checks in US$ and UK£. Open M-F 10am-2pm, Sa 10am-noon.

Market: Main Bazaar in Rishikesh, toward the river from the post office. There's a **didgeridoo** shop near the State Bank of India, with Hare Krishna tapes, ceramic *lingas,* and other indispensable souvenirs. Henna girls will paint you up in Lakshmanjhula. You can buy yoga books and ayurvedic herbs in Ramjhula and Swargashram.

Police: Main Rishikesh Office, Dehradun Rd. (☎430100). There's another branch (☎430228) on the south end of Lakshmanjhula. Both open 24hr.

Pharmacy: Asha Medical Agencies (☎432696). Opposite the Government General Hospital. Open 24hr.

Hospital: Government General Hospital (☎430402) and **Ladies' Hospital,** in the same bldg. on Dehradun Rd. Both are clean, well-staffed, and open 24hr.

Internet: Step Himalayan Adventures (see above). Rs30 per hr. **Blue Hill Travel** (☎433836), in Swargashram. Rs20 per hr. Open 7am-10pm.

Post Office: Main office (☎430340). In the center of town east of Lakshmanjhula Rd., next to the big Hotel Basera. **Ramjhula branch,** Swargashram. **Lakshmanjhula branch,** a 5min. walk south from the bridge. All open M-Sa 9am-5pm. **Postal Code:** 249201.

ACCOMMODATIONS

Seekers of the inner light may want to stay in an ashram around Ramjhula. The less spiritually inclined will find their best options in Lakshmanjhula on the eastern bank of the Ganga. Only those needing an early getaway should stay in the loud and congested center of Rishikesh near the railway station and bus stand.

HOTELS AND GUEST HOUSES

Most hotels in Rishikesh offer yoga and music lessons upon request. Check-out time is noon unless otherwise noted.

■ **High Bank Peasant's Cottage** (☎431167). From Ramjhula (west side), head toward Lakshmanjhula. Take Bypass Rd., which branches left; 50m later, turn right at the sign. Large, clean rooms with attached baths, valley views, and a lovely flower garden, perfect for a quiet retreat from the otherwise chaotic, spiritual town. Doubles Rs550. ❷

■ **Brijwasi Palace** (☎435181 or 435918). Behind Gita Bhavan, in Swargashram. Laundry, yoga classes (Rs100), and massages (Rs150 per hr.) to go along with clean rooms and bathrooms. Milk comes straight from the hotel cow who lives in the backyard. Doubles Rs200-300. ❶

■ **Green Hotel** (☎431242). One block from the Brijwasi Palace. Well-run place sails in seas of green. Immaculate rooms, seat toilets, hot showers, and a great Italian restaurant. Yoga classes Rs45 per session (8-9:30am) in winter. Internet access Rs40 per hr. Singles Rs100-150; doubles Rs200-1000. ❶

Yoga Niketan Guest House, Muni-ki-Reti, before the taxi stand. Has a well-groomed garden and steps leading down to the Ganga. Modern, clean, spacious rooms boast high-powered fans, white tile floors, seat toilets, and hot water. Convenient location near the Ramjhula bridge ensures easy access to Rishikesh proper and Swargashram. Free yoga and meditation classes at the nearby Yoga Niketan Ashram. For 3 meals at the ashram, add Rs50. Singles Rs300; doubles Rs400. ❷

Bhandari Swiss Cottage (☎432676). Just after High Bank. Small rooms offer valley views, seclusion, and a lovely garden. Common bath with cold shower. Balconies for contemplating the long hike back to town. Singles Rs100-200; doubles Rs200-300. ❶

ASHRAMS AND YOGA

No matter which yoga position you have managed to twist yourself into, an ashram is never far from sight in Rishikesh. Most Westerners head to Swangashram for ashram stays, which are often combined with yoga and meditation classes. Staying in an ashram is not like bunking up in a hotel—the meditative atmosphere comes with a series of rules that generally include: no meat, no eggs, no smelly food, no alcohol, no tobacco, no drugs, and no noise. Most demand daily bathing (always a good plan), request that menstruating women stay out of the ashram centers, and have strict curfews. Some are set up for pilgrims and Hindu worshippers and do not allow foreigners; most ashrams in the Ramjhula and Swargashram area, however, are very welcoming.

Ved Niketan (☎430278). At the south end of Ramjhula's east bank. Caged deities line the entrance to this yellow and orange ashram. The main guru, now in his 90s, still lives here, but others do the teaching. Day-long yoga (with donation) includes 7-8:30am meditation, 9-10:30am lecture (except in June), and 6:30-8:30pm yoga. Gates lock at 10pm. There are 150 singles and doubles (with bath) and 108 underground "cave" rooms with only floor mattresses. STD/ISD facilities offered. Payment by donation.

Yoga Niketan (☎430227). In the tranquil hills over Ramjhula. 15-night min. stay includes 3 meals, 2 yoga classes, and 2 meditation classes per day. Visible security force ensures compliance with the rules at this yoga boot camp. Doubles for married couples only; otherwise, buildings are single-sex. Squat toilets, no showers. Kitchen space in all rooms. Guests are expected to help with weekly cleaning. Curfew 9:30pm. Office open 8:30am-noon and 2-5pm. Rs250 per day.

Omkarananda Ganga Sadan (☎431473 or 430763). West side of Ramjhula, not to be mistaken for the Omarkananda Ashrani opposite the GMVN office, which takes no foreigners. Big, sterile-looking bldg. just outside the taxi/rickshaw stand. One of the swankiest ashrams in town—dazzling white rooms and bathrooms (some attached, all with squat toilets). Try for a river view. Yoga instruction Rs220 per week with 1 lecture/class each evening. 3-night min. stay. Breakfast (Rs20-25). Rooms Rs80-150.

Yoga Study Centre (☎433253). At the far south end of Haridwar Rd., on the river side of the road, practically outside of town. Well-known place to learn *iyengar yoga*, though it lacks the community feeling of the ashrams. Three classes per day on alternating days. General yoga classes M-Sa 6:30-8am. Lodging can be arranged Apr.-Aug. and Oct.-Jan. Pay on a donation basis.

Vanprastha Ashram (☎430811; fax 433125). Just before Ved Niketan. Spacious and well-lit flats surround a large and well-maintained garden. All rooms have attached bath and kitchen, sofas, and a double bed. Gas and utensils available Rs25 per day. 3-day min. stay. Open to foreigners Nov.-Mar. Book in advance from Calcutta (☎(033) 238 6701). Singles Rs150; suites Rs500.

UTTARANCHAL

◘ FOOD

Restaurants in Rishikesh don't serve meat or booze. They do serve delicious veg. *thalis*, though.

Amrita, on the western bank of the Ganga in Ramjhula, beneath the rickshaw stand. Outstanding fresh-baked raisin bread, jars of pure honey, cheddar cheese, lasagna with homemade noodles (Rs50), banana pancakes (Rs25), and spaghetti with a delicious, spicy marinara sauce (Rs50). ❶

Madras Cafe, in the Ramjhula rickshaw stand area. Indian food, California-style— lots of sprouts and whole wheat. Himalayan Health *Pullao,* with sprouts, curd, and ayurvedic herbs Rs50; hot lemon-ginger-honey tea Rs15. Open daily 6:30am-10:30pm. ❶

Chotiwala and Chotiwala Restaurant, in east Ramjhula near the bridge; impossible to miss, especially with the crowds that flock around the place. The 2 parts, side by side, were supposedly divided by 2 brothers. Both serve similar, standard Indian food. *Thalis* Rs35-50. Open daily 7am-11pm. ❶

Ganga View Restaurant, opposite Bombay Kshetra in Lakshmanjhula. This is where the foreign tourists staying in the Kshetra come together to enjoy good conversation, the Ganga view, and comfy rattan chairs. Peanut butter toast with honey Rs15; spaghetti Rs40; porridge with bananas, raisins, and coconut Rs20. Open daily 7am-9pm. ❶

Ganga Darshan, next to Ganga View, closer to the bridge. Cheap *thalis* (Rs20-30) and some special dishes (like "cheese chow mein") provide respite from the spice of most Indian food. *Dosas* Rs10-18. Balcony tables are great, but the service outside is slower. Open daily 5am-8:30pm; in winter 5am-8pm. ❶

◉ ♫ SIGHTS AND ENTERTAINMENT

Triveni Ghat, on the south end of Rishikesh, is believed to be the place where the Yamuna, Ganga, and Saraswati rivers meet, making it the most sacred spot in Rishikesh. The **arati** ceremony takes place here every evening at sundown. This is also a popular site at which to make river offerings at dawn. An ancient **Lakshman Temple** stands on the west bank. The 13-story **Swarga Niwas** ashram and cultural center has great views from the top. Their exhibits include images and statues of all the major Hindu deities. **Boats** head across the Ganga at Ramjhula, below Sivananda Ashram (Rs10). Another way to go with the flow is to **raft the rapids** along the Ganga. Companies toward the northern end of Rishikesh, such as **Step Himalayan Adventures** (☎432581), run 15km, 90min. rafting trips through four "good" and two small rapids. (Sept.-June, Rs390-700, depending on group size; transportation included.) Another good place is **GMVN ❶**, which provides accommodations at its rafting camp in Kaudiyalaj, north of Rishikesh. (Rooms Rs350; tents Rs100. Rafting trips Sept.-May: 3-4hr., Rs390 per person, all-day trip Rs1100.)

Not content with mere meditation and vegetation, many visitors also take **music lessons. Sivananda Ramesh Music School** (left at the sign on the far side of the bridge on Lakshmanjhula Rd., just after Tehri Rd.) will teach you to make the didgeridoo drone, the tabla ring, or the sitar gently weep. Only donations are accepted. **Hindi lessons** are offered by Mr. Tilak Raj at Ramjhula, Swargashram, behind the Ganga General Store. (Enquiries daily 9-10am. 10-day advanced course Rs1000; 5-day beginner course Rs500.) Settle in for a **massage** at the well-advertised Baba Health and Massage Centre in Rishikesh, 100m east of Hotel Shivlok. You can enjoy an ayurvedic, Swedish, Thai, or "general" full-body massage (they even massage your ears) in a dark, cool room complete with spacey music. (☎433339. Open daily 7am-

INSTANT KARMA When the Beatles came to Rishikesh to study Transcendental Meditation in February 1968, it was the culmination of several years of Western pop's infatuation with the Mysterious East. George Harrison-inspired sitar licks had been turning up in an increasing number of inappropriate places for several years, and the Beatles had already attended lectures by the Maharishi Mahesh Yogi during 1967. They recorded tracks for "The Inner Light," one of their most Indian-sounding songs, just before heading out for the Himalayan foothills.

In Rishikesh, George, John, Paul, and Ringo embraced the typical ashram experience —they eased off on the drugs, meditated, and mostly just hung out with other Westerners (including Mia and Prudence Farrow, the Beach Boys' Mike Love, and 60s pop anomaly, Donovan). They also wrote songs. Most of the "White Album," and much of what later became *Abbey Road* was written during the group's stay in Rishikesh. The most famous of these is "Dear Prudence," an entreaty to the latter Farrow to come out and join in the meditative fun: "The sun is up, the sky is blue/ It's beautiful and so are you/ Dear Prudence, won't you come out to play?"

Eventually, though, the blue skies clouded, and the Beatles became disillusioned with the Maharishi and his vegetarian diet. Less than a month after they left Rishikesh, John Lennon and Paul McCartney announced they'd ended their relationship with the guru. Some of the bitterness they felt comes through in the thinly veiled lyrics of a John Lennon song that appears on the second disc of the White Album: "Sexy Sadie, what have you done? You made a fool of everyone...."

10pm. Rs150 per session.) They also teach massage in a month-long course with 4 classes a day (Rs6000, lodging included). Complete ayurvedic treatment for general physical and mental well-being is offered for a minimum of a week (Rs3000 per week, lodging included).

DAYTRIPS FROM RISHIKESH

KUNJAPURI. Wait until the sun is up and the sky is blue before heading to the temple of Kunjapuri, on top of a nearby mountain. From here, you can see the whole region, including Haridwar and the snow-capped Himalayas. The temple itself is disappointingly modern and small, though the priest is friendly to visitors. To get there, take a bus headed for **Tehri** from the Yatra Bus Stand; tell the driver you want to get off at Hindolakhal (1hr., Rs15). From there, it's an hour's walk up the mountain along a paved road and up a surreal, narrow staircase at the top. Hop on a bus coming from Gangotri or Yamnotri to get back (last bus around 7 or 8pm).

NEEL KANTH MAHADEV. The trip to the temple at Neel Kanth Mahadev makes another good day-hike. The place is so popular with pilgrims bearing milk, *ghee*, and Ganga water that the *linga* has been eroded so that it is now just a few inches high. The jungle trail along the way, inhabited by wild elephants, is what really makes the hike worthwhile. Go early (5am) since it's a 4-5hr. climb with no stops, and the temple is more likely to be peaceful early in the day. Jeeps leave for the trailhead from the Laksmanjhula and Ramjhula taxi stands (12km; Rs40 per person, round-trip Rs70). Regular jeeps return to Rishikesh.

MANSA DEVI. About 10km from Rishikesh is the Mansa Devi, a temple that provides wall-less shelter for those seeking some distance from town. Camp for free and in relative isolation. Hindu pilgrims flood the site between the 7th and 10th of every month (especially Mar., Sept., and Oct.) for Navratri. Jeeps from the Yatra Bus Stand go to Mansa Devi (Rs25 per seat).

GLASSHOUSE ON THE GANGES. Twenty-three kilometers outside Rishikesh, on the road to Byasi, the Glasshouse on the Ganges is run by the Neemrana Hotels chain. Set in litchi orchards that were once part of the maharaja's garden, the Glasshouse overlooks the Ganga as it shoots down toward the plains. The resort is a cluster of four cottages with 12 luxurious rooms furnished in teak. The gardens and silver sand beach are home to rare birds and butterflies. (☎(011) 4616145, 4618962; fax (011) 4621112; sales@neemrana.com. Lunch and dinner Rs200 per person. Doubles Rs1500-2500. Book in advance; order meals on arrival.) ❺

GARHWAL PILGRIMAGES AND TREKS

Gods, sadhus, and saints have been coming to meditate among the snow-capped mountains of Garhwal and Kumaon since time immemorial. Until recently, just getting here was enough to test a person's faith—as recently as the 1960s, the northern pilgrimage sites could only be reached by foot from the plains. But new roads have made them more accessible, and a steady stream of package-tour pilgrims has made the peaceful isolation of the sites a distant memory. For true believers, the pilgrimage experience is suffused with a holiness that diesel, mud, and litter-strewn streets cannot spoil.

The temples at the pilgrimage sights are open from May to November, though it is dangerous to go during the monsoons, as frequent landslides and heavy rains often render the roads impassable. Rattling, non-A/C local buses are the only things that make the journey up the narrow roads from Rishikesh or Uttarkashi, so be ready to kiss comfort goodbye. Between pilgrimage sites and neighboring towns in the hills, you might find buses or shared jeeps going your way, if you're lucky. If not, you will have to either book a package tour or hire a taxi from one of the major cities (Rs2000 per day). Most *dharamsalas* do not welcome foreigners—you'd be well-advised to book a rest house room at least a month in advance.

UTTARKASHI उत्तरकाशी ☎01374

This busy town, on the banks of the Bhagirathi River, is the administrative center of the Uttarkashi District, as well as the last place to stock up on supplies or catch a Hindi movie before you head out for a trek. Uttarkashi is also a major transportation hub for the pilgrimage sites to the north. **Buses** head to: Barkot (for Yamnotri, in-season only, Rs45); Bhatwari (for treks to Sahasratal and Kedarnath, 1hr., Rs14); Gangotri (Rs50); Gaurikund (12hr., Rs97-110); Rishikesh (8hr., Rs80); Sayana Chatti (for Dodital trek, Rs14). Morning **taxis** to Rishikesh wait at the bus stand. The **tourist office** at the bus stand provides little help for trekking. Instead, try **Mt. Support Trekking**, BD Nautial Bhawan, Bhatwari Rd. (☎2419), about 10min. past the bus stand along Gangotri Rd., or the professional **Nehru Mountaineering Institute**, 5km out of town (ask anyone for directions). Mt. Support Trekking also **exchanges currency** for a hefty charge. (Open M-Sa 9am-7pm.) The **police roost** is on Gangotri Rd., 15min. from the bus station, on the right. The 24hr. emergency **District Hospital** is midway between Gangotri Rd. and the river, near the post office.

The **Bhandari Hotel ❷**, at the bus stand is a good place to spend the night before an early departure; a restaurant is inside. (☎2203. Doubles Rs600. Off season Rs300.) Another option is **Meghdoot ❶**, Main Market. (☎2278. May-June and Sept. singles Rs100; doubles Rs180. Oct.-Apr. and July-Aug Rs50/90.) **GMVN ❶**, has clean rooms with hot water and six-bed dorms. (☎2271. Apr. 16-June dorms Rs100; doubles Rs250-900; July-Nov. 15 dorms Rs80; doubles Rs200-720; Nov. 15-Apr. 15 dorms Rs50; doubles Rs130-450. For May, June, and Sept., book one month in advance.)

SNAKEBITE? Hashish and tobacco, smoked through a *chillum*, are a big part of the daily intake of most sadhus, but the really hip holy men try something else. A krait (an extremely poisonous snake) is rolled up between two unbaked *rotis* with its tail sticking out, and then shoved into the fire. When the *rotis* are fully baked, the sadhu removes the deadly sandwich from the fire and pulls at the snake's tail, ripping off the skin and bones. Then, preparing himself, he puts a jug of water by his side, takes two to three bites of the snake, and immediately goes into a coma. Every 8-10hr. the sadhu wakes up to drink some water and take another bite, sending himself back into a poisoned stupor. The whole process lasts three to four days. **Warning: this requires 30 years of practice—don't try this at home, or anywhere else!**

YAMNOTRI यमनोत्री

The source of the Yamuna River and the first stop on the Garhwal pilgrimage circuit, Yamnotri attracts 1500 pilgrims every day during the tourist season. The town essentially consists of a **temple** devoted to the goddess Yamuna and the 12-15 concrete buildings and numerous *dhabas* that surround it. The original temple was built by Rani Gularia of Jaipur during the 19th century but was soon worn down by heavy snowfall. The elements continue to erode away at the temple that took its place, making it essential to rebuild the structure every few years. The temple's architecture is not special—just a slapdash construction with dressed-up concrete walls and a corrugated metal roof. It is open from May to November, after which the image is carried to Kharsoli, a village opposite Janki Chatti.

Yamnotri is accessible only by a 14km trek from the town of **Hanuman Chatti** (2134m), which is well-connected by **buses** from Dehra Dun (163km) and Rishikesh (209km). The path angles gently upward for 8km to Janki Chatti (2676m), then turns steeply uphill until it reaches Yamnotri (3235m). From here, the source of the sacred river is an arduous 1km trek away, so most pilgrims pray at the temple itself. Start early in the morning—there is no shade for the first 10km out of Hanuman Chatti, and by then the higher altitudes and steep path will drain any energy you have left. **Horses** with guides can be rented for the 14km trek (Rs200-250). The path is lined with *chai* stalls and cold drink stands.

All major services, including **accommodations**, are available at Janki Chatti. The closest **hospital, post office,** and **communications** system (a wireless only for emergencies) are at Janki Chatti. A seasonal **police station** is set up every year at Yamnotri. There are **GMVN lodges** at **Sayana Chatti ❷**, 6km before Hanuman Chatti (Apr. 16-June Rs300; July-Nov. 15 Rs200. Closed rest of year.); **Hanuman Chatti ❶** (Apr. 16-June dorms Rs130; rooms Rs700; July-Nov. 15: Rs100/560. Closed rest of year.); and **Janki Chatti ❶** (Apr. 16-June dorms Rs130; rooms Rs350-600; July-Nov. 15 Rs100/280-520. Closed rest of year). Reservations can be made through the Rishikesh GMVN office. During the pilgrimage season, many of these accommodations are fully booked for package tours operated by GMVN; you might have to stay overnight at **Barkot,** 40km south, and take early morning transport to Hanuman Chatti. There are also several private hotels in Janki Chatti.

GANGOTRI गंगोत्री ☎ 013772

After Bhatwari, the road from Uttarkashi narrows and the surrounding mountains become more severe until the shimmering slopes of **Mt. Sudarshan** (6500m) finally come into view, towering above the small town of Gangotri. At an altitude of 3140m, Gangotri (sometimes called Bhagirathi), 98km northeast of Uttarkashi, is a major center for sadhus from all over India. It is here that the goddess Ganga made her descent from heaven and Raja Bhagiratha worshiped Shiva at the sacred stone

Bhagiratha Shilla. The present **temple,** near Bhagiratha's stone, was built by the Gorkha commander Amar Singh Thapa in the early 18th century as a replacement for an older structure. The temple is open only from May to November because of heavy winter snowfall. Steps lead down to the *ghat,* where pilgrims bathe. In the river sits a submerged rock that is considered a *linga,* marking the place where Shiva sat while the Ganga descended and cushioned her fall with his hair. A small bridge from the bus stand arches over to Gaurikund, where the Bhagirathi (yes, the river is called Bhagirathi in these parts) gushes out of the rock into a beautiful pool. **Gaumukh** (Cow's Mouth), an easy 17km trek from Gangotri, is the spot where the Bhagirathi emerges from the Gangotri glacier; there are excellent views of the peaks along the way. **Kedartal,** a spectacular lake with Thalaysagar peak in the background, is 18km from Gangotri. The trek is very difficult but well worth the effort. Hire a guide from Gangotri (Rs300 per day) and carry plenty of supplies since there is nothing but awe-inspiring views available along the way.

To get to Gangotri, take a **bus** or a **shared taxi** from Uttarkashi (see p. 650). The main bridge is next to Dev Ghat, where the Bhagirathi and the Kedar Ganga meet. In most accommodations, rooms are unpainted, the plaster is crumbling, and beds are dirty—bring a sleeping bag. Accommodations across the river from the temple are quieter. **Manisha Cottage ❷,** near the bus stand, has small doubles (Rs200-450). The **GMVN Guest House ❶,** next to Gaurikund, is spacious and clean, with a garden and a good restaurant. (Apr. 16-June dorms Rs130; rooms Rs350-800; July-Nov. 15: Rs100/280-640. Closed rest of year.) Most ashrams in Gangotri do not accept foreign guests, and there are few tourist services available here. A temporary **police station, health center,** and **post office,** are open during the pilgrimage season.

KEDARNATH केदारनाथ ☎ 01364

One of the 12 *jyotirlingas* in India, Kedarnath is also one of Shiva's chosen abodes. The Kedarnath **temple** was constructed thousands of years ago when the Pandavas, the heroic brothers of the *Mahabharata,* came here to serve their penance to Shiva. Viewing the Pandavas as sinners for having killed their own kin in battle, Shiva disguised himself as a bull to escape their notice. When the Pandavas discovered the ruse, Shiva turned to stone and tried to escape into the ground. But as his front half vanished, Bhima, one of the Pandavas, managed to catch Shiva's rocky rear end. Pleased with the Pandavas' diligence, Shiva appeared in his true form and forgave them. The back half of that stone form is now worshiped at Kedarnath. Shiva's front half broke off and re-emerged in Nepal, where it is venerated at the **Pashupati Temple** (see p. 792). Other parts of Shiva turned up at Tungnath (arm), Rudranath (face), Madhyamaheshwar (navel), and Kapleshwar (locks); together, they form the **Panch Kedar** (Five Fields) pilgrimage circuit.

Kedarnath remains open from May until late October and serves as the start point for many beautiful treks. **Buses** take pilgrims as far as Gaurikund, 216km from Rishikesh (Rs85). From there, it's a steep 14km, 4-6hr. trek. **Horses** are also available for hire (Rs250). Standard hotel rates are Rs100 for a single and Rs200 for a double in season. **GMVN ❶,** has two guest houses in Kedarnath, one on your left as you approach the town (☎6210) and a second across the river and below the hillside (☎6228). (Apr. 16-June dorms Rs130; rooms Rs300-700; July- Nov. 15: Rs100/240-560. Closed rest of year.) Many ashrams will not accept foreigners, but the **Bharat Seva Ashram** and the **Temple Committee** make exceptions on occasion.

BADRINATH बद्रिनाथ ☎ 01381

The temple town of Badrinath (3133m) is the northernmost compass-point (*dham*) in India's sacred geography. Once the abode of Lord Vishnu, it is the most famous of Garhwal's Hindu pilgrimage sites, attracting the faithful from all across

India during its summer season, May-Nov. Badrinath sits alongside the Alaknanda River, 297km from Rishikesh, not far from the Tibetan border, and it serves as one of the Ganga's 12 water channels. Its accessibility by road attracts growing numbers of pilgrims and tourists every year, who forego the austerity of a walking pilgrimage (once required) in favor of a harrowing bus ride. Badrinath can be reached by **bus** from Rishikesh via Srinagar, Rudraprayag, and Joshimath (12hr., 5 per day 3:30-6am, Rs170). Buses also come here directly from Kedarnath (Rs40).

The colorful Badrinath **temple** has a long main entrance gate (the Singh Dwara) that worshipers must pass through for *darshan* of the meter-high Badrivishal image inside. Probably a Buddhist temple in ancient times, the current temple is an unusual mixture of Buddhist and Hindu styles. Before visiting the temple, worshipers bathe in the **Tapt Kund** hot spring, often in preparation for a dip into the icy waters of the Alaknanda. Very basic **accommodations** are available at numerous *dharamsalas*, at the **Garhwal Hotel,** or at the **GVMN hotel ❶** (☎2212. Apr. 16-June dorms Rs50; cabins Rs150; doubles Rs280-400; July-Nov Rs50/80/230-720. Closed rest of year. Reserve 1 month in advance Apr.-July.)

JOSHIMATH जोशीमथ   ☎01389

As a stopping point for those on their way to Auli, the Valley of Flowers, Hemkund Saheb, and other local treks, Joshimath's tourist industry has burgeoned in recent years. It is now possible to find cheaper, cleaner places to eat and sleep here than elsewhere in the region. Plus, nestled into a mountain overlooking a roaring river and snow-capped peaks, Joshimath itself is an attractive destination for those seeking peace and quiet in the hills.

From Rishikesh, Joshimath is accessible via Badrinath-bound **buses** (11hr., 5 per day 3:30-6am, Rs152). From Almora, take a bus to Karnaprayag (7hr., 8am, Rs90) and then a jeep to Chamoli (Rs20) and a jeep from Chamoli to Joshimath (Rs35).

Transport drops you off near a fork in the road; the **upper (right) fork** leads to **Upper Bazaar,** which has most of the town's good hotels, restaurants, and supply shops. Buy as much food, water, and other essential goods as you can in Joshimath, because further along you will have to pay up to 2-3 times the maximum retail price for these items. For trekking and camping gear and guides, try **Eskimo Adventures,** in the middle of Upper Bazaar, across from Hotel Sriram.

Hotels in Joshimath generally charge Rs300-500 for clean rooms with good views. **Hotel Mount Elephant ❶,** in Upper Bazaar, has both a tidy six-bed dorm and private rooms. (☎22742. dorms Rs100; doubles start at Rs250.) **GMVN ❶,** operates two Rest Houses in Upper Bazaar (☎22118, 22226. Mid-Apr.-mid-Nov. dorms Rs130; doubles Rs230-650. Off-season 40% discount.)

For food, **Maharaja Restaurant ❶,** in Upper Bazaar has great, cheap chow mein (Rs20). The restaurant in **Hotel Sriram ❶,** offers the only pizza in town (Rs50).

AULI औली   ☎01389

Skiing? In India? What next? Home to 20km of seasonal (Jan.-Mar.) ski slopes, Auli has been the winter sports capital of UP since the 1970s, when the government decided that ski resorts were more fun than military training camps. **Equipment** can be rented (half-day Rs175, full-day Rs225) at the GMVN. The spectacular scenery (including views of Nanda Devi, which at 7820m is the second-highest peak in India) keeps Auli open in the summer for **cable car rides** up from Joshimath (4km, Rs300 round-trip). Alternatively, you can take the muddy 14km road (40 min., Rs300-350 per car round-trip). There is a **GMVN lodge ❶,** in Auli. (☎23208. Nov.-June dorms Rs70; rooms Rs840-1180; July-Oct. Rs60/670-950.) Accommodation is also available at Joshimath where you can take the ski lift to Auli.

VALLEY OF FLOWERS फूलों की घाटी

One of the most awe-inspiring sights in all of India, this alpine valley hidden high in the Himalayas has been attracting pilgrims and nature lovers ever since it was "discovered" by Frank Smith in 1937. Ten kilometers long, two kilometers wide, and enclosed by snow-capped peaks, the valley is cut in two by the Pushpawati River. Snow covers the valley floor from November to late May, when the area is inaccessible to visitors. In late May, the snow begins to melt, and the first flowers start to bloom in early June. The valley is usually opened to visitors in mid-June. Peak bloom is in late July and August, but it's worth it to come in late June or early July, when there are far fewer tourists, and you might even have the valley to yourself. There are over 500 species of flowers in the valley; many of them, such as the Himalayan blue poppy, are extremely rare. When the valley was first explored in the late 1930s, the plant species count was 5000. The serious ecological decline of the area has prompted the government to declare it a National Park; camping and cooking are prohibited. Be aware that the trail leading into the Valley of Flowers is narrow, muddy, and requires crossing streams and steep patches of ice. **Do not attempt this trek during or immediately after rainfall.** From Joshimath, take a shared jeep (Rs20) to Govind Ghat, 14km away. Try to leave early in the morning, around 5 or 6am. From Govind Ghat, it is a 13km uphill trek to Ghanghria. The walk takes 5-7hr.; alternatively, you can ride a horse up (3hr., Rs300). In Ghanghria, you must find a place to stay. This can be a frustrating experience because some of the hotels in town are dirty, overcrowded, and overpriced. If you stay at a private hotel, you can expect to pay Rs600 for a cramped cell with boards for mattresses. Furthermore, the town doesn't have power until 7pm (and even then, it's on-and-off), and the availability of running water leaves plenty to be desired. Hot water costs Rs20 per bucket everywhere. Fortunately, GMVN operates a **Tourist Rest House ❶**, here. While rooms are, again, overpriced (Rs650-850), dorms (Rs130) are reasonable. Reserve at least a week in advance through **GMVN Yatra Pilgrimage Tours and Accommodations Office** in Kailash Gate, Rishikesh (☎431783).

Ghanghria's tourism oligopoly is even more blatant when it comes to food. The **restaurants ❶**, in town have almost identical menus (even the same typos!) with a price disparity of Rs5 here and there. All serve up similar, bland Punjabi dishes (Rs35-55). It's even difficult to make your own meals, because scarcely available foodstuffs (such as bread, jam, and biscuits) cost 2-3 times what they do in Joshimath. The tough living in Ghanghria is sure to make you take your time on the trek to avoid returning to town too soon.

After spending the night in Ghanghria, set off the next morning on the Valley of Flowers trail (it branches off to the left after you pass the stream) and pay the hefty admission fee at the gate (Rs350 for foreigners, Rs30 for Indian citizens). After a 1½hr. climb, you will emerge into the splendor of the valley. Have a picnic, walk around, or just sit and stare at the 360 degrees of idyllic beauty, before returning to Ghanghria for the night.

HEMKUND SAHEB From miles around, Sikhs of all ages, from 8-year olds to octogenarians, make the pilgrimage to Hemkund Saheb, the temple that sits atop a 4500m mountain 6km from Ghanghria. On the Valley of Flowers trek, you'll be sharing paths and hotels with the thousands of Sikhs who make the 4hr. pilgrimage between June and August of each year, to witness waterfalls, mountain views, and a beautiful (but freezing-cold!) mountaintop lake in which the thick-skinned Sikhs bathe. For those who weather the climb, there is also a 1,000-bed *gurudwara* at the top where you can eat or snooze for free (donation suggested). Foreigners are allowed.

CORBETT NATIONAL PARK कोरबट

Corbett was India's first national park, founded in 1936 and named for James Corbett (1875-1955), a British gentleman renowned for his ability to kill tigers and other large animals with a shotgun. Corbett gave up killing tigers for kicks during the 1920s but was still called upon to shoot tigers and leopards from time to time when they threatened human lives. He became famous for his photographs of tigers and for the books he wrote, including *The Man-Eaters of Kumaon.*

In 1973, the Indian government, with support from the World Wildlife Fund, launched "Project Tiger" (see p. 367) in an effort to save the country's dwindling population of tigers. The 1319 sq. km Corbett Tiger Reserve, comprising the national park and the adjoining Sonandi Wildlife Sanctuary and Reserve Forest, was the first target area of this ambitious project. There are currently 138 tigers in the reserve. Sightings of the big cats are frequent, but even if you don't get that lucky, Corbett's other wildlife will make sure you don't leave entirely disappointed. The endangered gharial crocodile, herds of wild elephant, leopards, deer, over 500 species of birds, and monkeys coexist peacefully in the same habitat. The park's landscape, particularly around Dhikala, is as much a treasure as its wildlife.

> **! WARNING.** The animals here have enough problems already without your throwing things at them. Don't throw burning cigarettes around, don't feed the animals, and keep noise at a minimum. For your own safety (attacks by tigers are not unheard of), never walk outside the camp perimeter, and be careful at night.

⌐ TRANSPORTATION

The various zones of the park are accessed via **Ramnagar,** reachable from Delhi by **bus** (7hr., 12 per day 6am-9pm, Rs90). Buses to **Delhi** (8:30am-8pm) and **Nainital** (4hr., 2:30am and noon) leave from the government bus stand near the park office. If your next stop is **Ranikhet,** get off the bus at Dhangarhi and wait by the side of the road for buses headed north (4hr., last bus 2pm, Rs40). Private buses depart from below the bazaar to **Nainital** (2½hr., 4 per day 6am-1pm). Buses from Ramnagar run to **Delhi** (6½hr.; 9:30pm, return 11pm; Rs117) and **Varanasi** (21hr., 9:15pm, Rs200). You can hire **jeeps** from in front of the Park Office for Rs4.50-6.50 per km.

◼◪ ORIENTATION AND PRACTICAL INFORMATION

Corbett has five **zones** accessible to tourists. These zones are exclusive of each other, which means that you have to exit the park and pay another hefty fee to enter another zone. **Dhikala** is the most popular, offering a range of accommodations, two restaurants, film screening facilities, and a library. The other four zones offer greater solitude but fewer services. **Lohachavr** is the best place for birding; **Bijrani,** most frequented by jeeps on daytrips, contains the park's most diverse vegetation; **Jhirna** is an exceptionally beautiful area of the park; those looking for a more rugged experience and close encounters with wild elephants should head to **Halduparao.** Jhirna is accessible to visitors year-round, but the rest of the park closes during the monsoon (mid-June to mid-Nov.). The wildlife viewing is better during the summer (Mar.-June) than the winter (Nov.-Mar.).

Each zone has its own gated park entrance. **Dhangarhi Gate,** 16km north of Ramnagar, is the entrance to Dhikala. (Open 6am-6pm; in winter 7am-5pm. No entry after dark.) Here, you have to cough up the park entry fees. (Rs350 for three days plus Rs130 for your vehicle.) Before leaving Dhikala, all visitors must obtain a free **clearance certificate,** which should be turned in at Dhangarhi upon leaving.

Visitors must stop at the **Park Office,** opposite the Ramnagar bus stand, to secure a permit and to reserve and pay for accommodation within the park. (☎(05975) 51489. Open daily 8:30am-1pm and 3-5pm.) An all-inclusive package, including transport to and from the park and a 4hr. safari, costs around Rs1200. Show up at 8:30am at the office and wait for other visitors to share the cost. Ramnagar is your last chance to stock up on peanuts and insect repellent before trekking off into the great unknown. There is nowhere to change money here.

ACCOMMODATIONS AND FOOD

RAMNAGAR
Accommodations outside the park skyrocket in price and involve daily transport into the park. In Ramnagar, try the **Banbari Hotel ❶,** in Tesil Chowk, which has basic rooms with attached bath (☎05945; 51277. Doubles Rs150) and decent meals. The **Tourist Rest House ❶,** next to the park office, has dorms and private rooms, but you'll have to put up with the noise from the gas and bus stations next door (☎85225. Dorms Rs60; doubles Rs320-420). The big package-tour oasis, **Tiger Camp ❸,** 7km from Dhangari Gate toward Ramnagar, has two-person tents with mattresses and clean, warm blankets. (☎86088 or 87901; fax 85088. Tents Rs600.)For Indian, Chinese, and continental cuisine, head to **Govind Restaurant ❶,** one block past the bus station from the rest house. The owner is friendly and the food delicious. (Banana pancakes Rs25; fruit *lassis* Rs20. Open daily 8am-10pm.)

IN THE PARK
All lodgings within the park itself must be reserved through the Park Office in Ramnagar (see above). Log-hut dorms, **tourist "hutments"** (3 beds), and **cabins** (2 or 3 beds) are available in Dhikala. The **log hut ❶,** just one step away from the great outdoors, has austere bunks, stacked three-high and 12 to a room, and lockers (bring your own lock). Squat toilets and showers are in a separate building. Tourist hutments and cabins have attached bathrooms. (Check-out 11am. Log hut bunk Rs100, bedding Rs25; tourist hutment Rs500; cabin Rs900.) **Rest houses** outside Dhikala tend to have nothing much to offer except for good old-fashioned peace and quiet. **Old British hunting lodges ❸,** all come complete with fireplaces, carpets, and attached bathrooms. Cooking utensils and firewood are provided, but other essentials need to be brought from Ramnagar. (Lodges Rs300-900.) Visitors wishing to extend their stay are often told to wait until evening to see whether space is available, so it is possible you'll get stuck in Dhikala without accommodation, in which case you will have to hire a jeep out before the night curfew. Call ahead.

Dhikala has the only food available inside the park. Its two restaurants both serve all the usual items of international high cuisine. The government-run **KMVN Restaurant ❶,** is more expensive, with indoor seating. (Veg. *korma* Rs36. Open 7:30am-9:30pm.) At the other end of the camp, the privately owned **canteen ❶,** serves pretty much the same menu for less; it's next to a pleasant pagoda, from which you can look down on the plains while enjoying your vegetable curry. (Open daily 5am-2pm and 4-10pm.) No alcohol is allowed, and only vegetarian food is sold inside the park. A small **kiosk ❶,** at Dhangarhi Gate sells bottled water (Rs15) and munchies. Everything is more expensive inside the park, so stock up before you get here.

THE PARK

There *are* ways to get down and dirty in Corbett without breaking any rules. By far the best option is an **elephant ride.** For Rs100, visitors get bumped, shrugged, and shouldered for 2hr. across the prairie and through the jungle. This is the best way to try to see a tiger or to come close to wild elephants and other animals. Sign up for a ride at the station office at least a day in advance during the high season.

MAN BITES CAT Your *mahout* in Dhikala may be none other than Subradar Ali, the man that one man-eater of Kumaon will remember as the one who bit back. While gathering grass for his elephant Gunti on Valentine's Day, 1984, Subradar was attacked from behind by a tiger named Sheroo. The tiger leapt nearly 6m for his target, Subradar's head. As he was being dragged away by the neck, Subradar, taking a lesson from his striped assailant, began biting back. Forcing open the jaws of the beast, he yanked on Sheroo's tongue. This put an end to the dragging, and Sheroo pinned him squarely. Another guide appeared on the scene, distracting the tiger long enough for Subradar to roll down a nearby stream bank. With bleeding gashes on his head and arm, Subradar called his elephant to come and kneel so he could crawl on top. Gunti took him the 3km to Dhikala and, not wanting to disturb his family in Ramnagar, Subradar cleaned his wounds and changed his clothes himself. Both Rajiv and Indira Gandhi later visited him in the hospital. Rajiv asked if he desired fame and fortune—the event has since been the subject of several movies—but Subradar preferred to return to the elephants and tigers of Corbett. In fact, he views the whole experience as having bolstered his confidence, and he admits with a smile that he is sometimes more excited to find the tigers than the tourists he guides.

Tours depart at sunrise and sunset, approximately 6am and 4pm in the summer and 7am and 3pm in the winter. Sightings are equally likely at either time, but the weather is cooler in the morning. From your elephant, marvel at what seems to delight tourists most: yes, those are 3m-high cannabis plants, acres and acres of them. If you do spot a tiger, your guide will expect a modest "sighting" tip.

You can also hire a **jeep**—up to eight may ride with a guide around the Dhikala Station area. You cover more ground than you would on the elephants and can get all the way out to the reservoir, where the crocodiles play. While the crocs don't normally encroach on the compound, it's best to heed the sign that warns, "NO SWIMMING: Survivors Will Be Prosecuted." Jeeps are not guaranteed from Dhikala, as they operate from Dhangari and the park office in Ramnagar—it is possible (though not likely) to get stuck in Dhikala waiting for a jeep. *(The best times for jeep tours are 5-11am and 4-7pm. Rs500, plus Rs100 for a guide.)*

The only excursion permitted **on foot** outside the camp (and only before sunset) is to the nearby **Gularghati Watchtower**. Free **films** about nature and the park are shown behind the restaurant around 7pm; check the office for schedules. There are a few places where you can experience the natural beauty and wildlife outside the park, including the area of **Sitabani**, which has some excellent birdwatching spots and a decent rest house—ask at the Ramnagar office for details.

NAINITAL नैनीताल ☎ 05942

When the body of the goddess Sati broke into pieces and fell to earth after her self-immolation, one of her eyes landed here in the hills of what is now Uttaranchal, forming the stunning emerald lake of Nainital. Many lifetimes later, a certain P. Barron of Shahjahanpur, esquire, tilted up with his yacht to found what he called a "pilgrim cottage." Barron was the first of many Brits who came here to enjoy and exploit the area's lakeland beauty. Nainital soon became a popular British hill station and the summer capital of the United Provinces. The town is still one of India's most beloved hilltop hideaways and is the favorite fresh-air bolt-hole of the beleaguered UP masses. High season (May-June and Oct.) brings high prices and crowds and puts smiles on the faces of the town's residents, who make their living from tourism. The beautiful, shimmering, eye-shaped Naini Lake is the center of the town's activity, but in the autumn, after the rains have passed, Nainital has outstanding views of the Himalayas.

UTTARANCHAL

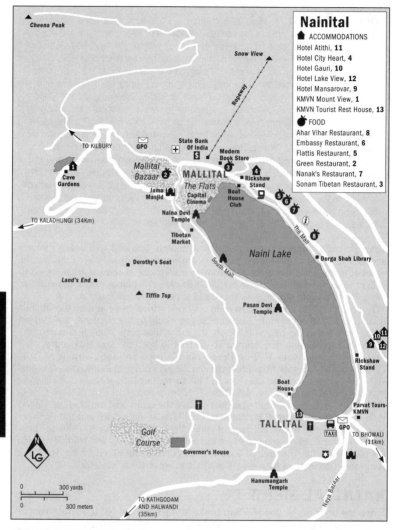

Nainital

🔺 **ACCOMMODATIONS**
Hotel Atithi, **11**
Hotel City Heart, **4**
Hotel Gauri, **10**
Hotel Lake View, **12**
Hotel Mansarovar, **9**
KMVN Mount View, **1**
KMVN Tourist Rest House, **13**
🍎 **FOOD**
Ahar Vihar Restaurant, **8**
Embassy Restaurant, **6**
Flattis Restaurant, **5**
Green Restaurant, **2**
Nanak's Restaurant, **7**
Sonam Tibetan Restaurant, **3**

▐ TRANSPORTATION

Trains: The nearest station is in **Kathgodam,** 34km away. From here, trains leave for **Delhi** (8:40pm) and return at 11pm.

Buses: Buses arrive at and depart from the lakefront in **Tallital.** Schedules change frequently. To: **Almora** (3hr., 4 per day 7am-4pm, Rs50); **Bareilly** (4½hr., 4 per day 1:30-6:15pm, Rs66); **Bhowali** (every 30min. 6am-6:30pm, Rs14); **Dehra Dun** (10hr.; 5:30, 6, 7am; Rs150; deluxe 4:30 and 8pm Rs188); **Delhi** (9hr., 7 per day 6am-7:30pm, Rs140); **Kathgodam** and **Haldwani** (2hr., every 15min. 5am-6:30pm, Rs30); **Ramnagar** (5hr., 5:30 and 7pm, Rs45); **Ranikhet** (3hr., 12:30 and 2:30pm, Rs43). Tickets to Dehra Dun and Delhi are sold at the travel agencies on The Mall; many also run deluxe buses to Dehra Dun (Rs300) and Delhi (Rs200). **Bhowali** is the major regional transportation center, and buses leave almost every hour from here for most mountain cities. Buses leave every 30min. from Haldwani to Nainital (6am-7pm). After 7pm, jeeps and taxis are available (Rs30-40 per person).

Local Transportation: Cycle-rickshaws charge Rs4 to drive the length of The Mall. Local **jeeps** and **taxi-vans** are available to go to other places at all times. During the high season, traffic is closed to motor vehicles and cycle-rickshaws from 6-9pm.

ORIENTATION AND PRACTICAL INFORMATION

The town of Nainital is split into two major parts—**Tallital** in the south and **Mallital** in the north. These are connected by **The Mall,** which runs along the east side of the lake. Buses arrive at Tallital, at the southern tip of the lake. From here, it's a 15-min. lakeside walk to Mallital. The main market is in Mallital. Most hotels and restaurants are on The Mall. The **Flats,** a common area used for football and field hockey, lies between Mallital and the northern part of the lake.

Tourist Office: (☎35337). The Mall, about two-thirds of the way to Mallital. Provides information for the town and region and arranges transport to nearby sights. Open M-Sa 10am-5pm; May-June and Oct. open daily 9am-6pm.

Budget Travel: Several travel agents along The Mall offer similar tours at similar prices. The tourist office also organizes tours. **Parvat Tours-KMVN** (☎35656). Just after Tallital on The Mall. Arranges day tours by taxi and bus to nearby resorts and lakes, including Bhimtal, Sat Tal, Hanumangarh (bus Rs100/taxi Rs500), and Mukteshwar (bus Rs150/taxi Rs1100). Most open daily 8am-8pm.

Currency Exchange: State Bank of India (☎35645). In Mallital, just beyond the Flats. Cashes AmEx traveler's checks. Open M-F 10am-2pm, Sa 10am-noon.

Market: The **Bara Bazaar,** in Mallital. The **Tibetan market,** in the western part of the bazaar, sells brand-name clothes (fake) and junk (real). Open M-Sa 9am-9pm.

Police: Mallital (☎35424) and Tallital (☎35525). In front of the Hotel Mansarovar at the Tallital end of The Mall.

Pharmacy: Indra Pharmacy (☎35139). By the bus stand in Tallital. Well stocked. Open M-Sa 7am-10pm, Su 7am-3pm. Another branch is in Mallital (☎35629), in Bara Bazaar. Open M-Sa 9am-10pm, Su 3-10pm.

Hospital/Medical Services: B. D. Pandey Hospital (☎35012). Near State Bank of India in Mallital. Open daily 8am-2pm. Dr. D.P. Gangola (☎35039) is a physician at **Indra Pharmacy;** he keeps hours in the Mallital (5-8pm) and Tallital (9am-2pm) branches.

Internet: Cyber Cafe, in Mallital, opposite the Flats. Connections are slow but reliable. Rs80 per hr. Open M-Sa 10am-8pm.

Post Office: The GPO is on the north side of Mallital, a few blocks up from The Mall's extension. There is another branch in Tallital, facing the bus stop. Open 10am-5pm. **Postal Codes:** Mallital 263002, Tallital 263001.

ACCOMMODATIONS

Hotel prices in Nainital tend to be higher and more subject to seasonal changes than anywhere else in Kumaon. Listed prices are peak-season rates, except where noted; outside of May, June, and October, expect a drop of anything from 25-75%. With over a hundred hotels to choose from, prices and services vary greatly from place to place. Most establishments along the hotel-crowded Mall are quiet and have beautiful views of the lake, though the air gets quieter and the views get better the farther up the hill you go. Most have 10am check-out, and will charge extra for hot water if you don't bargain your way out of it.

Hotel Lake View, Tallital (☎35632 or 36489; fax 35632; lakeview@nde.vsnl.net.in). Behind Hotel Mansarovar. Hidden at the back of Tallital, this friendly hotel is a bit pricey. Mr. and Mrs. Shah treat all their guests like family. Spacious rooms with clean bathrooms and balconies have superb views of the lake. Room service, laundry, TV, and restaurant. Doubles Rs400-850; 4-bed, 2-room suites Rs1400. ❸

Hotel Gauri (☎36617). Near Tallital. Behind Hotel Mansarovar, on the road parallel to The Mall. Newly renovated rooms with TVs and balconies offer views of the lake. Seat toilets and showers in some rooms. Doubles Rs400-800. Off season: Rs200-500. ❸

Hotel Atithi, Tallital (☎35080). Behind Hotel Mansarovar. Low-scale place offers rooms cheaper than most in this bracket. Restricted views of the lake from some rooms. Room service, laundry, TV, and restaurants. Doubles Rs350. ❷

Hotel Mansarovar, Tallital (☎35581). On a road parallel to The Mall. Small rooms with large clean bathrooms (squat and seat toilets). Room service, laundry, restaurant, and TV. Doubles Rs600-2000. Off season: Rs250-600. ❹

KMVN Mount View Tourist Rest House, Mallital (☎35400). A long, steep 2km walk from the Flats, this government-run rest house is cheap, clean, and uncontaminated by character of any kind. Dorms Rs100; doubles Rs650. Off season: Rs75/500. ❶

Hotel City Heart (☎35228). Near Mallital, on The Mall opposite the Nainital Club. Spectacular views of the lake from every room, as well as a courteous and well-informed staff. Room service, clean bedding, and spacious rooms, all with attached bath. Doubles Rs700-1400. Off season: Rs400-1000. ❹

KMVN Tourist Rest House, Tallital (☎35570). 200m from the Tallital bus stand toward the far side of the lake. Above the road and away from the noise, with grand views of the lake and hills. Hot water, showers, and seat toilets. Restaurant open 7am-10:30pm. Dorms Rs100; suites Rs1000. Off season: Rs75/800. ❶

◖ FOOD

All along The Mall are countless clean and well-priced restaurants with beautiful views of the lake—restaurants at either end of town in Mallital and Tallital are generally not as clean. Most restaurants have cheap outdoor seating—a must.

▧ **Embassy Restaurant,** between the library and Mallital, on The Mall. Classy yet inexpensive restaurant is packed with hip young *dilliwallahs* downing *rajma* (kidney beans), rice combo platters (Rs36), and cheap pizzas (Rs40–60). Open 10am-11pm. ❶

Nanak's Restaurant, between the library and Mallital, on The Mall. A wannabe Western fast-food place serving burgers (Rs40), "Jughead's trip in life" pizza (Rs70-125), milkshakes (Rs45-65), and mango sundaes (Rs80) in a dark room aglow with neon lights. Open daily 9am-11pm. ❶

Green Restaurant, Bara Bazaar, in the heart of Mallital; look for the large banner. The maroon, lamp-lit interior and colorful streamers overhead make up for the uncomfortable chairs and short tables. Curry rice (Rs25). Open daily 7am-11pm. ❶

Flattis Restaurant, between the library and Mallital, on The Mall. A large, dimly lit place that serves the largest variety of Indian and Western food in the area. Pizza Rs75-100, sizzlers Rs80, *dosas, thalis,* and a homesick Tuscan salad Rs30. ❶

Ahar Vihar Restaurant, near Mallital, upstairs from the well-lit variety stores on The Mall. A popular low-end restaurant with a homey kitchen feel. Large and delicious Gujarati and Rajasthani *thalis* Rs35-40. Open daily 10am-10pm. ❶

Sonam Tibetan Restaurant, by the Modern Bookstore, in Mallital. Meager choices but big portions of Tibetan food. Veg. noodles in broth (Rs25). Open daily 8am-10pm. ❶

👁 🏔 SIGHTS AND SCENERY

VIEWPOINTS. Any number of nearby hilltops and mountainside viewpoints offer views of the city. If the clouds cooperate, you can sometimes see Himalayan peaks as far away as the Tibetan border. The best way to take in the views is to rent a **horse** from one of Mallital's stables (at the mouth of Mallital before Bara Bazaar) and clip-clop up to the top. Expect the ride—which runs up steep, loose-stone trails against the honking chaos of the oncoming traffic—to be difficult. *(Round-trip Rs150, with the guide jogging alongside your milk-white steed. Expect to pay more if you want to stop and actually enjoy the view for more than 1hr.)*

The laziest way to get to the top of **Snow View** is to forsake horse and foot altogether and take the **ropeway,** which leaves from a clearly marked building 30m up from The Mall in Mallital. The low-effort nature of this little excursion makes it extremely popular during high season. Getting here at opening time (8am) is your best bet for ensuring tickets and people-free views. The last cable car leaves Mallital at 7pm. The last car returns from Snow View at 6pm. *(Round-trip Rs50, with a 1hr. stop at the top. KMVN has a cottage at the top. In season: doubles Rs600.)*

Another popular viewpoint around Nainital is **Naina Peak** (2611m), formerly known as Cheena Peak. Naina Peak is 6km away, roughly one hour by horse (Rs150) or three hours by foot. At the top is a snack shop and several places to sit and muse over the view. If the weather permits, you can see the peaks of Garhwal, including Nanda Devi (7817m). You can either start from Mallital or take a taxi to Tonneleay on Kilbury Rd., and walk from there. **Land's End,** behind **Tiffin Peak** (immediately west of the lake), has views over the valley to the west.

NAINI LAKE. The town's pride and joy is the lake itself. If you want to get out into the middle of Parvati's emerald eye, **boats** are available for hire *(paddleboats Rs40-60 per hr.; boatman-guided rides Rs30-50).* You can rent **yachts** from the Nainital Boat Club, though they will require membership *(yachts Rs60 per hr.; membership Rs150).*

OTHER SIGHTS. The road heading west from Tallital leads to the colonial-era **Governor's House** and a **golf course** that is open to visitors. Three kilometers along the road to Kathgodam is a small temple, **Hanumangarh,** home to a 6 ft. tall, bright orange statue of Hanuman. Just beyond the temple is an **observatory.** *(Open daily 3-5pm and 6-8pm. Admission Rs10.)* In 1880, a landslide killed 151 people and wiped out the city's largest hotel. The flattened area left behind was turned into a large, open public space. Today, the **Flats** are a favorite hang-out of snake charmers and musicians and are often busy with football and hockey games. In October, the **Autumn Festival** features sports competitions by day and cultural programs by night.

🎵 ENTERTAINMENT

On the banks of Sukhatal, by the KMVN Mallital, are the **Cave Gardens,** a recently opened underground attraction *(open daily 9am-7pm, admission Rs10).* **Capital Cinema** and **Ashok Cinema,** near the Flats, run Hindi movies regularly *(tickets Rs15).* A **stroll along The Mall** becomes more peaceful as darkness enshrouds the piles of chintz in the stores, but avoid the 6-9pm rush of tourists that arrives when the road is closed to traffic.

🗺 DAYTRIPS FROM NAINITAL

If you're looking for lake-side solitude, there are a number of places not far from Nainital that offer lovely views, and more peace and quiet than busy Nainital.

SAT TAL. Sat Tal contains a series of seven lakes hidden deep in pine and oak forests 21km from Nainital. It is possible to stay the night here and spend a day walking to all seven lakes, which are about 1km apart from one another. You can rent boats (Rs100 per hr.) and buy snacks from stalls along the lakefront, but most of the area around the lake remains undeveloped. Most tour agencies have buses to Sat Tal and the surrounding lakes (Rs100).

BHIMTAL. A smaller and cleaner version of Nainital, Bhimtal, 22km away, has a good reputation as a being a center for aquatic pursuits: water-skiing, sailing, and boating. The tourist value of the lake has made it a commercial destination, and these days there's more concrete than pine and blue-sky beauty. Bhimtal is also home to two environmental groups: Himalayan Man and Nature Institute (HIMANI) and the Action Group for Environment and Humanity, both situated at the Tallital end. One kilometer along the road to **Naukuchiya Tal** is a Kumaoni Folk Art Exhibition. (Open M-Sa 11am-6pm.) Tour buses don't stop here; you'll have to take a taxi. As usual, government accommodations are the cheapest. The **KMVN tourist bungalow ❶**, on the opposite side of the lake of Bhimtal, is about as quiet and cheap as Bhimtal lake-side hotels get. (☎47005. Dorms Rs100; tidy doubles Rs450.) One of the prettiest lakes, Naukuchiyatal , offers plenty of solitude and lots of opportunities to fish and spot migrating birds. The lake is said to have nine *(nau)* corners *(kuchiya)*, and good luck is supposed come to those who can see all nine at once. The **KMVN tourist bungalow ❶**, at Naukuchiyatal has a comfortable lounge and a beautiful garden in front. (☎47138. Dorms Rs60; doubles Rs400).

RAMGARH. The drive to Ramgarh, 32km from Nainital, is a beautiful journey through pine and oak forests. Although the town itself has little to recommend, the "snow viewpoint," 6km before town, commands clear views (well, sometimes) of peaks such as Nanda Devi and Nanda Kot. The best time to visit the region is during April, May, and October, when the weather has cooled, the sky is clear, and the rates have come down. The winter is also beautiful, but be sure to pack warm clothes, gloves, and boots to deal with the cold and snow.

RANIKHET रानीखेत ☎ 05966

At an altitude of 2000m, Ranikhet is surrounded by fields of pine and deodar forests that are inhabited by *kakar* (barking deer). Other than the loud silence of the forests and the overpowering views of Nanda Devi (7817m), the largest presence here is the military, which dates back to 1869, when British troops from UP arrived here for a bit of 19th-century R&R. With less traffic noise (you'll hardly hear a car horn after 8pm), and fewer travelers than the other hill stations, Ranikhet is a good place to sit back and relax. The "Queen's Field" is growing fast, though, and new resorts pop up every year. A local tourist brochure points out: "How long Ranikhet can maintain its virginity is a million dollar question." But for now, you can still enjoy Ranikhet's serenity relatively undisturbed.

▐▀ TRANSPORTATION

Buses: UP Roadways (☎20645) runs buses to: **Almora** (2½ hr., 5:30am, Rs30); **Dehra Dun** (12hr., 8:30am and 3pm, Rs170); **Delhi** (12hr., 4 per day 3-5pm, Rs180); **Haldwani/Kathgodam** (4hr., every 30min. 5:30am-5pm, Rs55); **Kausani** (3hr.; 6am, 12:30 and 2pm; Rs35); **Nainital** (3½hr., 7am, Rs28); **Ramnagar** (5hr.; 8:30am, 1 and 3pm; Rs60). **KMOU** (☎20609) has buses to: **Almora** (2½hr., 5 per day 6:30am-2:30pm, Rs30); **Haldwani/Kathgodam** (4hr., 7 per day 7am-2:30pm, Rs50); **Kausani** (3hr., 4 per day 6am-1:30pm, Rs35); **Nainital** (3hr., 11:30am, Rs40); **Ramnagar** (4hr., 5 per day 7am-3pm, Rs30).

Trains: Northern Railways Out Agency, above the UP Roadways Bus Stand, books tickets for the Kathgodam-Delhi train (Rs177). The price includes a one-way bus ticket from Ranikhet to Kathgodam. Reserve at least 3 days in advance. Open M-Sa 10am-2pm.

Local Transportation: Shared jeeps go to nearby destinations. For Chaubatia and The Mall, jeeps leave from above Alko Hotel (Rs5) or the KMOU stand (Rs5); for Dwarahat and Doonagiri, jeeps depart near Nainital Bank (Rs30). Most jeeps don't run after 5pm.

ORIENTATION AND PRACTICAL INFORMATION

Sadar Bazaar, the main road that anchors Ranikhet's meandering topography, is in the town center; most services and many of the hotels and restaurants are here. **Buses** arrive at either end of the bazaar; **UP Roadways** stops at the downhill end, while **KMOU** buses arrive and depart on the west end. The Mall area, 2km above the bazaar, is a tranquil setting for some of the better hotels. To get to The Mall, keep to your left along the road next to the **Alka Hotel** (up the mountains and away from the chaos). There is a mural-sized map of Ranikhet opposite the **Rajdeep Hotel** that also gives listings of area attractions. Monday is Ranikhet's **business holiday.**

Tourist Office: (☎ 20227). At the east end of the bazaar, up from the UP Roadways bus stand. Open M-Su 10am-5pm. Open May-June M-Sa 8am-8pm, Su 10am-5pm.

Currency Exchange: The nearest currency exchange is in Nainital or Almora.

Markets: Sadar Bazaar has stores selling traditional Kumaoni silver and gold jewelry.

Pharmacy: Mayank Medical Hall (☎ 21356). At the UP Roadways end of town. Open Tu-Su 8am-8pm.

Medical Assistance: The **clinic** of Dr. Prakash Srivastava (☎ 20101) is on the bazaar, uphill from the Mayank pharmacy. Open daily 9am-5pm.

Internet: Cyber Link, on Sadar Bazaar east of Moon Hotel. Has the only connection in town. Rs60 per hr.

Post Office: The main branch is along The Mall, 2km from town center. Another branch is near the tourist office. Open M-F 9am-5pm, Sa 9am-noon. **Postal code:** 263648.

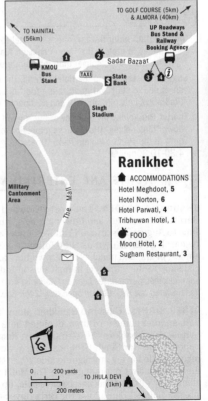

Ranikhet

🏠 ACCOMMODATIONS
Hotel Meghdoot, **5**
Hotel Norton, **6**
Hotel Parwati, **4**
Tribhuwan Hotel, **1**

🍎 FOOD
Moon Hotel, **2**
Sugham Restaurant, **3**

ACCOMMODATIONS

Hotels along the bazaar are noisier and less well-kept than those tucked into the hills along The Mall. In-season (Apr.-June and Sept.-Oct.) prices are higher in the bazaar, and rooms are harder to find. Most bazaar hotels have a 10am check-out and don't allow alcohol; those along The Mall have noon check-out and allow alcohol. In season rates are quoted. Off season expect a 40-60% discount. Always bargain a little before accepting a room.

Hotel Norton, just past Meghdoot. Colorful old British bungalow with cheapest rates for standard rooms. Much of the hotel's original antique furniture remains in place, adding to the atmosphere. Friendly staff. Doubles Rs300-600. Off season: Rs50 less. ❷

Hotel Meghdoot (☎20475), just past Kumaon Lodge in The Mall. Once a British officer's bungalow, with spacious rooms and huge bathrooms (seat and squat toilets). Balcony offers unobstructed views of the valley. STD/ISD service, cable TV, and restaurant. One standard double room Rs450; all others Rs625-900. Off season: 50% discount. ❷

Hotel Parwati (☎20325), above UP Roadways bus stop; look for large signs. The most elevated hotel in Ranikhet, it has clean rooms and super views from its lounge. Room service and hot water. Deluxe rooms have TVs. Singles Rs350; doubles Rs500; deluxe Rs700. Off season: 50% discount. ❷

Tribhuwan Hotel (☎20524), on the west end of town, just before the KMOU bus stand. A mighty beast composed of 3 bldgs. Isolated from most hotels, and a welcome change from the crowded main road. Balconies offer unobstructed views of the valley. Squat toilets and bucket showers. Carpeted rooms are larger and have small black and white TVs. Basic rooms Rs350; deluxe Rs600. Off season: 40% discount. ❷

FOOD

Moon Hotel, Sadar Bazaar, opposite Hotel Rajdeep. Has the nicest restaurant in town, with prices to match. The "Moon chicken Ala Numtaz" (Rs290) goes well with the dim lighting. The food is spicier than the standard regional fare. Open daily 8am-11pm. ❹

Sugham Restaurant, in the Hotel Parwati. The dimly lit interior isn't especially inviting, but an attentive staff and good, plain food make this a dependable restaurant. Chinese (Rs35-50), Indian (Rs35-70), and continental dishes (Rs40-80). Open daily 8am-9pm. ❶

Tourist Bungalow, far from town, but a good option for those in the Mall area. Munch down "fingar chips" (Rs18) or vegetable *pakoras* (8 for Rs18) while sipping tea (Rs5) in front of the TV. Chow mein Rs45. Open daily 7-8am (tea only), 8-10am, noon-2:30pm, 4:30-10:30pm. ❶

SIGHTS AND ENTERTAINMENT

CHAUBATIA GARDEN. The most renowned attraction in the area, the Chaubatia Garden features fruit and flower gardens, which are in full technicolor bloom from June to August. It is also a "Fruit Research Centre;" sneaky travelers sometimes do research of their own as they follow the trails through the forests. Apricots, apples, pears, and peaches are grown here and sold at reasonable rates at the official shop at the entrance. In high season Indian vacationers fill the garden. (*11 km from Ranikhet. Seven buses head to Chaubatia from the UP Roadways stand (40min., 8am-6pm, Rs5). Shared taxi Rs5. Garden open daily 24hr. Shop open M-Su 10am-4:45pm.*)

OTHER SIGHTS. Closer to Ranikhet, along The Mall, is the Hindu temple of **Jhula Devi,** another name for Durga, depicted here sitting on a swing (*jhula*). The small temple dates back to the 14th century. **Kumaon Regiment War Memorial Museum,** opposite the Nar Singh Grounds, houses ammunition from the Raj days and any recent battle having any significance. (*Open M-Sa 10am-5pm.*) A little farther down is the **Ram Mandir.** Continuing down The Mall toward Sadar Bazaar is the impressive, albeit new (1994) **Mankameshwar Temple,** up from the phone exchange and opposite the Nainital Bank. Near the Birla Boys School is the temple of **Hare Khan.**

FESTIVALS. The **Autumn Festival** in late September is Ranikhet's largest, with sports tournaments featuring hockey, cricket, and tennis as well as a potpourri of cultural exhibits from around Kumaon. For 10 days in June, you can stop in at the Nar Singh Stadium (also called the Nar Singh Ground) for the evening **Summer Festival.** A homey country fair, it features a ring toss, magicians, kiddie rides, a mini-zoo, Rs10 gambling, blaring music, and heartburn-inducing Chinese food.

GOLF COURSE. The **Kumaon Regiment Advanced Training Centre and Golf Course** (also known as "Upat Kalika"), is one of India's most scenic golf courses. Even if you're not keen on the game, the pine forests around the course are a pleasant place to wander. And where else can you find a 1000 ft. cliff as a course hazard? *(6km away. Shared taxis Rs5. Nine holes for Rs200; club rental Rs100; ball Rs120; tee Rs10; caddy Rs50 plus tip. Open M-Tu and F 7am-6pm, W-Th and Sa 7am-12:30pm.)*

🏔 DAYTRIPS FROM RANIKHET

Dwarahat, once the capital of Pandava kings, was abandoned when the river Kosi changed its course, leaving the city dry. The former capital is home to a cluster of Shiva temples built by the Chaud kings during the 14th century. Traditional Kumaoni wood work and *rangoli*, intricately designed paintings adorning walls and floors, can be seen in most houses here. The region's famous **Syalde-Bikhoti Mela** is held here annually from April 13-15. (21km from Ranikhet. Shared taxi Rs30.) Fifteen kilometers ahead is **Doonagiri**, where there is a **Vaishno Devi Temple** and, as usual, spectacular views of the Himalayas. (Bus Rs10, shared taxi Rs10.)

ALMORA अल्मोड़ा ☎ 5962

Legend has it that Almora was once the city of the gods. To proclaim their divine presence here, the gods left behind an abundant source of pure water, delivered to this mile-high city from over 120 underground wells. Almora is the most mystical of Kumaon's hill stations, having drawn peace-seekers from the likes of Gandhi and Nehru (who used to meet here to talk) to Swami Vivekananda and Timothy Leary. The most central hill station in UP, Almora was developed by Indians and not by the British—it was created as the seat of the Chanda dynasty 400 years ago. A stroll through the old bazaar evokes those bygone days—the buildings are fading, but colorful facades and cobbled streets echo centuries past. But the mountains, which offer opportunities for day hikes and exploration, remain oblivious to passing decades and dynasties. Amid the frenetic activity in the air, tranquility still survives. While nearby hill stations pursue the Western gods of finance and leisure, Almora is surrounded by modern and ancient Hindu temples and by the magnificent natural shrines of the cloud-piercing Himalayan peaks.

🚍 TRANSPORTATION

Almora's **bus stand** is on The Mall at the center of town. **KMOU,** before the UP Roadways stand along The Mall, sends buses to: **Kausani** and **Bageswar** (2½hr., 11 per day 6am-5pm, Rs30/35); **Kathgodam** and **Haldwani** (4½hr., 4 per day 6am-1pm, Rs40); **Nainital** and **Bhowali** (3hr., 5 per day 6:30am-1pm, Rs32/35); **Ranikhet** (2½hr., 4 per day 8am-3pm, Rs25). **UP Roadways,** down the steps, services: **Bhowali** (2½hr., every 30min. 5-8am and 1:30-5pm, Rs29); **Delhi** (11hr., 4 per day 7am-5pm, Rs180); **Dehra Dun** (12hr., 5am and 4pm, Rs170); **Kausani** (2½hr., 4 per day 7am-noon, Rs30); **Nainital** (3hr., 8am, Rs35); **Ranikhet** (2hr.; 6:30am, 1 and 2pm; Rs29). The **Dharanda Bus Stand** on the road below The Mall serves **Pithoragarh** (5hr., 4 per day, 7am-2pm, Rs50). Shared jeeps leave frequently from the main bus stand for most destinations listed above. They typically cost Rs5-10 more than a bus.

UTTARANCHAL

🔲 🔢 ORIENTATION AND PRACTICAL INFORMATION

The **town center** is on The Mall, the major thoroughfare for traffic and the site of most hotels and services; walking with the flow of traffic brings you to several restaurants and to the road to Kasar Devi. Most other services are southwest along The Mall. **Jauhari Bazaar,** the main bazaar, is the major parallel street up from The Mall. Sunday is Almora's **business holiday.**

Tourist Office: The **UA Tourist Office** (☎22180). By the post office, 800m southwest of the bus stand on the road veering up from The Mall. Carries information about Almora and Kumaon but keeps inconsistent hours. Try M-Sa 10am-5pm. A better bet for information is one of the local **trekking companies,** including **Discover Himalaya** (☎31470). Opposite the post office. The people at **High Adventure** (☎31445), on The Mall, a bit closer to town center, are also knowledgeable about the local sights.

Currency Exchange: State Bank of India (☎30048), on The Mall, near the town center. Changes only AmEx traveler's checks. Open M-F 10am-2pm, Sa 10am-noon.

Police: (☎30323). 10m along the road, opposite the post office.

Pharmacy: The best-stocked pharmacy in town is the **Prakash Medical Store,** as you enter the bazaar from The Mall. Open daily 7am-10pm.

Hospital: Civil Hospital (☎30025, emergency 30064). Up a short flight of stairs from the bazaar. Open daily 8am-2pm. Emergency open 24hr. **Base Hospital** (☎30012), 3km from town, is cleaner and less crowded. Open daily 8am-2pm.

Internet: The **STD booth** adjacent to Discover Himalaya charges Rs70 per hr. Open M-Sa 9am-10pm. **Hotel Sikha,** on the far end of the mall from the post office, has reliable connections. Rs80 per hr.

Post Office: (☎30019). On the downside of The Mall, 600m southwest of the bus stand. Open M-Sa 10am-6pm. **Postal Code:** 263601.

🔲 ACCOMMODATIONS

Almora has a limited choice of hotels. Most are along The Mall; dingier, cheaper places are clustered around the town center. More relaxed accommodations dotting the surrounding hills are difficult to reach (see **Daytrips from Almora,** p. 668). The off-season is July-August and November-March.

Hotel Savoy (☎30329). At the end of the ramp that veers upward opposite the post office. Those seeking comfort will be rewarded by large rooms with TVs, attached baths, and seat toilets. Rooms on the balcony are more expensive, but have good views; the lower ones have a lovely garden. Doubles Rs300-450. Off season: 25% discount. ❷

Kailas Hotel (☎30624). Opposite the post office, 10m above The Mall. The Kailas is run by the incomparably charming 83-year-old Mr. Shah (though the board says "run by housewives"), a marvelous source of all sorts of tales and wisdom about the Almora district and Indian history. The rooms could be cleaner, and the shared outdoor bathrooms are a pain, but Mr. Shah's relationship advice alone might be worth the Rs120-180 cost of a double room. Bargaining is futile. ❶

Hotel Surmool (☎30460). Mall Rd., 1 block from the post office away from the town center. Large, clean, well-run place with good views. Dorms Rs150; doubles Rs400-700. Off season: 25% discount. ❶

Hotel Shikhar (☎30238). At the end of The Mall. Shikhar has the most services of any of Almora's establishments—attached travel agency, general store, hair salon, restaurant, cyber-cafe, and STD/ISD. Rooms are spacious and well lit. The balcony above the restaurant has dramatic views of the valley. Doubles Rs250-1000. ❷

Hotel Pawan (☎30252). Opposite Trishul, closer to town center. Don't be fooled by the "Enjoy Billiards" sign; it's only for local members of the Billiards Club (don't bother asking about membership—you don't qualify). Well-kept and sufficient, with bright rooms, large mirrors, and clean bathrooms with squat toilets. Room service available. Checkout noon. Singles Rs200; doubles Rs250. Off season: Rs50 discount. ❶

KMVN Holiday House (☎22250). 1 km southwest of the bus stand, on the descending road. Set apart from the rest of the town, this pleasant and clean government hotel has its own garden and valley view. Combined seat/squat toilets. Dorms have bucket showers. Dorms Rs100; doubles Rs450. Off season: Rs70/300. ❶

🞄 FOOD

Sunrise Restaurant, past the post office, in Hotel Surmool. Enjoy creamy and heavy Punjabi and Chinese food as you contemplate the fish tank and rock sculpture decoration. *Shahi paneer* Rs45, *naan* Rs12. ❶

Glory Restaurant, opposite Mount View, up the road to the northeast. The 2nd floor's short ceilings and red lanterns lend this veg. restaurant an unusual amount of character. Try the Glory Special dosa (Rs30). Open daily 7am-10:30pm.❶

Sangam Restaurant, near the town center inside Hotel Himsagar. Has decent food at cheap prices. Great views and all-veg. food. *Dal makhani* Rs25, spicy chowmein Rs40. Open daily 8am-10:30pm. ❶

Swagat Restaurant, on the side of the Hotel Shikhar, down the steps. An airy place with a grand view. Veg. *thalis* (Rs35), *pakora* platter Rs15. Open daily 7:30-9:30pm. ❶

🞄 SIGHTS

KASAR DEVI TEMPLE. The main attraction near Almora is the Kasar Devi Temple, spectacularly positioned at the top of Kashyap Hill. Views from a giant, sloping mountaintop rock afford sweeping panoramas of the whole area, marred only slightly by the television antenna that shares the point. The temple is known as a center of spiritual energy—Swami Vivekananda came here to meditate, as have many soul-searching Americans and Europeans, some of whom still hang around the nearby tea stands. Follow the trail past the temple through town for the best views of the distant Nanda Devi mountain range. *(Near the hamlet of Kasar Devi, 7km from Almora. Reachable by a long hike upward past The Mall, which forks left after the Hotel Shikhar. One-way taxi Rs10 per person.)*

OTHER SIGHTS. A walk along the road above The Mall offers stunning views and a peaceful atmosphere. The walk is punctuated by the **Bhairav** and **Patal Devi** temples, which both offer terrific views of the sunset. Across the street is the small, government-run **G.B. Pant Museum,** which features tools and other artifacts from the Katyuri and Chanda dynasties. *(Open daily 10am-5pm daily. Free.)* Locals go to the locally important **Chitai Temple** to seek retribution if they feel they've been wronged. The King Golu Dev used to sit here as the administerer of justice. Today, plaintiffs paste or hang letters in the temple, describing their situation in hopes of finding resolutions to their problems. The **Nanda Devi Temple,** which pays homage to the goddess of newlywed brides, is a pretty place that draws religious and architectural enthusiasts alike. The **Nanda Devi Fair** is held here during the last week of August or the first week of September. The **Brighton End Corner,** at the south end of town, is a popular spot for sunset watching. Katermal is home to an 800-year-old **Sun Temple.** *(12½km from Almora or 1½km on foot.)* A 2km walk from town on Mall Rd. past the post office brings you to **Sunset Point,** the place where the locals gather each evening as the sun creeps behind the distant hills.

MARKETS. Even if you don't enjoy the bustling Indian markets, stroll through the cobblestone streets of Jauhari Bazaar above The Mall to catch a glimpse of the intricately carved wooden architecture. Also, drop by the **jewelers** past Raja stores to buy or look at traditional Kumaoni jewelry. Almora is the center of production of *tamtas*, silver-plated copper pots, which line the lower region of the bazaar. **Anokhe Lal** sells these pots, though they are pretty heavy to carry in a backpack.

◪ SCENERY NEAR ALMORA

TRANQUILITY RETREAT. Wedged between two hills and far from everything but its own splendor and jaw-dropping views, the Tranquility Retreat is a tiny getaway paradise for the short- or long-term visitor. Now in its fifth year, Tranquility has grown to seven rooms, with an organic garden and beehive. Armelle and Kishan, French expatriate and Indian farmer, busily tend the garden, bake bread (7 loaves per day) and steaming scones served with homemade honey, and cook up a vegetarian storm—French and continental mainstays with the occasional Indian touch—while exuding a warmth and compassion that keeps their contented guests from leaving the nest. There are two paths to Tranquility Retreat from the Kasar Devi road. If you are walking toward Kasar Devi, look for a blue sign high in a tree on the left 10min. after the Research Institute for Yoga Therapy. When walking away from Kasar Devi, there will be a sign on your right 15min. down the mountain from the Kasar Devi Temple. Write for reservations. *(Tranquility Guest House c/o Kishan Joshi, ☎ 263601 Saria Pina Estate, Almora, VPM. Food is available 7am-10pm for casual visitors as well as guests. Doubles Rs1500 per month.)*

◪ DAYTRIPS FROM ALMORA

JAGESHWAR AND SANDESHWAR. The temple complex of Jageshwar is 38km from Almora in a valley surrounded by deodar trees. Made up of 124 temples, the complex contains one of the 12 *jyotirlingas* of Shiva. The main temple features two statues of Deep Chand and Pawan Chand, two kings who were patrons of the complex. Photography is not allowed in the main temple. Two kilometers before Jageshwar is Sandeshwar, a smaller temple complex. *(Shared jeeps leave from the taxi stand in the center of town for Jageshwar and Sandeshwar about every 20 min. 1½hr., Rs30.)*

SURYA MANDRI KATARMAL. Built in the 8th century by the Katyuri dynasty, Surya Mandri Katarmal is the only sun temple in Kumaon. The main temple is surrounded by 44 smaller ones. *(12½km toward Kosi and a 1½hr. climb. Buses and jeeps leave frequently from Almora, Rs 5-10.)* The historical spot of **Lakhudiyar**, 15km toward Barechhina, features traditional rock paintings, some of the first examples of art in Kumaon. *(Take any bus or shared jeep headed for Pithoragarh or Jageshwar, Rs10.)*

BINSAR SANCTUARY AND JALNA. The Binsar Sanctuary, 30km from Almora, was the summer getaway of the Chand rulers; now, tourists come to lose themselves in the sanctuary's dense forests. Along with a handful of other hotels, there is a KMVN Tourist Rest House in the area. *(Doubles Rs300; 50% off season discount. Make reservations at the Almora tourist office.)* The picturesque town of **Jalna,** 32km toward Lohagat from Almora, is a perfect spot for a quiet afternoon. Wander about apple and apricot orchards with the snow-laden Himalayas as a backdrop.

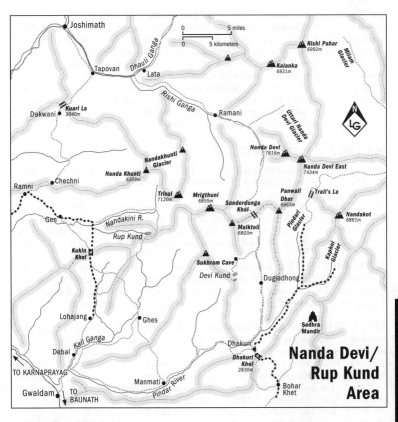

Nanda Devi/ Rup Kund Area

UTTARANCHAL

TREKKING

For further immersion in Kumaon's natural beauty, you might consider going on a **trek** to one of the towering glaciers in the Himalayas. **Discover Himalaya** (see p. 666) offers trekking packages that cost Rs500-1100 per person per day, depending on level of service. Expect to pay Rs50-70 for advice on planning high-altitude treks. Student discounts are often available. The most popular trek in Kumaon is the one to **Pindari Glacier** (90km). Rest houses line the trail at convenient distances along the six-day trek. The park begins in Loharkhket, 81 km by jeep from Kausani. Though the trek's popularity deters those seeking a true escape, there are some beautiful sights along the way (especially from Dhakusi to Phurkia). The 12-day trek to the **Milam Glacier** (200km), via stunning **Munsyari** in the Pithoragarh district, is ideal for those hoping to avoid the slow-moving glacial crowds, and willing to sleep in the cramped quarters of villages' huts. Because the Milam Glacier trek comes close to the Indo-Tibetan-Nepal border, taking a guide (Rs300-500 per day) is strongly recommended. Some adventurous trekkers combine the Pindari and Milam treks into a supersized glacial sweep through the difficult Pindari Kanda Pass (3820m). The 4-day **Kafni Glacier** trek (90km) is a good, short option for high-altitude trekkers. Discover Himalaya also runs a 4-day trek through the foothills of the Himalayas (200-2500m) to the **Barahi Devi Temple** at Devidhura, the site of the weird and wonderful **Rakshabandhan Festival,** which takes place around the third week of August. Two opponents equipped with baskets as shields throw lumps, stones, and rocks at each other. Blood from the wounds is collected and offered to the virgin goddess. (This and similar treks cost around Rs900 per person per day.) While Nanda Devi, the second-tallest mountain in India, is a tempting challenge to many trekkers, the Nanda Devi Sanctuary has been closed to all civilian traffic for several years because of its proximity to the Indo-Tibetan border. Those seeking views of the mountain must keep their distance. Vistas of Nanda Devi can be found from Kausani, Auli (see p. 653), or Rialkot along the Milam Glacier trek.

KAUSANI कौसानी ☎ 05962

Shortly after his two-week stay here in 1929, Mohandas Gandhi mused, "Why would Indians go to Switzerland when they have Kausani?" If you want to touch the snow-clad Himalayas, come to Kausani. This bus stop town, nearly 2000m above sea level, offers the most awe-inspiring views of peaks anywhere in the UP Hills. Not a typical hill station, Kausani has one main road, a few restaurants, and a few more hotels. It's a perfect spot for basking in the splendor of the Himalayas, well out of range of the honking cars and busy daily life of the larger hill stations.

◪ **TRANSPORTATION. Buses** stop in the center of Kausani, opposite the colorful Ram Krishnan and Saraswati temple. Buses and **jeeps** leave frequently from the town center for Bageswar, Almora, Gwaldam, Ranikhet, Bhowali, and Haldwani. Inquire at the tourist office or ask locals (more than one!) about departure times.

◪◪ **ORIENTATION AND PRACTICAL INFORMATION.** The center of town is marked by the three-way intersection of the main road from Ranikhet, another road that climbs up the mountain toward the KMVN, and the road leading down to Baijnath. The **tourist office** is on the main road where the buses stop. (Open daily May-June 8am-8pm; off-season: M-Sa 10am-5pm.) The nearest **currency exchange** is in Almora. The **Sunil Medical store** is on the road that climbs up the mountain (open daily 8am-8pm). The road continues, leading to the KMVN tourist rest house 2km away. The **post office** is near the KMVN tourist rest house (open M-Sa 8am-4pm). The travel agencies and restaurants are all in this area. Most hotels have **STD/ISDs,** but there is also a booth at the bus stop. **Postal code:** 263639.

◪◪ **ACCOMMODATIONS AND FOOD.** A large number of pricey resort hotels in Kausani advertise magnificent views of the Himalayas. The good news is that these hotels do not have a monopoly on nature's beauty. The rooms at the **Hotel Uttarakhand ❶,** have unobstructed mountain views, and are far enough away from the town center to offer a modicum of peace and quiet. Follow the stairs above the bus stand. (☎45012. Doubles Rs200-300. Off season: Rs50-150.) The attached restaurant is one of the best in town, with veg. fried rice for Rs35. (Open daily 6am-11pm.) Many of Kausani's nicer hotels are along one strip of road above the town center. Your best choice here is the ◪**Amar Holiday Home ❶,** which has modest-sized rooms, hot water, and a peaceful balcony. (☎45015. Open May-July and Sept.-Dec. Singles Rs150; doubles Rs300-500. Off season: Rs100/200-350.) On the same row of hotels is the **Anashakti Ashram ❶** (sometimes called "the Gandhi ashram"), one of the most serene spots around. Fees are paid on a donation basis, and the ashram is only for those interested in spiritual living. Guests are expected to help with daily cleaning, refrain from consumption of alcohol, eggs, and meat products, and attend daily prayer as often as possible. **KMVN tourist rest houses ❶,** are a safe bet in Kumaon, and the one in Kausani,

2km from town on a road that hugs the northern face of the mountain, is no exception. Book at least one month in advance during the high season (May-June and Oct.) The attached restaurant is open 7am-10pm. (☎45006. Dorms Rs60; doubles Rs300-800. Off season: 50% discount.)

Good cheap eats are much scarcer than cheap sleeps. Although you will probably end up just eating at your hotel, there are a few other options. **Hill Queen Restaurant ❶,** (not to be mistaken for name-usurper New Hill Queen Restaurant) offers cheap Punjabi (Rs35-50) food and some of the best views in town. They also have Internet (Rs60 per hr.). The **Kitchen Restaurant ❶,** next to the post office, offers reliable fare and serves *thalis* for Rs35. The **Ashoka restaurant ❶,** next to the Bhatt Clinic, serves up local dishes. The lentil-based *bara* dish (Rs35), accompanied by the local chutney, is a tasty treat after weeks of *dal* and chow mein. Kumaoni dishes take a while to cook, so order early.

◎⛰ SIGHTS AND DAYTRIPS. The main sights in Kausani are the sunrise and sunset; these are also the best times to see the distant mountains which are enveloped in clouds during the summer and monsoon season. There are also religious and historical towns within a 40km radius of Kausani. Hire a taxi (Rs1500 per day) and drive to as many as you like, making pit stops for the night at some. Most of them have only **KMVN or GMVN ❸,** accommodations available (Rs400-900).

If the views and treks start to get tiring, you can take a daytrip to **Baijnath** (18km), the site of a group of 18 ancient temples on the banks of the Gomti River. This complex features an intricately carved black granite statue of Parvati in the main temple. The priest from the Archaeological Survey of India will describe the statue for you in excruciating detail. The temple also features a large brass *linga* where *aarti* is held daily at 8am and 7pm. (Buses to Baijnath leave frequently from the town center. Rs8.) Yogi's Uttarakhand Cycle Tours (☎45012), next to the Hotel Uttarakhand, rents **mountain bikes** and organizes tours for Rs375 per day.

Twenty-two kilometers from Baijnath is a beautiful drive through terraced fields and thick pine forests to **Gwaldani,** where the Himalayan peaks seem closer than ever. Twenty-three kilometers from Baijnath lies **Bageshwar,** where the rivers Gomti, Saryu (Pinder), and Bhagirathi meet. There is an ancient Shiva temple, **Bagnath Mandir,** on the banks of the Gomti and Saryu, surrounded by smaller shrines of Ganga-ma, Hanuman, Durga, and the rest of the gang.

Fifty kilometers ahead is **Chaukori,** probably one of the best places to touch the Himalayan peaks. Up at 2410m, the sun sets later, creating a fusion of all shades of yellow, orange, red, and pink against the blue and white backdrop of the sky and peaks. The cliff top KMVN has superb views. On the road to Ranikhet are **Dwarahat** and **Doonagiri,** with Shiva temples built by the Chand and Katuriya dynasties.

Forty kilometers from Chaukori is the old and relatively unknown temple of **Patal Bhubneshwar.** Naturally sculpted by underground streams and earthquakes, the cave temple is an enchanting place. The cave is said to house over 33 deities in the form of these sculpted rocks. There are also smaller caves which are said to lead to Kalyug, Kailas, and Gangalihaat, though no one (except the five Pandavas, the *pujari* will insist) has explored them. (The tour lasts an hour. Wear loose comfortable clothes and go barefoot. Expect to tip the pujari who doubles as your guide—Rs50-100—and make a donation to the temple committee—Rs100.) Photography is not permitted.

UTTAR PRADESH
उत्तर प्रदेश

Uttar Pradesh, the "Northern State," is the true heartland of India, where parched plains spring to life with the coming of the monsoon. The state, which has been called "UP" for short ever since the British carved it out as the United Provinces, is India's most populous state, with 140 million residents. The cradle of Indian civilization from the time of the Aryan chieftains to the reign of the great Mughal emperors, UP gave India the *Ramayana*, the Hindi language, and since Independence, eight of its 12 prime ministers. It has also been the focus of bitter communal and inter-caste violence. In 1992, the state's BJP government encouraged the destruction of the Babri Masjid in Ayodhya, leading to thousands of deaths in communal riots across India. In the spring of 2000, a bicycle bomb went off in Ayodhya, injuring more than a dozen people. The state remains a flashpoint for Hindu-Muslim tensions. Radical affirmative action politics for Dalits (former Untouchables) also have a strong base in UP. Few people visit India without visiting UP, yet there is nothing here to photograph, slap on a postcard, and declare representative of the state—not its sacred city of Varanasi, nor the Taj Mahal in the Mughal capital of Agra, nor the old Muslim city of Lucknow. There is no quintessential UP, because UP is quintessentially Indian.

AGRA आगरा   ☎ 0562

Over the last decade, the average tourist's stay in Agra has declined from one and a half days to barely 12 hours. Everyone seems to be mumbling the same thing: Agra is a dump. It is not difficult to see why visitors who arrive expecting some kind of exotic, oriental Shangri-la—"the immortal city of undying love," according to the official literature—might leave feeling more than just a little bit disappointed. The monuments are every bit as magnificent as they are hyped up to be; the problem is that most of the tourist literature omits any mention of the parts of the city around and between its UNESCO-sanctioned sites. The main budget hotel center, Taj Ganj, is a powerful lesson in what happens when too many over-aggressive rickshaw-*wallahs* and rug vendors try to chase too many grungy backpackers down too few overcrowded streets. There *are* parts of Agra where visitors are treated to more than just urban grime and indigestion, but they are few and far between. In the Cantonment area there are wide, clean streets, upscale stores, and a string of parks maintained by the local Sheraton, which has a multi-million dollar stake in seeing that Agra puts

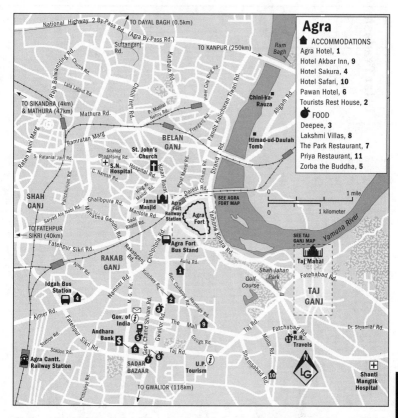

Agra

🏠 ACCOMMODATIONS
Agra Hotel, **1**
Hotel Akbar Inn, **9**
Hotel Sakura, **4**
Hotel Safari, **10**
Pawan Hotel, **6**
Tourists Rest House, **2**
🍎 FOOD
Deepee, **3**
Lakshmi Villas, **8**
The Park Restaurant, **7**
Priya Restaurant, **11**
Zorba the Buddha, **5**

its best foot forward. Luckily, Agra's real draw, the incomparably grand Taj Mahal, is still no less than breathtaking to behold, despite the mess of junky establishments that has sprung up outside its gates.

Agra's monuments were all built under the Mughals, who swept in from Central Asia early in the 16th century. At the Battle of Panipat in 1526, the Mughal warrior Babur crushed the ruling Lodi dynasty; as a direct result, the Mughals won a great South Asian empire, which included Agra, the Lodi capital. For the next 150 years, the site of the Mughal capital shifted between Delhi and Agra, leaving each city with a host of beautiful landmarks. With the slow decline of Mughal power in North India, Agra fell on hard times; the British made Calcutta (and later Delhi) their capital, and Allahabad rose to surpass Agra as the local political powerhouse.

Lately, Agra has worked hard to re-invent itself, funneling some of the hard currency it earns from tourists into smoggy industrial development. It sometimes requires great reserves of patience and magnanimity to rise above the temptation to scream and shout back at the persistent crowd that will follow your every step. But despite its irritations, Agra is well worth the effort. The monuments remain serene and beautiful, and memories of the Taj at dawn will remain with you long after you have forgiven and forgotten the rickshaw driver who refused to take you anywhere but his uncle's diamond warehouse.

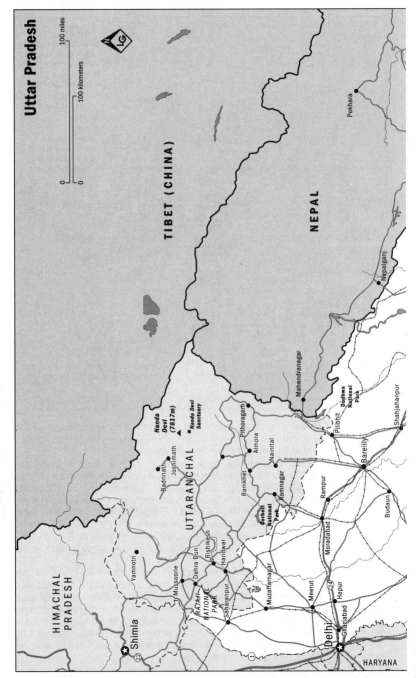

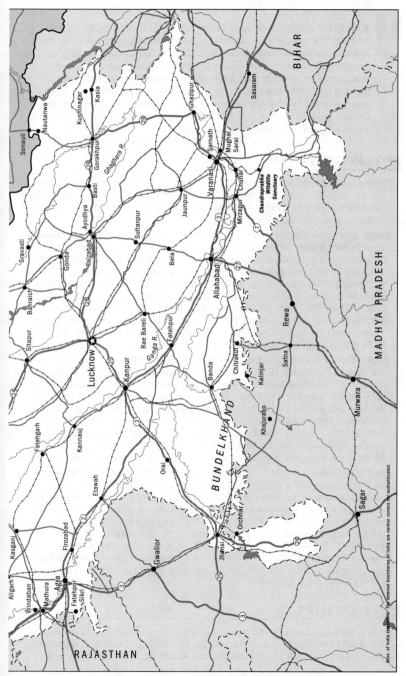

> ▲! **WARNING.** Agra, like all major tourist hubs in India, has a number of swindlers who'd love a chunk of your moolah. Rickshaw charges are excessive; the commissions incentive means drivers will often try to take you to the hotel or restaurant of their (and not your) choice. Be firm, be insistent, and be prepared to walk away. Also beware of crafty salesmen who persuade tourists with "parties," tea, and sweet talk to buy rugs and jewels to resell back home. Numerous schemes (credit card fraud, false identities, and even rape) can result from this, so don't get lured in. (See also **Touts, Middlemen, and Scams,** p. 17.) Walk away if the price you're quoted seems too high.

▐▬ TRANSPORTATION

Flights: Agra's **Kheria Airport** is 9km southwest of the city (enquiry ☎302274). To **Delhi** (1hr.; M, W, F, Su 7:20pm; US$60) and **Varanasi** (2hr.; M, W, F, Su 2:35pm; US$110) via **Khajuraho** (40min., US$85). **Indian Airlines** office (☎360190), in the Hotel Clarks-Shiraz complex. Open daily 10am-1:15pm and 2-5pm.

Trains: Agra has several rail stations, but most are of no use to tourists. **Agra Cantonment Railway Station** (enquiry ☎131), the main terminal, is southwest of the city, at the western end of Station Rd. A window at the computer reservation complex on the south side makes bookings for foreign tourists. To: **Bhopal** (7-10½hr., frequent 8:30am-12:50am, Rs 174; *Shatabdi Exp. 2002* 6hr., 8am, A/C chair Rs640); **Calcutta, Howrah Station** (30hr., 12:50pm, Rs312); **Delhi** (3-5hr., frequent 3am-1:10am, Rs54; *Shatabdi Exp. 2001* 2½hr., 8:18pm, A/C chair Rs390); **Gwalior** (1½-3hr., frequent 8:30am-12:50am, Rs84); **Lucknow** (6hr.; daily 10:45pm, Tu 7am; Rs81); **Mathura** (1-1½hr., several per day 6am-3am, Rs23); **Mumbai** (23-28hr.; daily 12:50 and 8:30am; M, Sa 8:50pm; Rs326); **Varanasi** (12-13hr., 8:45pm, Rs210).

Buses: Most leave from **Idgah Bus Terminal** (☎366588). Northeast of Agra Cant. Railway Station. To: **Bikaner** (12hr., 11pm, Rs198); **Delhi** (5hr., every 10min. 5am-midnight, Rs92); **Fatehpur Sikri** (1hr., every 20min. 6am-10pm, Rs17); **Gwalior** (3½hr., every 30min. 7am-6:30pm, Rs54); **Jaipur** (6hr., every 30min. 6:30am-10:30pm, Rs103) via **Bharatpur** (1½hr., Rs26); **Jhansi** (10hr., 4 per day 5am-8:30pm, Rs74); **Khajuraho** (14hr., 5:30am, Rs119); **Mathura** (1½hr., every 30min. 5am-8pm, Rs23); **Udaipur** (14hr., 6pm, Rs255). To get to **Varanasi,** catch a bus to **Allahabad** (18hr., 5 per day 2:30am-5pm, Rs199) from the **Agra Fort Bus Stand,** southwest of the fort. Deluxe buses leave from other places—contact a Taj Ganj area travel agent for details.

Local Transportation: Despite hassles, **rickshaws** are still the most convenient way to get around. Pay no more than Rs15-20 for a cycle-rickshaw or Rs25-30 for an auto-rickshaw going between the railway or bus stations and Taj Ganj or Agra Fort. Bicycles are another good option. **Raja Bicycle Store,** at the tonga stand, 100m south of Cyberlink, rents cycles (Rs10 per hr., Rs30-50 per day). Open daily 8am-6pm. You can also hire a **car and driver** from one of the places around the tourist centers. **R.R. Travels** (☎330055) Fatehabad Rd., Taj Ganj, organizes a 1-day tour that lasts 8hr. and includes Fatehpur Sikri (Rs800, Rs1000 with A/C). Open daily 7am-7:30pm. **UP Tourism** offers a similar tour of sights (Rs700) that starts at 9:30am from the Government of India Tourist Office (see below).

▄✦ ORIENTATION

Agra is a large and spread-out city, most of which sprawls west from the banks of the **Yamuna River,** along which are both the Fort and the Taj Mahal, separated by 1½km, and the **Shah Jahan Park. Yamuna Kinara Rd.** runs along the river's western banks from the Taj Mahal to **Belan Ganj,** a bustling neighborhood 1km north of **Agra Fort Railway Station,** where trains from eastern Rajasthan pull in. Tourist facilities cluster south of the Taj Mahal and Agra Fort. Bargain-basement backpacker dives crowd the streets of Taj Ganj, an unremittingly ugly and irritating rabbit-warren of hotels, restaurants, and souvenir shops that surrounds, chokes, and strangles the Taj Mahal from the southern side. **Mahatma Gandhi (MG) Rd., Gwalior Rd.,** and **General Cariappa Rd.** are three major thoroughfares that cross both **The Mall** and **Taj Rd.** From the upscale but none-too-beautiful **Sadar Bazaar,** which is squeezed between MG and Gwalior Rd., it's 2km due west to **Agra Cant. Railway Station;** 2km northwest along Fatehpur Sikri Rd. is the **Idgah Bus Stand.**

⚡ PRACTICAL INFORMATION

Tourist Office: Government of India Tourist Office (☎226378 or 226368). 191 The Mall. Opposite the post office. The most reliable and informative of Agra's tourist offices. Open M-F 9am-5:30pm, Sa 9am-4:30pm. The **UP Tourism Office,** 64 Taj Rd. (☎226341), near Clarks-Shiraz, offers maps and tour packages. Open M-Sa 10am-5pm. They also have an office at Agra Cant. Railway Station (368598), opposite the inquiry booth. Open daily 8am-8pm.

Currency Exchange: Andhara Bank (☎225026). Sadar Bazaar. In the black glass above the modern book depot. Exchanges currency and traveler's checks and gives credit card advances. Open M-F 10am-4pm, Sa 10am-12:30pm. **LKP Forex,** Fatehabad Rd. (☎331191). In the tourist complex area just left of Pizza Hut. Changes traveler's checks and major currencies for a 1% commission. Open M-Sa 9:30am-7pm. Outside these hours, black-market opportunists in Taj Ganj will be more than happy to take your dollars from you. Many of the larger luxury hotels will also change money for a fee.

Market: Taj Ganj is a high-pressure, hassle-a-minute hustlers' hang-out where you are constantly urged to buy everything from toilet paper to mini marble and plastic Taj Mahals. **Old Agra** is one big bazaar for buying belts, shoes, car parts, and plastic buckets. **Kinari Bazaar,** extending northwest from the fort, is especially well-stocked. Shop around, and always, always bargain hard (even if a sign claims fixed prices).

Police: City control room ☎361120; Taj Ganj branch ☎331015.

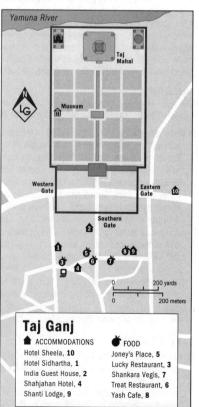

Taj Ganj

🏠 ACCOMMODATIONS
Hotel Sheela, **10**
Hotel Sidhartha, **1**
India Guest House, **2**
Shahjahan Hotel, **4**
Shanti Lodge, **9**

🍴 FOOD
Joney's Place, **5**
Lucky Restaurant, **3**
Shankara Vegis, **7**
Treat Restaurant, **6**
Yash Cafe, **8**

Pharmacy: Pharmacies are dotted around the major tourist areas and also cluster around Hospital Rd. and Sarojini Naidu Hospital. Some are open 24hr.

Hospital: Sarojini Naidu (S.N.) Hospital (☎361318). Hospital Rd. West of Old Agra, near Bageshwarnath Temple and Kali Masjid. **Shanti Manglik** (☎330038). Fatehabad Rd. Provides 24hr. emergency assistance and local ambulance service.

Internet: Cyberlink (☎333317). Thana Chowk, Taj Ganj. Just west of the hub at the first major crossing. Cyberlink has more computers than its rivals and is run by English-speaking staff. Rs60 per hr. Open daily 8am-11pm. **Cyber Space** (☎225532). Gopi Chand Shivare Rd. In the shopping arcade north of Zorba the Buddha, 1st fl. A good place with ISDN connections. Rs40 per hr. Open daily 10am-11pm.

Post Office: GPO (☎353674). The Mall. Opposite the tourist office. Massive and well-maintained, but notoriously inefficient. M-Sa 10am-6pm. **Postal Code:** 282001.

ACCOMMODATIONS

The area immediately south of the Taj Mahal testifies to how competition keeps prices in check. Rooms here are surprisingly cheap—except during peak times, there's no need to pay more than Rs100 for a decent double. This is where most budget travelers stay, and many cheap restaurants have sprung up to keep them watered and fed. This area also swarms with touts, con-men, and remarkably persistent rickshaw-*wallahs*. Most hotels have rooftop views of the Taj—often little more than a blurred glimpse of a marble minaret through the brown haze and electrical wires. There are, however, several good budget options outside of Taj Ganj, often closer to the real center of the city and usually a 10min. rickshaw ride from the world's most talked-about tomb. Prices vary by season; in December, the rates listed below may inflate by as much as 200%. Most check-out times are 10am.

TAJ GANJ

The best way to orient yourself is to start with the central hub, the area in front of Joney's Place; Taj Ganj splits to the north (toward the Taj), east, and west.

Hotel Sheela (☎331194 or 333074). East Gate. Just far enough from the noise of the hub without being more than a couple of minutes' walk away from the you-know-what. Strictly a no-commission, no-scams, no-rugs-or-knick-knacks zone. Pleasant rooms surround a garden patio restaurant. Singles Rs125-300; doubles Rs200-350. ❶

Shanti Lodge (☎330900), 50m on the left as you walk east from the hub. The tallest hotel in Taj Ganj, Shanti has a rooftop restaurant with a view of the Taj. The 2nd of its 2 buildings has better rooms with nice quilts and color TVs. 1st building: singles Rs80-120; doubles Rs150-200. 2nd building: singles Rs150; doubles Rs200-250. ❶

Shahjahan Hotel (☎331159). One of the oldest of the Taj Ganj budget places and still one of the more popular. The cushion-equipped rooftop chill-out area has good views of the Taj and a sunset swing. Restaurant serves the standard fare; the manager is very eager to please. Singles Rs60-120; doubles Rs150-250. ❶

Hotel Sidhartha (☎331238), 100m south of Western Gate. Clean, wall-papered rooms with sheets changed daily. Singles with attached bath Rs100; doubles Rs100-250. ❶

India Guest House (☎330909). On left side of street between the hub and the Taj, 25m from southern gates. Run by a friendly family. Rooms with twin beds from Rs30-45. ❶

CITY CENTER

Tourists Rest House (☎363961; fax 366910; dontworrychickencurry@hotmail.com). Kachahari Rd., near Meher Cinema off Gwalior Rd., northeast of the GPO. Agra's best budget deal by far—spotlessly clean rooms (with soap, toilet paper, and clean towels) around a green garden courtyard. 24hr. STD/ISD, email facilities, and a multi-lingual manager. Singles Rs95-300; doubles Rs120-350. ❶

Agra Hotel (☎363331; fax 265830). Field Marshal Cariappa Rd., within walking distance of the fort. Agra's oldest hotel still in operation (since 1926), it's beginning to show its age, but the friendly management and mellow atmosphere still make it a good deal. Attached restaurant. Singles Rs200-500; doubles Rs250-650. ❷

Hotel Akbar Inn (☎363212). 21 The Mall, halfway between Taj Ganj and the railway station. The Akbar feels a million miles away from the hassles of the outside world. Some rooms are a little small and stuffy. Singles Rs60-250; doubles Rs80-350. ❶

Pawan Hotel (☎225506). 3 Taj Rd., Sadar Bazaar. The only hotel in the main Sadar strip, this sprawling and slightly run-down hotel is well-placed for restaurants, bars, and auto-rickshaw tours of the world. All rooms have air-cooling. Singles Rs200-350, with A/C Rs500; doubles Rs250-500, with A/C Rs600-900. ❷

Hotel Sakura (☎369793). 49 Old Idgah Colony, 100m from the bus station. A fairly uninspiring place with rooms that run the gamut from luxurious to drab. The bathrooms are all very clean, however, and the hotel provides towel, soap, and toilet paper. Air-cooled singles with attached bath Rs100-350; doubles Rs150-400. ❶

Hotel Safari (☎333029). Minto Rd., opposite Hotel Swagat and near the All India Radio station. Spotless rooms, a pleasant rooftop patio, and free bicycles for those who want to cruise to the Taj (2km). Singles Rs150-250; doubles Rs300-350. ❶

◖ FOOD

Most of Agra's foreigner-friendly restaurants are clustered around Taj Ganj, Sadar Bazaar, and other tourist centers south of the old heart of town. Most travelers tend to stick to places close to (or inside) their hotels. If you simply can't face the thought of another banana pancake or plate of *dal bhat*, the best places to go for good meals are the restaurants in the five-star hotels south of Taj Ganj.

TAJ GANJ AREA

The restaurants near the Taj Mahal are notorious for poor hygiene; most who stay more than a few days get the "Agra aches," akin to "Delhi Belly." There have even been tales of restaurants deliberately poisoning guests and then pocketing a percentage of the charges levied by the dodgy doctor who helped the victim "recover." For the most part, though, you are unlikely to develop anything worse than a mild case of under-fed boredom.

Joney's Place, at the main hub of Taj Ganj. The original Taj Ganj Diner, Joney's Place has not grown much since its humble, one-table beginnings, but the place is as friendly and reliable as ever. Renowned banana *lassis* (Rs15). Breakfasts (Rs15) are also good, but the Indian dishes (Rs15-50) are somewhat variable. Open daily 5am-11pm. ❶

Yash Cafe, 75m east of the hub, next to Shanti Lodge. Red bricks, green paint, and Christmas lights make for a festive—if not just plain strange—atmosphere on this balcony restaurant. Standard menu of Western and Indian favorites. Pizza (Rs45-70) and *koftas* (Rs25-40). Open daily 7am-11pm. ❶

Shankara Vegis and The Door's Cafe, Chowk Haghzi, just east of the hub. The most popular of the rooftop gathering points. Games like Connect 4, tunes from Bob Dylan to Bob Marley, and decent views of the local all-marble dome cover up any awkward evening silences. Open daily 6am-11pm. Happy hour daily 6-7pm and 9-10pm.

Lucky Restaurant, west of the hub, near Cyberlink. A stereo and air-cooler create a temperate, unassuming atmosphere. Five-star "Danesh Farmoon," with coconut, chocolate, banana, and curd (Rs20). Open daily 6am-10:30pm. ❶

Treat Restaurant, at the Taj Ganj hub, south side, opposite Joney's Place. Tiny, wooden-benched place with four colors of light bulbs. Prompt service, dirt cheap. Serves *thalis* (Rs25-45), mini-breakfasts (Rs15), and the usual stuff. Open daily 6am-10:30pm. ❶

CITY CENTER

Deepee Veg. Restaurant, 1 Gwalior Rd., in the Meher Cinema complex. Part of the Dasaprakash family of high-quality, international restaurants, Deepee serves up excellent South Indian veg. meals and desserts. Well worth the fun atmosphere and unobtrusive service. Filling *thalis* Rs80-100. Open daily 10am-10:45pm. ❷

Zorba the Buddha, Gopi Chand Shivare Rd. In the shopping arcade north of the main part of Sadar Bazaar. Tiny, A/C dining room decked with photos of meditation meister Osho. No smoking, no meat, no hassles. Popular with the Euro-tourist crowd. Most dishes Rs60-120. Open daily noon-3pm and 6-9pm; closed May 1-July 5. ❷

The Park (Restaurant), Sadar Bazaar, just to the left of the main Sadar Bazaar strip. Airy, A/C dining room with tables set far apart on the marble floor. Listen to hits from 1980s flicks while deciding between Chinese and continental standards and excellent Indian food. *Dum aloo kashmiri* Rs60, spaghetti from Rs50. Open daily 9am-11pm. ❶

Lakshmi Villas, Taj Rd., just east of The Park Restaurant and the main strip of Sadar Bazaar. The only restaurant in town with a jewelry store in the foyer. Busy Lakshmi offers good South Indian veg. without fuss. Service is speedy for the 23 different *dosas* (Rs26-48) and a variety of milkshakes (Rs35-40). Open daily 7am-11pm. ❶

Priya Restaurant, behind Hotel Ratan Deep, off Fatehabad Rd. Large dining hall with kitschy posters of Plywood stars. Tasty Indian fare (from Rs60) including a Shah Jahan *thole* (Rs280) that could feed the royal tigers for a week. Open daily 7am-11pm. ❷

⦿ SIGHTS

While Agra contains several interesting monuments from the heyday of Mughal rule, most tourists come to see that marble jewel in India's crown, the Taj Mahal. Capitalizing on one of the most famous buildings in the world, the money-hungry folks at the Agra Development Authority and similarly minded bureaucrats at the archaeological survey of India have increased admission prices over the past two years, and so many a penny-pinching backpacker has had to settle for squinting rooftop views of the city's big draws. The Taj and the Fort both do not allow re-entry, so make the most of your one visit. Most sights charge Rs25 for cameras.

TAJ MAHAL

Open Sa-Th 6am-7:30. Rs500 for entry plus US$10 for foreigners.

Despite all the hype and hoopla, the sheer beauty of the place is so overwhelming that no amount of overexposure can diminish it. Especially at dawn and dusk, even the most jaded of globe-trotters often find themselves smiling in wonder as they behold the Taj. Emblazoned across the signs of a million-and-one restaurants, T-shirts, and biscuit tins the world over, this marble prima donna, unofficially crowned by her ardent fans as "the most beautiful building in the world," remains undeniably India's ultimate must-see.

The tale of the Taj is a sad, sweet love story. When he became Mughal emperor in 1628, Shah Jahan brought to the throne a great many virtues, among them intellect, political acumen, and a passion for fine architecture. Three years after becoming emperor, Shah Jahan received news that broke his heart: after 18 years of marriage, his favorite wife, Arjumand Banu Begum, had died giving birth to their 14th child. In his grief, Shah Jahan decided that his beloved should be buried in a tomb of timeless beauty. As the Bengali poet Rabindranath Tagore said, the Taj Mahal was designed to be a "tear [that] would hang on the cheek of time."

Work on the Taj began in 1632, one year after the death of Arjumand Banu Begum. Marble was quarried in Makrana, Rajasthan, and precious stones were brought to Agra from Yemen, Russia, China, and Central Asia. Architects were sent over from Persia, and French and Italian master craftsmen had a hand in decorating the building. In all, nearly 20,000 people worked non-stop on the construction of the Taj. By the time the tomb was completed in 1653, a great many things had changed—the Mughal capital had been moved from Agra to Delhi, the deceased Arjumand Banu Begum had become popularly known as "Mumtaz Mahal" ("Elect of the Palace"), and one of Shah Jahan's sons, Aurangzeb, had come to power. In 1658, Aurangzeb staged a coup, violently surmounting the opposition of his three brothers and imprisoning his father in Agra Fort. Shah Jahan lived out his days under house arrest, staring out across the Yamuna River at the Taj Mahal. When the deposed emperor died in the winter of 1666, his body was buried next to his wife's.

The path to the Taj from the original entry arch (now the exit) is one of the most well-designed architectural approaches in the world. The tomb building and the four principal minarets rest on a large pedestal of white marble. Up close, the Taj is hardly white at all: delicately inlaid precious stones create meandering floral patterns framed by elegant Arabic script (it is said that the entire Qur'an is written on the walls of the Taj). While much of the tomb's interior is off-limits, visitors can enter the dimly lit, domed chamber that contains the cenotaphs of Shah Jahan and Mumtaz Mahal; the latter is inscribed with the 99 names of Allah. The tombs themselves lie directly below in a room not accessible to the public. The **mosque** is to the west and the **Jawab** ("Answer"), its architectural mirror, is to the east. A popular local myth has it that Shah Jahan planned to construct a second Taj of black marble, to the north, on the other side of the Yamuna river. A small **museum** on the west side of the gardens showcases paintings of Shah Jahan and Mumtaz Mahal and some other curios, but few take the time to visit it. *(Open Sa-Th 10am-5pm. Rs2.)*

If you prefer a serene, private audience, show up at dawn—you'll have the place practically to yourself. At other times, the monument is crawling with tourists and security guards. Changing light patterns throughout the day affect the experience of viewing the Taj.

AGRA FORT

To the west of Yamuna Kinara Rd., 1½km up river from the Taj Mahal. Open daily sunrise-sunset. Rs50 for entry +US$10 for foreigners. With a Taj Mahal ticket US$10.

There aren't nearly as many restaurants named after Agra's fort, but it's a close second to the Taj on most visitors' check-list itineraries. Construction began under Emperor Akbar in 1565. Its fortifications were gradually strengthened over the years—the 2½km bulky, red sandstone walls that enclose it were not completed until the time of Emperor Aurangzeb. Of the three outer gates that lead through the walls and into the fort, only the **Amar Singh Gate**, decorated with colorful glazed tiles, is accessible to the public. The gate is named for the Rajasthani maharaja who killed the royal treasurer before the emperor's eyes and then jumped from the walls here in 1644 to escape the guards.

Due north of the Amar Singh Gate is the breezy **Diwan-i-Am** (Hall of Public Audience), a low three-sided structure that served as Shah Jahan's court while Agra was the Mughal capital. At the height of Agra's Mughal fame, the Diwan-i-Am was filled with nobles, courtiers, and regal accoutrements. Shah Jahan's throne sat on the platform at the east side of the hall. The low marble platform in front of the throne was reserved for his chief minister. The tomb at the center of the courtyard is that of a British officer who was killed here during the Mutiny of 1857.

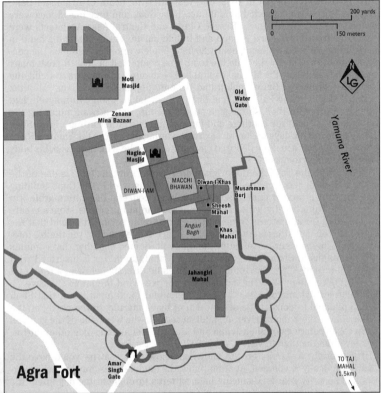

The **royal chambers** are between the eastern end of Diwan-i-Am and Agra Fort's ramparts; here the emperor's many needs were seen to in private. He also slept and prayed here from time to time. From Diwan-i-Am, the first chamber is the expansive **Michal Bhavan** (Fish Palace), which gets its name from the stock that was dumped into its water channels so that the emperor could amuse himself with rod and reel. Unfortunately, the chamber is missing blocks of mosaic work, and huge chunks of the royal bath have been pillaged over the centuries. In the northwest corner of the Michal Bhavan (left as you face away from Diwan-i-Am) is the **Nagina Masjid** (Gem Mosque), built by Shah Jahan for the women of his harem.

Southeast of the Macchi Bhavan is the fabulous **Diwan-i-Khas** (Hall of Private Audience), completed in 1637, where the emperor would receive visitors. The **terrace** just east of Diwan-i-Khas offers classic views over the Yamuna to the Taj Mahal. Just south of the terrace is the two-story **Musamman Burj** (Octagonal Tower), which features delicate inlay work. Legend has it that Shah Jahan spent his final hours here, as a prisoner, gazing wistfully at his Taj Mahal, which was reflected in mirrors positioned at every angle in his cell. The emperor, meanwhile, is said to have enjoyed watching as men, tigers, and elephants were pitted against one another in the cramped area between the inner and outer walls.

Heading south from the tower, it's a hop, skip, and a jump to the **Sheesh Mahal** (Palace of Mirrors), where the women of the court bathed. South of the Sheesh Mahal is an enclosure that includes the **Anguri Bagh** (Vine Garden). On the east side of the garden are three buildings. The **Khas Mahal** (Private Palace) is at the center, flanked by the **Golden Pavilions.** Rendered in cool marble, the Khas Mahal is supposedly where the emperor slept. The pavilions were women's bedrooms, with walls discreetly packed with jewelry. Note the pavilions' roofs, which were built to resemble roofs of Bengali thatched huts. The **Jehangir Mahal,** the large sandstone palace to the south, was designed for the Hindu queen Jodh Bai. In front of the palace is a large tub, thought to have been where Queen Nur Jahan took her baths.

OTHER SIGHTS

JAMA MASJID. The Jama Masjid (Friday Mosque), Agra's main mosque, is 100m west of Agra Fort Railway Station. Built in 1648 by Shah Jahan, out of sandstone spliced with ornamental marble in a big-zag pattern, the mosque complex was damaged during the Mutiny of 1857, when British forces deemed its main gate a threat to the strategically important Red Fort; the gate was promptly leveled along with some of the front cloisters of the mosque. For a while during the uprising, the Jama Masjid was, in a sense, held hostage—the mosque was planted with explosives, and the British authorities loudly proclaimed that if the Mutiny gained a large enough following in Agra, the Jama Masjid would suffer the consequences. The building remained standing, though it is in pretty bad shape today.

ITIMAD-UD-DAULAH. The so-called "Baby Taj," the Itimad-ud-Daulah, is a small, all-marble tomb that is always less crowded although possibly just as exquisite as its rival down the river. The tomb was built between 1622 and 1628 for Ghiyas Beg, a Persian diplomat who served as Emperor Jehangir's chief minister and was dubbed Itimad-ud-Daulah (Pillar of Government) for his exemplary service. Set in an intimate garden, the demolished tomb was designed by Ghiyas Beg himself but built by his daughter Nur Jahan, whom Jehangir married in 1611. The dazzling, semi-precious stone inlay work on white marble is perhaps the most beautiful in Agra. Several of Nur Jahan's relatives were subsequently buried in the central tomb. *(Cross the second bridge over the Yamuna and head north 300m; the tomb is on the left. Open daily sunrise to sunset. Foreigner entrance fee US$5 plus Rs10 tax).*

CHINI-KA-RAUZA AND RAM BAGH. Six hundred meters north of Itimad-ud-Daulah is the **Chini-ka-Rauza** (China Tomb), the decayed burial chamber of Shah Jahan's chief minister, Afzal Khan. Glazed tiles once covered the entire construction—the few that remain are severely dulled and weathered. *(Open daily sunrise to sunset. Free.)* Two hundred meters farther north and past the bridge intersection is **Ram Bagh,** a three-tiered garden said to have been designed by Babur. Once an amorous playground with water wheels and baths, today the grounds are an unimpressive tangle of weeds and stone. Only a few locals and some peacocks find the ruins a worthwhile respite. *(Open daily sunrise to sunset. Foreigner entrance fee US$5.)*

🔖 DAYTRIP FROM AGRA: SIKANDRA

A small town just outside Agra, Sikandra is famous as the home of **Akbar's Tomb.** Mughal emperor from 1556 to 1605, Akbar was a great patron of the arts and a respectful admirer of Hinduism. The most impressive structure at the complex is the **Buland Darwaza** (Gateway of Magnificence), embellished with geometric patterns and Qur'anic inscriptions. The central mausoleum is sparsely adorned with colonnaded alcoves and marble domes. A narrow passageway leads down to the remarkably simple crypt itself, with its flickering candlelight and smoking sticks of incense. The dome is a wonder of acoustics, and echoes reverberate for 10 seconds or more. Mornings and evening are less crowded, while the rest of the time the joint jumps with the usual mix of hawkers, hustlers, and picnickers. The grassy area between the northern wall of the mausoleum and the wall that encloses the entire complex is an interesting place—monkeys, deer, and peacocks enhance the architectural grandeur of the tomb. Resist the temptation to feed the animals, since they can be dangerous, especially when grabbing for food. People have been mauled by monkeys here. Sikandra is accessible by **auto-rickshaw** (Rs80-100 round-trip from Agra) or by one of the **buses** bound for Mathura, which board at the station and along Mathura Rd. *(Open daily dawn-dusk. Rs10 entry fee plus US$10.)*

FATEHPUR SIKRI फ़तेहपुर सीकरी ☎ 05613

Emperor Akbar, who ruled the Mughal empire from 1556 to 1605, was a man who had almost—but not quite—everything. Nothing could satisfy his most sought after wish: a male heir to succeed him. In time, Akbar became desperate and left Agra to wander across North India in search of help. His quest brought him to the village of Sikri, where he came across a Sufi mystic named Shaykh Salim Chishti, who consoled the ruler and promised him no fewer than three sons. When, a year

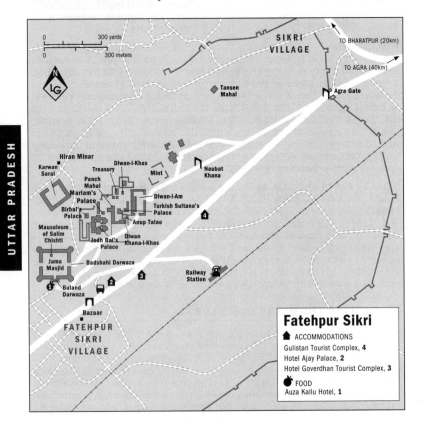

Fatehpur Sikri

🏠 ACCOMMODATIONS
Gulistan Tourist Complex, **4**
Hotel Ajay Palace, **2**
Hotel Goverdhan Tourist Complex, **3**

🍴 FOOD
Auza Kallu Hotel, **1**

later, the first foretold son arrived, Akbar repaid the saint by naming his son Salim (the future emperor Jehangir) and moving the entire court close to the saint's village of Sikri. To the surprise of the population of Agra, the palace of Fatehpur Sikri became the new capital of the Mughal empire.

Palaces, mosques, and battlements were hastily constructed, and Fatehpur Sikri served as the Mughal center for 15 years before the court shifted back to Agra. Exactly what made them return to Agra remains uncertain. Some say that drought forced the Mughals out, while others claim that the death of Shaykh Salim prompted the move. In any case, the decision left a pristine ghost-palace and abandoned city behind. Fatehpur Sikri casts a haunting spell on visitors, especially at dawn and dusk, as sunlight and shadows whirl across the barren palace buildings.

TRANSPORTATION AND PRACTICAL INFORMATION

Vehicles drive into Fatehpur Sikri from an access to the east of the palace complex. The deserted city is on a hilltop overlooking the modern village of Sikri to the south. From the bus or train stations, it's a 5min. walk up the hill to the ruins. **Buses** head to **Agra** (1hr., every 30min. 5:30am-7:30pm, Rs17) and **Bharatpur** (1hr., every hr., Rs11). **Trains** run daily to **Agra** (5:30 and 10:35am, 4:40pm, Rs8; express 8:20pm, Rs20). For **currency exchange,** head back to Agra or ask at one of the hotels.

ACCOMMODATIONS AND FOOD

Everything in Fatehpur Sikri is within walking distance of the palace. In peak season (Oct.-Mar.), hotels fill up, and prices may rise by 25%. The best budget option in town is the **Hotel Ajay Palace ❶**, just to the left as you come out of the bus station, which offers four very clean rooms. (☎882950. Singles with attached bath Rs75-100; doubles Rs150.) Down the road that heads toward Agra, on the right-hand side just before the turn-off for the railway station, the **Hotel Goverdhan Tourist Complex ❶** has spacious rooms and a friendly manager; amenities include towels, air coolers, and some TVs. (☎882643. Dorms Rs50; doubles Rs100-350.) East of the Goverdhan, 1km from the ruins, UP Tourism's **Gulistan Tourist Complex ❸** has luxurious rooms at luxurious prices, as well as a swanky restaurant around a gloomy bar. (☎882490. Singles Rs525-775; doubles Rs575-900. Off season discounts April-Sept.) For food, the restaurant in **Hotel Ajay Palace ❶** is your best bet. Homemade cheese and mineral-water ice put this place in a different league from roadside joints (Kashmiri *kofta* Rs40). The restaurant at the **Gulistan Tourist Complex ❸** has large lunch and dinner buffets (Rs260). Of the several stalls by the main gate to the old city compound, try the **Auza Kallu Hotel ❶**, in front of the gate (*thalis* Rs30-75).

SIGHTS

All sights open daily dawn to dusk. Entrance fee US$10.

Wherever tourists and their buses congregate, so do **guides** eager to offer tours of the deserted palace. Many of these "guides" falsely claim to be licensed; others insist they are students whose "duty" it is to show you around, only afterward whining for *baksheesh* or leading you into their handicraft shops. Ask to see proper ID. Official guides should charge around Rs40-50 for a tour of the monuments. Guides are rarely informative and the sandstone signposts can usually tell you more than they will.

UTTAR PRADESH

Coming from the east, you'll pass the **Naubat Khana** (Drum House), which was used to signal the emperor's arrival, and the ticket office for the palace complex. A path leads around into the **Diwan-i-Am,** the court where, from a throne between two sandstone slates, the emperor would hear the pleas and petitions of common men. To the west toward the throne is the main palace courtyard. To the right is the **Diwan-i-Khas** (Hall of Private Audience), where Akbar is thought to have met with VIPs and relatives. The hall is a massive chamber supported in the middle by one ornate column shaped like a budding flower. To the left is a meticulously carved gazebo, probably the sitting chamber of either the treasurer or royal astrologer.

On the south side of the courtyard is a tank called **Anup Talao,** the choice venue of legendary Mughal crooner Miyan Tansen (see also **Come On Baby, Fight My Fire,** p. 385). Finely carved columns and walls decorate the nearby **Turkish Sultana's Palace.** Near Anup Talao to the north stands the royal **banquet hall.** To the south of the tank sits **Diwan Khana-i-Khas,** the emperor's chambers. The whole courtyard is dominated by the five-story **Panch Mahal** tower that looms to the west of the Diwan-i-Khas. Steps lead up through scores of intricately carved stone columns to the fifth floor. Tourist access to the tower goes no farther than the base, however. The path from Panch Mahal leads west to the middle of another courtyard, which contains **Mariam's Palace,** once home to Akbar's Christian wife, where faded wall paintings are left over from the palace's glory days.

From Mariam's Palace, proceed south and cut right to the entrance of **Jodh Bai's Palace,** one of Fatehpur Sikri's largest and most evocative buildings. In the courtyard, symmetrical patterns and sandstone flowers carved into the walls surround a central fountain. This complex was probably used for the emperor's harem. Note the azure glazed tiles on the roof along the second story. Behind Jodh Bai's Palace is the **haremsara,** which once housed the palace's many servants and attendants. Nearby **Birbal's Palace** was the residence of either the minister's daughters or one of Akbar's queens. Leaving the palace complex and heading down past the Karen Saria, a path leads to the **Iran Minor,** a 22m tower with protruding tusk-shaped stones. The minaret was built as the memorial tomb for Akbar's favorite elephant, Iran. The 360° view from the top makes the dark and difficult climb worthwhile.

At the far western end of the complex, near the village, the base of the **Buland Darwaza** sits 13m above street level, and its gate stands 40m above that, making it the tallest doorway in Asia. The gate was added to the complex in 1595, following Akbar's triumph in Gujarat, and its style was copied in other Victory Gates around the country. As you pass through the gate, take off your shoes. The head of the **Jama Masjid** is off to the left, facing Mecca. In the middle is the pure white **mausoleum** of Shaykh Salim Chishti, the sage who prophesied the birth of Akbar's sons. The core of the tomb is made from mother-of-pearl. Visitors hoping for Shaykh Salim to intercede on *their* behalf hang threads from the marble latticework on the walls inside. Incense sticks burn inside the tomb, and musicians sometimes sit and play outside. Next to the mausoleum is a series of royal cenotaphs. The tiny white one holds the remains of the royal pigeon. The **Buddhas Darwaza** leads out of the courtyard; across the parking lot is the western end of the palace complex.

MATHURA मथुरा
AND VRINDABAN वृन्दावन ☎ 0565

The ancient, cultured city of Mathura, once known as the "Athens of India," is best known today as the temple-loaded birthplace of Krishna. Countless pilgrims come here every year for **Krishna Jayanti** (Aug. 31, 2002), the celebration of Krishna's birth, to pay homage to the blue-skinned hero of Hindu lore. Even outside the main festival season, Mathura hums with holiness. Thousands of pilgrims and priests crowd the city, mingling saffron and incense with the dust and grime of the streets.

While Mathura draws its fair share of devotees, the main religious center of this area is the nearby pilgrimage town of Vrindaban, where Krishna performed the deeds that made him famous: lifting up Mt. Govardhan, jamming on his flute, and cavorting with all the *gopis* (milkmaids) he could find. Krishna's favorite *gopi* Radha is also revered here; her name is painted on walls throughout the town, and residents greet each other with a jubilant "Radhe Radhe!" Ever since the Bengali teacher Chaitanya discovered the site's importance, Vrindaban has been a huge draw for pilgrims, whose ashrams are maintained by wealthy devotees and ISKCON, the International Society for Krishna Consciousness (Hare Krishnas). Devotees most prominently show their love for Krishna during Holi (Mar. 28, 2002), the Festival of Colors, when they satiate his playful spirit by throwing colored powder and water at each other. Watch out for mischievous monkeys: they grab for food and have been known to snatch eyeglasses from peoples' faces. Mathura and Vrindaban make an easy 1-2 day stopover between Delhi and Agra.

▐ TRANSPORTATION

Trains: Mathura Junction Station is a chaotic, non-English-speaking place 1½km south of the State Bank of India. To: **Agra** (45min.-1½hr., 17-20 per day 3:55am-11:44pm, Rs23); **Delhi** (3-5hr., 21-23 per day round the clock, Rs42); **Gwalior** (3-4hr., 9-11 per day 7:40am-11:44pm, Rs51); **Jhansi** (4-6hr., 8 per day 7:40am-11:44pm, Rs107); **Mumbai** (16-27hr., 5-6 per day 7:40am-12:10am, Rs329).

Buses: From the **new bus stand,** buses head every hr. or so (most frequent 6am-10:30pm) to: **Agra** (2hr., Rs23); **Bharatpur** (1hr., Rs19); **Delhi** (4hr., Rs68); **Jaipur** (6hr., every 30min. 5am-10:30pm, Rs95). From the **old bus stand,** UP Roadways buses head to **Haridwar** (10pm, 8hr., Rs155) and **Varanasi** (16hr., 6:30pm, Rs250).

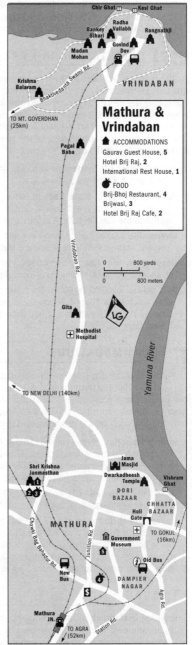

Mathura & Vrindaban

▲ ACCOMMODATIONS
Gaurav Guest House, **5**
Hotel Brij Raj, **2**
International Rest House, **1**

🍎 FOOD
Brij-Bhoj Restaurant, **4**
Brijwasi, **3**
Hotel Brij Raj Cafe, **2**

Local Transportation: Stretch **tempos** cruise from the New Bus Stand to Vrindaban (Rs5) and around town, as do **cycle-** and **auto-rickshaws** (Rs100 to Vrindaban). **Horse-drawn wagons** also peruse the streets and cost about the same as cycle-rickshaws.

■ ◪ ORIENTATION AND PRACTICAL INFORMATION

At the heart of Mathura is the bazaar, stretching north from **Holi Gate,** in the eastern part of town near the Yamuna River. The **old bus stand** is 500m south of Holi Gate, and the more frequently used **new bus stand** is on Chowki Bag Bahadur Rd., about 500m northwest of the State Bank of India. The town's most important landmark is the temple **Shri Krishna Janmasthan (Janmabhoomi),** built on the site of Krishna's birth, 2km northwest of the new bus stand. Vrindaban is 15km north of Mathura on the banks of the Yamuna.

Tourist Office: UP Tourism (☎405351), in the back, northwest corner of the old bus stand, 2nd fl. Open M-Sa 10am-5pm.

Currency Exchange: State Bank of India (☎407647). Junction Rd. crossing. Changes US and UK currency and traveler's checks. Open M-F 10am-4pm. SBI runs an extension branch at the ISKCON temple in Vrindaban.

Market: The **bazaar,** selling everything from chutneys to drums, extends just south and a long way north of Holi Gate. There is a **fruit market** next to the Jama Masjid.

Hospital: District Hospital (☎403006 or 500986), just north of the old bus stand. **Methodist Hospital,** Jaising Pura, Vrindaban Rd. (☎406032 or 730043).

Post Office: The GPO (☎403981) is 2km south of the old bus stand in the Civil Lines area. Open M-Sa 10am-4:30pm. There are more convenient branches in Vikas Bazaar, between the old bus stand and Holi Gate, and at the Shri Krishna Janmasthan complex. **Postal Code:** 281001.

▶ ACCOMMODATIONS

In Mathura, there are small restaurants, a few basic hotels, and tea stalls near the Shri Krishna Janmasthan for mid-worship munchies. The area around Holi Gate is the liveliest and noisiest part of town. Mathura has a few **ashrams,** including the **Keshvjee Gaudig,** opposite the district hospital (Rs30 per room). In Vrindaban, the only lodging options are ashrams, and the restaurant scene is not well developed.

International Rest House (☎423714), At the eastern end of the Shri Krishna complex. Cheap, simple rooms for pilgrims, as well as a garden where they can kick up their heels. Attached restaurant open 11am-3pm and 6:30-10:30pm for a "pious lunch and dinner." Singles Rs50; doubles Rs50-150. ❶

Hotel Brij Raj (☎424172), opposite Shri Krishna temple. Large, clean, rooms around a courtyard within chanting range of Krishna's birthplace. Doubles Rs200-450. ❶

Gaurav Guest House (☎406192). From the government museum traffic circle, head 100m south down the road with the cupola at its end. Look for the unmarked, blue and white hotel down an alley on the left. Uninspiring but clean rooms far from the temple ruckus. Singles Rs150-300; doubles Rs250-350. The **Gaurav Boarding House,** next door, offers more luxurious rooms. Singles Rs400-750; doubles Rs500-850. ❶

◪ FOOD

Brij-Bhoj Restaurant, inside Hotel Mansarovar Palace, 200m east of the State Bank of India. The cold interior is a welcome respite from the heat outside. Fine breakfasts Rs15-100, *paneer khoya* Rs55. Open daily 7am-midnight. ❶

Hotel Brij Raj Cafe, opposite the Shri Krisna complex, below and next to Hotel Brij Raj. Good *thalis* (Rs20), ice cream treats, and fresh coffee. Open daily 9am-11pm. ❶

Cyber Cafe, just south of Holi Gate. No computers yet, but an intimate cellar with hanging lamps and clay plates sets the ambiance for almost-romantic pizza (Rs50-80) and Chinese (Rs30-50) dinners. South Indian dishes Rs 20-50. Open daily 10am-10pm. ❶

Brijwasi, opposite the Shri Krishna temple, with another branch near Holi Gate. No real eats, but oodles of sweets. Open daily 7am-11pm.

🗲 SIGHTS

MATHURA

SHRI KRISHNA JANMASTHAN TEMPLE. Most of the sights in Mathura revolve around Krishna, whose birth here has given this otherwise unremarkable town its status as one of the holiest places in India. The most important site for pilgrims is the constantly buzzing Shri Krishna Janmasthan temple complex, which marks the spot of Krishna's appearance—the original temple, Kesava Deo, was destroyed by Aurangzeb and replaced with a mosque. The similar histories of the temples here and at the birthplace of Rama in Ayodhya have made the authorities particularly cautious—visitors must check all belongings (bags, cameras, etc.) at the cloakroom off to the left, pass through a metal detector, and undergo a zealous frisking. Scattered around the towering temple and amongst the souvenir shops are several small temples and shrines. The most important of these, at the back right side of the complex, is a small, dimly lit room believed to mark the exact site of Krishna's birth. The room is designed to represent the prison cell where the joyous god was born while the nefarious King Kamsa held his parents captive. Barbed wire and uniformed guards with guns stand around the complex between the temple and the mosque with its green and white domes. Back out the main gate and up the road is **Potara Kund,** where baby Krishna's diapers were supposedly washed. *(A straight, 1½km shot west from Holi Gate. Open daily 5am-noon and 4-9pm.)*

OTHER SIGHTS. The **Government Museum** houses a large collection of ancient Indian sculpture. Its pieces help shed light on Mathura's overall religious and cultural significance—for nearly 1200 years it was the artistic center for early Indian and visiting Hellenistic cultures. The museum contains several excellent examples of the mottled red sandstone sculpture for which the area is famous. *(600m west of the old bus stand. Open daily 10:30am-4:30pm. Rs25.)* Mathura's other attractions are on the east side of town. As you head north from the bazaar, the **Dwarkadheesh Temple** is 500m up on the left. Built in 1814 by local merchants, this temple is the main point of worship for local Hindus. The building's glossy, colorful exterior only hints at the decadence within; sparkling shrines, trickling fountains, and a trail of embedded coins brighten the interior. *(Open daily 6:30-10:30am and 4-7pm.)* Just 100m south of Dori Bazaar, the street forks off to the right toward the river and the sacred **Vishram Ghat,** where Krishna came to rest after slaying the menacing King Kamsa, and where many priests, guides, and beggars now congregate. From the *ghats,* **boats** take visitors on an overpriced, hour-long tour of the city's shore (Rs80-100), with a prime view of the dilapidated **Sati Bur,** built in 1570 and dedicated to the *sati* of Behari Mal. Sunset boat trips offer a unique view of the nightly *arati* ceremony, when priests bring fire to the sacred water amid the sound of gongs. The **Jama Masjid,** Mathura's main mosque, was built by Abo-in Nabir Khan in 1661. The mosque is unusually colorful, its teal and white facade brightening up the already striking bazaar and fruit market. *(A 1km walk northwest on the main road from Holi Gate through the bazaar.)*

UTTAR PRADESH

VRINDABAN

KRISHNA BALARAM TEMPLE. None of the holy places in Vrindaban draws more foreigners than the Krishna Balram Temple, the dazzling marble house of worship built by **ISKCON,** the International Society for Krishna Consciousness. The founder of the society, Srila Prabhupada, lived and worked here before embarking at the advanced age of 69 on a world tour to spread the word of "Krishna Consciousness." As you enter, the shrine to the left, with its curved marble staircase, houses a golden, life-sized replica of the *swami* sitting eternally peaceful over the site of his burial. An international congregation of Hare Krishnas mingles here and around the two other shrines, all extremely eager to chat with newcomers. The temple echoes throughout the day with the sounds of chants, drums, and clicking beads, though the pervasive atmosphere of serenity somehow manages to rise above all the chaos and commotion. *(Temple open daily in summer 4:30am-8:45pm, in winter 3:30am-8:15pm, with periodic breaks for meals.)* The Hare Krishnas serve a free meal of *dal* and rice mush in front of the temple at 10am and 5pm. There is also a **guest house ❷,** (☎442478) offering 45 clean doubles with attached baths (Rs200-500). The temple is likely to be full during August, September, and March. An attached **restaurant ❶** offers clean, sit-down dining, decent *thalis* (Rs40-60), and some Western fare. *(Open daily 8am-9:30pm.)* Outside the guest house, a small **museum** dedicated to Prabhupada displays the *swami's* rooms as he kept them, including books, clothes, jars of vaseline, and other bits of holy paraphernalia he used while still contained within his mortal body. *(Museum open daily 9:30am-1pm and 4:30-8:30pm. Free.)*

OTHER SIGHTS. In many of the town's temples, the original idols were removed to Jaipur when Aurangzeb attacked in 1670. Since the temples were pillaged by Muslims some are no longer considered fit for worship. Those that still invite worshippers are often brimming with pilgrims and closed to non-Hindus, making temple-touring a difficult undertaking. The large, thick-walled **Govind Dev Temple** is one of the oldest in Vrindaban. It lacks the characteristic *gopuram* of most temples, and the top four stories were destroyed by Aurangzeb and never replaced. *(Open daily 6am-noon and 4-8pm.)* One hundred meters northeast of the Govind Dev is the **Rangnathji Temple,** India's longest at over 200m. Seth Govind Das combined Rajput and South Indian designs when he built the temple in 1851. The 15m **Dhwaja Stambha,** the central column, is said to be plated in gold. Non-Hindus are not permitted inside, but can catch a glimpse through the back (eastern) entrance. Among the other more notable temples in Vrindaban, the **Madan Mohan Temple,** on the banks of the Yamuna, near Kali Ghat, has a small shrine in the base of its 19m sandstone tower, which is colored by a good amount of vegetation. Other popular sights include the dilapidated **Radha Vallabh Temple,** dating from 1626, and **Bankey Bihari,** literally "crooked Krishna," which is probably the most popular of Vrindaban's many temples. *(Open daily 9am-noon and 6-9pm.)* Launch off from **Chir Ghat** for a **boat ride** on the Yamuna river (Rs60-100). Evening cruises are especially picturesque, as the sun sets behind the glowing skyline of Vrindaban accompanied by the mellow *bhajans* echoing through its tangled streets.

LUCKNOW लखनऊ ☎ 0522

Although cycle-rickshaws and noisy scooters now screech and career their way through modern city streets overflowing with tires and stereo parts, Lucknow remains a city indelibly marked by its past. The skyline is dominated by crumbling monuments, attesting to the opulence of the nawab aristocracy of centuries past. Amid the ruins stand 10-story-high cement office buildings, as well as battered souvenirs of the British Raj. Now the capital of UP, Lucknow catapulted to its current status after it became the capital of Avadh in 1775. The local nawab rulers, keen to assert the authority they had recently wrested from the Mughals, embarked on a series of ambitious building projects that soon thrust Lucknow forward to challenge Delhi and Calcutta for the title of India's most sparkling city. Before long, the British reduced the nawabs to mere puppet rulers, though Lucknow continued to flourish under their patronage as a major center of Muslim poetry, music, and architecture. The British formally annexed Avadh in 1856, citing as their mandate the alleged "incompetence to rule" of the last nawab, Wajid Ali Shah, whom they accused of being a "debauched and capricious" king who squandered his wealth on courtesans. The nawab was sent into exile in Calcutta, and the ensuing British take-over was one of the sparks that ignited the Indian Mutiny the following year. The 1857 siege of the Lucknow Residency during the uprisings was to loom large in British legend until Independence.

Since Partition, when many of the city's Muslims fled to Pakistan, Lucknow's status as a major center of Muslim culture has come to an end, though many traditions live on. Local products such as *chikan* embroidery and *attar* perfume (see **Sniffing the Subcontinental Sublime,** below) endure, and it is still common to see signs written in Urdu rather than Hindi. The Muslim religious presence also survives; the most important event in Lucknow's religious calendar continues to be the Shi'a Muslim commemoration of Muharram (March 15, 2002)—a mourning for the martyrdom of Imam Husain (grandson of the Prophet) and his 72 companions. During the celebration, marchers wail laments as they carry replicas of Husain's tomb to the fire-walking ceremonies that take place in the *imambaras*.

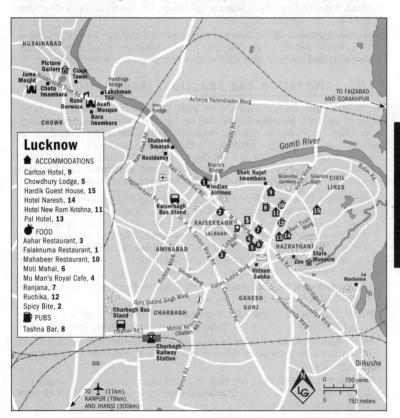

☞ TRANSPORTATION

Flights: Amousi Airport (☎436132 or 436327). 11 km from Charbagh. **Indian Airlines** (☎220927 or 224618), in the Clark's Avadh Hotel. Flies to: **Calcutta** (2½hr.; M, W, F, Su 7:20pm; US$160); **Delhi** (1hr., 1-4 per day US$95); **Mumbai** (3½hr., daily 5:20pm, US$255); **Patna** (1hr., daily 6:20 and 7:20pm, US$105); **Varanasi** (40min., daily 10:10am, US$75).

Trains: Charbagh Railway Station, Charbagh, 3km from Hazratganj. A rickshaw from the station to Hazratganj should cost around Rs15. To: **Agra** (6-15hr., 2-3 per day 10:15am-midnight, Rs120); **Allahabad** (4-8½hr., 4 per day 6am-10:25pm, Rs95); **Delhi** (6½-9hr., at least 12 per day 5:30am-1:30am, A/C chair Rs675); **Faizabad** (3-4hr., 7-8 per day 3:20am-7pm, Rs40); **Gorakhpur** (5-7hr., 11-15 per day Rs111); **Varanasi** (5-13hr., 7-8 per day 3:20am-11:15pm, Rs123).

Buses: The **Charbagh bus stand** is on Station Rd. From the railway station, walk to the main road. Take a left; the station is 300m down on the right. To: **Agra** (10hr., 7 per day 4:30-10:30pm, Rs153); **Allahabad** (5hr., every hr. 3:30am-10:30pm, Rs96); **Ayodhya** (4hr., every 30min. 5am-midnight, Rs60); **Delhi** (12hr., 7 per day 3:30-8:30pm, Rs216); **Faizabad** (3½hr., every 30min. 5am-midnight, Rs57); **Gorakhpur** (8hr., every 30min. 5am-midnight, Rs117); **Varanasi** (5 per day 6am-10pm, Rs120). The **Kaiserbagh bus stand,** northwest of Hazratganj, near the high court, is the main departure point for buses to **Delhi** (12hr., every hr. Rs213).

Local Transportation: Shared **taxis** and **tempos** run from Charbagh to Hazratganj and as far as Husainabad and usually cost about Rs4. City **buses** also ply the routes for Rs2-3. **Auto-rickshaws** are found mostly by the railway station and charge exorbitant prices.

☀ ❼ ORIENTATION AND PRACTICAL INFORMATION

Lucknow occupies the south bank of the **Gomti River** and extends far inland. In the center of the city is **Mahatma Gandhi (MG) Rd.** (referred to by locals as **Hazratganj**), along which are several bookstores, the police station, and most of the city's restaurants and shops. To the northwest is **Husainabad**, where many of the monuments are located. The main bus and railway stations are in the area of **Charbagh** to the southwest of Hazratganj. The areas of **Hazratganj, Husainabad,** and **Charbagh** form a sort of triangle around **Kaiserbagh** and **Aminabad,** an old bazaar area.

Tourist Office: UP Regional Tourist Office (☎638105). 10 Station Rd. From the intersection of Station Rd. and Vidhan Sabha Marg, head down Station Rd. 100m towards the railway station; the office is at the end of the alley just before the stationery store. Open M-Sa 10am-5pm. The **Tourist Reception Centre** (☎636173) inside the railway station is almost useless for foreigners. Open daily 24hr. **UP Tours** (☎212659), in Hotel Gomti, runs daily tours of the city on non-A/C buses (9:45am-2:15pm, Rs75). There must be at least 5 people for the tour to take place.

Currency Exchange: Bank of Baroda (☎202625). MG Rd. Opposite the turn-off onto Lalbagh Rd. Open M-F 10:30am-2:30pm and 3-4pm.

Market: Main bazaars at **Aminabad, Hazratganj,** and **Chowk.** Aminabad is a short rickshaw ride from Hazratganj (Rs15); Chowk is twice as far. Most shops open 10am-8pm.

Police: Hazratganj Police Station (☎222555). MG Rd. Turn left onto Hazratganj from Vidhan Sabha Marg. The police station is on the right side, next to the Kashmir Government Arts Emporium.

Hospital: Nishat (☎229674). 3JC Base Rd., Kaiserbagh. A small, private hospital that has many doctors on call. Go to **Balarampur Hospital,** Golaganj (☎224040) for emergency services. Both open 24hr.

Pharmacy: Atul Pharma Medicals (☎270519). 39/54 Ram Tirath Marg. Take the right-hand fork of Ram Tirath Marg after Hotel Naresh. Open daily 8am-10pm.

Internet: Cyberfast Internet Cafe (☎210592). 1st fl. Fast Business Centre. From MG Rd., turn down Lalbagh; FBS is the 1st major bldg. on the right. Rs50 per hr. Open 8am-midnight. Internet also available at the **GPO**. Rs30 per hr. Open 8am-10pm.

Post Office: GPO (☎222887). Vidhan Sabha Marg. Take a right from MG Rd. onto Vidhan Sabha. The GPO is the large yellow colonial bldg. with the clock tower. Open M-Sa 8am-7pm. **Postal Code: 226001.**

ACCOMMODATIONS

Most of Lucknow's budget hotels are in Hazratganj and around the Narhi Bazaar area along Ram Tirath Marg. Plusher options can be found in the northeast.

Carlton Hotel (☎222439 or 224021; fax 231886). Rana Pratap Marg. Turn left from Ashok Marg onto Rana Pratap Marg. The Carlton is 400m down on the left. This old palace maintains an air of forgotten luxury with huge furnished rooms, bathtubs, filtered water, and extensive porches. Bar, restaurant, and stuffed tiger downstairs. Free breakfast in the verdant courtyard gardens. Singles Rs500-1200; doubles Rs600-1500. ❹

Pal Hotel (☎229476). Ram Tirath Marg. 50m down on the right. In the heart of Narhi Bazaar, this no-frills, few-thrills hotel has reasonably clean, matrix-walled rooms with common or attached bath. Check-out 24hr. Singles Rs100; doubles Rs120-225. ❶

Hotel New Ram Krishna (☎286380). 17/2 Ashok Marg. A 5min. walk up past the main intersection with MG Rd., on the left. Popular, freshly painted, modern place that is trying very hard to replace the original next door. All rooms with attached bath and wall-to-wall carpeting. Check-out 24hr. Singles Rs180; doubles Rs230-600. ❶

Hotel Naresh (☎285298 or 275160). Ram Tirath Marg. From MG Rd., turn left onto Ashok Marg at the big intersection, then fork right onto Ram Tirth Marg at the fruit market. The hotel is 150m down on the left. Simple rooms with attached bath. Check-out 24hr. Singles Rs145-170; doubles Rs200-225. ❶

Chowdhury Lodge (☎221911 or 273135). 3 Vidhan Sabha Marg. Down an alley just before the main intersection with MG Rd. Basic rooms ideally situated in the heart of the city. Singles Rs90-160; doubles Rs170-350. ❶

Hardik Guest House (☎209497 or 209597). 16 Rana Pratap Marg. Turn left at the end of Ram Tirath Marg and then right at the traffic circle. Cool, quiet, clean, and personable. Restaurant downstairs. Check-out 24hr. Carpeted, air-cooled singles/doubles with color TV and attached bath Rs600-700. ❸

FOOD

Lucknow owes its reputation for rich and refined cuisine to the nawabs. For the famous Avadhi kebabs, you will either have to hit one of the big hotel restaurants or sift through the small kiosks in the old city. Lucknow is also well known for its mangoes—the fruit market on Ram Tirth Marg is open every day. If you are in Lucknow during June, check around for the *Avadhi Food Festival*, a twelve-day affair celebrating the city's gastronomic heritage.

▧ **Mu Man's Royal Cafe,** Hazratganj, in front of Capoor's Hotel. A long, dark, and hushed hall serves up tastefully presented meals from Rs55. Excellent *pakoras* (Rs30) and pizzas (Rs55-70), with shredded cheese and tomato (Rs30). Open daily 11am-11pm. ❶

Aahar Restaurant, Lalbagh. Turn left onto Lalbagh after the Mayfair Travels bldg. on MG Rd., and walk to the traffic circle; on the left. Cool place with an intimate atmosphere. Excellent food with a smile. Entrees Rs34-60. Open daily 10:30am-10:30pm. ❶

Mahabeer Restaurant, at the intersection of Sapru Marg and Ashok Marg. Quiet, classy restaurant serves sumptuous veg. food. The staff is very attentive. Great mini-meals Rs35-40. Open daily 10am-10:30pm. ❶

Falaknuma Restaurant, Clark's Avadh Hotel, 9th fl., on the MG Rd. traffic circle, after the cricket stadium. Luxury food at luxury prices, with unparalleled views of the city. Menu includes Lucknow classics and a full range of lamb and chicken kebabs (Rs145-295). A good place to play Avadh Nawab for an evening, if you can afford it (mineral water Rs40). *Ghazal* singing starts nightly at 8:30pm. Lunch 1-3pm, dinner 8-11:30pm. ❸

Moti Mahal, 75 Hazratganj. Opposite the police station. Look for the trademark golden arches. A/C restaurant upstairs serves Chinese food; ground and basement-level Mini Mahal serves breakfast, fast-food, and cakes. Open daily 8am-11pm.

Spicy Bite, MG Rd. In the Tulsi Theatre Bldg. near the traffic circle. A favorite with locals, Spicy Bite serves everything from fish and chips to pizza to Hong Kong style noodles. Dishes from Rs58. Open daily 11am-11pm. ❶

Ruchika, Ashok Marg, about 200m past the intersection with Ram Tirath Marg, on the right. The new veg. champion of Lucknow, this self-proclaimed paradise serves classy *paneers* and *koftas* in a modern, Asian, strangely geometric setting. Dishes from Rs32. Open daily noon-10:30pm. ❶

Ranjana, MG Rd., opposite Capoor's Hotel. Something of a Hazratganj institution, the once-popular eatery just got a much needed face-lift. Wallpaper, bright lights, and a single potted plant have replaced the restaurant's old character. But the food remains quite good. Indian and Chinese dishes Rs28-60. Open daily 10am-11pm. ❶

🔆 SIGHTS

Most of what remains of old Lucknow's glittering mosques and flamboyant palaces is concentrated around the older **Husainabad** area to the northwest of the city, a 20min. rickshaw ride from the din of Hazratganj.

THE RESIDENCY

Off MG Rd., northwest of Hazratganj. Open daily sunrise to sunset. Entrance fee US$5.

If the British Raj still governed India, the ruins of Lucknow's Residency would be one of its proudest monuments. One of the lengthiest struggles of the great uprising (the Indian "Mutiny" or "Revolt," depending on who's talking) took place when rebelling sepoys (Indians enlisted in the East India Company's army) besieged Lucknow's British residents from June to November of 1857 (see also **Mutiny and Aftermath,** p. 74). The against-the-odds defense of the Residency was to leave a lasting impression on the colonial psyche. Once they had retaken the city, the British left the ruins as a monument to the stiff-lipped stubbornness and resilience of the thousands trapped and killed inside. The battered remains of the Residency compound, still visibly scarred by the shots that pounded them 150 years ago, have been converted into a shady green park near the center of the city.

The siege began when news reached Lucknow of *sepoy* rebellions throughout the region. The Residency, a mansion for the East India Company's agent in Avadh, was turned into a fortress for the 3000 local British and Raj supporters seeking refuge there. After five months, the British finally succeeded in breaking the siege, and the remaining survivors—less than a third of the original population—were evacuated to Allahabad. Meanwhile, the battle to take back the rest of the city raged on, and Lucknow was not completely back under British control until March of the following year.

As you enter the complex through Ballie Gate, there are several buildings on the right and left that were used during the siege as hospitals and armories. The Residency building itself, with only one pock-marked tower still standing, sits at the top of the hill amidst palm trees and wide lawns. A museum/model **gallery** on its southern end houses a tatty miniature version of the complex, along with several old weapons, prints, and a copy of the florid, jingoistic poem Tennyson knocked off to commemorate the event. Below is the basement where many British women and children hid. Not far from the main building, the ruins of a small church and a cemetery hold the graves of the British "martyrs," including that of the unfortunate Sir Henry Lawrence who, according to his epitaph, "tried to do his duty."

HUSAINABAD

BARA IMAMBARA. Marking the resting place of Asaf-ud-Daula and his wives, the Bara Imambara was constructed in 1784 as part of a a food-for-work program instituted in the wake of a great famine. An *imambara* is a replica of the tomb of an *imam*, a martyred descendant of the Prophet Mohammed revered by Shi'a Muslims. Dedicated to Husain Ibn Ali, grandson of the Prophet, the Bara Imambara is the center of April's Muharram festival, which mourns his death. Chandeliers hang from the 15m high ceiling of the great hall, which, without a single pillar over its 50m length, still stands as one of the largest vaulted spaces in the world. A staircase to the left side of the main building leads up to the roof and into the **Bhulbhalaiya,** a multi-level labyrinth designed for the entertainment of the nawab's harem. A guide is not necessary, but proceed cautiously as dark, narrow passages turn suddenly and drop off into the great hall and its courtyard, 50 ft. below.

To the side of the Bara Imambara is the beautiful **Asafi Mosque,** built by Asaf-ud-Daula; it is closed to non-Muslims. Opposite the Asafi mosque is the **bauli,** once a spiraling series of water-cooled state apartments, now home to a green pool of algae and chattering bats. Straddling Husainabad Trust Rd. outside the *imambara* is the **Rumi Darwaza,** another work of Asaf-ud-Daula. This 20m-high gate, intended as a copy of the Sublime Port in Istanbul, is covered by a spine of trumpets. *(Open daily 7am-7pm. Rs10, includes entry to the bauli, the Rumi Darwaza, and the Picture Gallery.)*

OTHER SIGHTS IN THE HUSAINABAD AREA. Farther along Husainabad Trust Rd. after the Rumi Darwaza and the clock tower is the **Chota Imambara** (literally, "little *imambara*"), which was begun in 1837 by Nawab Mohammed Ali Shah. Two Taj-shaped buildings in the courtyard mark the tombs of the nawab's daughter and her husband. Ali Shah himself is buried below the main *imambara* structure. Inside are the nawab's silver-plated pulpit, religious regalia used during Muharram, and dozens of dusty mirrors and chandeliers. *(Open daily 7am-7pm. Rs1.)* Farther up, past the sights of Husainabad Trust Rd., on the left, is the **Jama Masjid,** Lucknow's largest mosque, and another conspicuous reminder of Ali Shah's legacy. The mosque is closed to non-Muslims. The **Picture Gallery,** inside a summer house built by the nawab during the 19th century, has a collection of portraits of all the nawabs along with forlorn-looking busts of Dante and Aristotle. *(Next to the clock tower. Open daily 8am-6pm. Entrance fee included in Bara Imambara ticket.)*

SIGHTS NEAR THE HAZRATGANJ AREA

SHAH NAJAF IMAMBARA. North of the Hazratganj area and just west of the Botanical Gardens is the Shah Najaf Imambara. The monument holds the tomb of Nawab Ghazi-ud-din Haidar (r. 1814-27) and served as base for the rebels of 1857. Its interior is decked with chandeliers; sparkling replicas of mosques cover the floor and platforms around the central domed room. Shi'a Muslims come here to express their devotion to Shah-i Najaf, the first Shi'a *imam*, and to the spiritual successor of the Prophet, Ali Ibn Abi Talib. On the fifth day of Muharram, firewalking takes place in the *imambara's* complex. *(Open daily 7am-7pm.)*

SNIFFING THE SUBCONTINENTAL SUBLIME

Mention India and odor in the same sentence, and you're likely to get a less-than-positive reaction. Indeed, for many a traveler, India is The Land of Don't-Breathe-Too-Deeply. In Lucknow, though, olfactory observation is more likely to run along the lines of *eau de toilette* than *eau de* toilet: this is a center for production of *attar*, India's finest class of perfumes. For centuries, *attar* has remained the scent of choice in both the secular and religious domains of Indian culture. The *attar* oil is extracted from pre-dawn flower buds and left in a large container of water. As the sun rises, the buds secrete an oily film which is then carefully preserved. There is an *attar* for every season and time of day: for summer, rose and Indian jasmine; for winter, musk. The undisputed raja of Lucknow's perfume biz is the **Azam Ali-Alam Ali Industry,** renowned for authentic *attars* since Mughal days. Their products are sold all over India and have been worn by the likes of Empress Nur Jahan and Princess Diana.

LA MARTINIÈRE. The Martinière school is one of Lucknow's most distinctive and intriguing architectural survivals. Frenchman Claude Martin, money-lender and architectural advisor to the nawab as well as military man and colonial entrepreneur *par excellence*, designed this building as his own mausoleum after deciding toward the end of his life that he would live out his days in India. Martin built and owned dozens of houses throughout India, but his final creation, built in the late 1700s, is the only one to have survived intact, thanks to its conversion into a school in 1840. Described by one observer as a product of "the heterogeneous fancies of a diseased brain," La Martinière is an eclectic mishmash of architectural styles and flavors. Startled-looking lions cling to colonnades, while a chorus of spritely figures congregates on the rooftop striking dignified, classical poses. A large turbaned pillar completes the ensemble. Report to the principal's office first if you come during school hours. *(Off Kalidas Marg, southeast of Hazratganj. Rickshaws cost Rs15-20 and take about 15min.)*

SIKANDRA BAGH. Once the site of Nawab Wajid Ali Shah's pleasure garden, this is where the final battle for the relief of the Residency took place. Across the street, the **National Botanical Research Institute** maintains lush gardens and nurseries, especially popular with early-morning, sneaker-clad walkers. *(At the intersection of Ashok Marg and Rana Pratap Marg. Gardens open daily 5-8am and 2-4:30pm. Free.)*

ENTERTAINMENT AND SHOPPING

Lucknow's history of self-indulgent rulers seems not to have trickled down to the commoners; the city's nightlife does not sparkle. A few **pool halls** hide on the upper floors of Hazratganj buildings, and budget **bars** are found along Station Rd. Pricier drinks are available in the **Falaknuma Restaurant** (see above). The only proper bar in Hazratganj is the pine-paneled **Tashna Bar,** Sapru Marg, in the Hotel Gomti. Full of chain-smoking, hard-drinking local businessmen crowded around a small TV, this small, dark, A/C place serves booze and basic munchies. (Beer Rs65-80; liquor from Rs50. Open daily 11am-10:30pm.) A little farther from the city center, the **Simbha Bar** at the Carlton Hotel has about the same stuff on tap, but the bar area is more informal, with couches, lounge chairs, and psychedelic paintings of animals on the walls. (Open daily 10am-10:30pm.) **Novelty Cinema,** on Lalbagh opposite Aahar's Restaurant, regularly shows English-language movies (Rs33 and Rs49). Lucknow is also home to the **Bhatkhande Music College,** one of the two major schools of **kathak dance** in India. Check newspapers or the tourist office for performance information.

Aminabad, west of Hazratganj, is one of Lucknow's old bazaar areas and the best place to shop for Lucknow crafts. Items of pastel clothing with white *chikan* embroidery cost Rs20-5000 per piece. To purchase *attar*, the local alcohol-free perfumes worn by Indian Muslims, head to **Chowk** and led your nose guide you. Tiny bottles of the flowery scents cost Rs30-6000.

FAIZABAD फ़ैज़ाबाद ☎ 05278

Once the capital of the kingdom of Avadh—until the nawab moved to Lucknow in 1775—Faizabad today serves as a stop-off for daytrips to neighboring Ayodhya. Several monuments remain from the city's heyday, including the mausolea of Nawab Shuja-ud-Daula and his wife Bahu Begum, the city's great patroness. These rarely touristed but impressive monuments are definitely worth a visit.

☐ TRANSPORTATION. Rickshaw rides from the bus and train stations to the Chowk area average ten minutes (Rs10). **Buses** head to: **Allahabad** (every 45min. 5:30am-12:30am, Rs70); **Delhi** (16hr., 2-3 per day 1:30-5:30pm, Rs301); **Gorakhpur** (4hr., every 45min. 5:30am-12:30am, Rs61); **Lucknow** (every 45min. 5:30am-12:30am, Rs56); **Varanasi** (6hr., 2-3 per day 5am-2pm, Rs90). Bus departures are erratic and unpredictable. **Tempos** to Ayodhya leave regularly from the Gurdi Bazaar, Chowk (Rs4), and the bus station (Rs6). **Trains** run to: **Delhi** (12½-14hr., 1-3 per day 3:50-10pm, Rs194); **Lucknow** (2½-4hr., 5-7 per day 3:15am-10pm, Rs39); **Varanasi** (4-5½hr., 3-5 per day 6:05am-9:20pm, Rs46).

☐ ☑ ORIENTATION AND PRACTICAL INFORMATION. Two main roads are in Faizabad. **Station Rd.,** from the railway station, becomes **Civil Lines** and leads to the **Chowk** area, where the sights and budget hotels are located. **National Highway (NH) 28** is the major bus route to Ayodhya and Gorakhpur. The **Regional Tourist Office** is in an alley off Civil Lines. With your back to the bus stand, turn left and then right after the Shane Avadh Hotel. The alley is just before Krishna Palace, on the right. (☎23214. Open M-Sa 10am-5pm.) The **State Bank of India,** Civil Lines, changes AmEx traveler's checks. Facing away from the bus stand, turn left, take the third right, just after the Shane Avadh Hotel, and turn right after Krishna palace, and the bank is on the right. (☎20430 or 22210. Open M-F 10am-2:30pm and 3-3:30pm, Sa 10am-1pm.) Faizabad's **post office** is off NH 28. With the bus stand behind you, turn left and walk toward the Chowk. Take the first main street to the left; the post office is on the right. (☎22301. Open M-Sa 10am-6pm.) A **cyber-cafe** is at the main civil lines intersection (Rs50 per hr.; open daily 10am-8pm).

☐ ☑ ACCOMMODATIONS AND FOOD. Budget lodgings are in the Chowk area and a couple of decent, clean hotels near the bus and train stations. Most of these have restaurants; otherwise, simple roadside *dhabas* are about the only place to eat. The well-appointed **Abha Hotel ❶,** in an alley with the Bank of Baroda in Motibagh (a 15min. rickshaw ride from the train station), is probably the best of the several small hotels in this area. All rooms have baths, and many have color TVs. (☎22550 or 22930. Singles Rs135-190; doubles Rs175-250.) The A/C restaurant downstairs serves decent food and ice cream. (Open daily 7am-10pm.) At the **Priya Hotel ❶,** down the same alley as the Abha, you get what you pay for. (☎23783. Singles Rs75; doubles Rs100.) The **Tirupati Hotel ❷,** Civil Lines, has spacious, well-furnished rooms with soap, towels, and attached bath (☎23231. Singles Rs145-550; doubles Rs195-650). A relaxed restaurant off the lobby serves the usual fare and *hakka* noodles (Rs48-55). **Mezbar Restaurant** (open daily 7am-10:30pm), in Shane Avadh, next to the Tirupati Hotel, has a classy restaurant.

UTTAR PRADESH

AYODHA अयोध्या ☎ 05238

In Ayodhya, a village dotted with dozens of temples and overflowing with *sadhus* and pilgrims, pious worship and a massive police presence have been forced into an improbable coexistence. Ayodhya has an ancient history as one of India's holiest cities. According to legend, the city was founded by the Hindu law-giver Manu, and it was also the birthplace of Lord Rama, hero of the *Ramayana* epic and the seventh incarnation of Vishnu, born into the ruling Surya dynasty. Many of Ayodhya's most important sites are devoted to him and his faithful servant Hanuman, the monkey god. Ayodhya catapulted into the limelight in 1992, when Hindu-Muslim unrest broke out over the controversial Babri Masjid (see **Sights**, below). Thousands were killed in the nationwide riots that followed, and Ayodhya has since remained a flash point for communal violence. Foreigners are unlikely to encounter any difficulties but should check the news before visiting, especially during the unpredictable **Ramanavami** festival celebrating Rama's birth.

A major pilgrimage destination for thousands of Hindus, Ayodhya today sees few foreign visitors—a stay here makes a welcome break from the stresses and strains of some of India's more popular tourist destinations. Off the main road, every street and alley is home to at least one temple, and usually a peaceful air of religious serenity pervades almost everywhere.

▐ **TRANSPORTATION.** Infrequent, sporadic **trains** depart from the **Railway Station,** 400m south of NH 28 and the Sri Ram Hospital. To: **Faizabad** and points west (30min.; Tu, Th, Su 8:30pm; Rs15); **Varanasi** (3½hr.; M, Th, Sa 5:30am; Rs53). It is much easier to catch trains from Faizabad. **Buses** between Faizabad and **Gorakhpur** (4hr., every hr. Rs64) stop briefly; catch them at the new **bus stand** near the bridge on NH 28. **Tempos** and **taxis** run the most convenient service to Faizabad (Rs4-6).

▓ ▐ **ORIENTATION AND PRACTICAL INFORMATION. National Highway (NH) 28** cuts through Ayodhya on its way from Faizabad to Gorakhpur. The **railway station,** tourist bungalow, and most of the major sights (including Hanuman Gardhi and Kanak Bhavan) are on either side of the highway, within walking distance of the bus station and tempo stop. Ayodhya is not a big city; it's not much more than a 20min. walk from one side of town to the other along the main highway. The best way to see Ayodhya is to escape as quickly as possible from the clamor of the built-up strip and walk north through the winding, climbing, temple-packed streets on your way to the *ghats*, or head in the opposite direction, into the more spaced-out but no-less-temple-filled south. The **tourist office** is a stand opposite the railway station. To get there, turn right with the bus station behind you, walk down NH 28 toward Faizabad, and take a left on the first road. The office is just before the station, on the left. (Open M-Sa 10am-5pm.) **Sri Ram Hospital** (☎ 32840) is 150m west of the bus stand. The **post office** is at Shrinagar Hat, on NH 28 as you head towards Gorakhpur. (☎ 32025. Open M-Sa 10am-5pm.) To change money, head to Faizabad.

▐ ▐ **ACCOMMODATIONS AND FOOD.** A few decent hotels have sprung up in the area south of NH 28, but, for the most part, ashrams, occasionally with single rooms (and attached bath and fan), are the more popular and sensible choice for the thousands of pilgrims who descend upon Ayodhya each year. Directly opposite the bus station, the **Birla Dharamsala** ❶ is located in a peaceful garden compound next to the quaint and serene temple. (☎32252. Singles with attached bath Rs100; doubles Rs150.) For more institutional comfort, the **Pathik Niwas Saket** (a.k.a. the **UP Tourist Bungalow**) ❶, 50m to the left of the train station, has uninspiring but clean rooms in a very quiet locale. (☎32435. Dorms Rs60; singles with bath Rs175; doubles Rs200-250.) The equally dull but reliable restaurant has a small menu and a vegetarian *thali* for Rs45 (open daily 7am-10pm). A better bet for some A/C and a sit-down meal is the **Shyam Restaurant ❶,** in the Ram Hotel, Dant Dhawan Kund; head 50m down the street opposite the Hanuman Fort off NH 28. The all-veg. menu includes *dosas* (Rs12-25) and Chinese for Rs19-45. (Open daily 8am-10pm.)

🔲 **SIGHTS.** Ayodhya is a temple-lover's paradise. There really does seem to be at least one sacred site around every street corner. *Sadhus* and pilgrims are everywhere, and fluorescent stalls selling sparkling bangles and cone-shaped piles of red and saffron *tilak* powder line the streets between temples. Many of the most important religious sites are within a 5-15min. walk of the bus and train stations, but Ayodhya is not the kind of town that comes with a convenient checklist of must-see attractions. The whole town is really one huge stretching temple complex, alive and vibrant with a continuous stream of holy hustle and bustle. The best way to drink in the atmosphere is to do as the *sadhus* do and let your footsteps lead you unhurriedly and at random from one shrine to the next.

The **Ram Janam Bhumi** (known as **Babri Masjid** to Muslims) is the contested holy site that led to Hindu-Muslim clashes in 1992 and brought international attention to Ayodhya. The trouble began over the location of a mosque, built during the 16th century by the Mughal Emperor Babur on a site that many Hindus hold to be the birthplace of Rama, hero-king of the Ramayana and incarnation of Vishnu. The mosque became a symbol for the resentment and prejudice many Hindus felt (and still feel) toward Indian Muslims. Hindu Nationalists, such as the Vishwa Hindu Parishad (VHP) used the Babri Masjid as a rallying cry, and the mosque was eventually closed due to the controversy. On December 6, 1992, religious fervor turned to violence when 200,000 VHP-led militant Hindus (most of them from outside Ayodhya) descended on the town, smashing through police barricades to destroy the Babri Masjid and erect a makeshift temple in its place. Today, devotee pilgrims of Rama and students of contemporary Indian politics huddle through a maze of cage-like fences surrounded by armed soldiers for a quick glimpse of the shrine, a glittering altar in a small military tent, and the mosque rubble below. Expect a thorough frisking and even a police escort. **Bring your passport.** No cameras or bags are allowed. *(From the bus stand, take the 1st major left off NH 28 into the north half of town; keep heading up and to the left. Open daily 7-11am and 1-6pm.)*

The **Hanuman Garhi,** in the white fort above the bus station, is one of Ayodhya's most important temples. It is abuzz with worshipers all day and into the night. Supposedly marking the spot where Hanuman sat guard in a cave overlooking Rama's birthplace, the main tile-covered shrine is at the top of a flight of over 75 steps. Leave your shoes at the bottom and look out for monkey droppings. The **Jain Temple** complex on Hanuman Rd. houses a 10m-high marble figure and curiously activated water fountains. To get there, take a right from the railway station and turn left at the end of the road; the temple is on the right after about 600m. *(Open daily 6am-8pm.)* Other temples include the **Kanak Bhawan** *(open daily 8am-noon and 4:30-9pm)*, off the main road farther up and east from the Hanuman Garhi, and the **Nageshwar Nath** temple, by the canal and river **ghats** over on the east side of town.

GORAKHPUR गोरखपुर   ☎ 0551

As the major transportation hub between India and Nepal, Gorakhpur is more often traveled through than to, and few people arrive here without definite plans to move on again as soon as possible. Buses leave regularly for the border, and the main railway station sends trains to major cities in India, so getting out is easy enough—a good thing, as Gorakhpur offers little to the visitor, though residents might try to convince you otherwise. Founded around AD 1400 and named for the

Hindu saint Gorakhnath, Gorakhpur still hosts the temple of the patron saint of the Natha Yogis, 4km from the railway station on Nepal Rd. Gorakhpur became an army town under the Mughals and again under the British, who used it as a base for recruiting Gorkha soldiers from Nepal; it is still a major military center today. Insect repellent is a must if you're going to be overnighting here; hungry mosquitos seem to penetrate even the most carefully netted hotel room windows.

▉ TRANSPORTATION

Trains: Railway Station, Station Rd. To: **Allahabad** (11hr., 5am and 10:30pm, Rs131); **Calcutta** (18-23hr., 1-2 per day Rs160-248); **Delhi** (13-18hr., 5 per day 1:05pm-midnight, Rs144-224); **Jhansi** (11½-17hr., 1-3 per day Rs186); **Lucknow** (4-6½hr., 9-14 per day 4am-12:45am, Rs104); **Varanasi** (6hr., 4 per day 5am-10:30pm, Rs97).

Buses: Gorakhpur Bus Station, 300m down the road from the railway station. To: **Faizabad** (4hr., every hr. 5am-9pm, Rs65); **Kushinagar** (1hr., every 30min.-1hr. 5am-8pm, Rs22); **Lucknow** (8hr., every 30min.-1hr. 5am-9pm, Rs117); **Sunauli** (2hr., every hr. 5am-10pm, Rs43). Buses to **Varanasi** (6hr., every 30min.-1hr. 5:30am-10pm, Rs90) and other points south depart from **Kacheri Bus Stand,** 1.5km south of the railway station. Regular buses (every 30min.-1hr. 6am-8pm) also run from the intersection before the railway station to the border with Nepal; make sure you are getting on a government bus. From the border, you will have to change buses and buy a new ticket. There are many **private buses** to the border operating from the same area, but they tend to charge up to twice as much for tickets through to **Kathmandu** or **Pokhara.** The so-called "direct" service offered on these buses is, in fact, no faster than the government bus route. Either way, you will have to spend several hours at the border arranging your visa and switching buses in Nepal. For more information, see **Sunauli,** p. 834.

▉ ▉ ORIENTATION AND PRACTICAL INFORMATION

Most of Gorakhpur lies south of its **railway station.** Inside the station is a small tourist information booth (open daily 10am-5pm). Budget hotels and restaurants are on **Station Rd.,** directly opposite the station. The downtown area, **Golghar,** on Jalkal Chawan Rd., also contains some cheap places to eat and spend the night. The road south from the railway station's entrance leads to the **main bus stand,** 300m away, before intersecting with Park Rd., which runs parallel to Station Rd. and marks the beginning of the **Civil Lines** region. The **State Bank of India,** on Bank Rd. downtown, cashes AmEx traveler's checks and exchanges US/UK currency. (☎338497. Open M-F 10am-2pm, Sa 10am-noon.) The **HPO** is located near the southern end of Bank Rd., by the district hospital. (☎333018. Open M-Sa 10am-6pm.) **Postal code:** 273001.

▉ ACCOMMODATIONS

Several decent budget hotels are directly opposite the railway station, beyond the swarm of young men competing to serve you breakfast or put you on a bus bound for Nepal. In the center of the city and at the western end of Station Rd. (Rs10-15 rickshaw ride from the station) are a couple of mid-range options, which are a bit quieter, but also a bit less convenient. Most places have 24hr. check-out, single-Hindi-channel black-and-white TVs, and great views of the station chaos.

Hotel Elora (☎200647). Station Rd. Opposite the railway station. Simple, clean rooms with attached bath and eager room service. Those at the back are away from most of the Station Rd. noise. Singles Rs110-350; doubles Rs150-450. ❶

Hotel Siddhartha (☎ 200976). Station Rd. Past Hotel Elora. Nothing to get excited about, but clean enough and enthusiastically run. Currency exchange available. Singles Rs100-150; doubles Rs150-200. ❶

Hotel Marina (☎ 337630). Golghar. On an alley off Jalkal Bhawan Rd., behind Hotel President in the center of town. Slightly more upscale and much groovier than most, its large, clean, carpeted rooms with attached baths are set amongst seashell curtains and sexy retro paintings. Singles Rs200; doubles Rs245-650. ❶

❐ FOOD

Plenty of small, open-air restaurants serve snacks and simple meals along the strip opposite the railway station. For anything more elaborate, sanitary, or comfortable, you'll have to make the trek into town.

Bobi's Restaurant, Jalkal Bhawan Rd. Across from Hotel President. A proper and popular place recently renovated. The menu includes burgers (Rs20-35), pizza (Rs40-60), and entrees (Rs30-90), as well as a variety of dessert pastries from the confectioners out front. Open daily noon-10:30pm; full meals served noon-3pm and 7-10:30pm. ❶

Vardan Restaurant, Station Rd., between Hotel Standard and Hotel Elora. Small, with occasional blasts of A/C, this is probably the best of the many places dotted around the station area. Food ranges from omelettes to *tandoori* dishes (Rs22-75) and spring rolls (Rs35-40). "Wine not allowed." Open daily 8am-11pm. ❶

Deluxe Bar, in Hotel Ganges Deluxe, on Park Rd. in Golghar. If you've just missed your train out of town and need something to knock you out until the Nepali border, then this dim and desolate bar's spirits (Rs16-125) and selection of beer (Rs60-70) might just do the trick. Cozy, semi-reclined seats for your languishing pleasure. Basic meals and snacks (Rs20-80) are also available. Open daily 7am-11pm. ❶

KUSHINAGAR कुशीनगर   ☎ 05563

"All things must pass. Decay is inherent in all things." With words to this effect, the Buddha preached his last sermon and then breathed his last breath here in Kushinagar, where he was cremated and went on to attain the ultimate happily-never-after of *parinirvana*. For centuries after the Buddha's death, Kushinagar flourished as a major religious pilgrimage destination. Foremost among the rulers who patronized the place was Ashoka, whose conversion to Buddhism helped the religion prosper and spread throughout India.

With the decline of Buddhism in India during the 12th century, however, Kushinagar faded from prominence, and its many temples and monasteries soon fell into forgotten jungle decay. It was not until the mid-19th century, when a group of archaeologists working under the auspices of the East India Company started exploring the area with spades, that Kushinagar again rose to widespread attention. The *stupas* and images they unearthed and the inscriptions written on them were enough to establish beyond doubt Kushinagar's holy heritage, and the tiny town was soon back on the map as a major religious center.

A lot of money has made its way west into Kushinagar since then. Today, the streets are paved, flat, and smooth, with Japanese financial backing, and lined with temples, stupas, and study centers built in most of the architectural styles of Buddhist East Asia. Very much a beggar-free, truck-free, cow-free zone, Kushinagar is a small village remarkable for its pervasive air of peace and prosperity. Though it is small enough to be visited on a daytrip from Gorakhpur, it is worth an overnight stay to enjoy its atmosphere of untouristed calm and quiet.

⊑ TRANSPORTATION. Small buses go regularly between Kushinagar and **Gorakhpur** (1¼hr., every 30min. 6:30am-8pm, Rs22). The **bus station** is in the town of **Kasia,** 3km from Kushinagar. Ask to be let off at Buddha Dwar gate; otherwise, you will have to get another bus back to the gate from Kasia station (Rs6). **Tempos** also make frequent runs between Gorakhpur and Kushinagar for a slightly higher fare than buses. Either form of transport can be caught from the post office on NH28.

■■ ⁊ ORIENTATION AND PRACTICAL INFORMATION. Fifty-one kilometers east of Gorakhpur, Kushinagar is on **National Highway (NH) 28.** All the places of worship, tourist attractions, and accommodations are on Kushinagar's L-shaped main road, **Buddh Marg,** which can be entered through the **Buddha Dwar gate** at the highway. The **Regional Tourist Office** is 200m down Buddh Marg, on the right, across from the Myanmar Temple and next to the Shree Birla Buddhist temple. (Open M-Sa 10am-4pm.) The **post office,** next to the **police station,** is a small, white building opposite the Buddha Dwar on NH 28. (Open M-Sa 10am-4pm.) **Postal Code:** 274403.

⁊▐ ACCOMMODATIONS AND FOOD. The main tourist season in Kushinagar runs from October to March; many hotels and restaurants close down completely in the offseason. Those listed below are open throughout the year. The **Linh-Son Chinese Rest House ❷,** at the Chinese Temple on Buddh Marg, next to the Myanmar Temple, maintains two stories of spotlessly clean, three-bed rooms with attached bath (☎71019. Rs250-350). The monks of the **Myanmar Buddhist Temple and Guesthouse ❶,** next door, offer simple dorms to pilgrims and visitors on a donation basis (☎71035. at least Rs50). **Hotel Pathik Niwas ❷,** Buddh Marg, 200m past the tourist office on the right, offers a wider range of accommodations. A white-walled complex built around manicured gardens and lined with paintings depicting the life of the Buddha, the Pathik Niwas' rooms and bathrooms are clean (toilet seats "sanitized for your protection"), and sheets and towels are changed daily. (☎05563 or 71038. Singles Rs400; doubles Rs500; A/C deluxe rooms Rs800/900; small, kitchen-equipped "American huts" Rs700/800.) The restaurant does everything from cheeseburgers (Rs30) to *malai kofta* (Rs40), as well as the obligatory chow mein menu. (Open 6am-10pm.) The **Yama Kwality Cafe ❶,** in front of the Myanmar Temple, is the only other restaurant open all year. Run by a friendly Bengali-Nepalese family, the cafe dishes out tasty noodles (Rs15-40), fried rice (Rs20-40), and tourist information (free) and maintains a good selection of newspapers and magazines.

◙ SIGHTS. Kushinagar's main attractions are the ancient *stupas* and images rediscovered here during the last century. These range along the main Buddh Marg stretch. Dotted between the historical remains are several modern temples and an expansive green **Meditation Park.** Next to the Myanmar Temple, set in beautiful lawns is Kushinagar's holiest site, the **Buddha Mahaparinirvana Temple,** said to mark the spot where the Buddha was liberated from the cycle of re-birth and attained the ideal state of *parinirvana.* Extensive traces remain of the original temple, and a 6m reclining Buddha survives inside the main temple building. Behind the image is a large, modern *stupa,* built to protect the age-weathered original beneath it. The original *stupa* is believed to contain a portion of the Buddha's cremated remains. Left out of the temple grounds and farther down Buddh Marg just as the road shifts left, the small **Matha Kunwar Temple** stands on the site of the Buddha's last sermon and contains a small, golden statue of the Buddha. One kilometer farther down the road, past the Japanese and Korean temples and the impressive Thai *wat,* is the remains of the **Ramambhar Stupa,** built on the site of the Buddha's cremation. Pay no attention to the Indian tourists: climbing on the *stupa* will do your karma no good. (*Stupas* open daily sunrise to sunset. Free.)

VARANASI वाराणसी   ☎ 0542

For Hindus, Varanasi (also known as Benares) is the holiest place on earth and the chosen residence of Shiva who, vowing never to leave, abides in every nook and cranny of the city. Hindus believe that Varanasi is a sacred zone, with a power so great that it permeates the city with its divine glow—hence the city's other name, Kashi (the Luminous). Those who die in Varanasi are guaranteed *moksha*, or liberation from the cycle of death and rebirth, and everyone here knows it. This otherworldly confidence has made Varanasi the chosen residence of many a mere mortal as well—over 1.2 million of them. In addition, countless thousands of pilgrims come here every day to bathe in the sacred waters of the Ganga and to pay their respects at the temples that stretch all along the riverside *ghats*.

The Old City is a maze of tortuous lanes smeared with cow dung and congested with animals and people. Small boys make small fortunes guiding foreigners to the Golden Temple through little-used alleys. Dead bodies, sometimes stretched between two bicycles or tied to the roof of a jeep, are delivered to the pyre to the traditional chant, "*Ram Nam Sata Hai*" (Ram is Truth). On the main street, buses bellow madly and spew exhaust over droves of shaven-headed pilgrims, their baldness an expression of earthly loss and the small pigtail of hair a hook for the gods to grasp should they decide to snatch them up. When the power goes out in the City of Light (as it does almost every night), the unprepared visitor must navigate the slippery narrow lanes of the old city by the teasing flicker of candlelight.

Due to five centuries (AD 1200-1700) of levelings at the hands of Muslims, no building in the city is more than 300 years old. But the attacks never really succeeded; they wiped out the city's temples and images but not the traditions that have kept Varanasi alive since at least as far back as the 6th century BC. In the early days of Aryan settlement in India, Varanasi, one of the world's oldest continuously inhabited cities, sat at the great ford where traders traversing North India would cross the Ganga. It gained fame as a bustling bazaar town and as a center of spiritual life. Teachers and ascetics came to mingle with the local deities in the ponds and rivers of Anandavana, the Forest of Bliss, that grew here before the city developed. The Buddha came to Sarnath, on the outskirts of Kashi, to preach his first sermon. Varanasi's Hindu priests were active in developing their religion through the millennia, and the city itself soon became an object of worship: a holy place inhabited by holy beings and bounded by a holy river.

Never a military or political powerhouse, Varanasi became a sanctuary for Indian culture, renowned for its silk brocades (Benares silk saris are still some of the best), its refined Sanskrit and Hindi, and its music. Especially since the founding of Benares Hindu University, Varanasi continues to support a thriving arts culture. But piety and devotion are what bring the millions who come for a brief *darshan* of the city, as well as the many who come to live, and die, in Varanasi.

UTTAR PRADESH

█ WARNING. Rickshaw-*wallahs* in Varanasi often collect commission from hotel owners for delivering guests. Beware of anyone who offers you a "ride anywhere" for "Rs5 only;" you will have very little control over your destination. Be firm about where you want to go, and don't believe your rickshaw-*wallah* when he tells you that the hotel you asked for is "full" or "closed." If you have any concerns or doubts upon arrival, call a hotel yourself from the train station, or ask the staff at the tourist office to do so for you.

UTTAR PRADESH

Varanasi

🏠 ACCOMMODATIONS
Ganges View Hotel , **11**
Hotel Arti, **8**
Hotel Arya, **7**
Hotel Relax, **3**
Hotel Temple on Ganges, **12**
🍎 FOOD
Bread of Life Bakery, **9**
Gazal Bar & Restaurant, **1**
Kamesh Hut Garden, **4**
Malika Restaurant, **5**
Mandarin Restaurant, **2**
Pizzeria Vaatika, **10**
Yelchico Bar & Restaurant, **6**

🚆 TRANSPORTATION

Flights: Babatpur Airport, 22km northwest of Varanasi Junction Railway Station. **Indian Airlines** (☎343746 or 345959), Cantonment. From the back exit of the railway station, head north 500m and turn left; go past the church; the office is on the left around the next turn. To: **Agra** (2hr.; M, W, F, Su 5pm; US$110); **Delhi** (2½hr.,4pm, US$130); **Kathmandu** (1hr., 11:55am, US$71); **Lucknow** (45min., 4pm, US$75); **Mumbai** (5hr., 4pm, US$240);

Trains: Varanasi Junction Railway Station. Rs10 by cycle-rickshaw or Rs30 by auto-rickshaw from Godaulia Crossing. To: **Allahabad** (2-3hr., 7-11 per day 4am-11:30pm, Rs39); **Delhi** (13½-19 hr., 3-5 per day 2:10-11pm, Rs231); **Gorakhpur** (5-8hr., 4 per day 12:15am-4:30pm, Rs92); **Lucknow** (4½-7½hr., 6-7 per day 5:10am-6:35pm, Rs120); **Mumbai** (29½hr., 11:30am, Rs340); **Patna** (4-6½hr., 4-6 per day 2:05am-9:10pm, Rs97); **Satna** (5½-9hr., 5-9 per day 4am-11:10pm, Rs97) from which a 4hr. bus ride takes you to **Khajuraho**.

Buses: Cantonment Bus Station, 300m to the left on Station Rd. as you exit Varanasi Junction Station. To: **Agra** (16-18hr., 5pm, Rs247); **Allahabad** (3hr., every 30min. 4am-11pm, Rs54); **Delhi** (18hr., 7pm, Rs309); **Gaya** (7hr., 6:30am, Rs91); **Gorakhpur** (6hr., every hr. 5am-7pm, Rs80); **Lucknow** (8hr., 8 per day 5-10:30am, Rs135); **Sonauli** (10hr., 10 per day 6:30am-6:30pm, Rs134).

Local Transportation: Auto-rickshaws from Varanasi Station to Godaulia or Cantonment cost Rs30. To **Sarnath** Rs45. Cycle-rickshaws go most places in the city. Don't take any nonsense from drivers; they make careers over-charging you. **Tempos** run from Lanka to Ramnagar Fort (Rs10). **City buses** connect Varanasi Station and **Sarnath** (Rs5).

ORIENTATION

Varanasi's city limits are marked by the **Varuna River** to the north and the **Assi River** to the south, hence the city's hybrid name. **Panch Koshi Rd.,** which circles the city's 16km radius, marks the boundary of the sacred zone of Kashi. Old Varanasi is stacked and squeezed up along the western banks of the Ganga at the point where the river begins to flow straight north. There is virtually nothing on the east bank, except for the old residence of the Maharaja. Steep steps from the river *ghats* lead into a labyrinth of narrow street and alleys lined with temples, shrines, budget hotels, and restaurants. Finding your way through this tangle may seem impossible at times, though many of the main backpackers' hang-outs are well marked, and the *ghats* are clearly labeled in English. Be wary of accepting offers of help in finding your way; lost-looking foreigners are easy targets for the hundreds of touts who prowl the streets. Also, be sure that the hotel you find is actually the one you're looking for. Fakes abound—as soon as one place becomes popular, half the hotels around it change their names to something confusingly similar.

Sticking to the river is the best way to navigate Varanasi, as most points of interest are along the waterfront. As long as the water level is not too high you can walk all the way from Assi Ghat, at the south end, to Raj Ghat in the far north. **Dasashwamedh Ghat,** the city's main *ghat*, is easily reached via **Dasashwamedh Rd.** from **Godaulia Crossing,** a central traffic circle. The surrounding area near the **Vishwanath Temple,** known as **Godaulia,** contains many of the budget hotels and is connected to the northern parts of Varanasi by **Chowk Rd.,** one of the few roads near the *ghats* wide enough for cars. Trains from the east cross the **Malaviya Bridge,** just beyond Raj Ghat; the railway and bus stations are inland in the northern part of the city. Things become more open and less chaotic in the far north, around the luxury hotel and tourist services of the leafy **cantonment,** as well as on the campus of Benares Hindu University, at the city's southern tip, near **Lanka Crossing.**

PRACTICAL INFORMATION

Tourist Office: The **UP Regional Tourist Office** (☎346370). In the main railway station. Quite helpful and sympathetic to travelers' problems. Open daily 6am-8pm. The **Tourist Bungalow** (☎343413), Parade Kothi, Cantonment. A short walk south of the railway station. Has nothing you can't find at the railway office. Open M-Sa 10am-5pm. The **Government of India Tourist Office** (☎343744), the Mall, Cantonment. Offers a variety of services and information. Open M-F 9am-5:30pm and Sa 9am-2pm.

Central Varanasi

▲ ACCOMMODATIONS
Golden Lodge, **4**
Hotel La-Ra India, **8**
Om House Lodge, **5**
Shanti Guest House, **1**
Trimurti Guest House, **2**
Vishnu Rest House, **12**
Yogi Lodge, **3**

🍎 FOOD
Keshari Restaurant, **6**
New Monga Restaurant, **9**
Yelchico Bar & Restaurant, **7**
♪ ENTERTAINMENT
International Music Centre, **10**
Triveni Music Centre, **11**

Currency Exchange: State Bank of India (☎343445), The Mall, Cantonment. Down the street to the right of the Best Western (or Kashika) Hotel. Open M-F 10am-2pm, Sa 10am-noon. **Bank of Baroda** (☎401471), Godaulia. On the left, just before Vishwanath Gali, as you head down Dasashwamedh Rd. towards the Ghat. May be more convenient, but gives advances only on MC and V. Open M-F 11am-3pm, Sa 11am-1pm.

Market: Most of your fruit needs can also be met around **Dasashwamedh Ghat.** Pilgrims' supplies and souvenirs are found along **Vishwanath Gali,** and sari sales take place in **Thajheri Bazaar** and **Kunj Gali,** both off the main **Chowk** drag.

Police: Dasashwamedh Police Station (☎321283).

Pharmacy: Heritage Hospital Pharmacy (☎367977 or 366726), Lanka Crossing. From Godaulia Crossing, take an auto-rickshaw (Rs25) toward Benares Hindu University. The hospital and its 24hr. pharmacy tower are on the left, just before Lanka Crossing. The entrance is on the opposite side, through the market complex.

Hospital: The best private hospital is **Heritage Hospital** (see above), where you can usually see an English-speaking doctor right away. **Sir Sunderial Hospital** at B.H.U. (☎310290 or 310292) is also reputable.

Internet: Zee Services (☎451800). 100m up Dasashwamedh Rd. from the south end of the ghat, on the left. Rs20 per hr. Open daily 6:30am-10:30pm. Other similarly priced options can be found in the alleyway maze behind 2EE. **Tiwari Travels** (☎366727), Assi ghat, to the left of Harmony. Rs40 per hour. Open daily 8am-9pm.

Post Office: **Head Post Office** (☎332090). 400m east of the intersection of Chowk and Kabir Chaura Rds., on the right. Open M-Sa 10am-6pm. **Postal Code:** 221001.

ACCOMMODATIONS

Dozens of budget hotels are packed into the winding maze of the Old City around Godaulia Crossing. Mid-range hotels can be found throughout Varanasi, especially along Vidyapith Rd., on top of the ghats, and on the main streets in Godaulia. Luxury hotels in the leafy cantonment area north of the railway station seem a world away from the traditional life of the city.

Hotel Temple on Ganges (☎368640 or 368703; hotel_temple@hotmail.com). Assi Ghat. A 20min. walk (or boat ride) down from Dasashwamedh, just off the road leading to the ghat. A spotlessly clean place whose offerings include massages, ISDN Internet hook ups, and free yoga lessons. The hotel restaurant's serves strictly vegetarian, strictly mineral water goodies to guests anywhere in the hotel. Nice rooftop terrace. All rooms have attached baths with hot water. Singles Rs100-350; doubles Rs350-650. ●

Golden Lodge (☎393832 or 328567). D 8/35 Kalika Gali. Head up Vishwanatha Gali and look for signs 150m on the right. Clean, simple, slightly shabby looking budget hotel offers "homely and comfortably staying." A/C and satellite TV. Attached Fagin's Restaurant serves Indian, Western, and Israeli favorites. Check out 10:30am. Singles Rs60-80; doubles Rs100-250. ●

Hotel Arti (☎313921). Harischandra Ghat. Just up the road from the 2nd of Varanasi's burning *ghats* on the right. Close enough for the morbidly curious, but far enough so *you* may rest in peace. Clean, carpeted rooms have attached bathrooms. Friendly staff does non-Ganges laundry. Doubles Rs200-250; single occupancy Rs150-200. ●

Vishnu Rest House (☎450206 or 450744). Pandey Ghat. From Dasashwamedh Ghat walk south 200m along the Ganges until you see "Pandey" written above the ghats. Not to be confused with the Vishnu *Guest* House, *Old* Vishnu Rest House, or any other variation. The most popular backpacker hang-out in town, this riverfront property fills up quickly. Colorful rooms and tye-dye sheets, but "not for drug addicts." Terrace restaurant offers superb views of the Ganga (open 7am-2pm and 6-9:30pm). Dorms Rs45; singles Rs70; doubles with bath Rs150-200. ●

Yogi Lodge (☎392588 or 401427). Kalika Gali. Around the corner from Golden Lodge and the Golden Temple. Centered around a comfy sitting lounge, this popular backpacker guest house feels a lot more like a home than most old city digs. Restaurant open daily 8am-3:30pm and 6-9:30pm. Dorms Rs50; singles Rs80; doubles Rs100. ●

Shanti Guest House (☎392568 or 400956). Near Manikarnika Ghat. Huge hotel that could pass for a small international city. Rooftop restaurant, which serves as Party Central for the Old City, has some of the best views in town. Below, freshly painted rooms of all shapes and sizes fill every corner. Reception changes money, rents motorcycles, and schedules boat rides. Singles Rs50-80; doubles Rs70-600. ●

Om House Lodge (☎392728). Nichi Brahmapuri, Bansphataki, Old City. Facing Dasashwamedh Ghat, turn left at Godaulia Crossing up the road to Chowk. Look for "Om Lodge" signs on the right and follow the arrows down the alley. Rooms are basic in this quiet place, but VCR, video games, and a library make up for it. Yoga classes Rs50 per hr. Music lessons Rs50 per hr. Dorms Rs25; singles Rs40-80; doubles Rs60-100. ●

Ganges View Hotel (☎313218). Assi Ghat. Next to the Harmony Book Shop. Live like a maharaja in this family-run home-cum-hotel. Each room is an exquisitely decorated work of art; glass chandeliers and velvet curtains dangle in the main dining room. Hosts free lectures and concerts during the regular season. Doubles Rs650-1200. ❸

Trimurti Guest House (☎323554). Saraswati Phatak, Old City. Head down Dasashwamedh Rd. towards the river; take the last left before the ghat (there will be signs for Trimurti and for Kashi Vishwanath "Golden" Temple); the guest house is 400m down on the left. Simple but adequate rooms spiral up to the roof. Dorms Rs30; singles Rs50; doubles Rs80-250. ●

Hotel Arya (☎276426). B 8/47 Sonar Pura. 1km south of Godaulia Crossing, on the main road to Assi ghat, near Harishchandra ghat. Convenient location and resourceful manager make (almost) everything easily accessible. Bike rentals, railway station pickup, and rooftop hut restaurant. Spacious rooms with attached bath, some with TVs and balconies. Singles Rs150-200; doubles 250-350. ●

Hotel La-Ra India (☎320323). Dasashwamedh Ghat Rd. 50m on your right after Godaulia Crossing, as you head down to the *ghats*. Slightly upscale, La-Ra provides clean, cool, marble-floor relief from the usual Godaulia grunge. All rooms with attached bath and telephone. Singles Rs225-525; doubles Rs275-650. ❷

Hotel Relax (☎343503). Parade Kothi, Cantonment. One hundred meters down the alley opposite the train station, on your right. Nothing special but comfortable, clean, and convenient for odd hour railway arrivals and departures. Rooms Rs75-250. ●

🏮 FOOD

Dining options in Varanasi range from the local, pilgrim-friendly, vegetarian eateries to those trying to satisfy the Western palate with interpretations of Italian, Mexican, Israeli, and oriental dishes; only a few of these are worth seeking out.

▧ **Keshari Restaurant,** off Dasashwamedh Rd. Near Godaulia crossing, down an alley opposite the La-Ra India Hotel, on the right. 2 floors offer rows and rows of booths for hungry shoppers. Quick and clean, Keshari satisfies with good *thalis* (Rs40-80) and countless other veg. dishes (Rs35-60). Open daily 9:30am-10:30pm. ●

▧ **Mandarin Restaurant and Bar,** in the Shivam Hotel, next to the Hotel Relax, near the railway station. This clean, calm restaurant serves a wider, tastier selection of Chinese dishes than most other places. Veg. Manchurian Rs40. Open daily 7am-11pm. ●

Pizzeria Vaatika, Assi Ghat, up to the right of the steps, in a garden. A slice of the Mediterranean on the banks of the Ganges. Mellow out over wood-oven pizza (Rs45-60), pasta (ravioli Rs45), and the distant sound of temple bells. Open daily 8am-10pm. ●

Bread of Life Bakery and Western Restaurant (☎313912). B3/322, Shivala, on the main road between Assi Ghat and Godaulia. The vision of an American interior designer and his German wife, this bistro is far removed from Varanasi's *dhabas*. Western favorites from tunafish sandwiches (Rs60) to mousaka (Rs80). Open daily 8am-9pm. ●

Malika Restaurant, in Hotel Padmini, 400m down Sigra Mahmoor Ganj Rd. from Sigra Crossing; look for the tall bldg. with flags. More kitsch than "classy," but miniature train seating is all too fun. All aboard for Western breakfasts (Rs70-95) and a good range of Indian/Mughlai dishes. *Jhal frezi* Rs70. Open daily 7:30am-10:30pm. ●

Shanti Guest House Rooftop Restaurant, near Manikarnika Ghat. With fantastic views of the Ganga and Manikarnika *ghat* and a pool table, this high-in-the-sky patio is the top backpacker hangout in town. The food itself is unremarkable, but no one seems to care. Guest house gate closes at midnight, but just knock loudly for entry.

New Monga Restaurant, Dasashwamedh Ghat Rd., just after Godaulia Crossing, on the right. Low-hanging wicker lamps, white tablecloths, bow-tie service and underground seclusion make for an almost romantic setting. Thumpin' Hindi pop keeps things lively. Veg. *thalis* Rs50-65. Open daily 10am-10pm. ●

Yelchico Bar and Restaurant, 2 branches in Varanasi. The first is near Godaulia Crossing. As you approach from the river, it's just past Mandanpura Rd., down a flight of stairs on the left. The only place in the Old City where you can get a glass of beer (Rs80). Open daily noon-10pm. The 2nd branch, at Sigra Crossing, is more of a civilized bar than a restaurant, though it serves meals. Open daily 11am-10:30pm. ❶

Kamesh Hut Garden Bar and Restaurant, Jagatganj. With your back to the Hotel Pradeep, walk right; turn right at the 1st alley. Green, open-air oasis has prompt service and a decent menu. Butter chicken Rs50. Beer Rs70. Open daily 7:30am-11pm. ❶

Gazal Bar and Restaurant, inside Hotel Vaibhav, 600m north of the main railway station, after the Hotel India. Cool basement air, beer (Rs60), and free peanuts, make this a good alternative to the railway waiting-rooms. Open 11am-11pm. ❶

🔾 SIGHTS

THE GHATS OF THE GANGA

A little religious imagination and some knowledge of what is going on at the city's countless sacred sites can help, but to experience the life and vibrancy of Varanasi—its crowded temples and teeming *ghats*—all you really need are your five senses and an open mind ready to be bent gently out of shape.

The holy Ganga is what draws millions of pilgrims to Varanasi, and the series of **ghats** (steps) that line the river are at the heart of city life; abuzz with crowds of people from before dawn until long after nightfall, the *ghats* are where the pounding pulse of the ancient city beats fastest. Thousands come at dawn to make offerings to the heavenly water, but the *ghats* are far from reserved for purely sacred activities. People stroll, meditate, play cricket, and make music along the banks. Dive-bombing teenagers crash into the river from the steps, while others bathe and wash their clothes in the waters. The Ganga draws all sorts of life and death as well, for in Varanasi, **cremations** are viewed as auspicious events (a reversal of traditional beliefs). They take place right on the *ghats* rather than out of town on inauspicious soil, as they do everywhere else. The bodies of those who can't afford cremation, as well as those of holy men, pregnant women, and children under 12, are dumped straight into the river and can sometimes be seen floating by. Water buffalo also bathe in the river, and sewers dump directly into the Ganga. *Let's Go* does not recommend bathing with buffalo.

The steps themselves are huge and sometimes number more than 100 from top to bottom, though some are hidden when the water is high. The name of each *ghat* is painted on the retaining walls in large letters in both Devanagari and Roman script. Memorizing the location of some of the major *ghats* will make finding your way around a lot easier. A **boat ride** along the river is one of the highlights of any Varanasi itinerary. The best time to do this is at dawn, when the *ghats* are their most crowded and the whole city shines like gold in the early-morning light. (A small boat seating four people should cost no more than Rs40 for an hour's trip from Dasashwamedh.) The *ghats* are presented here from south to north.

ASSI GHAT. The southern end of Varanasi's riverfront begins with Assi Ghat, a broad clay bank at the meeting point of the Ganga and Assi Rivers. Assi Ghat is one of the busiest and most important of all the bathing *ghats*. Its muddy banks are alive throughout the day with pilgrims crowding to pay their respects to the large Shiva *linga* that stands in the shade of a pipal tree just a few feet from the water's edge. Shops, drink-stalls, and restaurants make this a popular destination for non-religious travelers too. Assi Ghat is surrounded by temples, several of them among the most popular in the whole city (see **The Banks and Beyond,** p. 711).

TULSI GHAT. Tulsi Ghat, named for the famed 16th century Hindi poet, Tulsi Das, whose house sits at the top of the steps, is the next significant *ghat* after Assi (see **The Banks and Beyond,** p. 711). Back from the water above Tulsi Ghat is one of Varanasi's most ancient sacred spots, the **Lolarka Kund.** Sunk deep into the ground, this tank was at one time the site where early Hindus worshiped Surya, the sun god. Today, it is a major point of pilgrimage during the annual festival of Lolarka Shashthi (Aug. or Sept.), when thousands of couples come here to pray for sons.

HARISHCHANDRA GHAT. The next major *ghat* as you head north is Harishchandra Ghat, Varanasi's second most important cremation ground, distinguished by the spires of black smoke that rise throughout the day from the funeral pyres. The constant stream of mourners and attendants makes Harishchandra one of the busiest *ghats.* Though widely believed to be the oldest cremation site in Varanasi, it has not been accorded quite the same level of religious importance as Manikarnika farther north. **Photography is strictly prohibited.**

KEDAR GHAT AND CHOWKI GHAT. The *ghat* with the red, white, and green stripes is **Kedar Ghat.** Kedar means "field," and this is the field in which liberation is said to grow. The Kedar Temple, one of Varanasi's oldest and most important Shiva temples, is so holy that just resolving to come here is enough to liberate a person from the accumulated sins of two whole lifetimes. The stone mound that marks Shiva's presence here is thought to be the oldest *linga* in the city. **Chowki Ghat** has a fierce collection of *nagas*, early aquatic snake-gods at the top of its steps, around a central tree. From here to Dasashwamedh Ghat, a long stretch of *ghats* used for laundry is marked by a collage of colorful saris and *lungis* stretched out to dry. If you look up above at the walls on Raja Ghat, along the way, you can see just how high the monsoon-filled Ganga flooded in 1967 and '78.

DASASHWAMEDH GHAT. The next major bathing spot and the most crowded *ghat* in Varanasi, Dasashwamedh Ghat is often referred to as the **"Main Ghat."** Every morning, busloads of pilgrims make their way past the fruit stalls and flower sellers that line the wide road leading to the steps. Dasashwamedh is said to be the spot where the creator god, Brahma, performed 10 royal horse-sacrifices *(ashwamedhas)* with the mythical King Divodasa. Bathing here is supposed to bestow on pilgrims all the benefits of ten horse sacrifices. On the *ghat* is **Brahmeshwar,** the *linga* that Brahma established here after performing his sacrifices. Just south of Dasashwamedh Ghat, Shitala, the goddess of smallpox and other diseases, is worshipped in the **Shitala Temple.** Adorned with colorful paint, tinsel, and flags, this small box of a temple is more popular than any of the *lingas* of Dasashwamedh.

MAN MANDIR GHAT TO LALITA GHAT. Man Mandir Ghat is topped by one of the observatories built in the 18th century by Maharaja Jai Singh of Jaipur. Climb up on the right side of the building to see a collection of astronomical scales made of stone. Above **Mir Ghat** and **Lalita Ghat** are several important temples. The colorful **Vishalakshi Temple** belongs to a "Wide-Eyed" local goddess, but it is also a *Shakti pitha*—the eye of the goddess Sati (or in some accounts, her earring) is said to have landed here when she was chopped apart in the heavens. Nearby, a deep well, the **Dharma Kup,** marks the site where Yama, the god of death, paid homage to Shiva. At the top of Lalita Ghat, an ornate **Nepali Temple** contains erotic wood carvings (Rs10).

MANIKARNIKA GHAT. An axis of holiness runs between the **Vishwanath Temple** (see **The Banks and Beyond,** p. 711) and the next *ghat*, Manikarnika Ghat. This is the most sacred of all the *ghats* and the final stop on the popular *panchathirthi* pilgrimage, which leads devotees along the length of the city's riverside banks. Bathing here and worshiping at Vishwanath is a daily routine for many Benarsis and an essential part of any pilgrimage. Manikarnika Ghat takes its name from **Mani-**

karnika Kund, the small white tank just past the cremation grounds, which Vishnu is said to have dug out at the beginning of time and filled with his sweat. This first pool of water so delighted Shiva that he dropped his bejeweled earring *(mani-karnika)* in it. Vishnu's footprints are nearby, under a circular shelter.

The area just south of Manikarnika has become the city's **primary cremation ground.** Boats full of wood are moored here, and the pyres burn throughout the day and night, consuming the corpses of those lucky enough to have been liberated here. Bodies are carried on stretchers down the winding streets to the riverside, where they are dipped in the Ganga before being burned for three hours on fires lit from an eternal flame on the *ghat.* When the burning is complete, the eldest son of the deceased throws a pot of Ganga water onto the fire, and the ashes are sprinkled in the river. Above the *ghat* are hospices where the dying come to wait their turn. Visitors can watch the cremations from boats or buildings above the *ghat,* but you are likely to offend and upset mourners and workers if you linger too long or too conspicuously on the *ghat.* **Photography is strictly prohibited.**

SANKATA GHAT AND NORTHERN SIGHTS. Next is **Sankata Ghat,** above which is the blue and yellow temple of **Sankata Devi,** a powerful mother-goddess. The important bathing site is **Panchganga Ghat.** Five rivers are said to converge here: the Ganga, Yamuna, and Saraswati, which flow from Allahabad, and the Dhutapapa and Kirana, which have dried up. Vishnu chose this place as the greatest spot in Kashi, and his **Bindu Madhava** temple sits above the *ghat.* During the month of Karthik (Oct.-Nov.) the temple and the *ghat* are decked with lamps at night. For the rest of the year the most prominent feature of Panchganga Ghat is the **Dharhara Mosque** at the top, built over the ruins of an earlier Bindu Madhava temple by Emperor Aurangzeb. It is closed to visitors due to threats from Hindu zealots to "take it back." A statue of a cow at **Gai Ghat** watches over an array of Shiva *lingas.* Nearby is **Trilochan Ghat,** with the popular temple of the "Three-Eyed" Shiva. **Varanasi Devi,** the patron-goddess of Varanasi, also inhabits this temple.

Despite being in the oldest part of the city, the *ghats* farther north are more spaced out and less crowded those in the southern part of the city. The next *ghat* of visible importance is **Raj Ghat,** the last before the Malaviya Bridge. This is the crossing-point where, since ancient times, traders have ferried across the Ganga. The temple of **Adi Keshava** (Original Vishnu) sits on a high bank to the north of the bridge and marks the northern city limits. Vishnu washed his feet here, and the image inside the temple was shaped by Vishnu himself. Other than the Ganga and some pasture land, there is not much to see here nowadays.

THE BANKS AND BEYOND

THE VISHWANATH TEMPLE (GOLDEN TEMPLE). Up Dasashwamedh Rd. from the river and right through a temple-like archway, signs lead to the temple of Shiva as Vishwanath (Lord of All). Nicknamed the "Golden" Temple, it contains the Vishweshwar *linga,* the first one on earth and one of India's 12 *jyotirlingas,* which are said to have shot up from the ground as shafts of light. All of Varanasi is measured in circles around Vishwanath, making it the city's most important pilgrimage site. The temple is closed to non-Hindus, but shopkeepers across the road happily charge visitors for the view from their rooftops (Rs10). The temple's shining spire, encrusted with over 280kg of gold, soars up into the city, and bells chime at the many smaller temples that lead to it. There has been a Shiva temple on this site since ancient times, but the present building dates back only to 1777. Earlier temples here were repeatedly destroyed by waves of Muslim invasions; the last of these took place in 1669, when the temple was torn down at the command of Aurangzeb. The Jnana Vapi Mosque was constructed on top of the half-demolished ruins of an earlier Vishwanath Temple and still stands today, surrounded by soldiers and a cordon of barbed wire. Hindu extremists have made repeated threats to destroy the mosque and reclaim the old holy site.

JNANA VAPI. Under a pavilion, in between the temple and the mosque, is the **Jnana Vapi** itself, a "Well of Wisdom" said to have been in existence since the very beginning of the world. The waters that sprang up here when Shiva dug up the earth with his trident were the first pure waters anywhere on earth.

ANNAPURNA TEMPLE. The most important goddess temple in Varanasi is dedicated to Shakti, the divine embodiment of power or energy and Shiva's consort, in the form of Annapurna. Armed with spoons and saucepans, Annapurna is a provider of food; a **Mountain of Food Festival** occurs here in late October or early November. *(Opposite Vishwanath, just down the lane. Closed to non-Hindus.)*

KALA BHAIRONATH. Once an angry and sinful form of Shiva, Kala Bhaironath (also known as Bhairava) chopped off the fifth head of the god Brahma after he failed to recognize Shiva, embodied in a shimmering *linga* of light, as supreme among all the gods. As punishment, the rotting head stuck to his hand, and for years, Bhairava had to wander remorsefully around the whole of India, using the skull as a begging bowl for his food. It was not until he got to Varanasi that the head miraculously dropped from his hands, and Shiva appointed him the "chief justice" of the sacred city. He keeps an eye on Varanasi's residents, devours their sins as they are washed away by the Ganga's holy waters, and metes out instant retribution for the accumulated misdeeds of those who die here. The temple is often crowded with supplicant sinners offering incense, garlands, and all things orange to the image of this holy police chief. *(Just south of the HPO on Kabir Chaura Rd.; head up Chowk Rd. from Godaulia and turn right towards the post office. Open daily 5am-noon and 2-10pm.)* Not too far away, on the other side of the Chowk-Kabir Chaura Rd. crossing, is the temple of **Bare Ganesh,** the central Ganesh shrine in Varanasi.

DURGA TEMPLE AND KUND. The impressive red tower of this temple stretches up into the sky above its adjacent tank. It is believed that the goddess Durga rested here after saving the world from an otherwise "unassailable" demon, and she continues to be regarded as the protectress of Southern Kashi. The walls inside the temple, constructed in the 18th century, are inscribed with Tulsi Das's verses and adorned with paintings, the most notable of which depicts the love of Bharat, Rama's step-brother, who worshiped Rama's wooden sandals for the 14 years of Rama's exile. The shrine is also known as the "monkey temple." *(Straight west off Assi Ghat, a 5min. walk from the river. Open 5am-11pm.)*

TULSI MANAS MANDIR. Built of white marble and flanked by palm trees, this modern Vishnu temple was erected in 1964 in honor of Tulsi Das, the premier poet of the Hindi language who translated the Sanskrit epic, the *Ramayana*, into Hindi in the 16th century. The complete epic is inscribed on the inside walls in the poet's Hindi script, and painted depictions of scenes from the story line the temple walls. Toward the back of the temple, a collection of brightly painted mechanical figures acts out the timeless tale to the delight of parents and children passing through. *(Rs1 to enter.)* A mechanical mock-up of the great poet himself sits, book in hand, by the temple door. *(Just south of the Durga Temple. Open daily 5am-noon and 4-8:30pm.)*

SANKAT MOCHAN TEMPLE. The Sankat Mochan Temple, in a patch of trees southwest of Assi Ghat, is dedicated to Hanuman and is considered to be one of the most important temples in Varanasi; orange *sindur* smears attest this devotion. Each spring it is home to a popular music fair. *(Open daily 4:30am-10:30pm.)*

BENARES HINDU UNIVERSITY (BHU). Founded in 1916 by the reformer Madan Mohan Malaviya, the university was intended to merge modern ideas with traditional Hindu learning. The campus has two places suited to shorter visits. The **Sri Vishwanath Temple,** the largest temple in the city, has a large, white spire modeled on the one knocked down by Aurangzeb in 1669. *(Open daily 4am-noon and 1-9pm.)*

Bharat Kala Bhawan, the BHU museum, has an extensive collection of miniature paintings, artifacts, and sculptures. The second floor contains the sculptures and paintings of Alice Boner, the renowned Indophile who claimed to understand India "on its own terms." There is plenty here from Varanasi as well, from 19th-century etchings of the *ghats* to a statue of Krishna lifting Mt. Govardhana. The most stunning artifacts, a collection of coins, ornate jewelry, and emperor's jade dagger hilts, are kept in a safe room in the **Nidhi Gallery.** *(Lanka Crossing, at the south end of town. Museum open M-Sa 11am-4:30pm. Rs40.)*

RAMNAGAR FORT. The Ganga's eastern shore has one point of interest: Ramnagar Fort, the castle of Varanasi's maharaja. The fort contains a **royal museum;** while most exhibits are rather dilapidated, the royal family's sedan chairs, swords, and an extravagant astronomical clock are all on display. *(Open daily 9am-5:30pm; Rs7.)* Ramnagar is probably not worth the trip unless it's for the **Ram Lila,** the festive Ramayana pageant, held in September and October. *(In the village of Ramnagar opposite BHU at the south end of the city. Ferries at the end of Rawnagar Rd. cross the river for Rs2.)*

BHARAT MATA TEMPLE. A spirit of urbane and modernized Hinduism can be seen in the Bharat Mata Temple, on the city's western outskirts, south of the Cantonment. Mahatma Gandhi inaugurated this temple, which has a marble, swimming-pool-sized relief map of Mother India as its presiding "deity." If you can get one of the temple's "residents" to unlock them, the upper balconies provide the best views. *(A 15min. walk down Vidyapith Rd. from the railway station. Open daily 7am-6pm.)*

🎵 MUSIC

Varanasi is a center for Indian classical music (see p. 100), and many westerners come here to study the sitar or tabla. The best resource is the School of Performing Arts at **Benares Hindu University** (☎307641). Though the school itself only offers degree courses in Hindi and English, the faculty unofficially give **private music lessons.** These tend to be costly, so ask for recommendations of other reputable teachers. A good but touristy place to learn sitar or tabla is the **Triveni Music Centre** (☎452266), on Keval Gali in Godaulia, near the Vishnu Rest House. Instructor Nandu and his brother give lessons (Rs50-100 per hr.) and performances (M, Th, Su, 8-10pm, Rs40). They also sell instruments at inflated prices. The well-established **International Music Centre,** south of Dasashwamedh Rd., also offers private sitar and tabla lessons (Rs100-150/hr.), as well as evening concerts.

   Purchasing musical instruments can be a tricky business, for there are many sitar and tabla stores in the Old City. The faculty at BHU recommends one shop; the proprietor, **Mr. Nitai Chandra Nath,** is a sage of string instruments and a true artisan. From Godaulia Crossing, facing Dasashwamedh, turn right onto Madandura Rd., and turn down the third lane on your left (25m after Universal Book Co.); the Jangambali (Bengali Tola) Post Office will be on your left, and the unmarked sitar store is several doors down. If you cannot find the shop, ask in the street for **Nitai Babu,** and someone will show you the way. (Sitars Rs4000-7000.) **Imtiyaz Ali,** Siddh Giri Bagh, is a tabla shop recommended by Mr. Nath. Hop in a cycle-rickshaw and ask for the Maulavi Bagh Masjid in Siddh Giri Bagh; the store is to the right of the mosque. (Brass tablas Rs2000; copper tablas Rs2500.)

🛍 SHOPPING

Varanasi is famous for its silk, and the touts will never let you forget it. There are several shops in Varanasi with fixed prices and government-enforced quality control. Two of the oldest and most reputable stores are on Vishwanath Gali in the Old City: **Mohan Silk Stores** (☎392354), 5/54 Vishwanath Gali, and

Bhagwan Stores, D10/32 Vishwanath Gali, both on the right-hand side shortly after the main gate leading off from Dasashwamedh Rd. toward the Golden Temple. **J.R. Ivory Arts and Curios** (☎401772), D20 Vishwanath Gali, farther up Vishwanath Gali on the left, used to carry silk but now only stocks beautiful wood carvings and other fine art ranging in price from Rs80 to Rs45,000. Two other silk shops are in Sindhu Nagar, near the intersection of Aurangabad and Vidyapith Rds.: **M/S Bhagwanlila Exports** (☎222533) 41 Sindhu Nagar Colony, Sigra, and **Mahalakshmi Saree House** (☎221319) 10 Chandrika Nager, Sigra. Also recommended is "The King of Banares Sarees," **Chowdhary Brothers** (☎320469), Thatheri Bazaar, a short walk up Chowk from the police station, on the right. **Mehrotra Silk Factory** (☎345289), SC21/72 Englishia Line, Cantonment, with its seemingly infinite selection of silks, may be the best of these shops. The store carries shawls (US$9-8), tapestries (US$10-20), and raw fabric (US$5 per meter). To get there, walk up Vidyapith Rd., with the railway station in sight, make a right onto Station Rd., and then look for signs about 100m on the left. It's a good idea to visit these shops to get a sense of the prices of top-thread silk before bargaining in the Chowk or Old City. (Shops open daily 10am-8pm.) When buying silk, also remember to insist on buying both a horizontal and vertical thread. Real silk, when burned, has the odor of burning hair. Many fabrics in the market are woven with silk in one direction and a synthetic fiber in the other. When the fake thread is burned, it will smell like paper or plastic.

⚡ DAYTRIP FROM VARANASI

SARNATH

Auto-rickshaws putter wherever the money takes them (Rs40 to Varanasi). Buses go to the railway station (frequent 7am-7:30pm, 40min., Rs5). Tempos go to many different points in Varanasi, including the railway station (Rs8). To get to the temples, cross the intersection at the bus stand; the gate to the modern temple's park is 200m down Dharmapal Rd., on the right. Open daily 4-11:30am and 1:30-8pm. Entrance to stupa and ruins park US$5. Archaeological museum open Sa-Th 10am-5pm. Rs2. Chowkahndi Stupa is open dawn-dusk. Free.

In the wooded suburbs north of Varanasi lies Sarnath, a quiet and well-maintained site of ruins marking the location of Gautama Buddha's first sermon, the famous "Sermon in the Deer Park." After the Buddha attained enlightenment in Bodh Gaya, he walked the 200km to Sarnath, with lotuses blooming where his feet touched the ground. Gathering his former companions here, among the deer and peacocks, he revealed the Noble Eightfold Path. In later years, he occasionally returned to this quiet grove to meditate.

In the 3rd century BC, when the region was under the rule of the Mauryas, *stupas* were built to commemorate the Buddha's visits. This construction continued until the 4th century AD, when the Hindu Guptas rose to power and Buddhist influence began to wane. Sarnath's prestige as a center of Buddhism came to an abrupt end during the 12th century when it was demolished by Qutb-ud-din Aibak.

Sarnath makes for a pleasant stroll. Even in the time-tired state they are in today, the monuments here provide impressive evidence of the rich Buddhist culture that once flourished here and the importance that Buddhist philosophy once held throughout much of northern India. There has been little modern development in Sarnath since its monuments were excavated and explored during the 19th century by spade-*wallah* supreme, Sir Alexander Cunningham. With a bit of selective squinting, it is still possible to imagine Sarnath as it might have been when the Buddha himself walked through its woods more than 2000 years ago.

Sarnath is contained within a triangle of road. From the south, Sarnath Rd. comes from Varanasi and splits in two by the Rangoli Garden Restaurant. The branch heading northwest is **Ashoka Rd.** and runs past the Archaeological Museum. The branch going northeast goes past the UP Tourist Bungalow. Connecting these two roads after they diverge is the main road, **Dharmapal Rd.,** which runs east-west and contains almost all of the sights. The **bus stand** is at the intersection of Dharmapal Rd. and the road that passes the UP Tourist Bungalow. The **post office** (open M-Sa 8am-4pm) is near the bus stand and opposite the **UP Tourist Bungalow.** There's a small information counter in the bungalow, which gives out maps of the sites (open M-Sa 10am-5pm).

Most of Sarnath's points of interest are recently excavated piles of rubble: this is a place with more atmosphere and history than sights to write home about. However, the first stop on the way to the archaeological enclosure is intact. The sandstone spires of the modern Buddhist temple, **Mulgandha Kuti Vihar,** beckon from the main gate. Its peaceful interior was decorated by the Japanese artist, Kosetsu Nosi, with grandiose murals inspired by the *Buddhacarita* (The Acts of the Buddha). Nearby stands a pipal tree that is supposed to be a close relative of the tree under which the Buddha attained enlightenment. Behind the Mulgandha Kuti Vihar's grounds, a manicured garden leads to a small zoo and the **Deer Park.**

In the next enclosure over from the modern temple, the **Dhamekh Stupa,** the only ancient structure left intact by Qutb-ud-din's armies, looms above the trees. It commemorates the spot where the Buddha delivered his first sermon. Begun sometime during the 5th or 6th century, in the twilight of Buddhist predominance in North India, it remains unfinished. The bottom is made of decorated stone, with eight niches that once held images of the Buddha; the top is little more than clay bricks. Next to the Dhamekh Stupa lie the remains of the **Dharmarajika Stupa;** it must have been an impressive shrine in its day, but today only the foundations exist. It was built by the Mauryan emperor Ashoka in the 3rd century BC to house the relics of the Buddha; Ashoka himself is thought to have come here to meditate in what was once a major monastic center. The structure was reduced to rubble in the 18th century by hopeful locals hunting for treasure.

Next to the *stupa* are the remains of the **Main Shrine,** built by Ashoka to mark a favorite meditation spot of the Buddha. At the end of the ruined structure, down a shallow well, is the bottom portion of **Ashoka's pillar.** The column is engraved with Buddhist edicts in Brahmi script that warn Buddhist monks and nuns against creating rifts among the followers of the Buddha (the advice wasn't taken). The capital from Ashoka's pillar is one of the great masterpieces of early Indian art and is preserved at the **Archaeological Museum,** opposite the main entrance to the Dharmarajika Stupa compound and at the intersection of Dharmapal and Ashoka Rd. On display directly in front of the museum entrance are the famous four lions of the capital, whose design was adopted as the emblem of the Indian republic and appears on all national currency. The museum's collection is well-maintained and includes a number of excellent pieces, such as a perfectly wrought teaching Buddha from the Gupta period and two giant, umbrella-toting *bodhisattva* statues.

Beyond the main strip of Dharmapal Rd. shrines, 600m south of the Archaeological Museum on Ashoka Rd. rises the curious melange of Buddhist-Mughal architecture that is the **Chowkhandi Stupa.** The rectangular Gupta-period foundation commemorating the site where the Buddha met his five disciples is topped by a crowning tower in the octagonal Mughal style. It was built by either Emperor Akbar or Raja Govandhan, the local ruler, to mark the site where Emperor Humayun once spent the night. Also worth visiting is Sarnath's collection of temples dotted around town. Each displays a unique style of architecture and can make the aggravations of urban India seem years away.

ALLAHABAD इलाहाबाद ☎ 0532

The holy city of Allahabad stands at the sacred *sangam*, or confluence, of the Ganga and the Yamuna Rivers. Into these two rivers flows a third, the mystical Saraswati, river of wisdom. Lord Brahma called this spot Tirth Raj ("King of Pilgrimage Sites"), and all devout Hindus try to bathe in the waters at least once in their lives. Known for thousands of years as Prayag (Confluence), the city is nowadays more commonly known as Allahabad, the Perso-Arabic name meaning "Place of God" given to the city by the Mughal emperors.

The British declared Allahabad the capital of the United Provinces in 1901. The Indian Independence movement was strongly rooted here, thanks to the work of the Nehrus, the Allahabad family that forged a political dynasty after Independence. A relatively tourist-free city, Allahabad is well worth a couple of days, and it becomes the focus of national attention every 12 years when it hosts the **Maha Kumbh Mela,** the most important of all Hindu festivals in which millions of pilgrims converge at the Sangam. In May 2001, Allahabad was formally renamed **Prayagraj** to appease Hindu fundamentalists organizations who protested against the Islamic name given to the city by Mughal emperor Akbar.

⌐ TRANSPORTATION

Trains: Allahabad Junction Railway Station, Leader Rd. To: **Agra** (11½hr., 4:35am, Rs179); **Delhi** (8hr., 28 per day, 1am-10:55pm, Rs245; *Rajdhani Exp.* 2301 and 2309 7hr., Tu, W, Sa, Su 2:45am, A/C chair Rs975); **Gorakhpur** (9-11hr., 9:15pm, Rs151); **Gwalior** (11-15hr., 1-3 per day 6:35am-6:30pm, Rs169); **Kanpur** (32 per day, 4:40am-1:20am, Rs107); **Khajuraho** (7hr., 11 per day 6:20am-3:35am, Rs124); **Lucknow** (3-5hr., 4 per day 6:20am-10:30pm, Rs109).

Buses: Civil Lines Bus Stand, MG Rd., next to the Tourist Bungalow. To: **Ayodhya** (5hr., every hr. 6am-10pm, Rs72); **Gorakhpur** (8hr., 8 every hr. 6-10am, Rs124); **Lucknow** (6hr., frequent 4am-8pm, Rs86); **Varanasi** (3hr., every hr. 4am-5pm, Rs72). The **Leader Rd. Bus Stand,** opposite the main Allahabad Junction Railway Station, sends buses to **Agra** (13hr.; 11am, 3 and 7pm; Rs205) and **Delhi** (20hr., 6pm and midnight, Rs 268). **Zero Rd. Bus Stand** is north of Chowk.

Local Transportation: Cycle-rickshaws from the Allahabad Junction Railway Station to the Civil Lines area are Rs10. From Civil Lines to the Sangam: Rs20. **Tempos** wait at the bus or railway stations. To reach the Sangam, take a tempo to Daraganj Railway Station (Rs5) and walk south from the tracks.

✳ ⁊ ORIENTATION AND PRACTICAL INFORMATION

North of the railway tracks is the tree-shaded, British-built **Civil Lines** area, with all of its roads laid out in a grid; south is the congested and gritty **Chowk** area. The **Yamuna River** flows south of Allahabad until it reaches the sacred confluence point at the southeastern extremity of the city. The Ganga flows down along the eastern edge of the city. In Civil Lines, **Mahatma Gandhi (MG) Rd.,** with its hotels, restaurants, and ice cream stands, is the road to stick to for orientation; it is lined with tall and distinctive statues that make good landmarks. **Kamla Nehru Rd.** turns up from MG Rd. toward Allahabad University. **Leader Rd.** runs along the tracks on the Chowk side. The **Grand Trunk Rd.** streaks through the heart of Chowk. Triveni Rd. leads from the Grand Trunk Rd. to the **Sangam.**

Tourist Office: UP Tourism (☎ 601873). In the Hotel Ilawart complex, MG Rd. Just around the corner from the Civil Lines Bus Stand. These serious-minded pamphlet custodians dispense maps and advice in return for patience and smiles. Open M-Sa 10am-5pm.

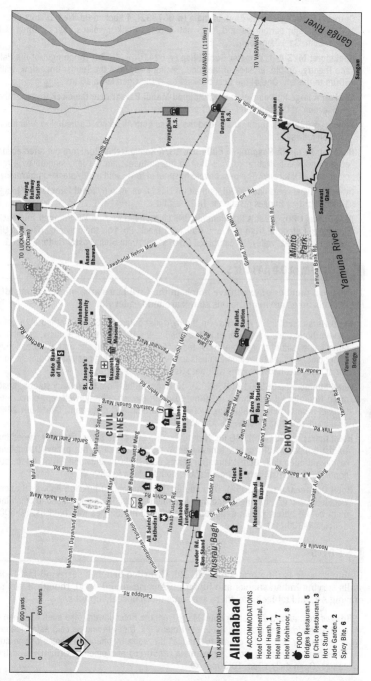

UTTAR PRADESH

Allahabad

♦ ACCOMMODATIONS
Hotel Continental, 9
Hotel Harsh, 1
Hotel Ilawart, 7
Hotel Kohinoor, 8

● FOOD
Bridges Restaurant, 5
El Chico Restaurant, 3
Hot Stuff, 4
Jade Garden, 2
Spicy Bite, 6

TO LUCKNOW (200km)

TO KANPUR (200km)

TO VARANASI (119km)

TO VARANASI

Ganga River

Yamuna River

Sangam

Saraswati Ghat

Minto Park

Fort

Hanuman Temple

Prayag Railway Station

Prayagghat R.S.

Daraganj R.S.

City Railrd. Station

Leader Rd. Bus Stand

Civil Lines Bus Stand

Zero Rd. Bus Station

Allahabad Junction

Anand Bhawan

Allahabad University

Allahabad Museum

State Bank of India

St. Joseph's Cathedral

Nazareth Hospital

All Saints' Cathedral

GPO

Clock Tower

Khuldabad Mandi Bazaar

CIVIL LINES

CHOWK

Khusrau Bagh

Bandh Rd.

Kacheri Rd.

Jawaharlal Nehru Marg

Mahatma Gandhi (MG) Rd.

Pannalal Marg

Kamla Nehru Rd.

Kasturba Gandhi Marg

Tejbahadur Sapru Rd.

Sardar Patel Marg

Clive Rd.

Muir Rd.

Tashkent Marg

Sarojni Naidu Marg

Maharshi Dayanand Marg

Pushpadevpades Tailoram Marg

Lal Bahadur Shastri Marg

Colvin Rd.

Nawab Yusuf Rd.

Smith Rd.

Leader Rd.

Dr. Katiu Rd.

Noorulla Rd.

Chhappa Rd.

Grand Trunk Rd. (NH2)

Beni Bandh Rd.

Fort Rd.

Triveni Rd.

Yamuna Bank Rd.

Lauder Rd.

Yamuna Rd.

Yamuna Bridge

Tilak Rd.

Shankar Ali Marg

A.P. Banerji Rd.

Zero Rd.

NSC Rd.

Swami Vivekanand Marg

Lala Sharan Rd.

Grand Trunk Rd. (NH2)

600 yards

600 meters

Currency Exchange: State Bank of India (☎607932). 4 Kacheri Rd. Near District Court. Changes major currencies and AmEx and Thomas Cook traveler's checks. Open M-F 10am-2pm, Sa 10am-noon.

Bookstore: M/S A.H. Wheeler Book Shop (☎624106). MG Rd. To the right of the Palace Theatre, on the left side of the road. Facing away from the Tourist Bungalow, walk 500m to the left. One of the best bookstores in UP. Open M-Sa 10am-7pm.

Market: A large fruit market is at **Khuldabad Mandi Bazaar** near the clock tower, at the intersection of Dr. Katiu and Grand Trunk Rd.

Police: (☎622592). On the main road that leads from All Saints' Cathedral to Allahabad junction railway station.

Hospital: Nazareth Hospital (☎600430). 13/A Kamla Nehru Rd. From the intersection of MG and Kamla Nehru Rd., it's 1km to the northeast, on the left, marked by a red cross and a Hindi sign. The best private hospital in town, with a fully stocked **pharmacy.**

Internet: Cyber-cafes line MG Rd. in the Civil Lines area. Also try **Modi Internet,** SP Marg. 1 block north of Bridges restaurant. Rs25 per hr.

Post Office: GPO, Queen's Rd. From the Civil Lines, head west on MG Rd. until you reach All Saints' Cathedral. Turn right and walk for 1 block. Possibly the only post office in UP with an attached "volleyball complex." Open M-Sa 10am-5pm. **Postal Code:** 211001.

ACCOMMODATIONS

There are a number of expensive hotels in the Civil Lines area, mostly along MG Rd. The cheapies are near the bus stand, around Leader Rd.

Hotel Harsh (☎622197) MG Rd. On the right just before All Saints' Cathedral. A colonial-era hotel once open only to *pukka sahibs,* the Harsh is today a dusty, crumbling ramshackle relic of times gone by. A team of friendly old men sits and waits patiently under creaking fans to welcome guests to musty old rooms big enough to house a couple of royal elephants. Rooms with bath Rs180-230. ❶

Hotel Kohinoor (☎655501 or 656323). 10 Noorulla Rd. From the railway station, head down Noorulla Rd.; the hotel is 300m down on the left. Classy, well-kept place with tasteful rooms, some overlooking a lawn and garden. A/C restaurant. Check-out 24hr. Singles Rs250-400; doubles Rs300-450. ❷

Hotel Ilawart (☎601440). MG Rd. Next to the Civil Lines Bus Stand. Formerly named the Tourist Bungalow, UP Tourism's newly-renovated hotel is clean but pricey. Downstairs restaurant open daily 6am-11pm. Bar serves beer (Rs80) daily noon-11pm. Check-out noon. Dorms Rs100; singles from Rs500; doubles from Rs550. ❶

Hotel Continental (☎652058). Dr. Katiu Rd. From Allahabad Junction Railway Station, walk to Leader Rd., turn right, and then left onto Dr. Katiu Rd. A good place to crash the night before an early train departure. Check-out 24hr. Singles with bath Rs250-500; doubles Rs300-600. ❷

FOOD

Dining outside is the norm along MG Rd. Crowded benches surround fast-food stalls serving Indian snacks and imitation American junk food, though if you're craving A/C and tablecloths, there are some more upscale options.

Bridges Restaurant, 22 Sardar Patel Marg. From the Hotel Ilawart, take a left and then a right at the four-way crossing; it's in the Hotel Vilas. Dimly lit and as cold as a Siberian funeral parlor, this place claims to "bridge" the world by offering a choice of fine cuisines from around the globe. Chow mein (Rs50-75) and omelettes (Rs40) lead the charge. Open daily 10am-10:30pm. ❶

Hot Stuff, Sardar Patel Marg. From the Hotel Ilawart, take a left and then a right at the four-way crossing; it's on the left after 300m. Allahabad's coolest fast-food joint. If you've just been dying for a "Boyish Burger" (Rs30) or a "Hot Stuff Special Foot-Long" (Rs50), then search no more. Open daily 10am-10pm. ❶

Jade Garden Restaurant, MG Rd. Opposite Hotel Harsh. Sparsely decorated and accented with dark red window frames and paintings, this restaurant feels like a ball-room with a lowered ceiling. A wide selection of veg. and non-veg. Indian and Chinese food. Veg. spring roll Rs45, *channa masala* Rs35. Open daily 10am-11pm. ❶

El Chico Restaurant, MG Rd. Take a left from the Hotel Ilawart; it's on the right after the 4-way crossing. No enchiladas here, just a fancy expensive restaurant. Good Indian (*dum aloo* Rs70) and continental dishes as well as delicious mushrooms and baby corn in garlic sauce (Rs100). Open daily 10am-10:30pm. ❷

Spicy Bite, left out of the Hotel Ilawart, and across the street. One of several good open air stalls on MG Rd. for late lunch and dinner. A lively atmosphere, and cheap, tasty Indian and Chinese dishes (everything Rs10-25). ❶

🗲 SIGHTS

TRIVENI SANGAM. Allahabad's chief attraction for millions of Hindu pilgrims is the Triveni Sangam, the meeting point of the rivers Ganga, Yamuna, and Saraswati, and the site of the **Maha Kumbh Mela.** The Yamuna skirts the south side of Allaha-bad; the Ganga flows to the east. The Saraswati, the mythical river of wisdom, is said to flow underground. For a negotiable fee (no more than Rs50) **boats** will take visitors from the fort side to the meeting place of the rivers. The difference in color between the muddy brown Ganga and the pale green Yamuna is plainly visible from the shore. In the summer, the water is warm and shallow, and it is sometimes possible to walk to the Sangam over the floodplains that spread out from the city. Millions of pilgrims camp here during the Kumbh Mela. At other times, especially at dusk, the banks along the Sangam offer good views of the fort, with the city in the background. Alongside the road approaching the Sangam is the **fort** built by Emperor Akbar in 1583. The Indian Army still finds the confluence strategically important, so the fort houses soldiers, and visitors are not allowed to enter.

HANUMAN TEMPLE. In the shadow of the fort's outer wall facing the Sangam is the Hanuman Temple, dedicated to the monkey god. The temple itself is only a shed with many red and gold flags out front, but it's extremely popular nonethe-less and is not to be confused with the Shankar Viman Mandapammulti, the multi-storied affair grinning out over the trees. A constant stream of chanting worship-ers snakes around the tiny temple, showering flower offerings on the image of the god that lies smeared with vermilion below ground level. The floodwaters are said to flow over Hanuman's feet each year before they recede. *(Open daily 4am-10pm.)*

ANAND BHAWAN. Once the mansion of the **Nehru family,** Anand Bhawan is now a museum devoted to their legacy. Independence leader Motilal Nehru, his son, Prime Minister Jawaharlal Nehru, and Jawaharlal's daughter and Prime Minister, Indira Gan-dhi, all lived and worked here, hosting meetings of the Independence movement. The Mahatma even had a room and working area in Anand Bhawan. The surprisingly mod-est Nehru showcase exhibits the family's passion for books—their bookshelves are stacked with everything from Roman Law to Tagore, and all the volumes can be peered at through glass panels. One of the most interesting, historically significant, and well-presented museums in UP, the Anand Bhawan is definitely worth a visit. *(At the northeast corner of the city, close to Allahabad University. Open Tu-Su 9:30am-5pm. Rs5.)* Next door is the **Swaraj Bhawan Museum,** the home of patriarch Motilal Nehru. This mansion has an excellent sound and light show in Hindi, which gives you a tour of the house while leading you through the events of the Independence movement. Apart from the show, however, there's not much else here. *(Open Tu-Su 9:30am-5pm. Show Rs5.)*

ALL SAINTS' CATHEDRAL. The boldest reminder of the British in Allahabad is All Saints' Cathedral, with its soaring Victorian gothic spires and stained glass windows. It was designed by Sir William Emerson, the architect who designed the Victoria Memorial in Calcutta. More weeds are on the lawn than when the English last prayed from these pews for God, King, and Country, and more bats screeching and squealing up in the belfry. However, it is not difficult to picture the old ghosts of the empire click-clacking their heels through the reverberant hall and into the sunshine for tea and cakes with the rest of Allahabad's Sunday-best expatriate crowd. *(In Civil Lines, at the intersection of Mahatma Gandhi Rd. and Sarojini Naidu Marg.)*

KHUSRAU BAGH. If All Saints' is the most Raj-reminiscent relic in Allahabad, then Khusrau Bagh is the most impressive reminder of Mughal rule. These gardens hold the speckled tombs of Khusrau (a son of Emperor Jehangir) and his mother. Following Mughal royal family tradition, Khusrau plotted against his father and was subsequently murdered in 1615 by his brother, the future emperor Shah Jahan. The gardens, shaded by fruit trees and lined with paths, are a popular place for people to come and relax. In the evenings, the place comes alive with games of cricket. *(In the Chowk area down Leader Rd., past the bus station.)*

OTHER SIGHTS. Beyond the fort, on the bank of the Yamuna, is **Saraswati Ghat**, where boats dock and evening ceremony lamps are floated down to the confluence. Follow Yamuna Bank Rd. away from the fort to reach **Minto Park** on the right, where Lord Canning proclaimed in 1858 that India would be ruled by the Queen of England. Independent India has reclaimed the historic site by renaming the park for Madan Mohan Malaviya (an Independence figure and critic of the caste system) and erecting a part-Mauryan, part-Italian monument. *(To reach the other side of the fort, take either a boat ride or detour through the fenced-off military installation behind the fort.)* The **Allahabad Museum,** Kamla Nehru Marg, has a large sculpture collection, including many terra-cotta figures from Kausambi, the ancient city and Buddhist center 60km from Allahabad. There is also a room with photographs and a few Nehru mementos. *(Open Tu-Su 10:15am-4:30pm. Rs150 for foreigners.)*

THE KUMBH MELA
The Maha (Great) Kumbh Mela at Allahabad in 2001 set the record for the world's largest human gathering. An estimated 20 million people came to the city to be present at Hinduism's greatest festival, which marks the holiest time to bathe in the Sangam. Every 12 years, at one precisely calculated moment, all the pilgrims splash into the water in a ritual act believed to undo lifetimes of sin. Columns of charging *sadhus,* often naked and smeared with ash, are among the most zealous bathers.

The story behind the Kumbh Mela concerns a *kumbh* (pot) that is said to have contained an immortality-bestowing nectar. The demons battled the gods for this pot in a struggle that lasted 12 days, during which time four drops of the divine nectar were spilled. One landed at **Haridwar** (see p. 639), one at **Nasik** (see p. 411), one at **Ujjain** (see p. 362), and one at **Allahabad.** The mythical 12-day fight translates into 12 human years, the length of the festival's rotation between cities. Every three years a Kumbh Mela is held in one of the four cities in January or February. The **Maha Kumbh Mela,** held at Allahabad every 12th year, is the greatest of all. Smaller *melas,* known as Magh Melas, are held in Allahabad in off-years during the month of Magh (Jan.-Feb.). In the sixth year, midway between Maha Kumbh Melas, an Ardha ("Half") Kumbh Mela is held. The next Kumbh Mela will take place in Hardwar.

WEST BENGAL

পশ্চিম বঙ্গ

West Bengal is India's most densely populated state, with nearly 800 people to every one of its 90,000 sq. km. With this crush of humanity comes a history and culture that has dominated India for hundreds of years and which continues to thrive today. In the 19th century, Bengal was at the center of literary and religious revival and a hotbed of national activism—the Bengali Renaissance produced India's finest writers, thinkers, and social reformers, including Rabindranath Tagore, India's first Nobel laureate for literature, and Swami Vivekananda, a spiritual leader who attempted to infuse Hinduism with Western ideas of material progress. As the state's capital, Calcutta still maintains its position as India's artistic and intellectual epicenter. Bengalis have developed a reputation of robust character, displayed by pride in their heritage, language, and unique religious traditions.

West Bengal's location, spanning the Gangetic delta, made it a rich agricultural and commercial region that attracted European plunderers during the 17th and 18th centuries. The province came to prominence after the Battle of Plassey in 1757, when Robert Clive defeated Nawab Siraj-ud-Daula and his French allies to claim Bengal for Britain. The British eventually made Calcutta their capital. The year 1905 saw the infamous Partition of Bengal, which divided the state along religious lines: East Bengal (later East Pakistan, then Bangladesh in 1971) and Assam held a strong Muslim population, and West Bengal, with Bihar and Orissa, was largely Hindu. The tragic, bloody partition paved the way for the bigger, bloodier tragedies that accompanied Partition in 1947. Today, Bengal revels in its enlightened Marxist traditions—the Communist Party of India has ruled since the 1960s.

West Bengal is home to a collage of landscapes and cultures. At its northern end, in the foothills of the Himalayas, is Darjeeling, India's most famous hill station. The southern end of the state drops right down to sea level at the swampy mangrove forests of the Sunderbans, home to the Royal Bengal Tiger. One hundred kilometers inland is the choked, crowded, yet utterly captivating city of Calcutta.

HIGHLIGHTS OF WEST BENGAL

India's most famous hill station, **Darjeeling** (p. 744), seduces heat-weary travelers with tea plantations, toy trains, and superb views of the Himalayas.

Calcutta's temples, monuments, museums, and parks (p. 732) are rivaled only by the unchecked exuberance of the city's denizens.

CALCUTTA কলিকাতা   ☎ 033

Oh Calcutta! Bursting at the seams with 13 million people, Calcutta is India's largest city area-wise, encompassing a mind-boggling 853 sq. km. Even to its own residents, Calcutta often seems like a human cyclone. You don't just walk down the street—you step into it, jump over it, and try to scoot your way around the worst parts of it. Wherever you go, you can't avoid breathing in layers of black soot. Street vendors hawking everything from *biryani* to "Galvin Gline" watches rule the sidewalks by day; families sleep by the thousands on

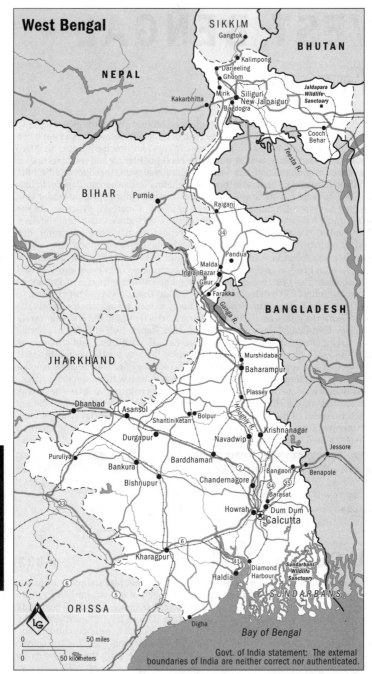

West Bengal

SIKKIM
Gangtok

BHUTAN

NEPAL

Kalimpong
Darjeeling
Ghoom
Mirik
Kakarbhitta
Siliguri
New Jalpaiguri
Bagdogra

Jaldapara
Wildlife
Sanctuary

Cooch
Behar

Teesta R.

BIHAR
Purnia

Raiganj

34

BANGLADESH

Pandua

Malda
Ingraj Bazar
Gaur
Farakka

Ganga R.

JHARKHAND

Murshidabad
Baharampur

Plassey

Dhanbad
Asansol
Shantiniketan
Bolpur

Hooghly R.

Krishnanagar

Durgapur
Navadwip

Jessore

Puruliya
Bankura
Barddhaman

Bishnupur
Chandernagore

2

Bangaon

35

Benapole

34
Barasat

33

Howrah
Dum Dum
Calcutta

6

Kharagpur

41

Diamond
Harbour

Sundarbans
Wildlife
Sanctuary

Haldia

6

5

ORISSA

N

SUNDARBANS

Digha

Bay of Bengal

0   50 miles
0   50 kilometers

Govt. of India statement: The external
boundaries of India are neither correct nor authenticated.

WEST BENGAL

the pavement at night. And yet the same people who lament the city's overpopulation and pollution also speak of their hometown as a "City of Joy" (the name of Calcutta's most famous slum). For years the city has enjoyed a position at the vanguard of Indian culture, dictating intellectual trends for the whole country. The city churns out poets, painters, and saints, and is deservedly proud of its magnificent parks and palaces.

The city's name derives from the word "Kalikshetra" (Ground of Kali), and the worship of Kali is an essential part of the city's character; the Durga Puja in October is the highlight of the year for many. Despite the scores of Indian temples scattered along the River Hooghly, Calcutta still bears the indelible imprint of the Raj. Competing with the temples for attention are monuments to monarchs, governors-general, and martyrs. In 1690, East India Company agent Job Charnock bought the land that is now Calcutta, helping to build it into a prosperous trading post and industrial base. Though captured in 1756 by Bengal's nawab, Siraj-ud-Daula, the fortified city became the centerpiece of British India soon after Robert Clive's victory at Plassey, and Calcutta became the capital of the Raj in 1773. Under the first governor-general, Warren Hastings (r. 1774-1785), Bengalis got their first taste of a British education. The new literati proved too proud to submit to assimilation under a foreign power, and the 19th century witnessed the elite-led Bengali Renaissance. Ram Mohan Roy (1774-1833) started the movement by pushing for social and religious reform with his Brahmo Samaj, a theistic movement calling for reform within Hinduism. Upper-class salons hosted a revolution in literature, music, dance, and painting, culminating in the work of Nobel Prize-winning poet Rabindranath Tagore. Calcutta also became a center for anti-British politics; when the British moved to partition Bengal in 1905, their efforts were met with bombs and boycotts.

By the end of the 19th century, Calcutta had plenty of critics, including the British colonialists who had built the city in the first place. A series of blows, from the transfer of the capital to Delhi in 1911, to the opening of the Suez Canal (which made Mumbai a much more prosperous port), to the disasters of Partition in 1947, gave the city a reputation for squalor and seediness. Increasing migration from Bangladesh and the rest of India and the silting of the increasingly unnavigable Hooghly have only made things worse. The Communist government has worked wonders in the countryside but has failed to rid the city of all its problems. In 1984, Calcutta opened its Metro, the first anywhere in India, and the government is currently developing Salt Lake to the east as a "second Calcutta." Untroubled by the rioting that has plagued other Indian cities, Calcutta's residents appear unified in their unmatched love for their home town.

■ INTERCITY TRANSPORTATION

FLIGHTS

Officially known as the Netaji Subhas Chandra Bose Airport, **Dum Dum Airport** (☎511 8070 or 511 8079) is 2km northeast of the city. The **pre-paid taxi** stand in the domestic terminal is the best place to catch a ride into downtown Calcutta (40min., Rs150-175). City buses #46, 303, and 510 (Rs4) and the less direct E3 (Rs5) all run between the Esplanade and the airport. Minibus #151 (Rs18) goes from BBD Bagh to the airport. The airport has a **currency exchange counter,** a **post office,** and **tourist offices.** The **train ticket counter** serves Delhi, Mumbai, and Chennai only. The Airport Manager in the domestic terminal can arrange beds in the waiting room for tired travelers with a layover of 24hr. or less.

WEST BENGAL

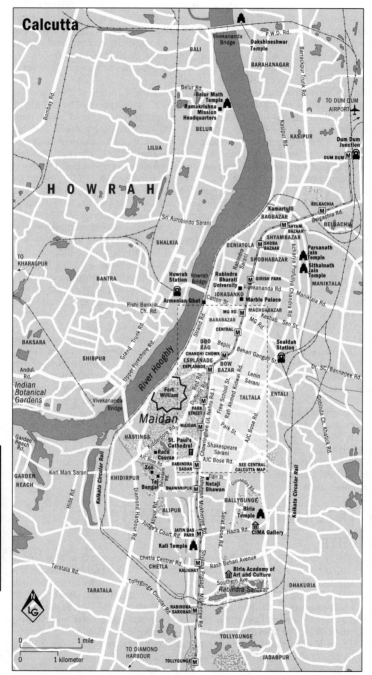

Calcutta

P.W.D. Rd.

Vivekananda
Bridge

BALI

Dakshineshwar
Temple

BARAHANAGAR

Barrackpur Trunk Rd.

TO DUM DUM
AIRPORT

Belur Rd.

Belur Math
Temple

Ramakrishna
Mission
Headquarters

BELUR

Kasipur Rd.

KASIPUR

Dum Dum
Junction

DUM DUM

Bombay Rd.

LILUA

H O W R A H

BELGACHIA

BELGACHIA

Belgachia Rd.

BELGACHIA

Sri Aurobindo Sarani

SHALKIA

Kamartulli
BAGBAZAR

SHYAM
BAZAR

SHYAMBAZAR

SHOBA
BAZAR

Parsanath
Jain
Temple

Sithalnath
Jain
Temple

TO
KHARAGPUR

BANTRA

BENIATOLA

SHOBHABAZAR

Achatya Profulya Chandra Rd.

Maniktala Rd.

MANIKTALA

Howrah
Station

Howrah
Bridge

Rabindra
Bharati
University

GIRISH PARK

Vivekananda Rd.

Rabindra Sarani

BAKSARA

Rishi Bankim
Ch. Rd.

Armenian Ghat

JORASANKO

Cotton St.

Marble Palace

MACHUABAZAR

Keshab

Strand Rd.

MG RD.

BARABAZAR

MG Rd.

Sealdah
Station

SHIBPUR

Grand Trunk Rd.

CENTRAL

Bepin Behari Ganguli Rd.

Dr. SC. Bannerjee Rd.

Andul
Rd.

Upper Foreshore Rd.

BBD
BAG

CHANDHI CHOWK

ESPLANADE

ESPLANADE

BOW
BAZAR

Lenin
Sarani

ENTALI

Indian
Botanical
Gardens

River Hooghly

Fort
William

Red Rd.

Dufferin Rd.

JL Nehru Rd.

Free School St.

Rafi Ahmed Kidwai Rd.

AJC Bose Rd.

TALTALA

Vivekananda
Bridge

Maidan

HASTINGS

Kidderpore Rd.

PARK
STREET

MAIDAN

Chowringhee (JL Nehru Rd.)

Park St.

Gobinda Ch. Khatick Rd.

Garden
Reach
Rd.

St. Paul's
Cathedral

Race
Course

Zoo

AJC Bose Rd.

RABINDRA
SADAN

Shakespeare
Sarani

AJC Bose Rd.

SEE CENTRAL
CALCUTTA MAP

Karl Marx Saran

GARDEN
REACH

KHIDIRPUR

Taj
Bengal

Belvedere Rd.

BHAWANIPUR

Netaji
Bhawan

Elgin St.

Gurusaday Rd.

Ashutosh Mukherjee Rd.

BALLYGUNGE

Birla
Temple

CIMA Gallery

Kolkata Circular Rail

Hide Rd.

ALIPUR

Diamond Harbour Rd.

Alipur Rd.

Judge's Court Rd.

JATIN DAS
PARK

Kali Temple

Sarat Bose Rd.

Hazra Rd.

Rash Behan Avenue

Taratala Rd.

Chetla Central Rd.

CHETLA

KALIGHAT

Shyam Prasad Mukherjee Rd.

Birla Academy of
Art and Culture

Southern Ave.

Rabindra Sarobar

DHAKURIA

TARATALA

Tollygunge Circular Rd.

RABINDRA
SAROBAR

Rabindra Sarobar Rd.

N
LG

0   1 mile
0   1 kilometer

TO DIAMOND
HARBOUR

TOLLYGUNGE

TOLLYGUNGE

JADABPUR

> ! **WARNING.** Many of Calcutta's taxis are operated by touts, who are attached to a specific hotel and receive a hefty commission for every tourist they deliver. **Insist on going to the hotel you want,** and ignore claims that it has been closed down or destroyed by floods. In the case of late arrivals, some travelers have even been known to spend the night in the airport and take a taxi the next morning when there is much less danger of muggings and other kinds of nastiness.

INTERNATIONAL AIRLINES. All carriers have offices at the airport, as well as downtown. **AeroFlot** 58 Chowringhee Rd. (☎242 1617). Open M-F 10am-1pm and 2-5:30pm, Sa 10am-1pm. **Air France** 41 Chowringhee Rd. (☎296 6161). Open M-Sa 9am-5:30pm. **Air India** 50 Chowringhee Rd. (☎242 2356 or 242 1187). Open daily 9:30am-5:30pm. **Alitalia** 230A AJC Bose Rd. (☎247 7394). Open daily 9:30am-5:30pm. **American Airlines** 2/7 Sarat Bose Rd. (☎747622). Open M-F 9am-1pm and 1:30-5:30pm, Sa 9am-1:30pm. **Air Canada, Gulf Air,** and **TWA** 230A AJC Bose Rd. (☎247 7783). Open M-F 9am-1pm and 1:30-5:30pm, Sa 9am-1:30pm. **Bangladesh Biman** 33C Chowringhee Rd. (☎293709). **British Airways** 41 Chowringhee Rd. (☎293450). Open M-Sa 9:30am-5:30pm. **Canadian, SAS, South African,** and **United Airlines** 2/7 Sarat Bose Rd. (☎747623). Open M-F 9:30am-1pm and 2-5:30pm, Sa 9:30am-1pm. **Cathay Pacific** 1 Middleton St. (☎240 3211). Open M-F 9:30am-1pm and 2-5:30pm, Sa 9:30am-1:30pm. **Delta** 13D Russell St. (☎246 3873 or 246 3826). Open M-F 9am-5:30pm. **Japan Airlines** 35A Chowringhee Rd. (☎226 7920). Open M-F 9am-1pm and 1:30-5:30pm, Sa 9am-1pm. **KLM** and **Northwest** 1 Middleton St., Jeevan Deep. (☎240 3151). Open M-F 9am-5pm, Sa 9am-1pm. **Kuwait Airways,** 2/7 Sarat Bose Rd. **Lufthansa** 30A/B Chowringhee Rd. (☎249 5777; fax 246 4010). Open M-F 9am-1pm and 1:30-5:30pm. **RNAC** 41 Chowringhee Rd. (☎298549). Open M-F 9am-1pm and 2-4pm, Sa 9am-1pm. **Singapore Airlines** 1 Lee Rd. (☎280 9898). Open M-F 9am-1pm and 2-5pm. **Swissair** 46C Chowringhee Rd. (☎282 4643). Open 9am-1pm and 2-5:30pm. **Thai Airways** 18G Park St. (☎229 9846). Open 24hr.; tourist window (#12) open M-F 9am-1pm and 2-5pm.

DOMESTIC AIRLINES. Indian Airlines and **Alliance Air** 39 Chittaranjan Ave. (☎236 0870 or 236 4433; fax 236 5391). Open 24hr. Great Eastern Hotel branch, 1-3 Old Court House St., 2nd fl. (☎248 0073 or 248 8009). Open M-Sa 10am-1:30pm and 2-5pm. **Jet Airways** 18D Park St. (☎229 2660). Open daily 9am-7pm. **Sahara Airlines** 2A Shakespeare Sarani. (☎282 8969 or 282 7686). Open M-Sa 10:30am-5pm.

Indian Airlines to: **Agartala** (1hr.; 1-2 per day; US$55); **Ahmedabad** (2½-4hr.; M-Sa; US$235); **Aizawl** (1hr.; M, W, F; US$95); **Bagdogra** (1hr.; M, W, F, Sa; US$85); **Bangalore** (3½hr.; daily; US$270); **Bhubaneswar** (1hr.; daily; US$90); **Chennai** (2hr.; 1-2 per day; US$225); **Delhi** (2hr.; 2-3 per day; US$205); **Dibrugarh** (1½hr.; Tu, Th, Sa, Su; US$100); **Dimapur** (2hr.; Tu, Th, Sa, Su; US$95); **Guwahati** (1hr.; daily; US$75); **Hyderabad** (3hr.; M-Sa; US$215); **Imphal** (2hr.; daily; US$85); **Jaipur** (2½-4hr.; M-Sa; US$225); **Jorhat** (1½hr.; Tu and Sa; US$95); **Lucknow** (2½hr.; M, Tu, Th, Sa; US$160); **Mumbai** (3hr.; 2 per day; US$235); **Nagpur** (1½hr.; M, W, F; US$170); **Patna** (1hr.; M, Tu, Th, Sa; US$105); **Port Blair** (2hr.; M, Tu, Th, Sa, Su; US$200). International service to: **Dhaka, Bangladesh** (1hr.; M, W, Th, F, Su; US$75) and **Kathmandu, Nepal** (1½hr.; M, Tu, W, F, Sa; US$96).

TRAINS

Calcutta has two stations: **Sealdah Station,** northeast on AJC Bose Rd., for trains going north, and **Howrah Station,** across the River Hooghly from Calcutta, for trains going to the rest of India. The best way to get to or from Howrah Station is by bus. If you're going to the Sudder St. area, take a bus to the Esplanade (Rs2) and walk five minutes. There is a **pre-paid taxi** stand at the station (Rs40 to downtown Calcutta)

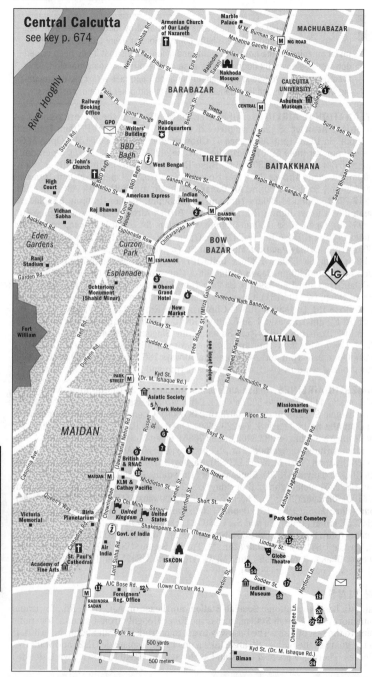

Central Calcutta
see key p. 674

River Hooghly

Armenian Church of Our Lady of Nazareth

Marble Palace

M.M. Burman St.

MACHUABAZAR

MG ROAD

Mahatma Gandhi Rd. (Harrison Rd.)

Biplabi Rash Bihari St.

Netaji Subhas Rd.

Ezra St.

Rabindra Sarani

Armenian St.

Nakhoda Mosque

CALCUTTA UNIVERSITY

Paiste Pl.

Kolutola St.

BARABAZAR

Ashutosh Museum

Railway Booking Office

Lyons' Range

GPO

Writers' Building

Police Headquarters

Bentinck St.

Tiretta Bazar St.

CENTRAL

College St.

Surya Sen St.

Sashi Bhusan Dej St.

BBD Bagh

St. John's Church

BBD Bagh E.

BBD Bagh W.

West Bengal

Lal Bazaar

TIRETTA

Chittaranjan Ave.

BAITAKKHANA

Bepin Behari Ganguli St.

High Court

Waterloo St.

American Express

Ganesh Ch. Avenue

Weston St.

Indian Airlines

CHANDNI CHOWK

Vidhan Sabha

Raj Bhavan

Old Court House Rd.

Esplanade Row

Chittaranjan Ave.

BOW BAZAR

Auckland Rd.

Eden Gardens

Curzon Park

ESPLANADE

Ranji Stadium

Garden Rd.

Esplanade

Ochterlony Monument (Shahid Minar)

Oberoi Grand Hotel

New Market

Lenin Sarani

Surendra Nath Banerjee Rd.

TALTALA

Red Rd.

Fort William

Lindsay St.

Sudder St.

see inset this page

Free School St. (Mirza Galib St.)

Rafi Ahmed Kidwai Rd.

Allimuddin St.

Dufferin Rd.

PARK STREET

Kyd St. (Dr. M. Ishaque Rd.)

Asiatic Society

Park Hotel

Ripon St.

Missionaries of Charity

MAIDAN

Russell St.

Royd St.

(Jawaharlal Nehru Rd.)

British Airways & RNAC

MAIDAN

KLM & Cathay Pacific

Middleton St.

Park Street

Camac St.

Hungerford St.

Short St.

Loudon St.

Casuarina Ave.

Queen's Way

Birla Planetarium

Ho Chi Minh Sarani

United Kingdom

United States

Shakespeare Sarani (Theatre Rd.)

Acharya Jagadish Chandra Bose Rd.

Park Street Cemetery

Victoria Memorial

Cathedral Rd.

Govt. of India

Air India

St. Paul's Cathedral

Academy of Fine Arts

ISKCON

AJC Bose Rd.

Lord Sinha Rd.

(Lower Circular Rd.)

Foreigners' Reg. Office

RABINDRA SADAN

Elgin Rd.

0   500 yards

0   500 meters

WEST BENGAL

Lindsay St.

Globe Theatre

Sudder St.

Indian Museum

Rawdon St.

Hartford Ln.

Chowringhee Ln.

Kyd St. (Dr. M. Ishaque Rd.)

Biman

N
LG

Central Calcutta

see map p. 675

🏠 ACCOMMODATIONS

Classic Hotel, 24
Gujral Guest Hosue, 16
Hotel Galaxy, 21
Hotel Plaza, 14
Modern Lodge, 20
Salvation Army Red Shield
Guest House, 18
Shilton Hotel, 19
YMCA, 13
YWCA, 7

🍴 FOOD

Abdul Khalique & Sons, 22
Aheli, 3
Amina, 15
Anand Vegetarian Restaurant, 2
Bar B-Q, 8
Flurys, 6
Haldiram Bhujiawala, 11
Hare Krishna Bakery, 10
How Hua, 23
Indian Coffee House, 1
Khalsa Restaurant, 17
Nizam's, 4
Tulika's Ice Cream Parlor, 9

♪ ENTERTAINMENT

Anticlock, 12
Someplace Else, 5
Tantra, 5

and a **West Bengal Tourist Office** (☎660 2518; open daily 7am-8pm). Tickets can be purchased at the **Railway Booking Office,** 6 Fairlie Pl. (☎220 3496), near BBD Bagh. The **Foreign Tourist Office** is on the first floor. Foreign currency or rupees with encashment certificate accepted. (Open daily 9am-1pm and 1:30-4pm.)

From **Howrah Station** to: **Bhubaneswar** (7½-9hr., 12 per day 8:25am-3:50am, Rs174); **Chennai** (28-34hr., 6 per day 1:15-10:20pm and 3:50am, Rs436); **Delhi** (23hr., 5-6 per day 9:10am-8:15pm, Rs377; *Rajdhani Exp. 2301:* 18hr., 5pm, Rs1450); **Mumbai** (32-36hr., 5 per day 10:40am-8pm, Rs430); **Patna** (8-10hr., 9 per day 9:15am-11pm, Rs202; *Rajdhani Exp. 2305:* 7hr., 1:45pm, 3-tier A/C Rs915); **Puri** (11hr., 6:05 and 9:45pm, Rs194); **Varanasi** (8-17hr., 5 per day 9:15am-11pm, Rs271). **Sealdah Station** to: **New Jalpaiguri** (13hr., 6 per day 6:25am-9:15pm, Rs206).

BUSES

Private buses go to Siliguri (12hr.), a departure point for Darjeeling. West Bengal Tourism runs the most direct bus, which leaves Calcutta at 6pm, reaching **Siliguri** at 6am (Rs205) and **Jalpaiguri** at 6:15am (Rs210). Buses also run to **Dingha** (6hr., 7am, Rs70) and **Jaigon** (19hr., 6pm, Rs250). Tickets must be purchased in advance at the booth at the Esplanade; to get there, take a left from Chowringhee Rd. onto SN Banerjee Rd. The booth is on the right just before the tram tracks. Other private bus company booths are to the left (follow the tracks).

BOATS

Two to three ships sail each month to **Port Blair** in the Andaman Islands; the exact schedule depends on the weather. Tickets and a tentative schedule for the month are available from the **Shipping Corporation Office** 13 Strand Rd., two blocks south of the Railway Booking Office. Enter through the mail entrance, go through the back door and up one floor. (☎246 2354. Open M-F 10:30am-1pm.) Arrivals and departures are announced about a week in advance. Ticket sales begin seven days before the scheduled departure, often selling out in the first couple of days. Bring three passport photos to purchase tickets. (3-4 days; Bunk Rs1000, 2nd class Rs2500, 1st class Rs3200. Food per day Rs50 in bunk, Rs100 in 1st and 2nd classes.) Boat conditions vary greatly.

🔀 ORIENTATION

Expansive as it is, Calcutta's layout is relatively straightforward; it shouldn't take you long to get your bearings. The **River Hooghly** cuts through town, separating Calcutta proper from **Howrah;** these areas are linked by one of the world's most heavily-used bridges, **Howrah Bridge,** and, farther south, by the new **Vivekananda Bridge.** Howrah's centerpiece is the frenetic **Howrah Station,** easily accessed from Calcutta by the Howrah Bridge. The main road in Howrah is the **Grand Trunk Rd.,** which runs parallel to the river and connects the Botanical Gardens in the south with the Belur Math up north.

WEST BENGAL

Flanking the river's eastern bank is the **maidan,** a grassy field transected by streets and dotted with monuments. The central city hugs the maidan; **Strand Rd.** cuts between the maidan and the river. At the maidan's northeastern corner is the **Esplanade,** the central bus and train terminus. A couple of blocks north is **BBD Bagh,** around which are the tourist office, GPO, railway and shipping companies, and several banks. To the east of BBD Bagh is **Old Court House Rd. Netaji Subhas Rd.,** north of the GPO, and **Chittaranjan Ave.** to the east, are the major thoroughfares leading to North Calcutta.

Running along the east side of the maidan is **Chowringhee Rd.** Several smaller streets wind their way east from Chowringhee. These include **Park St.,** with fancier restaurants, hotels, and shopping areas, and (two blocks north of Park St.) **Sudder St.,** home to the vast majority of budget accommodations. At the eastern end of Sudder St. is the north-south **Mirza Ghalib St.** (formerly **Free School St.**), with a range of eating and shopping facilities. Even farther east is **Acharya Jagadish Chandra (AJC) Bose Rd.,** which used to circle the city—to the south it curves back westward and leads to St. Paul's Cathedral and the Victoria Memorial, both at the maidan's southeast corner. East of it all is the clean and efficient **Eastern Metropolitan Bypass** (the Chief Minister's route to work, hence its excellent upkeep). This is the route taxi drivers should take to bring you into town.

In the south, Chowringhee Rd. becomes **Ashutosh Mukherjee Rd.,** which continues into southern Calcutta. To the west is the upscale area of **Alipur,** which also contains the zoo and the National Library; south of Alipur is the Kalighat Temple.

⨮ LOCAL TRANSPORTATION

Locals joke that the quickest way of getting around town is to walk. Traffic in Calcutta is chaotic, and going anywhere is frustratingly slow. New laws restrict traffic on most thoroughfares to one direction during the morning and the other in the afternoon. These and other confusing rules only add to the madness on the streets.

BUSES

Buses in Calcutta are cheap and always crowded. Most buses charge Rs3-5. It's important to let go of the "bus stop" concept; you can get on just about anywhere—just put your hand out and the driver will slow down. If the bus is moving too fast for you to feel comfortable running alongside and jumping aboard, shout *"asthe!"* The key to finding your bus is identifying a major destination that's in the same direction. When getting off, make your way to the door one stop before or else you'll never make it in time.

TRAMS AND SUBWAYS

Trams leave from the central Esplanade to major destinations throughout south Calcutta and to Sealdah and Howrah Bridges (Rs1-2). They are slow and sometimes crowded. A list of routes can be purchased at any bookstand. India's first **subway (metro)** extends in a virtually straight line from Tollygunge, up Chowringhee Rd., to Dum Dum Station. From this station, a taxi or auto-rickshaw to the airport takes 45min. with traffic (Rs70). The metro is relatively quick and uncrowded—the fastest and most reliable mode of transportation available. Be sure to buy a ticket at the counter before boarding. (Rs3-7. Open M-Sa 8am-9:30pm, Su 2-9:30pm. Trains leave approximately every 15min.)

TAXIS AND RICKSHAWS

Taxis are the most convenient way to cover long distances in Calcutta. Many drivers don't use the meters, and even those who do may have tampered with them.

Negotiating a price beforehand is a safe bet. Howrah to the Sudder St. area Rs40, rides within central Calcutta Rs15-25. The meter begins at Rs5, and the fare is 2.4 times the meter reading. The prepaid taxi counters at the airport have long lines, but they are worth the wait (Rs150-175). The city's fleet of **hand-pulled rickshaws,** the last in the world, is quickly dwindling. They are cheap, but you can usually walk faster than they can pull. Besides, hand-pulled and **auto-rickshaws** are banned from most major streets in most of central Calcutta and Howrah during most of the day, rendering them mostly useless to visitors.

◪ PRACTICAL INFORMATION

TOURIST AND FINANCIAL SERVICES

Tourist Office: Government of India Tourist Office 4 Shakespeare Sarani. (☎242 1402 or 242 5318). Provides maps and brochures, including the excellent *Calcutta This Fortnight,* a free pamphlet detailing cultural events such as dance and theater performances. The West Bengal Chamber of Commerce publishes *Calcutta: Gateway to the East* (Rs25), a smart and comprehensive introduction to the city and its sights. The office also provides a list of host families and *dharamsalas.* Open M-F 9am-6pm, Sa 9am-5pm. **Airport Branch** (☎511 8299). In the domestic terminal of Dum Dum Airport. **West Bengal Tourist Bureau** 3/2 BBD Bagh E. (☎248 8271). Provides city tours (full day Rs100), information and tours for all of West Bengal, and passes for wildlife parks and the Marble Palace. Open M-Sa 10:30am-1pm, Su and holidays 7am-1pm. Counters at the airport and Howrah Station (☎660 2518) open daily 7am-8pm.

Consulates: Bangladesh 9 Circus Ave. (☎247 5208). Open M-Sa 10am-5pm. **Bhutan,** contact **Bhutan Tourism** 35A Chowringhee Rd. (☎246 8370). Open M-F 10am-5pm. **Germany** 1 Hastings Park Rd. (☎479 1141). Open M-F 10am-5pm. **Nepal** 19 National Library Ave. (☎479 1224). Open M-F 9:30am-12:30pm and 1:30-4:30pm. **Sri Lanka** Nicco House, 2 Hare St. (☎248 5102). Open M-F 10am-5:30pm. **Thailand** 18B Mandville Gardens. (☎440 7836). Open M-F 9am-noon. **UK** 1 Ho Chi Minh Sarani. (☎242 5171). Open M-F 9am-noon. **US** 5/1 Ho Chi Minh Sarani. (☎242 3611). Open M-F 8:30am-12:30pm and 2-4pm.

Immigration Office: Foreigners Registration Office 237 AJC Bose Rd. (☎247 3301). Provides visa extensions and work visas only. Open M-F 9am-1pm and 2-4pm.

Currency Exchange: 24hr. **ATMs** are all over Calcutta, and all major banks have attached ATMs unless otherwise noted. **American Express,** 21 Old Court House St. (☎248 2133 or 248 9555; fax 248 8096). Has travel services and currency exchange. Open M-Sa 9:30am-6:30pm. **ANZ Grindlays,** 41 Chowringhee Rd. (☎248 3371). Open M-F 10am-3pm, Sa 10am-12:30pm. **Banque Nationale de Paris,** 4A BBD Bagh E. (☎248 2166 or 248 0197). Open M-F 10am-5pm, Sa 10am-2pm. **Citibank,** 43 Chowringhee Rd. (☎249 2484). Open M-F 10am-2pm, Sa 10am-noon. **HSBC,** 8 Netaji Subhas Rd. (☎248 6363). Also holds mail. Open M-F 9am-4pm. **State Bank of India,** Dum Dum Airport, international terminal. Open 24hr. **Thomas Cook,** 230A AJC Bose Rd. (☎247 4560; fax 247 5854). Chitrakut Bldg., 2nd fl., side entrance. Offers travel services and currency exchange. No ATM. Open M-Sa 9:30am-1pm and 1:45-6pm.

LOCAL SERVICES

Bookstore: Landmark, Emami, 17 Lord Sinha Rd., has the best selection of books. **Oxford Book Store** (☎297662). Below the Park Hotel on Park St. Maintains a space for author readings. Open M-Sa 10am-8:30pm. **College St.** is lined with book stalls. **Survey of India Map Sales Office,** 13 Wood St., has a good selection of trekking maps. Open M-F 10:30am-1pm and 2:30-5pm.

Library: National Library, Alipur Rd., near the zoo. India's largest library—2 million books in all of India's official languages. Open M-Sa 9am-8pm, Su 10am-6pm. **Asiatic Society of Bengal** (☎ 226 0355). 1 Park St. A Calcutta institution dating back to 1784 and the best place to study Persian manuscripts and 19th-century academic tomes. Adjacent museum contains paintings by Rubens and Reynolds. Open M-F 10am-6pm. **British Council** (☎ 282 5378). 5 Shakespeare Sarani. Open Tu-Sa 10:30am-6:30pm.

Cultural Centers: Alliance Francaise (☎ 282 8793). 24 Park Mansions, Park St. **British Council** (see above). **Academy of Fine Arts** (☎ 248 4302). Cathedral Rd. **Rabindra Sadan,** corner of Cathedral and AJC Bose Rd. Hosts Bengali plays and classical music.

Market: New Market, north of Lindsay St., is a huge indoor bazaar selling everything from Kashmiri carvings and *filmi* cassettes to fruit and animals. Open dawn-dusk. Don't miss the **flower market,** just before Howrah bridge, on the left. Open M-Sa 8-11am.

EMERGENCY AND COMMUNICATIONS

Police: Police Headquarters (☎ 479 1311-5), Lal Bazaar. **Emergency:** ☎ 215 5000.

Pharmacy: Dey's Medical Store, Ltd. (☎ 249 9810). 6A Nell Sengupta Sarani. On the left where Madge St. intersects New Market. Open M-F 8:30am-9pm, Sa 8:30am-5pm.

Hospital: B.M. Birla Heart Research Centre (☎ 479 4003, 4024, or 4012). 1/1A National Library Ave. Highly recommended English-speaking doctors. Open 24hr.

Internet: There are dozens of cyber cafes between Park and Sudder St., and most charge Rs20 per hr. **BQ's,** on Mirza Ghalib St. between Kyd and Park St., has good ISDN connections for Rs17 per hr.

Post Office: GPO (☎ 220 1451). BBD Bagh. Open M-Sa 7am-8:30pm. **Branch post offices:** Airport, Russell St., Park St., and Mirza Ghalib St. **New Market Post Office,** Mirza Ghalib St., opposite Sudder St. **Postal Code:** 700001.

▛ ACCOMMODATIONS

Prices in Calcutta tend to be high. Most of the budget accommodations in town are around the Sudder St. area. The location is central and the prices reasonable, though the hotels are a little shabby. There are other cheap hotels off Chittaranjan Rd., south of the Indian Airlines office, and to the northeast of New Market. Hotels often fill up before noon; most have noon check-out. Try to reserve in advance. Contact the Government of India Tourist Office for a list of host families willing to take in paying guests. (Rs200-400 per night with breakfast.)

Salvation Army Red Shield Guest House (☎ 245 0599). 2 Sudder St. Turn left after The Great Eastern Hotel (on J.L. Nehru Rd.); it's the big red bldg. on the right. One of the most popular hotels with the backpacker set and volunteers at Mother Teresa's Missionaries of Charity (see p. 738). Large, unappealing dorm rooms and bathrooms. Lights-out 10pm; gate closes at midnight. Check-out 10am. Reservations not accepted; rooms are usually available. Dorms Rs80; doubles Rs200-400. ❶

Hotel Galaxy (☎ 246 4565). 3 Stuart Ln., opposite the Modern Lodge. Only slightly more expensive than other budget places, Galaxy is a steal. The staff is very friendly. Huge rooms have color TV and wooden furniture. Doubles Rs450-650. ❷

Gujral Guest House (☎ 244 0392 or 245 6066). Lindsay St. Circle around the right side of Lindsay Hotel and turn left onto an alley behind it; look for the painted signs. Enormous, comfortable rooms await on the 3rd fl.; some doubles have Star TV. Common TV room. Tea and breakfast available. Singles Rs290; doubles with bath Rs300-1050. ❷

Classic Hotel (☎ 290256). 6/1A Kyd St. Just off Mirza Ghalib St., next to Mehfil restaurant. A marble-walled labyrinth of small, clean, windowless rooms with black and white TVs. Some rooms have seat toilets. Singles Rs150; doubles Rs300-660. ❶

Modern Lodge (☎244 4960). 1 Stuart Ln. By the east end of Sudder St., opposite Astoria Hotel and south down a street. Popular with Missionaries of Charity volunteers. Clean bathrooms. Check-out 10am. Singles Rs70; doubles with bath Rs100-220. ❶

Hotel Plaza (☎2446411 or 2492435). 10 Sudder St. At the street's western end. Medium-sized rooms with clean beds, baths, and carpets. Sweet tea and toast for breakfast. Doubles Rs400-900. ❷

Shilton Hotel (☎245 1512 or 245 1527). 5A Sudder St. Set back from the bustle on Sudder St.; look for signs. Huge rooms have clean bathrooms, good lighting, and desks. Dark but friendly TV room. Singles Rs175-220; doubles Rs300. ❶

YMCA (☎249 2192; fax 249 2234). 25 Chowringhee Rd. From Sudder St., turn right; it's immediately on the right. Enormous, clean rooms with attached bath; dorm rooms are also clean. Reserve 10 days ahead. Dorms Rs110; singles Rs370-610; doubles Rs540-820. Rates include breakfast and dinner. ❶

YWCA (☎297033; fax 292494). 1 Middleton Row (not St.). Off Park St. **Women only.** Simple, spacious, and clean rooms. Meals are included, as is access to table tennis and badminton tables (lawn tennis Rs20 extra). The staff is quite friendly. Reserve at least a week in advance. Singles Rs325-570; doubles Rs600-800. ❷

FOOD

Calcutta is the best place to enjoy authentic Bengali cuisine, with its street stalls vending mustard-seasoned rice and fish (avoid seafood in monsoon season). Calcutta's thriving Muslim population has seen kebab shops open up all over town, serving *kathi* roll (a *paratha* with a layer of egg and stuffed with spicy chicken, lamb, or egg). Try the tiny street shops on Chitpur Rd. or look out for more hygienic establishments. A thriving Chinese district is in Tangra near Salt Lake, the hottest place in town for Chinese food.

▨ **Aheli,** in The Peerless Inn, Chowringhee. The best Bengali *thalis* around (Rs225). Waiters don traditional *dhotis* and *kurtas*. Open daily 12:30-2:30pm and 6:30-10:30pm. ❸

▨ **Anand Vegetarian Restaurant,** 19 Chittaranjan Ave., between the Indian Airlines office and Chowringhee Rd. A haven for veggies among the mutton-and-beef stalls. Excellent South and North Indian food on 2 floors behind tinted glass. Popular with the bourgeoisie for post-cinema jaunts. Dishes Rs60-90. ❶

▨ **Nizam's,** 22/25 New Market, northeast of New Market, just southwest of the large red municipal bldg. Ask for directions—everyone knows where it is. The "pioneer of kebab rolls in India" sells chicken, mutton, paneer, and beef kebabs for Rs15-40. ❶

Amina, New Market, near Eliot Cinema. This joint is quickly displacing Nizam's as the best kebabs 'n' rolls joint. Excellent rose-water flavored *biryani* Rs35. ❶

Abdul Khalique and Sons Restaurant, 32 Marique Amir St., a block south of Sudder St., near Jamuna Movie Theatre. Squeeze onto a bench and watch your food being cooked. Beef stew Rs9, mutton *masala* Rs16, fish curry Rs10. Open daily 5am-11:30pm. ❶

Haldiram Bhujiawala, AJC Bose Rd., at the corner of Chowringhee Rd., next to the Aeroflot office. A neon sign advertises this eat-and-run sweet-and-snack chain, popular with Calcutta's middle class. Try the cutlets (Rs15) and puffs (Rs10-20). The *kulfi* (Rs20), which comes with *faluda*, is famous. ❶

Indian Coffee House, 15 Bankim Chatterjee St., 1st fl., just off College St., near Calcutta University. Popular haunt for students and Calcutta's intelligentsia. A portrait of Rabindranath Tagore presides over the scene. Coffee Rs7, chicken *hakka* Rs25. ❶

Flurys, 18 Park St., the large white bldg on the corner. A Calcutta landmark, popular with foreign tourists. Relaxed cafe with an enormous sweets shop specializing in sticky buns and chocolate pastries. Ask for a pastry assortment (Rs9) with your tea while you decide what to take back to the hotel. Open daily 7am-8pm. ❶

Hare Krishna Bakery, at the corner of Russell and Middleton St., two blocks west of the US consulate. No longer features *sadhus* and shaved heads; only the background music serves as a reminder that the profits go to the International Society for Krishna Consciousness. All the food—breads, pastries, samosas (Rs10-15)—is *prasad* (blessed), so don't leave any on your plate. Open daily 10:30am-8pm. ❶

How Hua, Mirza Ghalib St., opposite Hotel Paramount, south of Sudder St. Northern Chinese lovingly prepare their native cuisine in a classy, quiet, dining hall. Their specialty is *chimney soup,* which can be made with chicken, crab, or bean curd (Rs55). Delicious, freshly-made noodles. Open W-M 11am-11pm. ❶

Bar B-Q (☎ 299916). 43/47 Park St. This elegant, spacious restaurant with extensive Chinese and Indian menus rewards the weary backpacker with an escape from the grime. Don't order your food spicy unless you've got coolant in your belly. Szechuan chili chicken Rs125. Excellent bar upstairs. Reserve ahead on weekends. Open daily noon-3pm and 7-10:30pm. Major credit cards accepted. ❷

Suruchi, Elliot Rd., near Mallik Bazaar. Delicious mustard fish. Large seafood variety (Rs25-75). Open for lunch only. ❶

Khalsa Restaurant, Madge Ln., just north of the Salvation Army Guest House. Serves the best economy meals around. Thick *dal* Rs10, *parathas* Rs7, mixed vegetables Rs20. Open daily 4:30am-10pm. ❶

Tulika's Ice Cream Parlor, Russell St., opposite the Royal Calcutta Turf Club. Ice cream (Rs20-30) so good that locals wouldn't dream of going to that huge international chain down the street. Excellent *idlis* and *dosas* (Rs 20-30). Open daily 8am-11pm. ❶

◎ SIGHTS

The best way to experience Calcutta and to see the sights is by **walking.** If it's not too hot, equip yourself with a copy of Prosenjit Das Gupta's *10 Walks in Calcutta* and take to the streets for a few hours every day. Or, join renowned architect and conservationist Manish Chakrabovti on a guided walking tour of North Calcutta (contact **Footsteps;** ☎ 337 5757). If you're in a hurry, hop on West Bengal Tourism's **day tour** (Rs100). They rush you around the city in just 10 hours, but it's a good way to catch a glimpse of everything and decide what to revisit.

MAIDAN, PARK STREET, AND NEW MARKET AREA

VICTORIA MEMORIAL

Museum open Tu-Su 10am-4:30pm; Nov.-Feb. 10am-3:30pm. Foreigner price Rs150; Indians Rs10. Photography not permitted. Sound and light show Tu-Su 8:15pm. Rs10. Garden open 24hr.

The southern end of the maidan is dominated by the infamous Victoria Memorial, the most impressive (and outlandish) reminder of Calcutta's past as capital of the British Raj. The British spent 15 years (1906-21) putting together this strange cross between Buckingham Palace and the Taj Mahal, designed to stand in loving memory of the self-proclaimed "Empress of India." Untouched by the pollution and chaos of the rest of Calcutta, this overpowering monument to British imperialism seems quite out of place among the poverty-stricken streets of the "City of Joy." Four minarets surround a central dome of white marble, lugged at great expense from the same Rajasthani quarries that furnished the material for the Taj Mahal. But unlike Agra's great white monument, the "VM" is shaped by the angles and spheres of the Italian Renaissance, with a bronze winged statue of Victory on top of it. A statue of an aging Queen Victoria stands guard at the entrance to the complex, and a much younger Victoria sits inside the building, now a **museum** chock- full of British war memorabilia and state portraits. Much of the colonial artwork and finery on display still provokes resentment among Bengali tourists, but their malice doesn't extend to the ever-popular queen, whose name has remained affixed to the building despite decades of political efforts to change it. The most impressive exhibit is undoubtedly the **Calcutta Gallery,** a timeline that chronicles the city's history and features examples of artwork, literature, and craftsmanship by leading Bengali figures. Be sure to check out the letter written by Rabindranath Tagore that asks for revocation of his knighthood after the Jallianwallah Bagh Massacre (see p. 739). The entire monument is beautifully illuminated at night.

ST. PAUL'S CATHEDRAL

At the south end of Chowringhee Rd., on Cathedral Rd., opposite the Victoria Memorial. Open M-Sa 9am-noon and 3-6pm; services Su 7:30, 8:30, 11am, and 6pm.

This cavernous center of Anglican Calcutta was built by Maj. Gen. William Nairn in 1847. The white Gothic architecture is patterned on Norwich Cathedral. Old paintings of the Cathedral (at the Calcutta Museum) show a large spire, which fell during an earthquake in the 1930s. In its place, a new spire, modeled on the Bell Harry Tower at Canterbury Cathedral, was erected. There are some splendid stained glass windows; especially grand is the one overlooking the west portico.

BIRLA PLANETARIUM AND ACADEMY OF FINE ARTS

North of St. Paul's. Permanent collection open Tu-Sa noon-6:45pm. Rs10. Local artists' exhibition open M-Sa 3-8pm. Free.

For celestial viewing, head to the **Birla Planetarium,** a *stupa*-esque edifice just south of St. Paul's Cathedral. *(English show 1:30pm. Rs20.)* The **Academy of Fine Arts** is part of Calcutta's ongoing cultural buzz, holding exhibitions of local artists' work. The permanent collection here features many works by Rabindranath Tagore and the Bengal School of painters.

INDIAN MUSEUM

At the corner of Sudder St. and Chowringhee Rd. Open Mar.-Nov. Tu-Sa 10am-5pm; Dec.-Feb. Tu-Sa 10am-4:30pm. Rs50.

Housed in an Italian-style building, the nation's largest and oldest museum contains a remarkable collection of sculpture from around India. It's well worth the patience required to sift through the somewhat disorganized and enormous collection, which includes several Mauryan and Shunga capitals and a large section of railing from the *stupa* at Bharhut in Madhya Pradesh. The painting collection is usually closed, but a bit of persuasion and a little *baksheesh* can work wonders. The central courtyard, with flowers and fountains, is a welcome refreshment spot.

PARK STREET CEMETERY

Southeast end of Cemetery Rd., near AJC Bose Rd. Open daily 7am-4pm. Free.

The final resting place of British colonialists since 1767, the cemetery is one of the city's most serene spots. Among the most notable of the many huge gravestones here are those of Maj. Gen. Sir Charles Stuart (built like a small temple in black granite and replete with a *shikhara* and lotus motifs) and Rose Whitworth Aylmer adorned with spiralled obelisk and a romantic poem-epitaph by her admirer Walter Servage Landor. Also note the graves of Henry Vansittart, one of the first governors of the East India Company, and Sir William Jones, the first president of the Asiatic Society. Ask for the guidebook (Rs30) at the gate and remember to give a small donation in the box in the office.

WEST BENGAL

THE MAIDAN

Undeniably the best spot in town to experience Calcutta's public life, the maidan is a mix of unkempt nature and splendid gardens. Robert Clive cleared this vast field to give his soldiers a clear shot, and the old cannons dotting the maidan echo its military past. Unfortunately, **Fort William** itself remains closed to the public. During the Raj, the maidan was the site of a posh, year-round cocktail party, where the good ol' boys of the East India Company sat back and watched cricket games. These days it belongs to the masses. Tram and bus lines run straight through the maidan, which is also the site of daily community rallies of workers announcing various grievances and *bandhs* (strikes). At the northwest corner of the maidan, near the river, are the **Eden Gardens** *(admission free),* a pleasant respite from the crowds and congestion just outside its walls. The gardens sit in the shadow of the enormous **Ranji Stadium,** where ▩cricket is played before crowds that can top 100,000. The stadium has hosted World Cup matches and is notorious for the rowdy nationalistic fervor of the fans. The maidan also hosts local festivals and parades. Near the northern edge of the maidan is the **Shahid Minar** (Martyrs' Tower), built by the British in 1817 as the **Ochterlony Monument.** Originally built as a tribute to David Ochterlony, who led royal forces against Nepal in 1814-16, the obelisk—renamed in 1969—is now a symbol of fierce Bengali pride.

BBD BAGH (DALHOUSIE SQUARE) AREA

Most of Calcutta's historic buildings are near its center, north of the maidan. **BBD Bagh,** the area's hub, was renamed for Benoy, Badal, and Dinesh, three freedom fighters hanged by the British during protests following the 1905 partition of Bengal. The Lal Digha ("Red Tank"), sits in the center. Up Netaji Subhas Rd. to the left of the Writers' Building is Calcutta's financial district. On **Lyons Range,** *bakda-wallahs* sell stocks in the street. To the southwest of the Writer's Building is the GPO, alleged site of the infamous Black Hole of Calcutta incident of 1756, in which the Nawab of West Bengal imprisoned several Europeans in the penitentiary, dubbed the "Black Hole" for its tiny size (24 sq. m), and let many of them die, purely from his own negligence. The topic is still controversial; it's one of the few colonial incidents in which the Brits were not the bad guys. To the east of the Writer's Building is Lal Bazaar, home to music stores that sell everything from guitars to *ghungroo*s.

WRITER'S BUILDING

Spanning the north side of BBD Bagh is the red-brick caterpillar of the Writer's Building. No great literary figures toiled here, other than the clerks of the East India Company, for whom it was built in 1780. It's now the lair of the West Bengal state government—hidden inside are unthinkable catacombs of bureaucracy. The elevators recently got a full makeover after the Chief Minister got stuck in one.

ST. JOHN'S CHURCH

Government Place West. Open M-F 9am-noon and 4-6pm. Services M-F 9am, Su 8am.

With its clumsy-looking spire, St. John's is the oldest church in Calcutta. The octagonal mausoleum of Job Charnock, founder of Calcutta, is tucked away in the yard. Some belongings of Warren Hastings, the first governor-general of India, are kept inside the church.

RAJ BHAVAN AND HIGH COURT

Diagonally opposite St. John's.

Formerly home to British governors-general and viceroys, the vast grounds of Raj Bhavan (Government House) are the official residence of the Governor of West Bengal. The inside is suitably palatial, but it's not open to the public, so enjoy the walk in the shade of the barbed wire. Nearby, on the other side of Government Place West, are the State Legislature and the cheerful, tricolor Gothic High Court, where you can observe robed and wigged lawyers going about their business.

NORTH CALCUTTA

One of the oldest and most fascinating parts of the city, North Calcutta was home to the educated Bengali elite of Calcutta—the Tagores, Chakrabortis, Mullicks and Debs—during the colonial period. Tourists can visit many of the area's sprawling bungalows with permission from the owners. **Chitpur Rd.** (now officially Rabindra Sarani) is a narrow, crowded street lined with all kinds of shops—metal-workers, shoe-menders, wig-makers, and tailors. Just off the street is the red sandstone Nakhoda Masjid. The shops around the mosque sell *attar*, oil-based perfumes, and *surma*, a thick yet cooling eyeliner. There are also shops selling *sherwanis* and Lucknawi pajamas. At the end of Chitpur Rd. (a *long* way) is Kamartulli, a colony of craftsmen carving statues of your favorite Hindu deities.

MARBLE PALACE

Muktaram Babu Dr., off Chittaranjan Ave. Open Tu-W and F-Su 10am-4pm. Free.

Built in 1835 as a mansion for the *zamindar* Raja Rajendro Mullick Bahadur, the Marble Palace features 13 different types of marble in all kinds of colors, including green, grey, brown, and white. The Mullick family still lives in parts of the house. The guide will point out every single image of Victoria (and there aren't just two or three), including a massive wooden statue of the Empress on the ground floor. Highlights include the intricate ceiling and the solid gold clock on the first floor. Don't miss the sprawling lawns, where gray pelicans fish in the lake (on the right-hand side as you enter). You can get a free **gate pass** from the Tourist Office, on BBD Bagh, or the Government of India Tourism Office, on Shakespeare Sarani. A little *baksheesh* has been known to work just as well. Remember to leave the guide and the guards separate tips.

RABINDRA BHARATI UNIVERSITY

Near the Marble Palace. Museum open M-F 10am-5pm, Sa 10am-1pm. Free.

One of several universities founded by Bengal's most famous son, Rabindra Bharati University is built on the site of his lifelong home. The old mansion of the prolific Tagore family has been expanded and turned into an arts college, and the house itself has been preserved as the Rabindra Bharati **museum.** Beginning with the room where Tagore died, the museum traces the story of the Tagores and the Bengali Renaissance through a large collection of art and memorabilia. There is an entire section devoted to paintings by Rabindranath himself.

PARASNATH JAIN TEMPLE

Open daily 6am-noon and 3-7pm. Free.

Built by a jeweler in 1867, this shimmering palace is dedicated to Sithalnath, the 10th Jain *tirthankara*. The building is full of colored glass and mirrors, inlaid with sparkling and intricate designs. In one corner is an "ethereal lamp" that has been burning constantly since the temple was founded.

DAKSHINESHWAR TEMPLE

10km from the city center. Bus #32 from the Esplanade (Rs5.) Open daily 6am-9pm. Free.

It was here that the Hindu spiritual leader Sri Ramakrishna had his vision of the unity of all religions. One day, a brash, young agnostic walked into the compound, asking for proof of God's existence. Promising revelation, Ramakrishna led him into an adjacent chamber, where the young man was shown God—in his heart. Later, he came to be known as Swami Vivekananda, a spiritual leader who traveled around the world spreading the message of spiritual unity. The temple consists of three parts: the smallest chamber is devoted to Vishnu; the more impressive building next to the nearby sacrificial platform is dedicated to Shakti; opposite, built in traditional Bengali style, are five domes, each of which houses a Shiva *linga*.

NICCO PARK AND SCIENCE PARK

Off the East Metropolitan Bypass; Nicco Park is 2km from Science Park. Buses from BBD Bagh Rs5, taxis Rs40. Both open daily 9am-9pm. Nicco Park Rs35; Science Park Rs30. Nicco admission includes 10 ride tickets.

Amuse yourself at Nicco Park with all your thrill-seeking Indian friends—a collection of amusement park rides waits to jolt you out of India and into fantasy land. Science Park is a huge complex with several large buildings and exhibits. With a slew of hands-on toys and exhibits, this is India's finest science museum.

HOWRAH

BELUR MATH

Taxis from BBD Bagh Rs50. Open Apr.-Nov. Tu-Su 7-11am and 4-7pm; Oct.-Mar. 7-11am and 4-6pm.

This site served as the center of the movement founded in 1897 by Ramakrishna's disciple Swami Vivekananda (see **Dakshineshwar Temple,** above). The soaring temple dominates the grounds, but the most peaceful spot on the compound is at the end of the field, in the small cottage where Vivekananda spent his last days. His bedroom has been preserved, and an attached museum contains some of his belongings. Each one of the temples' four facades is designed to represent a different place of worship—church, temple, mosque, and *gurudwara.* Just before Belur Math is the headquarters of the Ramakrishna Mission.

BOTANICAL GARDENS

Ferries from Armenian Ghat Rs3. Open dusk-dawn. Free.

This is one of Calcutta's most relaxing spots—if you go during the week, you'll have few companions other than storks, cranes, insects, and an amazing range of plants from every continent. The **Great Banyan Tree** is supposed to be the largest in the world, with roots stretching out nearly a mile from the treetop. A series of storms killed the trunk decades ago, but its standing roots still survive and flourish under the expansive canopy.

SOUTH CALCUTTA

KALI TEMPLE AT KALIGHAT

Open daily 6am-10pm. Free.

Calcutta's most important temple, Kalighat, is where the goddess Sati's little toe is said to have fallen to earth after being hacked off by Vishnu. Pilgrims have streamed in and out of the temple since its construction in 1809, but the authorities have recently decided to close it to foreigners. Nevertheless, if you ask very nicely, this may be enough to get you inside the striking building, built in the medieval Bengali style. Inside, you can gaze into the goddess's wise and terrifying red eyes, reproduced on dashboards and refrigerators all over Bengal. Catch sight of a goat sacrifice or two, offerings to the bloodthirsty goddess during **Durga Puja** and **Kali Puja** in October.

NETAJI BHAVAN

Elgin St., near Chowringhee. Open Tu-Sa noon-4pm. Rs8.

For many, the peaceful tactics of Gandhi are no way to bring about real progress. Their hero is Subhas Chandra Bose, erstwhile leader of the Indian National Army, who sought to wrest control of the country from the British by force. Netaji Bha-

KALI MA, SHAKTI DE While the rest of the world has made a smooth transition into the 21st century, Bengalis, much like Indiana Jones in *The Temple of Doom*, continue to live in the age of Kali. Every October, the whole state's affairs come to a screeching halt to celebrate the coming of Durga, Kali's maternal alter-ego. Durga Puja is the most important festival for Bengalis, and it's a spectacle not to be missed by any visitor to the area. Preparations start with the onset of the monsoon; a small colony of idol-makers in Kumartulli (on Chitpur Rd., beyond Shyani Bazaar) starts hammering away at all the granite they can amass. By early September, the hammering has begotten a million renditions of the goddess. Most stores then have a month-long 20-50% off sale. People all over the city put together *pandals,* street shows, exhibitions, and *melas* as the excitement mounts and the anticipation rises. Finally, the four-day festival begins when Durga returns to earth with her children to visit her parents, Himalaya and Menake. Tied into this familial reunion is the story of the *Ramayana:* it was Durga who gave Rama the energizing *shakti* that helped him kill Ravana. The next two days are spent rejoicing and worshipping her arrival. On the fourth day, as Durga gets ready to bid farewell, the whole city heads to the river to send her off. At dusk, people launch their statues of Durga onto the water, adorned with candles and garlands of flowers, and watch as she makes her way to the sea.

van was the home of Bose, who collaborated with the Japanese and led troops against the British during WWII. It features a museum with Bose's belongings and a history of his achievements. Every January 23rd, his birthday is celebrated here.

ZOOLOGICAL GARDENS

Near the Taj Bengal. Taxi from Park St. Rs25. Open F-W 9am-5pm. Zoo Rs150; camera fee Rs250. Aquarium Rs2.

Calcutta's zoo contains India's foremost collection of predatory felines; the centerpiece is the large island home of the zoo's Bengal Tigers. Sightings are rare during the hot season, but don't fret—the lions and tigers are also on display in cages, where they laze in the open more frequently. Avoid weekends, when the zoo is absolutely swarming with visitors.

🔊 ENTERTAINMENT

The **Calcutta Information Centre,** in the same complex as the Nandan, provides information on theater, film, and other cultural events. (☎248 1451. Open M-F 1-8pm.) Check newspapers for listings and go early for tickets.

PERFORMING AND FINE ARTS. Calcutta supports a thriving performing arts scene. Bengali music, dance, and drama are staged throughout the city. The Drama Theater at the back of the **Academy of Fine Arts** has daily performances. (☎223 4302. Daily 6:30pm, Sa 10am and 3pm. Rs20-40.) On the corner of Cathedral and AJC Bose Rd. is **Rabindra Sadan** (☎223 9936 or 223 9917), an important concert hall dedicated to Tagore. **CIMA** (Center for International Modern Art), Sunny Towers, 43 Ashutosh Chowdhari Ave., regularly exhibits contemporary and traditional art.

CINEMAS. Although Calcutta is home to India's artsiest film industry, its cinemas, such as the **Globe Theater** on the corner of Madge and Lindsay St., and **Metro Cinema,** two blocks further north, tend to show the usual Indian and American fare. The gigantic **New Empire** and **Light House Cinema** movie theaters, side-by-side just west of New Market, both favor recent hits. **Nandan Theater,** south of the Academy of Fine Arts, has both English and Bengali films. (Shows 2, 4, and 6pm. Rs10-25.)

NIGHTCLUBS. Most nightclubs are full of boogying Calcuttans, even till early in the morning. **Tantra,** Park Hotel, Park St., plays new-age and techno. (Cover Rs350. Open 8pm-4am.) **Anticlock,** Hotel Hindustan, Calcutta's first disco, is still popular when Tantra gets too full. (Cover Rs350.) **Someplace Else,** Park Hotel, Park St., is a ritzy place to grab a drink. West Bengal law prohibits alcohol sales after 10:30pm, so be sure to drink early. (Beer Rs130. Cover Rs350. Open Th-Sa 7pm-2am.)

VOLUNTEER OPPORTUNITIES

Even after her death, Mother Teresa's organization continues to care for the destitute and dying. Now headed by Sister Nirmala, the **Missionaries of Charity** have bases around the city. Their **Mother House,** 54 AJC Bose Rd., has an excellent orientation program for foreigners interested in volunteering. While the Sisters always welcome those willing to help, they do expect a certain degree of dedication, commitment, and fortitude. Sister Nirmala registers all volunteers and is available before 9am and in the afternoon around 3pm. No prior arrangements have to be made, and you can volunteer for as long as you want, either for orphans at AJC Bose Rd. or at the home for destitute girls in Kalighat or Shishu Bhawan.

SILIGURI শিলিগুড়ি
AND NEW JALPAIGURI নব জলপাইগুড়ি ☎ 0353

Since Siliguri and New Jalpaiguri function as the main transit point to Nepal, Sikkim, and the Northeast, most travelers can't avoid stopping here at some point. Linked by urban sprawl, these joined-at-the-armpit cities have managed to capture all the congestion, noise, and filth of urban India with none of the beautiful scenery or fresh air that their location might seem to suggest. Because of their low elevation (114m), the climate of Siliguri and New Jalpaiguri has much more in common with Calcutta's scorching heat than with the cooler temperatures of nearby Darjeeling (80km north). This self-proclaimed "gateway to the Indian Himalayas" offers hardly a hint of the natural splendor that awaits just up the road.

▐▇ TRANSPORTATION

Flights: Bagdogra Airport, 16km west of Siliguri. Take the Hill Cart Rd. bus from NJP Station. It stops in front of Tenzing Norgay Bus Terminal before arriving in Bagdogra (Rs3). From Bagdogra hop on a rickshaw to the airport (Rs10). The trip takes 1hr. **Jeeps** also run to the airport from Hill Cart Rd. in front of the bus terminal (30min.; Rs30). **Indian Airlines,** 2nd fl., Mainak Hotel, Hill Cart Rd. (☎ 431493), a 5min. walk north from the bus station. Open M-Sa 10am-5:30pm. MC/V. Flights to **Calcutta** (1hr.; M and F 12:40pm, Sa 1:50pm; US$80) and **Delhi** (4hr.; M and F 1:05pm; US$185) via **Guwahati** (45min.; US$50). Prove you're under 30 and get a 25% discount. **Jet Airways** on Hill Cart Rd., (☎ 435876 or 538001), 200m south of the bridge on the west side of the street (look for the sign in the window of their 2nd floor office), has flights to **Calcutta** (2½hr.; M, F, and Sa 2:10pm; US$80) and **Delhi** (4hr.; M, F, and Sa 12:30pm; US$185) both via **Guwahati** (1hr., US$50). Open M-Sa 9am-6:30pm, Su 9am-5pm.

Trains: All trains stop at **New Jalpaiguri Station,** Hill Cart Rd., before continuing on to the Northeastern States. The **Central Rail Booking Office** (☎ 423333) is near the Hospital Rd./Hill Cart Rd. police traffic booth—the 3rd booth, a little more than 1km south of the bridge. Head 30m diagonally northeast from the booth. Open M-Sa 8am-8pm, Su 8am-2pm. To **Mumbai** (48hr.; Su and W 2am; Rs481) and **Calcutta** (12hr.; 4 per day 3:45-7:30pm; Rs210). All trains to **Delhi** run via Calcutta (Rs363). The **Toy Train** runs from NJP station to **Darjeeling** (9hr.; 6:30am and 9am; 2nd class Rs20, 1st class Rs200).

RABINDRANATH TAGORE

The Bengali poet Rabindranath Tagore (1861-1941) towers over modern Indian literature and Bengali life. The youngest son in the large family of the prominent *zamindar* and Brahmo Samaj leader Debendranath Tagore, Rabindranath dropped out of school at an early age and taught himself English and Sanskrit. He began writing poetry as a boy and, before long, broke new ground by introducing English forms previously unknown in Bengali. He traveled around Bengal looking after his family's estates; many of his poems and stories concern the lives of villagers in Bengal, and his songs draw from the melodies of Bengali folk music. Tagore translated many of his verses into rhythmic English prose, catching the attention of Western readers. In 1913 he received the Nobel Prize for *Gitanjali* (Song Offerings), a collection of poems expressing his longing to become one with God. Tagore was knighted by the British in 1915 but renounced his title after the 1919 Jallianwallah Bagh massacre in Amritsar. In his later years, Tagore experimented with novels, plays, and elaborate songs; toward the end of his life he took up painting as well. Gandhi and other political leaders considered Tagore an inspiration and frequently visited him at Shantiniketan, the school he founded in 1901. Verses by Tagore are now the national anthems of India and Bangladesh. His plays are widely produced, and his songs have become a genre of their own. The filmmaker Satyajit Ray has produced interpretations of several of Tagore's novels, including *Aparajito* and *Pather Panchali,* part of Ray's "Apu" trilogy. Bengalis are still fiercely fond of their poet-patriot; try quizzing anyone on the street on "Rabi Babu" and get a couplet or two in response.

Buses: Private buses congregate on the west side of Hill Cart Rd., about 250m north of the bridge. Government buses leave from the **Tenzing Norgay Bus Terminal,** just north of the private buses: the main entrance to the terminal is 50m up the side street running west of Hill Cart Rd. Government buses are cheaper and have more frequent departures to the north and northeast. You may prefer the extra comfort of private buses, especially for longer journeys. **Jeeps** gather in the square area, on the opposite side of the road, and run to the following destinations all day. They are the fastest but most expensive option. To: **Calcutta** (12-13hr.; 7:30pm; Rs225); **Darjeeling** (3hr.; every 30min. 5:30am-5pm; Rs55); **Kalimpong** (4hr.; every 30min. 6:15am-4:35pm; Rs45); **Kurseong** (1hr.; every 40min. 7am-5:20pm; Rs27); **Mirik** (2½hr.; every hr. 6:45am-4pm; Rs35). **Sikkim Nation Transportation (SNT) Centre** is on Hill Cart Rd., a short walk south from the bus station. To: **Gangtok** (4hr.; every hr. 7am-2pm; Rs70, deluxe Rs90); **Geyzing** (5hr.; 12:30pm; Rs78); **Pelling** (5hr.; 11:30am; Rs84). No buses to Pelling from June to Aug. Buses for **Kathmandu** leave from Kakarbhitta, Nepal. Take a jeep to the border at **Panitanki** (1hr.; Rs30), and then walk across the bridge or take a cycle-rickshaw (Rs10). *Touts* may claim they can put you on a bus going direct to Kathmandu. They can't. Don't believe them. You'll have to cross over to Kakarbhitta (see p. 848) on the Nepali side and buy a ticket there. Buses leave Kakarbhitta 3-6:30pm, so plan your jeep trip from Siliguri accordingly. To: **Gangtok** (3½hr.; Rs92); **Kalimpong** (2½hr.; Rs50); **Darjeeling** (3hr.; Rs55); **Kurseong** (1hr.; Rs26). Prices are negotiable.

✳🛈 ORIENTATION AND PRACTICAL INFORMATION

Everything you want to find in Siliguri is either on or near **Hill Cart Rd. (Tenzing Norgay Rd.),** with its blaring horns, kamikaze rickshaw drivers, and carbon monoxide fumes of truly Indian proportions. The most useful landmark is the **Mahananda River Bridge,** 250m south of the **Tenzing Norgay Bus Terminus.** Buses, jeeps, and budget accommodations are north of the bridge, while most shops and services line Hill Cart Rd. south of the bridge. Siliguri's twin city of **New Jalpaiguri,** 6km to the south, is home to the **New Jalpaiguri Railway Station** and little else. It's 30min. by auto-rickshaw between train station and bus terminus (Rs60).

WEST BENGAL

THE LITTLE ENGINE THAT COULD Recently declared a UNESCO World Heritage Site, the "toy train" that runs from Siliguri to Darjeeling is a feat of 19th-century engineering brilliance. Built between 1879 and 1881, the rail line was the first of its kind, employing a number of revolutionary techniques to make its steep ascent into the Indian Himalayas. Most notable are the famous "Z" turns, where the train reverses up a hill and then proceeds forward again at a higher altitude. The completion of the rail line cut travel time to Darjeeling from 5-6 days to less than 12 hours, thus making Darjeeling accessible as a hill station and summer retreat. At 7408ft., the station at Ghoom is second only to Cuzco in the Andes as the highest train station on earth.

Tourist Office: West Bengal Tourism (☎511974; fax 511979). In the big, orange bldg., 100m south of the bus terminal on the east side of the road. Makes advance bookings for Jaldapara Wildlife Sanctuary. Open M-F 10am-5:30pm. There's a smaller branch at the NJP Railway Station (☎561118). **Sikkim Permit: Sikkim Tourist Office** (☎432646), SNT Centre, 50m south of the bus station, on the other side of the street, issues **Sikkim permits** for free, but requires a passport photo. Open M-F 10am-4pm.

Passport Photo: Studio Ellora, Hill Cart Rd. (☎432028). 150m south of the bridge, next to the State Bank. Takes four photos for Rs60. Necessary for Sikkim permit and Nepal visa. Allow a day for developing. Open M-Sa 8:30am-8pm.

Currency Exchange: State Bank of India, Hill Cart Rd. (☎431364). 150m south of the bridge. Changes cash and Thomas Cook and AmEx traveler's checks. Rs20 commission for exchanges up to US$100. Currency exchange is on the 4th fl. Open M-F 10am-2pm, Sa 10am-noon. Many banks and hotels on Hill Cart Rd. change money.

Luggage Storage: Tenzing Norgay Bus Terminal, on the right as you enter (Rs2); or **NJP Station,** on track 4 (Rs3).

Police: (☎520453). On Hill Cart Rd. opposite the bus station and 50m north.

Pharmacy: Medical booths dot the city. Look around or ask a local. Most close by 10pm.

Hospital: North Bengal Clinic (☎510441 or 518667). Head 300m north from the bus terminal and turn right at Dipti's Bakery, just past Hotel Simla. Follow that road for 200m and take a right at the cluster of pharmacies: the clinic is the big, yellow bldg. 50m ahead. A private hospital with state-of-the-art facilities and a highly-trained staff.

Internet: There are many Internet cafes on Hill Cart Rd., especially south of the bridge. Most will charge Rs1-2 per min. **CyberSpace,** (☎432211). One floor above the Jet Airways office. Air-conditioned and offers an unbeatable Rs48 per hr. Open daily 9am-9pm.

Post Office: Head Post Office, Hospital Rd. (☎421950 or 530847). Turn left at the 3rd police traffic booth south of the bridge on Hill Cart Rd., and follow the road for 200m. Open M-Sa 7am-7pm, Su 10am-3pm. **Postal code:** 734401.

🏠🍴 ACCOMMODATIONS AND FOOD

"Come as a guest, go as a friend," proclaims the warm, family-like **Siliguri Lodge ❶.** North of the bridge on the east side of Hill Cart Rd. and opposite the bus station, this peaceful, alcohol-free establishment has a garden, complete with mini-gazebo, a TV in the lobby, and a choice of squat or Western-style toilets. (☎533290. Check-out noon. Singles Rs100; doubles Rs140-225; quads Rs200-350.) Two blocks north on the same side of the street is the more up-market **Hotel Mount View ❶,** Hill Cart Rd., which has large, institutional rooms, all with private bath and TV. The TVs range from hi-fi to diorama-in-a-microwave, so make sure to check what you're getting. Reservations are recommended. (☎425919 or 531958. Check-out noon. Dorms Rs100; singles Rs175-400; doubles Rs250-650. MC/V.)

There are a few decent restaurants on Hill Cart Rd., south of the bridge. The **New Ranjit Restaurant ❶**, in the Ranjit Hotel, less than 1km south of the bridge, on the west side of Hill Cart Rd., is popular for its all vegetarian dishes that cost Rs24-60. (Open daily 6am-10:30pm.) **Anand Restaurant ❶**, about 50m south of New Ranjit on the east side of the road, serves a solid variety of North Indian cuisine for Rs20-50. (Open daily 7am-10pm.)

🐘 JALDAPARA WILDLIFE SANCTUARY

Jaldapara is truly a site fit for kings—or so the kings of Bhutan and Coochbhear (now part of West Bengal) believed some 100 years ago, when each jealously coveted the land as a royal rhinoceros-hunting ground. The British arrived to "settle the dispute" in true imperial fashion by claiming the entire Dooras ("gateway") region as their own, and over time, they gradually converted thousands of acres of lush jungle into vast tea plantations. This ecological upheaval left only a few large pockets of dense forest; the well-preserved Jaldapara Wildlife Sanctuary, officially designated a national park in 1985, is one of them. Though it's one of India's smaller wildlife sanctuaries, Jaldapara is one of a handful of parks left in India with a sizable population of rhinos. It also contains over 100 species of birds and is home to an impressive community of monkeys, deer, buffalo, boar, and elephants.

Jaldapara is just about the only reason not to flee straight into the hills from Siliguri, and its well-run services ensure a comfortable wildlife-viewing experience. Best of all, the park is still relatively undiscovered by the tourists who flock to India's other wildlife sanctuaries. (In-season Oct.-Apr.; closed June 15-Sept. 15. Entrance fee Rs25. Camera fee Rs50.)

There are two lodges in the area. Both are excellent, though prices are very high. Rooms should be booked in advance through the tourist office in Siliguri. At the edge of Madarihat, the **Jaldapara Tourist Lodge ❷** has large, comfy rooms and a huge yard. All meals are included. The staff is friendly and attentive. (☎03563 62230. Dorms Rs300; doubles Rs615-1000.) The alternative is the **Hollong Forest Lodge ❸**, within the confines of the park. Spot the wildlife or the sunrise from your balcony overlooking a prim, colonial-era garden. (☎03563 62228. Doubles Rs850; with meals and elephant ride Rs1550.)

Visitors can cruise the park by taking an **elephant ride** (Rs120). These powerful pachyderms pack four people each and lumber through dense forest and open plain, giving you a 90min. tour of Jaldapara's wide variety of flora and fauna. Your long-trunked guides will likely be accompanied by several little ones who are just along for the ride. Tours leave at dawn from the Hollong Forest Lodge. If you're staying in the Tourist Lodge, they'll drive you up to Hollong for a fee (Rs235). **Elephant rides are not guaranteed.** If an elephant is sick or called off on other duty, or if there has been some activity among the wild elephants in the sanctuary, you might find yourself disappointed. There are also many more beds than there are seats on the elephants, so you would be wise to book ahead. If the elephant situation doesn't pan out, you can go for a drive (Rs200) and trek to the **tiger reserve,** where you'll be lucky to see a tiger. Next door to the Jaldapara Tourist Lodge, a number of leopards pace back and forth in cages. As the sign outside this **Rescue Center** points out, this is not a zoo. It is a sanctuary for spotted fellows who have been disturbed from their natural habitat and await a safe reintroduction into the wild.

Jaldapara is about 125km east of Siliguri, which provides the only major access point to the park. **Madarihat,** the town near the park's entrance, is accessible by **buses** running to and from Siliguri (4hr., every 2hr. 5:30am-5:30pm, Rs43). If direct buses to Madarihat are not available, frequent buses going to **Alipurduara, Hashimara, Joygoin,** or **Phuntsholling** can drop you there. There is an overnight bus from Madarihat to **Guwahati** (8hr., 9pm, Rs200).

ANIMAL HOUSE Tourists aren't the only ones starved for nightlife in early-to-bed, early-to-rise Northeast India. The natives are apparently getting restless as well. In fact, in recent years drunken gallivanting and late-night carousing are on the rise among local populations...of elephants. Last call at many of the popular pachyderm watering-holes comes in late November when Jaldapara's streams fall victim to the winter dry season. Rather than resort to a winter on the wagon, wild elephants have been hitting the human hot spots (usually people's huts) in search of *hariya*, a locally micro-brewed rice wine. But the hedonism does not stop there. With their booze-fed libidos primed, the wild male elephants cruise for chicks at the makeshift brothel which hosts domesticated female touring elephants. After having their way, the tuskers stagger back to the jungle—presumably to sleep the bender off.

SUNDARBANS NATIONAL PARK ☎ 03219

The 70-odd islands at the river-delta border between West Bengal and Bangladesh comprise the Indian portion of the Sundarbans, a 4000 sq. km wildlife sanctuary of mangrove islands and winding waterways. The park's most famous attraction—the Bengal tiger—shuns human contact, especially the thundering motorboats full of chattering Indian tourists who frequent the park on weekends. The other famous resident, the estuarine crocodile, makes himself a little less scarce, but you'll be very lucky if you see him, either. However, you will spot plenty of their prey, such as spotted deer, turtles, monkeys, and unlucky villagers. The birdsongs, along with the green of the mangroves and flow of the tides, are enough to make you feel you've taken a long, rickety ride to paradise after frantic Calcutta. The journey to the park—which is possibly more interesting than the park itself—takes you deep into the Bengali countryside, a place where few tourists venture and where unjaded locals may offer you their hospitality.

THE WILD RIDE TO SUNDARBANS NATIONAL PARK. The park is accessible from Sajnekhali, roughly 120km southeast of Calcutta. What follows is a trip through Indian bureaucracy, but trust us, it's worth it, and not as painful as it sounds. First, go to the **West Bengal Tourism office** in the southeast corner of Dalhousie Sq., Calcutta, and secure a **permit**. Permits are issued free within an hour, M-F 10am-4pm. With the permit safely in hand, you can continue over to the **Southern Railways terminal** at Sealdah station to catch a commuter train to Canning (1½hr., 17 per day, Rs10). In Canning, follow your fellow passengers through the bazaars to the **river**, which, depending on season and time of day, is either a raging waterway or a trickle. If it's raging, take a **ferry** to Dok Ghat (Rs1). If it's a trickle, **hike** up your sari and wade through 1km of mud and knee-deep water with the locals. **Don't wear clothes you care about.** In Dok Ghat, squeeze yourself a bit of breathing space in one of the **shared tempos** to **Somakhali** (45min., Rs8). Somakhali is a one-minute walk and 50 *paise* ferry from Basanti, where **tempos** run to **Mojit Bati** (30min., Rs10). Another **ferry** will take you to **Gosaba** (10min., Rs1), where **cycle rickshaws** head to **Pakhirala** (40min., Rs20). The park is at **Sajnekhali**, 10min. away by **ferry** (Rs3). The entire journey takes six hours and costs around Rs75. For Rs500-2100, the government will put you on a **group tour** that goes directly to the Sundarbans and eliminates most of the fun from the trip. The price includes food, accommodation, and three days of group sightseeing, minus time to get from Calcutta and back. Ask at the Dalhousie Sq. tourism office.

WEST BENGAL

🛏️🍴 ACCOMMODATIONS AND FOOD

In Sajnekhali, the only accommodation is the **Tourist Lodge ❶**, which needs to be booked in advance through any West Bengal Tourism Office. (☎03219). Dorms Rs220; double Rs550. Meals included.) Across the great divide in Pakhirala is the **Krishnakunja Hotel ❷**, where luxuries include concrete rooms with attached bath (Rs300-400). **Hotel Aram ❶** is considerably less luxurious. (Doubles Rs200.) If everything is full, turn back and return to Gosaba. In the bazaar here is the **Kamal Kamini Hotel ❶**, with simple rooms with fans and mosquito nets. (Rs50-80.) The **Anapuran Hindu Hotel ❶** has rock-bottom singles (Rs25) and doubles (Rs50), which share a miserable common toilet. There is also the semi-luxurious **Surya Tapa Lodge ❷**, where the rooms come with showers. The upstairs rooms are quieter and more comfortable. (☎52509. Rs300). The bazaar in Gosaba is the best place to stock up on food—there are a number of decent Bengali eateries and sweet shops. In Pakhirala, there are a few tea stalls and a store, but no restaurant. The hotels cook Bengali meals at high prices. The canteen in the Sajnekhali Tourist Lodge is over-priced. The nearest **pharmacies** selling ointments for tiger bites are in Gosaba as are the STD/ISDs to make those family-calls.

🐯 WATCHING FOR TIGERS

To do anything in the park, you need to obtain a clearance from the **Park Office** in Sajnekhali, open sunrise-sunset. This will be given upon display of your permit and payment of the daily Rs5 per person and daily Rs10 per camera fees. The only way to see the park is by taking a boat tour. Boats depart 7-8am from in front of the office. Half-day trips cost Rs400, full days are Rs800, and a Rs200 compulsory guide fee is charged for each trip. The biggest boats seat 35, but they have the loudest engines and can't get into the smaller estuaries. There is a Rs200 compulsory guide fee for each trip. Most groups consist of weekenders from Calcutta who are more interested in spending time away from smog and beggary than in waking up early in the prime tiger-spotting hours. Booking in advance with travelers serious about wildlife will pay off. Try to come on weekdays to avoid loud picnicking local tourists. February and March are quietest. **Sudharnokali** reportedly has the best chances of tiger sighting (4 hr.). **Burit Dabri** is the most popular with Bengali tourists and takes you within earshot of the Bangladeshi border (8½hr.). The **Natidupani** tour takes you through the heart of the park (8hr.). In **Sanjekhali,** there is a watchtower and a nature observation center (open 8am-5pm).

> # THE BIG CATS OF BENGAL
> Catching a glimpse of the Bengal Tiger, a majestic beast with a deep reddish tan, black stripes, and white-furred belly, is a rare event. Most of the tigers in West Bengal are found only in the swampy mangrove forests of the Sundarbans, though they have occasionally been known to stray. In 1974, a tiger made it all the way to a village 80km outside Calcutta, where it killed a local woman. Only about 4% of tigers are "man-eaters," but all will attack if disturbed. Forest guards wear fiberglass head and neck protectors—these are the parts most vulnerable to attack. Honey-gatherers wear masks on the back of their heads since tigers tend to attack only when people are looking away. Researchers are trying to train tigers to stay away from humans by positioning electrified dummies in the forest—a 300V shock is administered if the tiger attacks. The experiment has been successful so far, but some people refuse to enter the Sundarbans without being escorted by *fakirs*, religious men who have the power to ward off tiger attacks. West Bengal Tourism conducts tours to the Sundarbans; the best season to visit is October to March.

DARJEELING দার্জ্জিলিং डारजीलिंग ☎ 0354

Darjeeling has been a spoke in the wheel of the tourist industry since the 19th century, and it has grown very good at it over the years. The city of 350,000 manages to be both laid-back and cosmopolitan, with tasteful and well-priced hotels and restaurants, a lively city center, and significant amounts of greenery. Tottering on the brink of a knife-edged ridge, the city looks out over the Himalayan foothills and all the way up to Kanchenjunga, the third-highest mountain in the world. On the other side, the ridge drops away to the tropical valley floor thousands of meters below. When the British chanced upon this wooded ridge in 1828, they were so enraptured with the cool climate and majestic mountain views that they convinced the king of Sikkim to let them use the area as a health resort. Darjeeling's popularity as a getaway for heat-stricken colonials grew and grew, and by 1861, Sikkim was forced to cede this great playground of colonial India to the British.

Today, Darjeeling is famous not only for its spectacular scenery, but also for its role as the starting point for the earliest Everest expeditions and as a center for tea production. The region's Gorkha inhabitants, most of them brought by the British from Nepal as laborers, never abandoned their language, dress, or blend of Hindu and Buddhist beliefs. The Gorkha National Liberation Front's war for secession culminated in the 1958 formation of the Gorkha Hill Council, which now governs the area. Tensions persist, and the Council occasionally holds *bandhs* (strikes), during which the entire town and the road to Siliguri close for a day.

▐ TRANSPORTATION

Trains: The **Reservation Booth** (☎ 52774), at the **railway station,** issues quota tickets for major trains leaving NJP **(Siliguri)** Station. Open daily 8am-2pm. The station services the **Toy Train,** which traverses the route between Siliguri and Darjeeling (from Darjeeling 6hr.; 9:10am; 2nd-class Rs22, 1st-class Rs201) and also makes an overpriced daily "joy ride" to **Ghoom** and back (2hr., 11am, Rs200; 10min. stopover in Ghoom).

Buses and Jeeps: Most buses, including private ones, and jeeps heading out of Darjeeling leave from the main bus stand at the Chowk Bazaar on Hill Cart Rd. Other jeeps leave from the intersection of Laden La Rd. and Hill Cart Rd. and from the area around the clocktower. **Buses** to: **Gangtok** (5hr., 7:30am, Rs90); **Kalimpong** (3hr., 8am, Rs45); **Rimbik** (4hr., 7am and 12:30pm, Rs50) via **Manebhanjang** (1½hr., Rs15); **Siliguri** (3hr., every 30min. 6:30am-3:30pm, Rs33). **Jeeps** to: **Gangtok** (4hr., every 30min. 7am-2:30pm, Rs110); **Jorethang** (2hr., every 30min. 9am-2:30am, Rs80), where service is available to points in Sikkim; **Ghoom** (10min., frequent 6am-5:30pm, Rs10), available only from the jeep stand near the train station.

> **❗ WARNING.** Don't ride in cars bearing black license plates with white numbers; **they are not authorized to carry passengers** and may be detained by the police.

✳ ORIENTATION

Darjeeling is draped like a blanket on a clothesline over either side of a narrow, north-south ridge, and its steep, tangled streets, alleys, and stairways will strain both your legs and your sense of direction. Fortunately, locals are ready to offer assistance with directions. The town's belly is **Hill Cart Rd.,** on the west side near the bottom. The **railway** and **bus stations** are here, as is the motor entrance to town. This is the smelly, exhaust-filled part of town. Don't be discouraged—the rest of Darjeeling is quite nice. It's quite a climb from Hill Cart Rd. to **Chowrasta,** the town's central plaza near the top of the ridge. The Chowrasta intersection has a

DISORIENT EXPRESS Ninety kilometers in nine hours? Sounds like a fast-paced trek, but the toy train uses every minute to lug some 80 passengers up more than 2000m of vertical ascent from Siliguri to Darjeeling. This little engine that can (most of the time) hauls three cars and manages the climb (and descent) by traversing the main auto road at least 100 times. Service is sporadic, due to seasonal weather variations and constant mechanical problems. However, if the train is running, the breathtaking views make the experience one that should not be missed. The two time-saving alternatives are to ride the train to Kurseong, roughly the mid-point, and then catch a bus (2hr., Rs25) or a jeep (1½hr., Rs35) the rest of the way; you can also experience the train for the 1hr. ride between Darjeeling and Ghoom (although this may be the most boring part of the trip). And don't worry if part of the train slips from its 60cm tracks (this has been known to happen); locals will emerge from the woods bearing poles to lever the carriage back on course.

bandstand at the north end and a fountain and tourist office at the south. To the right of the fountain descends **Nehru Rd.** (also called **The Mall**), one of the town's main avenues filled with shops and restaurants. **Laden La Rd.** runs right below, connecting Nehru Rd. and Hill Cart Rd. At the intersection of Nehru and Laden La Rd. sits the **clocktower.** The road to the left of the fountain in Chowrasta (past the ponies) leads to the TV tower area, home to many of the area's budget hotels.

🛈 PRACTICAL INFORMATION

Tourist Office: West Bengal Tourist Office, Chowrasta (☎54050). On the south side, just above the Indian Airlines office; enter to the right, up the ramp. Friendly, English-speaking staff provides a map of Darjeeling (Rs3), helpful transportation info, and free luggage storage for trekkers. The **Darjeeling Gorkha Hill Council Tourist Office** (☎54879) is normally situated 50m north of Chowrasta on Mall Rd. W, but that office is under renovation until March 2002; until that time, the office will be in the Maple Tourist Lodge (☎54214). Head up Mall Rd. W from Chowrastra, and turn left at the Alice Villa; walk downhill through 200m of twists and turns to reach the Maple Tourist Lodge. The office also has maps and brochures and arranges rafting expeditions on the Rangeet and Teesta rivers. Open daily 10am-5pm.

Sikkim Permit: The process of securing a **Sikkim permit** (valid for 15 days) is a bureaucratic hassle that may take hours (it's much easier at the office in **Siliguri**—see p. 738). You need your passport at every step. First go to the **District Magistrate's Office,** 7min. down Hill Cart Rd., north of the bus stands; look for the "Sikkim Pass" sign. The office is on the 1st fl. of the central bldg. Open M-F 11am-1pm and 2:30-4pm. With the stamped form, go to the **Foreigners' Registration Office,** Laden La Rd. (☎54203), 10m down from ANZ Grindlays Bank, for an official "endoresement." Open M-F 10am-4pm. Then, return to the District Magistrate's Office for the final signature. The permit is free.

Currency Exchange: ANZ Grindlays Bank, Laden La Rd. (☎54681). Just down from the Nehru Rd. intersection. Changes traveler's checks, cash, and gives cash advances on MC and V (UK, US, and Australian currency only; Rs200 commission on traveler's checks). Open M-F 10am-5pm, Sa 10am-2:30pm; traveler's checks cashed only M-F 10am-3pm, Sa 10am-12:30pm. **State Bank of India,** Laden La Rd. (☎53589), 50m south of Grindlay's Bank, changes cash, AmEx and Thomas Cook US traveler's checks, and Thomas Cook UK traveler's checks. Open M-F 10am-3pm, Sa 10am-12:30pm. Rs100 commission on both cash and traveler's checks.

Luggage Storage: Free at the tourist office, most hotels, and trekking companies.

WEST BENGAL

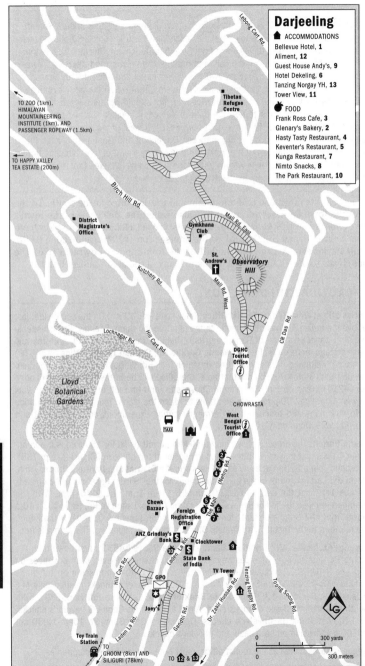

Darjeeling

🏠 ACCOMMODATIONS

Bellevue Hotel, **1**
Aliment, **12**
Guest House Andy's, **9**
Hotel Dekeling, **6**
Tanzing Norgay YH, **13**
Tower View, **11**

🍎 FOOD

Frank Ross Cafe, **3**
Glenary's Bakery, **2**
Hasty Tasty Restaurant, **4**
Keventer's Restaurant, **5**
Kunga Restaurant, **7**
Nimto Snacks, **8**
The Park Restaurant, **10**

TO ZOO (1km),
HIMALAYAN
MOUNTAINEERING
INSTITUTE (1km), AND
PASSENGER ROPEWAY (1.5km)

TO HAPPY VALLEY
TEA ESTATE (200m)

Lebong Cart Rd.

Birch Hill Rd.

Tibetan
Refugee
Centre

District
Magistrate's
Office

Kutchery Rd.

Gymkhana
Club

Mall Rd. East

St.
Andrew's

*Observatory
Hill*

Mall Rd. West

Lochnagar Rd.

Hill Cart Rd.

CR Das Rd.

DGHC
Tourist
Office
ⓘ

*Lloyd
Botanical
Gardens*

CHOWRASTA

West
Bengal
Tourist
Office ⓘ
1

TAXI

2
3
4

(Nehru Rd.)

Chowk
Bazaar

Foreign
Registration
Office

5
8 **6**
7

The Mall

ANZ Grindlay's
Bank 💲

Laden La Rd.

Clocktower

10

💲
State Bank
of India

9

Hill Cart Rd.

GPO
✚

Laden La Rd.

Gandhi Rd.

TV Tower

Tenzing Norgay Rd.

Toong Soong Rd.

11

Dr. Zakir Hussain Rd.

Joey's

WEST BENGAL

Toy Train
Station

TO
GHOOM (8km) AND
SILIGURI (78km)

TO **12** & **13**

N

0 — 300 yards
0 — 300 meters

Bookstore: Oxford Bookshop, Chowrasta (☎54325). Open M-F 9:30am-7pm, Sa 9:30am-2:30pm, Su in season. AmEx/MC/V.

Police: (☎54422). Police assistance booths are all over town; there's one in Chowrasta, one at the intersection of Nehru and Laden La Rd., and one opposite the GPO.

Pharmacy: Economic Pharmacy, Laden La Rd. (☎52174). Opposite the GPO, at the bend. Open daily 8am-8:30pm.

Hospital: Sardar Hospital (☎54218). The yellow bldg. above the north end of the main bus stand. Many pharmacies along Nehru Rd. have private doctors for consultation.

Internet: Compuset Centre, Gandhi Rd. On the right side, about 200m south of the clock-tower. Rs2 per min. Open daily 9am-6pm.

Telephones: Most STD/ISD booths are open 8am-11pm

Post Office: GPO, Laden La Rd. (☎54076). Halfway down the road, just after a sharp bend. Open M-F 9am-5pm, Sa 9am-3pm. **Postal Code:** 734101.

▛ ACCOMMODATIONS

Darjeeling is home to a wide array of high quality, cheap hotels; there's no need to settle for the wrong place or price. Off season (mid-June to Aug. and Dec.-Feb.), there's plenty of space, and discounts of up to 50% are sometimes available; in season (Sept.-Nov. and Mar.-May), you may have to hunt a bit for a room.

▉ **Aliment,** 40 Dr. Zakir Hussain Rd. (☎55068). From Chowrasta, take the road to the left of the fountain and bear right when it splits into three. After the TV tower (on the right), take a right up the hill and follow Dr. Z's around to the left. The owner's tips and the detailed tourist log are helpful in planning treks. All rooms have private bath. Laundry service and Internet access (Rs2 per min., Rs100 per hr.). Dorms Rs50; singles Rs70; doubles with bucket shower Rs150, with hot shower Rs200. ❶

▉ **Tower View,** 8/1 Dr. Zakir Hussain Rd. (☎54452; fax 54330). Just off Dr. Z's Rd. The friendly owner, a former Gorkha soldier, welcomes foreigners and shares his regional knowledge and the tourist log, which has good trekking tips. Rooms look out over Kanchenjunga, facing the sunrise. Backpacker-filled restaurant serves good meals. STD service. Dorms Rs50; singles Rs80-100; doubles Rs100-150. Off season: Rs40-120. ❶

Guest House Andy's, 102 Dr. Zakir Hussain Rd. (☎53125). Close to Chowrasta, 150m past the *puri* stalls. Run by an engaging and friendly Gurung woman, Andy's has a relaxed, family feel. Large, spotless rooms with seat toilets. Fantastic view from the roof. Top priced rooms have hot shower. Doubles Rs200-300. Off season: Rs150-250. ❶

Main Olde Bellevue Hotel, 1 & 5/1 Nehru Rd. (☎54178 and 53977). Just a few steps down Nehru Rd. from Chowrasta. This grand hotel has 2 separate bldgs.: the new wing has comfortable, though uninspiring rooms, while the 19th century "olde" wing, has slightly smaller, but beautifully furnished Raj-era suites. Phone ahead, and they will send someone to pick you up. Doubles Rs600-900. Off season: Rs300-600. ❸

Hotel Dekeling, 51 Gandhi Rd. (☎54159 and 53298; fax 53298). Above the Nehru-Laden La intersection. If you want to splurge, this is the best place to do it. Primped and carpeted, with a palatial lounge area, Dekeling will make you feel a lot richer than you probably are. Cozy beds, attached bathrooms with hot showers, and TV sets in most rooms. Doubles Rs600-1100. Off season: 30% discount. ❸

Bellevue Hotel, Chowrasta (☎54075). On the south side of the plaza. Although pricey, the ski-lodge atmosphere, central location, private baths, and fantastic views make it worth the extra rupees. For real decadance, snatch up the top-floor corner room, complete with panoramic views, a wood burning stove, and a bathtub (Rs1000). Doubles Rs550-1000; Rs100 less for single occupancy. Off season: Rs350-880. ❶

Tanzing Norgay Youth Hostel, Dr. Zakir Hussain Rd. (☎56794). 30m up the hill from the Aliment. Named after Everest's 1st Sherpa conqueror. The expansive balcony circling the bldg. compensates for sterile, institutional dorm rooms. Dorms Rs40; doubles Rs120; quads Rs200. ❶

🍴 FOOD

Darjeeling is crammed with restaurants; **Aliment** and **Tower View** are the best of the hotel variety. **Street stands** serving tasty food line Dr. Zakir Hussain Rd. just as it leaves Chowrasta, although you'll have to suffer the hungry stares and smelly deposits of the adjacent horses.

▨ **The Park Restaurant,** Laden La Rd. Opposite the State Bank of India. Everything from the music to the ivy-draped faux Ionian columns cries out "classy." Also serves the best Indian food you'll find in this part of Bengal. Open daily 11am-3pm and 6-9pm.

▨ **Hasty Tasty Restaurant,** 13 Nehru Rd. Line cooks prepare all-veg. fast food. The extensive menu covers a range of Indian, Chinese, Continental, and American fare. Service is quick and friendly. Entrees Rs25-80, ice-cream Rs14-20. Open daily 8am-8:30pm. ❶

▨ **Glenary's Bakery,** Nehru Rd. 100m uphill from the Hasty Tasty. This is the central branch of a chain that spans North Bengal. The self-proclaimed master baker lives up to his own billing. Donuts, scones, macaroons, and rolls for Rs10-40. American burger and pizza fare for Rs20-90. Open daily 7:30am-7:30pm. ❶

Kunga Restaurant, Gandhi Rd. Above the Nehru-Laden La intersection. Excellent Tibetan fare at competitive prices; quite popular with locals. *Thukpa* Rs28, *momos* (plate of 10) Rs30-55. Open daily 7:30am-8:30pm. ❶

Nimto Snacks, at the intersection of Nehru and Laden La Rd., opposite the police booth. A tiny eatery carved out of the wall, with an intimate, relaxed atmosphere. The all-veg. snacks and sweets are cheap and tasty. Excellent Tibetan *momos* (4 pieces with hot soup Rs6). Open daily 10am-7:30pm. ❶

Frank Ross Cafe, Nehru Rd. Just up the hill from the Hasty Tasty, is a good lunch stop, if only to see a menu offering tacos (Rs35) and enchiladas (Rs30). Standard Italian (Rs35-90) and American (Rs18-45) dishes are also served, as well as coffee drinks (Rs14-18). The portions aren't huge, but the food is good. Open daily 8am-9pm. ❶

Keventer's Restaurant, 9 Nehru Rd. Those in search of a taste of Raj-era Darjeeling need look no farther than "Kev's," famous for its hearty English breakfasts (Rs25-60). Their rooftop deck also makes for a fantastic brunch spot. Open daily 7:30am-8pm. ❶

🔘 SIGHTS

TIGER HILL. Darjeeling's most popular sight lies 11km out of town. A favorite with Indian tourists, early risers flock in droves to catch the sunrise from Tiger Hill, which offers the area's best views of **Kanchenjunga** (8586m), the world's 3rd-highest mountain. An observation tower on top of the 2590m rise offers views stretching from the flood plains of the Ganga delta to the snowcaps of the Himalayas, each peak lighting up in turn as the sunlight inches west. Everest is sometimes visible. The only drawback is the noisy crowd, but a little more seclusion is available in the upper floors of the observation tower for Rs20-40. The spring haze and summer monsoon clouds may also obscure the view. *(Most hotels and agencies organize morning excursions. Alternatively, catch a jeep from the hordes idling at the Nehru-Laden La intersection. Jeeps leave for Tiger Hill 4-5am, Rs30 1-way; Rs50 return. If you tire of sardine tourism, consider taking the comfortable 3hr. walk back via Ghoom.)*

HIMALAYAN MOUNTAINEERING INSTITUTE (HMI). Darjeeling has long been connected to mountaineering: when Nepal was a closed country, the earliest Everest trips took off from here. While the glory days of Edmund Hillary and Tenzing Norgay are now past, the HMI still functions as a training center for the Indian Army. The main appeal for tourists is the **Everest Museum** and the **Mountaineering Museum**, both choc-a-bloc with everything from butterflies to ice picks to relief models of the Himalayas. Around the corner, a telescope allows you to catch views of Kanchenjunga; it was a gift from Adolf Hitler to one of Nepal's prime ministers. Above the HMI is the cenotaph of **Tenzing Norgay,** a Sherpa from Darjeeling who summited Everest with Sir Edmund Hillary in 1953. Tenzing was the long-time director of the HMI, and his ashes now rest here. *(20min. walk from Chowrasta on Mall Rd. W, which becomes Birch Hill Rd., just beyond the zoo; see below. Museums open M-W and F-Su 8am-4:30pm. Rs5.)*

ZOOLOGICAL PARK. Darjeeling has more to offer than just mountains. The Padmaja Naidu Himalayan Zoological Park, though pitifully small, gives its animals much leafier spaces than most Indian zoos and has species rarely seen elsewhere, including Siberian tigers and Red pandas. Further down the ridge, the **Snow Leopard Breeding Center** is attempting to produce a sustainable population from a program that began with only two cats. *(Adjacent to the HMI. Both open M-W and F-Su 8am-4pm. Zoo entrance Rs5, camera fee Rs5. Breeding Center entrance Rs10.)*

HAPPY VALLEY TEA ESTATE. This is the best place to see a tea plantation where pickers work through the shrubs on the hills around you. The "factory" is also open to visitors. Except in the off-season (late June-Aug.), a worker will guide you through the tea leaves four-day metamorphosis from flora to flavoring. *(Walk along Hill Court Rd. 200m past the District Magistrate's Office, turn left at the sign, and walk down a winding road to the tea estate below. Open daily 8am-4pm. Free, but tip the guides.)*

OBSERVATORY HILL. A fine spot from which to take in Darjeeling's magnificent views, Observatory Hill is more importantly a sacred site for both Hindus and Buddhists. It is also believed to be the resting place of Indra's thunderbolt-casting scepter, or *dorje* (*Dorje-ling*, "land of the thunderbolt"). Protected by a grove of stately pines, woven together by thousands of prayer flags, and tirelessly guarded by an army of fearless monkeys that would make Hanuman proud, the hill is a world apart from commercial Chowrasta only minutes below. Don't miss the cave below and to the left, complete with carvings of Vishnu, Ganesh, and company. *(Stairs to Observatory Hill begin 50m north of Chowrasta on Mall Rd. E.)*

RANGEET VALLEY PASSENGER ROPEWAY. Clockwise around the ridge from the HMI is the starting point for the Rangeet Valley Passenger Ropeway. The cable car no longer makes the full trip to Singla Bazaar in the north, but it does go for a scenic 30min. dip over the tea shrubs. The cars won't operate until full (10-20 people), so service can be erratic. *(Cars run daily 10:30am-4:30pm. Round-trip Rs50.)*

GHOOM MONASTERY. Founded in 1850, Yiga Choling Ghoom is the region's most famous monastery. The Ghoom Monastery's large shrine contains a 5m golden statue of the Maitreya Buddha (the future Buddha). The murals inside have been recently refurbished and appear beautifully reborn. Don't confuse this with the new and not terribly interesting Samten Choling Ghoom Monastery below the road to Ghoom. *(In Ghoom, 8km from Darjeeling. Jeeps run here from the taxi stand near the train station between 6am and 5:30pm for Rs10. In Ghoom, turn onto the road opposite the "Ghoom Boys' H.S. School" gate and follow the road for about 1km to the monastery.)*

OTHER SIGHTS. The **Bengal Natural History Museum** has an extensive collection of stuffed creatures, particularly birds. *(Open F-W 10am-4pm. Rs2.)* Below the bus stand are the expansive and well-maintained **Lloyd Botanical Gardens,** specializing in alpine foliage. *(Open daily 9am-4pm. Free.)*

WEST BENGAL

SHOPPING

Darjeeling's main product is its excellent **tea,** available in shops and stalls all over town. The most reputable (though pricey) shops are **Nathmulls,** on Nehru Rd., near the State Bank of India, and the **Chowrasta Tea Shop,** in Chowrasta. Cheaper tea, along with everything else imaginable, is sold at the **Chowk Bazaar,** the market surrounding the main bus station. **Hayden Hall,** Laden La Rd. (☎53228), across the State Bank of India, is a women's cooperative that sells locally-handmade blankets, rugs, bags, and sweaters. Proceeds go to needy women in Darjeeling. (Open M-Sa 9am-5pm.) A larger collection of handmade goods is available at the **Tibetan Refugee Self-Help Centre,** beyond and below Observatory Hill. From Chowrasta, take CR Das Rd. (which starts near the police booth and runs below Mall Rd. E) north and west around the ridge. Follow the right fork, and descend to the right until you reach the center. Established by Tibetans who fled here in 1959, the center has a shop selling carpets, sweaters, and woodcarvings. The workshops are on the premises and open to the public for viewing. (Open M-Sa 9am-5pm.)

NIGHTLIFE

Darjeeling is mostly dead after 8pm. One exception is **Joey's Pub.** Joey, a Darjeelingite who spent two years in London in the 70s, has succeeded in recreating the British pub scene—Indian style. Beer options (Rs60-70) include San Miguel, Dansberg, and Guinness, among others. However, be forewarned that the Guinness is not the rich, creamy variety imported from St. James Gate, but is sadly the thin, watery variety imported from Nepal. (Open daily noon-3pm and 6-10pm.)

TREKKING AROUND DARJEELING

Trekking is the best way to get around the Darjeeling and Western Sikkim regions from October to early December and from March to early June. Treks consist of 6 or 7hr. hikes between villages, where small hotels (usually Rs35-50) and food are available. On the trail itself, provisions are unavailable and should be packed along with a sleeping bag, warm clothes, and rain gear. Trekkers must also bring their **passports,** which are required at Manebhanjang and sometimes at Sukia Pokhri. The routes are often old jeep roads bypassed in several sections by trails. For the most recent information, consult **West Bengal Tourism** (see p. 729) and tourist logs at the Bellevue, Tower View, and Aliment hotels.

The most common starting point for treks is **Manebhanjang,** a stop on the road from Darjeeling to Rimbik. **Buses** going to Rimbik (4hr., 7am and 12:30pm, Rs50) can drop you off (1½hr., Rs15). A popular two-day excursion starts at Manebhanjang and climbs steeply up to **Tonglu** (9km, altitude 900m), where lodging is available and the views are spectacular. The excursion returns to Manebhanjang on the following day or you may extend the trek into a loop that goes on from Tonglu to **Gairibas** (9km, -400m), and from there to **Bikhebhanjang** (6km, +400m) before climbing up to **Sandakphu** (6km, +600m). From Sandakphu, this trail heads to **Phalot** (23km, 0m) and from there to **Gorkhey** (15km, -600m), then to **Ramram** (9km, -400m), to the **Siri Khola River** (10km, -500m), and then ends in **Rimbile** (9km, +400m), where buses head back to Darjeeling (5hr., 6am and noon, Rs55). Another option is to head from Rimbik to Gorkhey, Phalut, Sandakphu, and back to Rimbik—each leg takes one day. The direct trail from Sandakphu to Rimbik has many bifurcations, and it's easy to get lost; it's better to go from Sandakphu to Rimbik via Gurdum and Siri Khola, which has a nice trekkers' hut. Consult West Bengal Tourism's free "Himalayan Treks" pamphlet when planning routes.

WEST BENGAL

KALIMPONG कालिमपं कालिम्पोगं ☎ 03552

Kalimpong's two chief claims to fame are its colorful flower nurseries and its numerous reputable schools, and if you're looking for peace and quiet, Kalimpong (1250m) makes an ideal getaway. The surrounding countryside meets the glorious expectations its location might inspire, and the town itself feels intimate and familial. Kalimpong is also a center of the Gorkha independence movement, and any *bandh* that shuts down Darjeeling also renders Kalimpong inaccessible.

▐ TRANSPORTATION

Buses and Jeeps: Buses and jeeps depart from Market Sq., with booking offices along the perimeter. **Buses** to: **Gangtok** (3hr., 7:30 and 8am, Rs50); **Panitanki,** on the Nepal border (3hr., 5:35am and 1:45pm, Rs55); **Siliguri** (2½hr., every 30min. 5:30am-4:30pm, Rs45); **SNT** runs 2 daily buses to **Gangtok** (3½hr., 8:30am and 1pm, Rs55). Open daily 7am-2pm. **Jeeps** run to: **Darjeeling** (2½hr.; frequent 7am-3:30pm; front Rs70, back Rs65); **Gangtok** (3hr., frequent 6:30am-3:15pm, Rs70); **Kakarbhitta** (3½hr., 6:30am and 2:30pm, Rs70); **Siliguri** (2hr., frequent 7:30am-5pm, Rs50).

▐ ORIENTATION

The **bus stand** occupies most of **Market Sq.** in the center of town. On the east of Market Sq. is Hotel Cosy Nook; on the west is a building with a corrugated roof. **Sikkim Nation Transport (SNT)** is just to the left of this building, and the Himilashree Lodge is to the right. Just south of Market Sq. is the old **football field,** also known as the **Mela Grounds. Ongen Rd.** crosses the square at the west end. Parallel to Ongen Rd. is **Main Rd.,** the town's major thoroughfare and primary axis. The 200m central stretch of Main Rd. is capped at both ends by traffic intersections. Main Rd. continues north and becomes **Rishi Rd.**

▐ PRACTICAL INFORMATION

Tourist Information: DGHC Tourist Office, 30m north of Main Rd.'s north intersection. Organizes sight-seeing tours of the area (Rs400 per vehicle of 4) and rafting expeditions on the Rengeet and Teesta Rivers (Rs350-650). Also sells photocopies of a well-drawn map of Kalimpong for Rs6. Open daily from 9am-5pm.

Budget Travel: Shangri-La Services, Rishi Rd. (☎55109; fax 55290). Fifty meters north of Main Rd.'s north intersection. An authorized agent for Jet Airways, Blue Dart Express, Sita World Travels, and FedEx, Shangri-La also organizes treks in Sikkim. Open daily 8am-6pm.

Currency Exchange: None of Kalimpong's banks change currency. The only legal place to change money is the **Soni Emporium** (☎55030), 100m north of the tourist office, just off Rishi Rd. to the right. Soni trades traveler's checks and US, UK, and French currencies at reasonable rates, and he will then invite you into his back room and persuade you to spend your newly acquired rupees on his collection of Indian and Tibetan art.

Bookstore: Kashi Nath and Sons, opposite the tourist office. Stocks a good selection of everything from Hardy to the Hardy Boys. Open daily 7:30am-7:30pm.

Police: (☎100 or 55268). On the corner at the south intersection of Main Rd.

Pharmacy: Shree Tibet Stores, Main Rd. (☎55459). Opposite Snow White Fashion. Open daily 8:30am-8:30pm. Doctor available 9:30am-1pm and 2-6:30pm. If it's an after-hours emergency, knock loudly on the door.

Hospital: Sadar Hospital (☎55415). Northeast of town. Heading north from Main Rd's north intersection, take a left just after the tourism office, then a left at the next fork.

Internet: Odyssey Internet Cafe, Main Rd. (☎58964). On the 1st fl. of the supermarket at Main Rd.'s south intersection. 8 terminals with access for Rs1 per min. Free soft drink with 1hr. of surfing. Open daily 9am-7pm.

Post Office: GPO, Main Rd. (☎55990). 30m south of the police station. Open M-F 9am-4:30pm, Sa 9am-3pm. **Postal Code:** 734301.

ACCOMMODATIONS

Deki Lodge, Tripai Rd. (☎55095; fax 56935; dekiloz@dtc.vsnl.net.in). From Main Rd.'s north intersection, head north on Rishi Rd. for about 600m; Tripai Rd. branches left, and Deki is visible from here. Deki's peaceful location, perpetually smiling staff, and relaxed, backpacker atmosphere set it apart from the rest. Spacious rooms, hot showers, and a small family of friendly cats and dogs. Laundry service and Internet (Rs1.50/min.). Singles Rs80-250; doubles Rs200-350; deluxe 2-person suites Rs650-750. ❶

Cloud 9, Rinkingpong Rd. (☎57034). Follow the main road 200m south of the post office, and take the left, upper road at the fork. Follow the road for 300m, continuing after Hotel Chimal for another 300m. Cloud 9 is a little pricier, but very much worth it. 5 rooms (and common room with TV), all pristine, well-furnished, carpeted, and with attached seat toilet and hot shower. The downstairs restaurant serves the best food in Kalimpong. On Saturday evenings, the owner brings together some musically- inclined friends for an informal jam session of mostly classic rock. Guests are welcome to join in. Doubles Rs600-800; single occupancy Rs475-675; 20% off season discount. ❸

Shangri-La Guest House (☎55109). Tripai Rd. This aptly-named hotel is worth the 45min. walk from town along the road to Deolo Hill. Beautiful and secluded, with kitchen facilities, private baths in each room, and a surrounding garden that provides fresh produce for meals. Check with Shangri-La Services (see **Budget Travel,** above) in town for info on availability and directions before trekking out. Doubles Rs300. ❶

Lodge Cosy Nook, Market Sq. (☎55541). On the east side of the bus stop. The betel-chewing owner offers advice on seeing the sights. Rooms are plain, but surprisingly clean and roomy, and all have attached bath (bucket hot water Rs4). Singles Rs150; doubles Rs200; triples Rs250; quads Rs300. ❶

Lodge Himalshree, Market Sq. (☎55070). Just to the right of the building with the corrugated roof. Run by a friendly family who disapprove of "hanky-panky," i.e. loud noise and alcohol. Hot water buckets Rs6. Doors lock at 9pm. "Dorms" (2 beds in the lobby) Rs70; doubles Rs130; triples with bath Rs250; quad without bath Rs200. ❶

FOOD

Kalimpong has a scant selection of good restaurants, but some Chinese eateries have popped up around Market Sq. Main Rd. is lined with veggie snack stalls.

Kalsang Restaurant, by the football field, 20m from Market Sq. Follow the road leading southeast away from the jeep stands, and descend the steps just past the football field into a Tibetan family's home. Cheap, delicious, and authentic Tibetan food. *Momos* Rs10, veg. *gyathuk* Rs15. Open daily 6am-7pm. ❶

Glenary's, Main Rd. and Rishi Rd. The master baker rears his doughy head at 2 locations in Kalimpong: one on Main Rd., 30m south of the southern intersection, the other on Rishi Rd., 100m north of the northern intersection. The same great pastries as in Darjeeling—swiss rolls Rs8, black forest cake Rs15, donuts Rs10. Open daily 8am-7pm. ❶

Fresh Bite, Rishi Rd. Opposite the tourism office. Speedy service and classic rock distinguish this Westernized lunch spot. Sandwich and burger fare Rs15-30, North Indian dishes Rs18-50, sumptuous sundaes and floats Rs40-60. Open daily 10am-7pm. ❶

Kalash Vegetarian Snacketeria, Main Rd. Opposite the State Bank of India. The best selection of veg. snacks in town. North and South Indian as well as continental favorites. Great *dosas* Rs15-30, curries Rs20-40, *momos* Rs15. Open daily 8am-7:30pm. ❶

👁 🎵 SIGHTS AND ENTERTAINMENT

One of the town's main attractions, Kalimpong's bountiful bouquet of orchids, amaryllises, roses, gladioli, and dahlias is most impressive from March to June. Several nurseries are scattered around the outskirts of town. **Ganesh Mani Pradhan Nursery,** 4km north of town on Rishi Rd., specializes in orchids; calling ahead is recommended. (☎ 57217. *Open daily 9am-5pm.*) The **Tharpa Choling Monastery,** a Geluk (Yellow Hat) monastery, was founded in 1892 and is still in the process of renovation; visitors are likely to see wood carvers and artisans at work. The monastery retains evidence of its Chinese influences, particularly in the temple on the hill. Above the main compound where Chinese script adorns the entry pillars, a distinctly Chinese statue (Ling Cesar) stands, and all the tools and texts necessary for Mo divination are present (see **One Mo Monastery,** below). *(Walk 20min. up Tripai Rd. from Deki Lodge. Just before another road joins from above, there's a small path leading off to the right which then curves left to a small white archway.)*

Kalimpong is well-known for its English-language schools. The oldest and most distinguished of these is **Dr. Graham's Homes,** which was built in 1900 when a Scottish minister set up a home for six orphaned students. The school eventually acquired the whole hilltop, and is almost entirely funded by alumni. It now has over 1200 students and is the model for many other schools devoted to poor and handicapped children. *(20min. beyond the Tharpa Chaling Monastery on the same road.)* If you continue farther on this road, it leads to the top of **Deolo Hill,** the highest point in the area. The views are peerless—from the top you can see Kanchenjunga, Darjeeling, Sikkim, Kalimpong, the confluence of the Teesta and Rangit rivers, and east to the border with Bhutan. The DGHC has built a number of free gazebos perfect for a picnic lunch. A 200m footpath leads to a more secluded side of the hill.

ONE MO MONASTERY Kalimpong's Tharpa Choling Monastery, of the *Geluk-pa* (Yellow Hat) sect, exhibits a particularly strong blend of Chinese and Tibetan influences. Most striking, perhaps, is the practice of Mo, a form of fortune-telling closely related to the I-Ching. Visitors are welcome to watch and join in. The first step is the casting of the Sho, a large seed split into two parts. While kneeling and thinking of a particular question or problem, the supplicant casts the seed onto the ground. If both sides land face up or face down, he or she isn't ready to continue; each person can take as many as three throws to get one side face up and the other face down. Next, the supplicant is given the Tonje, a large bamboo cup filled with 100 numbered bamboo sticks. The Tonje must then be shaken back and forth until one of the 100 sticks pops out. The number of this stick is then taken to the enormous Chinese (and corresponding Nepali) text, where the often-enigmatic fortune is read. Like the I-Ching, these fortunes are heavy on symbol and light on specifics. So if you can't decide what to do with your life, or maybe just where to go to dinner, Mo knows.

A 40min. walk beyond Dr. Graham's Homes sits the **Bhutanese Monastery,** or Thongsa Gompa. Established in 1630, the monastery is Kalimpong's oldest and the closest thing to Bhutanese culture you're likely to see without a US$200 per day visa. The monks and students are primarily Bhutanese, but the temple draws many local worshipers, particularly on Sundays. The monastery is in constant need of volunteers (see **Volunteer Opportunities,** below). *(Follow Rishi Rd. 100m past the turn-off for Tripai Rd. and Deki Lodge, where another road on the right will join it from below. Backtrack 20m down that road, take the 1st turn on your left, and head down this road for 100m until it ends at the monastery gate. Open to the public daily 5am-7pm).*

The **Kanchan Cinema Hall** often shows somewhat stale Hollywood films and standard Hindi attractions. *(On Rishi Rd. 300m north of Main Rd.'s north intersection. Showings 11am, 2, and 5pm. Rs6-15.)* The **Snooker and Pool Hall,** with its shiny new snooker table, is a local hangout. *(On Rishi Rd. 50m north of Main Rd.'s north intersection, next to Shangri-La Services. Open daily 7am-9pm. Pool Rs20 per frame, snooker Rs40 per frame.)*

VOLUNTEER OPPORTUNITIES

The **Bhutanese Monastery** (see above) is often in need of volunteers for everything from manual labor to medical care to teaching English, and gratefully accepts any help. Contact **Lama Kunzang** at the monastery or talk to **Chawang Nyima** or **Tsheltrum,** the resident Bhutanese painter, both of whom speak English.

NEPAL नेपाल

LIFE AND TIMES

LAND, FAUNA AND FLORA

The legends are true: Nepal has the most dramatic mountains in the world. The massive Himalayan range was thrust up 50 million years ago when India collided with the rest of Asia. Today, Nepal is nearly 75% mountain, and it contains eight of the world's 10 highest peaks.

At the northernmost reach of the Indo-Gangetic Plain, the relatively flat **Terai** is fertile, low-lying (200m), hot, and humid. This whole area was once covered in dense malarial forest that supported only wild animals and hungry mosquitoes, but recent years have seen vast deforestation, and today it is the hub of Nepal's growing population. Jutting 1500m out from the Terai, the forested **Chure Hills** run parallel to the 3000m Mahabharat Range farther north. Between the Chure and the Mahabharat Hills are the broad basins of the **Inner Terai,** cut by the deep, north-south river gorges of Nepal's three biggest rivers—the Karnali, the Narayani, and the Kosi. At altitudes of 500 to 2000m, the **Pahar** region, north of the Mahabarat, is marked by flat, fertile valleys, including the Kathmandu, Banepa, and Pokhara Valleys. This region has been inhabited and cultivated longer than anywhere else in Nepal. Over 40% of the population lives there today.

The **Himalayas** are inhabited only in pockets. Human settlements are sparse after 4000m. Nepal's plant life thins out as altitudes increase, with the dense timber forests yielding to alpine pastures of spruce, birch, and rhododendron. Beyond 4900m, nothing but mountains grow. Ten mountains in Nepal are higher than 8000m, including **Mount Everest** or *Chomolungma* (8848m), the highest point on earth. North of the peaks is the high desert plateau of the **Trans-Himalaya.**

The Terai is inhabited by tigers, leopards, *gaur* (wild ox), elephants, and deer. Many can be seen in the **Royal Chitwan National Park** (see p. 838), a UNESCO World Heritage Site. The Rapti Valley is one of the last refuges of the endangered Indian rhinoceros. The Himalayas are also home to the rare docile yeti *(Homo nivosus abominabilis)*, of four-toed footprint fame.

HISTORY

Nepal has a history and a culture as unique and diverse as its geography. Proximity to India has led to Indian influence in the Terai. The central hills and mountain valleys, including Kathmandu, have tended toward independence but not isolation. Deep in the mountains, life has gone on without much outside influence at all.

EARLY NEPAL (20,000 BC-AD 1200). Nepal's early history is shrouded in myth. Stone Age settlers arrived around 20,000 BC, and written references to the region appear in the 1st millennium BC. The **Kiratis,** a Mongol people who migrated into Nepal during the 8th century BC, were the first known rulers of the Kathmandu

c. 563 BC
Siddartha
Gautama (Buddha)
born in Lumbini

AD 464-733
Sanskrit inscrip-
tions record Lic-
chavi rule and
attest to the influ-
ence of North
Indian cultures

AD 1097
Chalukya lietenant
from Karnataka
pronounces him-
self king and rules
from his capital in
the Terai

Ari Malla (r. 1200-
1216) is the first of
the "Malla" ("wres-
tler") kings of the
Kathmandu Valley

Yaksha Malla (r.
1428-1482)
launches rare
attack on Indian
lands to the south

1743-1745
Rule of Prithvi
Narayan Shah,
conqueror of the
Kathmandu Valley
and first ruler of
united Nepal

Valley. Small kingdoms developed in the Terai region around 500 BC in response to the powerful Aryan kingdoms to the south. **Siddhartha Gautama,** the Buddha, was born into one of these early tribal confederations, the Sakya clan, during the 6th century BC. Three centuries later, the Indian Buddhist emperor **Ashoka** made a pilgrimage to the Buddha's birthplace, and built one of his famous pillars in **Lumbini** (see p. 834). Ashoka's Mauryan empire, greatly influenced local culture both politically and culturally (see p. 71).

Buddhism spread throughout Nepal during Ashoka's lifetime, and the concept of looking to the king for inspiration in fulfilling one's *dharma* came to play a major role in Nepal. Early kingdoms found it hard to guard their own borders and control their own land, and none expanded very far.

During the 4th and 5th centuries AD, the **Licchavis** arrived from the Indian plains and overthrew the Kirati kings. They brought Hinduism and the caste system to Nepal and set to work viciously oppressing the Buddhist masses. Under the Licchavis, the Kathmandu Valley enjoyed economic and artistic growth, which continued despite the wars and poor administration of the reign of the **Thakuris,** who rose to power in the 9th century.

MALLA KINGDOMS (AD 1200-1742). A new dynasty, the **Mallas** emerged in the Kathmandu Valley in 1200. After somewhat shaky beginnings, they ushered in a golden era in Kathmandu Valley culture and ruled for over 500 years. After the death of Yaksha Malla, the greatest of the Mallas, in 1482, the kingdom he had ruled from Bhaktapur was split among his three children. Kathmandu, Patan, and Bhaktapur developed into rival city-states. Despite constant feuding over trade with Tibet, all three kingdoms reached new heights in art and culture—the great wood-screened temples and the many cobbled **Durbar Squares** of the valley date from this time.

THE SHAH DYNASTY (1742-1816). It all began with the small hill-state of Gorkha, 50km west of Kathmandu. Gorkha was ruled by the **Shahs,** the most ambitious of the many immigrant Rajput clans that had come between the 14th and 16th centuries, driven out of India by Muslim invaders. In 1742 King **Prithvi Narayan Shah** ascended to the throne of Gorkha, and within two years he set out to conquer Nepal's richest region, the Kathmandu Valley. After 25 years of war and attrition, the three cities of Kathmandu, Patan, and Bhaktapur surrendered. When Prithvi Narayan Shah invaded Kathmandu, King Jaya Prakash Malla asked the British East India Company for help. "No," they said. The victorious Shah became the founder of the modern nation of Nepal, and his Gorkha army conquered the eastern Terai and hills. Prithvi Narayan closed the doors of his new nation to the outside world, a policy that kept Nepal isolated until the 1950s. Prithvi Narayan's kingdom deteriorated soon after his death in 1775, as the monarchy passed from one infant Shah to another, and nobles battled to act as regent.

NEPAL

Eventually the shrewd chief minister **Bhim Sen Thapa** took control and united Nepal by launching a war against the west, annexing Garhwal and Kumaon (now part of Uttaranchal) and Himachal Pradesh, in modern India. But the government mishandled its new lands. From 1788 to 1792 it fought a war with Tibet and China, and in 1814 its expansion into the Terai provoked the hostility of the East India Company.

The **Anglo-Nepalese War** was not the easy victory the British expected. In spite of superior numbers and weaponry, the British were repeatedly beaten by the Nepalese soldiers, who held their hilltop forts and charged at the redcoats with *khukuri* knives. It was two years before the British broke through and won in 1816. The **Treaty of Segauli** stripped Nepal of Himachal Pradesh, Garhwal, Kumaon, and much of the Terai, fixing the eastern and western borders of the country where they remain today. The prospect of another insurrection encouraged the British to adopt a more sensitive stance toward Nepal; it survived as one of the few countries in Asia that was never colonized. Eventually, the British Army recruited Nepalese soldiers for its new **Gorkha** (or Gurkha) regiments.

STAGNATION AND COUP D'ETAT (1816-46). Prime Minister Bhim Sen Thapa kept the country stable by strengthening the army, but chaos ensued when he fell from power in 1837, and several palace factions struggled to replace him. On September 14, 1846, a powerful minister was murdered, and the queen assembled the entire royal court in an attempt to discover the culprit. The personal guards of **General Jung Bahadur,** cabinet minister for the army, surrounded the court and opened fire, killing 32 of Kathmandu's most powerful nobles. Over the next few hours, Jung Bahadur and the queen came to a secret agreement, and the general was appointed prime minister.

RANA RULES (1846-1951). Jung Bahadur took the title of **Rana,** and under this name his family maintained an iron grip for 105 years, amid countless family feuds and outrageous nepotism. Jung Bahadur eventually stripped the king, Rajendra, of his power. After a visit to London in 1850, Jung Bahadur kicked off a series of reforms designed to drag Nepal into the modern world. He bureaucratized the government—he did away with patronage and started to keep track of who was spending what and why. Land tenure was registered, and landlords could no longer arbitrarily evict tenants from their land. In 1856, Jung Bahadur gave himself the ridiculous title "Super-Minister" and promoted himself to "Maharaja of Kaski and Lamjung," which gave him the right to overrule the king. The title was made hereditary, and the Shah kings became mere figureheads.

The Indian **Mutiny of 1857** provided an opportunity for Nepal to flex its muscles and win British support. Jung Bahadur sent 10,000 men to aid the British. In return, the British gave back the Terai lands they had taken in 1816. The British gave Nepal "guidance" on its foreign policy, but Nepal remained independent, scoffing at British demands for more trading rights and keeping strict tabs on Gorkha recruitment. The Rana prime ministers, however, proved to be more interested in advancing

1806-1837
Bhim Sen Thapa rules as chief minister, aided by ruthless regent queen Tripurasundari

1788-1792
War against Qing China in Tibet

1814-1816
Anglo-Nepalese War. Nepal loses Sikkim and much territory in the Terai and is forced to accept a British resident in Kathmandu

1837
Bhim Sen Thapa commits suicide in jail

1846
Gagan Singh, favorite of Queen Lakshimidevi, assassinated in court intrigue

1850-1851
Jung Bahadur travels to Britain

NEPAL

1857
Jang Bahadur fights alongside the British in Gora-khpur and Lucknow during the Sepoy Mutiny

1901-1929
Rule of Chandra Shamsher, marked by attempts to resolve unending family feuds over succession rights

1914-1918
Tens of thousands of Nepali soldiers fight on the British side during WWI

1918
Trichandra College founded, the first in the country

1935
Nepal's first political party, the Praja Parishad, founded by exiles in India

1959
First constitution; first elections held

their family fortunes than in helping their country. When Jung Bahadur Rana died in 1877, his successors turned out to be just as wicked, and a whole lot less competent.

Chandra Shamsher Rana, (r.1901-29), was a better administrator than most, but his motivation—social conscience or rampant egotism—is still the subject of controversy. He began his reign by building the enormous Singha Durbar palace for himself and his entourage. This project alone was enough to swallow the whole of the national public works budget for the first three years of his rule. During WWI, Chandra Shamsher implemented changes to appease Gorkha soldiers who had fought overseas and had returned home with revolutionary ideas. The introduction of a transportation system and a whole range of social reforms, such as the banning of slavery and *sati*, were among the first of the changes. Nepal's first college was founded, and tenant farmers were made the owners of the lands they had rented for centuries. **The Treaty of Friendship** with Britain formally recognized Nepal's independence in 1923. Fewer trade restrictions, however, made Nepal more dependent on imported British and Japanese goods. Prime Minister Judha Shamsher Rana (r.1932-45) returned Nepal to military rule, and dissatisfaction with Rana rule grew.

Indian Independence in 1947 gave Nepal a new neighbor to deal with. Indian Prime Minister Jawaharlal Nehru disapproved of the Rana regime. In 1947 the **Nepali Congress** was formed, in the tradition of the Congress that had led India to freedom. Several renegade members of the Rana family who favored democratization fled to India and joined the growing anti-Rana resistance. The turning point came in 1950 when **King Tribhuvan,** a palace figurehead since 1911, also fled to India. By this time, he had captured popular support. The king, the prime minister, and Congress leaders met in Delhi, where Nehru engineered the **Delhi Compromise of 1951,** effectively bringing the Rana regime to an end.

NEPAL AFTER THE RANAS (1951-1990). After the Ranas' defeat, Nepal's foreign policies underwent dramatic changes. The Delhi Compromise was replaced in 1959 by a new constitution that called for a democratically elected assembly. The Nepali Congress won a large majority in the elections, and its leader, **B.P. Koirala,** became prime minister. But the state of affairs was fragile. King Tribhuvan had died in 1955, and his son **Mahendra** was less enthusiastic about political reforms, claiming that Nepal wasn't yet developed enough to handle them. He dismissed the Congress government almost as soon as it took power, and threw its leaders in jail. In 1962, a new constitution replaced the national assembly with a system of *panchayats* (village councils) to elect members to district councils, which, in turn, elected a National Panchayat. Political parties were banned, and the new system, supposedly a "special" kind of democracy uniquely suited to Nepalese traditions, effectively marked a return to absolute monarchy.

NEPAL

King Birendra, who came to power in 1972 (for astrological reasons he wasn't crowned until 1975), supported the *panchayat* system. Early in his career Birendra declared Nepal a "Zone of Peace" (a declaration of neutrality that angered India) and tightened visa restrictions for foreigners. The *panchayat* system continued to provoke dissent, however, and resistance came to a head in 1979 with riots in Kathmandu and Patan. In response, Birendra called for a national referendum to decide between the *panchayat* system and multiparty democracy. The *panchayats* won by a narrow margin, and the monarchy hung on another decade, kept in place by censorship and police brutality.

THE LAST 10 YEARS (1990-2000). Inspired by revolutions in Eastern Europe and provoked by an economic blockade imposed by India, the outlawed opposition parties banded together in 1990, and pro-democracy demonstrations filled the streets of Kathmandu. When the king realized that mass arrests would not quell the uprising, he gave in and lifted the ban on political parties on April 8. A week later the major parties formed an interim government and wrote a new constitution. A parliamentary democracy came into effect, with Birendra as constitutional monarch.

Elections gave a majority to the Nepali Congress, which had led the democracy movement. The **Communist Party of Nepal-United Marxist-Leninist (CPN-UML)** became the main opposition. The new prime minister was **G.P. Koirala,** brother of the late B.P. Koirala. Rising inflation gave rise to general discontent (again), and an agreement with India over the Mahakali Dam project on Nepal's western frontier brought accusations of selling out to India. Unimaginative and stubborn, Koirala alienated many in his own party and was forced to resign in 1994.

The elections that followed brought the Communists to power in a minority government. Prime Minister **Man Mohan Adhikari** launched a series of populist schemes, including the "build-your-own-village" program, which gave large cash grants to local governments. Adhikari then resigned, hoping to gain a parliamentary majority for his government through another election. The king approved Adhikari's call for elections, but the Supreme Court ruled against the maneuver. No elections were held, and the Congress party took power by allying itself with the right-wing **National Democratic Party (NDP).** New Congress Prime Minister **Sher Bahadur Deuba's** efforts to bolster ties with the NDP were waylaid by intraparty dissent, and a March 1997 no-confidence motion brought the government down. The breakaway NDP faction led by **Lokendra Bahadur Chand** formed a coalition government with the CPN-UML, pushing Nepal into a new era of instability. In 1998, guerillas from the **Communist Party of Nepal (Maoist)** turned violent and killed several NGO workers, alleging that they had mishandled funds.

1960
The king dissolves parliament and assumes absolute power

1980
Referendum shows majority support for *panchayat* system

1990
Pro-democracy demonstrations lead to new constitution and parliamentary democracy

1998
Beginning of Maoist inurgency

2001
Crown Prince Dipendra massacres most of the royal family

2002
Maoist insurgency escalates

NEPAL

TODAY

THIS YEAR'S NEWS

Tourism slumped and Maoist activity increased in the aftermath of the **royal massacre** of June 2001, when a drunken Crown Prince Dipendra killed his father King Birenda and eight other members of the royal family before turning his gun on himself. The current king is **Gayendra Bir Bikram Shah Dev.**

The Maoist insurgency continues to gain momentum, and a national **state of emergency** was declared in November 2001 in response to a series of violent attacks on government facilites and personnel. The country was thrown into even greater turmoil just days before the state of emergency was due to end in late May 2002, when Prime Minister Sher Bahadur Deuba was expelled from his own party after he threatened to dissolve parliament.

> **❗ MAOIST INSURGENCY.** Nepal's **Maoist insurgency** is now in its sixth year, and violent activity has intensified over the past twelve months. As many as 3,500 people have lost their lives since the struggle began to overthrow the monarchy and install a Communist government. A state of emergency was declared in November 2001, **and as of May 2002, many governments were advising their citizens to stay away from the country until tensions subside.** Nationwide strikes *(bandh)* called by Maoist leader Baburam Bhattarai have repeatedly affected transport and communications across major tourist areas, and although foreigners are not normally the primary targets of violence, there have been several instances of armed attacks on foreign tourists or tourist facilities. Businesses and NGOs with American affiliations have been targeted on several occasions, and there has been an increase in anti-Western rhetoric in recent months. Tourists are advised to avoid all travel outside the Kathmandu Valley, and to stay clear of public gatherings.

GOVERNMENT AND POLITICS

Nepal became a constitutional monarchy with a parliamentary system of government on November 9, 1990. The power of the sovereign, a position held first by **King Birendra Bir Bikram Shah** (killed by his son the crown prince in June 2001), is limited, and real power is in the hands of the prime minister (currently **Sher Bahadur Deuba**), chosen by the 205-member House of Representatives. Members are elected by universal suffrage for a term of five years. An upper house, the 60-seat National Assembly, is made up of both appointed and elected members.

The main political parties in Nepal are the moderate Nepali Congress (NC), the Communist Party of Nepal-United Marxist-Leninist (CPN-UML), and the rightwing National Democratic Party (NDP). The Communist Party of Nepal (Maoist), led by **Baburam Bhattarai,** has been engaged since 1996 in a violent struggle to overthrow the government and impose Communist rule.

ECONOMICS

Nine of 10 Neplais depend on subsistence farming. Nepal is one of the poorest countries in the world. They use hillsides for terrace farming, but landslides and erosion wipe out crops regularly. In the more fertile Terai, where farming is more lucrative, high population growth makes even subsistence farming difficult. Many people's hopes for the future hinge on the hydroelectric potential of Nepal's raging rivers, but development stands at odds with the bankable tourist appeal of pristine valleys for rafting and hiking. Meanwhile, roads are expensive to build and maintain, and the Indian border is the only easily negotiable channel of trade. Heavy industry is concentrated in the Terai, and most manufactured goods and machinery have to be imported from India.

Nepal's biggest source of foreign exchange is the export of wool and international aid. Foreign assistance over the past four decades has been a mixed blessing. Aid donors have made many mistakes—development programs unsuited to the region, uneven distribution of aid, corrupt and unregulated rural NGOs.

PEOPLE

DEMOGRAPHICS

Nepal has 24 million people, representing 60 ethnic, linguistic, and caste groups. The country's cultural variety is largely the result of its rugged and often impassable terrain, which has kept areas isolated from each other. The cultures of Nepal have ancient roots in the land, but the country itself is young. Until two hundred years ago, a "Nepali" was somebody from the Kathmandu Valley, and it is still normal for people to identify themselves by their native region: *pahari, madeshi,* or *bhotia* (hills, plains, or northern-border dwellers), rather than Nepal.

Nepal is a nation of villages, and 90% of the population live in small market towns and rural settlements. Settlement is thickest in the fertile Terai, Nepal's bread-basket and a booming industrial region. Up in the highlands and the Trans-Himalayan valleys, almost no land is under cultivation, and these areas remain populated only by a few nomads.

Most Nepalis are Indo-Aryan Hindus, though Buddhism is also strong. The **Newari**, the earliest known arrivals in Nepal and the original settlers of the Kathmandu Valley, practice a blend of Buddhism and Hinduism. Only 4% of the total population today, the Newari have produced some of Nepal's most celebrated art. **Rais, Limbus,** and **Sunwars** live in the eastern hills, and the Terai is populated by **Tharus, Yadavas, Safars, Rajvanshis,** and **Dhimlas,** who speak dialects of Hindi (such as Bhojpuri and Maithili). The **Gurungs** and **Magars** of west central Nepal, are also thought to be among Nepal's earliest inhabitants. Today, 45% of the population claims Tibeto-Burmese descent. The Tibeto-Burmese settled mostly in the higher altitudes of the north, where Buddhist culture predominates. Among the most recent immigrants from Tibet are the **Tamangs,** the largest of Tibeto-Burmese ethnic groups, and the **Sherpas.**

LANGUAGE

The official language is **Nepali,** (also called Gorkhali). The mother tongue of half the population, Nepali is understood by nearly everyone. As a descendent of Sanskrit, like the languages of North India, it uses the Devanagari script. (For basic Nepali, see the **Phrasebook,** p. 886.)

The **Newari** language is Tibetan in origin, although it uses the Devanagari script and takes half of its vocabulary from Sanskrit. Recent large-scale migrations from Tibet have brought **Tibeto-Burmese** languages and Tibetan Buddhist culture to Nepal. Tibetan refugees continue to seek asylum in Nepal, and the use of Tibetan, with its Sanskrit-based script, is not uncommon. English is widely spoken, but at least remember *"namaste,"* a Sanskrit term meaning "I salute the God in you."

RELIGION

Nepal is the cultural crossroads between India and Tibet. About 90% Hindu and 5% Buddhist (with small Muslim, Christian, and Jain minorities), Nepalis its unique a mix-and-match of religious syncretism. Although Nepal is the only country in the world with Hinduism as state religion, most Nepalis follow some combination of Hinduism and Buddhism, with plenty of local traditions thrown in. Asked if they are Hindu or Buddhist, many Nepalis will reply that they "don't know," or that they're "both." That people can at once follow a religion of 33 million gods and one that originally recognized no gods at all baffles many visitors, but it seems to work pretty well nevertheless.

In general, northern regions near Tibet tend to be Buddhist, and areas closer to India are Hindu. Areas between (including the Kathmandu Valley) have the most complex blend of the two.

HINDUISM

Hinduism arrived in the Kathmandu Valley with the conquering Licchavi dynasty in the 4th and 5th centuries AD. It has long been Nepal's religion of status—**brahmins** (the priestly caste) and **chhetris** (the Nepalese warrior caste) have traditionally been at the top of the social hierarchy. Various legal reforms long ago tried to force lower-class Buddhists into an occupational caste system; this practice still survives, though few Buddhists accept the caste system.

Shiva is the most popular Hindu god; he is a fitting lord for this mountainous land, since he began his career as a Himalayan wanderer. He commonly appears as **Bhairava** or "Bhairab," a ghoulish figure who chases away demons, though he is also the compassionate **Mahadev,** worshiped out of love and devotion. In his form as **Pashupatinath,** the benevolent Lord of Animals, Shiva is Nepal's patron deity, and Nepal is often referred to as Pashupatinath Bhumi (Land of Pashupatinath). The temple of Pashupatinath near Kathmandu is the most important Hindu site in Nepal (see p. 792).

Vishnu, the cosmic "preserver," is also popular. In Nepal he is often called "Narayan," a name that comes from his role in the Hindu creation myth—he sleeps on the cosmic ocean while the creator god, **Brahma,** sprouts from his navel. Nepal's grandest festival, **Dasain,** is held in honor of the goddess **Durga.** Nepal also holds a special place for **Annapurna,** goddess of abundance and distributor of food. Each goddess is an individual in her own right, but the goddesses are also the consorts of male deities, embodying the female aspect *(shakti)* of each god. In the Nepalese religious tantras, this *shakti* is considered the most powerful and active force in the cosmos. (For a general introduction to **Hinduism,** see p. 85.)

BUDDHISM

Buddha was born during the 6th century BC in Lumbini, in modern Nepal. Although he left Lumbini as a young man and did most of his traveling and teaching in India, his doctrines are popular in the land of his birth.

Most Nepali Buddhists follow the **Mahayana** (Great Vehicle) school, which differs from the older **Theravada** (Way of the Elders) school. Mahayana Buddhism, with its doctrine of salvation for all, developed in India during the 1st century AD and predominated in Tibet, China, Japan, and other parts of East Asia. The more orthodox Theravada school persisted in Sri Lanka and Southeast Asia. HInduism beat out Buddhism in India, but an Indian-influenced Mahayana Buddhism survived in Nepal.

Mahayana Buddhism developed after a disagreement over monastic law *(vinaya)* in Buddhist communities. The Mahayana doctrines put less emphasis on the individual quest for nirvana, stressing instead the need for compassion for all beings. In the Mahayana tradition, the Buddha was not just a wise teacher and holy man—he was a cosmic being with magical powers and countless incarnations. The concept of a *bodhisattva*, who vows to put off his own enlightenment for the sake of saving all sentient beings, is very important in the Mahayana tradition, and a number of *bodhisattvas* are worshiped alongside the Buddha. (For a general introduction to **Buddhism,** see p. 92.)

TIBETAN BUDDHISM

In Tibet, a unique form of Buddhism developed when the Mahayana and Vajrayana (Thunderbolt Vehicle) traditions blended with the indigenous religion, **Bon** (see p. 551). Although Buddhism was originally brought to Tibet via Nepal, Tibetan traditions exerted a greater influence on the religion as it is practiced in Nepal than vice-versa. As a result of the Chinese occupation of Tibet, many Tibetan Buddhists have immigrated to Nepal, bringing prayer wheels and prayer flags blowing the mantra *Om Mani Padme Hum* ("Hail to the jewel in the lotus") all across Nepal's mountains and hills. Tibetan Buddhism divides the Buddha's nature into five "aspects," reflected in each of the five elements (earth, water, air, fire, and space). It is also noted for its monastic tradition—before the Chinese take-over, 25% of all Tibetans belonged to a religious order. Of the 6000 Tibetan monasteries in existence at the time of the occupation, only five remain. **Tibetan monasteries** are headed by teachers called lamas, addressed by the title *rimpoche* (precious one). Lamas are believed to have cultivated wisdom over many lifetimes, transmitting their knowledge to each reincarnation. The reincarnated lama is identified by astrologers who consult the Tibetan oracle and have the young candidates identify the former lama's possessions.

TANTRA

Tantra holds that polar opposites are merely two manifestations of the same consciousness, and that transcending these opposites leads to knowledge of the true nature of the mind. Consumption of meat, fish, and alcohol are off-limits. Tantric rituals also involve the harnessing and release of different energies in the body through sexual intercourse.

Tantra has much in common with the Hindu traditions of *shakti* and yoga. Between the 7th and the 9th centuries, tantra became popular throughout India as a part of both Hinduism and Buddhism, and its influence can still be seen today in Tibetan Buddhism, though it died out in India long ago. Some aspects of Tibetan Buddhism belong to the **Vajrayana** (Thunderbolt Vehicle) school, separate from both Mahayana and Theravada traditions. Vajrayana inherited much of its symbology from tantra—the major symbols of Vajrayana are the *vajra* or *dorje* (thunderbolt) and the *ghanti* (bell), which represent male compassion and female wisdom, respectively. The conscious release of bodily energy, achieved by meditation on goddess figures, is also prominent. These figures are often depicted in erotic poses, symbolizing reconciliation of dual energies.

INDIGENOUS TRADITIONS

Most people worship indigenous gods too, regardless of any other religion they might follow. Common in the Kathmandu Valley is the worship of the **Kumari,** a young girl recognized as an incarnation of the Hindu goddess Durga. The living goddess spends her entire childhood secluded in a palace, until she reaches puberty and

> **CLIMB (ALMOST) EVERY MOUNTAIN** Mountaineers sometimes climb within meters of a summit, then forgo the pleasure of those last few steps out of deference to the mountains' resident gods and sacred powers. Hindus believe mythical Mt. Meru to be the center of the universe and the axis of all power. Mt. Kailash in Tibet is Shiva's stomping ground, and the Gauri-Shankar and Annapurna mountains in Nepal are both named after gods. Most of the Himalayan peaks, including those with more mundane names—such as Macchapuchare, which means "fish tail," and Kanchenjunga, which means "five treasures"—are considered sacred. In fact, the Himalayan range itself is said to be the father of Shiva's consort, Parvati.

reverts to the status of a mortal (see **The Living Goddess: Kumari,** p. 785). The Newaris also worship **Macchendranath,** a god born of a fish and identified both with Lokesvara, Shiva's form as "Lord of the World," and with the *bodhisattva* of Compassion, Avalokitesvara. Macchendranath's towering chariot makes his festivals distinctive highlights of the religious calendar. The Newari craftsmen of the Kathmandu Valley have also turned **Bhima** (or Bhimsen), the hero of the *Mahabharata* epic, into their patron deity. Also prominent in the valley is **Manjushri,** the valley's creator god, associated with Saraswati, the Hindu goddess of learning.

Outside the Kathmandu Valley, different ethnic groups preserve many of their local beliefs despite the widespread acceptance of Buddhism and Hinduism. The local gods are worshiped in return for good harvests and healthy children, and animal sacrifices to the gods are common. Shamans lead many religions and mediate between the human and supernatural worlds.

CULTURE
FOOD AND DRINK

Dal bhat tarkari (lentils, rice, and curried vegetables) is the staple dish for most Nepalis. Indeed, *bhat*, the word for cooked rice, is often used as a synonym for *khana* (food). Food in Nepal differs little from Indian food, except for a few Tibetan dishes on Nepalise menus. Ravioli-like **momo** and **thukpa,** a noodle soup, are popular. Newari food is largely buffalo meat. **Choyala** is buffalo fried with spices and vegetables.

The most popular breads are **chappati,** identical to the ones you see in India. Most Nepalis don't really eat breakfast, though it is commonly served in tourist restaurants and hotels. Vegetarians will probably have a better time with the food than meat-eaters.

Milk, or **dudh,** is an important staple and is often served hot, making it safe to drink if you know it has been boiled. **Chiya** (tea) is served hot with milk and lots of sugar. Yogurt *(dahi)* forms the base for **lassis** and the Newari delicacy **juju,** made from yogurt, cardamom, and cinnamon. Most sweets, including **barfi** and **peda,** are milk-based.

Nepalis drink beer and *chang*, a homemade Himalayan brew. *Raksi* is a stronger *chang* that tastes and feels like strong tequila. *Tong-ba* is a Tibetan brew made from fermented millet and sipped through a straw.

THE ARTS

Nepali arts draw from a synthesis of regional styles. Absorbing Indian and Tibetan aesthetics, the Newari artisans of the Kathmandu Valley developed a distinct style, mostly in woodwork that has since disappeared, but many of the valley's masterpieces remain in their original settings. Nepalese art has been inspired by religion, funded by kings, and executed by anonymous craftsmen.

Thanks to the boom in tourism, just about anything made in Nepal can be bought in Kathmandu, but many handicrafts are cheaper and available in a better and wider selection in their place of origin. For woodcarving and pottery, head to Bhaktapur; for papier-mâché masks and puppets, go to Thimi; for metalwork, Patan; and for Tibetan crafts like *thankas*, the best place to go is Boudha.

ARCHITECTURE

The oldest remaining structures in the Kathmandu Valley are **stupas,** sacred mounds of earth layered with centuries of plaster. They are large hemispherical domes, usually marking Buddhist holy places or sacred relics. Nepalese stupas, such as the amazing **Boudhanath Stupa** (see p. 802) in the Kathmandu Valley, display distinctive symbols on the square, golden spire at their top. These **chakus** are painted with the Buddha's eyes surveying the four cardinal directions and a number one (?) to represent universal unity. Stupas are often accompanied by **chaityas,** small stone shrines holding written mantras or scripture.

The greatest architectural achievements of the Kathmandu Valley are wood-and-brick **pagodas,** many of which resemble elaborate *chakus;* from which they perhaps evolved. Nepal is the birthplace of the pagoda—a 13th-century architect named Arniko exported the pagoda form to Kublai Khan's Mongolia, where it later spread to the rest of Asia. Most of Nepal's pagodas are Hindu temple built around a central sanctum that houses the temple's deity. The sanctum is brick, with intricately carved wooden doors, window frames, and pillars. The pillars and struts on the outside support the tiered, sloping, clay-tiled roof. Despite appearances, the upper portions of the temple are not separate storeys; they are left empty because of a belief that there should be nothing above the deity except the roof and the heavens. The whole structure sits on a terraced stone base resembling a step pyramid.

The Newaris also planned and built **bahals,** blocks of rooms surrounding a rectangular courtyard. These compact community units were used either as monasteries or as blocks of houses. *Bahals* are designed to be perfectly symmetrical, and the main doors and windows usually appear along the group's central axis.

Despite their xenophobic foreign policy, the Rana prime ministers, who reigned from 1846 to 1951, embraced European neoclassical architecture for the buildings they put up as part of their various modernization drives, and some parts of Kathmandu's Durbar Square would not look out of place in Trafalgar Square.

SCULPTURE

Early work in the Kathmandu Valley was influenced by North Indian styles of stone sculpture. Newari artisans of the Licchavi period made devotional images of Vishnu and the Buddha that strongly resembled the work of the Mathura school. Written accounts indicate that wooden sculpture also flourished at this time, though none has survived.

Stone sculpture in Nepal reached its heights between the 7th and 9th centuries and virtually disappeared after the 10th. Metal became the medium of choice for medieval Nepalese sculpture, again as a result of Indian influence. During the 17th and 18th centuries, the dominant influence was Tibetan. Newari artisans made bronze images of tantric aspects of the Buddha, which were exported to Tibetan monasteries—many "Tibetan" bronze sculptures were actually made in Nepal. Nepalese artists of the Malla period also created fantastic wood sculptures as architectural ornaments. Temple roof struts and window grilles were made of wood ornately carved with plant and animal forms.

Over the last two centuries, the crafts of bronze-casting and wood-carving have declined because of a lack of patronage. Foreign-funded restoration projects have recently given sculptors some business, and the demand created by tourism has encouraged the mass production of consumer-oriented crafts.

NEPAL

PAINTING

The earliest paintings to have survived in the Kathmandu Valley were painted onto palm leaf manuscripts. A few examples have survived from as far back as the 10th century, but most are badly decayed. More common in Nepal today are Tibetan *thankas* (intricate scroll-paintings of deities) and *mandalas* (circles symbolizing the universe in Hindu and Buddhist art). During the medieval period, a distinctive Newari style of *thanka* developed, called a *paubha*. These were painted on coarser cloth and without the landscape background typical of traditional Tibetan *thankas*. Later paintings in Nepal were heavily influenced by the detailed miniatures of the Indian Mughal and Rajasthani styles.

MUSIC

Music in Nepal is a part of everyday life. The **gaine,** a caste of musician-storytellers, once wandered the hills, accompanying themselves on the *sarangi* (a four-stringed fiddle). Music of a traditional *panchai baja* (five-instrument) ensemble is often played for weddings, processions, and rituals. The women of most Indo-Nepalese castes are usually excluded from music-making, though they are allowed to sing in public during rice-planting and at the *teej*, an annual women's festival.

Several traditional styles of hill music still exist. Most popular is the *maadal*-based (double-sided drum held horizontally) *jhyaure* music of the Western Hills. The **Jyapu** farming caste developed an upbeat rhythmical style that uses numerous percussion instruments, including the *dhime* (a large two-sided drum) woodwinds to accompany nasal singing. The *selo* style, developed by the Tamangs but shared by others, keeps rhythm with the *damphu* (a flat one-sided drum).

Music is vital to Hindu and Buddhist ritual. In traditional Newari communities, most young men complete a musical apprenticeship that enables them to participate in festival processions. Newari Buddhist priests chant ancient tantric verses as part of meditation exercises, and on sacred occasions ritual dancing accompanies these hymns. The music of the Sherpas derives much of its character from the ancient rituals of Tibetan Buddhism.

The continued presence and influence of Indian classical music in Nepal is a relic of the days when it was all the rage at the court of the Malla kings. The Rana prime ministers were such fervent patrons of Indian classical musicians that they banned Nepalese folk performers from their courts altogether.

DANCE

Nepalese dance, in both folk and classical styles, is usually based on dramatic retellings of sacred Buddhist and Hindu stories. The Newaris of the Kathmandu Valley are the chief exponents of **classical dance.** Newari performers enter a trance and become vessels possessed by the spirit of the deity. They gyrate and gesture and generally put on quite a show, dressed in elaborate costumes and ornately painted papier-mâché masks. On the tenth day of the Dasain festival (in Sept. or Oct.), the *nawa* dancers of Bhaktapur perform the vigorous dance-drama of the goddess Durga's victory over the buffalo demon.

Tibetan Buddhism also uses music and dance in festivals, ceremonies, and sacred rites. Performances often involve intricate hand gestures, ritual objects, and the a number of unusual and symbolic musical instruments. **Cham** is a dance-drama specific to Tibetans and Bhotiyas, in which monks don masks and costumes to enact various Buddhist tales.

HOLIDAYS AND FESTIVALS

Hindu and Buddhist, and Jain festivals correspond to the lunar calendar, so the dates vary from year to year with respect to the Gregorian calendar; the dates given are approximate. Secular holidays in Nepal follow the official Vikram Sambat calendar. The dates given here are for 2003.

DATE	HOLIDAYS AND FESTIVALS
January 1	**New Year's Day.** This traditional Nepali festival culminates in drunken revelry at midnight. Held annually.
January 11	**Prithvi Narayan Shah's Birthday** honors the late king who united Nepal.
February 2	**Lhosar,** the Tibetan New Year, is a three-day festival celebrated by thousands of Tibetans and Sherpas who flock to Boudhanath Stupa in Nepal and to Dharamsala.
March/April	**Machhendranath Rath Yatra,** a popular festival, during which a massive chariot holding Lokesvar, a patron deity of Kathmandu, is pulled through the streets of Nepal by hundreds of worshippers.
April 14	**New Year's Day** of the Vikram Sambat Year 2060, celebrated throughout Nepal.
April 11	**Ramanavami** celebrates Rama's birth, with readings of the *Ramayana* in Hindu temples all over India and Nepal.
May 16	**Buddha Jayanti** honors the Buddha's birthday and his attainment of *nirvana.*
August 12	**Janai Purnima (Raksha Bandhan)** celebrates the Hindu sea god Varuna; the holiday is associated with brother and sisters.
September 9	**Indra Jatra,** when Kathmandu celebrates the capture of the King of Gods, Indra, in the Kathmandu Valley; processions and the annual blessing of the King of Nepal by the Living Goddess Kumari.
October 2-10	**Dussehra** (also known in some parts as **Navaratri**), a 9-10-day festival, celebrates the vanquishing of demons and honors Durga, the demon-slaying goddess. Known as **Dasain** in Nepal and **Durga Puja** in West Bengal.
October 25-27	**Tihar,** the Festival of Lights, an important holiday in Nepal.

ADDITIONAL RESOURCES

GENERAL

Culture Shock! Nepal, by Jon Burbank (1992). A guide to Nepali customs and etiquette aimed at those planning to live and work in Nepal.

Life and Death on Mt. Everest, by Sherry B. Ortner (1999). An exploration of the world of the Sherpas and their mountaineering culture.

Into Thin Air: A Personal Account of the Mount Everest Disaster, by Jon Krakauer (1998). Intimate first-hand account of the May 1996 Everest expeditions, in which 12 died.

Trekking in the Nepal Himalaya, by Stan Armington (1997). The most comprehensive trekking guidebook available. It includes maps, day-by-day descriptions, and altitude charts for the most popular treks.

Trekking in Nepal, by Stephen Bezrucha (1997). Detailed route descriptions and a comprehensive section on planning and health concerns. Especially rich in historical, cultural, and biological commentary on Nepal's trekking routes.

HISTORY AND POLITICS

Nepal: Growth of a Nation, by Ludwig Stiller (1993). An account of the period from the unification of Nepal until 1950. One of the few histories of Nepal that doesn't slobber all over the Shah dynasty.

Politics in Nepal: 1980-1990, by Rishikesh Shah (1990). Once banned by the government (always a good sign), these essays look at recent political history.

Nepal: Profile of a Himalayan Kingdom, by Leo E. Rose and John T. Scholz (1980). Covers the history, politics, culture, and economics.

RELIGION

Short Description of Gods, Goddesses, and Ritual Objects of Buddhism and Hinduism in Nepal. Published by the Handicraft Association of Nepal, this short but comprehensive book includes illustrations and is a valuable (and portable) reference. Available in Kathmandu bookstores (Rs80-100).

The Festivals of Nepal, by Mary M. Anderson (1988). A month-by-month description of the legends and practices surrounding Nepal's major festivals; you'll be in the right place at the right time.

LITERATURE

Himalayan Voices: An Introduction to Modern Nepali Literature, by Michael Hutt (1991). The best English anthology of Nepali poetry and prose.

Nepali Visions, Nepali Dreams: The Poetry of Laxmiprasad Davkota, translated by David Rubin (1980). A good introduction to Nepal's most prominent modern poet.

THE KATHMANDU VALLEY

Set against a backdrop of green hills and the awe-inspiring peaks of the Himalayas, the Kathmandu Valley is the heart of Nepal and the focal point of any visit. Before Prithvi Narayan Shah's unifying conquest in 1768, Kathmandu, Patan, and Bhakta-pur were individual city-states that vied for control of the valley. Today, each one retains traces of its days as a tiny kingdom with Durbar (Palace) Squares, each filled with towering temples, *sindur*-covered shrines, and the unrivaled metal work of the indigenous Newari people. Between the cities, exhaust-belching autos and urban development threaten to encroach on the Valley's dwindling fertile farmlands. Despite the continuous outward expansion of city limits, calm agricul-tural life does continue in the tightly packed, multi-storied Newari red-brick towns. The valley's hilltops have amazing views and a pollution-free quiet that seems to be a million miles away from the thriving anarchy of the country's cities. A network of trails winds through the hills, offering countless opportunities for short treks and bike rides. Though many travelers stay only long enough to get ready for a trek, the Kathmandu Valley is home to seven UNESCO World Heritage sites. It only takes a few days to see the valley's most popular sights, but those with the time and inclination to explore a little will be richly rewarded.

HIGHLIGHTS OF THE KATHMANDU VALLEY

Most cities in Nepal have a central square, but **Patan's Durbar Square** (p. 795), with its temples, palaces, and pavilions, sets the standard by which all others are judged.

The cobbled streets and restored temples of **Bhaktapur** (p. 805) are a window into val-ley life before backpackers and brownie sundaes arrived.

A visit to the monumental *stupa* at **Boudha** (p. 802) provides a glimpse into Tibetan Buddhism in Nepal.

KATHMANDU काठमाण्डु ☎ 01

Half a century after Nepal opened its borders to the world, Kathmandu has become a hippie haven, a mecca for trekkers, and a thriving cosmopolitan cultural center. Nepal's largest city, Kathmandu has a gravity that pulls together Tibetan refugees, work-seeking Nepalis, tourists, and cowboy bodhisattvas looking for spiritual salvation in linen shirts and endless hashish. For all its World Heritage sites, this bustling city is no fossil, nor is it just another anonymous South Asian metropolis. The indigenous Newari culture and centuries of turbulent history have left Kathmandu with an unmistakably Nepali fingerprint.

Founded as Manju-Patan around AD 723, Kathmandu was not always the val-ley's pre-eminent city. In Malla days, when it was known as Kantipur, it stood level with Patan and Bhaktapur, though it was more successful at controlling trade with Tibet. Prithvi Narayan Shah made Kathmandu his capital when he unified Nepal in the 18th century, and it has dominated the valley ever since. Bursting into the new millennium as the fast-growing capital of a desperately poor country, present-day Kathmandu bears the imprint of rapid economic growth: an array of imported goods, arts, institutions, diplomatic missions and foreign aid agencies, and, of course, planeloads of tourists. Despite the optimism inspired by the 1990 move-ment toward democracy, Kathmandu faces plenty of problems. The city suffers from oppressive pollution, a chronic shortage of resources, and a crippling lack of infrastructure, as its government languishes under ineffective politicians.

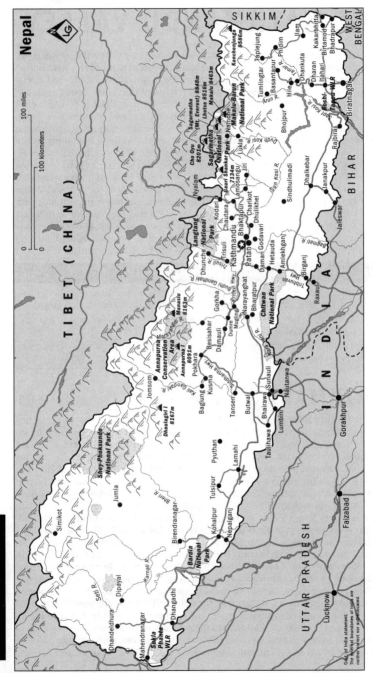

Nepal

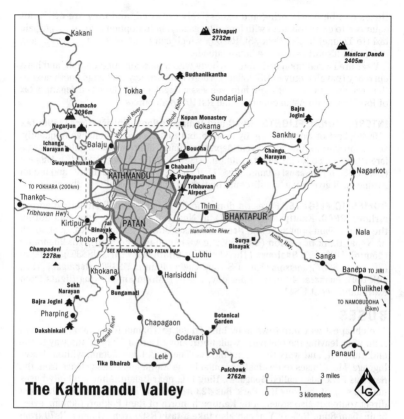

The Kathmandu Valley

For the tourist, Kathmandu is a fascinating city where pagodas crowd the traffic into narrow cobbled lanes and neighborhood boys kick soccer balls around dusty stone shrines. Myth and history intertwine at every corner—time-worn shrines stand alongside ancient shops, and the buses careening by bear murals of Shiva's beatific blue face. Of course, not everything in Kathmandu is quaint or mysterious; there's plenty of dust here too, as well as rancid trash and faceless concrete.

■ INTERCITY TRANSPORTATION

FLIGHTS
If you're flying into Kathmandu from the east, try to sit on the right side of the plane to get a good view of the mountains. Flights land at **Tribhuvan International Airport,** 5km east of the center of town. Planes are small, seats are limited, and facilities are so basic that even slightly bad weather can delay flights. Bring a book. As you leave the airport, you will find yourself at the left edge of a large parking lot; to get to the bus stop, walk to the far right and follow the downhill road through the huge archway to Ring Rd., where you'll wait for a bus heading to your left. **Bus #1** goes to **Ratna Park** (30min., frequent, Rs5), but not all buses are numbered and not all buses heading this way go to Ratna Park, **so be sure to ask the driver or conductor.**

Buses can be bewildering and excessively crowded, and they are often not equipped to carry travelers with lots of luggage. A better option is to take a **pre-paid taxi** (to Thamel Rs250; Freak St. Rs250), which can be arranged at a counter just before the airport exit or at a booth outside.

Visas are issued upon arrival to anybody with a passport, photograph, and hard currency (payable only in US dollars). There is a currency exchange booth next to the visa checkpoint. For more info, see **Visas: Nepal, p. 11.** There is a **departure tax** of Rs770 to South Asian countries and Rs1100 to all others.

INTERNATIONAL FLIGHTS. RNAC and **Indian Airlines,** Hattisar (☎414596; fax 419649), east of Durbar Marg, fly to **India,** but flight schedules change frequently, so call around to find out current departure times. International flights to: **Bangalore** (2½hr., US$257); **Calcutta** (40min., US$96); **Delhi** (1½hr., US$142); **Mumbai** (2hr., US$257); **Varanasi** (40min., US$71). If you're under 30, both RNAC and Indian Airlines will give you a 25% discount on tickets to India bought in Kathmandu.

DOMESTIC FLIGHTS. Fares on domestic flights are virtually identical across airlines. **RNAC,** Kantipath (☎220757), at New Rd. Open daily 9am-4pm during the winter, 9am-5pm summer. **Necon Air** has a branch near New Rd., just south of Nepal Bank of Ceylon (☎480565; resv@necon.mos.com.np). To: **Bhadrapur** (45min., US$109); **Bhairawa** (1hr., US$79); **Biratnagar** (1hr., US$85); **Janakpur** (20min., US$67); **Jomsom** (1hr., US $50); **Lukla** (40min., US$83); **Nepalganj** (1hr., US$109); **Pokhara** (40 min., 4 per day, US$67). Mountain-viewing flights from Kathmandu cost US$109.

BUSES

The cheapest way into town is by bus. To get to Thamel from Ratna Park, turn right after leaving the bus park, walk north along Durbar Marg all the way to the end, turn left, and walk three long blocks. The walk takes 20min. without heavy luggage. Most buses to destinations outside the Kathmandu Valley leave from the **New Bus Park** (also called **Gongabu**), Ring Rd., near Balaju. Almost all city buses make a stop at the New Bus Park. **Bus #23** from Ratna Park takes one of the most direct routes; it also stops along Kantipath, north of Rani Pokhari (30min., every 5min. 5am-8pm, Rs3-6). You can also take a **taxi** (Rs60 from Thamel, Rs70 from New Rd.). The departure bays are not labeled in English, but most of the ticket vendors speak English. Most buses that leave after noon are night buses—for these you should book 1-2 days in advance in season.

There are no express or deluxe distinctions here, and even tourist buses sometimes pick up locals along the way. Unless otherwise noted, prices are for morning/night buses.

PRIVATE BUSES. To: **Bhadrapur** (14hr., 4pm, Rs450); **Bhairawa** (every hr. 6:30am-8pm, Rs170/211); **Birganj** (8hr., every hr. 6am-7pm, Rs159/175); **Dharan** (12hr., 3-5pm, Rs353); **Gorkha** (6hr., every hr. 7-10am, Rs90); **Ilam** (20hr., 2pm, Rs505); **Janakpur** (11hr., 6 and 7am, Rs202/242); **Kakarbhitta** (16hr., 3-5pm, Rs107/211); **Pokhara** (7-8hr., frequent 6am-8:30pm, Rs155/210); **Tansen/Palpa** (11hr., 7am and 5:30pm, Rs173/327); **Tardi Bazaar** (frequent 7am-2:50pm, Rs110) for **Sauraha**.

GOVERNMENT BUSES. Sajha, the government bus corporation, is slightly cheaper and faster than private buses and runs mostly day buses; reserve two days in advance. To: **Bhairawa** (8hr., 7:15am and 7pm, Rs145/180); **Birganj** (8hr., 2am, Rs138); **Gorkha** (5hr., 6:30 and 7:45am, Rs75); **Lumbini** (9hr., 6:45am, Rs158); **Narayanghat** (4hr., 6:45am, Rs83); **Pokhara** (7hr., 7:30am and 7pm, Rs113/129); **Tansen/Palpa** (10hr., 7:30am, Rs159).

TOURIST BUSES. Tourist buses are slightly more expensive minibuses, with clear aisles and comfortable seats. Tickets for tourist buses to **Chitwan, Pokhara,** and **Nagarkot** can be booked through travel agencies in Thamel. Fares include a commission, but the stops are much more conveniently located on Kantipath at the intersection with Tridevi Marg. **Greenline Buses,** at the corner of Tridevi Marg and Kantipath, has A/C coaches to **Pokhara** (7hr., 8am, Rs750) and **Chitwan** (7am, Rs450; 8:30am, with A/C Rs600), with breakfast included. Tickets should be bought one day in advance. (☎257544. Open daily 10am-6pm. AmEx/MC/V.)

▲ ORIENTATION

Kathmandu is quite small, and navigation is pretty straightforward. The shrines of **Swayambhunath** and **Pashupatinath** are at the western and eastern edges of the city, respectively. Almost exactly halfway between them, the two main roads of **Kantipath** and **Durbar Marg** run parallel to each other, north to south. Kantipath has the the post office and banks; Durbar Marg is home to many airline offices, trekking agencies, luxury hotels, and upscale restaurants, as well as the **Royal Palace** at its north end. Between the two streets farther south is the **Tundikhel** parade ground, around which Kantipath and Durbar Marg become one-way streets.

Kantipath and Durbar Marg divide Kathmandu into two halves—most of the older, more interesting parts of the city are to the west of Kantipath. The area east of Durbar Marg is mainly new neighborhoods. West of Kantipath, in the northwestern corner of town, is the year-round tourist carnival that is **Thamel.** Thamel is joined to Kantipath and Durbar Marg by **Tridevi Marg.** Kathmandu's old center, **Durbar Sq.,** filled with magnificent architecture, is west of Kantipath, close to the banks of the **Vishnumati River. New Rd.,** built in 1934 out of the rubble left behind by an earthquake, runs east from Durbar Sq. to Kantipath. New Rd. is the city's commercial district, with rows of jewelers and electronics sellers. **Freak St.** runs north-south past the western end of New Rd., starting at the southern edge of **Basantapur Sq.** A nameless narrow lane that sprouts northeast from Durbar Sq. used to be the main trading center. It cuts through **Indra Chowk,** one of Kathmandu's most interesting neighborhoods, and **Asan Tol,** the center of Kathmandu's main bazaar.

Tripureswar Marg is the biggest road in the southern half of town, running east-west and leading to the **Patan Bridge.** The capital's twin city, Patan, is across the **Bagmati River,** the southern limit of Kathmandu. **Ring Rd.** encircles Kathmandu and Patan, connecting them with the suburbs that have grown up around them.

▐ LOCAL TRANSPORTATION

LOCAL BUSES

By far the cheapest means of getting around the Kathmandu Valley, the bus ensures that you rub shoulders with locals—just when you thought another wailing child couldn't possibly squeeze in, five more people and seven roosters climb on board. Though often overcrowded and maddeningly slow, Kathmandu buses do work; many are even painted with route numbers these days. **Always confirm that the bus is going to your destination.** The valley bus station is known as **Ratna Park** (named for the park across the street); Nepalis also call it *purano* (old) bus park. Listen for bus drivers shouting *"ranapa ranapa"* to find a bus heading that way. Bus #7 (to Bhaktapur) leaves from **Bagh Bazaar,** one block north of Ratna Park. Buses generally leave as soon as they're full.

#	DESTINATION	LENGTH	COST	#	DESTINATION	LENGTH	COST
1	Tribhuvan Airport	40min.	Rs5	12	Dhulikhel	2hr.	Rs17
2	Boudha (Boudhanath)	40min.	Rs5	14	Jawlakhel and Lagankhel	20min.	Rs5
2	Pashupatinath	30min.	Rs5	19	Swayambhu	45min.	Rs5
4	Sankhu	2hr.	Rs10	21	Kirtipur	1hr.	Rs5
5	Budhanilkantha	1hr.	Rs6	22	Dakshinkali	1½hr.	Rs15
7	Bhaktapur	45min.	Rs9	23	New Bus Park	30min.	Rs5
9	Old Thimi	30min.	Rs5	23	Balaju	30min.	Rs5
9	Bahaka Bazaar	1hr.	Rs6	26	Patan	30min.	Rs5

TROLLEYBUSES

Haggard, Chinese-built electric trolleybuses creak between Kathmandu and Bhaktapur (45min., frequent, Rs5). The first stop is on **Tripureswar Marg,** just south of the National Stadium. Trolleybuses tend to be less crowded than buses, and they are a far more pleasant (and environmentally friendly) ride.

TAXIS AND RICKSHAWS

Shiny new red, green, or yellow **taxis** are all metered, as are the older ones (identifiable by their black license plates). Rates typically start at Rs7-9. Fares within the city should be less than Rs150: Rani Pokhari to Swayambhu or Pashpatinath costs around Rs75; shorter trips like Thamel to New Rd. will cost around Rs40. An all-day sight-seeing tour around the valley costs about Rs1000. After 9pm, rates go up by over 50%, and drivers may be reluctant to take you where you want to go. Taxis queue on Tridevi Marg near the entrance to Thamel. **Auto-rickshaws** are cheaper than taxis, if you can persuade the driver to use his meter. Aggressive **cycle-rickshaw** drivers bargain hard, charging almost as much as auto-rickshaws. Rickshaws are not allowed on some major streets (e.g. Durbar Marg), and are only useful for short trips in the western part of the city.

TEMPOS

Tempos, either sturdier versions of auto-rickshaws or minibuses, can be flagged down anywhere along their routes; to request a stop, bang on the metal ceiling and honk like a mongoose. Tempos use the same route numbers as buses but leave from different places. Tempos leave from **Sundhara,** just outside the GPO: #2 to **Boudha** via **Pashupatinath** (30min., Rs6). Others depart from just north of **Rani Pokhari:** #5 to **Budhanilkantha** via **Lazimpath** (45min., Rs6); #23 to **Balaju** (40min., Rs6); #14 **Lagankhel** via **Jawalakhel** to **Patau** (20 min., Rs5).

BICYCLES AND MOTORCYCLES

Bicycles and motorcycles can be rented from shops in Thamel, especially around Thamel Chowk and Chhetrapati. Mountain bikes (Rs150 per day) are better for trips outside the city; heavier, bell-equipped one-speeders (Rs60 per day) are fine for the city. Motorcycles are Rs400 per day.

⛶ PRACTICAL INFORMATION

TOURIST AND FINANCIAL SERVICES

Tourist Office: The Nepal Tourism Board's main office, the **Tourist Service Center,** Bhrikuti Mandap (☎256909). South of Ratna Bus Park, just east of Durbar Marg. Open

Su-F 9am-5pm. They also have an office at the **airport** (☎470537). Open daily 9am-5pm. The **Thamel Tourism Development Committee** (☎429750). Has an office north on Thahity, near the small Bhagwati temple. Open Su-F 9am-4pm.

Trekking Information: Himalayan Rescue Association (HRA), P.O. Box 4944 (☎262746; hra@mail.com.np). In Thamel Mall at Jyatha-Thamel, just south of Kilroy's. Focuses on mountain safety, providing info on altitude sickness and free safety talks in the spring and fall. Talks Su-F 2pm. HRA also runs 2 clinics in Manang (Annapurna circuit) and Pheriche (Everest trek); they appreciate donations of medicine and money. **Kathmandu Environmental Education Project (KEEP),** P.O. Box 9178 (☎259567; fax 256615; keep@keepnepal.org.np), Thamel Mall, in the same complex as HRA. Has slide show presentations on low-impact trekking twice a week. Both offices keep logbooks for trekkers to record their experiences and to read about those of their predecessors. They also have informative bulletin boards posted with trekking tips and up-to-date info. Fill out an embassy registration form at one of these offices (or at your embassy) before you go trekking. Both open Su-F 9am-6pm; off-season 10am-5pm.

Budget Travel: Visit one of the well-established agencies on Durbar Marg: **Annapurna Travels, Everest Express,** or **Yeti Travels.** For bookings on tourist buses to places like Pokhara and Chitwan, most agencies offer similar prices—make sure you're getting the going rate. For plane tickets, go directly to the airline offices, as travel agencies charge commission on flights (see **Intercity Transportation,** p. 771). Most major airlines have offices on Durbar Marg, just south of the Hotel de l'Annapurna, or in Hattiswar, the area just east of Durbar Marg.

Immigration Office: The **Department of Immigration** (☎223590; fax 223127), which has recently moved to Bhrikuti Mandap, next to the Tourist Service Center. This is the place to get your **visa extended** or to purchase a **trekking permit.** Trekking permits can be bought in the white bldg. opposite the Dept. of Immigration just outside the Tourist Center's compound. Permits are no longer required for the major areas of Everest, Annapurna, Langtang, or Rara. For: **Humla** (US$90 for the 1st week, US$15 per day thereafter); **Lower Dolpa** and **Kanchenjunga** (US$10 per week for the 1st month; US$20 per week thereafter); **Manaslu** (US$90 per week for treks Sept.-Nov.; US$75 for treks Dec.-Aug.); **Upper Mustang** and **Upper Dolpa** (US$700 for the 1st 10 days, US$70 per day thereafter). Treks to Dolpa, Kanchejunga, Makalu, and Upper Mustang must be organized by a registered trekking agency. Visa extensions and trekking permits require a passport and a photo. Apply M-F 9am-3pm (9am-2pm in winter); pick up before 5pm (4pm in winter). There is an additional fee of Rs1000 for treks through a national park or conservation area (Rs2000 for Kanchenjunga and Annapurna). To avoid hassles during your trek, pay these entry fees in advance at the **Entry Fee Collection Centre** (☎222406). In the basement of the Himalayan Bank Bldg., by Fire and Ice. Open M-F 9am-4pm, Su 9am-2pm.

Currency Exchange: Exchange Centers are plentiful in Thamel, and many don't charge a commission for exchanging traveler's checks. The **Himalayan Bank** has a foreign exchange booth conveniently located on Kantipath, just south of the intersection at Tridevi Marg, but it only exchanges US dollars. Commission on traveler's checks Rs150 or 0.75%. **Moneygram** services are also available here for quick money transfers. Open M-F 8am-8pm. **Nepal Bank of Ceylon Ltd.,** New Rd. (☎231713). Takes a 1% commission on traveler's checks. Open M-F 9:30-5pm (limited service 5pm-8pm) and Sa-Su 10am-2pm. Rs100 for currency exchange. **Standard Chartered Bank Nepal Ltd.,** Kantipath (☎228474). Just south of the intersection at Tridevi Marg. Sells AmEx traveler's checks and gives cash advances on MC and Visa. Commission on traveler's checks Rs200 or 1.5%. Rs 100 for currency exchange. Open 9:30am-3:30pm. **Western Union,** Durbar Marg (☎223940; fax 222966). In Annapurna Travel and Tours, on the east side of the street. Money can be wired here in 1min. Open daily 9:30am-7pm. **American**

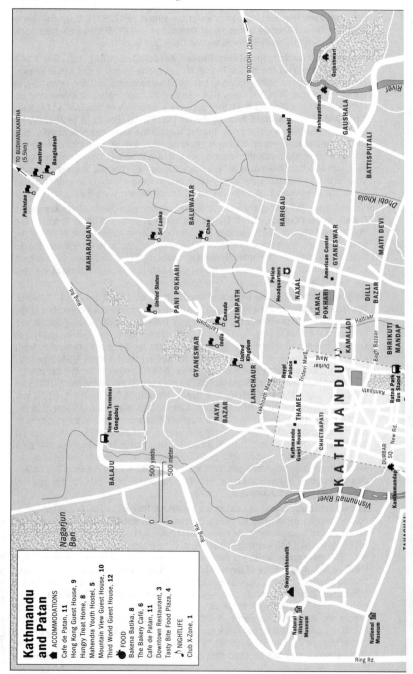

Kathmandu and Patan

▲ ACCOMMODATIONS
Cafe de Patan, 11
Hong Kong Guest House, 9
Hungry Treat Home, 8
Mahendra Youth Hostel, 5
Mountain View Guest House, 10
Third World Guest House, 12

🍴 FOOD
Bakena Batika, 8
The Bakery Café, 6
Cafe de Patan, 11
Downtown Restaurant, 3
Tasty Bite Food Plaza, 4

♪ NIGHTLIFE
Club X-Zone, 1

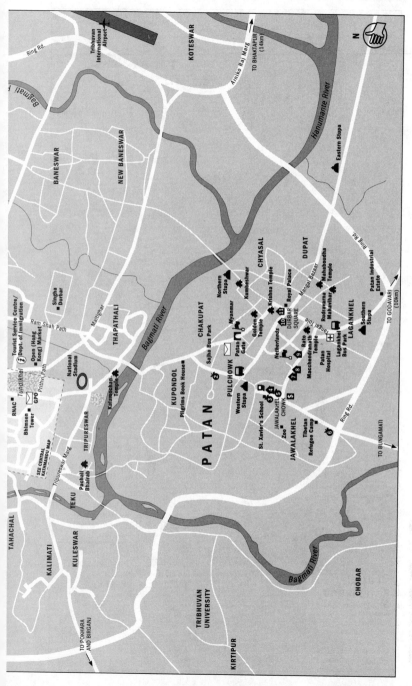

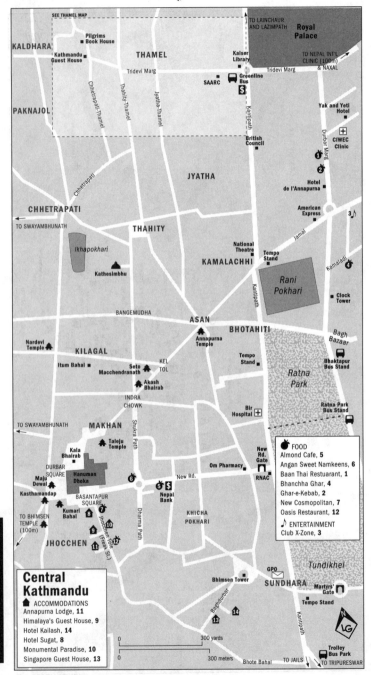

SEE THAMEL MAP

TO LAINCHAUR
AND LAZIMPATH

Royal Palace

KALDHARA

Pilgrims
Book House

Kathmandu
Guest House

THAMEL

Kaiser
Library

TO NEPAL INT'L
CLINIC (100m)
& NAXAL

Tridevi Marg

Tridevi Marg

PAKNAJOL

Chhetrapati-Thamel

Thahity-Thamel

Jyatha-Thamel

SAARC

Greenline
Bus

$

Kantipath

British
Council

Yak and Yeti
Hotel

CIWEC
Clinic

Durbar Marg

JYATHA

Hotel
de l'Annapurna

CHHETRAPATI

Chhetrapati

TO SWAYAMBHUNATH

THAHITY

Ikhapokhari

Kathesimbhu

American
Express

Jamal

3 ♪

National
Theatre

Tempo
Stand

KAMALACHHI

Kamaladi

4

Kantipath

*Rani
Pokhari*

Clock
Tower

BANGEMUDHA

ASAN

BHOTAHITI

Bagh
Bazaar

Nardevi
Temple

KILAGAL

Annapurna
Temple

Tempo
Stand

Bhaktapur
Bus Stand

Itum Bahal

Seto
Macchendranath

KEL
TOL

*Ratna
Park*

Akash
Bhairab

INDRA
CHOWK

Bir
Hospital

Ratna Park
Bus Stand

TO SWAYAMBHUNATH

MAKHAN

Shukra Path

Taleju
Temple

New
Rd.
Gate

Kala
Bhairab

🍎 **FOOD**
Almond Cafe, **5**
Angan Sweet Namkeens, **6**
Baan Thai Restuarant, **1**
Bhanchha Ghar, **4**
Ghar-e-Kebab, **2**
New Cosmopolitan, **7**
Oasis Restaurant, **12**

♪ **ENTERTAINMENT**
Club X-Zone, **3**

Om Pharmacy

RNAC

DURBAR
SQUARE

Hanuman
Dhoka

Maju
Dewal

6

$

New Rd.

5

Kasthamandap

BASANTAPUR
SQUARE

Nepal
Bank

Kumari
Bahal

8

7

TO BHIMSEN
TEMPLE
(100m)

9

10

Jhochhen Tole (Freak St.)

Dharma Path

KHICHA
POKHARI

JHOCCHEN

11

GPO

Tundikhel

**Central
Kathmandu**

🏠 **ACCOMMODATIONS**
Annapurna Lodge, **11**
Himalaya's Guest House, **9**
Hotel Kailash, **14**
Hotel Sugat, **8**
Monumental Paradise, **10**
Singapore Guest House, **13**

Bhimsen Tower

Baghdurbar

SUNDHARA

Martyrs'
Gate

Tempo
Stand

14

13

0   300 yards

0   300 meters

Bhote Bahal

TO JAILS

Trolley
Bus Park

TO TRIPURESWAR

NEPAL

Express: **Yeti Travels,** Hotel Mayalu, Jamal, P.O. Box 76 (☎226172; fax 226152). Sells traveler's checks. Open Su-F 10am-1pm and 2-5pm.

EMBASSIES AND CONSULATES

Australia, Bansbari (☎371678; fax 371533). On Maharajgunj, just past Ring Rd. Open M-Th 8:30am-5pm, F 8:30am-1:15pm.

Bangladesh, Maharajgunj (☎372843; fax 373265). On Chakrapath, near Hotel Karnali. 2 photos required for a 15-day tourist/transit visa, US$45. Open M-Th 9am-5pm, F 9am-noon and 2-5pm. Apply for a visa M-F 10am-noon, and pick it up the same day between 4:30 and 5pm.

Canada, Lazimpath (☎415389; fax 410422). Down the lane opposite Navin Books stationery shop. Open M-F 8:30-4:30pm.

China, Baluwatar (☎411740, visa services ☎419053). Visas Rs2200; bring your passport and 1 photo. Allow 4 days for processing. Visas to **Tibet** are available only to organized groups of 5 or more and obtainable only through a travel agency (see **Surrounding Countries,** p. 11). Open M-F 9am-noon and 3-5pm. Visa dept. open M, W, F 9:30-11am.

India, Lainchaur (☎410900; fax 413132). Walk north up Lazimpath and veer left before the Hotel Ambassador. 15-day transit visas require 1 photo and Rs350 and can be picked up the same day from 4:30-5:15pm. 6-month tourist visas require 1 photo and Rs2100, and you must wait to be cleared by your home embassy, which can take up to a week. US citizens must pay an additional Rs1400. Apply for visas M-F 9:30am-noon.

Myanmar (Burma), Chakupat, Patan (☎521788; fax 523402). Near Patan Gate. 1-month tourist visa requires 4 photos and US$20. Apply M-F 9:30am-1pm and 2-4:30pm; visas ready in 24hr.

Pakistan, Chakrapath (☎374024; fax 374012). Near the intersection of Ring Rd. and Maharajgunj, northwest quadrant. 3-month tourist visa requires 2 photos. Australia US$14; Ireland US$20; New Zealand free; US and Canada US$54; UK US$57. Apply M-F 10am-12:30pm; visas ready the next day.

Sri Lanka, Baluwatar (☎413623; fax 418128). Visas require 2 photos, and US$45, but some nationalities do not require visas for travel in Sri Lanka. Apply M-F 10am-12:30pm.

Thailand, Bansbari (☎371410; fax 371409). Turn east just north of the Australian Embassy. Visas require 2 photos and a copy of your plane ticket. 1-month transit visas Rs450; 2-month tourist visas Rs700. Apply M-F 9:30am-12:30pm; visas ready in 2 days.

UK, Lainchaur (☎410583; fax 411789). Open M-Th 8:15am-12:30pm, 1:30-5pm. Visas to **Malaysia** are administered through the UK's consular services (☎410583). A 3-month tourist visa (Rs2300) requires 2 photos, traveler's checks, plane ticket, and occasionally a hotel reservation slip. Apply M and W 2-3pm; processing takes 2 days. Many nationalities do not require visas for travel to Malaysia.

US, Pani Pokhari, Maharajgunj (☎411179; fax 419963). Open M-F 8am-5pm.

LOCAL SERVICES

Bookstore: Pilgrims Book House, Thamel (☎424942). Just north of the Kathmandu Guest House. Browsing here is one of the joys of being in Kathmandu. An enormous place that not only has every book you never knew you wanted, but also CDs, local handicrafts, classical music concerts, yoga classes, and limited mail services. Open daily 8am-10pm.

NEPAL

Market: Asan Tol, in front of the Annapurna Temple, has fresh fruits and vegetables. **Open Market** (also called Hong Kong Market), south of Ratna bus park, is a large tarpaulin congregation of food, clothing, and other products. Snacks, toiletries, and trekking supplies are at the **Best Shopping Centre,** where Tridevi Marg narrows into Thamel. Open Su-F 8am-8pm, Sa 10am-8pm, or in the million retail stores around Thamel.

Laundry Service: Almost all guest houses have laundry service, but independent establishments sometimes charge less. **The 1 Hour Laundry,** next door to the Khukuri House, north of the Kathmandu Guest House, also does dry cleaning and has the quickest service around. Open daily 8am-8pm.

EMERGENCY AND COMMUNICATIONS

Emergency: Ambulance, ☎228094. **CIWEC** (☎228531 or 241732). Has 24hr. emergency service.

Police: The **Tourist Police** handles petty thefts and rip-offs and can be reached at any of the city's tourist offices: Bhrikuti Mandap (☎247041 or 256231), Tribhuvan Airport (☎470537), and Thamel (☎429750). Contact the **city police** (☎226999) for more serious issues or emergencies (☎100).

Pharmacy: Om Pharmacy, New Rd. (☎222644). Near RNAC. Open daily 8am-8pm. Many common prescription medicines can be bought over-the-counter at the street-front clinics around Bir Hospital on Kantipath and Thamel.

Hospital/Medical Services: Kathmandu has numerous reliable clinics geared toward Westerners. In case of illness, visit one of these first. **CIWEC Clinic** (☎228531 or 241732). Off Durbar Marg, behind the Yak and Yeti sign, to the right. US$45 per consultation, US$65 after hours or on weekends. Open M-F 9am-noon and 1-4pm. On call 24hr. MC/V. **Nepal International Clinic** (☎434642; fax 434713). Opposite the Royal Palace, 3min. east of the main gates, down a lane to the right. Consultation US$35. Open Su-F 9am-1pm and 2-5pm. On-call 24hr. for emergencies. AmEx/MC/V. **Himalaya International Clinic,** Jyatha-Thamel (☎225455; fax 226980). Consultation US$20, US$40 house-call. Open daily 9am-5pm. **Patan Hospital,** Lagankhel, Patan (☎522266). Has a better reputation than the government-run **Bir Hospital** (☎221119, emergency ☎223807). On Kantipath north of New Rd. **Himalayan International Clinic,** Chhetrapati-Thamel (☎263170). South of Kathmandu Guest House on the east side of the street. Consultations US$25, house-call US$50. Open daily 9am-5pm.

Internet: Internet cafes are everywhere around Thamel and Durbar Sq. The **Easy Link Cybercafe** (☎416239). In Thamel; walk north on Thahity-Thamel and take a left at the small Bhagwati temple. Has fast connections, air-conditioning, low rates, and a standing offer of 10 free min. after your first visit. Rs40 per hr.

Telephones: Most STD/ISD booths have the same rates on outgoing calls but different deals on callbacks—shop around. Internet phones provide a much cheaper but slightly slower alternative to STD/ISD service. **Global Communications,** Tridevi Marg (☎228143). In the shopping center opposite Himalayan Bank. Has good rates (Internet phone Rs10 per min.) and charges a flat Rs25 for callbacks. Open Su-F 8am-8pm. The **GPO** charges Rs10 per page for faxes. Open Su-Th 10am-5pm, F 10am-3pm.

Post Office: GPO (☎227499). Near Bhimsen Tower; entrance just off Kantipath. Stamps sold Su-F 8am-7pm, Sa 11am-3pm. **Express Mail Service (EMS),** at the GPO, delivers within 3-7 days to pretty much anywhere in the world, but it's of dubious reliability. Open M-F 10:15am-3pm. To send a package abroad, visit the **Foreign Parcel Office,** around the corner on Kantipath, where it will be checked by customs. Open M-F 9:15am-2pm; in winter 9:15am-1:30pm. **FedEx, UPS, DHL,** and **Airborne Express** offer services in Thamel.

⌐ ACCOMMODATIONS

The majority of budget travelers head to Thamel, where increased competition has led to a general standardization of prices for similar accommodations. The prices listed are for in-season rates and do not include the 10% government tax. Rates are usually negotiable. **Beware of touts:** don't let anyone lead you to his friend's hotel; a hefty commission will appear on your bill.

Freak St. is Kathmandu's original tourist district. Ever since it hit its peak back in the 70s, Freak St. has been cheaper, less hectic, and less populated than Thamel; most of its hotels have been around for almost 25 years, growing old and musty as lodges in Thamel steal all their business. Located just south of New Rd., **Sundhara** is popular with Indian tourists; its accommodations are less conveniently located and pricier than the bargains found in Thamel, but they are a good option if you want to "find" the city before it finds you. The places below, unless otherwise noted, have hot water, seat toilets, laundry service, luggage storage, and a noon check-out, but no towels or toilet paper. Many places list room rates in the more stable US dollar, but you can pay in rupees; the manager will do a more or less arbitrary conversion using the going exchange rate of the day.

THAMEL

🖾 **Kathmandu Guest House** (☎413632; fax 417133; kghouse@wlink.com.np). All directions in Thamel are given in relation to this place, so you'd better figure out where Kathmandu's original "budget hotel" is. The old wing is darker and more worn but has the best access to the guest house's communication center, social and swanky lobby with satellite TV, ticket booking, bike rental, and barber shop. Reservations recommended. Old wing: singles US$2-10; doubles US$3-12. New wing: singles US$17-50; doubles US$20-60. 10% discount for stays of over a week and for HI/IYH. AmEx/MC/V. ❷

Hotel Potala (☎419159; fax 416680). Opposite K.C.'s, at the center of Thamel. Well-managed by a friendly Tibetan family, Potala has comfortable rooms with common baths. Though its low prices make it one of the best budget places in Thamel, its central location next to several bars makes it a bit noisy at night. Some rooms with fans. Singles Rs150; doubles Rs175-250. ❶

Hotel The Earth, Chhetrapati-Thamel (☎260312; fax 260763). South of Kathmandu Guest House, on the west side of the street. A range of large, clean, and generously furnished rooms at economical prices. Singles Rs200-350; doubles Rs300-500. 50% discount for students and volunteers; 20% discount for stays over 1 week. ❶

Hotel Garuda (fax 413614; garuda@mos.com.np). Around the curve north of the Kathmandu Guest House. Five-star service and spotless rooms for relatively low prices make Garuda popular with Himalayan expeditions. One of the few rooftop "gardens" in Thamel that is actually a garden. Attached baths with towels and toilet paper. Singles US$10-35; doubles US$15-40. 25% off-season discount. AmEx/MC/V. ❹

Mom's House Lodge (☎252492; fax 260094; h_karki@hotmail.com). Across from Hotel the Earth. Bare bulbs, bare-bones accommodations, but the rooms are clean and the management is ultra-accommodating. Try to get a room facing east, or you'll have to deal with the endless stream of pop music from the record store next door. Common and attached baths. Singles Rs150-250; doubles Rs250-300. MC/V. ❶

Prince Guest House, Satghumti-Thamel (☎414456; fax 220143; glocom@ntc.net.np). North of Kathmandu Guest House—turn left at the intersection. Pink n' purple decor and wall-to-wall carpeting in clean but smallish rooms with fans, phones, and attached baths. Rooftop garden and restaurant. Singles US$7; doubles US$10-15. ❷

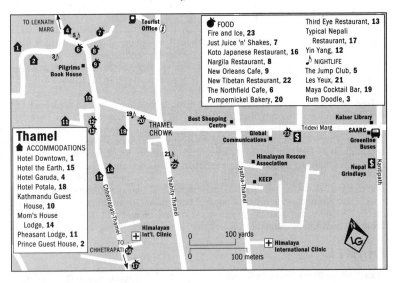

FOOD
Fire and Ice, **23**
Just Juice 'n' Shakes, **7**
Koto Japanese Restaurant, **16**
Nargila Restaurant, **8**
New Orleans Cafe, **9**
New Tibetan Restaurant, **22**
The Northfield Cafe, **6**
Pumpernickel Bakery, **20**

Third Eye Restaurant, **13**
Typical Nepali
  Restaurant, **17**
Yin Yang, **12**
♪ NIGHTLIFE
The Jump Club, **5**
Les Yeux, **21**
Maya Cocktail Bar, **19**
Rum Doodle, **1**

Thamel

ACCOMMODATIONS
Hotel Downtown, **1**
Hotel the Earth, **15**
Hotel Garuda, **4**
Hotel Potala, **18**
Kathmandu Guest
  House, **10**
Mom's House
  Lodge, **14**
Pheasant Lodge, **11**
Prince Guest House, **2**

THAMEL CHOWK

Best Shopping Centre

Global Communications

Himalayan Rescue Association

KEEP

Kaiser Library

SAARC

Greenline Buses

Nepal Grindlays

Tridevi Marg

Himalayan Int'l. Clinic

Himalaya International Clinic

100 yards

100 meters

Hotel Downtown, Satghumti-Thamel (☎430471; fax 261636; down-town@wlink.com.np). Opposite the Prince Guest House. Spacious rooms and immaculate bathrooms somewhat sheltered from the noise of central Thamel. Generous single beds big enough to sleep 2. Common or attached bath. 11pm lockout. Singles US$5-8; doubles US$8-12. ❶

Pheasant Lodge (☎417415). Down a short alleyway off Chhetrapati-Thamel, just south of the Kathmandu Guest House. Smack dab in the middle of things. Concrete floors, firm beds, clean sheets, and a choice of common toilets—squat or sit as you please. Often full—try right at the noon check-out time. Singles Rs100; doubles Rs150. ❶

FREAK STREET

Himalaya's Guest House, Basantapur, Jhochhen (☎246555; fax 258222; himal-got@mos.com.np). Take the 1st right off Freak St. as you walk from Basantapur Sq. Bright, clean rooms all have TV and fan. Managed by a friendly, accommodating family. Singles Rs200; doubles Rs300-500. ❶

Monumental Paradise, Freak St. (☎240876; mparadise52@hotmail.com). 50m from Basantapur Sq., on the east side of the street. Ambitious name, but this new kid on the block lives up to its title with large, spotless rooms and friendly service. Carpets, tinted windows, and seat toilets in all rooms. Somewhat upscale, but the dorms are a good deal. Dorms Rs150; singles Rs300; doubles Rs400-450. ❶

Hotel Sugat (☎245824; fax 221824; maryman@mos.com.np). Along the southern edge of Basantapur Sq., facing the royal palace. The rooftop garden has fantastic views. Spacious, carpeted rooms overlook Durbar Sq.; some have tubs and balconies. Fans, toilet paper, towels included. Singles Rs110-300; doubles Rs300-400. ❶

Annapurna Lodge, Freak St. (☎247684). Down the 2nd right as you walk from Basantapur Sq. Aging and simply furnished rooms are quiet and more or less clean. Seat toilets in attached baths; squat and seat toilets in common bath. Attached restaurant shows free movies. Singles Rs125-225; doubles Rs200-300. ❶

SUNDHARA

Hotel Kailash, Baghdurbar (☎268079). South of Bhimsen Tower, down a lane to the left. Bright, spacious rooms all with phones, fans, and attached baths. Singles Rs200; doubles Rs300; triples Rs400. ❶

Singapore Guest House, Baghdurbar (☎244105; fax 221703). South of Bhimsen Tower, on the left toward the end of the street. Large, elegant rooms with carpets, phones, TVs, fans, and attached bath. Attached restaurant (entrees Rs40-120). Singles Rs250-450; doubles Rs350-550. ❶

❏ FOOD

Beginning with the founding of Kathmandu's first luxury hotel in 1954, which featured chandeliers and fresh fish carried in by porters, to the advent of "Pie Alley," where 1960s overlanders gathered for apple pie and hash brownies, Kathmandu has achieved mythic status as an oasis of displaced delicacies. Today, Western favorites are *de rigueur* on tourist menus, but much of this food tastes blandly similar, borrowing most of its flavor from the *ghee* in which it has been ritually drowned. The Japanese, Thai, Tibetan, and Indian restaurants that elbow for room in neighborhoods frequented by foreigners and wealthy Nepalis generally offer more appetizing and less contrived fare. For a more authentic experience, you can always dig into the undisputed national dish, *dahl bhat tarkari* (rice, lentils, and vegetable curry) available on nearly every menu as the "Nepali Set Meal."

THAMEL

▨ **Typical Nepali Restaurant,** Chhetrapati-Thamel, south of Kathmandu Guest House, down an alley on the left. The singing, dancing manager, who identifies himself as J.J. (for "John Joker") persistently refills clay bowls of endless, free *raksi* (rice wine) while live Nepali music plays in the background. Complimentary bananas and popcorn accompany the all-you-can eat regional plates (Rs110-175), including *dahl bhat tarkari, roti,* and *momos.* Open daily 6:30am-10pm. ❷

▨ **New Tibetan Restaurant,** a short distance down Thahiti-Thamel, up the second set of stairs to your left. In addition to an admirable variety of *momo* (Tibetan dumpling) dishes (Rs40-75), the New Tibetan offers generous servings of delicious Nepali, Chinese, Tibetan, and continental food at down-to-earth prices. Nepali set meal Rs75, veg. chow mein Rs40. Try the uncommonly good yogurt with mixed fruit and honey (Rs40) for dessert. Open 7am-10pm. ❶

▨ **Just Juice 'n' Shakes,** down a lane to the right, north of Kathmandu Guest House. Friendly place with quite a reputation for thick, frozen smoothies and shakes (Rs50-90), hot espresso (Rs50), cappuccino (Rs50), and fresh juices (Rs25-60). A good place for breakfast—the fruit muesli with yogurt is delicious (Rs55). Check out the amusing visitors' wall. Open daily 6am-midnight. ❶

Third Eye Restaurant, just south of the Kathmandu Guest House, on the right. This quality Indian restaurant specializes in tandoori chicken (half-chicken Rs225, whole Rs375). The interior dining area is classy; the rooftop terrace has great views. Veg. dishes Rs120-180, *naan* Rs30-60. Open 8am-10pm. MC/V. ❷

Koto Japanese Restaurant, Chhetrapati-Thamel, near the Chhetrapati intersection (with another branch on Durbar Marg). Impeccable service, high-quality food, and simple bamboo furnishings. Tea refills and *yakis* will enliven the pizza-weary. Noodles, soups, meat, fish, and Japanese curries (Rs130-380). 10% tax. Open daily 11am-9pm. ❸

The Northfield Cafe, a few doors north of Kathmandu Guest House. A great place for homesick *gringos* to down chips and salsa (Rs120) and gnaw on spicy chicken wings (Rs135). Burritos Rs180-210, quesadillas Rs170, meat dishes up to Rs280, brownie sundaes Rs150. Blaring classical, jazz, and blues music. The breakfast menu is one of the best around. Open daily 7am-10pm. ❷

Pumpernickel Bakery, opposite K.C.'s. A Thamel institution. At breakfast time, the line to order freshly baked croissants, cakes, and cinnamon rolls (Rs20-40) spills onto the street. The pleasant garden patio and wicker furniture in the back make it a nice place to linger and people-watch. Open daily 7am-9pm. ❶

Fire and Ice, in the shopping center on Tridevi Marg, next to the Himalayan Bank. Wafting pizzeria smells will lure you in, and the opera music and great food will keep you (and plenty of other tourists) here. Pizza Rs130-300, delicate crepes Rs75-130, imported ice cream Rs65-105. Open daily 11am-10pm. ❷

New Orleans Cafe, just north of the Kathmandu Guest House. Bustling but low-key candlelit patio. Enjoy jambalaya, creole chicken, and other soul food, all with a generous helping of freshly baked, all-American Tibetan bread. Veg. dishes Rs80-170, non-veg. Rs90-250. Live music Th 7-10pm. Open daily 6:30am-11pm. ❷

Nargila Restaurant, north of Kathmandu Guest House, on the right. One of a few Middle Eastern restaurants around. Serves freshly made pita and hummus (Rs55), falafel sandwiches (Rs105), and other treats (Rs60-150) from its spacious, second-floor perch. ❶

Yin Yang Restaurant, just north of Third Eye. Experience Bangkok without the debauchery or pollution, on the shaded patio or interior dining area. Extensive but expensive Thai menu includes tasty *pad thai* (Rs180-210), veg. curries (Rs180), and fish dishes (Rs400-558). Open daily 10am-10pm. ❷

DURBAR MARG

Bhanchha Ghar, Kamaladi. From Durbar Marg, walk east at the clock tower; it's on the right. The name is Nepali for "kitchen," but there's a lot more than *dahl bhat* on the menu here—this is Nepalese *haute cuisine*. Specialties (Rs150-245) include wild boar and curried high-altitude mushrooms. The enormous set menu is pricey (Rs900) but includes a cultural show at night. 10% tax. Open daily 11am-10:30pm. AmEx/MC/V. ❷

Baan Thai Restaurant, just north of the Hotel de l'Annapurna on Durbar Marg. Authentic Thai food in a swanky, A/C setting. Watch Durbar Marg through lace curtains as you enjoy *pad thai* (Rs160-195) and seafood (Rs375-450). 10% tax. Open daily 11am-3pm, 6-10pm. MC/V. ❷

Ghar-e-Kebab, next to Baan Thai. Top-quality Indian restaurant, with delicious food and attentive service. Ravi Shankar impersonations nightly. Tandoori dishes Rs325-650. 8 course set meal US$12. 10% tax. Open daily noon-2:30pm and 7-10:30pm. AmEx/MC/V. ❺

NEW ROAD AND FREAK STREET

▨ **Angan Sweet Namkeens and Vegetarian Fast Food,** at the intersection of New Rd. and Dharma Path. Serves ice cream (Rs30-40), Indian sweets, *dosas* (Rs40-50), and other veg. treats (Rs20-65) on the go. Pay in front and shoulder your way into the back room to find a table. Free mineral water. Open daily 9:30am-8:30pm. ❶

Almond Cafe, New Rd., has a fast-food atmosphere but is cheap, clean, and frequented by Kathmandu's hippest high schoolers. Chow mein Rs40-60, pizzas Rs60-120. ❶

Oasis Restaurant, Freak St. Eat under the shelter of big leafy plants and rainbow umbrellas in the outdoor dining area. Mexican dishes Rs90-110, pizza Rs95, burgers Rs85-95. Open daily 8am-10pm. ❶

New Cosmopolitan Restaurant, on the Western edge of Basantapur Sq. One of the few restaurants with a view of the square. Extensive tape collection ranges from Pink Floyd to Portishead. *Crepes* Rs30-65, pizza Rs75-110. Open daily 8am-10pm. ❶

◉ SIGHTS

There are so many temples in Kathmandu that the word "templescape" has been coined to describe the city's skyline. The city's main attractions are in **Durbar Sq., Indra Chowk, Asan Tol,** and **Swayambhunath,** just west of the city. The best way to tour Kathmandu is on foot.

DURBAR SQUARE

Durbar (Palace) Sq. is the heart of the old city. The royal family moved about a hundred years ago to the north end of town, but the square retains its religious, social, and commercial importance. Many of Kathmandu's most interesting temples and historic buildings are located here in this bustling, wide-open space. A good way to explore the sights is to start from Basantapur Sq., the large open plaza by Freak St., and head west and then north in a clockwise arc; the sights are organized below in this manner.

KUMARI BAHAL. The first building you'll see at the western edge of Basantapur Sq. is the Kumari Bahal, marked by the two painted stone lions that stand guard outside. A traditional 18th-century Newari palace, the Kumari Bahal sports beautifully-carved window frames—the central one is covered in gold. This is where the living, earthly, human goddess of Kathmandu, the **Kumari,** resides, sometimes appearing at one of the windows in the courtyard to silently answer her devotees' questions with the look on her heavily made-up face (see **The Living Goddess: Kumari,** above). If she doesn't appear, plenty of touts in the square will offer their services to summon her appearance. *(No photography allowed.)*

TRAILOKYA MOHAN TEMPLE. Just outside the Kumari Bahal, this temple is a shrine to Vishnu, with an over-photographed dusty-black statue of Garuda (Vishnu's man-bird vehicle) kneeling reverently before the image and clasping his palms together in the *namaste* position.

THE LIVING GODDESS: KUMARI

A Newari Buddhist girl considered to be the living incarnation of the Hindu goddess Durga, the Kumari is a perfect example of the religious syncretism of the Kathmandu Valley. Kathmandu's Kumari, the most important of the 11 in the valley, is selected at the age of four or five from the Buddhist clan of the Newari *shakya* (goldsmith) caste. The Kumari-to-be must satisfy 32 physical requirements, including having thighs like a deer's, a chest like a lion's, eyelashes like a cow's, and a body like a banyan tree. She must remain calm in a dark room full of buffalo heads, frightening masks, and loud noises. Finally, her astrological chart must not conflict with the king's. If all these conditions are met, the Kumari is installed in the Kumari Bahal in Durbar Sq., where she leads the privileged, secluded life of a goddess until she reaches puberty. Several times a year she is paraded about town on a palanquin (the Kumari's feet must not touch the ground). As soon as the Kumari menstruates, or sheds blood in any other way, her goddess-spirit leaves her body, and she must return to her parents' home, where the transition to mere mortality can be difficult. Former goddesses often have difficulty finding a husband, since men who marry them are said to die young. Nepal's newest Kumari was chosen on July 11, 2001, when Preeti Shakya, a four-year-old from Kathmandu, assumed the traditional top knot and painted third eye that signify the living goddess.

KASTHAMANDAP. Continuing west past Trailokya Mohan, you will find the Kasthamandap, a gorgeous temple that (perhaps) gave Kathmandu its name. The wooden pavilion—built from the wood of a single tree—is Kathmandu's oldest existing building. Originally a *dharamsala* dating from the 14th century, it was eventually made into a temple and has been substantially altered over the centuries. Loitering porters now make the place feel a bit like a holy train platform. A central, *sindur*-smeared image of Gorakhnath, the deified Hindu saint who watches over the Shah dynasty, anchors this sacred space. Small Ganesh shrines sit in each corner; one of the idols' golden mouse-mounts points its nose at another Ganesh shrine, the **Maru Ganesh** (also known as **Ashok Binayak**), in its own metal-flagged enclosure near the eastern corner of the temple.

MAJU DEWAL. From the Kasthamandap, turn right and head north toward the main part of the square. The Maju Dewal Shiva Temple takes up the prime location, towering over everything on its 10-level step-pyramid. The temple was built in 1690 and makes a well-placed observation deck for Durbar Sq.—its height, however, does nothing to isolate it from the fray below. You could sit here for hours watching the square, if not for all the "guides," "English students," and kids asking, "Do you have one coin from your country?" A white *shikara* dedicated to Kayu Dev sits at the foot of the steps.

TEMPLE OF SHIVA AND PARVATI. As you continue north, you'll come to the Shiva and Parvati Temple. Painted white statues of the divine couple lean out from a tiny window above the entrance, leering eerily at the visitors who dare disturb their conjugal bliss.

TALEJU BELL. As you walk northeast past the Shiva and Parvati Temple, you'll see the Taleju (Great) Bell, put up by Rana Bahadur Shah in 1797. The bell, similar to the ones found in the other valley cities of Patan and Bhaktapur, rings for worship in the Degutaleju Temple.

KRISHNA TEMPLE. The octagonal Krishna Temple, just past the Taleju bell, was built in 1648 by King Pratap Malla. The temple houses images of Krishna and two goddesses that bear a curious resemblance to Pratap Malla and his wives. Next to the temple, a small hut shelters two enormous drums. Twice a year, a goat and a buffalo are sacrificed here.

KING PRATAP MALLA'S COLUMN AND THE DEGUTALEJU TEMPLE. In the center of this part of the square stands a column topped by a statue of King Pratap Malla, the architect of many buildings in this area. He sits facing his personal prayer room, housed in the Degutaleju Temple.

SWETA BHAIRAB. As you face the Degutaleju Temple, you'll see a large wooden screen just to the right that hides the figure of the scowling, fanged, golden face of an enormous Sweta Bhairab (White Bhairab). At the **Indra Jatra Festival** (Aug.-Sept.), the screen comes off and beer spouts from the mouth of this fearsome form of Shiva as devotees crowd in for a drink of the divine spittle.

JAGANNATH TEMPLE. Built in 1563, the Jagannath Temple (at Pratap Malla's left) is the oldest temple in this part of the square. Scandalously flexible couples are caught with their pants down in the carvings on the roof struts.

KALA BHAIRAB. Behind Pratap Malla, facing north, is the huge, garish monolith of Kala Bhairab (Black Bhairab), trampling an unfortunate demon underfoot. It is said that anyone who dares to tell a lie in front of this raging destroyer of evil will vomit blood and die. Don't even think about it.

TALEJU MANDIR. At the north end of the royal palace, the Taleju Temple's three-tiered golden pagoda towers over everything else in this part of the square. King Mahendra Malla built the temple in 1564 to honor Taleju, his dynasty's patron goddess. At 37m, the Taleju Temple was for a long time the tallest building in Kathmandu, a distinction preserved by building codes. But no more—the city, eager to modernize, has dispensed with this tradition. Ordinarily, the temple is open only to the king and a few priests, but on the ninth day of the October Dassain festival, lay Hindus are allowed to enter.

HANUMAN DHOKA DURBAR. The old royal palace takes its name from the statue of Hanuman that stands guard at the entrance, to the left of the Pratap Malla. The monkey-god lounges under a parasol. No one has lived in the palace for over a century, but it is still used for royal ceremonies, including King Birendra's coronation in 1975. Although the building has been evolving steadily since the time of the Licchavi kings of the 13th century, its art and architecture were influenced mainly by the patronage of King Pratap Malla (r. 1641-74). No Licchavi buildings remain, and the palace now has plenty of Shah-era whitewashing. Just inside the palace entrance is **Nasal Chowk,** a courtyard where the nobles of the kingdom used to assemble. It was here in 1673 that Pratap Malla danced in a costume of Narasimha, Vishnu's man-lion incarnation. Afraid that Vishnu would be angry about the stunt, Pratap Malla installed a Narasimha statue, to your left as you enter the courtyard, coyly fingering the snaking entrails of the demon he has just disemboweled. The main section of the palace open to the public is the **Tribhuvan Memorial Museum.** King Tribhuvan (r. 1911-55), who overthrew the Ranas in 1951 and restored Nepal's monarchy, is remembered here in a display of personal belongings including ceremonial outfits, newspaper clippings, and his stuffed bird clamped into its original cage. At the southern end of Nasal Chowk stands **Basantapur Tower,** a nine-story lookout erected by Prithvi Narayan Shah after he conquered the valley. It has great views of Durbar Sq. from above. The circuit around Nasal Chowk then leads to the **Mahendra Memorial Museum,** which isn't quite as impressive as Tribhuvan's. Outside the palace, along the wall past the Hanuman statue, is a **stone inscription** put up by Pratap Malla, which uses words from 15 different languages (including English and French). It's said that if anyone manages to read the whole text—a poem dedicated to the goddess Kali—milk will gush from the spout. *(Open Tu-Sa 9:30am-4pm; Nov.-Jan. 9:30am-3pm, F 9:30am-4pm. Rs250. Cameras prohibited.)*

NORTH OF DURBAR SQUARE

Kathmandu's most interesting street runs northeast from Durbar Sq. Without a name of its own, the street takes the title of whatever area it runs through. In earlier times, it was the beginning of the trade route from Kathmandu to Tibet, and it was Kathmandu's main commercial area until New Rd. was built after the earthquake of 1934. Today it is still a buzzing, temple-packed market area.

INDRA CHOWK. The second-story temple of **Akash Bhairab,** with its garish metal gargoyles, is unmistakable. Akash Bhairab's image, a large silver mask, is barely visible. During the Indra Jatra festival, it is put on display in the middle of the *chowk*, along with a *linga* specially erected next to it. *(The first crossroads on the diagonal street running northeast from Durbar Sq. is called Indra Chowk. Akash Bhairab is on the left side at this corner.)*

KEL TOL. The **Temple of Seto Machhendranath** is one of the most widely revered shrines in the valley. Both Hindus and Buddhists come here to pay homage to Machhendra, the valley's guardian, also considered to be an incarnation of Avalokitesvara, the *bodhisattva* of compassion. The white-faced image is paraded around town during the **Machhendranath Festival** in April, but the temple itself is

---

SOUTH ASIAN SEDER With 95% of Nepal's 20 million citizens claiming Hinduism, Buddhism, or both, as their religion, you'd hardly expect Kathmandu to host the largest *seder* (ritual Jewish Passover meal) in the world. Each year the Israeli Embassy puts on a *seder* for the 1300 or so young Jews who find themselves in Nepal during the week of Passover. Most of them have come to roam the Nepali wilderness following completion of their national military service, but at the *seder*, the trekking diaspora ditches *chappatis* and *dahl bhat* in favor of *matzos* and *maror*, in remembrance of the ancient Israelite exodus from Egypt. If you don't have an Israeli passport, you'll have to get your background checked by resident rabbis. For more information, contact the Israeli Embassy (☎411811).

---

covered by an unattractive iron fence to ward off thieves. *(Just off Kel Tol, down a passageway marked by a short pillar capped with a meditating Buddha.)* The pagoda in the middle of Kel Tol is dedicated to **Lunchun Lun Bun Ajima.** The road has been repaved so many times that this goddess' bathroom-tiled sanctuary is now sunk beneath street level. *(Kel Tol is the 2nd crossing north of Durbar Sq.)*

ASAN TOL. At Asan Tol, the next crossing, the road widens and is lined with vegetables. The **Temple of Annapurna** is on the right, draped with broad brass ribbons. The goddess of plentiful food, Annapurna, is depicted here as a silver pot.

BANGEMUDHA. The name of the square west of Asan Tol, Bangemudha, literally means "Twisted Wood." In one of the southern corners is a twisted lump of wood stuck to the wall, with an armor of coins nailed into it. The wood is dedicated to the god of toothaches, **Vaisya Dev,** and nailing a coin here is supposed to relieve dental pain. On the road north from Bangemudha you'll be greeted by jawfuls of grinning teeth. This is the dentists' quarter, and their signs all bear this happy smiling symbol. On the left side of this road, a lane leads to **Kathesimbhu,** a miniature model of the Swayambhunath *stupa* west of Kathmandu. Kathesimbhu, said to have been built with leftover earth from Swayambhunath, shares some of Swayambhunath's power. The elderly and those too weak to climb the hill to Swayambhunath can obtain an equal blessing here. Children seem to be the most devoted visitors, however, holding endless soccer games around its *chaityas*. *(The Bangemudha crossing is about 150m due west of Asan Tol.)*

OTHER SIGHTS. The **Rani Pokhari** tank and the temple at its center were built by King Pratap Malla to console his wife over the death of their son. The green-and-yellow fence around it is kept locked all year, except on Diwali (Nov. 4, 2002), the festival of light. *(On Kantipath, east of Asan Tol.)* The current **Royal Palace** is surrounded by an impenetrable, riot-proof fence that obscures all but the most unflattering views of the ugly, modern mansion, built in the 1960s. The building is open to the public only on the 10th day of Dasain, when the king and queen offer blessings to their subjects. *(At the north end of Durbar Marg.)*

SOUTH OF DURBAR SQUARE

BHIMSEN TEMPLE. The Bhimsen Temple is dedicated to the hero-god of Newari craftsmen—its bottom floor has been entirely taken over by shops. Next to it is a *hiti* (water tap) in a cellar-like depression, where jugs are filled from an elephant-shaped spout. *(On the lane that runs southwest of the Kasthamandap in Durbar Sq.)*

JAISI DEWAL TEMPLE. The Jaisi Dewal Temple is a large, dilapidated, step-pyramid Shiva temple covered with four centuries of pigeon dung. Painted with flowers and leopard-skin patterns, the temple is graced by a smooth figure of Shiva's bull mount, Nandi, at the base of the steps. Across the street from the entrance, a 2m high, uncarved *linga* promises fertility to those who pray to it. *(Continue to the end of the road from the Bhimsen Temple, turn left, and go up the hill.)*

BHIMSEN TOWER. The 59m-high Bhimsen Tower, also called Sundhara, is a useful landmark if you get lost along Kathmandu's streets. It looks like a run-down lighthouse with portholes, though Bhimsen Thapa, the prime minister who built it in 1832, was probably trying to imitate the Ochterlony Monument in Calcutta—ironic, considering that the British erected that monument to commemorate the defeat of Nepal in 1816. *(Off Kautipath in southern Kathmandu, next to the GPO. The tower is closed to the public.)*

TEKU. The junction of the Bagmati and Vishnumati Rivers at Teku is a sacred place often used for cremations. The wailing of the bereaved echoes around the temples and *chaityas,* and a tall brick *shikhara* stands over the confluence. The riverbanks might look like something out of a pastoral idyll, with buffalo munching hay in the shade, but the buffalo are in fact being slyly fattened for slaughter. *(In the southwest corner of the city. Be sensitive about photography.)*

PACHALI BHAIRAB. The area between Tripureswar Marg and the Bagmati might be wet and dirty and home to a big share of Kathmandu's slums, but its many temples make it an interesting part of town to explore. The shrine of Pachali Bhairab contains an image of Bhairab, decorated with coins under the spreading roots of a great pipal tree. Music from the nearby monastery jangles down into Bhairab's courtyard, where a golden human figure lies peacefully dead with its well-articulated golden toes morbidly sticking straight up. Don't fret; this is a *betal,* a representation of death meant to guard against the real thing. *(In a cluster of temples south of Tripureswar Marg, just east of the footbridge across the Bagmati.)*

KALAMOCHAN TEMPLE. The Kalamochan Temple is hard to miss, its architecture is a fusion of Mughal (onion domes), and Nepali (its dragons and doorways). On the exterior, Jung Bahadur Rana's beguilingly peaceful figure rises from a turtle's back. This Machiavellian prime minister built the temple in the mid-19th century. The ashes of the 32 noblemen he slaughtered in the Kot Massacre are supposed to be buried in the foundations. *(On Tripureswar Marg, close to the Patan Bridge.)*

TUNDIKHEL AND MARTYR'S GATE. The **Tundikhel,** or parade ground, is occasionally used for military marches and equestrian displays, such as the **Ghora Jatra Horse Festival** in late March, although you're more likely to find families picknicking here in Kathmandu's biggest open public space. *(East of Kantipath.)* Kathmandu's newer neighborhoods are to the east of the Tundikhel. **Martyrs' Gate** is a monument to four accused conspirators executed after a 1940 coup attempt. *(On a circle in the middle of the road, south of the Tundikhel.)*

SINGHA DURBAR. Until most of it burned down in a fire one night in July 1974, Singha Durbar was once the greatest of the Rana palaces. The off-white building, meant to rival the palaces of Europe, was built in three frantic years from 1901 to 1904 by Prime Minister Chandra Shamsher Jung Bahadur Rana—his monogram decorates the railings. The prime minister's household and entire administration fit into this complex, which, with 1700 rooms, claims to be the largest building in Asia. Ministries and departments are lodged in what's left of the palace, and their offices are off-limits to the public. *(East of Tundikhel.)*

NEPAL

WEST OF THE CITY

The west bank of the Vishnumati River is beyond Kathmandu's traditional city limits, but it has been brought into the metropolis by Ring Rd.

SWAYAMBHUNATH. The most prominent feature of the west bank is the hilltop *stupa* of Swayambhunath. More than 2000 years old, Swayambhunath is the holiest place on earth for Newari Buddhists, and it is the focus of the Kathmandu Valley's creation myth. Swayambhunath is also known as the "Monkey Temple," for the dozens of rhesus monkeys that clamber over the shrines, staining their behinds with *sindur* as they gobble up the daily rice offerings.

At the base of the hill is a large rectangular gateway flanked with prayer wheels—from here, the long crooked steps wind through the trees and Buddha-icons to the top where an enormous *vajra* stands; behind it is the *stupa*. From the golden cube on top, the Buddha's all-seeing eyes gaze out in every direction, as do the crowds of tourists ogling at the splendid panoramic views. What looks like Buddha's nose is actually the number "1," representing the unity of all things.

Each element of the *stupa* depicts part of the Buddhist cosmology. The dome itself represents the creative womb, while the 13 discs on the spire represent the steps toward nirvana. The nine gold shrines surrounding the *stupa* enclose images of the *dhayani* Buddhas, who portray the different aspects of the Buddha through the elements of earth, water, fire, air, and space. The four Buddhas, who occupy the shrines at the secondary points, also have female elements *(taras)*. Buddhist pilgrims circle clockwise around the *stupa*, turning the prayer wheels and meditating on this towering Buddhist symbol. *(3km from the city. A 30min. walk or bus #19 from Ratna Park leads you to Ring Rd., just west of Swayambhunath. Stupa Rs50.)*

BUDDHIST MUSEUM. Visitors baffled by Buddhist and Hindu iconography won't get much help from the unlabeled collection in this small museum, but the stone carvings are worth a look anyway. The small temple in front of the monastery is dedicated to Harati, the goddess of smallpox—it's not clear what she does now that smallpox is eradicated. *(On a platform west of the stupa. Open daily M and W-Su 10am-5pm. Free.)*

NATIONAL MUSEUM. Nepal's National Museum has an art gallery with a good collection of wood, stone, and metalwork. While excellent carvings can be seen on the houses and temples of the Kathmandu Valley, the museum allows you to get a closer, cleaner look. The Historical Museum building is at least as interesting as the art gallery. Its natural history section features the pelt of a two-headed calf, a set of bones from a blue whale, and an unusual abundance of stuffed deer heads. The Nepalese history section is an amusing tribute to rulers and their martial playthings. Organized by geographical region of origin, the recently-renovated Buddhist art gallery provides a decent introduction to different styles of Nepali Buddhist art. *(1km south of Swayambhunath, on the road from the river. Open Tu-Sa 9:30am-4pm; in winter 9:30am-3pm. Rs50; camera fee Rs50.)*

NATURAL HISTORY MUSEUM. A cramped brick building houses 14,000 specimens of Nepal's high-altitude critters, all shot, stuffed, skewered, or lacquered for your morbid viewing pleasure. *(Follow the motor road down the hill south of Swayambhunath. Open Su-F 10am-5pm. Rs20; camera fee Rs10.)*

🎵 🎭 ENTERTAINMENT AND NIGHTLIFE

When it comes to nightlife in Nepal, Kathmandu is ground zero, but it still isn't much in this early-to-bed country. Options include bars in tourist areas (which close by midnight), four casinos (the only ones on the subcontinent), and a few nightclubs (which also close around midnight). **Casino Royale** is in the Yak & Yeti, and **Casino Anna** in Hotel de l'Annapurna, both on Durbar Marg. **Casino Everest** is in The Everest Hotel in New Baneswar and **Casino Nepal** in the Soaltee Holiday Inn in Tanachal, at the western end of the city. All are open 24hr. **Hotel de l'Annapurna,** Durbar Marg, holds daily dance shows. (☎228787. 7pm. Rs350.) **Himachali Cultural Group,** Lazimpath, also has daily performances; call for reservations. (☎415280. 7pm. Rs350.) At least half a dozen establishments around Thamel—among them the **Twa Dewa,** Yaju's free movie restaurant—hold Video Nights in Kathmandu, showing recent film releases throughout the day. **Pilgrim's Book House** also has concerts of Indian music (Su, Tu, and F at 7pm, Rs300). In addition to the following pubs and discos, check-out the **New Orleans Cafe** (see p. 784).

The Rum Doodle 40,000½-Feet Bar and Restaurant, Thamel. Follow the turn in the road north of the Kathmandu Guest House; it's on the left. The bar's namesake is a 1956 literary spoof about a mountaineering expedition; the book is sold at the bar (Rs150). The walls are decorated with foot-shaped cut-outs signed and decorated by trekking and mountaineering parties. Live music F nights. Draft beer Rs75-140. Open 10am-10pm.

The Jump Club, north of the Kathmandu Guest House, next to Hotel Garuda. The latest favorite of the younger tourist crowd, this club/bar features snooker, black lights, and a small dance floor with the DJ spinning a schizophrenic mix of techno, R&B, rock, and reggae. Cocktails Rs100, beer Rs70-125. Open daily "6pm until you drop"; happy hour 5-9pm. No cover.

Maya Cocktail Bar and **Maya Pub,** Thamel. The cocktail bar is upstairs from the Pumpernickel Bakery; the pub is at the intersection by the Kathmandu Guest House. Both offer free popcorn and 2-for-1 cocktails 4-7pm. The dark pub is less crowded and has a mainstream pop music sound track; the funkier cocktail bar is bigger and more raucous. Beer Rs65-135, cocktails Rs130. Pool and snooker Rs40 per game, Rs250 per hr. Both open daily 3pm-around midnight.

Les Yeux, Thamel, on Thahity, just south of the intersection. In season, this bar and restaurant features nightly concerts by local rock and blues bands. Bring a guitar down and you might just get to play. Outdoor terrace with garden. Beer Rs120, cocktails Rs90-100. Open 8am-10pm.

Club X-Zone, in Kasthamandap Plaza, Kamaladi. Groove on the blacklighted dance floor or mellow out on the surrounding sofas. Beer Rs100. Open daily 9pm-1am. Cover charges Rs300-500, depending on who you are and whom you're with.

◨ SHOPPING

In Thamel or Durbar Sq., roving merchants hawk everything from flutes and chess sets to hash pipes and Tiger Balm. Just about anything made in Nepal can be bought in Kathmandu, though most crafts are better bought in their places of origin. For woodcarving and pottery, head to Bhaktapur; for papier-mâché masks and puppets, Thimi; for metalwork, Patan; and for *thankas* and other Tibetan crafts, Boudha. Bagh Bazaar is the best place for saris; cloth and beads can be found north of Indra Chowk.

The **Khukuri House,** in Thamel, at the zig-zag north of the Kathmandu Guest House, near Rum Doodle's, deserves special mention. This well-reputed knife shop is owned by a former Gorkha officer. (☎652435. Open Su-F 10am-7pm. MC/V.) **Didi's Boutique** and **Didi-daju,** both on Chhetrapati, east of Everest Steak House, carry a wide selection of handicrafts, many of which are produced by the Janakpur Women's Development Centre. (Open daily 10am-9pm. MC/V.)

VOLUNTEER OPPORTUNITIES

Expat prisoners in the central jail south of **Sundhara,** near the GPO, appreciate visitors who'll talk to them for a little while. Bring a little extra food or cash when you go—it's greatly appreciated. Walk south on Kantipath until you pass the Ministry of Finance on the right; the prisons are down the lane that forks south off Kantipath (see **Prisons** graybox, above). The **Sisters of Charity of Nazareth** (☎426453 or 419965), Navjyoti Center, Baluwatar, perform prison ministry, including assisting former women prisoners. **St. Xavier's School** (☎521050 or 521150), Jawalakhel, and **The Missionaries of Charity** (☎471810), Mitra Park, work with the destitute.

■ DAYTRIP FROM KATHMANDU

PASHUPATINATH पशुपतीनाथ

Pashupatinath is only nominally outside of Kathmandu, and it's easy to get there by bike—follow Tridevi Marg away from Thamel, and turn right at the first road after Durbar Marg. At the Marco Polo Business Hotel, turn left and follow the zig-zagging road east across a bridge. Watch for signs showing maps of Pashupatinath. Bus #1 from Ratna Park (45min., frequent, Rs4) stops along Ring Rd. at the turnoff to Pashupathinath; follow the signs from there. The #2 tempo from Sundhara (via Rani Pokhari) stops across the street, just inside Ring Rd. (30min., frequent, Rs6). Auto-rickshaws from Thamel cost about Rs60. Taxis cost Rs 80-100.

Dedicated to Shiva's incarnation as Pashupati, the gentle Lord of Animals and the guardian deity of Nepal, the temple complex of Pashupatinath, east of Kathmandu, is the holiest Hindu site in Nepal. In addition to the bathers who dip in the Bagmati on auspicious full-moon nights and on the 11th day after them, thousands of sadhus and Hindu pilgrims descend upon Pashupatinath during the full moon of late February or early March for the **Shivaratri** festival, a celebration of Shiva's birthday.

The **Pashupati Temple,** built in 1696, is right on the banks of the Bagmati. The brass backside of an enormous statue of Nandi can be seen from the entrance, but the rest of the temple is out of view and out of bounds for non-Hindus. Other viewpoints in the area afford over-the-wall glimpses of the gold-roofed pagoda. Away from the river and across from the main road is a cluster of five towering white cupolas known as **Panch Dewal,** whose compound has become a social welfare center. **Biddha Ashram,** operated by Mother Teresa's *Missionaries of Charity,* welcomes walk-in volunteers to help clients of the compound's hospice with basic domestic chores.

Two footbridges span the river. Between them on the near (west) bank is the 6th-century **Bacchareswari Temple,** reportedly once the site of human sacrifice during Shivaratri festivities. Eight ghats and precipitous stone walls line the river. Still frequently used for the 15 or so daily cremations, the smouldering ghats are aligned in caste order. The northernmost ghat is reserved for royal cremations, and the next is for VIP political and cultural figures. **If there are cremations in progress, be sensitive about taking pictures.**

Across the footbridges, on the east bank of the Bagmati, is a row of 11 small Shiva shrines, each housing the familiar stone Shiva *linga* and *yoni* icons. Not every show-stopping *linga* is made of stone, however—one of the sadhus dwelling in the cliff-carved cave houses (just north of Pashupati Temple on the west bank) can reputedly lift 75kg of rock with a string tied to his penis. Don't ask. The steps up the hill on the east bank of the river eventually level out at a wooded village of over 200 small Shiva temples; Nandi figures crouch along the main street. At the end of the village is a temple dedicated to **Gorakhnath,** an 11th-century saint revered as an avatar of Shiva. The steps continue downhill to the **Gujeshwari Temple,** locally considered to be the place where part of Sati's body fell when her flaming corpse was hacked to bits by Vishnu (the Kamakhya Temple in Guwahati, India, is more widely recognized as this site.) According to Buddhist lore, the temple's sacred well is a bottomless hollow left by the root of the lotus that blossomed and inspired the creation of the Kathmandu Valley. Non-Hindus may not enter, so many lotus-spotting tourists can only see the disappointing, rusty roofs of the buildings surrounding the temple. The road downstream in front of the temple leads to a bridge; once you cross it, stone steps lead over the hill and back to the Pashupati Temple. The road on the right heads to **Boudha** (see p. 802), a 30min. walk north through fields and small neighborhoods. *(Admission to the complex Rs75.)*

PATAN पाटन   ☎ 01

With only the Bagmati River lying between Kathmandu and its temple-dotted neighbor Patan, the two cities have practically merged. The legacy of their development as independent kingdoms lives on, however. Despite being the second-largest city in the valley, Patan has managed to retain the small-town sincerity that eludes its over touristed neighbor. Well-established as the valley's center for Newari handicraft production, Patan (also known as Lalitpur, or "City of Fine Arts") is a great place to stroll through alleys to observe metal smiths, woodworkers, thanka painters, and Tibetan carpet-weavers at work. Also a spiritual center, the city is graced with many small *stupas*, *shikharas*, and onion-domed temples. Some of these shrines languish in disuse and are invaded by weeds, but many still host daily *puja* for Patan's residents. Beauty doesn't come for free, however; the local government has recently begun charging visitors a Rs200 entry fee.

▐ TRANSPORTATION

Tempos (20min., frequent, Rs5-6) leave from Kathmandu's GPO. Most head to Jawalakhel and then Lagankhel, but some go to Mangal Bazaar—ask the driver. Tempos leave for Kathmandu from Patan's Durbar Sq. on Mangal Bazaar and can be flagged down anywhere on the main street. **Bus #26** runs from Kathmandu's Ratna Park to Patan Gate (25min., frequent, Rs5). **Bus #14,** also from Ratna Park, goes to Lagankhel via Jawalakhel (30min., frequent, Rs5). **Taxis** from Thamel to Patan's Durbar Sq. cost about Rs100, **auto-rickshaws** around Rs70. **Buses** depart for Kathmandu from Patan Gate and Lagankhel.

▟▐ ORIENTATION AND PRACTICAL INFORMATION

Patan is linked to Kathmandu by a bridge across the **Bagmati River** and bounded to the south by the same **Ring Rd.** that encircles Kathmandu. Patan's main road, which runs from Kathmandu, goes by the name of whatever neighborhood it's passing through: from the bridge south to Ring Rd. it is called **Kopundol,** then **Pulchowk,** and finally **Jawalakhel.** The **old city,** east of the main road, is loosely bounded by four **stupas** (supposedly built by Ashoka in the 3rd century BC). The eastern *stupa* is beyond Ring Rd.; the western *stupa* is along the main road in Pulchowk, opposite the turn-off to **Durbar Sq.,** the center of the oldest part of town. Several branches lead east from the main road. From north to south, the first leads to **Patan Dhoka** (Patan Gate), north of Durbar Sq. The second becomes **Mangal Bazaar,** the road at the south end of Durbar Sq. Finally, at **Jawalakhel Chowk,** the road leads toward **Lagankhel** and the **bus park.** See the Kathmandu and Patan map, in the Kathmandu section.

Tourist Office: There is a tourist info booth outside Patan Gate. Here you can pay the Rs200 **entrance fee** to receive an entry ticket, which you may be asked to show at other checkpoints throughout the city. Open daily 10am-5pm.

Currency Exchange: Nepal Grindlays, Jawalakhel Chowk (☎540566). Changes traveler's checks for 1.5% commission or minimum Rs200. Open M-F 9:30am-3:30pm.

Bookstore: Pilgrims Book House (☎521159). Has a huge branch on the main road in Kopundol. Open daily 9am-8pm. AmEx/MC/V.

Market: Fruit, spices, and fabrics are sold in Lagankhel, northwest of the bus park. There is a huge vegetable market just south of the bus park. **Namaste Supermarket,** along the main road in Pulchowk, sells a range of pre-packaged goods. Open daily 9am-8pm.

Pharmacy: There are many pharmacies in Mangal Bazaar, below Durbar Sq. **Alka Pharmacy** (☎535147) on the main road in Jawalakhel, north of St. Xavier's school, can arrange house calls. Open daily 7am-10pm.

Hospital: Patan Hospital, Lagankhel (☎522266). Clinic open Su-Tu and Th-F 8am-5pm; W and Sa emergencies only.

Police: (☎ 521350). In Jawalakhel, near the Central Zoo.

Internet Access: The Cybernet (☎521424), has a fast Internet connection (Rs1 per min.), and Internet phone for Rs7-10 per min. Open daily 8am-8pm.

Post Office: Outside Patan Gate, on the west side. Open M-F 9:15am-5pm.

■ ACCOMMODATIONS

Thamel's tourist explosion has put the squeeze on Patan's budget accommodations. Most people ride into Patan for the day and return to Kathmandu at night. Though Patan's budget hotels aren't as conveniently centralized as Thamel's, a night or two in Patan promises a respite from the morning racket of Kathmandu.

Cafe de Patan (☎537599; pcafe@ntc.net.np). Mangal Bazaar. Just southwest of Durbar Sq. Clean, comfortable, quiet rooms are available above this restaurant, just steps away from the sights. Balconies, abundant furnishings, and spotless bathrooms with seat toilets. Singles Rs300-500; doubles Rs400-600. ❷

Mountain View Guest House (☎538168). Kumaripati. 10min. from either Lagankhel bus park or Jawalakhel Chowk; on the north side of the street behind the Campion Academy. A bit removed from the older part of town, this family-run place has the feel of a warm and well-run household. Clean, modern, and well-furnished. Singles Rs200-250; doubles Rs300-380. ❶

Hungry Treat Home (☎534792 or 543360). A few minutes' walk east of Jawalakhel Chowk. Clean, amply sized rooms with large windows, fans, and carpeting. Tiled bathrooms with seat toilets and toilet paper. Attached rooftop restaurant with entrees for Rs35-100. Doubles Rs220, with attached bath Rs330. ❶

Mahendra Youth Hostel (☎521003). Jawalakhel Rd. As you walk north from Jawalakhel Chowk, it's down the second lane to the right, opposite St. Xavier's. Dorm rooms are worn, and facilities basic, but it's the cheapest around. Lockers. No hot water. Check-in 7am-10pm. Dorms Rs50-75; doubles with bath Rs200. 10% discounts for HI/IYHF members. ❶

Hong Kong Guest House (☎534337). Kumaripati. Just east of Hungry Treat House. Basic, cramped rooms with fans. Get chummy with locals in the 2nd-fl. snooker hall. Singles Rs200; doubles Rs350-600. ❶

Third World Guest House (☎522187; fax 526283; dsdp@wlink.com.np). Durbar Sq. On the east side of Durbar Sq., across from the Paton Museum. Classy place with spotless, well-furnished doubles and good views of the sq. Rooms US$15, with attached bath US$20. ❹

◖ FOOD

Patan's food selection is less varied than Kathmandu's, but it's also less tourist-oriented, with more *tarkari* (veg. curry) than teriyaki. Fast-food tandoori joints line the main road. More expensive places serve the same menu in more pleasant settings. For breakfast, **Hot Breads** on Jawalakhel Chowk offers a wide range of pastries, and the **German Bakery ❶**, has great cake and loaves of bread (Rs25-30).

▧ Downtown Restaurant, Pulchowk. Just north of the Sajha bus garage. Lace curtains screen the sights but not the sounds of the busy street. Deservedly popular for its extensive menu and low prices. Good selection of freshly baked *naan* and *rotis* (Rs12-40). Chicken *tikka masala* Rs85. Open Su-F 10am-9pm. ❶

Bakena Batika, Jawalakhel. Just inside Ring Rd., south of the Tibetan Refugee Camp. Though removed from the sights, this beautifully renovated Nepali house and tranquil courtyard make the perfect setting for light meals (Rs100), traditional Nepali courses (Rs150-200), and *risotto* (Rs200). Open daily noon-8:30pm. ❷

The Bakery Café, Jawalakhel Chowk. An All-American roadside diner atmosphere, and a menu to match. Popular with students, it's a good place to grab a bite while waiting for your bus. Burgers Rs60-105, 2 pieces of fried chicken Rs95, milkshakes Rs50. Open daily 7am-8pm. ❶

Tasty Bite Food Plaza, north of Jawalakhel. One of Jawalakhel's larger, cleaner places, with a standard Nepali/Chinese/Continental menu and a good selection of snacks. Newari dishes Rs35-125, burgers Rs30-60, french fries Rs30. Open daily 8am-8pm. ❶

Cafe de Patan, Mangal Bazaar. Southwest of Durbar Sq. Quaff the Square's best lassis (Rs40-55) in the ground floor dining area or the garden rooftop as Top 40 classics play in the background. Chinese (Rs60-95), continental (Rs70-140), and Nepali (Rs80-170) dishes. Open daily 8am-9pm. ❶

◉ SIGHTS

DURBAR SQUARE

A good approach to exploring Durbar Sq. is to start at the southern end of the **Royal Palace,** which sits on the eastern side of the sq., and continue north, circling around counter-clockwise. Although damaged during Prithvi Narayan Shah's 1768 conquest of the valley and the 1934 earthquake, the Royal Palace's three main courtyards have since been nearly restored to their 17th-century splendor.

THE ROYAL PALACE. The southern courtyard, **Sundari Chowk,** is not open to the public, but **Mul Chowk,** dating from the mid-17th century, can be entered between the two stone lions. On the southern wall, gilded statues of the Indian river goddesses Ganga (on a tortoise) and Yamuna (on a *makara*, a mythical snouted sea creature) guard the locked doorway to the **Taleju Shrine.** Dedicated to the patron goddess of Nepal's royal families, the shrine is open to Hindus one day a year during the mid-October **Dasain** festival. Other pagodas that rise around Mul Chowk are the **Degu Talle Temple,** an octagonal tower in the northeast corner, and on the north side, the **Taleju Mandir,** the tallest in the square. *(Mul Chowk open 9am-5pm.)*

The **Patan Museum** is in **Keshav Narayan Chowk,** the northernmost section of the palace; visitors enter through an elaborate golden doorway. The white-washed shrine inside is dedicated to Narayan. Beautifully restored with the help of the Austrian government and the Smithsonian Institute, the museum has been hailed as one of the best on the subcontinent. With its extensive collection of metal, wood, and stone sculptures, all accompanied by thorough and informative labels, the museum provides an excellent introduction to Hindu and Buddhist iconography. Don't miss the fascinating third-floor gallery dedicated to the sculpting processes. Cushioned window seats look out on the square below, and a courtyard cafe serves overpriced snacks. *(Museum open 10:30am-5pm. Rs250.)* Around the corner to the north of the palace is the water tank known as **Manga Hiti;** its mythical crocodile-like statues have been spouting water since the 6th century. The adjacent pavilion, **Mani Mandap,** was once used for coronations.

OTHER TEMPLES. Diagonal from the northernmost temple in the square is the three-tiered **Bhimsen Mandir,** with a lion-topped pillar in front of its recently added marble facade. Merchants toss coins onto the older, gilded first floor of this temple, which is dedicated to the god of trade. The next temple to the south is the **Vishwanath Mandir,** a double-roofed Shiva temple guarded by two stone elephants. The original structure dates back to 1627, but it collapsed in 1990 and has since been restored. The *linga* inside is said to replicate the Vishwanath *linga* in Varanasi (see p. 703). A Nandi faces the other side of the temple. As you continue south, the next temple is the stone, Indian *shikhara*-style **Krishna Mandir.** Supposedly the first all-stone *shikhara* specimen in Nepal, it is one of the few temples in Durbar Sq. still in active use. In the evenings, devotees set the building aglow with butter lamps. The upper floors, carved with friezes depicting scenes from the *Mahabharata* and *Ramayana*, are closed to non-Hindus.

Vishnu is the patron god of the square's oldest temple, the **Jagan Narayan Mandir.** The squat **Bhai Deval Mandir** is in the southwest corner of the square. Continuing around, you'll pass a fountain before arriving at the octagonal stone **Chyasin Deval,** which like the other Krishna temples in the square, was built in an Indian style. After Patan built the enormous **Taleju Bell** in front of the Sundari Chowk, Bhaktapur and Kathmandu were quick to commission similarly oversized bells. The next temple to the north is the **Hari Shankar Mandir,** an elaborately carved, three-tiered pagoda from the 18th century. The temple is dedicated to Vishnu (called Hari here) and Shiva (Shankar). Just north of the temple is a stone pillar topped with a golden statue of **King Yoganarendra Malla,** a monument with legends of its own.

SOUTH OF DURBAR SQUARE

Continuing along Mangal Bazaar east of Durbar Sq., you'll see signs for the **Mahaboudha Temple;** the right-hand turn-off is a 5min. walk from the square. The architect of this "temple of 1000 Buddhas" was inspired by the Mahabodhi Temple in Bodh Gaya, India, where the Buddha achieved enlightenment (see p. 140). Hemmed in by a ring of metalwork curio shops, the *shikhara*-style temple is covered with terra cotta tiles, each of which bears a sculpted figure of the Buddha. The temple was severely damaged in a 1934 earthquake, and the builders who reassembled it found themselves with so many bricks left over that they built a small shrine to the Buddha's mother Mayadevi, which stands nearby. To the right is the **Uka Bahal (Rudravarna Mahabihar),** the oldest monastery in Patan, is on the left at the next intersection. A pair of stone lions protects this former Buddhist monastery, while an ark full of brass beasts stands watch in the courtyard.

As you leave Uka Bahal, turn left onto **Tinker St.** The sound of metal being hammered fills the avenue, which ends at the wide market street running south from Durbar Sq. At the intersection of the two streets stands the **Ibaha Bahal,** a monastery dating from 1427 which was renovated in 1995 with the help of the Nippon Institute of Technology. Farther south along the same street, on the left, is the **Minnath Mandir,** with its garishly painted details. Minnath is often called *sanno* ("little") Machhendranath, in reference to the deity who inhabits another temple down a short lane across the street. This temple, the **Rato Machhendranath Mandir,** a 17th-century pagoda with an intricate, colorful, three-tiered roof, stands in the center of a big, grassy compound. A collection of brass animals, each one representing a month of the Tibetan calendar, poses on posts facing the temple. Machhendranath is a multi-purpose deity: he's an incarnation of Avalokiteshvara who is the *bodhisattva* of compassion, he is revered as the guru of a 7th-century saint, and he serves as the Newari god who controls the rains. In late May, the *rato* ("red") image of Machhendranath rides in a towering chariot that makes its rounds in Patan, followed by a smaller chariot carrying Minnath, who is considered to be his brother. Beginning in Pulchowk, the local residents tow the chariots to the next stop on the tour, having first fueled themselves with *raksi* and *chang.* The chariots are often halted along the way to wait for a suitably auspicious moment to move, and it can take them up to 60 days to reach Jawalakhel, their final destination. From here, the image of Machhendranath is removed from the chariot and carried to his temple in the nearby town of Bungamati. The enormous, rickety temple-chariots *(raths)* are destroyed and built anew every year, and the remnants remain around Jawalakhel Chowk, casually strewn between tempos and buses.

NORTH OF DURBAR SQUARE

GOLDEN TEMPLE. The Golden Temple, one of Patan's most famous buildings, is a 5min. walk north of Durbar Sq. Also known as **Hiranyavarna Mahavihar,** this ornate, gilded temple makes up the west side of the **Kwa Bahal,** a 12th-century Buddhist monastery that conducts daily morning *pujas.* The courtyard is marked by a small, but equally opulent, golden shrine. **No leather is allowed beyond the walkway around the edge of the courtyard—you can trade your shoes for flip-flops at the temple entrance.** The temple's facade contains images of Buddhas, *taras,* and mythological creatures. Gods supposedly slide down the *patakas,* the golden belts that hang from the roofs, to answer their worshippers' prayers. The stairs, in the northeast corner, lead to a collection of icons and Tibetan-style murals inside the monastery. *(Walk to the northern end of Durbar Sq., take a left at the Chimsen Temple, then take the next right. Open daily 8:30am-6pm. Rs25 for foreigners.)*

KUMBESHWAR MAHADEV. A few minutes north of the Golden Temple, Kumbeshwar Mahadev is the oldest temple in Patan. Though it had only two tiers when it was built in 1392, three stories were added later to make it one of two free-standing, five-roofed pagodas in the Kathmandu Valley (the other is the Nyatapola Temple in Bhaktapur). The deity-in-residence is Shiva, as indicated by the Nandi outside the temple and the stone *linga* inside. The water tank next to the temple is believed to be connected to the holy Himalayan lake of Gosainkund. A pilgrim is said to have dropped a *kumbh* (pot) in the lake, which then emerged in the tank in Patan, giving the temple its name. Thousands of devotees come to bathe in the tank during the **Janai Purnima festival** (held in August), when high-caste Hindus change their *janais,* sacred threads that Brahmins and Chhetris wear over their left shoulders. One block east of the temple, the road to the right leads back to the northern end of Durbar Sq., passing a number of smaller temples on the way.

JAWALAKHEL

The Jawalakhel neighborhood is notable for its foreign residents most of whom are Tibetan refugees and expats working for an ever-increasing number of foreign aid organizations.

CENTRAL ZOO. Just west of Jawalakhel Chowk is Nepal's only zoo. See that tiger that eluded you at Chitwan, dodge siamarg feces (they've been known to throw), and commune with swans on a paddleboat ride in the scummy pond. Or, spin yourself sick on the dilapidated merry-go-round, and queasily recover on an elephant ride around the zoo. (*Open Tu-Su 10am-6pm, tickets sold until 5pm. Rs60; camera fee Rs10; merry-go-round Rs10 per ride; paddleboat Rs40 per person; elephant ride Rs100.*)

JAWALAKHEL HANDICRAFT CENTER. A part of the Tibetan Refugee Camp, Jawalakhel Handicraft Center was established by the Red Cross and the Nepalese government in 1960 after the Chinese takeover in 1959 drove large numbers of Tibetan refugees to the area. The booming carpet industry, centered here, provides jobs to over 1000 Tibetans in the area. Proceeds from the souvenir shop go to the workers and to a social welfare fund that supports children's educational programs and provides a stipend to elderly Tibetans. Visitors are free to wander and observe the carpet-making process in the main room, which has over 40 huge looms. (☎521305. 5-10min. walk south of Jawalakhel Chowk. Open Su-F 8am-5pm.)

📷 SHOPPING

A lower-pressure sales atmosphere than Kathmandu (and an equally wide selection) make Patan an ideal place for souvenir shopping. Most of the items sold in Patan were actually produced here; prices and selection tend to be even better than in Kathmandu. The **Patan Industrial Estate,** just south of Lagankhel near Ring Road, houses showrooms catering to large tourist groups. It's a convenient place to find a wide variety of metalwork, wood carvings, and *thankas*, and you can see artisans at work. For carpets, head to the **Tibetan Refugee Camp** in Jawalakhel—they're made here. A standard quality (40 knots per sq. in.) 1m x 2m carpet will cost Rs6000-Rs9500. Patan is also full of non-profit outlets selling crafts from all over the country at fixed prices. Many benefit underprivileged workers—especially women—and ensure fair wages. They are found in the old Royal Palace on Durbar Sq. and in Kopundol. **Sana Hastakala,** Kopundol, opposite Hotel Himalaya, is sponsored by UNICEF. (☎522628; fax 526985; sanahast@wlink.com.np. Open Su-F 9:30am-6pm, Sa 9am-6pm. AmEx/MC/V.) **Mahaguthi,** sponsored by Oxfam, has branches in Kopundol, The Royal Palace, and Lazimpat. (Kopundol branch open M-F 9:30am-6:30pm, Sa-Su 10am-5:30pm. MC/V.)

🔆 DAYTRIPS FROM PATAN

GODAVARI गोदावरी

From Langankhel bus park, buses #13 and 14 continue up the hills to Godavari (1hr., Rs6), with spellbinding views of rice paddies along the way. Godavari bus park is the last stop.

If the dry, dusty city has you craving fragrant flowers, Godavari is the place to go. In this horticultural haven, on the valley's southeastern edge, you'll find the peaceful, expertly landscaped Royal Botanical Garden, the National Herbarium, and the nurseries that supply florists in Patan, as well as the Godavari Kunda and Pulchowki Mai, two local religious sites. The **Botanical Garden** is a 15min. walk from the bus park, up the road to the left; continue until the paved road comes to an end at the garden's entrance. The garden is big enough to get lost in, and the shady pavilions are a favorite picnicking spot for middle class Nepalis. (*Open daily 9am-5pm. Admission Rs25 for foreigners; camera fee Rs10.*) The small dirt road that branches off to the right before the entrance to the Botanical Garden leads uphill for 100m to the **Godavari Kunda,** a pool shrouded with faded prayer flags. Clear mountain water collects in an interior pool (closed) which then flows through spouts to the outer pool. Pilgrims come here every 12 years to purify themselves in the waters, but you might see kids swimming on any hot day. From the bus park, the road to the right leads uphill past St. Xavier's College to a marble quarry and **Pulchowki Mai,** a rather run-down temple. The temple houses images of Vishnu, Ganesh, and a tantric mother goddess, but most have been abraded into indecipherability. Outside the temple is a pool fed by nine sculptured spouts, symbolizing the nine streams that flow off Pulchowki, the nearby mountain for which the temple is named. A trail behind the temple starts the 3hr. climb to the peak, which, at 2762m, affords panoramic views of the valley.

BUNGAMATI बँगामथी

*The **bus** to Bungamati departs from Patan's Jawalakhel Chowk (30min., frequent, Rs5) and passes over a fantastic look-out point just before arriving at the turn-off to Bungamati, marked by a **police post.** To get to the temple, follow the stone path downhill from the police post. A labyrinthine network of agricultural trails winds around the terraced slopes; the intrepid visitor can head to the similarly untouristed town of **Khokana** known for its mustard oil production. The town is a scenic 15min. walk northwest*

Few tourists ever venture to **Bungamati's** cobblestone alleys which run between a jumble of red-roofed brick houses. Baby goats munching on weeds along car-free roads, women washing laundry in the communal fountain, and curious children greeting the village's rare visitors with wide-eyed stares–such sights and sounds allow the visitor to experience life in a typical Newari village.

The town's main claim to fame is its tall, *shikhara*-style **Rato Machhendranath temple.** Bungamati is revered as the birthplace of Machhendranath, the patron god of the Kathmandu Valley, also believed to be an incarnation of Avalokitesvara, the Bodhisattva of Compassion. Machhendranath's rainmaking prowess is vital to this self-sufficient agricultural community. During Patan's **Rato Machhendranath festival** in late May, the image of the deity is taken from a corresponding temple in Patan and pulled through the streets on a huge wooden chariot from Pulchowk to Jawalakhel. From here it is brought by palanquin to the temple in Bungamati, where it spends the remaining six months of the year before returning to Patan. Every 12 years (next in 2003), the immense chariots are pulled all the way to Bungamati, a colossal undertaking that sometimes requires the aid of the Nepali army.

KIRTIPUR किर्तीपुर

Sprinkled between ancient houses and hushed pedestrian streets, Kirtipur's Hindu shrines and Buddhist temples exemplify Nepal's fascinating religious syncretism. Kirtipur is a typical, impoverished Newari town simultaneously fighting off the encroaching development of nearby **Tribhuvan University** and inviting much-needed public funds for infrastructure within the town itself. Like Bungamati, Kirtipur is also largely ignored by tourists despite its ornate temples, hilltop views, and proximity to Chobar, which make it a worthwhile daytrip from Kathmandu.

The citizens of Kirtipur remain proud of the stand their ancestors took against Prithvi Narayan Shah's encroaching Gorkha forces during the 18th century (see **History,** p. 756). When Shah attacked for the first time in 1757, neighboring towns came to Kirtipur's aid and helped defeat the invaders. During a second battle in 1764, Shah's brother was shot in the eye with an arrow, and the Gorkhas again retreated. But the Gorkhas' superior weaponry turned the tide two years later, when Kirtipur finally surrendered after a six-month siege. The Gorkhas punished the men of the town by slicing off their noses, ears, and lips so that people throughout the country would recognize them as troublemakers from Kirtipur.

◪ ⁊ ORIENTATION AND PRACTICAL INFORMATION. To reach Kirtipur from Kathmandu, take a **taxi** (Rs200) or **bus #21** (30min., frequent departures, Rs5) from the Ratna Park bus station. The bus follows Dakshinkali Rd., passes through the gates of Tribhuvan University, and finally climbs a steep hill into town before taking a sharp left. Get off at the top of the hill, where you'll find a partially rusted but still-legible city map. The road extends to the left into the **Naya Bazaar,** home to several small shops offering **STD** and **Internet** services.

◙ SIGHTS. A walking tour of Kirtipur's sights can be completed in under two hours. A good place to start is the **Shree Kirti Vihara,** a Thai-style Theravada Buddhist temple built in 1989 and immaculately maintained by the resident monks. A small four-door gallery, stamped with the Thai Airways logo, depicts the four major stages in the life of the Buddha: his birth in Lumbini, his enlightenment at Bodh Gaya, his first sermon at Sarnath, and his death in Kushinagar.

From the rusty city map, take the steep, stone stairs to your right. Take a right at the top and a left when you reach a pool. The steps up to the ancient **Chilandeo Stupa** (also called Chilancho Vihara) are to your right, near a standard stone *shikhara*. This 1400-year-old *stupa* is surrounded by a number of stone shrines, some of which are very recent. The prayer wheel, to the right as you enter, is only six years old, but it is the largest in Kirtipur. Along the left side of the *stupa* is an abandoned 17th-century monastery, adorned with just one remaining *torano* arch on the center door, guarded by a sturdy Newari-crafted lock.

Facing the monastery, turn right and walk behind the *stupa*. At the second corner, a small stone path leads out of the *stupa* area. From the path, take your first right into an open area dominated by a towering stone **shikhara.** The upper level of the temple features representations of the Buddha, while the lower level is devoted to Hindu deities. This half-Buddhist, half-Hindu temple was built during the 17th century as a gesture of goodwill during a period of religious tension.

From the *shikhara*, turn left and follow the slate path down to a large courtyard with a pool. At the far end of the courtyard is the **Bagh Bhairab Mandir,** an 11th-century temple dedicated to Shiva the Destroyer *(Bhairab)* in the form of a tiger *(bagh)*. Mounted on the upper facade are Gorkhali swords and uniforms, commemorating Kirtipur's defeat by the Gorkhas. Worshipers and musicians visit Bagh Bhairab every morning and evening; there are chicken or buffalo sacrifices on Tuesdays and Saturdays. Bagh Bhairab is also the center of Kirtipur's December festival for the goddess Indrani, an offshoot of Kathmandu's Indrani festival.

Facing the entrance to the Bagh Bhairab Mandir, take the road to the left to the **Uma-Maheshwar Mandir.** Built in 1575, the temple overlooks the valley from the highest point in Kirtipur (1440m). Two stone elephants guard the temple which houses intricately carved images of Shiva and his consort Parvati. More noteworthy than the temple itself is its superb panoramic view. To the southwest looms one of the highest points of the Kathmandu Valley's rim, and to the northeast sprawls the city of Kathmandu. On a clear day, you can even see Everest.

CHOBAR चोभार

When Manjushri drained the Kathmandu valley with one legendary swing of his sword, the blow carved out the plunging cliffs of **Chobar Gorge.** A narrow Scottish-built **suspension bridge** spans the gorge. The choked, putrid Bagmati foams underfoot. From the bridge, the cliffside steps leading to South Asia's third-longest cave, **Chobar Gupha,** are visible on the west bank. Next to the bridge is the three-tiered **Jal Binayak,** a 950-year-old temple dedicated to Ganesh, who is represented here in the form of a large rock protruding from the back of the temple. Locals lean against this to harness its curative powers. Around the temple, a stylized Shiva *linga* dances with Parvati before the statue of a rabbit. Chobar Village spreads across a small hill which overlooks the gorge. At its peak is the 14th-century **Adinath Lokeshwar Mandir,** a half-Hindu, half-Buddhist temple covered with pots and pans—contributions of kitchenware to the temple are said to enhance the culinary skills of new brides as well as the strength of the marriage.

Bus #22 (30min., frequent, Rs5) heads to Chobar from Ratna Park in Kathmandu. Get off just before the bus turns west into the gates of Tribhuvan University, and continue along Dakshinkali Rd., the town's main road. As you pass the **Himalayan Bee Concern** on the right, stone stairs lead uphill to Chobar. The gorge can be reached either by continuing on Dakshinkali Rd. or from Chobar—turn right as you exit the temple, and follow the dirt path downhill. From the gorge, it's about 1hr. to Patan; cross the bridge, head straight along the uphill path, and turn left at the first intersection. From Kirtipur, Chobar is a 30min. walk away. Follow the main road through the Naya Bazaar; with the Buddhist temple on your left, turn left at **Ratna's Beauty Parlor,** take the next left, and follow the path until it meets the main road near a small temple with a gate. Turn left onto the main road, and follow the stairway up to Chobar.

NAGARJUN नागार्जुन AND BALAJU बालाजु

Many believe that the Buddha once meditated on Nagarjun; others maintain that the first Bodhisattva, Viswapa, stood on the peak to throw the lotus seed that would blossom into *swayambhu*. Crowned by an old *stupa* festooned with a canopy of aging prayer flags, Nagarjun (also called "Jamacho") is the closest summit to Kathmandu and offers a breathtaking panoramic view of the valley. Camping is permitted, but not easy, since the hillside is steep and covered in thick brush. Nagarjun sits in **Rani Ban** (also called Nagarjun Royal Forest), a well-preserved chunk of woods protected by the government (admission Rs10). After you enter Rani Ban, a well-marked trail on your right leads to the summit (5km, 2hr.). At the top is a lookout tower and the Buddhist shrine **Jamacho.** Jamacho is the center of April's full moon festival, **Balju Jatra,** when worshipers hold an all-night vigil at the summit and descend to Balaju the next day for a ritual bath in Baais Dhara.

Pleasant outdoor recreation can also be found in **Balaju Water Garden** in nearby Balaju, the industrial suburb just south of Nagarjun. Balaju is an easy 40min. climb from Thamel. Walk north from Kathmandu Guesthouse, turn left at Lekhnath Marg, and follow the congested traffic northwest past the rotary. **Bus #23** (30min., frequent, Rs5) leaves from Ratna Park and stops at the garden which is one of the few well-maintained public spaces around. Nepali families relax around manicured rose gardens, shaded benches, and fantastically garish fountains spraying water in all directions. (Open daily 7am-7:30pm, Rs5; camera fee Rs5.) During festival season, worshippers bathe in the water that courses from the 22 carved crocodiles of the **Baais Dhara,** to the right. Midway through the park is the **Bala Nilkantha,** a 7th-century contemporary of the more elaborate sleeping Vishnu, northeast of the valley in Budhanilkantha. Devotees crawl over the 12ft. long Vishnu and pour milk and honey over his face. Thamel-weary travellers can find respite in the noisy **swimming pool.** (Open daily 9am-12:30pm and 1-4pm. Rs40, students Rs35 with ID. Women only on Th.)

NEPAL

BOUDHA (BOUDHANATH) बौद्धनाथ   ☎01

The massive, whitewashed dome of Nepal's largest *stupa* draws Buddhists from far and wide to Boudha, east of Kathmandu. Nearly everybody here claims origins elsewhere. Many have fled Tibet since the Chinese crackdown in 1959, making Boudha the religious center of Nepal's growing Tibetan community; others have migrated from the northern peaks, and an increasing number are Westerners come to study at the many surrounding *gompas* (monasteries). Once you experience the serenity of monastic life, you may miss its simple charms—local children clamoring on the *stupa*, the smell of incense drifting in every direction, and every few hours, horns and drums announcing the rituals of the nearby monasteries.

✈ 🛈 ORIENTATION AND PRACTICAL INFORMATION

Boudha has expanded far beyond the confines of the **stupa compound,** but the *stupa* remains its symbolic center and the reference point for all other directions. The *stupa*, 5km east of Kathmandu, can be entered through a **gate** on the north side of **Tushal Rd.,** the main east-west road. The sprawling community north of the *stupa*, where you will find most of Boudha's monasteries, is accessible from two parallel lanes leading north out of the compound. **Phulbare Rd.** is a wide road that runs from the eastern edge of the compound past the Tashi Delek Restaurant and the Kailash Guest House. **Duratol Rd.** is a narrow path lying just to the west that leaves the compound opposite the entrance to the *stupa* itself. Small east-west lanes beside **Tusal Rd.** connect these two. **Always walk clockwise around the stupa.**

Buses: Bus #2 from **Ratna Park** (30min., frequent, Rs5) will drop you off a few yards before the gate. Blue **tempos** (#2, Rs8) leave from Jamal, the street running along the southern edge of **Rani Pokhari. Taxis** from **Thamel** cost around Rs100.

Currency Exchange: Mandala Money Changer, on the left, just inside the southern gates, changes traveller's checks for a Rs40 fee per check. Open Sun-Fri 9am-5pm, Sat 9-11am.

Market: Fruit sellers gather on Tusal Rd. outside the entrance to the *stupa* compound and in the lanes north of the *stupa*. Across the east-west road, about 25m east of the gate, is the well-stocked **Gemini Grocer.** Open daily 7:30am-7pm. MC/V.

Police: Tusal Rd. (☎470545). 100m west of the *stupa* entrance on the south side of the road.

Hospital: There are numerous storefront pharmacies and clinics on the two northern lanes. The largest and most modern is the **Shechen Clinic** (☎ 487924), on the road which branches left from Duratol upon leaving the Boudha *stupa*, next to the Shechen monastery which provides consultations for Rs500. Attached pharmacy sells condoms, as well as Western, homeopathic, and Tibetan medicines.

Internet and Telephones: The *stupa* is surrounded by Internet cafes. One of the best is **Dharana Cyberspace** (☎/fax 494178). Services include STD/ISD, fax, Internet phone, and Internet access (Rs1 per min.). Open daily 6:30am-9:30pm

☗ ACCOMMODATIONS

Boudha's clean and peaceful lodgings might make you want to stay a few extra nights. All of the guest houses listed here have seat toilets, hot water, and a noon check-out time. Those farther from the *stupa* tend to be quieter; many have private gardens.

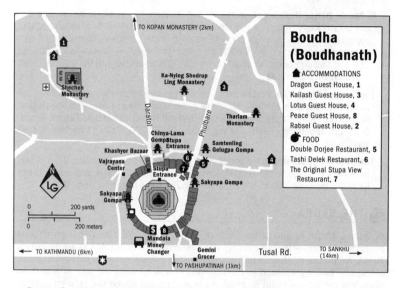

Dragon Guest House (☎/fax 479562). A 10min. walk from the *stupa*. Follow the signs from Duratol Rd. and walk behind the Shechen monastery. Remote but clean, with sparkling shared bathrooms and a large Western clientele. Terraces on each floor, a small library, and attached veg. restaurant. Breakfast Rs30-80, entrees Rs40-85; open daily 7am-10pm. Singles Rs250; doubles Rs350. ❶

Lotus Guest House (☎472432 or 472320). Beside the colorful Dobsang Monastery. From Phulbare Rd., take the first right after exiting the *stupa* compound. Motel-style layout, clean rooms, and a beautiful garden courtyard. Reservations recommended Oct.-Nov. Singles Rs250-290; doubles Rs350-390. ❶

Kailash Guest House (☎480741). Phulbare Rd. A 2min. walk from the *stupa*. Clean rooms furnished with mirrored locker and pleasant terraces on each floor. Singles Rs200; doubles Rs250-300. ❶

Rabsel Guest House (☎479009; fax 470215; rabsel@mes.com.np). On the way to Dragon Guest House. Clean rooms with private bath offer dazzling views of the nearby Khentse monastery. Central garden and common space on each floor. Continental breakfast in attached veg. restaurant included. Open 7am-9:30pm. Rs420 per person. ❷

Peace Guest House, on the right, just inside the southern *stupa* gates, has two well-worn dormitory rooms with a shared bath (no hot water). Padlocks with shared keys. Attached restaurant has separate Chinese and English menus. Guess which one features salted pig's tongue (open daily 7:30am-8pm). Rs100 per bed. ❶

🦋 FOOD

If you could build *stupas* from *momos*, Boudha would boast even more of these architectural wonders than it already does. The town's chorus line of hole-in-the-wall restaurants serves quality Tibetan treats alongside the standard tourist fare. A few *stupa*-side eateries will let you exchange romantic glances with Buddha's blue eyes as you eat; the cheaper, smaller places line Duratol and Phulbare Rd.

◪**Double Dorjee Restaurant,** on the right off Phulbare Rd., just past the Kamapa Service Society Nepal. A favorite with monks and ex-pats. Low tables, floral upholstery, and paper lanterns. Huge servings of mouth watering Tibetan, Chinese, Japanese, and continental dishes listed on the blackboard menu (Rs40-120). A Tibetan family provides slow and friendly service, so you'll have plenty of time to chat with the regulars. Open daily 7:30am-9:30pm. ❶

The Original Stupa View Restaurant, overlooks the *stupa* from the northern side of the compound. Not to be confused with same-name, different-place imposters, the Original Stupa View harbors a menu that manages to meld Nepali and Middle Eastern flavors. Small but appetizing selection of veg. dishes Rs120-200. Open 11am-9pm. Closed May 26-July 26. ❷

Tashi Delek Restaurant, on the corner of the *stupa* compound, at Phulbare Rd. A curtain marks the entrance to this 3-table, low-profile place. Fresh, tasty, and cheap meals Rs20-90. Their veg. *thukpa* is hard to beat (Rs25). Open daily 6am-8pm. ❶

⊙ THE STUPA

Boudha's *stupa* is one of the largest in the world. All kinds of legends surround its origins—the 5th-century date assigned by historians is really only a guess. A Tibetan myth tells of a poultry farmer's daughter who wanted to build a *stupa*. The king granted her permission to use an area the size of a buffalo skin. Not content to build so small a *stupa*, the girl sliced the skin into strips to trace the perimeter of the huge lot on which the *stupa* now stands. The Newari version tells the tale of a king who built taps from which no water would flow. Convinced that only the sacrifice of a great man would bring water, he ordered his son to go to the spouts and behead the shrouded man he found lying there. This, of course, turned out to be the king. Horrified by his deed, the regicidal, patricidal prince built the *stupa* to redeem himself. The *stupa* has inspired awe and reverence since ancient times, when its location along the Kathmandu-Lhasa trade route made it a popular pilgrimage site—people still pray here for safe passage through the Himalayas.

Each segment of the *stupa's* structure is supposed to correspond to one of the five elements: the three-leveled *mandala*-shaped base represents earth; the dome, water; the spire (with its 13 steps corresponding to the 13 steps to nirvana), fire; the parasol, air; and the pinnacle, ether. The red-rimmed, blue Buddha-eyes that gaze out from each of the four sides of the golden spire are unique to Nepali stupas, and the "nose" in between them is actually the number "1" in Nepali script. The whitewashed *stupa* is splashed with stripes of rust-colored wash to resemble the lotus shape. Niches in the wall contain prayer wheels and 108 images of the Buddha. At the entrance to the *stupa* itself is a shrine to the Newari goddess Ajima, protectress of children and goddess of smallpox. Visitors can climb onto the first three tiers of the *stupa*.

Monasteries usually welcome visitors as long as they observe the necessary etiquette (usually posted on signs outside). Dress modestly, take your shoes off before entering the *lhakang* (main hall), walk in a clockwise direction inside, and always ask before taking photos. As monasteries have traditionally relied on contributions from visitors and pilgrims, donations are greatly appreciated. If you visit a lama, present him with a white *khata* (prayer scarf). These are inexpensive and available at many shops around Boudha, where someone can show you how to fold them properly. In the *lhakang*, you'll find intricate wall paintings in overwhelmingly vivid colors and gold statues of notable Buddhist figures surrounded by offerings of food, incense, and butter-lamps.

The **Sakyapa** and **Sauntenling Gelugpa** *gompas* are right next to the *stupa* compound, and nearly 40 more *gompas* are spread out in the area to the north. The Shechen *gompa*, off Duratol Rd., features an immaculate and peaceful courtyard. In a small building northwest of the Shechen *lhakang* are three gargantuan 10ft. prayer wheels, one of the most impressive sets in the area.

The year's largest celebrations happen in February when thousands come to meet friends and family for **Losar,** the Tibetan New Year. The festivities begin with February's new moon and last for two weeks. During the first three days of the festival, monks at the local monasteries perform celebratory dances. The holiday ends with the full moon on a day known as the **Festival of Lights,** or Day of Offerings (*Cho-trul Duechen* in Tibetan) when worshipers circle the *stupa* amidst prayers and chantings of penance and thanksgiving.

The *stupa* is surrounded by **shops.** You don't need to come all the way to Boudha to buy the standard tourist junk, but it is *the* place for Tibetan antiques and cheap souvenirs like Tibetan head- and foot-gear and Buddhist prayer flags.

STUDY AND VOLUNTEER OPPORTUNITIES

The **Ka-Nying Shedrup Ling Monastery** (☎470993), known as the white monastery or *seto gompa*, is between Phulbare and Duratol Rd. and welcomes Westerners. To get there, follow Phulbare Rd., and take the left after you pass the Tashi Delek Restaurant. The monastery's leader meets visitors (daily 10am-noon) and holds a teaching session in English (Sa 11:30am-12:30pm). The monastery also hosts the Rangjung Yesha Institute Shedra (www.shedra.com), where visitors can enroll in four-month Tibetan language, cultural, and religious studies. **Kopan Monastery** (☎481268; www.kopan-monastery.com), on a hill 2km north of Boudha, holds several meditation courses throughout the year (seven-day course Rs4600-7000), organizes longer retreats in the hilltop facility designed for Westerners seeking Buddhist instruction, and offers lodging when courses aren't being held (dorms Rs110; with private bath Rs400; breakfast included). To get there from the *stupa*, follow Duratol Rd. for about 10min. until it meets a paved taxi road. Turn right, and continue a short distance to a dirt path leading off to the left. Follow the dirt road, keeping to the left, for about 30min. until it leads into Kopan; a map marks the entrance. Finally, the **Vajrayana Center** (☎481108; t_sherpavajra@yahoo.com) is a great place for English-speakers to teach English to Tibetans, for any length of time. The center also organizes free, ongoing Tibetan classes. To get to the center, follow Duratol Rd. from the *stupa* and take the first left onto a small road. Turn left at the first fork and again at the second; the center is on the left.

BHAKTAPUR भक्तपुर ☎ 01

The gods of city planning decimated Bhaktapur in 1934 with a disastrous earthquake, which proved to be a backhanded gift—diligent restoration and preservation efforts since then have returned the city to its 15th-century splendor and have made Bhaktapur the cleanest city in the Kathmandu Valley. Forking over the hefty entrance fee (Rs750) to stroll along the neatly paved pedestrian zone might remind you of being at a theme park, but Bhaktapur is not Mickey Mouse fairytown. Look between the magnificent temples and sacred landmarks of the Kathmandu Valley's third largest city, and you might see scenes from a medieval Newari town—armies of clay pots left in the sun to dry, kids clambering for rides on the backs of ancient stone griffins, and brick lanes lined with street vendors hawking their colorful wares. The entry fee continues to finance restoration projects and exciting civic programs such as trash collection.

Founded in the 9th century, Bhaktapur ("City of Devotees") was the capital of the Kathmandu Valley until the region was divided into three kingdoms in 1482. The town's prominence faded when the Gorkhas conquered it in 1768 and established the capital in Kathmandu (see **History, <u>p. 756</u>**). Many of its buildings are reconstructed versions of temples built between the 15th and 17th centuries. Restoration and rebuilding continue, encouraged by a German-funded development project begun in the 1970s. Attracted by the famous temples and museums (whose artifacts are of religious significance to Hindus and Buddhists alike), as well as by the town's strong sense of community, Nepali tourists constitute a large portion of Bhaktapur's non-resident population. For many visitors to the Kathmandu Valley, Bhaktapur is just a daytrip from Kathmandu. Those who stay overnight, however, get a chance to see multi-colored pagoda shadows lengthening across the twilight templescape of this vibrant city, long after most tourists have left.

▛ TRANSPORTATION

Buses: Bus #7 leaves from Kathmandu's Bagh Bazaar, just east of Durbar Marg and north of Ratna Park, and arrives at Bhaktapur's Minibus Park, near Guhya Pond (45min., frequent, Rs9). Less crowded than buses, **trollies** connect Kathmandu's Tripureswar, near the National Stadium, to Bhaktapur's **trolleybus park,** south of town (1hr., frequent, Rs5). Buses to **Nagarkot** (#7, 1hr., every 30min., Rs10) leave from **Kamal Binayak,** on the northeast edge of Bhaktapur, past Dattatraya Sq. Tourist buses arrive at the **Tourist Bus Park,** 5min. north of Durbar Sq. at the edge of town.

Local Transportation: To curb pollution, the city has banned heavy vehicles inside the gates; Bhaktapur is best explored on foot. **Bus #7** runs along the northern edge of town from the hospital to Kamal Binayak. **Taxis** wait just outside the main gate into Durbar Sq. **Bicycles** are available from a shop with no English name on the road that connects Guhya Pond and Durbar Sq. **Cycle Repair Center,** on the south side of the road, rents standard, one-speed bikes. Rs12 per hr.; Rs80 per day. Open daily 7am-7pm.

▟ ORIENTATION

Bhaktapur is bordered to the north and south by roads running to and from Kathmandu, 14km to the west. The southern half of the city is filled with fields, residential streets, and the *ghats* that line the **Hanumante River.** Bhaktapur's main sights are in the northern half of the city, in three squares strung together by a curving main street. **Durbar Sq.** is connected by a short lane at its southeastern corner to **Taumadhi Tol,** which, in turn, is connected to **Dattatraya Sq.** (also called **Tachapal Tol**) by a wide, shop-lined street known as **Sukuldhoka.** Minibuses from Kathmandu arrive near a large water tank called **Guhya Pond** to the west of Durbar Sq. Gate. The **trolleybus** stops in the southern edge of town, 15min. from Durbar Sq.

To enter the city, tourists must pay Rs750 or US$19 at the **Durbar Sq. Gate** or at the other checkpoints. If you sneak into town by another route and avoid these booths, you may still be asked inside for your ticket. The ticket can be used for multiple entries on different days as long as you notify the **Tourist Service Center.**

▟ PRACTICAL INFORMATION

Tourist Office: Tourist Service Center and Information Hall, Durbar Sq. Gate (☎612249). Run by the Bhaktapur Municipality, this is where you can pay the entrance fee for the city (see **Orientation,** above) and get a brochure and useful map. Keep your ticket and have it certified to re-enter if you leave. Public toilets with toilet paper are available. Open daily 6am-7:30pm.

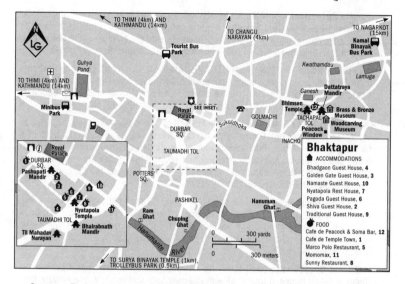

Bhaktapur

🏠 ACCOMMODATIONS

Bhadgaon Guest House, 4
Golden Gate Guest House, 3
Namaste Guest House, 10
Nyatapola Rest House, 7
Pagoda Guest House, 6
Shiva Guest House, 2
Traditional Guest House, 9

🍴 FOOD

Cafe de Peacock & Soma Bar, 12
Cafe de Temple Town, 1
Marco Polo Restaurant, 5
Momomax, 11
Sunny Restaurant, 8

Currency Exchange: Several shops around Durbar Sq. Gate, including **Layaku Money Exchange Counter** (☎ 613563). No commission. Open daily 8am-5pm.

Police: (☎ 610284). Just outside Durbar Sq., down the small street between the Palace of 55 Windows and Fasidega Temple. Open 24hr.

Pharmacy: Pharmacies line **Sukuldhoka,** the wide street connecting Taumadhi Tol and Tachapal Tol. There are also several opposite the hospital, including **Sewa Medicine Store** (☎ 613773). Open daily 6am-9pm; pharmacist on call 24hr.

Hospital: Bhaktapur Hospital (☎ 610676). West of the Navpokhu Pokhari Minibus Park, on the north side of the street. Not the cleanest, most up-to-date of medical clinics—if you're really ill you should probably head to Kathmandu for treatment. Many of the **pharmacies** have doctors affiliated with them who will see patients there during the day. For a simple consultation and/or prescription, this is your best bet.

Internet: Many businesses in Bhaktapur now offer Internet services; most of them are of the one-computer-in-a-room variety. **Cybertech Computers** (☎ 610581). West of the southwest corner of Taumadhi Sq. Rs70 per hour, Rs2 per minute. Open daily 6am-9pm.

Post Office: Next to the minibus park by Guhya Pond. Open M-F 9am-5pm.

🏠 ACCOMMODATIONS

All the places listed below have hot showers, convenient temple-side locations, and ultra-accommodating owners. Deciding which temple you want outside your window might be the toughest decision you have to make. Rates are always negotiable, especially during the off season (May-Aug.). Reservations are recommended in season (Sept.-Dec.). Noon check-out is standard everywhere, and most places lock up at 10pm. Prices listed here are in-season.

Pagoda Guest House, Taumadhi Tol (☎ 613248; fax 612685; pagoda@col.com.np). Right behind the Nyatapola temple. Bed and breakfast atmosphere and a unique location (practically on top of a 5-story temple) make this an inviting place. Squat and seat toilets. Singles US$6-25; doubles US$8-30. Off season: up to 50% discount. MC/V. ❸

Namaste Guest House, Sakotha Tol (☎ 610500; fax 225679; kumari@mail.com.np). On corner of Tibukchhen and Sakotha, leading into the northeast corner of Durbar Sq. Clean, spacious rooms with colorful bedsheets. Guests get 10% off at the **Sunny Restaurant** (see below). Singles Rs300, with bath Rs500; doubles Rs400/600. ❶

Shiva Guest House (☎ 613912; fax 610740; bisket@wlink.com.np). Opposite Pashupatinath Temple. Clean rooms, email (Rs2 per min.), in-house travel agency, and attached restaurant (entrees Rs85-250). All the sheets feature images of meditating Buddhas. Singles US$6, with bath US$15; doubles US$8/20; suite US$30. MC/V. ❷

Bhadgaon Guest House, Taumadhi Tol (☎ 610488; fax 610481; bhadgaon@mos.com.np). On the right after Cafe Nyatapola, as you leave Taumadhi Tol for Potters' Sq. Marble stairs and carefully kept garden courtyard make this one of Bhaktapur's most up-market hotels. Rooftop restaurant with terrific views (entrees Rs85-220). 9 rooms, all with attached bath, TV, fan, toilet paper, towels, and slippers. Singles US$25-35; doubles US$30-50. MC/V. ❺

Golden Gate Guest House, Bahatal (☎ 610534; fax 611081; goldengate@unlimit.com). On the left side of the street as you approach Taumadhi Tol from Durbar Sq. Duck through the doorway to reach the Golden Gate. Clean, characterless rooms with a view of both squares. Singles Rs250, with bath Rs500; doubles Rs350/750; top floor suites US$15. AmEx/MC/V. ❶

Traditional Guest House (☎ 611057; fax 612607; bcci@wlink.com.np). Opposite the Namaste Guest House. 8 rooms, all with attached bath and balcony, in a friendly, family atmosphere. In the evening, the staff prepares all-you-can-eat traditional Newari dishes just for guests (Rs120). Singles Rs250; doubles Rs350. ❶

Nyatapola Rest House, Taumadhi Tol (☎ 612415). Opposite Pagoda Guest House. Pink mosquito nets over all beds, rusted bar grates over windows, and views of a wooden fence, but the prices can't be beat. Has one of the few Internet phones in Bhaktapur (Rs10 per min. for calls to the USA). Attached restaurant with rooftop terrace (entrees Rs40-115). Singles Rs250; doubles Rs300. Off season: up to 50% discount. ❶

▐ FOOD

Most of Bhaktapur's restaurants whip up the usual Nepali-continental-Indian-Chinese food, though there are some less touristy places in the older, more residential areas of town where you can find Nepali cuisine for half the price but with twice the excitement. *Juju dhau* (king of curds), a creamy, sweet yogurt, is a local specialty that is sold almost everywhere.

▨ **Sunny Restaurant,** Taumadhi Tol. Near Nyatapola Temple. Glowing lanterns, sweet-smelling incense, knee-high tables, and a balcony with a splendid view of the square. Continental (Rs80-190), Newari (Rs110-140), and Nepali (Rs100-300) set meals. Open 7:30am-8:30pm. ❷

▨ **MomoMax,** Sakotha Tol. Off an alley at the intersection of Kibukchhen and Sakotha near Namaste Guest House. Low-lit, low-ceilinged, cheap hole-in-the-wall popular with locals. Devastatingly good *momos* (Rs20-25). Also serves Chinese and Tibetan dishes (Rs20-40). The veggie *pakoda* (Rs25) might make you declare Nepali citizenship. Open daily 11:30am-8pm. ❶

Cafe de Peacock and Soma Bar, Tachapal Tol. Faces Dattatraya Temple, 2nd fl. on the left. Indoor and outdoor seating make for great people-watching. Mexican, Italian, and Nepali dishes Rs100-300. Open daily 9am-9pm. AmEx/MC/V. ❷

Marco Polo Restaurant, Taumadhi Tol. Immediately to the left as you face Nyatapola Temple. A marginally cheaper alternative to other tourist restaurants. Tiny balcony overlooks the northwest corner of the square. Fairly extensive menu, including lasagna, burgers, and Indian and Nepali dishes (Rs60-100). Open daily 7am-8pm. ❶

Cafe de Temple Town Restaurant, Durbar Sq. Turn right after entering the Durbar Sq. Gate. A small garden around the patio tables obscures the sights but not the noise. Rooftop seating promises better views. Pizza Rs160-215, Indian and Nepali dishes Rs125-255. Open daily 9am-9pm. ❷

🜨 SIGHTS

DURBAR SQUARE. Bhaktapur has the oldest and least cluttered Durbar Sq. in the valley, with a wide-open pedestrian area surrounded by just enough architectural wonders to be imposing without also being overwhelming. The **Royal Palace** encloses the north side of the square. The current buildings date from the 16th and 17th centuries when Bhaktapur was the heart of Kathmandu Valley culture. Paintings, statues, and tapestries from this era still decorate the west wing of the palace, which now houses the **National Art Gallery.** The gallery displays intricate Newari *paubha* and Tibetan *thanka* paintings; its oldest objects are stone sculptures from as early as the 11th century. The gallery affords the best view of the palace's courtyards, most of which are closed to visitors. *(Museum open Tu-Sa 9:30am-4:30pm. Admission Rs20. No photography.)* East of the palace is the famous Garuda-crested **Golden Gate,** built in the early 18th century by King Bhupatindra Malla. The king's image caps a stone pillar facing the gate. On the other side of the gate sits the **Palace of 55 Windows**—each one of the intricately carved windows took a craftsman about 100 days to construct.

Like the palace, the temples in Durbar Sq. exemplify the remarkable craftsmanship of the Malla era. The westernmost temple in the Square, **Bansi Narayan,** is dedicated to Krishna, and its roof struts depict various incarnations of Vishnu. Across from the Golden Gate is the elephant-flanked, stone-carved **Vatsala Durga Temple.** Built in the mid-18th century in the *shikhara* style (see p. 96), this temple contains an impressive display of metalwork and carvings in wood and stone. To the left is the **Chayasilin Mandap** (Eight-Cornered Pavilion), a 1990 reconstruction based on a 100-year-old photograph of the *mandap.* Disguising the earthquake-resistant, steel reinforcements are fragments of the 18th-century original. Near the Chayasilin Mandap and opposite the Shiva Guest House, the **Pashupatinath Mandir,** the busiest of the Durbar Sq. temples, contains a 17th-century reproduction of the *linga* at Pashupatinath. Check out the especially creative erotic contortions of the couples on the roof struts. In the eastern section of the square, around the corner from the palace, are more temples and temple foundations. The most interesting of these is the 17th-century stone **Siddhi Lakshmi Temple,** with its procession of animals and people on either side of the stairs. Behind it is the larger, white, and somewhat unattractive **Fasideya Temple,** dedicated to Shiva. The two-story wood and brick buildings that surround this part of the square were once *dharamsalas.*

TAUMADHI TOL. Connected to Durbar Sq. by a short, bustling street, Taumadhi Tol, a place where architectural masterpieces and religious ceremony mingle with daily life, is Bhaktapur at its best. Musicians and daily worshippers converge on the square during the **Bisket Jatra,** Bhaktapur's renowned celebration of the new year in April. Nepal's tallest pagoda, **Nyatapola Temple,** dominates the square and can be seen from the outskirts of the city. The elegant, five-story, red pagoda was originally built in 1702 by King Bhupatindra Malla. Five pairs of stone creatures flank the stairs to the temple. Each pair is said to be 10 times stronger than the one

THANKAS FOR THE MEMORIES Hanging in shop windows, peering out at you from glass frames with their gold-painted eyes, *thankas* are everywhere in the Kathmandu Valley. Traditional *thankas* (pronounced TONG-ka, and meaning "something rolled up") are religious scroll-paintings that serve as aids for meditation in temples or at family altars. Colorful and elaborate, they are painted to comply with strict rules that dictate style and subject matter. Most *thankas* depict one of three main themes: the lives of the Buddha, *bodhisattvas*, saints, or lamas; the wheel of life; or the *mandala*. In representations of the Buddha's life, pictures start in the top left-hand corner and continue counter-clockwise. The wheel of life *thanka* depicts the various spiritual states of humankind, from sin (at the bottom) to enlightenment (at the top). The *mandala*, which shows the steps to enlightenment, is the most popular. A *thanka* might take anywhere from a week to six months to create. A *thanka* cannot be used, however, until it has been consecrated by a *lama*, who makes an inscription on the back. Most *thankas* that are sold have not been consecrated properly, and many don't meet the prescribed guidelines. If you're interested in buying one, shop around first, as sizes, quality, and prices (Rs100-40,000) vary widely.

below, starting with a pair of Malla wrestlers who look at least 10 times stronger than the average man. The image of **Siddhi Lakshmi,** the goddess to whom the temple is devoted, is locked inside and accessible only to priests. Visitors can still climb the steps for an unparalleled view of the square.

On the eastern side of the square is the bulky, three-story **Bhairabnath Mandir,** which was built as a single-story temple during the 18th century. A second floor was added later, but the 1934 earthquake leveled the structure and it was completely rebuilt with three stories. The tiny golden image over the entrance, often obscured by rice and dye offerings, is the frightful Lord Bhairab, God of Terror. Huge painted chariot wheels lean against the left side of the temple; Bhairab's head, which usually stays locked up in the temple, is carted around during Bisket Jawa celebrations. A doorway in the building at the south side of the square leads to a courtyard filled by the **Til Mahadev Narayan Mandir,** a 17th-century temple (on an 11th-century temple site) reminiscent of Changu Narayan, with its pillar-mounted painted Garuda, golden *chakra*, and *sankha*.

TACHAPAL TOL (DATTATRAYA SQUARE). A wide, curving street lined with shops links Taumadhi Tol to Bhaktapur's oldest square, Tachapal Tol. The wooden buildings that enclose the square were once *maths* (priests' residences), but they have all been converted for other uses. The ponderous **Dattatraya Mandir** presides over the eastern end of the square. Built in 1427, it is the oldest surviving building in Bhaktapur and was allegedly built from the trunk of a single gigantic tree. From the looks of it, that must have been quite a tree. Two hulking, eight-foot Malla wrestlers, gaudily painted during festivals, guard the entrance. Directly across from them, a stone cut Garuda figure kneels faithfully on a towering pillar, emphasizing the temple's connection to Vishnu. Dattatraya appeals to followers of Vishnu and Shiva as well as Buddhists, since he is considered an *avatar* of Vishnu, a guru of Shiva, and a cousin of the Buddha. At the other end of the square is the rectangular **Bhimsen Temple,** honoring a favorite god of Newari merchants.

Inside the two *math* buildings that flank the temple, there are two museums. To the left, the **Brass and Bronze Museum** displays a collection of 300-year-old functional objects such as lamps, cooking pots, hubble-bubble hookahs, spittoons, and carved ritual paraphernalia. Opposite, in the **Pujari Math,** is the **National Art Gallery Woodcarving Museum,** worth visiting more for its magnificent, sun-drenched courtyard than for its collection. Set into the eastern wall of the *math*, around the corner from the museum, is the famous **Peacock Window,** dating from the 17th century, often lauded as the paragon of Newari window-carving. It is surrounded on all sides by smaller, less ornate and sometimes decapitated fowl-themed woodcuttings. *(Admission to any one of the 3 museums allows entry to the other 2. Rs20. Open Tu-Sa 9:30am-4:30pm)*

OTHER SIGHTS. Just south of Taumadhi Tol is **Potters' Square,** where you can see potters at work behind enormous homemade wheels and hundreds of pots lined up to dry in the sun. Stroll south toward the river to see *ghats*, fields, and temples that, in contrast to those farther north, are more functional than decorative.

SHOPPING

Bhaktapur is home to some of the finest **pottery** in the valley, and while similar items are also available in Kathmandu, it's much more satisfying to purchase directly from the artisans here in Bhaktapur. The best place to meet up with potters and their collections of bowls, masks, and icons is the aptly-named **Potter's Sq.** Bhaktapur also has a long-standing reputation for fine **wooden handicrafts,** which are sold in Durbar and Tachapal Sq.

CHANGU NARAYAN चाँगु नारायण

Legend has it that many years ago a valley brahmin noticed that one of his cows was no longer giving milk. Suspicious, he kept his eye on the cow until one day, he saw a small boy materialize from a nearby *champak* tree, drink all of the cow's milk, and then disappear inside the tree again. Convinced that this was the work of a demon, the brahmin cut the tree down immediately. No sooner had he done so, however, than the tree began to bleed and the face of Narayan appeared and reprimanded him for what he had done. Mortified by his sin, the brahmin built a temple to Narayan where the tree had stood. To this day, the secluded temple has remained one of Nepal's most sacred sites.

Since its construction in the 4th century, worshipers have visited, adorned, restored, and revered this Vishnu shrine. Patched together and built upon over the centuries, the temple is a living time capsule revealing more than a millennium's worth of stylistic and artistic developments. Equally impressive are the large sculptures and polished black relief panels that cluster around the temple; these are considered among Nepal's greatest treasures. The hilltop town that surrounds this marvelous site has breathtaking panoramic views of the whole valley. The town now charges a Rs60 **entrance fee,** payable at a small shack to the left of the city gates (open daily 6am-6pm). In return for the fee, you receive a brochure containing information on the temple area.

 TRANSPORTATION. The main road into Changu Narayan leads into the new bus park. **Bus #7** departs from and arrives at Bhaktapur's minibus park, near Guhya pond (30min., Rs6). A **taxi** is the fastest way to reach Changu Narayan (Rs600 from Kathmandu; Rs300 from Bhaktapur). Otherwise, Changu Narayan is a strenuous, uphill, 45min. bike ride or 2hr. walk from Bhaktapur; follow the signs from the minibus park. Changu Narayan can also be reached via a 2hr. hike from the mountain viewpoint of Nagarkot to the east. Getting off the **Nagarkot #7 bus** at Telkot (30min., Rs5) and walking straight along the ridge will get you there in about 1½hr. You can also begin from the north side, off the road between Boudha and Sankhu, but only in the dry season (Oct.-Apr.) when the Manohara River is low enough to be forded. The **temple** is up the steps from the city gates.

⚏⚏ ACCOMMODATIONS AND FOOD. A visit to Changu Narayan works best as a day trip from Kathmandu or Bhaktapur; if for some reason you need to spend an unplanned night here, options are basic and uninspiring. The rustic **Changu Narayan Bed and Breakfast ❶,** is a harrowing 15min. hike from the temple; follow the steep set of stairs from the side of the temple farthest from town. (Rs200 per night.) A better bet is the **Changu Narayan New Hill Resort ❶,** 10min. from the bus park, along the road following the ridge. (Rs300.) Both offer basic backpacker-style accommodations. At the back of the Changu Narayan bus park sits the **Binayak Restaurant ❶.** Offering standard continental (Rs50-350) and Indian (Rs60-120) food as well as a range of drinks (Rs80-120), it's a good place to catch a light meal while waiting for your bus. Just inside the main gate sits the **Valley View Restaurant ❶,** offering dishes similar to the Binayak for Rs40-120 and great valley views.

◪ SIGHTS. Coming from town, you will enter the courtyard of the **Changu Narayan Temple** at the rear, under the gaze of two stone gryphons warning that the 7th-century golden image of Vishnu within is open to Hindus only. A brass doorway embossed with flower designs frames the entrance, and on either side of the temple, **pillars** bear the symbols of Vishnu. A life-wheel and a stone staff on the left represent brahmins and *chettris* respectively; a conch shell and lotus flower on the right represent the occupational and business castes. The inscription at the base of the pillar describes the victories of King Mahadeva. It is the oldest inscription in the valley, dating from AD 454. The **statue** of Vishnu's man-bird vehicle, Garuda, kneeling at the door with a cobra around his neck, was carved at about the same time. His face is said to be a likeness of King Manadeva himself, who reputedly said that he too was a vehicle for Vishnu. In the **birdcage** over Garuda's shoulder are two more recent figures, Bupathindra Malla and Bubana Lakshmi, the 17th-century king and queen of Bhaktapur who introduced metalwork to the temple by financing the ornate copper doorway.

The best sculptures are clustered around the **Lakshmi Narayan Temple,** past the pillar to the right of the main temple. In the central relief, Vishnu as Narasimha, half-man and half-lion, tears a hole in the chest of a demon. To its left, another relief shows the story of Vishnu as Vamana, the dwarf who grew to celestial size and crossed the earth and the heavens in three steps. On the **platform,** next to the Lakshmi Narayan Temple, is an image of Vishnu as Narayan, sleeping on a knotted snake. The ten-headed, ten-armed figure above Narayan depicts the universal face of Vishnu, showing each of his 10 *avatars.* Opposite the platform is an image of a ten-armed Vishnu, known as **Maha Vishnu,** with his consort Lakshmi sitting in his lap. Across the courtyard, near the temple's left pillar is the **sculpture of Vishnu** atop his *vahana,* Garuda. All of these sculptures date from the Licchavi period, before the Mallas took over in 1200 and when stone sculpture in the valley was at its height (see **Malla Kingdoms,** p. 756).

DHULIKHEL धुलिखेल ☎011

From its lofty position at 1550m, Dhulikhel routinely delivers spectacular Himalayan sunrises. But in contrast with its more touristy neighbor Nagarkot, Dhulikhel is also a living, breathing Nepali town, as its lively streets and squadrons of school-children attest. Hikers and bikers alike come to this eastern mountain town to explore the wilderness beyond. In the surrounding valleys are a number of scenic villages, including **Namobuddha** and **Panauti,** ideal one-day treks from town. Dhulikhel's comfortable accommodations and natural beauty make for a pleasant stay—even when monsoon clouds obscure the snowy mountains.

⚡🚹 ORIENTATION AND PRACTICAL INFORMATION. Dhulikhel is just off the Arniko Hwy., 32km southeast of Kathmandu. From Ratna Park in Kathmandu, take **bus #12** (1½hr., frequent, Rs18), which also stops at Bhaktapur's trolleybus park and at Banepa's bus park. Past the **bus park,** the road uphill forks. The right fork leads to the Rastriya Bunijya Bank and the hospital; the left fork leads to the **town center,** where a bust of King Mahendra stands next to a water tank. Facing the bust in the center of Dhulikhel, the road to the right leads to Dhulikhel's temples and the old part of town; the road to the left leads to the Nawarnuga Guest House, the Post Office, and the Kali Shrine. The **Rastriya Banijya Bank** changes currency (open Su-Th 10am-2:50pm, F 10am-1:30pm). The **hospital** (☎61497) is 10min. away from the bus park—follow the signs to the right. (Clinic open Su-Tu and Th-F 8:30am-5pm, W and Sa emergencies only.) There are several small pharmacies along the road to town, but the hospital's well-stocked **pharmacy** is the best place to get prescriptions filled (open daily 9am-10pm). The **police station** (☎62020) is a 5min. walk from the center of town, next to the **post office** (open Su-Th 10am-5pm, F 10am-3pm), on the road to the Kali Shrine. **Dhulikhel Communications** (☎61064), just before the Nawaranga Guest House on the road to Kali, has **Internet phone** and **email** services (Rs5 per min. Open daily 7am-7pm).

🏠🍴 ACCOMMODATIONS AND FOOD. 🖼**Nawaranga Guest House ❶,** a 5min. walk up the road to the right of King Mahendra's bust, is a backpacker's haven. It makes up for what it lacks in luxury with an uncommonly friendly and hospitable atmosphere. The superb restaurant serves authentic Nepali dishes (entrees Rs15-90) and doubles as an art gallery exhibiting the works of a local painter. (☎61226. Dorms Rs75; singles Rs125; doubles Rs200.) If you've come to see mountains, **Panorama View Resort ❶,** is your best bet. Up the hill below the Kali shrine (3km from the bus park), this place has large doubles with balconies and clean bathrooms with hot showers and seat toilets. The restaurant offers unrestricted views of the Himalayas from east to west. (☎62085. Doubles US$10, with attached bath US$12. Reservations recommended in season.) On the main road just north of the bus park is the **Dhulikhel Royal Guest House ❷.** The rooms vary in size and amenities, but they're all clean and comfortable. The attached restaurant doubles as a TV parlor; treat yourself to any of the movies in the guest house's obscure collection, which includes such neglected classics as "Lost in Siberia." (☎64059. Singles US$6-12; doubles US$10-20.) **Dhulikhel Lodge ❶,** 10min. down the hill from the bus park, has 20 large rooms with common bath and seat or squat toilets. (☎61753. Singles Rs300; doubles Rs500.) The restaurant serves Nepali, Chinese, and Italian meals (Rs55-160).

📷 SIGHTS AND SUNRISES. The spectacular sunrise over the mountains is the main draw in Dhulikhel, and the most popular place to watch it from is the **Kali Shrine.** To reach the shrine, follow the road past the post office, and then take the right fork up the hill; the hike takes about 45min. from the center of town. Dhulikhel's cobblestoned **main square** is also worth exploring. The square's two temples honor two different forms of Vishnu: the triple-roofed temple surrounded by a metal fence is dedicated to Harisiddhi, while the brightly tiled one in the middle of the square honors Narayan. Stumble a few steps northwest, past the brick and lumber construction rubble, to the pagoda-like **Bhagwati Mandir,** which is more interesting as a lookout than as a temple.

🔑 NEAR DHULIKHEL. Dhulikhel is the popular starting point for a number of one-day treks, the most established of which is the **Namobuddha circuit,** with the option of ending at **Panauti.** The Dhulikhel Lodge's helpful map can be picked up at almost any guest house for free. *Namobuddha* means "hail to the Buddha"—it is

NEPAL

the place where he supposedly offered his body as food to a starving tigress. In addition to a small but Swayambhunath-esque *stupa*, this area is also home to a number of monasteries and a small tea shop, making this an ideal place to take a break and observe the daily rituals of the local Buddhist monks. Namobuddha is 3hr. from Dhulikhel, 2hr. past the Kali Shrine along the same unpaved road. It's possible to take an alternative path back in Dhulikhel, but the 1hr. hike to **Panauti**, a quiet Newari village famous for its wood carvings, is equally rewarding. Its impressive array of temples and its idyllic setting at the junction of two streams make it a great daytrip. In the center of town is the **Indreshwar Mahadev Temple,** which, with its delicately carved roof struts and *toranos,* may be the oldest in Nepal. The triple-roofed **Krishna Narayan** temple sits at the junction of the town's two rivers. Across the river, by the suspension bridge, the 17th-century **Brahmayani Temple** honors the village's chief goddess. **Buses** run from Panauti to Banepa (20min., frequent, Rs4) and from there to Dhulikhel and Kathmandu, so a one-way trek is possible. The road along the hillside from Dhulikhel to Bhaktapur is ideal for **mountain biking.** From the bus park, follow the main highway away from town and then follow the signs to Bhaktapur. There are no bike rental facilities in Dhulikhel, so it is best to rent in Kathmandu. You can bring your bike on the bus (the driver will attach it to the roof for you) or put it in the back of a taxi.

NAGARKOT नगरकोट

Teetering 2175m above the eastern rim of the Kathmandu Valley, Nagarkot is the popular Himalayan viewpoint from which, in clear weather, you can see Mt. Everest. Tourism has spurred the development of Nagarkot beyond its origins as a military base. Today, hundreds descend upon the many guest houses, not to plot troop maneuvers, but to trace the path of the sun as it ascends over the Himalayas. There are several day treks down to neighboring villages that offer more authentic views of Nepali life than those in foreigner-filled Nagarkot. On the bus ride up, if you can bear to look out the window as the bus careens around hairpin turns, you'll see patterned rice and corn plots etched into the hillside next to uncultivated hills. Monsoon season is not the best time to visit unless you're a fan of cold air and averse to mountain views.

▐ TRANSPORTATION. Local **bus #7** travels from **Kathmandu** to Nagarkot via **Bhaktapur.** In Kathmandu, catch it at Bagh Bazaar (2hr., every 20min., Rs18); in Bhaktapur, from the Kamal Binayak bus stop in the northeast (1hr., every 30min., Rs10). The last bus leaves Nagarkot at 6pm. **Tourist buses** leave from Kantipath in Kathmandu (1½hr., 1:30pm, round-trip Rs180) and return from Nagarkot the next morning. Tickets can be bought at any agency in Thamel. **Taxis** from Kathmandu cost about Rs850, from Bhaktapur Rs500.

▐▌ ORIENTATION AND PRACTICAL INFORMATION. Nagarkot consists of an ever-growing cluster of guest houses grouped along a **ridge.** The road from Bhaktapur forks at the base of a hill, where a large **map** charts Nagarkot's guest houses. The road that curves to the right leads to **The Tea House, Club Himalaya,** and the **lookout tower.** The road that curves north around the left side of the hill leads to the bank, the rest of Nagarkot's guest houses, and the high point of the ridge marked by the tiny **Mahakal Shrine.** The **bus stop** is at the fork in the road. **Himalayan Bank Ltd.** exchanges currency and traveler's checks (☎680049. Open M-F 9:30am-3:30pm.) The nearest **hospital** is in Bhaktapur. **Club Himalaya** (☎680083) has Internet services for Rs15 per min., and international telephone services. **Sherpa Alpine Lodge** (☎680015) offers Internet services for Rs10 per min. The **tourist police** can be reached at ☎247041, 9am-5pm.

⚑⚐ ACCOMMODATIONS AND FOOD. As the hotel strip above the clouds expands, true budget lodges are becoming something of an endangered species, though prices are negotiable, especially off season. The following hotels cling to the ridge below the Mahakal Shrine. **The Hotel Madhuban ❷**, has a collection of compact A-frame cottages as well as larger and more expensive "standard" rooms. (☎ 680114. Rooms Rs448-746; cottages Rs300) The glassed-in dining room (entrees Rs40-200) has good views. **The Hotel at the End of the Universe ❷**, is one of Nagarkot's originals. The brick and bamboo bungalows are simple but comfortable. Reservations recommended in season. (☎ 680011; oasis@umpire.com. Doubles with common bath Rs600, attached bath Rs1120-1867.) **The Hotel Galaxy ❸**, offers clean, simple rooms with attached or common baths (☎ 680122, singles Rs374-746, doubles Rs523-1493) as does the **Sherpa Alpine Lodge ❷** (☎ 680015, all rooms Rs350). The newly-opened **Naked Chef ❸**, boasts sparkling facilities (☎ 680115, all doubles with attached baths Rs500-1000) and the fully-clothed waiters at the adjacent restaurant serve decent but pricey continental/Indian food (entrees Rs165-275).

Most hotels have adjoining restaurants serving identical, mediocre tourist food; marginally better grub tends to carry exorbitant prices. **The Tea House ❷**, just below Club Himalaya, is Nagarkot's most elegant place to eat. The plate-glass windows offer terrific views to compliment continental (Rs175-225) and Indian and Nepali dishes (Rs80-200). The **Restaurant at the End of the Universe ❶**, attached to the similarly titled resort, serves hitchhikers from all over the galaxy a typical continental variety of entrees. (Burgers, chicken, and rice Rs50-200.)

◪ SIGHTS. The hip thing to do in Nagarkot is to watch the sun rise above the hills and set behind the valley as it washs the mountain peaks in pink light. While all the guest houses have great views, there are some particularly fine lookout points in the area. You can walk up to the tiny **Mahakal Shrine,** right next to the **End of the Universe,** or sit at one of the benches in the brick-paved area between the Tea House and Club Himalaya. The best views are from the **lookout tower,** a leisurely 1hr. stroll south past Club Himalaya and the army base (ask around to make sure it's open). Alternatively, many hotels sell tickets for a pre-dawn tourist bus to the tower (Rs100). Lodge owners enthusiastically offer directions for walks to **Changu Narayan** (2hr.), **Sankhu** (2hr.), **Dhulikel** (5hr.), and **Shivapuri** (2-3 days).

SANKHU साँरव

A comfortable distance away from hectic Kathmandu, Sankhu is an otherwise uninteresting Newari town worth only the walk up to the nearby **Vajra Vogini Mandir.** The temple, built in the 17th century on an ancient Buddhist site, stands as a testament to Nepal's unique fusion of Hinduism and Buddhism. A fierce manifestation of Kali, Vajra Jogini has long been revered by Buddhists as a protector. Some say she convinced Manjushri to drain the water-filled Kathmandu Valley. Another legend suggests that she requested the construction of the Boudha *stupa* and sent a white crane to select its location. She has since been adopted as a tantric goddess, representing for Newari Buddhists the powerful female characteristics of the Buddha, while Hindus in the valley worship her as a form of Durga. The temple has three main copper roofs and a beautifully carved door with images from the Buddhist pantheon. The smaller two-tiered temple enshrines a replica of the Swayambhunath *stupa*. A cement cave used for tantric rituals lies at the end of a short trail near the entrance.

The 2km walk from town starts through the cement archway to the left of the bus stop and continues through the smaller archway at the town's edge, passing by ancient Newari brick houses covered in flamboyant woodcarving. About halfway to the temple, it continues to the right, while a stone-paved footpath leads straight ahead. While both lead to the temple, the dirt road is slightly longer though perhaps more scenic. The two meet again at the base of the long, steep stairway to the top of the hill. From the base of the stairs, it's an arduous 15min. climb to the top.

Bus #4 (1½hr., frequent, Rs10) departs Ratna Park in Kathmandu for Sankhu and also stops east of Boudha. Sankhu is also accessible by **bicycle** (the road from Kathmandu is flat, and fairly free of pollution beyond Boudha) or on **foot,** along a northwest trail from Nagarkot. It is also possible to walk between Sankhu and Changu Narayan in the dry season.

DAKSHINKALI दक्षिण काली

Most days of the week, "Southern Kali" looks pretty much like any other quiet little town on the fringes of the Kathmandu Valley. It takes on a very different personality, though, every Tuesday and Saturday morning, between 7-10am, when the town hosts the famous Dakshinkali **animal sacrifices,** bloody offerings to propitiate the patron goddess Durga (also known as Kali). Brightly clad women and men with doomed roosters, goats, sheep, and ducks queue up to offer their animals at the shrine, which is enclosed by a low metal railing and sits beneath a metal canopy suspended by four brass *nagas*. Inside the shrine, there is a small black image of Kali standing victorious atop a corpse, hardly visible to tourists who are allowed only on the walkways above. The image was installed in the 17th century by King Pratap Malla, purportedly on the orders of the goddess herself, though Durga worship had taken place at the site long before that. Piped Nepali pop music blasts cheerfully from loudspeakers, providing a surreal, pounding rhythm to the carnivalesque procession. Devotees wash their animal offerings in the stream behind the shrine before making the sacrifice. If the animals do not attempt to shake off the water poured over their heads (unlikely, really), they cannot be sacrificed. It's believed that animals killed in sacrifice will enjoy the reward of higher incarnation. Those offered during the eighth and ninth days of the festival of **Dasain,** the October celebration of the triumph of good over evil, are relieved from burdensome animal life and reincarnated as humans. When it reaches the image of Kali, the animal's throat is cut, and its blood splatters onto the idols. The animal's head is given as payment to the butchers—the body is considered *prasad* (blessed) and becomes the main course at a family picnic in the surrounding hills. Signs from the Dakshinkali temple lead to the nearby **Mata Temple,** which is unremarkable except for its view of the nearby hills.

Bus #22 runs from Ratna Park in Kathmandu to Dakshinkali (1½hr., Tu and Sa, Rs15). Huge crowds and small numbers of buses mean you'll have to get to the bus station very early if you want to see the sacrifices. Alternatively, the journey can be made by **taxi** (Rs500, round-trip). Either way, the tortuous ride up through hillside homes and fields has stunning valley views. Stay on the bus past Pharping, the deceptive Dakshinkali Cold Store, and the "Welcome to Dakshinkali" sign. Wait until the bus pulls into a parking lot filled with about 100 motorcycles. When the beleaguered busload of folks and fowl get off, you know you've arrived. If you've left your sacrifice back in Thamel, don't worry: the stands which line the walkway to the staircase down to the temple sell uncastrated roosters, the vegetables and spices that will later condiment them, and sacrificial accessories.

NEPAL

MET A YETI YET? Some believe he's the brutish lovechild of a lusty primate dominatrix and a hapless village man; others claim he's the missing link, a naked Hindu ascetic, a maligned *bodhisattva* whose head glows with a curious light, or a man-eating monkey marauding around the Himalayas. No one's really sure, but the elusive, hairy **Yeti** has been keeping tabloids, folk storytellers, and conspiracy theorists in business for years. Yetis have been spotted as far away as Indonesia and Mongolia–perhaps on their way to family reunions with their Western Wildman cousins, the Pacific Northwest's Bigfoot and Australia's Yowie–but they are most frequently spotted around Everest's Khumbhu region by the Sherpa villagers who gave them the name. "Yeti" may be a corrupt form of *Yati*, the Hindi word for "hermit," but the mysterious critter goes by at least a dozen different names. Newari myth tells of the *Khya*, a furry mischief-maker who lurks in dark rooms and tickles people to death. Likely to be seen throwing and eating yaks, the Yeti is unnaturally fond of imitating humans, giving rise to folktales telling of villagers who have tricked them into lighting themselves on fire or hacking each other to death with khukuri knives. Since a glimpse of a Yeti condemns the yeti-spotter to fatally bad luck, there seem to be few firsthand Yeti sightings, although the overeager Yeti-search teams of the 1950s and 1960s certainly tried hard enough to find one. In 1960, Sir Edmund Hillary brought a Yeti scalp to Western scientists, who promptly dismissed it as the rump of a Himalayan blue bear. Sightings are increasingly rare, however–the closest thing to abominable snowmen these days seems to be the hairy, yak-eating, big-footed western trekkers lumbering aimlessly in the mountains.

NEAR DAKSHINKALI

Tucked beneath an overhanging limestone cliff and surrounded by clear pools, the **Sekh Narayan Temple** is a roadside oasis just north from Dakshinkali. Built during the 17th century to honor Vamana (the dwarfish 5th incarnation of Vishnu), the temple has been dutifully maintained, and its bold, bright colors give it a surreal appearance. Next door is a 20th-century Tibetan Buddhist **monastery.**

To reach the Sekh Narayan Temple from Dakshinkali, walk on the main road out of the parking lot for 45min. A half-mile past Pharping, you'll reach a cluster of pools on your left, behind which are the stairs to the temple. You can catch the bus back to Kathmandu from Pharping, though it might be difficult to get a seat.

THE WESTERN HILLS

Modern-day Nepal was conceived in the hills west of Kathmandu, where 250 years ago King Prithvi Narayan Shah of Gorkha had a vision of a unified country. The central Himalayas, dominated by Machhapuchhare and the Annapurna range, provide a magnificent backdrop to one of the most popular regions of Nepal.

HIGHLIGHTS OF THE WESTERN HILLS

Nepal's second-most visited city, lakeside **Pokhara** (p. 824), lies in a beautiful subtropical valley overshadowed by the dazzling Annapurna massif.

The hill towns of **Tansen** (p. 821) and **Gorkha** (below) offer beautiful respite from Nepal's tourist mainstream.

Have your wishes fulfilled at the ridge-top temple of **Manakamana** (p. 820), now accessible by Nepal's first cable car.

NEPAL

GORKHA गोर्खा ☎ 064

A clutch of small residences scattered over a hillside, quiet and rural Gorkha seems an unlikely birthplace for modern Nepal, but it was from here that Prithvi Narayan Shah initiated the military rampage that eventually unified the nation. Spectacularly positioned on a hillside halfway between Pokhara and Kathmandu, Gorkha was ruled by a succession of small kingdom-states until Prithvi Narayan, a direct ancestor of the present king, left his home in Gorkha to conquer the Kathmandu valley. After 24 bloody years of fighting, he finally succeeded. Shah's mighty soldiers were the first to be called "Gorkha," a name that eventually came to be used for all Nepalese soldiers. These fierce fighters were recruited by the British Army and now make up a significant minority in the Indian Army. Gorkha's history is enshrined in the hilltop Gorkha Durbar, birthplace of Prithvi Narayan.

At the end of a paved road to the Kathmandu-Pokhara highway, Gorkha forms a link between many sleepy mountain villages and the outside world, and is a starting point for treks in the Annapurnas (see p. 854). Still comfortably untouristed, Gorkha's historic palace and sweeping mountain views make it a great place to take a break from a journey between Kathmandu and Pokhara.

📠 TRANSPORTATION

All **buses** from Gorkha go through **Anbu Khaireni,** a few kilometers west of Mugling, where the Gorkha road meets the Kathmandu-Pokhara highway. **Prithvi Rajmarg Bus Syndicate**, a private company that runs most of the buses, has a booth in the bus park marked by a red sign. (☎ 20323. Open daily 5:30am-5:30pm.) To: **Anbu Khaireni** (1hr., frequent 6am-6pm, Rs25); **Bhairawa/Sunauli** (7hr., 7am, Rs180); **Birganj** (7hr., 4 per day 6:30-11:20am, Rs145); **Kathmandu** (5hr., 9 per day 6:15am-2:30pm, Rs90-105); **Narayanghat** (3hr., 7 per day 8:45am-2:40pm, Rs50-65); **Pokhara** (3hr., 6 and 9:15am, Rs80); **Tandi,** for **Royal Chitwan National Park** (3hr., 3:10am and 3:40pm, Rs60). **Sajha Yatayat** (☎ 20106), next to the bus park, runs government buses to **Kathmandu** (5hr., 6:45am and 1:30pm).

🔆🛈 ORIENTATION AND PRACTICAL INFORMATION

Gorkha has evolved into three distinct sections. The newest part of town, only 15 years old, is centered on the **bus park.** The second area, about a century old, winds uphill from the bus park past three small shrines and into the **main street.** An hour's walk up the hill is the third section, which consists of the majestic **Gorkha Durbar.**

Currency Exchange: Rastriya Banijya Bank (☎ 20155). At the east end of the older part of town, just below the post office; its on your right as you follow the narrow street. Open Su-Th 10am-5pm, F 10am-1:15pm.

Police: From the bus park, walk downhill for 5min., turn right at the "Om Shanti Chowk" sign, and walk down the unpaved road; both forks in the road converge on the **police station** (☎ 20199), the white bldg. straight ahead.

Pharmacy: New Gorkha Medical Center (☎ 20116). Opposite Hotel Gorkha Prince. Open Su-F 7am-8pm, Sa 7am-noon.

Hospital: (☎ 20208). From the bus park, go 5min. downhill on the main road; after the Hotel Gorkha Bisauni, turn left onto the 1st paved road and walk 5min. uphill. The hospital (yellow with red stripes) has bare-bones facilities.

Telephone: Hotel Gorkha Prince and **Hotel Gorkha Bisauni** have free callbacks.

Internet: Sigma Communications, 20m down the road from the post office. Will type and send email (Rs25 per page). Open daily 6am-5pm.

Post Office: (☎ 20112). At the end of the older section of town; walk past the stone steps that lead to the palace and continue up the steep dirt road. Open Su-Th 10am-5pm, F 10am-3pm.

ACCOMMODATIONS

Hotel Gorkha Prince (☎ 20131). 100m downhill from the bus park; the hotel, marked by a red signboard, is on the left. Spacious rooms around a courtyard, friendly staff, STD/ISD service, a rooftop restaurant, and a tidy common room with MTV. Attached and common bathrooms. Dorms Rs80; singles Rs125-250; doubles Rs200-350. ●

Milan Guest House, 100m west of the bus park, down the asphalt road. A tad cleaner than the other cheapies around the bus park, Milan still has only concrete cells with barred windows. Singles Rs100; doubles Rs200. ●

FOOD

Fulpati Restaurant, at the Gurkha Inn, 120m down main road from bus park, on right. Great views, a beautiful garden, and tasty food make this Gorkha's best place to eat. Set breakfasts Rs90-160, Nepalese/Indian/Chinese food Rs35-140. The potato chili (Rs45) will bring tears to your eyes. 10% tax added to bill. Open daily 6am-10pm. ●

Gorkha Prince Rooftop Restaurant, at the Hotel Gorkha Prince. Rooftop setting, friendly service, and low prices on all your favorites. *Dahl bhat* set meal Rs75, veg. chow mein Rs30, and all the rest of the team Rs30-100. Open daily 7am-10pm. ●

Garden Restaurant, at the Hotel Gorkha Bisauni. Classy terrace, good views, and a decent tourist menu. Set meals Rs120-195, burgers Rs60-80, veg. curry Rs35. ●

SIGHTS

GORKHA DURBAR. Straddling the high ridge above Gorkha, this grand palace is where Prithvi Narayan Shah was born in 1722 after his mother had a dream in which she swallowed the sun. The ambitious prince was crowned at the age of 21, and within two years had set out to conquer the Kathmandu Valley, never to return to his birthplace. Though the exact date of its construction is uncertain, the palace is believed to have been built eight generations prior to Prithvi Narayan's birth, under the reign of Ram Shah (1606-1636). The city of Gorkha was ignored by the Shah Dynasty until King Mahendra returned here in 1958, although the same families of Hindu priests had continued to perform religious functions at the temples in the Durbar. The palace's present priests are direct descendants of those who served during (and before) Prithvi Narayan's rule. As you enter the palace complex, the first building on your left is the **Kalika Temple;** the cobblestones on the path leading to it are often sticky with the blood from the boisterous bi-monthly sacrifices. Just past it is the **main palace;** Prithvi Narayan's **throne** is visible through a tiny window, and the Shah dynasty's **eternal flame** supposedly burns inside; too bad the palace interior is closed to visitors. For all their martial prowess, the Gorkhalis sacrificed architectural flair; the palace was designed and built by Newars and carted in from Kathmandu. The Himalayas dominate the horizon, and you can see more of the mountains from the palace than you can from Pokhara. There's an even better view from the top of Upallokot, another 30min. up the stone stairway past the Hanuman Bhanjyang. *(Follow the main street through t he older section of town and take the stone stairway on the left. The road forks several times; stick to the right and you'll reach the palace in about 1hr. Open daily 6am-6pm. Cameras and leather articles, including belts and shoes, are not allowed inside the compound—you might want to bring flip-flops to walk around on the sticky floor.)*

NEPAL

OTHER SIGHTS. From the bus park, the wide, stone-paved street leads up to the **Rani Pokhari** (Queen's Pond), a terrace with a sunken pool. To the right of the pond are three small **temples.** The white onion-domed temple closest to the pond is dedicated to Vishnu. A statue of Prithvi Pati Shah, Prithvi Narayan's father, caps a stone pillar facing the temple. Just behind it is a two-tiered Krishna temple. The white *shikara*-style temple tucked behind the other two honors Ganesh. Continuing on the stone road past the temples, you will come to an open square. On the left is the **Bhimsen Mandir,** which draws crowds of pilgrims for the Janai Purnima festival in August. During the full-moon celebrations, Brahmins change their sacred threads (called *janai*) and others stick-dance and bathe at the communal water taps. The brown gateway on the right leads to the magnificent **Tallo Durbar Palace,** built between 1835 and 1839 by King Rajendra in a failed attempt to lure his older son away from Kathmandu to succeed him at the throne. A **museum park** honoring Prithvi Narayan and the Shah dynasty has been under construction for years. Ask to be shown the interior courtyard of the palace, full of exquisite woodcarving. The streets in the older part of the city are worth a wander. They're pleasantly clean, thanks to the Gorkha Youth Movement for the Environment and the strategic distribution of trash cans marked "Give me dust."

NEAR GORKHA

◪ MANAKAMANA मनकामना

It is claimed that the goddess Manakamana's choice of a remote, rugged hilltop for an earthly abode was her way of testing the resolve of her devotees. Her plan, however, has been foiled by the arrival of Nepal's first and only cable car system, US$6 million of Swiss engineering that runs from Cheres, 5km east of Mugling on the road to Kathmandu, to the top of the 1300m ridge where the temple stands.

The wife of Gorkha king Ram Shah (r. 1606-1636) had divine powers that she concealed from all but one of her devotees, Lakhan Thapa. Mr. Thapa was understandably distraught when she committed *sati* on the funeral pyre of her husband, but she had promised him that she would reappear soon, in fulfilment of his wishes. When, months later, a farmer came across a stone oozing milk and blood, Lakhan Thapa took this to be the promised reappearance. The stone is at the shrine of the **Devi of Manakamana** temple (it has stopped oozing), and its current attendant is a 17th-generation descendant of Lakhan Thapa. Because Manakamana Devi is known as the wish-fulfilling goddess, it's not surprising that she is pretty popular around these parts. Half a million visitors come here every year, sacrificing goats and chickens. (Inner sanctum closed to non-Hindus.)

The town itself is a sizable cluster of shops, and although many of the hilltop accommodations are geared to the local market, there are still plenty of mediocre guest houses with English-speaking staff. **Hotel Satkar ❶,** has pleasantly airy rooms. (☎60052. Doubles with squat toilet Rs200.) The **Hotel Minar ❶,** is friendly and has basic doubles. (☎29300. Doubles Rs200.) The **Alpine Hotel ❶,** has bigger rooms and a passable restaurant. (☎40002. Doubles Rs300. Restaurant open daily 6am-10pm.)

A visit to Manakamana can be done as a daytrip on the way between Kathmandu and either Pokhara or Gorkha: just ask the bus driver to drop you at the cable car. The ride takes about 3½hr. from Kathmandu or Pokhara and 1½hr. from Gorkha. Ascend the mountain in the **cable car,** which opened in November 1998. The 10min. ride to the top is positively surreal, gliding over terraced greenery and small hamlets untouched by the space-age incursion overhead. *(Open daily 9am-noon and 1:30-5pm. Round-trip Rs800. To return to Kathmandu, hop on any east-bound vehicle.)*

TANSEN (PALPA) तानसेन ☎075

It is hard to believe that a jewel like Tansen, 1370m up in the Mahabarat range, has remained untouched by the traffic between Pokhara and Sunauli. In this bustling town, with its remarkable architecture, amazing scenery, near-perfect climate, and cobblestone streets, simply going for a walk is a pleasant adventure. Tansen was once the capital of the mighty kingdom of Palpa, which first prospered under the 16th-century Sen kings and eventually grew to encompass most of the area from Mustang to the Terai. From its assimilation into the kingdom of Nepal in the early 19th century until the fall of the Ranas in 1951, Tansen served as an honorable place of exile for troublesome, power-hungry members of the royal family. Now simply the central marketplace of the Palpa district, Tansen is still one of Nepal's tidiest and most endearing hill towns, with exquisite views of the Chure hills to the south and the Himalayas to the north.

TRANSPORTATION

A counter in the northeastern corner of the **bus park** sells tickets to: **Butwal** (2hr., every 25min. 6:30am-5:30pm, Rs33); **Kathmandu** (10hr., 6am and 5:30pm, Rs227); **Pokhara** (8hr., 6 and 9am, Rs95). **Sajha Buses** sends daily buses to **Kathmandu** (10hr., 6:15am, Rs160). Their office is in Bishan Bazaar, 20m down the road to the left before Hotel the White Lake. (No phone, but dialing 20971 will get you the shop next door, which can get the bus people for you. Office open daily 5am-5:30pm.)

ORIENTATION AND PRACTICAL INFORMATION

Tansen is built on the southern slope of Srinagar Hill; uphill (toward the pine-covered peak) is always north. The **bus park** is at the southern (downhill) edge of Tansen. From here, the main road heads 10m north and then west past the **tourist office** and university campus; 500m after the university, the main road comes to a junction. Gauri Shankar Guest House is on the left; continuing right, you pass Hotel the White Lake, before reaching an intersection marked by a **police post** and the **post office**. A steep, unmotorable road leads downhill from here to the bus park. The main road continues north, becoming **Bank Rd.** At the end of Bank Rd., another lane leads downhill to **Amar Narayan Temple.** The main road curves left to **Shital Pati,** the town's central square, marked by a white gazebo-like structure.

Tourist Office: Tourist Information Center, just north of the bus park. Open Su-Th 10am-2pm. There are map signboards in the bus park and at Shital Pati.

Currency Exchange: Nepal Bank, Bank Rd. (☎20130). Near the post office. Cashes traveler's checks for a 0.5% commission (Rs50 minimum) and an additional Rs40 service charge. Open Su-Th 10am-2pm, F 10am-noon.

Police: The **main police station** (☎20255 or 20215) is in Durbar Sq.

Pharmacy: Sajha Swasta Sewa Pharmacy (☎20464). Opposite the post office, has a pharmacist on call 24hr. Open Su-F 8am-7pm, Sa 10am-5pm.

Hospital: Skip the district hospital west of Tansen in favor of the **United Mission to Nepal Hospital** (☎20111 or 20489), a 10min. walk northeast of town.

Internet: Pooja Computer, Bank Rd. (☎20462). Rs10 per min. Ouch. You may want to wait until you get someplace else. Open Su-F 7am-6pm.

Post Office: At the southern end of Bank Rd. Open Su-Th 10am-5pm, F 10am-3pm. **Postal Code:** 32501.

ACCOMMODATIONS

Hotel options in Tansen are limited. There are a few good places in town and a lot of cheap hole-in-the-wall places around the bus park. As you move higher up the hill, the views improve and the prices rise accordingly.

Hotel the White Lake (☎20291; fax 20502). Carpets, fans, and thick beds, along with attached baths (seat toilets), towels, soap, and toilet paper. Cheaper rooms have shared bathrooms, but are still nice. Restaurant serves one of the broadest menus in town—set breakfasts Rs50-150; pizzas Rs75-110; non-veg. dishes Rs100-140; and beer Rs75-90. Singles Rs200-500; doubles Rs300-1000. ❷

Gautam Siddhartha Guest House (☎20280). Take a left just before Hotel the White Lake and then left again at the square. Need some "lodging and fooding"? This homely place has bare, basic rooms, but it offers a cheap price and a magnificent view from the top floor. Doubles Rs150. ❶

Gauri Shankar Guest House, Shilkhan Tol (☎20150). Signs lead the way from the bus park. Follow the main road until it heads east uphill and instead go north downhill for 200m. Bright, well-maintained rooms with attached bathrooms. Good views from the rooftop terrace. Doubles Rs200-300. ❶

Hotel the Bajra (☎20443). 10m north of the bus park, is convenient for transportation but not as scenic as the other 2 places. The rooms are very clean, the staff is great, and it's far better than the hotels closer to the bus park. Attached restaurant. Dorms Rs50; singles Rs100-200; doubles Rs150-250. ❶

FOOD

The culinary scene in Tansen revolves around the magnificent Nanglo West. Other restaurants pale in comparison, both for atmosphere and food. There are plenty of cheaper options, particularly near the bus park, where simple meals are Rs25-40.

Nanglo West, Shital Pati. In a refurbished traditional bldg. Comfortable dining in the shady courtyard or on cushions in the elegant, traditional dining room upstairs. The bakery has freshly made croissants (5 for Rs25) and cinnamon danishes (Rs13), restaurant at the back has local exotica—*sukuti* (dried buffalo meat with garlic and ginger Rs50)—and international non-exotica—hamburger (Rs55). Bakery open daily 7:30am-7pm; restaurant open daily 10:30am-8:30pm. ❶

Hotel Srinagar, a 15min. walk northwest of town. On a clear day, it's money well spent—the patio dining area, on the ridge just west of Srinagar peak, has excellent views. Veg. *biryani* Rs100, chicken chili Rs110, spaghetti Rs180. Open daily 6am-11pm. ❶

Gyawali Restaurant, opposite the entrance to the Bhagwati temple under the "Hotel Deepak" sign. Serves Nepali meals at bargain prices; popular with locals. *Dahl bhat* Rs30, samosas Rs2, extraordinary veg. chow mein. Open daily 6am-10pm. ❶

SIGHTS

DURBAR SQUARE. Durbar Sq., in the center of town, can be entered from Shital Pati through **Baggi Dhoka,** a large whitewashed gate built by Palpa's first exile, Khadga Shumshere, who came here in 1891. One of the largest gates in Nepal, it was made to measure for Shumshere *and* his elephant—dismounting can be such a drag sometimes. Shumshere was also responsible for the Square's first palace, but the present blue and pumpkin-colored edifice was built by General Pratap Shumshere in 1927. You can enter less grandly through a small gate off Bank Rd. The **Tansen Durbar** currently houses Palpa's district secretariat.

AMAR NARAYAN TEMPLE. One of the oldest buildings in Tansen, the three-story Amar Narayan Temple serves as a stopover for pilgrims on their way to Muktinath. After annexing the city in 1804, Amar Singh Thapa imported Newari craftsmen and artisans and began to turn Tansen into a mini-Kathmandu. The Amar Narayan complex contains an image of Vishnu and exquisite wood carvings. It is surrounded by the 1m wide **Great Wall of Palpa,** a water tank with spouts fed by a natural spring, and a garden as popular with bats as it is with worshippers. *(From Shital Pati, follow the steep flagstone lane downhill and east through the old bazaar.)*

BHAGWATI TEMPLE. Commemorating an 1815 victory over the British, this temple hosts Tansen's largest festival, the **Bhagwati Jatra,** held in late August. An all-night celebration precedes the festival; in the morning, a chariot holding an image of Bhagwati is led through town. *(From Shital Pati. take the 1st road clockwise from Baggi Dhoka. The temple is 30m down on your left.)*

SRINAGAR HILL. The pine-forested ridge above Tansen, known as Srinagar Hill, is one of the most peaceful spots within walking distance, and the hilltop park boasts one of the longest mountain views in Nepal. The brilliant sunrises and sunsets during the week usually dazzle only a few hardy hikers. If the pre-dawn hike up the hill isn't enough to send you bouncing out of bed in the morning, consider spending the night in the park—there's an open-sided shelter and water spigot. The best place to watch the sunrise is at the east end of the park where a statue of the Buddha flanked by an elephant and a monkey stands. *(Either follow the signs up toward Hotel Srinagar, but head east instead of west when you arrive at the ridge, or follow the steps up to the park from behind the United Mission Hospital. It takes about 20min. to climb the hilltop from town and 20min. to traverse the ridge between the park and Hotel Srinagar.)*

OTHER SIGHTS. A few minutes south of Amar Narayan, the **Tundikhel,** a large field used for sports and big events, marks the southeastern edge of town. Next to it is the rose-filled **Birendra Park.** The town also has several other temples—of special note are the **Mahachaitya Bihar** and a **Ganesh Temple** with a beautiful brass door. *(Opposite each other, a 5min. walk west of Shital Pati. Follow the road past the Bhagwati Temple, and take a right up the cobblestone street when the road forks.)* The road directly north of Shital Pati leads to another **Ganesh Temple,** set into the hillside. A short, steep flagstone path leads past the **Jama Masjid Mosque** to the small red-and-white temple, which affords good views of the city below. *(Follow the road north of Shital Pati for 30m, but when the road curves left, just keep going straight up the narrow cobblestone street.)*

▟ SHOPPING

A few locally produced goods deserve special mention. Tansen's Newari craftsmen employ the lost-wax method in their remarkable **metalwork;** the Tansen *kuruwa,* a bronze water jar, is particularly well-known (Rs250-900). The *dhaka,* woven by women in Tansen and the surrounding hills, is also noteworthy. Several handicraft associations in town, especially along Bank Rd., sell shawls (Rs250-1000), *topis* (hats, Rs25-150), and handbags (Rs25-150) produced from this cloth.

▛ DAYTRIP FROM TANSEN

RANIGHAT

Follow the road up from Tansen toward Hotel Srinagar and then descend Srinagar Hill on the other side. You're bound to get a little lost heading down the mountain, but locals can point you in the right direction. It takes 2-3hr. to get to Ranighat and 3-4hr. to get back. The hike back uphill toward Tansen can be grueling; think of it as a warm-up for a trek.

NEPAL

Known as the "Taj Mahal of Nepal," Ranighat was built around the turn of the century by Khadga Shumshere as a monument to his wife and was designed by British planners. This opulent mansion is presently under restoration resulting in its half-crumbling, half-glistening white appearance. While the interior is mostly bare, there are plenty of rooms, doors, and balconies which make for some fun exploration. If Ranighat itself, set by the pebbly white shore of the Kali Gandaki river, is not enough to get you excited, the walk there is even better than the destination. The energetic hike leads you through a sub-tropical valley surrounded on all sides by looming mountains and populated by hardy Magar subsistence farmers.

POKHARA पोखरा ☎ 061

The starting point for treks in the Annapurna region, the heart of the country's river-rafting industry, and a stunning part of the world in its own right, Pokhara is second only to Kathmandu as Nepal's most popular tourist destination. Over 300 hotels, countless souvenir shops and trekking agencies, and a multitude of Westerners make Pokhara's Lakeside district a strange little world all its own.

It is difficult to grow accustomed to Pokhara's impossible skyline. Behind the local hills (which would count as mountains anywhere else) loom the gargantuan white peaks of the Annapurna Massif. But Pokhara isn't only about mountains: its name derives from the Nepali word for "pond," *pokhari*. Pokhara Valley, like the Kathmandu Valley, was once one huge lake. Today, only three lakes—Phewa, Begnas, and Rupa—remain. The Gurungs, the true "natives" of the region, used to live on the hilltops surrounding the valley. Only when Newari traders—traffickers of salt between Kathmandu, Bandipur, and Dhankuta—settled in Pokhara did a city begin to rise on the banks of the Seti River. They built the Bindyabasini Temple in the 16th century, by far the oldest structure in Pokhara. More recent development began with the construction of two highways during the 1970s—one connecting Pokhara to Kathmandu, the other linking it to India. With the infrastructure in place, hotels, restaurants, and adventure-seeking tourists soon followed.

⊠ INTERCITY TRANSPORTATION

Flights: The **airport** is on the Siddartha Hwy., between the bus park and the lake. Taxi fares from the airport to Lakeside are fixed (Rs100), but bargain for rides to the airport (Rs50-80). **Buddha Air** (☎21429; open daily 8am-6pm), **Mountain Air** (☎21834; open daily 7am-7pm), and **RNAC** (☎21021; open daily 10am-5pm) all have offices near the airport, on the road leading to Lakeside. **Gorkha Airlines** (☎25971; open daily 8am-6pm), **Cosmic Air** (☎32039; open daily 7am-6pm), **Yeti Airlines** (☎30016; open daily 9am-5:30pm), and **Necon Air** (☎25211; open daily 8am-6pm) are along the highway north of the airport. Private companies all fly to **Kathmandu** for the same rate (30min., frequent 9:20am-3:50pm, US$67). RNAC flies there cheaper (US$61), as well as to **Jomsom** (25min., 7am, US$50) and **Manang** (20min.; Sa-Su, Tu, and Th 8am; US$50). Cosmic also offers daily flights to Jomsom (7and 8am, US$61), and Necon flies to **Bhairwa** (20min., 3pm, US$61). Countless travel agencies on the main road in Lakeside sell tickets for all these companies at no additional charge.

Buses: The **bus park** is a muddy hell-hole when it's wet and a dusty hell-hole when it's dry. Follow the highway 1½km north from the airport to Prithvi Chowk, a rotary intersection; turn right and go 200m to the bus park (taxi Rs60). The **day bus office** (☎32773), in the center of the muck, has one blue and one red window. Open daily 4:50am-6pm. Day buses to: **Besisahar** (6hr.; 7:25, 8:35am, and noon; Rs85-105); **Bhairawa/Sunauli** (8hr., every 30min. 5-10:15am, Rs175-230); **Gorkha** (4hr., 7 and 9:30am, Rs80); **Kathmandu** (8hr., 9 per day 5:50-11:50am, Rs135-210); **Narayanghat** (5hr., 10 per

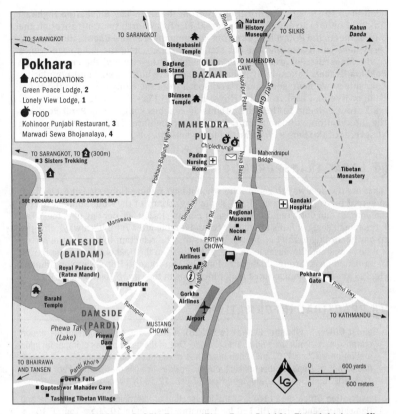

Pokhara

ACCOMODATIONS
Green Peace Lodge, **2**
Lonely View Lodge, **1**

FOOD
Kohinoor Punjabi Restaurant, **3**
Marwadi Sewa Bhojanalaya, **4**

TO SARANGKOT, TO **2** (300m)
■**3 Sisters Trekking**

SEE POKHARA: LAKESIDE AND DAMSIDE MAP

LAKESIDE (BAIDAM)

Manswara

Baidam

Royal Palace (Ratna Mandir)

Immigration

Ratnapuri

Barahi Temple

DAMSIDE (PARDI)

Phewa Tal (Lake)

Phewa Dam

Pardi Rd.

MUSTANG CHOWK

Pardi Khola

■ **Devi's Falls**
■ **Gupteshwor Mahadev Cave**
■ **Tashling Tibetan Village**

TO BHAIRAWA AND TANSEN

TO SARANGKOT

TO SARANGKOT

Bindyabasini Temple

Baglung Bus Stand

OLD BAZAAR

Bhim Bazaar

Natural History Museum

TO SILKIS

Kahun Danda

TO MAHENDRA CAVE

Nadipur Patan

Seti Gandaki River

Bhimsen Temple

MAHENDRA PUL

Chipledhunga **3**

Padma Nursing Home

Naya Bazaar

Mahendrapul Bridge

Pokhara-Baglung Highway

Tibetan Monastery

Simalchaur

New Rd.

Regional Museum

■ **Necon Air**

PRITHVI CHOWK

Yeti Airlines

Cosmic Air

i

Gorkha Airlines

Airport

Gandaki Hospital

Pokhara Gate

Prithvi Hwy.

TO KATHMANDU

Yagdhunga

N
LG

0   600 yards
0   600 meters

day 9:45am-3:20pm, Rs85); **Tansen** (7hr., 7am, Rs110). The **night bus office** (☎23564) is on the right when facing the bus park; it's up a set of stairs, under a white sign with a flag. Open daily 5am-3pm. Night buses to: **Bhairawa/Sunauli** (8-9hr., 4 per night 7:35-8:30pm, Rs205) via **Butwal** (7hr., Rs180); **Kathmandu** (8hr., every 15min. 6:30-8:45pm, Rs155). Buses heading out on the road to Baglung depart from the **Baglung Bus Stand,** at the far north end of town, north of **Mahendra Pul.** There is no such thing as a "tourist fare" no matter how much touts try to convince you that there is. To: **Baglung** (4hr., every hr. 5:30am-6pm, Rs60) via **Dhampus Phedi** (1hr., Rs30) and **Naya Pul** (2hr., Rs50); **Beni** (5hr., 5 per day 6-11am, Rs95). Travel agencies and hotels at Lakeside/Damside operate pricier and more comfortable coaches with morning departures (6:30-7:30am) from hotels. To: **Kathmandu** (Rs200); **Narayanghat** (Rs200); **Sunauli** (Rs250-300). Buses added or canceled according to demand. **Green Line Tours** (☎31472), Lakeside, is open daily 9:30am-6pm and operates luxury A/C buses (including breakfast) to **Kathmandu** (8am, Rs600) and **Chitwan** (8am, Rs480).

✦ ORIENTATION

For all its rustic feel, Pokhara is actually a huge, sprawling city. **Phewa Tal** (the lake) and **Pardi** (the dam) are the two major points of orientation—many travelers never get beyond **Lakeside (Baidam)** or **Damside (Pardi).** The residential

NEPAL

section of town is to the north, away from the lake. The **Siddhartha Highway,** linking Pokhara to India, forms a great arc from north to south through the city. It meets the **Prithvi Highway** from Kathmandu at **Prithvi Chowk,** the city center, where you'll also find the **bus station.** Farther north, the main road comes to the **Mahendra Pul** area, the historic heart of the city and the center of the **Pokhara Bazaar.** Lakeside overshadows Damside both in size and popularity. Lakeside's two main sections extend south from the campground to the Hotel Hungry-Eye and east from the Royal Palace to Fish Tail Lodge; it's a 30min. walk from one end to the other. Damside reaches south along **Pardi Rd.** from the intersection with the main Lakeside thoroughfare. There are **maps** posted at several of Pokhara's *chowks* and intersections.

📮 LOCAL TRANSPORTATION

Bikes are the best way to get around when it isn't raining. Shops in Lakeside/Damside rent bikes (Rs15 per hr., Rs40-50 per day). Many of the same shops also rent **motorcycles** and don't require a license or permit (Rs250-300 per day plus fuel). **Taxi** fares rise in season; fares are higher Sa and double after 7pm. It's always cheaper to pay according to the taxi meter. Drivers may be reluctant to turn on the meter, but be persistent. **City buses** leave every 30min. from the boat docks nearest Barahi Temple and pass through Mahendra Pul (Rs4) en route to Pritvi Narayan Campus (Rs8). Other buses run to most major locations in the city (5:30am-6:30pm).

⁇ PRACTICAL INFORMATION

Tourist Office: Siddhartha Highway (☎20028). A short walk northeast from the airport entrance or a 20min. bike ride from Lakeside. One of the best sources of impartial information on trekking. K.C., the office head, has a wealth of information on the Annapurnas as well as Nepal's other trekking routes. Provides free city maps. Open Feb. 13-Nov. 16 Su-Th 10am-5pm, F 10am-3pm; Nov. 17-Feb. 12 Su-Th 10am-4pm, F 10am-3pm.

Immigration Office: (☎21167). At the intersection of the main roads in Lakeside and Damside. Extends visas (US$50 for 1 month). Open Su-Th 10:30am-1pm, F 10am-noon; Nov. 17-Feb. 13, Su-Th 10:30am-12:30pm, F 10am-noon.

Annapurna Conservation Area Project (ACAP) Trekking Entry Permit Counter and Visitor Information: Opposite Grindlay's Bank in Lakeside. **You must purchase an entry permit (Rs2000) before trekking in the Annapurna Conservation Area.** Bring 1 passport-sized photo. The office also contains a well-informed, impartial staff as well as a number of maps, free pamphlets, and displays. The best source of information on trekking in the Annapurnas. Open mid-Feb.-mid-Nov. Su-F 9am-4:30pm and mid-Nov.-mid-Feb. Su-F 9am-3:30pm.

Passport photo: A number of places near the Trekking Entry Permit Counter will do 4 black and white photos for Rs150.

Currency Exchange: There are many authorized currency exchange counters in Lakeside and Damside. Most accept major currencies and AmEx, Visa, and Thomas Cook traveler's checks. **Nepal Grindlay's Bank** (☎20102), in northern Lakeside, just south of the campground, gives cash advances on MC and V (no commission) and cashes traveler's checks (Rs200 commission). Open Su-Th 9:45am-3pm, F 9:45am-12:30pm.

ATM: There is a 24hr. Grindlay's ATM near the Ultimate Descents office in central Lakeside. MC/V/Cirrus/Plus.

Market: The markets in the Lakeside/Damside area sell clothes, groceries, trekking equipment, and pharmaceuticals. Locals shop at the less expensive **Mahendra Pul** area (taxi Rs60-80 one-way; bike ride 20min.). **Saleway's,** in Mahendra Pul, has cheaper trekkers' food than Lakeside. Open Su-F 8am-8pm, Sa 10am-8pm.

Police: The **police station** (☎21087) is a 10min. bike ride south from the center of Lakeside; it's on the right just before the Immigration Office. There is also a frequently deserted 24hr. **Tourist Police Booth** in front of Moondance.

Pharmacy: Dozens of small pharmacies in Lakeside and Damside carry first-aid supplies for trekking; many have doctors on call. In Lakeside, the **Barahi Medical Hall** (☎22862) is well-stocked and has a doctor on call 24hr. If you need help after hours, ring the bell by the entrance. Open daily 7am-9pm.

Hospital: The **Padma Nursing Home,** New Rd. (☎20159), southwest of Mahendra Pul, has a large facility and many doctors. Open daily 7-9am and 3-7pm. For emergencies, go to the **Gandaki Hospital** (☎31954), east of Mahendra Pul, on the far side of the Seti Gandaki River. In Damside, Dr. Prakash Mishra is on call 24hr. at **Manish Medical Hall** (☎25650), on the main road 50m beyond Hotel Himali. Open daily 7am-9pm.

Internet: Internet access providers in Pokhara have formed cartels to prevent competition—the going rate is Rs5 per min. These cartels do not reach as far as Mahendra Pul, where you'll find **Cyber@City** up a little alley 30m east of Saleway's. Rs4 per min. and Rs180 per hr. Rs120 per hr. on Sa.

Post Office: The **main post office** (☎22014), on the main street in Mahendra Pul (30min. by bike; taxi Rs50-60). There is another post office nearer to Lakeside—head out of Lakeside and turn left immediately after the Immigration Office; it's on your left after 200m. Both open Su-Th 10am-5pm, F 10am-3pm. Most bookstores in Lakeside and Damside sell stamps and post letters. The **UPS Office** (☎27241), in Lakeside south of Tea Time on the side road, sends packages quickly, safely, and expensively worldwide. Open daily 8am-7pm.

▐ ACCOMMODATIONS

Lakeside bursts with travel agents, bookstores, money changers, supermarkets, and entertainment. Damside, a 15min. bike ride away, is quieter, smaller, cheaper, and has better mountain views. All hotels listed have luggage storage, laundry service, fans, STD/ISD, and noon check-out. Expect off-season discounts of up to 50%. In season, you may want to phone 2-3 days ahead. There will always be a hotel available, but you might not get your first choice.

LAKESIDE

▩ Butterfly Lodge (☎22892). Heading north on the main road, turn right at Pyramid Restaurant; on the right after 100m. A friendly atmosphere, gorgeous garden, and meticulous cleanliness right down to the shared (seat!) toilet. Not only is it the best place to stay in Pokhara, but all profits go to the Child Welfare Scheme, which runs day-care and health care centers in the Annapurnas. Dorms Rs100; doubles Rs200-1400. ❶

▩ Nature's Grace Lodge (☎27220). 50m beyond the Butterfly. Run by the same organization. Prices are the same, but the rooms are nicer. Though this place lacks the sprawling garden, a rooftop terrace and bar make up for it. All profits go to the Child Welfare Scheme. Doubles Rs200-300. ❶

Sacred Valley Inn (☎31792). On the main road, 150m south of Moondance. Excellent location—just a brief stroll to the heart of Lakeside. A slightly more upmarket option, but with big, airy rooms with rattan furniture on the balconies, you get what you pay for. Breakfast (Rs45-105) is worth the wait. Doubles Rs400-1000. ❸

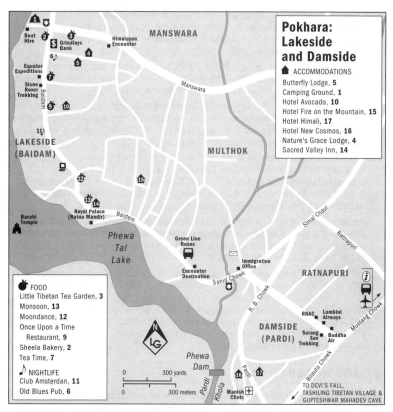

Pokhara: Lakeside and Damside

🏠 ACCOMMODATIONS

Butterfly Lodge, **5**
Camping Ground, **1**
Hotel Avocado, **10**
Hotel Fire on the Mountain, **15**
Hotel Himali, **17**
Hotel New Cosmos, **16**
Nature's Grace Lodge, **4**
Sacred Valley Inn, **14**

🍎 FOOD
Little Tibetan Tea Garden, **3**
Monsoon, **13**
Moondance, **12**
Once Upon a Time
Restaurant, **9**
Sheela Bakery, **2**
Tea Time, **7**

🎵 NIGHTLIFE
Club Amsterdam, **11**
Old Blues Pub, **6**

Hotel Fire on the Mountain (☎ 31461). A short walk from the main road, 250m south of Moondance. Peaceful, but close to the action. Beautiful garden, spacious rooms, and soft beds. Doubles Rs150-250. ❶

Hotel Avocado (☎ 23617). In the heart of Lakeside, behind Once Upon a Time. Helpful management, sparkling clean rooms, and an attractive little garden (no avocado tree). Hot water 24hr. All rooms have attached bath. Doubles Rs150-350. ❶

Hotel Cordial (☎ 25723). In north Lakeside. It's clean, has a friendly staff, a nice garden, and very cheap rooms. Doubles Rs100-500. ❶

Green Peace Lodge, about a 15min. walk north of Lakeside. Built on a small outcropping jutting into the lake, Green Peace offers the kind of serene isolation absent from central Lakeside. The rooms aren't spectacular, but the price is right and the lake view is stunning. Singles Rs100; doubles Rs150. ❶

Lonely View Lodge (☎ 26994). On a hill about 500m north of Grindlay's Bank. 4 bare rooms with soft beds in a very peaceful setting. Singles Rs130; doubles Rs180. ❶

Camping Ground (☎ 24052 or 21688). North end of Lakeside; turn left at the intersection north of Sheela Bakery and go 100m down toward the lake. Bordering the lake, with unobstructed mountain views, Pokhara's only campground is ideal in dry weather but sloppy during the monsoon. Squat toilets. Check-out 6pm. Hot showers Rs50, cold showers Rs30. Tents Rs40; vehicles Rs30-100. ❶

DAMSIDE

▧ **Hotel Himali** (☎25385). On the main road in Damside. Big rooms, a rooftop terrace, and mountain views. Also operates a trekking agency, **Fewa Treks.** Singles Rs100-150; doubles Rs150-200. ❶

Hotel Himalayan (☎21643). East off the main road in Damside, just past Manish Medical Hall. A meticulously well-kept garden, equally well-maintained rooms, and great mountain views from the balcony. Singles Rs150; doubles Rs200. ❶

Hotel New Cosmos (☎21964). Behind the main road in Damside. Great views of the lake and mountains. Try to get one of the 3 rooms with a view. Friendly, familial feel. All rooms have attached bath. Doubles Rs200-350. ❶

▟ FOOD

You won't find a lot of Nepalese food here—but with cinnamon buns, Swiss chocolate, garlic pizza, and steak *au poivre*, who's whining for *dahl bhat?*

LAKESIDE

▧ **The Little Tibetan Tea Garden,** 50m east of the main road, on the road just north of Grindlay's Bank. Authentic Tibetan food, a quiet bamboo garden, and reasonable prices put it leagues above the rooftop restaurants on the main road. Big, delicious *momos* Rs85-150, *thethuk* Rs80-120. Open daily 7am-10pm. ❶

▧ **Moondance,** central Lakeside, on the main road. Moondance is the best of Lakeside's mega-places; creative decor, good music, and board games contribute to the charm. The pub upstairs also wins top marks for after-dinner fun. Big menu ranges from pizza (from Rs120) to apple crumble (Rs80). Open daily 9am-10pm. ❶

Monsoon, on the main road, 150m south of Moondance, next to the Sacred Valley Inn. A quiet cafe run by British expats and stocked with reading material. Quiche Rs160. Only open for breakfast (Rs60-145) and lunch (Rs65-160) 7am-6pm. ❷

Tea Time, on the main road in central Lakeside. Very popular; the staff follows its "Live the life you love, love the life you live" motto. The cheapest and most subdued of the central Lakeside spots. Movies in the evening and a pool table (Rs50 per game). Big salads Rs65-190, chicken *masala* Rs160. Open daily 6am-midnight. ❷

Once Upon A Time, central Lakeside. Among the most popular restaurants in Lakeside. Bamboo motif pervades. Pleasant atmosphere and decent (if pricey) food. Entrees Rs79-199, beer Rs69-109, cocktails Rs99-149. Movies shown nightly with dinner in a barefoot sitting area (around 7pm). Open daily 7am-10pm. ❷

Sheela Bakery, in Lakeside, opposite Grindlay's Bank. Mainly serves sandwiches and pastries, but cheaper than other Lakeside bakeries. Well-garnished "cheese and tomato" sandwich Rs40, muesli Rs30, apple strudel Rs10. Open daily 6am-9pm. ❶

MAHENDRA PUL

▧ **Marwadi Sewa Bhojanalaya,** 50m east of Saleway's grocery store. Veg. Indian restaurant serving sublime *baingan bharta* (Rs35) and *masala dosa* (Rs40). Top it off with *ras malai* (Rs20) or *pera* (Rs5 per piece) for dessert. Open daily 6:30am-9pm. ❶

Kohinoor Punjabi Restaurant, in an alley behind Saleway's grocery; look for the "Club Ten" sign. Good Indian food. The chicken butter *masala* (Rs80) will have you scrambling to buy a Punjabi cookbook. *Aloo gobi* Rs40. Open daily 7:30am-10pm. ❶

👁 SIGHTS AND ACTIVITIES

A large part of Pokhara's old bazaar burned down in 1949 in a fire that spread from a *puja* at Bindyabasini Temple, so most of the architecture is very recent. Most lakeside agents (try **Encounter Destination,** ☎ 21963; open daily 8am-8pm) offer mini-bus tours of the valley. *(10am-1pm Rs130; 10am-5pm Rs150.)*

PHEWA LAKE. On an island in the middle of the lake is the **Barahi Temple.** Across the lake, the **Peace Pagoda** (still under construction) is on top of the hill. Row to the pink Hotel Fewa and take the trail behind it to the top. *(45min. hike.)* The view from this huge *stupa* is the best in the vicinity of Lakeside. Boat rental is available from a number of places in Lakeside. Largest and most convenient is the Barahi Ghat, down the road to the lake from Moondance. *(Rs130 per hr., Rs350 per day.)* The agency down the road to the lake from Tea Time also rents out kayaks *(Rs200 per hr.)* and sailboats *(Rs250 per hr, Rs800 for a half-day, Rs1200 for a full day).*

REGIONAL MUSEUM. The farmhouse-like Regional Museum showcases the cultural range of the Central Western region, like the **La Phewa** festival held every 12 years in the Thak Khola. The last one was in 1992. A number of very good displays on Nepal's diverse ethnography. *(On the road between Prithvi Chowk and Mahendra Pul, just uphill from the central Necon Air Office. Taxi from Lakeside Rs50-70; bike ride 25min. ☎ 20413. Open Sa-M and W-Th 10am-5pm, F 10am-3pm. Rs5; camera fee Rs10.)*

DEVI'S FALLS. The lake flows out at its southern end into the Pardi Khola, a stream that slices its way through the soft sedimentary rock and suddenly shoots down into a hole at Devi's Falls (known locally as **Patale Chhango** or Hell's Fall), 1km out of Pokhara, down the road toward the Indian border. Everyone agrees that the falls were named after a woman who was swept away in a 1961 flash flood, but accounts vary as to whether it was a Swiss Mrs. Devi or an American Mrs. Davis. To the left and behind the falls is a pool suitable for pre-monsoon swimming. Women should beware, however; groups of young men will insist on following. *(1km from Pokhara. Taxis from Lakeside Rs100 round-trip, 20min. by bike. Open daily 6am-6pm. Rs10.)*

GUPTESHWOR MAHADEV CAVE. Discovered in 1992, this cave contains ancient carvings and extends 3km into the earth. The first 100m are well-lit, at the end of which a large *linga* stands under cobra heads. To explore any farther you'll need a flashlight. After another 100m, the cave leads to the base of Devi's Fall. **Beware of falling rocks.** *(Across the street from Devi's Fall. Cave open daily 5am-6pm. Rs20.)*

BINDYABASINI TEMPLE. A long flight of steps leads up to Bindyabasini Temple, built during the 16th century by Newari traders who had just settled in the Pokhara Valley. The fire that engulfed Pokhara in 1949 started here. The main shrine, dedicated to Kali, is accompanied by a new Shiva temple. There is a small Buddhist monastery at the base of the steps. *(In a park at the north end of town, on the highway to Baglung. Taxis from Lakeside Rs80-90; 35min. uphill bike ride from Lakeside.)*

NATURAL HISTORY MUSEUM. There are two parts to this building. Half of it is the university's Natural History Museum with interesting displays on geology and animals the world over. There's a superb collection of Nepal's butterflies. The other half is home to the ACAP's public exhibits. It provides some valuable ethnographic detail and also highlights the hazards of over-population and heavy tourist traffic. *(At the north end of Pokhara on the Prithvi Narayan Campus. Open Su-F 10am-12:30pm and 1:30-5pm; Sept.-Feb.: 10am-12:30pm and 1:30-4pm. Free.)*

OTHER SIGHTS. The hilltop **Tibetan Monastery** ("Madepani Gampa") has excellent views of the valley. Nearby, on another hilltop, the **Bhadrakali Temple** is peaceful and shaded. *(To get to the Tibetan Monastery, cross the Seti Gandaki River at the Mahendra Pul Bridge. From the base of the Tibetan Monastery, head away from Mahendra Pul and turn right at 2 consecutive forks. Taxi from Lakeside Rs100. 1hr. by bike.)* North of Pokhara, outside the city limits, is a cave, **Mahendra Gupha.** Tunnels inside allow for a good 30min. of exploration; some parts of the cave have electricity, but take a flashlight anyway. *(Taxi Rs150. Cave Rs10. Open daily 7am-5pm.)* One kilometer up the dirt road from Mahendra Gupha is the more extensive **Bat Cave.** No batmobiles inside, but it makes for some fun climbing. *(Cave Rs10. Open daily 6:30am-6pm.)*

🔋 RAFTING AND TREKKING

Most people are drawn to Pokhara by the natural attractions beyond the city limits. Pokhara is teeming with agencies that can help you enjoy the great outdoors in safety and comfort and under the supervision of experienced guides.

Rafting expeditions run from a couple of days to nearly two weeks and generally cost US$35-60 per person per day. Rates should include equipment rental, guides, instruction, food, and transportation. Be wary of cheap deals; you get what you pay for. Routes on the challenging **Kaligandaki** (Class 3-4; 3 days) and the manic **Marsyangdi** (Class 4-5; 5 days) run only in season; monsoon rains make them unnavigable. The **Seti Khola** and **Trisuli** (Class 3-4; 2-3 days) are more fun during the high-water season from June to August. Some companies combine a Trisuli trip with a visit to **Chitwan National Park** (see p. 838). Others also do **kayaking** trips and offer beginner-level **kayak schools** (4 days, US$150-200, food transport, accommodation, and equipment included), which usually spend a day on Phewa Lake and then three days on the Seti Khola River.

Trekking agencies provide everything from equipment rental to guides to fully planned treks. Expect to pay US$12-15 per day for an English-speaking guide and US$6-9 per day for a porter. For more detailed information on planning a trek, see **Trekking in Nepal,** p. 851.

Equator Expeditions (☎20688; equator@mos.com.np). Opposite Tea Time. Honest and smart, Equator sends you rafting with safety kayakers and sends you trekking with knowledgeable guides. Kaligandaki US$100 for 3 days; Trisuli US$65 for 2 days. 4-day kayak clinics US$15-200. Office open daily 8am-8pm.

Himalayan Encounters (☎20873; raftnepl@himenco.wlink.com.np). 200m east of the main road from the intersection north of Grindlay's Bank. A British-run rafting and trekking agency that charges a little more than most, but makes up for it with professionalism and experience. Rafting on the Kaligandaki US$165 for 4 days; Trisuli US$80 for 2 days. English-speaking trekking guide US$20 per day; guide-cum-porter US$15 per day; porter US$11 per day. Office open daily 8am-9pm.

Ultimate Descents (☎23240; info@udnepal.com). In central Lakeside, 20m north of Moondance. Your best bet for rafting in Nepal, UD are pioneers in the field, with 15 years of international experience. Safety kayakers accompany every trip. Kaligandaki US$99 for 3 days; Marsyangdi US$250 for 5 days; Trisuli US$70 for 2 days. 4-day kayak clinic US$220. Office open daily 9am-8pm.

3 Sisters Adventure Trekking (☎24066). On the right side of the road, 600m north of Grindlay's Bank as the town begins to thin out. Female trekkers will appreciate this woman-run company that provides female guides (US$20 per day) and porters (US$10 per day). Office open daily 8am-8pm.

Mountain Way Trekking (☎20316; mountway@trekkin.mos.com.np). On the road with the median, 50m east of the immigration office. One of the oldest trekking agencies with grizzled veteran sherpa guides. The office also has informative free pamphlets. Organized trek US$45-70 per day; guide US$8 per day; porter US$6 per day.

Sisne Rover Trekking (☎20893; sisne@mos.com.np). Next door to Equator Expeditions. Covers both rafting and trekking and sends a safety kayak for every 2 rafts. Kaligandaki US$70 for 3 days; Seti Khola US$45-50 for 2 days; Trisuli US$18 for 1 day. 3-day kayak clinic US$100. Trekking guide US$10 per day; porter US$7 per day. Office open daily 8am-9pm.

Khampa Trek (☎21520; wwjte@cnet.wlink.com.np). Next to the UPS office in central lakeside. This guide-owned company offers guides (US$10-15) and porters (US$6-8) with a range of skill and experience.

🎵 ENTERTAINMENT

Entertainment in Pokhara consists mostly of eating, drinking, listening to music, and taking in the views from Lakeside's restaurants. Many restaurants feature **Nepali cultural shows** (e.g. **The Hungry-Eye, Boomerang**) or **movies** (e.g. **Once Upon a Time, Tea Time, Caffé Concerto**) during the evenings. Most movies start around 7pm and require that you have dinner. **Bars** are common along the main drags; Moondance and Maya are two of the best. **Musical entertainment** runs the gamut from Nepali dances to Indian pop bands; there's even a piano bar. **Club Amsterdam** in central Lakeside has live music, food, booze, a pool table (Rs50 per game), a TV, an outdoor sitting area, and "the cleanest toilet in Lakeside." (Beer Rs100-125. Open daily 11am-11pm. Live music W, Sa-Su.) The **Old Blues Pub**, at the center of Lakeside, has pool tables, dart boards, TV sports, and wallspace shared by Marilyn Monroe, U2, Ganesh, Jimi Hendrix, Count Basie, and a yak's head. (Soft drinks Rs20; beer Rs100-110; pool and darts free. Open daily from 5pm.) Of course it's not the real thing, but Pokhara's **Hard Rock Cafe** outdoes itself with live music nightly and "Hard Rock Cafe: Pokhara" t-shirts (Rs600. Beer Rs120-130. Open daily from 6pm.) If you're wondering what Nepali youths do after hours, check out the **Lotus Club,** 100m away from the main road by Tea Time. This is Pokhara's only dance club with lights, loud music; its closest thing to a hot local hang-out. (Beer Rs80; shots Rs60. Cover Rs200 for men (includes 1 free beer), Rs100 for women (includes 1 free coke); no cover for women M and Th. Open daily 6pm-1am.)

🎒 DAYTRIPS FROM POKHARA

SARANGKOT. Sarangkot (1592m) has some of the best views around. If you're feeling lazy, take a **taxi** up the road that runs most of the way to the top and walk up for another 30min. (Rs500-600 round-trip). Or, rent a **motorcycle** (See **Local Transportation,** p. 826) and head up the same road. You can simply walk up the road—when heading north, turn left off the Baglung Rd. at the "Sarangkot" sign, 1km north of the Baglung bus park. The walk from Lakeside (3hr.) is much nicer. It's easy to lose your way on the trails that criss-cross the hillside—guides will magically appear as soon as you start heading up the hill (Rs20-40). Dawn is the best time to come. To catch the morning light, it's easiest to stay at one of the places just below the hilltop. Many places are very cheap but expect (or require) you to eat your meals at the hotel. Water is also scarce, so make sure they have it and find out the cost of using it. The **Didi Lodge ❶,** has great views, but you must eat there (doubles Rs50). The cheapest place is the **Sarangkot View Point Lodge ❶,** just below the top of the hill. The two rooms are bare but cheap (doubles Rs20).

BEGNAS AND RUPA LAKES. Phewa, Begnas, and Rupa Lakes were all part of the huge body of water that once filled the Pokhara Valley. Phewa bears the burden of tourist traffic while Begnas and Rupa remain untouched. **Begnas Bazaar,** 15km from Mahendra Pul, is serviced by **local buses,** which leave from the main Prithvi Chowk bus park in Pokhara (1hr., every 15min. 5am-7pm, Rs12). The 2hr. **bike ride** to Begnas will certainly loosen up your legs before the trek. (From Pokhara, head east out the Prithvi Narayan Hwy. toward Kathmandu and turn left at Tal Chowk, 12km from Pokhara.) **Taxis** charge Rs500-600 round-trip. You can rent a **boat** and row to the other end of Begnas. From there, it's a 20min. hike to Rupa over Panchabhaiya Danda, but at Rs250 per hour, it's hard to lose track of time and enjoy it. *(Entrance fee to Begnas Lake Rs10, camera fee Rs20.)*

THE TERAI तराई

The most maligned of the country's regions, the Terai is the flat bit of Nepal to the south that dips into the Gangetic plain. Its flatness means that the Terai has many of Nepal's best roads, but travelers continue to see the region as a sweaty, mosquito-infested purgatory between India and the mountains, meriting no more than a few hours' frustrated transit. For Nepalis, however, the Terai produces the vast majority of the country's rice and hosts most of its industry, construction, and transportation infrastructure. The region was covered with impregnable malarial jungle until the 1950s and 1960s; eradication efforts prompted massive migrations from Nepal's hills and the bordering Indian states. Large chunks of land, such as the Royal Chitwan National Park, have been set aside to preserve some of the region's natural riches. There continues to be conflict between wildlife needs, the demands of a growing population, and now, a burgeoning tourism industry. The neighboring towns of Narayanghat and Bharatpur are the main gateway from the hills. The Mahendra Rajmarg Highway, running east-west from one corner of Nepal to another, connects the entire Terai. Lumbini, in the west, and Janakpur, in the east, are two of Nepal's main religious sites.

HIGHLIGHTS OF THE TERAI

The jungles, swamps, and plains of **Chitwan National Park** (p. 838) are proof that even the flatter parts of Nepal can be pretty beautiful.

Janakpur's temples (p. 844) offer a look at heavily Indian-influenced culture and architecture, without the headache of a border crossing.

The Buddha's birthplace, **Lumbini** (p. 834), is a pilgrimage site for many, and it has a number of enormous temples and monasteries.

⚐ BORDER WITH INDIA: BHAIRAWA भैरहवा

Just 5km north of the Indian border, Bhairawa (Siddharthanagar) has managed to avoid the nasty border-town grime that plagues its counterpart to the south, Sunauli. What the town lacks in sights, it makes up for in pleasant accommodations; it's a popular stop on the way to or from the border and for daytrips to Lumbini. Several carriers offer daily flights to **Kathmandu** (30min., 11:40am-4:35pm, US$79). **Buddha Air** (☎21893 or 23893; open daily 8am-6pm) and **Mountain Air** (☎21115 or 21116; open daily 7am-6pm) are just east of Bus Chowk, while **Necon Air** (☎21244 or 22798; open daily 8am-7pm), **Skyline** (☎23850; open daily 8am-6pm), and **Cosmic Air** (☎24219 or 20219; open daily 7am-6:30pm) are all 50 to 100m north of the bus chowk. Skyline also offers daily flights to **Pokhara** (20min., 3:30pm, US$61). From the **bus counter,** at the southwest corner of Bus Chowk (☎20351; open daily 5am-8:30pm), buses run to **Sunauli** (5min., frequent 6am-8pm, Rs4) and **Butwal** (1hr., frequent 5am-8pm, Rs15-20). Day and night buses run to **Kathmandu** (7-9hr.; 7, 8, 8:30am, 7, 8, 8:30pm; Rs168-228) and **Pokhara** (7-9hr.; 6:30, 8, 11am, 7, 8:30pm; Rs200-225). Many more connections are available at **Butwal.** Buses to **Lumbini** (1hr.; 6:35am, then every 20min. 7:45am-7:45pm; Rs15) depart from Lumbini Chowk. A **rickshaw** from Lumbini Chowk to Bus Chowk costs Rs10. **Private jeeps,** which can be hired from Bus Chowk, haul passengers to: the **airport** (Rs150); **Lumbini** (Rs500-600 round-trip); **Sunauli** (Rs70). There are frequent **public jeeps** to Sunauli (Rs5).

✠ BORDER WITH INDIA: SUNAULI सुनौली

The second-most popular entry point to Nepal (after the airport in Kathmandu), Sunauli has all the inevitable frontier grime but is much less of a hassle than Birganj and less dismal than Kakarbhitta. Don't get stuck here for long, though.

The **bus park** on the Indian side is about 500m south of the border. Purchase tickets on board the bus. Buses leave frequently for: **Delhi** (23hr., every 30min. 4:30am-6:30pm, IRs358) via **Lucknow** (9-10hr., IRs152); **Gorakhpur** (2½hr., every 15min. 4:30am-7:30pm, IRs43); **Varanasi** (10hr., every hr. 4:30-6:30am and 4-7pm, IRs134). Touts on the Nepali side will tell you that they can get you on board luxury buses or that you can purchase tickets only *before* you cross the border; none of this is true. The **bus park** (☎20194) on the Nepal side is about 100m from the border. Buses run to **Kathmandu** (11-12hr., 6 per day 4:30-10:30am, NRs170; 11-12hr., 8 per night noon-8:30pm, NRs211) and **Pokhara** (9hr., 9 per day 5:10-11:30am, NRs160; 9hr., 6:45 and 8:30pm, NRs200). All these buses pass through **Bhairawa** (10min., NRs5) and **Butwal** (1hr., NRs20). Kathmandu buses also pass through **Narayanghat** (4-5hr., NRs85). Change in Butwal for other connections throughout Nepal. **Jeeps** also run to **Bhairawa** (5min., frequent 5am-7:30pm, NRs5). You can also **walk** across the border or take a **rickshaw** (NRs10).

The requisite stops at both Indian and Nepali **customs and immigration** should take less than an hour. Nepalese visas can be obtained on the spot, but citizens of countries other than India or Nepal need visas to enter India (available only in Kathmandu). The border is open 24hr., as are both Nepalese and Indian immigration offices. The Nepali **tourist office** (☎20304; open Su-Th 10am-5pm, F 10am-4pm) and **police outpost** are just south of the big Nepali entrance gate, opposite one another. The **UP government tourist office,** next door to Hotel Niranjana, is run by the amazingly resourceful Mr. Zaidi, who has a wealth of information about both UP and Nepal. (Open M-Sa 10am-5pm; closed every second Sa.) There are several authorized **currency exchangers** on the Nepal side (most open 6am-6pm).

LUMBINI लुम्बीनी ☎071

Lumbini is a work in progress. Today's Lumbini is not a town, but a five sq. km plot of land set aside to honor the Buddha, who was reputedly born in the Sacred Garden at the south end. In ancient times, Lumbini saw its fair share of pilgrims and monuments, most notably the pillar erected in the 3rd century BC by the emperor Ashoka. By the 15th century, however, Lumbini's claim to fame had been forgotten, and it wasn't until 1896 that Ashoka's pillar was unearthed. The current halfhearted drive to raise the site's status from just an obscure spot in the Terai began in 1967 with a visit by U Thant of Burma, then Secretary General of the UN. It continues with the ambitious "Master Plan" of Japanese architect Kenzo Tange that envisions Lumbini as "an expression of Buddha's universal message of peace and compassion creating a sculpted landscape to make the teachings of Lord Buddha accessible to all humanity." A lack of funds has slowed progress, and the "maps" of Lumbini invariably reflect the Master Plan and bear little resemblance to reality.

▐ TRANSPORTATION

Frequent **buses** run between **Bhairawa** and **Mahilwar,** the small town adjacent to Lumbini. Buses leave from Lumbini Chowk at 6:35am and then every 20min. between 7:45am and 7:45pm (Rs15). Buses make the return journey every 30min. between 6:30am and 5pm (Rs15). **Bikes** are a great way to get around; **Lumbini Village Lodge** (see **Accommodations and Food,** below) has a few decent ones for hire (Rs20 per hr., Rs180 per day).

▚ ▐ ORIENTATION AND PRACTICAL INFORMATION

While Lumbini is laid out in a very precise and orderly fashion, everything is extremely spread-out; the road to enlightenment is long, and the road from enlightenment back to the bus stop is longer still. If you don't have a ride, rickshaw **Wallahs** will be eager to give you one. Lumbini is a 1½km by 5km rectangle enclosed by **Ring Rd.** and divided into three equal 1½ sq. km segments. The southernmost segment contains the **Sacred Garden,** where the Buddha was born. The middle segment is the monastic zone, cut through the middle by a canal. Mahayana temples and monasteries line the west side and Theravada temples and monasteries line the east side. The northernmost segment is mostly empty, though it contains a museum, research institute, and the impressive **Peace Stupa.** The town of **Mahilwar,** home to most of the accommodations and services, is just off the eastern side of Ring Rd., a short walk from the Sacred Garden. **Tourist information** is available from the **Lumbini Development Trust** information booth (☎ 80200; open daily 8am-5pm) on the edge of the Sacred Garden, north of the Tibetan temple, opposite the temporary bus park (for tourist buses only). **Currency exchange** is available in Mahilwar at the **Nepal Bank of Ceylon,** right at the entrance to town. (☎ 80152. Open Su-Th 10am-3pm, F 10am-1pm.) The **police station** (☎ 80171) is 150m southwest of the Sacred Garden. **Tara Medical Center,** in Mahilwar, has a **pharmacy** run by a trained medical adviser. (No phone, but dialing 80180 will get you the STD office across the street which will contact the pharmacy. Open daily 8:30am-7pm.)

▐ ▐ ACCOMMODATIONS AND FOOD

Most people visit Lumbini for the day and return to Bhairawa to sleep. There are a few good hotels in Mahilwar, a five-minute walk from the Sacred Garden, and there's usually space available, even in season. The cream of the crop is the **Lumbini Garden Lodge ❶,** on Mahilwar's main street. The rooms are clean and the prices are the lowest in town. (☎ 80146. Doubles Rs200-300.) More upscale is the brand-new **Lumbini Hotel ❶,** with bright, spacious rooms and attached toilets. (☎ 80142. Singles Rs300; doubles Rs500.) All hotels in Mahilwar serve decent and well-priced meals for guests only. The best place to eat in Lumbini is the restaurant in the Lumbini Village Lodge. Closer to the Sacred Garden, east of the Tibetan Temple, there are some small **food stands,** flanking the temporary bus park, that serve basic Nepali meals. Lumbini's only real restaurant, **Lumbini Garden Restaurant ❷,** 50m east of the turn to the Sacred Garden, serves a decent selection of Chinese, Indian, Nepali, and continental food at an exorbitant Rs70-225. (Open daily 7am-9:30pm.)

👁 SIGHTS

Lumbini's centerpiece is the **Sacred Garden,** which marks the birthplace of the Buddha. According to legend, Siddhartha Gautama, a prince in the Sakya royal family, was born in Lumbini in 623 BC, when the site was merely a forest grove near a water tank. Siddhartha's mother, Mayadevi, was on her way back from her husband's palace when she stopped for a bath in the water tank and then gave birth. The site of this event is now occupied by the **Mayadevi Temple.** Currently under renovation, it is swathed in an unsightly yellow tarpaulin and covered by a corrugated-metal roof. The main **Mayadevi sculpture** (3rd-4th century AD), which has long been worshipped by Hindus as a representation of a fertility goddess, was moved to the building at the entrance of the garden and will be moved back to the temple when renovations are complete. Another statue beside it bears a detailed depiction of the Buddha's birth. Beside the Mayadevi Temple is Nepal's oldest monument, the **Ashokan Pillar,** erected in 249 BC when Ashoka came to town to throw himself a party for the 20th anniversary of his coronation. South of the Ashokan Pillar is the **water tank** where Mayadevi bathed before giving birth to Siddhartha. Surrounding the Mayadevi Temple are half-excavated remains of monasteries, temples, and *stupas* dating from the 3rd century BC to the 9th century AD.

Just east of the Sacred Garden is the large yellow **Buddha Temple.** Constructed by King Mahendra in 1953, it contains statues from Burma, Thailand, and Nepal, including a large, gold Buddha at the main altar. Wall paintings depict the wheel of life, four *bodhisattvas,* and the major Hindu gods welcoming Siddhartha back to Nepal after his enlightenment. Immediately north of this complex is the **Tibetan Temple;** aside from the Buddha statue at its center, the most striking feature of the Temple is its well-kept rose garden. A 10min. walk north of the Sacred Garden, the **Eternal Flame** commemorates the 1986 International Year of Peace.

The Monastic Zone lies to the north of the eternal flame. The road forks here to flank the central canal. The first building on the west (Mahayana) side is the **Burmese Panditarana** center, which offers courses in **Vipassana meditation** (see **Meditation,** below). The most impressive of the Mahayana temples is the **Chinese temple,** which cost a whopping Rs7 crores to build. The **Nepali Monastery** is also finished, while temples for Korea, Vietnam, and Japan are still under construction.

The first building on the east (Theravada) side of the canal is also a Vipassana center: the **International Gautami Nun's Center.** The real eye-catcher on the Theravada side is the **Myanmar Golden Temple,** which looks like an enormous bell. The adjacent **monastery** houses a large community of monks. **The Maha Bodhi Society of India** also has a completed temple. The **Thai Monastery** is still under construction but is already home to a monastic community. The **Sri Lankan Temple** is still in the early stages of construction. North of the Theravada Monastic Zone are the **Lumbini Museum** and the **Lumbini Research Institute.** The museum houses a few relics of interest, and the research center has a largely untouched library, but both buildings are most interesting for Kenzo Tange's architecture. *(Free. Research Institute open Su-Th 10am-1:30pm and 2-5pm, F 10am-1pm and 1:30-3pm. Museum open W-M 10am-5pm.)*

At the far north end of Lumbini stands its largest monument: the colossal Japanese **Peace Stupa.** This 41m-high structure is expected to open November 2001. Next door is the **Fuji Gurujee Monastery.**

MEDITATION

There are two permanent centers for **Vipassana Meditation** in Lumbini. The **Panditarama** center (☎ 80118) runs regular courses—particularly in December and February—using the Pandita technique. Courses are taught by Pandita's pupil, Sayada Vivekananda, and Pandita himself occasionally shows up to lead a course. The **Gautami Nun's Temple** runs less frequent courses, following S.N. Goenka's teachings. To book a place, contact the Dharmashringa center in Kathmandu (☎01 371655). There is no charge for the courses, but a small donation is expected to defray food and lodging expenses.

NARAYANGHAT AND BHARATPUR ☎056

There are no two ways about it—Narayanghat is a big, noisy, smelly city. Most travelers will only pass through en route to Chitwan National Park, but if you're hoping to experience a taste of urban Nepal, you might actually like the place. The neighboring town of Bharatpur—which will interest you only if you're sick or flying to Kathmandu—is quiet and refreshingly laid-back. An hour's walk up river from Narayanghat brings you to the sadhu community of Devghat, where the Kali Gandaki and Trisuli rivers merge to become the sacred Narayani.

▐▄ TRANSPORTATION. A number of companies with offices on the highway, opposite the air terminal, offer daily flights from Bharatpur to Kathmandu (20min., 10:50am-12:40pm, US$61 + Rs110 airport tax). At press time, Bharatpur's airport was serviced only by **Cosmic Air** (☎20341), **Gorkha Air** (☎21093), and **Shangri-La** (☎25306), but **RNAC** (☎20326) may soon be offering slightly cheaper flights. **Buses** leave from the **Pulchowk Bus Park** to: **Birganj** (4hr., every 30min. 4am-1pm, Rs90); **Kathmandu** (5hr., every 30min. 5am-3pm, Rs95); **Pokhara** (4hr.; every 30min. 7am-5pm; Rs90, deluxe A/C bus Rs145); **Sunauli** (4hr., every 30min. 7am-4pm, Rs90). The bus park is intimidatingly chaotic, but it's not hard to find your bus. As a general rule, buses for a particular destination congregate in the part of the bus park closest to that destination: Pokhara to the north, Birganj to the east, Sunauli to the west, etc. At the eastern extremity of the crowd of buses, Chitwan-bound travelers can catch the local service to Tandi (Rs10). From **Pokhara bus park,** buses/minibuses go to **Gorkha** (2½hr., every hr. 7:30am-4:30pm, Rs45/65) and **Pokhara** (4hr., every 30min. 8am-2:30pm, Rs85/125). **Chitwan Sauraha Tours and Travel,** at the southwest edge of the Pulchowk Bus Park, sells tickets for tourist buses to Kathmandu. (☎21890. Open daily 7am-9pm. 4½hr., 10 and 11am, Rs500.) A **cycle-rickshaw** between Narayanghat and Bharatpur should cost Rs10-20.

▌▐ ORIENTATION AND PRACTICAL INFORMATION. Narayanghat and Bharatpur are on the east-west **Mahendra Rajmarg Highway.** Narayanghat sits on the east bank of the Narayani river, while Bharatpur is up the hill, 2km farther east. The center of Narayanghat is the **Pulchowk Bus Park,** at the chaotic intersection of the highway and the north-south road to Mugling. A 15min. walk north along this road leads to the **Pokhara Bus Park.** The most obvious landmark in Bharatpur is the **airport,** on the highway near the west end of town. **Nepal Bank,** on the road to Mugling, in the big, pink building 500m north of Pulchowk, changes currency and traveler's checks for a 2.5% commission. (☎20170. Open Su-Th 10am-3pm, F 10am-noon.) The **police** (☎20146) are in the red building off the dirt road two blocks south and one block west of Pulchowk Bus Park. There is a **hospital** (☎20111) in Bharatpur, north of the main square and a block west. On the main road north in Bharatpur is the private **Asha Hospital** (☎253516). There are a number of 24hr. **pharmacies** in the courtyard of the public hospital. **Pharmacies** also surround various other hospitals in town (most open 6am-9pm). **Hello Chitwan,** on the highway 200m east of the Pulchowk Bus Park, has **Internet access,** in the loosest sense of the word. (☎25777. Rs4 per min.) The **post office** is 25m east of the Pokhara bus park, just off the road to Mugling. (Open Su-Th 10am-5pm, F 10am-3pm.)

⟦⟧ ACCOMMODATIONS AND FOOD. All accommodations listed below are in Narayanghat, near one of the bus parks. **Quality Guest House ❶,** 20m north and 20m east of Pulchowk Bus Park, is close to the action but far enough from the bus park to afford some peace and quiet. (☎23488. Singles Rs130-200; doubles Rs250-300.) **Regal Rest House ❶,** opposite the Gulf gas station at Pulchowk Bus Park, has clean, spacious rooms with toilets, but it offers little protection from the dawn-till-dusk hubbub of the street below. (☎20755. Singles Rs250; doubles Rs350.) **The Satanchuli Inn ❶,** behind the Pokhara bus park is cozy and clean and opens up onto a refreshingly green garden. The river is just a stone's throw away. (☎21151. Singles Rs150-200; doubles Rs200-300.) The best places to eat in Narayanghat are the ramshackle **food stands ❶,** on the south side of Pulchowk Bus Park. (Curries Rs20-30; chow mein Rs30-40. Most open daily 7am-9pm.) For something more upscale, try the **Sangam Rooftop Restaurant ❶,** on the highway, 200m east of Pulchowk Bus Park. The food is cooked on a *taas*—a large, clay barbecue pit. (Veg. *thukpa* Rs35; chicken *tikka masala* Rs80. Open daily 8am-10pm.)

◙ SIGHTS. Devghat, 8km north of Narayanghat, honors the confluence of the Trisuli and Kali Gandaki Rivers, and is a popular sadhu hangout. A pink statue of the monkey god Hanuman sits in a small shrine in the square where the buses arrive. There is a Buddhist temple up the steps away from the river, and across the bridge are many shrines to various deities and saints, most prominently Mahadevi and Durga. Non-Hindus should refrain from entering the small temples. The real action comes around January 15, when thousands make the pilgrimage here. *(A 2hr. walk up the river from Narayanghat. Alternatively, buses from Pokhara Bus Station. 20min., every 30min. 7am-5pm, Rs5. Round-trip taxi ride plus 1hr. waiting time Rs250.)*

ROYAL CHITWAN NATIONAL PARK चिटवान ☎056

Royal Chitwan National Park is Nepal's largest and most touristed nature reserve. Its 932 sq. km—ranging from dense jungle to swamp land and grassland—are home to hundreds of species of animals and birds, including 21 protected species. While you'll be lucky to see a tiger, leopard, or sloth bear, sightings of rhinos, crocodiles, deer, and monkeys are almost guaranteed.

Until recently, Chitwan was the playground for Nepal's elite, and the sport was hunting big game. But things have changed, and Royal Chitwan National Park is now the most protected wildlife reserve in Nepal. In fact, the greatest threat to the wildlife came not from aristocratic rifles but from the area's 1950s malaria eradication program. The program's success indirectly led to the destruction of the local habitat as people moved down from the hills to take advantage of the fertile flatlands. Resettlement of these people began in 1964, and the area was declared a national park in 1973. Eleven years later, UNESCO designated the Royal Chitwan National Park as a Natural World Heritage Site.

The village of Sauraha, just north of the park on the bank of the dreamlike Rapti River, is the best base from which to explore the park. Sauraha now survives almost exclusively on tourism, and while there is something a little artificial about the rooftop restaurants and "safari" lodges, the place remains pleasantly tranquil.

⟦ TRANSPORTATION

Buses: Buses depart from **Chitrasari** for **Kathmandu** (5hr., Rs150); **Pokhara** (5hr., Rs170); **Sunauli** (5½hr., Rs150) between 10 and 11am. You can buy tickets at Chitrasari or you can book ahead at the **bus counter** (☎60667), in Tandi, east of the turn-off to Sauraha, marked "Prithvi Rajmarg Bus Syndicate." Open daily 7-9:15am and 1-5:30pm. You can also book tickets through your lodge in Sauraha or through one of Sauraha's many travel agents, but expect to pay a commission. To get to **Narayanghat,** where other connections are available, go to Tandi, and catch any west-bound bus on the highway (15min., Rs10).

Public Transportation: You can get a rickshaw between Tandi and Chitrasari for Rs20. Your rickshaw driver will want an additional Rs30 to cross the rickety footbridge and carry you to Sauraha. Jeeps wait on the other side of that bridge and will take you to Sauraha for Rs30, though they may ask as much as Rs100. Unless you're exhausted or weighed down excessively, it's probably worth your while just to walk from Chitrasari to Sauraha. Follow the right fork after you cross the bridge, and you'll be in Sauraha in 15min. Sauraha has lots of **bike rental shops** along the main road (Rs70-100 per day). **Chitwan Guide Office** (☎80081), on the main road, just north of the Moondance Restaurant, has good bikes (Rs15 per hr., Rs80 per day). Open daily 6am-9pm. A few places in Sauraha rent motorcycles, and for better or worse, don't require any kind of driver's license. **Chitwan Motorbike on Hire and Repairing Center** (☎80069), near the north end of town, rents for Rs140 per hr. or Rs500 per day, including a liter of petrol and a helmet. Open daily 6am-5pm.

▄▟ 🛈 ORIENTATION AND PRACTICAL INFORMATION

Chitwan National Park is at the center of the Terai. Its southern boundary is the Indian border, its northern boundary the Rapti River, and farther downstream flows the Narayani River. The Mahendra Rajmarg Hwy. runs almost parallel to the northern boundary of the park. The dirt road leading to the park entrance branches south off the highway in the town of **Tandi,** 20km east of Narayanghat. This dirt road heads south for 4km until it hits **Chitrasari,** a footbridge river-crossing that has developed into a little transportation hub. From there, it's 2½km farther south to **Sauraha,** the town that sits right at the park entrance. Sauraha is home to all the hotels, restaurants, and tour agencies that serve the park and its visitors. It's a small town and oriented almost entirely along the north-south **Main Rd.,** which runs all the way down to the river.

Tourist Office: The **Visitor Center** has a little museum with displays and information about the history and wildlife of the park, as well as the park **ticket office** (open daily 6-9am and 1:30-4pm). The center sells elephant rides (7:30am and 4:30pm; Rs1000) and **permits** (Rs500 per day) for entering the park. **Steep fines** await those caught in the park without a valid permit. **No one may enter the park at night.** In season, the wait to get park entry permits can be 3-4hr. Most of the time, the permit is purchased by whatever guide service you are using, so you don't have to go to the office yourself. To get to the Visitors Center, head down the main road toward the river, take a left at the Jungle View Restaurant, take your first right after about 50m on, and then turn right again at the end of the road. The Visitors Center is 20m ahead on your left.

Currency Exchange: A number of places in town change cash and traveler's checks for a 2% commission. The most central of these is **Sauraha Money Changer,** Main Rd. Open daily 7:30am-8pm.

Police: The **main police station** (☎80099) is a 20min. walk east of Sauraha along Tharu Village Rd.—take a left at the Jungle View Restaurant. The police station in **Tandi** is on the main highway, 300m east from the turn to Sauraha.

Pharmacy: Raj Medical Hall (☎80133). Opposite K.C.'s Restaurant, near the center of Sauraha. Open daily 7am-9pm. The nearest hospital (☎20111) is in Bharatpur.

Internet: Hotline Communication, Main Rd. (☎80030.) In front of the Jungle Tourist Camp, 1st fl. Internet Rs7 per min. for painfully slow and sporadic service. Open daily 7am-10pm. Only slightly more reliable and somewhat faster is the office near the bus park in Chitrasari, also RS7 per min.

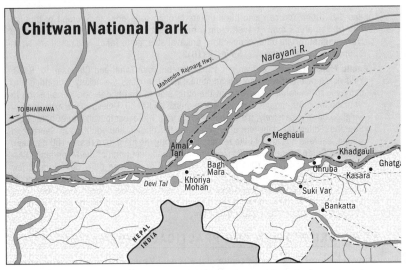

Chitwan National Park

🏔 ACCOMMODATIONS

Many tourists come to Chitwan on pre-paid package deals arranged in Kathmandu or Pokhara. If you arrive in Tandi without a reservation, head to Sauraha. Standard accommodations are free-standing cottages in garden compounds with solar-heated water. All hotels offer basically the same three-day, two-night package consisting of a jeep or elephant ride, half-day jungle walk, canoe trip, stick dance, lodgings, meals, and bus transportation from Kathmandu or Pokhara to any return city in Nepal. Be wary of bogus budget "deals," and ask to see a park permit. Also beware at cheaper hotels, as many are subsidized by their tour operations; if you opt to use a different tour company, you may find yourself harassed and even told to leave. Off season prices plummet (June-Sept., Dec.-Feb.); bargain hard, although some of the costs (park entry fee, government elephant ride) are fixed.

🦏 **Rain Forest Guest House,** Main Rd. (☎80007). Near the north end of town. Friendly staff, clean grounds, and reasonable prices make it the best deal in Sauraha. The dining room serves tasty spaghetti bolognese (Rs100). Doubles Rs100-300. ❶

🦏 **Tiger Wildlife Camp,** Main Rd. (☎80137). At the north end of town. Pleasant, tranquil, garden setting, large rooms, and the cheapest rates in town. What's the catch? Their tours cost about Rs100 more than the competition and they expect you to join them. Their guides are excellent, however, so you can't complain. Doubles Rs60-200. ❶

Wendy's Lodge, Main Rd. (☎80033). Near the Tharu Cultural Program, at the north end of town. A bit drab, but all four rooms have attached bath and fans, and the prices are reasonable. In-house tour operator offers well-run tours. Doubles Rs200-250. ❷

Travellers Jungle Camp, Main Rd. (☎80013). Beside the Chitwan Money Changer. One of Chitwan's oldest tourist lodges, the Jungle Camp has a wide range of accommodations and very clean, well-kept facilities. The restaurant is good, and there's a money changer next door. The mosquito nets are brand spanking new, and the affable owner speaks flawless English. Thatched-roof, mud-wall doubles Rs200-400, with bathtub Rs700. ❷

Riverside Hotel, Main Rd. (☎80008 or 80009). On the beach, at the south end of town. This upmarket hotel, under the same ownership as K.C.'s Restaurant, is simply luxuri-

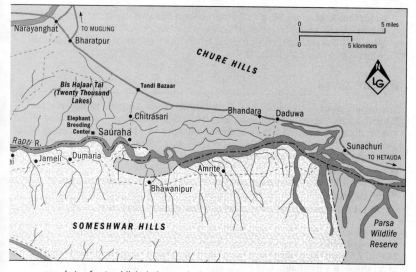

ous. Lots of natural light in large, nicely decorated rooms that come with towels, soap, and toilet paper. Proceeds go toward the education of local children. At press time, the hotel had recently opened and prices may since have gone up. Doubles Rs400-750. ❸

Jungle Tourist Camp, Main Rd. (☎80030). Close to the center of town. Basic but clean. Garden is dusty, but rooms are neat and well-priced, though they lack mosquito nets. All have attached bath. Email access available. Doubles Rs200-300. ❶

River View Jungle Camp, Main Rd. (☎80096). Near the center of town. With one of the nicest gardens in Sauraha, this upmarket lodge offers some decent budget options. Doubles Rs200-700. ❸

🍴 FOOD

Most lodges have attached restaurants, though the Chitwan culinary experience revolves around the **rooftop restaurants** in the center of town. A number of small establishments at street level offer Nepali fare. The rooftop places stay open well into the evening and join forces with the numerous beach bars on the river bank to bring you Bob Marley and cocktails with ridiculous names (Rs110-160). Baby don't worry: everything gonna be alright.

▨ **Jungle View Restaurant and Bar,** Main Rd. Smack dab in the middle of town. The best food and the best service of the rooftop restaurants earns this place an A+. Chicken curry Rs95, lasagna Rs110, delectable chicken enchilada Rs115. Happy hour 4-8pm. Open daily 6:30am-midnight. ❶

▨ **Namaste Cake, Pies, and Coffee,** Main Rd. Opposite Moondance Restaurant. The town's best (and cheapest) place for breakfast or a sweet treat. Run by a lovely family who makes you feel right at home. 2 boiled eggs Rs15, french toast Rs30, cake slices Rs35, pie slices Rs30. Open daily 6:30am-10pm. ❶

K.C.'s Restaurant and German Bakery, just around the corner from Jungle View Restaurant. The oldest and classiest of Chitwan's rooftop restaurants, with an experienced waitstaff. While the menu covers a little bit of everything, the chef's specialty is Mexican, and he lives up to his reputation. Delicious veg. enchiladas Rs130, cheese and bean burrito Rs130. Happy hour 5-8:30pm. Open daily 6am-10:30pm. ❷

Moondance Restaurant, Main Rd. In the middle of Sauraha. One of the most popular rooftop places, with good reason. Pleasant atmosphere, friendly staff, low prices, and good food. *Paneer* Rs99, amazing grilled fish Rs150, Nepali meal Rs115. Happy hour 4-8pm. Open daily 6am-10pm. ❶

🏞 THE PARK

The highlights of Chitwan National Park include the one-horned rhinoceros, the Bengal tiger, leopards, sloth bears, and wild bison. There are an estimated 56 mammalian species in the park and over 500 species of birds, nine species of amphibians, 126 species of fish, 150 species of butterflies, and 47 species of reptiles, as well as 107 of Nepal's 300 tigers. *(Park open sunrise-sunset. Rs500 per day.)*

> **⚠ WARNING.** Due mainly to rhino risk, the government requires visitors to Chitwan National Park to be accompanied by at least two guides at all times. **Let's Go does not recommend being bitten, gored, or trampled. .**

TOURS AND GUIDES. Since visitors to the park must be accompanied by guides at all times, it's inevitable that you'll end up booking a tour. Many people book **package tours** from Kathmandu or Pokhara, which include lodging, activities, and transportation. These packages are generally convenient and hassle-free; most tours are 3-days, 2-nights, and run US$55-65. In Sauraha, activities can also be booked a la carte through all hotels or independent tour operators. Hotels are generally slightly more expensive but are also more convenient since they can wake you up for early morning departures. Probably the best independent tour operator is the **United Jungle Guide Service,** under K.C.'s Restaurant, in the Jungle Guide Office. Guides are experienced and friendly, and tour prices are reasonable. *(☎80097. Open daily 7am-6:30pm.)* **Magic Reservation Office,** affiliated with Wendy's Lodge, is another option, though you don't need to be staying at Wendy's to book a tour. It's a small operation, but Gopal, the manager, is a knowledgeable veteran of the field. *(☎ 80033. Open daily 6am-9pm.)* When looking for a guide, ask other tourists for referrals; the number of years of experience should also be on the guide's permit certificate. For any fixed-rate activities, service charges should run Rs50-200 regardless of where you book. Be sure to tip the guide at the end of a good trip.

ELEPHANT RIDES. Plodding along on a ponderous pachyderm is the classic way to see Chitwan and is the most popular activity in the park. Elephant rides offer an opportunity to see the jungle animals at closer range than either walking or jeep tours afford—if you're lucky, you could end up just 2m away from a rhino. There are two kinds of elephant rides in Chitwan: government-run and private. **Government** elephant rides are the only ones that go into the park itself, across the Rapti River. These rides take 1hr. and leave from near the park ticket office at 7:30am and 4:30pm (see **Practical Information,** p. 839). You can book them directly from the park ticket office or through a tour operator. *(Rs1000 fixed rate, plus variable service charges.)* By far the better deal, **private** elephant rides stay on the near side of the Rapti River and traverse the still-wild Buffer Zone, a section of the park added in 1977 (so you still need a park ticket). These rides last 2hr. and leave from Main Rd. in front of the Tharu Cultural Program Building at 7am and 3pm. Private rides must be booked through a tour operator or hotel. *(Rs600-800.)* Either way, be sure to wear long pants and sturdy shoes, as the elephants seem to enjoy walking straight through patches of thick vegetation and even whole trees.

NEPAL

JUNGLE WALK/CANOE RIDE. A jungle walk is certainly the most exciting way to see the national park. All walking groups are accompanied by at least two guides, and trips wander along the park's trails in search of a rhino, tiger, or crocodile. Because walking groups are unprotected and guides are unarmed (except for a long stick), the rhinos do pose a real threat—in the fall of 1999, a guide was attacked by a protective mother rhino and was lucky to survive the encounter. However, groups go out every day without incident. Jungle walks come in three basic lengths: half-day (4hr.), full-day (12hr.), and two-day. The half-day walk usually includes a **canoe ride:** an hour floating down river, then a 2-3hr. walk back. Both the half-day and full-day trips explore the jungle from Sauraha, while the increasingly popular two-day trips stay overnight in a local village on the park's border farther downstream. If you're up to it, the two-day walk is a great way to see the park; it really covers a lot of ground and spends lots of time inside the park's boundary. Walks are privately operated and prices vary by season, tour operator, and number of people. *(Half-day walks Rs300-400 per person, full-day Rs500-700 per person, two-day Rs1200-1400 per person; canoe ride Rs300-400 per person.)*

JUNGLE DRIVE. The jungle drive offers a more expensive but more extensive tour of the park. Since jeep rides are long (4-5hr.), they cover more of the jungle, including the park headquarters at Kasara and the Gharial Conservation Project (where crocodiles are bred and released). But jeeps, unlike elephants, can't leave the road to follow animals or go through tall grass. Still, rhino sightings are practically guaranteed on any jungle drive. As the grass grows tall from June to the annual grass-cutting in January or February, animal spotting becomes increasingly difficult. Each jeep should come with a driver and a separate wildlife spotter. *(7:30am and 1:30pm; Rs700-1000, depending on season.)*

BIKE TO 20,000 LAKES. Because they're outside the park boundary, it's possible to visit the 20,000 Lakes without any tour guide supervision. While 20,000 is a bit of an exaggeration, there are a number of small watering holes in this peaceful wooded area. Bird-watching is the popular thing to do here, though if you're lucky, you may spot a gharial (long-snouted, non-dangerous crocodile) or a rhino. If nothing else, it's a pleasant place to sit back, relax, and watch the butterflies flutter by. The best way to reach this area is by bicycle, which you can rent from one of the many places in Sauraha. To get to the lakes, go north from Sauraha all the way to Tandi (6.5km). Head west along the main highway for 3km until you pass over a bridge. Immediately after the bridge, a dirt road branches to the left and follows alongside a small canal all the way to the lakes (4km). In all, the trip should take about an hour. *(There's a Rs25 **entrance fee** for this community forest, payable at the small checkpost on the road before the lakes. Guided trips also available; Rs300-500 per person incl. bike rental.)*

ELEPHANT BREEDING CENTER. Although it is better known for its rhino and tiger denizens, Chitwan is also populated by elephants. Just about every elephant in Chitwan is from India, where elephants still roam wild despite a millennium-old trade of capturing and training them. With elephant stomping grounds receding fast, elephant prices have sky-rocketed—they can cost up to one million Indian rupees. Chitwan has responded with its Elephant Breeding Centre, established in 1987. Training begins when an elephant turns two; both a human and a "role model" senior elephant are teachers. Each elephant has 3 attendants: the *phanet* is the elephant's driver and principal companion; the *mahout* is the one who takes the elephant to bathe and forage; and the *pachhewa* makes the food and also has the enviable task of cleaning out the stable. Most of the elephants are chained to posts, which may be upsetting to some, though the animals are given daily exercise. For Rs30, you can buy a bunch of 12 bananas and enjoy the peculiar experience of having an elephant eat out of your hand. *(To reach the stables, take the road near the north end of the town, opposite the Rain Forest Guest House, and walk west for 3km. The road ends at a shallow stream; the breeding center is on the far bank. Ferry across the river Rs10. Entrance fee Rs15, with park permit.)*

THARU VILLAGES. The **Tharu,** the indigenous people of Chitwan, have the dubious privilege of serving as an additional "attraction" alongside the tigers and the rhinos. A **guided walk** through the Tharu village along the road to the park entrance covers the culture, history, and religion of the people. *(2hr., Rs75 per person.)* The half-day walk to the village offers a more authentic introduction to Tharu culture. As the walk takes you through the park, a visit to the village can usually be tacked onto a regular half-day jungle walk. *(4hr., Rs 250-300.)* **Tharu stick dances** exuberantly invite participation. Dance troupes perform regularly at hotels and every evening at the Tharu Culture Program on Main Rd., north of Sauraha Bazaar. *(Programs start 7:30-8:30pm depending on season. Rs50 per person.)*

VOLUNTEER OPPORTUNITIES. The **Children and Women's Promotion Center,** opened in February 2000, provides education for underprivileged children and vocational training for women. It also serves as a boarding school which houses and feeds 12 children from nearby villages. The center relies exclusively on private donations, and it is deeply in need of not only financial help but also English-language instruction. *(From the park ticketing office, the center is a 10min. walk away from the river.)*

✠ BORDER CROSSING: BIRGANJ बिरगञ्ज

Birganj is the funnel through which traffic to India passes, narrowing at the border into a pot-holed, exhaust-filled artery clogged with trucks, rickshaws, bullock-carts, and tongas. Nepalis are the first to declare that Birganj is a miserable place; the only reason to come is to cross the border. For details on crossing the border, see p. 46. **Buses** run from Birganj to virtually every major city in the Terai; private companies serve **Kathmandu** (9hr., every 30min. 6am-noon and 8-9:30pm, Rs150); state buses run to **Pokhara** (6hr., every hr. 4am-7:30pm, Rs175). As many as four **airlines** charge US$55 for the short haul to Kathmandu (flights daily). Reserve at **Lumbini Airways** (☎27385), just off the main street two blocks south of the clock tower. A bus to the airport leaves from the office at 1:30pm (1hr., Rs50). To reach the border from the bus stand, you can either share a **tonga** (Rs5) or hire a **rickshaw** (Rs10). Rickshaws to **Raxaul** (including "waiting" charges) are NRs40 but can take hours to cross the clogged border bridge. You are better off walking the 200m across the bridge and getting another rickshaw on the Indian side.

Birganj stretches for long, cruel, and unusual miles along the road that leads over the Indian border. Buses bypass the main road and stop at the **bus park** directly east of the **clock tower,** at the north end of town. The **Nepal Bangladesh Bank,** just off the main street, two blocks south of the clock tower, changes traveler's checks and cash. (☎23689. Open Su-Th 11am-2:30pm, F 10am-noon.)

JANAKPUR (JANAKPURDHAM) जनकपुर ☎041

The scorching heat, dust storms, and mounds of deposits from the street-walking bovine population of Janakpur don't seem to deter the tourists here, many of whom are Indians making pilgrimages to the birthplace of Sita, the famous *Ramayana* heroine. Janakpur was the capital of the mythical kingdom of Mithila, which supposedly flourished between the 10th and the 3rd centuries BC. According to the *Ramayana,* it was here that the Mithila king Janaka found the baby Sita lying in a field and adopted her as his daughter. Despite its ancient associations, most of Janakpur's temples are modern constructions. Still, the city's skyline shines with the constant devotion of pilgrims, dominated by the flaking onion domes and triangular roofs of its many pilgrims' hostels, while the ground is pitted with *sagars* (artificial ponds) used for ritual baths. This quiet Terai city really comes to life during its festivals, particularly **Vivaha Panchami** (Nov.-Dec.), which features a re-enactment of Rama and Sita's wedding.

TRANSPORTATION

Necon runs daily **flights** to **Kathmandu** (30min., 11am, US$67). Their office is on Station Rd., south of Bhanu Chowk. (☎21900. Open daily 8am-6pm.) **Buses** go to numerous destinations, including: **Bhairawa/Sunauli** (8hr.; 6am and 10:30pm; Rs230, night bus Rs285); **Biratnagar** (6hr., 4:30am-8pm, Rs167); **Birganj** (4hr., every half hour 3:30am-4:20pm, Rs113); **Dharan** (7hr., 5:15am, Rs167); **Kakarbhitta** (8hr.; 4:30-11:15am and 5:30-8pm; Rs200, night bus Rs208); **Kathmandu** (11hr.; 6:15am and 8pm; Rs210, night bus Rs295); **Pokhara** (10hr.; 6am and 3:30pm; Rs236, night bus Rs295). However, catching a local bus from a major intersection—Itahari to Dharan, Hile, and other points north—is often the best way to get where you're going.

ORIENTATION AND PRACTICAL INFORMATION

Janakpur's network of curving alleyways makes it easy to get disoriented, but the city is small enough that a recognizable landmark is never far away. The bus park is at the southwest end of town. Both roads leading northeast out of the bus park eventually connect with **Station Rd.,** the main thoroughfare, at **Dhanush Sagar,** a large pool. From here, Station Rd. runs northeast past **Bhanu Chowk** (named for the Nepalese poet whose bust tops a pillar in the middle of the intersection) and continues to the **railway station,** at the northeast corner of town. Station Rd. also continues south of Dhanush Sagar to **Kuwa Village** and the **airport,** 2km from town.

The **tourist office** is on Station Rd., north of Bhanu Chowk. (☎20755. Open Su-Th 10am-5pm, F 10am-3pm.) The **NB Bank,** at Bhanu Chowk, exchanges Indian rupees and US dollars (☎21548. Open Su-Th 10am-2:30pm, F 10am-noon). There is a **hospital** (☎20033) just northwest of the Janaki Mandir, and **pharmacies** on Station Rd. The **haat bazaar** (Su, Tu, W, F) is west of Ram Mandir. Stores along Station Rd. south of Bhanu Chowk offer **Internet**. The **post office,** southwest of Dhanush Sagar, is hard to find; ask for directions or take a rickshaw. (Open Su-F 10am-4pm.)

ACCOMMODATIONS

Kathmandu Guest House (☎21753). Bhanu Chowk. A friendly and simple place with open hallways, ceiling fans, mosquito nets, and attached bathrooms with squat toilets. Singles Rs150; doubles Rs250. ❶

Hotel Welcome (☎20646). Station Rd. Northeast of Dhanush Sagar. Bright rooms that run the amenities gamut. The older rooms are basic; the more upscale ones are some of the nicest around. Singles Rs75-600; doubles Rs300-1500. ❷

Hotel Rama (☎20059). Mills Area Chowk. At Bhanu Chowk, follow the road to Bhanu's right to the next large intersection. Though slightly removed from the center, Hotel Rama has a wide range of comfortable rooms, and is surrounded by a well-groomed garden. All have attached bath. Singles Rs150-900; doubles Rs350-1000. ❷

Hotel Namaskar (☎22192). At the northeast corner of the bus park. Though the constant traffic makes it a bit noisy, the rooms are simple and clean, all with fans and mosquito nets. Attached or common bath. Singles Rs100-125; doubles Rs200-250. ❶

◖ FOOD

Janakpur's dining scene involves a choice between North Indian, North Indian, or North Indian food, but some of it is so tasty that you'll hardly notice that there's nothing else. Most meals run at similar prices as well (Rs30-90 for veg. curry dishes, *naan* Rs15-50). The restaurant at the **Hotel Welcome** is decent, but once all the fans get going, it's like eating next to a helicopter. **Ramailo Restaurant,** just east of Bhanu Chowk, offers private bamboo booths, and **Rooftop Restaurant,** just north of Dhanush Sagar, has a breezy and clean indoor dining area.

◉ SIGHTS

TEMPLES. There are few other things to do in Janakpur aside from temple-hopping. None of Janakpur's temples are very old, and all are still in use. A good walking tour begins at Station Rd. south of Bhanu Chowk at **Dhanush Sagar** and **Ganga Sagar,** Janakpur's largest and holiest ponds, and continues west and south through the city. The sights below are arranged in that order. On the west bank of Dhanush Sagar, through a faded yellow archway, is the **Ram Mandir,** Janakpur's oldest (built in 1882) and most typical Nepalese temple, hemmed in by a ring of small *shivalingas*. Built under a large banyan tree, the temple hosts the **Ram Navami Festival** to celebrate Ram's incarnation on earth. From the archway, turn left and walk north. After you pass a white, bee-hive-shaped shrine on the right, turn left and follow the road to the huge, white-and-primary-colored **Janaki Mandir.** The Janaki Mandir was built in 1911 on the spot where an image of Sita was found in miraculous circumstances in 1657 and where the infant Sita was discovered by her father-to-be. Her silver image is unveiled twice a day, once in the early morning and once in the evening. *(No smoking or photography inside the temple gates.)* Next door is the more stately, glassed-in **Ram Janaki Vivaha Mandap,** built 17 years ago to mark the place where Rama and Sita tied the knot. The colorful statues inside the twin-roofed pagoda represent Ram, Sita, and the friends and pilgrims present at their marriage. At each corner of the white-tiled platform are smaller temples, dedicated to each of the four couples married that day: Rama and Sita, and Rama's three brothers and their brides. *(Entrance Rs2; camera fee Rs5.)* During the **Vivaha Panchami Festival** in December, *sadhus* and brahmin priests re-enact the wedding ceremony. Follow the wide street northwest from the Ram Janaki Vivaha Mandap, past the hospital, until it intersects with the main highway at Ramanand Chowk, marked by a rotary with towering, interlocking arches. Opposite Ramanand Chowk, a brick path leads to the peaceful and sacred **Bihara Kund,** a shady pond surrounded by dozens of Rama and Sita temples. A 20min. walk south of Ramanand Chowk on the main highway is the **Hanuman Durbar,** a small temple that, until recently, housed the world's fattest monkey (55 kg), thought to be an incarnation of Hanuman, and known to be a victim of stomach cancer. The beloved rhesus, affectionately called Bauwa Hanuman, died at the age of 22 after a lifetime of continuous eating. The temple now houses his somewhat slimmer son, Punya.

JANAKPUR WOMEN'S DEVELOPMENT CENTRE. For an alternative to temples, the **Janakpur Women's Development Centre** (☎21080; women@jwdc.wlink.com.np) is a must for anyone interested in art or economic development. Almost an hour's walk south of Janakpur, the center can also be reached by rickshaw (Rs30); ask to be taken to the "development store." From the main road that runs

THE MURALS OF MITHILA Mithili women (from the areas of southern Nepal and northern India that once made up the Mithila kingdom) developed a painting tradition handed down for generations from mother to daughter. It originated with the bright designs that women paint on the walls of their thatch-roofed, mud and bamboo houses and has become known as **Madhubani.** These paintings often serve a ritual purpose as part of a festival or wedding—a woman may create paintings for her future husband as part of their courtship. The paintings are characterized by bold outlines filled in with bright colors; subjects vary from abstract geometric designs to scenes from everyday life. Images have different symbolic significance; pregnant elephants, parrots, bamboo, turtles, and fish represent fertility and marriage, while peacocks and non-pregnant elephants are good-luck symbols. The process and the purpose of the paintings are more important than the painting itself, which may be destroyed. Nowadays, of course, they're sold to tourists at hefty prices.

south along the west bank of Dhanush Sagar, the road to the airport, follow signs for a turn-off into the village of Kuwa. As you make your way through the village, you'll see Mithila paintings on the walls of the houses. Once in the village, take the first road to the right; when you come to a large temple, take a left, then an immediate right. Continue along the road until you come to open fields; the center is in a brick complex to your right. The artists use traditional motifs on hand-made paper, papier-mâché, ceramics, and textiles (see **Mithila Painting,** p. 847). The products are for sale here and at various non-profit outlets in Kathmandu and Patan. The center also trains women in literacy, mathematics, and business management. *(Open Su-Th 10am-5pm, F 10am-4pm.)*

STEAM RAILWAY. Janakpur is also the point of departure for Nepal's only **steam railway,** a slow and stately way of seeing the surrounding countryside. You can take the train to any of the villages between Janakpur and the Indian border and either walk back or wait for a return train. However, since there is no entry point here, be sure to **get off the train before the border; you may not be able to re-enter Nepal.** Trains leave Janakpur at 7 and 11:55am, and 3:30pm, and stop at **Parbaha** (20min., Rs12), **Baidehi** (40min., Rs9-18), and **Khajuri** (1½hr., Rs12-32), the last stop in Nepal.

DHARAN धरान   ☎025

At the point where the hellish plains meet the heavenly hills is the bazaar town of Dharan, where people from miles around converge to buy everything from cheap Walkmans to squat toilet bowls. The few foreign visitors who come here tend not to stay for long, but Dharan is a far more pleasant place to spend the night than many of the Terai's transportation hubs, although there isn't much to do in Dharan proper. **Chatara,** where river-rafters pull out onto the Sun Kosi, is 15km west; the trekking trailheads of **Hile** (p. 860) and **Basantapur** (p. 850) are to the north. Once the site of one of the British Army's Gorkha training camps, Dharan still hosts a number of Nepal's *khukuri*-smiths who now make knives for tourists. Buses arrive and depart from **Bhanu Chowk,** a busy rotary marked by a statue of the poet for whom it was named. **Chata Chowk,** the other major intersection, is a 10min. walk north, uphill on the same main street—it's easy to miss, as there is no landmark, but keep your eyes peeled for helpful English road signs. The closest **airport** is in Biratnagar; Necon Air and RNAC have several daily flights to Kathmandu. **Buses** go to: **Basantapur** (5½hr., every 30 min. 4am-5:10pm, Rs135) via **Dhankuta** and **Hile** (4hr., Rs83); **Biratnagar** (2hr., every 30min. 5:10am-6:20pm, Rs30); **Kakarbhitta**

(2½hr., every 30min. 4:30am-5:45pm, Rs90); **Kathmandu** (12hr.; 4:20am and 3-5pm; Rs295, night bus Rs353). Other bus connections can be made at **Itahari** (30min. frequent 4:25am-3:30pm, Rs15), at the junction of the area's two highways. The **Nepal Bank Ltd.**, just north of Chata Chowk, exchanges only Indian rupees. (☎20084. Open Su-Th 10am-3pm, F 10am-1:30pm.) **Cyberlink Communications** (☎/fax 23338), at Chata Chowk, has STD/ISD service, free callbacks, and Internet (Rs3 per min.).

A number of hotels are along Chatara Line, the lane running west from Chata Chowk. The friendly **Shristi Guest House ❶,** 200m down the Line on the left side, has well-maintained, large rooms with fans. (☎20569. Singles Rs150; doubles Rs250). The **Basil Hotel ❷,** has slightly more comfortable rooms with baths at significantly higher prices. (☎22412. Doubles Rs400.) Its real draw, however, is the attached **restaurant ❶.** (Entrees Rs30-115. Open 7am-9:30pm.) **Fresh Cafe ❶,** 100m south of Chata Chowk on the west side of the main road, serves decent Continental/South Indian/Tibetan vegetarian food at good prices (veg. *momo* Rs18, pizzas Rs70-185, *dosas* Rs15-50). Three doors to the north, the **Byanjan Bakery ❶,** doesn't have an English sign but it's worth trying to find–the samosas are plump and fresh (Rs5). Tie your shoes tightly before trying the *chat* (Rs15); it just might knock your socks off.

◤ BORDER CROSSING: KAKARBHITTA काकरभित्ता

At the border, Nepali visas are available to anybody with a passport photo (US$30 for 60 days). Nepali immigration, at the border crossing (☎62054) is open daily from 6am to 8pm. Indian immigration is open 6am-10pm. Indian visas, however, must be obtained from the Indian embassy in Kathmandu.

Kakarbhitta is a trading town on the India-Nepal border. Though not as oppressive as some of Nepal's other border towns, it is essentially a large, dusty mess of a bazaar centered on the bus station on the northern side of the east-west highway.

Buses run to: **Birganj** (7hr.; 4:10am, 4:45 and 6:45pm; Rs-290); **Birtamod** (20min., frequent 4:30am-6pm, Rs13); **Dharan** (2½hr., frequent 4:30am-4pm, Rs90); **Janakpur** (7hr.; 6 per day 3:30am-7:15pm; Rs190, night bus Rs208); **Kathmandu** (13 hr.; 11 per day 3:30-6:30am and 4-5pm; Rs350, night bus Rs454); **Pokhara** (13-15hr.; 4 per day 4am, 2:30-5:30pm; Rs420). **Rickshaws** run from the border to **Panitanki** in India (IRs3/NRs5), where there are buses to **Siliguri** (1½hr., frequent 5am-7pm, IRs10). Alternatively, you can take a **taxi** directly from Kakarbhitta to Siliguri (IRs40).

Most of the hotels and restaurants are in the market area, west of the bus park. Along the highway, east of the bus park, are the **banks** and the helpful **tourist office,** in a garden on the north side of the highway. (☎62035. Open Su-F 10am-5pm.) **Travel agencies** around the bus station charge NRs30-40 commission, which you can avoid by buying tickets at the ticket counters along the east side of the bus park. **Nepal Rastra Bank,** across the highway from the tourist information center, buys foreign currency and traveler's checks (1% commission) and is one of the last places to get rid of your Nepali rupees before you hop across the border. (☎62066. Open daily 7am-5pm for foreign exchange.) Kakarbhitta is packed with hotels, which surround the bus park. At the far left (northwest) corner of the bus park is the **Hotel Rajat ❸.** The spartan, older rooms have fans, mosquito mats, hot water, and common squat toilets. Rooms in the new building have clean attached baths with seat toilets, fans, TVs, phones, and mosquito nets. Some rooms have air-conditioning. (☎62033. Singles Rs150-1200; doubles Rs200-1600.) The attached garden restaurant—the only grass in Kakarbhitta—serves an impressive array of dishes. (Rs35-150. Open daily 7am-9pm.)

NEPAL

THE EASTERN HILLS

Eastern Nepal is home to some of the world's most jagged and otherworldly peaks. Six of Nepal's eight 8000-meter peaks, including Everest, tower over this part of the country and are a staggering prospect even for the most experienced of mountaineers, who spend lifetimes growing long beards and dreaming of lugging oxygen tanks to the top of the world. But you don't have to be a mountaineer to enjoy yourself here—the cool and misty foothills have a beauty all of their own. A journey to the small towns of the Eastern hills rewards with views of the Himalayas, spectacular day treks, and friendly chats with lodge owners over *dahl bhat*, even if you don't have the time or the energy (or the beard) for a monster trek.

JIRI जीरी ☎ 049

Keep the prayer-wheels turning, for the grueling bus ride to the main trailhead for the Everest trek might shake whatever faith you had in the Nepalese road system; at least the one-road town of Jiri (1935m) provides travelers with the rest, sustenance, and stable ground necessary for recovery from the bumpy ride from Kathmandu. **Buses** arrive from the Ratna Park bus station in Kathmandu (11hr., 5 per day 5:30-10am, Rs185; express 8hr., 7am, Rs215). From Jiri's **bus park,** buses run to **Kathmandu** (11hr., 5 per day 5:30-10am, Rs170; express bus 7am, 8hr., Rs200). Purchase tickets at the window opposite the Jiri Medical Hall (open 6am-6pm). Tickets for the **express bus** to or from Jiri must be purchased a day in advance, and you are expected to arrive at the bus park half an hour before departure.

From the bus park, backtrack up along the road to find accommodations. On Saturdays a **market** is held on the hilltop of **Naya Bazaar,** a 30min. uphill walk from the bus park. **Jiri Medical Hall,** at the bus park, is a well-stocked pharmacy. (☎29149. Open daily 5am-8pm.) The **hospital** is a 5min. walk from the bus park, along the unpaved path by the ticket window. (☎29155. Open Su-Th 9am-3pm, F 9am-1pm.) The **Jiri Helminth Project,** just down the hill from Naya Bazaar, is actually a research group studying intestinal parasites, but it also puts its knowledge to use by providing free medical care and ambulance service to Kathmandu. (☎29154. Open M, W, F 8:30am-noon; on-call 24hr.) The **police station** (☎29150) is 4km away on the road to Kathmandu. **Cherdung Lodge** charges Rs8 per min. for calls to Kathmandu and Rs180 per min. for international calls with free callbacks.

From the bus park, backtrack up along the road to find accommodations; lodges line the road into town. **Sagarmatha Lodge ❶** (☎29152; doubles Rs20), 50m from the bus park, and **Sherpa Guide Lodge ❶** (☎29158; doubles Rs10-50), farthest from the bus park, are the cheapest and most rustic. Near the Sherpa Guide Lodge, the **Hotel Jiri View ❶,** has small but brighter and cleaner rooms (singles Rs50-100; doubles Rs100). The nearby **Hotel Gauri Himal ❶,** is the most upscale place in town and also the cleanest. (☎29158. Dorms Rs100; singles Rs300; doubles Rs500.)

HILE होले ☎ 026

A cool, misty 1900m above the Arun Valley, Hile has spectacular mountain views and a unique ethnic mix of Bhotiyas, Rais, Newaris, and Indians. A trailhead for treks into the world's deepest valley, Hile hosts a colorful, bustling market, but the terraced villages below offset the bartering frenzy. Piles of *doka* (the conical, head-strapped baskets that porters use) wait to be filled and carried off into the hills. Most of Hile's visitors soon head for higher ground, but the town is worth a visit, even for non-trekkers, with several small *gompas* and tea estates on the way up to Basantapur. The real attention-grabber is the Himalayan range itself; there are great views from the hilltop north of town, a 45-minute walk away.

NEPAL

The **bus stand** is at the northern end of the north-south road that runs downhill through town. Tickets are sold at a small booth set back on the east side of the street. There are **buses** to: **Basantapur** (1½hr., every 30min. 6am-6pm, Rs50); **Biratnagar** (5hr., 11am, Rs115); **Dharan** (4hr., every 30min. 4:30am-5:30pm, Rs80); **Kathmandu** (18hr., 1pm, Rs405). **Global Telecommunication Service,** 300m south on the main road, has STD/ISD and fax. The **post office** is down the narrow alleyway next to the Himali Hotel. South of the bus stop are several trekking-style lodges, which have restaurants, electricity, showers, and hot water on request. Run by a friendly Tibetan family, **Hotel Himali ❶,** a few minutes south of the bus stop on the left, has large, bright rooms. (☎40140. Singles Rs60; doubles Rs100.) The more rustic **Bablu Hotel ❶,** opposite Himali, won't win any awards, but the dorms are the cheapest around. (Dorms Rs25; doubles Rs100.)

BASANTAPUR बसन्तपुर ☎ 026

At an elevation of 2200m, Basantapur is blessed with a beauty and peace spoiled only by impertinent roosters intent on rousing slumberers at 4am. This is the end of the road for buses but only the beginning for trekkers through the Eastern Hills. Whether or not you're planning a trek, if you've come as far as Dharan or Hile, it's worth making the trip to Basantapur to take in the cool atmosphere. The bumpy **bus** ride along an unpaved road from Hile terminates at Basantapur's southern tip, near the **police post.** A 5min. walk along the rutted road brings you to the other end of town, where the road continues east toward **Terhathum** (26km) and, in clear weather, has great mountain views. During monsoon season, however, an otherworldly fog shrouds most mountain views and leaves everything (and everyone) damp. Even summer days can get chilly, so bring your leg-warmers. **Buses** run to **Biratnagar** (7hr., 8:45am, Rs171) and **Hile** (1½hr., every 30min. 4:30am-5pm, Rs50) continuing on to **Dharan** (5½hr., Rs135). Basantapur's **post office** is just past Hotel Yak (toward Terhathum); look for a red-and-white sign and stairs leading to a letter box. (Open Su-F 10am-5pm, Sa 10am-1pm.)

Basantapur's lodges all offer similar tea-house accommodations: beds in wooden rooms, common squat toilets, and restaurants where you can spend the evening sipping *tong-ba* (Rs10-20) and watching people stare at you. **Hotel Yak ❶,** a few minutes past the bus park along the main road, offers some reprieve from the noise pollution of the buses and has clean rooms, showers, and a quality restaurant. (☎/fax 69047. Singles Rs65; doubles Rs100. Restaurant open 7am-10pm.) **Birat Hotel and Lodge ❶,** just past the bus park, has small sky-blue rooms. (☎69043. Singles Rs50; doubles Rs80.) The restaurant below is the only place around where you can devour *dahl bhat* under the watchful eyes of V.I. Lenin. Think twice before taking that third helping of *dahl bhat,* though; you might not fit into the slightly cramped but clean rooms at the **Laxmi Hotel ❶,** across the street from the Birat. The TV-equipped restaurant is where you'll find most of Basantapur's after-hours action. (☎69022. Singles Rs40; doubles Rs75.) All hotels listed have **STD/ISD** service.

ILAM ईलाम ☎ 027

Safely removed from the rest of civilization by a 20hr. bus ride, Ilam is one of Nepal's hidden gems. Its visitors are rewarded by crisp air, pleasant strolls, and amazing views of mountains and valleys. Ilam is a starting point for treks through the **Kanchenjunga** region, although daytrips through the countryside can be just as rewarding. The 4-6hr. walk to the pilgrimage site of **Mai Pokhari,** 12km to the north, winds past tea gardens and forests to the top of a ridge crowned by a temple and a sacred lake. To the northwest, a 3-hr. walk leads to the bazaar town of **Mangalbare.** The descent to **Mai Khola,** the river crossing on the road from Birtamod, is another breathtaking journey that takes only a few hours on foot. While recovering from long walks, you can join the mob at the **haat bazaar,** held near the post office every Sunday and Thursday, or stroll through Ilam's famous **tea estate,** which stretches across the hills above the bus park. Before they are drowned in a steamy cup of *chiya,* Nepal's finest tea leaves are harvested and dried here.

Getting a seat on the **bus** that winds its way up to Ilam can be difficult. Your chances are best from Birtamod, accessible by local bus from Kakarbhitta (20min. frequent 4:30am-6pm, Rs13). Most buses heading toward Kakarbhitta or Bhadrapus, the nearest airport, also stop in Birtamod. There are also direct night buses from Kathmandu's New Bus Park (20hr., 2pm, Rs505). From Ilam, there are frequent buses to: **Biratnagar** (5hr., 11:30am, Rs175); **Charali** and **Birtamod** (3½hr., every hr. 6am-1:30pm, Rs90) **Dharan** (5hr., 6am, Rs175); **Kathmandu** (18hr., noon, Rs505); **Phidim** (5hr., 6am, Rs120), a small town north of Ilam. The bus park is at the bottom of the hill, at the south end of town. Lodges and **pharmacies** line the main street, which leads north from the bus park up to the **town square,** marked by a large bust of King Birendra planted in an oversized plaster lotus flower. **Mechi Tours and Travels,** facing the bust in the square, arranges bus and domestic plane tickets, private vehicles and drivers, and has **currency exchange, STD/ISD** and fax service with free callbacks, and **Internet access** (Rs15 per min.). The owner is a good source of information about the surrounding areas. (☎20367. Open daily 9am-6pm.) Three lanes diverge from the square opposite the main street. The one to the right leads to the **post office** (open Su-Th 10am-5pm, F 10am-3pm) and the **haat bazaar** (Su and Th). The rudimentary **hospital** (☎20036) is at the end of the path. **Tea Town Lodge ❶,** 250m north of the bus park on the west side of the main road, has bright, clean rooms with common squat toilets. It is a small step up on the price ladder—the lodges next to the noisy buspark are slightly cheaper—but to minimize the possibility of a roach encounter, it's probably worth it. (Singles Rs150; doubles Rs250.) The restaurants attached to the lodges all serve (can you guess?) all-you-can-eat *dahl bhat* at pretty standard prices (Rs25-40).

TREKKING IN NEPAL

For many years, the **Annapurna, Langtang,** and **Everest** regions were the only zones open to foreigners, but in recent years there has been an explosive growth in trekking routes all over Nepal. Most trekkers, though, still stick to the original three areas. Fabulous treks in their own right, these three also have the benefit of a good trekking infrastructure—you can stay in tea houses, eat locally prepared food, and not worry about the leaking tents and freeze-dried breakfasts that have blighted many a trekking expedition.

BEFORE YOU GO

For more information on planning a trek in the Himalayas, see **Trekking, p. 32.**

GEAR. Gear requirements are pretty minimal—walking from lodge to lodge saves you the burden of carrying food, cooking utensils, and a tent. A **sleeping bag** is handy at low altitudes and necessary at high altitudes. If you're going reasonably high (over 3000m), you need decent **warm clothing.** Mountaineering equipment is not necessary on the Classic Three routes, but you should have a good pair of **boots** and perhaps also a pair of **snow gaiters;** check with people who've done your route recently to find out what the snow conditions are. Even people from cold countries are often surprised by how cold it is in the mountains; lodges don't have

NEPAL

> **ENTRY REQUIREMENTS.** There are several restricted trekking regions that require expensive permits which can take a while to obtain. The big three trekking regions of Annapurna, Langtang, and Everest only require easily-obtained "entry permits": Annapurna region Rs2000; Langtang Rs1000; Everest Rs1000. You can pick up entry permits at the Himalaya Bank in the Thamel district of Kathmandu, in the same building as the Annapurna Conservation Area Project (ACAP) office. Entry permits for Annapurna are also available in Pokhara (see p. 824). If you're found in one of the trekking regions without a permit, you can get one on the spot, but they'll charge you double.

central heating, and sitting around in sub-zero temperatures can be pretty miserable unless you're properly bundled up. A **scarf** is a great asset, as it can also protect your face from biting winds. Bring plenty of layers—trekking can take you through both sweaty jungle and knee-deep snow, so you'll need clothing appropriate to all sorts of weather extremes. You might also want to get some sort of **waterproof covering** for your backpack so that you won't be completely at the mercy of the rain. If you plan to trek through snow, **sunglasses** and liberally-applied **sunscreen** are necessities; they're also handy in lower, sunny regions.

Everything you need can be either bought or rented in Nepal (see p. 32). A lot of rental equipment is manufactured in Nepal and emblazoned with fake GORE-TEX, North Face, or Patagonia labels. Choose carefully, especially when it comes to a vital piece of equipment like a backpack—that's something you really don't want falling to pieces when you're halfway up the Thorung-La. Kathmandu is the best place to rent or buy (and sell) supplies, with Pokhara a respectable second.

WATER. Although it is now possible to buy bottled water even in the higher and more remote villages on the major routes, treating your own water is both cheaper and better for the environment. Some lodges have boiled and filtered water for sale, and a safe drinking water program is under development in the Annapurna region, but there will still be times when you'll need to treat your own water. **Iodine**-treated water tastes awful, but iodine is both widely available and very effective. Mixing in some Tang flavor crystals will usually kill off the bad taste. Bottles of iodine solution are available in pharmacies in Kathmandu and Pokhara (Rs25); add five drops per liter. A pricier, but much easier, alternative is iodine tablets (e.g. **Potable Aqua**), available in bottles of 50; add two tablets per liter. Tablets are available in Kathmandu (see p. 775) from the Kathmandu Environmental Education Project (KEEP) or from the Himalayan Rescue Association (HRA). They are also available for Rs500 on the trail at ACAP checkpoints (in Annapurna) and HRA offices (in Manang, Annapurna and Pheriche, Everest).

MAPS. It's easy to find maps of the main trekking areas, and they are an important part of your pre-trek shopping list. However, most maps produced in Nepal are approximate at best, and the information on them should be treated with skepticism. Still, these maps (such as those produced by Nepa Maps) are useful for letting you know vaguely where you are and where you're headed. More accurate and expensive maps, generally known as "Schneider maps," are also available in Kathmandu, but these may well be out-of-date. The National Geographic Society's map of Everest is excellent, as is the Himalaya Kartographisches Institut map of the Annapurnas. KEEP and HRA in Kathmandu (see p. 775) are good sources of information on trekking routes. Their bulletin boards may also be helpful if you're looking for trekking partners.

PORTERS AND GUIDES

"Tea house" trekking doesn't require you to carry very much, but your sleeping bag and fleece long johns can feel outrageously heavy when you're laboring up a hill at 5000m. Porters can be hired just about anywhere in Nepal, but be careful not to get ripped off. Paying the **surcharge** associated with hiring a porter through a hotel, lodge, or trekking agency is probably a good investment for the peace of mind it brings—your porter is less likely to abscond if he has a boss to whom he must answer. You might also consider hiring a guide: someone who speaks English and can fill you in on what you're walking through. Contrary to the insistence of trekking agencies, guides are by no means necessary on the major routes; the ubiquity of locals and other trekkers makes it almost impossible to get lost.

Having a porter and/or guide does a lot more than take a burden off your shoulders—it can also gain you access to local culture. They are probably familiar figures on the trail and often have many friends along the way. If you're lucky, you might even end up as a guest for a night in their home village. and you'll probably learn much more Nepali than you would otherwise. There is, however, a downside: they set the agenda. You go at their pace and end up staying at a lodge of their choice, either because it's owned by their sister-in-law or because the owner supplies them with a hefty commission for bringing you in. Either way, this might not be exactly what you had in mind. Women trekking in the Annapurna region might consider hiring **female porters and guides** from Pokhara's all-female trekking agency, **3 Sisters Adventure Trekking** (see p. 831).

It is your responsibility to ensure that your guide and/or porter is properly outfitted for the trek. Over-burdened and under-clothed porters have died of exposure and AMS at high altitudes. Many of them are lowlanders with no more immunity to cold and high altitudes than you.

ON THE TRAIL

Instead of sticking to a strict schedule, we suggest that you simply take as much or as little time over the trek as you feel comfortable with. Some people enjoy hurtling along the trail while others like to stop every 30 seconds to scrutinize yet another wildflower. Most people get up early and hike for 5-6hr. per day. This gives you plenty of time at the end of the day to wash your socks, take a shower, and hang out around your lodge's dining table. The social scene in lodges can be quite fun, and it is a good source of trekking companions for days to come.

ROUTE-FINDING. Route-finding on the major routes is straightforward; you are following the Himalayan equivalent of a highway. Since you are essentially walking from village to village, when in doubt, simply ask the way to the next village. It's not always a good idea to ask lodge employees even though their English may be good, because they've been known to exaggerate the distance to the next place in the hope that you'll give up for the day and stay at their lodge.

ACCOMMODATIONS AND FOOD. In the Classic Three trekking areas, whole villages were long ago converted into dense constellations of lodges. These were once the **tea houses** of "tea house trek" fame, but many are now fancy hotels, complete with single or double rooms, solar-heated shower systems, and extensive menus. Some of the fancier establishments even sport Western-style toilets. But there are still places—usually a village or two off the beaten track—where you can stay in the simplest of accommodations.

Food on the trail used to consist of *dahl bhat* three times a day, but it's now quite easy to avoid it altogether. Common food options include oatmeal, pizza, fried rice, apple pie, and chocolate cake. Food in many mountain villages tends to be prepared with reckless disregard for hygiene. A full range of bottled drinks, from Coke to Carlsberg, is also generally available, though prices skyrocket as you get farther away from the main roads.

Trekking becomes more expensive the higher you go: everything is carried up by donkey or porter, thus explaining the Rs100 bottles of Coke at 4000m. At lower altitudes you can travel comfortably at Rs300-500 per day, though you may find yourself dropping Rs700-900 per day as you hike higher. Planning a Rs600 per day budget should see you through your trek quite well. Lodge and restaurant rates are generally regulated by each town, which means that prices are effectively fixed.

LOCAL SERVICES. There are a few **banks** on the major routes (in Chame, Tatopani, and Jomsom in Annapurna, and in Namche on the Everest trek), but they offer poor exchange rates, and they *do not* handle credit cards. Change can be a problem, so bring plenty of small denomination bills. Some of the ritzier lodges will change US dollars, at miserable rates. **Film** and **batteries** are widely available along the major routes. **Pharmacies** are few and far between, and you should bring medications with you.

> **WARNING.** There have been occasional reports of **robberies** and **rapes** on the trails. Trekkers (especially women) should think twice before going alone, particularly off season, when the trails are less crowded.

THE ANNAPURNA REGION अन्नपुरण

The Annapurna Conservation Area is Nepal's most popular, and arguably most spectacular, trekking region. The ecological and cultural diversity is remarkable, and the vistas—notably at Annapurna Base Camp, Poon Hill, and around Manang—are peerless. Trekkers follow three main routes in the Annapurna region: the Annapurna Circuit, the Jomsom trek, and the Annapurna Sanctuary. These can be done separately, or combined into a single four-week mega-trek. If you've only got a few days, however, it's easy to get a good taste of trekking by connecting some of the routes out of Pokhara. A popular option is the 4-5 day loop from Pokhara to Ghorepani to Ghandruk and back. This route has fine views (from **Poon Hill** above Ghorepani) and provides the opportunity to spend some time in Gurung villages. Alternatively, you can trek through Birethanti, Ghandruk, Landruk, and Dhampus. Both of these routes involve cobbling together parts of the Jomsom (see p. 858) and Sanctuary (see p. 862) treks.

THE ANNAPURNA CIRCUIT

The Annapurna Circuit is a trekker's dream come true, with as rich a cross-section of Hindu and Buddhist culture, mountain landscapes, and exhilarating hikes as you can cram into a **16-21 day trek.** You might find yourself knee-deep in snow one day, crossing wind-swept desert the next, and strolling through forests of rhododendrons a few days after that. The exhausting challenge of the Thorung La (5416m) is well rewarded upon arrival in the holy town of Muktinath. Almost everybody walks it in the same direction, crossing the pass from Manang to Muktinath. The pass is easier to cross in this direction, and there are more accommodations high up on the Manang side than on the Muktinath side. But there's an additional advantage as the route seems much less crowded without traffic coming toward you.

ANNAPURNA CIRCUIT: BESISAHAR TO CHAME

TRANSPORTATION: Buses are the best way to get to the trailhead in Besisahar. From **Pokhara** to **Besisahar** (6hr.; daily 7:25, 8:35am; noon Rs85-105); from **Kathmandu,** take a Pokhara-bound bus to Dumre; from **Dumre** to **Besisahar** (3hr., frequent, Rs 35).

SERVICES: Food and lodging are available in numerous villages along this section of the trek. There are also post offices, police stations and check-points, some equipment stores (in Chame), and telephone booths along the way.

HIGHLIGHTS: Views of Himalchuli, Ngadi Chuli, Manaslu, Annapurna II and IV, and other snow-capped mountains. Various waterfalls surrounded by lush forest vegetation and rice terraces cut into the hillsides.

VILLAGE	ALTITUDE	TIME
Besisahar	820m	start
Khudi	790m	2hr.
Bhulbhule	840m	1hr.
Ngadi	920m	1hr.
Bahundanda	1310m	2hr.
Syange	1140m	2½hr.
Chamje	1410m	3hr.
Tal	1660m	2hr.
Dharapani	1880m	2½hr.
Bagarchhap	2100m	1hr.
Dhanakyu	2180m	30min.
Lata Marang	2350m	2hr.
Koto	2530m	2hr.
Chame	2620m	30min.

FEATURES: This portion of the hike leads first through verdant subtropical woods and rice paddies, then through rhododendron and pine forests and stands of bamboo. At higher elevations, rice cultivation gives way to corn, barley, and potato fields while evergreens replace tropical vegetation in the woods. Along the route, Buddhist and Tibetan influences begin to dominate the local architecture and culture. Altitude sickness is not a risk during this portion of the trek.

BESISAHAR TO CHAME. The circuit starts in **Besisahar,** at the end of a road heading north from Dumre on the Kathmandu-Pokhara road. Besisahar is a typical Nepali end-of-the-road town with plenty of accommodations, electricity, and phone service.

From Besisahar, the trail leads to **Khudi** and then heads north along the Marsyangdi, criss-crossing the river on suspension bridges. **Bhulbhule,** which has an ACAP office, and **Ngadi** are next. The first real climb of the trek up to **Bahundanda,** at a notch in the ridge high above the river, is child's play—both in terms of the exertion and the great views at the top—compared to what you'll get later on. You'll still be high above the river after the steep descent beyond Bahundanda, following a magnificent trail hewn out of the valley's rock walls. Of the many waterfalls along this trip, the most scenic is the one that comes crashing down the west wall of the valley close to **Syange,** where a suspension bridge takes traffic across the river. Beyond **Chamje,** a steep climb up through the rubble of a huge landslide brings you to **Tal,** a paradise on the dry lake bed left behind when a landslide dammed the river. There's an ACAP office here as well as a number of hotels.

There are three river crossings between Tal and **Dharapani,** where you'll find a police check-point, post office, and several telephones. Beyond Dharapani, the route follows the river left and takes you to the north of the main Annapurna massif. The villages start to look more Tibetan from this point. Next, you'll pass through **Bagarchhap,** a town that has bounced back from a devastating landslide in 1995, and **Dhanakyu** shortly thereafter. Unless you want an extra workout, you'll take the low route, which passes through **Lata Marang** and **Koto,** a spread-out town with a police check-point at the far end. **Chame,** not far from Koto, serves as the seat of government for the Manang district. It's the closest thing to a real town since Besisahar. Chame has everything—its own hospital, a bank, a post office, the district police headquarters, the last telephones before Manang, an information bureau, and stores where you can stock up on just about anything, including cold weather gear. As if that weren't enough, across the bridge, there's a hot spring that locals love to frequent. **Beyond Chame, altitude sickness becomes a serious risk.**

ANNAPURNA CIRCUIT: CHAME TO MUKTINATH

TRANSPORTATION: Flights leave from **Hongde** and head to **Pokhara** (Tu and Sa 8am, US$50). Check departure details at the RNAC office opposite the airstrip.

SERVICES: Food and lodging are not difficult to find, although the trail from Thorung Phedi to Muktinath is essentially barren, so be prepared. Manang contains a post office, an HRA clinic with pharmaceutical products for sale, several lodges, and some equipment shops. There is a police checkpoint at Hongde.

HIGHLIGHTS: Views of the Annapurnas. The icy, crystalline Tilicho Tal glacial lake. Tibetan-style villages with ancient *gompas* and herds of rugged animals, including yaks. Thorung-La, a breath-takingly high pass with spectacular views of the surrounding ridges.

VILLAGE	ALTITUDE	TIME
Chame	2620m	start
Thaleku	2720m	30min.
Bhratang	2850m	1½hr.
Dhukure Pokhari	3060m	2hr.
Pisang	3130m	1hr.
Hongde (low route)	3320m	2½hr.
Braga	3480m	1½hr.
Manang	3500m	30min.
Tengi	3640m	30min.
Ghunsang	3880m	1hr.
Yak Kharka/Letdar	4100m	1hr.
Thorung Phedi	4470m	1hr.
Thorung La (pass)	5416m	5hr.
Muktinath	3800m	3½hr.

FEATURES: As the trail ascends from Chame, it travels through deep woods and past enormous rock faces. Beyond Pisang, the trek enters the Nyesyang region, a dry area where the locals grow hardy crops and herd horses, yaks, and goats. The trail to Thorung La winds up moraines and has been used by herders for hundreds of years. This portion of the trek puts hikers at risk of **frostbite** and **altitude sickness**. Make sure that you have adequate clothing for snowy, cold conditions, and do not push yourself if you think you may have any symptoms of AMS (see p. 36).

CHAME TO MANANG. The route from Chame to Manang, following the increasingly deep Marsyangdi River valley, provides the best mountain views on the circuit trek. You're liable to go through a lot of film here—you'll stop to capture the perfect panorama of alpine green and rugged, white peaks only to find one even more perfect 30min. down the road. Heading west from Chame to Manang, the major peaks are: Lamjung Himal (6932m), Annapurna II (7939m), Annapurna IV (7525m), Annapurna III (7555m), and Gangapurna (7454m). The road west of Chame is dominated to the north by the "Great Wall of Pisang," a huge, smooth slab of slate that rises 1200m above the valley floor—to the Gurung people, it is the gateway to the land of the dead. You'll pass through **Thaleku** and **Bhratang** before crossing the river and ascending to picturesque **Dhukure Pokhari**, a breathless climb that serves as a friendly reminder of how high up you've come. **Pisang**, a popular resting point one day from Manang, is divided in two: New Pisang, on the south side of the river, is full of enormous lodges; Old Pisang, up the hill on the north side, is a dense tangle of flat-roofed stone buildings clustered around a *gompa* that hasn't changed much in the past 500 years.

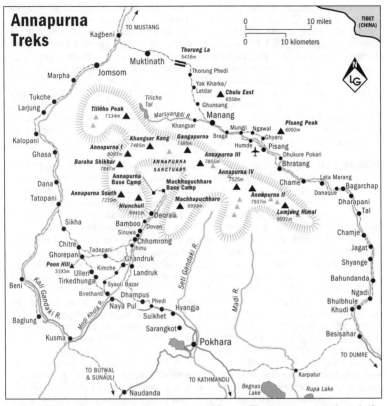

Annapurna Treks

From Pisang, you have a choice of routes to Manang. The low route is a short day's hike; the high route is a couple of hours longer. The **low route,** or **main trail,** from Lower Pisang is the main drag along the valley floor. It passes the airstrip at **Hongde** and heads to **Braga** and **Manang.** While the low route doesn't disappoint, the **high route** rewards the extra exertion a hundred-fold. Also, climbing higher and then descending to sleep is good for acclimatization. This route begins with a short, sharp ascent to Old Pisang and continues for a relatively flat first few kilometers before ascending steeply to **Ghyaru** (3670m), where the views of the Annapurnas to the south are unbeatable. From Ghyaru, the road stays high, following the valley wall to a promontory just above the ruined fort at Tiwol Danda before arriving at picturesque **Ngawal** (3650m).

From Ngawal, the route heads back down to join the low route in the main valley. Route-finding can be a little tricky here: pick up the trail dropping down the minor valley just beyond Ngawal, but avoid the major left fork (which leads to the airstrip). The high route follows the north bank of the river until the main trail crosses the river to join it at **Mungje** (3480m). **Braga,** 30min. farther, is an extraordinary village crowned with the region's oldest *gompa,* which is well worth a visit (open daily 7-10am and 1-5pm).

Manang, a medieval, Tibetan-style village, is the main destination of the Circuit trek. This is your last chance to make sure that your gloves are warm enough for the Thorung-La. Manang's HRA clinic has a free talk on altitude sickness at 3pm in season (Sept.-Dec. and Mar.-May). The HRA shop sells iodine, vitamin C, diamox, and has a small book exchange. There's also an ACAP office and a post office in town. Because Manang is a popular one- or two-day stopping point for acclimatization, the lodges (particularly the **Yak Lodge,** with its outstanding kitchen staff) are excellent, and there is plenty to do. There are a number of *gompas* and other attractions in the vicinity that make for popular daytrips, and if AMS is holding you back, you can chill out and watch movies at a number of places in Manang. **Khangsar** (3710m), an easy 2hr. walk away, is a popular acclimatization point for people on day hikes out of Manang. There are lodges here that can serve as a first step on the way to the great high-altitude lake, **Tilicho Tal** (5000m), first explored by Herzog's 1950 expedition; there's a seasonal lodge between Khansar and the lake.

MANANG TO MUKTINATH. Beyond Manang, thoughts turn to the **Thorung-La Pass** (5416m; 17,768 ft.). You'll want to spend 1-2 days acclimatizing in Manang and then 2-3 short days climbing to the foot of the pass to guard against altitude sickness. HRA recommends ascending no more than 450m in a day once you get above 3500m. Stops include **Tengi, Ghunsang,** and **Yak Kharka/Letdar.** There are plenty of opportunities for hikes up the flanks of **Chulu,** north of Ghunsang and Letdar.

Two routes go from Letdar to Thorong Phedi, neither of which is fully safe. The lower, easier route is prone to landslides and avalanches, which have proved fatal in the past; the higher route involves a steep, narrow descent into Thorung Phedi, which, when covered in snow or ice, can send you down a lot faster and more directly than you'd like.

Thorung Phedi, literally "foot of Thorung," is the last settlement before the pass, though there is a lodge at the **high camp** 350m higher up. Staying at high camp will save an hour off the big ascent to the pass. Set out from Thorung Phedi at first light. Severe conditions are common on the pass, and plenty of trekkers have left with frostbite as a souvenir. Come properly prepared, and be willing to sit out bad weather in a hut rather than pressing on. There is a stone hut at 5100m and another one at the pass itself, inhabited by a hardy entrepreneur who sells chocolate (Rs100) and much-needed hot drinks (Rs70-80). If everything goes well, crossing the pass can be a marvelous experience. It's a long, steep descent to **Muktinath;** the only settlement along the way is the lodge at **Chatar Puk** (4120m), not far above it.

ANIMAL INSIGHT In a land devoid of almost everything but rock and ice, animals are necessary for survival—they carry supplies, provide food for villagers, and have also served as inspiration for proverbs that run the gamut from droll to bizarre to utterly revolting. So, before you head out on the trail tomorrow, contemplate these words of wisdom from ancient Himalayan cultures.

When pride rides a donkey, her dainty feet dangle on the ground... When the horse is on the move, don't goad it with the stirrup; when a man is humility itself, don't treat him with arrogance... Just as a horse with a long jaw appears old, a man of patience may also look a fool... When falsehood is a hill, truth is only a yak... The miraculous: butter without a cow; an egg without a bird. The ridiculous: to load cargo upon a frog; to get milk from a tadpole... When a man nourishes a baby conch on milk, he hopes to use it to fend off crocodiles... For the tortoise living in a well, just hearing of the ocean's greatness will kill it... Donkey's dung: a person who is smooth on the outside, coarse and rough on the inside... A pigeon's anus cannot excrete a gold earring (huh?)... A bigger yak doesn't mean bigger dung.

MUKTINATH TO POKHARA. The rest of the Annapurna circuit trek is the Jomsom trek done in reverse (see below). After Thorung-La, this leg will be luxury. It's mostly downhill, rarely steep, and there is a lot of great apple pie along the way. Dig in: you've earned it.

🖪 JOMSOM TREK जोमसोम

This there-and-back route can be converted into a there-*or*-back route by flying one way between Jomsom (2710m) and Pokhara. Flying directly to high altitudes entails spending a day or two acclimatizing upon arrival. Hiking up to Muktinath from Pokhara should take around **6-9 days.**

JOMSOM TREK: BIRETHANTI TO MUKTINATH

TRANSPORTATION: RNAC, Cosmic, Shangri-La, and Skyline all **fly out of Jomsom** to **Pokhara** (20min.; all flights 7am, weather permitting; RNAC US$50, others US$61). Ask for a window seat and gawk at the closer-than-close mountain views. **Buses** run from Pokhara's Baglung Bus Stand to **Naya Pul** (2hr., every hr. 5:30am-6pm, Rs50). **Cars** will also make the trip for Rs600, 4 persons max. **Birethanti** is a 20min. walk from Naya Pul.

SERVICES: Food and lodging options abound on the trail. Tatopani offers all the essential shops and services: a post office, a bank, public phones, shoe-repair, book shops, etc. There are several police checkpoints along the trail.

VILLAGE	ALTITUDE	TIME
Birethanti	1100m	start
Ulleri	2080m	3hr.
Ghorepani	2820m	3hr.
Sikha	1980m	2hr.
Tatopani	1190m	2hr.
Dana	1400m	2hr.
Ghasa	2040m	4½hr.
Kalopani	2530m	3½hr.
Tukche	2590m	3hr.
Marpha	2670m	2½hr.
Jomsom	2710m	1½hr.
Kagbeni	2800m	2½hr.
Muktinath	3800m	4hr.

HIGHLIGHTS: Of course, amazing views of Himalayan giants, including Dhaulagiri and the Annapurnas. Deep canyons and graceful waterfalls. Great lodges with delicious grub. Soil containing fossilized mollusks, known as *shaligram,* that are believed to symbolize Vishnu. The complex of temples in Muktinath.

FEATURES: The beginning of the trail passes through bamboo stands and runs next to streams and waterfalls. After Ulleri, hardwood and rhododendron forests surround the path. Beyond Tatopani and its hot springs, the trail heads through Kali Gandaki Gorge, which becomes landslide-prone and frighteningly narrow at points. Near Ghasa, the plants are mostly subtropical species and gradually change to pine woods towards Kalopani; at Marpha, the climate becomes arid as the winds of the Trans-Himalaya buffet the land. The rest of the way to Muktinath, the countryside is barren and rocky, although locals have managed to cultivate some fruit trees and other crops. Beyond Kagbeni, **altitude sickness** becomes a risk, and if you plan to cross Thorung-La from this side, allot several days for acclimatization.

BIRETHANTI TO GHOREPANI. Trekkers typically start at **Birethanti,** a town at the confluence of the Bhurungdi and Modi Khola Rivers and a picturesque spot with plenty of lodges, a bank, a post office, an art gallery, and an ACAP checkpost that marks your entry into the Conservation Area.

NEPAL

The trail follows the Bhurungdi Khola to **Hille** and another dense cluster of lodges at **Tirkedhunga** (1580m). Now, the *real* climbing starts: it's basically uphill all the way to Ghorepani. The first, steepest section brings you through intricately terraced hillsides to the village of **Ulleri.** Beyond Ulleri, you move into increasingly dense forest. If you're trekking in the pre-monsoon season (Mar.-May), this area will probably reward you with spectacular floral displays of the arboreal rhododendrons of the Himalayas.

Ghorepani, or the pass **(Deorali)** just beyond it, is a major tourist center, and the surrounding area bears the ugly scars of deforestation. Ghorepani itself, a creation of the trekking business, looks like a bizarre hybrid of resort and shanty-town. There's an ACAP office here and a phone in the Nice View Lodge. A couple of book shop/exchanges can outfit you with reading material for your trek. There are a number of side trails through the nearby forests, and Ghorepani commands a magnificent panorama of Dhaulagiri and the entire Annapurna massif—the view is best seen at dawn from **Poon Hill** (3194m), 1hr. behind Ghorepani. It is possible to connect to **Ghandruk** via a forest path from Ghorepani.

> ■ **WARNING.** There have been several incidents of theft on the secluded forest trails around Ghorepani. Trekking in a group is recommended, particularly between Ghorepani and Tirkedhunga and between Ghorepani and Ghandruk.

GHOREPANI TO TUKCHE. From Ghorepani, the main trail heads gently downhill through Chitre, Phalate, Sikha, and Ghara to **Tatopani** and the Kali Gandaki Valley. From Chitre, there are trails via Tadapani to Ghandruk and Chomrong, on the way to the Annapurna Sanctuary. Trekking in the opposite direction, from Tatopani to Ghorepani, is 6-8hr. of blood, tears, toil, and sweat. Tatopani's famed **hot springs** (Rs10 entry fee) have been converted into two concrete, naturally heated hot tubs, flanked by a stand that serves soft drinks and beer (Rs120; happy hour 3-6pm has beer and popcorn for Rs110). This luxury, plus a number of great lodges with delectable food, make Tatopani an ideal rest stop. You can find the essentials here, including a shoe-repair shop, post office, bank, public phone, booksellers, and a police check-post. The quickest way to the hot springs by the river is to cut through the idyllic garden of the Dhaulagiri Lodge.

While most people heading south through Tatopani choose to head up toward Ghorepani, an alternative low-level route along the river to **Beni** (820m) and **Baglung** it is the quickest passage between Pokhara and Tatopani. Beni marks the endpoint of the road out of Pokhara, and is within a day's walk of Tatopani. Since part of the road is unfinished, you may need to take two buses from Beni to Pokhara (5hr., Rs70). A private vehicle will set you back Rs2500—contact the Yeti Hotel in Beni for jeep service.

Heading north out of Tatopani, start your journey through the Himalayas with Dhaulagiri to your left and the Annapurnas to your right. Houses range from the scattered, thatched homes of the Nepalese hinterland to the flat-roofed stone houses of the higher altitudes, which are often tightly clustered into dense, claustrophobic villages for protection against the brutal upland winds. Hindu shrines and iconography never disappear entirely, but prayer flags, wheels, and stones become the dominant religious motifs as you head north. Make sure to keep all shrines on your right as you pass them, in accordance with Buddhist custom.

The first major settlement north of Tatopani, **Dana** once thrived on salt trade taxation. From here to **Ghasa,** keep an eye open for langur monkeys. **Lete** and **Kalopani,** the next major settlements, have effectively fused into one and are linked by a flagstone trail. As you head north from Kalopani to **Tukche,** you will be immediately below the immense eastern buttresses of Dhaulagiri. Its magnificent ice fall dominates the view; a trail out of the valley will take you on a daytrip to the base of the ice fall. Navigation south of Tukche can be tricky in the dry season because the route heads to the stony valley floor, crossing the river on wobbly temporary bridges. Don't play Indiana Jones and ford the river; it's deep and the current is vicious. Head back to the bridges instead.

TUKCHE TO MUKTINATH. The next town north after Tukche, **Marpha** is a trekker favorite, with its neatly-clustered stone houses and elegantly-paved main street. Beyond Marpha is the high altitude desert of the Trans-Himalaya. Every afternoon this area (and everywhere north) is blasted by brutal winds that can whip the grit of the river valley into a blinding, flesh-stinging frenzy. Unless you want to be slapped around by Mother Nature, plan on being indoors by midday, especially if you're heading south *into* the wind.

Jomsom, the regional administration center, is a weird mix of traditional highland trading town, trekking mecca, and unpopular posting for bureaucrats. With its airstrip, it's also the beginning or end of many treks. Don't be misled, however, by the Jomsom trek's name—Jomsom is not the goal of the trek, it's merely the biggest town on the route. Jomsom has all the facilities you'd expect of an administrative center, including a hospital, bank, and post office. Many of these services, as well as a small cluster of lodges, are on the east bank of the river across the new suspension bridge. The airport and airline offices, police check-post, and most of the lodges and trekking supply stores (some of which sell books as well as toilet paper and biscuits), are on the west bank of the river at the south end of town.

Beyond Jomsom, the farther you go up the valley, the more you begin to feel that you are in Tibet, geographically, climatically, and ethnically. Keep going north (you need special and expensive permits to do this) and you will enter the ancient Buddhist kingdom of **Mustang,** a finger of Nepal that juts northward into Tibetan territory. It was this area that Kampa guerillas from western Tibet claimed as their own during the 60s when they waged war against the occupying Chinese. A regular trekking permit will take you as far as **Kagbeni,** a dusty cluster of Tibetan houses around an ancient *gompa* set in its own patch of irrigated green.

The real goal of the Jomsom trek is **Muktinath,** at the head of a valley to the east of the main Kali Gandaki Gorge. It can be approached from Kagbeni or more directly from Jomsom. While following the stony riverbed of the Kali Gandaki north of Jomsom, keep an eye open for fossil ammonites, the distinctively coiled long-dead mollusks that symbolize Vishnu. They were thrust up from their sea-bed graves along with the rest of the Himalayas when the Indian subcontinent collided with Asia. It's partly the abundance of these fossils, known locally as *shaligram,* that accounts for Muktinath's importance to Hindu and Buddhist pilgrims.

The brown and ochre desert hills, the snow-capped peaks to the south, the deep blue sky, the little patches of irrigated green in the valley floor, and the Tibetan villages scattered about the valley make Muktinath worth every drop of sweat and every aching joint. The complex of temples that draw many pilgrims to Muktinath includes 108 spouts of holy water and a sacred spot where a jet of natural gas sustains a small flame in a pool of water. Less spectacular, but nonetheless useful, are Muktinath's ACAP office and police check-post. While only the very fit or masochistic will try to cross the Thorung-La Pass from Muktinath (it's a very steep 7-8hr. climb), a daytrip part of the way up will reward you with great views and can help acclimatization. When the open road calls again, you can retrace your steps to Jomsom and then either fly or walk back to Pokhara.

NEPAL

◢ THE ANNAPURNA SANCTUARY

Pioneered by British climbing expeditions during the late 1950s, this **7-12 day trek** into the Annapurna Sanctuary up the Modi Khola Valley is the quickest and easiest route from Pokhara up to the Himalayan giants. The sanctuary itself is a gargantuan natural amphitheater with a 360 degree panorama of looming, white peaks.

ANNAPURNA SANCTUARY: BIRETHANTI TO ANNAPURNA BASE CAMP

TRANSPORTATION: The trek begins in **Birenthanti** (see directions for **Jomsom Trek,** above). A **bus** to the Baglung bus park in **Pokhara** leaves from **Dhampus Phedi** (2hr., every hr. 6am-6pm, Rs17), should you choose to end the trek here. **Taxis** make the trip to Lakeside, Pokhara, for Rs250, 4 passenger max.

SERVICES: There are lodges all the way up to Annapurna Base Camp, but the luxuries (satellite TV, equipment stores, telephones) stop after Chhomrong. Ghandruk and Chhomrong are the largest villages on the trek, and most services are available in them. **Lodges in the sanctuary often close during the winter,** so ask around to find out if they are open.

HIGHLIGHTS: Quaint Gurung villages with luxurious accommodations. Incredible Himalayan panoramas, including Machhapuchhare, Hiunchuli, and the Annapurnas. Sledding on the snowy slopes around Annapurna Base Camp.

LANDMARK	ALTITUDE	TIME
Birenthanti	1100m	start
Syauli Bazar	1150m	2½hr.
Kimche	1760m	1hr.
Ghandruk	2010m	2hr.
Kimrong Danda	2260m	2hr.
Chhomrong	2050m	3½hr.
Sinuwa	2320m	2½hr.
Bamboo	2350m	3hr.
Dovan	2610m	1hr.
Himalaya	2870m	1½hr.
Deorali	3230m	2hr.
Machhapuchhare base camp	3700m	3hr.
Annapurna Base Camp	4130m	2hr.

FEATURES: The trail moves uphill through forests and rice paddies. After Chhomrong, the last permanent settlement on the trek, the path passes through stands of bamboo and rhododendron. Beyond Deorali, the trail enters an avalanche-blasted gorge and emerges in the Annapurna Sanctuary, a windblown bowl enclosed by exquisite 7000-8000m peaks. **Avalanches** are a serious concern on portions of the trek. **Altitude sickness** is a risk around and after Deorali. If you are cooking your own food, be aware that **the use of firewood is not permitted beyond Ghandruk.**

BIRETHANTI TO DEORALI. The trek begins in **Birethanti** (also the starting point for the Jomsom trek) and goes north up the west bank of the Modi Khola. This pleasant riverside amble turns serious at the spread-out **Syauli Bazaar,** when the trail turns uphill to **Kimche,** and after many stone steps, leads to **Ghandruk.** For many years, the source of this well-heeled Gurung village's wealth was the British Army, which recruited heavily here for its famed Gorkha fighters. Now, however, the village is riding the crest of a major trekking wave, as its several grand concrete hotels suggest. As well as a police check-post, there are an ACAP office with a number of interesting displays and two "Gurung Museums," both of which are rooms crammed with traditional Gurung tools, clothes, and wares (Rs30 entrance fee for each). A number of hotels have phones. Ignore the signs for Jhinu hot springs here—it's a 2-3hr. walk away and better approached on your return journey (see below).

From Ghandruk, the route heads up to **Kimrong Danda** before descending steeply to a river crossing at **Kimrong Khola** (1830m) and ascending painfully to **Upper Chhomrong** (2180m). There are plenty of lodges, but try to resist the temptation to call it a day here. Instead, go down to **Chhomrong** proper, another large, handsome Gurung village, with a beautifully engineered stone staircase. Chhomrong is your last chance to stock up on supplies for the sanctuary; you can buy and rent gear here for non-negotiable rates. A number of lodges have telephones. The police check-point near the bottom of the hill is the last on your way up toward the sanctuary. ▓The Chhomrong Guest House wins the prize for "Best Lodge in the Annapurnas." It's friendly, efficient, and comfortable, and the cook has a golden touch: the chocolate cake is especially scrumptious. Their satellite TV and DVD player bring you daily movies and BBC World Service.

The road out of Chhomrong leads down across a river, and then steeply up to **Sinuwa,** which commands some impressive views of the surrounding countryside. From Sinuwa, a pleasant walk through the woods turns steeply downhill through a bamboo forest to the aptly-named **Bamboo,** a small collection of hotels. Beyond Bamboo, the path leads steadily upward, first to **Dovan,** and then to **Himalaya,** which is nothing more than a couple of lodges. The last stop-off in the valley is at **Deorali,** just beyond **Hinko** (3140m); a huge over-hanging boulder here has provided shelter for many a weather-beset party. There are also a number of non-boulder lodges in Deorali. Note that your rate of **altitude gain** should now be a serious consideration, especially if you've come straight up from Pokhara.

DEORALI TO ANNAPURNA BASE CAMP. The section between Deorali and **Machhapuchhare Base Camp,** or **MBC,** on the edge of the sanctuary, can be dangerous. It basically serves as a repository for avalanches coming off the upper slopes of Hiunchuli to the west, making it a bad place to be after heavy snowfall. In March 2001, four trekkers were killed in an avalanche just beyond Deorali. Pay attention to conditions and seek local advice; it's best to leave early in the morning and be past the avalanche tracks by 10:30am, before the sun and wind start unsettling heavy drifts of snow. There is an alternative route beyond Deorali that bypasses the most dangerous stretch. Five to ten minutes out of town, a small path cuts across the river on a rickety footbridge. The trail leads along the east bank of the river for 45min. before rejoining the main path on the west bank. Beyond this point, you still have to cross a couple of avalanche tracks.

As you emerge from the gorge of the Modi Khola, the first cluster of lodges is at what is inaccurately called Machhapuchhare Base Camp—the mountain is sacred and off-limits. The best views are farther into the sanctuary at the **Annapurna Base Camp,** or **ABC.** If you've come up from Pokhara and altitude sickness is a potential problem, consider spending two nights at MBC and doing an early there-and-back trip to ABC. Originally established by Chris Bonington's Annapurna South Face Expedition in 1970, ABC now consists of several lodges crouched in a very desolate, windblown spot (if you're trekking Jan.-Feb., check to see that the lodges are open). The view from ABC includes a whole series of Himalayan walls; clockwise from the south are: Hiunchuli, Annapurna South, Baraha Shikhar (Fang), Annapurna I, Singu Chuli (Fluted Peak), Tharpu Chuli (Tent Peak), Annapurna III, and Machhapuchhare. The snowy slopes around ABC are ideal for sledding: bring snow pants or a plastic sheet and you can slide all the way back down to MBC.

ABC TO DHAMPUS. The return trip backtracks to Chhomrong, from which it's possible to take a different route back to Pokhara than the one that starts in Birethanti. To continue to Dhampus from Upper Chomrong, drop down to **Jhinu Danda** (1730m), which is a 15min. walk away from idyllic **Jhinu hot springs.** Now a concrete-sided pool, the hot springs are located by the river in a cool, forested valley that is popular with both trekkers and langur monkeys. Continue across the Modi

Khola on the not-so-new **New Bridge** (1650m), which also contains a small cluster of lodges. From here, it's a matter of following the river until the ascent to the big bustling village of **Landruk** (1630m). **Tolka** (1730m) is strung out over 2km. A final reminder of the rigors of uphill hiking brings you to **Bhichok Deorali** (2100m). It's then a pleasant walk along the ridge to **Potana** (1970m). If you're heading from Potana up toward Landruk, keep right at both of the forks that come up shortly after Potana. If you're heading down from Potana, keep left at the fork 10min. after Potana. **Dhampus** (1690m) is the final settlement along the route. A big village stretched out along a ridge for a couple of kilometers, Dhampus used to have something of a reputation among trekkers as a den of thieves, but that dubious claim to fame seems to have been based on only a handful of incidents that occurred 20 years ago. The final descent from Dhampus to **Dhampus Phedi** (1140m), where you visit your final check-post, is long, steep, hot, and dusty. An alternative route out of Chhomrong takes you via Tadapani to Ghorepani and Poon Hill (see above). From there, it's a steep descent to Birethanti and Naya Pul.

THE LANGTANG REGION लाग्ंटाग्ं

The black sheep of the Classic Three, the Langtang region is often passed over by trekkers drawn by name recognition to Annapurna and Everest. The relative obscurity of the Langtang trek means that its trails are comparatively uncrowded, and with its majestic terrain and proximity to Kathmandu, Langtang is really quite an attractive trekking region. The general title "Langtang" actually covers three distinct but adjacent areas, the **Langtang Valley, Gosainkund,** and **Helambu.** Each of these areas can be visited alone, or they can be strung together into one longer trek. Individually, each area takes between 4-8 days to trek; collectively, the three regions can be hiked in **12-16 days.** The Langtang Valley has a straightforward trek up the valley and offers the chance for exploring some of the peaks and glaciers at its head; in Gosainkund, there is a series of frigid, high-altitude lakes, and plenty of alpine terrain; Helambu is lower and greener, winding through the jungled hills at the northern edge of the Kathmandu Valley.

THE LANGTANG VALLEY TREK

The Langtang Valley takes most people 5-6 days round-trip from Syabru-Besi; the trail is straightforward, following the Langtang River up the Langtang Valley, passing through the village of Langtang, and on to the Langtang Lodge for a few hours' Langtang lie-down. The return trip plods back down the same trail and back out to Syabru Besi. The stunning views, as well as the numerous opportunities for exploration from Kyanjin Gompa at the head of the valley, make this the most popular of the Langtang treks.

SYABRU BESI TO LAMA HOTEL. Treks in Langtang used to start in the town of **Dhunche,** but the development of this area has made **Syabru Besi,** a bit farther along the road by bus, a more attractive and convenient base. The town has a number of decent hotels catering to trekkers, including the **Buddha Guest House** and the **Northland Tibetan Guest House.** Besides telephone services, Syabru Besi has few other facilities. If you really want to escape the crowds, cross the river, and stay in one of the quieter but more basic hotels on that side of town.

From Syabru Besi, the trail starts just north of town; there's a small yellow "To Langtang" sign to point the way. The path crosses a steel bridge, passes through the other part of town, and heads east up the valley, along the northern (left) bank of the Langtang River. It soon crosses the river on a wood-and-stone bridge and continues along the southern bank. Within an hour, the trail passes a small tea

LANGTANG VALLEY: SYABRU BESI TO KYANJIN GOMPA

TRANSPORTATION: Buses leave from the New Bus Stand in Kathmandu and head to **Syabru Besi** (10hr., 6:30 and 7am, Rs140) via **Dhunche** (8hr., Rs110). Buses return from Syabru Besi to **Kathmandu** (10hr., 6:30 and 7am, Rs140). There is an airstrip near Kyanjin Gompa, but you would be very lucky to get a flight out from here.

SERVICES: Lodges and tea houses dot most of the region, and several have satellite telephone service, but beyond Kyanjin Gompa, you will have to camp on your own. There are several national park checkpoints where you will have to prove that you paid the **national park entrance fee.** Because this is a less-traveled region, you should arrive with all necessary equipment; you will likely not be able to buy it on the trail.

VILLAGE	ALTITUDE
Dhunche	2030m
Syabru Besi	1460m
Bamboo	1850m
Rimche	2250m
Lama Hotel	2380m
Ghora Tabela	3020m
Thangshyap	3110m
Langtang Village	3430m
Mundu	3550m
Singdom	3680m
Kyanjin Gompa	3850m
Langshisa Kharka	4160m
Kyanjin Gompa	3850m
Langshisa Kharka	4160m

HIGHLIGHTS: Wildlife from various birds to red pandas, wild boar, monkeys, and black bears. Views of Langtang Lirung (7245m), dramatic ice falls, and gargantuan glaciers.

FEATURES: The trail begins in terraced fields and hardwood and bamboo forests. Further along, there are many yak and cattle pastures, and yak dung is often used as a heating product in local houses. North of Kyanjin Gompa is a moraine whose higher reaches offer a spectacular vista of the surrounding mountains. Beware of **altitude sickness** beyond Ghora Tabela.

shop, and on the opposite side of the river, a pleasant **hot spring** set up for a refreshing bath. Continuing along the south side of the river, the trail hits a **T-junction,** where a sign points the way to Thulo Syabru (left to Kyanjin Gompa and Langtang). The trail then passes through **Bamboo,** a small settlement that makes a good lunch stop and also contains several hotels, including the **Old Bamboo Riverside Lodge.** If you want a more relaxing first day, stick around Bamboo. From here, the trail continues along the lush south side of the river until it hits a large steel suspension bridge. There are a couple of tea shops here that can provide lodging in a pinch. After the bridge the trail becomes steeper and drier, climbing up to the **Hotel Langtangview Lodge.** The trail continues up to the town of **Rimche,** home to a few lodges. The **Hotel Ganeshview Lodge** offers decent rooms and views. The **Sherpa Lodge** and the **Lama Guest House** are also good options in town. **Lama Hotel,** a 10-15min. walk from Rimche, is a pleasantly-sized tourist destination with more than six lodges and satellite phone service.

LAMA HOTEL TO LANGTANG VILLAGE. From Lama Hotel, the trail climbs steeply through the forest on the north side of the river, and after an hour or two reaches the **Gumnachok Lodge,** in a small clearing. There's another small settlement not far beyond. From here, the trail continues steeply until it reaches **Ghora Tabela,** home to a small tea shop and a national park check-post, where permits must be presented. After Ghora Tabela, the trail flattens somewhat and soon reaches **Thangshyap,** where accommodation is available at the **Hotel Tibetan Lodge.** Langtang Village comes into view around this point, but it's still more than an hour's walk to

NEPAL

town. The trail passes through several more settlements and tea shops before reaching **Langtang Village,** an attractive stone village with fantastic views of the mountains. The **Valleyview Lodge and Hotel** and the **Villageview Lodge and Hotel** are both fine places to stay; authorities have fixed prices in town at a flat rate, so pick your favorite view. As Langtang Village is above 3000m, **altitude sickness** can be a problem. It is theoretically possible to go from Lama Hotel to Kyanjin Gompa in a single day, but you probably shouldn't test the theory.

LANGTANG VILLAGE TO KYANJIN GOMPA. The path from Langtang Village to Kyanjin Gompa is fairly flat and reasonably short; the total gain in altitude is only 400m. Passing through sparse alpine terrain, the trail follows the north side

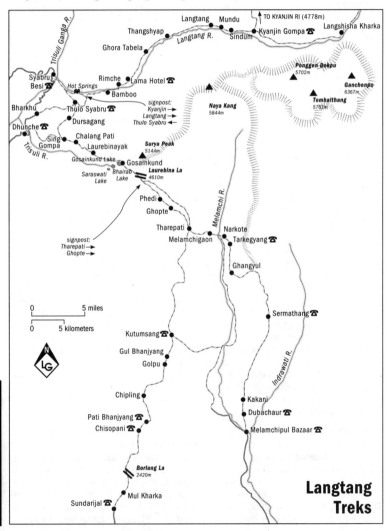

Langtang Treks

of the river past *mani* walls carved with Tibetan script. The first settlement after Langtang Village is tiny **Mundu**, home to the **Mundu Village Guest House.** After passing more *mani* walls, the trail leads to **Singdom**, where there are two lodges, including the **Singdom Village Hall and Lodge.** After Singdom, the terrain is dotted with increasing numbers of large boulders; these are the work of glaciers that hollowed out the upper part of the valley. From Singdom, the trail climbs through the boulder fields and soon reaches **Kyanjin Gompa,** the highlight of the trek. The best place to stay in town is the **Yeti Guest House,** which has solar-powered showers and satellite phone service. Another good option is **Yala Peak Guest House.** Check out the local **cheese factory** where the employees are generally glad to give a quick tour. (Cheese Rs275 per kg. Open daily 7am-5pm.)

Kyanjin is a great place to take in the splendid views and unwind on few daytrips. The most popular is the ascent of **Kyanjin Ri** (4773m), a hill to the north of town. The trail climbs up steeply from town to the prayer-flag-festooned first crest at 4350m and then continues up the ridge to the peak. The views of Langtang Lirung are incomparable, and the climb is fairly easy and generally free of snow. From here you can cross to the higher **Tsergo Ri** (4984m), though it's important to watch for signs of altitude sickness when attempting to climb either of these peaks. Another popular excursion is the hike up the valley to the settlement of **Langshisha Kharka,** which has glacier views. Finally, there are some more difficult options. **Yala Peak** (5500m) generally requires two days (including a high camp) and some equipment (ice axe, crampons, boots). The Ganja-La Pass (5130m) is another multiple-day affair that is an alternative way to reach Helambu from Kyanjin Gompa. The pass is difficult and requires several days of camping.

THE RETURN OR CONNECTING TO GOSAINKUND. To get back from Kyanjin Gompa, simply follow the same trail in reverse. People often go from Kyanjin Gompa to Lama Hotel in one day and from Lama Hotel to Syabru Besi the next.

If you're heading to Gosainkund from the Langtang Valley, make a detour after Bamboo and head to **Thulo Syabru** (2130m). Then take off the next day to **Sing Gompa** (see p. 868) or **Chalang Pati** (see below). There are two trails leading to Thulo Syabru from Langtang Valley; the first is marked by the yellow sign at the **T-junction** downhill from Bamboo, and the second is farther down the trail just past the hot springs. The second trail is shorter and easier. In Thulo Syabru the best places to stay are the **Yeti Restaurant and Hotel** and the **Eveningview Guest House.** The next day's hike connecting to the Gosainkund trail in Sing Gompa is steep but pleasant; the trail switchbacks uphill, passing the town of **Dursagang** (2720m), where accommodation is available at the **Himalay Hotel and Lodge.** The trail continues up the ridges to two tea shops at the crest (3210m) and then curves around the ridge to **Sing Gompa** (3250m), on the Gosainkund trail (see below).

▨ THE GOSAINKUND TREK गोसैनकुंड

The main connection between Langtang and Helambu, the Gosainkund trek is marked by a series of often-frozen high-altitude lakes. The approach to the lakes provides views from the Langtang Valley all the way west to Machhapuchare and the Annapurnas. Gosainkund Lake is famous as a watering hole for Shiva; each year the lake becomes a major pilgrimage site during **Janai Purnima,** which occurs around the July-August full moon. By itself, this is a short trek—it can be done round-trip in 3-4 days—but most people couple it with a trek up the Langtang Valley or continue on from the lakes down into Helambu.

GOSAINKUND TREK: DHUNCHE TO GOSAINKUND

TRANSPORTATION: Dhunche is the most convenient starting point for the Gosainkund trek, unless you are hiking in from another region (see **Langtang Valley,** above, for bus info).

SERVICES: There are several acceptable lodges along the path, though Dhunche is about the only place to stop for anything more than trail-side food and beds.

VILLAGE	ALTITUDE
Dhunche	2030m
Sing Gompa	3250m
Chalang Pati	3580m
Laurebinayak	3900m
Gosainkund	4380m

HIGHLIGHTS: High-altitude lakes with dramatic scenery all around.

FEATURES: The trek passes through evergreen and rhododendron woods, scrubby brush, and eventually leads to rather barren, rocky territory where **snow can be a risk;** if the path into Gosainkund is heavily inundated with snow, do not attempt to hike through to the lake. Around and after Sing Gompa, beware of **altitude sickness.**

DHUNCHE TO SING GOMPA. While Syabru Besi is now the most convenient starting point for the Langtang Valley Trek, **Dhunche** remains the best access point for Gosainkund. Dhunche has a number of lodges; the length of the bus ride means spending the first night here. Both the **Hotel Tibet Mountain View** and the **Hotel Thakali** are decent. There's also a small **pharmacy** in town (open daily 8am-5pm).

The trail for Sing Gompa departs from the road just north of town and follows the southern bank of the Trisuli River. It's quite steep, and you gain altitude quickly as you ascend toward the ridge. The trail crosses to the north side of the Trisuli and continues to climb up, up, and away. Just before Sing Gompa, the trail reaches a junction; the left path leads down to Thulo Syabru and the Langtang Valley and the right path to Sing Gompa and then Gosainkund. **Sing Gompa** is not far beyond this junction. The **Green View Hotel and Lodge** and the slightly more secluded **Red Panda Hotel and Lodge** are good. There's another **cheese factory** in town, where you can savor the taste of excellent yak cheese and curd. Be careful of altitude sickness since the ascent is over 1200m from Dhunche to Sing Gompa.

SING GOMPA TO GOSAINKUND. This leg of the trek can be done in a single day, but if you've come directly from Dhunche the previous day, you should be careful of altitude sickness and spend the night part way up in Laurebinayak. The trail from Sing Gompa winds around to the southern side of the ridge and follows the Trisuli River up the valley. After detouring briefly around the northern side of a small hill, the trail reaches **Chalang Pati,** where there are two small lodges, including the acceptable **Chalang Pati Hotel and Lodge.** Chalang Pati marks the end of the evergreen forest; from here, the terrain becomes increasingly alpine. The trail switchbacks up to **Laurebinayak,** home to a number of lodges and some fantastic Himalayan views. The **Hotel Mount Rest** is a good place to stay; if the altitude is a problem, there's no need to push on all the way up to Gosainkund in one day. From here, the trail shoots straight uphill past a large *stupa*, and farther uphill, a series of roof-less stone houses. Here, the trail rejoins the Trisuli River. The first lake you see is the Saraswati, far below the trail against the opposite ridge. The trail passes quite close to the next lake, Bhairab, where Gosainkund village comes into view. **Gosainkund** itself is a small windblown settlement on the shore of Gosainkund Lake. Both the **Peaceful Hotel and Lodge** and the **Lakeside Guest House** offer reliable, friendly accommodation. In town, there's not much to do except bundle up and drink tea; the more adventurous (and acclimatized) can walk around Gosainkund Lake or climb the surrounding hills.

THE RETURN/CONNECTING TO HELAMBU. The return trip to Dhunche can be done in one long day or two shorter, easier days; the route is the exact reverse of the one described above. If you're going from Gosainkund up to the Langtang Valley, take the right trail just below the Sing Gompa and head downhill to Thulo Syabru (see p. 867).

If you're doing the popular trek from Gosainkund into Helambu, you can connect to the Helambu circuit at Tharepati in one very long day or in two average-length days. The trail from Gosainkund skirts the eastern edge of the lake before ascending up toward the pass. This section of the trail is often snow-covered and is impassable at certain times of year and in bad weather conditions. **Laurebina Pass** (4610m) is marked by prayer flags and a *chorten;* to the south you can see the green foothills of Helambu, which lead into the Kathmandu Valley. The south side of the pass (descending into Helambu) is generally drier and easier to hike through. The trail descends steeply from there to a small tea shop where the path forks and a sign points downhill to Ghopte and Tharepeti. The lower trail is the one to take; the upper one is undeveloped and often snow-covered, and there are no facilities until Tharepati. The lower trail continues down from the tea shop all the way to **Phedi** (3630m), home to two hotels and a helipad. The **Taj Mel Lodge,** the lower of the two, is a pleasant, riverside accommodation. After Phedi, the trail imitates the up-and-down character of the Helambu area. It makes one steep ridge climb before reaching **Ghopte** (3430m), where there are another two lodges (both dorm-style). It is a fairly long day from Gosainkund to Ghopte, but some people push all the way to **Tharepeti,** on the Helambu circuit, to avoid the pile-up of pass-crossers in Ghopte (see p. 871).

⬛ THE HELAMBU TREK हेलम्बू

Unlike the Langtang Valley or Gosainkund treks, both of which wind mainly through high alpine country, the Helambu Trek is relatively low-altitude, thick-forested, and hot. Also, unlike the other two, Helambu is criss-crossed by trails running between villages, and there is no one particular route that must be taken or sight that must be seen; the entire area can be visited via any number of different routes. The route described below, a horseshoe-shaped trek starting in Sundarijal and ending in Melamchipul Bazaar, is one of the most common, but the variations are infinite, and the crowds disappear the minute you get off the beaten path.

SUNDARIJAL TO CHISOPANI. Sundarijal, the starting point, is very close to Kathmandu. The trail from Sundarijal begins ascending directly from the bus stop and follows a concrete path alongside a large black metal pipe that supplies water to Kathmandu. This part of the walk is well-developed; the concrete path becomes concrete steps, which climb past the Sundarijal Reservoir. The path crosses a dirt road after this and continues up the steep concrete steps to **Mul Kharka,** where the steps end. Above Mul Kharka is an army base, where permits are occasionally checked. The trail climbs up **Borlang Pass,** the high point of the day, and then makes a short descent to **Chisopani,** the site of numerous hotels. Both the **New BBC Hotel,** and farther on, the **Hotel Manakamana,** offer good facilities. Some people are inclined to go on down the hill to Pati Bhanjyang the same day, but unless you're in a hurry, the views and pleasant atmosphere make Chisopani a better option.

CHISOPANI TO KUTUMSANG. From Chisopani, the trail runs briefly along the dirt road; at the first sharp turn, the trail splits and heads north. It drops down through a number of steep gullies and finally merges with the dirt road again just before **Pati Bhanjyang.** It is possible to walk the dirt road all the way to Pati Bhanjyang, though this takes longer. The **Valley View Lodge,** south of town, is a peaceful

HELAMBU TREK: SUNDARIJAL TO MELAMCHIPUL BAZAAR

TRANSPORTATION: Buses go from Ratna Park bus station in Kathmandu to **Sundarijal** (1hr., every 30min. 6am-8pm, Rs20). Taxis to and from **Thamel** cost Rs200-300. Buses return from Melamchipul Bazaar to **Kathmandu** (4hr., every hr. 7am-3pm, Rs40). Buses from Kathmandu also continue up the road from Melamchipul Bazaar to **Talamarang**, about 10km further.

SERVICES: Numerous food and lodging options are available on the trail, and a few hotels have telephone service. There are some police and national park checkpost along the way, so be ready to prove that you've obtained your permits and paid your entrance fees.

HIGHLIGHTS: Stunning panoramas of the Helambu hills and the monstrous peaks of the Langtang Himal. Large Buddhist monasteries tucked in among the mountains and valleys. Sherpa agricultural settlements and villages. Endless possibilities for side-trail exploration and connections to other hiking regions, such as the Langtang Valley and Gosainkund.

VILLAGE	ALTITUDE
Sundarijal	1460m
Mul Kharka	1860m
Borlang Pass	2420m
Chisopani	2215m
Pati Bhanjyang	1170m
Chipling	2170m
Golpu	2130m
Gul Bhanjyang	2250m
Kutumsang	2470m
Kyuola Pass	3250m
Mangen Goth	3220m
Tharepati	3510m
Melamchigaon	2530m
Narkote	2000m
Tarkegyang	2740m
Ghangyul	2770m
Sermathang	2590m
Kakani	1996m
Dubachaur	1440m
Malamchipul Bazaar	870m

FEATURES: The trail passes through several different types of vegetation and topographical areas. As it winds up and down the hills, the trek goes through bamboo, oak, and rhododendron forests, up steep canyons, over high ridges, and through terraced fields. Unlike many other Himalayan treks, the Helambu circuit does not ascend to some high point and then descend to the finish; it climbs and drops throughout the hike, arriving at the crest of a ridge only to descend into a valley and then head up the next ridge. The only place where altitude sickness should be a worry is around Tharepati.

place to stay. From Pati Bhanjyang, one trail heads north to Kutumsang and another goes east to Tamalarang. Continuing north to Kutumsang, the trail climbs steeply again to **Chipling** and the **Chipling Lodge Hotel and Restaurant.** Beyond the ridge, the trail arrives at the village of **Golpu** and the **Himalaya Lodge and Restaurant.** The trail leads north, and halfway up the next (and final) ridge is the small settlement of **Gul Bhanjyang,** with a couple of lodges, including the **Hotel Dragon.** The trail ascends to the top of the ridge, and then makes a gentle dip into the saddle that holds **Kutumsang,** a pleasant village with good views on either side. The **Namaste Hotel and Lodge** and the **Sherpa Lodge,** at either end of town, are quiet accommodations. From Kutumsang, one trail heads east down the valley to **Mahankal** (1130m); the other heads north up the ridge to Tharepati, the highest point of the circuit.

KUTUMSANG TO THAREPATI. This is a relatively straightforward (though at times steep) trail, which follows the ridge all the way up from Kutumsang to Tharepeti. Heading north from Kutumsang, the trail approaches **Kyuola Pass,** which is visible from town. This section of the trail is heavily forested, but there are plenty of mountain views, which get better and better throughout the day. After the pass, the trail soon reaches **Mangen Goth,** the only large settlement on the trail; accommodation is available here. After Mangen Goth, the trail climbs steeply again, following the ridge all the way to **Tharepati.** High up on a crest, Tharepati shows off its spectacular views—to the east, west, and south are the staggered ridges and river valleys of Helambu; to the north are the snow-capped peaks of Gosainkund, and threading between them, the Laurebina Pass. In Tharepati are a number of lodges. On the very top is the **Gosainkund Hotel and Top Lodge;** lower down the hill is the **Jimmy Lama Mountain Hostel.** Tharepati is at the convergence of several different trails. To the north runs the trail up to Gosainkund (p. 869); to the east the trail runs down to Melamchigaon and Helambu.

THAREPATI TO TARKE GYANG. From Tharepati, the trail drops steeply off the eastern side of the ridge, losing altitude quickly. The vegetation becomes thick and lush once again and is dominated by bamboo and rhododendrons. Switchbacking down to the river valley, the trail crosses a small stream before leveling out somewhat. It drops down to a suspension bridge and then climbs briefly to **Melamchig-aon,** a lovely agricultural Sherpa village with a large Buddhist monastery and more spectacular views down the valley. It would make a short daytrip from Tharepati, but this is a good place to stay the night. Both the **Sun Lodge** and the **Wild View Hotel and Lodge** are friendly and have adequate facilities. The trail from here is unexciting and winds through the terraced fields in the lower part of town. It jumps sharply down to the Melamchi River, where there's a suspension bridge. The **Riverside Lodge,** just before the bridge, is another lodging option. After the bridge, the trail climbs to the village of **Narkote,** where there's another sizeable monastery. Just after Narkote, there's a large fork in the trail. The right (lower) fork leads down to Thimbu; the left fork heads up to Tarkegyang. Climbing the hill, the trail passes several small farms. The Sherpa Lodge is about halfway between Narkote and Tarkegyang. The trail continues to ascend to **Tarkegyang,** a large settlement with numerous accommodation choices. The **Mountain View Hotel** is big and clean and has telephone service. A number of trails converge in Tarkegyang. To the north is the trail up to **Yangri Peak** (3771m), then to the **Ganja La** (5130m), and into the Langtang Valley. Two trails leave from the south—one follows the ridge to Sermathang, the other (lower) trail drops down to Kaani and Kiul.

TARKEGYANG TO SERMATHANG. The trail to Sermathang follows the birds south from Tarkegyang. There are several forks, and the larger fork often leads downhill to Kakani, so be sure to ask along the way. The trail stays at roughly the same altitude, snaking along the ridge to the village of **Ghangyul.** There, the **Dolma Lodge** boasts clean, well-kept facilities. From Ghangyul, Sermathang is visible to the south—it's the cluster of houses in the notch at the top of the ridge. **Sermathang** is a pleasant place to stay; although only a short day's hike from Tarkegyang, the accommodation options beyond Sermathang are much less pleasant, and it's a long walk to go all the way to Melamchipul Bazaar in a single day. In Sermathang, both the **Mountain View Lodge** and **Yangri Lodge** offer decent rooms; Mountain View—surprise, surprise—has the best mountain views. There's a **Keep Office** in town that sells iodine tablets and also houses a tiny but lovely cultural **museum.** Sermathang also contains a **national park checkpost;** if you're coming from Melamchipul Bazaar, you can buy your park permit here. The town has several monasteries as well; pay a visit to the *stupa* on the knoll to the south of town.

SERMATHANG TO MELAMCHIPUL BAZAAR. The trek down from Sermathang to the road at Melamchipul Bazaar is long but gentle and can easily be completed in one day. The trail follows the top of the ridge the entire way down, passing through increasingly developed settlements as it nears the road. In the reverse

NEPAL

direction, this would be a lot of climbing to do in a single day, especially since the total change in altitude is 1720m. From Sermathang, the trail descends along the ridge to **Kakani**, where there are a couple of places to stay, including the **Himalyan Dorje Lakpa Guest House.** Kakani is a good overnight destination if you're coming up from Melamchipul Bazaar. After Kakani, the trail becomes a little harder to follow; it's a good idea to ask for directions. Continuing down the ridge, the trail comes to the dusty village of **Dubachaur** and the **Langtang Guest House.** The village is not worth spending much time in. From Dubachaur the trail crosses through more small settlements and farming terraces before dropping down and crossing the Melamchi River on a long suspension bridge to reach **Melamchipul Bazaar,** at the confluence of the Melamchi and Indrawati Rivers. Melamchipul is not a particularly scenic place, but if you need to stay here for the night, the best option is to cross back over the suspension bridge to the north side of the Melamchi River and walk 5min. up the trail to the **Jugal Himal Resort,** a secluded lodge away from the grime of the bazaar. Up the road several kilometers from Melamchipul Bazaar, **Talamarang** (960m) is quieter and cleaner than the bazaar, and home to the tidy **Talamarang Guest House.**

◊ LANGTANG-GOSAINKUND-HELAMBU COMBINATIONS

Most often, treks in the Langtang region combine the separate treks into one longer trek. A Langtang-Gosainkund-Helambu trek is usually done in around 12-15 days and normally follows roughly this route: Syabru Besi—Lama Hotel—Langtang Village—Kyanjin Gompa—Lama Hotel—Thulo Syabru—Sing Gompa—Gosainkund—Ghopte—Kutumsang—Chisopani—Sundarijal. This north-to-south direction is generally preferred over the others, as the Langtang Valley provides a better chance to acclimatize before crossing through Gosainkund and the Laurebina Pass (4610m). But the opposite route is also possible and is regularly done by trekking groups. The exit through Helambu is also flexible. From Tharepeti, you can head south to Kutumsang and out to Sundarijal (the most common route), or from Kutumsang you can branch east down the less-traveled trail to Mahankal and then Talamarang. Or you can head east from Tharepeti itself to Tarkegyang and on to Melamchipul, a scenic three-day route. There are myriad other options too, and perhaps your best bet is to let your feet and whims guide you around the trails.

THE EVEREST REGION

The Everest trek pays homage to the highest point on the planet. The trek up to Base Camp heads through the homeland of one of the most engaging and enterprising of all Nepal's ethnic groups, the Sherpas. The Sherpas migrated to the Solu Khumbu region south of Everest around 500 years ago, and they retain many Tibetan characteristics in their language, religion, and dress. The Sherpa capital, Namche Bazaar, long famous from accounts of expeditions to the region, is one of the most vibrant towns in all of Nepal.

A trip to Everest used to involve setting out on foot from Kathmandu, several hundred kilometers to the west, and necessitated a sequence of arduous ascents and descents of up to 2000m at a time. Not anymore. Today, a road extends approximately half of the way, to Jiri, connected by bus to Kathmandu. From Jiri, it still takes a solid 10 days to walk to Namche Bazaar, and another several days from Namche Bazaar to Everest. A trip to Everest by bus and on foot is a month-long undertaking. Most people save time by flying at least one way—there is an airstrip in Lukla, a two-day walk south of Namche Bazaar. If you decide to hike one way, rather than flying both in and out of Lukla, the logical choice is to walk in: the going will be easier, and you'll arrive in Namche already acclimatized. Many people do the reverse, walking from Namche to Jiri, because waiting for a flight out—particularly if you've got fixed international connections to make—can be extremely frustrating. The landing strip at Lukla is short, and weather conditions have to be pretty good before flights can take off and land. (Since trekking in the Everest region, especially on the approach to Namche Bazaar, involves climbing up and down ridges, the trekking charts include a column on altitude gained and lost during each leg of the trek.)

JIRI TO NAMCHE BAZAAR

JIRI TO BHANDAR. With the advent of plane service to Lukla, tourist traffic through Jiri has diminished sharply, and this stretch of the trek is much quieter than the areas above Lukla.

EVEREST TREK: JIRI TO NAMCHE BAZAAR

TRANSPORTATION: Buses run from Kathmandu's Ratna Park bus station to **Jiri** (11hr., 5 per day 5-10:30am, Rs185; express bus 8hr., 7am, Rs215) and from Jiri to **Kathmandu** (11hr., 5 per day 5-10:30am, Rs170; express 8hr., 7am, Rs200). Purchase tickets at the window opposite the Jiri Medical Hall (open daily 6am-6pm). Express bus tickets for either direction should be purchased the day before, and travelers are expected to arrive 30min. early.

SERVICES: Plenty of food and lodging options vie for hikers' attention. On this portion of the trail, there are not as many services (phone, pharmacy, police, etc.) available as in Namche Bazaar (see **Lukla to Everest Base Camp,** below).

HIGHLIGHTS: Hardwood and rhododendron forests in steep valleys. Traditional Sherpa villages with many *mani* walls. Glimpses of Everest, Makalu, and other colossal peaks.

VILLAGE	ALTITUDE	TIME	GAIN/LOSS
Jiri	1910m	start	
Chitre	2330m	1¼hr.	
Mali	2220m	30min.	
Shivalaya	1800m	1½hr.	490m/-600m
Sangabadanda	2240m	1¼hr.	
Deorali	2710m	1¾hr.	
Bhandar	2190m	1¼hr.	900m/-510m
Kenja	1640m	3½hr.	
Sete	2580m	2¼hr.	1040m/-650m
Dagchu	2850m	1hr.	
Goyom	3155m	45min.	
Lamjura La Pass	3530m	1¼hr.	
Thagtokbhug	2860m	1½hr.	
Junbesi	2710m	1¼hr.	990m/-860m
Salung	2960m	2hr.	
Ringmo	2720m	1¾hr.	
Trakshindo Pass	3070m	1hr.	
Trakshindo	2930m	30min.	
Nuntala	2190m	1hr.	820m/-1340m
Jubing	1680m	2¼hr.	
Khari Khola	2070m	1½hr.	580m/-700m
Bupsa	2350m	1¼hr.	
Puiyan	2780m	3hr.	

FEATURES: The trail climbs up and down ridges, through valleys and forests, and past numerous rivers, creeks, monasteries, fields, and pastures. Watch for wildlife along the way, including jackals and many species of birds. **Altitude sickness** becomes a concern only in the areas around Lamjura La Pass.

NEPAL

Everest Treks

The trail from Jiri begins south of town. From the bus park, follow the flat dirt road south for about 10min. to where a trail branches left up the hill. This trail climbs more or less straight up toward the ridge, passing small settlements and tea houses. The largest settlement before the ridge is **Chitre,** where you'll find the **Solu Khombu Lodge.** The trail climbs gently to the first pass (2400m), then drops down the opposite side to **Mali,** where a number of lodges, including the **Sherpa Lodge and Restaurant,** have sprung up. After Mali, the descent becomes steeper as the trail drops down to meet the Khimti River. It crosses a suspension bridge just before the river and then traverses another bridge that spans the river itself. Just across the river is **Shivalaya,** a common stop for trekkers at the end of their first (short) day. Both the **Tourist Lodge** and the **Trekking Guide Hotel and Lodge** are good options in town. Even if you don't stop here, you don't need to go all the way to Bhandar in one day—there are plenty of places to stay between Shivalaya and Bhandar. From Shivalaya the trail heads steeply uphill toward the ridge until **Sang-badanda,** where it levels off a little. At this point the trail forks; to the right is the direct route to Deorali and Bhandar, to the left is a longer side trail to Thodung. In Sangbadanda, the **Himali Lodge** is a decent place to stay. From here, the right trail continues toward the ridge, passing a number of newer settlements along the way. In **Khasru Bas** is the imposing **Uma Lama Lodge.** Farther along is **Buludanda** and the **Hill View Sherpa Lodge.** The trail reaches its highest point at **Deorali,** a wind-swept pass with several good lodges, including the **Highland Sherpa Guest House and Restaurant.** This is another good place to stop at the end of the first day, as it allows you to get acclimated to the higher altitude. Right after the pass is an easy-to-confuse fork in the trail; take the left fork (it almost looks like a switchback) to reach Bhandar. This is the most common stop at the end of the first day. The **Ang Dawa Lodge** and **Shoba Lodge and Restaurant** are decent.

BHANDAR TO JUNBESI. From Bhandar, the trail continues to drop down toward the Likhu River and gets confusing in a number of places. Immediately after the covered wooden bridge the trail forks; take the sharp left path. This drops steeply and brings you to a number of deceptive forks. Follow the left fork every time. As the trail nears the river, it crosses a small stream on a suspension bridge into the small village of **Tharo Khola** (1460m). From here the trail makes a sharp left and heads up the Likhu Valley along the west side of the river. There are a number of opportunities to cross the Likhu River on suspension bridges; you can take any of them. There are trails along both sides of the river heading up to **Kenja,** a booming community with a medical post, a police checkpost, and a good assortment of lodges, including the **Sherpa Guest House.** Above Kenja, the trail gets very steep as you begin to climb up toward the Lamjura Pass. The first big town is **Chimbu** (2150m), where you can nurse your blisters at the **Hill Top Lodge and Restaurant.** A short walk (30min.) uphill from Chimbu is **Sete,** where many trekkers spend the night to break the 2000m climb. The **Sherpa Guide Lodge** is well-kept. Sete is so popular, however, that those with the energy might want to go an hour farther to the **Maya Tamang Lodge** in **Dagchu,** to escape the crowds.

Beyond Dagchu, the trail continues its steep climb toward the ridge, passing through the villages of **Goyom** and **Lamjura** (3380m), the last town before the pass and home to the **Numbur View Lodge.** Just before the pass, the trail levels off significantly and follows the ridge north to the pass. The **Lamjura La Pass** is the highest point between Jiri and Namche. From the pass, the trail drops steeply into the Junbesi valley, passing through the village of **Thagtokbhug.** At the heart of the village is a *gompa* and, next to it, a huge *mani*-adorned boulder. **AM's Restaurant and Lodge,** with excellent views and clean rooms, is near the center of town. From here the trail runs along the northern side of the valley and turns slowly toward **Junbesi,** a prosperous community full of *gompas, stupas,* and lodges. The **Everestview Sherpa Lodge and Restaurant** has large, quiet rooms with fairly comfortable beds. There's a lot to see in and around Junbesi, making it a good place to stop for the night.

JUNBESI TO BUPSA. From Junbesi, the trail crosses the Junbesi River and climbs gradually up the next ridge. Just after the bridge is an important junction—the left (uphill) fork leads on to Namche Bazaar; the right (downhill) fork leads south to **Phaplu** where there's an airstrip (a half day's walk). Continuing on the left fork, the trail climbs to the top of the ridge at **Salung.** On clear days, this is where you'll catch your first views of Everest. The **Everest Panorama Lodge and Restaurant** has good facilities here. After Salung the trail drops down to the Ringmo River and makes a short, steep climb up to **Ringmo,** a welcoming little village surrounded by apple orchards. The **Apple House Lodge** in town serves apples with everything and has nice rooms. From Ringmo it's a short but sometimes confusing ascent to the **Trakshindo La;** ask as you go. On the far side of the pass, the trail passes through the village of **Trakshindo,** home to an impressive monastery and a number of lodges, including the **Mountain View Lodge and Restaurant.** The trail drops much more steeply after Trakshindo, down to the Dudh Kosi River. This is a long descent, and many stop for the night halfway down in the village of **Nuntala,** also called Manidingma. The **Naulekh View Lodge and Restaurant,** at the far end of town, has good rooms and a friendly staff.

NEPAL

After Nuntala the trail continues to drop, crossing the Dudh Kosi via a long bridge (1500m). A little past the river is the Rai village of **Jubing;** not many people stay here, but if you do, the **Gorkhali Lodge** is a good choice. Beyond Jubing the trail climbs gradually to **Chyoka.** Immediately past Chyoka is a series of forks in the trail—always take the right (uphill) fork, which should bring you directly over the top of the ridge rather than around it. On the far side of the ridge is **Khari Khola,** a large village with many lodges. The **Sagarmatha Khumbu Lodge and Restaurant** is run by a very friendly family and has decent rooms. A small, rickety bridge crosses the Khari Khola River, after which the trail climbs very steeply up the next ridge to **Bupsa,** visible from below. Bupsa, with its great views, is a popular place to spend the night. The **Yellow Top Lodge** stands out for its friendly atmosphere and relatively private rooms. To dodge the crowds, you can continue for another 30min. beyond Bupsa, where quieter accommodations are available.

BUPSA TO NAMCHE BAZAAR. The trail from Bupsa climbs steadily upward, weaving in and out between ridges and valleys. The next major settlement is **Puiyan,** home to the buzzing little **Bee Hive Lodge and Restaurant.** After Puiyan, the trail rounds another large ridge and Lukla comes into view—you can sit here and watch the planes land. The trail drops steeply down toward the valley floor, crossing a small river at **Surke.** The **Everest Trail Lodge** is a well-run establishment with an immaculate kitchen. Soon after Surke (just around the next bend) there's a fork in the trail; the right trail climbs steeply up to Lukla, the left one continues toward Namche Bazaar. Continuing along the left (lower) trail, the route climbs steadily up to **Chauri Kharka.** The **Tourist Guest House** has good food and is a pleasant place to stay; this is the last major settlement before the trail joins the much more crowded Lukla trail at **Cheplung.** To reach Namche from here, follow the directions for the Lukla to Everest Base Camp route. From Cheplung, it usually takes two days to reach Namche Bazaar.

🖳 LUKLA TO EVEREST BASE CAMP

LUKLA TO NAMCHE BAZAAR. Lukla, proud owner of Nepal's third-busiest airport, is a major tourist center with enough facilities and equipment to keep your grandmother happy. Many people skip the Jiri-Lukla section of the trek and fly in and out of Lukla, making a (roughly) two-week trip up to Base Camp. If you do fly straight here from Kathmandu, it is important to take at least one day to acclimatize before heading out on the trail. All sorts of equipment is available for purchase or hire, and there are plenty of agencies competing to outfit trekkers with guides, porters, and woolen socks. The **Panoramic Lodge** is by far the best accommodation in town, with big, clean rooms, hot water showers, and a huge dining room.

From Lukla, the trail heads north, dropping steeply downhill through a number of small settlements. The first big town on the trail is **Cheplung,** where the Jiri trail joins from below. The **Himalayan Rest House and Restaurant** is a large, clean place to stay, but most people opt to hike on to Ghat or Phakding on the first day. From Cheplung, the trail heads up the valley, meandering at an easy gradient to **Thado Kosi** (2500m), an attractive settlement on the Thado Kosi River. If you want to part ways with the crowds, stay for the night in **Saino Lodge and Restaurant.** You can still reach Namche the following day. Just around the next bend is the equally lovely (but more crowded) town of **Ghat** (2530m), with a very active monastery and a number of enormous *mani* boulders. The **Lama Lodge and Restaurant,** at the far end of town, is friendly and well-run. Coming from either Lukla or Jiri, Ghat makes a good overnight stop: it's more pleasant and less crowded than Phakding, and still within a day's walk of Namche.

EVEREST TREK: LUKLA TO EVEREST BASE CAMP

TRANSPORTATION: There is a very popular **airstrip** at **Lukla.** Unfortunately, flights are erratic, reservations are sometimes cancelled, and airline schedules change constantly. For the latest information and to make bookings, call RNAC in Kathmandu (☎220757); be sure to reserve well in advance of your intended departure; flights fill up quickly.

SERVICES: There are plenty of lodges and restaurants all the way to Gorak Shep. Namche Bazaar is a major administrative town and also the largest settlement on the way to Everest Base Camp, and basically everything needed for a trek can be bought here. This is also the place to send postcards, change currency, and get your wisdom teeth pulled. In Jorsale, be ready to present your passport and pay—or prove that you have paid—the **entrance fee for Sagarmatha National Park** (Rs1000).

VILLAGE	ALTITUDE	TIME	GAIN/LOSS
Lukla	2860m	start	
Cheplung	2660m	45min.	-200m
Phakding	2650m	2hr.	
Benkar	2790m	1hr.	
Chumoa	2780m	30min.	
Monju	2820m	45min.	320m/-160m
Jorsale	2810m	45min.	
Namche Bazaar	3450m	2½hr.	630m
Kyangsuma	3610m	1¼hr.	
Sanasa	3620m	15min.	
Tengboche	3860m	2¼hr.	760m/-350m
Deboche	3770m	20min.	
Pangboche	3860m	1¼hr.	
Shomare	3900m	1hr.	
Orsho	3970m	30min.	
Pheriche	4220m	1¼hr.	450m/-90m
Tukla	4620m	1½hr.	
Lobuje	4940m	2hr.	720m
Gorak Shep	5160m	1¾hr.	220m
Everest Base Camp	5350m	2½hr.	190m

HIGHLIGHTS: Sherpa villages and high-altitude monasteries. Chances to schmooze with world-class mountaineers as they prepare to tackle the world's highest mountain. And of course, the opportunity to gaze at some of the most rugged peaks on the planet: Mt. Everest, Lhotse, Makalu, Pumori, and Ama Dablam, among others.

FEATURES: The trek heads mainly through forested valleys until Pangboche, where the trail passes above tree line. Be aware that the trail out of Lukla goes through some areas where avalanches and floods have scarred the hillsides; consequently, the location of the trail changes from time to time. Beyond Pangboche, the vegetation is mainly scrub brush and wildflowers until Tukla, where the trail climbs up the Khumbu glacier's terminal moraine and, at various points, onto the glacier itself. While on the trail, adhere to **leave-no-trace waste disposal practices** since almost no toilet facilities are available and human refuse has made many camping sights both undesirable and unsanitary. **Altitude sickness** is a risk after Jorsale.

Phakding, 1hr. up the trail from Ghat, is a large town with many lodges. The town extends along the trail and across the river; if you do choose to stay here, the higher parts of town (across the river) are usually less crowded. The **Tashi Taki Lodge and Restaurant,** in central Phakding, and the **Kongde Peak Guest House and Restaurant** are both good places to stay. The trail continues up the opposite (west) side of the river to **Benkar,** a small village with a small waterfall. The peaceful **Waterfall View Lodge** here lives up to its name. Just beyond Benkar the trail re-crosses the Dudh Kosi River and leads up to the small settlement of

Chumoa, where you can dream of yeti safaris at the **Riverside Lodge and Restaurant.** A short way up the trail is **Monju,** which has a small monastery and a few good lodges, including the **Mount Kailash Lodge and Restaurant.** Beyond Monju, the trail drops down and crosses the Dudh Kosi River again on a long suspension bridge, then heads up to **Jorsale,** site of the official entrance to **Sagarmatha National Park,** where you must present your passport and pay the Rs1000 entrance fee, if you haven't already done so. Stop in the **Everest Guest House** and give your body a rest before pushing up the steep ascent to Namche. After Jorsale, the trail re-crosses the Dudh Kosi River on a rickety bridge, re-crossing it again on a much higher suspension bridge. From here the trail gets much steeper as it switchbacks its way up the hill, gaining altitude quickly. It's a good idea to take this hill slowly, as overexertion can easily lead to altitude sickness. **Namche Bazaar** is a sizable administrative center, offering more services than you're ever likely to need—currency exchange, bookstore, bakery, equipment shops, souvenirs, and a dentist. There's a **police checkpost** in town, where you'll have to present your park permit before leaving, and a **post office,** where you can off-load a few more of those Everest postcards. The **Buddha Lodge** in central Namche is as good a place to stay as any. Take a break by spending a day acclimatizing in Namche.

NAMCHE BAZAAR TO DINGBOCHE. The trail from Namche heads up past the police checkpost and along the right side of the hill, weaving in and out of the numerous ridges. You can see Everest from this section of the trail on clear days. The first village after Namche is **Kyangsuma,** a souvenir-filled settlement with several lodges, including the **Ama Dablam Lodge and Restaurant.** The trail stays fairly level beyond Kyangsuma, leading to **Sanasa** a short distance away, where the souvenir stalls will try to tempt you to weigh yourself down with junk. The **Khumbila Lodge and Restaurant** in Sanasa is clean and friendly. Beyond Sanasa, the trail heads downhill toward the Dudh Kosi River, passing a few small settlements along the way. The descent gets quite steep, finally crossing the river on a long suspension bridge at 3230m. From here it's a 1-2hr. climb up the ridge to **Tengboche,** where the stately Tengboche Monastery overlooks the Khumbu Valley and has views of many of the surrounding peaks. The monastery is well worth a visit, and tours are given daily. Tengboche can be a nice place to stay, although it gets crowded; the **Tashi Delek Lodge** has the best facilities.

Dropping off Tengboche's hilltop crest, the trail enters a lush forest and stays fairly flat until it re-crosses the Dudh Kosi River. Before crossing the river, the trail passes through **Deboche,** a quiet, attractive village lacking the crowds of Tengboche. The **Ama Dablam Garden Lodge** has large, comfortable rooms and plenty of privacy. The trail then crosses the Dudh Kosi River again on a high bridge. On the far side of the river, the terrain is more arid, and as the trail climbs, the vegetation becomes increasingly sparse and alpine. There's a fork in the trail here. The lower trail leads shortly to lower **Pangboche;** this is a good (though long) first day's stop after Namche, as it is less crowded than Tengboche. The **Ama Dablam Lodge** has clean rooms and is run by a very friendly family.

Above lower Pangboche, the trail passes through **Shomare,** a small Sherpa settlement. The **Pasang Lodge and Restaurant** has decent accommodations, although most people either stay in Pangboche or continue on to Dingboche or Pheriche. Above Shomare, the trail follows the river to a large boulder-strewn meadow and the tiny "village" of **Orsho.** At Orsho, the trail splits—the right fork drops down and crosses the river, then heads up to Dingboche; the left trail heads directly uphill to Pheriche. Both trails lead to base camp, but the right trail is more scenic and is a better way to get acclimatized. After crossing the river, the right trail climbs steeply uphill to **Dingboche** (4410m). This is a great place to spend a day acclimatizing, and there are a number of good short hikes. The **Taucheview Lodge**, at the far end of town, has clean, private rooms and a friendly staff. If you prefer to head to Pheriche (lower in altitude, with a health post and helipad), take the left trail uphill along the left ridge, crossing the river just before **Pheriche**, which stretches along the side of the river and is more protected than Dingboche. The **Himalayan Hotel** in Pheriche is a good place to stay. From Pheriche, the trail continues up the valley, meeting the right trail (from Dingboche) just before Tukla.

DINGBOCHE TO GORAK SHEP. From Dingboche the trail follows the upper ridge of the valley, climbing only slightly as it goes. At certain points you can look down at Pheriche and the lower valley. There's a short, steep descent to a small stream just before **Tukla**. Here the lower trail from Pheriche joins the upper trail. Tukla is at the bottom edge of the Khumbu glacier's enormous terminal moraine, that steep rocky hill looming over the settlement. This is a good place to stop for a while and check for altitude sickness—if you're feeling any symptoms, either stay here or descend. The **Yak Lodge** is the nicer of the two places to stay here. Immediately past Tukla, the trail begins to climb the moraine; the going is steep and rocky, and many a trekker has had to give up after trying to take it too fast. The trail follows the left side of the glacier at a much flatter grade to **Lobuje**. The **Alpine Inn** in Lobuje provides the nicest facilities, though everything here is dormitory-style. Many people spend a miserable night here and then push on to Gorak Shep and Base Camp; toward the top, people seem to rush to see the sights in misery and then head back down as quickly as possible. Some people make this their highest overnight camp and make daytrips from here to Kala Pattar and Base Camp. This means a *very* early start if you plan to be on top of Kala Pattar in time for sunrise. From Lobuje, the trail continues along the left side of the glacier and at times crosses onto sections of the glacier itself. The trail is rocky and often wet here. It's not too far to the highest overnight point of the trek, **Gorak Shep**, an even smaller settlement on a flat stretch of sand. The **Snow Land Inn** has the best food and lodging as well as a choice of private or dormitory rooms.

GORAK SHEP TO EVEREST BASE CAMP/KALA PATTAR. From Gorak Shep most people continue either to Kala Pattar, the large brown hill that looms above the village and has views of Everest, or to Everest Base Camp, the launching point for summit expeditions, or both. It's just about possible to visit both in one day.

The trail to **Kala Pattar** (5545m) is fairly straightforward, starting from the opposite side of the sand flat. It takes 1-2hr. to reach the summit from Gorak Shep. The trail to **Everest Base Camp** is less well-defined, and long stretches run along the glacier. It's best to follow a group of porters or expedition members rather than try to forge your own route across the glacier. Base Camp is less than overwhelming, but during climbing season (April-May) it becomes a sea of huge tents and ambitious would-be summiters. Everest itself isn't visible from Base Camp, but the chance to talk with expedition members (and see the spectacle) makes it worthwhile.

RETURNING FROM GORAK SHEP. Getting back down from Gorak Shep can be done very quickly. It's a short day to Pheriche, a medium day to Pangboche, or a very long day to Namche. Namche to Lukla is usually done in a day, and most people arrive in Lukla in time for the airline offices' afternoon opening hours (3-4pm). Those going back to Jiri usually go down at about the same pace as they came up—the trail is so up-and-down that it doesn't make much of a difference.

NEPAL

TREKKING IN OTHER REGIONS OF NEPAL

For information on treks through regions beyond the Classic Three, you'll have to go beyond this book. Consult a trekking company in Kathmandu (see p. 775) or in your home country. Some of the popular non-Classic Three treks include:

Lamjung. Starting in Dumre, this route takes trekkers up a minor peak, Rambrong (4400m), for fantastic views of the east end of the Annapurna massif.

Manaslu Circuit. The high point and highlight of this trip, starting in Gorkha, is the Larkya La Pass (5153m). Trekking permits cost US$90 per week Sept.-Nov. and US$75 per week Dec.-Aug.

Dhaulagiri Circuit. Starting from Beni, this trip around the world's seventh-highest peak takes you over two 5000m+ passes.

Dolpo and Mustang. An exploration of two remote and rugged regions north of Kagbeni where the awesome mountain scenery competes for attention with living vestiges of ancient cultures. Trekking permits cost US$70 per day, and you must be accompanied by an environmental officer and a registered trekking company.

Kanchenjunga Base Camp. Kanchenjunga's south face is the centerpiece of one of the planet's most awesome mountain vistas. Treks start from Tumlingtar or Taplejung. Trekking permits cost US$10 per week, and you must go with a registered trekking agency.

Simikhot to Kailash. Trek into the far northwest of Nepal, and cross the border into Tibet to join pilgrims paying their respects to holy Mt. Kailash and Manasarovar Lake.

NEPAL

APPENDIX

TEMPERATURE CHART (LOW/HIGH)

CITY	JANUARY		APRIL		JULY		OCTOBER		MONSOON	BEST TIME
	°C	°F	°C	°F	°C	°F	°C	°F		
Calcutta	12/26	54/79	23/35	73/95	25/32	77/90	23/29	73/84	June-Sept.	Nov.-Mar.
Chennai	20/29	68/84	23/34	73/93	25/36	77/91	24/32	75/90	Oct.-Dec.	Dec.-Mar.
Cochin	23/31	73/88	26/31	78/88	24/29	75/84	24/29	75/84	May-Aug.	Dec.-Mar.
Darjeeling	3/9	37/48	9/17	48/63	15/19	59/66	11/19	52/66	June-Sept.	Apr.-June; Oct.-Nov.
Delhi	7/21	45/70	17/32	63/90	26/39	78/102	16/35	61/95	June-Sept.	Nov.-Mar.
Guwahati, Assam	10/23	50/73	18/32	64/90	25/32	77/90	22/27	72/80	Apr.-Sept.	Oct.-Mar.
Hyderabad	16/29	1/84	24/36	75/97	22/31	72/88	19/30	61/86	June.-Sept.	Nov.-Feb.
Jaipur	8/22	42/72	19/33	61/92	26/35	78/95	15/31	59/87	July-Aug.	Nov.-Mar.
Kathmandu	2/18	36/64	12/28	54/82	20/29	68/84	13/27	55/80	June-Aug.	Oct.-Nov.
Mumbai	16/31	61/87	23/32	73/90	25/29	77/84	23/32	73/90	June-Aug	Nov.-Mar.
Panjim, Goa	19/31	66/87	23/32	73/90	24/28	75/82	21/32	70/90	June-Aug.	Dec.-Mar.
Shimla	3/9	37/48	10/17	50/63	15/21	59/70	8/19	42/61	July-Sept.	Apr.-July; Oct.-Nov.
Srinagar, Kashmir	3/4	37/39	7/20	45/68	17/31	63/87	6/22	42/72	None	Mar.-Sept.

GLOSSARY

adivasi: indigenous peoples of India

Agni: Hindu god of fire, messenger of the gods

ahimsa: non-violence

AIADMK: All-India Anna Dravida Munnetra Kazhagam, regional party in Tamil Nadu

air-cooling: low-budget air-conditioning—a fan blows air over the surface of water

Allah: literally, "the God," to Muslims

AMS: Acute Mountain Sickness

arati: Hindu candlelight ritual ceremony

artha: material wealth, one of the four goals of a Hindu's life (and most other people's, too)

ashram: hermitage for Hindu sages and their students

ASI: Archaeological Survey of India

atman: Hindu concept of individual soul, the breath of Brahman

attar: alcohol-free perfume

auto-rickshaw: three-wheeled, fire-breathing vehicle with the engine of a scooter and the soul of a demon

Avalokitesvara: Bodhisattva of Compassion

avatar: incarnation of a Hindu god on earth

ayurveda: ancient Indian system of medicine

azan: Muslim call to prayer, usually given from a minaret; Islamic alarm-call

bahal: Newari houses or monasteries forming a quadrangle with a central courtyard

baksheesh: tip, donation, bribe, or all of these at once

bagh: garden

ban: forest

bandh: general strike, often involves shop closings and transportation difficulties

basti: Jain temple

bazaar: market area of a town, good place to buy plastic buckets and spare tires

Bhagavad Gita: "Song of the Lord," philosophical scripture sung to Arjuna by the god Krishna; part of the *Mahabharata*

bhajan: Hindu devotional song

bhakti: personal, emotional devotion to a Hindu deity

bhangra: Punjabi folk music

Bharat: the Sanskrit word for India

bhavan: office or building

bidi: small cigarette made from a rolled-up tobacco leaf

bindi: forehead mark, worn mostly by Hindu women; symbolizes the third, all-seeing eye

BJP: Bharatiya Janata Party (Indian People's Party), the major Hindu nationalist party, symbolized by a lotus

bodhisattva: would-be Buddha who postpones his own enlightenment to help others

Bon: pre-Buddhist, animist religion of Tibet

Brahma: the Creator in the Hindu trinity

Brahman: the universal soul or spirit, embodied by Brahma

brahmin: member of the hereditary priesthood; highest of the four Hindu *varnas*

Buddha: Enlightened One

bugyal: high meadow above the treeline

cantonment: former British military district

caste: Hindu group that practices a hereditary occupation, has a definite ritual status, and marries within the group

chador: shawl

chaitya: Buddhist prayer hall or miniature stupa

chakra: Wheel of the Law in Buddhism; Vishnu's discus weapon in Hinduism

chalo: let's go

chappals: leather sandals

charbagh: traditional Mughal garden form, used particularly in tombs.

chattri: cenotaph; cremation monument

chillum: mouthpiece of a *hookah;* a pipe use to smoke *ganja*

chorten: Tibetan Buddhist memorial shrine

chowk (chauk): market area or square

chowkidar: watchman

coir: woven coconut fibers

communalism: religious prejudice, especially between Hindus and Muslims

Congress (I): party that grew from the Indian National Congress that pushed for Indian Independence; party of Jawaharlal Nehru and Indira Gandhi; "I" is for "Indira"

crore: 10 million, written 1,00,00,000

dacoit: armed bandit

Dalit: currently preferred term for former "Untouchables"

darshan: "seeing" a Hindu deity through his or her image

deodar: tall Indian cedar tree

dhaba: roadside food stand

dham: place, often a sacred site

dharamsala: resthouse for Hindu pilgrims

dharma: system of morality and way of life or religion (Hindu or Buddhist); one's duty and station in life

dhobi: washerman or -woman

dhoti: *lungi* with folds of cloth between the wearer's legs

dhow: boat of Arab origins

diwan-i-am: hall of public audience

diwan-i-khas: hall of private audience

DMK: Dravida Munnetra Kazhagam, regional party in Tamil Nadu

dorje: Tibetan Buddhist thunderbolt symbol

dowry: money or gifts given by a bride's parents to the son-in-law's as part of a marriage agreement; officially illegal but still practiced

dun: valley

dupatta: scarf warn as part of a *salwar kameez.*

durbar: royal palace or court

Durga: Hindu goddess who slayed the buffalo demon Mahisha

eve-teasing: cat-calling, sexual harassment

fakir: Muslim ascetic

ganj: market

ganja: dried leaves and flowering tops of female cannabis plant—smoke it and see what happens

Garuda: Vishnu's half-man, half-bird vehicle

ghat: riverbank used for bathing, often paved with steps

Ghats: ranges of hills on the east and west coasts of the Indian peninsula

ghazal: Urdu love song

godown: factory warehouse

gompa: Tibetan Buddhist monastery

gopis: Krishna's flirtatious milkmaid friends

gopuram: entrance tower of a South Indian Hindu temple

GPO: General Post Office

guru: religious teacher; in Sikhism, one of the 10 founding leaders of the Sikh faith

Guru Granth Sahib: Sikh holy book

gurudwara: Sikh temple

Haj: the pilgrimage to Mecca that all Muslims are required to make once in their lifetime if physically and financially able

Hanuman: monkey god, helper of Rama in the *Ramayana*

harmonium: air-powered keyboard instrument

harijan: literally, "child of God," Mahatma Gandhi's name for the Untouchables

hartal: general strike

haveli: Rajasthani mansion, traditionally painted with murals

hijra: eunuch; transvestite

hookah: elaborate smoking apparatus in which the smoke is drawn through a long pipe and a container of water

howdah: seat for an elephant rider

imam: prayer leader of mosque, or Shi'a Muslim leader descended from Muhammad

imambara: tomb of a Shi'a Muslim imam, or a replica of one

Indo-Saracenic: architecture merging Indian style with Islamic style from the Middle East

Indra: early Hindu god of thunder, king of the Vedic gods

jagamohana: audience hall or "porch" of a Hindu temple

jali: geometric latticework pattern in Islamic architecture

Janata Dal: political party based in U.P. and Bihar, supported by low-caste Hindus, symbolized by a wheel

Jat: large North Indian agricultural caste

jati: sub-division within the four Hindu castes

jauhar: Rajput custom of mass *sati*

-ji: respectful suffix added to names

JKLF: Jammu and Kashmir Liberation Front

juggernaut: corruption of the deity Jagannath's name; refers to large ceremonial carts used to transport the deity

jyotirlinga: a self-erecting *linga;* there are 12 in India

Kali: black-skinned Hindu goddess with lolling tongue who wears snakes and skulls

kama: physical love, one of the four goals of a Hindu's life. Have you heard of the Kama Sutra?

kameez: loose-fitting woman's shirt

karma: what goes around comes around, man

kata: silk prayer shawl, usually presented to a lama when visiting a monastery

khadi: homespun, handwoven cotton cloth

Khalistan: "Land of the Pure, " name of independent Punjab desired by Sikh separatists

khalsa: Punjabi for "pure;" a "baptized" Sikh

khukuri: machete-like Nepalese "Gurkha" knife

Krishna: blue-skinned Hindu god, who plays the flute and frolics with milkmaids; Arjuna's charioteer in *Mahabharata* who sang *Bhagavad Gita;* considered an avatar of Vishnu

kshatriya: member of the warrior/ruler caste, second highest of the four *varnas* of the Hindu caste system

kumbh: pitcher or pot

kurta: long men's shirt

la: moutain pass in the Himalayas and surrounding ranges

lakh: one hundred thousand (usually rupees or people), written 1,00,000

Lakshmi: Goddess of fortune and wealth, often considered the consort of Vishnu

lama: Tibetan-Buddhist priest or holy man

lila: Hindu concept of divine "play:" a god (usually Krishna) sporting with human worshippers, or theatrical production depicting a myth (usually *Ramayana*)

linga: also *lingam;* stone phallus that symbolizes Shiva

Lok Sabha: lower house of Indian parliament

lungi: sarong tied around a man's waist

Macchendranath: Newari rain god

maha: great

Mahabharata: Sanskrit epic about the five Pandava brothers' struggle to regain their kingdom

mahal: palace

mahout: elephant trainer

mandala: circle symbolizing universe in Hindu and Buddhist art, used in meditation

mandapam: colonnaded hall leading up to a Hindu or Jain temple sanctum

mandir: temple

mani: stone wall with Tibetan inscriptions

mantra: sacred word or chant used by Hindus and Buddhists to aid in meditation

marg: road

masjid: mosque; Muslim place of worship

math: residence for Hindu priests or sadhus

maya: the illusory world of everyday life

mehendi: painting of intricate, semi-permanent henna designs on the hands or feet

mela: fair or festival

moksha: Hindu salvation; liberation from cycle of rebirth

monsoon: season of extremely heavy rains

muezzin: crier who calls Muslims to prayer from the minaret of a mosque

mullah: Muslim scholar or leader

nadi: river

naga: Hindu aquatic snake deity

nagar: city

Nandi: Shiva's bull vehicle

Narayan: Vishnu sleeping on the cosmic ocean

nawab: Muslim governor or landowner

NDP: National Democratic Party, right-wing party in Nepal

neem: plant product used as an insecticide

Nepali Congress: centrist party that led the movement for democracy in Nepal, symbolized by a tree

nirvana: nothingness, the snuffing out of the flame, the goal of Buddhists

Om: ॐ; sacred invocation; mantra used by Hindus and Buddhists.

paise: 1/100 of a rupee

pagoda: Nepalese Hindu temple with tiered roofs

palanquin: hand-carried carriage

panchayat: traditional 5-member village

pandit: honored or wise person; Hindu priest

Parsi: "Persian; " Zoroastrians who migrated to India after Muslim conversion of Iran

Partition: 1947 division of British India along religious lines to create India and Pakistan

Parvati: mountain goddess; consort of Shiva through whom his power is expressed

peon: low-level worker

pipal: the Buddha meditated his way to enlightenment under one of these.

prasad: food consecrated by a Hindu deity and given out to worshipers

puja: prayers and offerings of food and flowers to a Hindu deity

pujari: Hindu priest conducting ceremonies in a temple

pukka: finished, ripe, complete

Puranas: Hindu mythological poems

purdah: Muslim practice of secluding women

qawwali: Sufi devotional or love song

qila: fort

Qu'ran: Muslim holy book containing God's revelations as told to Mohammed

Radha: milkmaid consort of Krishna

raga: melodic structure, the base for lengthy musical improvisations

raj: government or sovereignty

Raj: the British Empire in India

raja: king

Rajputs: medieval Hindu warrior-princes of central India and Rajasthan

Rama: Hindu hero-god of the *Ramayana* who defeats the demon Ravana; avatar of Vishnu

Ramadan: holiest month in the Islamic calendar, when Muslims fast from dawn to dusk

Ramayana: epic "romance of Rama" telling of Rama's rescue of wife Sita from Ravana

rani: queen

rath: cart, particularly one used in Hindu religious festivals

Ravana: villain of the epic *Ramayana*

RSS: Rashtriya Swayamsevak Sangh (National Volunteer Corps), Hindu nationalist paramilitary organization

sadhu: ascetic Hindu holy man

sagar: sea or lake

sahib: "master," Raj-era title for Europeans

salwar: women's baggy pants worn with kameez

sambar: large, dark brown deer

samsara: the endless cycle of life, death, and rebirth in Buddhism and Hinduism

sangam: meeting point of two rivers; also name of early gatherings of Tamil poets

sankha: Vishnu's conch shell

sannyasin: "renouncer," Hindu ascetic wanderer who has given up worldly life

sant: saint, holy man

sari: six(sometimes nine) yards of cloth, usually silk or cotton, draped around a woman's body, worn with a matching blouse

sati: ritual whereby widows burned themselves on their husbands' funeral pyres

Sati: Hindu goddess who landed in pieces all over India, forming *shakti pithas;* considered Shiva's consort

satyagraha: "truth force," Mahatma Gandhi's protest by non-violent non-cooperation

scheduled castes: official name for the former "Untouchable" groups, whose castes are listed in a "schedule" in the constitution

scheduled tribes: aboriginal groups recognized under the Indian constitution

sepoy: Indian serving in British Indian army under the Raj

Shaivite: follower of Shiva

shakti: divine feminine power in Hinduism

shakti pitha: Hindu holy place associated with the goddess Sati

Shankara: another name for Shiva

shanti: peace

shekari: an Orissan architectural style

Shi'a: Muslim sect which split from the Sunnis in the 8th century AD in a succession dispute; Shi'as look to imams in Iran as their spiritual leaders

shikhara: pyramid-shaped spire on a Hindu temple

Shitala: "cool" goddess of smallpox and other fever diseases in North India

Shiva: great god of Hinduism, known as the Destroyer in the Hindu trinity; usually depicted as an ascetic holy man

Shiv Sena: regional Hindu nationalist party in Maharashtra

shudra: member of the laborer caste, lowest of the four Hindu castes

sindur: vermilion paste used as an offering to Hindu deities

Sita: Rama's wife in the *Ramayana*, kidnapped by Ravana

sitar: 20-stringed instrument made from a gourd with a teakwood bridge

Sri: title of respect and veneration

STD/ISD: standard trunk dialing/international subscriber dialing. Nothing to do with sex

stupa: large mound, traditionally containing a Buddhist relic

Sufi: member of Islamic devotional and mystical movement

Sunni: largest Muslim sect; believes in elected leaders for the Islamic community

swadeshi: domestic goods; the Indian freedom movement called for their use rather than British imports

swaraj: self-rule, as demanded by the Indian freedom movement

sweeper: low-caste or Untouchable Hindu whose vocation is sweeping streets (hence the name) or cleaning latrines

tabla: two-piece drum set

tal: lake

tara: Tantric female companion to a dhyani Buddha

Terai: foothills at the base of the Himalayas

tempo: Bee-colored three-wheelers that screech and stink their way through cities like mechanised elephants on speed

thanka: Tibetan scroll-painting of a *mandala*, used as an meditation aid

thukpa: Tibetan noodle soup

tirtha: "crossing" between earth and heaven

tirthankara: one of 24 Jain "crossing-makers," a series of saints culminating with Mahavira, the founder of Jainism

tonga: two-wheeled carriage drawn (slowly) by an old horse or maltreated pony

topi: cap

trishul: trident, symbol of Shiva and originally a symbol of the Goddess

Untouchables: casteless Hindus, formerly shunned by high-caste Hindus because their touch was considered polluting; now known as scheduled castes, Dalits, or Harijans

Upanishads: speculative, philosophical Sanskrit Hindu hymns composed around 800 BC

utthapam: thick dosa made with onion

Vaishnavite: follower of Vishnu

vaishya: member of the merchant caste, third-highest of the four Hindu castes

vajra: Nepalese Buddhist thunderbolt symbol

varna: broad group of Hindu castes; *brahmins, kshatriyas, vaishyas,* and *shudras* are the four *varnas*

Vedas: sacred Sanskrit hymns composed between 1500 and 800 BC, forming the basis of the Hindu religion

Vishnu: one of the Great Gods of Hinduism, known as the Preserver in the Hindu trinity; frequently appears on earth as an *avatar* to save earth from demons

VHP: Vishwa Hindu Parishad (World Hindu Society), Hindu nationalist organization

wallah: occupational suffix, e.g rickshaw-wallah, *Let's Go-wallah*

yaksha/yakshi: early Hindu nature deity

Yama: early Hindu god of death

yoni: circular base, often accompanying a *linga*

zakat: almsgiving required of Muslims

zamindar: tax collector or landlord in Mughal India

FOOD AND DRINK

aloo: potato

am: mango

appam: South Indian rice pancake

arrak: fermented mash of malted rice, serious headache juice

badam: almond

baingan: eggplant

barfi: milk- and sugar-based Indian sweet

betel: red nut with mild narcotic properties when chewed; key ingredient in *paan.*

bhaji: vegetables dipped in batter and fried

bhang: dried leaves and shoots of the male cannabis plant

bhat: cooked rice

bhindi: okra (lady's fingers)

bidi: small cigarette made from a rolled-up tobacco leaf

biryani: rice cooked with spices and vegetables or meat

capsicum: bell pepper

chaat: snack

chai (chiya): tea, generally boiled with milk and sugar

chang: Himalayan rice wine

channa: chickpeas

chappati: unleavened, griddle-cooked bread

cheeni: sugar

chikki: peanut brittle

cutlet: meat or vegetable patty

dahi: yogurt

dal: lentil soup, a staple dish eaten with rice

dhaba: roadside food stand

dosa: South Indian rice-flour pancake
dudh: milk
dum: steamed
feni: Goan drink made from fermented coconuts or cashews
ganja: dried leaves and flowering tops of female cannabis plant—smoke it and see what happens
garam: hot
ghee: clarified butter
gosht: mutton or goat
gulab jamun: dry milk balls in sweet syrup
halal: food prepared according to Islamic dietary rules
idli: South Indian steamed rice-flour cakes
jalebis: deep fried, orange, syrup-filled sweet
kaju: cashew nut
kheer: rice cooked in sweetened milk, raisins, and almonds
kofta: meat- or vegetable-balls
korma: creamy curry
kulfi: thick pistachio-flavored ice cream
kumb palak: spinach
lassi: yogurt and ice-water drink
machli: fish
masala: a mix of spices, usually containing cumin, coriander, and cardamom
mirch: hot pepper
momo: Tibetan stuffed pastry similar to wontons or ravioli
murgh: chicken
mutter: green peas
naan: unleavened bread cooked in a tandoor

naryal: coconut
paan: betel leaf stuffed with areca nut
pakoras: cheese or other foods deep-fried in chickpea batter
palak: spinach
paneer: fermented curd; cheesy comestibles
pani: water
papad: crispy lentil wafer
paratha: multi-layered, whole-wheat bread cooked on a griddle
phal: fruit
pongal: rice item garnished with black peppers and chilies, often sweet
pulao: fried rice with nuts or fruit
puri: small, deep-fried bread
raita: spicy salad of vegetables and yogurt
raksi: strong Himalayan liquor
roti: bread
saag: pureed spinach or other greens
sabji: vegetables
sambar: South Indian lentil soup
samosa: deep-fried vegetable or meat pastry
thali: complete meal served on steel plate with small dishes of condiments
thukpa: Tibetan noodle soup
tiffin: snack or light meal
toddy: unrefined coconut liquor
tong-ba: Nepali grain liquor
utthapam: thick dosa made with onion
vadai: doughnut-shaped rice cake dipped in curd or sambar
vindaloo: very hot South Indian curry

PHRASEBOOK

ENGLISH	HINDI	ENGLISH	HINDI
	Hindi is understood in most of North India.		
Hello.	Namaste.	How are you?	Kaise hain, aap?
Sorry/Forgive me.	Maaf kijiyega.	Yes/No	Ha/Nahin.
Thank you.	Shukriya.	No thanks.	Nahin, shukriya.
Good-bye.	Phir milenge.	No problem.	Koi baat nahin.
When (what time)?	Kub?	What?	Kyaa?
OK.	Thik hai.	Why?	Kyoonh?
Who?	Kaun?	Help!	Bachao!
How much does this cost?	Kyaa daam hai?	Go away/Leave me alone.	Chale jao/Mujhe akela chor do.
Stop/enough.	Bas.	Is...available?	Yahand...milta hai?

ENGLISH	HINDI	ENGLISH	HINDI
	Hindi is understood in most of North India.		
Please repeat.	Phir se kahiye.	What's this called in Hindi?	Hindi mein kaise kehte hain?
Please speak slowly.	Kripya, dhire boliye.	I don't understand.	Mein nahin samajhta.
What is your name?	Apkaa naam kyaa hai?	My name is...	Mera naam...hai.
I like...	Mujhe...achaa lagta hai.	I don't like...	Mujhe...achaa nahin lagta.

Directions			
turn right	dayne hath muro.	turn left	bayne hath muro.
How do I get to...?	...kaise jayen?	How far is...?	...kitna dur hai?
near	paas	far	dur
Where is...?	...kahan hai?	out	baahar
below	neeche	at the back of	peeche
above	oopar	in front of	saamne

Food and Drink			
bread	roti, chappaati, naan	rice	chaaval
meat	gosht	water	pani
vegetables	sabzi	sweets	mitthai

Times and Hours			
open	khula	closed	bandh
What time is it?	Kitne baje hain?	morning	subah
afternoon	dopaher	evening	shaam
night	raat	yesterday	kal
today	aaj	tomorrow	kal

Other Words			
alone	akela	friend	dost
good	achhaa	bad	bura
hot	garam	cold	thunda
medicine	dawaii	alcohol	daru/sharaab

Numbers					
one	ek	१	ten	dus	१०
two	do	२	eleven	gyaarah	११
three	teen	३	twelve	baarah	१२
four	char	४	fifteen	pandraah	१५
five	paanch	५	twenty	bees	२०
six	chey	६	twenty-five	pachis	२५
seven	saat	७	fifty	pachaas	५०
eight	aath	८	one hundred	ek sau	१००
nine	nau	९	one thousand	ek hazar	१०००

ENGLISH	BENGALI	ENGLISH	BENGALI
	Bengali is spoken in West Bengal and Bangladesh.		
Hello.	Nomoshkar.	How are you?	Kemon achen?
Sorry/Forgive me.	Maf korben.	No problem.	Hoye jabe.
Thank you.	Dhonyobad.	Yes/No.	Ha/Na.

ENGLISH	BENGALI	ENGLISH	BENGALI
	Bengali is spoken in West Bengal and Bangladesh.		
Goodbye/ See you later.	Biday/Abar dekha hobe.	OK.	Achha/Thik.
Why?	Keno?	When?	Kathan?
Who?	Ke?	What?	Ki?
What is your name?	Apnar nam ki?	Stop/enough.	Bas.
How much does this cost?	Koto taka?	Go away/leave me alone.	Chere din/Birakto korben na.
Is...available?	...ache?	What's this called in Bengali?	Banglay eta ke ki bole?
Help!	Bachao!	Please repeat.	Aabar bolun.
My name is...	Amar nam...	Please speak slowly	Aste aste bolun.
I like...	Amar...bhalo lage.	I don't like...	Amar...bhalo lage na.
I don't understand.	Bujhi na.		

Directions			
(to the) right	dan dike	(to the) left	bam dike
How do I get to...?	...ki kore jabo?	How far is...?	...koto door?
near	kache	far	door
Where is...?	...kothai?	across	opar

Food			
bread	paoruti	rice	bhat
meat	mangsho	water	jol/pani
vegetables	shobji	fish	maachh

Times and Hours			
open	khola	closed	bandho
What time is it?	Koita baje?	morning	shokal
afternoon	bikel	evening	sondhya
night	raat	yesterday	gotokal
today	aaj	tomorrow	agamikal

Other Words			
alone	aka	friend (M/F)	bondhu/bandhobi
good	bhalo	bad	kharap
happy	khushi	sad	dukhi, mon mora
hot	gorom	cold	thandha
office	doftor	backpack	bojha
condoms	nirodh	pain	byatha

Numbers					
one	ak	১	twenty	bish	২০
two	dui	২	thirty	tirish	৩০
three	tin	৩	forty	chollish	৪০
four	char	৪	fifty	ponchash	৫০
five	panch	৫	sixty	shaat	৬০
six	choi	৬	seventy	sattar	৭০
seven	saat	৭	eighty	aashi	৮০
eight	aat	৮	ninety	nabbai	৯০
nine	noi	৯	one hundred	ek sho	১০০
ten	dosh	১০	one thousand	ek hajar	১০০০

ENGLISH	TAMIL	ENGLISH	TAMIL
	Tamil is spoken in Tamil Nadu.		
Hello.	Namaskaram.	How are you?	Yep padi irukkai?
Sorry/Forgive me.	Mannikkavum.	No problem.	Kavalai illai.
Thank you.	Nanri.	No thanks.	Illai, véndam.
Yes/No.	Amam/Illai.	OK.	Se ri.
Good-bye.	Poittu Varén.	When (what time)?	Yéppo?
Why?	Yén?	What?	Yénna?
Who?	Yaru?	Is...available?	...irukka?
How much does this cost?	Yenna velai?	Go away/leave me alone.	Yenna vidu.
Please speak slowly.	Medhuva pésungo.	What's this called in Tamil?	...Tamilla yenna?
I don't understand.	Puriyalai.	Help!	Kapathu!
Please repeat.	Thiruppi.	Stop/enough.	Porum.
I like...	Ennakku...pidikkum.	I don't like...	Ennakku...pidikkaathu.
What is your name?	Ungal péyar ennai?	My name is...	En peyar...
Directions			
(to the) right	valadu pakkam	(to the) left	idadhu pakkam
How do I get to...?	...eppadi poradu?	How far is...?	...evvalavu dooram?
near	pakkam	far	dooram
above...	...kku melai	below...	...kku kirai
in front of...	...kku munnadi	at the back of...	...kku pinnadi
Food and Drink			
vegetables	kari kai	rice	saadam
meat	maamsam	water	thanni
mango	maampazham	bread	roddi
Time and Hours			
open	tharandhu	closed	moodi
What time is it?	Yénna néram?	morning	kaathaalai
afternoon	madyaanam	evening	saayankaalam
night	raatri	yesterday	néthikku
today	innikki	tomorrow	nalai
Other Words			
alone	thaniya	friend	nanban
good	nalladhu	bad	kettadhu
hot	soodu	cold	aarinadhu
temple	kovil	doctor	maruthuvar
hospital	aaspathri	medicine	marunthu
Numbers			
one	onrru	1	twenty	iruvathu	20
two	eranndu	2	thirty	muppathu	30
three	moonrru	3	forty	naapathu	40
four	naanru	4	fifty	aiympathu	50
five	aiynthu	5	sixty	aruvathu	60
six	aarru	6	seventy	yerupathu	70
seven	yeru	7	eighty	yennpathu	80

ENGLISH	TAMIL		ENGLISH	TAMIL	
		Tamil is spoken in Tamil Nadu.			
eight	yettu	8	ninety	thonnoorru	90
nine	onpathu	9	one hundred	noorru	100
ten	paththu	10	one thousand	aayeram	1000

ENGLISH	NEPALI	ENGLISH	NEPALI
	Nepali is spoken in Nepal.		
Hello.	Namaste/ Namaskar.	How are you?	Kasto chha?
Sorry/Forgive me.	Sorry (maph garnus).	No problem./I'm fine.	Thik chha.
Thank you.	Danyabad.	No thanks.	Pardaina, danyabad.
Yes/No.	Ho/Hoina.	Good-bye.	Namaste.
When(what time)?	Kahile?	What?	Ke?
Who?	Ko?	Is...available?	...paincha?
Why?	Kina?	OK.	Huncha./La.
How much does this cost?	Kati ho?	Go away. (polite/ impolite)	Tapai januus ta./Jau!
I don't understand.	Bujina.	Please repeat.	Feri bhannus.
Please speak slowly.	Bistarai bolnus.	What's this called in Nepali?	Nepali ma ke bhanchha?
What is your name?	Tapai ko naam ke ho?	My name is...	Mero naam...ho.
Help!	Guhar!	My country is...	Mero desh...ho.
I like...	... man parcha.	I don't like...	... mar par dai na.
Stop/enough.	Pugyo.	Please give me..	Kripa garera malai...
Does anyone here speak English?	Yahan angreji bolne kohi chha?	I have a reservation.	Mero yahan reservation chha.
Directions			
(to the) right	daya, dahurie.	(to the) left	baya, debre.
How do I get to...?	...kosari janne?	How far is...?	...kati tada cha?
near	najik	far	tada
east	purba	west	paschima
Food and Drink			
bread	pauroti	rice	bhat
meat	masu	water	pani
vegetables	tarkari	food/meal	khana
Time and Hours			
open	khulcha	closed	bandha
What time is it?	Kati bajyo?	morning	bihana
afternoon	diooso	evening	sanjha
night	rati	yesterday	hijo
today	aaja	tomorrow	bholi
Other Words			
alone	eklai	friend	sathi
good	ramro	bad	naramro
happy	kushi	sad	dukhi
hot	garmi (weather)/tato	cold	jaado (weather)/chiso
newspaper	akhbar	magazine	patrika

ENGLISH	NEPALI		ENGLISH	NEPALI	
		Nepali is spoken in Nepal.			
		Numbers			
one	ek	१	twenty	biss	२०
two	dui	२	thirty	tees	३०
three	teen	३	forty	chaliss	४०
four	char	४	fifty	pachass	५०
five	panch	५	sixty	saathi	६०
six	chha	६	seventy	sattari	७०
seven	saat	७	eighty	asi	८०
eight	aathh	८	ninety	nabbe	९०
nine	nau	९	one hundred	ek saya	१००

ENGLISH	GUJARATI		ENGLISH	GUJARATI	
		Gujarati is spoken in Gujarat.			
Hello.	Namaste.		How are you?	Kem cho?	
Sorry/Forgive me.	Maaf karo.		Yes/No.	Ha/Na.	
Thank you.	Aabhar.		I am fine.	Hu majama chu.	
Good-bye.	Avjo.		No problem.	Kaye vandhon nathi.	
When?	Kyare?		I like...	Mane...gameche.	
Is...available?	...maleche?		Stop/enough.	Bas.	
What is your name?	Tamaru nam su che?		Help!	Bachao!	
My name is...	Maru nam...che.		My country is...	Maro desh...che.	
Go away/Leave me alone.	Jatore.		I don't like...	Mane...gamtu nathi.	
		Directions			
to the right	jamani baju		to the left	dabi baju	
How do I get to...?	...no rasto kayo che?		How far is...?	...ketlu dur che?	
		Time and Hours			
open	khulu		closed	band	
night	raat		yesterday	kale (gay kale)	
today	aaje		tomorrow	kale (avti kale)	
		Numbers			
one	ek	q	six	chah	૬
two	be	૨	seven	sat	૭
three	tran	૩	eight	aath	૮
four	char	૪	nine	nav	૯
five	pach	૫	ten	das	૧૦

ENGLISH	KANNADA	ENGLISH	KANNADA
		Kannada is spoken in Karnataka.	
Hello.	Ain samachar.	Good-bye.	Namaskara.
What is your name?	Ni nna he sa ru?	My name is...	Na nna he sa ru...
Please excuse me.	Da ya ma di na nna ksha mi si ri.	How much is this?	...nsu he ge?
Give me...	Ardha...	newspaper	varthapatrike
room	kone	address	vilasa

APPENDIX

ENGLISH	KANNADA	ENGLISH	KANNADA
	Kannada is spoken in Karnataka.		
Directions			
to the right	jamani baju	to the left	dabi baju
How do I get to...?	...no rasto kayo che?	How far is...?	...ketlu dur che?
front	munde	back	hinde
Time and Hours			
open	khulu	closed	band
evening	sayankala	night	rathri
noon	hagalu	early morning	...ketlu dur che?
Food and Drink			
bread	rotti	rice	akki
meat	mamsa	fruit	hannu
vegetables	tharakarl	water	niru
curd	mosaru	*dal*	thovve
Numbers			
one	ondu	six	aru
two	eradu	seven	elu
three	muru	eight	entu
four	nalku	nine	ombathu
five	aidu	ten	haththu

ENGLISH	MALAYALAM	ENGLISH	MALAYALAM
	Malayalam is spoken in Kerala.		
Hello.	Namaste.	How are you?	Enngane irikkunnu?
Sorry/Forgive me.	Kshemikkuga.	Yes/No	Ade/alla
Thank you.	Valara upakaram.	No thanks.	Véndá.
Good-bye.	Pogetté.	No problem.	Sárawilla.
When/What time?	Eppoýá/eppam?	OK.	Seri.
Who?	Árá?	I like...	Enikka ... istamá.
Go away/Leave me alone.	Pó, salyappadade.	Stop/enough.	Madi.
I don't understand.	Samajha nahin.	Use the meter!	Míteru kanakkáyitta!
What is your name?	Ninngade pér endá?	Help!	Onnu saháyikkámó?
My name is...	Enda péru ...	My country is...	Enda támassam ... ilá.
Directions			
How do I get to...?	... édu vazhiyá?	How far is...?	... ettara dúramá?
Where is...?	Ewidá?	above...	... ende molil
below...	... ende thara	in front of...	... munbil
behind...	... pinnil	inside	aahathe
outside	purethe		
Food and Drink			
bread	rotti	rice	córa
meat	eracci	water	vellam
meal	batchanam		

ENGLISH	MALAYALAM		ENGLISH	MALAYALAM	
	Malayalam is spoken in Kerala.				
Time and Hours					
open	torannu		closed	adaccu	
What time is it?	Ettara maniyá?		yesterday	innala	
today	innu		tomorrow	nále	
Numbers					
one	onnu	ഹ	six	aaru	൬
two	rendu	വ	seven	eru	൨
three	moonu	ന്വ	eight	ettu	൶
four	naalu	ർ	nine	onpathu	ൻ
five	anju	൭	ten	pathu	൰൦

ENGLISH	TELUGU		ENGLISH	TELUGU	
	Telugu is spoken in Andhra Pradesh.				
Hello.	Emandi		How are you?	Meeru ela unnaru?	
Sorry/Forgive me.	Kshaminchandi.		No problem.	Paravaledu.	
Thank you.	Krithagnatalu		No thanks.	Vaddandi.	
Yes/No.	Avunu/Kaadu		OK.	Sare.	
Good-bye.	Poyesta.		When(what time)?	Eppudu (time entha)?	
What is your name?	Mee peru emiti?		My name is...	Naa peru ...	
Directions					
How do I get to...?	... ki poye daniki dari emiti?		How far is...?	... entha duramu?	
near	daggara		far	dooramu	
Food					
vegetables	kooragayalu		rice	annamu	
meat	mamsamu		water	neeru	
Numbers					
one	okati	1	six	aaru	6
two	rendu	2	seven	eedu	7
three	moodu	3	eight	enimidi	8
four	naalugu	4	nine	tommidi	9
five	aidu	5	ten	padi	10

INDEX

A

abominable snowman,
  see yeti
accommodations 30–31
Achalgarh 521
acupuncture 239
Acute Mountain Sickness
  (AMS) 24, 36
Adalaj Vav 208
Adi Granth 90
aerogrammes 39
Agartala 449
Agni 70
Agonda 199
Agra 672–683
  Agra Fort 681
  Taj Mahal 680–681
ahimsa 91
Ahmedabad 201–208
Aibak, Qutb-ud-din 144
AIDS 27
Aihole 307
airports
  Agartala 449
  Agra 676
  Ahmedabad 202
  Amritsar 473
  Aurangabad 422
  Bagdogra 738
  Bangalore 274
  Bhairawa 833
  Bharatpur 837
  Bhopal 351
  Bhubaneswar 452
  Bhuj 219
  Calcutta 723
  Calicut 346
  Chandigarh 468
  Chennai 559
  Cochin 334
  Coimbatore 621
  Delhi 144
  Dharamsala 231
  Diu 211
  Guwahati 436
  Gwalior 381
  Hongde 856
  Jaipur 483
  Jaisalmer 528
  Janakpur 845
  Jomsom 859

Jorhat 443
Kathmandu 771
Khajuraho 369
Kullu 243
Leh 261
Lucknow 692
Lukla 877
Mangalore 297
Mumbai 389
Nagpur 431
Patna 131
Pokhara 824
Port Blair 108
Pune 414
Rajkot 209
Shimla 225
Silchar 444
Srinagar 271
Tirupati 128
Trichy 599
Trivandrum 315
Udaipur 508
Ajanta 72, 428–431
Ajmer 498–500
Akali Dal 82
Akbar 73, 97, 683, 719
Akbar's Tomb 683
Alappuzha, see Alleppey
alcohol 21, 211, 437
  beer spout 786
Alfassa, Mirra, "The
  Mother" 587
Allah 89
Allahabad 716–720
Alleppey 327–329
Almora 665–668
alternatives to tourism
  61–67
altitude, high 24
Amar Sagar 535
Ambedkar, B.R. 92
Amber Fort, Jaipur 493
American Express 14
  Calcutta 729
  Chennai 565
  Delhi 153
  Kathmandu 779
  Mumbai 398
Amritsar 75, 472–480
  massacre 479, 739
Andaman Islands 108–117
Andhra Pradesh 118–129

Anegundi 305
animal sacrifice 816, 820
animals 19
  Asiatic lion 216
  barking deer 662
  Bengal tiger 743
  camels 541
  four-toed yeti 755
  inebriated 742
  proverbs 858
  rhinos 842
  see also endangered
    animals
  tigers 332, 457, 655, 842
  wild ass 218
Anjuna 184–188
Annapurna Base Camp
  (ABC) 863
Annapurna Circuit 854
Annapurna region 854–
  864
Arambol 190–192
archaeological digs 64
architecture
  India 96
  Nepal 765
arts
  Nepal 764–766
Aryans 70, 84
Ashoka 71, 118, 138, 140,
  362, 451, 457, 756
  pillars 143, 216, 456,
    715, 836
ashrams
  Haridwar 643
  Nepal 792
  Pondicherry 587
  Rishikesh 647
Assam 434–445
Auli 653
Aurangabad 421–426
Aurangzeb 73, 421, 425,
  426, 483, 689
Aurobindo Ghose, Sri
  ashram 587
Auroville 588
auto-rickshaws 52
Ayodhya 698–699
  Babri Masjid 79, 699
ayurvedic medicine 124,
  324, 341

B

Babri Masjid 79, 699
Babur 73, 144, 381, 385, 673, 699
backpacks 35
backwater cruises
  Alleppey 329
  Cochin 341
  Kovalam 323
bad ideas
  jewel smuggling 18
  Operation Bluestar 477
  trekking near Srinagar 271
Bada Bagh 535
Badami 306–307
Badrinath 652
Baga 181–184
Baha'i Temple 164
Bajinath 671
Balaju 801
bandhani 496
Bandhavgarh National Park 368
Bangalore 273–284
Bangladesh 11, 46, 77
Barabar Caves 136
Baralacha La 258
bargaining 16, 17
Basantapur 850
beaches
  Anjuna 184
  Benaulim 196
  Calangute and Baga 181
  Colva 195
  Goa 181, 184, 188, 190, 192, 195, 196, 198, 199
  Gujarat 213, 223
  Kerala 320, 340, 348
  Mandrem 192
  Orissa 460, 464
  Palolem 198
  Tamil Nadu 569
  Vagator 188
Beatles 644
begging 18
Begum, Arjumand Banu 680
Belur 295
Benares Hindu University 712
Benares, see Varanasi
Benaulim 196
Bengali Renaissance 723, 735

Besisahar 855
Bhagwan Shree Rajneesh 418, 632
Bhairawa 833
Bhaja 420
Bhaktapur 805–811
Bharatiya Janata Party (BJP) 79, 80, 82, 672
bharatnatyam 101, 557
Bharatpur, Nepal 837
Bharatpur, Rajasthan 496–497
Bharmour 242
Bhimtal 662
Bhonsle, Shivaji 403, 418
Bhopal 349–353
Bhubaneswar 452–456
Bhuj 218–221
Bhutan 46
Bibi-ka-Maqbara 425
bicycles 54
Bihar 130–143
Bijapur 308–310
Bikaner 536–541
Binsar Sanctuary 668
birdwatching 497, 657
Birethanti 862
Birganj 844
Birla Mandirs
  Delhi 167
  Hyderabad 124
Bishnoi villages 527
boats 46
Bodh Gaya 92, 137–142
bodhi tree 140
Bollywood 100, 389, 407, 627
Bombay, see Mumbai
Bon 551
border crossings 46
  Bhairawa 833
  Birganj 844
  Pakistan 481
  Raxaul 143
  Siliguri and New Jalpaiguri 738
  Sunauli 834
Boudha 802–805
  stupa 765
Boudhanath, see Boudha
Brahma 87
Brahma Temple, Pushkar 503
Brahmaputra River 68, 439
Brindavan 284
Buddha 92, 130, 756
  ashes interred 142

death 701
enlightenment 137
first sermon 714
teachings compiled 135
Buddhism
  India 92
  Nepal 762–763
Buddhist art
  Aurangabad caves 425
  Karla and Bhaja caves 420
Buddhist sites
  East India 134, 141, 142, 465
  Kashmir 265
  Nepal 790, 796, 800, 836
  North India 236, 266, 702
  Sarnath 714
  South India 127
  Tabo Gompa 256
  Thong Wa Rang To Chorten 555
Bungamati 799
Bupsa 875
Burma 11, 46
Byalakuppe 291

C

Cabo de Rama 199
Calangute 181–184
Calcutta 721–738
  Indian Museum 733
  Victoria Memorial 732
Calicut 346–348
calling cards 39
car
  rental 52
car insurance 52
cash cards 15
caste 71, 79, 82
caves and cave temples
  Ajanta 72, 428
  Aurangabad 425
  Badami 306
  Barabar 136
  Elephanta Island 409
  Karla and Bhaja 420
  Mahabalipuram 582
  Nepal 801, 830, 831
  Rajgir 134
  Tabo 256
  Udaigiri and Khandagiri 456
caving 448
CDC 22

INDEX

MAP INDEX

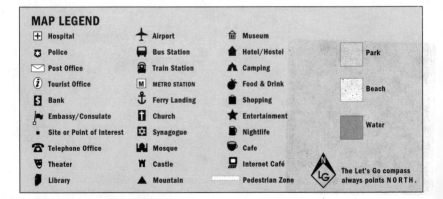

MAP LEGEND

⊞ Hospital	✈ Airport	🏛 Museum
✪ Police	🚌 Bus Station	🏨 Hotel/Hostel	Park
✉ Post Office	🚂 Train Station	⛺ Camping
ⓘ Tourist Office	M METRO STATION	Food & Drink
$ Bank	⚓ Ferry Landing	🛍 Shopping	Beach
⚑ Embassy/Consulate	✝ Church	★ Entertainment
■ Site or Point of Interest	☒ Synagogue	Nightlife	Water
☎ Telephone Office	🕌 Mosque	☕ Cafe
♥ Theater	♖ Castle	🖥 Internet Café
📖 Library	▲ Mountain	⋯⋯ Pedestrian Zone	The Let's Go compass always points NORTH.